THE OXFORD HANDBOOK OF
AGRICULTURAL HISTORY

THE OXFORD HANDBOOK OF

AGRICULTURAL HISTORY

Edited by
JEANNIE WHAYNE

Oxford University Press is a department of the University of Oxford. It furthers the University's objective of excellence in research, scholarship, and education by publishing worldwide. Oxford is a registered trade mark of Oxford University Press in the UK and certain other countries.

Published in the United States of America by Oxford University Press
198 Madison Avenue, New York, NY 10016, United States of America.

© Oxford University Press 2024

All rights reserved. No part of this publication may be reproduced, stored in a retrieval system, or transmitted, in any form or by any means, without the prior permission in writing of Oxford University Press, or as expressly permitted by law, by license, or under terms agreed with the appropriate reproduction rights organization. Inquiries concerning reproduction outside the scope of the above should be sent to the Rights Department, Oxford University Press, at the address above.

You must not circulate this work in any other form and you must impose this same condition on any acquirer.

Library of Congress Cataloging-in-Publication Data
Names: Whayne, Jeannie M., editor.
Title: The Oxford handbook of agricultural history / [edited by] Jeannie Whayne.
Description: New York, NY, United States of America : Oxford University Press, [2024] | Series: Oxford handbooks series | Includes index. |
Identifiers: LCCN 2023040465 | ISBN 9780190924164 (hardback) | ISBN 9780197685440 (epub) | ISBN 9780190924188
Subjects: LCSH: Agriculture—History.
Classification: LCC S419 .O94 2024 | DDC 630.9—dc23/eng/20230929
LC record available at https://lccn.loc.gov/2023040465

DOI: 10.1093/oxfordhb/9780190924164.001.0001

Printed by Sheridan Books, Inc., United States of America

Contents

Contributors   ix

Introduction: Agriculture from Pre-History to the Present   1
JEANNIE WHAYNE

PART I. TIMELESS ESSENTIALS

1. Making Sense of Land   25
   FRANK UEKÖTTER

2. Soil Fertility   41
   LAURIE E. DRINKWATER

3. A Short History of Seed Keeping   58
   HELEN ANNE CURRY

4. A History of Livestock and People   76
   CLAIRE STROM

5. Insects, Illness, and Other Biological Contestations   93
   MARTHA FEW

6. Agricultural Labor   113
   STEVE STRIFFLER

7. Peasants and the Peasantry   129
   JONATHAN RIGG

8. Women in Agriculture   146
   PAMELA RINEY-KEHRBERG

PART II. MODERN ESSENTIALS

9. Mechanization in Agriculture   161
   R. DOUGLAS HURT

10. The Growing Power of Agricultural Science 177
    J. L. ANDERSON

11. Expert and Knowledge Networks 196
    DEBORAH FITZGERALD

12. Commodity Frontiers as Drivers of Global Capitalism 211
    ULBE BOSMA AND ERIC VANHAUTE

13. Worker Health in Modern Agriculture 226
    MICHITAKE ASO

PART III. EXEMPLARY COMMODITIES

14. Corn 251
    ELIZABETH FITTING

15. Wheat 269
    THOMAS D. ISERN

16. Rice 286
    PETER A. COCLANIS

17. Soy 304
    ERNST LANGTHALER

18. Sugar 325
    SUZANNE MOON

19. Coffee 343
    STUART MCCOOK

20. Bananas 361
    EVAN P. BENNETT

21. Potatoes 374
    CHRISTOPHER SHEPHERD

22. Cotton 394
    JONATHAN ROBINS

23. Tobacco 411
    MELISSA N. MORRIS

24. Silk: A Reconsideration of "Failure" in Sericulture   424
    LISA ONAGA

PART IV. KEY TRANSITIONS AND CHALLENGES

25. Watershed Moments: Turning Points in Hydro-Agricultural
    Development   445
    CHRISTOPHER L. PASTORE

26. The Islamic Agricultural Revolution   463
    MICHAEL J. DECKER

27. Wet Rice in East Asia: A Long Revolution   477
    FRANCESCA BRAY

28. The Atlantic Plantation   499
    TREVOR BURNARD

29. Agriculture, the Atlantic Plantation, and the Environment in
    the US South   515
    JEANNIE WHAYNE

30. The British Agricultural Revolution   532
    RICHARD HOYLE

31. Frontier Agriculture and the Creation of Global Neo-Europes   552
    JONATHAN DALY

32. Contestations over Agricultural Production in Colonial Africa   570
    CASSANDRA MARK-THIESEN

33. The Global Green Revolution   585
    MARK B. TAUGER

34. Famine   603
    JENNY LEIGH SMITH

35. Forest Transition Theory   619
    BRETT M. BENNETT AND GREGORY A. BARTON

Index   637

Contributors

J. L. Anderson is Professor of History at Mount Royal University in Calgary, Alberta. Author of *Capitalist Pigs: Pigs, Pork, and Power in America*. He is past president of the Agricultural History Society and is currently the Alberta member of the Historic Sites and Monuments Board of Canada.

Michitake Aso is Associate Professor of the Global Environment in the Department of History at the University at Albany. He has been a fellow at the National University of Singapore, the University of Texas at Austin, and Kyoto University. His book *Rubber and the Making of Vietnam: An Ecological History* won the Agricultural History Society's Henry A. Wallace Award and the Forest History Society's Charles A. Weyerhaeuser Award. He has published articles in various scholarly journals and has taught courses on environmental, medical, and Asian history.

Gregory A. Barton is Professor of History at the University of Johannesburg and Western Sydney University. He is the author of *The Global History of Organic Farming* and three other books. He was a Fulbright Scholar to Bangladesh and has received grants from the Australian Research Council on the global history of organic farming and on global climate theory and desiccation.

Brett M. Bennett holds appointments as an Associate Professor of History at the University of Johannesburg, South Africa, and at Western Sydney University, Australia. He is the author, coauthor, or coeditor of four books, including *Plantations and Protected Areas: A Global History of Forest Management*.

Evan P. Bennett is Associate Professor of History at Florida Atlantic University where he teaches courses on Southern history, labor history, environmental history, and Florida history. He is the author of *When Tobacco Was King: Families, Farm Labor, and Federal Policy in the Piedmont* and coauthor of *Beyond Forty Acres and a Mule: African American Landowning Families since Reconstruction*.

Ulbe Bosma is Senior Researcher at the International Institute of Social History in Amsterdam and Professor of International Comparative Social History at the Free University in Amsterdam. He is the author of *The Sugar Plantation in India and Indonesia* and *The World of Sugar: How the Sweet Stuff Transformed Our Politics, Health, and Environment over 2,000 Years*. He coordinates the international network Commodity Frontiers Initiative (CFI).

Francesca Bray is Professor Emerita of Social Anthropology at the University of Edinburgh and former President of SHOT (Society for the History of Technology). Her books include *The Rice Economies: Technology & Development in Asian Societies*; *Technology and Gender: Fabrics of Power in Late Imperial China*; *Rice: Global Networks and New Histories*; and *Moving Crops and the Scales of History*.

Trevor Burnard is Wilberforce Professor of Slavery and Emancipation at the University of Hull and Director of the Wilberforce Institute. He is the author of fifteen books and is the editor in chief of the Oxford Online Bibliography in Atlantic History. His most recent books are *Jamaica in the Age of Revolution*, *Writing Early America*, *Writing the Global History of Slavery*, and the *Oxford Handbook of the Seven Years War*.

Peter A. Coclanis is the Albert Ray Newsome Distinguished Professor of History at the University of North Carolina, Chapel Hill, and a specialist in economic history. He is also the Director of the Global Research Institute and author of a number of books including *Time's Arrow, Time's Cycle: Globalization in South East Asia over La Longue Durée* and *The Shadow of a Dream: Economic Life and Death in the South Carolina Low Country, 1670–1920*.

Helen Anne Curry is Melvin Kranzberg Professor in the History of Technology at the Georgia Institute of Technology. She is the author of *Evolution Made to Order: Plant Breeding and Technological Innovation in Twentieth Century America*; *Endangered Maize: Industrial Agriculture and the Crisis of Extinction*; and coeditor of *Worlds of Natural History*.

Jonathan Daly is Professor of History at the University of Illinois, Chicago, and a specialist in Russian history. He has authored numerous books including *Hammer, Sickle, and Soil: The Soviet Drive to Collectivize Agriculture*.

Michael J. Decker is Professor of History at the University of South Florida, where his research focuses on the history and archeology of the ancient and medieval Middle East. He is the author of numerous publications including *Tilling the Hateful Earth: Agriculture in the Early Byzantine East*.

Laurie E. Drinkwater is Professor in the School of Integrative Plant Science-Horticulture Section at Cornell University. Her research program aims to reverse soil degradation trends and restore soil health and ecological integrity in agroecosystems. She has authored numerous articles on agroecology, biogeochemistry, and nutrient management including *Nutrients in Agriculture: Rethinking the Management Paradigm*.

Martha Few is Liberal Arts Professor of Latin American History and Women's, Gender, and Sexuality Studies at Penn State University. Senior Editor of the *Hispanic American Historical Review*, she is the author of a number of books, including *For All of Humanity: Mesoamerican and Colonial Medicine in Enlightenment Guatemala*, and coeditor of *Centering Animals in Latin American History*.

Elizabeth Fitting is Professor in the Department of Sociology and Social Anthropology at Dalhousie University in Nova Scotia, Canada. She is the author of numerous publications including *The Struggle for Maize: Campesinos, Workers, and Transgenic Corn in the Mexican Countryside.*

Deborah Fitzgerald is the Cutten Professor of History of Technology at the Massachusetts Institute of Technology's program in Science, Technology and Society. She is past president of the Agricultural History Society and author of *Every Farm a Factory: The Industrial Ideal in American Agriculture.*

Richard Hoyle was formerly Professor of Rural History at the University of Reading and Professor of Regional and Local History at the Institute of Historical Research at the University of London. He is now Visiting Professor of Economic History at Reading. He served as editor of *Agricultural History Review* for twenty years and is the author of numerous publications on tenancy, landholding, and land markets.

R. Douglas Hurt is Professor of History in the Department of History at Purdue University. A former editor of both *Agricultural History* and *Ohio History*, he has published two dozen books, most recently *The Green Revolution in the Global South: Science, Politics, and Unintended Consequences,* and *Agriculture in the Midwest, 1815-1900.*

Thomas D. Isern is Professor of History and University Distinguished Professor at North Dakota State University. He is the author of two books on the history of wheat harvesting—*Custom Combining on the Great Plains: A History* and *Bull Threshers and Bindlestiffs: Harvesting and Threshing on the North America Plains.*

Ernst Langthaler is head of the Department of Economic, Social, and Environmental History at Johannes Kepler University Linz and head of the Institute of Rural History in St. Pölten. He is the author of a number of books and articles, including *Agro-Food Studies* and "The Soy Paradox: The Western Nutrition Transition Revisited, 1950–2010," in *Global Environment.*

Cassandra Mark-Thiesen is head of a junior research group at the "Africa Multiple" Cluster of Excellence, University of Bayreuth. She is the author of *Mediators, Contract Men, and Colonial Capital: Mechanized Gold Mining in the Gold Cost Colony, 1879–1909.*

Stuart McCook is Professor of History at the University of Guelph. He is a specialist in global environmental history and author of *Coffee Is Not Forever: A Global History of the Coffee Leaf Rust.* The book received the Agricultural History Society's Wallace Prize for the best book on agricultural history outside the United States.

Suzanne Moon is Associate Professor of History of Science, Technology, and Medicine at the University of Oklahoma and a specialist in the history of technology. She is the author of *Technology in Southeast Asian, Technology and Ethical Idealism: A History of Development in the Netherlands East Indies,* and numerous articles. She is the former editor-in-chief of *Technology and Culture.*

Melissa N. Morris is Assistant Professor of History at the University of Wyoming and a specialist in early America and the Atlantic World. Her publications include "Spanish and Indigenous Influences on Virginian Tobacco Cultivation," in *Atlantic Environments and the American South: An Anthology.*

Lisa Onaga is Senior Research Scholar at the Max Planck Institute for the History of Science. Her work focuses on the ownership and authorship of knowledge at the material interface of animal and human life in agricultural, laboratory, health, and industrial settings. She has published extensively on the history of silkworm science and is currently completing a book about the entanglement of biology and silk farming in Japan during the nineteenth and twentieth centuries.

Christopher L. Pastore is Associate Professor of History at the University at Albany, State University of New York, and the author of *Between Land and Sea: The Atlantic Coast and the Transformation of New England.* While writing his chapter he was also a fellow at the Long Room Hub Arts & Humanities Research Institute, Trinity College Dublin, for a project cofunded by the European Union's Horizon 2020 program under the Marie Skłodowska-Curie Grant Agreement No. 713730.

Jonathan Rigg is Professor and Chair of Human Geography at the University of Bristol. Recently recognized with the prestigious Victoria medal from the Royal Geographical Society, he is the author of several works, including *More than Rural: Textures of Thailand's Agrarian Transformation* and *Rural Development in Southeast Asia: Dispossession, Accumulation and Persistence.*

Pamela Riney-Kehrberg is Distinguished Professor of History at Iowa State University and a specialist in rural and agricultural history. She is past president of the Agricultural History Society and has published several books, including *When a Dream Dies: Agriculture, Iowa, and the Farm Crisis the 1980s; Rooted in Dust: Surviving Drought and Depression in Southwestern Kansas,* and *Childhood on the Farm: Work, Play and Coming of Age in the Midwest.*

Jonathan Robins is Associate Professor of Global History at Michigan Technology University. He serves as book review editor for *Agricultural History* and is the author of *Cotton and Race across the Atlantic: Britain, Africa, and America, 1900–1920* and *Oil Palm: A Global History.*

Christopher Shepherd is Research Fellow at the Australian National University and specializes in the study of Latin America and Southeast Asia. His publications include *Development and Environmental Politics Unmasked: Authority, Participation, and Equity in East Timor; Haunted Houses and Ghostly Encounters: Animism and Ethnography in East Timor, 1860–1975;* and "Andean Cultural Affirmation and Cultural Integration in Context: Reflections on Indigenous Knowledge for the In Situ Conservation of Agrobiodiversity," in *Indigenous Knowledge: Enhancing Its Contribution to Natural Resources Management.*, ed. Paul Sillitoe.

Jenny Leigh Smith is an independent scholar based in Western New York. Her research focuses on the long-term environmental and human impacts of agricultural industrialization. She is currently completing a book about twentieth-century famines and leading a project that explores the history of refugee camps.

Steve Striffler is Professor of Anthropology and Director of the Labor Resource Center at the University of Massachusetts, Boston. He is the author of seven books including *Solidarity: Latin America and the US Left in the Era of Human Rights*.

Claire Strom is the Rapetti-Trunzo Chair of History at Rollins College in Florida. Her academic research focuses on the history of public health, both animal and human, but she writes on a wide variety of topics from pedagogy to race relations to wilderness kayaking. She is the author of many books and articles including *Making Catfish Bait out of Government Boys: The Fight against Cattle Ticks and the Transformation of the Yeoman South* and *Profiting from the Plains: The Great Northern Railway and Corporate Development of the American West*.

Mark B. Tauger is Associate Professor of History at West Virginia University, specializing in Russian/Soviet history and world agricultural history. He has published *Agriculture in World History* and two collections of articles on famines and agriculture in Soviet history: *Golod, Golodomor, Genotsid?* [in Russian in Kyiv] and *Famine et transformation agricole en URSS* [in French in Paris].

Frank Uekötter is Professor of the history of technology and environmental history at Ruhr University Bochum in Germany. He is the author of numerous articles, book chapters, and several books on a wide range of topics, including the history of soils and soil knowledge and the making of monocultures. Since 2021, he has been principal investigator of the ERC Advanced Grant project, "The Making of Monoculture: A Global History" (MaMoGH). In 2023, the University of Pittsburgh Press published his *The Vortex: An Environmental History of the Modern World*.

Eric Vanhaute is Professor of Economic and Social History and World History in the History Department at Ghent University in Belgium. He is the author of numerous publications on rural and agrarian history, including *Peasants in World History* (Routledge 2021). He is a member of the leadership of the Commodity Frontiers Initiative (CFI).

Jeannie Whayne is University Professor of History at the University of Arkansas and author, coauthor, or editor of eleven books, including her award-winning *Delta Empire: Lee Wilson and the Transformation of Southern Agriculture*. She is past president of the Agricultural History Society and a distinguished lecturer with the Organization of American Historians.

INTRODUCTION

Agriculture from Pre-History to the Present

JEANNIE WHAYNE

Two words – innovation and adaptation – sum up much of the agricultural history of this arable planet. At times, innovation in agricultural techniques required adaptation on the farm and in lifeways; at other times, both innovation and adaptation were in response to unanticipated forces like famines, natural disasters, and catastrophic plagues of locusts. Archeologists and anthropologists observed the tension between the two in exploring the origins of humans and the changes that occurred as hunters and gatherers slowly became more sedentary. As rudimentary forms of agriculture took shape, they noted transformations that occurred within their societies such as the development of formal hierarchies and conflicts over resources. Examinations of human skeletal remains provided evidence that a plant-based diet led to changes in human morphology, some of them negative.[1] As populations increased and urban centers arose, a complementary relationship developed between the countryside and towns/cities that gave rise to new forms of commercial interaction that frequently led to conflict over divergent interests. Beginning in the eighteenth century, industrial development in the West, accompanied by changes in agricultural methods, often resulted in destabilizing demographic shifts. The emergence of capitalism and the advent of colonialism created new challenges for the countries of the colonizers and for the colonized and forced or necessitated adaptations by both. The development of scientific agriculture and the use of a wide variety of chemicals, particularly in the twentieth century, resulted in improvements but also disrupted old lifeways associated with farming. By the twenty-first century, climate change caused by human activities made for floods and droughts that will test the ability of agriculturalists to adapt. The extent to which climate change will impact agriculture remains debatable among politicians and some of the public, but few farmers remain among the skeptics. Even minuscule shifts in temperature threaten the agricultural enterprise, but farmers will likely innovate and adapt.

At the end of the Pleistocene era, about 11,000 years ago, temperatures warmed sufficiently to permit sedentary living, and people in Asia and the Middle East began to cultivate plants for consumption. Thus began the Neolithic Revolution, a term coined by an Australian archeologist to describe the era when humans first departed their hunting and gathering lifestyle and began to practice rudimentary agriculture.[2] Anthropologist Graeme Barker in *The Agricultural Revolution in Prehistory: Why Did Foragers Become Farmers* takes a global view and brings together scholarship on diverse regions in his examination of the Neolithic Revolution. He suggests that it arose across continents independently. Regardless of continent or exact timing, the changes that shaped human history were foundational. As anthropologist Ian Kuijt in his *Life in Neolithic Farming Communities: Social Organization, Identity, and Differentiation* argues, the advent of agriculture created a particular set of social engagements that promoted the development of rural communities. The formation of village-centered rural communities also reinforced the necessity of agricultural production.[3]

For much of agricultural history, historians focused on distinct regions, but that began to change in the twentieth century. One of the most important developments came with Alfred Crosby's book *The Columbian Exchange*, which explored the means through which the world's agricultural systems began to become interconnected in the fifteenth century and that by the end of the early modern period had reached across the globe. This was an exchange not only of plants and animals but also of people. It entailed voluntary trade in items, the forced migration of Africans, and the introduction of new species of plants and animals to far distant points on the globe. While the Columbian Exchange enriched certain Europeans and traders, it led to the exploitation of Indigenous people and negatively impacted environments. The notion of the Columbian Exchange was widely adopted by historians and contributed to the development of the concept of the Atlantic plantation and a focus on the institution of slavery.[4]

In the twenty-first century, increasing concerns about globalization, the use of chemicals, the development of new forms of genetically modified seeds, and exploitative labor practices on corporate plantations stimulated the present generation of agricultural historians to raise new questions and return to old subjects with fresh perspectives. The preoccupation with environmental concerns has influenced recent books on world agriculture. Mark Tauger's *Agriculture in World History* makes an argument about "dual subordination," the idea that farmers have always functioned in a world where their enterprise was subordinate to urban civilization and the environment. A book by Marcel Mazoyer and Laurence Roudart, *A History of World Agriculture from the Neolithic Age to the Current Crisis*, describes agricultural systems across the globe, making a case for addressing the existing world political and environmental crisis that puts peasants at extreme risk. A book by Christopher Isett and Steven Miller, *The Social History of Agriculture: From the Origins to the Current Crisis*, provides a Marxist interpretation of the costs of profit-driven agricultural exploitation. Along the way, the book demonstrates the value of the comparative approach. Three books concerning agriculture and the environment also pose questions about the impact of the environment or climate change on agriculture across the world: *Agriculture and Environmental Change:*

Temporal and Spatial Dimensions by A. M. Mannion; *Climate Change and Agriculture: An Economic Analysis of Global Impacts, Adaptation and Distributional Effects* by Robert Mendelsohn and Ariel Dinar; and *World Agriculture and the Environment: A Commodity-by-Commodity Guide to Impacts and Practices* by Jason Clay.[5]

Any discussion of the effect of changes in the environment and climate must reckon with the Anthropocene. Although the concept remains controversial, there is a growing consensus that a new geologic era is in the process of arising because of the activities of humans. Precisely when this transformation began remains debatable. Paul Crutzen and Eugene Stoermer argue it began with the nineteenth-century Industrial Revolution when unprecedented pollutants were introduced into the environment. Others acknowledge the importance of the gasoline-driven automobile in increasing carbon monoxide levels in the atmosphere, and still others make a convincing case that it began in the mid-twentieth century as a result of several factors, including the explosion of the atomic and hydrogen bombs but also post–World War II modern agricultural methods: John McNeill and Peter Engelke in *The Great Acceleration* and Julia Adeney Thomas, Mark Williams, and Jan Zalasiewicz in *The Anthropocene: A Multidisciplinary Approach*.[6]

Agricultural history has thus expanded from its origins in anthropology and archeology to the twenty-first-century preoccupation of historians with issues of global importance. The evolution of the field has been greatly enhanced by the creation of agricultural history societies within countries and continents in the twentieth century and especially by organizations that meet internationally in the twenty-first century and explore issues of both parochial and international significance. The dialogue occurring at meetings of the Agricultural History Society and of the European Rural History Organization, for example, promises to lead to a flourishing new global agricultural historiography.

Timeless Essentials

The timeless essentials of agriculture have evolved, some of them almost beyond recognition, but they remain the fundamental features of agriculture. The basic elements are land, soil, and seed, three features that can be manipulated to serve a variety of purposes for humans. At the very basic level, they operate in beautiful yet simple symmetry to pull forth agricultural bounty to sustain life from the land. According to Frank Uekötter, the modern concept of land ownership seems self-evident in the twenty-first century but was largely unknown outside Western Europe until about 500 years ago. As European countries expanded in the Age of Discovery, misunderstandings about land use practices and the concept of land ownership contributed to conflict between Europeans and the Indigenous population in the Americas. For Western Europeans, land ownership was the foundation of inheritance, and the legal system was designed to strengthen it. The Indigenous peoples of the Americas had little or no concept of landownership, and together with other differences in culture and values, the arrival of the Europeans resulted in genocide and dispossession. By the early nineteenth century, colonialists in the Americas, Asia, and Africa had orchestrated the mobilization of land for agriculture. The rise of scientific agriculture and the reliance on expert knowledge in the twentieth century contributed to the growing concentration of landownership in fewer hands. Modern production methods both maintained and transformed agriculture and turned them into the tools of a twenty-first-century agricultural colonialism. Indeed, as Stefano Liberti observes in *Land Grabbing*, a new colonialism sponsored by distant governments and corporations has emerged, overturning traditional landholding patterns.[7]

It is impossible to know precisely how much early farmers struggled with soil fertility, but it is an ongoing issue in the modern era. Very early agriculturalists likely interacted lightly with the soil, but as humans became more reliant on agriculture, they settled in clusters that grew from villages into modern urban centers and demanded more from agriculture. As populations expanded even more and required greater acreage to be deployed to provide food for consumption, the use and misuse of soil by agriculturalists increased. Although scientific agriculture arose to address the problems, soil depletion and erosion remain major concerns, and scientific discoveries in the modern era have not fully resolved them. The twenty-first-century call to engage in more sustainable practices often runs counter to the demands of capitalist agriculture. As David R. Montgomery in *Growing a Revolution: Bringing Our Soil Back to Life* suggests, previous civilizations have fallen because of damage to soils done by over-cultivation.[8]

Until the late twentieth century, farmers relied on seeds from their previous year's crop that they preserved and planted. As scientific agriculture arose and directed farmers to hybridized seeds, seed varieties diminished, raising concerns about the vigor of the remaining favored few. Mauro Ambrosoli in *The Wild and the Sown: Botany and Agriculture in Western Europe, 1350–1800* establishes that the twenty-first-century problem with disappearing seed varieties is nothing new. However, biotech innovations in the laboratories of companies that devise genetically modified seeds have introduced more sophisticated ways to engineer seed varieties. These new seeds are designed to produce crops that are resistant to new pesticides and herbicides meant to kill pests, fungi, and grasses that might damage the crop. Using patent law to serve their interests, they have prosecuted those who would store and reuse such seeds, challenging the traditional practice of using last year's seeds on this year's crop. Controversy connected to the growing dominance of a new kind of seed known as genetically modified organisms (GMO) and the disappearance of heritage versions have encouraged the development of seed banks to preserve heritage seeds.[9]

Even before the onset of agriculture, animals began to interact with humans on an intimate scale. Whether they were raised for consumption or as work animals, they played an important role in promoting agriculture and food development. The relationship between humans and their domesticated livestock evolved significantly in the twentieth century as farmers employed selective breeding and the use of specialized feed to promote growth and maximize profits. In the modern era, feed lots for cattle and hog farms present environmental challenges, and the use of antibiotics to combat disease in chickens, for example, holds implications for human health. In *Porkopolis: American Animality, Standardized Life, & the Factory Farm*, Alex Blanchette explores the implications of modern pork production on animals and humans, suggesting that both have been bioengineered to satisfy the demands of industrial pork production.[10]

The problems of pests and other bacteria in human history have long been a preoccupation of historians, but J. R. McNeill in his masterful *Mosquito Empire: Ecology and War in the Greater Caribbean* makes a convincing case that lack of immunity to yellow fever both made and unmade empires from the Age of Discovery to the early twentieth century. Farmers have always had to contend with damage done to their crops by insects, fungi, bacteria, and viruses almost as a routine part of the practice of agriculture. Farmers in ancient Rome used folk remedies, but it was not until the seventeenth century that serious scholarly work was devoted to historicizing the problem. Perhaps the most dramatic and best-known blight suffered by farmers was the swarms of locusts that could lay waste to a region's crop, trigger famine, and lead to outbreaks of infectious diseases. The first record of locust infestation dates to ancient Egypt, and since then periodic plagues have arisen around the globe. A particularly destructive superswarm occurred in Central America in the early nineteenth century and moved across several countries, bringing devastation in its wake. In the twentieth and twenty-first centuries, increasingly serious locust swarms across the planet have arisen, in part because of climate change, and threaten crops and endanger global food security. Jeffrey Lockwood in *Locust: The Devastating Rise and Mysterious Disappearance of the Insect That Shaped the American Frontier* suggests that the biological controls and pesticides that have been deployed have been insufficient to address the crisis at hand.[11]

By interrupting the food supply, plagues of locusts created life-threatening issues for humans whether they were merely consumers or directly engaged as owners of land or those who labored for them. The emergence of farm laborers as a category accompanied the rise of agriculture, but one category of farm laborer that has attracted considerable scholarly attention is the peasantry. The term "peasantry" has been applied to the large mass of rural dwellers in the medieval period who worked the land. The peasantry included farmers who had some claim to the land as well as to landless laborers and many who were in some state of unfreedom, such as Russian serfs. Although scholars of the peasantry believe it to have been an essential element of rural and agricultural life, a lively debate has emerged over whether the term "peasants" accurately describes the vast and varied array of agriculturalists. Nevertheless, groups who have been identified by historians as representing the peasantry have been associated with political and social movements that challenged elites and attempted to assert certain rights associated with their status as agriculturalists. If Indigenous groups who engage in subsistence agriculture can be called peasants in the twenty-first century, their exposure to capitalist agriculture constitutes the challenge of a lifetime.[12]

Farm laborers, who might be categorized as peasants in some areas of the world, provide one of the most important services to agriculture by planting, cultivating, and harvesting crops. They have long been a factor in farm operations, providing necessary day-labor. David Moon in *The Russian Peasantry* and Eric Wolf in *Europe and the*

People without History both demonstrate their importance in Western history, but something fundamental occurred in the twenty-first century. With the advent of machines and chemicals after World War II in the United States and elsewhere, labor needs were greatly reduced, leaving farm labor with lower wages and only seasonal work. Foreign farm laborers were especially relatively powerless, but in the twenty-first century they constituted approximately half the farm labor supply in the United States and a sizable proportion of that in Europe. Even as most of the world's food supply continues to be produced by small holders around the globe in the twenty-first century, highly capitalized agriculture is expanding globally and relies on landless laborers who are often transient or temporary immigrants. Their exploitation is further guaranteed by corporate practices and government programs that support big agriculture. Laborers and farm labor unions continue to struggle in the face of seemingly insurmountable odds.[13]

Women farmers have largely been ignored by a profession that has assumed certain gender expectations. In other words, when earlier historians studied agriculture, they thought of its practitioners as male. As Linda Ambrose and Joan Jenson established in *Women in Agriculture: Professionalizing Rural Life in North America and Europe, 1880–1965*, women have not only been essential to agricultural production, but they have also played a crucial role in its transformation. In fact, women have been central to the farming enterprise from the Neolithic period to the present. In certain Indigenous societies like that in North America in the colonial era and before, women performed most of the agricultural tasks while men hunted. Historians have now recognized that female household activities in nineteenth-century farm households in the United States contributed to the farm's economic survival. Women also often worked alongside husbands in the fields when necessary, and, moreover, they played important roles in managing farming activities or even owned and operated their own farms. Modern machinery, meanwhile, makes many tasks that require strength less onerous. A woman can occupy an air-conditioned combine harvester—or manage the controls of a robot-operated tractor—as well as a man. Whether serving as important contributors to the farming enterprise by assuming expected gender roles or by operating their own farms, women have served an essential function in agriculture. Although the percentage of women farm operators on small farms has risen in the United States in the twenty-first century, the decline of small farms and trend toward corporate agriculture is likely to limit that expansion.[14]

Modern Essentials

Until the mid-nineteenth century, agriculture remained largely unmechanized, but innovations were already underway as early as the eighteenth century. The seed drill invented by Jethro Tull in England in 1701 had a dramatic effect on production levels. Although Mark Overton in *Agricultural Revolution in England* attributes the increase in productivity in England in the eighteenth century to a number of innovations, mechanization of agriculture there played an important role. Early versions of threshing machines were invented by the end of that century, but it was Cyrus McCormick's mechanical reaper, invented in 1831, that agricultural historians have identified as making a difference. However, according to Daniel Ott's *Harvesting History* published in 2023, McCormick's claim to deserve credit for the development of the new reaper rests on shaky ground. Regardless, reapers were in general use in the Great Plains of the United States by the 1850s, creating the first "breadbasket." Rather than deploying armies of laborers wielding scythes to the fields, farmers adopted the horse-drawn reaper with its vibrating blades that greatly reduced labor needs. Aside from wheat, however, much of agriculture remained relatively unmechanized. Cotton and tobacco farming, for example, two of the premier crops of plantation agriculture in the American South, continued to rely on labor-intensive practices. Cotton was one of the last to give way to modernization after the invention of a mechanical cotton picker during World War II transformed the process of cotton farming and, along with the use of chemicals to inhibit weed growth, led to a demographic revolution that accelerated the movement of Southerners away from rural areas. Although some agricultural products such as the berry industry remain unmechanized and much of the world continues to engage in labor-intensive practices, the mechanization of agriculture was a game-changer for the United States, the Soviet Union, and many European and Latin American farming sectors.[15]

Scientific agriculture originated with Justus von Liebig, a German chemist who pioneered the scientific method in science education and in agriculture in the nineteenth century. However, the term has come to be associated with mid-twentieth-century innovations described by historian James R. McNeill as part of the *Great Acceleration*. In agriculture, the Great Acceleration included culmination of centuries-long improvements in mechanization and the use of chemicals. The nineteenth century marked the period when laboratories began producing chemicals for use in agriculture, but a new understanding of their properties emerged in the late 1930s and 1940s. Dichlorodiphenyltrichloroethane (DDT), for example, had been created by an Austrian chemist in 1825 but its potential as an insecticide went unrealized until just before World War II. It was effective in eliminating pests, but insects developed resistance to them and thus more or different insecticides were applied; because it had harmful effects on humans and the environment, it was banned in the United States in 1972. Nevertheless, new categories of chemicals were created for use in agriculture, and by the twenty-first century, farmers had a wide array of chemicals to use as fertilizers, herbicides, and insecticides. A final scientific innovation involved the creation of seeds that had been genetically modified to withstand heavy chemical applications. Because of the heavy load of chemicals that accompany their use, they have raised serious health and environmental concerns.[16]

The modern farmer relies on the expert and knowledge networks that exist today, but agricultural knowledge in the past was almost entirely experience-based and was shared through generations. As Yves Segers and Leen Von Molle suggest in *Agricultural Knowledge Networks in Rural Europe, 1700–2000*, networks of agricultural knowledge took shape in the early eighteenth century. In the nineteenth and twentieth centuries, however, agricultural associations and more formal training in the agricultural sciences emerged in Europe and spread to some of its former colonies like the United States. There it was formalized through the creation of land-grant institutions charged with teaching the agricultural sciences. During and after World War II, chemical companies and agricultural equipment companies became prominent players as experts, but a host of middlemen, processors, and associations also connected the farmer to the many products that are necessary in modern agriculture and to the many actors who purchase, broker, or process farm products. Soil scientists and horticulturalists connected to universities train individuals to work with farmers rather than to farm, and chemical and implement companies provide information on and sell products to be used by farmers. The buyers and brokers who purchase what the farmer has to offer pass those products along to packing and processing plants long before they reach the consumer. In the age of modern scientific agriculture, farmers have become dependent upon these networks in a manner that would have been unthinkable in the past.[17]

Another modern essential is encapsulated in the notion of commodity frontiers. In the search for commodities to feed the global centers of capitalism, individuals from certain capitalist countries penetrated rural areas across the globe and promoted the production of agricultural (and mining) commodities and methodologies. From the fifteenth to the nineteenth centuries, the production of commodities for a world market involved the suppression and removal of Indigenous populations, the adoption of indentured servitude and slavery, and the expansion of the authority of the colonizers' home countries. In later years, the expansion of global commodities was promoted increasingly by corporations, often with the backing of their own home countries, which secured the assistance of local political and economic elites in the target country. These corporations sometimes advertised themselves as promoting development and guaranteeing higher standards of living for Indigenous people, but adoption of their products and the utilization of modern agricultural methods generally resulted in disruption of their rural lifeways as operators employed exploitative labor practices. In addition to eliminating biodiversity and sustainable agricultural practices, these corporations extracted precious resources and in the course of this did environmental damage. Indigenous peoples often—sometimes successfully—contested such exploitation, but agricultural corporations continue to reach into Africa, Asia, and Latin America. Ulba Bosma in *The Making of a Periphery* examines how one of the most productive areas in Southeast Asia became peripheral in the global economy as a result of its exploitation as a commodity frontier.[18]

With the emergence of modern capitalist agriculture, the threat to human health increased exponentially. Promoters of agribusiness operations claim that the plentiful food supply they have produced has improved health around the world, but critics point out that the availability of cheap and plentiful processed food has led to an obesity epidemic in the United States and elsewhere. In a pathbreaking study, *Rubber and the Making of Vietnam*, Michitake Aso demonstrates that a trend toward the use of machinery and of chemical herbicides and pesticides has presented unprecedented challenges to farm workers. Bodies could be mangled in the new machines, a factor that has not been eliminated in the twenty-first century. Lack of understanding about arsenic, the first new chemical introduced by agricultural scientists in the late nineteenth century, led to accidental overapplications that did damage not only to plants and orchards but also to the laborers who were applying them. Even after agriculturalists grew accustomed to the use of more sophisticated chemicals in the mid-twentieth century, their misapplication continued to have devastating effects on crops and humans. Agricultural laborers are at greater danger, and sometimes this danger increases along race and gender lines. In the cut-flower industry in Columbia, for example, women represent 60 to 80 percent of the work force and face exposure to the use of dangerous chemicals, all for the sake of the consumers in countries like the United States who crave fresh flowers. One chemical, Dichloropropene, is known to result in a host of medical issues including miscarriages.[19] While the general population in a given farm area may suffer the consequences by this wider spread of chemicals, the front-line agricultural workers suffer the greatest consequences.[20]

Exemplary Commodities

Alfred Crosby's *The Columbian Exchange* describes the exchange of crops and diseases between the Americans and the rest of the world and continues to serve as a useful way to understand how exemplary commodities linked continents during the so-called Age of Discovery. For thousands of years, three unique cereal grains had been cultivated in Asia, the Middle East, and the Americas and had served human populations in similar ways yet did not penetrate much beyond their region of origin. To be sure, rice, corn, and wheat expanded considerably *within* the regions where they were first cultivated prior to the Age of Discovery. Rice was domesticated in the Yangtze River Valley region of China sometime between 8,200 and 13,500 years ago. Recent evidence suggests that domesticated rice grew from a grass species *Oryza glaberrima* or *Oryza sativa*, spread throughout much of Asia, and was introduced to Africa between 1500 and 800 BCE. People in the Middle East, meanwhile, began to hybridize wheat about 12,000 years ago, it spread throughout the Middle East, and it was being grown in Europe between 5400 and 4900 BCE. Maize (corn), which originated as a naturally growing wild grass, teosinte, was domesticated in Mexico approximately 10,000 years ago and spread throughout North and South America, where it became a primary staple.[21]

Although they had been staples in their respective regions for thousands of years, rice, wheat, and corn each had a significant role to play in the Columbian Exchange. Rice, for example, became one of the most important crops along the Georgia and Carolina coasts in the seventeenth century. Because Africans had been growing it for approximately 2,000 years, they played a crucial role—as enslaved laborers—in the rice economy there. Wheat became one of the primary crops grown in Plymouth Colony, but it did not become prominent until it spread into the mid-Atlantic region in the late colonial period. Corn, meanwhile, a New World crop that was essentially alien to Europeans, Africans, and Asians, was quickly adopted because it could be grown in soils unsuitable for wheat and rice. Its introduction contributed to population growth and staved off famine in parts of Europe and China.[22]

Two other crops with distinct origins were also crucial elements of the Columbian Exchange. Tobacco was virtually unknown to the rest of the world but used widely in the Americas for ceremonial purposes. It was introduced to Europe by the Spanish but was first grown for export to Europe in Santo Domingo beginning in 1531. Gradually, the demand for it expanded, and by the end of the century, it was the world's first global commodity. Europeans initially appreciated it for its so-called medicinal qualities, but it was soon being used for recreational purposes. It virtually salvaged the British attempt to establish a foothold in Jamestown, Virginia, which was floundering badly, when the settlers began to cultivate it for export. Depending on which variety of tobacco the grower is producing, it does well on a variety of soils. Another storied crop originating in Peru was the lowly potato. A starchy tuber and root vegetable that grew in the wild, its domestication occurred around 8000 BCE. It spread from present-day Peru and Bolivia through the Americas. A hearty tuber that thrives in well-drained loamy soils, it is vulnerable to fungal and bacterial infections. In Europe, it is most famously connected to Ireland, where it became a staple after its introduction in the seventeenth century. But a potato blight beginning in 1844 led to crop failure, famine, and the departure of nearly two million Irish, many of them to Australia and the United States.[23]

Sugar and coffee, which were also important commodities in the Columbian Exchange, originated in the Southern Hemisphere and the Middle East respectively. It appears that sugar cane cultivation emerged almost simultaneously in two areas: in New Guinea and in South Asia. From India it was taken to China, and by the medieval period it was being grown in the Middle East and Europe. It was the Portuguese who brought it to Brazil where it became an important crop, but by the end of the sixteenth century it was being grown throughout the Caribbean. It grows well in a variety of soil types such as sandy, loamy, and clay soils but also does well in acidic and alkaline soils. Because of the use of machinery in the modern era, it can suffer damage through soil compaction and reduced yields. Coffee, meanwhile, was a latecomer to the pantheon of crops in the Columbian Exchange, having emerged in the fifteenth century in Yemen. Within a century it had spread throughout the Middle East, into India, Southeast Asia, and Europe. It grows well in subtropical and tropical regions like those of Asia, Africa, and the Americas and requires soils that are rich in humus, nitrogen, and potassium. From the beginning it was appreciated as a stimulant, and some have argued that it played a role in the Industrial Revolution. Because water quality was so poor, the British typically drank ale (beer) as an accompaniment to their meals. Coffee provided an alternative with verve. Although its connection to the Industrial Revolution may have been more as a heavily traded product rather than its effect on individual producers, the theory is provocative.[24]

Cotton has the distinction of having varieties that originated in the Old World as well as the New. On the one hand, its cultivation dated to between 5500 and 2300 BCE in Pakistan (South Asia) and spread into the rest of the Middle East, China, and India.

India, in fact, became known for its superb cotton fabrics in the common era. Though the various Asian versions were relatively well known and highly prized in Europe by the Age of Discovery, another cotton variety, also dating to approximately 5500 to 6000 BCE, followed its own expansionist direction in the New World from Peru, and by 3000 BCE was known to be grown in Mexico and even southern Arizona. The British Industrial Revolution, which owed much of its success to the cotton textile industry, drew its products initially though the British East India Company, but the growth of the plantation system in the southeastern United States supplanted the East Indian growers in the early nineteenth century. Like wheat and sugar cane, cotton grows well in loamy soil, but it can also thrive in alluvial soils, particularly in tropical and subtropical locations. Long-staple cotton, which produces a fine, long strand, could be woven into soft and expensive fabrics, but the discovery of a short-staple version called Petit Gulf cotton in the 1820s that was more easily processed in the newly created cotton gin (1791) played a role in its expansion into interior areas of the US South. Cotton robbed the soil of nitrogen, however, and by the twentieth century, agricultural experts began to promote rotating soy production, which restored nitrogen content, with cotton. According to the new history of capitalism, cotton was at the center of the global expansion of capitalism. However, cotton's heyday in the global marketplace lasted until World War II, after which demand for rice and soybeans supplanted it.[25]

Soy, which is classified as a species of legume, was domesticated in approximately 7000 BCE in central China, where it was used as a food and in medicines. By the first century of the common era, it was being grown in Japan and many other Asian countries. It was not widely known or appreciated outside of Asia, however, and apparently failed to make a showing in the Columbian Exchange. It is a hardy plant and grows well in a variety of soils but prefers a loose, well-drained loam. According to one often repeated anecdote, it first made its appearance in the Americas in the early nineteenth century as ballast aboard a ship. But by the end of the nineteenth century, it was being cultivated in Africa as an export commodity headed for Europe, which was then in need of oil. The dedication of Southern planters to cotton, together with the initial reluctance of Westerners to embrace soy as a food, slowed its adoption. Soy production in the United States was given a boost during the New Deal of the 1930s when planters were paid to take other crops—like cotton—out of production. Agricultural specialists had been promoting soy as a soil restorative crop for more than two decades, and the cotton-reduction program was a dream come true for them. Planters moved quickly into soy production, which accelerated after World War II, and by the twenty-first century was grown interchangeably with cotton. Soy continues to be grown widely in Asia and throughout the Americas and Africa. European countries have increased production of it in the twenty-first century as demand has grown among consumers for a wide variety of soy products.[26]

The banana, which originated in Malaysia in approximately 2000 BCE, also played an important role in the Columbian Exchange and was fated for an interesting economic and political history in the Americas. They had been introduced to Africa from southeast Asia sometime between the first and sixth centuries CE and became a staple food in the African Great Lakes region. It was from Africa that the banana traveled to the Caribbean in the sixteenth century. Infamously, the history of the banana is tied up with the multinational companies that began to buy up land in Central America in the late nineteenth century. Although the term "banana republic" originated with bananas grown in Jamaica and sold in the United States, it became associated with political regimes under the influence of multinational corporations. When corporate interests were threatened in Honduras by popular sentiment against foreign ownership, the American-owned United Fruit effected a coup d'état in the early twentieth century that was supported by the US government. With prices stabilized, consumption increased in the United States. In the late twentieth and early twenty-first centuries, consumption globally also increased in Eastern Europe but also in European Union (EU) countries, leading some to observe that the expansion violated EU trade agreements. A new kind of banana conflict seems to be brewing there.[27]

Silk, like cotton, can be turned to cloth, but its cultivation is entirely unique. It is formed by the larvae of insects undergoing a metamorphosis. Silk production originated in the Neolithic period in China and spread to India in approximately 140 CE. It is most famously associated with the so-called Silk Road that existed from the second century BCE to the eighteenth century CE. The Silk Road, a portion of which is now a World Heritage Site, linked Asia, the Middle East, Africa, and southern Europe. Like cloth made from long staple cotton, silk fabric was a luxury item and highly prized, leading to successful experiments to "grow" silk in the Middle East during the Byzantine period and in Italy in the eleventh and twelfth centuries. Silk might have played an important role in the Columbia Exchange, and it was certainly not for lack of trying that it did not.

The British monarch in the early seventeenth century, James I, promoted silk production in the colonies, but his subjects embraced rice and tobacco instead. There were sporadic and anemic further efforts to grow silk in the colonies in the eighteenth century, but it was only in the 1830s that an appreciable silk industry materialized in Connecticut, and then only briefly. China continues to lead in production of silk, with India a distant second. Although it is produced in villages on a small scale using traditional means, the silk industry has become much more "industrial" and been augmented by foreign investment in the twenty-first century.[28]

Key Transitions

Agricultural "development" is an ongoing process depending on environmental circumstances and the evolution of agricultural sciences, but there have been key transitions and watershed moments that stand apart from the ordinary adjustments that inevitably take place in agriculture. One of the most fundamental aspects of farming involves access to a sufficient water supply, and key transitions have occurred as early as the Neolithic period and as recent as the twentieth century's Green Revolution. They bookend the transformation that took place during the early modern Agricultural

Revolution. Indeed, hydro-agricultural development occurring in these distinct periods not only sustained existing agricultural practices but also allowed for a fundamental expansion of agricultural practices. In the Neolithic period, it was accompanied by a shift to more sedentary settlement patterns; in the early modern period, capitalism transformed feudal agricultural practices and, inspired by the profit motive, farmers replaced marshes and wetlands with productive farmland. In the twentieth century, with the Green Revolution, employing new technologies, farmers marshaled available water for use in agriculture. None of these innovations occurred without consequences. In the act of building dams, for example, environmental damage occurred, and people were displaced. Hydro-agricultural innovations required capital expenditures that increased public and private indebtedness in modern agricultural societies. Originally billed as a boon to agriculture and an important ally in the effort to feed an expanding revolution, the Green Revolution began to face scathing criticism. Vandana Shiva's *The Violence of the Green Revolution* recounts the devastating impact it has had in India.[29]

The Arab Agricultural Revolution, which occurred between the eighth and thirteenth centuries, included the introduction of the *sakai* (also known as *noria* or chain pumps) that provided for important innovations in irrigation practices. The pumps were powered either by animals or by moving water and, according to some scholars, helped propel an early "green revolution" that provided for a vast expansion of agriculture in the Middle East and an increase in the range of plants cultivated. Arab conquest of Spain and incursion into other regions introduced both new plants and different agricultural practices and thus played an important role in the region's agricultural revolution. The emergence of Arab scholars interested in understanding and promoting agriculture provided a key element, but so too did the collapse of the Roman Empire and the return of authority to Arab elites. Eager to expand agricultural production, these elites provided for greater access to landownership and promoted a renewed orientation to the market. Michael Decker, in fact, writes in "Plants and Progress" that it is time to rethink the benefits of this revolution.[30]

Although some scholars suggest 1000 CE as a watershed moment in wet-rice agriculture because it doubled the population in southern China, others suggest that insufficient data exist to confirm such a demographic revolution in that period. Instead, a key transition linked to wet-rice agriculture originated in 1127 with the defeat of the Northern Song state in China. Power shifted to the southern rice-growing region and led to the expansion of wet-rice agriculture in southern China and, later, the emergence and development of it in Japan. A vast expansion of wet-rice agriculture put China at the center of the expanding global economy in the Early Modern period and set Japan on a course of modernization. Some scholars describe what occurred as the "Song Agricultural Revolution" as it mimicked, in some respects, what occurred during the eighteenth-century British Agricultural Revolution. It led to urbanization and industrialization as well as important agricultural programs created by the state. Changes to the landscape were facilitated by vast irrigation and land reclamation projects and further augmented by government distribution of preferred rice seed varieties. Although intensive cultivation of wet-rice rice did not begin in Japan until around 1600, it fueled an equally impressive transformation that, for the most part, resembled what occurred in southern China.[31]

The Atlantic plantation emerged in the sixteenth century along the global expansion of European interests. Most of the literature focuses on the British role in the Caribbean and in the southeastern segment of the British colonies in North America, but the phenomenon is also associated with the Ulster Province in Northern Ireland. As Britain began its global expansion in the Age of Discovery, it planted settler colonists who soon became engaged in monocrop agriculture for export to a global marketplace. Not all British colonists created slave plantation societies, and not all slave plantation societies were founded by the British. The French, the Spanish, and the Danes also contributed to the Atlantic plantation complex. Whether growing tobacco in Virginia or sugar in St. Croix, the cultivation and export of such crops fueled the global economy. It laid the foundation for slave-based agriculture in the Western Hemisphere and propelled the Industrial Revolution in Britain, especially after the emergence of cotton plantations in the early nineteenth century in the US South. Plantation societies themselves, however, remained relatively anemic in terms of other economic enterprises, which resulted in inequalities of wealth and a marked delay in modernization.[32]

The environmental impact of plantation agriculture has been substantial. The Atlantic plantation involved costly practices such as deforestation, drainage of wetlands, elimination of biodiversity, and soil exhaustion and erosion. The drive to reap profits from New World colonies led to intensive cultivation, monocrop agriculture, the use of enslaved people and other forms of unfree labor, and the concentration of land ownership, all of which enriched a few individuals and left colonial regions environmentally damaged and underdeveloped. Even before the relatively new field of environmental history arose and inspired a new generation of scholars, historians of the US South recognized the impact of intensive cultivation of tobacco in colonial Virginia and the soil-depleting qualities of cotton plantations in the southern interior. Indeed, it has long been acknowledged that soil depletion played a role in the need for plantations to expand westward and led to the conflict over slavery that resulted in the Civil War. Until recently, much of the scholarship on the coming of the war focused on the political and economic crisis that roiled the nation. New studies—like that of Erin Stewart Mauldin in *Unredeemed Land*—probe the environmental angle while still centering the role of slavery and westward expansion as crucial factors in a new agro-environmental understanding of a devastating conflict that resulted in one undeniably positive development: the elimination of slavery.[33]

The British Agricultural Revolution occurred between the mid-seventeenth century and the late nineteenth century. Although there is some disagreement as to the dates and some historians question whether an agricultural revolution happened at all, a number of innovations took place that warrant attention. Indeed, the eighteenth century witnessed advances along several lines in Britain. The so-called Rotherham Plough was patented in 1730, and a threshing machine patent was issued in 1788. These inventions augmented improvements in farming, such as the introduction of the four-year crop rotation system in 1730, a system that restores and maintains soil fertility, avoids infestations of pests that are attracted to certain plants but not others, and results in an overall increase in productivity. Although crop rotation dates back to the Roman era, it had been unevenly employed in Britain because of the open field system. But with the Land Enclosure Act of 1773, the open field system was virtually eliminated, and though its elimination created social and economic stresses, it made improvements possible in animal husbandry and the adoption of the four-year-crop rotation more widely. The founding of agricultural societies that sponsored annual events—an early knowledge network—promoted and showcased best practices in farming to wider audiences. Regardless of whether a true revolution in agriculture occurred in Britain in this period, farm output and Britain's population increased significantly.[34]

Exploitation of a new frontier in agriculture dating to the late nineteenth century was made possible by the breadth of new machinery brought into use, a growing reliance on fertilizers that increased production, and the willingness of nation states to promote expansion of agriculture. Frontier agriculture developed globally, particularly in Russia, the United States, Canada, Argentina, and Australia. Indeed, these innovations made it possible for these countries to become the breadbaskets of the world. Crucial to their success was not only the fact that they possessed abundant grasslands but also that they were given a boost by a growing demand for wheat created by industrial development and the corresponding growth of urban centers. The making of these five breadbaskets differed in tempo and timing and did not occur without problems, but the growth of government sponsored programs typically—but not always—contributed to their success.[35]

Beginning in the late nineteenth century, several European countries claimed colonial possessions in Africa and began to promote agricultural development on the African continent to serve their own interests. Their efforts undermined traditional farming practices and led to agricultural contention in colonial Africa. In fact, agriculture had a long history in Africa, dating to approximately 5200 BCE. In spite of the disruption of the slave trade, Africa remained a pastoral and small-scale agricultural society (with a few exceptions). Between the late nineteenth century and the 1970s, Africa faced new challenges as European countries—Britain, Belgium, Germany, and France—that had laid claim to parts of Africa to profit from Africa's mining and agricultural potential. In introducing new cash crops like cotton, coffee, and cocoa, they drew on precious water resources, disrupted traditional farming practices, and engaged in forced labor. Dismissive of small-scale and subsistence farming, the "colonial masters" characterized their attempts as bringing more efficient and modern agriculture to Africa. They employed agricultural scientists and promoted agricultural education, but the attempts to reshape agriculture in Africa led to contestations and, increasingly, negotiations between African farmers and colonial representatives.[36]

In 1970, Norman Borlaug received the Nobel Peace Prize for his work in promoting a Green Revolution, one that involved marshaling all the forces of modern agriculture into play in order to promote the advancement of agricultural practices around the globe. This so-called revolution was founded in part on the view that agricultural production levels were insufficient given predictions of a vast expansion of the world's population. Fearing widespread famine in the face of this projected demographic disaster, proponents of the Green Revolution worked in concert with the Ford Foundation and Rockefeller Foundation to promote scientific agricultural methods, such as mechanization and the use of synthetic fertilizers and pesticides. Although lauded by many as achieving many of its goals and saving billions from starvation, the Green Revolution has its critics, and many Indigenous farming practitioners resisted all or parts of the program. Many small farmers objected to hybridized seeds and the use of expensive chemicals that would raise their cost of production and violate traditional practices. The so-called revolution remains contested and controversial.[37]

Famine is often a function of crop failure resulting from a variety of causes including weather conditions or swarms of locusts, and it mattered little whether agriculturalists were subsistence farmers or producing exclusively for the market. According to archeological evidence, the more reliant a society was upon agriculture, the more vulnerable it was to famine if crops failed. In other words, agriculture made possible a vast increase in population but was accompanied by the elimination of habitats and animal species that supported hunting and gathering. With the emergence of global capitalism in the eighteenth and nineteenth centuries, in fact, famines increased in frequency and severity, but new approaches to famines in the twentieth century have been successful in reducing both the number and ferocity of them. The work of humanitarian organizations and modern methods of supplying nutritional foods to famine sufferers have made the difference.[38]

The destruction of forest habitats was one factor in the elimination of alternative food supplies when famines occurred. Forest Transition Theory not only provides a convenient way to analyze the rise and fall—and rise again—of forests, but also serves as a way to observe the role and function of forests in agriculture. From the earliest days of agriculture, Indigenous forests provided important groundcover that provided nutrients to the soil. When farmers expanded into these forests, they had high-quality soil at their disposal. However, under certain circumstances, forests no longer enrich the soil in ways that serve agriculture. Forest Transition Theory has utility in providing a blueprint for what to expect as subsistence farmers transition to capitalist agriculture. The enticements of the market encourage deforestation and the cultivation of the cut-over land, but as economic development increases, a tendency arises on the part of rural dwellers in this setting to move to urban areas and sell out to larger operations. The final stage arises when tree farmers—usually large commercial operations—replace the Indigenous forests with fast-growing varieties that feed the market for lumber for building or other purposes. These new forests typically do not re-enrich the soil, and they are virtually always of single species. Serious ecological and environmental consequences can occur at every stage of deforestation, and the single-species tree farms often reduce Indigenous varieties that are more sustainable. Forest Transition Theory is likely to find applications in the era of climate change and the Anthropocene.[39]

In the twenty-first century, the warming climate has disrupted farming across the globe and required adaptation by agriculturalists, but just how far-reaching these changes will be remains speculative. Historians can draw examples of what might happen based on the Little Ice Age that occurred between the fourteenth and nineteenth centuries when mountain glaciers expanded. Average temperatures fell by only 0.6 degrees Celsius, but the drop led to crop failures and famines in Europe, and agriculturalists worldwide had to adjust to different crops as growing seasons shortened. Anthropologist Brian Fagan's *The Little Ice Age: How Climate Made History, 1300–1850* demonstrates the consequences of even slight changes in global temperature. Instead of a cooling earth that led to a drop in temperatures, the earth has warmed by more than 1.1 degrees Celsius since 1975, and glaciers are melting at alarming rates. Farmers have innovated and adapted to changes for thousands of years, but they are facing an unprecedented challenge that will test their ability to adjust.[40]

Notes

[*] The editor would like to thank Michitake Aso and Frank Uekötter for their invaluable assistance in thinking through the organization of a volume on agricultural history.
1. George R. Milner, "Early Agriculture's Toll on Human Health," *Proceedings of the National Academy of Sciences* 116, no. 28 (2019): 13721–13723, https://doi.org/10.1073/pnas.1908960116.
2. V. Gordon Childe, *Man Makes Himself* (New York: Oxford University Press, 1939).
3. Ian Kuijt, ed., *Life in Neolithic Farming Communities: Social Organization, Identity, and Differentiation* (New York: Kluwar Academic/Plenum Publishers, 2006).
4. Alfred W. Crosby, *The Columbian Exchange: Biological and Cultural Consequences of 1492* (Westport, CT: Greenwood, 1972); Philip D. Curtin, *The Rise and Fall of the Plantation Complex: Essays in Atlantic History* (New York: Cambridge University Press, 1990); Trevor Burnard and John Garrigus, *The Plantation Machine: Atlantic Capitalism in French Saint Domingue and British Jamaica* (Philadelphia: University of Pennsylvania Press, 2016)
5. Mark B. Tauger, *Agriculture in World History* (London: Routledge, 2011); Marcel Mazoyer and Laurence Roudart, *A History of World Agriculture from the Neolithic Age to the Current Crisis* (New York: Monthly Review Press, 2006); A. M. Mannion, *Agriculture and Environmental Change: Temporal and Spatial Dimensions* (Chichester: John Wiley & Sons, 1995); Robert Mendelsohn and Ariel Dinar, *Climate Change and Agriculture: An Economic Analysis of Global Impacts, Adaptation and Distributional Effects* (New Haven, CT: Yale University Press, 2009); and Jason Clay, *World Agriculture and the Environment: A Commodity-by-Commodity Guide to Impacts and Practices* (Washington, DC: Island Press, 2004).
6. Paul J. Crutzen and Eugene F. Stoermer, "The 'Anthropocene,'" *The International Geosphere–Biosphere Programme (IGBP) Global Change Newsletter* 41 (2000): 17–18; John Robert McNeill and Peter Engelke, *The Great Acceleration: An Environmental History of the Anthropocene since 1945* (Cambridge, MA: Belknap Press of Harvard University Press, 2014); and Julia Adeney Thomas, Mark Williams, and Jan Zalasiewicz, *The Anthropocene: A Multidisciplinary Approach* (Cambridge: Polity Press, 2020).
7. Frank Uekötter, *Die Wahrheit ist auf dem Feld: Eine Wissensgeschichte der deutschen Landwirtschaft* (Göttingen: Vandenhoeck & Ruprecht, 2010); Makyke Kagg and Annelies Zoomers, eds., *The Global Land Grab: Beyond the Hype* (London: Zed Books, 2014); and Stefano Liberti, *Land Grabbing: Journeys in the New Colonialism* (London: Verso, 2013).

8. David R. Montgomery, *Growing a Revolution: Bringing Our Soil Back to Life* (New York: W. W. Norton, 2017); Laurie Drinkwater, M. Schipanski, S. S. Snapp, and L. E. Jackson, "Ecologically Based Nutrient Management," in *Agricultural Systems: Agroecology and Rural Innovation for Development*, ed. Siglinde Snapp and Barry Pound (Amsterdam: Academic Press, 2017): 203–257; and Vaclav Smil, *Enriching the Earth: Fritz Haber, Carl Bosch, and the Transformation of World Food Production* (Cambridge, MA: MIT Press, 2000).

9. Mauro Ambrosoli, *The Wild and the Sown: Botany and Agriculture in Western Europe, 1350–1800* (Cambridge: Cambridge University Press, 1997); and Helen Curry, "Breeding Uniformity and Banking Diversity: The Genescapes of Industrial Agriculture, 1935–1970," *Global Environment* 10, no. 1 (April 2017).

10. Alex Blanchette, *Porkopolis: American Animality, Standardized Life, & the Factory Farm* (Durham, NC: Duke University Press, 2020); and Claire Strom, *Making Catfish Bait out of Government Boys: The Fight Against Cattle Ticks and the Transformation of the Yeoman South* (Athens: University of Georgia Press, 2009).

11. J. R. McNeill, *Mosquito Empire: Mosquito Empire: Ecology and War in the Greater Caribbean, 1620–1914* (Cambridge: Cambridge University Press, 2010); Jeffrey A. Lockwood, *Locust: The Devastating Rise and Mysterious Disappearance of the Insect That Shaped the American Frontier* (New York: Basic Books, 2004); and Martha Few, "Killing Locusts in Colonial Guatemala," in *Centering Animals in Latin American History*, ed. Martha Few and Zeb Tortorici (Durham, NC: Duke University Press, 2015): 62–92.

12. Jonathan Rigg, *More than Rural: Textures of Thailand's Agrarian Transformation* (Honolulu: Hawai'i University Press, 2019).

13. David Moon, *The Russian Peasantry, 1600–1930: The World the Peasants Made* (New York: Taylor & Francis, 1999); Eric Wolf, *Europe and the People without History* (Berkeley: University of California Press, 1982); and Steven Striffler, *In the Shadows of State and Capital: United Fruit, Popular Struggle, and Agrarian Restructuring in Ecuador, 1900–1995* (Durham, NC: Duke University Press, 2002).

14. Linda M. Ambrose and Joan M. Jenson, *Women in Agriculture: Professionalizing Rural Life in North American and Europe, 1880–1965* (Iowa City: University of Iowa Press, 2017); Katherine Jellison, *Entitled to Power: Farm Women and Technology, 1913–1963* (Chapel Hill: University of North Carolina Press, 1993); Pamela Riney-Kehrberg, *Rooted in Dust: Surviving Drought and Depression in Southwestern Kansas* (Lawrence: University Press of Kansas, 1994); and Riney-Kehrberg, *When a Dream Dies: Agriculture, Iowa, and the Farm Crisis of the 1980s* (Lawrence: University Press of Kansas, 2022).

15. Mark Overton, *Agricultural Revolution in England: The Transformation of the Agrarian Economy, 1500–1850* (New York: Cambridge University Press, 1996); R. Douglas Hurt, *American Farm Tools: From Hand-Power to Steam-Power* (Manhattan, KS: Sunflower University Press, 1982); and Daniel P. Ott, *Harvesting History: McCormick's Reaper, Heritage and Historical Forgery* (Lincoln: University of Nebraska Press, 2023).

16. McNeill and Engelke, *The Great Acceleration*; Joe Anderson, *Capitalist Pigs: Pigs, Pork, and Power in America* (Morgantown: West Virginia University Press, 2019); and Paul Brassley, Michael Winter, Matt Lobley, and David Harvey, *The Real Agricultural Revolution: The Transformation of English Farming, 1939–1985* (Woodbridge: Boydell Press, 2021).

17. Yves Segers and Leen Van Molle, eds., *Agricultural Knowledge Networks in Rural Europe, 1700–2000* (Woodbridge: Boydell Press, 2022); Deborah Fitzgerald, *Every Farm a Factory: The Industrial Ideal in American Agriculture* (New Haven, CT: Yale University Press,

2003); and Margaret Rossiter, *The Emergence of Agricultural Science, Justus Liebig and the Americans, 1840–1880* (New Haven, CT: Yale University Press, 1975)

18. Ulbe Bosma, *The Making of a Periphery: How Island Southeast Asia Became a Mass Exporter of Labor* (New York: Columbia University Press, 2019); and Eric Vanhaute, "Agriculture," in *Handbook Global History of Work*, ed. Karen Hofmeester and Marcel Van der Linden (Munich: De Gruyter Oldenbourg): 217–235.

19. V. Meier, "Cut-Flower Production in Columbia—A Major Development Success Story for Women?" *Environment and Planning A: Economy and Space* 31, no. 2 (1999): 273–289. https://doi.org/10.1068/a310273 (accessed August 30, 2023); and Keven Watkins, "Deadly Blooms: Columbia's Flower Industry is Based on the Exploitation of Women Workers," *The Guardian*, reposted by International Labor Rights Forum, August 29, 2001, https://laborrights.org/in-the-news/deadly-blooms-colombias-flower-industry-based-exploitation-women-workers-0 (accessed August 30, 2023).

20. Michitake Aso, *Rubber and the Making of Vietnam: An Ecological History, 1897–1975* (Chapel Hill: University of North Carolina Press, 2018).

21. Crosby, *The Columbian Exchange*; Douglas J. Kennett et al., "Early Isotopic Evidence for Maize as a Staple Grain in the Americas," *Science Advances* 6, no. 23 (2020).

22. Nathan Nunn and Nancy Qian, "The Columbian Exchange: A History of Disease, Food, and Ideas," *Journal of Economic Perspectives* 24, no. 2 (Spring 2010): 163–188; and Francesca Bray, Peter A. Coclanis, Edda L. Fields-Black, and Dagmar Schäfer, eds., *Rice: Global Networks and New Histories* (New York: Cambridge University Press, 2015).

23. Melissa Morris, "Cultivating Colonies: Tobacco and Upstart Empires, 1580–1640" (PhD diss., Columbia University, 2017); and Drew Swanson, *The Golden Weed: Tobacco and Environment in the Piedmont South* (New Haven, CT: Yale University Press, 2008).

24. Stuart McCook, *Coffee Is Not Forever: A Global History of the Coffee Rust* (Columbus: Ohio University Press, 2019); and Lynn Hollen Lees, *Planting Empire, Cultivating Subjects: British Malaya 1786–1941* (Cambridge: Cambridge University Press, 2017).

25. Jonathan Robins, *Cotton and Race across the Atlantic: Britain, Africa, and America, 1900–1920* (Rochester, NY: University of Rochester Press, 2016); Pete Daniel, *Breaking the Land: The Transformation of Cotton, Tobacco, and Rice Cultures since 1880* (Urbana: University of Illinois Press, 1985); and Sven Beckert, *Empire of Cotton: A Global History* (New York: Alfred A. Knopf, 2014).

26. E. Langthaler, "The Soy Paradox: The Western Nutrition Transition Revisited, 1950–2010," *Global Environment. A Journal of Transdisciplinary History* 11 (2018): 79–104; and Pablo Lapegna, *Soybeans and Power: Genetically Modified Crops, Environmental Politics and Social movements in Argentina* (New York: Oxford University Press, 2016).

27. John Soluri, *Banana Cultures: Agriculture, Consumption, and Environmental Change in Honduras and the United States* (Austin: University of Texas Press, 2005).

28. Lisa Onaga, "More than Metamorphosis: The Silkworm Experiments of Toyama Kametarō and His Cultivation of Genetic Thought in Japan's Sericultural Practices, 1894–1918," in *New Perspectives on the History of Life Sciences and Agriculture*, ed. Denise Phillips and Sharon Kingsland, Archimedes 40 (Cham: Springer International Publishing, 2015), 415–437; and Ben Marsh, *Unravelled Dreams: Silk and the Atlantic World, 1500–1840* (Cambridge: Cambridge University Press, 2020).

29. Vandana Shiva, *The Violence of the Green Revolution: Third World Agriculture, Ecology and Politics* (Lexington: University Press of Kentucky, 2016); Christopher L. Pastore, *Between Land and Sea: The Atlantic Coast and the Transformation of New England* (Cambridge,

MA: Harvard University Press, 2014); and Donald Worster, *Rivers of Empire: Water, Aridity, and the Growth of the American West* (New York: Pantheon, 1985).
30. Michael Decker, "Plants and Progress: Rethinking the Islamic Agricultural Revolution," *Journal of World History* 20, no. 2 (2009): 187–206; and Andrew M. Watson, "The Arab Agricultural Revolution and Its Diffusion, 700–1100," *Journal of Economic History* 34, no. 1 (1974): 8–35.
31. Bray et al., *Rice*; and David Biggs, *Quagmire: Nation-Building and Nature in the Mekong Delta* (Seattle: University of Washington Press, 2011).
32. Burnard and Garrigus, *The Plantation Machine*; and Richard S. Dunn, *A Tale of Two Plantations: Slave Labor in Jamaica and Virginia* (Cambridge, MA: Harvard University Press, 2014).
33. Frank Uekötter, *Apples, Oranges, and Cotton: Environmental Histories of the Global Plantation* (Frankfurt: Campus Verlag, 2014); Jeannie Whayne, "The Power of the Plantation Model of Development: The Sunk Lands Controversy," *Forest and Conservation History* 37 (April 1993): 56–67; and Erin Stewart Mauldin, *Unredeemed Land: An Environmental History of Civil War and Emancipation in the Cotton South* (New York: Oxford University Press, 2018).
34. Overton, *Agricultural Revolution in England*; Robert C. Allen, *Enclosure and the Yeomen: The Agricultural Development of the South Midlands, 1450–1850* (Oxford: Clarendon Press, 1992); and J. V. Beckett, *The Agricultural Revolution* (Oxford: Basil Blackwell, 1990).
35. Jeremy Adelman, *Frontier Development: Land, Labor, and Capital in the Wheat Lands of Argentina and Canada, 1890–1914* (Oxford: Clarendon Press, 1994).
36. Cassandra Mark-Thiesen, *Mediators, Contract Men, and Colonial Capital: Mechanized Gold Mining in the Gold Coast Colony, 1879–1909* (Rochester, NY: University of Rochester Press, 2018).
37. Mark Tauger, "Pavel Pateleimonovich Luk'ianenko and the Origins of the Soviet Green Revolution," in *The Lysenko Controversy as a Global Phenomenon, Vol. 1: Genetics and Agriculture in the Soviet Union and Beyond*, ed. William deJong-Lambert and Nikolai Krementsov (Cham: Palgrave, 2017): 97–127; and Nick Cullather, *The Hungry World: America's Cold War Battle Against Poverty in Asia* (Cambridge, MA: Harvard University Press, 2010).
38. Jenny Leigh Smith, "The Awkward Years: Defining and Managing famines, 1944–1947," *History and Technology* 31, no. 3 (2015): 206–219.
39. Brett M. Bennett, *Plantations and Protected Areas: A Global History of Forest Management* (Cambridge, MA: MIT Press, 2015); and Gregory Barton, *Empire Forestry and the Origins of Environmentalism* (Cambridge: Cambridge University Press, 2002).
40. Brian M. Fagan, *The Little Ice Age: How Climate Made History, 1300–1850* (New York: Basic Books, 2000)

Bibliography

Adelman, Jeremy Adelman. *Frontier Development: Land, Labor, and Capital in the Wheat Lands of Argentina and Canada, 1890–1914*. Oxford: Clarendon Press, 1994.
Ambrose, Linda M., and Joan M. Jenson. *Women in Agriculture: Professionalizing Rural Life in North America and Europe, 1880–1965*. Iowa City: University of Iowa Press, 2017.

Barton, Gregory. *Empire Forestry and the Origins of Environmentalism*. Cambridge: Cambridge University Press, 2002.

Beckert, Sven. *Empire of Cotton: A Global History*. New York: Alfred A. Knopf, 2014.

Bennett, Brett M. *Plantations and Protected Areas: A Global History of Forest Management*. Cambridge, MA: MIT Press, 2015.

Bosma, Ulbe. *The Making of a Periphery: How Island Southeast Asia Became a Mass Exporter of Labor*. New York: Columbia University Press, 2019.

Brassley, Paul, Michael Winter, Matt Lobley, and David Harvey. *The Real Agricultural Revolution: The Transformation of English Farming, 1939–1985*. Woodbridge, UK: Boydell Press, 2021.

Bray, Francesca, Peter A. Coclanis, Edda L. Fields-Black, and Dagmar Schäfer, eds. *Rice: Global Networks and New Histories*. New York: Cambridge University Press, 2015.

Burnard, Trevor, and John Garrigus. *The Plantation Machine: Atlantic Capitalism in French Saint Domingue and British* Jamaica. Philadelphia: University of Pennsylvania Press, 2016.

Crosby, Alfred W. *The Columbian Exchange: Biological and Cultural Consequences of 1492*. Westport, CT: Greenwood, 1972.

Fitzgerald, Deborah. *Every Farm a Factory: The Industrial Ideal in American Agriculture*. New Haven, CT: Yale University Press, 2003.

Kuijt, Ian, ed. *Life in Neolithic Farming Communities: Social Organization, Identity, and Differentiation*. New York: Kluwer Academic/Plenum Publishers, 2006.

Langthaler, E. "The Soy Paradox: The Western Nutrition Transition Revisited, 1950–2010." *Global Environment. A Journal of Transdisciplinary History* 11 (2018): 79–104.

Liberti, Stefano. *Land Grabbing: Journeys in the New Colonialism*. London: Verso, 2013.Mark-Thiesen, Cassandra. *Mediators, Contract Men, and Colonial Capital: Mechanized Gold Mining in the Gold Coast Colony, 1879–1909*. Rochester, NY: University of Rochester Press, 2018.

Marsh, Ben. *Unraveled Dreams: Silk and the Atlantic World, 1500–1840*. Cambridge: Cambridge University Press, 2020.

Mauldin, Erin Stewart. *Unredeemed Land: An Environmental History of Civil War and Emancipation in the Cotton South*. New York: Oxford University Press, 2018.

Mazoyer, Marcel, and Laurence Roudart. *A History of World Agriculture from the Neolithic Age to the Current Crisis*. New York: Monthly Review Press, 2006.

McCook, Stuart. *Coffee Is Not Forever: A Global History of the Coffee Rust*. Columbus: Ohio University Press, 2019.

McNeill, John Robert, and Peter Engelke. *The Great Acceleration: An Environmental History of the Anthropocene since 1945*. Cambridge, MA: Belknap Press of Harvard University Press, 2014.

Montgomery, David R. *Growing a Revolution: Bringing Our Soil Back to Life*. New York: Norton, 2017.

Pastore, Christopher L. *Between Land and Sea: The Atlantic Coast and the Transformation of New England*. Cambridge, MA: Harvard University Press, 2014.

Robins, Jonathan. *Cotton and Race across the Atlantic: Britain, Africa, and America, 1900–1920*. Rochester, NY: University of Rochester Press, 2016.

Shiva, Vandana. *The Violence of the Green Revolution: Third World Agriculture, Ecology and Politics*. Lexington: University Press of Kentucky, 2016.

Soluri, John. *Banana Cultures: Agriculture, Consumption, and Environmental Change in Honduras and the United States*. Austin: University of Texas Press, 2005.

Swanson, Drew. *The Golden Weed: Tobacco and Environment in the Piedmont South*. New Haven, CT: Yale University Press, 2008.

Tauger, Mark B. *Agriculture in World History*. London: Routledge, 2011.
Uekötter, Frank. *Apples, Oranges, and Cotton: Environmental Histories of the Global Plantation*. Frankfurt: Campus Verlag, 2014.
Wolf, Eric. *Europe and the People without History*. Berkeley: University of California Press, 1982.
Worster, Donald. *Rivers of Empire: Water, Aridity, and the Growth of the American West*. New York: Pantheon, 1985.

PART I
TIMELESS ESSENTIALS

CHAPTER 1

MAKING SENSE OF LAND

FRANK UEKÖTTER

"Buy land, they're not making it anymore"

—Mark Twain.[1]

INVESTMENT advice is often camouflage for a more complicated reality, and Twain's quip here was no exception. From an agricultural standpoint, the lands of the world were nothing if not extremely diverse. Topography mattered tremendously, as land values differed greatly depending on whether land was flat or hilly, close to sea levels or up in the mountains, or prone to hazards like flash floods. Soils varied enormously in terms of porosity, humidity, chemical composition, and the availability of plant nutrients, all of which mattered for agriculture. The geographic setting was equally significant, particularly if farmers sought to produce for markets. Beyond the material, societies developed complex webs of codes and routines that determined terms of use and transfer. Living in a capitalist society, Twain took for granted that buying land was a legitimate transaction, but that was anything but a given in world history. Furthermore, few of these things were static: cultural conventions changed, and so did land under the till, as soils could deplete or erode. Land may well be the world's most complicated natural resource.

In light of this complexity, it is useful to explore the history of agricultural lands through examining transnational trends. For all their diversity, we can identify some general patterns in the development of lands in modern history. They were subject to scientific research that sought to decode the mystery of soil fertility, and they were categorized and registered with government agencies. Lands reflected power relations in rural societies; they were bought, sold, and leased prolifically; they were subject to land reforms, both enacted and imagined. They were also potential carriers of diseases and often subject to use of unprecedented intensity while expert groups claimed distinct bodies of knowledge about soil nutrients or erosion risks. Land was shaped by a number of synchronous and overlapping trends, and a reasonable estimate of a land's value, commercial and other, requires attention to location, natural features, agricultural uses, cultural conventions, political contexts, and the vested interests of academic professions. Understanding land also requires a healthy distrust toward the modern infatuation with numbers.

Know Your Land

For most of human history, farmers have used fertile soils without a clear understanding of soil fertility. Throughout the ages, farmers cherished rituals and goddesses that revolved around plentiful harvests, but for those who did not want to leave it at religion and sought cognitive certainty in the absence of knowledge about atoms, molecules, and bacteria, all that was left was close observation. Scrutiny and experiments run through the history of agriculture, and today's laboratories and greenhouses are only the latest variations of a quest that is as old as the Neolithic Revolution. Through trial and error, farmers learned early on that adding water at certain times helped, that decomposing organic matter brought better harvests, and that plants grew best if the soil had a certain crumbling texture. It paid to watch fields and pastures closely and to learn from experience, but the deficiencies of cognitive and technological means implied significant limits for improvements. Premodern farmers would surely be amazed by the dramatic increases in productivity per acre that modern science and technology allowed, though it bears recognition that maximizing output was not always the top priority among farmers. Subsistence economies usually aimed for stable yields that were resilient to the vagaries of environmental conditions.

Traditional soil knowledge was bound to a specific place. In fact, the primary focus was often on the inherent diversity of one's possessions and not on how these possessions compared with others'. Premodern peasants, who were often unable to swap fields due to the constraints of feudal societies, gained the most when they learned about the growth potential of individual parcels of land. Extrapolating observations from specific fields was always fraught with uncertainties, and the unknowns inevitably grew with distance. This was a particular challenge in settler societies, where people struggled to make good use of previous experiences in places with different soils and climates. It sometimes helped to watch existing vegetation, though appearances could be deceiving. Tropical soils looked abundant in light of plant growth, and it took research from British pedologists and agriculturalists in the 1920s and 1930s to show that soils in much of tropical Africa were actually rather poor.[2] Colonialist tropes did not provide reliable guidance either. Diana Davis has noted for northern Africa that European agriculturalists showed "a poor understanding of arid-land ecosystems" because they were in thrall with the mythical "granary of Rome."[3]

For many settlers, the primary method of acquiring knowledge about new lands was trial and error. "The trend was to abandon land when it was considered 'tired,'" Reinaldo Funes Monzote wrote on sugar cane cultivation in Cuba.[4] Stuart McCook observed the same pattern on Brazilian plantations: "Once coffee yields had declined to the point where cultivation was no longer viable, Brazilian planters simply abandoned the exhausted plantations and moved on to establish new plantations in recently cleared areas."[5] To be sure, abandoned fields were not necessarily devastated and unfit for future agricultural use. They may have produced yields below expectations because they lacked some nutrients or because soil conditions did not match the settlers' preferred commodities, or they moved for reasons having little to do with the quality of the soil. James Belich has remarked on Virginia that "people emigrated at the same rate from good farmland as from exhausted tobacco land."[6] Either way, moving on was enticingly simple as long as land was abundant, and farmers were under no obligation to have afterthoughts. As a result, thriving agricultural regions could decline within a generation. On the Bay Islands off the coast of Honduras, an early center of banana production, it took less than twenty years to move from boom to crash.[7]

Careless land use came to an end when land in production grew and space came to look limited. Monzote found for Cuba "that beginning in the mid-nineteenth century the so-called exhaustion of land began to be the main reason for alarm."[8] However, advancing from concerns to action was a different matter, all the more as reliable knowledge was often hard to come by. In the United States, this became evident in the arid regions of the Great Plains when Hardy Webster Campbell developed a dry farming method that preserved moisture in the soil. Campbell went on speaking tours beginning in 1895 and promoted his method as the panacea for arid lands on the Great Plains, and although more than thirty years had passed since the creation of the US Department of Agriculture, authorities stood on the sidelines because they were unable to confirm or disprove the method. Railroads, banks, and other commercial interests stepped into the void and helped Campbell to spread his gospel because it promised to boost frontier agriculture.[9]

By 1900, scientific knowledge concerning the chemical dimensions of soil fertility was the most advanced. It was understood that plant growth hinged on certain nutrients. Nitrogen, potash, and phosphorus were the most important ones, but plants needed a range of other nutrients as well, and growth hinged on the least plentiful one: according to the Law of the Minimum, the scarcest resource was the limiting factor, as plants could not grow even if all other resources were present in abundance. The Law of the Minimum is commonly attributed to Justus von Liebig, but his contribution was not so much about discovery than about popularization, as Liebig drew strongly on previous work by Carl Sprengel. The nutrient theory of plant nutrition is best seen as an outgrowth of a seminal intellectual gestation period in early nineteenth-century chemistry.[10]

Throughout the nineteenth century, agrochemistry was much better at clarifying the fundamentals of plant nutrition than at providing specific advice for farmers. By itself, the Law of the Minimum said nothing about recommended doses, timing, or solubility, and agrochemists lacked the cognitive skills to offer exact recommendations. The vagaries of expert advice became obvious when Liebig developed and marketed a patent manure in the 1840s: it was a fiasco because it lacked nitrogen (Liebig initially thought that plants could obtain it from the air) and because the compound did not dissolve. Liebig's fertilizer "remained on the surface like a glass dressing," and the affair showed, in the judgment of his biographer, that "agricultural science was a good deal more complicated than Liebig had initially thought."[11]

Experimentation reduced the unknowns over time, and over the course of the twentieth century, soil testing methodology improved to a point where farmers could gain a rough understanding of the concentration of nutrients in their fields. Recent precision farming methods use high-tech solutions to analyze nutrition needs in real time and thus help to rediscover the real complexity of fields after a century of industrial methods that perceived them as homogeneous. However, chemical approaches were open to criticism because they were more or less oblivious of the biological and physical dimension of soil fertility. One of the critics was Albert Howard, who rallied against what he called the "NPK mentality" while compiling and studying compost heaps at the Institute of Plant Industry in Indore, India: "to-day the majority of farmers and market gardeners base their manurial programme on the cheapest forms of nitrogen (N), phosphorus (P), and potassium (K) on the market."[12] Howard was one of several enterprising spirits who sought to move beyond narrow agrochemical approaches in the twentieth century, and the net result of this quest was the organic farming movement. Today's alternative farmers stress their concern for healthy food and animal welfare, not least due to the predilections of urban consumers, but their historical origins lie in a transnational concern for the living soil.[13]

Agrochemistry remains the dominant paradigm for soil fertility worldwide, and only a minority of farmers refrain from mineral fertilizer on principles. Nonetheless, chemical approaches retain practical and cognitive ambiguities. Nutrients can wash away before roots pick them up, which has led to severe pollution problems and changes in the global nitrogen cycle.[14] To a significant extent, the hegemony of agrochemical approaches rests in its ability to guide farming practice in spite of cognitive simplifications, or perhaps because of it.[15] Scientific studies of soil microbiology often end in cataclysmic complications, as the inherent complexity of the living soil tends to defy scientific modeling and predictions. Ecologists have described soils as "the poor man's tropical rainforest" since a single spoon of earth holds a biological diversity on a par with Amazonia, and researchers continue to wrestle with the biological dynamism of soils.[16]

Own Your Land

Agriculture hinges on a certain idea of land ownership. Farmers would never go through the hassle of sowing, weeding, and tilling without a sense that, come harvest time, they are entitled to a share of what had grown. However, this sense of entitlement could take many different forms. The modern concept of property, with solitary owners and written titles of consistent nature on file at a government clearinghouse, is rather exceptional in world history. Many entitlements were unwritten and defined through human practices rather than formal rules, and claims often focused on use of the land rather than possession. In the place of one single authority that could use land as it pleased, multiple overlapping claims formed a disperse set of uses and users that could imply all sorts of tensions and contradictions. Overcoming this patchwork and simplifying ownership structures was a crucial step in the development of modern agriculture. As Jürgen Osterhammel wrote, "No state is 'modern' without a land registry and the legal right to dispose freely of real estate."[17]

Land titles were built on the Western tradition of written titles that people could invoke in an independent court of law irrespective of social status. They also drew on the modern faith in individual initiative: the idea was that farmers would make better use of their land if they were in full control. As the British agricultural reformer Arthur Young famously declared, "The magic of property turns sand to gold."[18] Collective ownership was invariably seen as wasteful and inefficient, and European governments sought to disband commons around 1800 in the quest for agricultural modernization.[19] The effort continued in the colonies: one of the first steps of French colonial rule in Morocco was to place all collective land in the public domain.[20] A distrust of collective use ran through the history of Western capitalism long before Garrett Hardin penned his article on "tragedy of the commons."[21] More recently, Elinor Ostrom suggested a more nuanced reading when she pointed out that commons could be sustainable and remarkably efficient with the right set of institutions.[22]

Land titles also hinged on the sovereignty of the modern territorial state. It is no coincidence that land registries are government institutions, as the credibility of written titles was built on state authorities who backed the claims and had the power to evict unlawful occupants. "Property and law are born together, and die together," Jeremy Bentham wrote on the interdependence of capitalist individualism and modern statehood.[23] However, states could also pursue their own fiscal interests when they surveyed land holdings within their realms. William the Conqueror commissioned the Domesday Book of 1086, the first comprehensive survey of landed wealth in medieval Europe, as an assessment of the resource base of his rule in England.[24] When Japan colonized Korea, it conducted a full cadastral survey and declared upon conclusion of the effort in 1918 that all unregistered land would henceforth belong to the colonial authorities.[25] The German state launched a comprehensive soil survey for taxation purposes in 1934 that ranked all fields on a scale of 1 to 100. Soil scientists found the approach exceedingly crude and argued for a more refined approach, but the project went ahead anyway. Characteristically, the authorities pointed out by way of defending the project "that single numbers fit more easily into existing tables than cumbersome words."[26] The numbers eventually entered farming language as the authoritative assessment of land values, a demonstration of modernity's infatuation with numbers in the face of environmental complexity.

Land titles were more than economic units. Control over land was a political asset beyond the age of feudalism. In the nineteenth century, revenues from agricultural estates underpinned the power of aristocratic elites, and conflicts over large landholdings were often proxy wars over political power. Wealth from landownership could underpin political careers even in the late twentieth century: Pakistan's prime ministers Zulfikar Ali

Bhutto and Benazir Bhutto, the latter known as the first female head of government in a Muslim country in modern times, came from the feudal landed gentry in the country's southeastern Sindh Province.[27] In Latin America, the power of United Fruit grew in part from landholdings far beyond economic needs: in the mid-1950s, United Fruit owned 1.7 million acres in Guatemala, Honduras, Costa Rica, Panama, Colombia, and Ecuador but planted only 388,000 acres with crops.[28] The power of large landowners began to fade when industrial societies gave citizens a chance to acquire wealth outside agriculture, but in the countryside, land remained a crucial lever of power that even colonialists were reluctant to tamper with. When Japan conducted its land survey in Korea, it allowed aristocratic landlords to retain their holdings and transformed them into contractual property rights, thus consolidating Japan's colonial power through an alliance with the old elite.[29]

Landholdings were an amalgam of political and economic power that few things could match in rural societies. Farmers sought to escape through migration long before the dawn of modernity. In the Middle Ages, Central European peasants moved eastward in search of less crowded realms. The medieval migrants are nowadays seen as inaugurating a general European process of land reclamation in peripheral regions that continued into the twentieth century.[30] For instance, Fascist Italy, bent on ruralizing an increasingly urban nation, launched numerous land reclamation projects in the 1920s and 1930s.[31] However, efforts within Europe paled in comparison with the hope for "free land" beyond the continent that underpinned the spread of white settler societies all over the globe. By way of justification, settler societies embraced a transnational trope that free farmers would form the backbone of new societies beyond the reach of feudal powers. As Daniel Bromley remarked, "Since the Enlightenment, few ideas about land have been as durable as those concerning land as a guarantor of individual liberty."[32] The yeoman farmers of Jeffersonian fame were just the US version.[33]

Land ownership patterns varied, of course, between countries and regions, as did the precise nature of land titles and how people came to acquire them. While settlers gained land for free in Algeria, they had to purchase it in neighboring Tunisia (which made Tunisian settlers fewer, but also attracted wealthier migrants).[34] Land conflicts could even run along gender lines: in the Gambia, women claimed usufruct rights to vegetable gardens that male landowners challenged, not least because they hated their wives' long absences and the measure of independence they gained.[35] It also bears recognition that the "virgin" land that settlers acquired was often anything but that, as settler societies were oblivious of Indigenous land use. But from the settlers' point of view, the greater concern was the nagging uncertainty of land titles. In the United States, land surveys and registration of sales lagged behind settlement throughout the nineteenth century, and corruption was endemic. Work at the General Land Office was so taxing that it turned Elijah Hayward, Andrew Jackson's land commissioner since 1830, into an alcoholic.[36] It showed the fundamental paradox in the modern experiment with land as a tradeable commodity. As a legal institution, the land title was remarkably resilient, but certainly not for lack of problems.

The Great Mobilization

Land serves as a transcultural icon of stability. Like most cultural tropes, it was never literally correct, but rarely was it less true than in the modern era. Since the late eighteenth century, agricultural lands experienced a mobilization without precedent in world history. One of the driving forces was the expansion of land under the plow that culminated in the nineteenth century as frontiers advanced in Argentina, the American West, the Russian south, and elsewhere.[37] In established agricultural regions, land markets gained a new dynamism since the early 1800s as commercially savvy farmers sought to acquire additional land. However, buyers were not necessarily from a farming background. The influx of non-agricultural investors has recently gained attention due to transnational concerns over "land grabbing," but the phenomenon is not new.[38] Diana Davis has observed that in Algeria, a French settler colony, land was increasingly in the hands of large corporations headquartered in Europe in the 1930s.[39]

The transport revolution of the nineteenth century added a second layer to the mobilization of land. A Prussian landowner, Johann Heinrich von Thünen, showed how distance from markets shaped agricultural land use. In his idealistic model, Thünen envisioned a market surrounded by concentric rings whose products depended on transport, with perishable goods and products that are heavy and bulky in relation to value being produced close to market and more extensive forms of agriculture farther out.[40] Thünen published the first edition of his *Isolated State* in 1826, almost a decade before the first German railroad, but the theory also worked on a grander scale when extensive railroad networks facilitated transportation. Thünen was one of the inspirations for William Cronon's *Nature's Metropolis*, which showed how Chicago channeled and transformed agricultural commodities in constant interaction with its hinterland.[41] The rise of fruit production in California hinged on extensive negotiations with railroads and middlemen over the speed and costs of rail transport and storage conditions.[42] In Costa Rica, a railroad to the Atlantic coast for the country's coffee elite became the launch pad for United Fruit's banana empire because the cash-strapped nation gave the American builder, Minor Keith, a ninety-nine-year lease on the railroad and some 7 percent of the nation's territory.[43]

However, land markets and transport conditions were just two of multiple mobilities that transformed agricultural production in the modern era. Nutrients circulated through soils with unprecedented speed, due to both the boom of commercial fertilizer use and the growing yields. After all, agricultural commodities are essentially stored nutrients from a chemical point of view, and commercial networks sent the precious elements to market in utter disregard for plant nutrition needs. Soils also hold and transfer pathogens such as Panama disease, a soil-borne fungus that caused wilting on Latin American banana plantations since the 1890s.[44] Concerns over soil-borne pathogens even inspired a mysterious question on US customs forms, which inquired about recent visits to farms because agriculturalists were worried about the dirt on people's shoes. Soil erosion is another type of unwelcome mobility that grew to staggering proportion in the wake of industrial farming methods. According to the 2007 National Resources Inventory, US croplands suffer an annual loss of 960 million tons of soil from water erosion and 765 million tons from wind erosion.[45] Critical observers have likened modern agriculture to soil mining, and some have even mined agricultural land in a literal sense: farmers dug holes on tea plantations in Sri Lanka in the hunt for cornflower blue sapphire, a treasured gemstone.[46] The great mobilization of the world's soils is also about energy flows, as vehicles and energy-intensive chemicals such as synthetic nitrogen turned agriculture, traditionally a net producer of energy, into a major consumer of fossil fuels.

In short, modern production methods did not just allow for greater yields per acre. They also brought a mobilization on multiple levels that followed different rationales and sometimes clashed: the transport revolution accelerated access to markets as well as the spread of pathogens. Somewhat counterintuitively, the great mobilization also made agriculture less flexible, as land became entangled in a multitude of networks that defied control even by powerful individuals. Welcome and detrimental types of mobilization go hand in hand: wheat cultivation in the Palouse, an agricultural region in the northwestern United States, produces among the highest yields and the highest rates of erosion.[47] The great mobilization of lands is a global experiment whose outcome is entirely open. We may remember it one day as a time of devastating soil mining or as a golden age when soil was used more efficiently for human needs than ever before. We may even end up with an uneasy coexistence of both readings.

Land Reform

Land titles were sacrosanct in Western law, but for those who lacked enough land to make a living, that was hard to reconcile with the individual pursuit of happiness. Inequality in rural societies was closely linked to unequal landholdings, and the quest to change land ownership by force, political fiat, or a combination thereof inspired people all over the modern world. A call for land reform could even prove popular in industrial societies. In Great Britain, where three-quarters of all land was owned by fewer than 5,000 people in the late nineteenth century, the Chancellor of the Exchequer David Lloyd George launched a "Land Campaign" in the fall of 1913 that included heavy taxation and a Ministry of Land that was to oversee rural regeneration and adjustments of rental agreements, a program that, in the words of David Cannadine, "put the fear of God into the landowning classes—which was exactly what Lloyd George intended."[48] However, World War I put an abrupt end to the campaign, and Lloyd George's attempt to revive the issue in the 1920s fell flat.[49] Views on land issues changed over time, sometimes with amazing speed, and outcomes differed greatly from country to country. Land reforms ranged from determined and ideological to lukewarm and aborted, but seen as a whole, land reform qualifies as one of modern history's great experiments in social engineering.

The French Revolution provided a first taste of the issue's volatility when rebellious Peasants prompted the National Assembly to abolish feudalism on August 4, 1789—a brilliant act of symbolic policy, for a good share of feudal privileges was actually transformed into titles under civil law.[50] Land reform became a more enduring concern in the late nineteenth century when the push for mass democracy gained momentum and boisterous government authorities looked increasingly able to master the complex task of land distribution. After all, it took a trustworthy, efficient, and well-informed administration to work toward more equitable ownership structures. Weak or corrupt bureaucracies produced insignificant or farcical efforts like those in Pakistan, where large landowners "evaded land reform regulations by dividing their estates among kin and by bribing and influencing officials responsible for land reforms."[51]

Some of the most significant land reforms took place in times of upheaval when previous authorities were gone or under pressure and people forged a new social contract. After the end of Ottoman rule, Bulgaria enacted a remarkably well conceived land reform in the 1880s.[52] Estonia started a land reform immediately after its declaration of independence in 1918. It helped that numerous Russians and Germans owned estates in the new country, and these landowners had typically abandoned their holdings due to the development of World War I. The endeavor was codified retroactively in October 1919 when the Estonian government was finally in control of the entire country.[53] In order to fulfill the promise of the Mexican Revolution, president Lázaro Cárdenas transferred 44 million acres of land to peasants in the 1930s.[54] After World War II, the American occupying forces in Japan enacted a comprehensive land reform to turn tenants into owners, end the peasant unrest that had destabilized Japan before the war, and thus create "a solid rural base for postwar politics."[55]

In the 1950s, Wolf Ladejinsky, the architect of Japan's land reform, faced baseless charges of communist sympathies.[56] This reaction demonstrated how land reform became a suspicious endeavor in the wake of the Cold War. Stalinist terror had forced the peasants of the Soviet Union to surrender their land to collective farms, thus launching the most ambitious but also the most brutal examples of land reform up to then. The role that collectivization played in the Soviet famines of the early 1930s, best known by the Ukrainian term "Holodomor," is one of the most divisive issues in post-Soviet historiography.[57] After World War II, the Soviet Union urged its communist satellites to collectivize their own agricultures, and that tainted land reform in the capitalist West. When Fidel Castro expropriated large landowners after the Cuban Revolution, it "was the turning point in the US relationship with Cuba."[58]

The Cold War framed the stance toward land reform in East and West, though ideological rigidity coexisted with the contingency of history. Unlike other Eastern European countries, Poland started slowly and ultimately abandoned collectivization, in part because Władysław Gomułka, Poland's leader since 1956, had been an eyewitness to the Ukrainian tragedy in the early 1930s.[59] Conversely, the United States saw the need to engage with the stark inequality of land holdings in Latin America after the Cuban fiasco, and the US-led Alliance for Progress of 1961 "set the basis for a continent-wide land reform movement."[60] After being born out of a concern for social equity, and becoming captive to ideological stances during the Age of Extremes, a third case for land reform focused on economic benefits for the individual farmer, and land reforms became part of development policy.[61] Technological enthusiasts hoped that the Green Revolution package of high-yield seeds and chemicals would make the drive toward land reform pointless, but that became one of the many disappointments of the Green Revolution.[62]

Land reform looks different depending on ownership structures, commodities, technologies, ethnic identities, and political regimes. Furthermore, much depends on tactics and related motives: recent efforts range from blueprints endorsed by the World Bank to land occupations by Brazil's Movement of Landless Rural Workers.[63] It certainly takes more than a good rationale. Few places in world history had a better case than Zimbabwe after independence in 1980—preserving white ownership of large estates was not a realistic option in a postcolonial world—but when land reform finally came in 2000, it was part of President Robert Mugabe's quest to stay in power, and the country suffered from the economic repercussions of an almost comprehensive shift from large export-oriented farms to small-scale production for domestic consumers.[64] Land reform is not dead, but it has lost a lot of its magic since the late nineteenth century, and few would see it as a panacea for rural development nowadays. However, interest is by far the strongest in the Global South. In urban societies and economies with strong industrial and post-industrial sectors, land reform has become a tough sell. Migration to the cities has probably done more to render the land question moot than all the efforts of the world's reformers combined.

Get Someone to Know the Land for You

The modern history of land is not just about material and commercial change. It also involved a fateful transition in the knowledge base of farming. For all the deficiencies of premodern understandings of soils, farmers could at least be confident that they knew more about their land than anyone else and that they would be the primary beneficiaries of that knowledge. However, modern agriculture brought new tools and new insights to the fields, and both were underpinned by experts from beyond the farmgate who often pursued their own commercial interests. For example, farmers bought mineral fertilizer along with recommendations for use from agrochemists that farmers could not check without a deep knowledge of soil chemistry. Manufacturers such as John Deere offered knowledge about the right crumbling structure of soil along with the implements to produce it. Drainage experts knew a lot about water problems and the technology to fix them. It took a degree in plant pathology to understand soil-borne diseases. Of course, farmers learned about the merits of expert advice upon harvest time and ignored recommendations from outsiders that were just a waste of money, but experience showed that some experts actually brought better yields. One of the most vexing questions that farmers faced in modern times was which experts to trust.

The rise of expert knowledge makes for a striking counter-narrative to the myth of farmer autonomy. Land ownership was a political and a socioeconomic asset, and farmers who retained possession of their land saw that as a matter of pride, but those who worked the land no longer controlled the knowledge that guided land use. Of course, farmers could seek academic training or conduct experiments of variable extent and depth, but time and money was limited, and a strong if not total reliance on specific experts became the norm. In many cases, experts were personal acquaintances that farmers met on a regular basis, which helped them to cope with the experience of intellectual dispossession.

Expert advice was not only ambiguous because commercial interests were in play. Modern soil knowledge was also fragmented along commercial and disciplinary lines. Agrochemists focused on plant nutrients, disease experts on pathogens, and so forth. Revealingly, it took the rise of a new field of expertise to think about the soil as a holistic whole. Soil conservation emerged as a new profession in the 1930s, with the United States of the New Deal years providing a particularly spectacular example. Four years after its creation, the US Soil Conservation Service had 952 employees in Washington, DC, and 12,379 in field services.[65] It was an inspiration for other countries, facilitated by international networking among soil conservationists. For example, New Zealand created a Soil Conservation and Rivers Control Council in 1941 after a domestic agricultural expert went on a study trip to the United States.[66] Beginning in the 1930s, European powers implemented soil conservation schemes in their African colonies.[67]

Scientific research has greatly expanded the knowledge that farmers can draw upon in the twenty-first century, and sustainable stewards of the land are no longer hampered by a lack of expertise. However, farmers have used available knowledge to widely divergent extents, and knowledge about soil conservation has shown to be one of the more difficult sells. Apocalyptic fears about the literal erosion of civilization run through the history of soil conservation, and for good reason. Fertile soil is similar to a bank account in that it allows for fluctuations and overdraft for some time, but in the long run, bankruptcy is inevitable if things get out of control. Soil erosion is a global challenge, but it is also a problem that people can ignore for a while, and negligence is particularly easy in a global economy: soil abuse is easier if the land is far away, owned by strangers, and different from soils at home. Few farmers would see the health of the land as a marginal issue, but it becomes a second-rate concern when they struggle to pay their bills.

Beyond Land?

Land has always been essential for agriculture. Whether that will be the case in the future is open to debate. Plants can also grow under controlled conditions in vertical stacks, an idea that has attracted more interest recently due to new energy-saving LED lights. Indoor or vertical farming also reduces food miles because it allows crop production to move into cities. Dutch agriculturalists have floated ideas about meat production in high-rises located close to the port of Rotterdam, with rearing conditions in these "pig towers" (*varkensflats*) that compare favorably with existing factory farms.[68] From a technological perspective, farming without land has become possible, but it remains to be seen whether vertical farming will provide a substantial contribution to feeding the world or whether it will enter the well-stocked agricultural pantheon of alluring panaceas that never really mattered.

But maybe modern societies have already moved beyond land, if only in practical rather than literal terms. In some respects, the *varkensflats* draw on an established business model. When grain imports from overseas became cheap and reliable in the late nineteenth century, German farmers near harbors and large rivers began to neglect crop production and focused on pork.[69] After World War II, large feedlots on the Great Plains grew into a local nuisance and a cornerstone of the American food system.[70] In both cases, farmers relied on feed that was produced elsewhere, and whether plant production in these places had contributed to erosion or soil depletion was none of their business. In a world of global resource flows, it was possible to produce food as if land no longer mattered. It is an experiment without precedent in world history, and arguably a rather risky one in the long run. After all, Mark Twain was right on one point: when it comes to the world's land, we have to work with what we have.

Notes

1. Tom Tietenberg and Lynne Lewis, *Environmental and Natural Resource Economics*, 10th ed. (New York: Routledge, 2016): 234.
2. Helen Tilley, *Africa as a Living Laboratory: Empire, Development and the Problem of Scientific Knowledge, 1870–1950* (Chicago: University of Chicago Press, 2011): 156.
3. Diana K. Davis, *Resurrecting the Granary of Rome: Environmental History and French Colonial Expansion in North Africa* (Athens: Ohio University Press, 2007): 171.
4. Reinaldo Funes Monzote, *From Rainforest to Cane Field in Cuba: An Environmental History since 1492* (Chapel Hill: University of North Carolina Press, 2008): 272
5. Stuart McCook, *States of Nature: Science, Agriculture, and Environment in the Spanish Caribbean, 1760–1940* (Austin: University of Texas Press, 2002): 22.
6. James Belich, *Replenishing the Earth: The Settler Revolution and the Rise of the Anglo-World, 1783–1939* (New York: Oxford University Press, 2009): 132.
7. John Soluri, *Banana Cultures: Agriculture, Consumption, and Environmental Change in Honduras and the United States* (Austin: University of Texas Press, 2005): 26.
8. Monzote, *Rainforest*, 152.
9. Cf. Mary W. M. Hargreaves, "Hardy Webster Campbell (1850–1937)," *Agricultural History* 32 (1958): 62–65; Mary W. M. Hargreaves, "The Dry-Farming Movement in Retrospect," *Agricultural History* 51 (1997): 149–165.
10. Cf. William H. Brock, *Justus von Liebig: The Chemical Gatekeeper* (Cambridge: Cambridge University Press, 1997).
11. Ibid., 123, 128.
12. Albert Howard, *An Agricultural Testament* (s.l.: Oxford City Press, 2010): 22.

13. Cf. Gregory A. Barton, *The Global History of Organic Farming* (Oxford: Oxford University Press, 2018); and Gunter Vogt, *Entstehung und Entwicklung des ökologischen Landbaus im deutschsprachigen Raum* (Bad Dürkheim: Stiftung Ökologie und Landbau, 2000).
14. Cf. Hugh S. Gorman, *The Story of N: A Social History of the Nitrogen Cycle and the Challenge of Sustainability* (New Brunswick, NJ: Rutgers University Press, 2013).
15. For more on this point see Frank Uekötter, *Die Wahrheit ist auf dem Feld: Eine Wissensgeschichte der deutschen Landwirtschaft* (Göttingen: Vandenhoeck & Ruprecht, 2010).
16. Cf. Paul S. Giller, "The Diversity of Soil Communities, the 'Poor Man's Tropical Rainforest,'" *Biodiversity and Conservation* 5 (1996): 135–168.
17. Jürgen Osterhammel, *The Transformation of the World: A Global History of the Nineteenth Century* (Princeton, NJ: Princeton University Press, 2014): 107.
18. Arthur Young, *Travels during the Years 1787, 1788 and 1789* (London: W. Richardson, 1794): 88.
19. Cf. Gérard Béaur, Philipp R. Schofield, Jean-Michel Chevet, and María Teresa Pérez Picazo, eds. *Property Rights, Land Markets, and Economic Growth in the European Countryside (Thirteenth–Twentieth Centuries)* (Turnhout: Brepols, 2013).
20. C. R. Pennell, *Morocco: From Empire to Independence* (Oxford: Oneworld, 2009): 148.
21. Garrett Hardin, "The Tragedy of the Commons," *Science* 162 (1968): 1243–1248.
22. Elinor Ostrom, *Governing the Commons: The Evolution of Institutions for Collective Action* (Cambridge: Cambridge University Press, 2015 [originally published 1990]): 26.
23. Jeremy Bentham, *The Theory of Legislation* (London: Routledge & Kegan Paul, 1931), 113.
24. Cf. Elizabeth Hallam and David Bates, eds. *Domesday Book* (Stroud: Tempus Publishing, 2001).
25. Marion Eggert and Jörg Plassen, *Kleine Geschichte Koreas* (Munich: Beck, 2005), 132n.
26. Jan Arend, *Russlands Bodenkunde in der Welt: Eine ost-westliche Transfergeschichte 1880–1945* (Göttingen: Vandenhoeck & Ruprecht, 2017): 220–242. Quotation at 231.
27. Anna Suvorova, *Benazir Bhutto: A Multidimensional Portrait* (Karachi: Oxford University Press, 2015): 31.
28. Stacy May and Galo Plaza, *The United Fruit Company in Latin America* (Washington, DC: National Planning Association, 1958): 81.
29. Bruce Cummings, *Korea's Place in the Sun: A Modern History* (New York: W. W. Norton, 2005): 151.
30. Cf. Walter Schlesinger, ed., *Die deutsche Ostsiedlung des Mittelalters als Problem der europäischen Geschichte: Reichenau-Vorträge 1970–1972* (Sigmaringen: Thorbecke, 1975); Peter Erlen, *Europäischer Landesausbau und mittelalterliche deutsche Ostsiedlung: Ein struktureller Vergleich zwischen Südwestfrankreich, den Niederlanden und dem Ordensland Preußen* (Marburg: Herder-Institut, 1992): 1.
31. Cf. Alexander Nützenadel, *Landwirtschaft, Staat und Autarkie: Agrarpolitik im faschistischen Italien (1922–1943)* (Tübingen: Niemeyer, 1997).
32. Daniel W. Bromley, "Private Property and the Public Interest: Land in the American Idea," in *Land in the American West: Private Claims and the Common Good*, ed. William G. Robbins and James C. Foster (Seattle: University of Washington Press, 2000): 23–36; "p. 25."
33. Cf. Daniel J. Boorstin, *The Lost World of Thomas Jefferson* (Chicago: University of Chicago Press, 1993 [originally published 1948]).
34. Davis, *Resurrecting*, 134.

35. Richard A. Schroeder, *Shady Practices: Agroforestry and Gender Politics in the Gambia* (Berkeley: University of California Press, 1999): 78–104.
36. Patricia Nelson Limerick, *The Legacy of Conquest. The Unbroken Past of the American West* (New York: W. W. Norton, 1988): 59n.
37. Osterhammel, *Transformation of the World*, 323.
38. Stefano Liberti, *Land Grabbing: Journeys in the New Colonialism* (London: Verso, 2013); Mayke Kaag and Annelies Zoomers, eds., *The Global Land Grab: Beyond the Hype* (London: Zed Books, 2014).
39. Davis, *Resurrecting*, 133.
40. Johann Heinrich von Thünen, *Von Thünen's Isolated State*, English ed. of *Der Isolierte Staat*, transl. Carla M. Wartenberg, edited with an introduction by Peter Hall (Oxford: Pergamon Press, 1966). For context see Gunther Viereck, *Johann Heinrich von Thünen: Ein Klassiker der Nationalökonomie im Spiegel der Forschung* (Hamburg: Krämer, 2006).
41. William Cronon, *Nature's Metropolis: Chicago and the Great West* (New York: W. W. Norton, 1991).
42. Steven Stoll, *The Fruits of Natural Advantage: Making the Industrial Landscape in California* (Berkeley: University of California Press, 1998): 63–68.
43. Jason M. Colby, *The Business of Empire: United Fruit, Race, and U.S. Expansion in Central America* (Ithaca, NY: Cornell University Press, 2011): 67.
44. Soluri, *Banana Cultures*, 53n.
45. U.S. Department of Agriculture. 2009. Summary Report: 2007 National Resources Inventory, National Resources Conservation Service, Washington, D.C., and Center for Survey Statistics and Methodology, Iowa State University, Ames, Iowa, p. 7 , available online at https://nam11.safelinks.protection.outlook.com/?url=https%3A%2F%2Fwww.nrcs.usda.gov%2Fsites%2Fdefault%2Ffiles%2F2022-10%2FSummary-Report-2007-National-Resources-Inventory.pdf&data=05%7C01%7Cjwhayne%40uark.edu%7Ce6a2cf5aa3914 4d3a54f08dba54odfe1%7C79c742c4e61c4fa5be89a3cb566a80d1%7C0%7C0%7C6382854 70421620050%7CUnknown%7CTWFpbGZsb3d8eyJWIjoiMC4wLjAwMDAiLCJQIjoiV 2luMzIiLCJBTiI6IkihaWwiLCJXVCI6Mno%3D%7C3000%7C%7C%7C&sdata=G8QrTn OeoKelgq1mXm7GvmcPlPpwo%2Bal2ZXVsNybmLM%3D&reserved=0 (accessed August 25, 2023).
46. Saleem H. Ali, *Treasures of the Earth: Need, Greed, and a Sustainable Future* (New Haven, CT: Yale University Press, 2009): 90.
47. Andrew P. Duffin, *Plowed Under: Agriculture and Environment in the Palouse* (Seattle: University of Washington Press, 2007).
48. David Cannadine, *The Decline and Fall of the British Aristocracy* (London: Papermac, 1996): 55, 70 (quotation).
49. F. M. L. Thompson, "Epilogue: The Strange Death of the English Land Question," in *The Land Question in Britain, 1750–1950*, ed. Matthew Cragoe and Paul Readman (Basingstoke: Palgrave Macmillan, 2010): 257–270; 259.
50. Hans-Ulrich Thamer, *Die französische Revolution* (Munich: Beck, 2006): 38.
51. Mohammad Abdul Qadeer, *Pakistan: Social and Cultural Transformations in a Muslim Nation* (London: Routledge, 2006): 45.
52. Russell King, *Land Reform: A World Survey* (London: Routledge, 2018 [originally published 1977]): 34.
53. Neil Taylor, *Estonia: A Modern History* (London: Hurst & Co., 2018): 37.
54. Robert Ryal Miller, *Mexico: A History* (Norman: University of Oklahoma Press, 1985): 319.

55. Marius B. Jansen, *The Making of Modern Japan* (Cambridge, MA: Belknap Press, 2000): 683.
56. Jeff Broadwater, *Eisenhower and the Anti-Communist Crusade* (Chapel Hill: University of North Carolina Press, 1992), 94. For Ladejinsky's views see Louis J. Walinsky, ed., *Agrarian Reform as Unfinished Business: The Selected Papers of Wolf Ladejinsky* (New York: Oxford University Press, 1977).
57. Cf. Stephan Merl, *Bauern unter Stalin: Die Formierung des sowjetischen Kolchossystems, 1930-1941* (Berlin: Duncker & Humblot, 1990); Robert Conquest, *The Harvest of Sorrow: Soviet Collectivization and the Terror Famine* (London: Hutchinson, 1986); Timothy Snyder, *Bloodlands: Europe between Hitler and Stalin* (New York: Basic Books, 2010): 21–58.
58. Richard Gott, *Cuba: A New History* (New Haven, CT: Yale Nota Bene, 2005): 180.
59. Norman Davies, *Heart of Europe: The Past in Poland's Present* (Oxford: Oxford University Press, 2001): 11.
60. King, *Land Reform*, 84.
61. Ibid., 3, 46.
62. Nick Cullather, *The Hungry World: America's Cold War Battle against Poverty in Asia* (Cambridge, MA: Harvard University Press, 2010): 106n.
63. Gabriel Ondetti, *Land, Protest, and Politics: The Landless Movement and the Struggle for Agrarian Reform in Brazil* (University Park: Pennsylvania State University Press, 2008).
64. Lionel Cliffe et al., eds., *Outcomes of Post-2000 Fast Track Land Reform in Zimbabwe* (London: Routledge, 2013); Ian Scoones et al., *Zimbabwe's Land Reform: Myths and Realities* (Woodbridge: James Currey, 2010).
65. For the author's take on US soil conservation see Frank Uekötter, "The Meaning of Moving Sand: Towards a Dust Bowl Mythology," *Global Environment* 8 (2015): 349–379. For the numbers see ibid., 362n.
66. Tom Brooking and Eric Pawson, *Seeds of Empire: The Environmental Transformation of New Zealand* (London: I. B. Tauris, 2011): 196.
67. Grace Carswell, *Cultivating Success in Uganda: Kigezi Farmers and Colonial Policies* (Oxford: James Currey, 2007): 49.
68. Jan Arend Schulp, "Reducing the Food Miles: Locavorism and Seasonal Eating," in *The Routledge Handbook of Sustainable Food and Gastronomy*, ed. Philip Sloan, Willy Legrand, and Clare Hindley (London: Routledge, 2015): 120–125.
69. Karl Eckart, *Agrargeographie Deutschlands: Agrarraum und Agrarwirtschaft Deutschlands im 20. Jahrhundert* (Gotha: Klett-Perthes, 1998): 51.
70. R. Douglas Hurt, *The Big Empty: The Great Plains in the Twentieth Century* (Tucson: University of Arizona Press, 2011): 190n, 204–206.

Bibliography

Barton, Gregory A. *The Global History of Organic Farming*. Oxford: Oxford University Press, 2018.

Béaur, Gérard, Philipp R. Schofield, Jean-Michel Chevet, and María Teresa Pérez Picazo, eds. *Property Rights, Land Markets, and Economic Growth in the European Countryside. (Thirteenth–Twentieth Centuries)*. Turnhout: Brepols, 2013.

Cronon, William. *Nature's Metropolis: Chicago and the Great West*. New York: W. W. Norton, 1991.

Cullather, Nick. *The Hungry World: America's Cold War Battle against Poverty in Asia*. Cambridge, MA: Harvard University Press, 2010.

Gorman, Hugh S. *The Story of N: A Social History of the Nitrogen Cycle and the Challenge of Sustainability*. New Brunswick, NJ: Rutgers University Press, 2013.

Kaag, Mayke, and Annelies Zoomers, eds. *The Global Land Grab: Beyond the Hype*. London: Zed Books, 2014.

King, Russell. *Land Reform: A World Survey*. London: Routledge, 2018 [originally published 1977].

Liberti, Stefano. *Land Grabbing: Journeys in the New Colonialism*. London: Verso, 2013.

Linklater, Andro. *Owning the Earth: The Transformative History of Land Ownership*. London: Bloomsbury, 2014.

Ostrom, Elinor. *Governing the Commons: The Evolution of Institutions for Collective Action*. Cambridge: Cambridge University Press, 2015 [originally published 1990].

Rosset, Peter, Raj Patel, and Michael Courville, eds. *Promised Land: Competing Visions of Agrarian Reform*. Oakland, CA: Food First Books, 2006.

Uekötter, Frank. *Die Wahrheit ist auf dem Feld: Eine Wissensgeschichte der deutschen Landwirtschaft*. Göttingen: Vandenhoeck & Ruprecht, 2010.

CHAPTER 2

SOIL FERTILITY

LAURIE E. DRINKWATER

LAND and the soil are the foundations of agriculture, and farmers produce food, fodder, and animal products under a variety of soil conditions. Farmers have used a variety of inputs and management strategies to address the challenges they face in maintaining the productive condition of their land. The sustainability of food production systems, for example, became a pressing concern during the period beginning with the transition to the Green Revolution to the present day. The shift to industrial agriculture and the widespread availability of synthetic fertilizers that ensued have had a major impact on how farmers manage soil fertility. Together, along with intensive crop breeding programs, the use of synthetic fertilizers enabled steady increases in crop yields per acre even with persistent declines in inherent soil fertility.

Since the emergence of the sustainable agriculture movement in the 1980s, views on soil fertility and soil management have broadened beyond the emphasis on soil chemistry and nutrient supply to include a variety of ecosystem processes that directly and indirectly support crop yields and agroecosystem health. As a result, the goals of soil fertility management extend beyond maximizing crop yields to include sustaining soil fertility, minimizing off-farm environmental impacts and mitigating climate change.

STATE OF SOILS AS A RESOURCE

Soil is an essential natural resource underlying productive agricultural systems. The extent of productive, arable land available on earth is limited. Less than three-quarters of the global land surface is considered to be habitable (Figure 2.1). We use half of the habitable area for agricultural production, and within that area arable land accounts for a relatively small proportion; only 23 percent, or 11 million km², is used to produce crops that supply the bulk of calories and protein for the global population. Fertile land that can be used to support the needs of humans is therefore a valuable, finite resource.

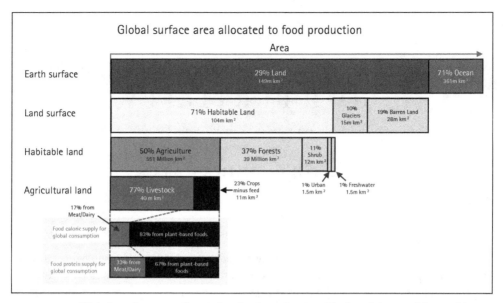

FIGURE 2.1 Global surface area allocated to food production. The breakdown of the earth's surface area by functional and allocated uses, including agricultural land allocation for livestock and food crop production, measured in millions of square kilometers as well as the relative production from livestock versus plant-based commodities. Area for livestock farming includes grazing land for animals, and arable land used for animal feed production. Redrawn from *Our World in Data*, https://ourworldindata.org/, accessed November 15, 2019.

Agriculture degrades soils over time, through several mechanisms, including erosion, loss of soil organic matter, nutrient depletion, desertification, salinization, and acidification. Worldwide, the fertility and health of formerly productive soils has declined in many regions, and as a result, farmers must compensate by increasing fertilizer additions in order to maintain yields. Once soils have been degraded, the restoration of soil fertility is difficult; in cases of severe erosion, desertification, or salinization, the damage often cannot be reversed. Even in situations where soil degradation is less severe, for example, soil that has become compacted due to excessive tillage and organic matter losses, additions of synthetic fertilizers alone cannot restore vigorous plant growth.

Soil degradation is a ubiquitous problem worldwide and substantial proportions of arable soils exhibit some degree of degradation. More than 75 percent of arable land in Africa is degraded, due to continuous cropping with minimal or no investment in maintaining soil fertility.[1] In China, with only 0.21 ha of agricultural land per capita, about half of the world's average, more than 40 percent of the arable land is degraded. The US Mississippi River Basin, a vast area of 1.1 million km² on some of the most fertile soils on earth known as the "Corn Belt," has lost half of the native soil organic matter and the rate of soil erosion is unsustainable, averaging 9.6 metric tons ha^{-1}. Other, indirect causes reduce the land available for food production. In the United States, between 1992 and 2012 almost 12.5 million hectares of agricultural land was irreversibly lost to development. This loss included almost 4.5 million hectares of the best land for intensive food and crop production. In areas that rely on irrigation to maintain high yields, land is being removed from production due to changing weather patterns and water limitations; 222,600 ha of prime agricultural land has been abandoned in California's San Joaquin Valley because of the recent severe drought that began in 2016.

Globally, agricultural production can be divided roughly into two distinct systems. The global food system is composed largely of industrialized agricultural systems that produce commodity crops that can be shipped long distances. This globalized food system feeds about 60 percent of the global population in industrial countries, mainly including the EU, United States, and Canada, and urban centers throughout the world. In industrialized agroecosystems, farmers use fertilizers and other agrochemicals to compensate for the loss of the ecosystem services once provided by plant species diversity. These inputs along with tillage and the lack of species diversity disrupt nutrient cycles and undermine the capacity of soils to supply and store nutrients. Farmers are caught in a vicious cycle where declining soil function requires them to use environmentally harmful levels of fertilizers to produce crops, which only reinforces the trend of fertilizer dependence and soil degradation.

At the other end of the spectrum are the smallholder, subsistence farming systems that feed the remaining 40 percent of the population, located largely in rural areas of developing countries including all of sub-Saharan Africa and other regions of Africa, South America, and Asia. For the most part, smallholder subsistence farmers do not have access to adequate resources to maintain soil fertility and yields. Subsistence farmers frequently respond to the reduced crop yields resulting from poor soil by intensifying their farming systems in ways that accelerate soil erosion and deplete soil organic matter. This creates a downward spiral of soil degradation that perpetuates food insecurity and poverty. The consequences of these declines in soil fertility and health have become even more severe as changes in precipitation patterns driven by climate change have increased the frequency and severity of droughts in the region.

Transition to Synthetic Fertilizers as the Dominant Source of Crop Nutrients

Soil Fertility Management

Soil fertility is an ancient concept and is broadly defined as the capacity of soils to support plant growth. This includes the ability of soils to supply major plant nutrients (nitrogen, phosphorus, and potassium) as well as micronutrients (calcium, magnesium, iron, sulfur, etc.). Soil pH is also an important factor, largely due to its effect on the availability of nutrients and the biological processes governing nutrient cycling and nutrient acquisition. Most crop plants require soils that are not too acid or basic and grow best when pH is 6.0–7.0. Beyond simply supplying nutrients, a number of other soil properties are essential for vigorous plant growth. Fertile soils need to be structured to allow infiltration of water and to store water in sufficient quantities that can be acquired by plants. Good soil structure or soil "tilth" results from aggregation of soil particles, which is largely dependent on biological activity and soil organic matter. Finally, a soil biota that is both abundant and diverse supports plant growth through a number of mechanisms, including the provision of nutrients, protection from pathogens, and production of compounds that increase plant resistance to pests and stimulate plant growth. Thus, soil fertility is dependent on a variety of complex, interacting soil processes that govern nutrient supply as well as chemical and structural properties.

Prior to the advent of manufactured fertilizers, farmers managed soil fertility primarily through crop rotation, nitrogen-fixing plants (legumes), recycling animal manures, and other cultural practices aimed at maintaining soil organic matter. Agricultural research on soil fertility focused on understanding how to manage soil organic matter and biological soil processes that mobilize nutrients to make them available to plants. In addition to serving as the source for nutrients that plants need in order to grow, soil organic matter supports plant growth through other key mechanisms related to maintaining and stabilizing soil tilth, soil water holding capacity, pH, and soil biota. Initially, many agronomists believed that synthetic fertilizers alone could not maintain yields. As a result, early fertilizer management guidelines recommended using synthetic nitrogen fertilizer in concert with organic nitrogen sources such as leguminous green manures and animal manure in order to maintain soil organic matter levels. The rise of manufactured fertilizers in the post–World War II era started a fundamental paradigm shift in the way agronomists approached soil management and nutrient supply to crops. The opinion that manufactured fertilizers could support high yields without additions of organic amendments gained support through the 1940s and 1950s to become the dominant perspective. The focus of soil fertility management shifted away from managing the more stable nutrient reserves in soil organic matter to emphasize delivering soluble forms of inorganic nitrogen and phosphorus to the crop through synthetic fertilizer additions. Nitrogen and phosphorus limitations are the most common in agricultural fields, so the vast majority of nutrient management efforts target these two nutrients.

As the use of synthetic nitrogen and phosphorus fertilizers became more widespread, agronomists developed recommendations based on empirical trials with varying fertilizer rates conducted on different soil types within each region. Efforts to improve fertilizer use efficiency were largely motivated by yield goals and economic considerations; agronomists sought to minimize fertilizer costs while maximizing yields and profitability through the development of soil tests that could measure plant-available nutrients. Agronomists developed dependable soil tests for predicting plant-available phosphorus, and these soil tests have been in common use since the 1960s. Predicting plant-available soil nitrogen proved more challenging, and efforts to improve predictions of the capacity of soil to supply nitrogen to crops continue. It is safe to say that for many decades over-application of fertilizers was common in the United States.[2] Even when farmers apply recommended fertilizer rates, significant losses to the environment can occur.

Soil Conditions under Industrial Agriculture

The strategy of using soluble fertilizers to supply major nutrients, combined with use of chemical weed controls, has led to a series of management changes that have restructured agroecosystems and disrupted the natural cycling of nitrogen and phosphorus through soil organic matter. Reliance on chemical fertilizers and herbicides made it unnecessary to grow cover crops and forages alternating with row crops and permitted the widespread adoption of the simplified rotations that are prevalent today.[3] These simplified rotations commonly include bare fallows (when land is maintained without any growing plants) alternating with cash crops in order to increase opportunities for early spring planting. As a result, the period of active plants and roots in temperate annual agriculture is limited to four to eight months per year, greatly reducing root-derived carbon inputs that play a major role in replenishing soil organic matter reserves. This reduction in organic carbon inputs, combined with tillage and the relatively labile composition of crop residues returned to the soil, has depleted soil organic matter stores in the vast majority of agricultural soils.

Besides reducing the capacity of soils to supply plants with major nutrients, these reductions in soil organic matter in combination with tillage alter soils in other ways. Normally, the top 15 to 25 cm of soil constitutes the plow layer and is subjected to regular mixing in preparation for planting followed by shallower mixing of the surface layers to control weeds. The most significant consequences of tillage include the reduction in vertical stratification, altered pore structure, and accelerated decomposition of soil organic matter. As a result, crop roots grow into a soil environment where the bulk density is temporarily reduced, pore structure from past roots and hyphae has been destroyed, and microbial communities and fungal hyphae networks are dispersed. Following tillage, the soil tends to settle and, compared to the original conditions found in native pre-tillage soil ecosystems, pore volume is significantly reduced. For instance, soil bulk density in cultivated prairie soils is nearly twofold greater compared to native prairies of the Midwest. This translates into pore volumes of approximately 45 to 50 percent for cultivated soils, compared to 60 to 70 percent in uncultivated prairie soils, and accounts for the reduced, infiltration, aeration, and water holding capacity of agricultural soils. Lastly, tillage and reduced soil organic matter also affect soil biota. Agricultural soils with lower levels of soil organic matter tend to have reduced abundance and diversity of decomposers and soil fauna. The effects of these changes in the communities of soil ecosystems for nutrient cycling and other processes that support plant growth are still under investigation; however, some evidence suggests that soils with larger, more diverse soil communities are more disease-suppressive and more efficient at retaining nutrients compared to those with depleted soil organic matter and reduced biological activity.

Environmental Consequences of Industrial Soil Fertility Regimes

During the 1970s, the substantial nutrient losses from agricultural lands gained attention when the impacts in aquatic ecosystems became apparent.[4] During the first two decades following the emergence of the environmental movement, the idea that agricultural fertilizers were causing nutrient enrichment and eutrophication of lakes and other aquatic environments was contested and quite a bit of research was devoted to tracking the fate of fertilizers and quantifying losses.

It is now clear that the unintended consequences of agriculture extend well beyond agricultural landscapes. Biogeochemical cycles have been profoundly altered at multiple scales, and agriculture is now recognized as a leading source of water pollution, nutrient enrichment, greenhouse gas emissions, and biodiversity loss. Current estimates suggest that human activities have doubled global nitrogen and phosphorus fluxes of biologically active forms of these nutrients, with agriculture being the major source for both.[5]

Phosphorus is lost mainly though runoff from agricultural lands, and the amount of phosphorus is greatest from bare soils or areas where fertilizer or manure are overapplied. In general, phosphorus fertilization rates have decreased in many regions with intensive agricultural production. However, the problem of manure overapplication is still widespread, largely due to the separation of livestock and crop production. Industrialized animal systems tend to concentrate animals in particular regions while importing feed. These areas are hotspots for excessive phosphorus and tend to leak substantial quantities of phosphorus into adjacent ecosystems.

Nitrogen loss pathways are more complex. Biologically active nitrogen is lost through two main pathways: nitrate leaching and release of gaseous nitrogen forms, particularly N_2 and nitrous oxide. Nitrate is highly mobile and moves through the soil profile with water during and after rain events. Depending on the soil profile and the hydrology of the landscape, this nitrate can end up in adjacent aquatic ecosystems such as streams and rivers, or it can move deeper into the subsoil and into groundwater and aquifers. The propensity of nitrate to move with water results in nitrogen pollution of drinking water and aquatic ecosystems. Nitrous oxide contributes to global warming and ozone depletion. Nitrous oxide is a potent greenhouse gas and on a 100-year timescale it is nearly 300 times more potent than CO_2. In addition, it is a strong ozone-depletion substance.

In response to the public pressure to reduce nutrient losses from agriculture, the aim of soil fertility management broadened to encompass both economic and environmental goals. These environmental consequences of relying on synthetic fertilizers also contributed to the sustainable agriculture movement that first took hold in the 1980s. Three distinct approaches to sustainable soil fertility management have emerged because of societal concerns about environmental degradation, agricultural sustainability, and the persistent problem of soil degradation.

Fertilizer Management using the 4Rs Nutrient Stewardship Framework

Fertilizer recommendations have undergone substantial refinement since the 1960s when synthetic fertilizers became widely used. Because soil tests that generally provide reasonable predictions of plant-available phosphorus are available, these are used as the basis for recommendations for phosphorus fertilizers. Compared to nitrogen, phosphorus is less mobile and environmental losses can largely be avoided when appropriate fertilization rates are used.

However, since a reliable test for plant-available nitrogen is lacking, nitrogen fertilizer recommendations are based on estimates of plant-available nitrogen generated by various algorithms and models. Optimizing nitrogen management to achieve yield goals while minimizing environmental losses has proven to be a considerable challenge, largely because the form of nitrogen added as fertilizer is highly mobile and extremely vulnerable to loss. The predictive models used to calculate fertilizer recommendations have become quite complex and are geared toward optimizing fertilizer use efficiency and yields, the assumption being that efficient fertilizer management will reduce environmental losses.[6] These efforts have reduced surplus fertilizer additions in some regions; that is, yields have generally increased per kg/N fertilizer added due to a variety of mechanisms.[7] Nevertheless, in the United States, farmer-reported nitrogen rates are still higher than recommended application rates for about a quarter of the acreage under major commodity crops such as corn, cotton, and wheat. Even in regions where fertilizer use efficiency has increased so that the average nitrogen surplus is reduced, improvements in damaged ecosystems are often not detectable. For example, despite indications that nitrogen use efficiency in the Mississippi River Basin has improved, the Dead Zone in the Gulf of Mexico has not shown any reduction in size or severity.

While best management practices (BMPs) for improving fertilizer use efficiency have been promoted for decades, a cohesive framework for simultaneously promoting synergistic BMPs has been lacking until recently. In 2009, a consortium of fertilizer industry groups introduced the "4Rs Nutrient Stewardship" framework to address the problem of nitrogen fertilizer management. Decades of research show that using multiple nutrient-management practices has greater potential to reduce the loss of nitrogen than using a single practice. This approach entails using a collection of BMPs designated as the "4Rs," which is shorthand for "the Right fertilizer source, at the Right rate, at the Right time, with the Right placement." The "4Rs," as the framework is commonly called, aims to provide a comprehensive conceptual model for integrating fertilizer BMPs in order to enhance environmental protection, increase production and profitability, and improve sustainability.

Practices That Are Promoted by the 4Rs

The 4Rs considers environmental goals and is an improvement over the piecemeal approaches to fertilizer management that predominated in the past. However, the conceptual framework that underpins the 4Rs is not fundamentally different from the one used to develop fertilizer management guidelines developed in the mid-twentieth century. Under this framework, the loss of soluble, plant-available nitrogen from agricultural systems is viewed primarily as a consequence of temporal asynchrony and spatial separation between applied nutrients and the crops. The 4Rs aims to mitigate nitrogen losses by increasing the proportion of nitrogen fertilizer taken up by crops by optimizing the application rate, chemical composition, timing, and placement of fertilizers.

Yield increase, even in the highest-yielding, intensively managed cropping systems, continues to be the major goal; environmental goals are included, but there are no quantitative goals relating to specific reductions in losses. Improvements in fertilizer management practices are largely based on improving the delivery of available nutrients directly to the crop. Improving the efficiency of fertilizer uptake by the crop is an important step toward reducing nitrogen and phosphorus losses; however, plant uptake alone does not control the fate of nitrogen and phosphorus in agroecosystems. Efforts toward managing microbially mediated processes rely on the addition of chemicals that inhibit microbial metabolic processes that promote nitrogen losses such as nitrification and denitrification. Sophisticated, computer-based management tools that estimate fertilizer needs are now available, although many of these tools still privilege economic outcomes over environmental considerations. For example, most of these models recommend increased applications of nitrogen fertilizer under conditions that are vulnerable to elevated nitrogen losses, such as excess spring rainfall or sandy soils. Nutrient budgets, which compare the amount of nitrogen added to the amount harvested in the crop, are not considered in developing or implementing fertilizer recommendations. As a result, in most agricultural systems, the difference between inputs and harvested exports remains unknown.

Prognosis for Implementing the 4Rs

Because the 4Rs Framework is a refined version of fertilizer management strategies that co-evolved with the development of high-yielding, fertilizer-based industrial agricultural systems, it is highly compatible with the conventional farming systems that dominate industrial countries. The 4Rs Framework is widely promoted by state and national agencies concerned with agriculture and environmental issues, universities, extension educators, and environmental conservation organizations. There are no data available on the number of farmers actually using the 4Rs to guide their fertilizer management. A recent project in the Western Lake Erie Basin targeted service providers who support farmers in the region by developing a 4Rs Certification Program. This approach, which was inclusive of diverse stakeholders in the region, was able to reach 35 percent of the farmers located in the watershed through training providers in 4Rs nutrient management.[8] Subsequent research will monitor the impact on farmer practices and water quality. In general, the potential for implementation of the 4Rs Framework in the United States will be largely dependent on extension and farmer outreach efforts. Policies that limit fertilizer application rates could be very effective in increasing fertilizer use efficiency and reducing environmental losses. These policies are in place in the European Union.

Soil Health

The emergence of soil health as a legitimate conceptual framework guiding soil management came after decades where soil fertility management was based largely on the use of soluble synthetic fertilizers. During this time, the concept of soil fertility became quite narrow; agriculturalists viewed soil fertility primarily in terms of the capacity of soils to supply plant nutrients and water. Furthermore, the soil fertility tests used by extensionists and farmers to evaluate soil fertility only measured extractable nutrients and other soil chemical properties such as pH. In contrast, the soil health concept is more in line with earlier, more holistic views of soil fertility that included properties such as soil tilth, soil organic matter content, and soil biological processes.

Prior to the 1980s, the terms "soil health" and "soil quality" appeared sporadically in the soil science literature, and it was not until the 1990s that a critical mass of soil scientists reached consensus on a soil quality conceptual framework.[9] Soil scientists frequently use these terms interchangeably; nevertheless, in the current soil science literature "soil quality" is the favored term and it appears in nearly three-quarters of the papers published on soil quality/health during 2017–2018. Until recently, "soil health" was used infrequently with <5 percent of the soil quality/health papers published during the 1990s using this term. Use of "soil health" has steadily increased and appears in the other 25 percent of soil quality/health publications during 2017–2018, probably reflecting the increasing acceptance among agricultural and soil scientists of a more holistic view of soil as an ecosystem.

During the 1990s, efforts to reach consensus on the definition, conceptual framework, and assessment strategies dominated the soil health discourse.[10] Many definitions of soil quality or health emphasized the concept of soil fitness to perform functions, and the capacity to support crop production was privileged over other ecosystem services and environmental outcomes. Eventually, influence from the emerging ecosystem services discourse led to the broader definitions in current use that embody an ecosystem perspective and consider sustainability to be an overarching goal. The US Natural Resources Conservation Service (NRCS) definition is widely used and states that "soil health, also referred to as soil quality, is defined as the continued capacity of soil to function as a vital living ecosystem that sustains plants, animals, and humans."[11]

Practices Promoted by Soil Health Advocates

The NRCS adopted soil health as a soil management goal in the 1990s. Since then, the NRCS has increasingly promoted the development of soil health indicators and management practices aimed at restoring soil health in agricultural systems. NRCS uses four management goals, listed below, to guide farmers in selecting management practices that will improve soil health on their farm. These goals reflect research results that identify the management practices that reduce soil vulnerability to erosion and have a positive effect on soil organic matter accrual. Soil organic matter is viewed as the keystone soil property supporting healthy soil function due to the many beneficial contributions of organic matter. These management goals serve as a basis for the specific practices recommended by the NRCS.

1. *Keep the soil covered as much as possible*: Keeping the soil covered by retaining crop residues, applying mulches or using rotations that minimize the length and frequency of bare fallows, has long been considered as essential for good soil stewardship, largely due to the potential for this strategy to reduce soil erosion. Following this principle has the dual benefits of protecting soil from erosion, while also having positive effects on soil organic matter cycling processes.
2. *Disturb the soil as little as possible*: This management goal aims to reduce tillage frequency and intensity, both of which reduce soil losses from erosion while also reducing the decomposition rate of organic matter, thus slowing down the rate of soil organic matter loss. In addition to using a strict no-till system, farmers can choose from a wide range of reduced tillage options that limit the depth or area of the field disturbed when fields are being prepared for planting and can also reduce tillage intensity by avoiding aggressive tillage practices such as moldboard plowing and rototilling. In terms of environmental impacts, tillage reductions result in environmental trade-offs because tillage contributes to weed control, and in systems with reduced tillage intensity the need for herbicides generally increases.
3. *Keep plants growing throughout the year to feed the soil*: Recent research on the role of living plant roots has revealed the monumental influence of roots and their associated microflora on soil organic matter formation and other processes that contribute to maintaining soil function and health. We now understand that the majority of organic material incorporated into soil organic matter is derived from plant roots and processed by the decomposers. Furthermore, extending the time that plants are growing in the soil helps to conserve nutrients, particularly nitrogen, therefore reducing environmental losses. A third mechanism that promotes soil health goals occurs through the influence of living roots on

beneficial soil organisms. Plant species that promote beneficial fungi and microflora that are able to suppress plant pathogens can be used as cover crop to enhance these benefits.
4. *Diversify as much as possible using crop rotation and cover crops*: The recognition that plant species diversity benefits agroecosystem function on many levels is another recent discovery, in this case, grounded in the ecological literature that studies natural, unmanaged ecosystems. The benefits of increasing plant species diversity are many, and include positive effects on soil organic matter accrual, nutrient cycling, and soil microflora. The inclusion of cover crops expands the opportunities for strategically increasing plant species diversity to support a high-functioning soil ecosystem, which is the basis of a healthy soil.

Challenges Facing Farmers Who Want to Manage for Improved Soil Health

From the perspective of farmers, the goal of managing soil organic matter to improve soil ecological functions and overall soil health is theoretically desirable but difficult to implement. The capacity to employ practices that will reverse soil organic matter losses and revitalize soil biota is limited by the need for farmers to produce profitable yields in the short term. The economic pressures that govern agricultural enterprises force producers to focus on crop yields and short-term soil productivity rather than broader soil contributions to agroecosystem function and long-term environmental sustainability. While a significant proportion of farmers have adopted management practices such as no-tillage and conservation tillage that reduce soil erosion, those practices that provide the greatest benefits for building soil organic matter are still rarely used. For example, in 2016, more than half the acreage of the three most widely grown crops in the United States was under some form of reduced tillage. In contrast, in 2017, cover crop usage was limited to <4 percent of the US crop acreage. While cover-cropping offers a plethora of benefits, there are many barriers to adopting this practice, and it is simply not compatible with most intensive production systems where bare fallows have enabled farmers to plant earlier in the spring. Furthermore, the summer annuals such as maize and soybeans that occupy vast acreages have been bred to tolerate earlier planting and continue growing later in the fall. For example, in 2005 the average planting date for corn in the Midwestern United States was nearly four weeks earlier compared to typical planting dates in the 1930s, when corn was commonly grown in rotation with perennial forages instead of an over-wintering fallow period. Thus, the entire corn-soybean system has been designed in such a way that using cover crops increases the risk of yield reductions due to delayed planting. The intensification of production leads to similar barriers across all industrialized farming systems, and farmers continue to rely on fertilizer inputs that compensate for reduced soil organic matter and enable them to maintain high yields. In spite of the known environmental consequences, the economic incentives created by government agricultural policies are tied primarily to crop yields.

Organic agriculture is unique in that it emphasizes soil health as the foundation of an ecologically sound production system; however, organic farmers face a different set of challenges to optimizing management to promote healthy soil. Organic farmers are required to use cover cropping and other practices to build soil organic matter, and studies comparing organic and conventional soil generally find greater levels of soil organic matter in fields under organic management regimes, particularly those fractions of organic matter that are most important for soil health functions. Organically managed soils also tend to have greater abundance and biodiversity of soil microflora and fauna. However, the Achilles' heel of organic soil management is the high tillage intensity required to control weeds in place of herbicides, which are forbidden under organic management. This trade-off between tillage intensity and weed control is a central dilemma in organic farming where the level of tillage required to produce crops without herbicides often undermines soil health gains that result from beneficial organic practices such as cover cropping and use of organic soil amendments. Although the allocation of research funding directed at improving organically farming system is still limited, many researchers are working on this problem and developing reduced tillage strategies that are compatible with organic management.

While improving soil health is widely promoted as a management goal, the farmer audience that can actually implement the suite of management practices outlined by the four NRCS management goals is limited. Many practices that improve soil health are incompatible with the structure of intensive, high-yielding production systems. Furthermore, due to these constraints, farmers tend to view soil health primarily from the perspective of the potential for soil health improvements to increase yields. This is problematic because it can take several years or even a decade before yield benefits from soil organic matter increases are realized. At the same time, soil scientists have increasingly embraced a broader soil health perspective that considers multiple ecosystem services that soil provides to humanity at large. For the time being, connections between soil health and crop yields must be made clearly apparent in order to get buy-in from farmers.

Ecologically Based Nutrient Management

Ecological nutrient management (ENM) is based on an ecosystem perspective and provides a conceptual framework grounded in ecosystem ecology.[12] Ecological nutrient management is a multifaceted approach to soil fertility management that aims to achieve acceptable yields, balance nutrient exports with additions, maintain soil nutrient reservoirs, and minimize losses of nutrients and soil to the environment. In agroecosystems with poor or degraded soils, an additional goal is to restore soil fertility and reverse the trajectory of soil degradation. Soil organic matter management is a central focus of the ENM framework, and this serves to integrate nutrient management and soil health goals; however, the theoretical underpinnings for this emphasis are distinct from those that inform the soil health conceptual framework. Likewise, ENM is not aligned with the traditional fertilizer-based approach that led to the 4Rs framework. Instead, ENM incorporates complex ecological processes into soil fertility management in the same way that integrated pest management applies ecological knowledge to pest control.

The nitrogen saturation conceptual framework, developed to explain changes in forest nitrogen biogeochemistry resulting from chronic anthropogenic nitrogen deposition, is the foundation of ENM.[13] According to this framework, ecosystems are nitrogen-saturated when primary productivity is no longer limited by nitrogen, and nitrogen additions exceed the capacity of the ecosystem to cycle or store nitrogen internally. Excess soil nitrogen tends to accelerate nitrogen-cycling processes, including nitrogen mineralization and nitrification, and as a result, nitrogen losses from the ecosystem increase. Under nitrogen-saturating conditions, nitrate leaching and greenhouse gas fluxes increase.

The nitrogen saturation conceptual model highlighted the importance of interactions between different elemental cycles and clarified the role of carbon-nitrogen coupling in determining whether nitrogen retention or loss pathways dominate. The theory led to major advances in biogeochemistry, and it influenced the way ecologists study and model nutrient cycling in natural ecosystems. Previously, it was common to focus on a single cycle and carbon, nitrogen, and phosphorus cycling processes were studied separately. The conceptual framework of coupled elemental cycles has been extended to phosphorus, and elemental cycling processes are now rarely studied in isolation.

Application of this conceptual framework to agricultural systems gives rise to a distinctly different nutrient management strategy; one seeks to enhance the naturally occurring processes governing elemental cycles. The goal of fertilizer management is to ensure that nutrients do not limit crop growth. As a result, in countries where farmers can afford to purchase fertilizers, agricultural systems are managed to achieve nitrogen and phosphorus saturation for the duration of crop production. In contrast, ENM aims to *avoid* nutrient saturation while providing adequate nutrients to crops.

Practices That Are Promoted by ENM

ENM starts with the assumption that recoupling elemental cycles will enable production and environmental goals to be achieved while enhancing the sustainability of soil resources. ENM entails five key principles:

1. *Nutrient additions should be equal to nutrients removed though crop harvests.* This simple mass balance approach ensures that soil mining, where greater amounts of

nitrogen and phosphorus are harvested than are being added, is avoided. Long-term removal of nutrients that exceeds nutrient additions undermines soil fertility and leads to soil degradation. This is the situation in many smallholder subsistence systems. On the other end of the spectrum, limiting the degree to which nutrient additions can exceed harvested removals reduces the risk of environmental losses. This is particularly true in the case of nitrogen. Excess nitrogen stimulates the biological processes that promote nitrogen losses.

2. *Minimize the size of nitrogen and phosphorus pools that are the most susceptible to loss.* Synthetic fertilizers are composed of soluble inorganic nitrogen (nitrate and ammonium) and phosphorus, both of which are vulnerable to being lost from the soil. Nitrate in particular is highly mobile and susceptible to loss through leaching or microbial transformations that convert nitrate to nitrous oxide. As the concentration of these forms of nitrogen increases in soils, the activity of loss pathways increases. Under ENM, flux through the inorganic nitrogen and phosphorus pools may be large; a central objective of this strategy is to reduce the concentration of these forms that are the most susceptible to loss.

3. *Build soil organic matter and other nutrient reserves that are least susceptible to loss.* Because plants can access many forms of nitrogen and phosphorus through partnerships with beneficial microorganisms living in the rhizosphere, ENM targets the full range of nutrient reservoirs and cycling processes. The basic strategy is to conserve and build nutrient pools that are less vulnerable to loss but can be accessed through plant- and microbially mediated processes. These reserves include labile and stabilized soil organic matter, microbial biomass, and sparingly soluble phosphorus. Management strategies that promote the accrual of nitrogen and phosphorus into these pools while minimizing those pathways that lead to nutrient losses are encouraged over those that directly add soluble nitrogen and phosphorus. In particular, the use of legumes rather than conventional fertilizers as the primary source of new nitrogen increases the incorporation of added nitrogen into soil organic matter reserves.[14]

4. *Maximize agroecosystem capacity to use soluble, inorganic nitrogen and phosphorus.* Plant and microbial acquisition removes soluble nutrients from the soil solution and prevents their loss from the soil. In addition to the benefits related to the formation of soil organic matter described under this chapter's section on soil health, maximizing living roots in space and time greatly increases the likelihood that soluble nitrogen will be captured before it is lost from soil through leaching or denitrification. Furthermore, when soil carbon is increased, the growth of soil organisms is stimulated, and they will also contribute to nutrient acquisition.

5. *Use functional and phylogenetic biodiversity to realize these goals.* Plant and microbial species differ in their capacity to carry out all these processes. Using plant diversity to promote a more functionally diverse soil biota can enhance overall productivity and nutrient cycling capacity of belowground communities.[15]

Examples of management practices that contribute to these outcomes include diversifying crop rotations and nutrient sources, cover cropping and intercropping, and legume intensification. Diversifying crop rotations and reducing bare fallows, particularly by adding cover crops or perennials as well as expanding reliance on legume N sources, are particularly effective for recoupling these elemental cycles through the multiple mechanisms outlined above. There is a growing literature supporting the efficacy of ENM for building soil organic matter and improving nutrient retention. For example, a meta-analysis investigating effects of diverse crop rotations compared to continuous monoculture found that diverse rotations increased total soil carbon by 3.6 percent and total nitrogen by 5.3 percent. When rotations included a cover crop, total soil organic carbon and nitrogen increased by 8.5 percent and 12.8 percent, respectively.[16] Another meta-analysis of 217 experiments using nitrogen tracer methods to study nitrogen management practices found that two practices—diversified crop rotations and organic nitrogen sources—significantly improved total nitrogen retention compared to more common 4Rs practices.[17] The particular suite of cropping practices used are site-specific and reflect the environmental characteristics of the agroecosystem (climate and soils), the crops that are being grown, the resources available to the farmer, and the livelihood goals of the household.

Challenges to Implementation

The barriers preventing broad adoption of ENM by farmers overlap to a large degree with those that impede the implementation of soil health management. However, while the structural incompatibilities between conventional industrial cropping systems and practices that are essential for improving soil health and implementing ENM are identical, there are some important differences in the way extension educators and farmers view these two management strategies. Soil health improvement is commonly promoted, but it is generally considered to be a desired but unnecessary management goal. In contrast, the 4Rs mindset itself is a formidable barrier to implementation of ENM. The focus on fertilizer management strategies that aim to maximize crop uptake of nitrogen and phosphorus excludes any consideration of how the reliance on soluble fertilizers affects carbon cycling. The 4Rs aims to optimize fertilizer rates to maximize yield or net income, while ENM seeks to reduce the amount of annually applied nitrogen and phosphorus required to maintain adequate yields over the long term. Thus, these two paradigms are at odds, and the agricultural establishment, which is deeply entwined with the agro-industrial complex that provides farmers with the inputs needed to manage industrial cropping systems, remains unconvinced that ENM is practical and necessary for sustaining long-term soil fertility.

Moreover, some practices, such as using legumes as the major source of new nitrogen, face obstacles that are even more intractable. The cropping systems of today co-evolved with reliance on synthetic fertilizers, and using fertilizers is a simple, easy, and effective strategy for reliably obtaining desired yields. In contrast, adding cover crops or diversifying nutrient sources and rotations is complicated and requires farmers to develop new management skills. Furthermore, legume seed can be expensive, and the cost of legume-derived nitrogen is greater than nitrogen provided through synthetic fertilizers. The underlying causes for these differences are complex, but government policies regulating energy production and agriculture play an important role.

ENM is highly compatible with organic agricultural systems, and some organic farmers do employ many ENM principles in managing soil fertility. However, like their conventional peers, organic farmers must prioritize short-term profitability goals. As a result, in order to maintain intensive crop production, many organic farmers find it difficult to include legumes in their rotations at the frequency needed to supply adequate nitrogen. These farmers rely heavily on composted manures, and due to the composition of these soil amendments, which contain too much phosphorus relative to nitrogen, they end up overapplying phosphorus.

Prognosis for Implementation of Sustainable Soil Fertility Management

Ultimately, the future of the soil resources that are essential to support humanity rests not in the hands of farmers but with the broader society. Consumers have the power to demand agri-environmental policies that can enable farmers to prioritize stewardship and sustainable soil management. Left to self-regulate, markets will not overcome the perverse agri-environmental policies that inadvertently promote continued soil and environmental degradation. The importance of soils that are healthy and provide diverse ecosystem services beyond food production needs to be made clear to the broader public. There are many opportunities to enact policies to incentivize ENM and soil health practices. For example, subsidies currently paid to farmers based on yields could be diverted toward sustainable soil and nutrient management outcomes. While there has been some progress in redirecting agricultural policies to support sustainable soil management, these changes have been insufficient to promote the substantial changes in soil fertility management needed to reverse the trajectory of soil degradation.

Notes

1. E. B. Barbier and J. P. Hochard, "Land Degradation and Poverty," *Nature Sustainability* 1 (2018): 623–631.
2. P. M. Vitousek et al., "Nutrient Imbalances in Agricultural Development," *Science* 324 (2009): 1519–1520.
3. A. N. Auclair, "Ecological Factors in Development of Intensive-Management Ecosystems in Midwestern United-States," *Ecology* 57 (1976): 431–444.
4. S. R. Carpenter, N. F. Caraco, D. L. Correll, R. W. Howarth, A. N. Sharpley, and V. H. Smith, "Nonpoint Pollution of Surface Waters with Phosphorus and Nitrogen," *Ecological Applications* 8 (1998): 559–568.

5. P. M. Vitousek et al., "Human Alteration of the Global Nitrogen Cycle: Sources and Consequences," *Ecological Applications* 7 (1997): 737–750; and Carpenter et al., "Nonpoint Pollution of Surface Waters with Phosphorus and Nitrogen."
6. N. K. Fageria and V. C. Baligar, "Enhancing Nitrogen Use Efficiency in Crop Plants," *Advances in Agronomy* 88 (2005): 97–185.
7. Vitousek et al., "Nutrient Imbalances in Agricultural Development."
8. Carrie Vollmer-Sanders, A. Allman, D. Busdeker, L. B. Moody, and W. G. Stanley, "Building Partnerships to Scale Up Conservation: 4R Nutrient Stewardship Certification Program in the Lake Erie Watershed," *Journal of Great Lakes Research* 42 (2016): 1395–1402.
9. J. W. Doran, M. Sarrantonio, and M. A. Liebig, "Soil Health and Sustainability," *Advances in Agronomy* 56, ed. D. L. Sparks (1996): 1–54.
10. E. K. Bunemann et al., "Soil Quality—A Critical Review," *Soil Biology & Biochemistry* 120 (2018): 105–125.
11. National Resource Conservation Service. Soil Health. Soil Health | NRCS (usda.gov). Accessed June 22, 2021.
12. L. E. Drinkwater, M. Schipanski, S. S. Snapp, and L. E. Jackson, "Ecologically Based Nutrient Management," in Agricultural Systems: Agroecology and Rural Innovation for Development, ed. S. S. Snapp and B. Pounds (2017): 203–257; L. E. Drinkwater and S. S. Snapp, "Nutrients in Agroecosystems: Rethinking the Management Paradigm," Advances in Agronomy 92, ed. D. L. Sparks (San Diego: Elsevier Academic Press, 2007): 163ff.
13. John D. Aber, K. J. Nadelhoffer, P. Steudler, and J. M. Melillo, "Nitrogen Saturation in Northern Forest Ecosystems," *BioScience* 39 (1989): 378–386.
14. L. E. Drinkwater, P. Wagoner, and M. Sarrantonio, "Legume-based Cropping Systems Have Reduced Carbon and Nitrogen Losses," *Nature* 396 (1998): 262–265.
15. B. J. Cardinale et al., "The Functional Role of Producer Diversity in Ecosystems," *American Journal of Botany* 98 (2011): 572–592.
16. M. D. McDaniel, L. K. Tiemann, and A. S. Grandy, "Does Agricultural Crop Diversity Enhance Soil Microbial Biomass and Organic Matter Dynamics? A Meta-Analysis," *Ecological Applications* 24 (2014): 560–570.
17. J. B. Gardner and L. E. Drinkwater, "The Fate of Nitrogen in Grain Cropping Systems: A Meta-Analysis of 15N Field Experiments," *Ecological Applications* 19 (2009): 2167–2184.

Bibliography

Drinkwater, Laurie E., M. Schipanski, S. S. Snapp, and L. E. Jackson. "Ecologically Based Nutrient Management." In *Agricultural Systems: Agroecology and Rural Innovation for Development*, edited by Barry Pound, 203–257. San Diego: Academic Press, 2017.

Drinkwater, Laurie E., and S. S. Snapp. "Nutrients in Agroecosystems: Rethinking the Management Paradigm." *Advances in Agronomy* 92 (2007): 163–186.

Montgomery, David R. *Dirt: The Erosion of Civilizations.* Berkeley: University of California Press, 2007.

Smil, Vaclav. *Enriching the Earth: Fritz Haber, Carl Bosch, and the Transformation of World Food Production.* Cambridge, MA: MIT Press, 2000.

Vitousek, Peter M., J. D. Aber, R. W. Howarth, G. E. Likens, P. A. Matson, D. W. Schindler, et al. "Human Alteration of the Global Nitrogen Cycle: Sources and Consequences." *Ecological Applications* 7 (1997): 737–750.

CHAPTER 3

A SHORT HISTORY OF SEED KEEPING

HELEN ANNE CURRY

SEED keeping—choosing and storing seeds from each season's harvest to serve as the starting point of the next—has been a routine task of farmers and gardeners across millennia. It is also a task that has changed profoundly over the past 150 years. In the twenty-first century, selecting seed on the farm, with an eye to maintaining or improving it, is associated mostly with farmers working outside of industrialized agriculture. This may be by necessity, as in the case of subsistence cultivators, or by choice, as with producers of heritage or heirloom vegetables and grains. In many circumstances, seed storage has also transitioned off the farm, although the extent to which farmers purchase seed, rather than saving it from their own harvest, varies according to the crop, country, regulatory context, and market expectations.

Although these transitions in seed keeping practices were associated with rising agricultural productivity, they also generated concern. Where farmers stopped selecting and storing seed, and where national regulations dictated what seeds could legally be sold, worries arose about the diversity of crops in cultivation. This uneasiness gave rise to a novel form of seed keeping, the seed or gene bank, tasked with ensuring the survival of diverse crop varieties well into the future. Today, state-run seed banks bear responsibility for reassuring governments and corporations that seeds will survive to serve as the source of future varieties. Their efforts are complemented by those of community or nongovernmental organizations, many critical of the industrial model of agriculture that first produced the need for seed banks, which have generated alternative approaches to keeping crop diversity alive.

Seed is central to contemporary debates about the perils of industrial agriculture and to aspirations for a sustainable future. The swift consolidation of the private seed industry from the 1970s onward and the decreased support for public plant breeding programs in the same period has caused growers and governments to question their exclusion from decisions about what seeds are good for them. The demand for sovereignty over seed is a key pillar of the global peasant movement, which has united rural communities in Africa, Asia, Europe, and the Americas. The rejection of crops grown from genetically modified seed and the popularity of heritage varieties and local seed exchanges mark a similar determination among middle-class farmers, gardeners, and consumers to reclaim control over seed.

In exploring these developments, scholars have rightly turned to histories of plant breeding as means of exposing contingencies in the seemingly inexorable trajectory of industrial seed production.[1] Meanwhile, social scientists have explored the role of seed saving among diverse farming and gardening communities as a means of resistance to that same trajectory.[2] A historical account of seed keeping unites these perspectives, highlighting this as a long-standing agricultural practice, a professionalized contribution to industrial production, and a contemporary means of community survival.[3]

Seed Storage and Selection on the Farm

For most of humans' history as agriculturalists, farming and gardening have involved producing seeds to plant in subsequent seasons, in addition to the grains, fruits, vegetables, fodder, and fibers destined for more immediate consumption. Agricultural communities around the world developed and used, and in some cases continue to use, different criteria for selecting seeds as well as diverse means of keeping these safe and viable. Their methods and tools have depended on the kind of seed being saved, prevailing environmental conditions, social circumstances, and community norms. Farmers may choose the most vigorous plants as the source of seed or simply draw from the grain store, or granary; they may search for a feature prized in cooking or craft, or for the healthiest-looking seed, or in desperate years use whatever remains available.[4] They may store their seeds in underground pits or aboveground granaries, often together with the grains destined for eating, or these may be brought inside the house to be hung from the rafters or stored in earthenware jars, woven baskets, cloth sacks, or plastic containers—typically in whatever fashion will best protect them from insects, rats, mold, and damp.[5]

The case of contemporary maize seed selection and storage among Maya farmers in Yaxcaba, in southeastern Mexico, illustrates key aspects of seed keeping as an on-farm activity.[6] These farmers cultivate a number of different types of maize, alongside beans, squash, and chili peppers, and most of them save seeds from each harvest to plant the following season. When choosing which ears of maize to harvest for seed, they select ones that are large and healthy, with uniform color and big grains. Size is considered a proxy for future yield: the bigger the ear and grain, the bigger the harvest. Selecting for color is an aesthetic choice that also maintains the visual distinctiveness of varieties preferred for different reasons, from use in a particular dish to hardiness in the face of drought or disease.

When it comes to storage, most farmers in Yaxcaba leave the ears selected for seed encased in the thick leaves that form the husk. These are placed in a granary with a thatched roof and elevated floor or stored in the family home in burlap sacks or along the rafters. Because insects pose a constant threat, farmers treat the ears with lime or commercial insecticides. There are exceptions to these general patterns, especially where different materials are available, whether plastic storage containers for seed or cardboard laminate for granary roofs, or when farmers grow varieties produced by state or commercial breeding programs.[7] These breeders' varieties can be more susceptible to insect damage after harvest, typically because they have not been selected for storability, and therefore demand different storage regimes.

This extended example calls attention to distinct aspects of seed keeping that cultivators have long attended to, from choosing which seeds are worthy of saving to the most appropriate methods of keeping them safe for future sowing. It also highlights innovation in practices. Farmers continually experiment, and practices of seed selection and storage are no exception. The variation in choices about seed keeping within even a small community of farmers, as seen among Maya farmers in Yaxcaba, highlights that these essential agricultural tasks are as much a matter of discussion, debate, and dynamism as of heritage or tradition. Growers exchange ideas informally with relatives and neighbors, and when possible source inspiration from further afield.[8] Above all, the example underscores the role of farmers as breeders, selecting traits that they feel are consistent with greater productivity, much as their counterparts in commercial seed production do, while also selecting for traits that those yield-focused counterparts might neglect, like storability.[9]

In many places, state investment in agricultural research, often in conjunction with commercial development, has transformed farmers' perspectives on seed selection and seed keeping. Initially this change was modest. State-led research produced new agricultural knowledge. It also created opportunities for professional experts—that is, individuals employed to develop that knowledge and deliver it to farmers. Wherever and whenever this happened, farmers gradually shifted from being experts in seed keeping to the recipients of expert advice.

Here maize offers another illustrative case, this time in the United States where maize, also known as corn, dominated (and still dominates) the agricultural economy. The late nineteenth century saw the establishment of a national infrastructure for agricultural education and research in the United States, including the creation of the US Department of Agriculture (1862) and legislation facilitating the establishment of state agricultural colleges (1862, 1890) and experiment stations (1887), with extension services (1914) following soon thereafter.

Among the many subjects addressed by government researchers and extension agents were best practices in seed selection and storage. These were assumed to be essential to ensuring the future productivity of seed, and therefore production more generally. According to typical advice, "Improvement of the quality of seed is the least expensive method of increasing the yield per acre."[10] For corn, experts in fields like plant physiology, crop production, and farm mechanics described how to select ears for seed in the field, the best dates to do so in different regions, the amount of seed to keep in reserve, methods of drying corn seed for better survival in storage, the ideal spaces for storage (and, conversely, the conditions that left seed most prone to damage), devices that would facilitate drying and storing, and systems of record keeping.[11] The first decades of the twentieth century also saw corn breeders (a nascent profession, discussed below) repeatedly revise the methods of seed selection they promoted to corn farmers.[12]

The engagement of agricultural researchers and extension agents in developing and delivering advice on seed selection and storage reflected their understanding that the typical practices of farmers might not be best practices. They also reflected differences between farmers and these professional advisers in defining the most desirable seed. A farmer might prize the cheapest seed, produced with the least investments in time, labor, or money. By comparison, researchers and extension agents, and the governments that employed them, were more likely to want seed that was maximally productive of good-quality grain. They therefore encouraged farmers to make investments in better seed keeping. These competing concerns became more evident when professional researchers began selecting seed and developing new varieties to market to farmers as improvements over those locally grown and traded. Farmers needed good reasons to pay a premium for seed, when it was ostensibly available at far less cost from their own fields.[13]

Privatization and Professionalization of Seed Production

Several trends conspired to take seed selection, and eventually some types of seed storage, off the farm. Chief among these was the expansion, at different times depending on the country and the kind of crop offered for sale, of the commercial seed trade.[14]

Seed selling as a business in Europe dates to at least the sixteenth century and typically tracked the growth in market gardening (producing vegetables to sell especially in urban markets) and the popularization of gardening and flower cultivation.[15] Seeds of forage crops also became a common commercial product earlier: as with many vegetables, harvesting and preparing the seeds of forage crops requires additional labor on the part of the farmer. Merchants added further incentives for farmers to purchase, rather than produce, fodder seed by marketing their own seed blends.[16] Selling the seed of grain crops as a business pursuit lagged behind because of the comparative ease of using stored grains from a granary as the subsequent season's seed. Nonetheless, grain markets have often served as seed markets, offering a route for farmers to obtain new varieties, and included kinds originating far afield as these markets internationalized in the eighteenth century.[17]

The increasing tendency of seeds to traverse distances initially caused problems. Farmers procuring a fresh seed stock from a fellow farmer or a local merchant would always have had to consider whether the seeds they invested in were of good quality: ready to germinate, weed-free, and truly of the type claimed. But new markets, increased demand, and extended trade networks created more opportunities for unscrupulous behavior. Accounts from the nineteenth century suggest that the mislabeling of seeds offered for sale was a common concern, whether with respect to the country of origin or, in the case of grain and vegetable crops, the variety of the seed being sold.[18]

Reports of adulterated, weed-ridden, spoiled, or otherwise unsatisfactory seeds being offered by merchants eventually brought about calls for quality control and regulation. These calls came from farmers who wanted to be certain of purchasing good seed, state agricultural administrators who wanted to increase farm output, and honest seed dealers who wanted to charge a premium for a high-quality product. The extension of seed markets therefore brought about seed certification schemes, seed testing stations (where quality and authenticity were assessed), and guidelines for farmers indicating how they could carry out their own tests of purity and germination.[19]

While seed analysts crouched over seeds in testing laboratories, a different group of experts exercised new authority over seeds in the field: professional breeders. The end of the nineteenth century saw increasing interest in the development of better crop varieties, especially within state agricultural institutions tasked with fostering national productivity. Nineteenth-century plant breeders in many countries undertook experiments in selection and hybridization, hoping to improve local varieties or adapt imported seed to new conditions.[20] The vigorous promotion of Mendelian genetics after 1900 depicted scientifically trained breeders as possessors of a powerful method for controlling the heredity of plants and animals through precise, predictable crosses. As a result, the early twentieth century saw the expansion of professional breeding alongside the new discipline of genetics.[21]

Rather than emphasize the education of farmers in best practices for seed selection, agricultural institutions gradually transitioned to emphasizing the need for farmers, who were often wary of paying a premium for a product they could produce cheaply themselves, to acquire seed from government sources or certified seed sellers. Only then, they were reminded, would they reap the rewards of scientific breeding.[22]

Although there were notable differences from one location to the next, the combination of privatization and professionalization in seed production and plant breeding in many industrial countries meant that, by the 1940s, farmers were no longer seen as playing the most important role in the creation of seed. This was largely a result of the transformation of seed keeping practices. Although most farmers still saved seed from one season to the next, they might now rely on—or be encouraged to rely on—state-run agricultural stations or private seed companies for advice on what seeds to plant, how to store them, and when to refresh farm-saved stocks with a supply of professionally bred, commercially sold, and state-certified seeds.

Genetic Erosion and the Rise of Seed Banking

The transition away from farmers' varieties made some observers nervous. When farmers opted for the creations of professional breeders, they sometimes stopped cultivating their own locally adapted types. Without anyone keeping the seeds of these varieties from season to season, they could easily disappear, together with the unique and potentially useful combinations of traits they might possess.

In the 1890s, German agronomists worried that the abandonment of farmers' varieties would deprive future breeders of valuable traits such as disease resistance, and they made a plea for these types to be systematically saved and studied.[23] In the ensuing decades, concerned researchers continued to demand systems for collecting and conserving farmers' varieties, often called landraces, and to do so on a more global scale. In one well-known assessment from the 1930s, two US scientists described the "world's priceless reservoir of germ plasm" of barley diversity in the Middle East and North Africa as "imperiled." The chief culprit was increased trade in seeds. As they observed, "A hundred years ago, when the grain crop of north Africa failed, the natives starved. Today, in years of shortage, the French supply their dependent populations with seed from California. Arab farmers in Mariout sometimes sell short to European buyers and import seeds from Palestine." Assuming that similar changes were taking place across the globe, they predicted extinction unless quick action were taken.[24]

These researchers recommended that agricultural institutions create extensive collections of crop landraces as a measure to prevent their loss, a proposal that echoed earlier suggestions. Many institutions already possessed such collections, but typically their extent was not as expansive nor their oversight as rigorous as concerned agronomists wanted. These collections ranged in size and content, from assorted materials gathered by individual plant breeders, to larger institutional collections used by multiple scientists and potentially including many more species, to a very few state-run collections worldwide that encompassed many distinct varieties representing tens, or even hundreds, of different species.[25] In the 1930s, the most impressive example of a state collection was that of the All-Union Institute of Plant Industry in Leningrad, which boasted some 250,000 crop varieties from around the world.[26]

Regardless of size, these collections, typically kept as seed (as opposed to living plants), served as immediate resources for agricultural development rather than long-term investments in the preservation of endangered types. It took truly rapid abandonment of local varieties, and recognition that seed samples were difficult to keep alive, to motivate a new kind of seed collection: seed banks, also called germplasm banks or gene banks, which aimed at permanent stewardship.

The crop species whose disappearance arguably did the most to catalyze the creation of conservation seed banks was maize. In the United States, geneticists and plant breeders had devised methods of producing hybrid corn seed economically in the 1920s.

This process resulted in seeds that were advertised as producing higher-yielding plants. However, the procedure of recombining inbred lines that generated these vigorous hybrids also entailed their producing genetically mixed seeds—seeds that when grown would not produce an equally vigorous second (or third, or fourth . . .) generation. This all but necessitated that growers return to a seed company each year for fresh stocks. A combination of corporate advertising, government regulation, and farmer experience drove a mass transition from established local varieties to new hybrid varieties in the United States by the early 1940s.[27]

The shift to commercial hybrid corn was so swift and so seemingly complete that some scientists wondered about the wisdom of letting the old farmers' varieties disappear.[28] Despite this, it took the expansion of US-led maize breeding activities to Mexico and Central and South America, typically as part of development aid, to provoke action. Anthropologists, breeders, botanists, and geneticists imagined another mass transition in which peasant and Indigenous farmers of these regions, possessors of incomparable diversity in maize, would soon abandon local varieties for commercial hybrids. In the 1950s, a committee of US maize experts, convinced that such a transition was underway, directed the collection of some 11,000 samples of "indigenous maize" from across the Americas. Crucially, they also arranged for the storage of these seed samples in purpose-built cold rooms, explicitly conceiving these collections for long-term preservation rather than near-term study and use.[29]

A decade later, concerns about rapid and widespread "genetic erosion"—the loss of genetic diversity resulting from extensive cultivation of the same or similar crop varieties—generalized to many more crops.[30] When experts gathered in Rome at the United Nations Food and Agriculture Organization (FAO) in 1967 to assess the need for plant exploration, utilization, and conservation, they declared international action in these areas "a great and urgent need" as a result of economic and industrial development. "The genetic resources of the plants by which we live are dwindling rapidly and disastrously," they warned.[31]

This sense of sweeping change was heightened further in 1968 by the declaration of a "Green Revolution" in agricultural production. Although increased yields seen in Latin America, the Middle East, and South Asia in the late 1960s arose from multiple factors, most attention focused on the development and spread of "miracle seeds": short-statured wheat and rice varieties bred by researchers at two international agricultural research centers.[32] The swift uptake of these seeds, largely at the insistence of governments and aid agencies, provoked concern about the survival of the farmers' varieties they displaced. Experts who gathered at FAO agreed that the only solution to the impending loss of these threatened varieties was to organize collecting missions, gather seeds, and arrange for their long-term storage as part of an "international gene bank."[33]

In Europe, where this specter created by commercial varieties was old news, the introduction of national lists provoked a similar narrative of loss. National lists restricted the sale of varieties to those officially registered, and registration required evidence of a variety's distinctiveness, uniformity, and stability, as well as the payment of a registration fee. Growers who preferred either unusual varieties for which there would be little market demand or landraces whose genetic variability rendered them ineligible for registration worried that these would disappear once national lists were enforced.[34]

Regardless of the precipitating cause, it proved easier to articulate the need for coordinated efforts to collect and conserve crop landraces than to agree on the form that these efforts ought to take. Thanks to scientists working within national and international agencies, the 1970s saw the creation of the International Board for Plant Genetic Resources, an institution dedicated to conserving the world's "plant genetic resources" by arranging for collection and long-term conservation of diverse crop varieties. It was besieged by conflict from the outset. Participants disagreed on which plants needed conservation attention, where seed banks ought to be located, and who would be placed in charge.[35]

Amid these disagreements, one element was largely agreed upon: most of the scientists and administrators involved considered long-term cold storage of seeds in purpose-built facilities such as seed banks, with ongoing maintenance by technical experts, to be the surest means of securing seeds, and the genetic diversity within them, for the future.[36] Working under the assumption that few growers would choose to maintain seeds of local varieties rather than purchase the products of professional breeding programs from commercial suppliers, they imagined and fostered a new form of seed keeping—seed banking—conducted in research facilities by technicians rather than in fields, granaries, and homes by farmers.[37]

Back to the Land

While scientists in the 1970s focused on building seed banks and devising technical standards for extending the life of seeds in cold storage, an alternative vision of conservation took shape to complement, and in some cases, to challenge, these activities. The trends in agriculture that caused plant breeders, explorers, and geneticists to worry about crop diversity disappearing, especially in countries undergoing economic development, also provoked worry among farmers and gardeners in wealthier nations who saw industrialized agriculture, and the varieties that accompanied this, as a threat to their preferred varieties of maize, beans, and broccoli—and to their way of life.

One early response of these concerned growers was to organize seed sharing networks. In the United States, the Missouri homesteaders Kent and Diane Whealy launched a grassroots seed exchange in 1975 as a means of both preserving vegetable diversity and ensuring access to it. The True Seed Exchange (soon renamed Seed Savers Exchange) connected growers with, or wanting, prized "heirlooms" or "old, reliable, superior vegetable varieties" through an annual members' listing.[38] In the Whealys' initial model, conservation of these varieties, treasured for their flavor, hardiness, or history, would be assured through their continued circulation and cultivation. Seed keeping at home was the linchpin of the entire enterprise: it supplied the seed that traversed the exchange network. In the 1980s, Kent Whealy began to feel apprehensive about the extent to which members circulated out of the exchange, taking precious seeds with them. This observation, plus the donation of a massive collection of bean seeds to Seed Savers Exchange, pushed Whealy to adopt a centralized collection—a seed bank—as an essential complement to the exchange network.[39]

This seed bank differed from state-run counterparts in its being accessible to the small-scale farmers and gardeners of the Seed Savers Exchange, and in its stewarding the varieties of most interest to that community. These were qualities that it shared with other community-led seed banks that appeared around the same time, in the United States and abroad. For example, the seed bank of Native Seeds/SEARCH of Tucson, Arizona, specialized in seeds of the arid southwestern United States, especially those associated with Native American agriculture. It was used to supply Native American farmers and other interested growers with seeds of these difficult-to-source varieties.[40] In the United Kingdom, where concerns about the introduction of a national seed list induced concerns among small-scale and especially organic growers about the loss of cherished vegetables, the Henry Doubleday Research Association established its Heritage Seed Library in order to preserve traditional varieties.[41] These and other early community-organized seed banks promoted two forms of seed keeping simultaneously: seasonal on-farm (or in-garden) cycles of selecting, saving, and sowing, and the more extended off-farm cycles of saving and regenerating in a seed bank.

Community seed banks became an agricultural intervention pursued especially by nongovernmental organizations (NGOs) in developing countries in the 1980s, thanks to two distinct but converging conversations: debates over the ownership of plant varieties and new accounts of the dynamics of seed introduction and exchange in agricultural communities.

The first of these was driven by the expansion of intellectual property protections in plant varieties from the 1960s onward and the subsequent consolidation of many small, independent seed companies into an ever-diminishing number of transnational corporations.[42] Activists who campaigned against these trends in the 1980s objected to the transfer of seeds from the farms and fields of the diversity-rich Global South to either the inaccessible fortresses of corporate crop development or the seed banks of the diversity-poor industrialized Global North. Both types of transfer disempowered farmers in poorer countries. The former allowed transnational firms to demand payment for access to "plant genetic resources" in the form of breeders' commercial varieties while retaining free access to farmers' varieties as a source of those same genetic resources. The latter placed diversity that was supposedly global heritage in the hands of foreign powers and into institutions whose track records on safe storage were subject to increasing scrutiny.[43] It also appeared to make these seeds easily accessible to the growing number of private companies experimenting with the possibilities of transgenic manipulation, an activity that many activists found troubling.[44]

In 1986, the Rural Advancement Foundation International (RAFI, today ETC Group), a key institutional player in activism related to the ownership of seed, released a "Community Seed Bank Kit." This folder of informational pamphlets provided a primer on the need for community seed banks and the potential role of NGOs in promoting these, as well as practical guidelines for how to establish a seed bank. In line with the goals of RAFI, the kit espoused self-determination and local decision-making over foreign control, and continuous engagement by growers rather than one-off technological solutions promoted by technical experts.[45] Following on the heels of RAFI's engagement, and with the support of international activists working with NGOs, the late 1980s and early 1990s saw the creation of many community seed banks in South and Southeast Asia, Latin America, and Africa.[46]

A second important prod to community seed banks came from agronomists' and social scientists' mounting observations that farmers' varieties were not disappearing in the way that scientists in the 1960s and 1970s had imagined they were. Surveys of peasants raising maize in Mexico, Peruvian potato cultivators, and Turkish wheat growers revealed that farmers, especially those existing on social or ecological margins, had good reason to continue sowing landraces rather than breeders' varieties.[47] These observations added fuel to existing critiques of Green Revolution varieties—and of the panoply of inputs that those varieties demanded—as causing more problems for peasant farmers than they resolved.[48]

They also stimulated new ideas about how to conserve crop diversity amid widespread agricultural change. Whereas the attention of biologists and breeders concerned about crop diversity had long centered on *ex situ*, or offsite, conservation in seed banks or other controlled facilities, new interest emerged among professionals in the possibilities of *in situ* conservation, that is, in onsite or on-farm programs, especially among peasant and subsistence cultivators. For these researchers, promoting on-farm conservation did not necessarily mean allowing farmers to continue in their established patterns of cultivation; instead it could (and probably would) involve new techniques and new alliances.[49] Community seed banking, an existing adaptation of the dominant *ex situ* approach that enabled farmers to access crop diversity and maintain this on farm, was one such technique.[50]

The promotion of on-farm conservation of crop diversity fostered interest in other interventions, ranging from enhancing the value of farmers' varieties through marketing, to hosting agricultural fairs, to educating farmers about regional diversity.[51] One approach that gained popularity, probably because of its simultaneous validation of both farmers' and researchers' knowledge, was participatory plant breeding. This approach recognized that farmers are more likely to cultivate particular varieties when these fulfill their needs as growers, consumers, and sellers of the eventual crop, but saw professional breeders, by virtue of their training, as best positioned to create varieties matching those needs. Participatory breeding programs of the 1990s and early 2000s therefore encouraged farmers and breeders to work together to select and maintain landraces, creating the most desirable versions of these in order to assure their continued cultivation. These programs took different forms depending on the particular cultural setting and institutional participants, but typically modified long-standing on-farm seed keeping routines of subsistence cultivators to make space for the interventions of professional collaborators.[52]

By the end of the twentieth century, community seed banks and participatory plant breeding had developed clear profiles among the range of solutions proposed to the loss of farmers' varieties and the genetic diversity they represented.[53] These solutions involved new hybrid forms of seed keeping, which validated the contributions of farmers and gardeners to the creation and maintenance of seed through their long-standing practices of seed keeping while also seeing value in the knowledge (e.g., genetics) and technologies (e.g., seed banks) of professional scientists.

CONCLUSION: SEEDING THE FUTURE

In the twenty-first century, disagreements over good seed have deepened. Objections to genetically modified (GM) organisms that date to the development of transgenic technologies in the 1970s, and intensified with the introduction of GM crops in the 1990s, persist in the rejection of gene-edited varieties.[54] The consolidation of corporate control over global seed stocks is more complete than ever before, a circumstance that provokes responses ranging from protests against intellectual property regimes to a surge in community-maintained seed libraries.[55] While the products of commercial breeding programs, typically selected for yield and uniformity, generate record global harvests and sustain an expanding world population, many more consumers and growers seek out types that are explicitly not the result of recent breeding investments.

The demand for food sovereignty—the ability to access nutritious, culturally appropriate foods and to determine the systems that produce these—increasingly incorporates the achievement of seed sovereignty. The global peasant movement La Via Campesina declares succinctly, "Seeds are an irreplaceable pillar of food production and the basis of productive social and cultural reproduction. Via Campesina promotes farmers' rights to use, develop and reproduce peasants' seeds and struggles against attempts by corporations to control our common heritage."[56]

Farther from the farm field, well-off consumers in many countries search grocery stores and farm stands for varieties they describe as heritage, heirloom, or traditional.[57] Their reasons for doing so are varied, ranging from flavor to health to nostalgia, but ultimately link back to an understanding of why, how, and by whom, the seeds of those varieties have been kept.

Multiple forms of seed keeping, and visions of good seed, come together in the most extensive, and iconic, seed keeping project of the twenty-first century: the Svalbard Global Seed Vault. Located on an Arctic archipelago, and dug deep into the permafrost, this seed storage facility promises to keep seeds viable longer, and more securely, than any other seed bank. The Global Crop Diversity Trust, or Crop Trust, the organization that coordinates deposits to the vault, declares it to be a "fail-safe" facility, providing the "final back up" of the world's crop diversity by protecting duplicate collections of many of the world's largest seed banks.[58] In 2021, it housed over one million samples representing more than 5,000 species of crops and their wild relatives.

These samples trace their origins to national and international agricultural research programs, most of which include landraces originally sourced from farmers as well as lines generated by professional breeders. In the case of the vault's duplicate collection of the Seed Savers Exchange seed bank, the samples represent the labor of home gardeners, too.[59]

To prevent unwanted appropriation of any seeds, for example by companies that might attempt to develop and patent them, all the deposits are "black boxed." This means that they are only accessible to those who deposited them. In this vision of seed banking, security means protection from unwanted exploitation as well as physical decay. The organizations who place seeds into the care of the Crop Trust are assured that these remain theirs alone, to develop according to their own understanding of what constitutes good seed.

The convergence in the Arctic of seed savers and professional breeders, state and international research institutions, and (in the case of the seed vault's funders) private philanthropies and transnational companies indicates the extent to which these diverse actors agree on at least one thing. Although crop seeds are the product of biological evolution, they are also created through human effort. The varied forms of seed keeping that arose in the twentieth century attest to the existence of multiple visions of good agricultural production, and to the knowledge that none would succeed without investments of labor, time, and care in the creation of seeds.

Notes

* I am grateful to Xan Chacko, Berris Charnley, and Jeannie Whayne for their feedback on earlier versions of this chapter.
1. Key contributions include Deborah Fitzgerald, *The Business of Breeding: Hybrid Corn in Illinois, 1890–1940* (Ithaca, NY: Cornell University Press, 1990); John H. Perkins, *Geopolitics and the Green Revolution: Wheat, Genes, and the Cold War* (Oxford: Oxford University Press, 1997); Jack Ralph Kloppenburg, Jr., *First the Seed: The Political Economy of Plant Biotechnology, 1492–2000*, 2nd ed. (Madison: University of Wisconsin Press, 2004); Berris Charnley, "Agricultural Science, Plant Breeding and the Emergence of a Mendelian System in Britain, 1880–1930" (PhD thesis, University of Leeds, 2011); Jonathan Harwood, *Europe's Green Revolution and Others Since: The Rise and Fall of Peasant-Friendly Plant Breeding* (London: Routledge, 2012); Courtney Fullilove, *The Profit of the Earth: The Global Seeds of American Agriculture* (Chicago: University of Chicago Press, 2017).
2. Key contributions include Virginia D. Nazarea, *Heirloom Seeds and Their Keepers: Marginality and Memory in the Conservation of Biological Diversity* (Tucson: University of Arizona Press, 2005); Virginia D. Nazarea, Robert E. Rhoades, and Jenna E. Andrews-Swann, eds., *Seeds of Resistance, Seeds of Hope: Place and Agency in the Conservation of Biodiversity* (Tucson: University of Arizona Press, 2013); Catherine Phillips, *Saving More than Seeds: Practices and Politics of Seed Saving* (London: Routledge, 2016). See also Thom Van Dooren, "Banking Seed: Use and Value in the Conservation of Agricultural Diversity," *Science as Culture* 18, no. 4 (2009): 373–395; Laura Pottinger, "Planting the Seeds of a Quiet Activism," *Area* 49, no. 2 (2017): 215–222.

3. An overview that complements the history sketched here is Marianna Fenzi and Christophe Bonneuil, "From 'Genetic Resources' to 'Ecosystems Services': A Century of Science and Global Policies for Crop Diversity Conservation," *Culture, Agriculture, Food and Environment* 38, no. 2 (2016): 72–83.
4. Stephen B. Brush, *Farmers' Bounty: Locating Crop Diversity in the Contemporary World* (New Haven, CT: Yale University Press, 2004), ch. 6. See also David A. Cleveland, Daniela Soleri, and Steven E. Smith, "A Biological Framework for Understanding Farmers' Plant Breeding," *Economic Botany* 54, no. 3 (2000): 377–94; T. Hodgkin et al., "Seed Systems and Crop Genetic Diversity in Agroecosystems," in *Managing Biodiversity in Agricultural Ecosystems*, ed. D. I. Jarvis, C. Padoch, and H. D. Cooper (New York: Columbia University Press, 2007): 77–116.
5. Emily Oakley and Janet Henshall Momsen, "Women and Seed Management: A Study of Two Villages in Bangladesh," *Singapore Journal of Tropical Geography* 28, no. 1 (2007): 90–106; P. S. Mehta, K. S. Negi, R. S. Rathi, and S. N. Ojha, "Indigenous Methods of Seed Conservation and Protection in Uttarakhand Himalaya," *Indian Journal of Traditional Knowledge* 11, no. 2 (2012): 279–282.
6. Luis Latournerie Moreno et al., "Traditional Maize Storage Methods of Mayan Farmers in Yucatan, Mexico: Implications for Seed Selection and Crop Diversity," *Biodiversity and Conservation* 15, no. 5 (2006): 1771–1795.
7. I refer to these as breeders' varieties, as distinguished from farmers' varieties/landraces. On the challenges of defining the latter, see Tania Carolina Camacho Villa, Nigel Maxted, Maria Scholten, and Brian Ford-Lloyd, "Defining and Identifying Crop Landraces," *Plant Genetic Resources* 3, no. 3 (2005): 373–384.
8. Mauricio R. Bellon, "The Ethnoecology of Maize Variety Management: A Case Study from Mexico," *Human Ecology* 19, no. 3 (1991): 389–418; J. R. Witcombe, R. Petre, S. Jones, and A. Joshi, "Farmer Participatory Crop Improvement. IV. The Spread and Impact of a Rice Variety Identified by Participatory Varietal Selection," *Experimental Agriculture* 35, no. 4 (1999): 471–487.
9. D. Louette and M. Smale, "Farmers' Seed Selection Practices and Traditional Maize Varieties in Cuzalapa, Mexico," *Euphytica* 113, no. 1 (2000): 25–41; Daniela Soleri, Steven E. Smith, and David A. Cleveland, "Evaluating the Potential for Farmer and Plant Breeder Collaboration: A Case Study of Farmer Maize Selection in Oaxaca, Mexico," *Euphytica* 116, no. 1 (2000): 41–57.
10. C. P. Hartley, "Seed Corn," *Farmers' Bulletin* 415, August 1917 revision (Washington, DC: US Government Printing Office, 1917): 3.
11. See, e.g., ibid.; W. L. Burlison and E. A. White, "Selection and Storage of Seed Corn," Circular no. 225, University of Illinois Agricultural Experiment Station, July 1918.
12. Deborah Fitzgerald, "Farmers Deskilled: Hybrid Corn and Farmers' Work," *Technology and Culture* 34, no. 2 (1993): 324–343; Fitzgerald, *The Business of Breeding*, 9–16, 49–56, 115–20.
13. Paul Brassley, "Crop Varieties," in *The Agrarian History of England and Wales*, vol. 7: 1850–1914, ed. E. J. T. Collins, Part I: 522–532.
14. Robert Tripp, *Seed Provision and Agricultural Development: The Institutions of Rural Change* (London: ODI, 2001), ch. 5.
15. Malcolm Thick, "Garden Seeds in England before the Late Eighteenth Century: I. Seed Growing," *Agricultural History Review* 38, no. 1 (1990): 58–71. On the United States, see Daniel J. Kevles, "A Primer of A, B, Seeds: Advertising, Branding, and Intellectual

Property in an Emerging Industry," *U.C. Davis Law Review* 47, no. 2 (December 2013): 657–678.
16. Mauro Ambrosoli, *The Wild and the Sown: Botany and Agriculture in Western Europe: 1350–1850*, trans. Mary McCann Salvatorelli (Cambridge: University of Cambridge Press, 1997), ch. 7.
17. John R. Walton, "Varietal Innovation and the Competitiveness of the British Cereals Sector, 1760–1930," *Agricultural History Review* 47, no. 1 (1999): 29–57; Josep Pujol-Andreu, "Wheat Varieties and Technological Change in Europe, 19th and 20th Centuries: New Issues in Economic History," *Historia Agraria*, no. 54 (August 2011): 71–103; Alan L. Olmstead and Paul W. Rhode, "Biological Globalization: The Other Grain Invasion," ICER Working Paper No. 9/2006, May 2006.
18. E.g., Gilbert H. Hicks, "Pure Seed Investigation," in *USDA Yearbook of Agriculture 1894* (Washington, DC: US Government Printing Office, 1895), 389–408; T. Johnson, "The Principles of Seed-Testing," *Science Progress in the Twentieth Century* 1, no. 3 (1907): 483–495.
19. Paolo Palladino, "The Political Economy of Applied Research: Plant Breeding in Great Britain, 1910–1940," *Minerva* 28, no. 4 (1990): 446–468; Kathy J. Cooke, "Expertise, Book Farming, and Government Agriculture: The Origins of Agricultural Seed Certification in the United States," *Agricultural History* 76, no. 3 (2002): 524–545; Dominic Berry, "Agricultural Modernity as a Product of the Great War: The Founding of the Official Seed Testing Station for England and Wales, 1917–1921," *War & Society* 34, no. 2 (2015): 121–139; Helen Anne Curry, "Wanted Weeds: Environmental History in the Whipple Museum," in *The Whipple Museum of the History of Science*, ed. J. Nall and L. Taub (Cambridge: University of Cambridge Press, 2019), 223–236.
20. Diane B. Paul and Barbara A. Kimmelman, "Mendel in America: Theory and Practice," in *The American Development of Biology*, ed. Ronald Rainger, Keith R. Benson and Jane Maienschein (Philadelphia: University of Pennsylvania Press, 1988), 281–310; Jean Gayon and Doris T. Zallen, "The Role of the Vilmorin Company in the Promotion and Diffusion of the Experimental Science of Heredity in France, 1840–1920," *Journal of the History of Biology* 31, no. 2 (1988): 241–262; Staffan Müller-Wille, "Early Mendelism and the Subversion of Taxonomy: Epistemological Obstacles as Institutions," *Studies in the History and Philosophy of Science Part C: Studies in History and Philosophy of Biological and Biomedical Sciences* 36, no. 3 (2005): 465–487; Thomas Wieland, "Scientific Theory and Agricultural Practice: Plant Breeding in Germany from the Late 19th to the Early 20th Century," *Journal of the History of Biology* 39, no. 2 (2006): 309–343.
21. Barbara Ann Kimmelman, "A Progressive Era Discipline: Genetics at American Agricultural Colleges and Experiment Stations, 1900–1920" (PhD thesis, University of Pennsylvania, 1987); Paolo Palladino, "Between Craft and Science: Plant Breeding, Mendelian Genetics, and British Universities, 1900–1920," *Technology and Culture* 34, no. 2 (1993): 300–323; Paolo Palladino, "Wizards and Devotees: On the Mendelian Theory of Inheritance and the Professionalization of Agricultural Science in Great Britain and the United States, 1880–1930," *History of Science* 32, no. 4 (1994): 409–444; Jonathan Harwood, "The Reception of Genetic Theory among Academic Plant-Breeders in Germany, 1900–1930," *Sveriges utsädesförenings tidskrift* 107, no. 4 (1997): 187–195; Charnley, "Agricultural Science, Plant Breeding and the Emergence of a Mendelian System"; Dominic Berry, "The Plant Breeding Industry after Pure Line Theory: Lessons from the National Institute of Agricultural Botany," *Studies in History and Philosophy of Science Part C: Studies in History*

and Philosophy of Biological and Biomedical Sciences 46 (2014): 25–37; Jonathan Harwood, "Did Mendelism Transform Plant Breeding? Genetic Theory and Breeding Practice, 1900–1945," in *New Perspectives on the History of Life Sciences and Agriculture*, ed. Denise Phillips and Sharon Kingsland (Cham, Switzerland: Springer, 2015): 345–370.

22. Charnley, "Agricultural Science, Plant Breeding and the Emergence of a Mendelian System."
23. Christian O. Lehmann, "Collecting European Land-Races and Development of European Gene Banks–Historical Remarks," *Die Kulturpflanze* 29, no. 1 (1981): 29–40.
24. H. V. Harlan and M. L. Martini, "Problems and Results in Barley Breeding," in *USDA Yearbook of Agriculture 1936* (Washington, DC: US Government Printing Office, 1936): 303–346, at 317.
25. Tiago Saraiva, "Breeding Europe: Crop Diversity, Gene Banks, and Commoners," in *Cosmopolitan Commons: Sharing Resources and Risks across Borders*, ed. Nil Disco and Eda Kranakis (Cambridge, MA: MIT Press, 2013), 185–212; Helen Anne Curry, "Imperilled Crops and Endangered Flowers," in *Worlds of Natural History*, ed. H. A. Curry, N. Jardine, J. A. Secord, and E. C. Spary (Cambridge: Cambridge University Press, 2018): 460–475; Christophe Bonneuil, "Seeing Nature as a 'Universal Store of Genes': How Biological Diversity Became 'Genetic Resources,'" *Studies in History and Philosophy of Science Part C: Studies in History and Philosophy of Biological and Biomedical Sciences* 75 (2019): 1–14.
26. I. G. Loskutov, *Vavilov and His Institute: A History of the World Collection of Plant Genetic Resources in Russia* (Rome: IPGRI, 1999).
27. Fitzgerald, *The Business of Breeding*, conclusion.
28. E.g., Edgar Anderson, "The Sources of Effective Germ-Plasm in Hybrid Maize," *Annals of the Missouri Botanical Garden* 31, no. 4 (1944): 355–361.
29. J. Allen Clark, "Collection, Preservation, and Utilization of Indigenous Strains of Maize," *Economic Botany* 10, no. 2 (1956): 194–200. See also Helen Anne Curry, "Breeding Uniformity and Banking Diversity: The Genescapes of Industrial Agriculture, 1935–1970," *Global Environment* 10, no. 1 (2017): 83–113.
30. Robin Pistorius, *Scientists, Plants, and Politics: A History of the Plant Genetic Resources Movement* (Rome: IPGRI, 1997); Robin Pistorius and Jeroen Van Wijk, *The Exploitation of Plant Genetic Information: Political Strategies in Crop Development* (Wallingford: CABI, 1999); Marianna Fenzi and Christophe Bonneuil, "From 'Genetic Resources' to 'Ecosystems Services.'"
31. FAO, *Report of the FAO/IBP Technical Conference on the Exploration, Utilization and Conservation of Plant Genetic Resources Held in Rome, Italy 18–26 September 1967*, Meeting Report No. PL/FO: 1967/M/12 (Rome: FAO, 1969): 1, 13.
32. Perkins, *Geopolitics and the Green Revolution*; Nick Cullather, *The Hungry World: America's Cold War Battle against Poverty in Asia* (Cambridge, MA: Harvard University Press, 2010). See also Akhil Gupta, *Postcolonial Developments: Agriculture in the Making of Modern India* (Durham, NC: Duke University Press, 1998); Tae-Ho Kim, "Making Miracle Rice: Tongil and Mobilizing a Domestic 'Green Revolution' in South Korea," in *Engineering Asia: Technology, Colonial Legacy, and the Cold War Order*, ed. Hiromi Mizuno, Aaron S. Moore, and John P. Dimoia (London: Bloomsbury, 2018): 189–208.
33. FAO, *Report of the Third Session of the FAO Panel of Experts on Plant Exploration and Introduction, Held in Rome, Italy, 25–28 March 1969* (Rome: FAO, 1969). Meeting Report No. PL: 1969/M/8; Otto H. Frankel and Erna Bennett, eds., *Genetic Resources in Plants— Their Exploration and Conservation*, IBP Handbook No. 11 (Oxford: Blackwell 1970): 15.

34. Valeria Negri, Nigel Maxted, and Merja Veteläinen, "European Landrace Conservation: An Introduction," in *European Landraces: On-Farm Conservation, Management and Use*, ed. M. Veteläinen, V. Negri, and N. Maxted (Rome: Bioversity, 2009): 1–22.
35. Pistorius, *Scientists, Plants, and Politics*; Helen Anne Curry, "From Working Collections to the World Germplasm Project: Agricultural Modernization and Genetic Conservation at the Rockefeller Foundation," *History and Philosophy of the Life Sciences* 39, no. 5 (2017).
36. Sara Peres, "Seed Banking as Cryopower: A Cryopolitical Account of the Work of the International Board of Plant Genetic Resources, 1973–1984," *Culture, Agriculture, Food and Environment* 41, no. 2 (2019): 76–86.
37. Xan Chacko, "Creative Practices of Care: The Subjectivity, Agency and Affective Labor of Preparing Seeds for Long-term Banking," *Culture, Agriculture, Food and Environment* 41, no. 2 (2019): 97–106.
38. *True Seed Exchange* 1976, copy consulted at the Robert Becker Memorial Library, Seed Savers Exchange, Decorah, Iowa. See also Diane Ott Whealy, *Gathering: Memoir of a Seed Saver* (Decorah, IA: Seed Savers Exchange, 2011).
39. Helen Anne Curry, "From Bean Collection to Seed Bank: Transformations in Heirloom Vegetable Conservation, 1970–1985," *BJHS Themes* 4 (2019): 149–167.
40. Chris Schmidt, "United States of America: Native Seeds/SEARCH," in *Community Seed Banks: Origins, Evolution and Prospects*, ed. Ronnie Vernooy, Pitambar Shrestha and Bhuwon Sthapit (Abingdon: Routledge, 2015), 172–175.
41. Helen Anne Curry, "Gene Banks, Seed Libraries, and Vegetable Sanctuaries: The Cultivation and Conservation of Heritage Vegetables in Britain, 1970–1985," *Culture, Agriculture, Food and Environment* 41, no. 2 (2019): 87–96.
42. Jay Sanderson, *Plants, People and Practices: The Nature and History of the UPOV Convention* (Cambridge: Cambridge University Press, 2017); Philip H. Howard, "Intellectual Property and Consolidation in the Seed Industry," *Crop Science* 55, no. 6 (2015): 2489–2495.
43. P. R. Mooney, *Seeds of the Earth: A Private or Public Resource?* (Ottawa: International Coalition for Development Action, [1979]); P. R. Mooney, "The Law of the Seed: Another Development and Plant Genetic Resources," *Development Dialogue* 1983, nos. 1–2 (1983); Cary Fowler, *Unnatural Selection: Technology, Politics, and Plant Evolution* (Yverdon, Switzerland: Gordon and Breach, 1994); Cary Fowler and Pat Mooney, *Shattering: Food, Politics, and the Loss of Genetic Diversity* (Tucson: University of Arizona Press, 1990).
44. Rachel Schurman and William A. Munro, *Fighting for the Future of Food: Activists versus Agribusiness in the Struggle over Biotechnology* (Minneapolis: University of Minnesota Press, 2010).
45. RAFI, *The Community Seed Bank Kit* (Rural Advancement Fund International, 1986).
46. Ronnie Vernooy, "In the Hands of Many: A Review of Community Gene/Seed Banks around the World," in *Community Seed Banks in Nepal: Past, Present, Future, Proceedings of a National Workshop, 14–15 June 2012*, ed. Pitambar Shrestha, Ronnie Vernooy and Pashupati Chaudhary (Pokhara, Nepal: LI-BIRD, 2013), 3–15. See also Ronnie Vernooy, Pitambar Shrestha, and Bhuwon Sthapi, eds., *Community Seed Banks: Origins, Evolution and Prospects* (London: Routledge, 2015).
47. Stephen B. Brush, "In Situ Conservation of Landraces in Centers of Crop Diversity," *Crop Science* 35, no. 2 (1995): 346–354. See also Mauricio R. Bellon, "The Dynamics of Crop Infraspecific Diversity: A Conceptual Framework at the Farmer Level," *Economic Botany* 50, no. 1 (1996): 26–39.

48. An influential series of early studies on this theme is summarized in Andrew Pearse, "Technology and Peasant Production: Reflections on a Global Study," *Development and Change* 8, no. 2 (1977): 125–159.
49. Stephen B. Brush, "The Issues of *In Situ* Conservation of Crop Genetic Resources," in *Genes in the Field: On-Farm Conservation of Crop Diversity*, ed. Stephen B. Brush (Boca Raton, FL: Lewis Publishers, 2000): 3–26. See also Brush, *Farmers' Bounty*.
50. E.g., M. Worede, "Ethiopian *In Situ* Conservation," in *Plant Genetic Conservation: The In Situ Approach*, ed. N. Maxted, B. V. Ford-Lloyd, and J. G. Hawkes (Dordrecht: Kluwer Academic Publishers, 1997): 290–301.
51. Brush, "The Issues of *In Situ* Conservation."
52. P. Eyzaguirre and M. Iwanaga, eds., *Participatory Plant Breeding, Proceedings of a Workshop on Participatory Plant Breeding, 26–29 July 1995, Wageningen, The Netherlands* (Rome: IPGRI/Bioversity International, 1996).
53. Esbern Friis-Hansen and Bhuwon Sthapit, eds., *Participatory Approaches to the Conservation and Use of Plant Genetic Resources* (Rome: IPGRI, 2000).
54. Ian Scoones, "Mobilizing against GM Crops in India, South Africa and Brazil," *Journal of Agrarian Change* 8, no. 2–3 (2008): 315–344; Schurman and Munro, *Fighting for the Future of Food*; Aleksandra Malyska, Robert Bolla, and Tomasz Twardowski, "The Role of Public Opinion in Shaping Trajectories of Agricultural Biotechnology," *Trends in Biotechnology* 34, no. 7 (2016): 530–534.
55. Craig Borowiak, "Farmers' Rights: Intellectual Property Regimes and the Struggle over Seeds," *Politics & Society* 32, no. 4 (2004): 511–543; Daniela Soleri, "Civic Seeds: New Institutions for Seed Systems and Communities—A 2016 Survey of California Seed Libraries," *Agriculture and Human Values* 35, no. 2 (2018): 331–347.
56. Via Campesina, "The International Peasant's Voice," https://viacampesina.org/en/international-peasants-voice/, accessed August 8, 2019: See also Annette-Aurélie Desmarais, "The Vía Campesina: Consolidating an International Peasant and Farm Movement," *Journal of Peasant Studies* 29, no. 2 (2002): 91–124.
57. Jennifer A. Jordan, *Edible Memory: The Lure of Heirloom Tomatoes and Other Forgotten Foods* (Chicago: University of Chicago Press, 2015).
58. Crop Trust, "The Svalbard Global Seed Vault," https://www.croptrust.org/our-work/svalbard-global-seed-vault/, accessed August 12, 2019. See also Cary Fowler, *Seeds on Ice: Svalbard and the Global Seed Vault* (Westport, CT: Prospecta Press, 2016).
59. Adrian Barnett, interview with Diane Ott Whealy, "Bank Your Edible Heirlooms," *New Scientist* 222, no. 2968 (May 10, 2014): 27.

Bibliography

Ambrosoli, Mauro. *The Wild and the Sown: Botany and Agriculture in Western Europe, 1350–1850*. Cambridge: Cambridge University Press, 1997.

Brush, Stephen B. *Farmers' Bounty: Locating Crop Diversity in the Contemporary World*. New Haven, CT: Yale University Press, 2004.

Curry, Helen Anne. *Endangered Maize: Industrial Agriculture and the Crisis of Extinction*. Oakland: University of California Press, 2022.

Fenzi, Marianna, and Christophe Bonneuil. "From 'Genetic Resources' to 'Ecosystems Services': A Century of Science and Global Policies for Crop Diversity Conservation." *Culture, Agriculture, Food and Environment* 38, no. 2 (2016): 72–83.

Fitzgerald, Deborah. *The Business of Breeding: Hybrid Corn in Illinois, 1890–1940*. Ithaca, NY: Cornell University Press, 1990.

Fullilove, Courtney. *The Profit of the Earth: The Global Seeds of American Agriculture*. Chicago: University of Chicago Press, 2017.

Gupta, Akhil. *Postcolonial Developments: Agriculture in the Making of Modern India*. Durham, NC: Duke University Press, 1998.

Harwood, Jonathan. "Did Mendelism Transform Plant Breeding? Genetic Theory and Breeding Practice, 1900–1945." In *New Perspectives on the History of Life Sciences and Agriculture*, edited by Denise Phillips and Sharon Kingsland, 345–70. Cham, Switzerland: Springer, 2015.

Harwood, Jonathan. *Europe's Green Revolution and Others Since: The Rise and Fall of Peasant-Friendly Plant Breeding*. London: Routledge, 2012.

Howard, Philip A. "Intellectual Property and Consolidation in the Seed Industry." *Crop Science* 55, no. 6 (2015): 2489–2495.

Jordan, Jennifer A. *Edible Memory: The Lure of Heirloom Tomatoes and Other Forgotten Foods*. Chicago: University of Chicago Press, 2015.

Kloppenburg, Jack Ralph, Jr. *First the Seed: The Political Economy of Plant Biotechnology, 1492–2000*. 2nd ed. Madison: University of Wisconsin Press, 2004.

Nazarea, Virginia D. *Heirloom Seeds and Their Keepers: Marginality and Memory in the Conservation of Biological Diversity*. Tucson: University of Arizona Press, 2005.

Nazarea, Virginia D., Robert E. Rhoades, and Jenna E. Andrews-Swann, eds. *Seeds of Resistance, Seeds of Hope: Place and Agency in the Conservation of Biodiversity*. Tucson: University of Arizona Press, 2013.

Perkins, John H. *Geopolitics and the Green Revolution: Wheat, Genes, and the Cold War*. Oxford: Oxford University Press, 2007.

Pistorius, Robin, and Jeroen Van Wijk. *The Exploitation of Plant Genetic Information: Political Strategies in Crop Development*. Wallingford: CABI, 1999.

Schurman, Rachel, and William A. Munro. *Fighting for the Future of Food: Activists versus Agribusiness in the Struggle over Biotechnology*. Minneapolis: University of Minnesota Press, 2010.

CHAPTER 4

A HISTORY OF LIVESTOCK AND PEOPLE

CLAIRE STROM

The history of livestock mirrors the broader history of human interaction with the natural world, which has seen a seismic shift from awe to arrogance. Initially, human relationships with livestock fundamentally rested on the animality of the creatures: in other words, on their ability to feed themselves, move themselves, and reproduce themselves. Over time, however, humans have found more efficient ways of achieving all these ends, which has turned livestock into another manmade product—one where animality is a net detriment. The human conceptual and actual manipulation of livestock to be more commodity and less animal has, however, not been uniformly beneficial, generating myriad new challenges from epizootics to environmental degradation.[1]

Animals became livestock through the process of domestication, which was, in essence, a form of interspecies cooperation. Domestication occurred when both humans and livestock benefited: from increased food and/or increased safety. Some animals were so advantaged by human settlements and the proliferation of bones (dogs), mice (cats), and garbage (pigs) that they basically domesticated themselves. Others, notably herd animals, were probably domesticated for sacrificial purposes long before humans realized the potential benefits of meat, motive power, fiber, and milk. These ruminants also benefited from human collaboration, gaining protection from predators, sustenance in lean times, and, at times, shelter against the elements. In this early narrative, the cooperation of humans and livestock maximized both species' biological survival.[2]

Nonetheless, the animality of livestock has always been a challenge, starting with the basic problem of finding sufficient food to sustain significant numbers of large creatures. Historically, three different systems of livestock management emerged, each reflecting environmental limitations as well as cultural expectations and legal strictures. In areas of the world with little water and limited vegetation, humans ensured that their animals received adequate nutrition through pastoral nomadism. Nomads have no permanent residence. Rather, their community location is dictated by the needs of their animals to find more pasture and water. Distances traveled also depend on the animal. Camels, for example, can go further than other animals without water. Another consideration is the stage of a particular herd, as a herd with many newborns travel more slowly than one composed of adult animals. Indeed, kids and lambs need, at times, to be carried by humans to avoid delays and animal exhaustion.[3]

The animality of livestock determines the lives of nomads and provides a net benefit. Traditionally, nomads used all of their animals. All herd animals provided motive power, carrying supplies or people or pulling carts. Milk—made into cheese, yogurt, or butter—and blood were the main food products. Women spun, cured, and tanned animal hides, hair, and wool to make tents, clothing, and bedding for their families. Indeed, sheepskin had a wide array of uses from wine bottles to parchment to bagpipes to flotation devices. Nor was the animal dung neglected; in fact, it was often the only possible fuel for cooking fires. Meat-eating was relatively rare because the lives of the animals were far more valuable to the nomads than their carcasses.[4]

On the continuum between nomadism and settled farming is transhumance. In much of sub-Saharan Africa, Central Asia, the Mediterranean world, northern Europe, and South America, pastoralists solved the problem of how to feed their animals by moving them seasonally between pastures. The key difference between nomadic and transhumant pastoralism is that transhumant herders have a permanent home. Most transhumance moves between various altitudes, either moving up to mountain pastures in the summer from villages at lower altitude—perhaps most famously captured with the movement of the Swiss goats in the children's classic *Heidi*—or moving down to the lowlands to escape the winter's cold and to sell stock, common in Navarre and Calabria in the sixteenth century. Generally, these movements of stock are more seasonally repetitive than the wanderings of nomadic groups. However, the mobility—intrinsic to the animality—of the stock is vital to the well-being of the animals and the livelihood of the herders.[5]

Transhumance is usually found in environments where some kind of sedentary agriculture can be practiced. The movement of the living animals, therefore, solves two problems. First, it frees fertile land for crop production, as in the southwest of England, where medieval farmers grazed their cattle on Dartmoor in the summer, allowing them to use the livestock's winter pastures to grow hay to feed the animals during the winter months. Second, it removes the animals from the ripening crops that they might eat or damage, allowing them to return in the fall to graze on the stubble. Movement was not always well-coordinated, however, resulting in conflicts between the grain raisers and the shepherds. As human and animal density increased, farmers protected their crops by fencing them, rather than by fencing their livestock because the advantage of animals was that they could move themselves to obtain sufficient fodder rather than being fed.[6]

On the other end of the spectrum from nomadic herding is sedentary agriculture. Farmers kept some livestock to augment production with motive power and fertilizer, and to provide some dietary protein—either as meat when animals had ceased to be useful or as dairy products. Most farmers did not own the amount of land necessary to feed their livestock and so utilized common land for at least some of the time. Common land appears in a wide variety of forms, from roadside verges in Java to the vast plains and prairies of North America to the *ejídos* of medieval Spain, and was used to pasture cattle, horses, sheep, and goats. Outside of Asia, most pigs were pastured in forests, which were often considered common land, to feed on the mast—the acorns, beechnuts, and other forage on the forest floor. Sometimes, as in colonial Virginia, the hogs roamed freely in the forest, becoming formidable, semi-feral beasts. At other times, hog movement was carefully managed, with swineherds being hired by farmers to drive animals into the woods in the fall. Indeed, although common lands declined throughout the twentieth century, they are still important in places as diverse as Romania, Mongolia, and Uganda. The ability of livestock to feed themselves with a minimum of human intervention was key in maximizing their usefulness to farmers.[7]

In agrarian societies, as human and animal population densities grew, animality became a problem. Wandering livestock damaged people and property. More animals in less space fostered epizootics, which undermined productivity and sometimes threatened human health. Thus, governments increasingly banned the keeping of livestock, except equids, from urban areas—even pigs that usefully consumed human waste—and required that animals in rural areas be fenced. For farmers to fence their animals, they had to own enough land to dedicate to fodder crop production, which made it impossible for many to continue to raise livestock. Such enclosure started in England in the sixteenth century and continues in various forms around the world to this day. The eradication of common lands resulted in poverty and destitution, as certain farmers—lacking political power for reasons of class or race or wealth—lost access to the resources necessary to cultivate and to pasture their animals. However, it offered significant advantages for other farmers who held the necessary land and had the power and means to protect and expand it. Enclosure fostered improvements in animal breeds by releasing fertile land for fodder production and making reproduction easier to control. Over time, this gave humans a greater ability to craft livestock to meet their needs, inherently shifting the interspecies dynamic to one where humans manipulated animals for their benefit.[8]

Humans understood their dominance over animals as intrinsic to their civilization. Building on this, the Europeans viewed livestock as a civilizing force that would tame both the land and the people. Thus, livestock became an important driver of imperialism, both intentionally and otherwise. From Hispaniola to New Zealand, domesticated animals helped Europeans take over new lands, dominate indigenous peoples, and realize vast profits. Colonizers brought Old World plants and animals to the New World that prospered, providing food, motive power, and cash crops to the new empires. Livestock—horses, mules, cattle, sheep, goats, pigs, and chicken—flourished in the new lands, getting fat on lush grasses and forests full of acorns and, in many cases, damaging or eradicating native flora and fauna. The native peoples found their traditional lifestyles challenged by these newcomers, but they also benefited, as they started to ride horses, run cattle, and eat hogs.[9]

Clearly, non-native species, when introduced to a new ecology, frequently fundamentally altered the environment. Their very animality impacted colonized ecosystems and indigenous economies, facilitating imperialism. For example, the introduction of sheep into the Valle del Mezquital in central Mexico in the sixteenth century contributed significantly to the transformation of the region from productive arable land surrounded by forest to bare soil punctuated by arid plants such as yucca and mesquite. Filipinos turned their horses—introduced by the Spanish—loose to graze on the mountainsides, destroying vegetation essential to soil health and stability. Similarly, free-range hogs and cattle virtually destroyed many of the canebrakes of the landscape in the southern colonies of North America. More dramatic was the introduction of ungulates to Australia, a land that had no hooved animals. The rapid introduction of sheep and cattle in the mid-nineteenth century caused immense damage to soil and native grasses that had never adapted to being trampled by hooves. This became all too apparent during the droughts of the 1870s when millions of stock animals died from starvation and thirst, twenty-four native species dependent on the grasslands became extinct, and millions of hectares of native grasslands were destroyed.[10]

Nonetheless, the ability of Western livestock to succeed in a wide variety of environments around the globe was not as inevitable. Some animals fared very well. Pigs, unlike most other livestock, are omnivores and can thrive in a wide variety of ecosystems. Travelers, explorers, and sailors left hogs on various islands throughout the Pacific and Caribbean to provide food for later voyagers. The pigs found a wide array of food—from fruit and tubers to birds and shellfish—and no predators, and they multiplied abundantly. Horses, introduced by the Spanish, flourished on the American Great Plains, spawning the Great Plains Indian horse cultures. They did not do so well, however, in South Africa, where African horse sickness, a lack of natural fodder, and predation by lions constantly challenged Dutch attempts to maintain adequate equine populations. Other livestock foundered in inhospitable climates or fell prey to indigenous predators, including humans. Probably sheep had the hardest time adapting, as they do not fare well in hot, humid environments and have few natural defenses. Moreover, both cattle and sheep were susceptible to epizootic diseases carried by indigenous ruminants and had trouble resuming normal breeding levels after the stress of being transported long distances by ship, although both eventually survived and flourished in a wide range of colonial lands.[11]

In many ways, therefore, deliberate actions of the colonizing humans proved vital in facilitating the biological irruption of Old World domestic livestock. Colonists were determined to establish familiar patterns of agriculture and profit-making in their new dominions, which often led to active intervention to benefit their livestock. For example, in the North American colonies, they aggressively hunted wolves and bears because of their tendency to prey on domestic animals. In 1656, Virginia passed a law offering a cow to any Native American tribe that produced eight dead wolves: aiming for the dual benefit of protecting their livestock and instilling the civilizing benefits of stock raising in the indigenous population. Colonizers also encouraged the killing of other native animals that competed with their livestock. Australian settlers classified kangaroos as vermin; white settlers offered bounties on jackals, lions, leopards, and hyenas in South Africa; and Americans shot bison from trains. Similarly, in New Zealand, settlers invested considerable time and money trying to make the islands into grassland pastures for their flocks. This required substantial environmental manipulation as land was cleared by fire and then reseeded with carefully bred grass seed, promoting an alien vegetation designed "for the conversion by cattle and sheep into dairy produce, wool and meat."[12]

Colonists also ensured the success of their livestock by cultural domination. As conquerors, the Europeans imposed their laws regarding land and stock. Conveniently, the colonists articulated that ownership of land was tied to intensive, "European-style" use of land. They did not recognize most of the land management practiced by indigenous peoples throughout the New World and Antipodes as agriculture and, thus, did not recognize the land as being owned. Such land—land that was not being "used"—could legally, in most European countries, be treated as common land. In Europe, the commons offered vital resources for raising livestock. Farmers owned some land but also grazed their animals on the verges, pastures, leas, and forests that they held in common with their neighbors. Thus, native resources were legally appropriated for Western livestock, enhancing these species' odds of survival.[13]

Where biological pressures and legal advantages proved insufficient, colonists ensured the domination of Old World livestock with violence. The histories of European expansion are rife with violence from official military campaigns to extralegal massacres. These frequently had the effect, either intended or ancillary, of benefiting stockraising. To mention just a few examples, in Hawai'i, internecine warfare for access to European resources, together with disease, made the local population less able to address the degradation wrought by cattle that arrived in 1793. From the 1830s, conflict arose between aborigines and squatters running sheep and cattle in Australia over access to water. Killing of native peoples continued for decades, declining only when many aborigines abandoned their traditional ways of life to labor on the squatters' livestock stations. In South Africa, the Dutch, and later the English, waged war against the pastoral Khoikhois and Nguni-speakers, seizing both their land and animals, while adopting indigenous stockraising techniques. And, in the 1870s and 1880s, the Argentines waged a number of military campaigns against indigenous peoples in the pampas. This so-called Conquest of the Desert gave Argentina control of 20 million hectares of valuable grazing land.[14]

Thus, over the course of four to five hundred years, Europeans succeeded in colonizing much of the globe. In many regions, livestock facilitated this process, which altered countless ecosystems and resulted in huge species loss and the disintegration of indigenous cultures. However, European livestock and conceptions of stockraising also changed. New environments dramatically altered animal breeds and colonists purposefully bred animals to prosper in local conditions and meet market requirements. Pigs and cattle left to forage in the backcountry of the American South eventually became new, semi-feral beasts with longer horns and tusks that were worth little but were hardy and took little effort to raise. Cattle in the Mato Grosso similarly developed large horns and aggressive temperament, effective at dealing with a wide range of predators. Meanwhile, in New Zealand, colonists crossbred sheep, first to maximize wool production, and then to develop a sheep that would thrive on colonial pastures but provide meat whose taste would be welcome on the British market.[15]

Colonists were forced to adapt their methods of stockraising to environmental imperatives. Where they did not, they failed. For example, in 1814–1815, the cost of maintaining the British-style stud farms established in India to provide horses for the East India Company was nearly twice the value of the stock. Arid lands in the Americas and Australia were not conducive to traditional European intensive agriculture, leading to the emergence of extensive systems, known variously as ranches, estancias, latifundias, and stations. Such extensive livestock operations relied once more on the animality of the stock to feed, breed, and transport itself to market. Importantly, though, in contrast to nomadism and transhumance, the objective was profit and the animal was the product: a product that was crucial to the global industrial transition.[16]

Livestock fostered the industrial revolution in three ways: it provided the motive power for moving industrial materials and operating early machinery, it supplied the protein necessary for urban labor, and it spurred many technological, scientific, and industrial advances. The haulage power of horses, and to a lesser extent, donkeys, mules, asses, and oxen, was key to the success of industrial nations. Their motive power from the Middle Ages on increased agricultural productivity, creating surpluses that fostered urban development. Such productivity soared in the nineteenth-century United States with the development of lighter, steel farm implements that could be pulled quickly and easily by horses or mules. Wheat acreage, for example, increased nearly 300 percent between the end of the Civil War and 1900, providing food for the nation's burgeoning cities. Equids were also used in industry, pulling coal carts in Europe, hauling mining supplies in the Rocky Mountains, and, by 1860, towing people along five hundred miles of horse-car lines in American cities. And, despite the advances in technology, animal power remained vital in warfare through World War II when they were used to transport supplies and pull artillery. Thus, in terms of equids' motive power, animality remained of key importance in fostering the industrial revolution.[17]

Animal protein was also crucial. People in cities cannot raise their own food, so urbanization necessarily created a market for agricultural products. This is not just a product of the modern world. The ancient Greeks had hog farms, as memorialized in the *Odyssey*, and farmers around ancient Rome kept herds of up to three hundred sows, capable of producing thousands of pigs for market every year. The availability of inexpensive protein for urban laborers proved a key factor in productivity and growth and required a good rural-to-urban supply chain. For example, in seventeenth-century Holland, the population grew dramatically in eight cities, all within a twenty-one-mile radius of each other. This density made intensive dairying feasible, supplying protein in the form of butter and cheese. Farmers reclaimed wetlands, fertilized them with manure—human and otherwise—exported from the cities, rotated crops, and reached a level of milk production not seen in the rest of the world until the nineteenth century. This surfeit of cheese helped the emergence of the Dutch as "a leading commercial power buoyed by a flourishing, well-fed population."[18]

Despite such early exceptions, in the early nineteenth century, protein transfer between cities and their hinterlands was limited by three intertwined issues: the ability of farmers to produce a sufficient surplus, the ease of moving protein to market, and the perishability of the product. Colonization solved the first problem, providing empires with vast grasslands around the world on which to raise cattle and sheep, and, in North America, with a heartland capable of growing almost limitless corn to fatten hogs. Colonial governments' visions of intensive arable agriculture gave way to ranching, as "it was land, rather than labour and capital, which was abundant."[19]

The living nature of animal protein had always facilitated moving it to market: livestock could walk. Over the course of at least five hundred years, men trailed cattle to market from Hungary to Italy, Denmark to the Netherlands, South Wales to England, Argentina to Chile, and Texas to Dodge City, Kansas. Pigs, goats, and sheep, too, were driven to market. Indeed, the number of hogs moved throughout the United States far outstripped the number of cattle, despite the fact that cattle drives have become an iconic American image while hog drives have faded into obscurity. But trailing animals was not ideal. For one, it was expensive. Speed was dictated by the walking pace of the animal, and time was lost for feeding and watering both animals and men. Secondly, while ruminants are fairly easy to drive, pigs are not, tending to seek out water and mud to wallow or scatter in woods to feed. Additionally, animals lost weight and, therefore, value along the trail, and many died, from drowning, predators, injury, or exhaustion—or were stolen on the journey.[20]

Technological advances in the nineteenth century facilitated more efficient movement of animal protein to market, reducing the time while extending the reach. Steamboats moved animals efficiently along rivers and canals, and, by the 1870s, steel-hulled steamships took live cattle from the United States to the United Kingdom. Railroads improved transportation even further and connected massive grasslands to urban markets throughout the Americas. However, it was still necessary to transport live animals so that they could be butchered close to market and their flesh would remain fresh. But moving live animals did not maximize profits. Cattle lost weight during sea and rail journeys and were at high risk of injury from the movement of the vessels/cars and from the other animals. Thus, the animality of the livestock resulted in lost profits. Clearly, transportation was not the only key. Moving meat would be preferable to moving animals, but that required preservation.[21]

Though preservation of meat—drying, salting, and smoking—and of milk (as cheese) dates back to at least ancient Greece, the imperial and industrial economies that situated substantial labor forces separate from food sources required a whole new level of protein preservation. Initially, ranchers in colonial Latin America converted their beef into three products: hides for export or domestic use; tallow, or refined animal fat, for candles and cooking; and dried or salted jerky. The jerky generally stayed within the New World, being eaten as a staple food or shipped to the gold and silver mines of the Americas or the sugar plantations of the Caribbean as a protein-rich, cheap food for the slave labor. Jerked beef did not taste good, however, which limited its market appeal in Europe. The same was true of canned beef, which was produced in abundance in the Chicago meatpacking plants in the late nineteenth century. This cheap protein was destined for consumption by another group of people whose freedom was circumscribed: the military. The US military, along with the British and the French, ordered millions of pounds of canned beef to fuel their operations around the world.[22]

Freezing technology eventually preserved mutton and beef for long-distance haulage and flavor retention, removing the necessity of taking live animals to market. In the 1870s, several attempts were made to move beef using iced railcars. In the 1880s, however, Gustavus Swift perfected a system whereby the beef was frozen while butchered and loaded into iced railcars, which were refilled along the route as the ice melted. This generated a whole new business of gathering, shipping, and preserving ice. Transoceanic shipments of meat soon followed. By the mid-1880s, Argentina's packing plants, or *frigoríficos*, were regularly shipping frozen mutton, the taste of which was less affected by freezing than beef, to Europe. And the first shipment of mutton reached London from New Zealand in 1882, prompting breeders to move away from merino wool sheep to animals that gave a higher quality of meat. Freezing meat effectively freed it from spatial constraints, allowing the butchering process to take place almost anywhere. It removed the importance of animals being animals, as they no longer had to arrive at market alive for the meat to be fresh. From this point on, the animality of livestock stopped being an overall benefit and increasingly became a net problem.[23]

To be sure, the fact that livestock were animals had presented problems long before the advent of refrigeration. To transform live animals into meat necessitates the messy and traumatic process of killing them. This mutated during the Industrial Revolution from a process with which everyone was familiar, to one that "must be as if it were not." Traditionally, the killing of domestic livestock was done either by their owners or by professional butchers who then sold the meat to the public. Before refrigeration, meat needed to be sold within ten to twelve hours of death, which limited the distance butchers could be from their customers. Such decentralized slaughter was problematic in cities, as live animals were driven through the streets to the various butchers, posing dangers to the general public. Additionally, slaughtering animals was noisy and generated noxious smells, which spread throughout the city as "soapmakers, bone boilers, fat renderers or tallow chandlers" bought the discards and transported them back through the streets to their establishments.[24]

Over time, governments assumed some responsibility for public safety and health. They regulated butchers through licensing or guilds, which offered a mechanism to curtail the sale of spoiled meat or unclean premises. Some governments built public slaughterhouses in large cities. These, such as the Grande Boucherie in Paris, contained both the live animals and the dead waste in one location, reducing the impact of both on the broader urban environment. By the late nineteenth century, however, continued urban growth combined with two other factors to necessitate changes in slaughterhouses. One change was a growing concern for public health. Population density made disease outbreaks caused by spoiled meat or unclean premises more problematic. Meanwhile, scientific advances offered explanations—such as better microscopes that showed the parasite responsible for trichinosis in the 1830s and Koch's germ theory, which helped explain milk contamination and the problems with dirty slaughterhouses in the 1880s. The second factor was the growing sensibilities of the urban middle classes.

Far removed from the farm, and increasingly enjoying animals for leisure, these people wanted slaughter to be painless and, more important, invisible. Indeed, they wanted to erase the connection between living animals and dead meat altogether.[25]

The progression of slaughtering animals in the United States was different from that in much of the rest of the developed world. Instead of transitioning from butchers to public slaughterhouses, the United States moved, in the 1820s, to large private packinghouses. These were initially situated on water networks to aid distribution in Cincinnati, and later, St. Louis, Milwaukee, Omaha, Kansas City, and Chicago, Carl Sandburg's "hog butcher for the world." Unlike the public slaughterhouses of Europe and Latin America, where individual butchers gathered to kill animals using age-old techniques, these private slaughterhouses used modern assembly-line technology to disassemble animals, deskilling the process to maximize speed and profits. Additionally, the meat created at these packinghouses was not sold fresh but preserved and sent to urban areas throughout the Northwest. Originally the focus was on large-scale hog butchering, as pork was easily preserved and shipped. Cattle moved through these stockyards, too, but their route was more complicated. Some were slaughtered, some were shipped to the Midwest for fattening, while others moved further east to feed the burgeoning cities on the coast. These large-scale operations undercut their competitors, often losing money on their meat. However, the economy of scale was such that they were able to profit from animal byproducts, selling pig fat, bristles, bones, and blood to produce a wide variety of other products from candles and explosives to dyes and margarine.[26]

US packinghouses, while being structured differently, also removed death from the public eye, completing the transformation of livestock from animal to product. From the late nineteenth century into the twentieth century, similar to slaughterhouses around the world, concerns about public health and humane slaughter combined with technology to alter livestock production. First, governments started to regulate the livestock business by passing laws that controlled all stages of meat/dairy production and sale. This dramatically augmented governmental authority. Second, the geographic freedom created by refrigeration led to the movement of slaughterhouses into rural areas where the animals were raised. This was economically sound, as only saleable dressed meat had to be transported to market. Thus, the livestock industry provided the protein necessary to feed the growing number of urban workers globally, fueling the labor for the Industrial Revolution and beyond. At the same time, the complexities of turning live animals into dead meat fostered technologies from fencing to railroads, from refrigeration to immunization, that, in turn, deeply influenced the development of the modern world.[27]

Despite the importance of livestock and animal protein in terms of innovation and growth, the changing relationship of humans and animals has also created significant problems. As humans struggled to counter the problems caused by livestock being animals, while at the same time maximizing the value of livestock as a product, they ultimately engineered diseases, damaged the environment, and created a morass of moral dilemmas. As animal density increased, and animals were transported across vast distances, the challenges of countering disease increased. In many cases, human action—rather than viruses, bacteria, or parasites—was the root cause of disease outbreaks and their consequences. For example, foot-and-mouth disease was prevalent among sheep and cattle in the United Kingdom from the early nineteenth century. Highly contagious, it rarely killed animals, but they lost some of their value in both weight and milk. Farmers in the early nineteenth century accepted the disease as "an unavoidable fact of life." However, the growth of the cattle industry in the late nineteenth century and the increase in international trafficking in livestock, in conjunction with scientific discoveries about the ways diseases spread, led to governmental intervention in the form of quarantines and mass slaughter of animals either infected or suspected of infection. Once such legislation was in place, foot-and-mouth disease became a huge problem, not for the disease itself, but for the potential human-imposed consequences.[28]

Human responses to babesiosis followed a similar trajectory. Babesiosis is caused by a tick-borne protozoan and causes only limited harm to cattle in areas where it is endemic. Animals that have never been exposed to it, however, face a mortality rate of up to 90 percent. As the cattle tick has a clear geographic range, the disease only became a problem when humans started moving livestock over significant distance, most notably with the trailing of southern US cattle north to the stockyards of Kansas City and Chicago. To counter the impact on northern herds, in 1906, the US government started a campaign to eradicate the cattle tick through the mandatory dipping of southern cattle in arsenic. This campaign, although ultimately successful, was hugely expensive and reduced the ability of many southern farmers to continue to own cattle. Again, a disease that presented only a minimal problem to cattle within its natural environment became a massive problem because of human intervention.[29]

In the modern arena, mad cow disease, or bovine spongiform encephalopathy, is a disease almost completely created by humans. The disease is caused by a prion, which is a protein. As a prion is not a living organism, it is impossible to kill. Similar prion-caused brain diseases in animals—most commonly Scrapie affecting sheep—were present in Europe as early as the eighteenth century. Mad cow disease, however—and transmission to humans as Creutzfeldt-Jakob disease, a terrifying and incurable destruction of the brain—only became an issue in the 1980s, following a series of human decisions. Since the late nineteenth century, farmers had supplemented cattle feed with protein derived from animal carcasses, some of which carried the prion. From the 1960s on, the amount of animal protein used increased, especially in dairy cattle, as intensive production techniques overstressed the cows. The physical toll on the cattle was exacerbated by farmers giving their cattle growth hormones—first natural and then synthetic—to spur milk production. The final human action came around 1980, when new techniques were adopted to process animal protein for feed that reduced costs and streamlined production. These techniques, however, failed to eliminate the prion, which was then consumed by cattle and subsequently, by humans. Thus mad cow disease, like babesiosis and foot-and-mouth disease, is a result of human manipulation of bovine lives.[30]

Humans control many other aspects of animal lives, countering facets of animality that impact profit margins, including the time that it takes an animal to reach slaughter weight and the land and labor necessary to achieve the final product. Since the early twentieth century, humans have utilized a combination of confined animal feeding operations (CAFOs) and scientific advances to maximize productivity and profit. Confined animal feeding operations started in the United States in the early 1920s with chickens. Chickens mature fast and can be grown indoors with little trouble. By the end of World War II, much of the American South was raising chicken in the "broiler belt." As production increased, the price of chicken fell drastically, making chicken more accessible and leading to a tripling of consumption between the war and the 1990s. In the postwar years, pigs followed chickens into confinement. With a fast growth rate, and easily fed on corn, the main problem with hog confinement was the challenge of manure. Once that was solved with slatted floors, the industry boomed. At the beginning of the century, humans generated 80 percent of the world's pork and chicken in CAFOs. Cattle, because of longer pregnancies and slower growth, adapted less well to CAFOs. Instead, modern production centers on feedlots, often attached to packinghouses, where the animals are "finished" with grain and soybeans before slaughter. By 1973, commercial feedlots generated two-thirds of American beef. CAFOs have also spread around the world, as meat consumption in much of the developing world has increased. By the early 2000s, China had three times as many factory farms as the United States.[31]

Treating animals as other agricultural products to be grown, not raised, required scientific innovation. Animals in feedlots and CAFOs no longer feed themselves, move, or reproduce independently. They are fed carefully designed diets, often made up of foods that they would never experience in the wild or even in the pasture. Basic diets of feed grains have been augmented with a wide variety of human food byproducts from citrus pulp to almond husks. The incredible animal density in CAFOs makes disease a huge risk, so, as early as the 1950s, producers put hogs and poultry on a regular prophylactic diet of antibiotics—half of all antibiotics in the world go to animals—while they dosed cattle with artificial hormones to promote growth. Most breeding now is done through artificial insemination, which is quicker and safer for the humans, although presumably less satisfactory for the animals. Finally, animals are mutilated to conserve the end product, with piglets having their incisors and tails clipped to prevent damage.[32]

Along with removing most of the definitional traits of animals from modern livestock, CAFOs degrade the environment in many ways. One-third of the world's farmland, some of it previously devoted to producing food for human consumption, now grows animal feed. Intensive cultivation methods required the application of fertilizers that have contaminated both fresh and salt waters. Additionally, much of the deforestation of the Brazilian Amazon since 2000—which led to massive fires in 2019—has been to supply soybeans for feed. Large concentrations of animals produce large quantities of manure, which poses human health risks ranging from respiratory infections to depression and brain damage. Hog manure is particularly problematic, and spills and leakage have contaminated water supplies with nitrogen and phosphorus. Developed countries have tried to address this problem, with Spain, for example, spreading more manure on fields and Denmark requiring it be stored in sealed vats. China, however, with its growing number of CAFOs, still discharges most of its hog manure into the watersheds, causing large-scale die-offs in freshwater lakes and the South China Sea, as well as threatening the health of humans who consume the water. While cattle manure is less problematic, cattle, especially those raised on artificial feed, emit methane, a powerful greenhouse gas. Livestock, in general, contribute 65 percent of nitrous oxide—a greenhouse gas that is at least two hundred times more damaging than carbon dioxide—to the atmosphere.[33]

Turning livestock from animals into products, reducing their animality as much as possible, has created numerous serious and unforeseen consequences. While meat is cheaper than ever, the dangers posed to human health and to the planet have increased exponentially. Additionally, the separation that humans sought for so long between the animal and the flesh is beginning to dissipate. In some parts of the globe, a growing concern about animal welfare has started to shift the pendulum. In 2003, for example, Germany passed a law requiring that hogs have access to sunlight and toys, and in 2008, California banned single-animal pens for sheep and poultry cages. The next stage, however, is unclear and the options span a sizable continuum from continued growth of CAFOs, to artisanal meats, to Impossible meat (the name of one brand of meat-flavored plant-based food). Most radical is cultured meat—either from stem cells or synthetically generated. Together with vegetarianism, this removes the need for animals at all, creating an imagined future where livestock will perhaps become undomesticated. Without such drastic change it is apparent that the relationship between humans and livestock will become more imbalanced still, with more collateral damage to the health of people, animals, and the planet.

Notes

1. This article focuses exclusively on ungulates, as the most significant livestock throughout history. Thus, there is no discussion of poultry, which has had a large impact on modern history, or other smaller livestock such as rabbits and guinea pigs. Overall, the focus is on cattle and hogs as the most important livestock in terms of meat production and global presence. The author would like to thank Tom Brooking, Jim Norris, Bob Smither, Phoebe Strom, Sandra Swart, and Shawn Van Ausdal for their help and insights. Parts of this text appeared in my earlier article, "Cattle and Cultures," *Agricultural History* 88, no. 3 (Summer 2014): 426–427.
2. M. Ryder, *Sheep & Man* (London: Duckworth, 1983): 17–27; Juliet Clutton-Brock, "Introduction to Pastoralism," in *The Walking Larder: Patterns of Domestication, Pastoralism, and Predation*, ed. Clutton-Brock (London: Unwin Hyman, 1989): 115–118; Laurie Carlson, *Cattle: An Informal Social History* (Chicago: Ivan R. Dee, 2001): 18–32; Mark Essig, *Lesser Beasts: A Snout-to-Tail History of the Humble Pig* (New York: Basic Books, 2015): 33–41; Richard Bulliet, *Hunters, Herders, and Hamburgers: The Past and Future of Human-Animal Relationships* (New York: Columbia University Press, 2005).
3. Valentin Shilov, "The Origins of Migration and Animal Husbandry in the Steppes of Eastern Europe," in *The Walking Larder*, 123; Meike Meerpohl, "Pastoralism and Trans-Saharan Trade: The Transformation of a Historical Trade Route Between Eastern Chad and Libya," in *Pastoralism in Africa: Past, Present and Future*, ed. Michael Bollig et al. (New York: Berghahn, 2013): 422; Terry Jordan, *North American Cattle-Ranching Frontiers: Origins,*

Diffusion, and Differentiation (Albuquerque: University of New Mexico Press, 1993), 60; Ryder, *Sheep & Men*: 231, 240.
4. Ryder, *Sheep & Men*, 720-735; John Richards, *The Unending Frontier: An Environmental History of the Early Modern World* (Berkeley: University of California Press, 2003), 282; Carlson, *Cattle*.
5. Ferdnand Braudel, *The Mediterranean and the Mediterranean World in the Age of Philip II* (New York: Harper & Row, 1972): 85-86; C. Devendra and G. Haenlein, "Animals That Produce Dairy Foods: Goat Breeds," in *Encyclopedia of Dairy Sciences,* ed. John Fuquay (Amsterdam: Elsevier, 2011), 310-324; Monideepa Mitra et al., "A Note on Transhumant Pastoralism in Niti Valley, Western Himalaya, India," *Pastoralism: Research, Policy and Practice* 3 (2013).
6. Harold Fox, *Dartmoor's Alluring Uplands: Transhumance and Pastoral Management in the Middle Ages* (Exeter: University of Exeter Press, 2012): 217; Carla Rahn Phillips and William Phillips, *Spain's Golden Fleece: Wool Production and the Wool Trade from the Middle Ages to the Nineteenth Century* (Baltimore: Johns Hopkins University Press, 1997): 21-22; Álvaro Aragón Ruano, "Relaciones ganaderas entre Navarra y Guipúzcoa durante la Baja Edad Media y el cominenzo de la Edad Moderna," *España medieval* 38 (2015): 27-31.
7. Martine Barwegen, "Browsing in Livestock History: Large Ruminants and the Environment in Java, 1850-2000," in *Smallholders and Stockbreeders: History of Foodcrop and Livestock Farming in Southeast Asia,* ed. Peter Boomgaard and David Henley (Leiden: KITLV Press, 2004): 288; Jordan, *North American Cattle-Ranching Frontiers*; Karl Butzer, "Cattle and Sheep from Old to New Spain: Historical Antecedents," *Annals of the Association of American Geographers* 78 (March 1988): 44; Timothy Silver, *A New Face on the Countryside: Indians, Colonists, and Slaves in the South Atlantic Forests, 1500-1800* (Cambridge: Cambridge University Press, 1900): 173; Essig, *Lesser Beasts*, 81; John Hare, *A Prospering Society: Wiltshire in the Later Middle Ages* (Hatfield: University of Hertfordshire Press, 2011), 50-51; Laura Sutcliffe et al., "Pastoral Commons Use in Romania and the Role of the Common Agricultural Policy," *International Journal of the Commons* 7, no. 1 (2013): 58-72; Robin Mearns, "Community, Collective Action and Common Grazing: The Case of Post-Socialist Mongolia," *Journal of Development Studies* 32, no. 3 (1996): 297-339; Maia Call and Pamela Jagger, "Social Capital, Collective Action, and Communal Grazing Lands in Uganda," *International Journal of the Commons* 11, no. 2 (2017): 854-876.
8. For concern about livestock, see Joanne Bowen, "To Market, To Market: Animal Husbandry in New England," *Historical Archaeology* 32, no. 3 (1998): 137-152. For enclosure, see Claire Strom, *Making Catfish Bait out of Government Boys: The Fight against Cattle Ticks and the Transformation of the Yeoman South* (Athens: University of Georgia Press, 2009); Liz Wily, "The Global Land Grab: The New Enclosures," in *The Wealth of the Commons: A World beyond Market and State,* ed. David Bollier and Silke Helfrich (Amherst, MA: Levellers Press, 2012). Vaclav Smil, *Should We Eat Meat? Evolution and Consequences of Modern Carnivory* (New York: Wiley-Blackwell, 2013): 61.
9. John Fischer, *Cattle Colonialism: An Environmental History of the Conquests of California and Hawai'i* (Berkeley: University of North Carolina Press, 2015): 15; Mart Stewart, "From King Cane to King Cotton: Razing Cane in the Old South," *Environmental History* 12, no. 1 (2007): 67; Alfred Crosby, *The Columbian Exchange: Biological and Cultural Consequences of 1492* (Westport, CT: Greenwood Press, 1972); William Cronon, *Changes in the Land: Indians, Colonists, and the Ecology of New England* (New York: Hill & Wang, 1983): 128-132.

10. Elinor Melville, *A Plague of Sheep: Environmental Consequences of the Conquest of Mexico* (Cambridge: Cambridge University Press, 1997): 34–39, 53; Greg Bankoff, "Colonizing New Lands: Horses in the Philippines," in *Breeds of Empire: The "Invention" of the Horse in Southeast Asia and Southern Africa, 1500–1950*, ed. Bankoff and Sandra Swart (Copenhagen: NIAS Press, 2007): 102–103; Silver, *A New Face*, 179–180; Stewart, "From King Cane," 59–79; Cameron Muir, *The Broken Promise of Agricultural Progress: An Environmental History* (Abingdon: Routledge, 2014): 9–31.

11. Essig, *Lesser Beasts*, 22, 121–122; Fischer, *Cattle Colonialism*, 14; Crosby, *Columbian Exchange*, 75–94; Pekka Hämäläinen, "The Rise and Fall of Plains Indian Horse Cultures," *Journal of American History* 90, no. 3 (2003): 833–862; Sandra Swart, "Riding High—Horses, Power, and Settler Society in Southern Africa, c. 1654–1840," in *Breeds of Empire*, 129; Elizabeth J. Reitz, "The Spanish Colonial Experience and Domestic Animals," *Historical Archaeology* 26, no. 1 (1992): 84–91.

12. Virginia Anderson, *Creatures of Empire: How Domestic Animals Transformed Early America* (Oxford: Oxford University Press, 2004): 107; Melville, *Plague of Sheep*, 65; Richards, *Unending Frontier*: 284–285; Maureen Ogle, *In Meat We Trust: An Unexpected History of Carnivore America* (Boston: Houghton Mifflin Harcourt, 2013): 17; Joshua Specht, *Red Meat Republic: A Hoof-to-Table History of How Beef Changed America* (Princeton, NJ: Princeton University Press, 2019): 24; William Cronon, *Nature's Metropolis: Chicago and the Great West* (New York: W. W. Norton, 1991): 216; Tom Brooking and Eric Pawson, eds., *Seeds of Empire: The Environmental Transformation of New Zealand* (London: I. B. Taurus, 2011): 159.

13. Anderson, *Creatures of Empire*, 80; Melville, *Plague of Sheep*, 75–76, 117; Essig, *Lesser Beasts*, 134; Cronon, *Changes in the Land*: 54–81.

14. Fischer, *Cattle Colonialism*, 31, 58–60; Muir, *Broken Promise*, 9–31; Geoffrey Blainey, *A Land Half Won* (Melbourne: Sun Books, 1983): 72–98; Richards, *Unending Frontier*, 293–94; Roy Hora, *The Landowners of the Argentine Pampas: A Social and Political History, 1860–1945* (Oxford: Clarendon Press, 2001): 41–42.

15. Rebecca Woods, *The Herds Shot Round the World: Native Breeds and the British Empire, 1800–1900* (Durham: University of North Carolina Press, 2017): 38, 110, 130–132; Anderson, *Creatures of Empire*, 122; Strom, *Making Catfish Bait*, 58; Robert Wilcox, *Cattle in the Backlands: Mato Grosso and the Evolution of Ranching in the Brazilian Tropics* (Austin: University of Texas Press, 2017): 201.

16. Saurabh Mishra, "The Economics of Reproduction: Horse-breeding in Early Colonial India, 1790–1840," *Modern Asian Studies* 46, no. 5 (2012): 1125; Wilcox, *Cattle in the Backlands*; Melville, *Plague of Sheep*; Muir, *Broken Promise*.

17. R. Moore-Colyer, "Aspects of the Trade in British Pedigree Draught Horses with the United States and Canada, c. 1850–1920," *Agricultural History Review* 48, no. 1 (2000): 44; P. Edwards, "The Horse Trade of the Midlands in the Seventeenth Century," *Agricultural History Review* 27, no. 2 (1979): 92; Larry Sawers, "US Army Procurement of Draft and Pack Animals in the Civil War Era," *Eastern Economic Journal* 29, no. 1 (2003): 62; R. DiNardo and Austin Bay, "Horse-Drawn Transport in the German Army," *Journal of Contemporary History* 23, no. 1 (1988): 129–142.

18. Essig, *Lesser Beasts*, 73–74; Deborah Valenze, *Milk: A Local and Global History* (New Haven, CT: Yale University Press, 2011): 86–92, 84.

19. Essig, *Lesser Beasts*, 154–155; Muir, *Broken Promise*, 9; Hora, *Landowners of the Argentine Pampas*, 10.

20. Strom, "Cattle and Cultures," 428–429; Ian Blanchard, "The Continental European Cattle Trades, 1400–1600," *Economic History Review* 39 (1986): 427–460; Thomas Wigham, "Cattle Raising in the Argentine Northeast: Corrientes, c. 1750–1870," *Journal of Latin American Studies* 20 (1988): 313–335; Caroline Skeel, "The Cattle Trade between Wales and England from the Fifteenth to the Nineteenth Centuries," *Transactions of the Royal Historical Society* 9 (1926): 135–158; Richard W. Slatta, *Gauchos and the Vanishing Frontier* (Lincoln: University of Nebraska Press, 1983); Ernest Osgood, *The Day of the Cattleman* (Chicago: University of Chicago Press, 1929); Essig, *Lesser Beasts*, 161–165; Ogle, *In Meat We Trust*, 7–8; Specht, *Red Meat Republic*, 134–143; Richards, *Unending Frontier*, 400; Benjamin Orlove, "Meat and Strength: The Moral Economy of a Chilean Food Riot," *Cultural Anthropology* 12, no. 2 (1997): 234–268; Jordan, *North American Cattle-Ranching Frontiers*.

21. Essig, *Lesser Beasts*, 169; Ogle, *In Meat We Trust*, 15; William Zimmerman, "Live Cattle Export Trade between United States and Great Britain, 1868–1885," *Agricultural History* 36, no. 1 (January 1962): 46–52; Hora, *Landowners of the Argentine Pampas*, 48–49, 42; Wilcox, *Cattle in the Backlands*, 68; Ogle, *In Meat We Trust*, 15, 39–40; Carlson, *Cattle*, 116–17; David Surdam, "The Antebellum Texas Cattle Trade across the Gulf of Mexico," *Southwestern Historical Quarterly* 100, no. 4 (1977): 478; Specht, *Red Meat Republic*, 159–161; Peter Rivière, *The Forgotten Frontier: Ranchers of North Brazil* (New York: Holt, Rinehart & Winston: 1972): 71.

22. Richards, *Unending Frontier*, 347, 368, 400–1; Hora, *Landowners of the Argentine Pampas*, 10; Wilcox, *Cattle in the Backlands*, 49; Jonathan Brown, "A Nineteenth-Century Argentine Cattle Empire," *Agricultural History* 52, no. 1 (1978): 174; Samuel Amaral, *The Rise of Capitalism on the Pampas: The Estancias of Buenos Aires, 1785–1870* (Cambridge: Cambridge University Press, 1998): 281–282; Specht, *Red Meat Republic*, 232.

23. Ogle, *In Meat We Trust*, 40–43; Carlson, *Cattle*, 119–21; Cronon, *Nature's Metropolis*, 233–235; Brooking and Pawson, *Seeds of Empire*, 17, 105; Hora, *Landowners of the Argentine Pampas*, 48–49; Woods, *Herds Shot Round the World*, 119–130.

24. Noélie Vialles, *Animal to Edible* (Cambridge: Cambridge University Press, 1994): 22; Jared Day, "Butchers, Tanners, and Tallow Chandlers: The Geography of Slaughtering in Early-Nineteenth-Century New York City," in *Meat, Modernity, and the Rise of the Slaughterhouse*, ed. Paula Young Lee (Durham: University of New Hampshire Press, 2008): 180, 186.

25. Sydney Watts, "The Grande Boucherie, the 'Right' to Meat, and the Growth of Paris," in *Meat, Modernity*: 14; Ogle, *In Meat We Trust*, 33–35; Dorothee Brantz, "Animal Bodies, Human Health, and Reform of Slaughterhouses in Nineteenth-Century Berlin," in *Meat, Modernity*: 74–75; Chris Otter, "Civilizing Slaughter: The Development of the British Public Abattoir, 1850–1910," in *Meat, Modernity*, 93; Vialles, *Animal to Edible*, 120–124; Ian MacLachlan, "Humanitarian Reform, Slaughter Technology, and Butcher Resistance in Nineteenth-Century Britain," in *Meat, Modernity*, 107–150; Francesco Buscemi, "From Killing Cows to Culturing Meat," *British Food Journal* 116, no. 6 (2014): 952–964.

26. Carl Sandburg, "Chicago," *Poetry: A Magazine of Verse*, (1914); Essig, *Lesser Beasts*, 169–173, 176; Ogle, *In Meat We Trust*, 21–22; Specht, *Red Meat Republic*, 181; Cronon, *Nature's Metropolis*, 228–229.

27. Specht, *Red Meat Republic*; Vialles, *Animal to Edible*; Ogle, *In Meat We Trust*.

28. Abigail Woods, *A Manufactured Plague: The History of Foot-and-Mouth Disease in Britain* (London: Earthscan, 2004): 3.

29. Strom, *Making Catfish Bait*.

30. Wilson Warren, *Meat Makes People Powerful: A Global History of the Modern Era* (Iowa City: University of Iowa Press, 2018): 167; Maxime Schwartz, *How the Cows Turned Mad: Unlocking the Mysteries of Mad Cow Disease* (Berkeley: University of California Press, 2003): 146–149; Carlson, *Cattle*, 150–54.
31. Donald Stull and Michael Broadway, *Slaughterhouse Blues: The Meat and Poultry Industry in North America* (Belmont: Wadsworth, 2013): 44–46, 68; Essig, *Lesser Beasts*, 214–17; Warren, *Meat Makes People Powerful*, 149; Ogle, *In Meat We Trust*, 135; Smil, *Should We Eat Meat?*, 124; Mia MacDonald and Sangamithra Iyer, "China and Industrial Animal Agriculture: Prospects and Defects," *FoodFirst Backgrounder* 15, no. 1 (2009).
32. Ogle, *In Meat We Trust*, 135, 143; Essig, *Lesser Beasts*, 213, 227, 217; Peter Dauvergne, *The Shadows of Consumption: Consequences for the Global Environment* (Cambridge, MA: MIT Press, 2008): 151; Smil, *Should We Eat Meat?*, 131–32.
33. Smil, *Should We Eat Meat?*, 53–157; Warren, *Meat Makes People Powerful*, 155–157; Linden Ellis, "Environmental Health and China's Concentrated Animal Feeding Operations," A China Environmental Health Project Research Brief, 2007, https://www.wilsoncenter.org/sites/default/files/media/documents/publication/factory_farms_feb28.pdf; MacDonald and Iyer, "China and Industrial Animal Agriculture"; Dauvergne, *Shadows of Consumption*, 152.

Bibliography

Bankoff, Greg, and Sandra Swart, eds. *Breeds of Empire: The "Invention" of the Horse in Southeast Asia and Southern Africa, 1500–1950*. Copenhagen: NIAS Press, 2007.

Bulliet, Richard. *Hunters, Herders, and Hamburgers: The Past and Future of Human-Animal Relationships*. New York: Columbia University Press, 2005.

Crosby, Alfred. *The Columbian Exchange: Biological and Cultural Consequences of 1492*. Westport, CT: Greenwood Press, 1972.

Essig, Mark. *Lesser Beasts: A Snout-to-Tail History of the Humble Pig*. New York: Basic Books, 2015.

Jordan, Terry. *North American Cattle-Ranching Frontiers: Origins, Diffusion, and Differentiation*. Albuquerque: University of New Mexico Press, 1993.

Melville, Elinor. *A Plague of Sheep: Environmental Consequences of the Conquest of Mexico*. Cambridge: Cambridge University Press, 1997.

Ogle, Maureen. *In Meat We Trust: An Unexpected History of Carnivore America*. Boston: Houghton Mifflin Harcourt, 2013.

Schwartz, Maxime. *How the Cows Turned Mad: Unlocking the Mysteries of Mad Cow Disease*. Berkeley: University of California Press, 2003.

Smil, Vaclav. *Should We Eat Meat? Evolution and Consequences of Modern Carnivory*. New York: Wiley-Blackwell, 2013.

Specht, Joshua. *Red Meat Republic: A Hoof-to-Table History of How Beef Changed America*. Princeton, NJ: Princeton University Press, 2019.

Strom, Claire. *Making Catfish Bait out of Government Boys: The Fight against Cattle Ticks and the Transformation of the Yeoman South*. Athens: University of Georgia Press, 2009.

Stull, Donald, and Michael Broadway. *Slaughterhouse Blues: The Meat and Poultry Industry in North America*. Belmont: Wadsworth, 2013.

Valenze, Deborah. *Milk: A Local and Global History*. New Haven, CT: Yale University Press, 2011.

Vialles, Noélie. *Animal to Edible*. Cambridge: Cambridge University Press, 1994.
Warren, Wilson. *Meat Makes People Powerful: A Global History of the Modern Era*. Iowa City: University of Iowa Press, 2018.
Wilcox, Robert. *Cattle in the Backlands: Mato Grosso and the Evolution of Ranching in the Brazilian Tropics*. Austin: University of Texas Press, 2017.
Woods, Abigail. *A Manufactured Plague: The History of Foot-and-Mouth Disease in Britain*. London: Earthscan, 2004.
Woods, Rebecca. *The Herds Shot Round the World: Native Breeds and the British Empire, 1800–1900*. Durham: University of North Carolina Press, 2017.
Young Lee, Paula, ed. *Meat, Modernity, and the Rise of the Slaughterhouse*. Durham: University of New Hampshire Press, 2008.

CHAPTER 5

INSECTS, ILLNESS, AND OTHER BIOLOGICAL CONTESTATIONS

MARTHA FEW

IN early June 1801, alarming reports began to circulate in colonial Central America and southern Mexico that locusts had invaded the agricultural fields around the town of San Salvador, feasting on cacao trees, indigo plants, and staple food crops of corn and wheat. Nearby valley towns of Olocuilta, San Vicente, and San Miguel reported that the insects had also infested their farms, haciendas, and the surrounding forested mountains.[1] Eyewitnesses noted that the locusts—*chapulín* or *langosta* in Spanish—were on the move again, beginning to take flight as the giant swarm headed in a northwesterly direction toward Sonsonate, an area known for cacao and balsam production.[2] On June 18, the colonial newspaper *Gazeta de Guatemala* updated its readers with news that the insects had "laid waste" to Sonsonate and the surrounding countryside.[3]

The swarm continued to move north and west along Central America's Pacific coastal plain, arriving in late June to Escuintla Province. Residents there reported that female locusts deposited eggs sacs or tubes called *cañutillos* in the agricultural fields and in the forests of the volcanic mountain chain that traversed the region.[4] From there, huge locust clouds again took flight, continuing to move northwest, a heading that political officials worried would take the swarm on a direct route to the agriculturally important Suchitepéquez region. By early August the insects reached this area of Guatemala's Pacific coastal plain, where again they blanketed the landscape.[5] At this point the swarm apparently split into two groups: one remained in Suchitepéquez, while the other continued north into Chiapas and Tabasco in what today is southern Mexico. In early September, Tabasco's governor alerted the viceroy of New Spain in Mexico City that the locusts had indeed arrived. The swarm was not as large or as devastating as expected, however, because recent heavy rains had impeded the insects' travel.[6]

The locusts that had remained in Suchitepéquez Province when the swarm split spent the winter of 1801–1802 there. By early May 1802, their numbers had increased: political officials estimated that huge patches of the insects now covered some 600 square miles.[7] The president of the Audiencia of Guatemala judged that unseasonably strong winds had "blown" some of the swarm over into Soconusco, where they infested the area by late spring. Another eyewitness claimed that this was in fact a separate swarm that had originated in Nicaragua.[8]

Whatever their origin, the locusts' arrival reminded older residents of a swarm that had attacked the same area some thirty years earlier in the 1770s, unnerving them because they still remembered the resulting food shortages, widespread hunger, and disease outbreaks that emerged in the swarm's wake.[9] At this point, the swarm split again; one group flew east into the Guatemalan highlands, while the other continued in a northwesterly direction into the province of Chiapas.

In the face of the swarm's seemingly unimpeded movement from El Salvador and Nicaragua, through Guatemala, and into southern Mexico, the intendent of Oaxaca penned a letter to the viceroy in Mexico City in which he broke the news that the "practical methods" of locust extermination used in Guatemala had failed.[10] These methods, typical of other areas facing a locust plague in the eighteenth century,

MAP 5.1 The Audiencia of Guatemala in the eighteenth century. Source: Commissioned by author and appears in Martha Few, *For All of Humanity: Mesoamerican and Colonial Medicine in Enlightenment Guatemala* (Tucson: University of Arizona Press, 2015).

included the removal of chapulín egg sacs from agricultural fields using both human and animal labor, driving the insects into pits to crush or bury them alive, and setting them on fire. The intendent called on colonial officials and clergy to resort to "heavenly assistance" (*auxilio divino*) to repel the insects, such as nine-day prayers called *novenarios* dedicated to particular saints known for their locust-repelling powers, and for religious processions to carry these saints' images through towns and farmed fields.[11] Even so, neither practical nor religious methods worked, as clouds of locusts again took to the air, landing in early June in the fields in Oaxaca in the area around Tehuantepec.[12]

This timeline of two consecutive years of locust swarms and the geography of their movements across colonial Central America and southern Mexico are part of a superswarm of nine consecutive years of locust plagues (or *plagas* in Spanish, as they were often called at the time) that lasted from 1798 to 1806. Rather than a series of smaller locally or regionally focused infestations, that is, swarms that emerged and then receded after one to two years as they had in previous decades, this superswarm was different. Locusts repeatedly afflicted a significant portion of the Viceroyalty of New Spain for the better part of a decade and had economic, food supply, and biological effects on human populations far beyond the areas of the swarms' physical and temporal presence. Yet despite the dire effects of this and other multiyear swarms that intensified in the late eighteenth and early nineteenth centuries here and elsewhere in the Americas, many have focused on locusts only in supporting roles in a greater narrative describing the history of agriculture and public health.[13] More recent interdisciplinary work connects periodic intensifications of locust swarms in Latin America and Spain to climate events such as the Little Ice Age and sustained drought, and spans the pre-Columbian and colonial eras.[14] Other scholars have argued that insect populations such as mosquitos, locusts, ants, and caterpillars shape, and are shaped by, empires and environmental transformation of the colonial Americas.[15]

The 1798–1806 superswarm emerged from the frequent smaller local and regional swarms in the fifteen or so years that proceeded it, and that encompassed diverse landscapes, ecologies, and methods of agricultural production is used here as a case study for colonial food security.[16] These earlier swarms, though smaller in geographic scope, had already stressed export agriculture, food production, and supply to urban areas, and had led to food shortages among the region's Indigenous peoples, multiethnic poor, and other vulnerable populations. They also intersected with significant outbreaks of epidemic disease in this region, including smallpox, measles, and typhus, during the same time period.[17]

This multiyear perspective, covering a broad area of hundreds of square miles that stretched from colonial Central America to southern Mexico on the Pacific coast, across the isthmus of Tehuantepec to the Yucatán peninsula on the Atlantic, shows how and why locusts and their swarms were something that the colonial state had to react to and attempt to control. For the colonial project to continue to remain stable, Spain had to protect its subjects, including its majority tributary Indigenous populations, whose labor and taxes sustained colonialism in these regions.[18]

Archiving Locusts

Locust swarms, especially multiyear swarms, triggered the production of extraordinary rich paper trails of archival materials in their wake—in manuscript and printed form—that documented the political, economic, and medical devastation that they wrought. Much of this material tends to be elite or government-generated, written by political officials, priests, large landowners, Indigenous elites, scientists, medical physicians, and European travelers, in a time of severe ecological and social crisis. These writers included some of the most important officials in the Viceroyalty of New Spain: provincial intendents and governors; Audiencia presidents, bishops, and archbishops; and the viceroy. They shared information on swarm locations, movement, and speed. They provided information about grain prices, extant supplies, price gouging, and requests for food aid to stave off hunger and famine. And they presented fine-grained details and progress (or lack of it) on locust-extermination campaigns and accompanying religious rituals and processions.

This information made its way to the public through word of mouth, meetings of local scientific societies, as well as in regular updates published in newspapers in Guatemala, Mexico, and Spain.[19] This material was generated and collected at the local, regional, and viceregal levels, so the source base remains scattered across local and national archives in Central America, Mexico, Spain, and in multiple research libraries in the United States, Great Britain, and elsewhere. Thus, creating a transregional history of locust infestations, and following a succession of swarms over hundreds of miles over consecutive years, proves challenging for researchers interested in larger comparative regional frameworks of analysis. Moreover, sources relating to locust swarms and the devastation they wrought are not catalogued as such. Instead researchers find their traces bundled in with agricultural records, records of epidemics and famine, tax rolls and tribute records, colonial investigations of Indigenous idolatry and other religious crimes of interest to the Church, and when specific Indigenous communities requested tribute reduction or relief in the aftermath of agricultural devastation that brought epidemic disease and hunger in their wake.

When we follow locusts over space and time, the swarm emerges from the archives as a living entity containing millions of insects that transformed over time. The swarm of 1801 is not one but a series of swarms that emerged, flew together, and split apart to move into different directions as locusts made their way from the rich indigo fields of El Salvador and Nicaragua north and west though the cacao groves, sugar plantations, and *milpa* corn fields of Guatemala and Chiapas, across the isthmus of Tehuantepec, and into Oaxaca. The swarm wintered together and laid eggs to renew its insect members, and at times joined with other swarms. In the process, despite the widespread and multiple efforts at local and regional levels of colonial society to discipline the land and its peoples in order to exterminate the locusts, the diversion of colonial resources and labor to fight and kill locusts on the ground, and the best efforts of scientists and botanists to invent new locust-killing methods or identify and introduce locust-resistant food crops, humans in colonial Spanish America, as elsewhere, had to reconcile and adapt to locust swarm behavior.

Modern entomology classifies all locusts as grasshoppers, but not all grasshoppers as locusts. Some dozen species of grasshoppers have the ability to swarm.[20] Locusts eat by moving their jaws from side to side to remove and consume plant materials.[21] Swarms can reach sizes of up to 400 square miles, contain some several billion insects, and travel as far as 3,000 miles from their point of origin.[22] Swarming occurs when the insects crowd around remaining food sources, in response to drought and other weather or environmental changes or anomalies. This causes locust phase polyphenism: as the grasshoppers begin to swarm, their bodies repeatedly molt and transform with bigger wings, stronger legs, and a distinct color change.[23]

Both European and Mesoamerican cultures share a deep history with locusts. In European cultures, locusts have long figured in the imagination and practical experience of various societies as an important and potentially ominous species. Islamic cultures attribute important roles to insects, including locusts, as part of their sacred texts.[24] Key Judeo-Christian religious texts also give locusts prominent roles in their sacred history from. The Old Testament is filled with references to locust plagues, as is the New Testament with its references to locusts in Revelation as literal harbingers of the apocalypse.[25] Into modern times, Christian cultures in Europe and the Americas have read locust plagues as evidence of divine punishment or signs of apocalypse and have used a variety of religious strategies including religious processions, public prayers, and even locust excommunication in efforts to halt the insect swarm's spread.[26]

At the same time, locusts were not completely alien to Indigenous colonial Central America and southern Mexico, which comprise a large area of the historical and cultural region of Mesoamerica and its Indigenous societies. In 1454 the Mexica Empire (also referred to as the Aztec Empire) experienced a devastating succession of locust swarms in the Valley of Mexico that contributed to widespread famine.[27] Furthermore, Mesoamericans have included chapulín and other insects as important parts of their diets from the ancient past to the present day. A number of Mesoamerican codices reference locust swarms and include them in their annals. The *Codex Mexicanus*, a Nahuatl-language manuscript that dates to the late sixteenth century, depicts locusts in its calendric, genealogical, historical knowledge and images.[28] The historical section references the most important events for that community over many decades. On the date 6 Rabbit, in the year 1466, a chapulín appears above the chronogram, on top of what looks like a hill, with three humans next to it. Below the chronogram, there appears to be a sketch with two chapulín below and above ground.[29] Similarly, the sixteenth-century Codex Aubin depicts a locust image to signify a chapulín invasion in 1403 in the Valley of Mexico, described in the text as "Here the chapulín descended."[30] The inclusion of chapulín images in the historical section are significant in showing that locust plagues were considered among other events critical to Mexica history, including remarkable natural and celestial events (floods, eclipses), important migrations, the first smallpox epidemic, and the arrival of the Spanish to the capital city Tenochtitlan.

The sixteenth-century Florentine Codex, an encyclopedic work of Mesoamerican knowledge that includes natural history, has a section devoted to insects in general information, specifically on chapulín.[31] These pages record Indigenous knowledge of multiple types of grasshoppers, their Spanish and Nahuatl designations, the colors and physiology, and information on when they swarm and what plants they prefer to eat. The codex records that the *Acachapolin*, for example, "flies like an arrow," while the *Xopan Chapolin* are large and slow-moving, recognized by their colors (black, green or "multi-colored") and for their preference for eating bean plants.[32] Each of these Mesoamerican sources depicts individual locusts, and also locusts described as parts of swarms, showing that the insects prey on humans and agriculture by eating their foodstuffs.

FIGURE 5.1 Locust swarm depicted in the Codex Mexicanus. Source: Bibliothèque National de France, http://gallica.bnf.fr/ark:/12148/btv1b55005834g.

Locusts, Flying

When locusts swarmed into the huge, mobile clouds and flew together across southern Mesoamerica, they literally transformed the environment, forcing humans to react and adapt. Following in the archival wake of historical locust swarms reveals how colonial communication networks of warning worked in times of stress and threat to spread the most up-to-date information on their movement over hundreds of miles. This occurred when political officials in different colonial cities regularly shared data with each other. On May 27, 1802, the intendent of Chiapas, located in Ciudad Real, wrote to the viceroy in Mexico City with specific, detailed information on the geographic movement of the swarm:

> However the *la plaga* (the plague) has again returned to the province and covered Soconusco. It started in the provinces of Quetzaltenango and Suchitépeques, then [travelled] to the Tonalá curate adjacent to the Intendency of Oaxaca. If they are not exterminated again, then they will continue on to Tehuantepec.[33]

Even this short paragraph conveys much information. The writer called the swarm a plague, reflecting the frequent use of disease metaphors when referencing a locust swarm in archival sources. The swarm "again returned," indicating a multiyear swarm, and that earlier locusts killing methods had not succeeded. Lastly, the intendent provided a detailed description of movement of swarm for hundreds of miles through a large section of colonial Central America and southern Mexico, and he gave a prediction, based on previous experience with swarms, for where that year's swarm would travel next. In the process, the detailed observations and reporting by Chiapas's intendent recorded one leg in a longer narrative history of this particular swarm that can be pieced together from multiple colonial sources and geographical viewpoints such as this one.

Looking further into this multiyear outbreak reveals the ways that regional political authorities whose jurisdictions historically fell in the path of locust swarms in this region shared information with each other for where the swarm will go next. Here the writer shared the details with the viceroy of the colonial capital of Mexico City as the most important political official in the Viceroyalty of New Spain. The day after the Chiapas intendent updated the viceroy he sent a second update, to the governor of Oaxaca, who governed the area where he believed the swarm would head next. In this report, the Chiapas intendent wrote that he received news that the swarm had invaded Soconusco and predicted that "it is clear that the locusts will also infest all of New Spain."[34] He also reported the development of feelings of hopelessness and helplessness among the area's residents, an atmosphere that he feared might affect the resilience of the towns under his jurisdiction: "The pueblos have lost heart, and are driven to despair because they cannot win the fight against the swarm."[35]

As the swarm worked its way from its origin in San Salvador up the Pacific coastal plain, more and more colonial officials began to contribute to the ongoing communication network tracking the swarm's size and movement and assessed its destructive potential. At this point the captain general of Yucatán entered the discussion.[36] On June 10, 1802, he too wrote to the viceroy and told him that he had been closely following the swarm's movement through Guatemala. He wanted to alert him that at the beginning of the year, locusts had also arrived in the area around the Atlantic port city of Mérida, and that they had originated from "the ocean," implying that the locusts had come to Yucatán from somewhere in the Caribbean.[37]

Such detailed archival sources record the life histories of a specific locust swarm in time and space—where and when they emerged from indigo fields, cacao groves, or forested mountains rich in volcanic soils, and where they traveled. Eyewitnesses noted what types of plants and crops they ate along the way, including indigo, cacao, corn, corn, beans, yuca, bananas, and sugar.[38] They also provide detailed observations of the kinds of landscapes where locusts wintered and laid their eggs, and how weather in the form of winds and rains either promoted or impeded the swarm's travel.[39] Collectively the sources provide a history of the life cycle of the swarm from its emergence to its dissolution, even through consecutive generations when dealing with multiyear super swarms such as this one.

In addition to assessing the movements of swarms, colonial observers had for many years noted direct causal connections among locusts, famine, and epidemic disease. In a report from Dominican friar Antonio Molina, who had witnessed multiyear locust swarms of the late seventeenth and early eighteenth centuries in Guatemala, connected the arrival of a locust swarms with food shortages and epidemic disease: "The locust causes woeful widespread damages, such as famine. They take over the land, destroying the fields and preventing sowing. Famine is usually followed by an epidemic [outbreak]."[40]

Eyewitnesses in the early nineteenth century made these connections as well during the superswarm. On September 20, 1801, the governor of Tabasco notified the viceroy that heavy rains and flooding earlier that month had caused extensive damage to the maize and bean crops. An epidemic of fevers called *tercianas* broke out in the towns and pueblos in the aftermath of the flooding, causing sickness and death. At that point the locusts arrived.[41] Archival sources documenting public health efforts against epidemics, smallpox inoculation and vaccination campaigns and census materials, and letters from tributary Maya communities requesting the deferment or cancellation of taxes because of high mortality rates from a range of infectious illnesses like typhus and measles outbreaks also show evidence that locust swarms frequently preceded or followed these and other disease outbreaks.[42]

Because of the broad recognition among colonial elites that the emergence of locust swarms appeared linked to famine and disease outbreaks, practical and scientific information about the insects and how to combat their swarms shows that these events were of interest not only to colonial officials, botanists, and scientists but also to an interested, literate public in this Enlightenment era. Residents of colonial Central America and southern Mexico eagerly consumed news about locust swarms found in colonial newspapers published in Guatemala, Mexico, and Spain that circulated in the capital and important regional towns. People generated and read new ideas and innovations of the day used to combat them, from books, pamphlets, and colonial newspapers, and even wrote letters to the editor sharing this type of information.[43] These sources provided short reports on the emergence of swarms and their movements, as well as information on the most up-to-date extermination methods. Moreover, the University of San Carlos, established in 1680 and located in Guatemala's capital, produced a small but influential number of Guatemalan-born scientists and medical doctors during the eighteenth century.[44] The university provided science and agriculture professionals, and its graduates formed a key sector of the public that bought, read, and wrote for newspapers, how-to pamphlets, books, and printed short instructions from the colonial government produced at the time.[45]

Colonial newspapers show evidence of the public's engagement with, and participation in, news of locust plagues when readers wrote letters to colonial newspapers with helpful news or information to share about a particular swarm. This included José Rossi y Rubí of Suchitepéquez Province, who wrote a letter in early June to the *Guatemala Gazette*.[46] The newspaper deemed it important and published it in the June 7 issue:

> I have multiple, trustworthy reports that the *Langosta*, or *Chapulín*, are heading toward this province (Suchitepéquez). After they [the insects] ravaged the town of Sonsonate and its surrounding districts, they laid eggs in the mountains of Moyuta and in Escuintla, and then took flight, heading northeast. This will put them on a direct course to our countryside and farmland.[47]

Scientific and ecological knowledge on how to kill the insects spread not only in colonial newspapers, but also through the publication of locust-killing handbooks such as José de Valle's *Guide to the Plague of Locusts, and the Methods Used to Exterminate them, or to Lessen Their Effects, and Prevent Food Scarcity. Prepared by Order of the Government of Guatemala*, published in Guatemala in 1804.[48] Handbooks devoted to the cultivation of important export crops included sections devoted to insect pests such as locusts, as did the indigo/*xiquilite* cultivation guide written in 1799 by Don José Mariano Moziño, the botanist of the Royal Expedition to New Spain, titled *Treatise on Xiquilite and Indigo of Guatemala, Dedicated to The Royal Economic Society*.[49] This guide on how to cultivate indigo using the most up-to-date scientific knowledge of the time contains a chapter dedicated locusts, who liked to eat *xiquilite*, the Nahuatl name for the tender young indigo shoots.

The cornerstone of colonial responses to locust swarms were locust-killing campaigns, described in archival sources using the language of annihilation, measures that aimed to "kill and destroy the langosta," and described a killing event as a "massacre" (*matanza*).[50] Local colonial officials drew on the tributary labor system to organize Indigenous Maya workers at the town level to kill locusts. This colonial labor force of Indigenous men, women, and children applied the available technologies to kill the locusts: fire to burn the insects and agricultural tools to crush and bury them. They also set their domesticated animals loose—flocks of turkeys and chickens, pigs, cattle, sheep, and goats—onto fields infested with locust egg sacs or with newly hatched locusts with undeveloped wings called hoppers (*saltónes*) or fetuses (*fetos*).[51] Pigs rooted out and ate the locust egg sacs; turkeys and chickens ate the young locusts, and all of the domesticated animals trampled on the eggs and crushed newly hatched locusts, as they made their way across the infested fields.

As Guatemalan botanists and scientists understood locust eradication strategies, these early stages were seen as a critical point for intervention to kill the locusts before they could develop wings and swarm.[52] Historian and naturalist Francisco Ximénez, writing in 1722, explained that locusts had to be killed before they developed wings: "First [the locusts] eat up everything, later they begin to procreate their *hijuelos* (little children) and send them forth, and they cannot fly because they have not yet grown wings. And the [people] drive them so that they fall together into pits, and then burn them."[53] One official warned, "This is an opportune moment to stop them by killing *la pequeña semilla* [lit., the little seed, that is, the young locusts] before they grow the wings that they need to fly and destroy the fields."[54]

Campaigns to kill locusts show the ways that Spanish administrators, who represented colonial authority and power, uprooted villagers and farmers to fight and kill locusts. Indigenous Maya villagers became caught between locusts and the colonial state, represented by local authorities, who pooled community resources through cooperation and through coercive colonial labor institutions to kill the insects.[55] Spanish colonial officials organized and managed colonial subordinates to kill locusts, mostly Indigenous Mayas, including men, women, and children. Colonial officials put Spaniards seen as experienced hands in charge of organizing and directing systematic locust-killing and other anti-locust measures during infestations. The majority of firsthand accounts of anti-locust measures focus on the arsenal of weapons—especially fire, agricultural implements, and suffocation by driving and burying locusts into pits—that were applied to the task of destroying the locusts quickly and efficiently. Here and elsewhere, these remained the primary extermination tools for the entire colonial period and into the nineteenth century.

While political officials, hacienda owners, farmers, and Indigenous elites did search for new extermination methods, no new innovative technology for killing locusts in large numbers emerged during the colonial period. In the meantime, colonial elites argued for adjustments to fit local ecologies of how, when, and where locusts infested particular areas. These efforts in part focused on the diversification of food crops and other agricultural innovations as a way to deprive locusts of food and as a hedge against hunger and famine. The decree written during the superswarm by the president of the Audiencia in May 1801 to regional officials areas afflicted by locust plagues illustrates this nicely: "I must dedicate all my efforts/foresight to prevent this affliction as soon as possible," he wrote.[56] He ordered that they ensure that farmers "double cultivation of wheat and corn," and "add cassava (*yuca*), yams (*batatas*), and potatoes (*papas*)," food plants considered to be locust-resistant because the food source of the plant grew beneath the soil and at the same time healthful for local populations.[57] This issue of locust-resistant crops was also taken up by Guatemala's Enlightenment-era scientific society.[58]

Various regional corregidores and alcaldes mayores in charge of implementing these changes at the local level responded in writing in June and July of that year that they would obey the president's order to diversify their crops, including Francisco Guerra, who governed Totonicapán and Quetzaltenango Province; Tadeo Cerda, corregidor of Chimaltenango; the interim head of Sololá Don Carlos Yndiz; and also political representatives from Verapaz and Sacatepéquez.[59] It remains to be seen, however, if these recommended changes were adopted.

The president of the Audiencia summed up his decree with the observation that the locust-killing campaigns had overburdened and exhausted local populations. Moreover, an even more dire threat loomed: "a deadly famine (*un hambre mortal*) that experience shows us will be even worse" than the locusts.[60] This meant that he and other colonial officials were willing to entertain almost anything in the search for a strategy to exterminate locusts and stop the swarms, even if they came from unlikely people and places.

The Tale of a Secret Locust-Killing Recipe

That is in fact what happened. That same year, 1801, a man named Don Miguel de Acosta languished in Nueva Guatemala's city jail. He heard rumors circulating among the prisoners of the locust swarm's imminent arrival, again threatening the rich agricultural towns in and around the capital. After hearing the news, Acosta somehow obtained pen, ink, and paper and wrote a letter to the city council in which he made what seemed like a tantalizing claim: Acosta wrote that he knew of a secret botanical method used by the Indigenous peoples of Siam (now Thailand) to repel and kill locusts. Acosta wrote, "I have obtained a secret way that planted fields can be protected from the ravenous bleakness and death caused by the langosta, here called chapulín."[61] Acosta proposed that if only the city council would release him from jail, he promised to gather the necessary plants and other materials from the surrounding countryside and apply the method himself. He guaranteed success only when the materials were gathered, mixed, and applied by an expert, as he claimed to be, in "the art and exactitude of what those Native Peoples (*naturales*) of Siam do."[62]

The two letters that Acosta wrote to the city council do not provide any clues on how he learned of this secret so-called Siamese locust-killing method, whether he had traveled to Asia himself, or if he had acquired the information from someone else who had, or some other way. Nor does he ever name or describe the plants, herbs, and other materials in this locust extermination recipe. Finally, these documents provide no further biographical information on Acosta himself, or information on why and how long he was in jail. We can infer, however, that Acosta was elite because of the "Don" he used as part of his name. And we can infer that he was highly educated for the time from the content of the two letters that he sent to the city council, where, among other clues, he cited a number of key natural history thinkers, including Carl Linnaeus. Ultimately, however, Guatemalan colonial officials decided not to take Acosta up on his offer.

Nevertheless, Guatemala's colonial scientists and political officials took Acosta's claim seriously by bringing his letters before the city council. This is instructive of how Acosta and other learned men operating in colonial New Spain during the Enlightenment era claimed Indigenous knowledge for colonial ends. Acosta made the argument that his "secret" locust-killing recipe fit into ideas of Indigenous knowledge as a category or body of knowledge as something worthy to explore. Acosta promised, "The effect of this secret is almost foolproof if carried out correctly."[63] Acosta drew on well-worn, imperial/colonial tropes of Indigenous knowledge as "secret" that needed to be "discovered" and at the same time emphasized the locust eradication method's exotic Asian origin that those in Guatemala likely would not be familiar with as they would, say, Maya botanical knowledge. Because Acosta was the only one who had gained access to this secret Indigenous knowledge, this made him the only one who could and must apply the plant-based locust repellent:

> This method obliges me to be the only one who guides it and puts it into operation, . . . so as to gather the materials necessary to bring about the proposed effect [killing locusts], and the use of these materials in the places that you wish to rescue and protect, fields of wheat, corn (*milpas*), vegetables, and other important agricultural fields.[64]

The subtext here is that this kind of specialized knowledge, gleaned from Indigenous peoples of Asia, needed a colonial intermediary to translate the method culturally and practically in order to properly utilize it. Acosta's claim to know what the Siamese called the plants, their New World cognates, and how to recognize them in local ecological contexts granted Acosta the status of expert. Acosta made this clear to his readers:

> The Indigenous peoples (*Naturales*) of the Kingdom of Siam in the East Indies in part gave birth to the method that I offer to you, their sown fields provide the materials needed, and these plants are also grown here and have the same features so that I know how to recognize them and harvest them, even though there is some difference in the names that they are known by the Siamese.[65]

Acosta was clearly motivated by self-interest. He had spent time jail in the capital for an undisclosed crime, and surely he would have liked to be released. This is an interesting strategy to pursue to write a letter himself, directly to city council members. They read it and took his proposal seriously, seriously enough, for example, to have the renowned medical physician and scientist Don Narciso Esparragosa provide his learned opinion on Acosta's proposal. Esparragosa headed the Protomedicato, the colonial bureaucracy that regulated medicine and public health in colonial Central America, regularly wrote columns on science and medicine for the newspaper, and he also held the title of professor and first chair of medicine at Guatemala's San Carlos University.[66]

In addition to self-interest, Acosta explicitly drew on the language of humanitarianism, that fighting the swarm helped humanity: "My natural love for humanity compels me to wish for its preservation, and exterminate all that can threaten [humans], even ... given my unfortunate situation [of being imprisoned]."[67]

Similar language of humanitarianism underpinned discussions of the application to colonial populations of new medical innovations at the time, seen in archival sources that documented the first state-directed public health campaigns in colonial Central America against smallpox, typhus, and measles that were concurrent with state-directed locust-extermination efforts.[68] This is not surprising. Colonial observers referred to locust infestations as plagues. Moreover, people associated locust swarms with illness outbreaks and famine, threats as much to human health as to local and regional economies. Reports from the field described locust swarms as epidemics, plagues, and contagion (e.g., *epidemia de langosta*, *plaga de langosta*, and *el contagio de dicho langosta*) and called for *remedios* (cures) to fight against their spread, as if the swarm were a disease.[69]

Acosta buttressed his claims of humanitarian goals by associating locusts with biblical references that many would have been familiar with, a way to underscore the fight against them within a Christian worldview. He made the argument that this Indigenous Siamese method should not be dismissed as sorcery or misguided folk belief:

> Locust plagues are one of the three greatest horrors with which God has punished the world, and that only in heaven can one find a cure. But also we know that to stop other similar miseries God has provided material or natural things, according to [His] sacred plans that there are natural methods (*medios naturales*) and the use of them is an absolute miracle.[70]

Yet at the same time, he wondered at the contradiction of why native peoples knew this secret miraculous method, and not Christians:

> To this I add that when God permitted/gave free will to the Pagans of Siam, and other barbarians in Asia, to locate [the] (plant) materials to use to drive off and free themselves from the locust, why did he deny them to the Catholics, who always dedicate themselves to study, meditation, observances, and industries (on how to kill the locusts)?[71]

Even though Acosta obtained the method from others, no space existed in his intellectual framework to see "the Indigenous peoples of Siam" as innovators in the way he considered himself an innovator. Acosta compared what he did combining plants and other materials into a locust-killing recipe to the experimental methods used by the world's cutting-edge scientists of the Enlightenment: "Many *luces* [Enlightened men] utilized the physics of combinable ingredients to the same end, as has affirmed these learned men (*profesores*)."[72] In the process, Acosta stripped this method of its Indigeneity, confirmed the botanical recipe's effectiveness based on scientifically sound principles of Enlightenment investigation, and finally cloaked the method in biblical legitimacy as a miracle that protected humanity.

Conclusion

Locusts, by periodically joining to create massive swarms and traveling hundreds of miles, and lasting for consecutive years, played a significant role in the history of colonial Central America and Mexico. Residents there considered locusts to be significantly embedded in a wide range of colonial economic, political, and religious processes, processes that historians have deemed central to research on the history colonialism in Latin America. The locust superswarm that afflicted Central America and southern Mexico at the turn of the nineteenth century offers a window into late colonial responses to the insects and provides a case study in colonial food security, where various regions in Spanish America shared information on swarms and their movements and came to each other's aid with food supplies and seeds. Local elites and members of scientific societies attempted agricultural innovation strategies and searched for new locust-killing methods amid this multiyear swarm.

The superswarm forced colonial authorities to divert significant amounts of tributary Indigenous labor to locust-extermination campaigns for a period of years, further stressing local populations and food supply networks. Indigenous peoples, especially Mayas from rural areas who lived through the swarms, described outbreaks of physical illness (in particular, interlinked aspects of hunger and epidemic disease), coupled with what we would call today psychological illnesses (described in the sources as melancholy, fear, and the like), which followed in the swarm's wake. Archival sources additionally provide a window onto Enlightenment understandings of Indigenous knowledge of locusts from the colonial perspective, that is, what colonial authorities thought was Indigenous knowledge about locust-extermination "recipes." Reshifting the focus from locusts as agricultural "pests" to following locusts and their swarms in the archives and on the landscape reveals the ways that the insects formed interactive relationships with humans that both shaped, and were shaped by, colonial geographies and ensuing environmental transformations in the colonial Americas.

Notes

1. *Gazeta de Guatemala*, June 15, 1801, "Langosta, o Chapulín," 489–491, at 489. Olocuilta is a town in El Salvador, known in the colonial period as San Juan Olocuilta. Olocuilta was built on the site of a Postclassic town called, in Nahuatl, Ulucuilta. See the town's webpage: http://www.olocuilta.gob.sv/index.php, accessed August 5, 2020.
2. Murdo MacLeod, *Spanish Central America: A Socioeconomic History, 1520–1720* (Berkeley: University of California Press, 1973), 82–83. For more on Sonsonate, see Ana Margarita Gómez and Sajid Alfredo Herrera, eds., *Mestizaje, poder y sociedad: Ensayos de historia*

colonial de las provincias de San Salvador y Sonsonate (San Salvador, El Salvador: Facultad Latinoamericana de Ciencias Sociales, 2003).

3. *Gazeta de Guatemala*, June 18, 1801, "Suchitepeques," 495.
4. Ibid., 496. The article refers to the location as "las montañas de Moyuta" (the mountains of Moyuta), referring to the mountains and valleys around the Moyuta volcano, a stratovolcano located near the town of the same name in the Santa Rosa Department of what is now modern Guatemala. The volcano has an elevation of 5,451 feet. Currently approximately 400,000 people live within 20 miles of the volcano. See Global Volcanism Program, 2013; Moyuta (342130) in "Volcanoes of the World," v. 4.6.6. E. Venzke, ed., Smithsonian Institution, https://dx.doi.org/10.5479/si.GVP.VOTW4-2013, accessed March 1, 2018.
5. *Gazeta de Guatemala*, June 18, 1801, 497.
6. Bancroft Library, University of California, Berkeley (hereafter BL); Luis Chavez Orozco, ed., *Papeles sobre la plaga de langosta de 1801–1804*, Vols. 5–9 (Mexico City: Publicaciones del Banco Nacional de Crédito Agrícola y Ganadero VIII, 1954): 2: letter from governor of Tabasco to the viceroy of New Spain, September 20, 1801. For the rains that impeded the locust swarm, see Virginia García Acosta, Juan Manuel Pérez Zevallos, and América Molina del Villar, *Desastres agrícolas en México: Catálogo histórico*, Vol. 1: *Épocas prehispánica y colonial (958–1822)* (Mexico City: Centro de Investigaciones y Estudios Superiores en Antropología Social, Fondo de Cultural Económica, 2003): 423.
7. While the locusts likely covered many square miles of fields and forests in this area, it is important not to take this estimate at face value.
8. Archivo General de Centro América (hereafter AGCA), Guatemala City, Guatemala, A1.1-21-602, Decree from the President of the Audiencia of Guatemala, May 27, 1801, ff. 1–7v.
9. Archivo General de Indias (hereafter AGI), Seville, Spain, Estado L. 49, E. 106, 7 de mayo 1802, letter from José Mariano Valero, Intendent of Ciudad Real, to Don Pedro Zeballos, Ministro de Estado, n.p. In this letter, Valero refers to a communication dated October 31, 1801, from José Rosí Rubi in Suchitepéquez reporting on the swarm.
10. That year in Oaxaca became known as "el año de hambre," the year of hunger. García Acosta et al., *Desastres agrícolas en México: Catálogo histórico*, Vol. 1, 423.
11. For more detail, see Martha Few, "Killing Locusts in Colonial Guatemala," in *Centering Animals in Latin American History*, ed. Martha Few and Zeb Tortorici (Durham, NC: Duke University Press, 2015): 62–92.
12. BL, Orozco, ed., *Papeles sobre la plaga de langosta*, letter from governor of Tabasco to the viceroy of New Spain, September 20, 1801. During the 1801–1802 season, locusts traveled north and east into the Cuchumatán mountains, reaching all the way to Verapaz. McCreery, *Rural Guatemala*, 31.
13. For examples of research that focuses on insect infestations in supporting roles in the history of agriculture in colonial Central America, see Bernabé Fernández Hernández, "Problemas de la agricultura de Honduras a comienzo del siglo XIX," *Americanistas* 7 (1990): 63–72; David McCreery, *Rural Guatemala; 1760–1940* (Stanford, CA: Stanford University Press, 1994); Germán Romero Vargas, *Las estructuras sociales de Nicaragua en el siglo XVIII* (Managua, Nicaragua: Vanguardia, 1987); Robert S. Smith, "Indigo Production and Trade in Colonial Guatemala," *Hispanic American Historical Review* 39, no. 2 (May 1959): 181–211.
14. This is currently an active area of research. See especially Luis Alberto Arrioja Díaz Viruell, *Bajo el crepúsculo de los insectos: Clima, plagas y trastornos sociales en el Reino de Guatemala (1768–1805)* (Michoacán, Mexico: El Colegio de Michoacán, 2019); Luis Alberto Arrioja

Díaz Viruell and Armando Alberola Romá, eds., *Clima, desastres y convulsiones sociales en España e Hispanoamérica, siglos XVII–XX* (Alicante, Spain: Universidad de Alicante, 2017); C. Contreras, "Conexión climática del fenómeno de 'El Niño' con la plaga de la langosta centroamericana (*Schistocerca piceifrons piceifrons*, Walker)," *Entomología mexicana* 8 (2009): 347–351; Alejandra García Quintanilla, "Saak' y el retorno del fin del mundo: La plaga de langosta en las profecías del katun 13 Ahua," *Ancient Mesoamérica* 16, no. 2 (Fall 2005): 327–355; and Giovanni Peraldo Huertas, ed., *Plagas de langostas en américa latina. Una perspectiva multidisciplinaria* (San José, Costa Rica: Editorial Nuevas Perspectivas, 2015), http://hdl.handle.net/10669/11262.

15. See J. R. McNeil, *Mosquito Empires: Ecology and War in the Greater Caribbean, 1620–1914* (Cambridge: Cambridge University Press, 2010); Few, "Killing Locusts"; and Matthew Mulcahy and Stuart Schwartz, "Nature's Battalions: Insects as Agricultural Pests in the Early Modern Caribbean," *William and Mary Quarterly*, 75, no. 3 (July 2018): 433–464.

16. There are a growing number of recent works that address food security that historicize its relation to climate change, ecology, and natural disasters in the eighteenth- and early nineteenth-century world. See Geoffrey Parker, *Global Crisis: War, Climate Change, and Catastrophe in the Seventeenth Century* (New Haven, CT: Yale University Press, 2013); and John Lidwell-Durnin, "Cultivating Famine: Data, Experimentation and Food Security, 1795–1848," *British Journal for the History of Science* (2020), doi:10.1017/S0007087420000199. This area of research owes much to the pioneering work of agricultural historians. For Latin America, see Enrique Florescano, *Precios del maíz y crisis agrícolas en México (1708–1810)* (México: El Colegio de México, 1969); Romero Vargas, *Las estructuras sociales de Nicaragua*; and William Taylor, *Landlord and Peasant in Colonial Oaxaca* (Stanford, CA: Stanford University Press, 1972).

17. For more detail, see Martha Few, *For All of Humanity: Mesoamerican and Colonial Medicine in Enlightenment Guatemala* (Tucson: University of Arizona Press, 2015).

18. For earlier locust swarms in this region for the late seventeenth and early eighteenth centuries, see Few, "Killing Locusts"; and Luis Alberto Arrioja Díaz Viruell, "Nociones, creencias e ideas sobre plagas de langosta en Guatemala y Nueva España, siglo XVIII," *Revista de historia moderna. Anales de la Universidad de Alicante* 35 (2017): 214–253. Later locust plagues also occurred as multiyear events with extended geographic ranges, such as from 1882 to 1884 when a drought and locust plagues extended from Yucatán to Campeche, Tabasco, Veracruz and the Gulf of Mexico, and to Chiapas and Oaxaca and the Pacific Ocean. See García Quintanilla, "Saak' y el retorno del fin del mundo," 327, fn. 1.

19. These include the *Gazeta de Guatemala*, *Gazeta de México*, and the *Gazeta de España*.

20. "Texas A&M Entomologist Wants to Control Harmful Locust Swarming Behavior," July 19, 2017, *Texas A&M Today* (online edition), accessed December 7, 2017, http://today.tamu.edu/2017/07/19/texas-am-entomologist-wants-to-control-harmful-locust-swarming-behavior/.

21. United Kingdom Research and Innovation, Biotechnology and Biological Sciences Research Council, https://bbsrc.ukri.org/, "How Does a Locust Eat?," www.bbsrc.ac.uk/documents/how-do-locusts-eat-pdf, accessed August 20, 2020,

22. May R. Berenbaum, *Bugs in the System: Insects and Their Impact on Human Affairs* (New York: Basic Books, 1995): 111. For reference, the swarm that opened this chapter that traveled from El Salvador into Chiapas covered a distance of around 430 miles according to Google Maps, which judges that to be the length of a trip by car along the Pan American Highway from San Salvador, El Salvador, to Tonalá, Chiapas.

23. Martina E. Pocco, M. Marta Cigliano, Bert Foquet, Carlos E. Lange, Eliana L. Nieves, and Hojun Song, "Density-Dependent Phenotypic Plasticity in the South American Locust, *Schistocerca cancellata* (Orthoptera: Acrididae)," *Annals of the Entomological Society of America* 112, no. 5 (September 2019): 458–72, https://doi.org/10.1093/aesa/saz032.
24. Olfat S. El-Mallakh and Rif S. El-Mallakh, "Insects of the Qur'an," *American Entomologist* 40, no. 2 (1994): 82–84.
25. From the Old Testament: "And the locusts came up over all the land of Egypt, such a dense swarm of locusts as had never been before, nor ever shall be again. For they covered the face of the whole land, so that the land was darkened, and they ate all the plants in the land and all the fruit of the trees which the hail had left; not a green thing remained, neither tree nor plant of the field, through all the land of Egypt" (Exodus 10:14–15), quoted in Lockwood, *Locust*, 20. From the New Testament: "Then over the earth, out of the smoke, came locusts, and they were given the powers that earthly scorpions have" (Revelation 9:3), quoted in Gene Kritsky and Ron Cherry, *Insect Mythology* (New York: Writers Club Press, 2000): 76.
26. See E. P. Evans, *The Criminal Prosecution and Capital Punishment of Animals* (New York: E. P. Dutton, 1906); Alexandra Parma Cook and Noble David Cook, *The Plague Files: Crisis Management in Sixteenth-Century Seville* (Baton Rouge: Louisiana State University Press, 2009); Few, *Killing Locusts*, 74.
27. Ross Hassig, *Time, History, and Belief in Aztec and Colonial Mexico* (Austin: University of Texas Press, 2001): 60.
28. This codex is painted on *amate*, a Mesoamerican-style bark paper, but bound together as a Western-style book; s.v. "Mexicanus, Codex," in *The Oxford Encyclopedia of Mesoamerican Cultures*, ed. David Carrasco (New York: Oxford University Press, 2000), 2:302–3.
29. The Codex Mexicanus is held at the Bibliothèque National de France, with the digitized version available here: http://gallica.bnf.fr/ark:/12148/btv1b55005834g. For a general study of this codex, see Lori Boornazian Diel, *The Codex Mexicanus: A Guide to Life in Late Sixteenth-Century New Spain* (Austin: University of Texas Press, 2018).
30. S.v. "Aubin, Codex," in *The Oxford Encyclopedia of Mesoamerican Cultures*, 1:60–66.
31. Bernardino de Sahagún, *Florentine Codex; General History of the Things of New Spain*, ed. and trans. Arthur J. O. Anderson and Charles E. Dibble, 13 parts (Santa Fe, NM: School of American Research; Salt Lake City: University of Utah Press, 1950–1982). The Florentine Codex is held by the Medicea Laurenziana Library in Florence, Italy; the author worked with the digitized version available via the World Digital Library, https://www.wdl.org/en/search/?additional_subjects=Florentine%20Codex#10096, accessed August 16, 2020. For a good general study of this codex, see Jeanette Favrot Peterson and Kevin Terraciano, *The Florentine Codex: An Encyclopedia of the Nahua World in Sixteenth-century Mexico* (Austin: University of Texas Press, 2019).
32. Bernardino de Sahagún, *Florentine Codex*, sixteenth century.
33. BL, Chavez Orozco, ed., *Papeles sobre la plaga de langosta de 1801–1804*, 4.
34. BL, Chavez Orozco, ed., *Papeles sobre la plaga de langosta de 1801–1804*, 4–5.
35. BL, Orozco, ed., *Papeles sobre la Plaga de Langosta*, 5.
36. Ibid., 13–14.
37. While I have not yet been able to confirm or deny the governor of Yucatán's assertion, modern research shows that hurricanes, for example, can serve as vectors for the transportation of locusts from Africa to the Caribbean. C. Howard Richardson and David J. Nemeth, "Hurricane-Borne African Locusts (*Schistocerca gregaria*) on the Windward

Islands," *GeoJournal* 23, no. 4 (April 1991): 349–57. I thank Stuart Schwartz for alerting me to this source.

38. AGI, Guatemala 669, "Expedientes sobre añil y su reglamento, 1783–1809," n.p., and "Testimonio del expediente sobre señalamiento de precios del añil cosechado en este año corriente en las Provincias de San Salvador, 1802," n.p., 1802; *Gazeta de Guatemala*, September 4, 1797, f. 247; *Gazeta de Guatemala*, November 15, 1802, "Añil y langosta," 297–98 and "Estado de las siembras," 299; AGCA, A1-6106-55878, letter from Don Mariano Aguayo, owner of the *trapiche* San Francisco (here meaning sugar plantation) to Prudencio de Cozar, alcalde mayor of Huehuetenango y Totonicapán, May 20, 1803, n.p.; and AGCA A1-6106-55880, letter from Antonio González, Nueva Guatemala to Prudencio Cozar, alcade mayor of Huehuetenango y Totonicapán. June 3, 1803, n.p.

39. AGI. Estado, L. 49, E. 106, letter from José Mariano Valero, Ciudad Real to Don Pedro Zeballos, Ministro de Estado, Madrid, May 7, 1802, n.p.

40. AGCA, A1.2.5-3099-29833, 1706, "Exposición del ayuntamiento de Guatemala elevada al Superior Gobierno sobre ayuda para el extermino de la langosta," ff. 1–1v; Molina, *Antigua Guatemala*, 106. Antonio Molina (1628–1683) was a Creole (born in the Americas) Dominican friar and chronicler.

41. BL. Orozco, ed., *Papeles sobre la plaga de langosta*, 2.

42. Few, *For All of Humanity*.

43. *Gazeta de Guatemala*, August 30, 1802, letter to the editors from "J. L. R," Villa de Teguantepeque, dated August 1, 1802, ff. 209–212. The letter writer included a copy of an edict from the bishop of Oaxaca, Antonio de Bergosa y Jordán, about the methods he and others used their to fight against the locusts and help his parishioners meet their basic needs in the swarm's aftermath that year, which the *Gazeta* also published.

44. Between 1704 and 1821, the University of San Carlos conferred bachelor's degrees in medicine to thirty persons, the licentiate to twelve, and the doctorate to twelve. Lanning, *The Eighteenth-century Enlightenment*, 211.

45. The university's graduates numbered 1,300 from 1775 to 1821. Jordana Dym, "Conceiving Central America: A Bourbon Public in the Gaceta de Guatemala (1797–1807)," in *Enlightened Reform in Southern Europe and its Atlantic Colonies, c. 1750–1850*, ed. Gabriel Paquette (Burlington, VT: Ashgate, 2009): 105.

46. *Gazeta de Guatemala*, June 18, 1801, "Suchitepeques," 495–97. Rossi y Rubí had spent an earlier part of his career in Lima, where he was active in local Enlightenment scientific cultures, and in the newspaper *Mercurio peruano*. I thank G. Antonio Espinoza for bringing Rossi y Rubí's Peru connections to my attention.

47. "Tengo noticias seguras y multiplicados de que la Langosta, o *Chapulín*, se va acercando a esta provincia. Despues de haber as asolado la de Sonsonate, y sus comarcanas, ha deshovado en las montañas de Moyuta, en la de Escuintla, y tomado su vuelo al Nor O Este, que es justamente la linea de direccion que lo conduce a estas campiñas." *Gazeta de Guatemala* 209, 18 June 1801, "Suchitepequez," 495. Capital letters in the original.

48. José de Valle, *Instruccion sobre la plaga de langosta; medios de exterminarla, o de disminuir sus efectos, y de precaber la escasez de comestibles* (Nueva Guatemala: Ignacio Beteta, 1804).

49. John Carter Brown Library, Brown University (hereafter JCBL), José Mariano Moziño, *Tratado del xiquilite y añil de Guatemala* (Nueva Guatemala, 1799).

50. Respectively, AGI, Guatemala 219, March 1706, "El oidor D. Pedro de Ozaeta," ff. 1–1v; AGCA, A1-1781-11781, Libro de cabildos, March 2, 1706, ff. 9v–10.

51. AGI, Guatemala, carta Oficiales Reales a su Magestad, July 3, 1665, n.p.

52. Gage, *A New Survey of the West-India's*, 163.
53. Ximénez, *Historia natural del Reino de Guatemala*, 227.
54. AGCA, A1.2.5-1772-25239 (1772), f. 3.
55. Cook and Cook describe a locust-killing campaign in late sixteenth-century Seville, Spain, where city authorities recruited community members to collect tubes/sacs of locust eggs (*cañutillos*) by offering to pay one *real* for each *almud* collected (an almud equaled roughly 27.75 liters). Officials would then burn the eggs. If an inadequate number of paid volunteers offered to perform this labor, city officials would compel each of Seville's parishes to contribute a certain number of locust-egg collectors. See Cook and Cook, *The Plague Files*, 19–21.
56. AGCA A1.1-21-602 (1801), ff. 1–7v, f. 1v.
57. Ibid. See JCBL, Moziño, *Tratado del xiquilite*, for a list of food plants considered locust-resistant, and broader efforts to include these crops among more traditional staple crops of wheat, corn, and beans.
58. See, e.g., JCBL, Moziño, *Tratado del xiquilite*, who dedicated his handbook to Guatemala's scientific society, Real Sociedad Económica. For more on this organization and its role in agricultural innovation, see Few, *For All of Humanity*, 9, 22, 207; Sophie Brockmann, "Surveying Nature: The Creation and Communication of Natural-Historical Knowledge in Enlightenment Central America" (PhD diss., Cambridge University, 2014); and Scott Doebler, "The Chinese Cotton Contest: The Royal Economic Society of Guatemala, Maya Farmers, and the Struggle over Enlightenment-Era Agricultural Science, 1796–1798," *Colonial Latin America Review* 30, no. 1 (2021): 137–60.
59. AGCA A1.1-21-602 (1801), ff. 1–7v: f4; ff. 6–7.
60. AGCA A1.1-21-602 (May/June 1801), ff. 1–7v: f. 1.
61. AGCA A1.2-2214-15850, "Don Miguel de Acosta, presó en las carceles públicas, propone usar de ciertas yerbas para la destrucción."
62. This evidence is helpful to tease out what people thought Indigenous knowledge was during the Enlightenment. I do not have the space here in this short chapter, however, to examine Mesoamerican/Maya perspectives and knowledge about locusts. AGCA A1.2-2214-15850 (1801–1803), "Don Miguel de Acosta" ff. 1–20v.
63. AGCA A1.2-2214-15850 (1801–1803), "Don Miguel de Acosta," f. 1v.
64. Ibid., f. 1. It is interesting that Acosta used the term *milpa* because of it specifically refers to traditional Maya agricultural fields of corn, beans, and squash in colonial Guatemala (and today).
65. Ibid., f. 1.
66. Few, *For All of Humanity*, 113–14, 122–24, 190–91.
67. AGCA A1.2-2214-15850 (1801–1803), "Don Miguel de Acosta," f. 1v.
68. For colonial Central America, see Few, *For All of Humanity*.
69. For references to *epidemia de langosta*, *plaga de langosta*, and *el contagio de dicho langosta*, see, respectively, AGI, Guatemala 219, March 1706, "El oidor D. Pedro de Ozaeta y Oro acompaña certificación por donde parece que habiendose experimentado en diferentes territorios de aquellas provincias por marzo del año de 1706 epidemia de langosta," f. 1; AGCA, A1-1783-11777, Libro de Cabildo, October 6, 1665, ff. 113–13v; and AGI, Guatemala 219, March 1706, "El oidor D. Pedro de Ozaeta," f. 1v, and Molina, *Antigua Guatemala*, 106.
70. AGCA A1.2-2214-15850 (1801–1803), "Don Miguel de Acosta, f. 2.
71. Ibid.
72. Ibid., f. 2v.

Bibliography

Arrioja Díaz Viruell, Luis Alberto. *Bajo el crepúsculo de los insectos: Clima, plagas y trastornos sociales en el Reino de Guatemala (1768-1805)*. Michoacán, Mexico: El Colegio de Michoacán, 2019.

Arrioja Díaz Viruell, Luis Alberto, and Armando Alberola Romá, eds. *Clima, desastres y convulsiones sociales en España e Hispanoamérica, siglos XVII-XX*. Alicante, Spain: Universidad de Alicante, 2017.

Contreras, C. "Conexión climática del fenómeno de 'El Niño' con la plaga de la langosta centroamericana (*Schistocerca piceifrons piceifrons*, Walker)." *Entomología mexicana* 8 (2009): 347-51.

Few, Martha. *For All of Humanity: Mesoamerican and Colonial Medicine in Enlightenment Guatemala*. Tucson: University of Arizona Press, 2015.

Few, Martha. "Killing Locusts in Colonial Guatemala." In *Centering Animals in Latin American History*, edited by Martha Few and Zeb Tortorici, 62-92. Durham, NC: Duke University Press, 2015.

Florescano, Enrique. *Precios del maíz y crisis agrícolas en México (1708-1810)*. Mexico City: El Colegio de México, 1969.

Lidwell-Durnin, John. "Cultivating Famine: Data, Experimentation and Food Security, 1795-1848." *British Journal for the History of Science* (2020). doi:10.1017/S0007087420000199.

McCreery, David. *Rural Guatemala; 1760-1940*. Stanford, CA: Stanford University Press, 1994.

McNeil, J. R. *Mosquito Empires: Ecology and War in the Greater Caribbean, 1620-1914*. Cambridge: Cambridge University Press, 2010.

Mulcahy, Matthew, and Stuart Schwartz. "Nature's Battalions: Insects as Agricultural Pests in the Early Modern Caribbean." *William and Mary Quarterly* 75, no. 3 (July 2018): 433-64.

Peraldo Huertas, Giovanni, ed. *Plagas de langostas en América Latina. Una perspectiva multidisciplinaria*. San José, Costa Rica: Editorial Nuevas Perspectivas 2015.

Romero Vargas, Germán. *Las estructuras sociales de Nicaragua en el siglo XVIII*. Managua, Nicaragua: Vanguardia, 1987.

Smith, Robert S. "Indigo Production and Trade in Colonial Guatemala." *Hispanic American Historical Review* 39, no. 2 (May 1959): 181-211.

Taylor, William. *Landlord and Peasant in Colonial Oaxaca*. Stanford, CA: Stanford University Press, 1972.

CHAPTER 6

AGRICULTURAL LABOR

STEVE STRIFFLER

THE production of crops and animals for food and other products has been and remains one of the most fundamental sites through which human beings labor. Working the land has consumed the daily lives of the majority of people for most of human history. Even today, when in relatively wealthy countries like the United States less than 2 percent of the population works in agriculture, about one-third of the world's economically active population still relies on agriculture for its livelihood. Millions of small-scale farmers and pastoralists in Asia, Africa, and Latin America produce most of the world's food, often on relatively small plots of land. And millions more work as wage laborers on landholdings of various sizes.[1]

And yet, although agricultural labor has been and remains central to how people survive, how they relate to one other, and how they organize politically, culturally, and economically, there has never been anything simple, uniform, or constant about agricultural labor itself. The multiplicity of ways in which people have sought to produce not only food, but a range of other agricultural products, have varied tremendously across time and space. More than this, just as the methods through which people work the land shape the foods and products they generate, the changing nature of the foods and products that people envision transforms systems of labor within and beyond agriculture. In other words, agricultural labor is an ever-changing and uneven social process that has deeply shaped history.

What the history suggests, then, is that labor is not only central for understanding agricultural history, but that agricultural labor provides a particularly compelling lens through which to understand human history. By focusing on agricultural labor, we are able to understand not only how labor interacts with nature to produce food, clothing, and other products, but how this complex process of meeting human needs generates social, economic, and political forces that shape hierarchies of race, class, and gender, propel large-scale migrations, and continually transform daily life. In a very real sense, almost everything we associate with the modern world, including cities, states, religious systems, and advanced technology, rests on foundations laid by agricultural labor.

All the major features we associate with modern agriculture emerged unevenly through hundreds of years of struggle between those who work the land and those who rule over them. There was nothing natural or inevitable about the emergence of large-scale industrial agriculture, and in fact subsistence farmers throughout the world initially resisted creating and turning over surpluses to elites, then resisted efforts to reorient their production toward markets, and then continued to struggle against the competitive, exploitative, logic of agrarian capitalism.[2] That is, they resisted forms of agriculture that all too frequently left those who worked the land with little to show for their efforts and beholden to a political and economic class who lived off of (or benefited from) their labor. The exact nature of this process varied tremendously across time and place, but the deepening integration of agriculture into markets has been a conflict-laden one that has left agricultural labor subordinate to the ruling classes and urban centers who depend on the wealth and food they produce.

Early Origins of Agriculture and States

Agriculture in the form of cultivating crops either through slash-and-burn techniques or through more settled farming developed about 10,000 years ago. Although its emergence and spread developed unevenly in the centuries to come, it nonetheless represented a significant change in the way food was produced and society organized. Indeed, for the prior 190,000 years of human existence, people had subsisted on non-domesticated sources of food through hunting and gathering. They lived in relatively small groups, working cooperatively and with minimal hierarchy to acquire and consume the food and other products needed to subsist. Farming was not part of the equation.[3]

Although the arrival of agriculture represented a fundamental shift in how people labored to meet their needs, it nevertheless spread slowly and unevenly across time and space. Humans began domesticating plants and animals sometime prior to 10,000 BCE, but they did not really start to rely on farming until about 9,000 years ago in the Near East. As a method for acquiring subsistence, its benefits were by no means self-evident. Agriculture generally involved more work, brought with it a variety of health hazards, exposed populations to new forms of food insecurity, and required more complex systems of social organization. By contrast, hunting and gathering required less time and energy, and hunter-gatherers themselves lived healthier and longer lives.[4]

However, about 13,000 years ago global temperatures started to rise, decreasing the quantity of grazing lands, which in turn reduced the number of animals available to hunter-gatherers. This led people in many regions to search for alternative ways of acquiring food, which did not always lead down the path of settled agriculture but did encourage humans to store more of the food they hunted and gathered. This, in turn, made them more sedentary, created new types of labor, and led to population growth and urban settlements. Even then, agriculture did not automatically spring forth. People in northern Peru lived in relatively dense settlements for at least a millennium without agriculture, and those in the northwest of North America lived in villages without ever relying on farming.[5]

Yet agriculture did spread unevenly across the globe, coexisting alongside traditional methods of gathering food. No single system captured how people across the world labored to meet their material needs through the 1500s. Depending on climate and geography, people relied on a mix of agriculture, hunting/fishing, foraging, and herding to meet subsistence needs, trading when they needed to or had a surplus. Unless they were located near larger urban settlements, say, in the lower Yangzi, near Paris or southern England, around Delhi, or by Tenochtitlan, most people were not directly affected by high-yielding agriculture, which was slow to spread beyond certain areas.[6]

However, settled agriculture ultimately ushered in deep transformations in labor processes and the social, political, and economic systems shaping them. Perhaps most significant, agriculture facilitated the development of agrarian settlements, which, in turn, laid the groundwork for the broader emergence of cities and towns. With greater urbanization came more elaborate political and economic systems.

In this sense, the growth in agriculture and the early emergence of states were closely intertwined. Large-scale agriculture allowed a sector of the population to no longer directly work the land, freeing them up for other productive activities or to develop and oversee political and religious systems. At the same time, the development of large-scale agriculture itself required some sort of centralized entity to coordinate production and distribution, including the creation of irrigation systems, modes of transportation, and even markets. It made possible a sector of the population who did not work the land but oversaw those who labored as agricultural producers.[7]

This revolutionary transformation frequently entailed deep changes in gender relations as well, often to the detriment of women. Prior to the emergence of agriculture men typically hunted while women gathered. There was little gender dominance, and women participated equally in decision-making. Even with slash and burn, gender relations remained relatively equal, with men clearing the land and women farming it. Yet settled agriculture brought with it both more work and more diverse forms of labor. Fields not only had to be cleared, plowed, irrigated, planted, cared for, and harvested, but agriculture also created additional domestic work, which contributed to a more clearly defined division of labor. The push of women away from plowing or herding was further encouraged by the benefit of having larger families within agricultural communities, which led women to spend more time at home bearing and caring for children.[8]

Feudalism and Its Discontents

The rise of agriculture, then, had paradoxical consequences for those who labored. Increasing centralization, as well as improved methods of farming, irrigation, breeding, storage, and transportation, allowed for greater "efficiency" and could dramatically increase production. But it did not necessarily mean less or easier work, let alone more leisure time, for those who labored on the land. Peasants had to produce not only for themselves, but for an expanding non-farming population. Even as fewer people were able to grow and raise far greater amounts of agricultural products, those who worked the land often found themselves working under labor systems and political economies that required more of their labor to simply ensure basic survival. Indeed, the ruling political classes that emerged on the foundation of agriculture were often much more interested in securing political control over peasants than they were in improving or even increasing production.[9]

What this meant is that peasant households and communities around the world struggled to simultaneously produce enough for their own consumption while meeting their obligations to elites who used their power to extract wealth from those who worked the land. This feudal struggle, defined by elite efforts to coerce peasants to hand over their labor or crops, in many ways drove world history up to and through European colonialism beginning in the 1400s. Peasants resisted, and rulers turned to various forms of coercion to gain access to labor and surplus production. Their success in doing so allowed ruling classes to enrich themselves, urban centers to develop, and the modern world to emerge.[10]

Indeed, it has often been argued that once cities and towns emerged, and markets for agricultural products appeared, peasants saw an opportunity and slowly moved away from subsistence production, willingly reorienting their production toward the market. And, that once they did so, they necessarily began to innovate, specialize in profitable commodities, compete against one another, work to reduce costs and increase production, and otherwise become budding capitalists. There is some truth to this narrative about the early origins of agrarian capitalism, but as Christopher Isett and Stephen Miller convincingly argue, as long as peasants had access to enough land to provide for their own subsistence, they had no need to work for others and were resistant to elite overtures to either hand over surplus production or produce for the market. This held true with remarkable consistency across time and space.[11]

As a result, peasants developed all sorts of methods for resisting attempts by landlords and political elites from gaining direct control over their labor or its fruits. In the case of Europe, for example, starting in the late Roman Empire, variations of serfdom spread across the region, with serfs cultivating food crops for themselves while also giving a portion to the noble family or providing labor on land directly operated by the nobility. This was not done willingly. Extracting surplus required lords to impose taxes, rents, and fines, and otherwise deprive households and communities of basic rights and customary access to land. It also required considerable investment in armies and political systems to monitor and discipline rural populations. Such efforts were continually challenged by those who worked the land.

Feudal rule, in this sense, was accomplished through the ever-present threat of physical violence. Elite power was frequently challenged, and the political order occasionally broke down. At times, peasants openly rebelled, as they did in England toward the end of the thirteenth century, when elites intensified efforts to restrict access to what had traditionally been collective lands while at the same time increasing taxes and servile obligations. Yet, although such rebellions could represent serious threats to elite power in particular moments, they were difficult to sustain and were typically repressed with a brutality intended to send a clear message to would-be rebels.[12]

A not entirely different process played out in the Andes under Inca rule beginning in the late 1430s. Markets existed prior to the imperial expansion of the Incas, but production was oriented around subsistence. As Inca rule expanded, eventually encompassing some 20 million people from southern Chile to Ecuador, the conquerors imposed onerous taxes and labor obligations, in effect forcing households to work longer and harder to maintain themselves while supporting elites and the apparatus of rule. The Inca claimed all land, leaving their subjects with just enough resources to survive. Peasants resisted, and the rulers responded in a variety of ways, from open violence and the resettlement of entire communities to co-opting local leaders and developing systems of surveillance.[13]

In a broader sense, then, much of what we came to associate with civilization, including cities, roads, urban infrastructure, and religious and political systems, was built on the foundation of coerced agricultural labor. The exact form of rule varied from locale to locale. Whereas the Incas deeply disrupted preexisting relationships between land and labor, elites in other places—such as ancient China and Rome—were willing to leave existing systems of production largely in place, relying more on controlling trade and extracting taxes. In parts of Africa prior to the twelfth century, some regions were controlled by complex state systems rooted in agriculture—but even here, geography made it difficult for elites to exert too much control over production itself, leaving them content to control trade. In other regions of Africa, people managed to remain free of states altogether, engaging in farming and other methods for ensuring subsistence.[14]

At the start of European colonial expansion in the 1400s, then, agricultural labor systems were characterized by considerable variation, but subsistence production rooted in households that relied primarily on the labor of family and community members was the norm. Generally, they labored on land they controlled. Where present, ruling elites were largely forced to respect customary claims to both land and labor. There were, not surprisingly, instances where these traditional systems had broken down or were being seriously challenged, as in feudal Europe. And almost everywhere that political systems emerged there was an ongoing struggle over who owned or controlled the land, in what ways it could be utilized, and how labor would be accessed, controlled, and obligated. But, in general, elites found it difficult to simply eliminate or ignore customary rights, leaving production in the hands of households while developing political systems designed to levy taxes, fees, and other methods of extracting labor and wealth from those who worked the land. Peasants controlled the basics of farming, held property in common, bartered with other communities when need required, and diversified their production with the primary goal of ensuring subsistence, not selling for the market.[15]

The Uneven Emergence of Agrarian Capitalism

The process of commercialization by which agricultural production became increasingly oriented toward markets slowly intensified from the 1400s onward. Not only did it tend to produce greater inequality and insecurity for larger numbers of agricultural producers, and in fact would push many off the land altogether, but the process itself underwrote and intensified European colonialism. The uneven transition from agricultural production aimed primarily for subsistence toward one oriented around markets was not one that most peasants willingly made. Even when presented with accessible and potentially profitable markets, most recognized that increased specialization was risky in that it exposed them to market forces they did not control while diverting time and resources away from the crops that ensured their survival.

In this sense, although the commercialization of agriculture would happen at different times, in different ways, and with varying levels of state involvement and coercion across the globe, it was almost always the byproduct of political conflict between those who ruled and those who worked the land. It was rarely as simple as peasants seeing an opportunity and willingly opting into the market to maximize returns.

England in the early 1400s is a good example of this process, though not because it would become the model that others would follow on the path to agrarian capitalism. To the contrary, increased commercialization and the emergence of agrarian capitalism would look quite different in China, the Americas, Africa, Asia, and even other European countries such as France. But how this transition played out in rural England highlights the central place that conflict played in driving the process forward and, in this case, how it helped lay the groundwork for both industrial capitalism and a form of colonialism that would forever change the nature of agricultural labor and its relationship to the land.[16]

England could be distinguished from most of Europe in the early 1400s by both the size of its landholdings and its relatively low level of population density. Increasing land concentration during the medieval period meant that the countryside was defined by great inequality, and population decline meant that English lords struggled to gain access to labor. Lords had to compete with each other to acquire agricultural labor, which in turn allowed households and communities to eliminate the bonds of serfdom. This did not mean that peasants gained possession of the land. In fact, such security around access to land was partially lost as they were no longer bound to a particular lord. But it did mean that they had much greater freedom to move around and secure the best terms for gaining access to land from English lords.[17]

It also meant, however, that peasants increasingly entered into leases that required money to meet their obligations. With access to land no longer acquired by providing labor services to a local lord, peasant households had to produce commodities for the market in order to earn money to make good on their leases. Now competing with other farming families, and hence trying to cut costs, become more efficient, and increase productivity and profit, peasants increasingly specialized in agricultural commodities that were in demand and provided the greatest return. This shift, characterized by an increasing concern with efficiency, cost, and profit, brought with it a whole series of consequences, impacting family size, forcing households to meet more of their basic food needs through the market, exposing them to the vagaries of market forces, and increasing differentiation between those who successfully navigated this changing world and those who did not. Peasants increasingly found themselves "freed" from the legal constraints of feudalism, but in so doing risked losing access to the land altogether.[18]

By forcing a portion of the rural population off the land and out of agriculture, the emergence of agrarian capitalism laid the groundwork for urbanization and industrialization by creating urban populations of consumers dependent on cheap food and landless migrants forced into wage labor in England's emerging factories. In so doing, the development of agrarian capitalism also helped make European colonies profitable by establishing the two principle sources of demand for colonial commodities: European working classes with the spending power to purchase "tropical" products and an emerging factory system that itself consumed raw materials from all over the world. This process, in turn, would transform agricultural labor across the globe.

COLONIALISM AND THE GLOBAL TRANSFORMATION OF AGRICULTURE

Colonialism came in a variety of forms, but on a broad level it entailed dispossessing the colonized from the land in ways that transformed agricultural labor throughout much of the world. In settler colonies such as the United States and Australia, colonizers removed Indigenous populations from the land through a combination of forced dislocation and extermination. Once the land was cleared of people, agricultural labor came in a range of forms. In the United States, around 350,000 indentured workers made their way from Europe in the 1600s to work in cotton, tobacco, sugar, and other crops. Indeed, prior to US independence (1776), about half of white colonists worked as servants. With so much money to be made, however, demand for labor was greater than even the poorer regions (and prisons) of Europe could provide—and European immigrants did not prove to be a reliable long-term labor solution for planters since they had the annoying tendency to serve out their indenture and establish their own farms.[19]

This led large landowners to turn to slave labor from Africa, with the US South becoming thoroughly dependent upon slaves for agricultural labor through the 1700s and first half of the 1800s. Indeed, on the eve of the Civil War (1861–1865) there was no reason to think that slavery was about to disappear on its own or evolve into capitalist agriculture based on free labor. Southern planters were completely reliant on slavery, and it would require a war followed by decades of struggle around sharecropping to transition out of an agriculture rooted in racialized forms of labor coercion.[20] By contrast, agricultural labor in New England and the Midwest looked quite different. Relatively cohesive communities emerged around subsistence farming and resisted becoming dependent on commercial crops before eventually succumbing to market pressures. In both cases, the transition to capitalism was riddled with conflict.[21]

In other regions, such as Latin America and Africa, colonizers did not want simply the land, but access to Indigenous labor. In Latin America, the Spanish and Portuguese ruled through massive grants (*encomiendas*) that gave them control over Indigenous populations. In order to retain access to land for their own subsistence production, Indigenous communities had to deliver "surplus" agricultural production to the colonizers while also working directly on Spanish farms, mines, infrastructure projects, and the like. Under such conditions, and especially as Indigenous communities were ravaged by disease, labor relations could be extremely exploitative. Indigenous people had to neglect their own lands and subsistence needs in order to work in mines or to produce foods for elites.[22]

As the population declined under the weight of disease and exploitation, and as new generations of landed elites sought even more direct control over the land, many Indigenous people found themselves more thoroughly dispossessed as elites privatized large swaths of Latin America in the 1700s and 1800s. The encomienda system gave way to haciendas and plantations, and as the process unfolded most Indigenous people either retained access to land through various forms of indentured servitude or lost access completely and became landless workers on plantations. In other regions, such as the Caribbean and Brazil, where Indigenous populations were wiped out, dwindled to few in number, or were able to escape, colonizers depended on slave labor for sugar and coffee plantations. Regardless of the exact form that colonialism took, access to land (and hence food) became more precarious and labor exploitation tended to intensify as large landowners increasingly focused production on a handful of products for the export market.[23]

Europeans followed a broadly similar pattern in Africa and Asia in the late 1800s, justifying rule through racist narratives while gobbling up the best land and establishing large monoculture plantations with export crops—tea in Assam, coffee in Kenya, tobacco and rubber in Sumatra, and so on. The particulars varied from region to region, but colonizers came up with creatively exploitative ways of accessing labor across the globe that were rooted in notions of racial superiority and involved contrived types of taxes or debt. This disruption upended the lives of millions who had survived on subsistence agriculture grounded in village customs that regulated the exchange of goods, controlled access to land and labor, and put a check on elite machinations. Colonial rule and foreign capital reached deeper into communities, and colonists sought labor and land to produce commodities and raw materials for profits that were sent back to Europe for consumption. As elsewhere, peasant households and communities in Africa and Asia resisted efforts to undermine their subsistence base and force them to produce crops for the market or work on plantations for wages. Labor, coercion, and racism were part and parcel of colonial agriculture.[24]

In the case of Africa, for example, British colonists established the infamous "hut tax," which effectively required Africans to sell their labor (in order to pay the tax), thereby providing the British with a labor force for mines and agriculture. Similar tactics were imposed on the colonized elsewhere. In general, as traditional land use rights eroded, Indigenous communities lost access to land in relation to large landowners. And within Indigenous communities themselves, women were often on the losing end as men more frequently acquired formal titles to now privatized holdings.

Colonialism, then, entailed the deeper integration of Indigenous populations into wider economies as well as the greater specialization of agricultural production aimed toward markets, increasingly global ones. This process intensified as Europe industrialized, and "tropical" crops like sugar, bananas, rum, cocoa, tea, and coffee became commonplace in European diets. Consumption in the Global North increasingly depended on unfree and/or highly exploited labor in the Global South. As demand for tropical products exploded in Europe, and as export-oriented plantations displaced smallholdings in Latin America, Asia, and Africa, smallholders in those regions struggled to hold on to land, with many becoming landless laborers or migrating to urban areas.[25] As we saw, this phenomenon was familiar to Europeans as well, who themselves were displaced by the thousands from the land and forced to migrate to cities in search of wage work beginning as early as the 1400s.

As should be clear, the orientation of agricultural production toward markets did not automatically lead to an agrarian capitalism characterized by free labor, cost-cutting, and continual innovation. Many continued to produce food as they had, intensifying their work in order to meet elite demands for labor and production. Even on plantations, which were typically oriented toward global markets, landowners relied on agricultural labor that was deeply unfree (e.g., slavery, indentured servitude, etc.) and generally preferred to increase output by squeezing more out of those who worked the land rather than innovating or investing in agricultural improvements. Colonial agriculture was deeply commercialized and undermined subsistence production in all sorts of ways, but it was not necessarily capitalist—nor automatically headed in that direction.

Agriculture Meets Industry

The broader push toward the deeper commercialization of agriculture and the development of agrarian capitalism continued through the 1800s and early 1900s. Land devoted to crops rose by about 75 percent between 1850 and 1920 on a global level, with some of the greatest increases in Latin America and Southeast Asia. Much of this increased production came in the form of capital-intensive export agriculture, which continued to put pressure on smallholders and landless workers alike. Part of what made this massive expansion of agriculture possible were technological advances in transportation, machinery, and other areas.[26]

For peasants, the net effect was that they competed with their counterparts on entirely different continents, were exposed to market forces well beyond their control, and frequently struggled to hold on to their land. Although many continued to rely largely on household labor, it was increasingly difficult to retreat to subsistence. Most were now compelled to produce for markets, and thus had to continually look for ways to cut costs and become more efficient. For landless workers, who labored on landholdings that were also subject to competitive pressures, life was invariably precarious, as access to land and subsistence production disappeared and landowners sought to continually squeeze labor to increase profits.

The deeper industrialization of agriculture during the twentieth century, especially after World War II, propelled these processes forward. Farms across the world became increasingly specialized in particular crops destined for the market. More farmers became dependent on large corporations for chemical fertilizers, pesticides, and scientifically bred seeds, plants, and animals. Yields, and in some cases the ability to farm, became more dependent on the ability of farmers to buy specialized equipment, fertilizers, pesticides, and seeds.

This broader development of industrialized agriculture, including its timing, nature, and depth, varied across space. Even in the United States, a country that came to define corporate-capitalist agriculture, the process played out quite differently from region to region. In the US South, the struggle between planters and agricultural labor intensified after slavery ended and Reconstruction drew to a close. With slavery off the table and capital in short supply, Southern planters doubled down on cotton and sought to access black and white agricultural labor through sharecropping arrangements, whereby large landowners gave farmers access to land in exchange for a portion of the crop (cotton, tobacco, etc.). The terms of the arrangement were fairly one-sided, however. When it came time to settle up after the harvest, tenant farmers typically had little to show for their efforts, and they could quite often owe money for the credit they had borrowed. Although sharecropping gave farmers access to land and considerable control over their labor, the system was rigged in such a way that it made it very difficult to survive, let alone get ahead. Planters profited handsomely, while the system of sharecropping effectively kept blacks and poor whites politically and economically marginalized.[27]

Not surprisingly, this oppressive system generated organized resistance from sharecroppers, with perhaps the most significant examples coming from the Alabama Sharecroppers Union (ASU) and the Southern Tenant Farmers Union (STFU). Formed in 1931, and openly communist, the ASU was a union of black sharecroppers—eventually including some thirty locals—who advocated for better wages, prices, rights, and contracts for sharecroppers.[28] The biracial STFU formed in Arkansas in 1934 with the help of the Socialist Party, ultimately organizing thousands of white and black sharecroppers across a number of Southern states who struck against planters and pushed the federal government to improve conditions.[29] Both unions faced severe repression and neither lasted long, but they succeeded in not only organizing thousands of rural poor at a time when the balance of forces were severely stacked against them. They also carried out mass actions that led to (moderately) improved wages, prices, and contracts against a powerful planter class and an unsympathetic federal government.

In contrast to the US South, agriculture in the western United States, and particularly California, was fairly thoroughly capitalist from its birth. Here, agrarian capitalism did not emerge out of slavery, feudalism, or small-scale production, but was dominated by fairly large-scale agribusiness that sought to capitalize on the economic growth of the 1850s by investing in land and agriculture. Focused on profit from the start, California agribusiness constantly invested and innovated, switched from one crop to another as demand shifted, and incessantly explored more efficient, profitable, and vulnerable sources of labor. After the Civil War, US-born whites, recent arrivals from Europe, and Chinese made up the bulk of the labor force, followed quickly by infusions of Japanese, Hindustanis, and Filipinos. After racist immigration policy curtailed Chinese immigration, planters increasingly turned to Mexican labor.

Regardless of nationality, but because of their "race," agricultural workers in California labored under extremely difficult conditions. Long hours, low wages, and unsanitary labor camps were the norm. Here again, agricultural labor resisted. In 1903, for example, Japanese and Mexican workers in California staged one of the earliest agricultural strikes in the United States—an episodic rebellion that would be repeated over and over again by agricultural workers throughout the state during the coming decades. More prolonged efforts to organize larger movements, however, proved difficult to sustain, in part because California agribusiness was particularly adept at continually seeking out more vulnerable sources of agricultural labor. The most conspicuous and well-known example of this was the Bracero Program, a series of laws and diplomatic agreements begun in 1942 that allowed agribusiness to contract with Mexican workers in order to address labor "shortages" associated with World War II. Agribusiness succeeded in extending the program far beyond the end of the war and brought in millions of Mexican workers until 1964. Controversial from the beginning, and a constant source of conflict between the US and Mexican governments, as well as workers, farmers, and state authorities, the Bracero Program was plagued by strikes and scandals associated with the horrid working and living conditions experienced by migrant workers.[30] It was not until the end of the program in the mid-1960s that the United Farm Workers union was able to gain traction, organizing tens of thousands of agricultural workers across California in the 1960s and 1970s. Even then, organizing and improving conditions for farm workers has been an uphill struggle.[31]

In less wealthy regions, such as Africa, Asia, and Latin America, beginning in the 1950s, the Green Revolution brought industry to agriculture in a different way through the introduction of high-yielding varieties of staple foods, especially wheat and rice. By dramatically increasing the production of particular crops, this revolution was intended to reduce hunger, poverty, and political unrest (i.e., communism) in the Third World. Promoted by the US government, the World Bank, and major foundations such as Ford and Rockefeller, the Green Revolution did have some success in limiting rural rebellion, but its track record on hunger and poverty has been less impressive.

It did, however, open new markets for agribusinesses looking to profit from new seed varieties, fertilizers, pesticides, and equipment. By extending high-input agriculture to more parts of the world, the Green Revolution made producers and entire countries dependent on particular forms of agriculture that required relatively high levels of spending on fertilizers, pesticides, seeds, and systems of irrigation. In many cases, this revolution led to environmental degradation and increased debt while further undermining subsistence production and exposing small producers to the insecurities associated with global markets.[32] Many lost their land, either migrating to cities (and other countries) or joining the millions of landless agricultural workers.

Agriculture under Neoliberalism

Most of these trends, including the growing influence of foreign companies over agriculture in Latin America, Asia, and Africa, as well as the deepening exposure of agricultural labor to market forces, were further stimulated by the intensified push for free trade and privatization beginning in the late 1970s and 1980s. In broad terms, policies and agreements aimed at liberalizing trade and removing agriculture from government control have led to declining prices and farm income for farmers throughout the world, including in the United States, and are tied to the growth of large-scale farming at the expense of small-scale producers. For many communities, who are often serviced by poor roads, have poor-quality land, and have limited access to credit, the competition brought by free trade has made agriculture untenable.[33]

This deepening exposure to global markets has been compounded by the fact that at the same time that small producers in Asia, Africa, and Latin America have been left vulnerable to global markets, they have been forced to compete against farmers in wealthier countries (particularly those in the United States) who receive massive government subsidies to produce agricultural commodities on a large scale. During the same period that family farms in the United States have struggled with bankruptcies and foreclosures, the US government has subsidized American agriculture to the tune of over $10 billion a year for decades, with 90 percent of that going to large producers of corn, cotton, wheat, rice, and soybeans. These crops are then sold (or dumped) globally at below the cost of production. The consequence of these depressed prices, aside from massive profits for US agribusiness, is the destruction of farming in many places in Africa, Asia, and Latin America. US agribusiness has not made life easier for small-scale producers, who make up three-quarters of the world's poor.[34]

The system of free trade has also left small producers almost completely exposed to the market. Forced to continually increase yields while cutting costs, they are often left dependent upon chemicals, fertilizers, and technology—upon global agribusiness. Without the government subsidies available to large industrial farms, this dependence leaves them particularly vulnerable when market prices inevitably drop—which in turn leads to increased farm bankruptcies and greater concentration of land ownership. This has been no less true in the United States, where the number of farms has dropped dramatically at the same time as their size has grown. Similar processes have played out in countries as diverse as France, India, and Mexico, further concentrating poverty in rural areas around the world.

The demise or destabilization of small farms leads not only to greater rural poverty and large scale migration, but to increased inequality as many small farmers join the ranks of the landless. Numbering well over 100 million in India and Brazil alone, landless agricultural wage laborers are among the poorest of the world's poor—with many living on less than three dollars a day. Many face some form of racial, gender, or ethnic-national discrimination. Wages are exceptionally low, often not paid, and rarely subject to meaningful minimum wage laws. A living wage for agricultural workers is largely unheard of. Millions are forced to continually migrate, existing in nearly impossible living conditions while working under extremely difficult circumstances. And few are part of unions, other labor organizations, or really even have a meaningful right to organize. To make matters even worse, the expansion of high-input, industrial agriculture has left millions of agricultural workers increasingly exposed to dangerous chemicals. In the United States alone, billions of pounds of pesticides are applied to agricultural fields every year, with tens of thousands of workers experiencing both immediate effects, such as headaches, nausea, and even seizures, as well as more chronic problems, such as cancer, infertility, and respiratory problems. With this model of agriculture spreading across the globe, workers throughout the world are now facing the negative consequences associated with greater exposure to pesticides and other chemicals.[35]

This process has been and is being contested around the globe, by agricultural workers, small farmers, and their allies among consumers, policymakers, labor unions, social movements, and the like. There is increasing recognition that industrial agriculture does not work particularly well for workers, farmers, consumers, the environment, and even the animals involved. But thus far it has been difficult for the world's agricultural workers and small farmers, many of whom produce food in much more sustainable ways than big agriculture, to exert enough power upon the state and other regulatory entities to protect them from the market forces that drive down wages for workers and leave farmers under-resourced, dependent on agribusiness, and exposed to the market. Likewise, efforts to create alternatives to industrial agriculture, ranging from fair trade and organic to urban gardening and community supported agriculture, have yet to produce significant benefits for the millions of small farmers and agricultural workers who labor on the land. In this sense, the central problem for those who work the land has remained the same—namely, how to retain enough money and produce to live sustainably, with dignity, and with a certain degree of security. This is precisely why agricultural labor continues to be a compelling lens through which to understand human history.

Notes

1. Food and Agriculture Organization, *World Food and Agriculture: Statistical Pocketbook 2018* (Rome: FAO, 2018).
2. I use the term elite(s) throughout the essay to refer to relatively small groups of people who control economic wealth and political power in a given society. We might now refer to them as the upper or dominant class.

3. Christopher Isett and Stephen Miller, *The Social History of Agriculture: From the Origins to the Current Crisis* (Lanham, MD. Rowman & Littlefield, 2017): 8–11.
4. Isett and Miller, *The Social History of Agriculture*, ch. 1; Brian Fagan, *World Prehistory: A Brief Introduction* (New York: Prentice Hall, 2006).
5. Isett and Miller, *The Social History of Agriculture*, ch. 1.
6. Kenneth Pomeranz, "Advanced Agriculture," in *The Oxford Handbook of World History*, ed. Jerry H. Bentley (Oxford: Oxford University Press, 2011): 247–250.
7. This section on the development of agriculture prior to the 1400s draws from Isett and Miller, *The Social History of Agriculture*, particularly chs. 1–3.
8. Isett and Miller, *The Social History of Agriculture*, ch. 1; Sarah Shaver Hughes and Brady Hughes, eds., *Women in World History*, Vol. 1: *Readings from Prehistory to 1500* (New York: Routledge, 2015).
9. Isett and Miller, *The Social History of Agriculture*, ch. 2; Harilaos Kitsikopoulos, *Agrarian Change and Crisis in Europe, 1200–1500* (New York: Routledge, 2012).
10. Isett and Miller, *The Social History of Agriculture*, ch. 2.
11. Isett and Miller, *The Social History of Agriculture*.
12. Ibid.; Spencer Dimmock, *The Origins of Capitalism in England, 1400–1600* (Chicago: Haymarket Books, 2015).
13. Thomas C. Patterson, *The Inca Empire: The Formation and Disintegration of a Pre-Capitalist States* (Oxford: Berg Publishers, 1997).
14. Isett and Miller, *The Social History of Agriculture*, ch. 2.
15. Ibid., chs. 1–3; Eric Wolf, *Europe and the People Without History*, 2nd ed. (Berkeley: University of California Press, 2010).
16. Isett and Miller, *The Social History of Agriculture*; Dimmock, *The Origins of Capitalism in England*.
17. Isett and Miller, *The Social History of Agriculture*; Dimmock, *The Origins of Capitalism in England*.
18. Robert Brenner, "The Rises and Declines of Serfdom in Medieval Europe," in *Serfdom and Slavery: Studies in Legal Bondage*, ed. M. L. Bush (London: Longman, 1996): 247-276; Isett and Miller, *The Social History of Agriculture*, 74–83; Shami Ghosh, "Rural Economies and Transitions to Capitalism: Germany and England Compared (c. 1200–c. 1800)," *Journal of Agrarian Change* 16, no. 2 (April 2016): 255–290.
19. Isett and Miller, *The Social History of Agriculture*, 125–127.
20. Edward. E. Baptist, *The Half Has Never Been Told: Slavery and the Making of American Capitalism* (New York: Basic Books, 2016).
21. Isett and Miller, *The Social History of Agriculture*, 168.
22. James Lockhart and Stuart B. Schwartz, *Early Latin America: A History of Colonial Spanish America and Brazil* (Cambridge: Cambridge University Press, 1983).
23. Lockhart and Schwartz, *Early Latin America*; Mark A. Burkholder and Lyman L. Johnson, *Colonial Latin America*, 10th ed. (New York: Oxford University Press, 2018).
24. Pomeranz, "Advanced Agriculture," 252–253; Wolf, *Europe and the People without History*, 2010.
25. Wolf, *Europe and the People Without History*, 2010.
26. Pomeranz, "Advanced Agriculture," 252–253.
27. Isett and Miller, *The Social History of Agriculture*, ch. 10; Baptist, *The Half Has Never Been Told*; Edward Royce, *The Origins of Southern Sharecropping* (Philadelphia: Temple University Press, 2010).

28. Robin D. G. Kelley, *Hammer and Hoe: Alabama Communists during the Great Depression.* (Chapel Hill: University of North Carolina Press, 1990).
29. James D. Ross Jr., *The Rise and Fall of the Southern Tenant Farmers Union in Arkansas* (Knoxville: University of Tennessee Press, 2018); Donald Grubbs, *Cry from the Cotton: The Southern Tenant Farmers' Union and the New Deal* (Fayetteville: University of Arkansas Press, 2000).
30. Deborah Cohen, *Braceros: Migrant Citizens and Transnational Subjects in the Postwar United States and Mexico* (Chapel Hill: University of North Carolina Press, 2013); Mireya Loza, *Defiant Braceros: How Migrant Workers Fought for Racial, Sexual, and Political Freedom* (Chapel Hill: University of North Carolina Press, 2016).
31. Isett and Miller, *The Social History of Agriculture*, ch. 10; Matt Garcia, *From the Jaws of Victory: The Triumph and Tragedy of Cesar Chavez and the Farm Worker Movement* (Berkeley: University of California Press, 2012).
32. Vandana Shiva, *The Violence of the Green Revolution: Third World Agriculture, Ecology, and Politics* (Lexington: University Press of Kentucky, 2016); Nick Cullather, *The Hungry World: America's Cold War Battle against Poverty in Asia* (Cambridge, MA: Harvard University Press, 2010).
33. Philip McMichael, *Food Regimes and Agrarian Questions* (Black Point, Canada: Fernwood Books, 2013).
34. E. Wesley F. Peterson, *A Billion Dollars a Day: The Economics and Politics of Agricultural Subsidies* (New York: Wiley-Blackwell, 2009).
35. Farmworker Justice, *Exposed and Ignored: How Pesticides Are Endangering our Farmworkers* (Washington, DC: Farmworker Justice, 2013); Adam Tompkins, *Ghostworkers and Greens: The Cooperative Campaigns of Farmworkers and Environmentalists for Pesticide Reform* (Ithaca, NY: ILR Press, 2016).

Bibliography

Brenner, Robert. "Agrarian Class Structures and Economic Development in Pre-Industrial Europe." *Past and Present* 70 (1972): 30–75.

Edelman, Marc. *Peasants against Globalization: Rural Social Movements in Costa Rica.* Stanford, CA: Stanford University Press, 1999.

Federico, Giovanni. *Feeding the World: An Economic History of Agriculture, 1800–2000.* Princeton, NJ: Princeton University Press, 2005.

Genovese, Eugene D. *Roll Jordan Roll: The World the Slaves Made.* New York: Vintage, 1976.

Isett, Christopher, and Stephen Miller. *The Social History of Agriculture: From the Origins to the Current Crisis.* Lanham, MD. Rowman & Littlefield, 2017.

McMichael, Philip. "The Land Grab and Corporate Food Regime Restructuring." *Journal of Peasant Studies* 39, no. 3–4 (2012): 681–701.

Moon, David. *The Russian Peasantry, 1600–1930: The World the Peasants Made.* London: Addison Wesley Longman, 1999.

Scott, James C. *Weapons of the Weak: Everyday Forms of Peasant Resistance.* New Haven, CT: Yale University Press, 1987.

Shiva, Vandana. *The Violence of the Green Revolution: Third World Agriculture, Ecology, and Politics.* Lexington: University Press of Kentucky, 2016.

Street, Richard Steven. *Beasts of the Field: A Narrative History of California Farmworkers, 1769–1913.* Stanford, CA: Stanford University Press, 2004.

Taylor, J. Edward, and Diane Charlton. *The Farm Labor Problem: A Global Perspective.* Cambridge, MA: Academic Press, 2018.

Weber, Eugene. *Peasants into Frenchmen: The Modernization of Rural France, 1870–1914.* Stanford, CA: Stanford University Press, 1976.

Wolf, Eric. *Europe and the People Without History.* 2nd ed. Berkeley: University of California Press, 2010.

CHAPTER 7

PEASANTS AND THE PEASANTRY

JONATHAN RIGG

THE peasantry has been a major object of study by rural sociologists and anthropologists since the mid-1960s. Shakespeare wrote of peasants ("O what a rogue and peasant slave am I!" [*Hamlet*, II, 2]) and the peasantry ("How much low peasantry would then be glean'd from the true seed of honour!" [*Merchant of Venice*, II, 9]), but it took some centuries more for the subject to take root in scholarship. Today, the *Journal of Peasant Studies* has one of the highest impact factors of any journal in the field, peasant studies is a vigorous area of academic work, and peasant political movements are vital and influential.[1]

Even with more than a half century of sustained academic attention, however, peasants and the peasantry remain hotly contested. Scholars continue to debate who or what peasants and the peasantry are, even whether they have ever been a distinct and identifiable social reality. Partly this is because peasants are so diverse—representative of "overwhelming heterogeneity," as Jan Douwe van Der Ploeg puts it.[2] Moreover, for many scholars considering contemporary rural conditions, whether they existed or not is somewhat beside the point: agrarian change and modernization have rendered the peasantry a historical artifact.[3] At the same time as there has been this current of de-peasantization, there is also a thread of scholarship that has tracked peasants through to the contemporary era, writing of processes of re-peasantization wherein "new" or "neo-peasants" have emerged, blending some of the "old" peasant mentalities and approaches with new technologies and sensibilities, informed by contemporary political aims.[4]

This means that whether peasants are truly "out there" in the twenty-first century countryside, to be surveyed, interviewed, and interpreted—as one might a smallholder rice farmer, for instance—is a matter of debate and dispute. In consequence, tracking and tracing the intellectual development of peasant studies is a necessary starting point for any review, such as this one.

The Sedimentations of Peasant Studies

The contemporary study of the peasantry owes much to the publication of two books in 1966, *Peasants* by Eric Wolf and *The Theory of Peasant Economy*, the first English-language translation of a substantial proportion of Alexander Chayanov's classic 1925 work *Organizatsiya krest'yanskogo khozyaistva* or *Peasant Farm Organization*.[5] Five years later, a third highly influential volume in the field was published, Teodor Shanin's edited *Peasants and Peasant Societies*.[6] This was to become a key teaching text. Finally, two years after this, in 1973, the first issue of the *Journal of Peasant Studies* (*JPS*) was published under the editorship of Terence J. Byres, Charles Curwen, and Shanin.[7]

Thus, over seven years between 1966 and 1973, contemporary peasant studies took shape. While Chayanov's book was published in 1925, it remained largely unread and unappreciated until its translation into English in 1966. In the preface to the translation of Chayanov's work, the editors write: "In contrast to their reputation in Japan, Chayanov's name and works have slipped into obscurity in both Europe and America. He is rarely cited in his native country or language and, to the best of our knowledge, has not been translated during the past 35 years into any other European language."[8]

What these three studies and, over subsequent years, the issues of *JPS* did was both to de-exoticize and de- (or re-) historicize the peasantry. No longer were peasants exotic subjects of study by anthropologists nor, equally, were they objects of purely historical analysis. They were active and vital agents in the contemporary rural—and even urban—landscape.

Who Are the Peasantry?

The issue of whether the peasantry exist, indeed whether they have ever existed, rests in part on a question of definition: who are peasants, and what do we mean by *the* peasantry?

Scholars have approached the peasantry, broadly speaking, in four ways: as a class;[9] as a production category (peasant *farming* or peasant *economics*);[10] as an object of historical interest;[11] and as a process.[12] Teodor Shanin considers the peasantry to have four defining features:

- Social organization based on the family farm;
- farming (or "land husbandry," as he termed it) as the main contributor to livelihood;
- a distinct cultural identity based around the village-community; and
- domination (and marginalization) by outsiders.[13]

Wolf uses the last of these features—which he refers to as subordination[14]—to define the peasantry as a "microclass" (or, rather, microclass*es*) shaped by local geographical conditions ("eco-types") and particular historical processes. Wolf explains as follows:

> [P]easantries are always localized.... And this is perhaps why it is difficult or impossible to speak of the peasantry as a class.... [P]easantries are never macroclasses at the level of the total system, always microclasses at the level of locality and region. It follows from this that we cannot know much about them unless we understand them historically, how they developed in that niche, and how that niche developed, in turn, in relation to forces beyond it. But I would doubt that it does any good to speak of *the* peasantry.[15]

For Wolf, then, while there are peasants there is no peasantry, in the sense of there being an internally coherent and identifiable class that we can call *the* peasantry. Peasants have evolved, in Wolf's view, in quite distinct ways in particular places, shaped by diverse environmental conditions and varied histories of oppression and subordination.

Chayanov's (1925) *The Theory of Peasant Economy* focuses, as the title suggests, on the peasant economy and on peasant economic behavior. His interest is less with peasants as a social group or class than with peasant *farming*. For Chayanov, a peasant farm should not be viewed as a business; farming for a peasant family farm was a way of life.[16] Chayanov's focus on the family farm is an indication that there are other terms that come, at least in the manner of their use, quite close to peasant and the peasantry. The family farm, for Chayanov, is a farm that relies on family labor and does not employ any hired help.[17] His definition of a family farm is, therefore, narrow and close to a peasant farm. Two other terms employed by scholars, often interchangeably, are smallholder and small farmer. While it is problematic to set a particular size cut-off for smallholders and small farmers—land varies enormously in productivity, from triple-cropped wet rice land to arid drylands suitable for grazing—two hectares has come to be adopted by many agencies as just such a cut-off.[18] Not content with a single category of peasant, some scholars subdivide this further into poor peasant, marginal peasant, even middle-income peasant. There is also the linked term peasant-community, with community being an equally historically rich and contested term.

Scanning the literature and the terms that scholars use to refer to small farmers hints at the object of their attention. The term "family farm" focuses on the provision and use of labor, and on labor relations; "smallholder" and "small farmer" pay attention to matters of land access, ownership, and scale (usually less than 2 ha); "peasant" and the "peasantry" betray a concern with peasant identity and issues of subordination; while "peasant-community" emphasizes the norms of reciprocity and sharing that characterize the peasant social condition and context. There is considerable overlap between these terms; that said, the terms "peasant" and the "peasantry" do mark out a distinctive space in terms of the attention that they bring to the political position of the objects of their attention—namely their marginal or subordinate position. Farming a small area of land does not make a peasant.

The Peasantry and the Present

In *The Age of Extremes*, the historian Eric Hobsbawm wrote, "The most dramatic and far reaching social change of the second half of this [twentieth] century, and the one which cuts us off forever from the world of the past, is the death of the peasantry."[19] For him, the peasantry is dead. For van der Ploeg, by contrast, the peasantry is alive and well and, importantly, not just in the fields of the rural South: "peasant studies is not about the past and the 'truth' that is supposedly anchored in it. It is, instead, about understanding a constantly moving process. Peasant studies is, more than ever, a journey of discovery."[20] These two points of view encompass the range of positions held by scholars concerning peasants and the peasantry today.

Those who subscribe to the end of the peasantry position do so on the straightforward grounds that globalization has, indeed, brought an end to the peasantry, probably during the 1970s in many parts of the world. "It makes little sense," Henry Bernstein writes, "to refer to 'peasants' in the world(s) of contemporary capitalism."[21] There is, therefore, no contemporary peasant "question," because there are no peasants. They have been extinguished by processes of social and economic transformation, or modernization. It is wishful thinking to imagine otherwise.

The way around this dilemma for some contemporary scholars of the peasantry is to argue that peasants need to be defined and understood in processual terms.[22] There is no need, then, to make the case that peasants persist, in a backward-looking sense, but rather to delineate how peasants are changing and adapting under the forces of contemporary change. Rather than arguing that peasants have died under the forces of modernization (as Hobsbawm does), they have been remade. Such an approach also means that peasant transition paths will be necessarily different as these forces operate in varied national and geographical contexts. There is no singular and simple peasant category, but many forms thereof, each wrought by the particularities of place and the exigencies of historical transformations. In this way, van der Ploeg echoes Wolf, although while Wolf was focusing on how peasants historically emerged as microclasses, van der Ploeg is concerned with contemporary emergence paths.

The countryside has been profoundly changed by processes of neoliberalization, mechanization, deregulation, globalization, chemicalization, and migration. All have squeezed and reshaped peasants whether defined as a class, production category, or social entity. Yet, and here is the rub, there are still some 475 million farms smaller than 2 ha across the world, arguably representing the globe's single largest social formation, economic "sector," employment category, and (potentially) political movement. This is one of the core puzzles of the study of the peasantry: the forces of modernization appear to be working thoroughly against the survival of the peasantry, and yet units of production that look very much like peasant farms in terms of their size and operation—and even in terms of the peasant identities of those who work such farmers—persist in very large numbers indeed. The persistence of such large numbers of smallholders, and the failure of the farm-size transition to take hold, raises the question of whether the agrarian transition in countries of the rural South will take a different course from the historical experience of the rural North. This relates to debates over the peasantry because if smallholders do still dominate the rural landscape, at least in terms of numbers, then there is greater scope for peasants to persist, even if only as neo-peasants.

Van der Ploeg,[23] a peasant transformer, provides a useful table that sets out how the neo-peasantry (although he does not use that term) link to, but at the same time are differentiated from, the peasantry of old (Table 7.1). Implicit here are the processes that have propelled and shaped the shift from left to right in the table. Central are the commodification of land, the commercialization of production, the recasting of labor relations, and the spatial integration of populations into broader national and global processes. It is these processes which some scholars suggest have (inevitably) led to the extinguishing of the peasantry (the peasant eradicators), while others have looked to the means and mechanisms by which some rural actors have resisted and pushed back against this inexorable tide of change, with the result that peasants have persisted, but differently (the peasant transformers). Van der Ploeg falls into the latter camp, Hobsbawm into the former, while Bernstein is "very skeptical of re-peasantization,"[24] seeing it as just a political project.

Surprisingly, the peasant transformers often work on agrarian change in the rural North. Processes of "re-peasantization" in the North are being driven, in part, by changing perspectives on farming. Post-productivist tendencies[25] and the revaluing of local and Indigenous knowledge, ecological and organic agriculture, integrated pest management, farmers markets, and diverse farming systems all play into the contemporary peasant movement. This should not, however, be regarded as any sort of "return" but, rather, a remaking for the contemporary world. In some instances, this can be seen as a neo-peasant movement working against and resisting the forces of rural and agricultural modernization, but at other times, it is redolent of and embedded in modernization processes.

Table 7.1 Linking and dividing the past and the present

From the traditional peasant condition	To the neo-peasantry
Land and land husbandry	Ecological capital and ecological stewardship
Subsistence and family labor	Self-provisioning
Partial market integration	Active distantiation from dominant socio-technical regime
Routine	Co-production involving ecological and economic exchange
Subordination and domination	Multiple resistance
Community and local exchange	Networked relations and new marketplaces

Source: Van der Ploeg, Jan Douwe, "The Peasantries of the Twenty-first Century: The Commoditisation Debate Revisited," *Journal of Peasant Studies 37*, no. 1 (2010): 1-30.

A final useful way to think of the peasant reform process is provided by Ben White, whose reputation is based mainly on his work in Indonesia.[26] White, taking an ethnographic approach, identifies three types of such new peasantries, termed here persisters, returners, and entrists (he does not use these terms). Persisters are those farmers who have taken over the family farm, having worked it with their parents during their youth and early adulthood. Returners are those who have left the family farms to take on other work, often as young adults, and who return and inherit or take over, in their middle age, the farm from their aging parents. Entrists are those with no prior experience or connection with farming, who have purchased land to take up farming as a departure and new venture. This last group comes quite close to the neo-peasants identified by some scholars in the countries of the rural North.

The Peasantry as a Political Force

A major impetus behind the sustained interest in peasants—not to mention the extension of interest in the peasantry from anthropology to political science—is the belief that peasants are an influential and growing political force across the globe, North and South. Food and land matter, and therefore smallholders, or peasants, do too. The political significance of land can be seen in the debate over land grabbing, and that of what we eat in the proliferation of work and attention paid to food sovereignty and food security. Almost half a billion farms of less than 2 ha, supporting around 2.5 billion people, represent a potent political force and social movement, just so long as they can be mobilized. La Vía Campesina—"The Peasant Way"—is the best known of numerous rural political movements, formally constituted in 1993 at a meeting in Mons, Belgium, and established to defend the peasant model in the face of the forces of neoliberalization. This transnational movement has been claimed to be the world's largest social movement.

The challenge is that given growing inter-penetration of rural and urban, escalating occupational multiplicity as farmers do more than just farm, and growing engagement with commercial activities, how does a peasant political identity persist? Within peasant studies, there is an animated debate over whether peasant farming is inherently ecological and capitalism's "other" or, rather, an essentialization that does not do justice to the realities and varieties of small-scale farming. It has become a hollow trope.

We see this in scholarly debates over the Vía Campesina movement and the engagement of the movement with food sovereignty. For Philip McMichael, the global food crisis has produced a peasant-based countermovement reflected in La Vía Campesina.[27] He observes that this "countermovement expresses a positive antithesis to corporate industrial agriculture: re-envisioning the conditions necessary to develop resilient and democratic forms of social reproduction, anchored in sustainable management of food systems by land users," part of a "broader vision of how to rethink the ecological conditions and scale at which human communities can live, and survive."[28] Though he does not claim that this is *just* a peasant movement, peasants—or an *idea* of the peasantry—do lie at the heart of the movement, reflected not least in La Vía Campesina's annual reports and other publications.[29]

Anyone who intends to study the peasantry cannot simply enter the field and "find" peasants. Peasants emerge as part of an intellectual-cum-political project, rendered visible through a set of contested framings.

Peasants and the Peasantry in Thailand

How do these debates within peasant studies play out in practice and in places? As two key scholars of the peasantry, Wolf in 1966 and van der Ploeg in 2010, have argued, the peasantry are neither singular nor unchanging. With this in mind, how have debates over the peasantry evolved, and what traction do they have in one country—Thailand?

In 1892, Prince Damrong Rachanuphap, Siam's first minister of the interior, instituted a series of reforms to create the administrative units that continue to exist today: villages (*mubaan*), subdistricts (*tambon*), districts (*amphoe*), and provinces (*changwat*).[30] Until that time, most rural settlements and populations were functionally remote from the capital, Bangkok, and the hand of the Siamese state seems to have rested lightly on the shoulders of countryfolk.[31] Taxes were levied directly (land tax, head tax) and indirectly (export taxes on rice), rice was requisitioned from time to time, and corvée (forced, unpaid) labor was demanded, but agriculture was regarded as a matter for farmers, not a concern of the state. As Han ten Brummelhuis says of the Central Plains region in the nineteenth century, the most commercialized and integrated part of the country:

> In the water state of Old Siam, the absence of state control over water management for rice growing is amazing. Rice was the most important staple by far for its inhabitants and wet rice cultivation depends on water first of all. Still, here we find a state that could afford not to concern itself with rice growing even though the lives of the people depended on it.[32]

The first in-depth studies of rural conditions and life in Siam/Thailand date from the late 1940s, with fieldwork for the Cornell University Thailand Project getting underway in Bang Chan in the Central Plains in 1948.[33] The great majority of these early studies use the term "peasant" as the collective noun to describe the kingdom's rural farming population, as do two key books that did much to shape such debates in the Southeast Asian region, James C. Scott's *The Moral Economy of the Peasant: Rebellion and Subsistence in Southeast Asia* (1976), and Samuel L. Popkin's *The Rational Peasant: The Political Economy of Rural Society in Vietnam* (1979).[34]

The first sustained attempt to bring a Marxist interpretation to the study of the Thai peasantry was Jit Poumisak's *The Face of Thai Feudalism Today*, published in Thai in 1957 and translated into English in 1987. In the study, he argued that Siam's *sakdina* system of land ownership, wherein all land was owned by the king and allocated by him to members of the royal family, made the country's peasants in effect a slave class, tied in and subordinate to an exploitative (Asiatic) mode of production.

In Thailand, we also see a strong localist debate centered on the work of the influential professor of economic history Chatthip Nartsupha and his book *The Thai Village Economy in the Past*, published in Thai in 1984 (*Sethakit mubaan Thai nai adit*) and translated into English in 1999. His book is not a peasant study (the term is only intermittently used), but it does have a peasant inflection:

> [T]he Thai village economy in the past was a subsistence economy. Production for food and for own use persisted and could be reproduced without reliance on the outside world. Bonds within the village were strong. Control of land was mediated by membership of the community. Cooperative exchange labor was used in production. Individual families were self-sufficient. . . . People cooperated in social activities and there was no class division, except for the existence of slaves who were accepted as part of the family. There was no class conflict within the village.[35]

The fact that Chatthip should use "villager," "village-community," and "farmer" rather than "peasant" or the "peasantry" (remembering that his book was written in Thai), raises the question of whether there is an equivalent word to "peasant" in the Thai language.

In much official literature, *kasetakon raiyoi* or "small-scale farmer" is used to refer to agriculturalists working small farms and is equivalent to smallholder. It does not, however, capture many of the other defining characteristics of "peasant," and in particular the sense of subordination. More usual in everyday conversation, is *chao rai chao na*, which translates as "field cropper, rice farmer," often abbreviated to just *chao na* (rice farmer). Implicit in this term, and especially the abbreviated version, are both small-scale farming and a farming "way of life," and some scholars translate *chao na* as peasant-farmer.[36] Notwithstanding the absence of a straightforward equivalent term in the Thai language, English-language books have often used the term "peasant," including both early ethnographic studies but also more recent publications such as Andrew Walker's *Thailand's Political Peasants: Power in the Modern Rural Economy* (2012). Studies of the peasantry, and peasant studies, have an intellectual pedigree in Thailand that can, in this way, be traced back to the 1950s.

Thailand's Peasants: Peasant Eradicators and Peasant Transformers

Just as there are scholars who argue that peasants globally are close to extinction, as well as those who see peasants persisting into the third millennium, so too in Thailand.

The view of the peasant eradicators is reflected in the work of Robert Dayley and Attachak Sattayanurak. They argue that "inertia tied to the notion of 'peasant' lives on even as observers awkwardly seek to reconcile this once useful class category with actual changes on the ground."[37] Two things are evident in this quotation. First, the authors take a backward-looking approach to the peasantry asking, in effect: do traditional notions of the peasant still have traction and relevance in contemporary Thailand? And second, they implicitly pose this question against the backdrop of contemporary transformations. In the light of prevailing conditions, Dayley and Sattayanurak conclude, echoing Hobsbawm (1994), that "Thai peasants, as individuals, as households, as a class, or as a unit of analysis no longer meaningfully exist."[38] For them, peasants have not evolved into some new form of peasantry, but taken up "wholly new and multiple occupational, social, group, and generational identities."[39] The peasant as process argument simply does not adequately capture the degree to which rural lives and livelihoods have been transformed in Thailand, and smallholders or small farmers cannot be seen as just another term for the peasantry.[40]

Figure 7.1 is adapted from Dayley and Sattayanurak's heuristic model of generational and temporal change in Thailand.[41] This illustrates the degree to which peasants have differentiated, under the forces of capitalism, into a wealth of very different social classes and production categories. It is instructive to compare Table 7.1 and Figure 7.1. Table 7.1 is adapted from van der Ploeg's attempt to show how peasant-like action has emerged even in the context of neoliberalism;[42] Figure 7.1 is based on Dayley and Sattayanurak's model and seeks to show, by contrast, how any semblance of the peasantry has been left far behind by contemporary transformations. Both use the same style of transition argument, but the former to demonstrate how peasants have been remade, and latter how they have been dissolved.

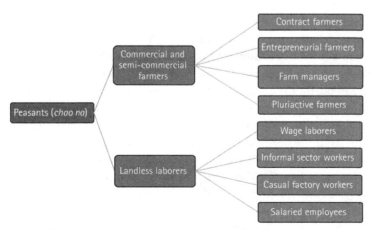

FIGURE 7.1 Peasants to workers and points between. Note: linking and dividing the past and the present. Source: adapted from Robert Dayley and Attachak Sattayanurak, "Thailand's Last Peasant," *Journal of Southeast Asian Studies* 27, no. 1 (2016): 64.

One scholar of Thai agrarian change who has adopted a peasant transformer position is the anthropologist Andrew Walker, who writes:

> I don't accept these predictions about the disappearance of the peasantry and the triumph of neo-liberalism. Recent rural sociology has shown us that peasant societies encountering capitalist development do not follow any clear trajectory towards social bifurcation, proletarianization, or impoverishment. Peasantries have proven to be remarkably resilient.[43]

In other words, Walker challenges the implications of the sequencing in Figure 7.1. The processes of transition and division do not, in his view, capture what is happening in the Thai countryside. For Walker, the puzzle is that notwithstanding Thailand's progress toward upper-middle-income status, a peasant mentality and identity persists, but against a backdrop of considerable material prosperity. Hence his term: middle-income peasant. Other scholars have adopted a somewhat similar position. Charles Keyes in his study in the Northeastern region—Walker was working in the North—writes of "village cosmopolitans";[44] Naruemon Thabchumpon and Duncan McCargo in their work on the Thai capital Bangkok, "urbanized villagers."[45] All three, like Walker, struggle with the continuing connections and resonances between the past and the present, and with the degree to which defining elements of the peasantry, not least the continuing prevalence of smallholder production, continue to be a dominant presence in the Thai countryside. This also makes the "peasant" smallholder a potent political force in Thailand, as explored toward the end of this chapter. For them, therefore, there is real and continuing salience of peasants and the peasantry in twenty-first-century Thailand, even in a "miracle economy" that has experienced deep and rapid structural change.

Proliferating Thai Peasantries

As with wider debates over the peasantry, in Thailand scholars have identified all manner of peasant processes and groups: "de-peasantization," "re-peasantization," and "post-peasantization," as well as "post-peasants." While on occasion, scholars have felt the need, theoretically, to nail their colors to one or other of these peasant masts, when they are grounded empirically it becomes evident that the processes and their identification are not mutually exclusive. This is evident in Tubtim's study of Nam Jam, a village around 10 km from the northern Thai provincial capital of Chiang Mai where, in 2012, she identified eight different village "classes": landed villagers; landless villagers (wage laborers); Thai in-migrants ("dormitory people"); Hmong tenant farmers; Burmese in-migrants (wage laborers); "city people" resident in the village; academics resident in the village; and foreigners resident in the village.[46] In this single village there are, then: peasants (landed villagers), post-peasants (wage laborers), and neo- (or new) peasants (academics resident in the village). These different peasantries can, in turn, be associated with processes of: de-peasantization, re-peasantization, and post-peasantization.

And, using Ben White's typology (introduced above), they can also be seen as examples of: peasant persisters, peasant returners, and peasant entrists.

Whether, then, peasants are gradually disappearing in the wake of Thailand's socioeconomic transformation, are being rewrought into some new peasant type under these processes, or are coming into being as new peasants in the countryside may not be much of an issue; it is possible to have it all, so to speak. This is reflected in how smallholders talk about themselves and their children's futures, seemingly peasants at one moment and a post-peasantry at another. Mae Thong, a sixty-three-year-old farmer in Ban Lao, a village in Thailand's Khon Kaen Province, explained in an interview: "[Ban Lao] is still a rice-farming village. Once a rice farmer, always one, no matter whether you earn money in other ways. Even with factories surrounding the village, some prefer to farm. They love farming, as their parents taught them how to farm. It's a tie to their roots."[47]

This sentiment was echoed by a fellow villager, Dao: "[I continue to farm] so we don't have to buy food! We want to have a store of rice to eat and secure our food needs. If we have to buy just one kilogram of rice it's gone so quickly and if one day we don't have any money, where would we find our food? But if we have a granary full of paddy, we feel comfortable and have peace of mind."[48]

But when we asked about the future, Mae Thong painted a rather different picture of the likely persistence of the Thai peasantry: "My sons grew up in our rice fields. But today's [young] just look down at their phones and stay at home all of the time. They don't even know where the rice field is! And they will sell out [the land] as soon as their parents die!"[49]

What has not (yet) disappeared in the wake of this proliferation of processes and groups (or microclasses), arguably, is peasant politics. Indeed, and rather surprisingly, peasant politics over the years of this millennium have been more contentious than at any point since the peak of the communist insurgency in Thailand in the 1970s when there were fears that, like Laos and Vietnam, the kingdom would "fall" to communism. Paradoxically, just as peasants appear to be disappearing in Thailand, peasant politics is on the rise. This is not to say, however, that the peasant politics of the twenty-first century is the same as that which galvanized peasant cultivators in the 1970s. The twenty-first-century peasant movement is not, mainly, about resisting capitalism's embrace but rather about clamoring for fair access to it. Whether this can, then, be counted a peasant movement is moot.

The Contemporary Politics of the Thai Peasantry

With this in mind, Andrew Walker argues that contemporary peasant politics in Thailand is very different from the peasant politics of the 1970s.[50] The state's support for smallholders through various interventions from universal health coverage to rice price support policies and micro-credit schemes have supported smallholder (peasant) livelihoods and "in this sense, state support tends to preserve the peasantry rather than fundamentally transform it."[51] A novel but notable feature regarding the future of the smallholder in Thailand relates to debates over the "sufficiency economy" (SE).

The sufficiency economy or *sethakit porpiang* has its roots in the localism discourse of the 1980s, and with Chatthip's work (see above). But it was much more than just a thread of academic debate. It was underpinned by the community culture school (*watthana chumchon*), and this informed the practical work of nongovernmental organizations. The movement emphasized local knowledge, production for consumption rather than sale (or, at most, local sale or exchange), self-reliance, community participation, and Buddhist notions of moderation. In 1997, in the midst of the Thai financial crisis, the former King Bhumibol Adulyadej of Thailand set out his interpretation of the problems facing Thailand and his vision for their solution. This came to be known as the King's New Theory of the Sufficiency Economy, based upon three key principles: "moderation," "reasonableness," and "self-immunity." It has putatively provided the inspiration for each of Thailand's Five-Year National Economic and Social Development plans from the Ninth (2002–2006) through to the Twelfth (2017–2021) plans.

The key point is that critics[52] find the SE to be hopelessly out of touch with the conditions and aspirations of many rural people in Thailand. It is seen as an urban vision of rural futures that draws on a romantic agrarian myth of peasant identity. Tubtim writes that the organizations and celebrities who lend their support to the SE "do not earn their main income from farming . . . [and the] practices of these groups often bear little resemblance to the realities faced by smallholders."[53]

The yawning gap between the urban vision of the countryside and the smallholder (or peasant) experience of the rural came to a head in the color-coded upheavals that pitted "yellow shirts" against "red shirts," culminating in the military crackdown of red shirt protests in Bangkok in 2010. Farmers in Thailand have traditionally been counted the "backbone of the nation" (*kraduk san lang khong chaat*). More recently, they have been labeled "buffalo"—dim, and easily led astray by venal and unprincipled politicians, not least the governments of former prime ministers Thaksin Shinawatra (2001–2006) and his sister, Yingluck Shinawatra (2011–2014). While the red/yellow conflict cannot be reduced to a simple rural/urban battle, there is little doubt that much red shirt support was centered in rural areas of the North and Northeast, and among (relatively) poor smallholders or, for some, "peasants" (Figure 7.2).

Squaring the Peasant Circle

In 1894, Friedrich Engels published *The Peasant Question in France and Germany*. He thought the future of the small peasant in industrializing and capitalizing Europe to be desperate, arguing that "our small peasant [in France], like every other survival of a past mode of production, is hopelessly doomed," adding, "He is a future proletarian."[54] The surprise is that more than a century later, peasant studies—and peasants—remains a recalcitrant presence, certainly in academic and political debates, and perhaps in the countryside too.

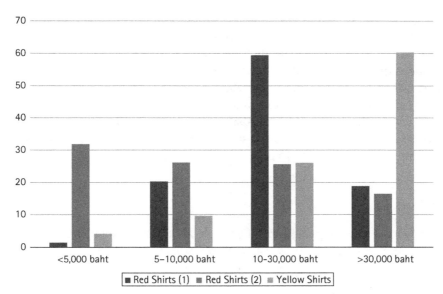

FIGURE 7.2 Monthly household income of Red and Yellow Shirts supporters. Note: the data for "Red Shirts (1)" and "Yellow Shirts" is based on a survey by the Asia Foundation. The sample was small (Red Shirts, n = 69; Yellow Shirts, n = 73). The data for "Red Shirts (2)" rests on a larger sample (n = 402) and is taken from a survey by Thabchumpon and McCargo. Source: date extracted from Thabchumpon and McCargo (2011): 1003; Phongpaichit (2016): 17.

Where scholars stand on the question of the peasantry rests, in no small part, on the question of definition. Peasant "purists" define the peasantry in historically rooted terms and come to the conclusion that, in the context of globalization and the emergence of late capitalism, it makes little sense to write of peasants persisting into the modern era. The demise of the peasantry, therefore, has also led to the passing of the peasant "question." Even where farmers working small areas of land—smallholders—persist, these producers cannot be counted as peasants. Indeed, it is a distraction from the processes and conditions that we need to understand if we are to address poverty and wellbeing in the countryside, especially in the rural South. Protecting and insulating peasant livelihoods may, in this line of argument, actually perpetuate low incomes and poverty among smallholders, rather than raising their living standards.

There are also scholars who argue that rather than taking a backward-looking view of the peasantry, we need to adapt and adjust our definitions to contemporary conditions. Van der Ploeg, taking this more expansive view, argues that the peasantry have not so much persisted in the guise of smallholders, but *re-emerged* in recent years.[55] Over much of Asia, for instance, while structural change has been deep, broad, and rapid, smallholders (or peasants) have not, in large part, been separated from the land.[56] Households embrace both rural and urban, farm and non-farm activities and occupations to sustain their livelihoods, through livelihood bricolage. This, then, opens up a space for new considerations of the peasantry, as neologisms such as re-peasantization, de-peasantization, neo-peasants, and post-peasants make evident.

Where there is no dispute is that agrarian transition paths are multiple, rural populations diverse, and rural political movements vigorous. Whether these multiple paths signal de- or re-peasantization, whether rural populations with connections to the land can be counted as peasants or semi-proletarians, and whether rural political movements can be viewed as peasant-based is disputed—and will remain so. What is equally clear, however, is that peasant studies remains a vibrant, even growing area of scholarship and peasant politics a potent force in many countries.

Notes

1. The journal's 2017 Impact Factor of 3.815 placed it 4/85 in Anthropology and 2/57 in Planning & Development. In 2019 the journal was in its 46th volume.
2. Henry Bernstein, Harriet Friedmann, Jan Douwe van der Ploeg, Teodor Shanin, and Ben White, "Forum: Fifty Years of Debate on Peasantries, 1966–2016," *Journal of Peasant Studies* 45, no. 4 (2018): 694.
3. Eric J. Hobsbawm, *Age of Extremes: The Short Twentieth Century, 1914–1991* (London: Abacus, 1995).
4. See Jan Douwe van der Ploeg, "The Peasantries of the Twenty-first Century: The Commoditisation Debate Revisited," *Journal of Peasant Studies* 37, no. 1 (2019): 1–30.
5. Bernstein et al., "Fifty Years of Debates," 689.
6. Teodor Shanin, *Peasants and Peasant Societies* (Oxford: Blackwell, 1971).
7. In 2001, Terry Byres and Henry Bernstein, the latter also a later editor of *JPS*, founded the *Journal of Agrarian Change*, which also has a strong peasant intellectual lineage.
8. D. Thorner, "Chayanov's Concept of Peasant Economy," in A. V. Chayanov, D. Thorner, B. H. Kerblay, R. E. F Smith, and B. Kerblay, *A. V. Chayanov on the Theory of Peasant Economy* (Homewood, IL: R. D. Irwin, 1966), v.
9. Eric R. Wolf, *Peasants* (Englewood Cliffs, NJ: Prentice-Hall, 1966).
10. Chayanov et al., *Theory of Peasant Economy*.
11. Hobsbawn, *Age of Extremes*.
12. Shanin, *Peasants*.
13. Teodor Shanin, "Peasantry: Delineation of a Sociological Concept and a Field of Study," *European Journal of Sociology* 12, no. 2 (1971): 289–300.
14. Wolf, *Peasants*, 13.
15. Eric R. Wolf, *Pathways of Power: Building an Anthropology of the Modern World* (Berkeley: University of California Press, 2001): 254–55.
16. This partly explains why some scholars regard peasant "economics" as a non sequitur.
17. "And since, on the family farm which has no recourse to hired labor, the labor force pool, its composition, and degree of labor activity are entirely determined by family composition and size, we must accept family makeup as one of the chief factors in peasant farm organization." Chayanov et al., *Theory of Peasant Economy*, 53.
18. Jonathan Rigg, Albert Salamanca, and Eric C. Thompson, "The Puzzle of East and Southeast Asia's Persistent Smallholder," *Journal of Rural Studies* 43 (2016): 118–33.
19. Hobsbawn, *Age of Extremes*, 289.

20. Jan Douwe van Der Ploeg's reflections on five decades of peasant studies. Bernstein et al., *Fifty Years of Debates*, 694.
21. Henry Bernstein, "Is There an Agrarian Question in the 21st Century?" *Revue canadienne d'études du développement (Canadian Journal of Development Studies)* 27, no. 4 (2006): 453.
22. Van der Ploeg, "The Peasantries of the Twenty-first Century." In fact, this was also Shanin's position in his 1971 paper (Shanin, "Delineation of a Sociological Concept," 298–300).
23. Van der Ploeg, *Peasantries of the Twenty-first Century*, 2.
24. Bernstein, *Fifty Years of Debates*, 713.
25. The shift from intensive and industrially driven farming (or productivist systems) to a post-productivist era characterized by disintensification, an emphasis on quality over quantity of production, a concern for environmental sustainability and animal welfare, and the need to see the countryside as places to be "consumed" rather than sites for production.
26. Bernstein, *Fifty Years of Debates*, 708.
27. Philip McMichael, "Historicizing Food Sovereignty," *Journal of Peasant Studies* 41, no. 6 (2014): 933–57.
28. Ibid., 936–37.
29. See https://viacampesina.org/en/.
30. Siam was renamed Thailand in 1939. It is the only country of Southeast Asia not to have been colonized.
31. It is worth noting here that for Eric Wolf a key aspect of a peasant, as distinct from a "primitive" or a farmer, is their subordinate position within the structures of a state; following this line, for farmers in Thailand to be counted as peasants they must be tied to the state at some level or other.
32. Han ten Brummelhuis, *King of the Waters: Homan van der Heide and the Origin of Modern Irrigation in Siam* (Leiden: KITLV Press, 2005): 14.
33. Lauriston Sharp, Hazel M. Hauck, Kamol Janlekha, and Robert B. Textor, *Siamese Rice Village: A Preliminary Study of Bang Chan, 1948–1949* (Bangkok: Cornell Research Centre, 1953). The preliminary report of the study stated: "no other study of an actual Thai community of any kind had ever been made" before the initiation of the Bang Chan project (4).
34. Samuel Popkin, *The Rational Peasant: The Political Economy of Rural Society in Vietnam* (Berkeley: University of California Press, 1979); J. C. Scott. *The Moral Economy of the Peasant: Rebellion and Subsistence in Southeast Asia* (New Haven, CT: Yale University Press, 1976).
35. Chatthip Nartsupha, *The Thai Village Economy in the Past*, trans. C. Baker and Pasuk Phongpaichit (Chiang Mai, Thailand: Silkworm Books, 1999 [1984]): 73.
36. Robert Dayley and Attachak Sattayanurak, "Thailand's Last Peasant," *Journal of Southeast Asian Studies* 47, no. 1 (2016): 44.
37. Dayley and Sattayanurak, *Last Peasant*, 43.
38. Ibid., 63.
39. Ibid., 63.
40. See also Bernstein, "Is There an Agrarian Question," 454.
41. Dayley and Sattayanurak, *Last Peasant*, 64.
42. Indeed, arguably *because* of neoliberalism, in the sense that these actions are often counter-movements.
43. Andrew Walker, *Thailand's Political Peasants: Power in the Modern Rural Economy* (Madison: University of Wisconsin Press, 2012): 36.

44. Charles Keyes, *Finding Their Voice: Northeastern Villagers and the Thai State* (Chiang Mai, Thailand: Silkworm Books, 2014).
45. Naruemon Thabchumpon and Duncan McCargo, "Urbanized Villagers in the 2010 Thai Redshirt Protests," *Asian Survey* 51, no. 6 (2011): 993–1018.
46. Tubtim Tubtim, *Rural Crossroads: Class and Migration in Peri-urban Chiang Mai* (PhD thesis, Sydney University, 2014).
47. Jonathan Rigg, *More than Rural: Textures of Thailand's Agrarian Transformation* (Honolulu: University of Hawai'i Press, 2019): 232.
48. Jonathan Rigg, *Rural Development in Southeast Asia: Dispossession, Accumulation and Persistence* (Cambridge: Cambridge University Press, 2020): 28.
49. Rigg, *More than Rural*, 233
50. Walker, *Thailand's Political Peasants*, 21–24.
51. Ibid., 22.
52. ibid.
53. Tubtim Tubtim, "Thailand: The Political Economy of Post-Peasant Agriculture," in *Asian Smallholders in Comparative Perspective*, ed. E. C. Thompson, J. Rigg, and J. Gillen (Amsterdam: Amsterdam University Press, 2019): 291–94.
54. Fredrick Engels, *The Peasant Question in France and Germany*. First published in *Die neue Zeit*, Bd. 1, No. 10, 1894–1895. English translation available: https://www.marxists.org/archive/marx/works/download/Engles_The_Peasant_Question_in_France_and_Germany.pdf.
55. Van der Ploeg, "Peasantries of the Twenty-first Century."
56. Rigg et al., "The Puzzle."

Bibliography

Bernstein, Henry. "Is There an Agrarian Question in the 21st Century?" *Revue canadienne d'études du développement (Canadian journal of development studies)* 27, no. 4 (2006): 449–60.

Bernstein, Henry, Harriet Friedmann, Jan Douwe van der Ploeg, Teodor Shanin, and Ben White. "Forum: Fifty Years of Debate on Peasantries, 1966-2016." *Journal of Peasant Studies* 45, no. 4 (2018): 689–714.

Brummelhuis, Han ten (2005). *King of the Waters: Homan van der Heide and the Origin of Modern Irrigation in Siam*. Leiden: KITLV Press, 2005.

Chayanov, Alexander V., Daniel Thorner, Basile Kerblay, and R. E. F. Smith. *A. V. Chayanov on the Theory of Peasant Economy*. Homewood, IL: Published for the American Economic Association by R. D. Irwin, 1966.

Dayley, Robert, and Attachak Sattayanurak. "Thailand's Last Peasant." *Journal of Southeast Asian Studies* 47, no. 1 (2016): 42–65.

Engels, Friedrich. "The Peasant Question in France and Germany." First published in *Die neue Zeit* 1, no. 10 (1894–1895). English translation available at https://www.marxists.org/archive/marx/works/download/Engles_The_Peasant_Question_in_France_and_Germany.pdf.

Hobsbawm, Eric J. *Age of Extremes: The Short Twentieth Century, 1914–1991*. London: Abacus, 1995.

Keyes, Charles. *Finding Their Voice: Northeastern Villagers and the Thai State*. Chiang Mai, Thailand: Silkworm Books, 2014.

McMichael, Philip. "Historicizing Food Sovereignty." *Journal of Peasant Studies* 41, no. 6 (2014): 933–57.

Nartsupha, Chatthip. *The Thai Village Economy in the Past*. Translated by Chris Baker and Pasuk Phongpaichit. Chiang Mai, Thailand: Silkworm Books, 1984.

Phatharathananunth, S. (2016). "Rural Transformations and Democracy in Northeast Thailand." *Journal of Contemporary Asia* 46(3): 504–19.

Popkin, Samuel L. *The Rational Peasant: The Political Economy of Rural Society in Vietnam*. Berkeley: University of California Press, 1979.

Rigg, Jonathan. *More than Rural: Textures of Thailand's Agrarian Transformation*. Honolulu: University of Hawai'i Press, 2019.

Rigg, Jonathan. *Rural Development in Southeast Asia: Dispossession, Accumulation and Persistence*. Cambridge: Cambridge University Press, 2020.

Rigg, Jonathan, Albert Salamanca, and Eric C. Thompson. "The Puzzle of East and Southeast Asia's Persistent Smallholder." *Journal of Rural Studies* 43 (2016): 118–33.

Scott, James C. *The Moral Economy of the Peasant: Rebellion and Subsistence in Southeast Asia*. New Haven, CT: Yale University Press, 1976.Shanin, Teodor. "Peasantry: Delineation of a Sociological Concept and a Field of Study." *European Journal of Sociology* 12, no. 2 (1971): 289–300.

Shanin, Teodor. *Peasants and Peasant Societies*. Oxford: Blackwell, 1971.

Sharp, Lauriston, Hazel M. Hauck, Kamol Janlekha, and Robert B. L. Textor. *Siamese Rice Village: A Preliminary Study of Bang Chan, 1948–1949*. Bangkok: Cornell Research Centre, 1953.

Thabchumpon, Naruemon, and Duncan McCargo. "Urbanized Villagers in the 2010 Thai Redshirt Protests." *Asian Survey* 51, no. 6 (2011): 993–1018.

Tubtim, Tubtim. "Rural Crossroads: Class and Migration in Peri-urban Chiang Mai." PhD diss., Sydney University, 2014.

Tubtim, Tubtim. "Thailand: The Political Economy of Post-Peasant Agriculture." In *Asian Smallholders in Comparative Perspective*, edited by E. C. Thompson, J. Rigg, and J. Gillen, 269–303. Amsterdam: Amsterdam University Press, 2019.

Van der Ploeg, Jan Douwe. "The Peasantries of the Twenty-first Century: The Commoditisation Debate Revisited." *Journal of Peasant Studies* 37, no. 1 (2010): 1–30.

Walker, Andrew. *Thailand's Political Peasants: Power in the Modern Rural Economy*. Madison: University of Wisconsin Press, 2012.

Wolf, Eric R. *Peasants*. Englewood Cliffs, NJ: Prentice-Hall, 1966.

Wolf, Eric R., et al. *Pathways of Power: Building an Anthropology of the Modern World*. Berkeley: University of California Press, 2001.

CHAPTER 8

WOMEN IN AGRICULTURE

PAMELA RINEY-KEHRBERG

Rosa Ise was a Kansas farmer. In 1873, the seventeen-year-old married a Civil War veteran many years her senior, and the two of them homesteaded land in north central Kansas. She plowed, milked cows, planted a garden, and managed her family's finances. She bore twelve children and raised eleven to adulthood. Those children made up the workforce of their growing agricultural operation. Throughout her years on the farm she saved and scrimped, and she used her money to buy more land and educate her children. When her husband died, she carried on managing her farm, leaving the land only because of the combined pressure of her largely grown brood, who saw their futures in the city, rather than the countryside. Though she might not have called herself a farmer, rather a farm wife, or a wife, Rosa Ise's work inside and outside of the home was absolutely essential to the running of the farm; as both wife and widow, she was, by any measure, a farmer.[1]

Antoinette Blachon, like Rosa Ise, became a farm manager. Born in 1880, her parents made their home in south central France. She grew up in a family led by a strong woman; while her father earned next to nothing trading horses, her mother managed the family property. Antoinette was not terribly fond of farm labor. She spent much of her childhood working as a shepherdess, a task she found unpleasant. Maintaining control of the sheep was often beyond her. For a time, she left agriculture for work in the silk industry. Eventually, she made her way back to farming, not as a laborer but as the proprietor of a small manor, which included two farms. Her husband, however, was unsuited to supervising the family's lands. While managing sheep had been beyond her, managing farms was not. Antoinette took over handling the business of the family estate. Antoinette Blachon was a woman in agriculture— she was a farm manager.[2]

Although she was not born to agriculture like Antoinette Blachon, Josephine McCarthy Waggoner was a farmer and a chronicler of her people. A Lakota woman, born in 1872, she lived in several locations on North America's northern Great Plains. During her childhood, her parents fed their family by combining hunting and gathering with government rations. The Lakota resisted agriculture, because of the environmental limitations of the northern Great Plains. The US government had other plans for the

Lakota people, however. As a child, Josephine was sent to St. Benedict's Agricultural Boarding School, or Farm School, as she called it. She received further education at Hampton Normal and Agricultural Institute. As a young woman she watched the lifestyle of her people change as the government forced them to take up farming. She wrote about the women working in the fields, tending to their allotments. After Josephine married, she bore ten children and ranched along with her husband. Life was a round of losses and struggles, in part because of the Dust Bowl years, which made sustaining a ranch especially difficult; they lost their ranch as a result. Near the end of her life, she and her husband recovered their land and raised a garden and goats, in addition to crops.[3] Josephine Waggoner lived many productive years as a farmer.

Rosa Ise, Antoinette Blachon, and Josephine Waggoner were not historical anomalies. They were, in fact, more the rule than the exception. Throughout human history, most people in most places at most times have supported themselves by agriculture. It is only very recently that the majority of the world's people have ceased to farm, and supported themselves through alternative employment. Many of these farmers in the past were women, who toiled next to, or in conjunction with, male partners, or who may have farmed independently. Some of these women called themselves farmers. Some called themselves farm wives, or wives. Some claimed that they only "helped," while their husbands did the primary work of farming. No matter what they may have called themselves, these women were farmers, too, and definitely women in agriculture. Women have played an integral role in agriculture across societies and across years. Even as agriculture itself has changed, women have continued to do much of the work that feeds the world.

WOMEN IN INDIGENOUS AGRICULTURE

Some of the world's first farmers were women. In Indigenous cultures, as groups made the transition from hunting and gathering to agriculture, the division of labor followed lines that usually placed women in agriculture. Hunting, in most cultures, was men's work. It required a good deal of mobility to follow animals. Women, made more sedentary by pregnancy and the demands of breast-feeding infants and tending to small children, applied themselves instead to gathering plants and tending crops. Women contributed as much to the caloric needs of their families as men, and sometimes more.[4] Anthropologist Barbara Roth has shown that it was women who initially adopted and cultivated maize in what would become the southwestern United States. As she wrote, "The productivity and reliability of maize would have been particularly attractive to women who were responsible for bringing in a significant component of the diet. Maize did not require new technologies for processing or drastic changes in scheduling, and it was similar to wild grass plants already in use." She further commented, "agriculture was successfully incorporated into the diet because of women's efforts in harvesting, processing, and storing the new plants."[5] Women's role in agriculture could also be a cause for conflict when Indigenous peoples came into contact with incoming European settlers. In British colonies in North America, colonizers interpreted the Native American division of labor as a gross dereliction by men of their duties as providers. In England, hunting was a leisure activity of the upper classes. Because Indigenous men spent the majority of their time hunting, rather than in the fields, colonizers interpreted their behavior as improper and unmanly, and used it as part of their justification to expropriate native lands.[6] Because it was farmed by women, British colonizers argued, the land was not being used as it should be.

English Agriculture, 1700–1850

Even though incoming English settlers in North America claimed to disdain the idea of women working in the fields, they came from a culture whose women regularly contributed agricultural labor on family farms. Historian Nicola Verdon researched the work that English women did on farms between 1700 and 1850. In the early period, which would have been much like the England that the colonists left, it was easy to find women in agriculture. She described the work of men and women in the eighteenth century as "complementary but distinct." Men had their work, and women had theirs, and women's work took them out of the house and into the "garden, dairy, and farmyard." Pigs, bees, fowl, and the dairy all fell to women.[7] The dairy was particularly important, with women's work producing products for home consumption as well as sale. Earlier historians argued that when dairies became larger and more commercialized, the role of the farm wife was diminished. Verdon, however, found that many women continued to work beside the dairy maids, and that their supervisory tasks were significant. Additionally, having more servants working in the dairy meant that women had to care for and supervise more laborers within the household. Even women on some of the largest farms were not exempt from agricultural laborer. Verdon cited the story of Elizabeth Cotton, who lived with her husband and large family on a 400-acre Suffolk farm. Although she was quite well-to-do, the list of her labors was significant. Cotton "attended to business callers, opened her kitchen to labourers, was expected to take charge of the farm in her husband's absence, supervised the dairy and had to deal with the transgressions of her light-fingered maid."[8] Although Cotton's social activities and servants might have made it look as if she was not a worker, a careful examination of her life revealed otherwise.

Women as "Invisible Farmers"

Women were invisible farmers for numerous reasons. Men more often handled the work that linked farm to town, acting on behalf of the whole family. Much of the work women did occurred inside the home or close to it. While it was easy to find a man in the field behind a plow, it was harder to discern what went on in the kitchen or the barnyard. She was less visible. This was true of Elizabeth Cotton in the 1850s and 1860s, and it was also true of many farm women more than a hundred years later. As sociologist Carolyn Sachs noted in her 1983 book, *Invisible Farmers*, women's invisibility also stemmed from their lack of power within the agricultural economy. For the most part, they lacked control over land, the proceeds from crops, and the hired labor. Because of this powerless position, women became invisible.[9] When the US Department of Agriculture surveyed farm women in 1980s, researchers also discovered that few farm women identified themselves as farmers. On the family's tax forms, 60 percent self-identified as "wife, mother, housewife," rather than "farmer, rancher, producer." Even so, 55 percent claimed to be one of the main operators of the agricultural enterprise, and 60 percent said they either definitely or probably could operate the farm without help from their husband. As sociologist Rachel Rosenfeld has noted, "Farming . . . is a less well defined occupation, especially for women, because it often takes places in the context of a family operation. Taking on this title, then, is not automatic for women even when they do the work of farming."[10]

It is unclear, however, that farm women throughout much of the past would have recorded their roles differently, given the opportunity. When anthropologist Deborah Fink studied Iowa farm women in the 1980s, she discovered that many did not see their work on the farm as a distinct occupation, separate from that of their husbands. Women who had milked cows, raised chickens, and managed a household full of people claimed that they "had not worked." They saw themselves as "helpers." As Fink commented, "Women did specific activities that we tend to call work, but that, within the family economy, were not considered work. Had nonfamily people been hired to do the same tasks, they would have been called workers. Women's work might have been invisible in the family economy, but it was a factor of production and it shaped relations both within the household and among households."[11] Women worked in agriculture, but their labors often disappeared into the collective activities of the family, headed by a man.

Invisible or not, the tasks women performed on farms were myriad. Those tasks have varied by the location of the farm, the ethnicity of the farmers, and the level of capitalization of the operation. The crop or crops the farm produced also affected the way in which the individuals on the farm worked. Women have milked, raised fowl, gathered eggs, and raised sheep, goats, cattle, and swine. They have planted, cultivated, and harvested crops, and then preserved the harvest. Women have also fulfilled the labor needs of farms by bearing and raising the next generation of agricultural workers. They have acted as managers, sometimes because of talent or inclination, but at other times out of necessity. Women have performed every job that agriculture demands.

The Southern United States

In the American South before the Civil War, agricultural labor was no respecter of the biological differences between men and women. Women labored on farms of various sizes and shapes, doing a range of chores. Women on small farms did a wide variety of work. Tobacco was highly labor-intensive, and both enslaved and poor white women worked in the fields, tending the crop. It was hand labor, and much of the work, such as pulling worms off the plants, could be done by women as easily as by men.[12] Cotton was also a labor intensive crop, requiring repeated cultivation during the growing season, called chopping, and hand-picking during the long harvest season beginning in August or September and continuing throughout the fall. While enslaved girls and women did all of these agricultural chores, so did white women on poor to middling farms. The combination of labor-intensive crops with a lack of available labor, or funds for labor, meant that many white women worked in the fields, along with enslaved laborers. Enslaved women carried significant additional burdens, including bearing children, who did not belong to them but rather became the saleable property of their owners.[13]

For Southern white women on plantations, their work was more likely to be domestic, although it could extend into farm management as well. Historian Jessica Parker Moore described the life of Matilda Fulton, whose husband served as a US senator for Arkansas in the 1830s and 1840s. In her husband's absence, she showed herself both willing and able to do all of the work necessary to running a small plantation. She stepped out of domestic space into public space and supervised her family's property: managing money and crops and directing workers. She regularly negotiated with men. She was willing to buy slaves, sell slaves, and assert her authority over their lives and labor.[14] When her husband died at age forty-nine, Matilda Fulton was left to manage the property on her own. Despite heavy debts, she continued, selling some slaves and land in order to finance her continued residence at Rosewood plantation. At the time of her death in 1879, she had managed the plantation for more than forty years.[15] While the extent of her managerial role was somewhat unusual, Fulton was one of a myriad of Southern women who were essential to the operation of farms and plantations.

From the end of the Civil War well into the twentieth century, Southern women continued to be the backbone of their families' agricultural operations. For many families, both black and white, tenancy became a way of life. In these families, women's labor was absolutely essential to maintaining crops and families. When sociologist Margaret Jarman Hagood visited 254 white Southern tenant women in the 1930s, she discovered that nearly all were deeply interested in agriculture, possessed a good knowledge of the inner workings of their farms, and had more than a casual acquaintance with the work required. She also observed, "In the matter of work preference, an overwhelming majority—seven-eighths—of the mothers like field work (including work in tobacco barns) better than housework." She also commented that "there is a great deal of pride in the ability to work like a man."[16] In spite of large families and pressing housework, the fields were where these women wanted to be.

THE UNITED STATES BEYOND THE SOUTH

The South was the most agricultural of all of the regions of the United States, but agriculture was a major part of the economies of many of the states, and wherever agriculture existed, women found roles within it. Women did every kind of labor. Some of the work they did was the accepted and stereotypical work of women: bearing and raising children, cooking, cleaning, sewing, preserving food for future use, and other indoor chores. Although this work took place within the home, it was essential to the survival of farms, which often continued to exist because women were willing to scrimp and save.[17] Women processed dairy products, but whether or not they milked was based on local culture. Chickens and other fowl were the province of women. The care of large animals often fell to men, but women and girls also acted as herders. Gardens belonged to women and their child helpers. Caring for hired laborers also fell to women. This usually included cooking for threshing and harvest crews, a task that involved a full year's planning for immense and complicated feasts. In other places, families hired out their threshing. Women might also hire themselves out to work for threshing crews. This could involve a short but intense season of twenty-hour days, cooking endless meals. In the very early years of the twentieth century, Carrine Gafkjen, a Norwegian immigrant to North Dakota, spent part of the summer for eight years working in a cook car, feeding two to three dozen men employed as threshers. She worked alone and earned between three and four dollars a day, an unheard-of sum for a woman. Gafkjen used her money to pay the expenses of her homestead and to buy another section of land. When she married one of those threshermen, another Norwegian immigrant, he gave up his own homestead and came to live on her land.[18]

The question of whether white Northern women should do field work greatly concerned observers in the years from the end of the Civil War to the middle of the twentieth century. Everyone, from writers of popular fiction to the officials at the USDA, seemed to believe that this was work that they should not do. The Country Life Commission also chimed in on the issue and argued that women's workloads should be lightened, in order to encourage girls and women to remain in agriculture. If they could live more like their city sisters, they would not be tempted to stray from rural life.[19] The USDA and Country Life Commission were arguing against rural realities. Immigrant women from Europe regularly engaged in field work, especially those of German and Scandinavian heritage, and observers criticized this practice as unchivalrous. Cultural prejudices, however, could not stop families from doing what was necessary.[20] During peak times, such as harvest, no one who was physically able was exempt from doing what needed to be done. The same conditions applied when there was plowing, raking, planting, or other field work that needed to be completed. While many families would have preferred to keep women and girls confined to work in the house and the barnyard, conditions did not permit it. And there were some jobs, such as corn planting, that fathers might prefer to have their daughters do, because they would be careful and precise.[21] Concerns about protecting white women from too arduous agricultural labor made their way into other areas colonized by the British, such as Australia and New Zealand, but women there, too, undertook whatever the demands on the family required. Historian Kate Hunter found many young Australian women who were their "father's right hand man."[22] And while reformers fretted about the propriety of field labor for white women, they generally did not worry about African American women working in cotton fields, or Mexican American women working as migrant farm laborers.

Women in Global Agriculture

The flexibility with which farm families in the United States organized their labor is similar to that experienced in families in many other parts of the world. Agriculture required large amounts of physical labor. In most places around the globe, farm families, except for those with far greater than average resources, lacked the wherewithal to draw strict gender lines between women and agricultural labor. Many had no desire to do so, seeing agriculture as part of the gendered work of women. In many places, women always had been, and continued to be, agricultural laborers. Families in continental Europe regularly employed female labor in the fields. Women in Mexico tended corn fields through all stages of production. East Asian women labored in the rice fields. It is only in the last fifty years since the second half of the twentieth century that many agricultural processes have yielded to mechanization, and the extent of mechanization varies enormously across crops and regions of the world.[23]

The mechanization of agriculture throughout the Western world has had a paradoxical effect on the working lives of women. On the one hand, mechanization has decreased the need for labor in general, and often, family labor specifically. Prior to the use of internal combustion engines on farms, a farm of 160 acres (the amount allotted to farmers under the Homestead Act in the United States) required the labors of a man, a woman, and their many children. There was plenty of work for all, and often too much work to easily accommodate children's very real needs for education and recreation. Work had to come first. With the development of more and larger machinery, very few families in the United States remained on 160-acre farms. Those farms are now significantly larger, and the application of mechanical power means that a single individual, at most times of the year, can manage the field labor. Dairy farms are notoriously labor-intensive, but with milking machines, it takes far less family labor to manage a herd of cows. Women's work, once integral to so many tasks and to caring for the many individuals who provided much of the essential labor on farms, had become less of a necessity.

On the other hand, mechanization had the capacity to overcome many of the strength requirements of traditional farm labor, thereby reducing the barriers to women doing more varieties of farm labor. Breaking land, plowing, and a number of other tasks associated with working the soil were arduous in the extreme when the only power available was human power, and the power of horses, mules, and oxen, which had to be controlled by their handler. When the power could come from internal combustion engines and hydraulics, a broader range of people became capable of the work. In the 1980s, sociologist Rachel Rosenfeld discovered that machines had encouraged some women to enter the field more consistently than they had in the past. Other forms of machines, such as automobiles and computers, also increased the participation of farm women in the running of their family enterprises. Automobiles allowed farm women to easily and quickly make trips into town to do the business of the farm, whether it was picking up a part or signing papers at the bank. The computer and various software packages designed for agricultural accounting allowed women to handle the business end of the farm more efficiently, while continuing their other tasks around the property.[24]

The automobile had another effect as well: it made it possible for farm women to support the family's business by working off the farm. This became increasingly critical in the late twentieth century as many farm families in the United States struggled to hold on to their land and their operations. During the farm crisis of the 1980s, roughly a third of US farms edged near, or fell into, economic ruin. In the 1970s, many families had taken advantage of high land prices to borrow against their equity and expand their operations. They had purchased new machines, new buildings, and, sometimes, more land. While crop and land prices remained high and interest rates reasonable, this was a relatively painless strategy. In the late 1970s, however, the situation began to change. Crop prices fell, interest rates soared, and land prices collapsed. By the middle of the decade, one-third of the farm families in the United States were facing the loss of their farms. In this situation, lenders and agricultural professionals suggested (and sometimes insisted) that the best solution to a family's financial woes would be to send someone, often the wife, out to work. Off-farm labor offered the possibility of a steady wage, and of benefits that farm families might not otherwise have had, like health insurance. Because women now had access to automobiles, traveling 10, 20, or even 30 miles a day to take a job in town seemed like a more reasonable proposition.

Migration and Women's Roles

In the twentieth century, migration played an integral role in the lives of women in agriculture. In the United States, this took the form of women leaving agriculture. Women had long felt the pinch of their economic position on the farm. Daughters did not generally inherit land and had fewer opportunities to earn their own money than their brothers did. As taste became increasingly homogeneous and consumer culture extended even into the countryside, they had less of a chance to participate. They also knew the kind of work that awaited them, should they decide to marry a farmer and remain in the countryside. The long round of milking, gardening and food preservation, and myriad other chores, punctuated by regular childbearing, allowed their mothers little time for themselves. Young women increasingly questioned whether or not that was a life that they wanted. Moving from countryside to city, for many young women, was the answer to the discontent they felt about agricultural life. As Joan Jensen explored in *Calling This Place Home*, cities such as Minneapolis and St. Paul beckoned young farm women away from a life in agriculture. They might not have opportunities for employment beyond domestic service or clerking in a department store, but the lighter labor and regular wages those jobs offered seemed preferable to the long hours and unremunerated labor represented by their parents' farms. Hence, young farm women chose to leave.[25] This trend did not reverse itself as the twentieth century progressed. Although many attitudes about the place of women changed over time, it was still the rare daughter who inherited the family farm. Additionally, urban employment opportunities for women multiplied, giving women who wanted to enter the paid workforce many more avenues to pursue.

In other parts of the world, large numbers of men have migrated away from farms. When times are hard, and when there is the promise of a job in another part of the country or the continent, men leave home and send money home to their wives and children. In many places, men have far greater access to paid employment and fewer social restrictions on their mobility. This has been the story true in places as diverse as China, India, and sub-Saharan Africa. Industrialization in China created a boom in opportunities in the nation's cities. Men migrated by the millions to places like Beijing and Shanghai, looking for work in construction and other trades. Wives and children stayed behind to tend the family plot and to care for the elderly in the countryside.[26] Throughout sub-Saharan Africa, men engaged in seasonal labor migrations to major cities, while women remained on farms in the hinterlands. AIDS then migrated from the cities to the countryside, with returning men, adding to the burdens of rural women.[27] In early twenty-first-century India, the situation has been particularly grim. Severe droughts have swept southern India, and the monsoon rains have failed to materialize. Men have migrated to cities looking for work, or killed themselves out of desperation. They have left women and children in the countryside, to grow support themselves as best they can, given the extreme environmental situation.[28]

Women's Land Ownership

In the United States of the twenty-first century, the migration might be going back in the other direction. In 2012, women owned 14 percent of the United States' 2.1 million farms. In the area of ranching, for example, women have increasingly moved into the role of owner and manager. In response to this trend, Beth Robinette, of Cheney, Washington, began operation of what she called New Cowgirl Camp, a five-day intensive course that teaches women the basics of animal husbandry, management, finances, and other necessities of managing ranchland. Because technology has eased the brute strength requirements of the job, women have been increasingly willing and able to take over operations as their brothers have chosen to abandon agriculture. New women ranchers cite changes in attitudes and technology, as well as the support of other women, as reasons for their choice to take up what is thought of as a traditionally male occupation.[29]

In the American Midwest, women have become an economic power to be reckoned with, as much of the land in this area has passed into the ownership of women. Traditionally, men inherited farmland. Today, much of it is in the hands of women, many of whom inherited it as widows. Some farm the land themselves, but many rent the land to tenants. In many cases, their own children have opted out of agriculture, taking jobs and pursuing careers in towns and cities. In the state of Iowa, more than 60 percent of rented land is in the ownership of women. As landlords, women could be instrumental in shaping the future of agriculture. Researchers found that many women held on to the land for sentimental reasons, and as such, had a strong commitment to its long-term health. In the early 2000s, a coalition including the Women, Food, and Agricultural Network, the USDA, and Iowa State University surveyed 1,500 women landholders. Those surveys showed that soil conservation was a strong priority. This may change the conditions owners set for tenants in the future. As one expert claimed, "women often are willing to give on finances to gain a half inch of topsoil. . . . Women totally get the idea of leaving a legacy."[30] To what degree the changing face of ownership will change the way that the United States farms remains to be seen. If the values that many women landholders claim are translated into action, it could have a powerful effect on the way in which land is managed and maintained.

Women and Agricultural Advocacy

Women have also been a strong voice for farm families in the United States, especially in the years since World War II. American farmers faced a cost-price squeeze that drove tens of thousands of them out of business. The cost of the goods they needed to run their farms was increasingly difficult to meet, given the low prices they received for their products. In the face of this situation, women organized to save their family farms. Most farm women did not describe themselves as feminists and felt unsure about becoming a public voice for agriculture. They were sure of their place within the structure of the family farm, and as concerned as their husbands about the pressing problems facing farm families. Women became active in more traditional agriculture groups, such as the Farm Bureau, as well as producer groups that promoted a single product. Whether they were promoting pork or talking about the agricultural economy in general, they found their voices promoting the health and success of their farms.[31]

This emphasis on advocacy extended into the difficult days of the 1980s, when the farm economy crashed to depths unseen since the Great Depression. Women were at the forefront of various heartland agricultural advocacy groups, such as PrairieFire and the Iowa Farm Unity Coalition. They were also at the forefront of telling the Farm Crisis story to the nation, even appearing in women's magazines, such as *Ladies Home Journal*, to explain to the magazine's readers why farm families were applying for food stamps. The problems of the decade demanded that women draw on their strengths and do what they had traditionally done—which was anything that was necessary to keep their family operations afloat. Sometimes that meant working harder on the farm, while men worked off, or working off the farm themselves. It could also mean organizing a crisis hotline, building a food bank, or helping register their neighbors for food aid.[32] When the crisis was behind them, they continued to advocate for change in agriculture, including the creation of new groups focused on women's role in the business of agriculture, such as the Women, Food, and Agriculture Network, an organization that provides networking and leadership opportunities, as well as education, for women interested in sustainable agriculture. Since 2011, the organization has sponsored a "Plate to Politics" program that helps to prepare farm women for leadership roles in local, state, and national politics, whether as farm advocates, or elected representatives.[33] They are training the next generation of agriculture's advocates.

Women in agriculture, past and present, number in the millions. They are and were agricultural laborers of all varieties. They worked for their husbands and fathers, and on their own behalf. They worked with their families, and on their own. Some were enslaved, while others owned their own bodies and their own labor. Many women have managed farms, some for husbands, but others for themselves. Few have owned their own land, but even so, because of their commitment to agriculture as a family enterprise, they have organized on behalf of farmers. As populations have moved and shifted, the number of women taking responsibility for farms has shifted as well. For some this has meant empowerment, while for others it has meant desperation. The story of agriculture is incredibly complex, and without the labor of women, entirely incomplete.

Notes

1. John Ise, *Sod and Stubble* (Lawrence: University Press of Kansas, 1996).
2. Deborah Reed-Danahay, "Sites of Memory: Women's Autoethnographies from Rural France," *Biography* 25, no. 1 (Winter 2002): 98–100.
3. Josephine Waggoner, *Witness: A Hunkpapha Historian's Strong-Heart Song of the Lakotas*, ed. Emily Levine (Lincoln: University of Nebraska Press, 2013): 238.
4. R. Douglas Hurt, *Indian Agriculture in America: Prehistory to Present* (Lawrence: University Press of Kansas, 1987): 34–37.
5. Barbara J. Roth, "The Role of Gender in the Adoption of Agriculture in the Southern Southwest," *Journal of Anthropological Research* 62, no. 1 (Winter 2006): 529–30.
6. William Cronon, *Changes in the Land: Indians, Colonists, and the Ecology of New England* (New York: Hill & Wang, 1983): 54–81.
7. Nicola Verdon, "'. . . Subjects Deserving of the Highest Praise': Farmers' Wives and the Farm Economy in England, c. 1700–1850," *Agricultural History Review* 51, no. 1 (2003): 27.
8. Ibid., 39.
9. Carolyn Sachs, *The Invisible Farmers: Women in Agricultural Production* (Totowa, NJ: Rowman & Littlefield, 1983).
10. Rachel Rosenfeld, *Farm Women: Work, Farm, and Family in the United States* (Chapel Hill: University of North Carolina Press, 1985): 245–46.
11. Deborah Fink, *Open Country, Iowa: Rural Women, Tradition, and Change* (Albany: State University of New York Press, 1986): 34–35.
12. Rebecca Sharpless, "Southern Women and the Land," *Agricultural History* 67, no. 2 (Spring 1993): 33.
13. Daina Ramey Berry, *Swing the Sickle for the Harvest Is Ripe: Gender and Slavery in Antebellum Georgia* (Urbana: University of Illinois Press, 2007): 82–86.
14. Jessica Parker Moore, "'Keeping All Hands Moving': A Plantation Mistress in Antebellum Arkansas," *Arkansas Historical Quarterly* 74, no. 3 (Autumn 2015): 258–59.
15. Ibid., 274–76.

16. Margaret Jarman Hagood, *Mothers of the South: Portraiture of the White Tenant Farm Woman* (Chapel Hill: University of North Carolina Press, 1939): 89.
17. Mary Neth, *Preserving the Family Farm: Women, Community, and the Foundations of Agribusiness in the Midwest, 1900–1940* (Baltimore: Johns Hopkins University Press, 1995): 17–39.
18. Carrie Young, *Prairie Cooks* (New York: HarperPerennial, 1997): 13–15.
19. Neth, *Preserving the Family Farm*, 102–3.
20. Ibid., 17–39.
21. Pamela Riney-Kehrberg, *Childhood on the Farm: Work, Play, and Coming of Age in the Midwest* (Lawrence: University Press of Kansas, 2005): 40–41.
22. Kate Hunter, *Father's Right-Hand Man: Women on Australia's Family Farms in the Age of Federation* (Melbourne: Australian Scholarly Publishing, 2004).
23. Useful resources on women in international agriculture, e.g., include Alan De Brauw, Qiang Li, Chengfang Liu, Scott Rozelle, and Linxiu Zhang, "Feminization of Agriculture in China? Myths Surrounding Women's Participation in Farming," *China Quarterly*, no. 194 (2008): 327–48; Ritu Agarwal, "Women Farmers in China's Commercial Agrarian Economy," *Economic and Political Weekly* 42, no. 42 (2007): 4261–67; Claudia Radel, "BECOMING FARMERS: Opening Spaces for Women's Resource Control in Calakmul, Mexico," *Latin American Research Review* 46, no. 2 (2011): 29–54; Marit S. Haugen and Berit Brandth, "Gender Differences in Modern Agriculture: The Case of Female Farmers in Norway," *Gender and Society* 8, no. 2 (1994): 206–29.
24. Katherine Jellison, *Entitled to Power: Farm Women and Technology, 1913–1963* (Chapel Hill: University of North Carolina Press, 1993): 182–84; Rachel Rosenfeld, *Farm Women: Work, Farm, and Family in the United States* (Chapel Hill: University of North Carolina Press, 1985): 144–47, 279.
25. Joan Jensen, *Calling This Place Home: Women on the Wisconsin Frontier, 1850–1925* (St. Paul: Minnesota Historical Society Press, 2006): 401–42.
26. Huifang Wu, Jing Rao, Baoyin Ding and Keyun Zhang, "Left-behind Women: Gender Exclusion and Inequality in Rural-Urban Migration in China," *Journal of Peasant Studies* 43, no. 4 (2016): 910–11.
27. Mark N. Lurie and Brian G. Williams, "Migration and Health in Southern Africa: 100 Years and Still Circulating," *Health Psychology and Behavior Medicine* 2 (2014): 34–40.
28. "India's Farmer Suicides Severely Affect Rural Women," *Deutsche Welle*, 2019, https://www.dw.com/en/indias-farmer-suicides-severely-affect-rural-women/a-46631519. accessed March 4.
29. Amy Chozick, "Female Ranchers Are Reclaiming the American West," *New York Times*, January 11, 2019.
30. Cheryl Tevis, "This Land Is Her Land," *Successful Farming*, September 5, 2012, https://www.agriculture.com/family/women-in-agriculture/farm-families/this-l-is-her-l_339-ar26202, accessed February 23, 2019..
31. Jenny Barker Devine, *On Behalf of the Family Farm: Iowa Farm Women's Activism since 1945* (Iowa City: University of Iowa Press, 2013).
32. Ibid., 137–38; Mark Friedberger, *Farm Families & Change in 20th-Century America* (Lexington: University of Kentucky Press, 1988), 218; Mark Friedberger, "Women Advocates in the Iowa Farm Crisis of the 1980s," *Agricultural History* 67 (Spring 1993): 224–34; "Harvest of Tears," *Ladies' Home Journal*, August 1985, 173.
33. Women, Food, and Agriculture Network, accessed February 23, 2019, http://www.wfan.org/.

Bibliography

Barker-Devine, Jenny. *On Behalf of the Family Farm: Farm Women's Activism since 1945.* Iowa City: University of Iowa Press, 2013.

Berry, Daina Ramey. *Swing the Sickle for the Harvest Is Ripe: Gender and Slavery in Antebellum Georgia.* Urbana: University of Illinois Press, 2010.

Fink, Deborah. *Open Country, Iowa: Rural Women, Tradition and Change.* Albany: State University of New York Press, 1986.

Hagood, Margaret Jarman. *Mothers of the South: Portraiture of the White Tenant Farm Woman* Chapel Hill: University of North Carolina Press, 1939.

Hunter, Kate. *Father's Right-Hand Man: Women on Australia's Family Farms in the Age of Federation.* Melbourne: Australian Scholarly Publishing, 2004.

Jellison, Katherine. *Entitled to Power: Farm Women and Technology, 1913–1963.* Chapel Hill: University of North Carolina Press, 1993.

Jensen, Joan. *Calling This Place Home: Women on the Wisconsin Frontier, 1850–1925.* St. Paul: Minnesota Historical Society Press, 2006.

Neth, Mary. *Preserving the Family Farm: Women, Community, and the Foundations of Agribusiness in the Midwest, 1900–1940.* Baltimore: Johns Hopkins University Press, 1998.

Osterud, Nancy Grey. *Bonds of Community: The Lives of Farm Women in Nineteenth Century New York.* Ithaca, NY: Cornell University Press, 1991.

Osterud, Grey. *Putting the Barn before the House: Women and Farming in Early Twentieth-Century New York.* Ithaca, NY: Cornell University Press, 2012.Rosenfeld, Rachel Ann. *Farm Women: Work, Farm and Family in the United States.* Chapel Hill: University of North Carolina Press, 1985.

Sachs, Caroline. *The Invisible Farmers: Women in Agricultural Production.* Totowa, NJ: Rowman & Littlefield, 1983

Sharpless, Rebecca. *Fertile Ground, Narrow Choices: Women on Texas Cotton Farms, 1900–1940.* Chapel Hill: University of North Carolina Press, 1999.

Verdon, Nicola. *Rural Women Workers in 19th Century England: Gender, Work and Wages.* New York: Boydell Press, 2002.

Walker, Melissa. *All We Knew Was to Farm: Rural Women in the Upcountry South, 1919–1941.* Baltimore: Johns Hopkins University Press, 2000.

PART II
MODERN ESSENTIALS

CHAPTER 9

MECHANIZATION IN AGRICULTURE

R. DOUGLAS HURT

AGRICULTURAL technology includes mechanized implements, but not all agricultural technology is mechanized, that is, not all farm equipment consists of machines with moving parts. Many aspects of American agriculture are mechanized, but the most important innovations have been the gasoline tractor and small grain harvesting and threshing equipment that culminated with the self-propelled grain combine. Tractor technology affected farmers across the nation, while harvesting and threshing machines primarily influenced agriculture in the Midwest and Far West during the late nineteenth and early twentieth centuries and the South after 1950. These hardware technologies also influenced the adoption, duplication, licensing, manufacturing, and distribution of American-made tractors and combines abroad. The development and adoption of these technologies depended on cumulative knowledge, perceived need, and affordability.

Since the classical age in Western Civilization, farmers have sought ways to harvest and thresh their grain crops more efficiently. Farmers could cut only about a half-acre of grain per day with a sickle and only two to three acres per day with a cradle scythe, as well as only thresh about 7 bushels of wheat and 18 bushels of oats with a flail during a ten-hour day. Two or three men, however, could thresh at least 30 bushels per day by treading the grain from the heads with horses. After threshing, farmers had to separate the chaff from the grain, usually with a winnowing basket. Harvesting, threshing, and winnowing proved to be hard, time-consuming work.[1]

The mechanization of the grain harvest occurred slowly and incrementally. By the American Revolution, some farmers used British fanning mills. American-made fanning mills became available by 1800. Fanning mills consisted of wooden paddles attached to a rod in an enclosed box. Farmers fed the threshed grain and chaff into the top. As the farmer turned the crank, the revolving fans blew away the chaff and the grain fell through screens to a basket below. By the late 1830s, hand-powered fanning mills had become standard implements wherever farmers raised wheat for sale. A fanning mill required three men for operation, one to turn the crank, one to pour the grain and chaff into the mill, and one to sack the grain. Farmers could clean 400 to 600 bushels in a ten-hour day.[2]

Farmers wanted a machine that would thresh, not merely winnow the grain from the chaff. During the 1820s, a few small, hand- and horse-powered threshing machines appeared on the market. Boston inventor John Pope built the most efficient threshing machine during that decade. This machine had a revolving belt that fed the cut grain into a cylinder with iron teeth that rotated and beat the grain from the heads. This threshing machine did not separate the grain from the straw and chaff, all of which fell to the ground ready for winnowing with a fanning mill. Although his machine was hand-powered at first, Pope added gearing that enabled farmers to use a treadmill or sweep to transfer horsepower to the threshing machine to drive the movable parts.[3]

In 1837, Hiram A. and John A. Pitts built a machine that threshed, separated the straw, and winnowed the chaff at once. The clean grain emptied into bags through a spout. A two-horse treadmill powered the machine. With the Pitts threshing machine, four men could thresh about 100 bushels per day with a two-horse team, a rate more than twice the threshing speed and capacity of the earlier machines. By the 1850s, grain farmers commonly used threshing machines, some of which threshed as many as 500 bushels per day. Threshing machines saved time, labor, and overall harvesting expense as well as prepared the crop for market as quickly as possible.[4]

Although fanning mills and threshing machines sped the grain harvest and reduced labor, farmers wanted an implement that cut grain. Small grains are time-sensitive for harvesting. In the case of wheat, the crop ripens in approximately ten days before it shatters from the heads. Consequently, the wheat acreage that a farmer can raise depends on the amount that he can harvest, not on the amount planted. Without a mechanical reaper, farmers could not substantially increase their grain crops in the absence of considerable harvest labor.

Mechanization of the grain harvest proved difficult because a cutting device had to slice through the stalks without clogging and shattering the grain heads. Not until 1831 did the age of mechanical grain harvesting begin when Cyrus Hall McCormick tested a reaper in Rockbridge County, Virginia. McCormick's reaper had a knife-like blade that oscillated and sawed through the grain stalks as the machine moved forward. Projecting fingers on the cutter bar guided the stalks to the sickle. The grains stalks fell onto a platform, and a worker raked them off for the binders that followed, tied the grain into sheaves, and placed them in shocks ready for threshing. On June 21, 1834, McCormick patented his reaper, but he did not offer it for sale until 1840.[5]

In the meantime, on July 2, 1833, Obed Hussey tested a reaper near Carthage, Ohio, which he patented on December 31. Hussey's reaper differed from McCormick's machine because it did not have a pickup reel to gather the stalks before the cutter bar, which consisted of a series of triangular steel plates riveted to a flat iron bar. The cutter bar reciprocated between slotted, spike-like fingers. Two horses provided draft power for the ground wheels that drove the gearing. The cut grain fell onto a platform for removal.[6]

By the early 1840s, both reapers cut cleanly, but Hussey's cut approximately one-fourth to one-third more per day. Both machines required relatively level fields free from obstructions, such as stumps or rocks. Hussey and McCormick continued to make technical improvements to their machines, and although Hussey's sickle, or cutter bar, proved superior, McCormick's reaper had a better design for draft and handling the cut grain. By the early 1850s, the mechanical reaper had become a viable, not experimental, harvesting machine. As early as 1858, tsarist Russia began importing McCormick reapers.[7]

Manufacturers continued to improve the reaper, particularly by adding a set of revolving rakes that oscillated and swept across the grain platform. These self-raking reapers eliminated one more worker from the grain harvest. With the driver now riding the reaper, only binders and shockers followed along to tie the sheaves and shock the crop before threshing. During the 1860s, the manufacture of mechanized, agricultural implements, particularly reapers, became transnational enterprises. Agricultural implement companies made American-style reaping machines in London, Berlin, Leipzig, Prague, Warsaw, Vienna, and Christ Church, among others, through licensing or pirating.[8]

Reapers enabled grain farmers to harvest larger crops faster and with less labor than with a cradle scythe. A reaper roughly replaced two to seven cradlers, who cut at a rate of two acres each per day. Two binders usually followed each cradler and several shockers trailed them. Fewer workers reduced labor costs. Reapers did not shatter the grain from the heads as readily as cradle scythes, and reaping machines cut the stalks close to the ground, which saved more straw for other uses. Farmers believed that reapers would pay for themselves in a year due to saved grain and reduced expenses for hired workers. By 1855, reapers had become a common sight in the wheat fields at harvest time. Wartime labor shortages and increased grain prices during the Civil War further encouraged farmers to adopt reaping machines. By the end of the war, reapers had reduced the number of workers required to harvest, bind, and shock from fourteen to eight. With a reaper, a farmer could harvest from 12 to 15 acres per day.[9]

The reaper, however, only cut grain; although some inventors had experimented with a mechanism that automatically bound the cut grain into sheaves by 1850, this problem proved difficult to solve because it required developing a mechanism that would either tie a knot in twine or twist a wire to hold a sheaf together. The first commercially successful binder did not appear until 1872, when Sylvanus D. Locke of Janesville, Wisconsin, developed an implement with a mechanism that cut a piece of wire from a spool, wound it around a sheaf, and twisted the ends to tie the band. In 1876, McCormick began manufacturing wire binders. These machines quickly became popular because they limited the need for binders.[10]

Mechanical binders could not harvest more acreage per day than a reaper given the horsepower requirements, and the wire created a disposal problem at threshing time. Other inventors continued their attempts to develop a mechanism that would tie a knot in a piece of twine strong enough to hold a gavel for shocking. As early as 1858, John

Appleby of Whitewater, Wisconsin, developed a knotting device, though he did not patent it until 1874. William Deering licensed it and added the mechanism to his binders in 1878. In 1881, McCormick began making twine binders and stopped manufacturing wire binders two years later. By the end of the decade, farmers used twine binders to harvest almost the entire wheat crop. The farm implement companies continued to improve the binder and added a bundle carrier. This device collected several sheaves until the operator tripped a lever that deposited them in a pile on the ground ready for shocking. This innovation saved steps for the shockers, reduced the number needed, and sped the harvest.[11]

Mechanical reapers in various forms saved time and labor expenses, but they did not increase the grain acreage that a farmer could harvest in a day. Between the widespread adoption of the hand-rake reaper in the 1840s and the twine binder in the 1880s, horses could not provide the consistent speed necessary to increase substantially the total acreage that a farmer could harvest in a day. Farmers would wait until the early twentieth century, when gasoline tractors provided the draft power to expand the binder's daily cutting capacity. Only then could grain farmers risk planting more acres with as much assurance as possible that they could harvest the crop in a timely fashion. By the late nineteenth century, many grain farmers also wanted to eliminate their need for shockers and threshing men. Farm women, who traditionally and culturally fed hired workers at harvest and threshing time, equally anticipated the further mechanization of the grain harvest.[12]

Large-capacity threshing machines also required more power than horses could provide for the smooth, consistent operation of the mechanisms that made these machines operate. Steam power resolved this problem for a brief period. During the early 1870s, movable steam engines began powering threshing machines. No one can precisely say when someone first used a steam engine for farm power. By the Civil War, Southern planters used steam engines to operate rice and sugar cane mills and cotton gins. Prior to the 1850s, farmers who used steam engines could not move them easily. Usually bolts held them to the floor and a belt linked them to the machines requiring power. Portable steam engines did not reach the market until the 1850s, thereby enabling grain farmers to adopt new power sources to make their work more efficient and easier, but not necessarily at a lower cost. By the late 1860s, some grain farmers used portable steam engines to operate threshing machines in the field. A steam-powered threshing machine could clean more than 100 bushels per hour. By 1880, farmers in all sections of the nation increasingly used steam engines to power threshing and milling equipment. At the turn of the twentieth century, steam engines powered machines that threshed as many as 3,000 bushels of wheat and 6,000 bushes of oats per day. These threshing machines and steam engines, however, proved too expensive for a farmer to purchase, but contract owner-operators with itinerant threshing crews circulated among farms at harvest time to thresh a farmer's crop. By 1900, however, steam power proved less than satisfactory, but it provided another important transition in the mechanization of the grain harvest.[13]

Tractors

Although steam engines increased the speed and efficiency of threshing machines, they could not at first move under their own power. Threshing crews had to pull them from place to place with horses, and farmers could only use them to power threshing, grinding, milling, and ginning machines. In 1873, the Battle Creek, Michigan, firm of Merritt and Kellogg produced the first traction steam engine in the United States. A decade later, most of the threshing machine manufacturers also built steam traction engines. These steam engines weighed from 10 to 20 tons, far beyond the support capacity of many bridges, while their lugged, iron wheels damaged roads. By the mid-1880s, however, self-propelled steam engines met the threshing needs of most grain farmers.[14]

The early self-propelled steam traction engines were not strong enough to pull a plow. Farmers in the Great Plains and Far West wanted steam engines that would speed tillage by pulling a gang of plows. Although steam traction engines could move from field to field relatively easily, agricultural implement companies had difficulty building a steam engine for tillage. Engineers used the steam engine's weight to generate traction, but the cast iron gears could not withstand the strain when plowing. During the 1870s, implement manufacturers began using Bessemer steel for the gears, which enabled the transfer of more power to the wheels for pulling equipment. Implement manufacturers touted their steam-traction engines for their power, speed, and performance with advertisements hailing them as the "Conqueror," "Little Giant," and "Champion," among others.[15]

By the 1890s, giant steam-traction engines plowed the wheat lands of large-scale farms in the American West. Some steam engines weighed as much as 25 tons and with 120-horsepower easily plowed from 35 to 45 acres per day. On the largest wheat farms in the West, often called Bonanza farms, giant steam-traction engines pulled plows, harrows, and seed drills at the rate of 3 or 4 miles per hour and covered 100 acres per day. These implements easily replaced forty to fifty teams of horses and accompanying men and implements. Steam traction engines, as would be true with the later development of gas tractors, however, required implement manufactures to redesign tillage implements with steel. Horse-drawn implements could withstand draft power of about one and a half miles per hour. The comparatively high speed of steam traction engines easily caused wood and iron implements to break or scatter the furrow slices when plowing.[16]

By the turn of the twentieth century, implement manufacturers produced more than 5,000 steam traction engines annually, with the J. I. Case and Huber Companies building the most implements, but steam-traction engines did not meet the tillage needs of small-scale grain farmers. The steam-traction engine peaked in popularity between 1908 and 1915, but only one in twenty farmers owned a steam tractor. By World War I, then, steam-traction engines proved superior to horses but they remained too large, heavy, and un-maneuverable in small spaces as well as expensive. Fortunately, for the

American farmer the development of a light, affordable gasoline-powered tractor had reached a marketable stage of development. Steam-traction engines had always been iron dinosaurs in size, now they, too, became extinct for farm work.[17]

Farmers needed more consistent power than what horses and mules could provide and more suitable and economical draft power than steam tractors. They needed a power source that would not tire during the day while consistently driving the gears of large threshing machines or pulling tillage and seeding equipment. In 1889, the Charter Gas Engine Company of Sterling, Illinois, produced the first internal combustion tractor in the United States, but it could not pull a plow. Three years later John Froelich, an Iowa inventor, mounted a gasoline engine on a wood and steel frame and attached traction gearing. This implement became the first mechanically successful gas tractor produced in the United States, and it powered a threshing machine that year. By the turn of the twentieth century, mechanical engineers worked to replace steam boilers with internal combustion engines. No other power source influenced American agriculture more than the internal combustion engine and gas tractor.[18]

Froelich's gas tractor introduced fundamental change to the mechanization of American agriculture. Steam engines required two to three workers to operate, while a gas tractor required only one, the driver. Gas tractors carried their own fuel and water. At first, gas engines merely replaced the boiler on a steam traction engine. The heavy iron frame, often weighing 10 tons, made the gas tractor as difficult to maneuver as steam traction engines. Even so, farm implement manufacturers sold gas tractors soon after the turn of the twentieth century. In 1905, the Hart-Parr Company began using the term "tractor" to replace the designation of "gasoline traction engine." Farmers, implement dealers, and manufacturers soon adopted the term. The Hart-Parr Company led the competition in tractor development during the first decade of the twentieth century.[19]

The early gas tractors built by any company proved unreliable, expensive, and gigantic. Farmers sensibly took a wait-and-see approach to tractor development and used their horses for farm power. While they waited, implement manufacturers worked to reduce the weight and improve the gearing. In 1910, the International Harvester Company built about one-third of these implements. These tractors were "shop made." Mass, assembly-line production remained in the future. High costs, design problems, and size limited these gas tractors to large-scale wheat farms in the Great Plains and Far West. Although gas tractors proved suitable only for drawbar work, that is, pulling, and powering threshing machines, they did not meet the needs of small-scale, row-crop farmers. Most farmers harvested fewer than 50 acres of grain annually. Soon these mammoth gas tractors went the way of the traction steam engine.[20]

In 1913, the Bull Tractor Company built a tractor that it hailed as the "Bull with a Pull." It produced 12 horsepower for belt work and 5 horsepower for drawbar work, with models ranging from $395 to $400. At this time, the Wallis "Cub," a tricycle-designed tractor, became the first "frameless" tractor because the manufacturing company replaced the heavy iron frame by using the crankshaft and transmission housing to hold the engine. By 1915, farm implement manufacturers had reduced the weight of some tractors to 3,000 pounds. These tractors could pull two plows and replace three horses. Still, gas tractors remained too expensive and unsuitable for row-crop farming. Agricultural engineers looked to the automobile manufactures to help solve their problems. Small-scale farmers needed a tractor for plowing, cultivation, and powering various implements, such as threshing machines. They had a need, and cumulative knowledge helped engineers improve gas tractor technology and reduce the price of the implement.[21]

Henry Ford now entered the field of tractor development. Ford believed that he could adapt assembly-line, automobile technology to tractor production and tap a new market. Ford built his first tractor between 1906 and 1908 with parts cobbled from various automobile designs, but it did not have enough power to pull a plow. Success did not come quickly. Not until April 1917 did Ford market a lightweight, low-cost, two-plow tractor, which he called the Fordson. Weighing only 2,500 pounds and standing less than five feet tall with an affordable price of $750, the Fordson achieved immediate success. Ford used his automotive dealerships to sell the tractors, and a farm labor and workhorse shortage stimulated purchases after World War I.[22]

In 1917, Ford established a tractor manufacturing plant in Cork, Ireland, where workers assembled tractors from imported parts. A safe port, cheap and available labor, and easy transport to England gave him the opportunity to expand tractor production abroad. The first Fordson built in Cork came off the assembly line in July 1919. During the war, Canadian farmers began using American tractors, though not in great numbers. Even though the government imported and distributed Fordsons for the wholesale price of $795, prairie farmers preferred the reliability and lower cost of horses. The British government also imported Fordson tractors for only £150, plus freight. It also bought several thousand American binders. By the mid-1920s, Ford controlled 75 percent of the tractor market in the United States, and the frameless Fordson became the first mass-produced tractor.[23]

Still, the Fordson had many flaws. It proved too light and underpowered for farmers who wanted to pull three or four plows instead of two. Most important, the front end reared up and sometimes caused the tractor to overturn whenever the drawbar encountered moderate resistance. Even so, the Fordson showed the viability of small, affordable tractors that met the power needs of small-scale farmers. Moreover, as farmers substituted tractor power for horse power, they could raise more commercial grain crops instead of forage and feed crops because a horse required about 5 acres for hay, oats, and forage during the year. Unlike a horse, if a tractor did not operate it did not need food, that is, fuel. In addition, tractors did not require rest or much care, although repairs often required skilled mechanics. Tractors started easier than steam traction engines, shut off easily, and did not emit sparks that could set a grain field on fire.[24]

Tractors, however, still proved inadequate for most row-crop farmers who needed to cultivate corn, cotton, or vegetables. Farmers found that they could not easily use it to pull a cultivator and turn at the end of a field without smashing the plants. They needed a tractor whose wheels could move between the rows without damaging the crop. As a result, by the early 1920s, gas tractors remained primarily restricted to the Midwest and Great Plains, where farmers used them for plowing and powering threshing machines.

Farmers still awaited a tractor that could plow, pull a cultivator between crop rows, and power threshing machines and other equipment, all at an affordable price.[25]

In 1924, the International Harvester Company (IHC) produced the technological breakthrough that soon made the Fordson obsolete for many farmers. IHC called this tractor the Farmall and designed it for row-crop agriculture with its tricycle design and low cost. Two small front wheels traveled between the plant rows while the high axle permitted the larger rear wheels to straddle the furrows and plants. The Farmall could turn sharply, and it soon proved a favorite of small-scale farmers. Tractor manufacturers quickly offered all-purpose tractors such as the Farmall. The Farmall did more to prove the value and versatility of the tractor to mechanize farming than any other implement nationwide.[26]

During the 1920s, four important innovations improved the performance and versatility of tractors. In 1922, the International Harvester Company under the McCormick-Deering trade name marketed an implement with a power-take-off (PTO) system. This gearing transferred the tractor's engine power to various implements whose moving parts required considerable and consistent power. The PTO drove the mechanisms of binders, corn pickers, and mowers. In time, the PTO also drove the gears of combines. Power-take-off gearing made tractors truly "all-purpose" implements. In 1927, farm implement manufacturers standardized the size and shaft fittings, speed, and rotational direction of the gearing so that tractors and implements would be interchangeable.[27]

In 1928, the mechanization of agriculture further advanced when John Deere added a power lift that enabled the driver to raise plows, discs, and cultivators from the ground without leaving the seat of the tractor. This improvement made turning easier at the end of a crop row and the tractor more maneuverable in small fields. The power lift also lessened a farmer's physical labor from getting up and down from the tractor to raise and lower an implement at the beginning or end of each row to make a turn. In 1932, Allis-Chalmers added pneumatic tires to replace the iron, lugged wheels. Farmers could now use tractors to pull wagons and other equipment on public roads without damaging the surface. Pneumatic tires also produced a smoother ride, reduced fuel costs, and further eliminated the need for draft horses on the farm. In 1939, Henry Ford became the first American manufacturer to use the "three-point hitch" of Belfast inventor Harry Ferguson. This hitch used hydraulic power to keep the plow or cultivator at a preset depth. It also regulated the downward thrust on the rear wheels and enabled more efficient use of the engine's power.[28]

On the eve of World War II, the corn and cash grain farmers in the Midwest and Great Plains primarily used tractors because the relatively level terrain enabled the complete mechanization of grain farming from pulling plows, grain drills, and corn pickers to powering threshing machines and later combined harvester-threshers or "combines." Southern farmers more slowly adopted tractors because they had an affordable, cheap labor supply, and tobacco and rice crops proved particularly challenging for the use of tractors. By the end of World War II, the gas tractor had become the undisputed source of motive power on British, Canadian, and American farms. As a result, tractors also contributed to the reduction of workhorses on American farms. In 1955, the number of tractors on farms exceeded horses, and the federal government soon stopped counting horses because their numbers had become insignificant for draft power.[29]

The tractor enabled farmers to plant and harvest more acreage with less labor than with horse-powered implements. Farmers perceived a need and, if they operated on a large enough commercial scale to afford a tractor, they readily purchased this implement, which they then used to mechanize further their farming operations. Tractors became symbols of progressive farming. Farm mechanization with tractors, however, also brought problems of soil compaction and overextension of credit for investments in this new technology and for the purchase of more land on which to use it. The time that farmers saved by using a tractor did not usually transfer into leisure time. Rather, it merely made more time available for other work. With tractors, farmers increasingly specialized in one or two crops. By planting more acres of one crop, farmers also created surpluses, which lowered grain prices and their income unless they could increase production by planting more acres or, after 1933, by participating in various price-support programs of the federal government. Diversified farming disappeared. Tractors also decreased the need for hired workers, tenants, and sharecroppers. Whether those agricultural workers improved their economic positions after being tractored off the land, no one can precisely say. Tractors, however, equalized the gender divisions of farm work. Many farm women enjoyed tractor work, and thereby freed their husbands and sons for other farm tasks. Farm sizes also increased and the agricultural population declined. The farmers who remained generally agreed that tractors save their legs from traipsing in a plowed furrow behind a horse, and it extended their working lives as farmers. The tractor did not solve the problems of agriculture, and it created new challenges, but it played the major role in the mechanization of farming.[30]

Combines

Once farmers had access to efficient reapers and later binders as well as threshing machines, they anticipated an implement that would mechanize the grain harvest and threshing process in one combined operation. Nearly a century would pass, however, before implement companies developed an affordable, efficient combine. On June 28, 1836, not long after Hussey and McCormick patented their reapers and about the same time that the Pitts brothers experimented with their threshing machine, Hiram Moore patented the first relatively successful combine. This huge machine extended 27 feet from the end of the cutter bar and pickup reel to the outside of the machine. Moore's combined reaper thresher required twenty horses to power the working parts and six men to operate the machine with other workers needed to haul the grain bagged on the combine to the barn or granary. By 1843, Moore believed that he had perfected his combine to cut and thresh 25 acres of grain per day. Moore's combine, however, proved too large, unwieldy, and inefficient for small-scale grain agriculture in the Midwest, where farmers could use a two-horse reaper to cut 12 to 15 acres per day in humid conditions. Reapers and binders also cost about $150, while Moore offered his combined for $500.[31]

At the turn of the twentieth century, inventors and farm implement companies continued to develop a combine that would be suitable for wheat farmers in the Midwest, California, Oregon, and Washington. By the end of World War I, some Great Plains farmers began using combines that made a 12–16 foot cut with the gears powered not by a ground wheel and horses but by an auxiliary gasoline engine attached to the machine to drive the working parts. The gas engines generated consistent and uniform power that horses could not provide. The postwar agricultural recession slowed adoption of these small combines, but Great Plains wheat farmers had already made a commitment to mechanization with the adoption of threshing machines and tractors. They had a need for more efficient harvesting, and they adopted combines if they could afford them.[32]

Combine harvesting required a three-man crew—a tractor driver, combine operator, and a grain hauler. By reducing the number of workers required for harvesting and threshing, farmers reduced their hired labor costs. With a tractor and combine, a farmer no longer required hired help to gather the binder's sheaves into shocks and a crew at threshing time. Midwestern wheat farmers, however, needed at least 100 acres of grain by the mid-1920s to make the combine affordable. Combines, however, collected more grain than any other machine, and its combined labor costs for harvesting and threshing averaged about three times less than for harvesting and threshing separately in 1925. More grain at the elevator and less labor expense meant an increased income for farmers. Moreover, a 15-foot combine could harvest from 35 to 40 acres per day. The combine's harvesting speed reduced the chance of loss from bad weather as well as encouraged farmers to expand production by planting more acres because they could harvest a larger crop. Wheat farmers believed that these advantages merited investment in combines. By 1929, observers expected Great Plains farmers to harvest about 75 percent of their winter wheat crop with combines.[33]

The mechanization of Canadian agriculture corresponded to the lengthy American transition from steam engines to gas tractors. In 1912, several Alberta farmers used tractor-powered Holt combines imported from the United States to harvest wheat and a year later flax. Combines with pickup reels that collected a swath of grain from windrows improved threshing performance with grain cut not fully ripe and damp given the climate. During the early 1920s, the American firms of J. I. Case and International Harvester tested and sold combines in Saskatchewan, and tractors and combines eventually became the leading implements of Canadian agriculture.[34]

Although the Great Depression and World War II slowed tractor and combine sales, more farmers purchased these implements when the war ended. High wartime prices gave farmers disposable income, and tractors and combines saved physical labor and expenses as well as guarded against labor deficiencies at harvest time. During the mid-1940s, self-propelled combines eliminated the need of a tractor, auxiliary gas engine, or power-take-off to operate the machine. By removing the tractor from the harvest, farmers gained another implement for other work. Tractors also used more fuel than the less powerful combine engines. Self-propelled combines proved more maneuverable than tractor-pulled machines, both in the field and down country roads. Most important, only two people could now harvest the crop, one to drive the combine and another to haul the gain to a storage bin or the local elevator for sale. Farmers saved labor expenses because family members usually provided this unpaid labor, often with the wife serving as the truck driver.[35]

The mechanization of Soviet agriculture occurred at a slower pace due to wars, revolution, and a political system that collectivized farms. During the mid-1920s, American agricultural experts demonstrated the use of tractors in the Soviet Union. The first Fordsons arrived in 1923 and, in 1925 the Soviets purchased American tractors in record numbers. They also increasingly bought combines. More purchases followed primarily from the International Harvester, Ford, John Deere, Case, and Allis-Chalmers companies until 1933, when imports practically ceased, although American firms continued to provide technical assistance to help the Soviet Union to mechanize its agriculture. Tractors sped the process of collectivization but not Soviet grain production. Until the mid-1930s, most tractors in the Soviet Union had been manufactured in the United States or the Russians tried to build American tractors from copied models.[36]

Change came slowly. The relatively high cost of investments in tractor-dawn combines slowed the wide-scale adoption of self-propelled combines. Although most American wheat farmers harvested their crop with combines by the end of World War II, tractor-drawn models predominated until 1960. Whether tractor-drawn or self-propelled, however, combines became more versatile. Soybeans, for example, primarily served as a forage or nurse crop to return nitrogen to the soil. When cut with a binder or combine, however, the beans shattered from the pods. By the early 1930s, improved cutter bars and pickup reels began to solve this problem, but combined harvesting of soybeans did not become efficient until 1977, when seed losses fell to about 1 percent.[37]

Mechanization of the corn harvest also took time to overcome technical difficulties. Combines had to cut and thresh tough, large plants. This required considerable power and a cutting and threshing mechanism that would not clog. The Great Depression and World War II slowed innovation and large-scale production of corn combines that picked, husked, and shelled. Until self-propelled combines for harvesting corn appeared in 1946, farmers continued to cut the stalks by hand or use a tractor-driven corn picker that snapped the ears from the stalk for mechanical shelling later. In 1954, however, the Deere & Company developed a corn head for attachment to a combine. It enabled farmers to cut two rows at once, but corn combines required as much as five times more power than machines that harvested small grains. The chassis also required greater strength, all of which increased costs. By the late twentieth century, however, farmers used combines to harvest wheat, grain sorghum, soybeans, and corn, as well as sunflowers and other small grains. Moreover, tractors and combines had become symbols of capital-intensive, technologically sophisticated, mechanized agriculture. By the early twenty-first century, manufacturers had equipped tractors with GPS satellite guidance systems to regulate automatically plowing, seeding, and fertilizer applications based on changing soil structures and conditions.[38]

Demographic change also encouraged farmers to adopt mechanized agricultural technology. In 1900, 29.8 million people, or approximately 42 percent of the American population, lived on farms. The farm population declined further until the Great Depression caused many men and women to return to their family farm until employment opportunities improved. By 1940, wartime industrial and military demands, however, began luring many from the farms, and most did not return. The farm population fell to 24.4 million, or 17.5 percent of the population, by the mid-1940s. In 2000, it had declined to 4.4 million, or 1.6 percent of the total population. The decline continued and, by 2012, only 1 million people declared farming as their primary occupation, although another million remained part-time farmers.[39]

Those who stayed on the farms particularly after World War II increasingly used new or improved technologies to replace departed farm workers. As many farmers moved to urban areas for better economic opportunities, others purchased their land and expanded operations, which required more labor. Agricultural technology proved more readily available than human labor, and farm wages proved too low to keep many workers engaged in agricultural work. Moreover, farmers could purchase agricultural technology on credit, amortize the cost over time, and thereby eliminate the need for ready cash to pay wages. Agricultural technology did not alone cause the decline of the farm population, but it served as a contributing factor.

The mechanization of American agriculture also brought worldwide recognition to the United States as the leader in the development of agricultural technology. Mechanized implements such as tractors and combines eased the physical work of farmers, saved labor costs, expanded cultivated acreage, and sped the harvest, as well as made many agricultural jobs more efficient. Mechanized farm implements also helped encourage the consolidation of farms, but it also contributed to increased farm indebtedness, among other problems. In time, farms became larger and fewer in number. Farms also became more specialized and less diversified, particularly in the Great Plains and Midwest. When the farm population declined, small-town businesses, churches, and schools suffered from the loss of customers, members, tax money, and students.

In addition, mechanized agriculture created a mindset on the part of manufacturers, farmers, and politicians that American technological superiority could be exported to make other nations modern and, in some cases, civilized. In this context, the world needed mechanized farming. The international adoption of American agricultural technology would inevitably bring progress and prosperity to other nations. Mechanized agricultural equipment had transformed the American farm economy and helped create a modern nation. American mechanized farm implements represented science, progress, and transnational assistance that would lead to economic independence for those nations that acquired it as well as corporate profits for those who sold it. The global reach of American agricultural technology and the companies that manufactured it became a form of economic "global manifest destiny," a matter of historical inevitability that would contribute to the positioning of the United States as the world's leader in economic and political affairs. American mechanized agricultural technology, then, could help modernize "underdeveloped" countries and promote the establishment of capitalist market economies dominated by the United States that would, in turn, provide resources, discourage communism, and promote political and economic ties with the United States.[40]

The mechanization of American agriculture with gasoline tractors and ultimately self-propelled grain combines are not the only mechanized implements that have helped make American farmers the most productive and prosperous in the world. Cotton pickers, tomato and sugar cane harvesters, and grain drills, among other implements, have helped meet the needs of farmers. In terms of hardware technology, however, the gasoline tractor and combine have influenced American agriculture on the broadest scale. For large-scale farmers with sufficient capital and credit to afford them, mechanized implements have improved their productivity and efficiency and benefited the quality of farm life.

Notes

1. John T. Schlebecker, *Whereby We Thrive: A History of American Farming, 1607–1972* (Ames: Iowa State University Press, 1975), 113; R. Douglas Hurt, *American Agriculture: A Brief History*, rev. ed. (West Lafayette, IN: Purdue University Press, 2002): 58–60.
2. Leo Rogin, *The Introduction of Farm Machinery in Its Relation to the Productivity of Labor in the Agriculture of the United States during the Nineteenth Century* (Berkeley: University of California Press, 1931), 155–57; Peter D. McClelland, *Sowing Modernity: America's First Agricultural Revolution* (Ithaca, NY: Cornell University Press, 1997): 190–91.
3. Rogin, *The Introduction of Farm Machinery in Its Relation to the Productivity of Labor*, 162–63.
4. Ibid., 165–66, 168, 170; Schlebecker, *Whereby We Thrive*, 119.
5. McClelland, *Sowing Modernity*, 152–55; Rogin, *The Introduction of Farm Machinery in Its Relation to the Productivity of Labor*, 72–74, 85.
6. Rogin, *The Introduction of Farm Machinery in Relation to the Productivity of Labor*, 85–87; Percy Wells Bidwell and John I. Falconer, *History of Agriculture in the Northern United States, 1620–1860* (New York: Peter Smith, 1941): 287.
7. Rogin, *The Introduction of Farm Machinery in Relation to the Productivity of Labor*, 87–91; Schlebecker, *Whereby We Thrive*, 114–15; Cyrus McCormick, *The Century of the Reaper* (Boston: Houghton Mifflin, 1931): 56, 122, 133; Dana G. Dalrymple, "American Technology and Soviet Agricultural Development, 1924–1933," *Agricultural History* 40 (July 1966): 192.
8. Rogin, *The Introduction of Farm Machinery in Relation to the Productivity of Labor*, 95–100; Gordon M. Winder, "A Trans-National Machine on the World Stage: Representing McCormick's Reaper through World's Fairs, 1851–1902," *Journal of Historical Geography* 33 (April 1, 2007): 359–63, 375.
9. Schlebecker, *Whereby We Thrive*, 117–18.
10. Ibid., 117; Rogin, *The Introduction of Farm Machinery in Relation to the Productivity of Labor*, 111.
11. Rogin, *The Introduction of Farm Machinery in Relation to the Productivity of Labor*, 115–18; Schlebecker, *Whereby We Thrive*, 190.
12. Hurt, *American Agriculture*, 197.

13. Schlebecker, *Whereby We Thrive*, 193–94; Reynold M. Wik, *Steam Power on the American Farm* (Philadelphia: University of Pennsylvania Press, 1953): 5, 24, 39–42.
14. Wik, *Steam Power on the American Farm*, 75–76.
15. Ibid., 181.
16. Ibid., 87, 94; Schlebecker, *Whereby We Thrive*, 248–49.
17. Jeremy Adelman, "The Social Basis of Technological Change: Mechanization of the Wheat Lands of Argentina and Canada, 1890 to 1914," *Comparative Studies in Society and History* 34 (April 1992): 287–88, 294–95.
18. Schlebecker, *Whereby We Thrive*, 201–2; C. H. Wendel, *Encyclopedia of American Farm Tractors* (Sarasota, FL: Crestline: 1975): 2.
19. Schlebecker, *Whereby We Thrive*, 202; R. B. Gray, *The Agricultural Tractor, 1855–1950*, pt. 1 (St. Joseph, MI: American Society of Agricultural Engineers, 1975): 18, 23, 28; Philip Rose, "Farm Tractors: A Review of Their History, Condition of Use and Methods of Construction," *Scientific American Supplement* 18 (April 29, 1916): 282; Robert C. Williams, *Fordson, Farmall, and Poppin' Johnny: A History of the Farm Tractor and Its Impact on America* (Urbana: University of Illinois Press, 1987): 17; Reynold M. Wik, "Henry Ford's Tractors in American Agriculture," *Agricultural History* 38 (April 1964): 81. The first use of the word tractor occurred in an 1890 patent.
20. Rose, "Farm Tractors," 282; Schlebecker, *Whereby We Thrive*, 204; Williams, *Fordson, Farmall, and Poppin' Johnny*, 18–19.
21. Williams, *Fordson, Farmall, and Poppin' Johnny*, 9–10, 25; E. I. Baker, "A Quarter Century of Tractor Development," *Agricultural Engineering* 12 (June 1931): 206.
22. R. M. Wik, *Henry Ford and Grassroots America* (Ann Arbor: University of Michigan Press, 1972): 92; Williams, *Fordson, Farmall, and Poppin' Johnny*, 48; Wik, "Henry Ford's Tractors," 80, 83; Wendel, *Encyclopedia of American Farm Tractors*, 113; John T. Schlebecker, "Henry Ford's Tractor," *Smithsonian Journal of History* 2 (Summer 1967): 63, 55.
23. D. S. Jacobson, "The Political Economy of Industrial Location: The Ford Motor Company at Cork, 1912–26," *Irish Economic and Social History* 4 (December 1977): 36, 43–45, 50, 53, 55; Robert E. Ankli, H. Don Halsberg, and John Herd Thompson, "The Adoption of the Gasoline Tractor in Western Canada," *Canadian Papers in Rural History* 2 (1980): 12; Peter Dewey, *"Iron Harvests of the Field": The Making of Farm Machinery in Britain since 1800* (Lancaster, UK: Carnegie Publishing, 2008): 175–78; John Herd Thompson, *The Harvests of War: The Prairie West, 1914–1981* (Toronto: McClelland & Stewart, 1978), 63–65.
24. Ankli, Halsberg, and Thompson, "The Adoption of the Gasoline Tractor in Western Canada," 13–15; Wik, *Henry Ford and Grassroots America*, 94–95; Wik, "Henry Ford's Tractors," 83–84, 86; Williams, *Fordson, Farmall, and Poppin' Johnny*, 49, 54.
25. Williams, *Fordson, Farmall, and Poppin' Johnny*, 71–72, 76–77; D. C. Heitshu, "The Requirements of the General Purpose Farm Tractor," *Agricultural Engineering* 10 (May 1929): 155.
26. Gray, *The Agricultural Tractor*, pt. 2, 9; Williams, *Fordson, Farmall, and Poppin' Johnny*, 90.
27. Williams, *Fordson, Farmall, and Poppin' Johnny*, 62–65; Alan I. Marcus and Howard P. Segal, *Technology in America*, 3rd ed. (London: Palgrave, 2018): 195; Heitshu, "The Requirements of the General-Purpose Farm Tractor," 155. In 1922, the McCormick-Deering Company marketed the 15-30 model tractor with a PTO. This tractor probably was the first implement designed specifically with a PTO system.

28. Gray, *The Agricultural Tractor*, pt. 2, 15–16; Colin Fraser, *Tractor Pioneer: The Life of Harry Ferguson* (Athens: Ohio University Press, 1973): 67–73, 109–19; Williams, *Fordson, Farmall, and Poppin' Johnny*, 91, 93, 103.
29. Gilbert C. Fite, *American Farmers: The New Minority* (Bloomington: Indiana University Press, 1981): 70; Schlebecker, *Whereby We Thrive*, 251–52; *Historical Statistics of the United States: Colonial Times to 1970*, pt. 1 (Washington, DC: Government Printing Office, 1975): 511, 517, 519; Williams, *Fordson, Farmall, and Poppin' Johnny*, 96.
30. Fite, *American Farmers*, 184; Williams, *Fordson, Farmall, and Poppin Johnny*, 131–34, 137, 157, n178–79; 205; John L. Shover, *First Majority—Last Minority: The Transformation of Rural Life in America* (DeKalb: University of Northern Illinois Press: 1976): 149.
31. Rogin, *The Introduction of Farm Machinery in Relation to the Productivity of Labor*, 120–23.
32. Thomas D. Isern, *Custom Combining on the Great Plains: A History* (Norman: University of Oklahoma Press, 1981): 13, 15; L. A. Reynoldson, "The Combined Harvester-Thresher in the Great Plains," US Department of Agriculture, *Technical Bulletin*, no. 70 (1928): 3.
33. Reynoldson, "The Combined Harvester-Thresher in the Great Plains," 37, 51–52; W. F. MacGregor, "The Combined Harvester-Thresher," *Agricultural Engineering* 6 (May 1925): 103; W. E. Grimes, "The Effect of the Combined Harvester-Thresher on Farming in a Wheat-Growing Region," *Scientific Agriculture* 9 (August 1929): 773.
34. R. Bruce Shepard, "Tractors and Combines in the Second Stage of Agricultural Mechanization of the Canadian Plains," *Prairie Forum* 11 (Fall 1986): 253–63, 266; Ankli, Halsberg, and Thompson, "The Adoption of the Gasoline Tractor in Western Canada," 9, 35.
35. Schlebecker, *Whereby We Thrive*, 297.
36. Dana G. Dalrymple, "The American Tractor Comes to the Soviet Union: The Transfer of Technology," *Technology and Culture* 5 (Spring 1964): 191, 193–96, 213; Debora Fitzgerald, *Every Farm a Factory: The Industrial Ideal in American Agriculture* (New Haven, CT: Yale University Press, 2003): 163; Norton T. Dodge and Dana G. Dalrymple, "The Stalingrad Tractor Plant in Early Soviet Planning," *Soviet Studies* 18 (October 1966): 65, 168; Dalrymple, "American Technology and Soviet Agricultural Development," 192–98.
37. Tom Carroll, "Basic Requirements in the Design and Development of the Self-Propelled Combine," *Agricultural Engineering* 29 (March 1948): 101; Schlebecker, *Whereby We Thrive*, 297; Graeme Quick and Wesley Buchele, *The Grain Harvesters* (St. Joseph, MI: American Society of Agricultural Engineers, 1978): 225–32.
38. Schlebecker, *Whereby We Thrive*, 252; Quick and Buchele, *The Grain Harvesters*, 221–22.
39. United States Department of Commerce, Bureau of the Census, *Historical Statistics of the United States Colonial Times to 1970*, Bicentennial Edition, pt. 1 (Washington, D.C.: Government Printing Office, 1975): 457; United States Department of Agriculture, *Agricultural Statistics, 2001* (Washington, D. C.: Government Printing Office, 2001): IX-2; United States Department of Agriculture, *Census of Agriculture*, vol. 1, table 1 (Washington, D. C.: Government Printing Office, 2014): 7.
40. Mona Domosh, "International Harvester, the U.S. South, and the Makings of International Development in the Early 20th Century," *Political Geography* 49 (November 2015): 18–20, 27; Winder, "A Trans-National Machine on the World Stage," 353–54; Anand Mehta and Andrew C. Gross, "The Global Market for Agricultural Machinery and Equipment," *Business Economics* 42 (October 2007): 66–73; Carroll Pursell, *Technology in Postwar America: A History* (New York: Columbia University Press: 2007): 46–47.

Bibliography

Danhof, Clarence H. *Change in Agriculture: The Northern United States, 1820–1870*. Cambridge, MA: Harvard University Press, 1969.

David, Paul A. "The Mechanization of Reaping in the Ante-Bellum Midwest." In *Industrialization in Two Systems: Essays in Honor of Alexander Gerschenkron*, edited by Henry Rosovsky, 3–39. New York: John Wiley, 1966.

Fitzgerald, Deborah. *Every Farm a Factory: The Industrial Ideal in American* Agriculture. New Haven, CT: Yale University Press, 2003.

Gray, R. B. *The Agricultural Tractor, 1855–1950*. St. Joseph, MI: American Society of Agricultural Engineers, 1975.

Hurt, R. Douglas. *American Agriculture: A Brief History*. Rev. ed. West Lafayette, IN: Purdue University Press, 2002

McClelland, Peter D. *Sowing Modernity: America's First Agricultural Revolution*. Ithaca, NY: Cornell University Press, 1997.

Olmstead, Alan L. "A Reappraisal of the Mechanization of Reaping and Mowing in American Agriculture, 1833–1870." *Journal of Economic History* 35 (June 1975): 327–52.

Quick, Graeme, and Wesley Buchele. *The Grain Harvesters*. St. Joseph, MI: American Society of Agricultural Engineers, 1978.

Rasmussen, Wayne D. "The Mechanization of Agriculture." *Scientific American* 247 (September 1982): 76–89.

Rogin, Leo. *The Introduction of Farm Machinery in Its Relation to the Productivity of Labor in the Agriculture of the United States during the Nineteenth Century*. Berkeley: University of California Press, 1931.

Schlebecker, John T. *Whereby We Thrive: A History of American Farming, 1607–1972*. Ames: Iowa State University Press, 1975.

Wik, Reynold M. "Henry Ford's Tractors in American Agriculture." *Agricultural History* 38 (April 1964): 79–86.

Wik, Reynold M. *Steam Power on the American Farm*. Philadelphia: University of Pennsylvania Press, 1953.

Williams, Robert C. *Fordson, Farmall, and Poppin' Johnny: A History of the Farm Tractor and Its Impact on America*. Urbana: University of Illinois Press, 1987.

CHAPTER 10

THE GROWING POWER OF AGRICULTURAL SCIENCE

J. L. ANDERSON

THE story of agricultural science is a story of power over plants, animals, microbes, elements, minerals, and the land itself. Armed with scientific expertise and the products of scientific research, farmers have transformed much of the world's surface area and much of the flora and fauna to meet human needs. These changes are comparatively easy to quantify. Animals and plants produce much more and at a faster rate than ever before thanks to genetic manipulation, carefully formatted rations or fertilizers, pharmaceuticals or pesticides, and a host of other scientific interventions. The power to grow food and fiber has grown dramatically over the past several hundred years, thanks in large part to the application of scientific discoveries.[1]

But while agricultural science is most often framed in terms of increased yield, hardiness, pest or drought resistance, and faster or more efficient weight gain, it is about much more. The story of agricultural science is about power over individuals, groups, and institutions. It is about bureaucratic struggles within and between government institutions, imperial centers and colonies, capital and labor, as well as corporations and consumers. Finally, agricultural science is also the struggle among and between hemispheres. Scientists have articulated laudable goals such as reducing hunger, cutting costs, and easing labor, to name a few, but the development and use of power, regardless of how well-intentioned, is never neutral: there are always winners and losers in the exercise of power. The growing power of agricultural science, then, is often contested, with debates about who creates science and how, who benefits from it, and what role users, institutions, and states play in deploying or controlling it.

Historians of agricultural science began with the study of public institutions and individuals, in large part because those parties developed large caches of records that were often publicly available. More recently, though, new lines of inquiry have focused more on less formal knowledge creation. The emphasis on laboratories and credentialed scientists failed to account for knowledge creation when labs and scientists were rare, ignoring the important work of altering farm practice from the ground up.

Historians have accepted that there are multiple sites of knowledge creation and that, for better or worse, the production of knowledge and its deployment are forms of power.[2]

Creating Scientific Knowledge

Historian Jeremy Vetter observed that one of the most important questions in the history of science in general and agricultural science in particular is who creates knowledge. Scholars have shown that in Europe there was a significant transformation in agricultural practice after 1350. By the seventeenth century, farmers demonstrated interest in agricultural reform, even though there was little systematic experimentation until the eighteenth century. Agricultural knowledge or, as historian Francesca Bray labeled it, agronomic science, was part of the imperial Chinese state during the period from 1250 to 1650. Bray examined how several agricultural texts (*nongshu*) authored by state bureaucrats compared with the writings of private landowners. For much of this period, agricultural knowledge was co-produced by the state, landowners, and small farmers. While recognizing the power of the state over agricultural production, Bray contended that in imperial rice production, peasants and landowners shaped the knowledge that shaped the land.[3]

In Britain and Europe, educated elites and academicians rather than peasants participated in creating knowledge in the early eighteenth century. Chemists in France, Scotland, England, and the German states published treatises linking cultivation and chemistry, a trend that accelerated during the food and agriculture crisis of the Napoleonic Wars. Sir Humphry Davy was part of a broader movement when he published *Elements of Agricultural Chemistry* (1818), his landmark synthesis of contemporary scientific knowledge. The Prussian chemist Sigismund Friedrich Hermbstädt began publishing *Archiv der Agriculturchemie für denkiend Landwirthe* (*Archives of Agricultural Chemistry for Thinking Farmers*) in 1804. Albrecht Thaer is remembered as one of the earliest systematizers in agricultural science, presiding over an agricultural school near Berlin in 1804 and publishing his *Grundsätze der rationellen Landwirthschaft* (*Principles of Agriculture*) between 1809 and 1812.[4]

Chemists were not the only people interested in how and why crops grew better under particular conditions and on some lands than others. In the German states, interest in nature study, or *Naturwissenschaft*, dates to the mid-eighteenth century. Farmers and educated elites formed local nature societies. These *Naturforscher* (nature researchers) and their improvement societies did not generate data, but they prepared the way for the rise of dedicated scientific institutions that arose in the nineteenth century. In the United States, a dedicated group of farmers also began to study the soil to improve agriculture and communities. Knowledge production depended on these intellectually curious rural people who were interested in health and fertility long before anyone would label their activities as scientific inquiry.[5]

Members of rural elites such as Edmund Ruffin of Virginia read Davy's work and used soil chemistry to amend acidic soil with locally mined marl to lower pH and enable nutrient uptake by crops. For Ruffin, the owner of an aging plantation with tired soil, improved productivity and agricultural diversification were means to create a self-sufficient Southern slaveholding republic. Ruffin's failure to convince Southern farmers to diversify and marl their land was a defeat for his political project, but his farm publications and efforts to create a state board of agriculture were widely discussed across the region and beyond.[6]

Some reformers just wanted faster horses. English elites imported Arabian horses in the early seventeenth century and published the first *General Stud Book* for thoroughbred horses in 1791. The *General Stud Book* was a record of pedigree, reflecting the concern about parentage that created animals that conformed to defined set of characteristics, not least of which was speed. They lamented the practice of inbreeding, or the breeding of parent stock to offspring or siblings. The book was a form of insurance that the purebred animal was what it alleged to be, an important concern in a world of inherited titles and estates.[7] Though horse breeders eschewed inbreeding, other amateurs found it to be a useful tool in making breeds. Robert Bakewell of Dishley, a tenant farmer who experimented most famously with sheep, was the most noted of these and made significant contributions to breeding. Bakewell emphasized the careful selection of males and females rather than emphasizing only the males. Second, he pursued inbreeding, with parent stock and offspring bred to each other to express the desired traits. Finally, he emphasized progeny testing rather than pedigree, focusing on the results of breeding rather than simply parent stock. Bakewell succeeded in fixing characteristics over generations and, consequently, created distinct breeds or types, practices that were taken up for both plant and animal breeding.[8]

By the early nineteenth century, a more formal study of agriculture emerged in Europe. Justus von Liebig's laboratory in Giessen and the Rothamstead Experimental Farm in England were early examples of this movement. Liebig's experiments began in 1826, followed by John Bennet Lawes at Rothamstead in 1843. Both were concerned with fertility, with Liebig theorizing that it was possible to understand the chemical composition of soil and amend it to enhance production. Lawes studied the relationship between fertilizer and crop yields on actual experimental plots.

Americans were particularly inspired by Liebig and his laboratory at Giessen. Liebig's *Organic Chemistry in Its Applications to Agriculture and Physiology* (1840) sparked discussion in the United States over how to explain both real and perceived declines in soil fertility. Americans who studied at Giessen returned to the United States to establish their own privately funded laboratories. Two of these labs, one at Harvard and the other at Yale, were the sites of research that advanced the study of soil science in ways that were far more practical than Liebig's. Margaret Rossiter, the leading historian of Liebig's legacy in the United States, concluded that Liebig's direct influence on farmers was comparatively modest. His real influence was the chemists he inspired, the labs that they built, and the new understanding of soil chemistry that emerged at the new agricultural experiment stations.[9]

Building Institutions for Agricultural Science

Agricultural reformers readily accepted science and hoped to spread the ethic of experimentation, turning to governments to support new institutions for research. That knowledge was often contested, as scientists, farmers, and policymakers vied for control over institutions and the knowledge itself.

In his classic *First the Seed*, Jack Kloppenburg explained that during the early nineteenth century in the United States, taxpayer-supported public institutions dominated agricultural science. The US Patent Office began distributing seeds to farmers in 1839. Several states established agricultural colleges in the 1850s, and in 1862 Congress authorized the creation of the USDA and passed the Morrill Act to provide federal support for the agricultural colleges, although there was comparatively modest body of agricultural science to teach. Farmers wanted more practical solutions to local problems, which led to the creation of agricultural experiment stations authorized by the Hatch Act of 1887.[10]

While the United States established a commitment to agriculture at the federal level between the 1840s and the 1880s, other countries pioneered similar pathways. The Dutch government created positions at the nation's universities dedicated to agricultural research and teaching by the mid-nineteenth century. Various German states developed experiment stations in the late nineteenth century to develop new plant varieties and soil fertility. Jonathan Harwood claimed that these institutions, especially in Bavaria, were "peasant-friendly," focused on plant breeding to benefit the smallholder.[11]

Agricultural experiment stations in the United States were under pressure to prove their worth to farmers. In Kansas, wheat research during the 1880s and 1890s focused on identifying the varieties that had the highest yield, ripened earliest, and survived harsh winters. By the 1920s, both experiment station and private sector scientists worked hard on developing hybrid corn, although the promised increased yields of hybrid corn only threatened to exacerbate the problem of chronic surplus during that period. For the plant breeders who worked on hybridization, helping farmers boost yield was just one concern. Plant breeders at the experiment stations were often more interested in the science than farm conditions. The rise of Mendelian genetics boosted their status and influence in the scientific community.[12]

Imperial Russia's state-sponsored experiment stations emerged after those of Germany, the Netherlands, and the United States. After the abolition of serfdom, wealthy landowners organized for agricultural reform and often pursued advanced education in chemistry. One notable example was Aleksandr Engel'gardt. After a military career, this nobleman paid for his own chemistry lab and was subsequently appointed professor at the St. Petersburg Agricultural Institute. He used his own estate to conduct fertilizer experiments, creating one of the first experiment stations in Russia.[13]

The Russian government did not organize scientific endeavors in agriculture until the famine of 1891–1892. Much of this experimental work focused on the cultivation of the arid steppes, which had been settled as part of Catherine the Great's expansion program. The steppes, however, were fragile, deteriorating quickly under cultivation, provoking scientific discourse over the relationship between land, vegetation, and climate. Soil scientist Vasilii Dokuchaev concluded that soil was not an independent variable in farming, that it must be considered in context. During the Russian Civil War, the Bolsheviks continued the work of agricultural modernization to boost production, utilizing nationalized estates for experimentation and establishing the Lenin Academy of Agricultural Sciences in 1929 in Leningrad.[14]

The French attempted to reorient research away from German model toward an American one. Paul Marchal, an economic entomologist, visited several American universities and experiment stations in 1913 and admired what he saw. In 1916, he issued a 300-page report that emphasized the results Americans achieved in boosting food production through science. He lamented that French agricultural education had centered on several specialized agricultural schools (dairy, horticulture, etc.), with divided authority between teaching at the Écoles Nationales d'Agriculture and research at the Institut National Agronomique, creating a turf war over research and experimentation. Government scientists and policymakers heeded Marchal and began a centralization effort that continued until the Great Depression.[15]

For all the work to develop institutions for agricultural science, there were important examples of farmers either modifying the knowledge they received from scientific experts or even creating their own understanding. In some cases, farmers in the American Midwest after World War II defied government and chemical company fertilizer guidelines in hopes of increasing production. Scientists belatedly endorsed those modifications as legitimate practices. Furthermore, in the Great Plains, pesticide applicators developed their own understanding of the role of chemicals in shaping the land, a perspective that differed from that of those in the labs and working the experimental plots.[16]

The Problem of Authority

Having established institutions dedicated to agricultural science, there were multiple conflicts over authority within those institutions and between scientists. The rediscovery of Gregor Mendel's work was a challenge and opportunity for plant breeders. The varying responses of agricultural scientists in the United States, Great Britain, Germany, and France reveal that there was no inevitable outcome. American scientists used Mendelian genetics to open distance between the scientist and farmer, not to mention to challenge the authority of the chemists. Many German scientists accepted Mendelism, although varietal crosses continued to enjoy support among plant breeders. Like the Americans, they also saw genetics as a means to establishing distance between other scientists as well as producers. French scientists saw value in a Mendelian approach but, like Luther Burbank in the United States and most British plant breeders, they continued to view mass selection as a valuable tool for developing commercial verities. Indeed, the triumph of Mendelism in America may have had more to do with the convenience of conceptualizing the gene as a discrete unit to facilitate profit than it did with science.[17]

One of the most renowned turf wars in agricultural science took place in the Soviet Union, acted out by two men who both served as directors of the Lenin Academy. Nikolai Vavilov was a pioneering geneticist who became the first director of the Academy of Agricultural Sciences in 1929. That year, he organized a conference on genetics and plant and animal breeding to showcase the promise of genetics for alleviating the problems of food scarcity in the Soviet Union. While the emphasis of the conference was the potential of genetics, other plant scientists such as Trofim Lysenko rejected genetics. Lysenko's approach, labeled agrobiology, was neo-Lamarckian in its view of acquired characteristics rather than inherited traits. Over the next several years, both theories coexisted within Soviet agricultural science, although Vavilov ultimately fell victim to a scientific turf war in which the dispute was not settled in scholarly journals but by politics. Vavilov fell out of favor when he was unable to deliver on the promise of genetics. Bureaucratic obstacles and inefficiencies that slowed research made his opponents look good by comparison. Stalin was impressed with Lysenko and his promises of new, productive varieties and in 1940 ordered the arrest of Vavilov, who died in prison of starvation in 1943.[18]

Just five years after Vavilov's death, the Central Committee of the Communist Party denounced classical genetics and officially approved Lysenko's agrobiology theory of inheritance. It was a victory but, as historian Michael Gordin has shown, it was not a total victory. Many of the heretical geneticists conducted their work at the provincial level rather than the Academy, often by reframing it in new terms. Furthermore, as Gordin points out, after 1948 Lysenko and the agrobiologists saw the tenuous nature of their victory over genetics. The rapid re-emergence of genetics after Khrushchev was forced out in 1965 indicates that despite the Central Committee's imprimatur, Lysenko's agrobiology was never fully secure.[19]

Indeed, it was difficult to remove national politics from agricultural science. In Mexico, agronomists who hoped to reshape farm practices of the peasants were enlisted for political purposes. They participated in land reforms of the post-revolutionary period and attempted to convince farmers to change their ways. When these reforms collapsed, scientists were eager to re-establish a place in public life, which they were able to do with the Green Revolution.[20]

Even in the scientific community, power was unevenly distributed across the disciplines. Soil chemists dominated in Liebig's day and the plant breeders were ascendant in the early twentieth century, but entomologists experienced a rise in prestige and power after World War II. Even then the entomologists were divided. For decades, insect control relied on the combination of cultural techniques, biological control, and chemicals. Cultural practices such as managing habitat by limiting host species, crop rotation, and barnyard sanitation were more important than chemicals. Yet the rapid acceptance of synthetic insecticide led to a reprioritization among entomologists. Historian John Perkins contended that after the commercial introduction of DDT, chemicals were the new go-to for control. DDT boosters did not advocate abandoning mechanical, biological, or cultural techniques, but they pushed them to the background. The comparative ease of application and low cost of chemicals, not to mention the stunning effectiveness of chlorinated hydrocarbon insecticides in those early years, were difficult to resist. The consequence of chemical confidence was the contemplation of eradication strategies rather than just control.[21]

The success of plant breeders in the United States was reflected in the political economy of the seed industry. The Plant Variety Protection Act of 1970 elaborated new rules for the ways in which germplasm would be monetized. This act allowed private breeders to protect intellectual property by conveying a twenty-five-year patent on new varieties of sexually reproduced plants, paving the way for the patenting of genes. Corporations rather than farmers gained the most, although other regimes constructed their own political economy of seeds and science. Fascist powers in Europe utilized agricultural science to meet the needs of the state rather than the market.[22]

SCIENTIFIC AGRICULTURE AND IMPERIALISM

The empires that created scientific knowledge were eager to export it for profit, exploiting resources and people around the world. Scientists engaged in bioprospecting and engineering not only to make commodity plants adapt to local conditions in the colonies but also to bring germplasm back to the seat of empire. These efforts reveal multiple sites of knowledge creation.

Colonial Spanish officials in the Caribbean hoped to use science to enhance the productivity of coffee and sugar. They established research stations patterned on those created in Germany, the Netherlands, and the United States. These colonial elites desired not only the economic benefits of imperial science but also political and ideological benefits. Agricultural science, historian Stuart McCook contended, promised "order and progress" in addition to profit. Colonial elites and scientists cooperated to create a simplified commodity landscape, a world of displaced native flora and fauna that generated profit that allowed them to consolidate power. The new landscape, however profitable, was one of constant threats from blight and pest species that required further scientific intervention.[23]

The Dutch imperial effort also included scientific agriculture. In 1817, the newly installed director of Agriculture, Arts, and Science in the colony of Java established the Lands Plantentuin, a section of the palace garden dedicated to agricultural experimentation. Ultimately, they brought additional land into use for agricultural experimentation as part of the botanical garden project to develop jute, corn, peanuts, soy, and rice. The Dutch also created a Government Chinchoa Estate and laboratory in the 1850s, which became a major research center in its own right. By 1905 the colonial government created a department of agriculture to support commodities as well as rice production to feed the colony.[24]

In Bengal, scientific agriculture and indigo production were a blend of Western imperial science and Indigenous knowledge. During the nineteenth century, there were many coexisting sources of knowledge regarding indigo production including Europe, the Caribbean, and the subcontinent. After German scientists developed synthetic indigo in 1897, the British reinvested in natural indigo research for production and processing. By the 1920s, however, synthetic indigo had become a feature in the British industry, leaving the colonial industry in decline.[25]

Imperial outposts shaped the construction of knowledge in other ways, too. Dual-purpose British livestock breeds reflected the mixed agricultural system and consumer demand of the British Isles. But increased specialization in much of the world during the twentieth century meant that British breeds were in decline. The solution from the outposts was to remake the animals. In New Zealand, breeders utilized European breeds such as the Spanish Merino and English Lincoln to develop Corriedale sheep, an animal adapted to local conditions and market demand. Similarly, Hereford cattle were not stable artifacts. In the Americas, Herefords were bred to be larger, while the authority to define the breed shifted from Britain to America. Similarly, the role of Karakul sheep in German South-West Africa in the early twentieth century reveals the problems and potential of agricultural science in the colonies. Karakul sheep imported from the Turkmenian steppes of Russia failed to thrive in Africa, leading German scientists to begin a Mendelian breeding program utilizing domestic African sheep. Germans envisioned Africa as a blank slate, but the reality was more complex.[26]

In North America, "foreign" seeds were the foundation of much farm prosperity, with Turkey wheat, a non-native species, as a signal example. The Kansas State Agricultural College began studies and tests on winter wheat varieties (sown in autumn) in the 1880s that continued under the auspices of the Agricultural Experiment Station in Manhattan after the Hatch Act. Station scientists conducted extensive tests on multiple wheat varieties, often with geographical names that included "Russian," "Odessa," "Bulgarian," "Hungarian," and "Turkey," although the true physical origins of these varieties can only be surmised. Researchers focused on identifying varieties with the highest yield, but many of those varieties were susceptible to winter-kill. High yield did not matter if the crop could not survive the winter. Turkey wheat emerged as a favorite in the mid-1890s because it was both high-yielding and hardy. In the words of one Kansas official, by 1898 Turkey wheat was accepted as "our standard hard wheat."[27]

Grain production on America's Great Plains, however, never supplanted the place of grazing in the region, with scientists focused on exploring the potential and limits of the range. In the early twentieth century, Professor Frederic E. Clements of the University of Nebraska developed a theory of grassland management rooted in the concept of succession, the idea that ecosystems moved through phases until they reached a climax state of relative stability. For Clements, studying the grasslands would help scientists establish optimal carrying capacities for American rangeland. Government bureaucrats largely accepted this view and embarked upon pest eradication projects and introducing non-native species. While the diverse conditions of the Western range undermined this project, the most important disruption was the drought of the 1930s, revealing that change and dynamism rather than climax and stasis were normal conditions.[28]

While American scientists developed understanding of domestic problems, they also carried their work abroad. Scientists at land-grant universities and their Chinese colleagues, many of whom trained at those institutions, hoped to transform Chinese agriculture in a North American image. These scientists at Cornell University, the USDA, and Rockefeller Foundation hoped to rescue the rural Chinese peasant from poverty, just as missionaries of the period hoped to save souls. Agricultural evangelicals failed, however, to fully understand the place and people they hoped to help, just as Christian missionaries did not fully understand local conditions and culture. The missionary project failed, due in part to the immensity of the task and modest resources dedicated to it, the biases and weaknesses of the missionary scientists, and their pursuit of misguided projects.[29]

The Quest for Control: Successes

Success stories of agricultural science are legion. Scientists at experiment stations, land-grant schools, private institutes, and corporate laboratories generated much of that work, ranging from plant breeding and animal nutrition studies to pesticide and fertilizer research. Popular narratives of these stories often suggest that the line from scientific innovation to increased production was straight, but the reality was often much more complicated.

For example, the Haber-Bosch process for ammonia synthesis ranks as one of the most celebrated developments in agricultural science, but alone its effects were limited. While numerous scientists had experimented with synthesizing nitrogen, they failed to develop a process that was commercially viable until 1910, when Fritz Haber, a leading German chemist, developed a working model to synthesize nitrogen. Carl Bosch, a BASF chemist, was tasked with scaling up the model to produce it commercially. Their technique, which became known as the Haber-Bosch process, allowed for increased yield across time and multiple continents.[30]

Yet Alan Olmstead and Paul Rhode argue that stories of nitrogen fertilizer have obscured the importance that biological innovation played in accounting for productivity gains. They contend that biological innovation not only preceded important developments in labor-saving machinery and the widespread use of fertilizers, but that the gains from fertilizer were not possible without the biological innovation such as hybridization. New plants maximized the benefits of nitrogen fertilizer, not to mention pesticides.[31]

The "rediscovery" of Mendel's work on heritability of traits in 1900 inspired scientists to undertake extensive experimentation with inbreeding that resulted in major breakthroughs. Through inbreeding, specific traits could be isolated and, when crossed with other inbred lines, the resulting hybrids would result in a magnification of those traits from yield to drought resistance. The work that resulted in hybrid corn began with George Shull at the Carnegie Station, along with Edwin East and Donald Jones of the Connecticut Experiment Station, but it was ultimately a product of private industry, individuals, and public research institutions. Even though the first commercial hybrid corn was marketed in the 1920s, there was slow uptake by farmers. The US government's acreage reduction programs of the Roosevelt administration provided the impetus for boosting yield at a time of low corn prices.[32]

As with the case of hybrid corn, other biological innovations took place in an array of settings, a few of them unexpected. After World War I, the United States was interested in rubber research in response to both real and perceived vulnerabilities to a rubber shortage. The loss of Southeast Asian markets prompted wealthy American industrialists to find alternate sources. Japanese expansion in the region in the 1930s reignited interest in alternate rubber sources on the part of the US government, which created the Emergency Rubber Project to develop substitute plants and synthetic alternatives not only in the labs and in the field, but also in Japanese internment camps. Although the wartime research did not result in an economically viable substitute, the search for rubber substitutes revealed the limits of private research as well as the multiple sites of knowledge creation.[33]

A host of livestock diseases have been controlled through scientific innovation and practice. In the United States, much of that work took place through the US Department of Agriculture's Bureau of Animal Industry (BAI). Scientists of the BAI responded to the growing threats of rinderpest, Texas fever, hog cholera, and numerous other diseases. They have done so despite conflicts among scientists as well as between government scientists and producers. Resistance was common. During Iowa's Cow War of 1931, farmers resisted tuberculin testing. In the American South, yeomen frequently opposed the long campaign for tick eradication to control Texas fever. In Ghana, colonial officials and scientists attempted to contain the outbreak of Cocoa Swollen Virus in 1936 by cutting diseased trees, which provoked resistance by small-scale farmers who hoped to preserve their cash crop. When nationalist critics of the cutting policy came to power under Kwame Nkrumah in 1951, they reversed their position. Research into chemical and biological control demonstrated that destroying and replacing trees with resistant varieties was the only viable solution to maintaining cocoa production.[34]

The research on animal nutrition and synthetic growth hormones allowed producers to maximize the payoff from developments in genetics, just as the growth of synthetic fertilizers gave hybrid seed the optimal chance for success. The 1948 "Chicken of Tomorrow" campaign is a good example of the confluence of multiple scientific developments in breeding, the use of antibiotics to promote growth, and new feeds resulted in a bird that was larger, matured faster, and required less gain to fatten, all of which were successes that subsequently influenced the cattle and hog industries.[35]

The Quest for Control: Problems

Success stories aside, scientific contributions to the extraordinary growth in farm productivity are only part of the story. The application of that knowledge has been uneven and has sometimes resulted in negative, unintended consequences. In many cases, agricultural scientists and policymakers behaved like the boy with the new hammer. For the boy, the old saying goes, all the world is a nail. Scientific discourse was a special kind of hammer that privileged certain solutions, many of which failed to address farmers' long-standing concerns about their position in society that were often more important to them than science.

Farmers often desired solutions to farm "problems" that were market-based, including government-regulated railroad freight rates, farmer-owned cooperatives, and government-owned grain elevators and banks. Farmers resented middlemen who sometimes profited regardless of the price of farm products. They railed against corporate agriculture control that made it difficult for individual family farms to compete for credit, land, and market share. In short, what many farm families hoped for was a realignment of economic structure to level the playing field. These kinds of solutions, however, were often ignored or disparaged by political leaders. When market reforms were enacted, they were frequently limited in scope, scale, and duration. Changing the political and economic structure of agriculture was extremely difficult, especially as farmers moved from majority to minority status in North America.

Part of the appeal of scientific agriculture was that it shifted the focus from structural reform to the farmer. Rather than tear down and rebuild the dominant social, economic, and political institutions that contributed to low commodity prices, it was easier to promote increased production and efficiency through science and technology. Farmers, confronting the challenges of structural change, could accept scientific agriculture in the field and barnyard as a temporary or partial solution, even as it became more entrenched over time. The prescriptions of the agricultural experiment stations and scientists, then, often focused on reforming producers and their farms rather than the regional, national, or global economy.[36]

The research stations themselves were tools of social control. In Germany's Baltic provinces in the late nineteenth century, elite landowners actively created their own institutions for agricultural science. These institutions were often more about distributing information to buttress existing production patterns and social hierarchy rather than experimentation and outside expertise that might lead to political and economic change at the expense of elites.[37]

The hybrid corn story is also a story of winners and losers. For generations, farmers had practiced mass selection to produce the seed for next year's crop. They picked the ears of corn that performed best, whether it be yield (i.e., ear size or multiple ears per stock), a deep tap root, or resistance to a particular pest. This optimal seed, selected from across the field, constituted a more traditional form of agricultural knowledge in which the farmer was the expert. Farmers who purchased hybrids ceded control over the selection process in the interest of yield. But those who planted seed from the previous year's hybrid crop found that the vigor dissipated in the next generation. Agricultural science promised increased yields but also committed farmers to increased expense for seed, fertilizer, and pesticides and resulted in the de-skilling of farm labor as well as declining genetic diversity.[38]

The spread of chemical agriculture that accompanied the rise of hybrid seed led to numerous problems. Only a portion of the nitrogen fertilizer that is applied can be taken up by plants. Some of it dissipates upon application or, more commonly, is washed away into surface waters. A large portion of the fertilizer from the Mississippi Valley ends up in the Gulf of Mexico, where it has resulted in a large dead zone. Furthermore, resistance to those chemicals on the part of target species revealed the limits of chemical control. Within just a few years of use, experts and some users found that DDT and other pesticides were less effective than they had been. Organisms that survived the chemical onslaught reproduced with other survivors, illustrating the validity of natural selection theory and the reality of chemical limits. Users and scientists recognized the problem, discussing it in scientific literature as well as farm publications.[39]

Furthermore, the widespread and often indiscriminate application of those chemicals meant that non-target species were injured or killed. Rachel Carson raised this issue in *Silent Spring*. The problem of "drift," the spread of aerially applied chemical beyond the intended target, plagued farmers who lived downwind. Drift killed or damaged crops that were sensitive to herbicides, poisoned livestock, and even injured people. In the American West and South, chemical applicators made little attempt to avoid farm workers, spraying while farm workers labored in vineyards, cottonfields, orchards, and fields of vegetables. Chemical plants that produce fertilizer and pesticides have been the source of significant pollution and harm, ranging from the explosion at the Union Carbide pesticide plant in Bhopal to plants along the Mississippi and its tributaries that discharged contaminants directly in the rivers, resulting in fish kills and other large-scale disruptions to ecosystems.[40]

Green Revolutions

The end of the colonial era did not end the projection of imperial agricultural science around the world. By the mid-twentieth century, the United States and fading European powers envisioned what in 1968 a US Agency for International Development official labeled the "Green Revolution" to improve agricultural production in developing nations. In much of the world, drought, monsoon, and pests limited agricultural potential. These environmental threats and the structural obstacles that the colonizers had put in place over generations, combined with the predominance of small-scale producers who lacked credit and technology, caused widespread hunger in much of the world. Improved crop varieties along with synthetic nitrogen fertilizer, pesticides, and irrigation promised relief. Scientists and policymakers in Europe and the United States were confident. Their domestic experiences with what Jonathan Harwood labeled their own green revolutions taught them about the potential of agricultural science.[41]

Traditional interpretations of the Green Revolution emphasize the Cold War context, in which Western science could stave off communist gains in the non-aligned "third" world. More recently, historians have emphasized that the roots of the Green Revolution were deeper than the Cold War period. The geopolitical ambitions of Western powers and the desire to reduce the threat of famine, however, were not mutually exclusive. In sub-Saharan Africa, British colonial officials recognized by the 1930s that colonial monocultures were destructive to the colonized. The call for more scientific attention to health and agriculture coincided with the movement for independence. Experts from the colonial office subsequently became technical advisers in the Green Revolution. Similarly, in the 1940s Rockefeller Foundation Mexican Agriculture Program, scientists conducted plant breeding in Mexico to develop dwarf wheat and disease-resistant varieties.[42]

The Green Revolution yielded mixed results. World food production rose faster than population growth during the second half of the twentieth century, due in part to the Green Revolution. Despite those productivity gains in some cases, most of the benefits of such gains flowed to larger farmers who were already in a positive market position. They already had larger tracts of land and better access to water and sources of credit. Unlike Europe's late nineteenth- and early twentieth-century green revolutions, these were not peasant-friendly. It was difficult for peasants to participate due to the high costs for seed and fertilizer and the development of irrigation infrastructure. The fact that many of the new plant varieties were bred for yield also meant that other valuable traits such as milling or baking properties were absent. In some cases, the new varieties were fussier than the varieties they displaced. Claims by Green Revolution promoters that millions of lives have been saved and enhanced by reducing food insecurity are true, but they are not the only true claims about it.[43]

The loss of local knowledge and landraces has been the subject of much discussion. In southern Africa, a handful of companies eventually controlled the seed corn market due to trade agreements that compelled economic liberalization. Zimbabwe enjoyed a mixed record of success in providing seed varieties for farmers before the 1980s, drawing on the colonial network Seed Maize Association (SMA). Liberalization of the economy during the 1980s, however, meant increasing market share for foreign biotech companies, which were not able to meet the needs of smallholders any better than the old SMA.[44]

Western liberal democracies were not the only proponents of the Green Revolution, they were not the only parties. The People's Republic of China had its own Green Revolution, although it was designed to be compatible with the political goals of a Red Revolution. Chinese scientists and bureaucrats independently forged an agricultural revolution that rejected liberal capitalism, framing scientific innovation to reinforce the peasant class rather than challenge it. They presented new scientific techniques as extensions of folk knowledge, a sleight of hand that allowed the party to praise the importance of noble peasants, even in a rapidly urbanizing and industrializing nation.[45]

For all the success of the Green Revolution in reducing hunger, much of it has resulted in the consolidation of power by those who were already powerful. De-skilling as well as increased capital and operating costs were the price of agricultural science. Economic liberalization, a condition of support from the International Monetary Fund and World Bank, has furthered that consolidation by opening markets to Western biotech companies. In many cases, the resulting commodification of the gene has lessened hunger but reduced autonomy of producers in underdeveloped nations.

Conclusion

The place of science in agriculture has been repeatedly reified and reinforced since the emergence of modern scientific inquiry. Scientists working in laboratories and on experimental farms posited a new soil science, cultivated new crop varieties, and developed theories of inheritance, activities that have been repeated and expanded throughout the generations by scientists working on their own property, in government-funded research facilities, or even in privately funded labs.

Western societies doubled down on science. Agricultural scientists still labor in comprehensive research universities, corporate laboratories, government laboratories, and experiment stations. The products of those labs and facilities are omnipresent, so much so that it is far more difficult to find landraces that have not been crossed, either accidentally or deliberately, with improved varieties from commercial or government sources. Even farmers who eschew modern inputs of industrial agriculture still rely on science for seed selection, assessing soil fertility and carrying capacity, livestock breeding, and veterinary medicine.

The growing power of agricultural science, then, has found full expression on the land. It is so thoroughly part of global agriculture that science itself is part of the rural landscape. That knowledge contributed to significant increases in productivity as well as problems. Scientists, however, leveraged their successes to exercise even more control over the countryside, creating a feedback loop in which each new scientific advance, even if contested, contributes to greater power of agricultural scientists over every living thing in the countryside.

Notes

1. Alan L. Olmstead, "Historical and Institutional Perspectives on American Agricultural Development," *American Journal of Agricultural Economics* 102, no. 2 (March 2020): 400–18.
2. Deborah Fitzgerald, Lisa Onaga, Emily Pawley, Denise Phillips, and Jeremy Vetter, "Roundtable: Agricultural History and the History of Science," *Agricultural History* 92, no. 4 (Fall 2018): 569–604.

3. Mauro Ambrosoli, *The Wild and the Sown: Botany and Agriculture in Western Europe, 1350–1850* (Cambridge: Cambridge University Press, 1997); Francesca Bray, "Science, Technique, Technology: Passages between Matter and Knowledge in Imperial Chinese Agriculture," *British Journal for the History of Science* 41, no. 3 (September 2008): 319–44.
4. Peter Jones, *Agricultural Enlightenment: Knowledge, Technology, and Nature, 1750–1840* (Oxford: Oxford University Press, 2015): 161–65.
5. Denise Phillips, *Acolytes of Nature: Defining Natural Science in Germany, 1770–1850* (Chicago: University of Chicago Press, 2012), x; Jones, *Agricultural Enlightenment*, 165; Benjamin R. Cohen, *Notes from the Ground: Science, Soil, and Society in the American Countryside* (New Haven, CT: Yale University Press, 2009); Emily Pawley, *The Nature of the Future: Agriculture, Science, and Capitalism in the Antebellum North* (Chicago: University of Chicago Press, 2020).
6. Steven Stoll, *Larding the Lean Earth: Soil and Society in Nineteenth Century America* (New York: Hill & Wang, 2002); David F. Allmendinger, *Ruffin: Family and Reform in the Old South* (Oxford: Oxford University Press, 1990).
7. Margaret Derry, *Masterminding Nature: The Breeding of Animals, 1750–2010* (Toronto: University of Toronto Press, 2015), ch. 1.
8. Derry, *Masterminding Nature*, 17–19; Nicolas Russell, *Like Engend'ring Like: Heredity and Animal Breeding in Early Modern England* (Cambridge: Cambridge University Press, 1986).
9. Margaret W. Rossiter, *The Emergence of Agricultural Science: Justus Liebig and the Americans, 1840–1880* (New Haven, CT: Yale University Press, 1975): 172.
10. Gladys L. Baker, Wayne D. Rasmussen, Vivian L. Wiser, and Jane M. Porter, *Century of Service: The First 100 Years of the United States Department of Agriculture* (Washington, DC: US Department of Agriculture, 1963); Alan I Marcus, *Agricultural Science and the Quest for Legitimacy: Farmers, Agricultural Colleges, and Experiment Stations, 1870–1890* (Ames: Iowa State University Press, 1985); Jack Ralph Kloppenburg, *First the Seed: The Political Economy of Plant Biotechnology, 1492–2000* (Cambridge: Cambridge University Press, 1988).
11. Harro Maat, *Science Cultivating Practice: A History of Agricultural Science in the Netherlands and Its Colonies, 1863–1986* (Wageningen: Ponsen & Looijen, 2001); Jonathan Harwood, *Technology's Dilemma: Agricultural Colleges between Science and Practice in Germany, 1860–1934* (Bern: Peter Lang, 2005); Harwood, *Europe's Green Revolution and Others Since: The Rise and Fall of Peasant-Friendly Plant Breeding* (New York: Routledge, 2012).
12. Deborah Fitzgerald, *The Business of Breeding: Hybrid Corn in Illinois, 1890–1940* (Ithaca, NY: Cornell University Press, 1990): 72.
13. Olga Elina, "Planting Seeds for the Revolution: The Rise of Russian Agricultural Science, 1860–1920," *Science in Context* 15, no. 2 (2002): 214.
14. David Moon, *The Plough That Broke the Steppes: Agriculture and Environment on Russia's Grasslands, 1700–1914* (Oxford: Oxford University Press, 2013); Elina, "Planting Seeds for the Revolution," 209–37.
15. Stéphane Castonguay, "The Transformation of Agricultural Research in France: The Introduction of the American System," *Minerva* 43 (2005): 265–87.
16. J. L. Anderson, *Industrializing the Corn Belt: Agriculture, Technology, and the Environment, 1945–1972* (DeKalb: Northern Illinois University Press, 2009); David D. Vail, *Chemical Lands: Pesticides, Aerial Spraying, and Health in North America's Grasslands since 1945* (Tuscaloosa: University of Alabama Press, 2018).
17. Paulo Palladino, "Wizards and Devotees: On the Mendelian Theory of Inheritance and the Professionalization of Agricultural Science in Great Britain and the United States,

1880–1930," *History of Science* 32, no. 4 (December 1994): 409–44; Palladino, "Between Craft and Science: Plant Breeding, Mendelian Genetics, and British Universities, 1900–1920," *Technology and Culture* 34, no. 2 (April 1993): 300–23; Christophe Bonneuil, "Mendelism, Plant Breeding, and Experimental Cultures: Agriculture and the Development of Genetics in France," *Journal of the History of Biology* 39 (2006): 281–308; Thomas Wieland, "Scientific Theory and Agricultural Practice: Plant Breeding in Germany form the Late 19th to the Early 20th Century," *Journal of the History of Biology* 39, no. 2 (2006): 309–43; Garland E. Allen, "Origins of the Classical Gene Concept, 1900–1950," *Perspectives in Biology and Medicine* 57, no. 1 (Winter 2014): 8–39; Charles Lawson and Berris Charnley, eds., *Intellectual Property and Genetically Modified Organisms: A Convergence in Laws* (London: Routledge, 2017).

18. Eduard I. Kolchinsky, "Nikolai Vavilov in the Years of Stalin's 'Revolution from Above' (1929–1932)," *Centaurus* 56, no. 4 (November 2014): 330–58.
19. Michael D. Gordin, "Lysenko Unemployed: Soviet Genetics after the Aftermath," *Isis* 109, no. 1 (March 2018): 56–78.
20. Joseph Cotter, *Troubled Harvest: Agronomy and Revolution in Mexico, 1880–2002* (Westport, CT: Praeger, 2003).
21. John H. Perkins, *Insects, Experts, and the Insecticide Crisis: The Quest for New Pest Management Strategies* (New York: Plenum Press, 1982): 11–12.
22. Tiago Saraiva, *Fascist Pigs: Technoscientific Organisms and the History of Fascism* (Cambridge, MA: The MIT Press, 2016).
23. Stuart McCook, *States of Nature: Science, Agriculture, and Environment in the Spanish Caribbean, 1760–1940* (Austin: University of Texas Press, 2002): 8.
24. Maat, *Science Cultivating Practice*, 47–48, 52, 55; Arjo Roersch van der Hoogte and Toine Pieters, "Science in the Service of Colonial Agri-Industrialism: The Case of Chinchona Cultivation in the Dutch and British East Indies, 1852–1900," *Studies in History and Philosophy of Biological and Biomedical Sciences* 47 (2014): 12–22.
25. Prakash Kumar, *Indigo Plantations and Science in Colonial India* (New York: Cambridge University Press, 2012).
26. Rebecca J. H. Woods, *The Herds Shot Round the World: Native Breeds and the British Empire, 1800–1900* (Chapel Hill: University of North Carolina Press, 2017); Robrecht Declercq, "Building Imperial Frontiers: Business, Science, and Karakul Sheep Farming in (German) South-West Africa (1903–1939)," *Journal of Modern European History* 14, no. 1 (2016): 53–77.
27. James C. Malin, *Winter Wheat in the Golden Belt of Kansas: A Study in Adaption to Subhumid Geographical Environment* (Lawrence: University Press of Kansas, 1944): 187; Courtney Fullilove, *Profit of the Earth: The Global Origins of American Agriculture* (Chicago: University of Chicago Press, 2013).
28. Nathan F. Sayre, *The Politics of Scale: A History of Rangeland Science* (Chicago: University of Chicago Press, 2018); Ronald C. Tobey, *Saving the Prairies: The Life Cycle of the Founding School of American Plant Ecology, 1895–1955* (Berkeley: University of California Press, 1981).
29. Randall E. Stross, *The Stubborn Earth: American Agriculturalists on Chinese Soil, 1898–1937* (Berkeley: University of California Press, 1986).
30. Vaclav Smil, *Enriching the Earth: Fritz Haber, Carl Bosch, and the Transformation of World Food Production* (Cambridge, MA: MIT Press, 2004); Hugh S. Gorman, *The Story of N: A Social History of the Nitrogen Cycle and the Challenge of Sustainability* (New Brunswick, NJ: Rutgers University Press, 2013).
31. Alan L. Olmstead and Paul W. Rhode, *Creating Abundance: Biological Innovation and American Agricultural Development* (Cambridge: Cambridge University Press, 2008).

32. Diane B. Paul and Barbara A. Kimmelman, "Mendel in America: Theory and Practice, 1900-1919," in *The Development of American Biology*, ed. Ronald Rainger, Keith R. Benson, and Jane Maienschein (New Brunswick, NJ: Rutgers University Press, 1988); Olmstead and Rhode, *Creating Abundance*.
33. Mark R. Finlay, *Growing American Rubber: Strategic Plants and the Politics of National Security* (New Brunswick, NJ: Rutgers University Press, 2013).
34. Ole H. V. Stalheim, *The Winning of Animal Health: 100 Years of Veterinary Medicine* (Ames: Iowa State University Press, 1995); Claire Strom, *Making Catfish Bait out of Government Boys: The Fight against Cattle Ticks and the Transformation of the Yeoman South* (Athens: University of Georgia Press, 2009); Alan L. Olmstead and Paul W. Rhode, *Arresting Contagion: Science, Policy, and Conflicts over Animal Disease Control* (Cambridge, MA: Harvard University Press, 2015); Francis K. Danquah, "Sustaining a West African Cocoa Economy: Agricultural Science and the Swollen Shoot Contagion in Ghana, 1936-1965," *African Economic History* 31 (2003): 43-74.
35. William Boyd, "Making Meat: Science, Technology, and American Poultry Production," *Technology and Culture* 42, no. 4 (October 2001): 631-64; Roger Horowitz, *Putting Meat on the American Table: Taste, Technology, Transformation* (Baltimore: Johns Hopkins University Press, 2005); Mark R. Finlay, "Hogs, Antibiotics, and the Industrial Environments of Postwar Agriculture" in *Industrializing Organisms: Introducing Evolutionary History*, ed. Susan R. Schrepfer and Philip Scranton (London: Routledge, 2003).
36. Marcus, *Farmers, Agricultural Science and the Quest for Legitimacy*.
37. Mark R. Finlay, "International Science and Local Conditions on the Ground: The Agricultural Sciences and Baltic German Identity," *Journal of Baltic Studies* 44, no. 3 (September 2013): 339-62.
38. Fitzgerald, *The Business of Breeding*; Helen Anne Curry, *Endangered Maize: Industrial Agriculture and the Crisis of Extinction* (Oakland: University of California Press, 2022).
39. Thomas Dunlap, *DDT: Scientists, Citizens, and Public Policy* (Princeton, NJ: Princeton University Press, 1981); David Kinkela, *DDT and the American Century: Global Health, Environmental Politics, and the Pesticide That Changed the World* (Chapel Hill: University of North Carolina Press, 2013); Frederick Rowe Davis, *Banned: A History of Pesticides and the Science of Toxicology* (New Haven, CT: Yale University Press, 2014).
40. Pete Daniel, *Toxic Drift: Pesticides and Health in the Post-World War II South* (Baton Rouge: Louisiana State University Press, 2005).
41. Tore C. Olsson, *Agrarian Crossings: Reformers and the Remaking of the US and Mexican Countryside* (Princeton, NJ: Princeton University Press, 2017); Harwood, *Europe's Green Revolution and Others Since*.
42. Prakash Kumar, Timothy Lorek, Tore C. Olsson, Nicole Sackley, Sigrid Schmalzer, and Gabriela Soto Laveaga, "Roundtable: New Narratives of the Green Revolution," *Agricultural History* 91, no. 3 (Summer 2017): 397-422; John H. Perkins, *Geopolitics and the Green Revolution: Wheat, Genes, and the Cold War* (Oxford: Oxford University Press, 1997); Joseph Morgan Hodge, *Triumph of the Expert: Agrarian Doctrines of Development and the Legacies of British Colonialism* (Athens: Ohio University Press, 2007); Olsson, *Agrarian Crossings*.
43. Raj Patel, "The Long Green Revolution," *Journal of Peasant Studies* 40, no. 1 (2013): 1-63; Harwood, *Europe's Green Revolution and Others Since*, 120-22; Nick Cullather, *The Hungry World: America's Cold War Battle against Poverty in Asia* (Cambridge, MA: Harvard University Press, 2010); R. Douglas Hurt, *The Green Revolution: Science, Politics, and Unintended Consequences* (Tuscaloosa: University of Alabama Press, 2020).

44. Noah Zerbe, "Seeds of Hope, Seeds of Despair: Towards a Political Economy of the Seed Industry in Southern Africa," *Third World Quarterly* 22, no. 4: 657–73.
45. Sigrid Schmalzer, *Red Revolution, Green Revolution: Scientific Farming in Socialist China* (Chicago: University of Chicago Press, 2016).

Bibliography

Cohen, Benjamin R. *Notes from the Ground: Science, Soil, and Society in the American Countryside*. New Haven, CT: Yale University Press, 2009.

Cotter, Joseph. *Troubled Harvest: Agronomy and Revolution in Mexico, 1880–2002*. Westport, CT: Praeger, 2003.

Curry, Helen Anne. *Endangered Maize: Industrial Agriculture and the Crisis of Extinction*. Oakland: University of California Press, 2022.

Derry, Margaret E. *Masterminding Nature: The Breeding of Animals, 1750–2010*. Toronto: University of Toronto Press, 2015.

Fitzgerald, Deborah. *The Business of Breeding: Hybrid Corn in Illinois, 1890–1940*. Ithaca, NY: Cornell University Press, 1990.

Fullilove, Courtney. *The Profit of the Earth: The Global Origins of American Agriculture*. Chicago: University of Chicago Press, 2017.

Hurt, R. Douglas. *The Green Revolution in the Global South: Science, Politics, and Unintended Consequences*. Tuscaloosa: University of Alabama Press, 2020.

Jones, Peter M. *Agricultural Enlightenment: Knowledge, Technology, and Nature, 1750–1840*. Oxford: Oxford University Press, 2016.

Kloppenburg, Jack Ralph. *First the Seed: The Political Economy of Plant Biotechnology, 1492–2000*. Cambridge: Cambridge University Press, 1988.

Maat, Harro. *Science Cultivating Practice: A History of Agricultural Science in the Netherlands and Its Colonies, 1863–1986*. Wageningen: Ponsen & Looijen, 2001.

Marcus, Alan I. *Agricultural Science and the Quest for Legitimacy: Farmers, Agricultural Colleges, and Experiment Stations, 1870–1890*. Ames: Iowa State University Press, 1985.

Moon, David. *The Plough That Broke the Steppes: Agriculture and Environment on Russia's Grasslands, 1700–1914*. Oxford: Oxford University Press, 2013.

Olmstead, Alan L., and Paul W. Rhode. *Arresting Contagion: Science, Policy, and Conflicts over Animal Disease Control*. Cambridge, MA: Harvard University Press, 2015.

Olmstead, Alan L., and Paul W. Rhode. *Creating Abundance: Biological Innovation and American Agricultural Development*. Cambridge: Cambridge University Press, 2008.

Perkins, John H. *Geopolitics and the Green Revolution: Wheat, Genes, and the Cold War*. Oxford: Oxford University Press, 1997.

Perkins, John H. *Insects, Experts, and the Insecticide Crisis: The Quest for New Pest Management Strategies*. New York: Plenum Press, 1982.Rossiter, Margaret W. *The Emergence of Agricultural Science: Justus Liebig and the Americans, 1840–1880*. New Haven, CT: Yale University Press, 1975.

Saraiva, Tiago. *Fascist Pigs: Technoscientific Organisms and the History of Fascism*. Cambridge, MA: MIT Press, 2016.

Sayre, Nathan F. *The Politics of Scale: A History of Rangeland Science*. Chicago: University of Chicago Press, 2018.

Schmalzer, Sigrid. *Red Revolution, Green Revolution: Scientific Farming in Socialist China.* Chicago: University of Chicago Press, 2016.
Smil, Vaclav. *Enriching the Earth: Fritz Haber, Carl Bosch, and the Transformation of World Food Production.* Cambridge, MA: MIT Press, 2004.
Woods, Rebecca J. H. *The Herds Shot Round the World: Native Breeds and the British Empire, 1800–1900.* Chapel Hill: University of North Carolina Press, 2017.

CHAPTER 11

EXPERT AND KNOWLEDGE NETWORKS

DEBORAH FITZGERALD

IN the 1988 documentary *The Goddess and the Computer*, American anthropologists working in Nepal were amazed at the highly complicated yet seemingly unscientific nature of rice farming in the steep mountains. Nepalese farmers followed a very ritualized practice of honoring the water goddess, she who brought plentiful water supplies to the temples and to the rice paddies dotting the terraced mountainside. Many scientists felt that this old-fashioned system was out of date and would benefit from the application of new computer modeling techniques. The anthropologists set out to do just this. Using principles of hydrology, soil science, and ecology, they developed the perfect combination of factors—seeds, water, climate, altitude—to ensure maximum yields of rice. And they discovered that the Nepalese farmers needed no Western advice at all; their system was already based upon the best practices dictated by their environment. It may have been pre-industrial, but because it was based on farmers' experience over generations, it was perfectly aligned with the region's history and ecology. It reflected the hard-won expertise of Nepali farmers.[1]

Our ideas about expertise are somewhat paradoxical. We tend to think of expertise as the end result of deep and specialized training in a particular field, training that typically is based in scientific and technical theory. Experts have training in scientific fields, such as biology or soil science; they have been certified by both an educational institution and a professional association as capable of understanding and solving a particular class of problem. Yet in an arena as experience-based as agriculture, such theoretical training can only get one so far. A soil scientist with only laboratory and book training might be an expert on soil theory but would have a difficult time growing things without the practical experience of farming in a particular location. Indeed, the idea of expert knowledge or mastery of a specialty certainly predates the rise of scientific expertise. Although the rise of science-based expertise and official certifications of ability are the norms today when we evaluate someone's credentials, we still expect such people to have mastered the practical and experience-based skills that such certifications promise.

Today there is an enormous range of experts whose business, directly and indirectly, is agriculture. While not farmers themselves, they depend entirely upon the existence and success of farmers for whom they usually act as brokers of some kind. Agricultural chemists, pathologists, veterinarians, soil scientists, agricultural economists, geneticists, horticulturalists, agricultural engineers, and many other college-educated experts make up one part of this population. Another part is the middlemen who sell seed for planting and feeds for livestock to farmers each year, the livestock breeders who sell the animals, the implement dealers who sell farm machinery to farmers, the auction houses that buy finished livestock, the packing and processing industries that turn plants and animals into food, the bankers who loan farmers operating funds each year, the traders at the Chicago Board and other exchanges who buy and sell stocks in farm products and inputs, the food industry that buys dairy products, meats, grains, fruits, and vegetables from farmers and other brokers and turns those raw materials into frozen, canned, dried, and all manner of time-insensitive foods, and the professors of agricultural sciences who train generations of young students to become not farmers, but people who work in one of the above roles. Each of these people claims an expertise in something related to farming, and while farmers have come to rely upon and trust many of them, the relationship has not been an equivalency. Farmers depend upon these experts more than the experts rely upon farmers. Put another way, when a farmer fails it can destroy his family and devastate his rural community. When an agribusiness suffers a setback, the company redirects their efforts or abandons the division. But rarely is a company's bottom line even undermined.

Improvers and Teachers

How did this system come to be? As long as farmers have tilled the soil and raised animals for food, they have had a market relationship with someone. The business of simple buying and selling did not rely upon scientific theories at first, but only upon supply and demand. And in the nineteenth century, one did not need to be a scientist to do practical experiments relating to drainage, breeding, or soil improvement, to name but a few. Especially in Europe, many landowners formed agricultural societies devoted to providing a forum for discussing such ideas and exploring agricultural matters. As early as 1777 the Bath and West of England Society (it became the Royal Bath and West of England Society in 1977) was established, along with several others, and the Board of Agriculture was formed in 1793 with the aim of collecting information on current agricultural conditions. Voluntary societies became quite common in the early to mid-nineteenth century, often specializing in, for example, cattle breeding or wheat growing. Other countries also followed this path. The Society for the Advancement of Agriculture was established in Amsterdam in 1776.[2]

British and Dutch colonists who immigrated to North America had to learn how to farm all over again when they encountered new soils, climates, and seeds in the mid-seventeenth century. As every American schoolchild learns, it was not the colonists who were the experts, but Native Americans, who showed them how to plant a dead fish with their grain seeds for best results. By the mid-nineteenth century, American farmers had learned a great deal about variations in soil types, not only in New England, but reaching out across the country. Their knowledge was still very much experience-based, but it was becoming more elaborate. And like the Europeans, they began forming agricultural societies to enable them to compare notes.[3]

It was through this banding together that successful farmers became aware that, in Germany, organic chemists were studying the composition of farm soils. Justus von Liebig's *Organic Chemistry in Its Applications to Agriculture and Physiology*, published in 1840, caused a sensation in America. A soil chemist at Giessen, Liebig found that soils were much more complex than previously known, but that poor soil could be emended with a specific and tailor-made application of appropriate nutrients. Liebig developed a winning combination of theory (chemistry) and practice (applications to the soil) that appealed to Americans desperate for a solution to their "worn-out" soils in New England, the mid-Atlantic, and Southern states where repeated cropping had severely depleted the soil. American publishers, scientists, and farmers alike received Liebig's scientific approach with great enthusiasm.[4]

Liebig's contribution was not only his development of a way to test and emend soils. Indeed, his more lasting effect was to introduce the Americans to a system of doing research. Liebig's book came out in 1840, and Americans studied it very carefully, necessitating many editions of the book in its first few decades. In addition, some Americans traveled to Germany to study with Liebig himself and to see his approach firsthand. What they learned had a profound effect on American education and American agriculture. Why? Liebig approached the classification and improvement of soils from a scientific point of view, that is, he and his staff organized research around a question that could be addressed systematically. He understood the importance of institutionalized research, ideally in a university setting. This allowed scientists to develop research programs over time with guaranteed funding and disinterested oversight. Liebig supported the dissemination of these research results to farmers themselves, who would be the ultimate beneficiaries of university-based studies. And university students would be trained in scientific methods applied to agriculture so there would be a new generation of agricultural experts going forward.[5]

In Europe, the development of science-based agriculture based on the German university was highly admired, and many countries made progress over the century. In the United Kingdom the Cirencester (later Royal) College of Agriculture was established in 1842, and its design and standards were the model for all such agricultural colleges that followed. In the Netherlands, the earliest successful agricultural colleges dated from 1821, when a veterinary school was started as a response to the repeated outbreaks of rinderpest; in 1876 the State Agricultural School in Wageningen was founded and used scholarships to attract students, a tactic that proved very successful in increasing enrollments. In France the École Nationale Supérieure Agronomique started in 1848 in Montpelier, and in Denmark the Royal Veterinary and Agricultural College opened in 1856. In Sweden, what is now the Swedish Agricultural University dates back to 1775, when it was the Veterinary Institute at Skara. Spain created a Central School of Agriculture in 1858, and the Norwegian College of Agriculture opened in 1859. In most cases, these universities and colleges were founded to address urgent local or regional farming problems, such as an outbreak of pests or persistent disease, and at a time when emerging scientific approaches were promising real solutions. But the growth and success of agriculture depended not only upon science. It relied as well on the creation of new generations of students who would use their knowledge in supervising estates or in further research or in agricultural business firms.

The American Land-Grant System

In the United States, Liebig's approach to scientific research and education led agricultural enthusiasts to increased agitation for a national system of agricultural research, teaching, and dissemination of timely information to farmers. In the 1840s and 1850s, hundreds of new agricultural societies were founded, and several states established laboratories in their existing universities or began building new colleges of agriculture. In 1862, the federal government created the US Department of Agriculture to conduct research and develop regulatory mechanisms for improving agricultural production across the country. Congress also passed the Morrill Land-Grant Act of 1862, which required each state to build a college of agriculture, using the funds released by the sale of federal land, and each dedicated to serving the farming interests of that state. It took another several decades for all the states to actually build and occupy these colleges; indeed, historically black agricultural colleges were not mandated until 1890, and those for Native Americans not until 1994. It is very difficult to imagine Congress creating such a grand scheme today. But at the time, on the eve of the Civil War, Congress ratified the ideas that farming was absolutely crucial to the health and economic success of the country; that farmers were believed to have the values and experiences most emblematic of this experiment in democracy; and in a country built on immigration, that there needed to be a way to bring new citizens into this new world and equip them with the skills and understanding of successful farming. Although the funding model for this system was not perfect, in effect providing far less funding to the Southern states and less populous Western states, it amounted to a radical and bold approach to solving the problems of feeding the country and creating a class of virtuous yeoman.[6]

The land-grant system was not established all at once but rather over the course of about fifty years. The first issue was building the colleges of agriculture, creating curricula, and hiring professors and technical staff. The problems involved with this were several. First, there was no body of learned professors of agriculture in America at that time, so hiring was a challenge. Nor was there a body of systematic knowledge of agriculture in general for them to teach. The fields of basic science could be taught, but the applications of science to practical agricultural problems had not much been done. Moreover, the conditions of soil, climate, and aridity varied widely, and most farm families did not see agricultural education as necessary or worthwhile; non-farm families had no interest in agriculture, preferring to send their offspring to study law or medicine. There was very little support for agricultural research and education in the countryside. Further, many state governments did not agree with the federal government that states needed to spend some of their own money on the colleges, which was mandated in the Morrill Act; they often felt that there were more pressing local and regional needs. Slowly but surely, however, the agricultural colleges came into view. The Hatch Act (1887) and the Adams Act (1906) established the agricultural experiment stations at each college and ensured that staff would conduct original research. And in 1914 the Smith-Lever Act established the extension services at each college, which funded outreach efforts to farm and non-farm families throughout the state.[7]

The third leg of the land-grant system was the dissemination of knowledge to practicing farmers. Called the "extension service" in the United States, this was the means by which the fruits of agricultural practice were put into effect on the farms across the country. Divided into county units, extension agents tried to cultivate good relationships with every farmer in his county: he visited farms, helped farmers identify pests and diseases in their crops, offered advice on livestock issues, and tried to encourage the farmers to operate in a businesslike fashion. Experimenting with new seeds, creating a system for field drainage, keeping track of bills and receipts, building structures to store grains, and much more was the agent's gospel. The goal was not only to get farmers to improve their practices, but to improve them through the application of scientific knowledge and often, science-based products. Rather than using dung or compost on their fields, farmers could buy synthetic fertilizers. Instead of feeding their pigs table scraps, they could give them specialized feeds. Instead of waiting for the onslaught of pests and diseases, farmers could apply generous doses of herbicides and pesticides. And instead of hiring seasonal labor and depending upon farm animals to pull plows, farmers could buy machinery to do just about every job on the farm. To the county agent, it was just common sense that farmers should embrace science- and technology-based practices that would make farming experience less risky, less arduous, and more rewarding.[8]

But this was only part of the agent's thinking. The modernization of farming introduced problems as well as solutions. Though science and technology offered many benefits to farm families, the land-grant system itself, and especially the agricultural colleges, were often more appealing to rural youth than staying on the farm. Civic leaders and government officials worried about a rural brain-drain as young people headed for college, never to return to the farms. Even with science and technology, farm life was difficult, and calamitous weather or markets could discourage even good farmers. County agents were often the key people trying to keep farmers from moving or retiring and trying to persuade young people to bring their college learning back to their family farm. One tactic was to make farm life more fun and more similar to town life—consolidating schools, providing electric and telephone service as well as indoor plumbing—and was key to this effort. Another tack was the creation of rural youth clubs, especially the 4-H (1902) and Future Farmers of America (1928). The "H" in 4-H stood Head, Heart, Hands and Health: "I pledge my head to clear thinking, my heart to greater loyalty, my hands to larger service, and my health to better living, for my club, my community, my country and my world. The program was designed to engage young people in raising food and animals and competing for prizes at state fairs each year, activities that showed youth some of the business of farming and instilled responsibility and pride in their work. The FFA was in many ways a continuation of 4-H. It was geared to high school and college students from farm backgrounds and helped them stay interested in rural life through service projects, formal education, and leadership training. These organizations were unable to stem the flow of young people away from farms, but they probably did help build a phalanx of young people keen to make farming a modern science-based industry.[9]

Thus, it took about 100 years for the earliest glimmerings of scientific ideas applied to agriculture to lead to the stabilization of agricultural institutions throughout Europe and North America. This effort grew out of the remarkable expansion of scientific experimentation and knowledge production, and the state's growing belief that only with consistent scientific and financial commitment would national food security be realized. With this framework in place, other forms of expertise and controlling influence in agriculture continued to develop.

Agribusiness Takes the Lead

By the early twentieth century, the number of people offering advice to farmers was expanding rapidly. Whereas formerly the county agent was the farmers' primary source of information and advice, by the 1920s they had other options. Most important were brokers, or middlemen, who represented trade associations and businesses focused upon agricultural inputs such as seeds, livestock, chemicals, insurance, machinery, and so on. These were the people with whom farmers developed relationships, an interdependence born of science, technology, and advertising. The earliest brokers were businesspeople who sold raw materials, primarily seeds and animals, to farmers. Before hybridization of fruits, vegetables, grains, and livestock, many farmers could save their best seeds from one year to the next for planting, obviating the need to buy fresh seed each year. For corn growers this was the norm until the late 1920s. Corn farmers carefully chose seed from the harvest to plant the following year, kernels and ears that demonstrated the qualities he thought were most promising. But once hybrid corn was developed, farmers had to buy seed each and every year because hybrids could not be replanted without severe production losses. Eventually, nearly all farm crops became proprietary due to genetic breeding, and farmers had to pay for something—seed—that had been free just two generations earlier. And as farmers became dependent upon hybrid seeds, they became dependent upon the scientific explanations of seed salesmen, which expanded the knowledge chasm between farmers and experts to a large degree.

Hybridity was a difficult concept, and invisible, which put most farmers at the mercy of seed salesmen.[10]

Trade associations were another kind of broker. Virtually all plants and animals grown for commercial sale were governed by trade association guidelines. Before fruit was shipped fresh or vegetables were sold to the cannery or frozen food factory, it was graded for size, color, shape, and conformity to an agreed-upon norm for that food. Trade associations and cooperatives set these standards for growing, shipping, and selling virtually everything farmers produced. One of the earliest examples of this was the California Fruit Growers Exchange, an organization started in the late 1880s in Southern California that tried to increase sales of oranges throughout the country by improving orange quality through breeding and grading, managing the thousands of independent growers, and creating advertising campaigns that persuaded Americans to eat lots of oranges. These campaigns were wildly successful and demonstrated to skeptical growers that the art of visual and psychological persuasion could be the difference between poor or excellent markets. Other fruit and vegetable growers took note in the early twentieth century, including the Blue Diamond almond growers, who formed their cooperative in 1910; Sun Maid Growers of California, which launched its raisin promotions in 1912; and the Humboldt Creamery in northern California, which organized in 1929.[11]

It may not seem obvious that the creation of cooperatives and associations introduced new expertise into the farming operation. We often think of early co-ops as humble organizations operated by ordinary farmers pooling their resources to get better prices. And in some parts of the United States this was the case. But California was another story. Here, these organizations functioned like super-specialized agricultural experiment stations and extension services, focused on only one fruit or vegetable. And in this regard, it became clear that this was a big opportunity for experts to become more prominent in farming. First, individual growers had little recourse if they had too much produce to sell and not enough buyers; they were each too small to find new buyers further away from local markets, especially given the time-sensitivity of fresh fruit. By banding together into cooperatives, they could hire marketing experts to figure out how to expand their markets and commandeer transportation networks. The organizations worked with agricultural scientists and engineers to develop the best strains of fruits and vegetables to grow and ship, and the best forms of mechanization and labor practices to use as they increased their output. These experts found that shipping fresh fruit was risky and required very precise packing designs, which then led to the breeding of standardized shapes and sizes of produce. The cooperatives also created a huge demand for transcontinental rail traffic in cold train cars, a system that was subject to continual improvement for decades. And they oversaw the graphic design campaigns that, in the case of oranges, created an exciting new advertising style that inspired many other products as well.[12]

Another form of expertise and control existed in the Southern plantation economy of the nineteenth century. The slave plantations concentrated almost entirely on lucrative commodity crops—tobacco in Virginia and North Carolina, cotton in the Deep South, rice in the South Carolina Sea Islands, and sugar in Louisiana. These depended heavily upon complex systems of expertise; tobacco in particular was a crop that demanded careful and experienced treatment, from planting to harvesting to curing to marketing. Into the early twentieth century, most of this expertise belonged to the grower and his slaves, who learned from each other how to know when to harvest or when the cure was finished. The subtlety of these judgments was a challenge to those keen on industrializing the operation in the twentieth century. But as with other commodity crops, both cotton and tobacco were controlled by outside brokers, which organized and maintained systems of grading and marketing that pushed back on the grower's decisions and prerogatives.[13]

In the Midwestern United States, where grain farming and livestock raising dominated the farm economy, the experts who controlled the system were different still. There things were decided locally by the grain elevators, which dictated the price farmers could get for their grain on any given day; the stock market, which set those prices based on global production and trade; the railroads, which dictated when and where trains cars would be available and at what rate; and the buyers, who paid more for certain breeds and strains and thus encouraged farmers to grow that. Here the expert was the one who controlled the economy, local or beyond, regardless of whether he or she had a PhD in soil science or economics.

The city of Chicago concentrated expertise in livestock and grain in the nineteenth century. Thanks to the westward flow of new immigrants as well as the completion of the transcontinental railroad in 1848, Chicago sat at the center of a vastly changing landscape. Farming and food processing became the engines of Midwestern prosperity, as new farmers broke ground for crops and began raising livestock, both on a larger scale than was possible in the Eastern states. All of this grain and pork and beef ended up in Chicago, where stockyards and meatpacking plants grew in numbers and power beginning in the 1860s. Both Swift and Company and Armour and Company became dominant in the meat market, partly through concentrating the entire process, from owning the feedlots to butchering the cattle and pork to "dressing" it, that is, packing it for sale to individuals rather than local butchers. Swift was closely involved in the creation of refrigerated train cars, which allowed the company to ship meat products around the country safely. Both companies also adopted the "disassembly line," a highly mechanized way of cutting carcasses up quickly. And both companies, thanks to their large scale, became essential purveyors of meat for the government starting in the Civil War and continuing through the twentieth century. Although most farmers never met an Armour representative, such middlemen set the prices and conditions of sale for virtually all farmers in America.[14]

The same kind of thing happened with grain. In the Midwest, corn was by far the dominant crop in the nineteenth century, while wheat was king further west. Before 1850, farmers sold their grain by the sackful to a local merchant, who moved it by river to a larger grain market such as Chicago. With the coming of the railroad, however, this system was upended, as farmers sold their grain to specialized local grain elevators, which could store the grain if necessary and then pour it into a train car for shipment. As William Cronon describes it, grains became "golden streams that flowed like water," a metaphor that aptly captures many of the transformations that mechanization made possible. The Chicago Board of Trade, which was created in 1848 in large part to deal with this huge increase in grain and meat, also became the chief regulator of these trades, creating classes and grades of wheat and corn. Standards of quality became regulations that governed the prices paid according to the grain's cleanness, weight, and color. Farmers could not afford to remain indifferent to the quality of the grain he sold, because now it would cost him dearly. But grain became even more abstracted as grain traders adopted the telegraph in 1848, effectively creating futures markets not in today's actual grain, but in the hypothetical grain of tomorrow. Here again, the application of expertise and technology had several possible outcomes. It allowed farmers to sell much more grain more easily. Yet it also constrained the conditions under which farmers operated and the quality decisions that were once his alone. Some farmers must have wondered if they, too, had become abstractions.[15]

One of the biggest outside influences on what farmers produced was the economic and strategic demands of wars. Beginning with the Civil War, and continuing into World Wars I and II, military demands created a highly concentrated degree of focus among farmers, middlemen, and the federal government. In a variety of ways, the government established guidelines that dictated what farmers would grow, how it would be sold and to whom, what prices it would fetch, and which food companies would receive contracts for the military market. The demand for safe, increasingly time-insensitive food galvanized the food industry to become ever more creative in meeting the government's needs and possibly establishing a continuous client. But it could also close down production traditions that did not fit the military's requirements. For example, many small farmers all over the United States grew vegetables for the canning industry, which had a large role in feeding troops. These farmers did well. But other farmers, who had been supplying the government with chickens, or fruits, or cheese, were cut out of the equation when the government decided to concentrate its purchases in just a few locations. Where once they bought chickens from a variety of locations, they decided to buy only from one or two to save time and trouble. Thus, the wartime markets could cut both ways for farmers. Again, decisions made by the Quartermaster could reach all the way back to the farm. When the Quartermaster inspected canned beef stew submitted by Armour and decided that the grade of beef was too fatty or tough, Armour stopped buying beef from those farmers who supplied the beef. And if canned peaches had a weird texture, or an off color, Del Monte might bypass the farms producing them in the future. Thus, the production chain developed for military provisioning had a powerful effect on all aspects of food production and processing.[16]

Postwar Consolidation

Following World War II, it became very clear that the world was a bigger, more interconnected place than it had been in the early 1940s. Agricultural commodities traveled vast distances as countries tried to reclaim markets they had controlled before the war's blockades and attacks wreaked havoc with shipping lanes. The war had destroyed nearly all agricultural capacity in much of Europe as well as Japan, and other countries scrambled to re-create markets there. American farmers had tremendous surpluses once they did not need to provide for the war effort, and this was scooped up by the lend-lease program and others designed to help Europe rebuild following the war. But few things returned to normal following the war. Rather, those in American agriculture experienced a set of changes that further eroded the independent and diversified farming tradition and increased the role of agribusiness in setting the rules of the farming game.[17]

There were many ways in which this played out. One was the extraordinary growth of the processed food industry during and after the war years. National Biscuit grew by 26.4 percent, Borden by 27.7 percent, General Foods by 21.6 percent, and Corn Products by 23.6 percent. This expansion was due to growth in the study of food chemistry, the military's need for easily shipped food for the troops, and the idea to turn mountains of grain and dairy into time-insensitive foods, what became the "convenience foods" of the 1950s and 1960s. These factors changed both the way people ate and the way farmers understood their markets. Another aspect of this change was the decision of some food industries to vertically integrate their production process. For example, during World War II, meat rationing led people to eat less beef and more chicken, accelerating a trend in the poultry industry toward concentrating production in a few places and hiring former chicken farmers on contracts. These contracts were little better than sharecropping arrangements; farmers lost money, lost their independence, and had few other options. A similar phenomenon occurred in the pork industry in the 1970s as the big corporate buyers of pork for processing forced small farmers into "contract or nothing" arrangements in which, as with poultry farmers, they were required to invest heavily in automated equipment, sheds, specialized feeds, and other accoutrements of the industrial livestock pattern.[18]

Farming under contract has been a global phenomenon since the 1960s, common in nearly every food chain. Coffee in Africa and Latin America, baby vegetables in Burkina Faso and Zambia, fruit in Chile—all are produced within a highly integrated system of contracts and markets that are very tightly coupled and leave little room for farmers to exercise their own expertise. Indeed, in some places, "farmers," in the early twentieth century sense, have rarely existed. Rather, agricultural operations are conducted by growers, who supervise the business, and their laborers. Much of California agriculture is of this sort, as well as much of the Caribbean fruit trade. It is a system without sentimentality. Agricultural products are commodities, like so many others, even though they are more delicate, often grown at the mercy of weather and natural cataclysms, and whose quantities tend to be either in excess or in shortage. Contract farming is as close to industrial production as agriculture can get. This kind of farming increased the distance between consumers and producers more and more, leading most consumers to lose track entirely of where their food came from.[19]

Perhaps the most profound way that the war changed things, and the climax to date of agricultural expertise trumping local knowledge, was the Green Revolution.

Launched in Mexico by the Rockefeller Foundation in 1943, this effort (then called the Mexican Agricultural Program) was an effort to develop vigorous strains of hybrid corn and wheat resistant to stem rust disease that would yield far more than indigenous varieties, making Mexico more self-sufficient than before. The system was designed to exploit and export the land-grant model of agricultural research, education, and extension. Mexican agricultural colleges and experiment stations were beefed up, and many young Mexican agricultural students traveled to land-grant colleges in the United States to receive training in scientific plant breeding, plant pathology, and other scientific areas deemed essential to fundamentally change Mexican agricultural practice. A key feature of using hybrid seeds was the simultaneous use of scientific "inputs"—fertilizers, pesticides, and irrigation—without which the hybrid seed would not perform well. Over a decade, Mexican farmers were producing vastly more of these crops, and the program was seen as a potential cure for world hunger and rural despair all over the world.[20]

This method of growing and managing crops was transplanted around the world, particularly to developing countries, and nowhere more dramatically than India. Long considered an agricultural failure, despite a robust export trade in grains as late as 1965, India was seen as the obvious recipient of what was considered an agricultural revolution. American organizations—the Rockefeller Foundation, Ford Foundation, and USAID, to name a few—poured scientific, technical, and managerial resources into the country, confident that it would fundamentally transform the lives of its people. And it did do that, but not entirely in the ways the leadership had hoped. "Green Revolution" crops were not necessarily ones that most Indians ate. Wheat, for example, was primarily an export crop in India, as it was in Mexico. But for American breeders, wheat was considered a top crop because it was so popular among American and European countries, and because it was amenable to breeding improvements. Corn was also not an Indian priority but was a priority in Mexico, and importantly it was the first commodity crop to be hybridized. What many Indians ate—rice, millet, lentils—was less interesting to the scientists and thus not a big part of the Green Revolution. This kind of agricultural operation relied on huge quantities of fertilizers, pesticides, and irrigation, items that were extremely expensive and continuously required. Indian farmers were not equipped to invest in this kind of thing, and once the international funding was reduced, it left farmers in a terrible position. These "inputs" were environmentally very toxic, and they accumulated over the years. Waterways were contaminated and soils were rendered useless after a decade of operation. The costs of the Green Revolution in India are now considered much worse than the gains by many analysts.[21]

Conclusion

The development of agricultural expertise through history, ultimately, bears a striking resemblance to the development of capitalism itself. This should come as no surprise.

While we tend to think of expertise as a virtuous, education-based acquisition of specialized knowledge, which it typically was, it was also a means of getting ahead, of exploiting other people's ignorance, and of widening the gap between those who struggle to make a living and those who tell them how to do it better. There is a dark side to expertise, in agriculture as elsewhere, because as this review has suggested, even the best-intentioned experts have been unable to foresee the future and the ways that their advice and improving schemes will play out. Agricultural chemicals can increase a farmer's crop yields quite substantially, but they are expensive for the farmer to buy and harmful for the environment to survive. Agricultural education provided rural youth with a systematic understanding of nature and economics, but it also led them to abandon the rural life and drained the countryside of future leaders. Applying scientific practices between countries, such as the United States and India, was generous and well-meaning, yet it was done without an adequate understanding of its people, history, politics, dietary and labor habits, and intentions.[22]

Ironically, those farmers who have pushed back against the agribusiness-based farming practices have developed a different kind of expertise. As Thomas Fleischman shows, East German villagers who kept pigs, feeding them table scraps and allowing them to forage, had far fatter and healthier pigs than those who agreed to convert to confinement hog operations. There the pigs were stressed by tight quarters, infections were contagious and often fatal, and the farmers paid a high price for a system that was oddly precarious. In France, we see something similar. The government decided to vigorously support industrial-style agriculture in the post–World War II period, pressuring small farmers to expand their acreages, adopt hybrid varieties of plants and animals, and invest in fancy outbuildings, chemicals, and marketing schemes. While many farmers obliged, a large number came to believe that this system was irrational and overly expensive, and they returned to the old ways. Although the old ways were once considered unscientific and ignorant, they could now be called organic, allowing these farmers to tap into a lucrative market and return to a more relaxed and independent farming business. As a final irony, organic farming has developed its own kind of expertise and has become part of the agricultural education system itself.[23]

Thus we come full circle. Institutions for agricultural research and education have grown and spread across the globe since the nineteenth century, but they have often reflected quite contemporary concerns. Although each state in the United States still supports a robust agricultural college, those in England have shifted almost entirely to vocational education, that is, training for jobs rather than researching scientific problems. In the Southern Hemisphere, agricultural education and research came only in the postwar period and was heavily shaped by the rosy prognostications of agribusiness, American foundations, and American agricultural scientists. Like India, many African countries have struggled with this legacy. On the one hand, they are ever eager to become self-sufficient in food production as well as capable of developing export markets. On the other hand, the tools and logics they have been offered by well-meaning experts has often not suited their ecology or their ambitions. They find themselves dependent upon the wrong expertise, caught on a "technological treadmill" that never pays off. It will be up to future generations to come up with new paradigms of agricultural sustainability and security, ones that heed the lessons of the past.[24]

Notes

1. John Stephen Lansing and Andre Singer, "The Goddess and the Computer" (Watertown, MA: Educational Documentary Resources, 1988).
2. Lord Ernle, *English Farming, Past and Present* (London: Longmans, Green & Co., 1932).
3. Steven Stoll, *Larding the Lean Earth: Soil and Society in 19th Century America* (New York: Hill & Wang, 2002).
4. Margaret Rossiter, *The Emergence of Agricultural Science: Justus Liebig and the Americans, 1840–1880* (New Haven, CT: Yale University Press, 1975).
5. Ibid.
6. Alfred C. True, *A History of Experimentation and Research in the United States, 1607–1925, Including a History of the United States Department of Agriculture* (Washington, DC: Government Printing Office, 1937).
7. Charles Rosenberg, *No Other Gods: On Science and American Social Thought* (Baltimore: Johns Hopkins University Press, 1976; repr. 1997); Deborah Fitzgerald, *Every Farm a Factory: The Industrial Ideal in American Agriculture* (New Haven, CT: Yale University Press, 2003).
8. David Danbom, *The Resisted Revolution: Urban America and the Industrialization of Agriculture, 1900–1930* (Ames: Iowa State University Press, 1979).
9. Gabriel Rosenberg, *4-H Harvest: Sexuality and the State in Rural America* (Philadelphia: University of Pennsylvania Press, 2015).
10. Deborah Fitzgerald, *The Business of Breeding: Hybrid Corn in Illinois, 1890–1940* (Ithaca, NY: Cornell University Press, 1990).
11. Steven Stoll, *The Fruit of Natural Advantage: Making the Industrial Countryside in California* (Berkeley: University of California Press, 1998).
12. Susanne Freidberg, *Fresh: A Perishable History* (Cambridge, MA: Harvard University Press, 2010).
13. Barbara Hahn, *Making Tobacco Bright: Creating an American Commodity, 1617–1937* (Baltimore: Johns Hopkins University Press, 2011).
14. William Cronon, *Nature's Metropolis: Chicago and the Great West* (New York: W. W. Norton, 1991)
15. Ibid., 113.
16. Deborah Fitzgerald, "World War II and the Quest for Time-Insensitive Foods," *Osiris* 35 (2020).
17. Lizzie Collingham, *The Taste of War: World War II and the Battle for Food* (New York: Penguin, 2011).
18. On growth see Laurence M. Marks and Co., "Food and Dairy Profits and Security Prices," January 13, 1950 (Wilmington Trust Papers, acc 2118, box 20, Hagley Library); Monica Gisolfi, *The Takeover: Chicken Farming and the Roots of American Agribusiness* (Athens: University of Georgia Press, 2017). On pork, see Thomas Fleischman, *Communist Pigs: An Animal History of East Germany's Rise and Fall* (Seattle: University of Washington Press,

2020); Jim Hightower, *Hard Tomatoes, Hard Times: The Failure of the Land-grant College Complex* (Washington, DC: Agribusiness Accountability Project, 1972).
19. "Contract Farming and Vertical Integration in Agriculture" (Washington, DC: US Department of Agriculture, 1958); Richard Walker, *The Conquest of Bread: 150 Years of Agribusiness in California* (New York: The New Press, 2004); Steven Striffler and Mark Moberg, *Banana Wars: Power, Production, and History in the Americas* (Durham, NC: Duke University Press, 2003).
20. John Perkins, *Geopolitics and the Green Revolution: Wheat, Genes, and the Cold War* (New York: Oxford University Press, 1997); E. C. Stakman, Richard Bradfield, and Paul C. Mangelsdorf, *Campaigns against Hunger* (Cambridge, MA: Belknap Press of Harvard University Press, 1967).
21. Nick Cullather, *The Hungry World: America's Cold War Battle against Poverty in Asia* (Cambridge, MA: Harvard University Press, 2010); Akhil Gupta, *Postcolonial Developments: Agriculture in the Making of Modern India* (Durham, NC: Duke University Press).
22. James C. Scott, *Seeing like a State: How Certain Schemes to Improve the Human Condition Have Failed* (New Haven, CT: Yale University Press, 1998).
23. Fleischman, *Three Little Pigs*; Venus Bivar, *Organic Resistance: The Struggle over Industrial Farming in Postwar France* (Chapel Hill: University of North Carolina Press, 2018).
24. On Africa, see, e.g., African Academy of Sciences, *Enhancement of Agricultural Research in Francophone Africa* (Kenya: African Academy of Sciences, 1991). On the treadmill, see Willard W. Cochrane, *The Development of American Agriculture: A Historical Analysis* (Minneapolis: University of Minnesota Press, 1993).

Bibliography

Cochrane, Willard W. *The Development of American Agriculture: A Historical Analysis.* Minneapolis: University of Minnesota Press, 1993.

Cronon, William. *Nature's Metropolis: Chicago and the Great West.* New York: W. W. Norton, 1991.

Cullather, Nick. *The Hungry World: America's Cold War Battle against Poverty in Asia.* Cambridge, MA: Harvard University Press, 2010.

Danbom, David. *The Resisted Revolution: Revolution: Urban America and the Industrialization of Agriculture, 1900–1930.* Ames: Iowa State University Press, 1979.

Daniel, Pete. *Breaking the Land: The Transformation of Cotton, Tobacco, and Rice Cultures since 1880.* Urbana: University of Illinois Press, 1985.

Fitzgerald, Deborah. *Every Farm a Factory: The Industrial Ideal in American Agriculture.* New Haven, CT: Yale University Press, 2003.

Gupta, Akhil. *Postcolonial Developments: Agriculture in the Making of Modern India.* Durham, NC: Duke University Press, 1998.

Harwood, Jonathan. *Europe's Green Revolution and Others Since: The Rise and Fall of Peasant-Friendly Plant Breeding.* London: Routledge, 2012.

Moser, Peter, and Tony Varley, eds. *Integration through Subordination: The Politics of Agricultural Modernization in Industrial Europe.* Turnhout, Belgium: Brepols, 2013.

Perkins, John. *Geopolitics and the Green Revolution: Wheat, Genes, and the Cold War.* New York: Oxford University Press, 1997.

Pollan, Michael. *The Omnivore's Dilemma: A Natural History of Four Meals*. London: Penguin, 2006.

Rossiter, Margaret. *The Emergence of Agricultural Science: Justus Liebig and the Americans, 1840–1880*. New Haven, CT: Yale University Press, 1975.

Stoll, Steven. *The Fruits of Natural Advantage: Making the Industrial Countryside in California*. Berkeley: University of California Press, 1998.

CHAPTER 12

COMMODITY FRONTIERS AS DRIVERS OF GLOBAL CAPITALISM

ULBE BOSMA AND ERIC VANHAUTE

TODAY, widely divergent socio-ecological regimes face different, yet related, challenges. Agrarian societies, largely located in the poorest areas in the world, struggle to secure food, resources, and local livelihoods in the context of an increasingly globalized, extractive, and uneven world. Post-industrial societies, on the other hand, face the challenge of reducing their ecological footprint and "greening" their consumption. Concepts such as circularity, resource efficiency, sustainable development, and social metabolism have entered policy documents to signal that wealthy, post-industrial countries have become aware of the need to reduce their dependence on imports of huge quantities of biological and mineral resources, which come mostly from poorer countries. Despite these good intentions, the fact remains that core countries massively extract and import raw materials from peripheral regions, while they export their most polluting industries, thus externalizing the social and environmental impacts of mass consumption onto more vulnerable peoples and places.[1]

This story is not new; it is inexorably part of how the global economy has developed over the past seven centuries. It has been marked by a global capitalist expansion, in which core societies, colonial powers usually, compensated for their ecological deficits by imperialist exploitation. The proliferation of extractive economies in geologically and climatically distinct ecosystems, at ever greater distances and across ever broader space, has been an indispensable element of global economic expansion. Frontier expansion, in other words, has long been a driver of economic growth. Economist Edward Barbier defines frontier expansion, or frontier-based development, as "exploiting or converting new sources of relatively abundant resources for production purposes."[2] We learn from his encompassing study that over the past centuries and even millennia, many frontier zones collapsed under social and ecological pressures, whereas others apparently reached a temporary socio-ecological balance. Whereas such equilibria can exist at local levels for some time, at a macro or world scale, the extractive commodity frontier system is inherently unstable. In most cases, the pressure to produce more against ever declining prices, preferably far below reproduction costs, leads to ecological degradation and severe exploitation of labor.

While frontiers of commodity production are not necessarily capitalist, the extensive cotton frontiers of the USSR are a case in point; the concept of commodity frontiers is embedded in a specific historical understanding of capitalism as a historical system, developed by scholars such as Werner Sombart, Fernand Braudel, and Immanuel Wallerstein.[3] Capitalism is understood as a historical process of commodification of labor and nature through private property and one driven by the intrinsic need to permanently open up new opportunities for accumulation. The profit-driven character of capitalism leads to an unstinting quest for the cheapest answers to environmental and resource problems. This applies both to the micro level of individual sites of commodity production as to the global political economy of resource management. Solutions typically pivot on richer and more powerful countries exporting their problems to poorer countries, by opening new frontiers of commodity cultivation, extraction, and even waste disposal. David Harvey refers to this process as capital's "spatial fix," which can include robber capitalism, the extraction of resources by dispossession of local communities, and highly uneven development.[4]

Harvey's spatial fix is a central mechanism in the history of capitalism. Or, following Jason W. Moore, capitalism is a radical new approach by which societies coped with resource scarcities or crises. It emerged at the end of the European Middle Ages as an answer to ecological degradation by relocating entire production systems. This was "Capitalism's genius," according to Moore: instead of the ecology setting limits to economic and political expansion, merchant capital financed the extraction of resources elsewhere.[5] Moore developed his notion of the moving and expanding commodity frontier through the well-known example of the spatial movement of cane sugar production. The sugar frontier moved from India toward Persia in the sixth century CE, and it arrived in Egypt in the eighth century. There it emerged as an important item of trade both within the Arabic world and with Venetians and Genoese merchants.[6] Sugar cultivation became part of European expansion in the twelfth century, when the Crusaders took over sugar estates after their conquest of Lebanon and transferred this cultivation to Cyprus.

European colonial sugar production moved across the Mediterranean, entered the Atlantic Ocean in the fifteenth century, and reached the American continent with the voyages of Christopher Columbus. This expansion was usually accomplished below reproduction costs, through the massive enslavement and exploitation of Africans, and through land grabbing. At the same time, this frontier expansion externalized big chunks of the social and environmental costs of extraction, production, and circulation. Thus, production costs could be reduced and profitability increased. Ecological destruction, social contest, as well as growing demand of European consumers forced the frontier to move on to new uncommodified venues. In the case of sugar, the ecological degradation of the Mediterranean islands and Madeira drove European sugar production across the Atlantic into a prodigious sugar production in Brazil.[7] While being the largest sugar producer until the 1760s, its output stagnated because of deforestation near the sugar estates, competing demand for labor by the gold mines and lack of investment. Saint-Domingue succeeded Brazil as the largest sugar producer of the Atlantic world. However, the hundreds of thousands of enslaved men and women rebelled and overturned this commodity frontier that had yielded immense profits for France for decades. The revolution of Haiti of 1791 cleared the path for Cuba to emerge as the world's largest cane sugar producer, seconded by Java. Cuba´s success was based upon large illicit slave imports that continued well into the 1860s and flouted the bilateral treaty it had signed with Britain on the abolition of the slave trade. However, the supplies of labor were never enough to keep pace with the growth of the Cuban sugar industry. The island's sugar factories could only survive by economizing on field labor, which resulted in an ecologically rapacious agricultural system that devoured large tracts of new fertile land. Java's trajectory went the opposite direction. Here, rapid population growth provided an abundance of labor, and this allowed for an agricultural system that enmeshed cane growing in the existing rice production. This system was more ecologically sustainable thanks to a very high labor-intensive cultivation system. In 1925, Cuba produced 5 million tons of cane with fewer than 400,000 workers; Java produced half of this with 1.4 million workers.[8]

This example shows that contemporaneous frontiers that produce the same commodity under the comparable ecological conditions can widely diverge in terms of labor relations and land use. The exploitative character of these frontiers sustains their profitability as well as exacerbates their vulnerability. The collapse of large commodity frontiers can exert a shock to entire capitalist system. The Civil War in the United States (1861–1865), for example, forced the British textile industry to open new locations of cotton cultivation almost overnight. They were found in India, which entailed an immense geographical transfer of production.[9]

Commodity Frontiers as Processes of Extraction and Contestation

The emergence and growth of capitalism involves a history of accelerating and sprawling expansion of commodity production across the globe, meeting and overcoming many hurdles. Increasing quantities of commodities have been shipped and traded over ever larger distances: wheat, sugar cane, tobacco, cocoa, coffee, and cotton from plantations and estates, and products from forests, marine zones, and mines. It started with the relatively small-scale wheat and timber frontiers in the Baltics and has culminated, among others, in the massive soy frontier in Brazil today. New "uncommodified" spaces were opened, and new natural supplies of land, labor, and energy were made available to the centers of capital and power. The Baltics provided Western Europe with wheat and timber, and the Americas supplied tropical agricultural products, whereas enslaved labor was procured from Africa. This expansion was not a singular event but turned out to be permanent, cumulative, and violent. On the eve of World War I, Europe and its settler offshoots controlled 80 percent of the world's land and resources. This massive territorial expansion enabled the growth of a capitalist world system and fueled its absorptive, adaptive, and transformative capacity. It generated new forms of accumulation that degraded resilience, increased vulnerability, and exposed societies to new ecological hazards.[10] While capitalism has been externalizing the cost of its growth, it unavoidably generated consecutive social and ecological crises. In fact, crises are inherent and systemic to capitalism, as are the movements of resistance and the counter-narratives they generate. These conflicts and tensions have been shaping commodity frontier expansion over the last seven centuries.

The concept of frontier may create some confusion for those who associate it with the classical Turner thesis. Frederick Jackson Turner advanced the notion of the frontier in 1893 as "land free to be taken," not compounded by institutional constraints and entering a territory in which a completely new society could emerge.[11] The Turner concept showed a blatant disregard for the original inhabitants of the frontiers. Frontiers usually did not emerge in completely inhabited regions and thus new sites of conflict, negotiation, accommodation, or even assimilation emerged. The frontiers became venues of war, resistance, lawsuits, intolerance, plunder, extraction, sabotage, ecological degradation and segregation, even sometimes genocide. More accommodating situations also occurred, including biological symbiosis, marriage, economic partnership, political bonds and treaties, celebration, conversion, and gifts. The modes of their embedding in global capitalism varied widely depending upon the kind of products they yield, the forms of political authority, military power, labor relations, information flows, etc. Detailed local studies have abundantly described and analyzed these frontier processes.[12] However, due to their limited scope and theoretical heterogeneity, most had little impact on the dominant neoclassical and structuralist approaches.

Over the past decades, global historians and social scientists have tried to overcome this predicament by studying the expansion of commodity production and extraction using commodity-centered and commodity chain approaches. These considerations and approaches have driven the current socio-ecological turn in the study of capitalism, as well as a growing historical interest in the subject. Transnational movements, political ecologists, local NGOs, and historians borrow from each other's vocabularies, and some of these concepts have become highly appreciated transdisciplinary currency. Concepts such as ecological economics, environmental justice, world ecology, and commodity frontiers have taken center stage in these conversations.[13] They are embraced by a widening circle of academic authors and public intellectuals as they cover a narrative that offers a comprehensive explanation for how capitalism has been transforming the global countryside. At the same time, it is important not to reify a structuralist perspective and be aware that capitalism is not a predictable but a nonlinear historical process and to remain sensitive to the crises and resistances it has provoked.

REGIMES OF COMMODITY FRONTIER EXPANSION

Capitalism's dependence on new resources increased over time, as it required more and more land, labor, and energy to reproduce itself. As long as capitalism did not encompass the entire globe, natural limits could be overcome by geographical expansion into hitherto un- or under-appropriated spaces. This has happened historically not in a linear or even exponential way, but through highly unequal and convoluted trajectories. The accumulation strategies that worked through particular forms of science, technology, territoriality, and governance created widely divergent forms of expansion and exploitation. Studying capitalism through the lens of such cycles, or regimes, allows us to understand it as a historical process whose structures of accumulation and power have changed immensely over space and time. It also enables us to discern the contradictions and dialectical relations within the capitalist system.

Over time, structures of power, technology, and scale of the capitalist global economy have changed enormously, making capitalism in 1500 very different from capitalism in 1800, 1900, or 2020. To make sense of the enormous variety of places and the dizzying number and scale of changes over time, the work of Harriet Friedmann and Philip McMichael on successive "food regimes" introduced almost thirty years ago is particularly helpful.[14] As Friedmann and McMichael specified, food regime is foremost an analytical device to pose specific questions about the structuring processes in the global political economy. The food regimes approach views agriculture and food in relation to the development of capitalism on a global scale and argues that social change is brought about by struggles among social movements, capital, and states. Regimes are methodological tools to specify changing relations between "world ordering" and local agency. A genealogy of regimes shows that episodes of restructuring and transition are bounded by more stable periods of regulation and organization, albeit in a non-determined way. The genealogy of commodity regimes provides a genuine, global comparative-historical lens to look at the social, economic, political, and ecological relations within global capitalism. It aims at a non-hierarchical, non-evolutionary, and non-deterministic interpretation of global social change.[15]

We use the concept of commodity regime as a meta-historical device that allows us to capture the ways in which different societal domains on commodity frontiers (ecological, technological, social, and political) are organized and related to one another. Every commodity regime is characterized by particular labor relations, particular patterns of land ownership, particular forms of the insertion of capital, as well as particular sets of technologies and state policies. By and large, one can identify three, perhaps four, different regimes in the advancement of global commodity production: an early capitalist regime until the Industrial Revolution gained traction (by the mid-nineteenth century), an industrial regime marked by the prominent roles of industrial markets and the state from the mid-nineteenth century to the 1970s, a corporate regime dominated by a new market ideology and transnational businesses, and, conditionally, a still unfolding contemporary regime from the early 2000s onward. Each regime over the past six hundred years had its own trajectory of labor relations, property relations, technological progress, roles of the state, degrees of vertical integration between countryside and end producers, and movements of reaction and resistance. The two key transformations demarcating these regimes were the Industrial Revolution as it became transnational by the mid-nineteenth century, and the emergence of exceptionally powerful transnational businesses beginning in the 1970s. The two transitions coincided with the changing role of the state, which was more prominent in economic life between the 1850s and 1970s than either before or since.

The first regime, which lasted from the 1450s to the 1850s, was characterized by direct and violent dispossession of people from land and nature, as well as unfree labor systems with a proliferation of chattel slavery, peonage, and subcontracting. Its forceful expansion was sanctioned by states, but its principal expansionary driver was merchant capital, which could be organized as trading companies such as the Dutch and English East India companies. In the second regime, which lasted from the 1850s to the 1970s, industrial markets and interventionist states gained prominent roles, as did multinational capital, global bulk commodity markets, and new transport and communication technologies. These factors thoroughly reinforced the infrastructural capabilities, such as railways, steamship lines, and telegraph and telephone, to shape the conditions under which frontiers expanded. In the 1970s a new so-called corporate commodity regime emerged, driven by a refurbished ideology of free commodity markets and the concentration of transnational corporate power. Corporate power was reinforced by the changing role of the state vis-à-vis transnational corporations and financial institutions, and new global political divisions among and between North and South, reproducing and in some ways remapping imperial, colonial, and Cold War political geographies. The concentration of power in the hands of a few producers took a quantum leap as commodity trade and financial institutions became tightly connected from the 1980s. Since the early 2000s, firms and financial actors looking for new investment opportunities have come to own or finance increasing amounts of land around the world, largely through dispossession, and often with the assistance of state power. Rising authoritarianism around the world is pressuring people and environments on commodity frontiers in South America, the United States, Southeast Asia, and elsewhere. Companies, often with the state's assistance, are expanding into radically new production and information technologies. As a still-unfolding regime, many questions remain about which processes and relations will be most important in this phase of capitalism, which will spur or encounter the most resistance, and what forms that resistance will take.

Clearly, there are overlaps between the different regimes, which underscores the fact that each regime sets at least some of the conditions for the one that follows. Over time, these historical movements became increasingly interwoven, revolutionizing the preceding production systems and incorporating new commodity frontiers.

This continual process of frontier expansion transformed former rural societies and configured the world of today.

Commodity regimes have been the subject of profound social and political contests. Together with physical limits to further expansion, contestation has been a destabilizing force, eventually leading to a transition toward a new regime. This speaks against a teleological or linear interpretation of capitalist expansion and urges us to try to uncover its historical and spatial logic. Historical research shows us that each commodity regime exhibits particular frictions in the realms of nature, land, and labor, inciting resistance and counter-narratives. It also reveals that so far capitalism at a global scale has overcome these frictions by various fixes, or particular sets of solutions to capitalist social and ecological crises. We already mentioned the spatial fix, but economists have also pointed at the increasing impact of technological fixes, particularly since the Industrial Revolution. They include the mechanization of planting, harvesting, haulage, and processing of mass commodities such as sugar or wheat immensely reducing labor inputs. Another strand of technological fixes pertains to botanical knowledge that has led to higher yields per acre. Further, historians and political scientists have abundantly studied state-led fixes, especially with the rise of nineteenth-century bureaucracies. State-led fixes include physical infrastructure such as roads and railways, the maintenance of public safety, as well as the institutional arrangements that, for example, guarantee banks that they have leverage over their debtors. Nineteenth-century plantation colonialism such as in Cuba and Java would have been impossible without active support of the state to create the necessary infrastructure and institutional settings. Since the 1970s, growing criticism toward the interventionist state has given rise to a complex of market-oriented fixes, also described as a neoliberal or corporate fix. While states have become less inclined to use their regulatory power, private enterprise has become increasingly globalized. Transnational corporations became in less need of the state to prepare the ground for their expansion and produce massive volumes of goods and commodities while continuously reducing their operational costs.

The history of commodity frontiers is therefore more than just a series of spatial fixes, as it is attended by increasing technological, state, and economic power. States continue to exert immense economic power, while professing a belief in a retreat from the realm of economic life. Global inequalities are preserved, and even exacerbated, by the national interests of the economically more powerful core countries. In the 1980s and 1990s, the World Bank and IMF forced governments of the Global South out of their national food markets, while at the same time protection of farmers in the United States and the European Union reached staggering heights. Meanwhile, the high-income industrialized countries still import far more biomaterial than they export, and in addition they tend to export their most polluting industries. This approach of historical regimes through the lens of multiple frictions and a cumulative series of fixes surpasses single-factor explanations. This in turn is pivotal to an understanding of present socio-ecological conditions and contestations and the future options we have toward more equal societies.

Commodity Frontiers as a Comparative-Historical Lens

We have argued that the concept of commodity frontiers can offer a unique historical lens to study the expansion of global capitalism. Commodity frontiers studies aims to cover by and large three major fields or research questions: how global integration or global capitalism, fueled by technological change and economies of scale, transformed rural societies and agricultural systems worldwide; how successive regimes of appropriation of nature, land, and labor developed; and how resistance against these processes of appropriation was instigated.[16]

Global Integration

Capitalism has been driving global integration over the past six hundred years, yet the relationship between commodity frontiers and end producers has changed immensely over the course of that time. In the early phases of capitalism, technology could only enhance the productivity of land and labor to a limited extent and postpone decreasing resilience. As early as in the seventeenth century, however, technological innovations could avert ecological exhaustion, as was the case in the sugar industry in the Caribbean. Erosion was combated by new planting techniques, more fuel-efficient batteries of cauldrons were developed, windmills supplied free energy for the mills reducing the need for cattle, and stronger mills squeezed the cane to such an extent that it could be used as fuel to boil the sugar. The Industrial Revolution, however, brought about a qualitative change in this respect, expanded commodity frontiers in a differentiated manner, and increased rural inequalities despite rapidly increasing productivity. The application of steam technology accelerated the processing of crops immensely through steam-powered threshing machines, centrifuges separating molasses from sugar, and so on. A worldwide infrastructure of steamships and railways provided the necessary infrastructure for a global commodity market. Agricultural science produced a range of leaps in agricultural productivity, in which experimental agricultural stations both in the temperate zones and tropical dependencies played a crucial role. Starting in the late nineteenth century, these stations generated a chain of spectacular increases in yield per acre for a broad range of crops. The most famous and consequential success was the Green Revolution, or the Third Agricultural Revolution of the 1950s and 1960s, which reportedly saved a billion lives. However, there is also a darker side of this story. Differential access to technology, and the ways in which capitalist agriculture creates new commodified inputs (seeds, fertilizers, pesticides, etc.) increased dependency of the farmers. Agronomic innovations led to further concentration of power at the commodity frontiers. The current stage of biotechnology enables the integration of the food and energy sectors, and a profound appropriation of life through seed patents and intellectual property protections, leading to large-scale processes of dispossession. This concentration was speeded up by rapid integration of commodity trade and financial institutions in the 1980s, which in turn was furthered by neoliberal emphasis on market institutions. International reports confirm that the vast majority of the world's smallholders are at risk. Globally, this has led to unabated urban migration. In sub-Saharan Africa, 14 million people move to cities each year, a migration that is second only to the massive rural-to-urban shift happening in China.[17]

Since the 1980s, countries in the Global South, for example, have simultaneously become massive importers of food and exporters of cheap industrial manufactures, as well as agro-industrial inputs. Hastened by International Monetary Fund (IMF) and World Bank structural adjustment programs and by uneven trade rules, scores of local food markets across the Global South have been destroyed, leaving household and community food security vulnerable to the vicissitudes of global food and agricultural markets. Together with enclosures by large agro-industries, these contemporary developments have led to the weakening and dispossession of peasants across the Global South. The governance of commodity chains that has concentrated in the hands of a limited number of powerful transnational corporations, and local-level dispossession in the global countryside are often two sides of the same coin. At present a limited number of transnational corporations control much of global commodity chains. The most well-known name is Monsanto, now taken over by the German firm of Bayer, reportedly for $66 billion. Started in 1901 as producer of saccharine for companies such as Coca-Cola, it gained notoriety for its production of pesticides and is now widely criticized for its role in the plant seeds and their genetic manipulation. Today, the big corporations of the past that were involved in commodity production are no longer necessarily controlling the commodity frontiers through ownership but through control of the circulation of the commodities, through encapsulating the agricultural side of the production process, or through consultancy and management services. Big corporations might supply seeds, fertilizer, and agricultural advice, while further down the chain they own processing and refining plants.

Access to Nature, Land, and Labor

Over the past six hundred years, commodity frontiers have engendered a shift from reciprocal labor relations and patron-client relationships into a proliferation of chattel slavery, peonage, and subcontracting. Wage labor did expand as well but was for the large masses of workers in the commodity frontier zones just nominal; most labor regimes were marked by debt-bondage and coercion.[18] Within the variety of labor regimes that have existed, the boundaries between different types of labor relations shift easily and are often blurred. Moreover, individual labor relations are embedded in household-based and group-based networks. "The partiality of wage labor" (i.e., wage labor combined with other types of remunerated and non-remunerated labor) is especially clear from a household perspective since a large majority of households have never been solely dependent on wage labor income. Non-wage labor has been an essential part of capitalist reproduction. Processes of incorporation create dynamic frontier zones where land and peoples are freshly absorbed in the capitalist system. Obviously, these communities develop strategies of adaptation, differentiation, and resistance. If peasantries are able to keep some degree of economic independence and are capable of producing cash crops on their own terms in combination with food crops, they might benefit from their interaction with the capitalist global economy. Many small rubber farmers and small coffee producers across the Global South have managed to do this.

In the nineteenth century, increasingly capable state bureaucracies and improving infrastructure facilitated a fundamental restructuring of land and labor regimes. In general, one can say that the expansion of global capitalism is articulated in a fundamental transformation of land rights. While the forms that this transformation took were complex and varied across time and space, some central features can be distinguished: the transformation of a complex system of customary rights to land usage and to legal and written titles to land ownership; and the transformation of the concept of property from jurisdiction and ambiguously defined areas to concretely defined, and possibly enclosed, physical spaces. Colonial governments converted communal into individual property, creating land markets that enabled the expansion of corporate plantation enterprise. This process culminated in the privatization of large parts of the earth's surface through dispossession and displacement of peasants and Indigenous populations. Regulations pertaining to land use have been a primary tool for opening access to labor and commodity production, albeit in very different ways. The intensification of commodified land rights since 1850 has been fueled by colonial (a massive land grab transforming communal and peasant land rights) and developmental (state-sponsored collectivization schemes including expropriation and displacement) projects and by the global enclosures, massive contraction of land rights, and accelerated de-peasantization on a world scale. A global land grab, unprecedented since colonial times, is currently underway as states and speculative investors acquire millions of hectares of land in the Global South. Over the past decades, agribusiness companies have been increasing their production of palm oil. Between 2000 and 2015 more than sixty-five large-scale land deals for oil palm plantations in Africa were signed, covering more than 4.7 million hectares. Especially, community lands have been a main target for the expansion of the plantations. However, not all of these projects worked out as planned. Partly due to increasing resistance by local communities, the area under concession concessions have been turned back to almost half.[19]

Resistance and Counter-narratives

Commodity frontier expansion is neither straightforward nor uncontested. As capital expands into new territories, new productive activities, and new bodies, its ongoing attempts to externalize the social and environmental "costs" of production and reproduction are met with resistance. People struggle against exploitation, social inequalities, and degraded environments. Together with demographic and ecological change, and in the context of broad political economic transformations, some resistances prefigure and compel regime change: they push capital to seek new frontiers for expansion. For instance, until the early nineteenth century, revolt and desertion (marronage) were responses to enslavement and servitude, underlying the shift to wage labor. In the heydays of Western colonialism, rebellion and escape were joined by labor resistance aligning with anti-colonial movements.

Despite the overall trend of weakening social and ecological resilience, we still see different outcomes. There is a substantial peasantry worldwide still in control of their land and ecology; conditions of production and reproduction are often predicated on peasants' position in global, regional, or local commodity chains.

As transnational commodity chains replaced the colonial division of labor over the course of the twentieth century, resistance today has also acquired a transnational character. Workers struggle against capital's global "wage race to the bottom," Indigenous communities struggle against the polluting and degrading activities of transnational corporations that operate in local spaces with near legal impunity, and peasants struggle against the incursions of transnational capital into agrarian spaces and practices. In some cases, resistances provide counter-narratives to capital for different ways of organizing political, economic, ecological, and social life. Studying resistance within historical regimes and periods of tension between regimes, therefore, is a crucial part of defining and analyzing regimes themselves. Desertion of enslaved and servile populations were a permanent feature of the frontier zones during the early capitalist commodity regime. Slavery, indeed, became increasingly untenable as a result of slaves' resistance, such as the revolution in Saint-Domingue in 1791 and the large-scale uprising in Jamaica in 1832, as well as the emergence of an abolitionist movement. Labor shortages continued to be a perennial problem for commodity frontiers.

THE URGENCY OF A COMMODITY FRONTIERS ANALYSIS OF THE COUNTRYSIDE

Rural and agrarian worlds have been vital frontiers of civilizations, empires, and globalizing capitalism. The incorporation of rural zones and the creation of new peasantries have been central to the expansion of village societies, early states, agrarian (tributary) empires, and global capitalism in its different forms. In most societal settings, these zones were integrated as loci of appropriation of the produce of land and labor and as peripheral spaces of production, exploitation, contestation, and re-creation. Peasantries thus have been primary frontiers in societal expansion. Their partial incorporation as producers of new surpluses instigated mixed, complex, and often opposing processes of restructuring, generating a multiplicity of frontier zones. There are, for example, immense dissimilarities in the way how peasantries in Java have become incorporated in the colonial plantation economy and how in the adjacent island of Sumatra peasantries maintained much of their autonomy while growing, for example, coffee or rubber for the global market. The commodity frontiers can both be driven by smallholder and plantation systems and many mixed forms in between.

Global capitalist expansion since the long sixteenth century demanded a drastic increase in the world-ecological surplus. Along the margins of social and economic systems, hybrid cultures originated; social groups and social zones were incorporated or excluded. As we have argued, rather than lines, frontiers must be envisioned as historical and dynamic processes of both incorporation and differentiation that created and reorganized spatial settings or frontier zones. This shows how the frontier perspective grasps the imbalances of incorporation processes, emphasizing the role of the margins and friction zones, and integrating nature and ecology as a defining part of the global economy.[20]

Attempts to further the cause of global sustainability are hopelessly flawed if they circumvent, as ecologist Alf Hornborg claims, "the distributive political and cultural dimensions of the global environmental problems."[21] Historical configurations rather than objective physical conditions and technological limits endanger our common future. As agronomists have argued, technological innovation can prevent nightmarish scenarios, in which the future of the world hinges on keeping the majority of the world population poor. However, the recent scramble for land in Africa, Latin America, and Russia may seem inevitable to avoid food shortages in the world's mega cities; the ensuing dramas of dispossession and destruction within local rural societies are just tragic.

There are compelling reasons to shift academic attention to the global countryside: global poverty is overwhelmingly concentrated in rural areas; a considerable share of the global heating is caused by agriculture; and loss of biodiversity leads to a decreasing capacity of ecological regeneration. Current debates on sustainability are unduly optimistic, as they underestimate the historical resilience of capitalist commodity regimes and tend to overlook the fact that centuries of global commodity production have seriously weakened the institutional capabilities in the global peripheries. Meanwhile, structural and systemic approaches tend to homogenize the global countryside, ignoring agency that might change these regimes. To disentangle the complexities that may derail today's attempts to frame a "global agenda of sustainable growth," we ought to know in much more historical depth the dynamics of enclosures of land, regimes of labor control, and transfers of capital and knowledge. At the same time, we need to historically internalize the concepts of sustainability and resilience. Sustainable systems and resilient communities are two very different things; systems can be very resilient while putting large groups of people at risk.

There is an urgent need to uncover the consecutive commodity regimes in all their aspects in a history of seven centuries of global capitalism, which have created unequal power relations and massive inequalities. The historical and spatial complexities of this global condition require an historically informed and comparative analytical approach that unites the myriad case studies about how local rural societies resist, accommodate, or even benefit from capitalism, containing fragments of knowledge spread over disciplines. The commodity frontier concept invites us to study processes of incorporation and transformation of the countryside in a historical, interconnected, and dialectical way. Through the concept of commodity frontiers, we have identified historical capitalism as a process rooted in a profound restructuring of rural societies and their relation to nature. The commodity regime framework will enable us to connect core processes of extraction and exchange with degradation, adaptation, and resistance in rural peripheries. It provides a bottom-up perspective on economic and ecological change, giving space to agency on the margins.

Notes

1. Alf Hornborg, "Footprints in the Cotton Fields: The Industrial Revolution as Time-Space Appropriation and Environmental Load Displacement," *Ecological Economy* 59 (2006): 74–81.
2. Edward B. Barbier, *Scarcity and Frontiers. How Economies Have Developed through Natural Resource Exploitation* (Cambridge: Cambridge University Press, 2011): 7.
3. Werner Sombart, *Der moderne Kapitalismus*, 3 vols. (Leipzig: Duncker und Humblot, 1902); Fernand Braudel, *La méditerranée et le monde méditerranéen a l'époque de Philippe II* (Paris: Colin, 1966); Immanuel Wallerstein, *The Modern World-System*, 3 vols. (San Diego: Academic Press, 1974–1989).
4. David Harvey, "The Spatial Fix: Hegel, von Thünen, and Marx," *Antipode* 13, no. 3 (1981): 1–12.
5. Jason W. Moore, *Capitalism in the Web of Life: Ecology and the Accumulation of Capital* (London: Verso, 2015): 61–62.
6. Mohamed Ouerfelli, *Le sucre production, commercialisation et usages dans la Méditerranée médiévale* (Leiden: Brill, 2008).
7. Stefan Halikowski Smith, "The Mid-Atlantic Islands: A Theatre of Early Modern Ecocide?," *International Review of Social History* 55 (2010): 51–77.
8. Ulbe Bosma, *The Sugar Plantation in India and Indonesia. Industrial Production 1770-2010* (New York: Cambridge University Press, 2013): 159–60.
9. Sven Beckert, *Empire of Cotton: A Global History* (New York: Alfred A. Knopf, 2014).
10. We define resilience as the capacity of societies to protect their members from suffering, and vulnerability as a decreasing capacity to do so. Differential vulnerability to ecological disaster is inherent in capitalism rather than, for example, a cultural trait of certain societies. See Tim Soens, "Resilient Societies, Vulnerable People. Coping with North Sea Floods before 1800," *Past and Present* 3 (2018): 143–77.
11. Frederick Jackson Turner, *The Frontier in American History* (New York: Holt, 1920).
12. See, among others: Sabrina Joseph, ed., *Commodity Frontiers and Global Capitalist Expansion: Social, Ecological and Political Implications from the Nineteenth Century to the Present Day* (Cham: Palgrave Macmillan, 2019). Individual contributions examine agricultural and pastoral frontiers, natural habitats, and commodity frontiers with fossil fuels and mineral resources located in various regions of the world.
13. Joan Martínez-Alier and Roldan Muradian, eds., *Handbook of Ecological Economics* (Cheltenham: Edward Elgar, 2015).

14. Philip McMichael, *Food Regimes and Agrarian Questions* (Halifax: Fernwood Books, 2013).
15. Eric Vanhaute and Hanne Cottyn, "Into Their Land and Labours: A Comparative and Global Analysis of Trajectories of Peasant Transformation," *ICAS Review Paper Series*, no. 8 (2017).
16. Sven Beckert, Ulbe Bosma, Mindi Schneider, and Eric Vanhaute, "Commodity Frontiers and the Transformation of the Global Countryside: A Research Agenda," *Journal of Global History* (2021): 3.
17. *Food and Agriculture: The Future of Sustainability. A Strategic Input to the Sustainable Development in the 21st Century (SD21) Project* (New York: United Nations Department of Economic and Social Affairs, 2012).
18. An extensive investigation of these changing labor relations is conducted by the Global Collaboratory on the History of Labour Relations, based at the International Institute of Social History in Amsterdam: https://collab.iisg.nl/web/labourrelations.
19. Alliance Against Industrial Plantations in West and Central Africa, "Communities in Africa Fight Back against the Land Grab for Palm Oil," September 19, 2019, https://www.grain.org/en/article/6324-communities-in-africa-fight-back-against-the-land-grab-for-palm-oil.
20. The ecological distribution conflicts are currently mapped by the *EJAtlas*; see https://ejatlas.org.
21. Alf Hornborg, "Zero-Sum World. Challenges in Conceptualizing Environmental Load Displacement and Ecologically Unequal Change in the World-System," *International Journal of Comparative Sociology* 50, no. 3–4 (2009): 255.

Bibliography

Barbier, Edward B. *Scarcity and Frontiers. How Economies Have Developed through Natural Resource Exploitation.* Cambridge: Cambridge University Press, 2011.
Beckert, Sven. *Empire of Cotton: A Global History.* New York: Alfred A. Knopf, 2014.
Beckert, Sven, Ulbe Bosma, Mindi Schneider, and Eric Vanhaute. "Commodity Frontiers and the Transformation of the Global Countryside: A Research Agenda." *Journal of Global History* 16, no. 3 (2021): 435–50.
Bernstein, Henry. *Class Dynamics of Agrarian Change.* Halifax: Fernwood, 2010.
Bosma, Ulbe. *The Making of a Periphery. How Island Southeast Asia Became a Mass Exporter of Labor.* New York: Columbia University Press, 2019.
Edelman, Marc, Carlos Oya, and Saturnino Borras, eds. *Global Land Grabs: History, Theory and Method.* New York: Routledge, 2015.
Gereffi, Gary, and Miguel Korzeniewicz, eds. *Commodity Chains and Global Capitalism.* Westport, CT: ABC-Clio, 1994
Hornborg, Alf, John R. McNeill, and Joan Martinez-Alier, eds. *Rethinking Environmental History. World-System History and Global Environmental Change.* Lanham, MD: Altamira Press, 2007.
Martínez-Alier, Joan, and Roldan Muradian, eds. *Handbook of Ecological Economics.* Cheltenham: Edward Elgar, 2015.
McMichael, Philip. *Food Regimes and Agrarian Questions.* Halifax: Fernwood, 2013.
Moore, Jason W. *Capitalism in the Web of Life: Ecology and the Accumulation of Capital.* London: Verso, 2015.

Moore, Jason W. "Sugar and the Expansion of the Early Modern World-Economy: Commodity Frontiers, Ecological Transformation, and Industrialization." *Review* (Fernand Braudel Center) 3 (2000): 409–433.

Rural Economy and Society in North-western Europe, 500–2000, 4 vols. CORN Publication Series. Turnhout: Brepols, 2010–2015: Erik Thoen et al., eds., *Struggling with the Environment: Land Use and Productivity* (2015); Eric Vanhaute et al., eds., *Making a Living: Family, Income and Labour* (2012); Bas van Bavel et al., eds., *Social Relations: Property and Power* (2010); Leen Van Molle et al., eds. *The Agro-Food Market: Production, Distribution and Consumption* (2013).

Soens, Tim. "Resilient Societies, Vulnerable People. Coping with North Sea Floods before 1800." *Past and Present* 3 (2018): 143–177.

Vanhaute, Eric. "Agriculture." In *Handbook the Global History of Work*, ed. Karen Hofmeester and Marcel Van der Linden, 217–35. Berlin: De Gruyter, 2015.

Weis, Tony. *The Global Food Economy. The Battle for the Future of Farming*. London: Zed Books, 2007.

Wolf, Eric. *Peasants*. Englewood Cliffs, NJ: Prentice Hall, 1966.

CHAPTER 13

WORKER HEALTH IN MODERN AGRICULTURE

MICHITAKE ASO

WELL into the twentieth century, the health of agricultural laborers has correlated highly with rural conditions. The major causes of ill health among mobile and settled farmers alike were infectious disease, physical injury, malnutrition, and starvation. The most important determinants of the health of agricultural laborers were the social and economic conditions of the countryside: Was there enough to eat? How was food distributed? How much control did people have over their labor and the land? The growing prominence of machines, chemicals, and capital in agriculture during the nineteenth century altered the conditions of agricultural laborers in Europe and the United States. For much of the world, political projects including colonialism and nationalism and economic systems such as capitalism and communism did more to transform the living and working conditions of agricultural laborers than did technological change. Even those not directly employed by transnational companies were affected by tighter integration into empires, nation states, and world markets.

In the twentieth century, newly created work and migration patterns in the countryside aggravated many of the threats that agricultural laborers faced. During this process, agricultural labor emerged as a distinct occupation and thus garnered more attention. In the 1920s and 1930s, the International Labour Organization (ILO) turned to the health of agricultural laborers, even if it had a difficult time defining exactly who was an agricultural laborer. Louise Howard's trail-blazing study moved the debate forward by considering the work of agricultural laborers in terms of occupational health. After World War II, the health of agricultural laborers received sustained attention from the ILO and the United Nations (UN) and its specialized agencies such as the World Health Organization (WHO). In the 1980s and 1990s, global agricultural labor became an issue in the United States largely due to public concerns about pesticide residues on food. In the late 1990s and 2000s, scientific journals and textbooks on agricultural medicine appeared even as agricultural labor retained its ambiguous position in occupational health concerns.[1]

Because agriculture has become more reliant on machines and external inputs such as capital, chemicals, and a non-family workforce, as well as grown more conceptually detached from non-human nature, it has become an increasingly hazardous occupation for laborers. This argument depends somewhat on the type of farm, although several issues affect a significant cross-section of agricultural laborers. This general argument must also be qualified with discussions of citizenship, race, class, gender, and environment. Moreover, health hazards facing workers have not gone unchallenged and there have been attempts to understand inequalities and to combat oppression and worker ill health coming from laborers and their allies. Governments, too, have at times played a role in establishing legal protections for agricultural laborers. Yet, even for owner-operators who tend to be white, male citizens of developed nations, and who are often healthier than surrounding populations, farming per se is a relatively hazardous occupation. And for migrant and seasonal workers, mostly non-citizens, people of color, and women, and those facing neoliberal policies in places without strong legal protections, farming presents an increasingly precarious livelihood.[2]

Agricultural laborers are defined broadly as people who produce, through contact with plants, animals, and other non-human life, goods for sale, including food, fibers, and fuels. These laborers constitute a notable part of the world's population.[3] Even defined in a narrower sense as those who sell their own labor, and not the goods produced by it, on a market, agricultural laborers remain important both numerically and for their role in society. According to US Department of Agriculture (USDA) data, in 2000 there were 1.13 million hired farmworkers. An ILO report from the early 2000s estimated that there were 4.5 million seasonal workers in agriculture in the European Union. In industrialized countries overall, migrant and seasonal workers make up about 50 percent of agricultural labor. While agricultural laborers constitute only 2.5 percent of the total labor force in industrial countries according to one economic historian, they continue to account for almost 50 percent of the global labor force. These are substantial numbers, and higher still if those who work informally or part-time in agriculture and those who work for little or no pay, such as youth, are included. In Europe and North America, women often contribute to the viability of the farm through outside work even if they account for only a small percentage of operator-owners.[4]

Agricultural laborers work on a wide variety of farms and food-processing locations, but those selling their labor on managerial and tenant estates and large family farms employing full-time and seasonal labor are particularly vulnerable. Putting responsibility on individual agricultural laborers for their ill health has masked the ways that political economy influences health outcomes. The concept of structural vulnerability helps shift the focus away from individual agency onto structural forces that shape worker health. It is most useful in analyzing the health of paid labor in land-based plant cultivation, animal husbandry, forest harvesting, fisheries, and aquaculture. It also provides some insight into understanding situations of unpaid labor such as enslaved peoples in the Americas.[5]

In many cultures, agriculture has long been a respected social activity, with farmers viewing their livelihoods in a holistic manner. In this way, the health of agricultural laborers and the hazards they tolerated have depended on ambient rural conditions even if their products have been integrated into short- and long-distance markets. A common cause of farmer ill health has been famine. These famines have had many causes, from the extension of imperial rule and free market ideology as in Ireland and British India in the nineteenth century to wartime conditions in French Indochina and state oppression in communist-controlled China and Cambodia in the twentieth century. Sometimes the principal cause of malnutrition and death has been distribution, at other times price, and occasionally absolute quantity. In all cases, certain groups in rural society have been blocked from access to subsistence levels of food and suffered tremendously. Thus, lack of access to resources has been the most common factor determining agricultural laborers' health, especially during times of general insecurity.[6]

Outside of famine conditions, there have been many reasons for ill health among family farmers and agricultural laborers. Diseases such as malaria, hookworm, and others have been common, though until population growth and other recent disruptions subsistence farmers had often learned to deal with such problems either through avoidance or through adaptation. Moreover, the health needs of rural residents and agricultural laborers were addressed by village healers and through collective rituals. Such traditional medicines were often accessible and affordable, if not always effective. By imposing markets or enacting strategic concerns, businesses and states pressured farmers to move to areas that had not been traditionally given over to agricultural pursuits or altered the timing of such pursuits, thereby increasing exposure to infectious diseases.[7]

One important form of traditional agriculture affected by tighter integration into world markets has been the harvesting of forest products. During the nineteenth century, many gathering activities that had been aimed at local consumption were pulled into global markets. The collecting of latex, for example, which was a centuries-old practice, became associated with the worst excesses of capitalism and colonialism. In the Belgian Congo, Europeans dismembered or killed Africans who did not meet arbitrarily set quotas of latex collected from wild vines. Tapping latex from *Hevea brasiliensis* trees in the Amazon consisted of a tenant farming–like situation. Soaring rubber prices in the nineteenth century added many more laborers, and much more brutality, to the region. In this system, tappers gathered latex and sold it to middlemen who then sold it to world markets, often making large fortunes. These tappers sometimes purchased equipment, food, and other supplies with loans that were paid back at high interest rates. Tappers encountered poisonous snakes, insect bites, and other dangers of working alone in forests. Most of all they met with human violence, from other tappers and from their bosses. This system continued even after the collection of latex collapsed when South and Southeast Asian plantations started to produce rubber.[8]

Not surprisingly, this system provided no organized healthcare, apart from Henry Ford's ill-fated rubber plantation project called Fordlandia. This situation changed somewhat during World War II when the US government sought to partially meet its military's need for rubber through increased collection in the Amazon. The United States worked with the Brazilian government to transport to the region thousands of men who benefited somewhat from the work of sanitary engineers and public health personnel. Other types of harvesting linked to agriculture have included the mining of guano in the Pacific, where poor pay and dangerous working conditions (e.g., dust-caused illnesses and physical injuries) greeted migrant workers. Finally, killing of wild animals for meat consumption and sale has exposed hunters to infectious diseases ranging from HIV/AIDS to Lyme disease. Like the tappers in the Amazon, harvesters around the world have rarely enjoyed access to state or company-sponsored healthcare.[9]

Agricultural laborers have been commonly associated with settlement, but mobility has also been an important aspect of their lives. Mobility is, for example, integral to nomadic pastoralism. Pastoralists have developed sheep and cattle grazing practices that followed spatiotemporal patterns of rains and worked symbiotically with settled agriculturalists. Thus, when European powers imposed arbitrary national borders in, say, sub-Saharan Africa, and market incentives for producing more cattle for export in the nineteenth century, they disrupted the rhythm of this system. The effects of the shift to settled agriculture remain to be considered, but the newly constricted pastoral system tended to degrade soils, with many pastoralists and their herds subsequently suffering poverty and ill health. Mobility has been intrinsic to swidden agriculture as well. Although the early history of swidden agriculture may have involved state avoidance, the history of the past two hundred years is more complex, with swidden agriculturalists at times benefiting from access to resources through complementary relationships with states and markets. As with pastoralists, growing restrictions on mobility and integration into nation states have had mixed results for swidden agriculturalists. A limited increase in access to rural health has often been offset by clashes with states and growing populations that strain local resources.[10]

Farm workers on large family farms and tenant estates have also experienced unique challenges. Despite industrialization, urbanization, and other social transformations, people who engage in farming at least part of their lives remain vital to understanding much of the world. Many of these agricultural laborers have worked on tenant estates, or large plots of land rented out to tenants who have some say in the running of the farm. California's industrial agriculture has included many such estates leasing land to farmers, who often themselves have hired migrant and seasonal labor. Post-slavery cotton and tobacco sharecropping in the US South was a system in which poor black and white people farmed an owner's land in exchange for a portion of the harvest. Paid seasonal and permanent laborers have also worked on large family farms, with a single family owning and managing the land. This type of farm can be seen from the fruit farms of the US West to Asian rice farms. These neat analytic categories disguise a complex reality involving much overlap and blending.[11]

On tenant estates and large family farms in capitalist economies, laborers' health remains largely an individual concern. Agricultural laborers on tenant estates and large family farms often confronted similar hazards as those on managerial estates, although their health has been more closely tied to prevailing rural conditions. Broad attempts to address worker health have come about only recently through government programs aimed at improving general rural conditions. The health of laborers on family farms and tenant estates has depended on a nearly infinite combination of factors including crop, ecology, and geography, but a brief review of rice monocultures in Asian river deltas serves as a case study.

For centuries, rice agriculture has occupied an important place both symbolically and materially in Asian countries.[12] In China, Japan, Korea, and Vietnam, farmers have played a fundamental role in society and Confucian-inspired social hierarchies. In fact, one of the principal functions of centralized states in Asia was the construction and maintenance of vast irrigation and flood control systems. The health of agricultural laborers, however, does not seem to have been a specific government concern, and most communities relied on religious and medical traditions for disease prevention and cure in the countryside.[13]

The nineteenth and twentieth centuries saw two common challenges for Asian rice farmers: capitalist colonialism and the Green Revolution. While these crises differed in many respects, in both cases their proponents sought to transform long-established practices and to replace labor with capital (machines, fertilizers, pesticides, and credit). Moreover, as Francesca Bray has pointed out, enthusiasts of progress sought to replace human muscle with other energy sources.[14] In other words, advocates of development often spoke of industrial, rather than industrious, agriculture. In many places this process has been incomplete, leaving laborers exposed to the dangers of capital without the protections of preexisting moral economies or newly created state-run social safety nets. One often-noted exception is post–World War II Japan, where land redistribution successfully reduced the numbers of tenant farmers and enabled new owners to mechanize their farms.[15]

In the main, colonialism encouraged unhealthy practices in agricultural labor. For example, the rice farmers of Southeast Asian deltas were greatly affected by the European, American, and Japanese empires. In the Mekong Delta, French colonialism increased the scale of canal construction and Vietnamese settlement that had been started by the Nguyen dynasty. Like the Nguyen rulers, the French colonial state initially attempted to increase rice production using unpaid corvée labor on irrigation and road-building projects. Eventually, the economic and political imperatives of colonialism and global markets encouraged state officials to turn increasingly to paid labor. Colonial state projects contributed to greatly increased rates of malaria, cholera, and other diseases. The bodies of these hired laborers were subject to limited state health interventions at best while the growing demand for, and supply of, polished rice resulted in nutritional diseases such as beriberi. Moreover, French colonialism created large populations of landless tenants who had little protection against ill health.[16]

In capitalist economies, many health risks present during the colonial period continued into the era of nation states. Increased food production via new rice strains and chemical inputs could offer some measure of protection against famines at the national scale. But without attention to distribution and issues of inequality, this increased production has often led to decreased individual productivity and growing poverty. In many rice-producing societies, Bray argues, "technical improvement perpetuates subsistence-level agriculture, and while this allows for demographic growth it cannot improve rural living standards, nor can it contribute to the general development of the national economy."[17] In other words, populations have grown while national wealth and individual well-being has not.

The link between increasing agricultural outputs and growing national economies and their effects on agricultural laborers has played out differently in societies with socialist economies. In the People's Republic of China, for example, the process of collectivization profoundly altered the experience of labor in the countryside. One aspect of this transformation was that women became a prominent, sometimes dominant, presence in the farm workforce. "The expanded mobilization of women during the Great Leap Forward," Gail Hershatter argues, "consolidated a trend towards a long-term feminization of agriculture."[18] This shift meant that different sets of issues, including maternity and family care, became significant in agricultural health. This process of collectivization coincided with Mao Zedong's "war against nature." During this period, famine ravaged many communities in China, and women's ability to labor meant the difference between life and death.[19]

As with colonial capitalism and socialist revolution, the Green Revolution has destabilized agricultural laborers and communities around the world. Chemical technologies prominent in the Green Revolution, including synthetic fertilizers and pesticides, have had a profound impact on the health of agricultural laborers. Adding fertilizers via green and organic manure (night soil) is a very old practice; yet, before high-yield varieties (HYVs) of rice there was little need to add nitrogen to wet rice fields.[20] Those defending the use of chemical fertilizers have argued that night soil can spread parasites contained in human and animal excrement (though traditional treatment methods usually rendered it safe for use) and have pointed to the high human costs of mining natural fertilizers such as guano. In the second half of the twentieth century, synthetic fertilizer use in Africa, Asia, and South America grew, although it has recently leveled off worldwide.[21] The heavy application of such fertilizers has also been associated with, among other things, health problems caused by elevated nitrogen levels in rural waters, which has negatively affected agricultural laborers and their families.

Synthetic pesticides have a more direct effect on the health of agricultural laborers. Attempts to limit "pests," including insects, weeds, fungi, and nematodes, in agriculture dates back centuries, from the spread of chemicals such as whale oil and pyrethrum, to the practice of intercropping techniques such as the "three sisters" and crop rotations.[22] In the early nineteenth century, pesticides incorporating sulfur and copper (e.g., Bordeaux mixture) were developed, with heavy metal (including arsenic and lead) compounds coming soon after (e.g., Paris green). These pesticides presented problems of acute toxicity (rapid effects) to agricultural laborers charged with applying them to crops. Beginning in the late 1930s, and increasingly during World War II, organochlorines (such as Dichlorodiphenyltrichloroethane, commonly known as DDT, and aldrin) and organophosphates (cholinesterase inhibitors including carbamate, parathion, and malathion) came into widespread use.[23]

Unsurprisingly these pesticides had known human health effects, as they were originally developed as chemical weapons meant for the battlefield. When they entered civilian use through agriculture and public health campaigns, promoters sought to downplay concerns over health impacts and highlight the benefits of these technologies. But awareness of their negative effects never disappeared, and in 1962 Rachel Carson's *Silent Spring* brought toxicological concerns about overuse of pesticides to a global public. While *Silent Spring* is more famous for its examination of the effects of DDT on the environment, birdlife in particular, it also covered the effects of pesticides on agricultural labor.[24]

In the 1980s, US consumer fears about chemical exposures helped bring more attention to the impact of pesticides on "Third World" agricultural laborers. The publication of the *Circle of Poison* and subsequent US congressional hearings helped highlight the manufacture and export of hazardous pesticides that were then coming back to the American public through imported food.[25] Studies of migrant laborers from Central and South America have shown that while the banning of DDT was good for the birds and other life sensitive to bioaccumulation, it had the unintended consequence of increasing the exposure of agricultural laborers to organophosphates and their higher acute toxicity. From Mexico to South Asia to California, some farmers facing impossible debt have committed suicide using the very organophosphate pesticides that were supposed to improve their lives.[26]

Pesticide exposure has been a problem for agricultural labor in Southeast Asia as well. The region is projected to soon have a higher urban than rural population, yet a significant number of people continue to farm as wage laborers and lead increasingly precarious lives.[27] These marginalized people have little control over when, where, and how they work for wages and are thus highly exposed to employment hazards. Chemicals have become more common because of their labor-saving value and their existence outside of prevailing social relations. As Tania Li shows, landowners "quickly adopted chemical herbicides when they became available around 1996, significantly reducing their need to employ the women of Sipil who used to do their weeding." Li continues that although landowners recognized the social disruption caused by the herbicides, their low price and effectiveness made them attractive for those who could afford them. Moreover, Bray suggests that under some conditions family farms with no hired labor might invest most in biochemicals, including herbicides and pesticides, to fill the same role as laborers employed by others.[28]

Several factors appear to put female agricultural laborers at particular risk for pesticide poisoning and make them less likely to be treated. Women have grown as a percentage of the agricultural workforce as pesticide use has increased. According to Food and Agricultural Organization (FAO) statistics, in 2000 women made up nearly 44 percent of the agricultural workforce worldwide. Even in developed countries, women do the triple duty of farming, family care, and work off the farm, with the United States and Europe slowly catching up to the rest of the world in terms of gender balance in the farming sector. These women often contend with general oppression and have been, moreover, viewed as temporary workers, which means that they have received less training and protection from exposure than other workers. Moreover, medical studies have pointed to biological factors, including higher levels of body fat and potential reproductive consequences, that result in greater pesticide burdens for women.[29]

Analyzing the effects of pesticides should not mask other health hazards, and physical injuries remain an important risk faced by all agricultural laborers. Two sources of illness in California agriculture, for example, are heat and sunstroke, and farmers everywhere still get caught in and crushed by machinery.[30]

An important source of injury and death for agricultural laborers remains handling animals on farms. As with the mechanization of plant-based agriculture, new technologies such as refrigeration opened the way to the long-distance shipping of meat, milk, and other animal products. This industrialization of animal production has introduced sources of danger for laborers through physical injury, exposure to toxins used in chemicals to disinfect livestock, and other production processes. Medical researchers have traced the source of many human diseases back to human and animal interactions, and animal husbandry continues to expose laborers to infectious diseases. Q fever, an emergent zoonotic disease, was first identified in Australia among those working with animals. Dealing with sea life in aquaculture can present its own hazards, and the overuse of antibiotics has not helped those in either industry.[31]

Reminiscent of eighteenth-century views of agriculture, those referring to the agrarian ideal often argue that agriculture has a beneficial effect for mental health. This can be far from the case. Although Upton Sinclair's 1906 book *The Jungle* is better remembered for its success in bringing about laws aimed at protecting consumers, it also tried to call attention to the situation of immigrant workers in the meatpacking industry. In an update to Sinclair's trenchant critiques of this industry, Timothy Pachirat has shown that the daily violence exerted on animals in the meat-processing industry in the US Midwest has often severe consequences for the mental health of agricultural workers. While owners deal more directly with questions of crop failure and world market prices, agricultural laborers suffer when they lose benefits and accept employment with low wages. Moreover, they enjoy neither the feeling of control of being an owner, nor the subsidies and rights that come with farm ownership. The stresses of migrant life, including discrimination based on race, class, gender, and nationality, compound the effects of ill health due to agricultural activities.[32]

Managerial Estates

The expansion of monoculture farms and vast plantations, the predominant forms of industrialized agriculture over the past two hundred years, has brought profound changes to worker health. Most of these estates have been run by professional managers with absentee owners, either individual or corporate. One of the most important consequences of the creation of plantations was the desire for vast amounts of cheap agricultural labor. In the Americas during the nineteenth century, first enslaved and then indentured peoples supplied this labor. While the rice and cotton plantations were deadly places, they were also contact zones for healing traditions and motivated some of the earliest attempts at agricultural medicine. Elsewhere in the world, imperial officials helped create extensive migration networks both within and among colonies and empires. For example, South Asians went to British Malaya to work on rubber plantations, Javanese traveled in the Dutch East Indies to work on sugar cane and rubber plantations, Vietnamese from northern and central French Indochina went to Cochinchina, New Caledonia, and elsewhere to work for agricultural enterprises, and Chinese and Japanese laborers traveled around the world for work.[33]

The imperial plantation altered the processes affecting the health of agricultural labor.[34] From a social, legal, economic, and political perspective, migrant laborers were extremely vulnerable as they were far from family and friends and had few formal protections. Furthermore, plantation agriculture operated on and through human and nonhuman life. To manage large migrant populations, plantations created racialized hierarchies of labor. Those on the bottom, both migrant and indigenous populations, suffered daily violence through physical abuse, horrible working conditions, and low pay. Not surprisingly they often sickened and died. Plantation managers also instituted gendered practices that structured the economies of violence. At certain times, plantation managers sought to employ exclusively male labor but there was often an interest in female migrants who could both "domesticate" male workers and reproduce the labor force. The loosely regulated conditions of commodity frontiers created dangerous conditions for women. With little oversight, male sexual violence was always a possibility. Moreover, health issues related to reproduction were rarely addressed. Racializing and gendering processes continue to have consequences for job hierarchies on plantations and related access to healthcare. Those perceived as other by management and owners tend to receive the fewest resources. Independence movements challenged some of these hierarchies but left other structural determinants of health in place.[35]

In terms of how specific plantation activities influenced health, one of the worst has been the preparing of land for cultivation through deforestation, clearing, plowing, irrigation, and infrastructure building. Both social and environmental factors have contributed to the danger. These factors have included inexperienced, untrained workers living far from population centers, combined with harsh conditions and underfunded medical care. Plantation managers have sought the cheapest possible labor, which in areas with low populations and abundant land has meant relying heavily on migrants. Companies have invested little in training or providing for safety measures, resulting in physical accidents, illness, and death.

While agricultural development has sometimes been linked to decreases in certain diseases, plantations tended to increase exposure to other diseases, at least in the short run. Malaria, beriberi, hookworm, tuberculosis, dysentery, and others, combined with malnutrition and overwork, has led to high levels of morbidity and mortality among agricultural laborers. During the 1920s, for instance, the rubber plantations of French Indochina saw an explosion in malaria as primary and secondary forests were cleared on red earth lands. On some plantations, during some months, annual mortality rates reached 45 percent of the workforce. Infant mortality rates were another sign of deadly workplace conditions. Tran Tu Binh, a Vietnamese communist revolutionary, wrote that he heard no sounds of babies during his time on the Phu Rieng plantation of French colonial Vietnam.[36]

Once plantations were producing crops, inadequate diets, in both quality and quantity, often led to malnutrition. Furthermore, substandard housing exposed workers to the elements. Yet, the plantations were also some of the first sites to provide a modicum of healthcare for agricultural labor, and colonial states created the first health standards with plantation labor in mind. In addition, plantation medical doctors served as an early model for the specialty of agricultural medicine, even as in practice estate care was often minimal and worker health was usually worse than that of surrounding rural populations.

The struggles of plantation labor continued into the postcolonial world. In Vietnam, nationalist and socialist political regimes concerned with improving workers' conditions did make significant improvements. In 1960, rubber workers signed a collective agreement that set out the conditions for plantation labor and created a model for contracts in other industries. Even so, the Vietnam War delayed the implementation of many of its provisions for improved pay and working conditions. The post-1975 Socialist Republic of Vietnam celebrated the contributions of rubbers workers to national independence, but the economic situation made higher standards difficult to reach. In the 2000s, by contrast, the privileged position of rubber has shielded workers in the industry from the worst consequences of neoliberal policies, which have weakened a once robust national healthcare system.[37]

The roots of agromedicine, or the application of biomedicine to agricultural labor, are rather shallow. In 1789, an English physician published an essay that described the causes of disease among agricultural laborers and suggested some means to keep them healthy. Health at that time was understood within a humoral framework, and the illnesses that afflicted agricultural laborers largely arose from too much heat, cold, moisture, and overexertion. According to this framework, rural English air was generally healthy, especially during the day, but there were several dangers to be avoided. Both falling asleep in wet clothes on the ground and the emanations of southern England's marshes were an important source of illness. For this physician, contagion too represented a threat and he urged isolation to stop the spread of disease. Finally, he moralized about the laboring class and their "intemperance," including excessive drinking and eating.[38]

In terms of keeping laborers healthy, he counseled paternalistic landowners to make sure that workers had proper clothing. He recommended Peruvian bark, especially when mixed with wine and spices, as a useful treatment for the recurrent fevers that could strike those working outdoors. Moreover, he advised giving workers Sundays off so they could keep clean and rested, as tired laborers worked less effectively. This physician's knowledge of agricultural laborers was based on hospital observation, anecdotes, and common assumptions, not systematic study, and it suggests that the European medical profession still viewed agricultural labor as a comparatively healthy "way of life."[39]

At the turn of the nineteenth century, European medical doctors began to make several discoveries that helped to extend their professional authority over more of society, including rural populations. In the 1790s, Edward Jenner developed a smallpox vaccination based on his observation of the immunity that cowpox gave to those, mostly women, working with cattle. By the early nineteenth century, medical doctors from the Dutch East Indies to the US South were making links between stagnant water and fevers. Later in the nineteenth century, Louis Pasteur, a French medical scientist who had strong agricultural ties, developed his ideas about microbes and an eponymous process to render them harmless. Despite these changes, the health of most agricultural laborers was still dependent on ambient rural conditions and local healers.[40]

Medical science has had interests that sometimes coincided, sometimes conflicted, with capital and the state concerning the health of agricultural laborers. The results of the interplay of professional medicine, farm owners, and the state have been mixed for laborers. Ironically, some of the first steps to address the health of agricultural laborers came from those running managerial estates and a body of law, medicine, and scholarship developed around Southeast Asian plantations. In response to high death rates, the colonial government of British Malaya considered measures to provide healthcare in the late nineteenth century. These measures, and perhaps more important the shift from clearing work to established monocultures, helped gradually to reduce worker deaths due to malaria, tuberculosis, and malnutrition. In French Indochina, the colonial government enlisted the Pasteur Institute to counteract outbreaks of malaria on rubber plantations during the expansion of the 1920s.[41]

These tentative measures reflected the paternalistic attitudes of the colonial states. They, and more general labor codes in the late 1910s and 1920s, aimed to provide a steady supply of workers for plantations and limit worker unrest as much as possible. Octave Homberg, a financier involved with the rubber industry in French Indochina, noted how "a maternity ward, a vaccination center established today in the brush will give us each day a work force of a powerful factory, a vast agricultural exploitation." In Homberg's view, investment in rural healthcare was justified because it would increase profits, strengthen the French nation, and, as an added benefit, improve the health of the colonized. His view also reflected changing demographics, as the large flows of immigrants that had initially sustained the rubber plantations began to slow and owners tried to keep more laborers alive through better healthcare.[42]

Colonial governments, however, were too often ineffective in improving the conditions of agricultural laborers. Many medical doctors simply assumed that workers were faking complaints about pain and disease. Moreover, plantation medicine could also be used as a weapon against workers. Tran Tu Binh, who worked as a nurse on the Phu Rieng plantation, recounted how medical personnel were ordered to deny workers' requests for rest. Such alliances between medical doctors and agricultural management and ownership continues to be documented.[43]

Plantation medicine has intersected with twentieth-century internationalism, first of the League of Nations (LON) and the ILO and then of the UN and the WHO. With a few exceptions, the earliest attempts to improve agricultural laborers' health concentrated on rural healthcare. In 1931, the LON discussed agricultural labor in Europe, and in 1937 it held the Intergovernmental Conference of Far-Eastern Countries on Rural Hygiene.

The 1930s saw the "marriage of health and agriculture" more generally. With regard to the ILO, the first permanent agricultural committee emerged from discussions begun in the 1920s though it only held its first session in 1938. After World War II, the WHO and the UN continued to address the health of agricultural labor, efforts that helped create the specialization of agromedicine.[44]

While admirable in theory, agromedicine as practiced in the United States still treats white and colored bodies differently. One of the standard textbooks in the field, citing an article published in the journal *Agromedicine*, writes of "the probable heritability of an agrarian type of psychosocial make-up." Of course, agrarian livelihoods cannot be passed on genetically; yet, further discussion of principal operators, that is, owners, and farm workers does not make clear the psychological or social factors that might make "an agrarian type" an inheritance. Instead, the textbook continues to refer to genes by stating that "the vast majority (over 95%) of the U.S. family farm workforce is Caucasian, primarily of Northern European descent." "Indigenous" farm workers, which are defined here as white, "may have the same culture and socioeconomic status as the owner/operator. . . . These workers may be exposed to the same hazards as other workers but do not have the same inherent lower socioeconomic status as migrant or seasonal or foreign-born workers." Finally, the reader learns that "in North America, migrant and seasonal workers are largely Hispanics from Mexico. However, Central and South America contribute workers as well as Bosnia, Asia, Africa, and the Caribbean Islands." While this account may represent an accurate snapshot of a racialized understanding of contemporary farming demographics, it omits the history of the racializing processes entwining land and labor that, as Leah Penniman argues, excluded people of color from farm ownership. This discussion of white ownership of farmers without mention of the violence of settler colonialism and the continued dispossession of indigenous and people of color farmers of land perpetuates views of colonial planters who depicted whites as the "brains" and natives or non-whites as the "hands" on farms. Not surprisingly, medical doctors working in such a context often adopt unwarranted assumptions that can lead to malpractice in the treatment of agricultural laborers.[45]

In terms of class, agricultural laborers have generally had less bargaining power than industrial laborers, and farm workers have not benefited from the same legal protection as factory workers. For instance, the US National Labor Relations Act of 1935 specifically excluded agricultural laborers from its coverage. Recent activism has focused on passing basic labor laws that cover agricultural labor.[46]

Since most agricultural laborers could not rely on owners, governments, or biomedical doctors to improve their working conditions, they have resorted to other means to stay healthy. Many workers consumed "traditional" medicines and gathered what they could find on the land. Others sought to improve conditions through workers' movements. In French Indochina, rubber workers carried out strikes throughout the twentieth century that sought concrete improvements in working and living conditions. Even though these strikes fed into broader political movements, including the anti-colonial and communist movements, rubber workers have had to continue to fight for improved conditions under Vietnamese national governments. In other Southeast

Asian countries during the Cold War, agricultural labor often relied on foot dragging and other "invisible" means of protest to improve working conditions.[47]

Workers' movements have been entangled with other political projects. In the United States, farm worker organizers drew from the civil rights movements of the 1960s and developed their own tactics such as boycotts that appealed to consumers to help improve agricultural labor conditions. One of the best-known campaigns was run by Cesar Chavez and others in the National Farm Workers Association (NFWA), which became the United Farm Workers Union (UFW) in 1966. Even though many activists were not farmers themselves, these groups successfully fought for better working conditions and higher pay for agricultural laborers.[48] In socialist countries such as the People's Republic of China and the Democratic Republic of Vietnam, improving health was often part of broader state goals to mobilize farmers for political ends. The patriotic hygiene movements in East and Southeast Asia, for example, looked to combat American and European imperialism by eliminating diseases and pests in the countryside. Barefoot doctors and other traditional healers were employed to provide low-cost, accessible healthcare for farmers who, in the case of the Democratic Republic of Vietnam, provided the food and recruits that the state needed to fight its wars.

Finally, workers' responses to hazardous conditions have been influenced by their understandings of labor and the environment. Agricultural laborers have often spoken of being pitted against nature by an exploitative system. In the sugar cane fields of Brazil, workers pointed to animals, insects, and the cane itself as the causes of their injuries and illness. Similarly, a common saying coming from the rubber plantations of French Indochina stated that beneath every tree, fertilizing it, was buried a worker's body. But, as Tran Tu Binh made sure to emphasize, what workers feared most were the violent managers and rapacious owners. In other words, these workers have recognized that they were abused by other humans but have often conceived of that oppression in naturalistic terms.[49]

ORGANIC, SUSTAINABLE, URBAN, AND FAIR TRADE FARMING

Recent thinking about agricultural practices is riddled with ironies and largely falls into two camps. In one camp stand defenders of industrial agriculture. These stalwarts tout industrial agriculture's benefits as increased production of nutritious food. By some measures, agricultural change in the last two hundred years has been a success story. One economic historian argues that agricultural during this period "has succeeded in feeding a much greater population a greater variety of products at falling prices, while releasing a growing number of workers to the rest of the economy." In numerical terms, between 1800 and 2000 the world population grew six to seven times as large while agricultural output grew at an even faster pace of ten times as large. This growth is one reason why famines are no longer a regular occurrence and undernourishment results mostly from "poor entitlements," that is, not enough money to buy food or instability that interrupts distribution. For advocates of industrial agriculture, pesticides, herbicides, and biotechnology have played an essential role in this increase in food production.[50]

In the other camp stand those who have challenged the dominance of industrial agriculture. For defenders of so-called alternative agriculture, including practices labeled organic, sustainable, urban, and fair trade, thinking about ideal agriculture has circled back to practices that would be familiar to the eighteenth-century English physician cited above. These advocates point to the benefits of decreased chemical use and practices that are better for the health of the land and its people. They, too, point out that distribution, and not simply production, are key factors causing malnutrition and starvation, and obesity arises not from too little food but from too much of the wrong kind of food. The organic farming movement, and later sustainable farming, grew out of similar concerns for the health of soils and of communities as a whole.

Both defenders of industrial agriculture, and even many of its critics, have tended to ignore the health and well-being of those hired to work in the field. The organic farming movement, for instance, initially focused on consumer health. Early proponents such as Albert Howard argued that plants and animals raised organically were healthier for those eating them, not for those producing them. In Howard's 1943 publication *The Agricultural Testament*, he addressed the question of "how does the produce of an impoverished soil affect men and women who have to consume it?"[51] Yet, from fruit picking in North and Central America to palm oil harvesting in Southeast Asia, recent controversies show that the health of agricultural labor remains a contentious issue. A growing number of scientific studies have pointed to the risks that people undergo when they use herbicides and pesticides for farming and landscaping, and even staunch defenders of industrial agriculture admit that "people applying pesticides . . . seem to have higher cancer rates than people who rarely encounter pesticides." In the past few years, juries have awarded huge settlements against chemical companies such as Monsanto/Bayer and its herbicide Roundup Ready.[52]

In the post-1945 world, organic and industrial agriculture first came into direct conflict over the application of chemical fertilizers. Concerns about global food supplies, and nationalistic concerns about food security, encouraged political leaders to promote greatly increased production, which relied on prodigious amounts of chemical fertilizers. Later, organic farmers' manipulation of ecological relationships for pest control meant that they stood against the use of pesticides and herbicides. While initial support for organic farming drew heavily from an agrarian ideal, organic farming has the potential to improve labor conditions for laborers as well. Organic farming and complementary direct-marketing strategies such as community support agriculture (CSA) have called into question many of the assumptions and practices of industrial agriculture including those related to worker health.[53]

As the term "organic" has entered the mainstream and become a government-regulated label, however, organic and industrial farming practices have converged in certain respects. Now organic farming can present many of the same health hazards for workers as other forms of industrial agriculture. These hazards are sometimes exacerbated by the return to human labor to carry out tasks that chemicals and machines had taken over. Thus, deindustrializing agriculture can have mixed results for laborers. Similarly, sustainable farming is almost exclusively discussed in terms of the three legs of environment, equity, and economy (or profit, people, and planet). While laborers may be implicitly included in equity (people), their concerns are often unaddressed in practice.[54]

Although focused on land ownership rather than agricultural labor per se, urban agriculture and people of color farmers' movements have historically been aimed at survival. Furthermore, they have sought to heal the wounds of past and current exploitation of agricultural laborers.[55] In the case of active black farmers, land ownership in the United States has decreased from 16 million acres in 1920 to about 2 million acres in 1997.[56] Scholarship shows that owning a family farm brings many benefits, which proponents of urban agriculture are attempting to reproduce for both landowners and laborers. Other groups have also viewed agricultural labor as a key healing practice. Drawing on consumer-focused movements of the past, recent fair-trade efforts have aimed to use the power of the purse to improve global agricultural labor conditions, often with mixed results.[57]

Over the past two hundred years, agriculture has become a distinct occupation, with laborers' health diverging from that of surrounding rural populations. Although a few agricultural laborers (owner-operators) have enjoyed improved health outcomes, most others (migrant and seasonal farmers) have encountered increasingly hazardous conditions with only uneven protection.

The hardships facing these laborers seem to be worsening as the planet warms. In all agricultural settings, from family-owned farms to managerial estates, climate change is poised to increase the number and severity of agricultural hazards.[58] Fruit pickers on the US West Coast will endure more extreme weather conditions (both hotter and colder, drier and wetter), which will increase physical stresses. Those hired on tropical plantations will be exposed to more pesticides and herbicides as well as emerging and re-emerging infectious diseases. These effects will likely continue to be unevenly distributed across socioeconomic groups.[59]

Notes

1. For interwar years, see Louise Howard, *Labour in Agriculture: An International Survey* (London: Oxford University Press, 1935); and Amalia Ribi Forclaz, "A New Target for International Social Reform: The International Labour Organization and Working and Living Conditions in Agriculture in the Inter-War Years," *Contemporary European History* 20, no. 3 (2011): 307–29. For the post–World War II era, see Virginia Thompson, *Labor Problems in Southeast Asia* (New Haven, CT: Yale University Press, 1947); and Amy Staples, *The Birth of Development: How the World Bank, Food and Agriculture Organization, and World Health Organization Changed the World, 1945–1965* (Kent, OH: Kent State University Press, 2006). For an example of recent work on occupational health dealing with

agriculture, see Christopher Sellers and Joseph Melling, eds., *Dangerous Trade: Histories of Industrial Hazard across a Globalizing World* (Philadelphia: Temple University Press, 2011), which includes a chapter by Amarjit Kaur on labor on Southeast Asian managerial estates.
2. For the idea that increased exploitation can lead to responses to protect people from deadly processes see Karl Polanyi, *The Great Transformation* (Boston: Beacon Press, 1944). For data related to the health of owner-operators, see Table 1.4 in Kelley J. Donham and Anders Thelin, *Agricultural Medicine: Rural Occupational and Environmental Health, Safety, and Prevention* (Hoboken, NJ: John Wiley & Sons, 2016), 23. For a recent discussion of precarity, see Oliver Tappe, "Patterns of Precarity: Historical Trajectories of Vietnamese Labour Mobility," *TRaNS: Trans-Regional and -National Studies of Southeast Asia* 7, no. 1 (2019): 19–42.
3. For a similar definition, see Donham and Thelin, *Agricultural Medicine*, 1.
4. USDA, "Farm Labor," Economic Research Service, https://www.ers.usda.gov/topics/farm-economy/farm-labor/#legalstatus, accessed November 21, 2019. According to the same source, the National Agricultural Statistical Service (NASS) Farm Labor Survey (FLS), in 2000, there were 2.06 million family farmworkers, down from 7.6 million in 1950. In 2017, about 400,000 hired farmworkers were not US citizens, according to the USDA. ILO, "Towards a Fair Deal for Migrant Workers in the Global Economy" (Geneva: ILO, 2004): 50, cited in Donham and Thelin, *Agricultural Medicine*, 20. Data are best for agricultural workers in developed countries since 1950 but it is still hard to count immigrants classified as illegal. Giovanni Federico, *Feeding the World: An Economic History of Agriculture, 1800–2000* (Princeton, NJ: Princeton University Press, 2005). For women on North American farms, see Donham and Thelin, *Agricultural Medicine*, 19–20.
5. For definitions of estates and family farms, see Federico, *Feeding the World*, 122. For concepts of structural violence and structural vulnerability, see, e.g., Paul Farmer, "On Suffering and Structural Violence: A View from Below," *Daedalus* 125 (1996): 261–83; and more recently Sarah Horton, *They Leave Their Kidneys in the Fields: Illness, Injury and Illegality among U.S. Farmworkers* (Oakland: University of California Press, 2016). For an account of the "Neo-Europes" created by settler colonialism, see Alfred Crosby, *Ecological Imperialism: The Biological Expansion of Europe, 900–1900* (New York: Cambridge University Press, 2004).
6. Mike Davis, *Late Victorian Holocausts: El Niño Famines and the Making of the Third World* (New York: Verso, 2001); Geoffrey C. Gunn, *Rice Wars in Colonial Vietnam: The Great Famine and the Viet Minh Road to Power* (Lanham, MD: Rowman & Littlefield, 2014); Frank Dikötter, *Mao's Great Famine: The History of China's Most Devastating Catastrophe, 1958–1962* (New York: Walker, 2010).
7. For collective rituals aimed at health, see Paul Katz, *Demon Hordes and Burning Boats: The Cult of Marshall Wen in Late Imperial Chekiang* (Albany: State University of New York Press, 1995).
8. Barbara Weinstein, *The Amazon Rubber Boom, 1850–1920* (Stanford, CA: Stanford University Press, 1983); Warren Dean, *Brazil and the Struggle for Rubber: A Study in Environmental History* (New York: Cambridge University Press, 1987); Bradford Barham and Oliver Coomes, "Wild Rubber: Industrial Organisation and the Microeconomics of Extraction during the Amazon Rubber Boom (1860–1920)," *Journal of Latin American Studies* 26, no. 1 (1994): 37–72.
9. For the Amazon, see Greg Grandin, *Fordlandia: The Rise and Fall of Henry Ford's Forgotten Jungle City* (New York: Metropolitan Books/Henry Holt, 2009); and Seth Garfield, *In Search of the Amazon: Brazil, the United States, and the Nature of a Region* (Durham, NC: Duke

University Press, 2013), inter alia 72–74. For labor and guano, see Edward Melillo, "The First Green Revolution: Debt Peonage and the Making of the Nitrogen Fertilizer Trade, 1840–1930," *American Historical Review* 117, no. 4 (2012): 1028–60; Gregory Cushman, *Guano and the Opening of the Pacific World: A Global Ecological History* (New York: Cambridge University Press, 2013); and G. Samantha Rosenthal, "Life and Labor in a Seabird Colony: Hawaiian Guano Workers, 1857–70," *Environmental History* 17, no. 4 (2012): 744–82. For zoonotic disease, see Nathan D. Wolfe, Peter Daszak, A. Marm Kilpatrick, and Donald S. Burke, "Bushmeat Hunting, Deforestation, and Prediction of Zoonotic Disease," *Emerging Infectious Diseases* 11, no. 12 (2005): 1822–27.

10. For pastoralists, see Diana Davis, *The Arid Lands: History, Power, Knowledge* (Cambridge, MA: MIT Press, 2016): 98–102, 126–31; and Matthew Turner and Eva Schlecht, "Livestock Mobility in Sub-Saharan Africa: A Critical Review," *Pastoralism* 9, no. 1 (2019): 13. For swidden agriculture, see James Scott, *The Art of Not Being Governed: An Anarchist History of Upland Southeast Asia* (New Haven, CT: Yale University Press, 2009); Michael Dove, *The Banana Tree at the Gate: A History of Marginal Peoples and Global Markets in Borneo* (New Haven, CT: Yale University Press, 2011); and Tania Li, *Land's End: Capitalist Relations on an Indigenous Frontier* (Durham, NC: Duke University Press, 2014).

11. Linda Nash, *Inescapable Ecologies: A History of Environment, Disease, and Knowledge* (Berkeley: University of California Press, 2006).

12. Inter alia, Francesca Bray, *The Rice Economies: Technology and Development in Asian Societies* (Berkeley: University of California Press, 1994). For an examination of rice consumers, see Seung-joon Lee, *Gourmets in the Land of Famine: The Culture and Politics of Rice in Modern Canton* (Stanford, CA: Stanford University Press, 2011).

13. Inter alia, Mark Elvin, *Retreat of the Elephants: An Environmental History of China* (New Haven, CT: Yale University Press, 2004).

14. Bray, *The Rice Economies*, 3.

15. Ibid., 57–59.

16. Michael Adas, *The Burma Delta: Economic Development and Social Change on an Asian Rice Frontier, 1852–1941* (Madison: University of Wisconsin Press, 1974); Pierre Brocheux, *The Mekong Delta: Ecology, Economy, and Revolution, 1860–1960* (Madison: University of Wisconsin Press, 1995); David Biggs, *Quagmire: Nation-Building and Nature in the Mekong Delta* (Seattle: University of Washington Press, 2010); Francesca Bray, Peter A. Coclanis, Edda L. Fields-Black, and Dagmar Schaefer, eds., *Rice: Global Networks and New Histories* (New York: Cambridge University Press, 2015).

17. Bray, *The Rice Economies*, 155; Nick Cullather, *The Hungry World: America's Cold War Battle against Poverty in Asia* (Cambridge, MA: Harvard University Press, 2010).

18. Gail Hershatter, *The Gender of Memory: Rural Women and China's Collective Past* (Berkeley: University of California Press, 2011): 237.

19. Judith Shapiro, *Mao's War against Nature: Politics and the Environment in Revolutionary China* (New York: Cambridge University Press, 2001). For a more nuanced view, see Sigrid Schmalzer, *Red Revolution, Green Revolution: Scientific Farming in Socialist China* (Chicago: University of Chicago Press, 2016).

20. See the Vietnamese saying: "Nhất nước, nhì phân, tam cần, tứ giống," that is, first water, second fertilizer, third labor, and fourth seeds. Bray, *The Rice Economies*, 13.

21. For worldwide use of fertilizer, see Table 4.15 in Federico, *Feeding the World*, 55. For a discussion of fertilizers in sugar cane fields of Southeast Asia, see G. Roger Knight, "A

Precocious Appetite: Industrial Agriculture and the Fertiliser Revolution in Java's Colonial Cane Fields, c. 1880–1914," *Journal of Southeast Asian Studies* 37 (2006): 43–63.
22. Jakobina Arch, "Whale Oil Pesticide: Natural History, Animal Resources, and Agriculture in Early Modern Japan," in *New Perspectives on the History of Life Sciences and Agriculture*, ed. Denise Phillips and Sharon Kingsland, 93–111 (Cham, Switzerland: Springer, 2015).
23. See James Whorton, "Insecticide Spray Residue and Public Health, 1865–1938," in *Sickness and Health in America: Readings in the History of Medicine and Public Health*, ed. Judith Walzer Leavitt and Ronald Numbers, 459–72 (Madison: University of Wisconsin Press, 1985); John Wargo, *Our Children's Toxic Legacy: How Science and Law Fail to Protect Us from Pesticides* (New Haven, CT: Yale University Press, 1996); Edmund Russell, *War and Nature: Fighting Humans and Insects with Chemicals from World War I to Silent Spring* (New York: Cambridge University Press, 2001); David Kinkela, *DDT and the American Century: Global Health, Environmental Politics, and the Pesticide That Changed the World* (Chapel Hill: University of North Carolina Press, 2011); Frederick Davis, *Banned: A History of Pesticides and the Science of Toxicology* (New Haven, CT: Yale University Press, 2014).
24. Rachel Carson, *Silent Spring* (Boston: Houghton Mifflin, 1962).
25. David Weir and Mark Schapiro, *Circle of Poison: Pesticides and People in a Hungry World* (San Francisco: Institute for Food and Development Policy, 1981); United States Senate, *Circle of Poison: Impact of U.S. Pesticides on Third World Workers: Hearing before the Committee on Agriculture, Nutrition, and Forestry, United States Senate, One Hundred Second Congress, First Session, on the Impact on Third World Workers Who Use U.S. Made Pesticides, June 5, 1991* (Washington, DC: Government Printing Office, 1991). See also Susanna Bohme, *Toxic Injustice: A Transnational History of Exposure and Struggle* (Oakland: University of California Press, 2015).
26. Angus Lindsay Wright, *The Death of Ramón González: The Modern Agricultural Dilemma*, rev. ed. (Austin: University of Texas Press, 2005); See also John Soluri, *Banana Cultures: Agriculture, Consumption, and Environmental Change in Honduras and the United States* (Austin: University of Texas Press, 2005); Akhil Gupta, *Postcolonial Developments: Agriculture in the Making of Modern India* (Durham, NC: Duke University Press, 1998); James McCann, *Maize and Grace: Africa's Encounter with a New World Crop, 1500–2000* (Cambridge, MA: Harvard University Press, 2005).
27. See Figures A.6, A.7, and A.10 in Appendix 2.1, Jonathan Rigg and Peter Vandergeest, eds., *Revisiting Rural Places: Pathways to Poverty and Prosperity in Southeast Asia* (Honolulu: University of Hawai'i Press, 2012): 306–7, 310.
28. Li, *Land's End*, 147; Bray, *The Rice Economies*, 163–64.
29. See Table 4.19, Federico, *Feeding the World*, 62; Sarojeni V. Rengam, *Resisting Poisons, Reclaiming Lives!: Impact of Pesticides on Women's Health* (Penang, Malaysia: Pesticide Action Network Asia and the Pacific, 2007).
30. Along with Nash, *Inescapable Ecologies*, see Seth Holmes, *Fresh Fruit, Broken Bodies: Migrant Farmworkers in the United States* (Berkeley: University of California Press, 2013); Horton, *They Leave Their Kidneys*; see also the story of Peter Benson's father-in-law in *Tobacco Capitalism: Growers, Migrant Workers, and the Changing Face of a Global Industry* (Princeton, NJ: Princeton University Press, 2012).
31. Kenneth Kiple, ed. *The Cambridge World History of Human Disease* (New York: Cambridge University Press, 1993), does not list agriculture as an entry in its index, yet many diseases

are of agricultural origin. For Q fever see Kiple, ed., *Cambridge*, 957–61. See also Kendra Smith-Howard, "Antibiotics and Agricultural Change: Purifying Milk and Protecting Health in the Postwar Era," *Agricultural History* 84 (2010): 327–51; Julia Martínez and Adrian Vickers, *The Pearl Frontier: Indonesian Labor and Indigenous Encounters in Australia's Northern Trading Network* (Honolulu: University of Hawai'i Press, 2017).

32. Upton Sinclair, *The Jungle* (Cambridge: R. Bentley, 1972); and Timothy Pachirat, *Every Twelve Seconds: Industrialized Slaughter and the Politics of Sight* (New Haven, CT: Yale University Press, 2011). See also Benson, *Tobacco Capitalism*; Holmes, *Fresh Fruit, Broken Bodies*; Bohme, *Toxic Injustice*.

33. Sidney Mintz, *Sweetness and Power: The Place of Sugar in Modern History* (New York: Viking, 1985); Philip Curtin, *The Rise and Fall of the Plantation Complex* (New York: Cambridge University Press, 1990); Mart Stewart, *"What Nature Suffers to Groe": Life, Labor, and Landscape on the Georgia Coast, 1680–1920* (Athens: University of Georgia Press, 1996); G. Roger Knight, "Gully Coolies, Weed-Women and Snijvolk: The Sugar Industry Workers of North Java in the Early Twentieth Century," *Modern Asian Studies* 28 (1994): 51–76; Suzanne Moon, *Technology and Ethical Idealism: A History of Development in the Netherlands East Indies* (Leiden: CNWS Publications, 2007); Lisa Yun, *The Coolie Speaks: Chinese Indentured Laborers and African Slaves in Cuba* (Philadelphia: Temple University Press, 2008). For Brazil, see Thomas Rogers, *The Deepest Wounds: A Labor and Environmental History of Sugar in Northeast Brazil* (Chapel Hill: University of North Carolina Press, 2010).

34. Piya Chatterjee, Monisha Das Gupta, and Richard Cullen Rath, "Imperial Plantations: Past, Present, and Future Directions," *Journal of Historical Sociology* 23 (2010): 1–15.

35. Pierre Brocheux, "Le prolétariat des plantations d'hévéas au Vietnam méridional: aspects sociaux et politiques (1927–1937)," *Le mouvement social* 90 (1975): 55–86; Philippe Bourgois, *Ethnicity at Work: Divided Labor on a Central American Banana Plantation* (Baltimore: Johns Hopkins University Press, 1989); Shobhita Jain and Roda Reddock, *Women Plantation Workers: International Experiences* (New York: Berg, 1998); Piya Chatterjee, *A Time for Tea: Women, Labor, and Post/Colonial Politics on an Indian Plantation* (Durham, NC: Duke University Press, 2001); and Amarjit Kaur, *Women Workers in Industrialising Asia: Costed, Not Valued* (New York: Palgrave Macmillan, 2004).

36. Martin Murray, "'White Gold' or 'White Blood'?: The Rubber Plantations of Colonial Indochina, 1910–40," in *Plantations, Proletarians, and Peasants in Colonial Asia*, ed. E. Valentine Daniel, Henry Bernstein, and Tom Brass (London: Frank Cass, 1992): 41–67; Michitake Aso, *Rubber and the Making of Vietnam: An Ecological History, 1897–1975* (Chapel Hill: University of North Carolina Press, 2018): 111 for mortality rate and Chapter 3 in general; Amarjit Kaur, "Rubber Plantation Workers, Work Hazards, and Health in Colonial Malaya, 1900–1940," in *Dangerous Trade: Histories of Industrial Hazard across a Globalizing World*, ed. Christopher Sellers and Joseph Melling (Philadelphia: Temple University Press, 2012): 29.

37. Aso, *Rubber*, 215–17.

38. William Falconer, *An Essay on the Preservation of the Health of Persons Employed in Agriculture, and on the Cure of the Diseases Incident to That Way of Life . . .* (Bath: R. Cruttwell, 1789).

39. Ibid.

40. Stewart, "What Nature Suffers to Groe"; Peckham, *Epidemics in Modern Asia*.
41. J. Norman Parmer, "Estate Workers' Health in the Federated Malay States in the 1920s," in *The Underside of Malaysian History: Pullers, Prostitutes, Plantation Workers*, ed. Peter J. Rimmer and Lisa M. Allen (Singapore: Singapore University Press, 1990): 179–92; Ann Laura Stoler, *Capitalism and Confrontation in Sumatra's Plantation Belt, 1870–1979*, 2nd ed. (Ann Arbor: University of Michigan Press, 1995); Kaur, "Rubber Plantation Workers"; Aso, *Rubber*, 140–46.
42. Octave Homberg, *La France des cinq parties du monde* (Paris: Plon, 1927), 6; Lenore Manderson, *Sickness and the State: Health and Illness in Colonial Malaya, 1870–1940* (New York: Cambridge University Press, 1996).
43. Tran Tu Binh and An Ha, *The Red Earth: A Vietnamese Memoir of Life on a Colonial Rubber Plantation*, trans. John Spragens Jr. (Athens: Ohio University Press, 1985): 27, 37; Aso, *Rubber*, 119–20; Holmes, *Fresh Fruit, Broken Bodies*; Horton, *They Leave Their Kidneys*, 99–101.
44. Forclaz, "A New Target," 324; International Labour Office, *Social Problems in Agriculture: Record of the Permanent Agricultural Committee of the I.L.O.* (Geneva: ILO, 1938).
45. Donham and Thelin, *Agricultural Medicine*, 18–21; Leah Penniman, *Farming While Black: Soul Fire Farm's Practical Guide to Liberation on the Land* (White River Junction, VT: Chelsea Green, 2018); and Holmes, *Fresh Fruit, Broken Bodies*.
46. U.S. National Labor Relations Act of 1935, https://www.nlrb.gov/how-we-work/national-labor-relations-act. For recent legislation at the state level, see "The Farm Laborers Fair Labor Practices Act" passed in 2019 in New York State.
47. James Scott, *Weapons of the Weak: Everyday Forms of Peasant Resistance* (New Haven, CT: Yale University Press, 1985).
48. Matt Garcia, *From the Jaws of Victory: The Triumph and Tragedy of Cesar Chavez and the Farm Worker Movement* (Berkeley: University of California Press, 2012).
49. Rogers, *The Deepest Wounds*; Tran, *The Red Earth*; Aso, *Rubber*.
50. Giovanni, *Feeding the World*, Preface, xiii, 1; Robert Paarlberg, *Food Politics: What Everyone Needs to Know* (New York: Oxford University Press, 2010).
51. Greg Barton, *The Global History of Organic Farming* (Oxford: Oxford University Press, 2018): 118.
52. Oliver Pye and Jayati Bhattacharya, eds., *The Palm Oil Controversy in Southeast Asia: A Transnational Perspective* (Singapore: ISEAS, 2013); F. Bailey Norwood, Pascal A. Oltenacu, Michelle S. Calvo-Lorenzo, and Sarah Lancaster, *Agricultural and Food Controversies: What Everyone Needs to Know* (New York: Oxford University Press, 2015): 16.
53. Julie Guthman, *Agrarian Dreams: The Paradox of Organic Farming in California* (Berkeley: University of California Press, 2004). See also Andrew Case, *The Organic Profit: Rodale and the Making of Marketplace Environmentalism* (Seattle: University of Washington Press, 2018).
54. Leo Horrigan, Robert S. Lawrence, and Polly Walker, "How Sustainable Agriculture Can Address the Environmental and Human Health Harms of Industrial Agriculture," *Environmental Health Perspectives* 110 (2002): 445–56.
55. Monica White, *Freedom Farmers: Agricultural Resistance and the Black Freedom Movement* (Chapel Hill: University of North Carolina Press, 2018); Penniman, *Farming While Black*. See also Kristin Reynolds, *Beyond the Kale: Urban Agriculture and Social Justice Activism in New York City* (Athens: University of Georgia Press, 2016).

56. Jess Gilbert, Gwen Sharp, and M. Sindy Felin, "The Loss and Persistence of Black-Owned Farms and Farmland: A Review of the Research Literature and Its Implications," *Southern Rural Sociology* 18, no. 2 (2002): 1–30, cited in Penniman, *Farming While Black*, 7. Gilbert et al. note that the acreage of black farm ownership is higher than the 1997 USDA Census of Agriculture indicates.

57. For a Potawatomi Nation perspective, see Robin Wall Kimmerer, *Braiding Sweetgrass* (Minneapolis: Milkweed Editions, 2013). For fair trade, see Sarah Lyon and Mark Moberg, *Fair Trade and Social Justice: Global Ethnographies* (New York: NYU Press, 2010); and Sarah Besky, *The Darjeeling Distinction: Labor and Justice on Fair-Trade Tea Plantations in India* (Berkeley: University of California Press, 2014).

58. Donham and Thelin, *Agricultural Medicine*, 29.

59. Maia Call and Samuel Sellers, "How Does Gendered Vulnerability Shape the Adoption and Impact of Sustainable Livelihood Interventions in an Era of Global Climate Change?," *Environmental Research Letters* 14, no. 8 (2019): 1–15.

Bibliography

Besky, Sarah. *The Darjeeling Distinction: Labor and Justice on Fair-Trade Tea Plantations in India*. Berkeley: University of California Press, 2014.

Bohme, Susanna. *Toxic Injustice: A Transnational History of Exposure and Struggle*. Oakland: University of California Press, 2015.

Bray, Francesca. *The Rice Economies: Technology and Development in Asian Societies*. Berkeley: University of California Press, 1994.

Dean, Warren. *Brazil and the Struggle for Rubber: A Study in Environmental History*. New York: Cambridge University Press, 1987.

Forclaz, Amalia Ribi. "A New Target for International Social Reform: The International Labour Organization and Working and Living Conditions in Agriculture in the Inter-War Years." *Contemporary European History* 20, no. 3 (2011): 307–29.

Hershatter, Gail. *The Gender of Memory: Rural Women and China's Collective Past*. Berkeley: University of California Press, 2011.

Holmes, Seth. *Fresh Fruit, Broken Bodies: Migrant Farmworkers in the United States*. Berkeley: University of California Press, 2013.

Li, Tania. *Land's End: Capitalist Relations on an Indigenous Frontier*. Durham, NC: Duke University Press, 2014.

McCann, James. *Maize and Grace: Africa's Encounter with a New World Crop, 1500–2000*. Cambridge, MA: Harvard University Press, 2005.

Nash, Linda. *Inescapable Ecologies: A History of Environment, Disease, and Knowledge*. Berkeley: University of California Press, 2006.

Rogers, Thomas. *The Deepest Wounds: A Labor and Environmental History of Sugar in Northeast Brazil*. Chapel Hill: University of North Carolina Press, 2010.

Sellers, Christopher, and Joseph Melling, eds. *Dangerous Trade: Histories of Industrial Hazard across a Globalizing World*. Philadelphia: Temple University Press, 2011.

Soluri, John. *Banana Cultures: Agriculture, Consumption, and Environmental Change in Honduras and the United States*. Austin: University of Texas Press, 2005.

Staples, Amy. *The Birth of Development: How the World Bank, Food and Agriculture Organization, and World Health Organization Changed the World, 1945–1965*. Kent, OH: Kent State University Press, 2006.

Stewart, Mart A. *"What Nature Suffers to Groe": Life, Labor, and Landscape on the Georgia Coast, 1680–1920*. Athens: University of Georgia Press, 1996.

Stoler, Ann Laura. *Capitalism and Confrontation in Sumatra's Plantation Belt, 1870–1979*. 2nd ed. Ann Arbor: University of Michigan Press, 1995.

Wright, Angus Lindsay. *The Death of Ramón González: The Modern Agricultural Dilemma*. Rev. ed. Austin: University of Texas Press, 2005.

PART III
EXEMPLARY COMMODITIES

CHAPTER 14

CORN

ELIZABETH FITTING

As the quintessential Indigenous crop of the Americas and fundamental to far-reaching changes to agriculture under capitalism, corn has helped shape human societies. Agrarian political economy and food regime approaches to food and agriculture permit the analysis of several key processes through which corn or maize (used interchangeably here) went from being a staple crop of the Americas, to a global commodity and a ubiquitous, industrial "flex" crop found in products ranging from ketchup to ethanol. The physical and physiological characteristics of the corn plant, and its adaptability and transportability, are instrumental factors in why humans took up maize cultivation and how it became a global staple.

Certain crops, like corn, have always had uses beyond food: for centuries, maize has provided not just a key food staple, but it was used for making alcohol and as animal feed, in addition to a plethora of other uses for the various parts of the plant, such as leaves for *tamal* wrappers or in decorations and cobs for fuel. During the twentieth century, these uses multiplied as corn became an ingredient in processed foods, ethanol, sweeteners, and bioplastics. In the twenty-first century, however, there has been a global trend toward multipurpose agriculture or "flex crops," and corn has played a central role in this shift. Corn is the most established, and among the most significant, flex crops due to the physiological and physical characteristics of the plant, and its early and pivotal role in plant breeding science, industrial agriculture, and agricultural biotechnology.

The food regime approach, informed by agrarian political economy, provides a helpful framework for understanding the significance of corn for capitalist, industrial, and later, multipurpose agriculture. The food regime approach historicizes the role of food in an emerging global food order and focuses our attention on policies and practices (such as international trade, food aid, regulation and labels, and agricultural subsidies, among others) related to food production, provisioning, and consumption. Agrarian political economy asks questions about the ways in which capitalism unevenly inserts itself in agriculture, how agriculture contributes to capitalist accumulation and industrialization, and how these processes shape social relations in different places. Since agriculture entails harnessing biological processes (e.g., through photosynthesis and cultivation and gestation cycles), it poses "natural" obstacles to capitalist development and accumulation; however, in the twentieth and twenty-first centuries agri-food capital has successfully sought ways to overcome some of these challenges, particularly, through mechanization and the production of industrial inputs such as synthetic fertilizers and pesticides.

Maize is an important part of the story of the industrialization of agriculture and how capital overcame natural barriers to accumulation. David Goodman, Bernardo Sorj, and David Wilkinson (1987) delineate two processes that surmount some of the natural barriers to capitalist accumulation in agriculture—what they term "appropriationism" and "substitutionism." What these processes do is separate agricultural production into specialized sectors, industrialize them, and relink them through national and international supply chains. When an aspect of farm production is undermined, converted into an industrial process, and reincorporated back into the farm as an input, it is referred to as a process of appropriationism.[1] For example, appropriationism refers to the replacement of manual labor by machinery or of manure with synthetic fertilizer.

Substitutionism refers to a situation when an agricultural end product is transformed into standardized, homogenized inputs by industrial processing, such as flour milling, sugar refining, and oilseed pressing, or when the end product is replaced with a new end product made from less expensive industrial raw materials, such as margarine as a replacement for butter. These transformations in farming and agriculture—some of which began in the late nineteenth century and took off with the industrialization of farming in the mid-twentieth century—were uneven, but, in general terms, they entailed a shift toward more specialized production around particular commodities, more capital-intensive farming, and created economic conditions much less favorable to small family farms. In effect, what was previously an integrated system of energy and nutrient recycling controlled by farmers became a process of buying and selling industrial inputs and outputs, reducing the control farmers had in the process, while leveraging the influence of agribusiness corporations.[2]

From Mesoamerica to the Colonial World

> "Enlightened [colonial] elites used corn in this sense: as a contemptible object subject to discrimination. Corn carried the stigma of being alien, strange, poor. The wealthy judged corn and declared it to be guilty. The poor, on the contrary, opened their doors to it, embraced it, adopted it.... Corn was an adventurer, a settler of new lands, one of those that helped fashion the modern world from the distant sidelines."
> —Arturo Warman, *Corn and Capitalism* (1988), xiii

Food and agriculture were central to colonial projects in the Americas, which entailed attempts to eradicate Indigenous peoples and to "civilize" them into European customs, including dietary and agricultural practices, while also keeping them separate and inferior. European explorers and settler colonists were often suspicious of Indigenous foods. Sixteenth-century Europeans argued that the Indigenous diet was dangerous for Europeans, despite the fact that most explorers, fur traders, and early settlers reported eating local staples such as maize.[3]

Mexican anthropologist Arturo Warman traces the history of maize from Mesoamerica to its emergence as a global staple crop. He demonstrates that corn was a key player in the expansion of colonialism and the capitalist world system, and that by following the crop's history of adoption around the world, we have insight into how local farmers, and their environments, fared under various colonial and capitalist relations. Although corn was often held in disdain in colonial narratives, it became a staple crop of colonial diets and of the Atlantic slave trade, because corn is easily and efficiently stored for food and feed. In other words, thanks to its botanical characteristics, maize not only helped transform Mesoamerican civilizations and societies, but helped "fashion the modern world."

Corn is a particularly flexible plant in the sense that it can be grown in a vast array of environments. It can be eaten as a vegetable by those who grow it or dried and stored by farmers to be used for animal feed or to be prepared as foods like tortillas, polenta, porridge, and beverages. This ability to grow in an array of environments and the ease with which corn can be stored and transported meant that as maize traveled from the Americas to Europe, Asia, Africa, India, and elsewhere, it was often recognized by small-scale farmers for its adaptability, and in some cases as a means to remain relatively self-sufficient. Corn became one of the world's most important staple food crops, alongside wheat and rice. Today, corn is the most cultivated cereal grain worldwide, grown on every continent except Antarctica. It is also the most important cereal grain used for food in Latin America and Africa, where white varieties of corn are preferred for human consumption. In 2022, the world produced 1.2 billon metric tons of corn.[4]

Zea mays comes in five phenotypes—sweet, pop, floury, dent, and flint—and is a member of the grass family, but unlike other grasses, the maize plant relies on humans to remove the tightly covered kernels from the husk and plant them. In other words, maize is a plant that coevolved with humans and can be considered a "companion species." For this reason, Warman refers to corn as "our plant kin" explaining that "people and corn depend upon each other in order to subsist and survive as a species" (1988, 27).

The biological origins of maize were for a long time a mystery, but we now know it was domesticated from a single ancestor, a wild grass called teosinte, nine thousand years ago in south-central Mexico. Both the Maya and Aztec civilizations, among other Mesoamerican groups, cultivated the descendants of that ancestor and became "people of corn" developing cultural practices, myths, and legends about the crop. In the seventeenth century, Carl Linnaeus's work in taxonomy included using a binomial nomenclature for biological organisms, and he redundantly added *Zea*, the Greek word for "life-giving," to "mays," the Latinized version of *mahiz*, which in Taino meant "life-giving seed."[5] The word *Zea* is from ancient Greek and refers to grains and cereals in general, and the English referred to maize as "Indian corn" because corn was the generic term for cereal grains.

In the Americas, maize was traditionally intercropped with squash and beans, both of which are plants that do not compete with corn for sunlight. Squash lowers the evaporation of ground moisture around the corn and impedes the growth of weeds with its foliage, while beans grow up the stalk of the maize plant and, like all legumes, help take nitrogen from the air, where it is abundant, and make it available to the plant. The "three sisters," as these companion crops are called among Indigenous nations of North America, or the "milpa" in Latin America (which refers to the cornfield plus these two other plants), are also nutritional complements.

In addition to the nutritional complementarity of the companion crops, the technique of nixtamalization developed in Mesoamerica, and practiced by various Indigenous peoples of the Americas, also enhances the nutritional content of maize. This technique entails soaking and cooking corn kernels in water with alkali (with mineral lime, or in some places, wood ash lye), and after rinsing, the kernels are hulled, making them easier to grind and make masa (or corn dough). The word "nixtamal" has Nahuatl origins, combining the term for ashes (*nextli*) with tamal (*tamalli*). Nixtamalization is still widely practiced in parts of Mexico and Central America and is also used in the industrial production of some corn-based foods. Nixtamalization increases the calcium content of corn and makes niacin available for absorption when eaten, helping to prevent pellagra, a disease caused by severe niacin deficiency. When maize traveled from the Americas to Europe, Asia, and Africa, it was introduced without the technique of nixtamalization, making those populations reliant on corn diets susceptible to pellagra. Unfortunately, because the technique of nixtamalization did not accompany corn on its global travels, as cornmeal became "the poor man's staple everywhere—*mamaliga* in Romania, *puliszka* in Hungary, *sofki* in Ghana, *mealies* in South Africa, *fungie* in Zaire— it lost an important source of nourishment."[6]

Spanish ships brought maize from the Caribbean to Seville, and then the crop made its way through Italy, Egypt, and Africa. The first reference to maize in Africa was by an anonymous Portuguese ship pilot who described its cultivation on the Cape Verde islands between 1535 and 1550.[7] Corn cultivation also made it to China via the Portuguese, but its cultivation was quite limited until 1700. Maize had become one of China's major crops by the early twentieth century, and during the twenty-first century, for the first time in Chinese history, corn production surpassed that of rice.[8]

In West Africa, flint maize adapted well where sorghums and millets had been cultivated, and corn was grown because its quick maturity let some of the varieties escape drought; but floury maize became more popular than flint corn with its hard starch and lower yields. Outside of West Africa, corn was adopted as a novelty or niche crop. For example, in Ethiopia it was not until the twentieth century that corn went from a garden vegetable to a field crop.[9] In colonial southern Africa, maize offered clear advantages in yield and labor requirements over the African cereal crops of sorghum and millets; it had higher yields and a shorter growing cycle than sorghum. Corn began to replace these African subsistence crops among Black farmers who embraced planting maize earlier than white settlers. Farmers cultivated floury and white flint maize, which was preferred for food. However, when the American white dents arrived—which had higher yields than flint corn and softer starch making it more suitable to mechanized mills—white farmers began to treat maize as an important cereal crop. In *Maize and Grace* (2005), James McCann explains that as American dent corn was adopted and cultivated in southern Africa it was treated as a commodity grain and was part of a larger shift toward industrial and export agriculture in the region. American white dent corn provided the economic base for the growth of settlers' rule in southern Africa.[10]

The story of how American maize became both an African subsistence crop and an industrial cash crop illustrates key changes in the international food system or "regime." The food regime approach explores connections between capitalist accumulation and the international relations of food production and consumption. The first international food regime occurred from about 1870 to the 1920s, the era of imperialism, when colonial policies consolidated specialized export zones: while tropical imports were produced to export to European consumers, settler colonists focused on farming wheat in places like Canada, Australia, and Argentina. Settler colonies helped resolve the social and economic difficulties posed by land dispossession when peasants were displaced from their land: it enabled some to leave and become settler colonialists and, in the process, provided food for the empire.[11] By 1930, maize surpassed wheat in colonial Africa as the most important cash crop and sorghum as the major food crop. And yet, despite maize's growing importance in colonial Africa, agricultural research focused on cash crops like coffee and cotton, cocoa, and other crops that linked African economies to the emerging world commodity markets. Investments in African maize varietal improvement largely focused on high yield as the most important trait to advance. Unlike most elsewhere in the world, the vast majority of the maize grown in Africa is white maize consumed directly by humans instead of being fed to livestock or used as an input in industrial processing.[12]

At the turn of the twenty-first century, countries of the Global South—that is, low- and middle-income countries, the majority of which are former colonies—that once grew their own maize as a key food staple are dependent on corn imports, as a result of market-oriented neoliberal policies. Although maize is Africa's most important crop, grown both in large industrial mono-cropped fields, as well as by small-scale subsistence farmers, the continent has become a net importer of the crop.[13] Notably, Mexico, too, a center of domestication and biological diversity for maize, now imports one-third of its corn from the United States. Most of the world's maize that is used for direct human consumption is consumed in Africa and Latin America. White corn is preferred in countries like Mexico and Guatemala for human consumption in order to make tortillas and other corn-based foods; however, US imports tend to be yellow, genetically engineered varieties used for feed and industrially processed foods.

World War I interrupted trade, and a new regime stabilized in the years following World War II. The second food regime, centered on US hegemony, was driven by industrial agriculture, development policies and banks, and a shift in US policy and trade relations. In the post–World War II period, for example, the US Public Law 480 created international food aid through which the United States sent subsidized food and agricultural products to other nations. Food consumption patterns shifted in many places with the industrialization of agriculture and the move toward meat-heavy diets.

While the history of corn's migration around the globe points to the diverse ways it was adopted by farmers in different locations and contributed to an increased number of varieties of corn through crossing and free pollination, in contrast, the popularity of hybrid corn in the United States reduced the number of corn varieties grown in modernized and industrial agriculture.[14]

From Staple to Industrial Crop

> "With the advent of the F-1 hybrid, a technology with the power to remake nature in the image of capitalism, *Zea mays* entered the industrial age and, in time, it brought the whole American food chain with it."
> —Michael Pollan, *The Omnivore's Dilemma* (2006), 31

Corn was the first crop to be transformed into an industrialized commodity in the nineteenth century. By the 1950s, industrial commodity corn had changed farming in North America. Several technologies were fundamental to this shift toward modernized, industrial corn agriculture, notably the John Deere steel plow of the late 1830s, grain elevators, the tractor of the 1920s, advances in milling, the technique of hybridization, synthetic fertilizer, and the expansion of the railroad system. These technological advances were often supported by government policies, and capital pursued both technological and social avenues to overcome barriers to accumulation. Industrial corn became an American success story, remaking the landscape of the American Midwest with high-yielding hybrids increasingly cultivated on monocropped farms using industrial inputs.

The hybridization of corn was a turning point for capitalist accumulation in agriculture and entailed a process of appropriation.[15] In the nineteenth century, the US government undertook germplasm collection and research and distributed high-quality seed without fee to farmers. Varietal development was a process of simple selection that could be undertaken by farmers into the twentieth century; however, with the increased knowledge of hereditary differences in the early twentieth century, plant breeding shifted from the collection of sought-after plant varieties to the collection of plant varieties with sought-after traits. This began to pay off in the 1930s when hybrid corn became commercially available and US corn yields increased.

Although maize is a naturally hybridizing plant, a maize "hybrid" refers to a variety that results from the crossing of two different varieties, each of which has first been inbred to the point of being genetically uniform. The first generation of a hybrid variety (called F-1 by plant breeders) has an increased yield or hybrid vigor. Unlike open-pollinated varieties developed by scientific plant breeders, though, the second generation of hybrid corn (F-2)—that is, the generation that appears after the seed is saved and replanted—exhibits a considerable reduction in yield. Hybrid corn overcame what sociologist Jack Kloppenburg (1988) has called the "biological barrier" to commodification because farmers interested in maintaining good yields must purchase hybrid seed for each planting. By the 1940s, hybrid corn was grown throughout most of the Corn Belt, a decade after it had first been introduced.[16] Bred for thicker stalks and stronger root systems to remain standing, hybrids withstand mechanical harvesting and have yields higher than open-pollinated varieties largely because they can be planted closer together. Hybrid corn was a remarkable innovation, but one of its downsides for farmers is what makes it an early example of appropriationism; in other words, an aspect of the agricultural production process, in this case the reproduction of seed, was no longer in the hands of the farming household or community but produced offsite and reincorporated back into the farm as a purchased input. Hybrid corn also entailed, as Deborah Fitzgerald (1993) has shown, a process of de-skilling, as it "effectively locked farmers out from an understanding of their own operations without the aid of experts."[17] Not surprisingly, hybrid corn played a key role in the establishment and success of seed companies in the United States in the early twentieth century aided by policies that prioritized hybrids over open-pollinated varieties, which could be replanted.

In the US Corn Belt, hybrid corn yields improved significantly with the invention and commercial availability of chemical fertilizers in the 1950s. While average yields were 22 bushels per acre in the 1930s, by the 1970s, yields increased to 95 bushels. Today US yields are close to 200 bushels per acre. The average yield in the Global North (or higher-income countries) is 8 tons per hectare and in Global South it is less than 3.[18] Synthetic nitrogen meant that farmers no longer had to rotate their crops with legumes, which add nitrogen to the soil. By 1965, more than 95 percent of US corn acreage was planted with hybrids, largely relying on synthetic nitrogen.[19] The production of synthetic nitrogen requires fossil fuels. From a biological perspective, the reliance on synthetic fertilizer has transformed corn agriculture, together with the widespread adoption of the tractor, from a process of capturing sunlight and turning it into food "to converting fossil fuels into food."[20] Every acre of industrially produced corn requires at least 50 gallons of oil.[21] The ecological costs of producing industrial corn entails not only increased fossil fuel consumption, but nitrogen runoff from the synthetic fertilizer applied to farm fields that makes its way into water supplies, among other issues.

In Mexico, during the 1940s, the Rockefeller Foundation's research and training project, named the Mexican Agricultural Program (MAP), was set up in order to raise the productivity of maize and wheat, among other crops, in the hopes of alleviating hunger, raising the nutritional levels of the average diet, and reducing Mexican dependency on basic food imports. The Foundation worked in collaboration with the Mexican Ministry of Agriculture and Animal Husbandry (now SADER) and the Office of Special Services, a semiautonomous office of the ministry. As a result of this project, Mexico was the first developing nation to undergo an agricultural Green Revolution, which took place primarily in the country's irrigated regions of the north. When the project ended in the 1960s, Mexican wheat yields were among the highest in Latin America—and became a model for the development of semi-dwarf, high-yield, disease-resistant wheat varieties in India and elsewhere—but maize yields remained low.[22] This Green Revolution favored wheat over corn and benefited larger, commercial farmers over more subsistence-focused, smaller-scale peasant farmers because the project's varieties often required irrigation, synthetic fertilizers, and other commercial inputs.

The project's varieties helped transform the uncultivated areas of Mexico's north and northwest states into wheat-producing farmland. The government financed roads and irrigation works, agricultural banks and credit, and guaranteed wheat prices for large-scale farmers. These policies and subsidies contributed to the postwar industrialization of Mexico, and in some areas, maize was displaced for more remunerative crops. Small landholdings became sources of cheap labor for expanding industries and agro-exporters. Mexico would soon need to import corn again—as had happened during a food crisis in the late 1930s, when the supply of cereal grains and beans became a serious problem due to crop shortfalls and transportation problems.[23]

As more profitable crops replaced maize in the north of Mexico and the government imported yellow corn from the United States to supply urban consumers, corn became a nostalgic symbol of middle-class nationalism. In his history of Mexican cuisine, Jeffrey Pilcher (1998) demonstrates that during the 1940s, a period marked by rapid urbanization and industrialization, import substitution, and the "Mexican Miracle" of economic growth, corn-based foods that had formerly been considered poor, nutritionally deficient, and backward were appropriated by the growing middle and urban classes as "authentically" Mexican. In the same period, but increasingly from the 1960s, the diet of the poor incorporated sugar and fat, especially in the form of soft drinks and processed foods.[24] Meat consumption also rose among wealthier Mexicans, resulting in an increase in sorghum cultivation for cattle feed during this period.[25] The cultivation of sorghum, and later corn, for animal feed was increasingly linked to industry, both national and international. The interest and demand for artisanal, "authentic" tortillas among middle-class Mexicans (and North Americans) would again increase following the neoliberal reforms of the 1980s, and the North American Trade Agreement (NAFTA) of the mid-1990s, when Mexico's reliance on US corn imports grew, and these imports were increasingly genetically engineered varieties.

From Livestock-Feed and HFCS to Flex Crop

> "Corn's triumph is the direct result of its overproduction, and that has been a disaster for the people who grow it."
> —Pollan, *The Omnivore's Dilemma* (2006), 118.

In 1970, approximately 85 percent of US corn was planted with hybrid varieties that had cytoplasmic male sterility (CMS-T), which was popular because it eliminated the need for the labor-intensive process of de-tasseling. Unfortunately, CMS-T varieties were also susceptible to the southern corn leaf blight, which became an epidemic that same year. Because fields were sown with the same crop (monocropped) and with varieties that shared a genetic component susceptible to the blight, 15 percent of the total US corn crop was destroyed, hitting the Corn Belt the hardest. The impact of the blight highlights the need to maintain a degree of genetic variation in major crops when planted, and also in the genetic materials available *in situ* and *ex situ* for breeding purposes.

Corn harvests recovered in 1971—thanks to better weather, the reduced use of CMS-T varieties, and the employment of students to de-tassel the female plants by hand in the corn seed fields—and in the fall of 1972, Russia purchased 30 million tons of US corn after experiencing a huge shortfall. This helped boost the price of US corn, temporarily, and enticed farmers to plant the crop or expand the land devoted to it. In 1973, the US Farm Bill started to pay farmers directly rather than using support prices and government grain prices. This was a key policy shift. As Michael Pollan explains, the Farm Bill "removed the floor under the price of grain. Instead of keeping corn out of a falling market, as the old loan programs and federal granary had done, the new subsidies encouraged farmers to sell their corn at any price, since the government made up the difference."[26] Most subsequent government Farm Bills, however, have lowered the price of corn. Facing corn prices lower than the cost of production, US farmers looked for ways to raise yields and grow more corn in order to keep up with their expenses, but many faced rising debt and bankruptcy.

The increased yields with corn hybrids and synthetic fertilizer in the United States also facilitated the expansion of large feedlot operations where animals, in more confined spaces, are fed diets of corn. For cattle, this change of diet from grass requires the use of antibiotics for the animals to remain healthy. When the 1973 Farm Bill allowed corn prices to fall below cost of production, it became profitable to feed inexpensive corn to cattle, pork, and chicken. The most popular variety of corn for feed and industrial processing is yellow dent "field corn," which is different from the sweet corn consumers eat as a vegetable. This overproduction of corn has rippled out to many aspects of agriculture and the food chain in the United States and abroad: the United States exports up to 20 percent of its corn harvest to places like Mexico.[27]

This second food regime was also characterized by agri-food capital investments in increasingly complex forms of appropriationism and substitutionism including the replacement of traditional foods produced in the tropics like cane sugar and peanut oil with derivatives that could be produced in more temperate climates such as soybean oil and high-fructose corn syrup (HFCS). The replacement of cane sugar with HFCS and gasoline with ethanol-blended "gasohol" are both part of the process through which capital overcomes obstacles to accumulation in agriculture.[28]

The market for HFCS grew rapidly in the 1970s after a breakthrough in the wet milling process with the use of enzymes, shortening the time needed. Wet mills convert corn into the basic component parts of processed foods and are thus a significant technology in the industrial food chain. In the wet milling process, the corn kernel is separated into three main parts: the hull or outer skin, the germ, which contains most of the oil, and the endosperm for gluten and starch. In the 1840s, wet milling was used to make corn starch and by the 1860s, acids were included in the milling process to produce glucose from corn starch, enabling corn syrup to hit the market. Corn syrup was the main product of wet milling processing until Japanese chemists discovered that using an enzyme instead of acid transforms glucose into the even sweeter fructose molecule, thus paving the way for the rise of HFCS.

Large buyers of corn, like Cargill and Archer Daniels Midland (ADM), began exercising influence on the direction of US policy in the 1980s, which often reflected their interests above that of farmers.[29] The price of sugar rose after the US government increased support for domestic sugar farmers and extended an import quota on sugar thanks to the lobbying efforts of ADM, among others. In 1984, both Pepsi and Coca-Cola announced they would no longer use sugar in their soft drinks, replacing sugar with HFCS. The consumption of the sweetener soared in the United States, and other countries followed the uptake in consumption, most notably in Canada, Mexico, Hungary, Slovakia, Bulgaria, Belgium, Argentina, Korea, and Japan. Growing health concerns about this new sweetener followed.

As gas prices rose in the 1970s and there was increasing concern over foreign oil dependency, ADM hoped that the same wet mills the company used for HFCS could be used to produce ethanol in the summer when soft drink sales were lower.[30] At the time, ADM was producing one-third of the HFCS in the United States and lobbied the US government to secure some protections for the sector, like a tax exemption and a tariff imposed on Brazilian ethanol. Alcohol blends from the fermentation of plant materials for transportation fuel gained popularity in the nineteenth century, but it was not until the 1970s that a food/fuel complex emerged.[31] The first generation of biofuels converted the sugar and oils from food and feed crops, including corn, into fuel. The market for ethanol took off at the turn of the twenty-first century alongside a decrease in the per capita intake of HFCS in the United States.

The boom in biofuels during the 2000s, as an alternative to fossil fuels, was a key moment in the transition toward "flex crops," or multipurpose agriculture. Between 2000 and 2016, annual global biofuel production surged from 18 billion to 135 billion liters, primarily using maize, sugar cane, and oil palm.[32] Corn is the among the most established and significant flex crops, alongside soybean, sugar cane, and oil palm, in the global expansion of multipurpose agriculture.

Championed for their versatility, flex crops can be used for food, fuel, and as an industrial material. Crops are flex crops in two ways: first, the same crop can be used for different purposes and in making different products; and second, they have the capacity (or perceived capacity) in different and changing economic and technological conditions to be redirected or substituted from one use to another. Flex crops have a greater capacity than other crops to replace farm-based produce with industrially produced substitutes (the process of substitutionism) and they are, or are thought to be, more easily substituted into gaps in a supply chain.[33]

Current research on flex crops shows that the benefits of this boom are primarily accrued by the agro-industries that control the value chains and seldom by the farmers who grow the crops.[34] Flex crops appeal to financial investors because investment in such crops is similar to having a diversified portfolio; it helps reduce uncertainty and stabilize or increase profits.[35] Unfortunately, corn is one of the more energy-intensive crops—if not the most inefficient—from which to produce biofuels, and when corn is channeled away from the food chain into biofuel production, it is also disruptive to global food prices.[36] Due to the concern and controversy around whether first-generation biofuels adversely affect the food supply and raise the price of food, a second generation of biofuel technologies that do not rely on food crops for biofuel feedstock, or only rely on the non-edible parts of food crops, are in development.

The third international food regime that began to take shape in the late twentieth century was characterized not only by the establishment of a food/fuel complex, but also by the rise of genetic engineering as a key technology for capitalist agriculture and by changes in regulation in relation to this technology. Genetically engineered corn was first commercially available in 1996 and constitutes over 90 percent of all corn grown in the United States.

GMOs and the Neoliberal Food Regime

> "Without corn there is no country" (*sin maiz, no hay país*).
> —Slogan from Mexico of the anti-GM corn network
> In Defense of Maize (2001)

The 1980s brought a wave of structural adjustment policies to countries facing economic crisis. These policies, informed by a neoliberal agenda, included austerity measures and widespread cuts to public services, as well as agricultural and food price supports and subsidies as conditions for the loans provided by the World Bank and International Monetary Fund (IMF). Mexico was the first country to implement structural adjustment policies as part of its loan package with the IMF in an effort to refinance its foreign debt. In addition to cuts to subsidies and price supports, these policies promoted liberalized trade agreements, often via the World Trade Organization.

In general terms, the emergent food regime is characterized by neoliberal policies and a further consolidation of corporate power in the food and agriculture sectors. This period also witnessed a rise in nontraditional food exports from the Global South such as fruits, vegetables, and meat, the expansion of supermarket chains, the financialization of markets, and the rise of flex crops. While countries in the Global North like the United States continued to export subsidized grain, agricultural subsidies were cut in the Global South. Together these policies and processes have pushed small-scale farmers and agricultural laborers into a casual global workforce.

After a drop in oil prices, an economic crisis hit Mexico in the early 1980s and there were peso devaluations, inflation, and debt renegotiations. The country brought its policies in line with the structural adjustment agendas of the World Bank and the IMF implementing cuts to rural subsidies and counter-agrarian reform policies (such as those which enable communal landholders to sell land). Agribusinesses expanded operations in Mexico, increasing exports of fruits and vegetables to Canada and the United States largely based on conventional, capital-intensive agriculture. As part of the project to liberalize trade, NAFTA went into effect in 1994 and Mexican imports of US corn dramatically increased. It is a bitter irony of the neoliberal food regime that countries of the Global South, like Mexico, import basic foods that they themselves have historically produced, and in this case, such a culturally significant one.

These policy changes were extremely difficult on rural Mexicans who faced enormous challenges in maintaining rural livelihoods without state subsidies and price supports, among other factors, including environmental ones such as soil erosion and drought, and who also faced a loss of employment in agriculture—half a million agricultural workers were displaced between 1995 and 2005.[37] Farming remains important to rural Mexican households, as in many parts of the world, but often in conjunction with other income-generating activities, such as labor migration within Mexico and across national borders into the United States, and to a lesser extent Canada.

Neoliberal agricultural and trade policies have facilitated the growth in the cultivation of genetically engineered crops, and this has involved market concentration in the food system, notably among seed corporations. Three corporations, Bayer (which bought Monsanto), Corteva Agriscience (which merged Dow and DuPont), and Syngenta (owned by ChemChina), control more than 60 percent of the world's commercial seed market, and the top ten corporations control over three-quarters.[38] Yet despite this market concentration, many of the world's small-scale farmers do not rely on the corporate seed industry but rather save, use, and improve local or "traditional" varieties of seed. They do so for a variety of reasons: for example, farmers may not be able to afford industry seed and the associated input costs; they may prefer the taste and texture of local varieties; they may not reside near a reliable seed distributer and trust the quality of local seed over industry seed; or they may not want to relinquish control over their on-farm seed saving practices with intellectual property rights (IPRs) that accompany genetically engineered seed.

Genetically modified organisms (GMOs) or transgenic plants are the products of recombinant DNA techniques that use organisms, their parts, or their processes to modify or create living organisms with particular traits. This includes plants whose genomes contain inserted DNA material from other plants or species. Conventional plant breeding and farming practices also produce new gene characteristics in plants, but what makes plant breeding and farming different from genetic engineering is that they work at the level of the whole plant. In contrast, genetic engineering has the capacity to overcome the sexual incompatibility of different species and to identify, isolate, and relocate any gene from one organism to a recipient plant's genome. Genetically engineered crops include different types of varieties: herbicide-tolerant (Ht) varieties, pest-resistant (Bt) varieties, stacked varieties (which are both herbicide-tolerant and pest-resistant), and those with other characteristics such as added nutritional content (e.g., "golden rice" with vitamin A). A recent advance in genetic engineering is gene editing with CRISPR (clustered regularly interspaced short palindromic repeats) technology. Unlike other genetic engineering techniques, CRISPR does not insert foreign genes into plants but uses the protein Cas9 enzyme to edit DNA sequences and modify gene function in a more targeted and less expensive manner. Because CRISPR-Cas9 does not insert foreign genes into plants, but rather edits DNA sequences, the US Department of Agriculture has decided that the use of this technology for plants does not need to be regulated. It is unclear, currently, whether CRISPR gene-edited plants will face regulation in other countries.

With the advance of biotechnology, plant biodiversity is valued as a source of genes for the development of new technologies, crop varieties, and pharmaceutical products. Agricultural biotechnology extends the commodification of seed because much of genetically engineered seed is accompanied by intellectual property rights, requiring users to pay a licensing fee in addition to the initial seed purchase. This fee runs counter to the widespread practice of peasants and farmers to select, save, and even exchange seed for replanting. Most attempts to enforce intellectual property restrictions on seed have thus far taken place in the Global North. A notable and well-publicized case of patent enforcement grew out of Monsanto's claim that a Canadian farmer, Percy Schmeiser, was growing Roundup Ready canola without a license. By charging a fee to use seed saved by farmers, intellectual property provides another way to overcome the free reproduction of seed, or seed's "biological barrier to commodification." The commercialization of seed, including IPRs, is one way that public resources or "the commons" are undergoing privatization or enclosure; it contributes to what David Harvey calls "accumulation by dispossession," or the accumulation of capital by undermining a group's access and control over the resources that it needs to maintain its livelihood.[39] Legislative and regulatory changes to protect intellectual property also erode farmer control over inputs and the farming process.

In first two decades of the twenty-first century, the United States was the country with the most biotech crops grown, followed by Brazil, Argentina, Canada, and India. In the Global South, Latin America is the region with the largest area devoted to biotech crops.[40] The cultivation of biotech crops has transformed agricultural practices and agrarian relations in those countries where it has been widely adopted. However, associated regulations and trade of GMOs have also influenced regions where they are not commercially grown on a large scale.[41]

In Mesoamerican countries—the center of biodiversity, and where maize originated—transgenic corn has been the focus of anti-GMO activism. In Mexico, an anti-GMO network and movement formed around the controversial finding of transgenic corn growing in traditional cornfields, despite the fact that the testing and commercial cultivation of GM corn was prohibited at the time. The commercial cultivation of transgenic corn in Mexico remains prohibited today except in authorized test plots.

Evidence of genetically engineered corn growing among traditional cornfields was found in the highlands of Oaxaca in 2001. Although there was a de facto moratorium on the scientific field-testing of genetically engineered corn at the time, and growing it was prohibited, the country imported transgenic corn from the United States for use as animal feed, grain for tortillas, and industrial processing. Small-scale Mexican cultivators likely encountered these imports in regional markets. At the time, most of this corn was a Bt variety that expresses the bacterial toxin *Bacillus thuringiensis*, which is poisonous to the European and Southwestern corn borers. These pests burrow into the stem of the corn plant, causing them to fall over. In the United States, once transgenic corn has been harvested there is no mandatory labeling or segregation of it from conventional corn.

In response to the controversy, pro-maize and anti-biotech campaigns and networks, such as In Defense of Maize and Sin Maíz No Hay País (Without Corn, There Is No Country), emerged and expanded, drawing together environmental, food activist, independent peasant, and Indigenous rights organizations. Numerous academics, researchers, and scientists are also involved in these networks. Scientists who participated in the early years of the In Defense of Maize network were not against agricultural biotechnology per se, but rather against the testing and cultivation of transgenic corn, which was, at the time a Bt variety, designed to attack pests not found in Mexico. Concerned scientists and activists have also emphasized that Mexico is a center of biological diversity of maize, and that traditional maize has enormous cultural significance. Biotech crops like cotton have been grown in Mexico without the same degree of public attention or concern that has been given to maize. Since 2012, however, GM soybean has generated concern for Mayan honey producers in the Yucatán because GM pollen was found in honey samples destined for export.

Maize is the main crop grown throughout the country, the cornerstone of rural livelihoods, a key ingredient of culinary traditions and the national diet, and a powerful and longtime symbol of the Mexican nation. At times, maize invokes elements of shared culture across different scales of place, ranging from the small rural community or region to the nation state, but also beyond the borders of Mexico to Indigenous and rural Latin America. Anti-GMO activists focus on the risks of transgenic corn in particular, in other regions of Latin America such as Guatemala and Colombia.[42]

Supporters and advocates of biotechnology argue that GMOs provide an important tool for increasing food production and the nutritional content of crops, particularly as our climate changes and the world population increases. Debates over GMOs can be very polarized, but supporters and critics may have more complicated and nuanced positions on the topic—for instance, in opposition to (or support of) a *particular* type of genetically engineered crop, as is the case in Mexico with transgenic corn.[43] Additionally, much like with the Green Revolution, the benefits and problems of GMOs are unevenly experienced and distributed.

The neoliberal food regime has not only involved the growth of transnational agribusiness and food conglomerates, but also transnational networks of resistance and social movements as well. In Western Europe, early campaigns against GMOs were quite effective in mobilizing consumers around issues of food safety, ideas about preserving rural society, and ethical concerns about genetic engineering as defiling the natural boundaries between species. In the Global South, resistance to this technology focuses on the effects of GMOs on the environment and small-scale farmers' livelihoods, as well as the interconnected issues of property rights and biopiracy—or the appropriation of traditional knowledge and biological resources.[44] These issues have increasingly been adopted among activist networks spanning the Global South and North.

Conclusion

> "It would be accurate to say that corn is a central character in the history of capitalism, but it would be unjust to suggest that the migration and spread of corn is its only conceivable circumstance; resistance to the encroachment of corn is another. Corn is also so much more than that. It is a unique resource for the construction of a new reality, for change and social transformation."
> —Warman, *Corn and Capitalism*, 233–34

The once humble Mesoamerican staple has become a ubiquitous ingredient found in every aisle at the supermarket and a "flex crop" of global importance. Maize has always been a versatile crop with multiple uses, a key factor in why it was adopted and celebrated by small-scale farmers in vastly different ecological and climatic regions. Along with humans, our "plant kin" has shaped the direction of agricultural change. The plant's physical and physiological characteristics, and its adaptability and transportability, have also meant that maize was an ideal crop for commodification, industrial processing, and multipurpose agriculture. The overproduction of corn in the United States during the latter part of the twentieth century has had ripple effects across the US food chain and beyond, affecting the livelihoods of maize farmers and consumers in Mexico and elsewhere. In this way, the triumph of industrial corn presents challenges to smaller-scale farmers and subsistence producers. While agrarian political economy and the food regime approaches focus on policies, practices, and social relations of food, trade, and agriculture, these approaches can also draw our attention to the agency of farmers and consumers, as well as of the maize plant itself, in shaping agricultural practices.

The story of maize—from a traditional companion crop to hybrids and genetically engineered varieties—tells us a great deal about the transformation of agriculture under different periods of capitalism from mercantile and colonial, industrial to neoliberal. Maize is also an important part of the story when social movements and activist networks challenge GMOs, neoliberalism, and the global food system.

Notes

1. David Goodman, Bernardo Sorj, and John Wilkinson, *From Farming to Biotechnology: A Theory of Agro-Industrial Development* (Oxford: Basil Blackwell, 1987), 2.
2. Joseph Baines, "Fuel, Feed and the Corporate Restructuring of the Food Regime," *Journal of Peasant Studies* 42, no. 2 (2015): 299.
3. Rebecca Earle, "'If You Eat Their Food . . .': Diets and Bodies in Early Colonial Spanish America," *American Historical Review* 115, no. 3 (2010): 688–713 See 698 on archeological studies of Spanish settlements in Florida that had squash and maize, 688 on diets, and 704 on admired foods, such as pineapple and cacao. In the sixteenth century, Juan de Cárdenas, a doctor from Seville, wrote about corn's virtues (Arturo Warman, *Corn and*

Capitalism: How a Botanical Bastard Grew to Global Dominance, trans. Nancy L. Westrate [Chapel Hill: University of North Carolina Press, 2003], ch. 2). See also Robert Launay, "Maize Avoidance? Colonial French Attitudes toward Native American Foods in the Pays des Illinois (17th–18th Century)," *Food and Foodways* 26, no. 2 (2018): 92–104.
4. USDA, FAS Grain, "World Agricultural Production" Circular Series WAP 11-23 Nov (2023), p. 25 https://apps.fas.usda.gov/psdonline/circulars/production.pdf.
5. Betty Fussell, "Translating Maize into Corn: The Transformation of America's Native Grain," in "Food: Nature and Culture," special issue, *Social Research: An International Quarterly of the Social Sciences* 66, no. 1 (1999): 42.
6. Ibid., 51.
7. Warman, *Corn and Capitalism*, 61.
8. CropLife Staff, "Chinese Growing More Corn than Rice," *CropLife*, 11-23 Nov (2023), p. 25 https://apps.fas.usda.gov/psdonline/circulars/production.pdf.
9. James McCann, *Maize and Grace: Africa's Encounter with a New World Crop, 1500–2000* (Cambridge, MA: Harvard University Press, 2005), 28–29.
10. Ibid., 106–10.
11. Harriet Friedmann and Philip McMichael, "Agriculture and the State System: The Rise and Fall of National Agricultures, 1870 to the Present," *Sociologia Ruralis* 29, no. 2 (1987): 93–117. These authors introduced and revised the food regime approach, which has also been taken up by other food scholars.
12. McCann, *Maize and Grace*, 1.
13. Ibid., 208.
14. Warman, *Corn and Capitalism*, 234–35.
15. Goodman, Sorj, and Wilkinson, *From Farming to Biotechnology*, 12.
16. Jack Kloppenburg Jr., *First the Seed: The Political Economy of Plant Biotechnology* (Cambridge: Cambridge University Press, 1988): 91.
17. Deborah Fitzgerald, "Farmers Deskilled: Hybrid Corn and Farmers' Work," *Technology and Culture* 34, no. 2(April 1993): 342.
18. McCann, *Maize and Grace*, 11.
19. Kloppenburg, *First the Seed*, 91.
20. Michael Pollan, *The Omnivore's Dilemma: A Natural History of Four Meals* (New York: Penguin, 2006): 45.
21. Ibid.
22. Cynthia Hewitt de Alcántara, "Economic Restructuring and Rural Subsistence in Mexico: Corn and the Crisis of the 1980s," Ejido Reform Research Project (San Diego: Center for U.S.-Mexico Studies / UNRISD, 1994): 26.
23. David Barkin and Billie DeWalt, eds. *Food Crops vs. Feed Crops: Global Substitution of Grains in Production* (Boulder, CO: Lynne Rienner 1990): 35; Joseph Cotter, "Before the Green Revolution: Agricultural Science Policy in Mexico, 1920–1950" (PhD diss., University of California, Santa Barbara, 1994): 258.
24. Jeffrey Pilcher, *"Que vivan los tamales!": Food and the Making of Mexican Identity* (Albuquerque: University of New Mexico Press, 1998): 116.
25. Barkin and DeWalt, *Food Crops vs. Feed Crops*.
26. Pollan, *The Omnivore's Dilemma*, 52.
27. Ibid., 53–55.
28. Baines, "Fuel, Feed and the Corporate Restructuring of the Food Regime," 303. See also Sean Gillon, "Flexible for Whom? Flex Crops, Crises, Fixes and the Politics of Exchanging Use Values in US Corn Production," *Journal of Peasant Studies* 43, no. 1 (2016): 117–39.

29. Pollan, *The Omnivore's Dilemma*, 52.
30. Baines, "Fuel, Feed and the Corporate Restructuring of the Food Regime."
31. Ibid.
32. Mairon G. Bastos Lima, "Toward Multipurpose Agriculture: Food, Fuels, Flex Crops, and Prospects for a Bioeconomy," *Global Environmental Politics* 18, no. 2 (May 2018): 144.
33. Saturnino Borras Jr., Jennifer C. Franco, S. Ryan Isakson, Les Levidow, and Pietje Vervest, "The Rise of Flex Crops and Commodities: Implications for Research," *Journal of Peasant Studies* 43, no. 1 (2016): 93–115.
34. Bastos Lima, "Toward Multipurpose Agriculture."
35. Borras et al., "The Rise of Flex Crops and Commodities."
36. Although most yellow dent corn is for animal feed, the price of different types of corn are linked. See Timothy Wise, *Eating Tomorrow. Agribusiness, Family Farmers and the Future of Food* (New York: The New Press, 2019): 152.
37. Mamerto Pérez, Sergio Schlesinger, and Timothy Wise, *The Promise and Perils of Agricultural Trade Liberalization. Lessons from Latin America* (Washington, DC: Washington Office on Latin America, 2008).
38. Pat Mooney, *Blocking the Chain: Industrial Food Chain Concentration, Big Data Platforms, and Food Sovereignty Solutions* (Val-David, Québec: ETC Group, 2018), 8, accessed February 21, 2019, http://www.etcgroup.org/sites/www.etcgroup.org/files/files/blockingthechain_english_web.pdf; ETC Group. *Putting the Cartel before the Horse ... and Farm, Seeds, Soil, Peasants, etc. Who Will Control Agricultural Inputs*, Communiqué No. 111 (Val-David, Québec: ETC Group, 2013), 4, www.etcgroup.org/putting_the_cartel_before_the_horse_2013.
39. David Harvey, *The New Imperialism* (Oxford: Oxford University Press, 2003), 147–48.
40. ISAAA (2018), http://www.isaaa.org/resources/publications/annualreport/2018/default.asp.
41. Elizabeth Fitting, "GM Crops and the Remaking of Latin America's Food Landscape," in *Food and Place: A Critical Exploration*, ed. Fernando Bosco and Pascale Joassart (London: Rowman & Littlefield, 2018): 52–65.
42. Fitting, *The Struggle for Maize*, 2011. See also Elizabeth Fitting, "Cultures of Corn and Anti-GM activism in Mexico and Colombia," in *Food Activism: Agency, Democracy and Economy*, ed. Carole Counihan and Valeria Siniscalchi (London: Bloomsbury, 2014): 175–92.
43. This is discussed in greater depth in Fitting, *The Struggle for Maize*, chs. 1 and 2.
44. Rachel Schurman, "Introduction: Biotechnology and the New Millennium," in *Engineering Trouble: Biotechnology and its Discontents*, ed. Rachel Schurman and Dennis Doyle Takahashi Kelso (Berkeley: University of California Press, 2003): 9–11.

Bibliography

Fitting, Elizabeth. *The Struggle for Maize: Campesinos, Workers and Transgenic Corn in the Mexican Countryside*. Durham, NC: Duke University Press, 2011.
Friedmann, Harriet, and Philip McMichael. "Agriculture and the State System: The Rise and Fall of National Agricultures, 1870 to the Present." *Sociologia Ruralis* 29, no. 2 (1987): 93–117.
Fussell, Betty. "Translating Maize into Corn: The Transformation of America's Native Grain," in "Food: Nature and Culture," special issue, *Social Research: An International Quarterly of the Social Sciences* 66, no. 1 (1999): 41–66.

Goodman, David, Bernardo Sorj, and John Wilkinson. *From Farming to Biotechnology: A Theory of Agro-Industrial Development*. Oxford: Basil Blackwell, 1987.

Kloppenburg, Jack, Jr. *First the Seed: The Political Economy of Plant Biotechnology*. Cambridge: Cambridge University Press, 1988.

McCann, James. *Maize and Grace: Africa's Encounter with a New World Crop, 1500–2000*. Cambridge, MA: Harvard University Press, 2005.

Otero, Gerardo, ed. *Food for the Few: Neoliberal Globalism and Biotechnology in Latin America*. Austin: University of Texas Press, 2008.

Pechlaner, Gabriela. *Corporate Crops: Biotechnology, Agriculture and the Struggle for Control*. Austin: University of Texas Press, 2012.

Pilcher, Jeffrey. *"¡Que vivan los tamales!" Food and the Making of Mexican Identity*. Albuquerque: University of New Mexico Press, 1998.

Pollan, Michael. *The Omnivore's Dilemma: A Natural History of Four Meals*. New York: Penguin, 2006.

Staller, John E., Robert H. Tykot, and Bruce F. Benz. *Histories of Maize in Mesoamerica: Multidisciplinary Approaches*. Walnut Creek, CA: Left Coast Press, 2010.

Warman, Arturo. *Corn and Capitalism: How a Botanical Bastard Grew to Global Dominance*. Translated by Nancy L. Westrate. Chapel Hill: University of North Carolina Press, 2003 [1988].

CHAPTER 15

WHEAT

THOMAS D. ISERN

The authors of the chapter on wheat in Bailey's *Cyclopedia of American Agriculture* (1907), agricultural educator E. E. "Dad" Elliott and soil scientist Thomas Lyttleton Lyon, declare that wheat is "a plant of vast economic importance, widely distributed over the civilized world and having a history coincident with that of the human race."[1] Their tone is imperial, hearkening to antiquity. Wheat, Elliott and Lyon make clear, was a crop of colonization, but a junior partner to humankind. Its key contribution to the partnership was protoid, the gluten that made leavening and bread possible. To this partnership there adhered a complex of technological and cultural practices constituting commodity cultures, maturation of which not only propelled wheat to rank among the top three grains produced worldwide (along with corn and rice) but also established definite, long-standing wheat belts in far-flung parts of the world. Elliott and Lyon do not foresee the foreboding consequences that lay ahead, as expansionist wheat culture would be blamed for environmental catastrophes on several continents.[2]

From its emergence parcel to the Neolithic Revolution some 10,000 years before present (BP) to its current status as one of the big three grain crops of the world, wheat has had prominence and consequence in agricultural history. This chapter charts the global history of wheat in three aspects: its role as a crop for the colonization of temperate regions, establishing cereal networks vital to vast empires; its status as the basis of commodity cultures in wheat belts of the world, as typified by those of the Great Plains of North America; and its importance to environmental history, whereby wheat culture historically has been blamed for ecological catastrophes in semiarid lands. The history of wheat suggests that a plant may have agency—that wheat, a cereal grain with agency, has made history.

ORIGINS AND QUALITIES OF THE CULTIVAR

To Elliott and Lyon, the origin of wheat was a mystery. The contemporary work by Peter Tracy Dondlinger, *The Book of Wheat*, confesses an ignorance of genesis: "The geographical origin of wheat has never been certainly determined."[3] Wheat culture spanned hemispheres and nourished empires but had only myths of origin, and no history. Such history was to come from scientists dedicated to the discovery of the wild progenitors, as detailed by the Israeli plant scientist Moshe Feldman. The quest required sorting known wheat plants into their three classes, defined by the numbers of their sets of chromosomes: diploids, comprising einkorn; tetraploids, comprising emmer, durum, and several others; and hexaploids, comprising spelt, bread wheat, and others. Bread wheat and the other hexaploids, it turned out, had no wild progenitors. They resulted from hybridization of tetraploid cultivars with wild einkorn.[4]

It was the Israeli agronomist Aaron Aaronsohn who fixed the identity of wild einkorn, finding it near the Sea of Galilee in 1906. The tetraploids, specifically emmer, were found in subsequent years at multiple Middle Eastern sites. The polyploid wheats were capable of innumerable recombinations, the plotting of which defined what came to be called the "cradle of agriculture" in the "Fertile Crescent" east of the Mediterranean. It was the very emergence of wheat cultivars that defined these terms. The quern stone for grinding grain became the symbol of Neolithic material culture; the discovery of querns at other sites across Eurasia and beyond mapped the dissemination of wheat husbandry.[5]

Wheat was amenable to positive evolutions. Wheat possesses, as Feldman says, "blurred boundaries between species and even between genera."[6] Early farmers mixed genotypes in their fields. Selections promoted several especially valued traits: first, spikes that held together, to be threshed out after gathering; second, ready germination; and third, threshability. Other selections defining modern wheats induced erect habit, simultaneous ripening, and larger grains. The sum of selections was a plant unable to live in the wild, a cultivar requiring husbandry.[7]

Early scholars of wheat regarded it, the cerealist Dondlinger confessed, as a gift of god "since time immemorial."[8] It was, however, humankind that disseminated wheat cultivars from their points of origin. Wheat moved with farmers through Anatolia to Greece by about 8000 BP, thence across the rest of Europe. Wheats reached both Scandinavia and England by 5000 BP. Other paths led via the Caucasus into South Russia by 6000 BP, via Egypt into North Africa also by 6000 BP, across Iran to Pakistan by 6500 BP, to southwest India by 5000 BP, and along the Silk Road to the Yangtse valley by 4000 BP. In subsequent millennia, Europeans would carry wheat into distant parts of the globe through colonization.[9]

The persistent extension of wheat culture evidenced the grain's virtues. In the first place, as the cereal scholar P. R. Shewry remarks, "bread wheat shows sufficient diversity to allow the development of over 25,000 types."[10] The *Cyclopedia* in 1907 outlined eight general types of wheat grains:[11]

1. Einkorn, heavily bearded, little valued by farmers.
2. Spelt, "a very ancient form," superficially resembling modern varieties.
3. Emmer, similar to spelt, well adapted to dry regions and often raised for livestock feed.

4. Common wheat, or bread wheat, "grown all over the world where wheat is produced."
5. Club wheat, comprising soft white wheat varieties.
6. Poulard, closely related to durum.
7. Durum, or macaroni wheat, a tall wheat with heavily bearded heads bearing large grains.
8. Polish wheat, which also could be used for pasta.

Dondlinger in 1916 accepts the eight general types but warns, "The classification of wheat seems always to have been in a more or less chaotic state." This problem for systematic classification was a virtue in the field, making wheat able "to embrace practically every kind of environment." Dondlinger thus hails wheat, in all its exasperating variety, as the "prime necessity of civilized life."[12] By the early twentieth century, wheat was, among Western peoples, a mark of civilization and had taken on overtones of race superiority. As the famed chemist from North Dakota, Edwin F. Ladd, allowed in 1920, "Wheat is the greatest staple for the Caucasian race."[13]

The habits of wheat commended it to farmers and equipped it for expansion. Tillering, or stooling, was a key virtue. "Wheat, like other cereals, has the characteristic of throwing out side shoots," each of which might bear a spike, Dondlinger declares. Tillering and multiple heads led to impressive records as to multiplication. A selection of Red Fife spring wheat named Minnesota 163 was reported to have multiplied over ten years in the 1880s and 1890s from a single grain to 300,000 bushels. Moreover, wheat was adapted to culture as either a spring crop or a winter crop, planted in fall to overwinter and be harvested by midsummer. Winter wheats had the advantage in the lower latitudes of temperate regions, but spring wheats prevailed in the higher.[14]

Once threshed out of the field, wheat exhibited other virtues. The crop was eminently portable and stable; it could be handled in containers or in bulk. Storage in granaries was good for years, so long as vermin were excluded or controlled. Trans-oceanic transport required no refrigeration. Once placed before consumers, wheat met a range of nutritional needs. It was a major source of carbohydrates, energy for working people, but wheat's protein content was significant where meat was not in dietary abundance. Wheat was an important source of iron, zinc, B-vitamins, and selenium. Its fiber content offset the glycemic responses to carbohydrates. The whole-grain movement, which began with London's Bread Reform League in 1880, promoted the nutritional and fiber benefits of a grain too often stripped of them by processing.[15]

Still, no such granular attributes were so appealing as the almost magical virtues of what Shewry calls wheat's "key characteristic," the "unique properties of doughs formed from wheat flours." He counts, as of 2009, more than 20,000 scholarly papers devoted to the subject of gluten since 1945. "It is the gluten contained in the starchy parts of this wheat grain which distinguishes it," he declares. "When fermentation sets in, or, to use the common phrase, the bread begins to rise, carbonic acid gas . . . forms an open, porous loaf. The dough owes this elastic quality to the presence of the gluten."[16] Shewry appropriates much of his praise of gluten from the *Cyclopedia*.[17]

Wheat as a Colonizing Cultivar

The positive qualities and imperial freight of wheat made it the point of the share for Europeans entering temperate zones of colonization. Like wool, wheat filled the bill for an agricultural commodity that could be produced in the wide temperate zones of colonization. Commonly raised in remote places of sparse population, wheat was mainly grown for shipment to metropolitan centers. Unlike meat, fruits, or vegetables, grain traveled well by sea or rail, and it stored indefinitely. Wheat was a crop familiar to the diasporic peasantry of European lands fanning out to global frontiers, and it met the desires of consumers in their global community. Industrializing European nations required grains to energize their people. Historians of sugar rightly emphasize its importance in providing calories for the working classes. With the prevalence of sugared jams, sugar was commonly consumed with bread products, which not only augmented caloric intake but also provided essential fiber.[18]

Colonization typically transitioned from extractive activities to permanent settlement—what historians have come to call settler colonialism.[19] Wheat provided profitable employment for colonists, nourishment for countrymen, and profits for investors. (Its effects on Indigenous peoples in the path of wheat culture were less benign.) Wheat farming staked places on what the geographer Isaiah Bowman has termed the "pioneer fringe" of world agriculture. This marginal zone of light rainfall was a place of risk and often tragedy, but also of great potential.[20] The apparent over-extension of wheat culture on the pioneer fringe retained a longer-term rationale, as historian Mary W. M. Hargreaves explains. Such rains as came commonly fell during the growing season, followed by drier summer weather favorable for ripening. Such weather bolstered the protein content of grain, improving its milling and baking qualities and earning farmers premium payments.[21]

Marginal wheatlands were the contentious edge of larger wheat regions formed up by colonization. Colonizing enterprises long have been characterized by historians through an iteration of central place theory writ large that depicts a world divided into center and periphery. There arose in the late twentieth century two revisions in old views of center-periphery with particular pertinence to the history of wheat. First, environmental historians infused ecological considerations into the relationships of core and periphery. Alfred W. Crosby framed environmental change in imperial terms with his 1986 book, *Ecological Imperialism*. Crosby reckons not only with intentional transport of animals and plants but also with collateral exchange in what he calls "portmanteau biota." Wheat traveled with baggage, from microscopic fungi to huge draft animals. The other notable revision in historical views was a matter of decentering: historians discovered that all lines did not connect from periphery to center, that indeed, many important connections were forged among peripheral points. Thus, historically significant ties might have developed among the wheatlands of the world independent of direction from the metropolis.[22]

In one leading wheat-producing nation, Canada, the dynamics of metropolis and hinterland caused wheat to loom large in national definition. Staples theory as propounded by economic historian Harold Innis made commodities the drivers of the national narrative. Wheat and the prairie provinces assumed outsize positions in history and public affairs. Thus in 1897 the Canadian government established the Crow Rate for prairie grain headed to Pacific markets. In the 1920s, Canada built the Port of Churchill on the Hudson Bay Railway to carry prairie grain to Atlantic markets. In Canada the periphery had clout. On the other hand, scholars such as Vernon Fowke argue that grain producers felt historically disadvantaged, embedding a long-standing sense of grievance in Canada's wheat country.[23]

The extension of wheat culture into new lands occupied by Indigenous peoples offered both opportunity for culinary exchange and danger of cultural suppression. In South America, colonial authorities argued for the primacy of wheat breads on both cultural and religious grounds. Indigenous peoples accustomed to maize culture resisted, resulting in retention of preferences by both parties, but also appropriation of one another's grains. As Luis Millones Figueroa observes, "Even though wheat was indispensable for those who wanted to reproduce European lifestyles, 'Indian breads' were necessary."[24]

North American indigenes suffered under a wheat regime. Confined on reservations, they were dependent on annuities; white wheat flour figured as the basic staple. Some Indigenous advocates say the encounter with gluten was toxic. Concrete evidence of either celiac disease or gluten sensitivity afflicting unusual numbers of Native Americans is lacking. What is certain, however, is that commodity issues imposed white flour into native foodways at the very time white European Americans had come to value whole grains. American Indians adopted high-carbohydrate foodways. Frybread evolved from makeshift necessity into cultural symbol of reservation life—with disastrous effects on public health. One Indian scholar refers to frybread as "die bread." Having taken the interior of North America by military conquest for the sake of Euro-American wheat farmers, American authorities thrust upon surviving indigenes a fatal culinary regimen.[25]

The most comprehensive description of center-periphery dynamics on the wheat frontier is William Cronon's *Nature's Metropolis*. Cronon chronicles Chicago as the metropolis of the prairies and offers fifty pages under the section title "Pricing the Future: Grain."[26] His narrative details how one city in North America, strategically situated, not only dominated its own hinterland but also rationalized the commodification of wheat worldwide.

Chicago arose with water transportation advantages as a center of the prairies. With the building of railroads west, the city's influence extended over the developing territories, then states, of the northern plains. Wheat, "the classic crop of western farming," was vital to trade centered on Chicago. Until the mid-nineteenth century, the spine of the grain trade was water transport. Farmers and merchants packed wheat into sacks and delivered them to a wharf. Working men shouldered sacks at every exchange point. Shippers retained ownership of grain. "Sacks," writes Cronon, "were the key to the whole water-based transportation system."[27] Grain in trade was no abstraction; it was a physical object.

"Railroads changed all this," Cronon observes. They opened new lands to grain culture and encouraged farmers to raise more grain. Receipts at Chicago multiplied, they arrived by rail, and they were reckoned by carloads rather than sacks. The invention that made possible bulk handling of grain was the steam-powered grain elevator, the first of which in Chicago appeared in 1848. An elevator was a tall, compartmentalized warehouse wherein endless conveyor belts fitted with buckets delivered grain from a delivery pit to the various bins and compartments. When it was time to ship, workers opened chutes, and grain was gravity-fed into a ship or a car. Grain elevators were massive, constructed of two-inch lumber nailed flat to form walls 10 inches thick. Material changes led to intellectual transformations of the grain trade by the Chicago Board of Trade. The board asserted regulatory authority over key aspects of the trade, in 1856 defining grades of wheat and standards of quality. With bulk handling and grain grading, it was no longer necessary or desirable to retain shippers' ownership over physical grain—a development "with a host of unanticipated consequences," Cronon remarks.[28]

One of these was the futures market. Bulk handling obscured the relationship of trade with physical nature, while the telegraph changed the "market geography" of the trade. These changes concentrated the grain trade, making Chicago one of the great grain entrepôts of the world by the late 1850s. Parties commenced contracting to sell short, that is, sell grain they did not yet own. Chicago became a futures market, a center for contracting the future delivery of grain perhaps not even in existence. This created openings for manipulators to corner the market, distorting market movements. Moreover, grain grading, and the mixing of grain grades to create gain in which farmers did not share, fomented discontent in wheat country. All this constituted what Cronon calls a "second nature" divorced from farming and physical commodities but affecting them gravely.

The frustrations of wheat farmers marginalized by this second nature found voice in the 1903 film directed by D. W. Griffith, *A Corner of Wheat*. There still existed a first nature of wheat, as farmers established themselves in expansive settlement regions on multiple continents. In the Northern Hemisphere the two great areas of wheat expansion were the Russian Empire and North America. As historian David Moon has disclosed, the two northern wheat frontiers were directly related. That story commenced on the Russian steppe, which spans semiarid grassland for some five thousand miles east and west.

Extensive settlement of the steppe by Slavic settlers from the forest regions of the empire commenced with Russian victories over Tatar khanates in the eighteenth century. The conversion of pastoral lands to arable involved deliberate adaptations, including important Ukrainian introductions such as the hardy wheat varieties Gurkha and Arnautka. The pace of expansion picked up with rising demand for grain from the 1840s, partially caused by the repeal of Corn Laws in Britain. The Black Sea port of Odessa emerged as a principal shipping point. Another important development was the arrival of German colonists invited to settle on Russian steppe lands, prominent among them the Mennonites who settled near the Black Sea. They practiced crop rotation and the black fallow, and they embraced the hard red winter wheat varieties they found available in their new homeland.[29]

Of all the connections between the Russian steppe and the American plains, most striking is the transfer of wheat culture instigated by the Mennonites. When the Mennonites found their agricultural opportunities constrained by land base and their culture pressured by Russification, they commenced emigration to the agricultural frontiers of distant lands, including the chernozem soils within the Santa Fe Railroad land grant in central Kansas. Mennonite parties mobilized from Russia to Kansas in 1873–1874. According to tradition, they brought with them seed of a hard red winter wheat known as Turkey Red, which vitalized the wheat industry on the central plains. The traditional story has long been doubted by historians. The great historian of winter wheat culture, James C. Malin, concluded that "exclusive credit" for Turkey Red could not be conferred on the Mennonites. Malin said the story was a product of "provincialism and the wisdom born of hindsight."[30] Russian historian Norman E. Saul echoed Malin's doubts.[31]

It fell to Moon to sort out the Russian connection. Moon finds the traditional story merely "plausible," but then details the larger, significant role of Mennonite wheat culture. A Mennonite miller, Barnhard Warkentin, was sourcing hard red wheat seed from Odessa for the settlers by the late 1870s. Increase of seed propelled four Mennonite-settled colonies to prominence for success in wheat farming, and they sold seed to neighboring farmers. Warkentin also established a cooperative relationship with Kansas Agricultural College, chiefly with a Kansas farm boy turned mycologist, Mark A. Carleton. Carleton was attracted initially to the Russian wheats because they were rust-resistant.[32]

After joining the staff of the US Department of Agriculture, Carleton made two plant exploration expeditions to Russia, in 1898 and 1900. In 1898 he entered the empire via Odessa but did not concentrate his seed collection efforts in the winter wheat regions nearby, as they were in a drought; nevertheless, he traveled broadly in the steppe and came home with an unexpected find: the durum wheat he called Kubanka, a "macaroni wheat," for making semolina and pasta. Carleton went on to wage a public-relations campaign focusing both on Western millers, who considered durum too hard for convenient milling, and the American public, which disdained pasta. Meanwhile, on his return to Russia in 1900, Carleton focused his attention in the Crimea, returning with seed that he called Kharkov—his term for what was known in Kansas as Turkey Red. Carleton's continued collaboration with Warkentin resulted in general adoption of hard red winter wheats in central plains agriculture.

No other venue of substantial wheat colonization in the temperate zones acquired the mythic cast of the Kansas Mennonite connection. Historical experiences in wheat colonization zones of the Southern Hemisphere, such as the pampas of Argentina, are instructive. In the pampas, livestock industries preceded arable agriculture. *Estancieros* (holders of great estates devoted to cattle culture) controlled the land. When the government passed a homestead act in 1884, estancieros used it to solidify their holdings. With favorable markets for grain in the early twentieth century, landholders secured tenants to break ground for wheat. The tenants moved on as either the land was depleted or it was laid down to forages, thus improved for grazing. Always the wheat-farming tenants operated in what their historian terms the "outer regions," on the edge of livestock country, extending it.[33]

The settlement situation in South Australia, a planned colony on the Wakefield model, was quite different. Here, observes the geographer Donald W. Meinig, authorities privileged crop husbandry over livestock raising. Conservative land laws gradually loosened to allow more extensive settlement. Wheat farming surged north into the interior, approaching Goyder's Line—the perimeter of diminishing rainfall beyond which the state said grain farming was not feasible. Blessed with a few humid years, wheat farmers pushed past Goyder's Line—until severe drought in the early 1880s stopped the advance of agriculture. As elsewhere in Australia, the expansion of wheat culture inland reached a dry point where it failed, leaving a marginal wheat belt.[34]

Commodity Cultures and Ecological Catastrophes

The word "wheat" does not appear in the index to *Dust Bowl*, Donald Worster's history of the southern plains in the 1930s. This seems odd, first, because in public memory of the Dust Bowl, wheat and wheat farming figure prominently; and also, because the work spends considerable time analyzing the culture that caused the environmental catastrophe of the 1930s, and it would seem that wheat might have had something to do with that. Worster declares, "there was no opportunity for an indigenous culture to take firm root here."[35] Lamenting the lack of a constructive cultural ecology, the author dichotomizes the material and the cultural. It is possible to break that dichotomy, characterizing producers according to their work and their stuff. The concept of a commodity culture emerges from such works as *Breaking the Land*, Pete Daniel's history of cotton, tobacco, and rice cultures in the American South.[36]

Hiram Drache's classic history of bonanza farming, *The Day of the Bonanza*, might be taken as evidence of the sort of heedless capitalism Worster finds on the southern plains. To accept such characterization uncritically is to forget that Drache's companion work to *The Day of the Bonanza* is *The Challenge of the Prairie*, the story of the family farmers who raised wheat and made homes in the same region. These folk spent winter nights patching the sacks in which they would bag their crop and possessed a cultural ecology grounded in the silty soils they worked.[37]

Craig Miner, a historian of wheat in Kansas, is the biographer of John Kriss, a "self-made man with minimal formal education" who, in a fortunate alliance with grain magnate Ray Garvey, farmed tens of thousands of acres of wheat land in northwest Kansas for most of the twentieth century. The businesslike postures of Garvey and Kriss, says Miner, raised fundamental questions about wheat farming on the plains. He acknowledges that both journalists and scholars lay blame for the Dust Bowl on large-scale, commercial farmers. Yet he argues that "the American farmer, especially on the Great Plains, has a dual nature," and that "John Kriss represented that impossible mix about as well as an actual person could."[38] Through the struggle to raise wheat, Kriss acquired an environmental sensitivity and feel for the land that was undeniable.

Like Drache, Miner makes homage to the ordinary farmers who made wheat work for family farms. His two books, *West of Wichita* and *Next Year Country*, are portraits of such folk and their communities. Miner's farmers, including many from the Russian steppe, learned that wheat, not corn, was the best potential basis for long-term prosperity; they took the measure of multiyear drought; they battled clouds of migratory locusts; notwithstanding all of which, they established communities striving for "civilization and culture." Their struggle to reconcile "western Kansas as a commercial enterprise and at the same time as a way of life," Miner pleads, must be understood by "the dynamics of total human experience."[39] "Wheat always survived and its scope always expanded," says the historian; eventually, "The high prairie environment gave dignity to the sufferings and strivings of its inhabitants. It connected them with the elemental and the ancient."[40] This is not the description of a people without a culture.

Wheat historians like Drache and Miner write in the tradition of James C. Malin, author of the 1944 classic *Winter Wheat in the Golden Belt of Kansas*. Malin brings his narrative to its first climax with the soft winter wheat boom, from 1872 to 1882. He is concerned first with the relationship of wheat culture with the subhumid environment, then with mechanical adaptations, choice of wheat varieties, and complementary cropping systems. As he quotes a farmer from Dickinson County in 1881, "We have got to adapt ourselves to the country we are living in."[41] After detailing the transition to hard red winter wheat varieties, 1882–1902—the story on which David Moon would elaborate—Malin goes granular with an examination of the inventions and techniques farmers devised to work the land. Concluding a narrative replete with homely drawings of ridge busters and subsurface tillage devices, Malin renders prosaic material culture significant with a passage worthy of Bailey's *Cyclopedia*:

> The bread-eating civilization and the rice-eating civilization have largely divided the world between them and the rice-eaters have been rapidly becoming bread-eaters.... High gluten wheats are the best bread wheats and as Carleton so often pointed out, aridity and high gluten quality seem to be inseparable. So far as the North American continent is concerned, the Plains region ... is the only source of supply of such wheat.[42]

Malin establishes a material culture integral to the commodity culture. Wherever investigators follow his lead, they find similar material evidence of the commodity culture of wheat. For instance, a study of agricultural folklife on the Canadian prairies details the grassroots efforts of farmers to address their problems of tillage and of harvest. The discer was a folk invention developed by handy shop men with welders during long winters in Saskatchewan during the 1930s and 1940s. They wanted a tillage implement that would control weeds but bury only part of the wheat crop residue. They fashioned a disc-type implement that became the standard implement for tillage and seeding across the Canadian plains for a generation. A similar culture of folk invention produced the header stack-barge for wheat harvesting by the 1930s. Folk inventors during the 1910s and 1920s devised tractor-drawn barges that could be drawn through the harvest field and receive cut grain from harvesting implements. The barges then dumped the stacks onto the ground, to be threshed by combines taken from stack to stack. The header stack-barge was invaluable in times of short crops. Folk invention grounded in common need is evidence of a commodity culture at the grassroots.[43]

Given the crucial and time-sensitive nature of harvesting and threshing small grains, it is not surprising that more powerful evidence of a commodity culture emerges from the history of these operations. *Bull Threshers and Bindlestiffs*, a history of harvesting and threshing of wheat on the Great Plains in the days before combined harvesters, focuses on the wheat culture snapshot by Elliott and Lyons in Bailey's *Cyclopedia*—the early twentieth century. The work meticulously outlines the handling of grain harvested with binders and headers. There were ingrained habits involved with placing sheaves into stooks or constructing grain stacks that would stand. Threshing grain from the stook or stack involved more elaborate folkways comprising roles and expectations of every member of a threshing crew, from skilled separator man to lowly straw monkey. A code of steam whistles signaled communications in the field, and all participants knew what they meant.[44]

The combine pushed aside this web of harvesting culture, but it enabled the formation of a new one that spanned the length of the Great Plains—interstate, international custom wheat harvesting. Because of the shortage of both machinery and labor during World War II, thousands of custom harvesters from the United States and Canada took to the road, harvesting their way from Texas to Saskatchewan, hailed as home-front war heroes. Many custom harvesters continued operating after the war, and they do so to the present, although in diminished numbers. This business is a family enterprise passed down through generations. Asked why they persist in the business, despite its logistical challenges, participants commonly say, "It gets in your blood."[45]

The idea that wheat lacks a culture is reverse-engineered from catastrophic events in environmental history—the Dust Bowl of the 1930s on the Great Plains of North America and similar developments on other continents. Two notable instances of Dust Bowl–like eruptions associated in memory with wheat farming are the Soviet Dust Bowl, as some have termed it, in the Virgin Lands developed by the Soviet Union during the 1950s, and the Australian Dust Bowl, beginning in the 1890s and continuing for decades.

The Soviet Dust Bowl is not a clear-cut case as to how to regard the historical expansion of wheat culture. In 1954, Premier Nikita Khrushchev dictated a major initiative of grain production in northern Kazakhstan and adjacent states. Managers came in with impressive machinery to plow and plant 40 million acres to spring wheat, resulting in, as David Moon says, "dust storms like those of the American Plains."[46] One view of what ensued is that despite environmental setbacks, the Virgin Lands Campaign augmented the food supply of Soviet peoples and made the Soviet Union, later Kazakhstan, a major exporter of wheat; the other view considers the Soviet Dust Bowl an unmitigated disaster. Environmental historian Marc Elie says the difference in views resembles that among American scholars as to the progressive or declensionist tropes of Great Plains history. He chronicles the role of Canadian prairie conservationists from the prairies advising Kazakhstan in its "dangerous race" between "grain monoculture" and "improved understanding."[47]

Circumstances of the Australian Dust Bowl, sometimes linked to wheat culture, seem less pertinent to the subject. A historian of southeastern Australia from the 1890s to the 1940s argues that the situation there was like that in America in the 1930s, only more episodic. The narrative discloses dust storms predated wheat culture in the region. Dating from the 1880s, there had been degradation of vegetation due to overstocking with sheep and infestations of rabbits. The major expansion of wheat culture, in the mallee (scrub) lands, took place well into the twentieth century—whereas Dust Bowl-like conditions had descended on the land during the Federation Drought of 1895–1902.[48]

The implication of wheat culture in environmental catastrophe wants critical examination in the place where wheat culture exhibited its greatest historical efflorescence, the Great Plains of North America. Here wheat figured prominently in popular explanations for the Dust Bowl. Such beliefs were reinforced by Pare Lorentz's 1936 documentary film *The Plow That Broke the Plains*, which may have focused on machines, but they were machines tilling for planting and harvesting wheat. The Dust Bowl memoir of Lawrence Svobida, a wheat farmer in Meade County, Kansas, is downright confessional, closing, "My own humble opinion is that, with the exception of a few favored localities, the whole Great Plains region is already a desert that cannot be reclaimed."[49] Timothy Egan's popular treatment of the Dust Bowl, *The Worst Hard Time*, points an accusing finger at wheat farmers who "tore out the sod and then walked away, leaving the land naked."[50]

Scholarly interpretations span the spectrum as to the causes of the Dust Bowl and the role of wheat therein. Counterpoint to Worster's critique of capitalism is the work of Paul Bonnifield, *Dust Bowl*. Bonnifield has no patience with systemic explanations and celebrates the resilience of the farmers who stuck it out. It falls to a more measured scholar, R. Douglas Hurt, in his 1981 book, *The Dust Bowl*, to fashion a comprehensive explanation involving multiple causation. Underlying and precipitating factors, Hurt says, included unstable soils, especially southern dark browns; the long-term climate of the Great Plains; suitcase farming, with failure to attend to conservation needs; general inattention to soil conservation; and excessive breaking of grasslands for wheat, facilitated by mechanization. Finally, there was the multiyear drought of the 1930s, which exposed the vulnerability of wheat. In better years, winter wheat, with its tillering habits, made good ground cover. If it lacked fall moisture, wheat offered no protection against the destructive winds of late winter to early spring. Black blizzards were a failure of wheat.[51]

While wheat bore the opprobrium of citizens and scholars, there were important scholarly dissenters such as Malin and Miner. Malin is philosophically committed to the *longue durée*. For him the Dust Bowl is a passing problem that would be worked out, as "man was able to maintain a rate of discovery sufficient to reharness natural forces to new uses as rapidly as already known natural resources were exhausted."[52] Miner essentially accepts dust storms as a cost of doing business and argues that wheat farmers like John Kriss did as well as could be expected.[53]

The work that punctures all pat explanations as to origins of the Dust Bowl is the 2005 book by Geoff Cunfer, *On the Great Plains*. Cunfer deals with the span from settlement to present, patiently mapping data as to land use, county by county. This compilation reveals that contrary to popular and scholarly assumptions, most of the land base of the Great Plains remains grassland—the great plow-up was not so great after all. The data reveal enough stability in land use that it might well be termed sustainable. Within this long-term situation, says Confer, "Wheat was and is the quintessential cash crop of the Great Plains." Farmers "adapted their commercial ambitions successfully to fit environmental imperatives. The worst drought in a century brought them up short in the 1930s, but with the return of rain farmers quickly resumed their land-use system with little change and then maintained it for another fifty years."[54]

Cunfer zeroes in on the Dust Bowl and its causes, noting that he is weighing into a long debate of the question, "What natural and human factors contributed to the dust storms of the 1930s?"[55] His core finding is that there is no strong correlation between land use—wheat farming—and dust storms. Many of the worst dusters swept into the croplands after arising in unbroken rangelands. Cunfer writes, "It is time for environmental historians to consider the possibility that dust storms, rather than being evidence of human ecological failure, are instead normal forms of ecological disturbance on the southern plains that happen whenever the region experiences extended periods of low rainfall and high temperatures."[56] Cunfer's work offers absolution to the unity of humankind and wheat as to the worst environmental catastrophe of the historic era on the Great Plains of North America.

Wheat culture in the twenty-first century, as illustrated by production totals for the top ten nations in 2018, extends to lands and continents far beyond the wheat belts of a century ago (Table 15.1). Most notable here are the positions of China and India at the top, as well as Pakistan further down on the list. These are not countries that wheat scholars a century ago considered part of the "civilization" of wheat.

Table 15.1 Wheat production in metric tons, 2018

China	133,596,300
India	103,596,230
Russia	74,452,692
United States	52,257,620
France	40,604,960
Canada	32,347,900
Ukraine	28,370,280
Pakistan	24,348,983
Germany	23,062,600
Argentina	19,459,727

Source: Food and Agriculture Organization of the United Nations, http://www.fao.org/faostat/en/#rankings/countries_by_commodity.

The explanation for the Asian nations in the global leadership for wheat production lies in the late twentieth-century Green Revolution, an attempt to satisfy the nutritional needs of burgeoning populations through crop improvements. The catalytic figure of the Green Revolution was an Iowan educated at the University of Minnesota, the agronomist Norman Borlaug.[57] In the mid-1940s, Borlaug went to work for the Rockefeller Foundation in Mexico, concentrating on wheat improvement. Borlaug developed a remarkable generation of high-yielding dwarf wheats embraced not only by Mexico but also by nations across Latin America and Asia, wherever wheat culture was feasible. China and India became not only the world's leading producers of wheat but also the leading consumers of it. This is the most striking expansion of wheat culture since the age of European colonization.

THE AGENCY OF WHEAT

In the cereal history of humankind, the *longue durée* demands reflective consideration of plants, especially cultivars such as wheat, in terms deeper than those accorded to them heretofore. It prompts recognition of the agency of plants. Agency is the capacity of a person or entity to affect the course of events—to make history. During the final decades of the twentieth century, historical thought laid aside social-scientific determinisms and recognized human agency. Attention turned to the making of decisions, the taking of actions, and the reckoning with consequences by human individuals and groups. An unintended consequence of this line of thought was to demote non-human entities—animals and plants—from the status of historical actors to lesser positions as tools, materials, appendages, or even just background.[58]

Before long, historians commenced to reinsert animals into the narrative as more than bit players. A sticking point had to do with intelligence and consciousness. Animals might not possess the human-like intelligence to be historical actors; certainly they were not conscious of intent and consequence in the way of humankind. A groundbreaking article by David Gary Shaw punched through the problem. He argued there were other types of intelligence than that of humankind; efficacy, rather than consciousness, was the measure of agency. By making an example of a particular horse—Wellington's battle horse, Copenhagen—Shaw made the case for agency of not only species but also particular animals in history. The most important outcome of this line of thought was a fallback position for animal agency: what Shaw calls a unity. A unity of a person and an animal—Wellington and Copenhagen—or humankind and a species—say, Scottish shepherds and their border collies—might achieve a type of agency impossible for either party on its own.[59]

From ethnobotany and other academic places on the border between the humanities and the natural sciences came a movement to put forward plants, too, as agents. John Charles Ryan points out that although plants have been "integrally connected" with humankind for ages, "plants are regarded ordinarily in scientific and social scientific discourses as passive." Ryan asks, "What if we were to consider how plants *act upon* us, contributing to the co-generation of our cultural practices?"[60] Indeed, what if we were to consider wheat in such terms?

Wheat asserted influence on human affairs long before the best minds of humankind devised means even to inquire into its origins. It attached itself to humankind through the assertion of peculiar virtues making it mutually interdependent with humankind. As a unity, wheat took active part in global historical movements, energizing colonization, empire, subjugation, science, and modernization. Wheat permeated human cultures, defined geographic places, even shaped human bodies. It received credit and blame for its contributions to history. Wheat demonstrated agency. Recognition of such plant agency is an essential consciousness for contemporary agricultural historians.

Notes

1. E. E. Elliott and T. L. Lyon, "Wheat," in *Crops*, vol. 2 of *Cyclopedia of American Agriculture*, 4 vols., ed. L. H. Bailey (New York: Macmillan, 1907): 660.
2. Ibid., 660–70.
3. Peter Tracy Dondlinger, *The Book of Wheat: An Economic History and Practical Manual of the Wheat Industry* (London: Orange Judd, 1916): 1–2.
4. Moshe Feldman and Abraham A. Levy, "Origin and Evolution of Wheat and Related Triticeae Species," in *Alien Introgression in Wheat: Cytogenetics, Molecular Biology, and Genomics*, ed. Márta Molnár-Láng, Carla Ceoloni, and Jaroslav Doležel (New York: Springer, 2015), 21; Moshe Feldman, "Origin of Cultivated Wheat," in *The World Wheat Book: A History of Wheat Breeding*, coordinators Alain P. Bonjean, William J. Angus, and Maarten van Ginkel (London: Lavoisier, 2016): 2:3–7.
5. Feldman and Levy, "Origin of Cultivated Wheat," 7–10; Ken-ichi Tanno and George Wilcox, "How Fast Was Wild Wheat Domesticated?," *Science* 311, issue 5769 (2006): 1886.
6. Feldman and Levy, "Origin and Evolution of Wheat," 24.
7. Ibid., 21–24, 54–58; Feldman, "Origin of Cultivated Wheat," 24–39; P. R. Shewry, "Wheat," *Journal of Experimental Botany* 60, no. 6 (April 2009): 1537–1538.
8. Dondlinger, *Book of Wheat*, 6.
9. Shewry, "Wheat," 1537–39; Feldman, "Origin of Cultivated Wheat," 39–41.
10. Shewry, "Wheat," 1539.
11. Elliott and Lyon, "Wheat," 664–665.
12. Dondlinger, *Book of Wheat*, 6–8.
13. Foreword to Thomas Sanderson, *The Bread Value of Wheat*, North Dakota Agricultural Experiment Station Bulletin 127 (1920): 3.
14. Dondlinger, *Book of Wheat*, 17, 21–22; W. M. Hays and A. Boss, *Minnesota No. 163 Wheat*, Minnesota Agricultural Experiment Station, Class Bulletin No. 8 (1900); Elliott and Lyon, "Wheat," 661, 662.
15. Shewry, "Wheat," 1541–44; Peter R. Shewry and Sandra J. Hay, "The Contribution of Wheat to Human Diet and Health," *Food and Energy Security* 4, no. 3 (2015): 178–202.
16. Shewry, "Wheat," 1539–1541.
17. Elliott and Lyon, "Wheat," 661.

18. Sidney W. Mintz, *Sweetness and Power: The Place of Sugar in Modern History* (New York: Viking, 1985); James Walvin, *Sugar: The World Corrupted: From Slavery to Obesity* (New York: Pegasus, 2018).
19. James Belich, *Replenishing the Earth: The Settler Revolution and the Rise of the Anglo-World* (Oxford: Oxford University Press, 2009).
20. Isaiah Bowman, *The Pioneer Fringe* (New York: American Geographical Society, 1931), 8, 34, 42, 112, 143.
21. Mary W. M. Hargreaves, *Dry Farming in the Northern Great Plains: Years of Readjustment, 1920–1990* (Lawrence: University Press of Kansas, 1993).
22. John A. Hobson, *Imperialism: A Study* (New York: James Pott, 1902); Walter Christaller, *Die zentralen Orte in Süddeutschland: Eine Ökonomisch-geographische Untersuchung über die Gesotzmässigkeit der Verbreitung und Entwicklung der Siedlungen mit städtischen Funktionen* (Jena: Gustav Fischer, 1933); D. K. Fieldhouse, *Economics and Empire, 1830–1914* (Ithaca, NY: Cornell University Press, 1973); R. E. Dumett, ed., *Gentlemanly Capitalism and British Imperialism: The New Debate on Empire* (Harlow: Longman, 1999); D. Arnold, *The Problem of Nature: Environment, Culture and European Expansion* (Oxford: Oxford University Press, 1996); Alfred W. Crosby, *The Columbian Exchange: Biological and Cultural Consequences of 1492* (Westport, CT: Greenwood, 1972); Alfred W. Crosby, *Ecological Imperialism: The Biological Expansion of Europe, 900–1900* (Cambridge: Cambridge University Press, 1986); Tom Brooking and Eric Pawson, *Seeds of Empire: The Environmental Transformation of New Zealand* (London: I. B. Tauris, 2011).
23. Harold Innis, "The Wheat Economy," in *Essays in Canadian Economic History*, ed. Mary Q. Innis (Toronto: University of Toronto Press, 1979): 273–79; Gerald Friesen, *The Canadian Prairies: A History* (Toronto: University of Toronto Press, 1984); Vernon C. Fowke, *The National Policy and the Wheat Economy* (Toronto: University of Toronto Press, 1957).
24. Luis Millones Figueroa, "The Staff of Life: Wheat and 'Indian Bread' in the New World," *Colonial Latin American Review* 19, no. 2 (August 2010): 315.
25. Carlo Catassi, "Gluten Sensitivity," *Annals of Nutrition and Metabolism* 67, no. 2 (2015): 16–26; Roxanne Khamsi, "The Trouble with Gluten," *Scientific American* 310, no. 2 (2014): 30–31A; Patty Talahongva, "No More 'Die Bread': How Boarding Schools Impacted Native Diet and the Resurgence of Indigenous Food Sovereignty," *Journal of American Indian Education* 57, no. 1 (Spring 2018): 145–53.
26. William Cronon, *Nature's Metropolis: Chicago and the Great West* (New York: W. W. Norton, 1991): 97–147.
27. Ibid., 108.
28. Ibid., 116.
29. David Moon, *The Plough That Broke the Steppes* (Oxford: Oxford University Press, 2013), 3–19; David Moon, *The American Steppes: The Unexpected Russian Roots of Great Plains Agriculture* (Cambridge: Cambridge University Press, 2020).
30. James C. Malin, *Winter Wheat in the Golden Belt of Kansas: A Study in Adaptation to Subhumid Geographical Environment* (Lawrence: University of Kansas Press, 1944): 166.
31. Norman E. Saul, "Myth and History: Turkey Red Wheat and the 'Kansas Miracle,'" *Heritage of the Great Plains* 22, no. 3 (Summer 1989): 1–13.
32. Moon, *American Steppes*, 148–59; Thomas D. Isern, "Wheat Explorer the World Over: Mark Carleton of Kansas," *Kansas History* 23, no. 1–2 (Spring–Summer 2000): 12–25.
33. Jeremy Adelman, *Land, Labour, and Capital on the Wheatlands of Argentina and Canada, 1890–1914* (Oxford: Clarendon Press, 1994).

34. D. W. Meinig, *On the Margins of the Good Earth: The South Australian Wheat Frontier, 1869–1884* (Chicago: Rand McNally, 1962).
35. Donald Worster, *Dust Bowl: The Southern Plains in the 1930s* (Oxford: Oxford University Press, 1979): 168.
36. Pete Daniel, *Breaking the Land: The Transformation of Cotton, Tobacco, and Rice Cultures since 1880* (Urbana: University of Chicago Press, 1985).
37. Hiram M. Drache, *The Day of the Bonanza: A History of Bonanza Farming in the Red River Valley of the North* (Fargo: North Dakota Institute for Regional Studies, 1964); Hiram M. Drache, *The Challenge of the Prairie: Life and Times of Red River Pioneers* (Fargo: North Dakota Institute for Regional Studies, 1970).
38. Craig Miner, *Harvesting the High Plains: John Kriss and the Business of Wheat Farming, 1920–1950* (Lawrence: University Press of Kansas, 1998): 186–89.
39. Craig Miner, *West of Wichita: Settling the High Plains of Kansas, 1865–1890* (Lawrence: University Press of Kansas, 1986), 211, 238, 231.
40. Craig Miner, *Next Year Country: Dust to Dust in Western Kansas, 1890–1940* (Lawrence: University Press of Kansas, 2006): 290, 300.
41. Malin, *Winter Wheat*, 107.
42. Ibid., 254.
43. Thomas D. Isern, "The Discer: Tillage for the Canadian Plains," *Agricultural History* 62, no. 2 (Spring 1988): 79–97; Thomas D. Isern, "The Header Stack-Barge: Folk Technology on the North American Plains," *Social Science Journal* 24, no. 4 (Autumn 1987): 361–73. Both these articles are chapters in the book *Of Land and Sky: History at the Grassroots of the Canadian Prairies*, forthcoming from Texas A & M University Press.
44. Thomas D. Isern, *Bull Threshers and Bindlestiffs: Harvesting and Threshing on the North American Plains* (Lawrence: University Press of Kansas, 1990).
45. Thomas Isern, *Custom Combining on the Great Plains: A History* (Norman: University of Oklahoma Press, 1981); Thomas D. Isern and Suzzanne Kelley, "'Done for Another Year': The Resilience of Canadian Custom Harvesters on the North American Plains," in *Farming across Borders: A Transnational History of the North American West* (College Station: Texas A&M University Press, 2017): 371–392.
46. Moon, *American Steppes*, 399.
47. Marc Elie, "The Soviet Dust Bowl and the Canadian Erosion Experience in the New Lands of Kazakhstan, 1950s–1960s," *Global Environment* 8, no. 2 (October 2015): 259–92.
48. Stephen R. Cattle, "The Case for a Southeastern Australian Dust Bowl, 1895–1945," *Aeolian Research* 21 (2016): 1–20.
49. Lawrence Svobida, *Farming the Dust Bowl: A First-Hand Account from Kansas* (Repr., Lawrence: University Press of Kansas, 1986): 255.
50. Timothy Egan, *The Worst Hard Time: The Untold Story of Those Who Survived the Great American Dust Bowl* (Boston: Houghton Mifflin, 2006), 113.
51. R. Douglas Hurt, *The Dust Bowl: An Agricultural and Social History* (Chicago: Nelson-Hall, 1981).
52. James C. Malin, *The Grassland of North America: Prolegomena to Its History* (Lawrence, KS: The Author, 1947): 335.
53. Miner, *Harvesting the High Plains*.
54. Cunfer, *On the Great Plains*, 99–101.
55. Ibid., 150.
56. Ibid., 163.

57. See Leon Hesser, *The Man Who Fed the World: Nobel Peace Prize Laureate Norman Borlaug and His Battle to End World Hunger* (Dallas: Durban House, 2006).
58. The rise of human agency in historical writing is surveyed in Thomas D. Isern, "Agency, Complexity, Memory: A Scholarship for Western Places," *Social Science Journal* 51 (March 2014): 1–5. See also Rod Aya, "The Third Man; or, Agency in History; or, Rationality in Revolution," *History and Theory* 40, no. 4 (December 2001): 143–152.
59. David Gary Shaw, "The Torturer's Horse: Agency and Animals in History," *History and Theory* 52, no. 4 (December 1913): 146–167.
60. John Charles Ryan, "Passive Flora? Reconsidering Nature's Agency through Human-Plant Studies (HPS)," *Societies* 2, no. 3 (2012): 104.

Bibliography

Adelman, Jeremy. *Frontier Development: Land, Labor, and Capital on the Wheatlands of Argentina and Canada, 1890–1914*. New York: Oxford University Press, 1994.

Cronon, William. *Nature's Metropolis: Chicago and the Great West*. New York: W. W. Norton, 1991.

Cunfer, Geoff. *On the Great Plains: Agriculture and Environment*. College Station: Texas A&M University Press, 2005.

Drache, Hiram. *The Day of the Bonanza: A History of Bonanza Farming in the Red River Valley of the North*. Fargo: North Dakota Institute for Regional Studies, 1964.

Elliott, E. E., and T. L. Lyon. "Wheat." In *Crops*, edited by Liberty Hyde Bailey, 660–70. Vol. 2 of *Cyclopedia of American Agriculture*. London: Macmillan, 1907.

Fowke, Vernon C. *The National Policy and the Wheat Economy*. Toronto: University of Toronto Press, 1957.

Hurt, R. Douglas. *The Dust Bowl: An Agricultural and Social History*. Chicago: Nelson-Hall, 1981.

Innis, Harold. "The Wheat Economy." In *Essays in Canadian Economic History*, edited by Mary Q. Innis, 273–79. Toronto: University of Toronto Press, 1979.

Isern, Thomas D. *Bull Threshers and Bindlestiffs: Harvesting and Threshing on the North American Plains*. Lawrence: University Press of Kansas, 1990.

Malin, James C. *Winter Wheat in the Golden Belt of Kansas: A Study in Adaptation to the Great Plains Environment*. Lawrence: University of Kansas Press, 1944.

Meinig, D. W. *On the Margins of the Good Earth; The South Australian Wheat Frontier, 1869–1884*. Chicago: Published for the Association of American Geographers by Rand McNally, 1962.

Miner, Craig. *Harvesting the High Plains: John Kriss and the Business of Wheat Farming, 1920–1950*. Lawrence: University Press of Kansas, 1998.

Moon, David. *The American Steppes: The Unexpected Russian Roots of Great Plains Agriculture, 1870s–1930s*. Cambridge: Cambridge University Press, 2020.

Shewry, P. R. "Wheat." *Journal of Experimental Botany* 60, no. 6 (2009): 1537–53.

CHAPTER 16

RICE

PETER A. COCLANIS

Introduction

ALONG with maize and wheat, rice is one of the three leading cereal grains in the world, and it is the staple food for more people than any other crop. Rice cultivation utilizes more land than any other grain, feeds more of the world's poor than any other crop, is the single most important source of rural employment and income in the world, and constitutes almost 20 percent of total human caloric intake worldwide. In other words, rice is a big deal, not only in Asia, where 90 percent of the world's rice is produced, but also in many other parts of the world. Indeed, it is consumed by nearly half of the world's population, has long been central to the diets in various parts of Africa, and is the most important food grain in tropical regions of Latin America and the Caribbean.

Its importance in the material world is mirrored by its significance in the cultural realm, particularly in Asia. This has been the case for thousands of years and in certain ways is still true even today in that rapidly changing region. For example, the name of the Buddha's father, Suddhodana, king of Nepal in the sixth century BCE, literally means "pure rice," and in traditional Chinese society the idiomatic expression "Have you eaten your rice today?" was a polite way of saying hello. All over Asia, "Mother Nature" is depicted as or used synonymously with the Rice Goddess—known as Dewi Sri on Java and Bali and Mae Po Sop in Thailand—and now iconic Japanese names such as Toyota (Toyoda) and Honda are also associated with rice, the literal meaning of the former being "fertile rice field" and the latter "main" or "original rice field."

Origins and Early History of Rice Cultivation

Clearly, for many in Asia rice still *embodies* life, which is not altogether surprising given its importance to the region over the millennia and the fact that Asia was the place where rice domestication first began somewhere around 9,000–10,000 years ago. Like other aspects of the Neolithic Revolution narrative—the story of the beginning of agriculture and animal domestication—much remains unknown or at least unclear about the origins of rice cultivation. Although scientists are confident that rice was first domesticated somewhere in southern China/northern Southeast Asia, the details are still murky. Recent bioarcheological work suggests that rice was being cultivated near the Shangshan area of the lower Yangzi River in southern China at least 9,400 years ago, but there is also genetic evidence to suggest that rice may have been domesticated more than once in Asia, with some rice researchers making claims for at least three independent episodes of domestication.[1] It is likely that further research will yield new evidence and that the rice origin story will continue to evolve. Whatever the case, Asia will remain the setting.

Although many species of wild rice exist (even today), only two rice species have ever been domesticated: *Oryza sativa* in Asia and *Oryza glaberrima* in West Africa much later, probably around 4,000 years ago. *O. sativa* and *O. glaberrima* look much the same but are considered different species because they do not cross or interchange their genes easily in nature.[2] In parts of the world where they have historically coexisted—in West Africa beginning in the sixteenth century CE and, a bit later, in the Western Hemisphere–varieties of *O. sativa* have generally come to dominate, particularly because yields are generally higher and *O. sativa* grains are less susceptible to shattering.

There is great morphological variation in *O. sativa* rice, but in terms of genetics, most rice scientists recognize two principal types: *japonica* rice and *indica* rice. Although both types likely originated in southern China, over time *japonica* rice spread mainly to northern China, Japan, and Korea, and *indica* rice across southern China, Southeast Asia, and Southern Asia. It should be noted that some scientists recognize other types of Asian rice such as *javanica*, but *javanica* rices are now seen by most researchers as tropical forms of the *japonica* type.

From their places of origin in southern China and elsewhere, rice gradually radiated outward, spreading to other parts of southeastern China, Southeast Asia, and South Asia, as well as to Japan—evidence suggests that rice was being cultivated there 6,000 years ago—and to Taiwan, Korea, the Philippines, and other parts of insular Asia. Cultivation of Asian rice extended westward to the Indus River region over 4,000 years ago, and later spread to Persia, Asia Minor, and Egypt. Both the Greeks and the Romans were familiar with rice and its cultivation, encouraging production in parts of the Middle East. This said, its most impressive period of expansion came later, not via the Greeks or Romans, but from Arab and other Muslim traders as part of the so-called Arab agricultural revolution, which spanned the period between the eighth and thirteenth centuries CE. It was through the efforts of such traders—often gaining entrée following Muslim military probes and/or conquests—that a great deal of scientific knowledge about agriculture and horticulture spread from the Middle East/Levant to various parts of Africa and the western part of the Eurasian supercontinent. Among the knowledge transferred was information pertaining to both the production and uses of *O. sativa*, which information gained traction both in Africa and Mediterranean Europe, in the latter case, in Greece, Italy, and Spain especially.

To be sure, there were other routes and modes of transmission for scientific knowledge regarding agriculture, with a good amount of knowledge either developed or creatively adapted *in situ* in various places. Moreover, it is possible at once to simplify technology transfer and overstate the significance of the Arab agricultural revolution by placing too many discrete developments under this interpretive umbrella. Nonetheless, it is impossible to gainsay the fact that considerable knowledge transfer regarding many major crops (including rice) and their uses accompanied Islam as its adherents spread west (and east) from the religion's birthplace in the Middle East.

Cultivation and Cultivation Practices

The fact that rice can be grown in a variety of ways and in a vast number of geographical settings helps to explain the successful diffusion of knowledge regarding risiculture around the world. Indeed, in the vast stretch of the planet between the latitudes of about 53 degrees north and 40 degrees south, rice can be grown almost anywhere, assuming a sufficient supply of sunlight and adequate stocks of water. Although the plant grows best in areas of high temperatures—especially in sub-tropical or warm-temperate climates—historically, it has in fact been grown successfully as far north as the Amur River Valley along the border area between Russia and China and as far south as southern Australia. Similarly, it can be grown at various altitudes, depending on latitude. If rice cultivation is often associated with low-lying river deltas in the tropics and sub-tropics, it has been grown at 10,000 feet in the Himalayas, at 6,000 feet in Luzon in the Philippines, and at high altitudes in the Andes. Just to complicate matters further, some of the highest yields in the world today are achieved in desert areas in Egypt. The keys, again, are sun and water.

Though sun and water are *sine qua nons* for rice cultivation, these resources must be combined with others before rice can be grown. To use modern economic parlance, labor (human and often non-human) and capital (in the forms of tools and the like) are needed. Although hydroponic risiculture, whereby rice is grown in nutrient solutions of one type or another, has existed in various forms since ancient times, the vast majority of rice has always been grown in soil, with some types of soil better suited for rice than others. Land, labor, and capital, then, were the variables in play as rice was domesticated and began slowly and unevenly to evolve and fan out from the places where it had originated.

As it did so, different farmers and farming populations selected rice genotypes that did well in, or successfully adapted to, different ecosystems, and diverse rice cultivars began to develop. As they did, different farmers and farming populations began to modify, however modestly and incrementally, both cultivation methods and the tools and implements employed.

Climate and climatic differences obviously shaped risiculture in decisive ways, with considerations such as length of day, temperature, altitude—other things being equal—helping to determine which rice cultivars would be grown where. Soil characteristics were closely related to the considerations mentioned above, and they too played important roles in shaping a given rice regime, although, as D. H. Grist pointed out long ago, the soils considered suitable for rice cultivation depend more on the conditions under which rice is typically grown than upon the physical characteristics of the soils themselves.[3] And the principal soil "condition" at issue is the ability to hold and retain water, which condition farmers and farming populations recognized early on was instrumental to successful rice production.

Rice grows in a wider variety of soils than any major food crop, and it is produced in soils in almost all of the "orders" in the most commonly used soil taxonomy scheme. Generally, though, it grows better in heavier clay soils than in lighter sandy soils, in large part because the clay hardpans are better suited for water retention. Similarly, almost all good rice soils are acidic rather than alkaline, with pH values between about 5.5 and 6.5. In studies undertaken in both Asia and other parts of the world, soil acidity has been found to help both mineral absorption and the character of the root system, and it is generally associated with higher yields. Rice can grow in alkaline soils, but more water is needed, and more labor too, as the rice generally needs to be transplanted. Rice can even be grown in soils with moderately high levels of salinity—common in areas close to seacoasts, for example—but soils containing large amounts of sulfides are often toxic to rice plants.

Just as rice can be grown in many different climes and in many different types of soils, the plant can be grown—and, indeed, has been grown—in many different ways. Given that there are today more than 40,000 different rice cultivars, it is unsurprising that there is no one way to grow rice. Even extending our gaze far back in time to periods when there were far fewer cultivars, there was no one "standard" way to grow rice, for different cultivars responded differently to different production practices and protocols. However, some common technological patterns have informed risiculture over time.

First, farmers and farming populations must have realized relatively soon after rice domestication began that the plant seemed to do better—larger yields, fewer labor requirements, more predictability—with adequate, even abundant supplies of water during the growing season. Hence, the long-term correlation between rivers and rice cultivation. This is not to say that rice cannot be grown without manipulation of water supplies by humans. The first domesticated rice cultivars were grown "dry." So-called upland rice, common in hilly areas, especially in Asia, is often grown "dry"—dependent for water only on rainfall—even today, and rice is still sometimes grown "dry" even in low-lying areas, particularly in LDCs (less-developed countries). Indeed, so plentiful was water in some tropical low-lying areas that rice-export complexes emerged therein even before serious irrigation efforts began. Despite its long history, dry rice has not received a lot of scholarly attention, although such neglect may soon be a thing of the past, as climate change and water scarcities get more farmers everywhere to think more about the water intensity of the rice they produce.

Being "thirsty" crops, most rice cultivars do much better when supplied with water in appropriate amounts at appropriate times during the growing season. From early on, therefore, we see attempts by rice farmers to manipulate the ecosystems wherein they plant by devising means to ensure that water is in fact available in desired amounts when appropriate (and removed when desired). Said manipulation of water by humans is known as irrigation, which has perhaps been more closely associated historically with rice than with any other food crop.

Over time, the irrigation works devised have become increasingly sophisticated as well as more efficient in both economic and environmental terms, but the basic rationale behind irrigation has remained the same across many millennia, to draw controlled amounts of water onto and off of croplands at planned intervals in order to improve the cultivation process in some way. Irrigation obviously can help to ensure that plants receive the moisture needed to grow, but, when water is applied to fields at properly scheduled times during the growing season, it can also significantly reduce uncertainty, retard the growth of weeds, and limit damage done by biotic pests and abiotic disorders such as drought stress, sunscald, etc. In so doing, the labor requirements per unit of land are also lessened.

Irrigation works of one type of another go back a long way, perhaps seven or eight thousand years. The earliest works were established in rain-scarce areas in what is now Iran, employing impounded water for use in agriculture. Beginning around 4500 BCE, the Indus River civilization in what is now Pakistan and northwest India began developing larger and more sophisticated irrigation systems, which included reservoirs, irrigation canals, and the like. Until recently, scholars did not believe that farmers in this Bronze Age civilization grew rice, but important bioarchaeological findings published in 2017 demonstrated that rice was in fact being grown along with other small grains and legumes in the Indus River region well before 2000 BCE.[4]

So close was this connection between rice and irrigation over the millennia that a rich scholarly literature came into existence exploring the relationship between irrigated rice production and "despotic" governing systems, the idea being that the need for massive irrigation works for crop production and flood control mandated the mobilization by governing authorities of large labor forces to work on said irrigation works, which led over time to increasingly centralized and despotic governmental regimes, particularly in irrigation-dependent areas in Asia, but also in other parts of the world.

Strictly speaking, this interpretation, which had many adherents in the middle decades of the twentieth century, is no longer widely endorsed. On the empirical level, it has often been found wanting. Even so, scholars today often invoke the "oriental despotism" thesis, mainly associated with the Sinologist Karl Wittfogel, for heuristic purposes.

Although it is difficult to generalize about "rice" production practices because of the cereal's deep and varied history, it is possible to observe that there are some common characteristics, one of which is the importance of irrigation. A second involves the intensive use historically of animate power. There are exceptions to both of these generalizations. Rice can be grown "dry," that is, dependent only on rainfall, and often has been in temporary "swidden" plots in Asia. Such plots are generally found on hilly forest lands that, after being cleared by slash-and-burn techniques, serve as rice grounds until their fertility wanes, and producers shift to other grounds. Another exception: with the so-called rice revolution, which began in the mid-1880s in Louisiana, it became clear that under certain conditions rice could be grown on large units of land in capital-intensive rather than labor-intensive ways. Today in places such as the United States and Australia, such capital-intensive production is the order of the day.[5] But, by and large, rice production has meant both lots of water and lots of human and animal labor in flooded paddy fields.

The labor-intensity of rice production is not only well documented historically, but also has led some of the leading scholars of risiculture in Asia to focus on such labor-intensity as one of the keys distinguishing Asia's developmental trajectory over the *longue durée*. The arguments put forth by these scholars regarding the effects of labor intensity in rice production in various parts of Asia differ, and are still being debated by specialists, even if their emphasis on labor intensity per se is generally accepted. Indeed, the labor intensity of traditional forms of rice cultivation can be seen elsewhere in the world as well, as can various forms of labor coercion, whether we look at production schemes in Asia, Africa, or the Americas.

In highly stylized form, one can say that paddy rice is typically grown in small, bunded fields ranging in size from considerably less than 1 acre to about 5 acres (from about 0.4 hectares to about 2 hectares). Once the structural integrity of the bunds (small embankments of clay, mud, weeds, etc.) is assured, the grounds embanked need to be prepared for sowing. This generally means allowing water onto the field, plowing, harrowing, tilling, or hoeing in order to bring fresh nutrients to the surface, remove weeds, break down the soil into finer, looser units, and create furrows/seedbeds. Historically, plowing has been done with or without draft animals, and later sometimes with small mechanized tractors powered by steam or internal-combustion engines. When animal power or mechanized tractors are employed, plowing is generally rendered more efficient, though it should be remembered because paddy fields in Asia are generally very small, human and animal power predominated in most areas until the late twentieth century, and even today mini-tractors are far more common than standard-size machines. When draft animals were used in rice cultivation, water buffalo and oxen were commonly used in Asia, but horses, donkeys, and mules as well as oxen were used elsewhere. In the early twenty-first century, labor historians began paying more attention to the labor exerted by animals in behalf of humans, and in few economic activities was this more true than in rice cultivation, particularly field preparation. Regarding field preparation: because of the onerous labor requirements involved in preparing rice fields for planting, in most cultivation schemes such activities are gendered, involving mostly male laborers.

Once the paddy fields were ready for planting, sowing could begin. In Asia, myriad sowing strategies were and are employed. Rice seed can be broadcast or drilled into paddy lands, or seed may be cultivated first in wet nurseries, then transplanted into paddy fields when the seedlings are deemed to have developed sufficiently. Fertilizers are often used on the seedlings in the nurseries to facilitate development. Once in the paddy fields, which are either kept flooded throughout the growing season or drained and flooded intermittently, the principal labor task is weeding, generally done by female laborers.

The rice harvest, including drying and threshing, historically has been extremely labor-intensive particularly in Asia, where, again, because of the small size of paddy fields, mechanization has proven difficult, even today. Labor intensity is exacerbated in rice harvesting when the rice plant becomes lodged—bent over with the stems near the ground—which commonly occurs in risiculture. Lodging, moreover, often leads to drastic cuts in yields, making the backbreaking work of hand-harvesting via sickle or rice knife more frustrating still.

In comparison to the modern era, yields in rice, in other cereals, indeed, in all cultigens were very low, in large part because agricultural science had not yet developed. If we deploy the term "industrialization" as do many historians of technology, that is, as a process entailing the institutionalization of high levels of productivity through the increasingly systematic employment of scientific knowledge in economic life, it is easier to understand the constraints impeding agriculture before said process took on steam. This said, rice had certain advantages yield-wise in comparison to other cereals that help to explain how and why rice-based societies, particularly in Asia, were able to support and sustain relatively large, dense populations.

Yield-to-seed ratios—one standard, if rough way to measure the performance of agricultural systems in preindustrial times—were low for all cereals, but said ratios were much higher for rice than for small grains such as wheat, barley, and rye.[6] One reason for this was related to the fact that a rice panicle contains many more grains than appear on the heads of other small grains, allowing, all things being equal, for more rice to develop from a single plant than is the case for other small grains. Moreover, rice cultivars in Asia often allow for double—and sometimes triple—cropping in one year, which compounds this cereal's yield potential. The fact that marginal labor productivity in rice declines very slowly, as Clifford Geertz demonstrated long ago, meant that close attention to the plant during the growing season—whether via closely monitored fields, extra weeding, and/or pest control—could prove rewarding at harvest time, however onerous the harvest was itself. These factors are important in understanding both Asian population dynamics and in many cases rice's role in facilitating the same.

Rice Geography

Asia has always been the epicenter of world rice production, but the cereal has been grown in other parts of the world for a long time, particularly in Africa. During the premodern era, rice was grown in several parts of Africa, in various parts of what is now the Middle East, in southern and southeastern Europe, and, as an early manifestation of the so-called Columbian exchange, in the Western Hemisphere, especially in the southeastern part of what later became the United States, in Brazil, and in the Caribbean Basin.

Although the documentary record leaves much to be desired, creative scholars have used a variety of methods to suggest that in West Africa domestication of rice (*O. glaberrima*) may have begun sometime late in the first millennium BCE, and rice was certainly being cultivated in the region by the middle of the first millennium CE. Uncertainty about dating exists because, although we know that West Africans were using rice late in the first millennium BCE, we are not sure if the rice being used was cultivated. In any case, *O. glaberrima*, which bears resemblance to a wild species of rice known as *O. barthii*, was likely first domesticated out of *O. barthii* in the inland delta of the upper Niger River (probably in what is now Mali). Once domesticated, the primary cultivation zone for *O. glaberrima* in West Africa was relatively narrow, constrained to portions of what is known today as the Upper Guinea coast, that is the region of tropical rainforest stretching from today's Senegal through the Gambia, Guinea-Bissau, Guinea-Conakry, Sierra Leone, Liberia, Côte d'Ivoire, and southwestern Ghana. Unlike other cereals first domesticated in West Africa such as pearl millet and sorghum, production of *O. glaberrima*, somewhat surprisingly, never expanded in Africa much beyond this area. This, despite the fact that there were few barriers to further expansion and the fact that rice cultivation later spread into other parts of West Africa and central Africa. Today, for example, Nigeria is the largest producer of rice in West Africa, mostly *O. sativa*.

Within the primary zones of cultivation along the Upper Guinea coast, rice was eventually grown in a variety of ways, some of which were quite ingenious, in a wide variety of ecological settings, ranging from upland swamps to tidal swamps and even in brackish mangrove swamps near the coast. In West Africa, *O. glaberrima* was traditionally grown mostly for domestic or local consumption, and, unlike *O. sativa*, which was introduced much later than *O. glaberrima*, never attained major commercial importance.

The origins of *O. sativa* or Asian rice in West Africa are, if anything, even more unclear than the origins of domestication of *O. glaberrima* in the region, with several different "origin" stories on offer. Some scholars hypothesize that *O. sativa* arrived with traders from North Africa in the ninth century CE in the trans-Sahara trade to West Africa. Others suggest that it crossed overland from East Africa or Madagascar, where Asian rice was being grown late in the first millennium CE. Others date its entrance into West Africa considerably later, in the sixteenth century CE, by virtue of a number of discrete introductions by Iberian traders and ship captains doing business at various sites along the West African coast. Erik Gilbert's work, based on genetic evidence, suggests that said introductions of *O. sativa* into West Africa were extremely complex, mainly the result of Iberian seafarers in the period after 1500 CE, but likely involving some Asian rice introduced into West Africa from the Americas. The relationship between Africa, rice, and the Americas has emerged as an interesting and important topic of debate in its own right. First, however, it is worth a brief look at rice production in the Middle East, Levant, North Africa, and Europe before the modern era.

Asian rice (*O. sativa*) spread via various routes of transmission and dissemination into sundry parts of the Middle East, the Levant and Egypt, the Indian Ocean, and East Africa (Madagascar in particular) during the first millennium CE, although some specialists make cases for limited production in Egypt, the Levant, as well as Sicily even earlier. Cultivation spread into this vast region as a result of contacts with South and Central Asia as well as with Malagasy peoples from Southeast Asia, but it was the spread of Islam throughout this region beginning in the eighth century CE that proved most important. By the thirteenth century CE, rice production had spread along the Mediterranean littoral through parts of North Africa and onto the southern European mainland—into Greece, for example, but more importantly into the area around Valencia in eastern Spain. By the fifteenth century, rice had been introduced into northwestern Italy—into the rich alluvial valley of the upper Po River—which was to become the leading production site in Europe for centuries thereafter. Production spread later to other parts of Europe—Portugal and France, most notably—but Italy is even today the leading rice producer in Europe, with Spain a distant second.

For several centuries after its introduction into northwestern Italy, that region was the leading supplier of rice in the West. By the middle of the eighteenth century, however, Italian rice was superseded in most markets in the West by rice from another source, one that would have seemed not merely unlikely but implausible when the rice industry in the valley of the upper Po was established in the fifteenth century: America. Indeed, the same process that sent Europeans to Asia, and, according to Erik Gilbert and other scholars, Asian rice to West Africa—which is to say, the outward economic expansion of parts of Europe in the late medieval and early modern periods—was responsible for the transmission of rice to the Western Hemisphere as well.

Details of said transmission process are at once murky, complicated, and controversial. Over the past half century or so, but particularly since the publication in 2001 of Judith A. Carney's influential study *Black Rice: The African Origins of Rice Cultivation in the Americas*, it has become increasingly common for scholars and students alike to attribute the origins of rice cultivation in the Americas largely to enslaved West Africans already familiar with rice cultivation, who, naturally enough, began cultivating both *O. sativa* and to a lesser extent *O. glaberrima* once in the New World. According to Carney and others, once Euro-Americans became cognizant of the economic possibilities opened up by rice, they found ways to appropriate and redeploy African rice technology for their own purposes, in so doing, eventually setting up rice-export complexes in several parts of the Western Hemisphere, most notably in Portuguese Brazil—first in the northeast and later in the south—but more emphatically along the southeastern coast of British North America in what later became the United States, particularly in coastal areas of South Carolina and Georgia. As part of the acts of appropriation and redeployment, Euro-American actors and their scholarly descendants largely reduced or elided the African contribution to technology transfer in rice for generations.

However influential, the revisionist West African "rice story" has not convinced everyone. Three eminent scholars of the Atlantic slave trade—Philip D. Morgan, David Richardson, and David Eltis—have raised important questions about the thesis, particularly about the degree of concordance between the major areas of rice production in the Americas and the enslaved labor forces employed therein. They point out, for example, that many, if not most of those labor forces did not have experience in rice cultivation in

West Africa, that non-rice-growing parts of the Americas imported similar proportions of slaves from "rice" regions in West Africa, and that at the times when the major rice-cultivating areas in the Americas began to grow rice, relatively few of the African slaves therein came from rice-growing regions in West Africa.

Similarly, other scholars have argued that knowledge about rice cultivation is one thing, and creating a rice *industry* and formidable rice-export platforms is quite another. Whatever knowledge Africans may have had about growing rice, it was Europeans and Euro-Americans—and their capital, contacts, and entrepreneurship—that rendered rice extremely important economically in parts of the Americas, differentiating the plant markedly in importance from certain other crops said to be transferred by Africans to the Americas—sorghum, for example.

The complex origins and path of rice to—and from—the Americas are also noted, as we have seen, by Gilbert, whose work in the genetics of rice suggests that various rice cultigens moved back and forth between Africa and the New World. Then there is the often discredited "white" origin story for rice in South Carolina, the so-called seed from Madagascar narrative, in which white merchants and ship captains figure prominently by introducing *O. sativa* to Carolina via the Indian Ocean island. Recent research by Jane Hooper and others relating to rice-producing Madagascar as a major rice-provisioning center for European vessels traveling between Europe and Asia raises once again the possibility that there may be something after all to the old "tale."

Similarly, while it is likely that rice technology from West Africa was important to cultivation practices in the Americas, it should also be noted that Europeans were familiar with both rice and sophisticated irrigation systems in both Europe and Asia, and likely contributed to the technological "package" regarding rice in the Americas. None of this is to suggest that the transfer of West African technology regarding risiculture was not important, but that technology transfer is very complicated, and the role of West Africa was not singular.

In the Western Hemisphere, rice was grown as a subsistence crop in various places in the Caribbean Basin but emerged as an important industry in only a few areas: Portuguese Brazil and British North America. The rice industry proved especially important in the latter area, and in the half century after its establishment in South Carolina around 1700 CE the colony became the leading supplier of rice in the West. In South Carolina and Georgia—the leading rice-producing areas in British North America—the cereal was generally produced for export by enslaved African and African American laborers on large plantations. On these plantations, which were established on drained swamp lands near the coast, rice was grown in large irrigated fields, subdivided into paddy "squares." A variety of drainage and irrigation schemes were employed, the most sophisticated of which eventually used tidal flows to draw water onto and off of freshwater rice fields near the coast. By premodern standards, productivity via such schemes was high.

Once European and Euro-American planters and merchants rendered rice production into a rice industry, and, more to the point, into an export platform, rice from South Carolina and Georgia dominated the principal rice markets in the Americas and Europe for almost a century before being superseded by competitors in Asia. During the height of the industry in South Carolina and Georgia, considerable wealth was generated, the vast preponderance of which went to the planters and merchants overseeing the industry rather than to the enslaved producers themselves. The forces responsible for the decline of the industry in this area—the expansion, elaboration, and increasing integration of global capitalist markets—signaled a new era in the history of rice.

Markets and Trade

The role of and demand for rice are exceedingly complicated, *moving* targets, which have long varied and continue to vary over space and time. As a result, it is exceedingly difficult to generalize about the grain's (many) uses. For example, although it is well known that rice is the key cereal for the world's poor, it has at various points in time and in various places behaved—and been viewed as—a luxury or superior good, the demand for which rises more than proportionately as income increases. Some studies have suggested that in the United States in the late twentieth century demand for rice, long an "inferior good"—declining as incomes rose—had in fact become a superior good. More intriguingly, it is possible, that rice at times may have behaved as a "Giffen good"—that is, one for which demand, counterintuitively, rose with increases in price. Examples of true Giffen goods have proven rare in history. People are generally able to find a close substitute for the good in question rather than to consume it in greater quantities as its price rises. That said, historical evidence has been found to suggest that rice at times has behaved as a Giffen good for the poor in Hunan Province in China.[7]

Although rice consumption has long been associated with Asia's poor, scholars have pointed out that historically in various parts of Asia—China and Indonesia are cases in point—the poorest groups by and large could not afford rice but subsisted rather more on tubers, sago, maize, "coarse" grains, etc. Even when the poor are in fact consuming most of the rice, in some places—northern Europe and the United States in the eighteenth and nineteenth centuries come to mind—part of this demand for rice among the "poor" actually arose because of the emergence of an interest in welfare work among other better-positioned groups and social formations (as well as the state). In a sense, then, the rising demand for rice resulting from this enhanced social preference for provisioning lumpen groups and the marginalized can be viewed as part of the demand for a larger income-elastic "product" known as altruism, benevolence, or charity.

Rice, moreover, is also found in the pharmacopeia of various cultures around the world, has played important roles in religions, and served numerous ritualistic and ceremonial functions. Its most important economic functions historically were not pharmaceutical, ceremonial, or ritualistic, however, but more elemental, to wit: as a basic foodstuff for feeding large portions of the world's human (and animal) populations, and as a cheap, useful, and versatile intermediate or final non-food product. The importance of such functions, which go back to time immemorial, intensified and concatenated in the modern era as an integrated world market for rice gradually came into existence and the cereal in time was transformed into a global commodity.

In addition to its principal historical role as the grain of choice (or necessity) for large proportions of the world's population, rice has had an array of other alimentary and industrial uses. Rice and/or its many byproducts has long served as an animal feed in both the East and the West, and it has also long been used in the production of alcoholic beverages. Rice is used in the production of various oils, vinegars, and syrups, and it has long been used in the manufacture of starch, pastes, and paper. Rice straw and various byproducts have myriad other uses as well. Thus, if its principal use for millennia has been as a source of complex carbohydrates for meeting basic human (and animal) needs, it also served other important purposes.

No cereal anywhere in the world has played a more dominant dietary role than has rice, particularly in parts of Asia. Even in the early twentieth-first century, with grain consumption falling as a percentage of total caloric intake, rice accounts for almost 20 percent of total human calorie intake. In Asia, the percentages for rice are even higher. Data from 2009 to 2011 reveal, for example, that rice still accounted for between 45 percent and 70 percent of total calories consumed in Bangladesh, Cambodia, Vietnam, Myanmar, and Indonesia. Rice accounts for a high percentage of total caloric intake in various other parts of the world, including Africa, especially in Nigeria, Egypt, and Madagascar. In the Caribbean and tropical parts of Latin America it plays a more important role in human diets than both cereals such as wheat and maize and tubers such as potatoes and root vegetable crops such as cassava.[8]

On balance, rice is a very nutritious grain, providing more energy in kilocalories than does wheat, for example. One hundred grams of dry rice converts into about 362 kilocalories, while the same amount of dry wheat grain provides about 348. Similarly, rice contains more carbohydrates and calcium than does wheat. On the other hand, wheat provides more phosphorus, iron, and protein than does an equivalent amount of rice. The protein content of wheat is about 12 percent on average, while the protein content of (unmilled brown) rice on average is only about 9.5, although it should be noted that the protein content of rice cultivars in the International Rice Research Institute's vast germplasm collection range from 4.3 percent to 18.2 percent. It seems fair to say that both rice and wheat are nutritious cereal grains, with rice supplying lots of kilocalories and complex carbohydrates per unit and wheat more protein. Not for nothing are these two cereals ranked first and second in the world in terms of *direct* consumption by humans. The qualifier *direct* is critical, however: maize is by far the leading cereal grain produced worldwide—in the second decade of the twenty-first century it has sometimes been the leading cereal grain produced even in China—but most maize is used as animal feed or as a source of ethanol rather than to feed humans directly.[9]

The vast preponderance of the world's rice has always been produced in Asia. Nine of the top ten rice-producing nations in the world in crop year 2019–2020 were in Asia—Brazil, which placed tenth, is the only non-Asian nation among the leaders—with China and India far ahead of all other producers, and with other nation states in South and Southeast Asia claiming spots three through eight and Japan number nine. By and large, the earliest centers of rice production are still the leading producing areas. In crop year 2019–2020 global (milled) rice production reached a record 497.69 million metric tons, with China and India alone accounting for over 53 percent of the total. The nine leading producers in Asia—China, India, Indonesia, Bangladesh, Vietnam, Thailand, Myanmar, the Philippines, and Japan—accounted for 83 percent of the rice produced in 2019–2020, with total Asian production amounting to about 90 percent of the world production. *Plus ça change, plus c'est la même chose*: Between 1911 and 1915, Asian producers accounted for almost 96 percent of total global production.[10]

Since 1960, world rice production has increased by 330 percent while the amount of land in production, measured in hectares, has grown by only 35 percent. The tremendous growth in rice produced per unit of land was due to numerous factors, most notably to an increased commitment to, and better use of, scientific knowledge in risiculture. One of the most important, high-profile manifestations of said commitment was the so-called Green Revolution package—the employment of high-yielding varieties, mechanized equipment, improved irrigation, synthetic fertilizers and pesticides, etc.—which package, beginning in the 1960s, helped dramatically to rationalize and modernize, and, in so doing, to render more productive rice-production practices in various parts of Asia, India being a notable case in point. Although this package of practices was hardly perfect—indeed, it not only failed to address some long-standing problems, but also introduced some new ones—its achievements, on balance, were positive.

Whether grown in small plots in labor-intensive ways without a greater deal of mechanization or on huge farms employing massive amounts of expensive capital equipment and virtually no human beings, rice meets up and competes in markets, local, regional, and international. To understand the history of rice trading, one must recognize that throughout history the vast majority of the world's rice was either not traded at all or traded only locally, within a few miles of where it was grown. Historically, rice has been treated as a subsistence crop by most growers as meeting household food needs was the first priority, and only if a surplus remained over subsistence needs would "leftover" rice be exchanged or sold. Most such transactions took place near the sites of production because of the small-scale, intermittent, and often ad hoc nature of the "markets" for rice.

To be sure, some merchants and traders in the past were able to exchange rice in more regular and routinized way over greater distances. For example, during the middle Qing period internal rice markets in China were well developed and trading practices were often quite sophisticated. Similarly, by the early eighteenth century CE, forward contracts were being employed in the Dojima rice exchange in Osaka, Japan. Over the millennia, small portions of such trade were also transacted internationally, often from areas with rice surpluses in a given season or period to areas suffering from rice deficits during the same. Tiny amounts were even shipped long distances, sometimes to feed armies, navies, and merchant sailors, and occasionally in some markets even as luxury products.

At various points during the Common Era, for example, rice traded regularly and sometimes predictably by sea over long distances in Asia, most notably in the Indian

Ocean, the South China Sea, and the East China Sea. Certainly, the rice trade generally constituted only a small part of the trade conducted in intra-Asian trade networks, but as an article of trade, it was not uncommon. Some Asian rice also found its way to the Middle East and Europe. Elsewhere in the world, though, rice was traded mainly locally, when it was traded at all.

Europe's outward economic thrust in the fifteenth and sixteenth centuries—a thrust related to the rise of capitalism in the West—led over time to important changes in the long-distance trade in rice. Over the course of the three hundred years between roughly 1500 and 1800 CE, European merchant capital, aided and abetted by the techno-military power of various European nation states, succeeded in establishing in embryonic form the rudiments of a global economy, a loosely, even vaguely connected world system, as it were, wherein capital (including intellectual capital), technology, goods and products, and even labor began to circulate or at least move more readily around the globe.

Rice initially did not much partake in such global mobility: it was too heavy and bulky, given its price and the state of transportation and communications technology at the time. Rice markets developed and widened—agricultural complexes set up in British North America and Brazil began to supply Europe with rice—but distinct and relatively independent regional rice markets still prevailed both in the East and West.

This situation changed over the course of the "long" nineteenth century, however. Demand for rice (among other foodstuffs) in the West was growing rapidly as a result of rising incomes, urbanization, and industrialization. At the same time, transportation and communications improvements, the intensification of European and Euro-American economic penetration of non-Western areas, the enhanced ability of Western nation states to project power in non-European areas, and the active, sometimes decisive initiatives of Asian merchant capital, taken together, linked Asia more closely to the West, facilitating the establishment or reorientation of portions of Asian rice production and trade complexes toward the West, in some cases dramatically.

According to political economist David Macpherson, writing in the 1790s, rice was the first "necessary" shipped to the West from India, all previous trade consisting of items "rather of ornament and luxury than of use."[11] And useful rice certainly proved to be in the West. Between the time Macpherson wrote and 1914, Asian rice broke out of Asia, swamping Western markets, and—on the basis of price—outcompeting producers in other supply sources. Although the early Asian "movers" were located in Bengal in eastern India and Java in the Nederlands Oost-Indië (Dutch East Indies), during the second half of the nineteenth century, the rice-exporting giants of mainland Southeast Asia—Burma, Siam, and Cochinchina—overwhelmed other Asian suppliers of rice to the West, indeed, to other parts of Asia as well. That the developmental effects of the transformation of these three areas into export platforms were mixed at best testifies amply to both the problems and the ironies of capitalism and linkage to capitalist markets for suppliers of cheap, basic food commodities.

Within Asia itself, population growth, swelling cities, the establishment of specialized, food-deficient plantation and mining zones in parts of the region—particularly in Sumatra, British Malaya, and Borneo—and periodic food shortages and famines, some of which were caused by El Niño–Southern Oscillation (ENSO) climatic shocks, brought about surges in rice demand. And by the time of World War I, not only had world demand for rice (and other cereal grains) grown vigorously, but an integrated global market for rice was also coming into existence, with prices moving in concert worldwide, and the law of "one price" becoming closer to reality.

Once established, the global rice market displayed—and continues to display—certain characteristics that distinguish it from global markets for the other great cereal grains. Compared to the markets for wheat and maize, the global rice market is much smaller as a percentage of total output, thinner, less articulated, and marked by less frequent recourse to financial intermediation via derivative products, etc. Although the ratio of rice exports to total rice production—usually about 7 to 9 percent—has grown since the 1960s, it is today still considerably lower than the ratios for maize (around 12 percent) and especially wheat (almost 20 percent).[12] Rice is still largely grown for subsistence and local consumption, often by poor people, unlike the cases for maize and wheat.

The global rice trade, not surprisingly, has been dominated by Asian suppliers ever since it came into existence. The trio of rice-export giants in Southeast Asia that led the Asian "breakout" in the second half of the nineteenth century—Burma (Myanmar), Siam (Thailand), and Cochinchina (Vietnam)—dominated the newly integrated world market in the 1920s and 1930s, and Thailand has remained a dominant player ever since. Indeed, since the 1980s it has generally been the world's leading exporter. Internal disorder and dislocations as well as state policy preferences set back the export sectors in Myanmar and Vietnam for a time during the postwar period, but both nations (especially Vietnam) are again among the leading exporters, along with some surprising Asian suppliers in the early twenty-first century such as India, Pakistan, China, and even Cambodia, and non-Asian suppliers such as the United States, Italy, Brazil, and Uruguay. Regarding the United States: once the industry was transformed into a capital-intensive system in the late nineteenth century as a result of the "rice revolution," the United States began to regain its international competitiveness and by the second quarter of the twentieth century again became a major exporter. Although the United States grows only a small proportion of the world's rice, it has generally been among the top five exporters, and for a time in the postwar period was often number one.

World rice exports are dominated by a small number of nations, but the import market for rice is much more diffuse. Asian nations such as the Philippines and Indonesia are typically major importers, as are a number of nations in Africa and the Middle East, but significant demand often emanates from the EU and the Americas as well. The global rice trade, like the trade in other foodstuffs, particularly commodities, is powerfully affected today by governmental policies (subsidies, tariffs, NTBs, etc.), weather shocks, and currency fluctuations, etc., but the overall shape of the market, especially the export market, generally follows a more-or-less consistent pattern.

The Future of Rice

Such patterning might diminish as the twenty-first century proceeds, for the rice industry faces powerful challenges. Any short list of such challenges would include an array of issues related to the environment: diminishing/degraded water supplies, overuse of synthetic fertilizers and pesticides, problems posed by methane released on flood rice fields, and adapting to climate change more generally. And the difficulties facing the rice industry go well beyond those relating to the environment. Rice lands are being lost as urban and peri-urban development increases, the growth rate in rice yields is slowing, and farming is losing its appeal among younger population cohorts. Perhaps the most serious problem of all, however, relates to the relative shift of research funding away from agriculture since the 1980s, as other sectors became trendier. It is only in the last few years that funding levels have begun to increase again, which is heartening, for without new scientific breakthroughs—and the diffusion of the results of such breakthroughs—the future of risiculture and the rice industry more generally is uncertain.

Notes

1. Xinxin Zuo et al., "Dating Rice Remains through Phytolith Carbon-14 Study Reveals Domestication at the Beginning of the Holocene," *PNAS* [*Proceedings of the National Academy of Sciences of the United States of America*] 114 (June 20, 2017): 6486–6491.
2. S. D. Sharma, "Domestication and Diaspora of Rice," in *Rice: Origin, Antiquity and History*, ed. S.D. Sharma (Enfield, NH: Science Publishers, CRC Press, 2010), 1.
3. D. H. Grist, *Rice*, 3rd ed. (London: Longmans, Green & Co., 1959), 11.
4. J. Bates, C. A. Petrie, and R. N. Singh, "Approaching Rice Domestication in South Asia: New Evidence form Indus Settlements in Northern India," *Journal of Archaeological Science* 78 (2017): 193–201.
5. Peter A. Coclanis, "White Rice: The Midwestern Origins of the Modern Rice Industry in the United States," in *Rice Global Networks and New Histories*, ed. Francesca Bray et al. (New York: Cambridge University Press, 2015): 291–317.
6. Francesca Bray, *The Rice Economies: Technology and Development in Asian Societies* (Oxford: Basil Blackwell, 1986), 15.
7. Robert T. Jensen and Nolan H. Miller, "Giffen Behavior and Subsistence Consumption," *American Economic Review* 98 (2008): 1553–1577.
8. Global Rice Science Partnership (GRiSP), *Rice Almanac*. 4th ed. (Los Baños, Philippines: International Rice Research Institute, 2013): x.
9. https://www.statista.com/statistics/263977/world-grain-production-by-type/, accessed August 24, 2021; Peter A. Coclanis, "Challenging Times Ahead: A Historical Look at the Future of Food and Agriculture," *Agricultural History of China* 37, no. 1 (2018): 43–56.
10. https://www.statista.com/statistics/255945/top-countries-of-destination-for-us-rice-expo rts-2011/ , accessed August 25, 2021; Randolph Barker, Robert W. Herdt, with Beth Rose, *The Rice Economy of Asia*, 2 vols. (Washington, DC: Resources for the Future, 1985), 1:39.

11. David Macpherson, *Annals of Commerce, Manufactures, Fisheries and Navigation* (London: Nichols & Son, 1805), 4:362.
12. Global Rice Science Partnership (GRiSP), *Rice Almanac*, 4th ed., 40, https://www.statista.com/statistics/263977/world-grain-production-by-type/, accessed August 25, 2021.

Bibliography

Barker, Randolph, Robert W. Herdt, with Beth Rose. *The Rice Economy of Asia*. 2 vols. Washington, DC: Resources for the Future, 1985.

Bates, J., C. A. Petrie, and R. N. Singh. "Approaching Rice Domestication in South Asia: New Evidence from Indus Settlements in Northern India." *Journal of Archaeological Science* 78 (2017): 193–201.

Bray, Francesca. *The Rice Economies: Technology and Development in Asian Societies*. Oxford: Basil Blackwell, 1986.

Bray, Francesca, Peter A. Coclanis, Edda L. Fields-Black, and Dagmar Schäfer, eds., *Rice: Global Networks and New Histories*. New York: Cambridge University Press, 2015.

Carney, Judith A. *Black Rice: The African Origins of Rice Cultivation in the Americas*. Cambridge: Harvard University Press, 2001.

Chauhan, Bhagirath S., Khawar Jabran, and Gulshan Majahan, eds., *Rice Production Worldwide*. New York: Springer, 2017.

Coclanis, Peter A. "Distant Thunder: The Creation of a World Market in Rice and the Transformations It Wrought." *American Historical Review* 98 (1993): 1050–1078.

Coclanis, Peter A. "The Rice Industry of the United States." In *Rice: Origin, Antiquity and History*, edited by S. D. Sharma, 411–31. Enfield, NH: Science Publishers, CRC Press, 2010.

Coclanis, Peter A. "White Rice: The Midwestern Origins of the Modern Rice Industry in the United States." In *Rice: Global Networks and New Histories*, edited by Francesca Bray et al., 291–317. New York: Cambridge University Press, 2015.

Eltis, David, Philip D. Morgan, and David Richardson. "Agency and Diaspora in Atlantic History: Reassessing the African Contribution to Rice Cultivation in the Americas." *American Historical Review* 112 (2007): 1329–1358.

Food and Agriculture Organization of the United Nations [FAO]. FAOSTAT [Food and Agriculture Data for 245 nations and territories from 1961 until the most recent data available] [http://www.fao.org/faostat/en/#home]. Accessed August 6, 2019.

Gilbert, Erik. "Asian Rice in Africa: Plant Genetics and Crop History." In *Rice: Global Networks and New Histories*, edited by Francesca Bray et al., 212–28. New York: Cambridge University Press, 2015.

Global Rice Science Partnership (GRiSP). *Rice Almanac*. 4th ed. Los Baños, Philippines: International Rice Research Institute, 2013.

Grist, D. H. *Rice*. 3rd ed. London: Longmans, Green, 1959.

Jensen, Robert T., and Nolan H. Miller. "Giffen Behavior and Subsistence Consumption." *American Economic Review* 98 (2008): 1553–1577.

Knapp, Seaman Asahel. *The Present Status of Rice Culture in the United States*. Washington, DC: United States Department of Agriculture, Division of Botany, 1899.

Latham, A. J. H. *Rice: The Primary Commodity*. New York: Routledge, 1998.

Linares, Olga F. "African Rice (*Oryza glaberrima*): History and Future Potential." *PNAS* [Proceedings of the National Academy of Sciences of the United States of America] 99 (December 10, 2002): 16360–16365.

Owen, Norman G. "The Rice Industry of Mainland Southeast Asia 1850–1914." *Journal of the Siam Society* 59 (1971): 75–143.

Sharma, S. D. "Domestication and Diaspora of Rice." In *Rice: Origin, Antiquity and History*, edited by S.D. Sharma, 1–24. Enfield, NH: Science Publishers, CRC Press, 2010.

United States Department of Agriculture, Economic Research Service. *Rice Yearbook* 2019 [https://www.ers.usda.gov/data-products/rice-yearbook/rice-yearbook/#World%20Supply,%20Utilization,%20and%20Trade], last updated March 2023.

Zuo, Xinxin, et al. "Dating Rice Remains through Phytolith Carbon-14 Study Reveals Domestication at the Beginning of the Holocene." *PNAS* [Proceedings of the National Academy of Sciences of the United States of America] 114 (June 20, 2017): 6486–91.

CHAPTER 17

....

SOY

....

ERNST LANGTHALER

WE live in a world of soy.[1] Nearly each of us takes some of the bean's ingredients again and again—either directly, as tofu in a veggie burger, or indirectly, as a chop of meat on the grill. Since the main sites of consumption and production are widely spread, soy's trade flows span the globe. Indeed, soy is the world's leading agricultural commodity. Since 2009, soybeans have ranked first in trade value, followed by wheat and wine. Together with the bean's products, the extracted oil and the residual cake, soy's top position in agricultural trade, amounting to $86 billion in 2016, becomes even more impressive, compared to wheat ($36 billion) and wine ($32 billion). Soy's dominance is astonishing, given that wheat was the undisputed leader in agricultural world trade for a long time. In 1929, for instance, wheat with a trade value of 3.43 billion *Reichsmark* (RM) surpassed soybeans (0.46 billion RM, excluding oil and cake) more than sevenfold, followed by sugar (3.02 billion RM) and coffee (2.35 billion RM). Before the onset of the world trade after the turn from the nineteenth to the twentieth century, soybeans, soyoil, and soycake were solely produced, distributed, and consumed in East and Southeast Asia. Soy had only attracted Western travelers, writers, and scientists as an exotic plant from the Far East. For instance, the Austrian botanist Friedrich Haberlandt envisioned the transfer of the soybean plant to Central Europe as a basis of domestic agriculture and nutrition in the 1870s. Since then, however, soy has emerged as a global cash crop, affecting large tracts of society and nature. With regard to its tremendous socio-natural impacts, it is far from an exaggeration to call the late Anthropocene "Soyacene."[2]

Soy's emergence as a global commodity involved a multitude of conditions, drivers, and actions. From an anthropocentric perspective, soy was inserted in global food regimes that coordinated capital accumulation along transnational commodity chains "from farm to fork," regulated by actors such as nation states, capitalist enterprises, or social movements. Food regimes tended to expand their frontiers to labor and natural resources not yet incorporated in commodity chains. Commodity frontiers were expanded *externally*, through extensive incorporation of new spaces ("broadening," e.g., conversion of grasslands into fields), *internally*, through more intensive incorporation of already occupied spaces ("deepening," e.g., adoption of more productive technologies), or *flexibly*, through combinations of both modes. The conditions and consequences of capital accumulation, including disruptions of society and nature, were often contested and needed to be regulated according to the interests and values of powerful and wealthy actors. Once the contradictions within a regime could not be contained anymore, it fell into crisis and was transformed into another regime. Agro-food globalization comprised the British-centered food regime (1870–1929), the US-centered food regime (1947–1973), and the WTO-centered food regime (since 1995).[3]

From a postanthropocentric perspective, soy emerged as a global commodity not passively, but it played an active role. Through its properties as a plant domesticated in East Asia some millennia ago, *Glycine max* both enabled and limited interaction with the rest of the "socio-nature," the hybrid networks of human and non-human actors. Soy's properties comprised both strengths (e.g., nitrogen fixation in the soil in symbiosis with bacteria) and weaknesses (e.g., vulnerability to weeds due to slow maturation). Given its unique combination of nutrients—25 to 45 percent protein and 15 to 20 percent fat—the crop resisted any clear definition. Depending on the dominant usage, its classification oscillated between "pulse" and "oilseed." In connection with other elements (crop rotation, farm technologies, labor relations, management strategies, market links, etc.), soy shaped specific styles and more general modes of farming: peasant, entrepreneurial, or capitalist. Because of its versatility, the "miracle bean" also served political and economic powers (e.g., as "flex crop" used for food, feed, or fuel) or allied with civic counter-movements (e.g., as sustainable, ethical, and healthy "whole food"). In short, soy's role in such "more-than-human" networks involved opposing descriptions.[4]

Soy contributed heavily to the Great Acceleration of the social appropriation of nature since the mid-twentieth century (Figures 17.1 and 17.2). Though world trade of soy had already taken off during the 1910s and 1920s, it contracted through the economic and military crises of the 1930s and 1940s, the Great Depression and World War II. The 1950s to 1970s saw an unprecedented rise in volume that, after stagnation during the 1980s, has continued from the 1990s until today. These waves of globalization involved frontier expansions of three major commodity chains around soy: from East Asia to Western Europe (1910s–1930s); from North America to Western Europe and East Asia (since the 1950s); and from South America to Western Europe (since the 1970s) and East Asia (since the 1990s). The global commodity web around soy connected diverse world regions of production and consumption. The earliest commodity chain linked the northeast of China as the world's leading soy producer to consumer societies in Northwest Europe. The following commodity chain connected the US Midwest and South as major suppliers of soy in the divided world market in the Cold War with livestock complexes in Western Europe and Japan. The latest commodity chain integrated the South American producers as well as European and Chinese consumers into the global soy complex. During the long twentieth century, regional soy expansion occurred as waves of agro-food globalization in China, the United States, and Brazil.[5]

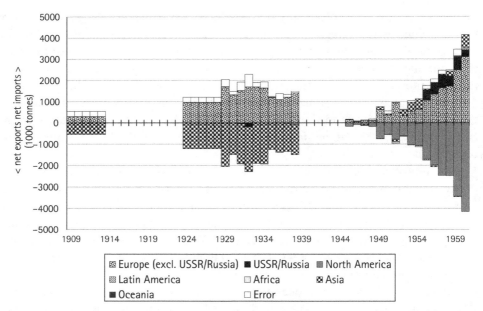

FIGURE 17.1 World trade in soy products (beans and oil), 1909–1960. Data source: Lois B. Bacon and Friedrich C. Schloemer, *World Trade in Agricultural Products* (Rome: International Institute of Agriculture, 1940), 264–71; Food and Agriculture Organization, *Yearbook of Food and Agricultural Statistics, Part 2: Trade, 1948–1961* (Rome: FAO, 1949–1962); Food and Agriculture Organization, "Faostat."

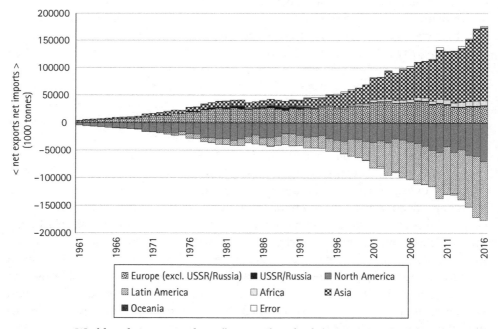

FIGURE 17.2 World trade in soy products (beans, oil, and cake), 1961–2016. Data source: Lois B. Bacon and Friedrich C. Schloemer, *World Trade in Agricultural Products* (Rome: International Institute of Agriculture, 1940), 264–71; Food and Agriculture Organization, *Yearbook of Food and Agricultural Statistics, Part 2: Trade, 1948–1961* (Rome: FAO, 1949–1962); Food and Agriculture Organization, "Faostat."

Chinese Soy in the British-Centered Food Regime

Soy entered the global stage in the British-centered food regime. The Great Divergence of economic growth in the United Kingdom compared to China and India in the nineteenth century involved commodity frontier expansions in both vertical and horizontal directions: the exploitation of the "subterranean forest" (i.e., coal as fossil energy) through steam-engine technology and "ghost acres" (i.e., agricultural land in European settler colonies) through long-distance trade of staple food. Thereby, European industrial classes, especially capitalists and wage laborers in the British "workshop of the world," got underground and overseas access to cheap energy, raw materials, and foodstuffs. In order to facilitate global sourcing at falling transport costs, the United Kingdom and other European nation states adopted free-trade policies, based on the gold standard and legitimized by classical-liberal economics. At the turn of the century, the sparsely populated northeast of China was incorporated in global resource flows. The Chinese Empire promoted Han Chinese migration to these provinces for fiscal and geopolitical reasons. Imperialist Japan outpaced Russia in the quest for economic and military influence in the region, implemented through railroad construction and the occupation in 1931. From 1908 onward, surplus production of soybeans by settler farms and estates, previously sold to mainland China and Japan, flowed via Japanese trading companies to consumer goods industries in Northwest Europe. In the West, the exotic crop from the Far East was soon labeled "miracle bean," indicating its multiple uses. European manufacturers replaced scarce vegetable oils through soyoil as cheap ingredient of processed foodstuffs (e.g., margarine) and utility items (e.g., soap). Moreover, the German Hansa Mill pioneered the extraction of soy lecithin, used as emulsifier in the food and feed industry. The cake as by-product of soyoil extraction was advertised as protein-rich animal feed, against farmers' initial reservation. Besides separation of oil and cake, the food industry processed whole beans into full-fat soy flour as a cheap substitute for animal protein for poor households hit by the Great Depression. Despite its euphemistic brand name, "Edelsoja" had limited success due to consumers' reservations. The regulatory foundations of the British-centered regime, suspended in World War I, eroded in the post-1925 world agrarian crisis and finally collapsed in the post-1929 Great Depression, when national protectionism restrained free trade and major countries, even the United Kingdom, abandoned the gold standard.[6]

Northeast China, called "Manchuria" in colonialist jargon, emerged as the leading producer and exporter in the world market of soy at the beginning of the twentieth century. The Manchurian supply of soy, driven by Chinese, Japanese, and European demand, took off in the late 1900s and peaked in the early 1930s, before political turmoil, economic crisis, and natural adversities terminated it (Figure 17.3). Available data suggest that the 98 percent increase in soybean production from 1924 to 1931 resulted solely from the enlargement of cultivated land by 151 percent, since yields per unit of land steadily declined by 21 percent. These figures indicate an external shift of the soy frontier.

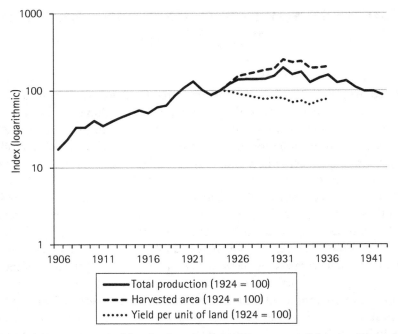

FIGURE 17.3 Soy expansion in Manchuria, 1906–1942. Data source: Johannes Langenberg, *Die Bedeutung der Sojabohnein in der Weltwirtschaft* (Pinneberg: Beig, 1929), 20; John R. Stewart, "The Soya Bean and Manchuria," *Far Eastern Survey* 5, no. 21 (1936): 221–26; G. F. Deasy, "The Soya Bean in Manchuria," *Economic Geography* 15, no. 3 (1939): 303–10; Kang Chao, *The Economic Development of Manchuria: The Rise of a Frontier Economy* (Ann Arbor: University of Michigan Press, 1982), 44.

The doubling of land devoted to soybeans involved the conversion of near-natural grasslands and extensive farmland in the Manchurian plain into fields used more intensively. Declining land productivity reflected nutrient mining on existing fields and plowing-up poorer soils at marginal locations. Throughout this period, soy occupied a central place in the Manchurian economy, amounting for about three-quarters of total exports.

Land, labor, and technology for the Manchurian soy expansion unfolded in the crisis of late-imperial and early-republican China. The three northeastern provinces, Liaoning, Jilin, and Heilongjiang, were of utmost importance for the rulers. In political terms, the region at the intersection of China, Russia, Korea, and Japan was considered as the "cockpit of Asia." In economic terms, it emerged as Beijing's breadbasket thanks to the rich land reserves and the favorable monsoon climate with warm, wet summers and cold, dry winters. From the mid-nineteenth century onward, the Qing dynasty promoted Han Chinese settlement as well as the reclamation and cultivation of land in their homeland, formerly prohibited for immigration. They opened the Manchurian frontier not only to raise revenues from land sales and leases for financing military efforts, but also to strengthen defense against imperialist powers by settling a larger population on the borders. As debts and threats worsened at the turn of the century, the New Policies of 1902 reinforced these efforts.

This initiative coincided with the opening of railroads through Manchuria with access to the sea in 1903, financed by foreign capital: the Chinese Eastern Railway to Vladivostok and the South Manchuria Railway to Dairen. While initially both lines were in Russian hands, the southern track section came under Japanese control following the Russo-Japanese War of 1904–1905. Consequently, foreign imperialist and commercial strategies ruled the exploitation of Manchuria's rich resources, channeled through the ports of Dairen and Vladivostok by the Japanese trading company Mitsui Bussan. As famine and warlordism spread throughout China in the 1920s, voluntary migrants to Manchuria, primarily male, joined with refugees, many of them women and children, forced to search for a safer home. From 1891 to 1942, 25.4 million people moved from northern China to Manchuria and 16.7 million returned, leaving a net transfer of 8.7 million. Rather than adapt to the unfamiliar world around them, the new villages became extensions of the old ones in China mainland, bound together by the ties of family and peasant community. Serial migration from south to north enabled social upward mobility, as former laborers and tenants invested their earnings to become landowners and start families.[7]

With the crisis-driven reclamation and cultivation of land by Han Chinese settlers, the soy frontier expanded rapidly from south to north along rivers and railroads. Soy was part of the cultural luggage settlers carried with them. Whole beans had been used in East Asia for centuries for foodstuffs in non-fermented (tofu, soy milk, okara, etc.) and fermented (soy paste, soy sauce, natto, etc.) forms. Manchurian peasants usually planted soybeans once within a three- or four-year cycle of crop rotation. They tediously cultivated the plants almost entirely by hand methods: the soil was broken in April, using a single-handled, steel-tipped plow, drawn by a mixed team of oxen, mules, or donkeys. The seed was sown and covered by hand and fertilized, if at all, with a compost of manure and soil. Since the plant matured very slowly and fertilizer was in short supply, weeds had to be removed several times through carefully turning and breaking the ground with a heavy hoe. People harvested the beans in September by pulling the plants up by the roots or cutting them with a sickle before they had fully ripened. After drying, the seeds were separated from the pods using a stone roller, dragged by a mule. Winnowing was done by throwing the mixture of beans and chaff against the wind. Once dried and separated, the soybeans were ready for household self-consumption and for market sale as a whole or, after crushing, as oil and cake.[8]

The "more-than-human" network around soy shaped peasant styles of farming that combined family self-provision and market linkages. According to a survey taken in the mid-1930s, landed property was highly concentrated, with a gradient running from the more equal south to the more unequal north. On average, the property of the biggest owners (56.8 ha) was tenfold the property of the others (5.3 ha). However, leases of nearly half of the landed property by the biggest owners alleviated the inequality (biggest owners: 33.9 ha; other owners: 4.6 ha; tenants: 6.2 ha). With the land rents paid by tenants, the biggest owners hired twice the amount of labor capacity provided by their own family members. The wage laborers came from the households of landless workers. The other owners relied predominantly on family labor, while the tenants ran pure family farms. Whereas crop selection showed some differences by farm size, the share of the acreage sown with soybeans was similar, at one-fifth of the cultivated land. The uniformity of land use reflected predominant farming styles, involving locally financed simple technology, small, but diversified business activities with a preference for low risks, and market linkages deeply embedded in family and community relations. Since the peasant mode of farming relied on small-scale technology, large farmers did not enjoy advantages due to economies of scale. The basic equipment, comprising two draft animals and a plow, was commonly available on medium-sized and even on small farms as well. Conversely, family farms with their rather intrinsically motivated workforce enjoyed a cost advantage over farms employing more extrinsically motivated wage laborers, who had to be monitored to ensure the quantity and quality of work—for instance, manual weed control in order to protect slowly maturing soybean plants.[9]

US Soy in the US-Centered Food Regime

Soy found enlarged rooms of maneuver in the US-centered food regime that evolved in the economic and political turmoil from the late 1920s to the early 1940s. The closing of the westward-moving "American frontier" in 1890 reoriented US agricultural development from the extension of European-style farming, based on nutrient mining on former prairie grasslands, to more intensive and sustainable land uses. The transition to capital-intensive farming based on fossil energy opened a window of opportunity for soy in rotation with corn. Moreover, state management of the economic and ecological crisis of US agriculture in the 1930s, namely the Great Depression and the Dust Bowl, promoted soy as a counteragent to the erosion of both farm prices and dried-up soils. Henry Ford's obsession with soy as a raw material for automobile manufacturing caused a sensation in the press but never proceeded far beyond the experimental stage. More important, the government's management of agriculture and food in World War II encouraged farmers to grow price-subsidized oilseeds for food purposes in order to save scarce tropical oils for military use.[10]

Although state support for soy was quite low in the postwar decades, making the commodities markets the main determinant of its price, rising revenues fueled domestic surpluses. The expanding oilseed crushing industry channeled soyoil to manufacturers of margarine and other foodstuffs and the residual cake to livestock feeders. The expansion of the livestock complex in connection with the diffusion of animal-based diets as well as the substitution of organic by synthetic oils in the manufacturing sector reversed the hierarchy between soyoil and soycake, positioning the latter as main product and the former as by-product. Beyond the US market, soy, wheat, and other crops served as weapons of the Western regime of "cheap food," fighting both poverty and communism with American-style development. US processors and traders supplied soycake as part of compound feed free of duties in the framework of the 1947 General Agreement on Tariffs and Trade (GATT) to Western Europe and Japan. There, livestock complexes met rising middle-class demand for meat that was valued in consumer culture as a male-gendered symbol of "wealth" and "strength." The remaining stocks of soyoil unmarketable in the domestic market were sold to food-deficient "Third World" countries in their own currencies according to the 1954 Agricultural Trade Development and Assistance Act (Public Law 480), thereby strengthening neocolonial dependency. In the "cheap food" regime, soy became an ingredient of the Western nutrition transition, combining the "meatification" and "oilification" of popular diets. Despite its invisibility to ordinary customers, soy's transatlantic and transpacific commodity webs served not only geopolitical, but also agribusiness interests. Though Cargill and other US companies rose as key players in the global soy business under the US-centered food regime, they pushed for liberalizing the protectionist framework in the crisis following the "oil shock" and the dissolution of the Bretton Woods system in 1973.[11]

The United States as a soy powerhouse dominated the world market until the 1970s, with Western Europe and Japan as main customers. After take-off in the 1930s and acceleration in the 1940s, the US soy frontier expanded rapidly from the 1950s to the 1970s and, after stagnation in the farm debt crisis of the 1980s, has continued to shift further since the 1990s (Figure 17.4). The 313-fold growth of production from 1924 to 1973 resulted mainly from the 36-fold enlargement of cultivated land devoted to soybeans, but also from the 8.7-fold rise in yields per acre. These figures indicate a predominantly

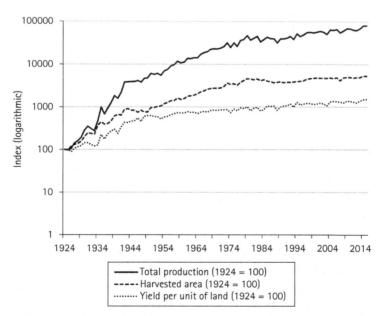

FIGURE 17.4 Soy expansion in the United States, 1924–2015. Data source: US Department of Agriculture, "National Agricultural Statistics Service,", http://www.nass.usda.gov., accessed October 1, 2019.

internal shift of the soy frontier. Though total farmland decreased, soybeans increasingly displaced grains such as oats, barley, and wheat in the Midwest and cotton in the South. Land productivity improved through the application of technologies such as high-yielding varieties, agrochemicals, and moto-mechanization.

Driving forces of the US soy expansion unfolded through the management of the crisis of Midwestern agriculture. From the mid-nineteenth century onward, the Corn Belt, covering the states of Ohio, Indiana, Illinois, Iowa, and Missouri, emerged as a specialized region for commercial corn-livestock production. The region was endowed with a mid-continental climate with cold winters and warm summers as well as former grassland soils rich in nutrients. However, overexploitation of soils and overproduction of commodities in general and in World War I in particular depressed yields and prices, thereby plunging the region's farming community into debt. Solutions to the agrarian crisis involved two intertwined crop innovations that became pillars of Midwestern agriculture from the 1930s onward: on the one hand, high-yielding hybrid corn as a key element of American-style capital-intensive farming; on the other hand, nitrogen-fixing soy deriving from Asian-style labor-intensive farming. Though the exotic plant was previously known to natural scientists, religious minorities, and Asian immigrants only, soy's evolving network established a niche in Corn Belt agriculture in the 1920s. It involved multiple actors: the US Department of Agriculture (USDA) that organized the collection of seed samples in East Asia in cooperation with agricultural colleges and experiment stations that selected location-adapted varieties and distributed them to farmers; the American Soybean Association that organized soy growers and represented their political and economic interests; and the regional oilseed crushing industry that incentivized soy production through price guarantees such as the Peoria Plan.[12]

Soy's transition from niche to mainstream in Midwestern and Southern agriculture accelerated in the 1930s and 1940s, as a set of institutional and technological developments promoted the cultivation for beans sold in the market instead of hay fed to the farm's livestock. The New Deal's Agricultural Adjustment Administration addressed the economic and ecological crisis of Midwestern and Southern agriculture through programs for setting aside corn, cotton, and other price-depressed crops and introducing soil-improving plants on eroded fields. Subsequently, the government's management of agriculture and food in World War II, struggling with the scarcity of tropical oils from Southeast Asia, supported the domestic production of oilseeds. These institutional arrangements led farmers to integrate nitrogen-fixing soybeans in rotation with nitrogen-depleting hybrid corn in their crop mix. The transition to capital-intensive technology based on fossil energy facilitated soy's entrance into farming systems in regionally different ways: in the Corn Belt, the plant profited from the moto-mechanization of corn farming, since acreage for horse feeding on tractor-equipped farms became available for cash crops and combines also operated soybeans. In the Mississippi Delta, soy, in combination with corn, rather drove the adoption of new technologies, since most cotton farms had yet to be motorized with the aid of state-subsidized credits. Within a few decades, the soy frontier expanded in the newly-labeled

"Corn-Soy Belt" and the Mississippi Valley, where infrastructure for processing and trading emerged along the waterway and railway network.[13]

Soy's integration into Midwestern and Southern farming systems shaped entrepreneurial styles of farming, combining family labor with integration into factor and product markets. Besides land and labor, technology became the crucial productive force, as depicted by the instructional film *Soybeans for Farm and Industry* from around 1940. It demonstrates the application of a multitude of tractor-drawn machines: soil preparation with the disc harrow, fertilizing with the manure distributor, sowing with the seed drill, weeding with the rotary hoe, harvesting and threshing beans with the combine, and so on. The only human being that appears on the field is the tractor driver. The film's notion of a fully mechanized one-man farm was exaggerated, since neither family labor nor hired labor disappeared. In Iowa, for instance, the average number of hired laborers per family farm even rose from 1.2 in 1950 to 1.4 in 1964, reflecting the growth of average farm size from 68 to 89 hectares. However, the film accurately foresaw the vanishing point of the ongoing transition from labor-intensive to capital-intensive farming in the Midwest and South. With the advent of large-scale machinery such as self-propelled combines, soybean farming, along with corn cropping, faced economies of scale. Iowa in the mid-1960s provides a telling case: although the acreage covered by soybeans was slightly below or above one-fifth for all classes (except for the smallest farms), the percentage of farms planting soybeans correlated positively and the number of combines per acre cropland correlated negatively with farm size. However, technological innovation was closely connected to family relations: saving money and easing labor motivated the farming families to purchase or rent machines, based on the willingness to experiment with unfamiliar technologies. On the one hand, the decision to invest in farm equipment reflected priorities of family life. Apart from the general motive of reducing bodily strain, farm women particularly welcomed machines that reduced the need to engage seasonal workers and feed them at home. On the other hand, farm mechanization changed the gendered division of labor among family members. Contrary to the women's multiple roles in agricultural production, the adoption of the fully mechanized farm model, hailing farmers and their sons as "masters" of modern technology, relegated women to the reproductive sphere. Thereby, farm enterprise and household began to disintegrate but still were connected in everyday work and life.[14]

Corn-soy farming involved experimenting not only with risky machinery, but also with even more risky agrochemicals. Though agricultural scientists, extension professionals, and farm journalists advised against fertilizing the nitrogen-fixing soybean crop, farmers challenged received wisdom by applying synthetic fertilizers in the same way as they did to corn. Moreover, pesticides in general and herbicides in particular promised an effective response to weeds as the soybean plant's deadly enemy. The herbicide 2,4-D, initially developed as a biological weapon during World War II, provided a simple and cheap tool for eliminating weeds, causing the plant to literally grow itself to death. However, excessive application of 2,4-D effectively eliminated broadleaf weeds but simultaneously created selection pressure in favor of herbicide-tolerant weeds, thereby aggravating rather than alleviating the problem. Farmers saw themselves forced to apply ever more 2,4-D and alternative herbicides developed by the chemical industry, thus rendering weed control more complex and expensive. By the 1960s, farmers were caught in a vicious cycle of intended actions to raise the farming system's productivity and nature's unintended reactions. However, they embraced herbicides and experimented from day to day to shape their use in order to avoid the effort and expenses associated with mechanical weed control.[15]

Brazilian Soy in the WTO-Centered Food Regime

Soy's alliances multiplied after the economic crisis of the 1970s and the political reactions to it, characterized by the amalgamation of elements of old and new food regimes. While maintaining a central position, the United States found itself in a more polycentric setting, co-determined by transnational corporations (TNCs) and the Cairns group of export-oriented emerging countries. Their neoliberal agenda regarding agricultural world trade materialized in the Uruguay round of the GATT from 1986 onward, institutionalized by the World Trade Organization (WTO) in 1995. New Agricultural Countries (NACs) from South America challenged the US dominance in the global soy market, shaken by a supply crisis due to weather-induced harvest failures, massive purchases by the USSR, and a US trade embargo in 1973. In Brazil, soy played a key role in the ambitious project of "conservative modernization," implemented by the military regime in the mid-1960s for fiscal and geopolitical reasons. State-led development programs expanded the national agribusiness from the core regions in the very south of the country to more peripheral areas in northern direction, where near-natural biomes were converted into "agricultural deserts." Political and economic restructuring in the late 1980s and early 1990s according to the neoliberal agenda in the Mercosur free-trade zone permitted TNCs to acquire large tracts of the soy complex. The "ABCD-companies" (Archer Daniels Midland, Bunge, Cargill, and Dreyfus), which controlled three-quarters of the world market of grains and oilseeds, adopted a highly flexible global business model based on soy as a standardized commodity, regardless of origin and quality. Transnational agribusinesses and export-taxing state governments in South America profited from the price-induced global boom of soycake from the 1990s onward, driven by demand from livestock complexes in other world regions: in reunified Europe, where the mad cow disease provoked the shift from animal-based to plant-based feed, and in post-reform China, where the emerging urban middle classes adopted prestigious diets rich in meat. Mounting surpluses of soyoil were processed to biofuels, thereby enabling agribusiness corporations to flexibly switch between different sources of capital accumulation. However, the dominating commodity web around "food from nowhere," based on cheap resources such as soycake and soyoil, faced counter-movements in favor of "food from somewhere," hailing whole soybeans as alternative to the "neoliberal diet." "Green-capitalist" supermarkets took advantage of this tension by stretching their strategies of capital accumulation to both market segments, thereby exploiting the dietary preferences of low- as well as high-income classes.[16]

Among the countries of the South American "soylandia," Brazil emerged as the leading producer and exporter. The Brazilian soy expansion unfolded in two bursts of growth: the first one from the 1960s to the 1970s, driven by state-led development and an international supply crisis of US soy, and the second one from the 1990s onward, reflecting neoliberalism as well as rising European and Chinese demand (Figure 17.5). The expansion of production by a factor of 320 from 1961 to 2014 mainly resulted from the 126-fold extension of the soybean area, for the most part through conversion of near-natural savannah grasslands and forests (*cerrado*). Meanwhile, the 2.5-fold rise in yields per land unit, accomplished through more productive technology adapted to (sub-)tropical conditions, played a minor, though increasingly important, role. These figures indicate a flexible mode of frontier expansion, combining external and internal shifts.

Land, labor, and technology for the early Brazilian soy expansion were mobilized through "conservative modernization" by the military regime, backed by foreign investments, in order to fix fiscal, geopolitical, and social concerns: gaining foreign currency for import substitution industrialization through agricultural exports as well as colonizing "empty" spaces in the vast territory by impoverished and riotous settlers from populous regions. After US and Japanese soybean varieties had entered mixed

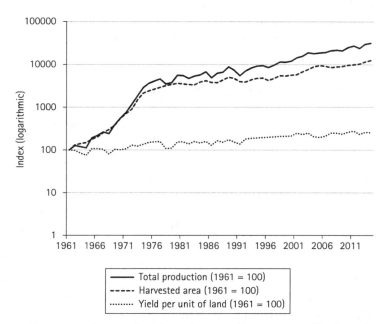

FIGURE 17.5 Soy expansion in Brazil, 1961–2014. Data source: Food and Agriculture Organization, "Faostat."

farming systems in the very south of the country by the 1960s, the savannah biome in the center-west region moved into the technocratic planners' focus from the 1970s onward. According to the strategic articulation of public and private agendas, domestic and foreign capital invested in the mobilization of productive resources: newly constructed highway connections to ports cross-cut the Amazonian rainforest in south-north direction; commercial farms run by white immigrants from southern states converted vast tracts of "virgin lands"; and the public research agency Embrapa in cooperation with US universities developed site-specific productive technologies such as soybean varieties adapted to acid soils, tropical climate, and smaller latitude (e.g., FT Cristalina). As the shifting soy frontier crossed boundaries between the moderate South and the tropical Midwest, moving from Rio Grande do Sul though Paraná, Mato Grosso do Sul, and Goiás to Mato Grosso, legal and illegal land grabbing displaced or exterminated Indigenous communities as well as animal and plant species, thereby impoverishing socio-natural diversity.[17]

Economic and political instability in the 1980s, accompanied by hyperinflation and the transition from military dictatorship to parliamentary democracy, weakened state-led development programs and opened the country for transnational agrobusiness. Neoliberal forces, unleashed by both right-wing and left-wing governments, pushed forward the Brazilian soy frontier since the 1990s: former public domains (rural planning, agricultural research, farm credit, etc.) were subordinated to well-organized agribusiness interests, privileging cash crop export to distant markets as source of corporate profits and state revenues. The socio-natural exploitation of savannah and rainforest biomes, radicalized through substitution of the biotechnological package for farm labor, threatened both human and non-human habitats. The mass media mystified agribusiness as expression of the "common interest," which delegitimized criticism to social and environmental injustice.[18]

While the state-led frontier expansion in Mato Grosso had opened rooms of maneuver for entrepreneurial styles of farming by market-oriented settler families with strong rural ties, a financial-capitalist approach to farming advanced in the slipstream of agro-neoliberalism. In response to shifting economies of scale, investors created "network firms" that pooled financial capital from different sources, leased huge tracts of land cultivated by subcontractors, and split returns among themselves. The capitalist mode of "farming without farmers" depended on factor and product markets, but it was disconnected from social ties of family and neighborhood as well as from metabolic cycles of regional ecosystems. Typically, agro-capitalists hired farm managers or outsourced cultivation to subcontractors while living with their families in distant towns. Similar to the mindset of the European settlers in nineteenth-century North America, both entrepreneurial and capitalist soy croppers shared a sort of "frontier mentality," obsessed with replacing "chaotic wilderness" through "well-ordered civilization." Large-scale machinery conquered the fields both directly, through application of machine power, and indirectly, through devices for applying agrochemicals. Moto-mechanization of soy farming involved strong scale effects: both the share of farms growing soybeans and the acreage covered by soybeans were positively correlated with farm size in the 2000s.

Conversely, the number of combines per unit of cropland was negatively correlated. In short, the larger the farm, the higher the machinery's efficiency—and the bigger soy's share. As a consequence, the farm concentration in soy farming, and hence income inequality, progressed faster than in other branches of agriculture.[19]

Applications of moto-mechanical and agrochemical high-technology on soy fields went hand in hand. Soy's general vulnerability to weeds during its early growth phase was particularly pronounced in the savannah and rainforest biomes, since monocultures and soy-grain rotations in combination with the tropical climate opened up niches for a multitude of weeds. Therefore, most farmers welcomed the introduction of herbicide-tolerant transgenic soy by the US biotech company Monsanto in 1996, despite the loss of their property rights to seeds. Monsanto's seeds were genetically manipulated in order to insert resistance to glyphosate, an efficient plant killer less toxic than most other herbicides. Monsanto's technological package of the glyphosate Roundup and glyphosate-tolerant Roundup Ready (RR) seeds, softening pressure of weeds, in combination with low- and no-tillage cultivation, reducing soil erosion, simplified and cheapened soy farming. Through illegal transfer from neighboring countries and legalization in Brazil in 2005, RR seeds rapidly conquered the farmland devoted to soy. In contrast to marketing slogans that highlighted simplicity and cheapness, transgenic soy accelerated the "metabolic rift" between human actions and non-human reactions. What worried soy farmers most was the appearance of glyphosate-tolerant "superweeds" on their fields, created through genetic and epigenetic mutations due to strong selection pressure for resistance among wild plants from over-application of glyphosate. Combating "superweeds" such as Palmer amaranth ('pigweed') through application of more and stronger herbicides made soy farming more troublesome and costly. The agrochemical industry reacted to this shift of demand by supplying mixtures of glyphosate and 2,4-D for eliminating both conventional and glyphosate-tolerant weeds. Caught in the "transgenic treadmill," soy farmers did not apply less herbicides—as promised by the biotech industry—but even higher doses.[20]

Brazil's soy expansion not only was a burden on nature, leading to deforestation, greenhouse gas emission, biodiversity loss, soil erosion, and water pollution, but also affected rural society. What undermined livelihoods most was the transfer of collective land assets of rural communities into individual property of agribusiness enterprises. As farmland became a highly valued commodity, capital-rich commercial farms, mostly owned by farmers of European or US descent, accumulated it at the expense of Indigenous and peasant communities that lacked registered property rights. Besides escalating prices in the booming land market, extra-economic pressures drove the displacement of small landowners as well: social isolation due to enclosure by large soy farms pressed peasants to abandon their land; collateral damage of agro-industrial farming such as agrochemical drifts harmed neighboring people as well as their livestock and crops; cases of brute violence by ranchers and soy planters, including murders, were documented in large number. Displaced peasants (*campesinos*) partly resorted to rural-urban migration to make a living; others stayed in the countryside, often lacking a roof over their heads, as underpaid wage laborers or even slave-like workers in labor-intensive branches of agriculture; and yet others joined the Landless Workers' Movement, which integrated rural emigrants into communities oriented toward agroecological farming.[21]

Besides the commodification of land that led to vast concentration, the replacement of labor through labor-saving technology shook rural society as well. While production on Brazilian soy farms nearly tripled between 1985 and 2004, employment fell by more than three-quarters, from 1.7 million to 335,000 workers. Most employment opportunities in the soy complex emerged off-farm in upstream and downstream agribusinesses. Soy expansion impacted on working and living conditions not only quantitatively, but also qualitatively. The decimated rural labor force was segmented into a majority of underpaid and unskilled helpers for laying out new fields and a minority of well-paid and skilled crafters for operating the technical devices. While employees in the upper segment only worked on the farm and lived in nearby cities with good infrastructure, workers in the lower segment regularly faced dire conditions such as low wages, dirty dwellings, and social isolation. Wages amounted to only 2.6 percent of total costs of soy production in Brazil around 2000, compared to 5.0 percent in the United States. However, soy farming was less susceptible to unfree labor than sugar cane production or cattle ranching, since capital-intensive soy farming was labor-extensive, on the one hand. On the other hand, the exclusion of employers included in the "dirty list of slave labor" from public subsidies acted as a deterrent; only 10 out of 583 listed farms in 2014 produced soy. Thus, soy expansion brought about unfree labor indirectly, through dismissal of laborers who ended up in slave-like relations in other agricultural branches, rather than directly, through on-farm exploitation.[22]

Soy's Multiple Movements under Global Capitalism

Following soy as a commodity through time and space, both from an anthropocentric perspective on food regimes and from a postanthropocentric perspective on "more-than-human" networks, reveals multiple movements. During the twentieth century, soy expanded externally, internally, and flexibly at regional commodity frontiers, thereby advancing from the margins to the cores of global agro-food chains. As a standardized commodity, it became a major source of revenue, especially for transnational corporations and export-taxing nation states. However, soy-based globalization also placed a heavy burden on society and nature. Soy's pathways emerged within the "Great Transformation" of global capitalism and its aftermaths, involving a series of double movements of market liberalization and state-led protection. The initial double movement comprised the dis-embedding of the "self-regulating market" from society through liberal nation states from the mid-nineteenth century onward and its re-embedding during the Great Depression after 1929 through protective regimes as diverse as Soviet Bolshevism, the US New Deal, and German Fascism. Another double movement emerged around the marketization wave according to the neoliberal agenda from the 1980s onward and its progressive and reactionary counter-movements following the post-2007 Great Recession.[23]

Soy's emergence as a commodity was driven by a series of regimes and transitions of agro-food capitalism. Marketization integral to the British-centered food regime paved the way for soy to enter the global stage. Japanese trading corporations met the demand of European industrial classes for overseas resources through supplying cheap soy from the externally expanding Manchurian frontier. Among the counter-movements to classical-liberal capitalism–with Nazi Germany promoting soy as a cornerstone of food autarky—the United States and the USSR rose to hegemons of bipolar food regimes in the Cold War. Cheap soy from the internally expanding frontier in the US Midwest and South served as a weapon of American-style development in Western Europe, Japan, and parts of the "Third World." Transnational agribusinesses in coalition with export-oriented NACs undermined state-organized capitalism and enforced another wave of marketization, culminating in the WTO-centered food regime. Cheap soy from the flexibly—both externally and internally—expanding frontier in South America challenged US dominance in global markets, especially in reunified Europe and post-reform China. Simultaneously, soy expansion in near-natural biomes disrupted human and non-human habitats and provided counter-movements to neoliberal hegemony—for instance, victims of agrochemical drifts lodging claims against soy farmers and throwing herbicide-resistant "superweeds" into their fields.[24]

Soy not only was driven by multiple (counter-)movements, but also acted as a driver of state and corporate projects of agro-food globalization. Soy derived its crucial strength in "more-than-human" networks from the flexibility as both fat- and protein-supplying commodity, enabling quick adaptations to changing market situations. In the first food regime, Manchurian soyoil switched from a by-product of regional soycake trade to a main product for the European market. Attempts to exploit the residual cake succeeded in the second food regime, when soy-based compound feed from the United States emerged as a main product for overseas markets. In the third food regime, when soy-exporting NACs successfully competed for markets for soycake as animal feed, the food and biofuels industries exploited the residual oil. Besides soy's strengths, its weaknesses affected the crop's commodification as well. Most important, the plant's vulnerability to weeds during early maturation paved the way for technological optimization of commercial soy farming: from machinery and herbicides for mechanical and chemical weed control to the biotechnological package around transgenic seeds, inappropriately promoted as an easy and cheap way to raise profitability.

However, soy's versatility not only enabled it to serve key actors of the prevailing food regime, but also to ally with countervailing forces. For instance, the counter-culture to Western lifestyles in the late 1960s and early 1970s, represented by Frances Moore Lappé's manifest *Diet for a Small Planet* of 1971, hailed vegetarian soyfoods as an alternative to meat-rich diets. Soy-oriented utopias by the hippie culture were not only successors of earlier alternatives such as the dietary doctrines of the Seventh-day

Adventists in the late nineteenth century, but also forerunners of later alternatives such as middle-class vegetarianism in the early twenty-first century. These examples highlight soy's considerable agency within "more-than-human" webs that reached beyond state and corporate projects. The "soy paradox"—the crop's dual role as both protagonist and antagonist of the prevailing food regime—indicates alternative routes of soy-based agro-food globalization. To what extent the "Soyacene" and its severe burden on society and nature can be countered by movements envisioning a more responsible way of connecting with soy in the face of the multiple (climate, health, energy, etc.) crises in the twenty-first century remains to be seen.[25]

Notes

* The author would like to thank the editor of this handbook, an anonymous reviewer, and his collaborators in the research project SoyChange.
1. Apart from some precursors, the making of soy as a global commodity only recently gained attention in social sciences and humanities. Historical approaches have been complemented by the efforts of anthropologists, sociologists, geographers, economists, and political scientists: Christine M. Du Bois, Chee-Beng Tan, and Sidney Mintz, eds., *The World of Soy* (Urbana: University of Illinois Press, 2008); Richa Kumar, *Rethinking Revolutions: Soyabean, Choupals, and the Changing Countryside in Central India* (New Delhi: Oxford University Press, 2016); Pablo Lapegna, *Soybeans and Power: Genetically Modified Crops, Environmental Politics, and Social Movements in Argentina* (Oxford: Oxford University Press, 2016); Mariano Turzi, *The Political Economy of Agricultural Booms: Managing Soybean Production in Argentina, Brazil, and Paraguay* (Cham: Palgrave Macmillan, 2017); Matthew Roth, *Magic Bean: The Rise of Soy in America* (Lawrence: University Press of Kansas, 2018); Christine M. Du Bois, *The Story of Soy* (London: Reaktion Books, 2018); Jia-Chen Fu, *The Other Milk: Reinventing Soy in Republican China* (Seattle: University of Washington Press, 2018); Robert Hafner, *Environmental Justice and Soy Agribusiness* (New York: Routledge, 2018); Kregg Hetherington, *The Government of Beans: Regulating Life in the Age of Monocrops* (Durham, NC: Duke University Press, 2020); Amalia Leguizamón, *Seeds of Power: Environmental Injustice and Genetically Modified Soybeans in Argentina* (Durham, NC: Duke University Press, 2020); Claiton M. da Silva and Claudio de Majo, eds., *The Age of the Soybean. An Environmental History of Soy during the Great Acceleration* (Winwick: White Horse Press, 2022); Matilda Baraibar and Lisa Deutsch, *The Soybean through World History: Lessons for Sustainable Agrofood Systems* (London: Routledge, 2023); Ines Prodöhl, *Globalizing the Soybean: Fat, Feed, and Sometimes Food, c. 1900–1950* (London: Routledge, 2023).
2. Friedrich Haberlandt, *Die Sojabohne: Ergebnisse der Studien und Versuche über die Anbauwürdigkeit dieser neu einzuführenden Culturpflanze* (Wien: Carl Gerold's Sohn, 1878); Claiton M. da Silva and Claudio de Majo, "Towards the Soyacene: Narratives for an Environmental History of Soy in Latin America's Southern Cone," *HALAC—Historia Ambiental, Latinoamericana y Caribeña* 11, no. 1 (2021): 329–356; data source: Lois B. Bacon and Friedrich C. Schloemer, *World Trade in Agricultural Products: Its Growth, Its Crisis, and the New Trade Policies* (Rome: International Institute of Agriculture, 1940), 510; Food and Agriculture Organization, "Faostat," http://www.fao.org/faostat, accessed February 1, 2020.

3. Philip McMichael, *Food Regimes and Agrarian Questions* (Halifax, Nova Scotia: Fernwood, 2013); Jason W. Moore, *Capitalism in the Web of Life: Ecology and the Accumulation of Capital* (London: Verso, 2015); Sven Beckert, Ulbe Bosma, Mindi Schneider, and Eric Vanhaute, "Commodity Frontiers and the Transformation of the Global Countryside: A Research Agenda," *Journal of Global History* 16, no. 3 (2021): 435–450.
4. Christine M. Du Bois and Sidney Mintz, "Soy," in *Encyclopedia of Food and Culture*, ed. Solomon H. Katz (New York: Charles Scribner's Sons, 2003), 3:322–326; Ernst Langthaler, "The Soy Paradox: The Western Nutrition Transition Revisited, 1950–2010," *Global Environment* 11, no. 1 (2018): 79–104; Jan Douwe van der Ploeg, *The New Peasantries: Rural Development in Times of Globalization*, 2nd ed. (London: Routledge, 2018).
5. Ernst Langthaler, "Broadening and Deepening: Soy Expansions in a World-Historical Perspective," *HALAC—Historia Ambiental, Latinoamericana y Caribeña* 10, no. 1 (2020): 244–77; Ernst Langthaler, "Soy Expansions: China, the USA and Brazil in Comparison," in *Commodity Chains and Labor Relations*, ed. Andrea Komlosy and Goran Musić (Leiden: Brill, 2021), 55–80; Ernst Langthaler, "Great Accelerations: Soy and Its Global Trade Network, 1950–2020," in *The Age of the Soybean. An Environmental History of Soy during the Great Acceleration*, ed. Claiton M. da Silva and Claudio de Majo (Winwick: White Horse Press, 2022), 65–90.
6. Kenneth Pomeranz, *The Great Divergence: China, Europe, and the Making of the Modern World Economy* (Princeton, NJ: Princeton University Press, 2009); James Reardon-Anderson, *Reluctant Pioneers: China's Expansion Northward, 1644–1937* (Stanford, CA: Stanford University Press, 2005), 171–251; David Wolff, "Bean There: Toward a Soy-Based History of North East Asia," *South Atlantic Quarterly* 99, no. 1 (2000): 241–252; Ines Prodöhl, "Versatile and Cheap: A Global History of Soy in the First Half of the Twentieth Century," *Journal of Global History* 8, no. 3 (2013): 461–82; Hiromi Mizuno and Ines Prodöhl, "Mitsui Bussan and the Manchurian Soybean Trade: Geopolitics and Economic Strategies in China's Northeast, ca. 1870s–1920s," *Business History* 61 (2019): 1–22; Ernst Langthaler, "The Great Depression as Great Transformation? Global Food Regime Crisis and (Inter-National Transition Pathways, 1925–39," in *Agriculture and the Great Depression. The Rural Crisis of the 1930s in Europe and the Americas*, ed. Gérard Béaur and Francesco Chiapparino (London: Routledge, 2023): 21–38.
7. Reardon-Anderson, *Reluctant Pioneers*, 127–59; Thomas R. Gottschang and Diana Lary, *Swallows and Settlers: The Great Migration from North China to Manchuria* (Ann Arbor: University of Michigan Press, 2000), 43–68; Mizuno and Prodöhl, "Mitsui Bussan and the Manchurian Soybean Trade."
8. Reardon-Anderson, *Reluctant Pioneers*, 179–188; Imperial Maritime Customs, *The Soya Bean of Manchuria* (Shanghai: Inspectorate General of Customs, 1911), 4–5.
9. Reardon-Anderson, *Reluctant Pioneers*, 218–242.
10. Prodöhl, "Versatile and Cheap"; Roth, *Magic Bean*, 86–199.
11. Ray A. Goldberg, *Agribusiness Coordination: A Systems Approach to the Wheat, Soybean, and Florida Orange Economies* (Cambridge, MA: Harvard University Press, 1968), 103–147; Bill Winders, *The Politics of Food Supply: U.S. Agricultural Policy in the World Economy* (New Haven, CT: Yale University Press, 2009), 31–158; Langthaler, "The Soy Paradox."
12. See R. S. Loomis, D. J. Connor, and Kenneth G. Cassman, *Crop Ecology: Productivity and Management in Agricultural Systems*, 2nd ed. (Cambridge: Cambridge University Press, 2011), 459–470; John C. Hudson, *Making the Corn Belt: A Geographical History of*

Middle-Western Agriculture (Bloomington: Indiana University Press, 1994), 151–72; Du Bois, *The Story of Soy*, 53–69; Roth, *Magic Bean*, 15–40; Prodöhl, *Globalizing the Soybean*, 138–150.

13. See Joseph Leslie Anderson, *Industrializing the Corn Belt: Agriculture, Technology, and Environment, 1945-1972* (DeKalb: Northern Illinois University Press, 2009), 152–167; Jeannie M. Whayne, *A New Plantation South: Land, Labor, and Federal Favor in Twentieth-Century Arkansas* (Charlottesville: University Press of Virginia, 1996), 157–175; Ines Prodöhl, "From Dinner to Dynamite: Fats and Oils in Wartime America," *Global Food History* 2, no. 1 (2016): 31–50.

14. Anderson, *Industrializing the Corn Belt*, 152–90; Jane H. Adams, *The Transformation of Rural Life: Southern Illinois, 1890-1990* (Chapel Hill: University of North Carolina Press, 1994), 243–253; film source: "Soybeans for Farm and Industry," Wisconsin Historical Society, International Harvester Company Film Collection, AC 741, http://archive.org/details/0914_Soybeans_for_Farm_and_Industry_00_21_44_29, accessed October 1, 2019; data source: US Bureau of the Census, *Census of Agriculture 1964—Iowa* (Washington, DC: US Government Printing Office, 1967).

15. Anderson, *Industrializing the Corn Belt*, 33–63.

16. Antonio Augusto Rossoto Ioris, *Agribusiness and the Neoliberal Food System in Brazil: Frontiers and Fissures of Agro-Neoliberalism* (London: Routledge, 2018), Herbert S. Klein and Francisco Vidal Luna, *Feeding the World: Brazil's Transformation into a Modern Agricultural Economy* (Cambridge: Cambridge University Press, 2019), 405–13; Turzi, *The Political Economy of Agricultural Booms*, 1–77; Gerardo Otero, *The Neoliberal Diet: Healthy Profits, Unhealthy People* (Austin: University of Texas Press, 2018), 26–57; Matilda Baraibar Norberg, *The Political Economy of Agrarian Change in Latin America: Argentina, Paraguay and Uruguay* (Cham, Switzerland: Palgrave Macmillan, 2019), 117–49; Maria Eugenia Giraudo, "Taxing the 'Crop of the Century': The Role of Institutions in Governing the Soy Boom in South America," *Globalizations* 65, no. 1 (2020): 1–17.

17. Philip F. Warnken, *The Development and Growth of the Soybean Industry in Brazil* (Ames: Iowa State University Press, 1999); Loomis, Connor, and Cassman, *Crop Ecology*, 476–82; Claiton M. da Silva, "Between Fenix and Ceres: The Great Acceleration and the Agricultural Frontier in the Brazilian Cerrado," *Varia Historia* 34, no. 65 (2018): 409–44; Cassiano de Brito Rocha, Claudio de Majo, and Sandro Dutra e Silva, "A Geo-historical Analysis of Expanding Soybean Frontiers in the Brazilian Cerrado" *HALAC—Historia Ambiental, Latinoamericana y Caribeña* 12, no. 2 (2022): 117–149.

18. Ioris, *Agribusiness and the Neoliberal Food System in Brazil*, 78–170; Klein and Luna, *Feeding the World*, 232–72.

19. Andrew Ofstehage, "Farming Is Easy, Becoming Brazilian Is Hard: North American Soy Farmers' Social Values of Production, Work and Land in Soylandia," *Journal of Peasant Studies* 43, no. 2 (2015): 442–460; Turzi, *The Political Economy of Agricultural Booms*, 83–97; Mateo Mier y Terán Giménez Cacho, "Soybean Agri-Food Systems Dynamics and the Diversity of Farming Styles on the Agricultural Frontier in Mato Grosso, Brazil," *Journal of Peasant Studies* 43, no. 2 (2015): 419–441; Baraibar Norberg, *The Political Economy of Agrarian Change in Latin America*, 6–21; data source: Instituto Brasileiro de Geografia e Estatística, *Censo Agropecuário 2006: Brasil, Grandes Regiões e Unidades da Federação* (Rio de Janeiro: IBGE, 2012), tab. 1.2.14, 1.2.23, 1.6.73.

20. Du Bois, *The Story of Soy*, 116–172; Lapegna, *Soybeans and Power*, 25–51; Katarzyna O. Beilin and Sainath Suryanarayanan, "The War Between Amaranth and Soy," *Environmental Humanities* 9, no. 2 (2017): 204–229.
21. Turzi, *The Political Economy of Agricultural Booms*, 91–97; Ioris, *Agribusiness and the Neoliberal Food System in Brazil*, 140–170.
22. Mamerto Pérez, Timothy A. Wise, and Sergio Schlesinger, eds., *The Promise and the Perils of Agricultural Trade Liberalization: Lessons from Latin America* (Washington, DC: Washington Office on Latin America, 2008); Raj Patel, *Stuffed and Starved: Markets, Power and the Hidden Battle for the World Food System* (London: Portobello Books, 2008), 204–12; Rachael D. Garrett and Lisa L. Rausch, "Green for Gold: Social and Ecological Tradeoffs Influencing the Sustainability of the Brazilian Soy Industry," *Journal of Peasant Studies* 43, no. 2 (2016): 461–493.
23. Karl Polanyi, *The Great Transformation: The Political and Economic Origins of Our Time* (Boston: Beacon Press, 2010); Ernst Langthaler and Elke Schüßler, "Commodity Studies with Polanyi: Disembedding and Re-Embedding Labour and Land in Contemporary Capitalism," *Österreichische Zeitschrift für Soziologie* 44, no. 2 (2019): 209–223.
24. Joachim Drews, *Die "Nazi-Bohne": Anbau, Verwendung und Auswirkung der Sojabohne im Deutschen Reich und Südosteuropa (1933–1945)* (Münster: Lit-Verlag, 2004); Prodöhl, *Globalizing the Soybean*, 97–130; Beilin and Suryanarayanan, "The War between Amaranth and Soy"; Karin Fischer and Ernst Langthaler, "Soy Expansion and Countermovements in the Global South: A Polanyian Perspective," in *Capitalism in Transformation*, ed. Roland Atzmüller et al. (Cheltenham: Edward Elgar, 2019), 212–227.
25. Frances Moore Lappé, *Diet for a Small Planet* (New York: Ballantine Books, 2011); Warren Belasco, "Food and Social Movements," in *The Oxford Handbook of Food History*, ed. Jeffrey M. Pilcher (Oxford: Oxford University Press, 2012), 481–498; Langthaler, "The Soy Paradox."

Bibliography

Baraibar, Matilda, and Lisa Deutsch. *The Soybean through World History: Lessons for Sustainable Agrofood Systems*. London: Routledge, 2023.

da Silva, Claiton M., and Claudio de Majo, eds. *The Age of the Soybean. An Environmental History of Soy during the Great Acceleration*. Winwick: White Horse Press, 2022.

Du Bois, Christine M. *The Story of Soy*. London: Reaktion Books, 2018.

Du Bois, Christine M., Chee-Beng Tan, and Sidney Mintz, eds. *The World of Soy*. Urbana: University of Illinois Press, 2008.

Hetherington, Kregg. *The Government of Beans: Regulating Life in the Age of Monocrops*. Durham, NC: Duke University Press, 2020.

Ioris, Antonio Augusto Rossoto. *Agribusiness and the Neoliberal Food System in Brazil: Frontiers and Fissures of Agro-Neoliberalism*. New York: Routledge, 2018.

Kumar, Richa. *Rethinking Revolutions: Soyabean, Choupals, and the Changing Countryside in Central India*. New Delhi, India: Oxford University Press, 2016.

Langthaler, Ernst. "Soy Expansions: China, the USA and Brazil in Comparison." In *Commodity Chains and Labor Relations*, edited by Andrea Komlosy and Goran Music, 55–80. Leiden: Brill, 2021.

Langthaler, Ernst. "The Soy Paradox: The Western Nutrition Transition Revisited, 1950–2010." Global Environment 11, no. 1 (2018): 79–104.

Lapegna, Pablo. *Soybeans and Power: Genetically Modified Crops, Environmental Politics, and Social Movements in Argentina*. Oxford: Oxford University Press, 2016.

Leguizamón, Amalia. *Seeds of Power: Environmental Injustice and Genetically Modified Soybeans in Argentina*. Durham, NC: Duke University Press, 2020.

Prodöhl, Ines. *Globalizing the Soybean: Fat, Feed, and Sometimes Food, c. 1900–1950*. London: Routledge, 2023.

Roth, Matthew. *Magic Bean: The Rise of Soy in America*. Lawrence: University Press of Kansas, 2018.

Turzi, Mariano. *The Political Economy of Agricultural Booms: Managing Soybean Production in Argentina, Brazil, and Paraguay*: Cham, Switzerland: Palgrave Macmillan, 2017.

CHAPTER 18

SUGAR

SUZANNE MOON

The cultivation of sugar as a global commodity has had profound consequences for the lives of those who labor to grow and process it, for the environments in which it is grown, and for the health of human consumers. Sugar's cultivation stretches back to antiquity, and its abundant use in medicine, food, livestock feed, and fuel has embedded it deeply in human societies. Global sugar production currently stands at roughly 181 million metric tons annually from both cane and sugar beets, a relatively stable number (plus or minus 10 mt) since the turn of the twenty-first century.[1] It is among the most productive of crops in terms of yield per hectare in the world, thanks to centuries of experimentation. Demand continues to grow, especially in countries experiencing economic growth, with annual global demand at 175 million metric tons.[2] Efforts to expand the uses of sugar for fuel production and electricity co-generation help to maintain already extraordinary levels of demand for this commodity.[3]

Sugar's present-day ubiquity makes it seem mundane and its growth inevitable. Over the last five hundred years, it transitioned from a rare medicine and luxury item to an indispensable consumer good. Yet the ways that sugar is taken for granted can obscure the extraordinary efforts it took over the long term to create the global system of sugar production and the ongoing efforts required to maintain it. The history of sugar cultivation and production offers us dual interpretive perspectives. Looked at in one way, the history of sugar production is one in which the mutual development of sugar growing and wider systems of labor, environmental use, and scientific and technological development stabilized, for better or worse, resulting in the establishment of a complexly interconnected, and by some measures, highly efficient system of agricultural production.

But a gestalt shift offers us a different and telling perspective—that of sugar's fragility. Recent work on the history of sugar production highlights sugar's perpetual vulnerabilities to labor disruption, to environmental problems, and to changing economic conditions. This perspective highlights the diverse and interconnected social, agricultural, environmental work performed throughout sugar's history to both make and maintain sugar as a viable global commodity. Establishing systems of industrial-scale sugar production simultaneously created fierce systemic problems with maintenance, as producers cyclically solved, and then created, new forms of social, economic, and environmental problems. Although few scholars explicitly use the concept of maintenance in their studies of sugar, it nevertheless allows us to understand the global system of sugar production less as a finished accomplishment than as an ongoing challenge. Thinking of global sugar production in terms of maintenance allows us to unite the two interpretive approaches above of solidity and fragility, by bringing to the fore the constant work and diverse forms of maintenance on which the viability of the system of sugar production rest.

Growing Cane and Making Sugar

The social history of sugar cane production cannot be disentangled from the natural characteristics of the plant and the physical sites of production. Yet it is important not to fall prey to deterministic narratives of its history. Although approaches to growing and processing sugar cane were certainly limited by the nature of the plants and the sites of cultivation, diverse methods developed over time and place. Sugar was indeed co-produced with the natural environment, the shape of markets, and the social organization of societies.[4]

Sugar cane (*Saccharum officinarum*) was first cultivated in New Guinea. In prehistoric times sugar was transported great distances, with cultivation subsequently taken up in Africa, South Asia, Southeast Asia, and China. It has since spread around the world to subtropical and tropical areas where water availability and warm temperatures make its cultivation possible.[5] Although the vast majority of current worldwide production is grown on a large scale using industrialized processes, cultivators working on a small scale continue to thrive in some parts of the world, including Africa and India.

Several natural characteristics of sugar cane have significant impacts on the human and natural context of its cultivation. It is a demanding crop in terms of soil nutrients, depleting soils on which it is grown if not heavily fertilized, and it requires considerable amounts of water.[6] Although it varies by variety, sugar cane usually requires a lengthy growing season of at least eleven months. Left on its own, sugar can "ratoon," or regrow from the roots after harvest, although ratooned fields generally need to be entirely replanted after two years due to declining yields.[7] Continuous cane cultivation can therefore only work successfully when the land is fertilized regularly, usually through organic or synthetic fertilizers, or plant rotation, and provided with ample water, timed properly across a long growing season.

The natural characteristic most consequential for sugar's social history is the fact that once harvested, the amount of sucrose available for extraction declines precipitately in a brief time. Harvesters generally have no more than forty-eight hours to cut the cane and get it into the milling process.[8] Harvest and processing is therefore frantic, non-stop, and extraordinarily labor-intensive. After being harvested, the cane has to be crushed in a rolling mill, and the liquid carefully evaporated to extract and crystallize the sugar.

As the scale of production grew from the early modern through the modern period, so too did the growth of harsh, compelled labor regimes including but not limited to slave labor, to undertake the difficult, fast-paced work required to bring in a successful crop. Sugar cane cultivation, whether on a small or large scale, places great demands on water and soil and requires intense labor, requirements that create innate vulnerabilities that growers had to manage. Large-scale production, especially in those places where planters used exploitative labor practices to address these natural dilemmas, produced enduring social tensions, which themselves constituted a new form of vulnerability in sugar production.

Labor

The history of sugar production has been closely associated with compulsory labor. European sugar plantations in the Caribbean, Brazil, the United States mainland, and elsewhere relied on a constant influx of African slave laborers to make sugar production viable.[9] The reasons for this may seem obvious—work on sugar plantations was backbreaking and during harvest operated around the clock. Even when slavery was not used, laboring on sugar plantations was undesirable work, to say the least. Records of runaway slaves and indentured workers, as well as globally consequential slave rebellions, abound in the literature. It is a commonplace to ascribe this link between compulsion to the growing demand from, and thus profitability of, changing sugar markets, especially between the eighteenth and twentieth centuries. Yet the Atlantic plantation model was only one approach to devising profitable systems of labor.[10] To understand better the place of compelled labor in the history of sugar cane production, it is helpful to first explore the smallholder practices in which the labor compulsion common to estates was largely much reduced, or even absent.

A case in point is the smallholder sugar production in China.[11] Sugar cane cultivation in the southern areas of China expanded during the Tang Dynasty (618–907 CE) because of the upsurge of Buddhism, as sugar was an object of both medical and ritual significance in Buddhist practice. By the Song dynasty, a maritime trade in sugar had evolved, including both refined white sugar and cheaper brown sugars being exported regularly to Southeast Asia and later to Japan.[12] Sugar cultivation and processing was performed by peasant farming families with holdings generally of no more than a few hectares, many of whom were also engaged in subsistence farming. In the Pearl Delta region, peasant sugar cane cultivation continued to expand into the nineteenth century.[13]

Mazumdar shows that officials in the Yuan period (1279–1368) wrote and used instructional manuals to promote good agricultural practices among farmers. They stressed such labor-intensive practices as fertilization and crop rotation, intensive weeding, and transplantation of seedlings from cane nurseries to fields, demonstrating that peasant production in China was subject to constant efforts to improve yields and farmer incomes.[14] Most labor was provided by farm families and day laborers, with women handling transplantation and weeding and men and hired hands handling field preparation, irrigation, harvest, and processing. Families typically balanced labor requirements by practicing ratooning for at least two years after the first crop, making less frequent the effort involved in planting. Likewise, rotating crops with bananas, as was common in the Pearl River Delta, maintained the soil and saved labor. Mazumdar estimates that two men (along with female family members and occasional day laborers) would be sufficient to grow and harvest sugar cane on a field of 15 *mu* (roughly 1 hectare of land). For Chinese farmers as for other planters, milling technology like cane crushers was a considerable expense both to obtain and to maintain. Chinese farmers solved this problem either through the slow accumulation of capital resources, or by setting up cooperatives. Cooperative organizations might share equipment and provide labor for each other at harvest time, thus ensuring even the smallest producer would be able to profit from their cane fields.[15] The combination of family labor, day labor, and cooperatives meant that such smallholder production was unlikely to produce labor unrest (although it is likely that not all laborers were treated fairly) because so many laborers were deeply invested in the harvest and tied to production by strong social expectations. Similar forms of smallholder sugar production exist elsewhere, often producing brown sugars for local markets, including gur or jaggery in India and panela in Latin America.

Smallholder sugar at times has also been used to supply sugar companies in the modern period, as was the case in early twentieth-century Taiwan. Peasant farmers in Taiwan grew sugar as part of their multi-cropping practices. They used waste materials from cane to feed livestock, for example, and rotated cane with other crops in the traditional Chinese way. When Japanese colonial authorities wanted to increase production of sugar for the Japanese market, they could not simply convert sugar to a plantation crop. Instead, they used a variety of "soft" methods, from propaganda to focused agricultural extension, to persuade farmers to adopt new practices that would increase sugar yields. Although not without significant tensions, Japanese extension agents eventually looked for ways to harmonize market requirements with the needs of peasant farmers, as efforts at harsher compulsion routinely failed.[16]

The adoption of plantation labor practices, by contrast, usually involved significant forms of labor compulsion, all of which tended to either introduce or exacerbate social tension and conflict. The combination of large crops to harvest and process, with the short timeline consistent with high yields of processed sugar, meant that plantations needed readily available laborers, willing or forced to work long hours for little or no pay. Ulbe Bosma argues that compulsion appears again and again, in a variety of guises in the history of industrialized sugar production, because successful planters had to have guaranteed control over both labor and land to be able to produce a successful crop.[17] Whether compelling farmers to provide their land on good terms, as was the case on Java during the colonial period, or importing slave labor to the United States, compulsion provided security to planters. Slave labor was used not because it was necessarily cheaper than free labor, but because it offered so much control over the laborers themselves. Planters often asserted their right to control labor as a necessary condition of successful sugar production.[18] Even after abolition, indentured laborers in sites like

Mauritius and British Malaya often toiled under conditions barely better than those of slaves, as planters sought to restrict labor rights and labor mobility.[19] This ability to dictate horrifying labor conditions appears to be a measure of the power of sugar planters. But the instability of compulsory regimes over the long term was also a weakness built into the system, constantly threatening the sustainability of production. Industrial-scale sugar production may have been able to produce sugar in record quantities but adopted labor practices that harmed its long-term resilience.

Pioneering efforts to grow sugar on a large scale occurred in Asia and the Caribbean. Chinese sugar producers, capitalizing on demand for Chinese sugar, opened overseas sugar plantations as early as the thirteenth century on the island of Java, and over time in the present-day countries of Taiwan, Vietnam, Thailand, and the Philippines. They operated on an entirely different basis than did Chinese peasants. Chinese entrepreneurs frequently owned both cane land and the mills where cane was extracted and processed, using labor gangs made up of bachelor workers (Javanese or Chinese) who were normally paid a small portion of the proceeds.[20] By the seventeenth century, European and Chinese entrepreneurs sometimes collaborated in these enterprises. Yet racially charged tensions emerged as more Chinese laborers immigrated, swelling their population. Europeans, feeling economically threatened by the shifting demographics, attempted to deport Chinese laborers and provoked massacres of Chinese populations, setting off long-term ethnic discrimination that continues in the region to the present day.[21]

In the Atlantic regions, especially in North America, the Caribbean, and Brazil, European-owned plantations, after experimenting unsuccessfully with indentured white laborers, turned to African slaves to provide labor in the fields and factories. The story of the Atlantic slave trade is well known, as sugar became a central element of the so-called triangle trade, in which the British traded finished goods to Africa for slaves, who were then traded to the plantation owners in exchange for sugar. Slave populations not only labored in the cane fields, they frequently had to grow food to feed themselves, construct and maintain their own housing, and take care of their own medical needs.[22] Slavery in the Americas was a brutal affair, and sugar plantations were particularly harsh. In Louisiana, planters used so-called drilled-gang labor, featuring long hours of intensively supervised work with few breaks and little autonomy, enforced by corporal punishment.[23] Owners made handsome livings, even given the complexity and riskiness of sugar production. Yet the extremity of compulsion and the denial of basic human freedoms, which they treated as essential to the process, were in fact a point of significant frailty in plantation sugar production, even given the difficulties involved in abolishing slavery. The cultures of exploitation that emerged in many (although not all) of these areas made sugar cultivation then and now a tense battleground between planters/owners and workers.

When Haiti's slave revolt delivered the first shock to the Atlantic plantation system, its entire sugar economy collapsed. Yet that outcome to abolition was relatively rare. The advantages that planters had in land ownership, wealth, and access to political power meant that planters continued to exercise considerable control over ostensibly free workers. To be sure, former slaves who could did much to free themselves, by simply leaving the plantations or demanding better pay for their essential labor. In both the Caribbean and North America, some planters attempted to recruit Asian immigrants to replace them, with mixed results.[24] However, even after emancipation, cultures of patronage and traditions that allowed planters absolute authority over their workers made compulsion durable, as it reappeared in new forms. In Louisiana, for example, after the American Civil War, the Union occupation tended to reinforce the use of labor gangs, albeit with the requirement of (low) wages. In the Caribbean, poll taxes, vagrancy laws, and required "apprenticeships" for former slaves made it difficult for emancipated slaves to gain true economic freedom. In Brazil, many freed workers continued their earlier roles, now as tenants, in which they exchanged labor in the cane fields for access to a house and garden. The quality of the land on offer would be based on an individual's relationship with the landowners, thus reinforcing the power of the patrons, and requiring workers to keep their heads down to benefit even modestly from their freedom.[25] Having lost the right to own their laborers, plantation owners did their best to make sure that any alternative economic opportunities were rare, and that workers would have little choice but work on planters' terms. In Louisiana, planters' associations held down wages, among other practices. In British Malaya, planters sought legal rights to reclaim "runaway" indentured laborers.[26]

The continuity of coercive practices may at first seem like an unfortunate example of the stability or, in more deterministic readings, the necessity of labor coercion in sugar production. But the very instability of these arrangements suggests instead inherent weaknesses. Coercive practices were constantly shored up through political manipulation, police power, union-busting, and social violence. Worker strikes in nineteenth-century Louisiana were answered with virulent white supremacy that has dogged the region ever since. In twentieth-century Brazil, efforts to unionize were accompanied by violence against workers.[27] Compelled labor thus has a Janus-faced quality. On the one hand, compulsion has been remarkably difficult to unseat. On the other, its evident injustices lead to constant social conflict, exacerbated by the efforts employed to maintain coercion.

The story of Atlantic slavery and its long-term consequences has tended to overshadow the fact that compulsion in sugar production came in many forms.[28] These other forms of compulsion, if (at times only marginally) less brutal than slavery, nevertheless also created unrest and conflict. The use of poorly paid, often indentured, immigrant labor was a common practice in British Malaya, and the island of Mauritius, for example.[29] British planters in Malaya routinely recruited immigrant laborers, many from South Asia, to work on sugar plantations in the nineteenth century. Yet wages were low, living conditions were bad, and in Malaya workers were tied by extortionate contracts to the plantation itself, albeit with narrow, but legal ways to escape.[30] A similar contract labor situation reigned in Hawaii, with the work of native Hawaiians supplemented, and eventually overwhelmed by, Asian immigrants from Japan, China, and the Philippines. Contract laborers had the cost of their transportation from their homeland deducted from their paychecks and, unlike Hawaiians, were forced to rely on the plantation for overpriced food and shelter. Racist practices meant that Asian workers were paid less than non-Asians and Hawaiians and were more likely to be subject to corporal punishment. Here, too, occasional outbursts of violent protests against unequal wages and the provision of food were common.[31]

A more subtle form of compulsion, but one that nevertheless led to significant unrest, was the relationship between rice and sugar cultivation on the island of Java under Dutch colonial rule. Sugar planters obtained land by setting up lease agreements with Javanese farmers such that sugar and rice would rotate on a three-year cycle. This plan actually benefited cane growers significantly as they paid for the land based on the price of rice, not sugar, and the regular rotation with flooded rice irrigation allowed the land to regain some of its fertility. Yet under this system many farmers were underpaid, as sugar planters made deals with village leaders (some of whom were paid a consideration) rather than individuals. Over time, farmer indebtedness became a notable problem in sugar areas; some farmers or farm family members turned to occasional work in the cane fields, although planters continued to favor the use of gangs made of landless laborers.[32] The problem of poor compensation for sugar land meant that although Javanese farmers were far less likely to experience the horrible working conditions of their contract laboring peers in places like Hawaii and Malaya, or even the tenants in Brazil, their economic circumstances suffered noticeably. Farmer debt in sugar regions was taken up by anti-colonial activists as concrete evidence of the unjust character of colonial rule.[33]

The history of labor has frequently and understandably focused on the plight of cane cutters and those most harmed by the production of sugar. Yet sugar production involved highly skilled laborers too, especially sugar masters who oversaw the evaporation processes that resulted in crystallized sugar, and engineers who built and maintained the machines essential to these processes. Unexpectedly, even workers whose skills were well-remunerated and highly valued could become embroiled in social or political conflict. In the Atlantic plantation system, many, but not all, sugar masters were enslaved people, who thus suffered many of the same difficulties as other slaves, albeit with a few of the perks common to slave artisans. The engineers who developed and maintained the machinery in sugar mills were generally highly educated, free people, located in a social continuum somewhat below the elite planters but well above the slaves they so often worked with.[34] Engineers enjoyed considerable privileges and became increasingly important as new equipment, such as steam-powered crushing mills and vacuum pan evaporators, began to be taken up in the early to mid-nineteenth century. By the early twentieth century, most sugar processing facilities required the help of skilled engineers.

Their value or status as free people did not, however, always protect them from the conflicts that emerged around compulsory labor. In fact, as Jonathan Curry-Machado points out for the case of Cuba, their value could at times make them vulnerable to suspicion. In nineteenth-century Cuba, as sugar milling and processing equipment became increasingly expensive, Cuban plantation owners found themselves at the mercy of foreign capital to finance their operations, and foreign engineers to keep their equipment running. After several failed efforts to train local engineers, Cuban planters relied on expatriate engineers from Spain or the United States.[35] Feeling threatened by their dependency on foreigners, and resentful that these engineers were generally unwilling to train local competitors, some planters accused engineers of sabotaging cane fields or stimulating slave uprisings, a curious accusation given that engineers would be undercutting their own careers if they did so. Yet suspicions attached to these foreign engineers because they worked side by side with slaves, and because foreign abolitionist movements were active in condemning slavery. For the most part innocent of such charges, engineers were made scapegoats for the anxieties planters felt as they increasingly lost much of their economic autonomy.

Bosma's point that successful industrial-scale sugar production has always required consistent security of land and labor rests on the facts of sugar's natural characteristics, especially the need to harvest and process quickly to high yields of sucrose. Yet as Bosma emphasizes, planters achieve this control in different ways in different places, denying overly deterministic narratives about labor and sugar.[36] Certainly, demand for a highly controlled labor force increased with the scale of production. But strategies for controlling labor were diverse, from the use of slavery or indentured labor to varieties of partnerships with peasant producers. In most industrial-scale production, however, the very economic power of sugar producers meant that high-level political connections, patterns of land ownership that privileged planters, and the ability to control access to economic opportunities in areas long planted to sugar tended to make the use of compulsory tactics easy, and the harsh conditions of labor made work in cane fields consistently undesirable work. Planters may have guaranteed themselves high levels of production, but at the cost of constant, unresolved, and sometimes violent conflicts with laborers. To maintain coercion, or control over labor, thus required considerable and constant forms of social maintenance, which in many cases produced enduring social problems.

Environment

Some early planters viewed the tropics as a land perfectly suited to sugar cane production, and indeed a tropical or subtropical climate was necessary, especially before the development of frost-resistant cane varieties. But no environment subjected to industrial-scale monocropping remains "perfectly suited" for long. Although sugar cultivators around the world long understood the depleting effects of sugar on the soil, industrial-scale production put especially heavy demands on both the soil and the surrounding environment, as planters deforested surrounding woodlands to fuel the mills. To make plantation-style sugar production work involved both transformations of local environments, and significant efforts to maintain lands and water supplies in order to sustain crop yields. Such work to maintain sugar land as sugar land had far-reaching, and often irreversible, consequences for the surrounding environments and the people who lived in them.

Small-scale sugar producers understood from early times the need to intensively fertilize land planted to sugar under continuous cropping. Japanese extension agents in the early twentieth century noted that Taiwanese sugar growers were reluctant to introduce intensification practices in part because they would disrupt other aspects of the multicropping peasant economy.[37] However, this knowledge seems to have been forgotten or ignored by plantation operators, perhaps because sugar plantations were often established on virgin lands. Chinese planters on Java, for example, although managing to maintain soil fertility for a time, nevertheless did not do enough to revitalize the soils, and the earliest sugar plantations, in the area surrounding the present-day city of Jakarta, were exhausted after only forty years.[38]

Early modern European planters in the Caribbean were hampered not only by inexperience with the crop, but also by a false ideal about the innate fertility of the tropics.[39] Early planters viewed the lush tropical rainforests as sites of inexhaustible fertility, in contrast to contemporary ecologists who stress the extreme fragility of tropical rainforests, especially those located on islands. It did not take long for sugar planters to discover that not only did these soils get depleted, but that the deforestation that accompanied sugar production also brought drought, erosion, and compromised water supplies. In other places, however, such as northern Brazil, the myth of endless fertility could be sustained longer. Faced with a million acres of trees in northern Brazil, early sugar planters confidently declared that the land could never be exhausted, and planters could hold more land than they could reasonably operate, allowing some rotation of the sugar crop. Indeed, as Thomas Rogers points out, at least for the first hundred years of exploitation in the region, inefficient modes of production meant that planters made relatively small inroads on the forest. By the later nineteenth century, however, most of the massive forest had disappeared, either to power the mills or to make way for sugar cultivation.[40]

The response of large-scale planters and governments to the environmental problems created by sugar production varied, but all sought joint transformations of land and cultivation practices to make sugar yields sustainable over the long term. European planters and botanists traded information about fertility problems in their writings comparing the results of conventional methods for restoring soil fertility, including applying the bagasse (the leftover plant matter after sugar production) back to the fields, utilizing manure, and introducing plant rotations.[41] By the mid-nineteenth century, advocates and followers of Liebig's work on fertilizers argued about which fertilizers, including guano, would benefit sugar the most. The context of this debate was an underlying question about how best to improve yields of sugar: by improving cultivation in the field? Or the efficiency of the factory? Thus work on soil fertility, although unavoidable for most planters who had no virgin land to turn to, might in some cases be seen as only one of several paths toward achieving the profits planters aimed for.[42]

A second major environmental consequence of sugar production, as already mentioned, was deforestation. This was not merely an unintended side effect of plantation production. Plantations were routinely sited in or near forests precisely because the fuel was need to power the mills during harvest. As sugar planting expanded, severe deforestation accompanied it in nearly every place that sugar was introduced on a large scale, even in continental sites like the southern United States and northern Brazil.[43] Deforestation had numerous negative consequences including the growing prevalence of drought (or greater vulnerability to drought), erosion, and deteriorating water supplies. Deforestation was in some cases irreversible, as forest cover was replaced by invasive grasses that were difficult to eradicate.[44] All these problems put sugar cultivation at risk.

The combination of sugar monocropping and the affiliated deforestation had far-reaching consequences. The wholesale transformation of ecologies, as well as the pressure to produce as much cane as possible, affected the quality of local food supplies. Although seen most dramatically in small island environments, the problems were evident elsewhere as well. Many sugar islands imported considerable quantities of food, even as slaves were often required to grow their own food on garden plots to supplement their diet. Yet planters always balanced using any labor, land, or water for food production against the economic value of sugar. Hawaii, for example, which during its peak years of sugar production had a population not much bigger than the self-sustaining population of Polynesians hundreds of years earlier, was a net importer of food as native food crops lost their ecological niches and the water needed to produce them as sugar spread.[45] In Brazil, planters engaged in cynical calculations about how to balance the availability of land or resources devoted to food, and the desire to ensure that laborers would not have a real economic alternative to working in the sugar fields. Rogers notes that some planters opposed restoring fish stocks in local rivers because it might make potential workers too independent of the sugar plantations.[46] Even on Java, where sugar and rice grown in rotation allowed local food supplies to stay relatively healthy throughout the nineteenth and early twentieth centuries, the ecological consequences of sugar cultivation could do periodic damage, as when disease attacked rice plants growing in soil that was depleted from sugar cane cultivation.[47]

Planters had to protect, modify, or otherwise intervene in the environment to make sugar production viable. In Hawaii, for example, powerful sugar planters created forest preserves in the early twentieth century to protect their watersheds, in effect privatizing what had previously been a public resource. They also built extensive and expensive irrigation works, to bring water from the naturally wet side of the island to the naturally dry side. They used artesian wells to draw groundwater, albeit unsustainably. Carol MacLennan notes that Hawaii pumped 314 million gallons of water daily to feed its sugar cane in the 1930s.[48] One consequence for such projects was the passing of public resources into private hands, leaving it to the discretion and priorities of planters to determine how the water could be used, a decision that had consequences especially for native Hawaiians.

Although less obvious thanks to sugar's location in areas long under cultivation on the island of Java, irrigation practices there also had far-reaching consequences for the use and maintenance of water resources. In areas where sugar and rice were both grown (as was true in most sugar areas), sugar planters generally had priority for water use. Laws aiming to regulate water usage dictated water sharing, usually through day-night divisions, allowing sugar planters to draw water during the day, and relegating rice farmers to working in the dark to irrigate their crops. In some parts of Java, cisterns were used instead to store the water that flowed at night so that farmers could use it during daylight hours. But the all-important silt carried in the water, which was responsible for the impressive, continuous fertility of Java's rice lands (and indeed, responsible for the success of the sugar-rice rotation), tended to settle to the bottom of the tanks, making the water less able to revitalize the soils.[49]

Although planters suffered serious problems as a result of deforestation, the practice of denuding land to facilitate sugar production is not a problem only of the past. In contemporary Latin America, for example, sugar cane cultivation is responsible for significant forest loss in virgin land, as the continuously growing demand for sugar keeps prices high enough to make forest clearance, especially illicit forest clearance, remunerable. The ecological costs of sugar production therefore need to be understood as emerging not merely from ignorance, or unintended consequences, but as part of particular cultures of resource exploitation associated with sugar cane production. The environmental consequences of monocropping of any crop are well understood, and sugar's industrial history is no exception. Far from being an "ideal" location for sugar, tropical and sub-tropical locations were highly vulnerable sites, and made even more so by planting practices. Sites of sugar production had to be made suitable for sugar and then maintained through significant and constant environmental interventions.

Technology and Science

Sugar production, even in the distant past, when it was grown in relatively small quantities, was always a site of experiment as cultivators developed knowledge of the crop, its response to water and soil conditions, and devised equipment and techniques to extract the most sucrose possible, and refine it into desirable forms. Such efforts intensified in the nineteenth and twentieth centuries as planters looked to make the most of their sugar lands, improving the efficiency and reliability of both the crop and the factories.

However, the use of science and technology as a source of improvement (in yield, in efficiencies, and the like) tells only part of the story. Scientific and technological work was also vital to the maintenance of sugar production in the face of the environmental and labor problems that monocropping itself created. By the twentieth century, with some sugar areas in decline, scientific and technological investigation sought new uses for sugar, apart from traditional use as food and feed, to bolster economies grown entirely dependent on sugar production. And just as technological and scientific efforts worked to solve some problems, they created new problems in their wake.[50]

The twin problems of maintaining soil fertility and maximizing sucrose extraction were the core challenges of sugar cultivation, especially under the conditions that prevailed in most plantations. For European planters, a central question well into the nineteenth century was the question of whether sugar was "made" in the field or in the mill. To increase yield or improve quality, should they look to improve the growing conditions or the variety of cane? Or should they focus on extraction, maximizing the amount of sucrose you could obtain from any plant?[51] There were advocates on both sides of this question, and ultimately significant developments on both fronts. By the late eighteenth and early nineteenth centuries, agronomists, botanists, and planters all contributed internationally circulating publications on these topics, drawing on current scientific theories like those of Liebig or experiences working on cane plantations in places like Barbados, Cuba, Mauritius, Java, and Hawaii.[52] The merchant George Porter, for example, advocated the rigorous application of scientific principles and best agronomic practices to improve yields in declining British sugar colonies in the late eighteenth century. He recommended (among other things) how to space sugar cane plants, when to harvest, and the use of fertilizers.[53] Among the best known of the agronomists who followed the findings of Justus von Liebig, the German researcher who used chemistry to investigate the workings of fertilizers, was Alvaro Reynoso. Trained in chemistry and born in Cuba, Reynoso developed a so-called integrated approach to sugar cane, urging planters to take into account a diverse array of factors to perfect and make most efficient the production of sugar in the field, including the depth and spacing of furrows, the amount and timing of irrigation and drainage, fertilization, and the use of machinery. Reynoso's labor-intensive system of production was never adopted in Cuba where labor was relatively scarce, but in modified form was taken up on Java (as well as Brazil) and later dubbed the "Java" system of production.[54] For Reynoso as others, growing sugar required careful understanding of sugar as an interlocking system.

Scientific investigations were also crucial to resolving one of the key problems that emerged in large-scale cultivation, the apparent degradation of varieties, which showed up as serious and irresolvable declines in yields after a number of years of planting. Sugar cane (like other plants) may, when monocropped, become especially vulnerable to insects and bacteria that evolve to take advantage of this food source. In most of the Atlantic sugar areas, the so-called creole canes were the most widely used in the early modern period. However, over time, as cane performance degraded, new cane varieties were imported from diverse locations, including the Otaheite canes from Tahiti, and the noble canes from New Guinea. As Storey points out, when Europeans imported the noble canes, they benefited from centuries of selection work done by the people of New Guinea.[55]

Some planters, such as those on the island of Mauritius in the eighteenth century, sought to breed their own canes to resolve the problems of degradation.[56] Eventually, success with sugar cane breeding and the formulation of the idea of hybrid vigor—the understanding that hybrid plants may be more vigorous and productive than their non-hybridized parents—stimulated considerable scientific attention to plant breeding over the course of the nineteenth century and up to the present day. Mauritius became an important center for both sugar production and the production of canes that could be sold to sugar planters the world over, as planters pushed for both the creation of scientific research institutions and research that would serve their own operations.[57] As sugar cane production spread to different parts of the world, scientific sugar cane breeding became essential to the maintenance of individual plantations and the larger industry. The introduction of sugar cane breeding stations meant that sugar planters would rely for their survival more on the scientists that they (sometimes directly, sometimes indirectly) employed, rather than on voyaging botanists and Pacific Islanders. Research was in some places supported by the state, as for example in the Netherlands East Indies in the late nineteenth century, but was also supported by planter associations, such as the Hawaiian Sugar Planter Association, which ran its own experiment station and became a significant contributor to international sugar science.[58]

Government sponsorship of sugar science was especially visible where economic dependence on sugar was so significant that declines or stagnation of sugar production posed a significant existential threat. For example, in Trinidad after World War II, British researchers sought to stimulate the market for Trinidadian sugar by exploring alternate uses of sugar beyond food or feed, including the creation of Dextran (a medical product) and bio-fuels.[59] Although the Trinidadian bio-fuels project did not really take off, in Brazil, sugar became a key input for the production of ethanol after experiments in the 1970s, and it is widely used within that country, which makes extensive use of sugar-based ethanol as fuel for vehicles.[60]

One of the most frequently cited characteristics of the industrialization of sugar was the change over time in both milling and evaporation technology. The nineteenth century in particular saw dramatic shifts in how sugar was extracted from cane. Bigger and more efficient milling technology, including horizontal rather than vertical cane crushers, and the introduction of steam power meant that larger crops could be processed and more sucrose could be extracted. Vacuum pans allowed for more precise and less wasteful sugar processing than open kettles and used less energy besides. Some sugar producers could now run the evaporation process on bagasse rather than wood.[61] Such improvements addressed both the efficiency of the operation and the ease with which sugar could be refined into its most desirable forms.

Yet these growing efficiencies came at a cost, in terms of not just the cost of the equipment, but in their dependency on machinery manufacturers and engineers. As David Singerman has argued, when plantations invested in more sophisticated machinery, they also had to make considerable investments of time and effort to maintain those machines, particularly when steam power became the norm. The machinery used for sugar production was often customized to particular needs, and both machinery companies and planters had to keep detailed records and maintain ongoing relationships to make sure that the equipment was kept in good repair. Singerman documents a steady stream of expert representatives from machinery companies venturing to sugar producing regions to observe, fix, and install equipment, the failure of which could have devastating effects for producers. Growing efficiencies became important for maintaining competitiveness in global sugar markets, but they came at the price of increasing their embeddedness in wider networks over which they had little control.[62]

Motivation to adopt these improvements increased in the 1860s with the spread of sugar beets, the first major challenge to sugar cane's dominance as the cultivar of choice.[63] With the crash in global sugar prices, improvements in efficiency and economies of scale become very important for cane planters. In Mauritius, for example, it was mainly large-scale operations, financed or owned by joint-stock companies that could afford the best technology, positioning the larger estates to become the more significant players. This change resulted in a steady centralization of the milling and refining processes as fewer and fewer independent operators could afford to buy their own equipment. In the Louisiana sugar industry in 1860, a planter would have needed to invest about $12,000 in equipment, a not inconsiderable sum, but by 1907 that figure had grown to $170,000.[64] By the 1880s, most milling and processing was done by such centralized concerns. The change in business models that resulted was significant. Some smaller planters shifted from making sugar to growing cane or went out of business entirely, and the larger companies expanded in size, putting an end to the autonomous plantation.[65] Instead of planters reaping the most benefits from the sugar industry, it was now larger, eventually multinational, corporations that reaped the greatest profits.

Science and technology provided tools that allowed the expansion of sugar production in some places or protected its investment in others. Yet this is not a simplistic story of technology or science determining the fate of sugar production. The Hawaiian sugar industry declined in the 1970s, as multinational owners decided to put their efforts elsewhere, despite the tremendous efforts put in by Hawaiians over more than a century to provide an ideal environment—scientific, environmental, and economic—for sugar production. In other places, late adoption of new technologies seems to have had little bearing on the long-term success of the operation. Taking advantage of continually cheap labor and extensive land, Brazilian producers were slow to take up some of the improvements in technology and technique, while Louisiana planters upgraded desperately, only to see the loss of domestic subsidies finally forced them to a marginal position in world production. Yet for all of this, continuous scientific and technical work became deeply embedded in efforts to maintain the global viability of industrial-scale sugar production.

Conclusion

In 1985, Sydney Mintz wrote, "The track sugar has left in modern history is one involving masses of people and resources, thrown into productive combination by social, economic and political forces that are remaking the entire world."[66] The global expansion of sugar production over the course of five hundred years has all the appearance of a juggernaut. Yet the historical development of industrial sugar production also created significant, enduring vulnerabilities. The history by which sugar production became global is as much one of ongoing maintenance as one of innovation, with a constant struggle to make sugar viable in the face of changing business models, damaged environments, and social tensions inherent in the sugar industry's labor practices.

Notes

1. United States Department of Agriculture, Foreign Agricultural Service, "Sugar: World Markets and Trade Report 2019–2020," May 2019, accessed October 1, 2019, https://apps.fas.usda.gov/psdonline/circulars/sugar.pdf.
2. Ibid.
3. Ibid.
4. Sydney Mintz, *Sweetness and Power: The Place of Sugar in Modern History* (New York: Penguin Books, 1985), although dated, remains an excellent integrative study of sugar's history.
5. FAOSTAT, http://www.fao.org/faostat/en/#home, accessed October 1 2019.
6. H. Bakker, *Sugar Cane Cultivation and Management* (Boston: Springer, 1999): 81–86.
7. John B. Rehder, *Delta Sugar: Louisiana's Vanishing Plantation Landscape* (Baltimore: Johns Hopkins University Press, 1999): 18–19.
8. Bakker, *Sugar Cane Cultivation*: 234–235.
9. For a useful overview of the American experience see Richard Follett, Sven Beckert, Peter Coclanis, and Barbara Hahn, *Plantation Kingdom: The American South and Its Global Commodities* (Baltimore: Johns Hopkins University Press, 2016): 61–90.
10. Ulbe Bosma, "The Global Detour of Cane Sugar," in *Colonialism, Institutional Change, and Shifts in Global Labor Relations*, ed. Karin Hofmeester and Pim De Zwart (Amsterdam: Amsterdam University Press, 2018).
11. Sucheta Mazumdar, *Sugar and Society in China: Peasants, Technology, and World Markets* (Cambridge, MA: Harvard University Press, 1998).
12. Ibid., 60–119.
13. Ibid., 269–94.
14. Ibid., 269–72.
15. Ibid., 269–94.
16. Shuntaro Tsuru, "Embedding Technologies into the Farming Economy: Extension Work of Japanese Sugar Companies in Colonial Taiwan," *East Asian Science, Technology and Society* 12, no. 1 (2017): 3–32.
17. Ulbe Bosma, *The Sugar Plantation in India and Indonesia: Industrial Production, 1770–2010* (Cambridge: Cambridge University Press, 2013). See also Bosma, "The Global Detour of Cane Sugar."
18. Richard Follett, "The Rise and Fall of American Sugar," in Follett et al., *Plantation Kingdom*, 61–90; and Thomas D. Rogers, *The Deepest Wounds: A Labor and Environmental History of Sugar in Northeast Brazil* (Chapel Hill: University of North Carolina Press, 2010): 64–69.
19. Ibid. See also Lynn Hollen Lees, *Planting Empire, Cultivating Subjects: British Malaya 1786–1941* (Cambridge: Cambridge University Press, 2017); and William Kelleher Storey, *Science and Power in Colonial Mauritius* (Rochester, NY: University of Rochester Press, 1997).
20. Bosma, *The Sugar Plantation in India and Indonesia*, 13–16.
21. Ibid.
22. Judith Ann Carney and Richard Nicholas Rosomoff, *In the Shadow of Slavery: Africa's Botanical Legacy in the Atlantic World* (Berkeley: University of California Press, 2009): 100–38.
23. Follett, "The Rise and Fall of American Sugar," 61–90.
24. Ibid. See also Moon-ho Jung, *Coolies and Cane: Race, Labor, and Sugar in the Age of Emancipation* (Baltimore: Johns Hopkins University Press, 2006).

25. Rogers, *The Deepest Wounds*, 77.
26. Follett, "The Rise and Fall of American Sugar," 61–90; and Lees, *Planting Empire, Cultivating Subjects*.
27. Rogers, *The Deepest Wounds*: 125–54.
28. Bosma, "The Global Detour of Cane Sugar."
29. Storey, *Science and Power*, 32–42; Lees, *Planting Empire, Cultivating Subjects*, 21–61.
30. Lees, *Planting Empire, Cultivating Subjects*, 62–100.
31. Carol MacLennan, *Sovereign Sugar: Industry and Environment in Hawai'i* (Honolulu: University Hawai'i Press, 2014): 132–135, 170–175.
32. Bosma, *The Sugar Plantation in India and Indonesia*, 87–128.
33. Suzanne Moon, *Technology and Ethical Idealism: A History of Development in the Netherlands East Indies* (Leiden: CNWS Publications, 2007).
34. Jonathan Curry-Machado, *Cuban Sugar Industry: Transnational Networks and Engineering Migrants in Mid-Nineteenth Century Cuba* (New York: Palgrave Macmillan, 2011): 23–71.
35. Ibid. See also Jonathan Curry-Machado, "Privileged Scapegoats: The Manipulation of Migrant Engineering Workers in Mid- Nineteenth Century Cuba," *Caribbean Studies* 35, no. 1 (2007): 207–245.
36. Bosma, "The Global Detour of Cane Sugar."
37. Tsuro, "Embedding Technologies in the Farming Economy."
38. Bosma, *The Sugar Plantation in India and Indonesia*, 87–128.
39. Leida Fernández-Prieto, "Mapping the Global and Local Archipelago of Scientific Tropical Sugar," in *Global Scientific Practice in an Age of Revolutions, 1750–1850*, ed. Patrick Manning and Daniel Rood (Pittsburgh: University of Pittsburgh Press, 2016), 181–198.
40. Rogers, *The Deepest Wound*, 21–44.
41. Fernández-Prieto, "Mapping the Global and Local Archipelago."
42. Ibid.
43. See Follett, "The Rise and Fall of American Sugar," 61–90; and Rogers, *The Deepest Wound*, 21–44.
44. MacLennan, *Sovereign Sugar*, 208–213.
45. Ibid., 103–144.
46. Rogers, 54–78.
47. Suzanne Moon, "Empirical Knowledge, Scientific Authority, and Native Development: The Controversy over Sugar/Rice Ecology in the Netherlands East Indies, 1905–1914," *Environment and History* 10, no. 1 (2004): 59–81.
48. MacLennan, *Sovereign Sugar*, 145–169.
49. Moon, *Technology and Ethical Idealism*.
50. Ulrich Beck, *Risk Society: Towards a New Modernity* (London: Sage Publications, 1992).
51. Fernández-Prieto, "Mapping the Global and Local Archipelago."
52. Ibid. See also Storey, *Science and Power*; and MacLennan, *Sovereign Sugar*.
53. Fernández-Prieto, "Mapping the Global and Local Archipelago," 187.
54. Ibid. See also Ulbe Bosma and Jonathan Curry-Machado, "Two Islands, One Commodity: Cuba, Java, and the Global Sugar Trade (1790–1930)," *New West Indian Guide* 86, no. 3 (2012): 235–262.
55. Storey, *Science and Power*, 11–96.
56. Ibid.
57. Ibid.

58. MacLennan, *Sovereign Sugar*, 220–248. For the role of scientists in sugar breeding see Storey, *Science and Power*.
59. Sabine Clark, *Science at the End of Empire: Experts and the Development of the British Caribbean, 1940–1962* (Manchester: University of Manchester Press, 2018).
60. Arnaldo Walter and Pedro Gerber Machado, "Socio-Economic Impacts of Bioethanol from Sugarcane in Brazil," in *Socio-Economic Impacts of Bioenergy Production*, ed. Dominik Rutz and R. Janssen (Cham, Switzerland: Springer, 2014).
61. Storey, *Science and Power*, 11–36, offers a useful overview of these developments. For the introduction of steam see Curry-Machado, *Cuban Sugar Industry*, 23–47.
62. David Singerman, "Sugar Machines and the Fragile Infrastructure of Commodities in the Nineteenth Century," *OSIRIS* 33, no. 1 (2018): 62–84. See also David Singerman, "Inventing Purity in the Atlantic Sugar World, 1860–1930" (PhD diss., Massachusetts Institute of Technology, 2014).
63. Storey, *Science and Power*, 39.
64. Follett, "The Rise and Fall of American Sugar," 61–90.
65. Ibid. See also Storey, *Science and Power*, 11–36.
66. Mintz, *Sweetness and Power*, 211.

Bibliography

Bosma, Ulbe. "The Global Detour of Cane Sugar." In *Colonialism, Institutional Change, and Shifts in Global Labor Relations*, edited by Karin Hofmeester and Pim De Zwart, 109–133. Amsterdam: Amsterdam University Press, 2018. https://doi.org/10.1515/9789048535026

Bosma, Ulbe. *The Sugar Plantation in India and Indonesia: Industrial Production, 1770–2010*. Cambridge: Cambridge University Press, 2013.

Clark, Sabine. *Science at the End of Empire: Experts and the Development of the British Caribbean, 1940–1962*. Manchester: University of Manchester Press, 2018.

Curry-Machado, Jonathan. *Cuban Sugar Industry: Transnational Networks and Engineering Migrants in Mid-Nineteenth Century Cuba*. New York: Palgrave Macmillan, 2011.

Fernández-Prieto, Leida. "Mapping the Global and Local Archipelago of Scientific Tropical Sugar." In *Global Scientific Practice in an Age of Revolutions, 1750–1850*, edited by Patrick Manning and Daniel Rood, 181–198. Pittsburgh: University of Pittsburgh Press, 2016.

Follett, Richard, Sven Beckert, Peter Coclanis, and Barbara Hahn. *Plantation Kingdom: The American South and Its Global Commodities*. Baltimore: Johns Hopkins University Press, 2016.

Jung, Moon-ho. *Coolies and Cane: Race, Labor, and Sugar in the Age of Emancipation*. Baltimore: Johns Hopkins University Press, 2006.

Lees, Lynn Hollen. *Planting Empire, Cultivating Subjects: British Malaya 1786–1941*. Cambridge: Cambridge University Press, 2017.

MacLennan, Carol. *Sovereign Sugar: Industry and Environment in Hawai'i*. Honolulu: University of Hawai'i Press, 2014.

Mazumdar, Sucheta. *Sugar and Society in China: Peasants, Technology, and World Markets*. Cambridge, MA: Harvard University Press, 1998.

Mintz, Sydney. *Sweetness and Power: The Place of Sugar in Modern History*. New York: Penguin, 1985.

Rogers, Thomas D. *The Deepest Wounds: A Labor and Environmental History of Sugar in Northeast Brazil.* Chapel Hill: University of North Carolina Press. 2010.

Singerman, David. "Sugar Machines and the Fragile Infrastructure of Commodities in the Nineteenth Century." *OSIRIS* 33, no. 1 (2018): 62–84.

Singerman, David Roth. "Inventing Purity in the Atlantic Sugar World, 1860–1930." PhD diss., Massachusetts Institute of Technology, 2014.

Storey, William Kelleher. *Science and Power in Colonial Mauritius.* Rochester, NY: University of Rochester Press, 1997.

Tsuru, Shuntaro. "Embedding Technologies into the Farming Economy: Extension Work of Japanese Sugar Companies in Colonial Taiwan." *East Asian Science, Technology and Society* 12, no. 1 (2018): 3–32. https://doi.org/10.1215/18752160-4129327.

CHAPTER 19

COFFEE

STUART MCCOOK

AMONG the world's cultivated plants, coffee is a comparative newcomer. Its history as a major crop stretches back just five centuries, as opposed to other crops that have been around for millennia. During these five hundred years it has, by many measures, been wildly successful. Coffee cultivation has spread from a small corner of Africa across the global tropics, and it is now cultivated in at least fifty countries. According to some estimates, coffee farming contributes to the livelihoods of about 125 million farmers across the global coffeelands, most of whom are smallholders. Historically, coffee has appealed to farmers because—unlike many other tropical crops—there have rarely been any significant economies of scale. It can be produced profitably both as a monoculture on large estates, or as part of diverse smallholder agroforestry systems—and in many other combinations and permutations. And the plant produces a drink that is the delight of consumers around the world. The history of coffee is intimately tied with the history of globalization; farmers have mostly cultivated it for distant markets and consumers. This global fact has decisively shaped the history of coffee farming. At some moments this global commodity chain has created tremendous opportunities for farmers in the Global South, and at other moments it has been a poverty trap and sometimes driven farmers out of the countryside altogether.

THE BIRTH OF COFFEE

The drink we now know as "coffee" is made from the roasted, ground seeds of the coffee plant. Botanically, coffee more properly, *Coffea* is a genus, which contains more than one hundred species. They can be found in a wide range of ecological niches across tropical Africa and Madagascar. Only a handful of these species have ever been cultivated on any significant scale.[1] And of this handful, two species have dominated: arabica coffee *C. arabica* and robusta coffee *C. canephora*. The native range of arabica coffee is small, mostly concentrated to the mountain forests of southwestern Ethiopia, where it grows as an understory crop. Whereas arabica coffee is primarily a highland plant, robusta is primarily a lowland plant. Unlike arabica, robusta is a highly diverse and wide-ranging species, but most robusta varieties do best in Africa's warm lowlands. Most histories of coffee focus almost exclusively on arabica coffee, but any complete history of global coffee farming must consider both species.[2]

The early history of arabica coffee consumption in Ethiopia remains unclear, but it is possible that local peoples first consumed the wild plant's leaves. These were dried and roasted, and then used in a tea-like infusion in boiled water. Arabica leaves are also used in other infusions such as *chamo*, which includes garlic, ginger, and other seasonings gathered from the forest. At some point, Ethiopian peoples likely started experimenting with ways to cook and process the tree's fruit—the cherries and the beans within. Even then, the fruit were not, at first, used as a drink. Among other things, the Oromo of Ethiopia used coffee as an ingredient in portable, high-energy snacks to be eaten on long journeys—ground coffee mixed with honey or butter and formed into balls. Dried coffee beans were also used as gifts and as tribute to local rulers. In this way, people across Ethiopia started consuming coffee. As demand rose, people started harvesting more wild coffee, and managing the forest (for example, by reducing shade) to increase the yields of wild coffee. They also brought coffee trees out of the forest and planted them in domestic gardens alongside other crops. Coffee cultivation gradually spread across much of Ethiopia, along domestic trade routes.[3]

The consumption of robusta coffee began somewhat later, and several hundred kilometers to the south. The peoples who lived around the Great Lakes of Africa (in modern-day Uganda and Tanzania) started cultivating and consuming robusta coffee, possibly as early as the sixteenth century. The habit of coffee consumption may have been introduced by invaders from Ethiopia, but arabica coffee was not. Instead, they cultivated robusta coffee—which may have been introduced to the Great Lakes region from the Congo River basin. They cultivated robusta coffee along the northern and western shores of Lake Victoria, and on the Sese Islands. In the Bukoba district, the coffee beans were dried whole, with spices. Among the Haya people, these dried beans were used in rituals, as tribute, to cement relationships of blood brotherhood. These cured robusta beans slowly became an important item of trade within the Great Lakes region.[4]

THE FOUNTAINHEAD: YEMEN

Arabica coffee (both as a plant and a commodity) spread eastward in Ethiopia, reaching parts of the country where Islam predominated, and which were tightly linked to Islamic religious and commercial networks along the Red Sea and beyond. Two other coffee-based preparations became popular among Islamic consumers: *quishr*, an infusion made from the dried skin of the coffee cherries, and *qahwa*, an infusion made from the roasted and ground seeds (which is the drink we now know as coffee). The habit of coffee drinking was spread by traveling Sufi monks who drank coffee to sustain themselves during their long nighttime rituals, and also by students. A new social institution, the coffeehouse, also enhanced the drink's popularity outside of religious and academic circles. Coffee consumption spread along the Red Sea, up the Yemeni coast up to the holy cities of Mecca and Medina, and into Egypt. After the Ottomans conquered Egypt in the early sixteenth century, coffee drinking spread through the leading cities of the Ottoman Empire, in the Eastern Mediterranean and the Middle East. Muslim pilgrims returning from the Haj also spread the habit of drinking coffee along the islands and coasts of the Indian Ocean.[5]

Coffee cultivation also spread across the Red Sea. Arabica coffee was brought across the Red Sea to Yemen some time before the mid-1500s. This transfer was part of a broader flow; for millennia, people had moved crops and agricultural technologies across Africa, Asia, and the Mediterranean. Yemen was a linchpin that connected these three areas.[6] Arabica coffee might have been initially brought to Yemen for purely domestic consumption. The Yemenis consumed coffee—typically as *quishr*. The Yemenis were "so passionate about this drink," noted the French botanist Nicolas Bréon, "that they would prefer to do without food and clothing." He suggested that "without this particular taste [for *quishr*] the Arabs would be little interested in cultivating coffee."[7] Still, growing coffee for *quishr* was perfectly compatible with producing for markets outside Yemen; the husks and skin could be used locally, and the dried seeds could be sold onto the global markets. The farmers were acutely sensitive to global demand. As demand grew, wrote one French observer in 1709, "[the Yemeni farmers] have not fail'd to encrease its Species, which they do more and more every Day, in Proportion to the Consumption and Profit of it; insomuch that, at present, there are Coffee-Trees in many of the Mountains and other places of *Yaman* which, till of late, had never borne any."[8]

The landscapes where arabica coffee was cultivated In Yemen looked nothing like its home in the forests of Ethiopia. It was cultivated on steep highland terraces overlooking the Red Sea, and in mountain valleys. The coffee plants had to be irrigated during Yemen's long dry season. The plants also had to be protected from the full sun, and from the seasonal cold (and occasional snow) that affected some areas. So the farmers introduced shade trees, which formed a "perfect umbrella" that protected the plants. Although some of Yemen's coffee was grown on large estates, most of it was produced on small family farms. The farmers tended their trees with care, which contributed to Yemen's long-standing reputation for producing coffee of high quality. They could also produce a lot of coffee; from the mid-fifteenth century to the early eighteenth century, Yemen had a near monopoly on global coffee production and remained a significant producer until the early nineteenth century. As late as the 1820s, Yemeni smallholders produced eight thousand tons of coffee per year, using techniques that had changed little for centuries.[9]

The development of Yemen's coffee frontiers foreshadowed several key trends in coffee cultivation. Coffee frontiers were sometimes established in areas that were ecologically marginal for the arabica coffee plant. But with the proper farming techniques—such as the irrigation and artificial shade in Yemen—these ecologically marginal areas could be made highly productive. Even so, such areas remained vulnerable to changes in temperature, rainfall, or other key environmental factors. Successful coffee frontiers had ready access to trade and transportation routes that linked producers and consumers. These linkages help explain why Yemen, not Ethiopia, was the fountainhead of the global coffee industry. Coffee prospered where land, labor, and capital were available (or could be made available). And perhaps most important, coffee could be farmed profitably—and sustainably—both as an estate crop and as a smallholder crop.

Yemen's coffee farms also shaped the genetic structure of the global coffee industry. Unlike most species of coffee, arabica coffee plants can self-pollinate. The offspring of an arabica plant will be genetically similar, if not identical, to the parent. From an agricultural perspective, self-fertility offers some critical advantages: it is easy to propagate countless plants with the same characteristics. It is also easier to move self-fertile plants over long distances, since a new population could be built on a single seed or a single plant. The population of wild arabicas in Ethiopia was, and remains, comparatively variable. But only a small subset of that population were taken across the Red Sea to Yemen. Farmers there likely selected the varieties best adapted to Yemen's landscapes. This had global implications, since the founding of the world's cultivated coffee came from Yemen. Foreigners who wanted to establish coffee farms elsewhere obtained seeds and seedlings from Yemen's already narrow arabica populations—further limiting the diversity of cultivated coffee. The world's coffee industry was based on a perilously narrow, twice-filtered genetic base.[10]

At first, the plant moved through long-established networks of exchange in the Indian Ocean Basin. According to legend, in the seventeenth century a monk named Baba Budan took coffee seeds from Yemen to India's Malabar Coast, where cultivation was established in the hills that now bear his name. From India, the plant was later introduced to Ceylon and Java, quite possibly by Muslim pilgrims doing the Hajj, although this part of coffee's history remains unclear. Arab traders likely took coffee seeds from India to Ceylon near the end of the seventeenth century. Traders and Sufi monks might have introduced coffee to West Sumatra around the same time. Coffee in South and Southeast Asia was, at first, primarily destined to local rather than global markets.[11]

Coffee and the Plantation Complex

Late in the seventeenth century, European powers started to get involved in the coffee trade and in coffee production. This followed the growing popularity of coffee and coffeehouses in Europe. Europeans had learned about coffee drinking through commercial and political exchanges with the Ottoman Empire, and also through the involvement of European trading companies in trade networks in the Indian Ocean Basin. The British East India Company started shipping coffee from Yemen to the Indian port of Surat in India in the mid-seventeenth century. The Dutch East India Company (VOC) promoted coffee cultivation in its Asian colonies. The VOC spread coffee plants and encouraged coffee cultivation in Java and its other island colonies in Asia. The French East India Company established coffee farms on Île Bourbon (now Réunion) in the western Indian Ocean.[12]

The European monopoly companies—and European settlers—often resorted to coercion to produce coffee. In the early 1720s, the Dutch established a system that required local peoples in West Java to plant coffee, which would be sold at a fixed price to Dutch buyers in Batavia. But their attempts to control coffee production in this period were largely unsuccessful. In any case, coercion was not necessary; local smallholders produced coffee without compulsion, both for domestic and international markets. Coffee was first produced as plantation crop—using African slaves—on Réunion. In 1735, just twenty years after coffee was first introduced to the island, enslaved Africans accounted for 80 percent of the population. Official exports reached 1,200 tons in 1745, and as much as 3,000 tons on the eve of the French revolution.[13] These European-controlled coffee frontiers in the Indian Ocean quickly eroded Yemen's dominance over global coffee production; as early as 1726, the Dutch imported 90 percent of their coffee from Java. But even as Asian production grew, production in the Americas grew even faster.

Early in the eighteenth century, Europeans moved arabica coffee to the Americas, via Europe. The Dutch took a single coffee plant from Batavia to Amsterdam. This was an arduous trip; the route took the ship around the Cape of Good Hope, where the weather could be close to freezing. Miraculously, the plant survived the voyage and was cultivated and propagated in the Amsterdam Botanical Garden; in 1714 the magistrates of Amsterdam sent the king of France "a Coffee Tree at perfect Growth, loaded with Fruit."[14] French botanists duly cultivated and propagated the tree in hothouses at the Jardin du Roi. These scientific institutions played a vital role in the networks that relayed arabica coffee from Asia to the Americas. Gardeners and botanists learned how to cultivate and propagate the plant, increasing the amount of raw planting material available for the difficult transoceanic journey. This process was not unique to coffee; these and other botanical gardens propagated and circulated many tropical crops and commodities.[15]

In the late 1710s and early 1720s, the Dutch took offspring of this tree to their New World colony of Guyana (now Suriname), and the French introduced it to Martinique. These oceanic voyages were another major genetic bottleneck; the founding populations of coffee in the New World were all descended from a single tree. This original variety of cultivated arabica is now commonly known as "Typica" coffee. From Dutch Guyana, people took coffee southward into Brazil; from Martinique, people spread it through the West Indies and the Central American mainland.[16]

Within two decades, the global center of coffee production shifted from the Indian Ocean Basin to the West Indies. There, coffee was primarily a plantation crop, grown by enslaved Africans. Most West Indian colonies produced at least some coffee, but by the second half of the century the French colony of Saint-Domingue dwarfed all others. The coffee plant had been introduced to the island early in the eighteenth century; the first official export was in 1738. In 1755 it exported roughly 3,400 metric tons of coffee, easily surpassing Réunion. By 1790 it exported nearly 37,000 metric tons. This coffee boom was not the result of official policy; the island's coffee industry developed spontaneously in the shadow of the sugar industry. Settlers from France and *gens de couleur* established farms on hillsides and other lands that were unsuitable for sugar cane. Coffee plantations required considerably less labor and capital than sugar plantations, so they attracted the less affluent members of the European elite and also the more affluent *gens de couleur*. By the last decade of the eighteenth century, Saint-Domingue was the world's largest producer of both sugar and coffee—at its peak, it produced 60 percent of the world's coffee. This dominance did not last; the island's plantation economy was destroyed in the 1790s, during the slave revolt that overturned the colonial government.[17]

Green Waves of Coffee: Mass Production

The global coffee trade languished for a few decades, disrupted in particular by the Haitian Revolution and the Napoleonic Wars. But it started to recover after about 1820. The recovery was driven in part by rising demand in the industrializing economies of Europe and North America. But it was also driven by producers in colonial Asia and the newly independent nations of Latin America. While production grew almost everywhere, by mid-century production in the Americas had decisively overtaken that in Asia. The Americas have, collectively, remained the world's dominant coffee-producing zone ever since. The center of coffee production in the Americas shifted from the West Indies to the mainland. Coffee had remained economically insignificant until Spain and Portugal's mainland colonies gained independence between 1810 and 1825. The leaders of the newly independent nations searched for export commodities with which to earn hard currency. Coffee production opened up in two main places: Central America and Brazil. In Central America, farmers in Costa Rica developed the first significant export trade. Most coffee in Costa Rica was produced on small and medium-sized farms using family or wage labor. In the following decades, other countries in Central America also opened new coffee frontiers, using a range of free and coerced labor.[18]

Brazil's coffee boom transformed the global coffee trade. In 1822, Brazil declared independence from Portugal. Seeking new sources of revenue, the government encouraged coffee cultivation, which could fill the gap that the Haitian Revolution had left in the global markets. Over the following decades, Brazilians did just that, taking advantage of slave labor and abundant forested land. Over the century, new railroads and steamship networks connected Brazil's vast and expanding coffeelands to global markets. By mid-century, Brazil produced half of the world's coffee; by the early twentieth century, it produced more than 80 percent. Brazil's exploding production drove global coffee prices downward, helping stimulate demand in the industrializing countries of the Global North—especially the United States. By the end of the century, the United States had surpassed all other countries to become the world's single largest market.[19]

To varying degrees, the expansion of cultivation in the rest of the world also involved the frequently ruthless exploitation of labor and forests. Outside of Brazil, slave-based coffee production continued in Cuba and Puerto Rico for much of the nineteenth century, although Cuba's coffee plantations lost many of their slaves to the booming sugarcane industry. In Java, the Dutch developed a supposedly humane system of coffee production, the "Culture System," which forced every household to cultivate a specified number of coffee trees and to sell the coffee to government buyers. The buyers would deduct a fixed "land rent" from the purchase price, which could amount to 40 percent of the total. In an attempt to increase yields, colonial officials also forced locals to cultivate coffee more intensively, often on farms distant from their villages. Beyond this, coffee planters in British colonies often turned to nominally "free" Indian laborers, who often worked in dire conditions, as did Indigenous laborers on coffee farms in Central America and Mexico.[20]

But the most egregious of the systems of forced cultivation proved to be expensive and unwieldy over the longer term. The Dutch gradually abandoned the Cultivation System and other forced cultivation schemes, and by the 1890s, the Brazilians had abandoned slave-based production in favor of migrants from southern Europe. In any case, coerced labor was never universal. In many places, smallholders and medium-sized farmers produced coffee freely and profitably. In Ceylon and India, local smallholders grew coffee alongside European estates, and even in remote corners of Mexico smallholder coffee and estates coffee grew in tandem.[21]

In the mid-nineteenth century, new crop diseases changed the global dynamic of coffee farming. A previously unknown disease, the coffee leaf rust, struck Ceylon in 1869. This fungal disease could defoliate the trees and thus disrupt the development of the coffee tree's branches and fruit. It spread through Ceylon in the 1860s, eventually driving estate planters to abandon coffee en masse for tea; many local smallholders abandoned coffee for commercial coconut production.[22] By 1900, the rust had gradually spread from Ceylon to Asia and the Pacific. This spread reflected the deepening horizontal connections across the world's coffeelands, which were linked by steamships and railroads. It caused particularly severe losses on coffee farms in the humid lowlands, where the fungus flourished. It devastated coffee production in much of Southwestern India, the Philippines, and the Dutch East Indies—especially on Sumatra and Java, whose names had once been synonymous with coffee. Later in the century, planters and scientists found that the rust could be controlled by copper sprays. But while these sprays could control the rust, in most places they were too expensive to be commercially viable.[23]

The coffee rust was just one of a growing range of environmental problems that coffee farmers encountered, as they exhausted the fertile soils of newly cleared forests (the "forest rent"), encountered new diseases and pests, and grappled with soil erosion and other consequences of poor agricultural practices. In places, they established new agricultural experiment stations and hired scientists who, they hoped, would help solve these problems. British botanists at the Royal Botanic Garden in Peradeniya, Ceylon, helped coffee planters try to cope with the rust. But it was the Dutch who established the first important coffee research centers in the 1870s. Scientists on Java and Sumatra did pioneering work on the coffee rust, and on the botany and breeding of coffee. In 1885, Brazilian farmers in the State of São Paulo founded an agricultural experiments station and hired an eminent Austrian agronomist, Franz Dafert, to study the problems of Brazilian production. Scientists at these and other stations made important discoveries about coffee and coffee farming, but they rarely had a decisive impact on coffee production. Dafert was aghast at the wasteful practices of the São Paulo planters, which he described as committing "robbery," but he was powerless to change them. The scientists often struggled to find scientific solutions to problems that were as much economic as ecological.[24]

Overproduction and Differentiation

Coffee farming in the twentieth century was transformed by the changing global economy. In the early years of the century, global coffee production (largely driven by Brazil) began to exceed demand regularly, driving global prices downward. This general trend was complicated by a biennial production cycle common in plantation coffee (again, typical of Brazil). Coffee farms would bear a heavy crop one year; the following year the exhausted trees would bear much less. Brazilian governments enacted a series of schemes to prop up the global price of coffee. During years of high production, they borrowed money to buy "surplus" coffee stocks. This coffee would be warehoused and released onto global markets in years where production was lower. Brazil's valorization schemes did succeed in their short-term goal of increasing and stabilizing the global price of coffee. But the policies also had the unintended effect of stimulating coffee production outside of Brazil.[25]

Brazil's commodity-grade arabicas faced challenges from both higher-quality and lower-quality coffees. No other country could compete with Brazil on volume, but they could compete on quality and price. Over the 1910s and 1920s, producers opened new arabica pioneer fronts in India, in Colombia and Central America, and in Kenya and Tanganyika (which had been brought under European colonial control).[26] The high quality of the coffee rested partly in the *terroirs*—the particular soils, topographies, and climates in which the coffee was cultivated. These new frontiers were in highland areas that were similar to Arabica coffee's native range in Ethiopia. The quality of the coffee produced in these regions also resided in the how the coffees were harvested and processed. Producing a high-quality coffee required capital and know-how; these mild arabicas were typically more expensive to produce than commodity-grade arabicas. But they also fetched correspondingly higher prices.[27]

Brazil's arabica also faced competition from an unexpected quarter: robusta coffee from Africa and Asia. This was the other species of coffee that had been cultivated by Africans. As Europeans colonized Africa during the latter half of the nineteenth century, they encountered new coffee species. They collected some of these plants and shipped them to botanical gardens and commercial nurseries in Europe; in 1900, some Dutch planters shipped robusta seeds and seedlings to Java. Unlike arabica, robusta coffee was well-adapted to lowland landscapes. It also, unlike arabica, proved to be resistant to the coffee leaf rust. Between 1900 and 1910, plant breeders in Java developed commercially viable selections of robusta. From 1910 onward, farmers in Java and Sumatra quickly replaced their rust-stricken arabica farms with robusta.[28]

Robusta's main disadvantage was commercial; it did not have the taste that buyers prized. But with the support of the Dutch government, it could compete successfully against the low-quality Brazilian arabicas. Robustas found a place in the roast and ground coffee blends popular in the United States and Europe. Its share of the global coffee market continued to grow over the twentieth century. The commercial success of robusta drove the opening of new coffee frontiers in the Dutch East Indies, Uganda, the Belgian Congo, and other parts of Africa and Asia where arabica production was not viable. These robustas, which could often be produced more cheaply than Brazilian arabicas, began to undercut Brazilian production from below.[29] Brazilian control schemes, then, ultimately aggravated the problem of global overproduction that it had intended to solve. Ironically, valorization reduced Brazil's share of global coffee production in the process. By 1937, Brazil's coffee defense schemes were no longer sustainable, and Getúlio Vargas's government abandoned them, flooding the market with coffee and driving global prices downward.

During the uncertain years of the 1930s, governments in exporting countries around the world began supporting (and often regulating) coffee production to ensure that their coffees could find markets. During these years, many colonies and countries established coffee institutes to help manage coffee production and trade, and to protect farmers from the worst excesses of the volatile global markets. For example, the Colombian Federation of Coffee Growers was founded in 1928 to promote Colombian coffee. Financed by a tax of ten cents on each sack of coffee exported, the federation brought the country's coffee growers into a single organization, which worked with national banks and government agencies. It offered extension services to farmers and sold them equipment and supplies at cost. The association also systematically promoted Colombian coffee in international markets. In Africa and Asia, the European imperial powers set tariffs and import quotas on "foreign" coffee to protect coffee production in their colonies. Such protections continued through the war and into the late 1950s.[30]

Coffee's Partial Green Revolution

The global coffee economy was disrupted by World War II. As production and consumption gradually resumed after the war, coffee prices in the mid-1950s skyrocketed as global demand exceeded supply. The price booms encouraged planters around the world—especially in in southern Brazil, Central America, and West Africa. Brazilian farmers extended Brazil's coffee frontier southward into the state of Paraná, whose rich red soils were ideal for the coffee plant, but whose climate was sometimes susceptible to devastating frosts. Farmers in western Africa, in an arc running from the Ivory Coast to Angola, expanded new robusta coffee frontiers to fuel growing global demand for instant coffee. By the end of the 1950s, one of these robusta producers—the Ivory Coast—was the world's third largest coffee exporter. By the mid-1950s, it became apparent that the planting boom would lead once again to an oversupply of coffee and prices would fall once again.[31]

In the Cold War context of the late 1950s, a collapse in global coffee prices was not just a financial problem, but also a geopolitical one. The NATO countries (which included most of the leading coffee-consuming nations) feared that communist insurgencies in the Global South would spread. To help promote political and economic stability in the Global South, the world's leading producing and consuming countries signed the International Coffee Agreement (ICA) in 1962. The agreement's goal was to balance global production and consumption, thereby stabilizing the price of coffee. This was to be achieved through a system of export quotas assigned to each producing nation. The quota system was far from perfect, in part because coffee production remained highly variable. A particularly bad frost in southern Brazil in July 1975 killed hundreds of millions of trees and reduced the next coffee harvest by half, sending prices skyrocketing. The quota system was suspended for several years after the frost, and other producing countries increased production to take advantage of the higher prices. As production recovered, quotas were reimposed. The ICA was an imperfect, contentious agreement, but it did manage to prevent the catastrophic price collapses from earlier in the century. On the other hand, it never solved the problem of chronic overproduction.[32]

In the decades following World War II, the Green Revolution gradually came to coffee. Colonial and national coffee institutes encouraged their farmers to "rationalize" or technify coffee production. Until the mid-twentieth century, most arabica farmers around the world still grew either the "typica" or "Bourbon" arabicas. Both were varieties from Yemen, which had been cultivated globally for two centuries. Both worked well in small diverse plots and on large estates, and they had good cupping potential. So why change? The main impetus was to increase farm productivity; in principle, a technified coffee farm could produce significantly more coffee per hectare than a traditional farm. Diseases and pests provided another impetus; the typica and Bourbon cultivars were susceptible to some of the main diseases of coffee, especially the coffee rust, which made its way through West Africa in the 1950s and 1960s, and Latin America in the 1970s and 1980s.[33]

Most technification programs were built around new, high-yielding cultivars. These cultivars were the product of local and global knowledge. Coffee plants would occasionally develop mutations or spontaneously cross with neighboring coffee cultivars and species. Farmers would notice these new plants and propagate the ones that looked interesting. Often, these plants would come to the attention of scientists, who would then take specimens to plant in a botanical garden or agricultural experiment station. The plants would be propagated and studied for a range of botanical and ecological characteristics (adaptation to local ecosystems, disease resistance, and productivity); the promising ones were often crossed with existing coffee cultivars. Coffee institutes might release the most promising improved selections to farmers and also circulate them to experiment stations around the world. In Brazil, the Instituto Agronômico de Campinas had developed an improved selection of a cultivar called Mundo Novo, which produced 240 percent more coffee than the traditional Typica cultivar. The Caturra cultivar had a "dwarf" mutation discovered in Brazil; it was smaller than traditional cultivars but just as productive. Producers outside Brazil benefited from this innovation. It did particularly well in landscapes with adequate rainfall, so while it was not widely adopted in Brazil, it flourished in Colombia and Central America.[34] On the other side of the world, in Timor, farmers found a spontaneous hybrid of arabica and robusta. This was taken to a new institution, the Coffee Rust Research Center in Portugal, where breeders crossed it with arabica cultivars (including Caturra), in the hopes of generating a high-yielding, rust-resistant arabica.[35] These new coffees, however, were just one part of the technification.

Full technification, as promoted by national coffee institutes and international research centers, was a package that involved restructuring the ecology and economy of traditional coffee farms. The new coffees were supposed to be planted more densely than the traditional cultivars; shade was to be reduced or eliminated altogether, since sunlight would stimulate growth. Chemical fertilizers were to be used to ensure soils could sustain these higher yields, and fungicides and pesticides to keep diseases and pests at bay. These additional yields and technology required much more labor than traditional farms. Experts assumed that the increased production would more than offset the costs of renovation and the costs of added labor. Some farmers, especially in Brazil, Colombia, and Costa Rica, did embrace full technification, especially as the coffee leaf rust made its way through Latin America in the 1970s and 1980s.[36]

The technification initiatives were most widespread in places with strong coffee institutes, which offered farmers financial and technical support. Large and medium-sized farms were more likely to technify, while many smallholders were not. Many farmers balked at the additional expense and labor the technified farms required. Others did not technify because they were illiterate and could not read the complex technical literature, or because technical support was inadequate. Even so, the farmers who did not fully technify were not necessarily opposed to innovation. They often adopted pieces of the technological package, but not the package as a whole. Depending on their circumstances a farmer might, for example, plant the new Caturra coffees but not eliminate shade. Or they might start using chemical sprays but continue cultivating Bourbon or Typica arabicas. By the 1990s, some two-thirds of the coffeelands of northern Latin America had been fully or partially technified.[37]

Neoliberal Coffee

The ICA's quota system broke down after 1989. It had been under pressure since the 1980s, as the World Bank and other organizations promoted structural reform programs in the Global South. In exchange for loans, borrowing countries were required to reduce government control over their economies and liberalize the national markets. As the Cold War drew to an end, the International Coffee Agreement lost its geopolitical rationale. Internal tensions among the producing countries had also grown over the 1980s. When the quota system broke down, producing countries quickly flooded the markets with their stocks of "excess" coffee, sending prices immediately into a tailspin. Since the 1990s, the global coffee trade entered a new phase of booms and busts, which have proven difficult to control collectively. At some moments—in 2002, and again in 2019—the benchmark prices for coffee have fallen below the costs of production for many farmers, who have been struggling to survive in these newly volatile markets.[38]

The global geography of coffee production continues to evolve. Brazil continues to dominate world's coffee production, but the center of domestic production in Brazil has shifted northward to the state of Minas Gerais. Brazilian production increased by a further 10 percent and continues to grow steadily. Colombian production has also grown, after a massive renovation program promoted by the National Federation of Coffee Growers. Farmers are opening new coffee frontiers in Peru and Honduras, on the fringes of Latin America's traditional coffee belt.

But perhaps the most significant story of the post-ICA years has been the explosion of coffee production in Vietnam, which by the mid-1990s became the world's second largest coffee producer—almost all of which was robusta. This boom was the result of a deliberate strategy of the Vietnamese state, aimed at resettling people into a forest region. Some critics have argued that this boom explains the problems of oversupply; but while Vietnam may have contributed to the problem, it was not its only cause. Coffee production elsewhere in Southeast Asia is also recovering; smallholders in Sumatra are largely responsible for reviving coffee production in Indonesia, which is also mostly robusta. It is once again the world's fourth largest coffee producer, regaining the place it had more than a century before. In the past decade, some farmers in China's Yunnan Province have started abandoning tea production for arabica. Chinese production may still be relatively small, but as of 2019 it ranked thirteenth globally, ahead of traditional coffee producers such as Costa Rica, Tanzania, and El Salvador.[39]

Some farmers are dealing with the volatile markets by producing high-quality coffees for specialty coffee buyers. The rise of the specialty coffee industry, the "Starbucks Revolution," has driven global demand for high-quality "mild" arabicas, most of which come from two major highland regions whose *terroirs* are suited to producing this kind of coffee: along the American Cordillera from Peru to Mexico, and in eastern Africa, from Tanzania to Ethiopia. Coffee farmers in these regions have started planting desirable arabica varies, like the Ethiopian Gesha coffee, by harvesting the beans only when they are ripe, and by taking great care in processing the cherries. The Specialty Coffee Association (SCA, founded in 1982) has set standards for quality, and any coffee that scores at least 80 points can be classified as specialty coffee. In principle, the specialty market allows farmers to break from the volatile commodity markets, sometimes by a significant amount. Gesha coffee from the Panamanian Hacienda la Esmeralda, with a score of 95 points, fetched $130 per pound at auction; others have sold for considerably more. But even more ordinary specialty coffees can sell for double or triple the price of commodity coffee.[40]

Certified coffees offered another way for farmers to cope with volatile prices and declining institutional support. These certification systems were typically defined and promoted by international NGOs. The Fair Trade movement sought to empower small farmers, helping them organize cooperatives and promote community development. Fair Trade coffee would sell for a premium over the price of conventional coffee. The early leaders of the Fair Trade movement hoped that the system would become an alternative to the conventional coffee markets. The other major certification system was certified organic coffee, and related certifications such as the Smithsonian's Migratory Bird Center's certified Bird Friendly coffee. The organic coffee certifications aimed to promote sustainable livelihoods and ecosystem health in the coffeelands. As with Fair Trade coffee, certified producers of organic coffee would receive a premium price for their coffee. Interest in certification schemes grew after the 2002 coffee crisis, when global overproduction drove coffee prices below the cost of production in many parts of the world. Since then, NGOs and businesses have developed a number of other certification schemes—including Rainforest Alliance Certified Coffee, and Starbucks' in-house Coffee and Farmer Equity (C.A.F.E.) certification. Although certified coffees have made a difference to many farmers, they are not a panacea. For example, farmers have often produced more coffee than the Fair Trade market can absorb, forcing them to sell the excess on the conventional market at commodity prices.[41]

The priorities of coffee research have evolved since 1990, reflecting the changing economic and ecological context of coffee production. For most of the twentieth century, researchers had emphasized productivity. But the particular model of technification promoted from the 1960s onward proved to be ecologically and economically unsustainable for many farmers, and also catastrophic for the broader ecosystems. In many places, farmers lost the economic and technical support that had made technification possible or were unable to afford the cost of inputs in the face of volatile or declining coffee prices. Farmers and others started to express concern about soil erosion, the loss of biological diversity, and contamination from the chemicals used on the farms.[42]

Since 1990, research has also started to emphasize cup quality, disease resistance (especially to the coffee rust), and economic and ecological sustainability more generally. A new industry-funded research organization, World Coffee Research, is working with coffee institutes to develop sustainable, rust-resistant coffees that can flourish in shaded systems as well as full-sun systems. These are known as F_1 coffees, which are crosses between traditional arabica cultivars and wild coffees collected in Ethiopia in the 1950s and 1960s. These F_1 coffees are helping to reinsert some badly needed genetic diversity into the world's cultivated arabicas. Other researchers are doing innovative work on coffee agroecology, in the hopes of developing more sustainable coffee farming.[43] And they are starting to confront the largest existential threat to coffee farming: climate change.

Coffee Futures

The future of coffee, like the future of all life, is already being transformed by climate change. Its impact will only grow in the years to come. Warming temperatures are, in places, forcing arabica farmers to abandon their crops, to move their farms, or to switch to robusta. Some forecasts suggest that climate change will drive coffee cultivation to higher altitudes; one forecast suggests that Brazil could lose 95 percent of its landscapes suitable for arabica by the end of the century.[44] In Ethiopia a combination of warming temperatures and deforestation is threatening the forests were wild arabica grows. This is a global problem since these wild coffees have been—and could be—an important course of diversity for breeding programs that could help breeders develop climate-resilient coffees.[45] Climate change is also triggering new outbreaks of diseases and pests—the coffee berry borer and the coffee rust. A major outbreak of the disease—known as the "Big Rust"—swept across the Americas between about 2007 and 2015, damaging coffee production across the region and driving some people out of farming altogether. These people have joined the flow of migrants heading north to the United States.[46]

The pressures of climate change are compounded by chronically and often catastrophically low prices, which make it difficult for farmers to respond effectively. The problem of almost chronic oversupply, which has plagued the coffee industry for more than a century, has yet to be solved. But this historical problem may be entering a new phase as climate change threatens all of the world's coffeelands. For all of the economic and environmental problems that coffee producers face, though, coffee remains an essential crop—for farmers perhaps even more than consumers. In the tropical landscapes where coffee flourishes, there are few alternatives that offer farmers the same kind of livelihood—even if that livelihood is now more precarious and difficult than ever. The challenge for the future is to work at developing models of coffee cultivation that are both ecologically and economically sustainable.

Notes

1. Aaron P. Davis et al., "An Annotated Taxonomic Conspectus of the Genus *Coffea* (Rubiaceae)," *Botanical Journal of the Linnean Society* 152, no. 4 (2006): 465–512, https://doi.org/10.1111/j.1095-8339.2006.00584.x.
2. F. Bart, "Café des montagnes, café des plaines," *Études Rurales*, no. 2 (2008): 35–48.
3. Jeff Koehler, *Where the Wild Coffee Grows: The Untold Story of Coffee from the Cloud Forests of Ethiopia to Your Cup* (New York: Bloomsbury, 2017): 45–60.
4. Brad Weiss, *Sacred Trees, Bitter Harvests: Globalizing Coffee in Northwest Tanzania* (Portsmouth, NH: Heinemann, 2003); T. S. Jervis, "A History of the Robusta Coffee in Bukoba," *Tanganyika Notes and Records* 7–12 (1941 1939): 47–58.
5. Michel Tuchscherer, "Coffee in the Red Sea from the Sixteenth to the Nineteenth Century," in *The Global Coffee Economy in Africa, Asia and Latin America, 1500–1989*, ed. W. G. Clarence-Smith and Steven Topik (Cambridge: Cambridge University Press, 2003): 50–52; Jonathan Morris, *Coffee: A Global History* (London: Reaktion Books, 2019): 47–50.

6. Haripriya Rangan, Judith Carney, and Tim Denham, "Environmental History of Botanical Exchanges in the Indian Ocean World," *Environment and History* 18, no. 3 (August 1, 2012): 311–342.
7. N. Bréon, "Mémoire sur la culture, la manipulation et le commerce du café en Arabie," *Annales maritimes et coloniales* 2 (1832): 566.
8. Jean de LaRoque, *A Voyage to Arabia Felix through the Eastern Ocean and the Streights of the Red-Sea* (London: E. Symon, 1732): 246.
9. Bréon, "Mémoire," 565.
10. F. Anthony et al., "The Origin of Cultivated *Coffea Arabica* L. Varieties Revealed by AFLP and SSR Markers," *TAG Theoretical and Applied Genetics* 104, no. 5 (2002): 894–900; J. Berthaud, "L'origine et la distribution des caféiers dans le monde," in *Le commerce du café avant l'ère des plantations coloniales. Espaces, réseaux, sociétés (XVe–XIXe siècle)*, ed. Michel Tuchscherer (Cairo: Institut français d'archéologie orientale, 2001): 361–370.
11. W. G. Clarence-Smith, "The Spread of Coffee Cultivation in Asia, from the Seventeenth to the Early Nineteenth Century," in *Le commerce du café avant l'ère des plantations coloniales. Espaces, réseaux, sociétés (XVe–XIXe siècle)*, ed. Michel Tuchscherer (Cairo: Institut français d'archéologie orientale, 2001): 371–384.
12. Clarence-Smith, "Coffee Cultivation in Asia."
13. Gwyn Campbell, "The Origins and Development of Coffee Production in Réunion and Madagascar, 1711–1972," in *The Global Coffee Economy in Africa, Asia and Latin America, 1500–1989*, ed. W. G. Clarence-Smith and Steven Topik (Cambridge: Cambridge University Press, 2003): 68–69.
14. LaRoque, *A Voyage to Arabia Felix*, 249.
15. Londa L. Schiebinger and Claudia Swan, *Colonial Botany: Science, Commerce, and Politics in the Early Modern World* (Philadelphia: University of Pennsylvania Press, 2005).
16. Anthony et al., "Origin of Cultivated *Coffea Arabica*"; Auguste Chevalier, *Les caféiers du globe* (Paris: Paul Lechevalier, 1929): 56–57.
17. Michel-Rolph Trouillot, "Motion in the System: Coffee, Color, and Slavery in Eighteenth-Century Saint-Domingue," *Review (Fernand Braudel Center)* 5, no. 3 (1982): 331–388. Weights have been converted from the pre-Revolutionary Livre de Paris (489.5 gr) to metric tons.
18. Steven Topik et al., eds., "The Latin American Coffee Commodity Chain: Brazil and Costa Rica," in *From Silver to Cocaine: Latin American Commodity Chains and the Building of the World Economy, 1500–2000* (Durham, NC: Duke University Press, 2006): 117–46.
19. Steven Topik and Michelle Craig MacDonald, "Why Americans Drink Coffee: The Boston Tea Party or Brazilian Slavery?," in *Coffee: A Comprehensive Guide to the Bean, the Beverage, and the Industry*, ed. Robert W Thurston, Jonathan Morris, and Shawn Steiman (Lanham, MD: Rowman & Littlefield, 2013): 234–47.
20. W. G. Clarence-Smith, "The Impact of Forced Coffee Cultivation on Java, 1805–1917," *Indonesia Circle*, no. 64 (1994): 241–64; James L. A. Webb, *Tropical Pioneers: Human Agency and Ecological Change in the Highlands of Sri Lanka, 1800–1900* (Athens: Ohio University Press, 2002).
21. Webb, *Tropical Pioneers*; Casey Marina Lurtz, *From the Grounds Up: Building an Export Economy in Southern Mexico* (Stanford, CA: Stanford University Press, 2019).
22. Stuart McCook, *Coffee Is Not Forever: A Global History of the Coffee Rust*, Ecology and History (Athens: Ohio University Press, 2019), ch. 3.
23. McCook, *Coffee Is Not Forever*, chap. 4.
24. Warren Dean, "The Green Wave of Coffee: Beginnings of Tropical Agricultural Research in Brazil (1885–1900)," *Hispanic American Historical Review* 69, no. 1 (February 1989):

91–115; Stuart McCook, "Managing Monocultures: Coffee, the Coffee Rust, and the Science of Working Landscapes," in *Knowing Global Environments: New Historical Perspectives on the Field Sciences*, ed. Jeremy Vetter (New Brunswick, NJ: Rutgers University Press, 2011): 87–107; P. J. S. Cramer, *A Review of Literature of Coffee Research in Indonesia*, Miscellaneous Publications Series, No. 15 (Turrialba: SIC Editorial, Inter-American Institute of Agricultural Sciences, 1957).

25. Robert H Bates, *Open-Economy Politics: The Political Economy of the World Coffee Trade* (Princeton, NJ: Princeton University Press, 1997), ch. 2; V. D. Wickizer, *The World Coffee Economy with Special Reference to Control Schemes*, Commodity Policy Studies 2 (Stanford, CA: Food Research Institute, Stanford University, 1943), ch. 10.

26. Bates, *Open-Economy Politics*, ch. 3; Mario Samper-Kutschbach, "Trayectoria y viabilidad de las caficulturas centroamericanas," in *Desafíos de la caficultura en Centroamérica*, ed. Benoît Bertrand and Bruno Rapidel (San José, Costa Rica: Agroamerica, 1999): 1–68; Antonio Di Fulvio, *Le café dans le monde* (Rome: Institut international d'agriculture, 1947).

27. Mario Samper-Kutschbach, "The Historical Construction of Quality and Competitiveness: A Preliminary Discussion of Coffee Commodity Chains," in *The Global Coffee Economy in Africa, Asia and Latin America, 1500–1989*, ed. W. G. Clarence-Smith and Steven Topik (Cambridge: Cambridge University Press, 2003): 120–53.

28. Stuart McCook, "The Ecology of Taste: Robusta Coffee and the Limits of the Specialty Revolution," in *Coffee: A Comprehensive Guide to the Bean, the Beverage, and the Industry*, ed. Robert W Thurston, Jonathan Morris, and Shawn Steiman (Lanham, MD: Rowman & Littlefield, 2013): 248–61.

29. McCook, "The Ecology of Taste."

30. Bates, *Open-Economy Politics*, ch. 3; Benoît Daviron and Stefano Ponte, *The Coffee Paradox: Global Markets, Commodity Trade, and the Elusive Promise of Development* (London: Zed Books, 2005): 85–86.

31. Daviron and Ponte, *The Coffee Paradox*, 85–86; Gavin Fridell, *Coffee* (Cambridge: Polity Press, 2014): 57–63.

32. Daviron and Ponte, *The Coffee Paradox*, 86–88; John Talbot, *Grounds for Agreement: The Political Economy of the Coffee Commodity Chain* (Lanham, MD: Rowman & Littlefield, 2004), ch. 4.

33. McCook, *Coffee Is Not Forever*; Robert A. Rice, "A Place Unbecoming: The Coffee Farm of Northern Latin America," *Geographical Review* 89, no. 4 (October 1999): 554–570; David Conrad Johnson, "The International Coffee Agreement and the Production of Coffee in Guatemala, 1962–1989," *Latin American Perspectives* 37, no. 2 (March 2010): 34–49, https://doi.org/10.1177/0094582X09356957.

34. E. A Graner and C. Godoy, eds., *Manual do cafeicultor* (São Paulo: Edições Melhoramentos, 1967), 34–39.

35. C. J. Rodrigues Jr. et al., "Importância do hibrido de Timor para o territorio e para o melhoramento da cafeicultura mundial," *Revista de ciências agrarias* 27 (2004): 203–216.

36. Rice, "A Place Unbecoming"; Wilson Picado Umaña, Rafael Ledezma Díaz, and Roberto Granados Porras, "Territorio de coyotes, agroecosistemas y cambio tecnológico en una región cafetalera de Costa Rica," *Revista de historia*, no. 59–60 (2009): 119–165.

37. Rice, "A Place Unbecoming"; Picado Umaña, Ledezma Díaz, and Granados Porras, "Territorio de coyotes, agroecosistemas y cambio tecnológico en una región cafetalera de Costa Rica."

38. Steven Topik, John M. Talbot, and Mario Samper, "Introduction: Globalization, Neoliberalism, and the Latin American Coffee Societies," *Latin American Perspectives* 37, no. 2 (2010): 5–20; Daviron and Ponte, *The Coffee Paradox*, 88–95.
39. Topik, Talbot, and Samper, "Introduction: Globalization and the Latin American Coffee Societies"; International Coffee Organization, "Coffee in China" (London: International Coffee Organization, August 10, 2015).
40. Price Peterson, "Strategies for Improving Coffee Quality," in *Coffee: A Comprehensive Guide to the Bean, the Beverage, and the Industry*, ed. Robert W Thurston, Jonathan Morris, and Shawn Steiman (Lanham, MD: Rowman & Littlefield, 2013): 13–19.
41. Robert A. Rice, "Noble Goals and Challenging Terrain: Organic and Fair Trade Coffee Movements in the Global Marketplace," *Journal of Agricultural and Environmental Ethics* 14, no. 1 (March 1, 2001): 39–66, https://doi.org/10.1023/A:1011367008474; Gavin Fridell, *Fair Trade Coffee: The Prospects and Pitfalls of Market-Driven Social Justice* (Toronto: University of Toronto Press, 2007); Sarah Lyon, *Coffee and Community: Maya Farmers and Fair-Trade Markets* (Boulder: University of Colorado Press, 2011); Maria Martínez-Torres, *Organic Coffee: Sustainable Development by Mayan Farmers* (Athens: Ohio University Center for International Studies, 2006).
42. Carlos E. Fernández and R. G. Muschler, "Aspectos de la sostenibilidad de los sistemas de cultivo de café en América Central," in *Desafíos de la caficultura en Centroamérica*, ed. Benoît Bertrand and Bruno Rapidel (San José, Costa Rica: Agroamerica, 1999): 69–96; John H. Vandermeer and Ivette Perfecto, *Breakfast of Biodiversity: The Political Ecology of Rain Forest Destruction* (Oakland, CA: Food First Books, 2013).
43. Ivette Perfecto and John H. Vandermeer, *Coffee Agroecology: A New Approach to Understanding Agricultural Biodiversity, Ecosystem Services, and Sustainable Development* (London: Routledge, 2015).
44. Christian Bunn et al., "Multiclass Classification of Agro-Ecological Zones for Arabica Coffee: An Improved Understanding of the Impacts of Climate Change," ed. Juan A. Añel, *PLoS ONE* 10, no. 10 (October 27, 2015): 2, https://doi.org/10.1371/journal.pone.0140490.
45. Aaron P. Davis et al., "The Impact of Climate Change on Indigenous Arabica Coffee (Coffea Arabica): Predicting Future Trends and Identifying Priorities," *PLoS ONE* 7, no. 11 (2012): e47981, https://doi.org/10.1371/journal.pone.0047981.
46. Juliana Jaramillo et al., "Some Like It Hot: The Influence and Implications of Climate Change on Coffee Berry Borer (*Hypothenemus hampei*) and Coffee Production in East Africa," *PLoS ONE* 6, no. 9 (September 14, 2011), https://doi.org/10.1371/journal.pone.0024528; McCook, *Coffee Is Not Forever*.

Bibliography

Bacon, Christopher M. *Confronting the Coffee Crisis: Fair Trade, Sustainable Livelihoods and Ecosystems in Mexico and Central America*. Cambridge, MA: MIT Press, 2008.
Bates, Robert H. *Open-Economy Politics: The Political Economy of the World Coffee Trade*. Princeton, NJ: Princeton University Press, 1997.
Clarence-Smith, William, and Steven Topik, eds. *The Global Coffee Economy in Africa, Asia and Latin America, 1500–1989*. Cambridge: Cambridge University Press, 2003.
Daviron, Benoît, and Stefano Ponte. *The Coffee Paradox: Global Markets, Commodity Trade, and the Elusive Promise of Development*. London: Zed Books, 2005.

Fridell, Gavin. *Coffee*. Cambridge: Polity Press, 2014.
Koehler, Jeff. *Where the Wild Coffee Grows: The Untold Story of Coffee from the Cloud Forests of Ethiopia to Your Cup*. New York: Bloomsbury, 2017.
Lurtz, Casey Marina. *From the Grounds Up: Building an Export Economy in Southern Mexico*. Stanford, CA: Stanford University Press, 2019.
McCook, Stuart. *Coffee Is Not Forever: A Global History of the Coffee Rust. Ecology and History*. Athens: Ohio University Press, 2019.
Morris, Jonathan. *Coffee: A Global History*. London: Reaktion Books, 2019.
Perfecto, Ivette, and John H. Vandermeer. *Coffee Agroecology: A New Approach to Understanding Agricultural Biodiversity, Ecosystem Services, and Sustainable Development*. London: Routledge, 2015.
Samper-Kutschbach, Mario. "The Central American Coffee Commodity Chain." *Oxford Research Encyclopedia of Latin American History*, May 23, 2019. https://doi.org/10.1093/acrefore/9780199366439.013.606.
Talbot, John. *Grounds for Agreement: The Political Economy of the Coffee Commodity Chain*. Lanham, MD: Rowman & Littlefield, 2004.
Thurston, Robert W., Jonathan Morris, and Shawn Steiman, eds. *Coffee: A Comprehensive Guide to the Bean, the Beverage, and the Industry*. Lanham, MD: Rowman & Littlefield, 2013.
Tuchscherer, Michel, ed. *Le commerce du café avant l'ère des plantations coloniales*. Cairo: Institut français d'archéologie orientale, 2001.
Wintgens, Jean Nicolas. *Coffee: Growing, Processing, Sustainable Production: A Guidebook for Growers, Processors, Traders and Researchers*. Weinheim: Wiley-VCH, 2004.

CHAPTER 20

BANANAS

EVAN P. BENNETT

BANANAS are among the oldest food crops cultivated by humans and are today the most-consumed fruit in the world. But their place in the diets of billions of people is not the result of a straight line of historical development. The popularity of these ancient fruits is, instead, the product of modern industrial capitalism. The organization of labor in banana production, the control of the banana trade by a few multinational companies, and even the fact that one variety rules the world market when dozens of other cultivars are produced worldwide are evidence of the connection between bananas and capitalism. Such capital-intensive production has resulted in a flood of healthy fruit that has been anything but healthy for the environment, workers, and democracy in the tropical nations where banana production dominates.

Bananas appear to grow on trees, but the large-leafed plants are actually a perennial herb. What appears to be the tree's trunk is a shoot known as a pseudostem that grows out of the bulb-shaped heart of the plant called a corm, which lies under the soil. From the corm spread shallow but far-ranging roots that collect the large amount of water the plants require for growth. Banana plants are known for their large flower, which usually appears about six months after the development of the pseudostem, but they do not reproduce sexually. Instead, each corm produces additional corms that are genetically identical to the original, which then produce their own pseudostems—identified as suckers, but often called daughters because of the way they will sprout around the base of the original corm and pseudostem. The flower produces the bananas, but the fruit is sterile and famously lacks seeds. A pseudostem will produce only one flower and bunch of fruit; its daughters rise in succession, replaced in time by their daughters.

These strange plants, at least the ones that produce fruit people consume, are the product not of normal plant evolution, but of human intervention. Wild bananas exist but are different from the more familiar versions. The plants look similar and their fruit is similar in shape, they are generally less sweet and, more noticeably, have a multitude of hard seeds that can produce new plants. They can be found throughout South and Southeast Asia, Indonesia, and Oceania, the result of human-aided expansion. Anthropologists conjecture that humans first desired the edible corms, not the fruits, of wild banana varieties, and developed methods for transplanting and cultivating them. Over time, the seeds disappeared when human cultivators began to select plants with mutations that inhibited seed growth.

The development of seedless varieties, both of sweet bananas and starchier plantains, created something of a Neolithic revolution in agriculture. Cultivators developed hundreds of varieties of bananas over thousands of years as they carried plants throughout southern and southeastern Asia to the Pacific Ocean and across the Indian Ocean to Africa, where they arrived in multiple waves separated by millennia. In Asia and the Pacific, the genetic diversity of the plant expanded as growers selected for plants that fit their ecological conditions. The diversity declined, however, as people carried the fruit west. In the tropical lowlands of sub-Saharan Africa, the plantain became the most widespread variety, while in the highlands the African Great Lakes, the East African Highland banana is a regional staple.

A third variety of banana, this one from the Indian Ocean coast, arrived in North Africa via the Middle East as Muslim trade routes expanded after the seventh century CE. These Indian Ocean Complex bananas gave rise to both the scientific and popular names for the plants: *mauz*, the Arabic word for the fruit, became, in Linnaeus' hands, *Musa*. Two stories have been given to explain the banana's common name. Some have suggested the Arabic word for "finger," *banan*, is the source. It is more likely Europeans picked the word up from West African sources. . The latter name followed as European traders carried them to colonial outposts on the West African coast, where they planted them to make food for the millions of Africans they enslaved and dispersed across the Atlantic basin and beyond. Bananas followed this trade as well, and from the sixteenth to the nineteenth centuries, banana agriculture spread all around the Caribbean Basin and throughout the American tropics. Bananas encircled the world like a belt.

Despite their widespread distribution, banana consumption remained localized to the regions that grew them. Since it takes between nine months and a year for a single plant to produce mature fruit, the relative slowness of the plants limits the volume of production. Individual cultivators could produce enough fruit for local consumption, but not for large markets. More critical, however, was that bananas, unlike the other staple crops that stitched together early modern trade routes, did not travel well. Once cut from the plant, green bananas naturally accelerate the ripening process by releasing ethelyne gas. In the unventilated heat of a ship's hold, even the greenest bunches will become overripe within days. Sometimes bananas made it to cities outside the tropics, but they were an expensive novelty.

Transportation revolutions in the nineteenth century enabled the development of the trade in bananas. In the 1870s, Massachusetts-based shipowner Lorenzo Dow Baker proved that with fair winds, ships could get bananas safely from Jamaica to the burgeoning cities of the northern United States, and in the process whetted American appetites for the fruit. In 1885, Dow and his partners formed the Boston Fruit Company to feed this demand. Abandoning sail for steam, they loaded ice in the holds to cool the precious fruit and slow its ripening. Soon, they shipped bananas just about anywhere in the United States. Eventually renamed the United Fruit Company, the company rushed to monopolize the market. Equally quickly, competitors adopted their methods to block them. A few small importers took some of the business, but only the Standard Fruit Company, which began by importing bananas into New Orleans, could ultimately stand toe-to-toe with United Fruit. By the early twentieth century, the two companies monopolized the banana market in the United States and Latin America. They not only controlled the flow of most bananas going to the United States, but they competed in the European market too. Today, the modern iterations of the companies, Chiquita (United Fruit) and Dole (Standard Fruit), remain the largest banana companies in the world.

In the earliest phases of the business, importers purchased available crops at the markets of Caribbean ports. Over time, they encouraged local farmers to grow more bananas. Since this did not require a significant amount of work or investment, farmers obliged. All they had to do was cut a daughter away from its mother plant to spur its growth and flowering; the plants largely took care of themselves until they fruited. In the 1880s and 1890s, a revolution in agriculture spread across the Caribbean as smallholders in Jamaica, Cuba, the other islands, and the Caribbean coasts of Central and South America began planting bananas and selling them to American buyers.

The companies recognized that this model was not ideal for long-term growth and control, so they purchased large tracts of land on which to grow their own fruit. This gave them control of not only the largest distribution networks, but the means of production as well. They owned the land on which they grew bananas, the railroads that carried them to port, the ships that carried them to North America, and the distribution networks that carried them to corner markets across the nation.

The American Minor Keith was one of the first businessmen to build a plantation empire. Invited to Costa Rica in 1871 to help his uncle complete a railroad from the capital in San José to the Caribbean port of Limón, Keith inherited the project when his uncle died on the job in 1874. Pushing thousands of workers to and beyond their physical limits, he oversaw completion of the railroad in 1890. Over that time, he accumulated thousands of acres of land as payment. Needing a way to make the railroad profitable, he formed the Tropical Trading and Transport Company to ship bananas (he had begun growing them in Costa Rica as a way of feeding the workers on the project). Over the following years, he expanded his landholdings in Colombia, including in the territory that would eventually become Panama, and in Guatemala. In 1899, Keith sold his holdings to the partners of the Boston Fruit Company, who made him a vice president and renamed the company the United Fruit Company. Overnight, United Fruit owned not only tens of thousands of acres in Central and South America, it also controlled railroads and ports. From this base, the company expanded its grip, buying land, building plantations, importing, and dictating terms to the political leaders of Costa Rica, Colombia, and Guatemala. A similar pattern followed in 1929 when United Fruit bought Sam Zemurray's Cuyamel Fruit Company, which owned large tracts of land in Honduras. By 1930, the United Fruit Company alone owned more than 3.4 million acres across the Caribbean lowlands. The story was similar for the Standard Fruit Company, which pushed into Ecuador as well as the Caribbean.

By the early twentieth century, they had carved much of Central America and northern South America into vast zones in which the companies controlled the entire economy. These zones consisted of thousands of planted acres as well as thousands more in reserve. No mere outposts, these were planation complexes that had several tiers of housing, from management down to workers, commissaries, and even recreational facilities for the white American managers who resided there.[1]

Workers labored long hours in dangerous conditions. Establishing a stand of banana plants required workers to clear tropical forests, dig canals for irrigation and drainage (bananas require a lot of water but cannot survive in standing water), and transplant thousands of plants, called "suckers," to the fields. Once the suckers were planted, the ground had to be hoed for weeds and the plants mulched with organic material (often dead banana leaves). After the plants reached sufficient height to shade the ground, workers pruned leaves and dug out excess daughters to keep the plants' energy focused on fruit production. (Some number of daughters were kept to allow for plant succession.) Once the fruit developed, workers cut the massive bunches with machetes. Bunches weighed between 80 and 100 pounds, so this was usually a two-person job. This job also had to be done quickly, in the brief window between when the bananas reached their optimal size and the beginning of the yellowing process. Foremen pushed workers to keep a fast pace despite the dangers of swinging machetes and venomous snakes and spiders. Workers rushed bananas to the packing sheds for shipment since the ripening process accelerated as soon as their machetes separated the bunches from the plants. Once they harvested the bunches, workers returned to the fields to cut down the now-useless pseudostems so that the next daughter could rise in its place. This cycle continued for a few years until the soil was exhausted and the company moved on to newly cleared lands.[2]

To grow the bananas, companies imported workers from all over the Caribbean, especially the impoverished British Caribbean, because of the difficulty of obtaining sufficient numbers of local workers. Executives also liked imported workers because they could exert greater control over their lives. Single male workers lived in rough barracks, while families lived in ramshackle cottages. Malaria and other tropical diseases were common. Companies often paid workers in scrip, forcing them to buy their food and supplies from company stores at inflated prices. They also maintained close oversight of surveilled workers and repressed any attempt workers might make to organize themselves. Not only could the fruit companies rely on local political leaders to safeguard their interests, they regularly relied on the military and diplomatic support of the US government to keep both workers and recalcitrant political leaders in line.

Booming demand for bananas in the United States fed the rapid expansion of banana plantations. Between 1892 and 1911, banana imports into the United States increased from 12 million bunches to nearly 45 million bunches annually, and demand only increased throughout the twentieth century.[3] Bananas, it seemed, were on every breakfast table and every dessert tray in North America. What had been a novelty was, by the early twentieth century, a staple of American diets. Modern advertising campaigns helped spur demand. Banana companies helped extol the health benefits of the fruit.

They published recipe books and guides for educators to encourage consumption. All this publicity fed a cultural revolution of sorts. So familiar were bananas that they figured into comedy routines, popular music, and, with Carmen Miranda's tutti-frutti hat, even fashion.

Americans fell in love with the cheap fresh fruit that was available all year round thanks to an expansive network of trains that delivered the bananas around the country as soon as they came off the ship. By 1905, New Orleans had become the largest fruit port in the world thanks to the banana trade.[4] The Standard Fruit Company monopolized the ice business in New Orleans in order to supply its trains. In time, New York City; Baltimore, Maryland; Tampa, Florida; Mobile, Alabama; and Galveston, Texas, also became important banana ports. The unlikely town of Fulton, Kentucky, became the "Banana Capital of the World" because five railroad lines carrying bananas met there and dispatchers for the fruit companies found it a convenient place from which to direct the fruit across the nation. The gleaming ships of United Fruit's Great White Fleet, the name taken in imitation of the fleet of American battleships that symbolized US expansionist policy in the late nineteenth and early twentieth centuries, themselves became familiar in their own right since they doubled as cruise ships to Caribbean ports of call. Providing first-class service, they even allowed passengers to cool their rooms using chilled air brought up from the ships' holds (where ice was stored to slow the ripening process.

In Europe, demand similarly expanded, but the delivery network differed. Colonial administrators, not corporate moguls, controlled the banana trade. In the early twentieth century, British policymakers encouraged the expansion of banana planting in their colonial possessions of Jamaica and Belize, as well as in Dutch-controlled Suriname. Rather than turning over large amounts of land to large corporations, they established an organization through which small-scale growers could coordinate shipping and distribution with the company that came to be called Fyffes. Fyffes, in turn, had guaranteed control of three-quarters of the British market. After World War II, the British government essentially duplicated this model in the Windward Islands, giving the Geest Corporation exclusive rights to banana shipping from these islands. The French government, meanwhile, followed this model, nurturing smallholder banana production on their colonies of Martinique and Guadeloupe through state-supported growers' organizations.[5]

The expansion of banana agriculture across the tropical lowlands of Latin America and the Caribbean was not simply a function of expanded demand, corporate greed, or state policy, though. The threat of plant disease also drove banana companies to buy land and remake the landscape of Latin America. Monocrop agriculture creates conditions in which pests and diseases can spread rapidly across the landscape because of a lack of barriers in preventing their movement. Plantation crops thus regularly teeter on ecological collapse. Beginning in the 1890s, a fungal infection caused by a fungus called *Fusarium cubense* attacked banana crops across the Caribbean basin and beyond. The fungi traveled up the root structures and vascular tissues of infected plants, causing the leaves to wither and, in severe cases, prevent the plants from producing fruit. As an infected plant decayed, the fungus released spores into the soil that would then germinate when they came into contact with the roots of other plants. Since the plants were genetically virtually identical to one another, the disease could spread especially quickly once the fungus appeared in the soil. One infected plant could then infect all of the plants around it; within a relatively short time, an entire plantation could be dead.

"Panama disease"—as it was called because of where it was first noted—spread rapidly in the early twentieth century. Costa Rican plantations bore the brunt of the disease by the turn of the twentieth century, and major outbreaks occurred in Suriname, Cuba, Trinidad, Puerto Rico, and Jamaica over the next decade. Honduras noted its first outbreaks in the 1910s.[6] As plants died, exports fell, and companies scrambled for more land.

For banana companies, the problem was compounded by the fact that they grew only one variety of bananas, the Gros Michel ("Big Mike"), first recognized as a distinct variety in the 1830s by a French planter originally from Saint-Domingue (Haiti) who noticed it growing on Martinique and took a sample to grow on his plantation in Jamaica. Over the next half-century, government officials in search of new export crops and workers hoping to bring foods from home as they moved around the Caribbean in the wake of emancipation spread the variety across Jamaica and around the Caribbean Basin. By the 1890s, the combination of consumer preferences and shipping requirements encouraged companies to focus their attention on growing this variety. Large and sweet, the Gros Michel attracted consumers with its beautiful color and tantalizing aroma. But it was other physical qualities that made it irresistible to shippers. The long fruit did not ripen too quickly, and its thick skin resisted easy bruising. The individual fingers also nested together on the bunch in a way that protected the fingers from breaking off easily.

Gros Michels proved particularly vulnerable to Panama disease, but agricultural practices compounded whatever inherent susceptibility the plants had to infection. The fungus had been extant in the Caribbean and Central America for centuries before the outbreaks of the early twentieth century, but its effects were so diffuse as to be barely noticeable. Spores (and therefore disease) faced roadblocks in their movement so long as a mosaic landscape of small farms and jungle remained in place. Plants might carry or die from the disease, but their farmers would have had little reason for concern. However, historian John Soluri explains, clearing thousands of acres of forests and planting them with Gros Michel bananas made the pathogen a significant problem.[7] Gros Michel had an Achilles' heel in *Fusarium cubense*, but banana companies' decision to grow them as a monocrop was the fundamental problem.

It took scientists more than two decades to isolate the fungus that caused Panama disease. A cure proved elusive. Quarantine became the preferred tool, but it was ineffective because of the very mobility of the banana industry. Every aspect of the banana economy was built on motion. Companies transplanted banana plants from farm to farm and from one country to another. Workers similarly crossed land and sea to wherever there were jobs. Company-built irrigation and drainage canals moved water from where it was not wanted to where it was needed, while their railroads carried bananas and everything needed to grow them across long distances. Spores of the fungus followed all of these vectors, attached to soil, clothing, tools, and anything else they could cling to. Even the ample tropical rains, so critical to the growth of bananas, ferried the disease from place to place as it carried soil from the mountains to the sea.

In the 1920s, United Fruit, at their own private research farms, and the British government, at the Imperial College of Tropical Agriculture in Trinidad, each began hunting for a variety of banana that could resist Panama disease. The work proceeded very slowly. Scientists first tried but failed to cross-pollinate the Gros Michel with wild, seeded varieties in hope of producing offspring that resisted disease while maintaining the qualities that made it popular. The Gros Michel had been selected for its low fertility—its lack of seeds—so cross-fertilizing with anything was nearly impossible. When they were able to obtain seeds from their experiments, the plants almost all failed to bear fruit. Attempts with other varieties failed, too, but for commercial, not scientific reasons: consumers in the Unites States simply would not purchase bananas that did not look and taste like Gros Michels. Standard Fruit and Cuyamel Fruit both attempted to import the Lacatan variety in place of Gros Michels, but distributors refused to buy them because they differed from the banana American consumers recognized.[8]

Since they could not overcome Panama disease, US banana companies tried to outrace it. Abandoning infected plantations, they cut new ones out of the tropical forests they owned and rushed to buy more reserve land. By the 1920s, United Fruit operated businesses in thirty-two countries and owned more than 1.6 million acres of land.[9] They built new docks, moved railroads, and moved workers by the thousands to build these new plantations. In their wake, they left rotting wharves, abandoned towns, and fields infected with *Fusarium cubense*. The companies, so focused on bananas, saw little reason to plant anything else on them.

Building new plantations and controlling holdings this large required significant support from local governments. The writer O. Henry first used the term "Banana Republic" in 1901 as a title for a short story based on the political corruption he had seen in Honduras; the term remained apt for most of the following century. Banana companies, most notoriously the United Fruit Company, gained functional control of the economies and politics of entire nations in their rush to secure unimpeded access to land, cheap, pliable labor, and low taxes. Political leaders across the banana-growing regions of Latin America and the Caribbean complied with the demands of American executives in order to retain their own power and build personal fortunes. Those that refused soon lost their offices.

Two notable examples of the power of the banana companies to shape local politics in this era stand out. The first took place in Colombia. In the 1920s, a changing political landscape brought public criticism of United Fruit and a formal investigation into its history of land acquisition. Banana workers took advantage of the opportunity to protest the company's labor practices. In October 1928, tens of thousands of workers walked off the job to demand improved treatment by the company. They hoped to secure higher wages, more sanitary working conditions, curtailment of the practice of hiring workers through labor contractors who shielded the company from labor laws, and an end to the company's practice of paying workers in scrip redeemable only in United Fruit–owned stores.

Political leaders in Colombia's ruling Conservative party recognized the threat to the existing order and the economic calamity that would follow if United Fruit felt its interests were threatened and decided to move operations to another country. They also feared that the US embassy, encouraged by United Fruit executives to see worker activism as a threat to American interests in Colombia, might convince President Calvin Coolidge to send in the US military to put down the strike. Convinced of the need to take decisive action to avoid the embarrassment of being invaded by the United States, the Colombian government dispatched troops to the town of Cienaga, where the strikers had their strongest support, in December 1928. The troops corralled the community, strikers and non-strikers alike, into the town square and opened fire. Accounts vary, but soldiers killed upwards of several thousand in the Banana Massacre (Matanza de las Bananeras). The massacre broke the strike but also helped to destabilize Colombian politics for decades to come.

The overthrow of President Jacobo Árbenz in Guatemala in 1954 proved an even clearer example of the power of United Fruit in the countries where it grew bananas. United Fruit began building plantations in Guatemala around 1900. Over the next half-century, with the help of autocratic political leaders, the company amassed 4 million acres of land (70 percent of the nation's arable land), on which it paid little to no taxes. The company built railroads across the nation's difficult terrain, but it pressured government officials not to build other roads in order to prevent competition. It also built port facilities but paid no customs duties. Government leaders enforced no labor laws and repressed any attempt by banana workers to organize themselves. These workers, most of them Maya Indians, were among the most destitute and brutalized in the world. By the 1930s, when General Jorge Ubico led Guatemala, United Fruit could count on compulsory labor laws that mandated Mayas work a minimum of one hundred days a year for United Fruit or its subsidiaries. Meanwhile, the law cleared the way for company foremen and managers to use violence, up to and including homicide, to punish workers who failed to obey orders. United Fruit, Guatemala's small, but growing middle class complained, was simply one large banana plantation.[10]

Nearly a decade of reform followed a 1944 popular uprising by urban workers and military leaders that overthrew Ubico's government. In the early 1950s, President Árbenz extended these to the nation's relationship with United Fruit. He pressed United Fruit to pay export duties, pay fair prices for land it acquired, accurately report the value of its land holdings, and respect Guatemalan law with regard to the treatment of its workers. In 1952, he took aim at United Fruit's massive landholdings by issuing Decree 900, which called for the government to confiscate all unused or abandoned farms larger than 223 acres and redistribute these to peasants. United Fruit stood to lose millions of acres it had abandoned because of Panama disease. Despite the seeming worthlessness of the land, the company, understanding its potential value if a cure for Panama disease could be found, was loath to see its land redistributed. Adding to company leaders' anger,

Árbenz's government offered to pay only a small fraction of what the land was worth because it turned to the valuations the company had provided in its tax returns.[11]

United Fruit turned to the US government for help in keeping their land. Company executives labeled Árbenz a communist and employed a massive disinformation campaign to convince US political leaders that the Soviet Union was behind his land reforms. In an era when United Fruit's Chiquita brand—introduced in 1944 as a way to distinguish its fruit from that of its competitors in the minds of American consumers— seemed as American as apple pie and anticolonial uprisings had brought a wave of nationalized industries, building support for US action against Árbenz was relatively easy. Diplomats from the US State Department pressured Árbenz to cede to United Fruit's demands. When he refused, the US Central Intelligence Agency (CIA) began an operation to overthrow him. When an invasion of US-backed insurgents and a naval blockade failed to effect his ouster in December 1953, CIA operators used United Fruit's Miami-based radio network to broadcast a disinformation campaign. Threatening a US invasion and accusing the Árbenz government of atrocities against its supposed internal enemies, the CIA was able to turn the Guatemalan military against Árbenz. In June 1954, Árbenz resigned and fled Guatemala. His departure closed the door on reforms and brought on a long period of political instability and violence. As in Colombia, banana companies were not to blame entirely for the chaos that followed, but they certainly bore a large portion of responsibility. The economic power of companies like United Fruit left workers in poverty, while support for repressive governments undermined attempts to create durable, honest government institutions. The nations where United Fruit and its competitors operated paid dearly for cheap bananas.

Whatever help the American government could give the company in overcoming political opponents, it could do little to help United Fruit and its competitors battle its more insidious foe, Panama disease. By the 1950s, researchers had turned up no way to control the spread of the disease, and the banana companies were nearly out of places to run from it. Meanwhile, attempts to develop a variety of banana that could resist Panama disease and match the Gros Michel's qualities as a shipping banana while appealing to a mass market had proceeded only slowly since the 1920s. "Big Mike" was hard to replace.

There was one contender: the Cavendish. First developed in the nineteenth century on the English estate of William Cavendish, Sixth Duke of Devonshire, the variety had several cultivars of different sizes. All had been exported to South and Southeast Asia, Australia, and the islands of the South Pacific throughout the second half of the nineteenth century, but the popularity of the Gros Michel had limited their planting in the Caribbean and Central America. Banana scientists knew the variety well and understood that it held promise. Most important, the Cavendish appeared not to be susceptible to Panama disease. It did not taste just like the Gros Michel, but the flavor was fairly close when ripened properly. Also, Cavendish plants were shorter that Gros Michel plants, a benefit both in terms of ease of harvest and wind-resistance, a critical concern in a region prone to tropical cyclones. Only one characteristic made banana shippers reluctant: Cavendish bananas had thinner skins and, thus, existing shipping methods left them prone to bruising. Unlike the Gros Michel, massive bunches could not simply be piled on one another in the holds of the banana fleet.

In the early 1950s, Standard Fruit, running out of new land to clear, took a chance with the Giant Cavendish cultivar. They called it the "Golden Beauty" to build its appeal.[12] It was not immediately popular, but neither did distributors and consumers reject it outright. For a couple years, the company imported the Cavendish alongside the Gros Michel, but in 1958, it abandoned the latter entirely in favor of the former. Growers in the British Caribbean, also short on new land and encouraged by scientists, colonial agents, and exporters, made a similar transition at around the same time. The industry's transition away from Gros Michels remained incomplete, however, until the mid-1960s. Distributors and consumers continued to show a preference for Gros Michel bananas when placed next to Cavendish varieties. United Fruit, with its massive landholdings, was less eager for this reason to dump the Gros Michel and continued planting it. This proved futile in the long run, though, and the company, faced with rapidly declining profits, made the switch to a Cavendish variety known as Valery in the early 1960s.

By 1965, the Cavendish had replaced the Gros Michel on plantations across Latin America and the Caribbean as United Fruit followed Standard Fruit's example in planting the variety. Its ascendance was followed by a change in how companies shipped bananas. Faced with the problem of bruising, shippers experimented with cutting up the giant stems and placing smaller bunches of the fingers in boxes for shipping. By the mid-1960s, this method had become the dominant practice. This change came just as shipping generally moved away from break-bulk cargo and toward containerization. In 1955, American trucking company owner Malcom McLean built the first container ship, the *Ideal X*, and proved that ships could efficiently carry cargo loaded into steel containers that could be loaded directly onto trucks. A revolution in shipping all kinds of cargo took place seemingly overnight, and so did the nature of work on the docks. No longer did longshoremen clamber down into ships' holds and unload pallets of one thing and bags of another. Instead, they used cranes to move the containers from stacks on the ships' decks to waiting semi-trucks. The adoption of the boxed banana coincided perfectly with this change. Across the ports of the United States and Europe, images of large men carrying hefty bunches of bananas disappeared, replaced by longshoremen operating cranes and forklifts.

The boxes offered an opportunity for banana companies to market their products, too. United Fruit had labeled their fruit with the Chiquita name in the 1940s as a way of distinguishing their bananas from those grown and imported by other companies. They had created an entire advertising campaign with Carmen Miranda as a spokesperson. Standard Fruit had followed this model in branding when they introduced the Cavendish. Boxing allowed both companies to further distinguish their bananas, reclassifying them as branded consumer items. Standard Fruit started it by printing the brand name "Cabana" on its boxes. United Fruit followed a few years later by reviving the Chiquita brand name.[13]

Branding bananas was a double-edged sword, however. The 1960s was a period of increasing brand identification in American grocery stores. Consumers, primed by massive advertising campaigns, sought out name brand items, including bananas. This was boon for both companies, who spent large sums on convincing consumers on the healthiness of their fruits. Brand identification, however, placed significant pressure on companies to show why their fruits were better and, as important, avoid any negative associations in consumers' minds. Neither company wished for consumers to find fruit objectionable in appearance. Pressure increased for larger, cleaner fruit, and, as a result, banana companies increased their use of chemical fertilizers, insecticides, and fungicides. These all carried consequences for both workers and the environment. Runoff from nitrogen-rich fertilizers spoiled water supplies while workers found themselves exposed to a wide range of toxic chemicals.[14]

The Cavendish offered banana companies relative stability even as the region where they grew them convulsed with political upheaval. Guatemala, Honduras, and Colombia all endured repressive governments and internal strife—some of it related to the power of the banana companies in this era. The companies themselves, too, went through a period of upheaval in the late 1960s and 1970s, as a wave of corporate mergers reshaped the US banana markets. Castle & Cooke, owner of the Dole pineapple brand, purchased Standard Fruit in 1967 and placed its Dole brand on the bananas it shipped. Not long after that, Del Monte, better known as a producer of canned vegetables, purchased the relatively small West Indies Fruit Company, giving it access to Caribbean banana lands. And in 1969, Eli Black purchased United Fruit, rechristened it United Brands, and made it part of his larger business holdings. United Brands faltered almost immediately under the weight of increased competition, investigations by the US government, and a 1972 earthquake that devastated production in Honduras. Black committed suicide in 1975, and the company traded hands several times before being renamed Chiquita Brands in 1985. Today, Chiquita is a privately held subsidiary of the Brazilian companies Safra Group and Culturale.

These large companies continue to dominate the production of what are often called "dollar bananas"—bananas intended for US and other non-European markets and thus traded on the open market for American dollars. Taking advantage of economies of scale, these corporations own massive plantations that are often larger than 12,000 acres in size, and they control distribution from the fields to the grocery stores. In the countries where they are present, they are often the largest employers, hiring tens of thousands of men and women. Working conditions, while better than in the early to mid-twentieth century, remain problematic. Cutting bananas is still done manually, workers still face exposure to chemical pesticides and fungicides, and the work is often seasonal and done by temporary employees, many of whom are imported and therefore lack the protections of citizenship.[15]

These conditions differ markedly from those on the farms in the so-called ACP (Africa, Caribbean, Pacific) network, which, as of 2003, accounted for about a third of the world banana trade. In the ACP system, farmers in former European colonies in the three regions grow bananas on contract for European distributors through state-sponsored growers' associations. Most of these growers are small to medium-sized Caribbean landowners. Growing bananas on these farms is far more labor-intensive because most lack the size necessary to pay for equipment that is commonly used by the large corporations that control the dollar banana business. Most also use fewer fertilizers and chemical pesticides as well. However idyllic these farms may seem in comparison to the large plantations of Central America, they face problems of profitability and sustainability because of the high costs of shipping bananas from numerous points to Europe.[16]

The ACP system faced an additional challenge in the form of competition from the Dollar Banana companies, led by Chiquita. In the early 1990s, recognizing that the newly formed European Union (EU) would streamline importing bananas and responding to increased demand for bananas across Europe, the Dollar Banana companies increased the amount of bananas they shipped to Europe. In response, the EU placed higher tariffs on the non-ACP bananas. The so-called Banana Wars ensued. Led by the United States, individual Latin American banana-producing countries took the EU before the World Trade Organization (WTO) to contest the duties. Despite the ACP system's purpose of supporting the growers of former European colonies, the WTO found in favor of the Dollar Banana countries, forcing the EU to negotiate new trade deals with the Latin American countries under the watchful eye of the United States. Figuring out how maintain a balance that will allow the smaller growers of the ACP nations to survive in the face of the oligopolistic power of the Chiquita, Del Monte, and Dole has been of significant concern for European diplomats and activists for Fair Trade bananas for the past two decades. It has become only more complicated as the leading banana exporters have themselves become subsidiaries of larger multinational corporations.[17]

In the end, it may be nature that has the final word on the future of banana exports. In the 1990s, Taiwanese farmers began seeing signs of rot on their Cavendish plants. Another variety of *Fusarium* was to blame. Scientists called it Panama disease Tropical Race 4, and like its namesake, there is no cure at hand. The disease soon spread throughout Southeast Asia and Australia, then moved to Africa. In 2019, government officials in Colombia announced that it had been found along that nation's Caribbean coast. As they did a century earlier, banana companies and government scientists recognize the threat the disease poses to their primary fruit and have begun the search for a new variety that will withstand the disease. Varieties like the Goldfinger and the Mona Lisa have shown promise, but they are not quite ready for widespread planting. Unlike in the last battle with Panama disease, the companies have nowhere to run. The future of the banana as an export crop and as a cheap food for so many around the world will depend on the development of a new variety, another step in the banana's long human history.

Notes

1. James Wiley, *The Banana: Empires, Trade Wars, and Globalization* (Lincoln: University of Nebraska Press, 2008): 23–39.
2. William Fawcett, *The Banana: Its Cultivation, Distribution, and Commercial Uses* (London: Duckworth & Co., 1913): 20–47.
3. John Soluri, "Accounting for Taste: Export Bananas, Mass Markets, and Panama Disease," *Environmental History* 7 (July 2002): 388.

4. Virginia Scott Jenkins, *Bananas: An American History* (Washington, DC: Smithsonian Institution Press, 2000): 51.
5. Laura T. Raynolds, "The Global Banana Trade," in *Banana Wars: Power, Production, and History in the Americas*, ed. Steve Striffler and Mark Moberg (Durham, NC: Duke University Press, 2003): 27–28.
6. John Soluri, *Banana Cultures: Agriculture, Consumption, and Environmental Change in Honduras and the United States* (Austin: University of Texas Press, 2005), 53–55.
7. Ibid., 54.
8. Ibid., 55–56, 65–67.
9. Dan Koeppel, *Banana: The Fate of the Fruit that Changed the World* (New York: Hudson Street Press, 2008), 75.
10. Ibid., 121.
11. Ibid., 127–28.
12. John Soluri, "Banana Cultures: Linking the Production of Consumption of Export Bananas, 1800–1980," in *Banana Wars: Power, Production, and History in the Americas*, ed. Steve Striffler and Mark Moberg (Durham, NC: Duke University Press, 2003), 71.
13. Ibid., 72–73.
14. Ibid., 74–75.
15. Raynolds, "The Global Banana Trade," 32–37.
16. Ibid., 29–32, 35–37.
17. Ibid., 39–45.

Bibliography

Bucheli, Marcelo. *Bananas and Business: The United Fruit Company in Colombia, 1899–2000*. New York: New York University Press, 2005.

Chapman, Peter. *Bananas: How the United Fruit Company Shaped the World*. New York: Canongate, 2007.

Floyd, Joseph. "Seeing the Southland: Travelers on United Fruit's Great White Fleet." *Southern Studies* 22, no. 1 (Spring/Summer 2015): 100–116.

Frundt, Henry J. *Fair Bananas: Farmers, Workers, and Consumers Strive to Change an Industry*. Tucson: University of Arizona Press, 2009.

Jenkins, Virginia Scott. *Bananas: An American History*. Washington, DC: Smithsonian Institution Press, 2000.

Koeppel, Dan. *Banana: The Fate of the Fruit that Changed the World*. New York: Hudson Street Press, 2008.

Martin, James W. *Banana Cowboys: The United Fruit Company and the Culture of Corporate Colonialism*. Albuquerque: University of New Mexico Press, 2018.

Moburg, Mark. *Slipping Away: Banana Politics and Fair Trade in the Eastern Caribbean*. Oxford: Berghahn Books, 2008.

Pianni-Farnell, Lorna. *Banana: A Global History*. London: Reaktion Books, 2016.

Soluri, John. *Banana Cultures: Agriculture, Consumption, and Environmental Change in Honduras and the United States*. Austin: University of Texas Press, 2005.

Striffler, Steve, and Mark Moberg, eds. *Banana Wars: Power, Production, and History in the Americas*. Durham, NC: Duke University Press, 2003.

Wiley, James. *The Banana: Empires, Trade Wars, and Globalization*. Lincoln: University of Nebraska Press, 2008.

CHAPTER 21

POTATOES

CHRISTOPHER SHEPHERD

Scores of collected or cultivated plants yield a starchy, edible tuber beneath the surface of the soil. Only one, however, carries the distinction of growing in more than 150 countries in all kinds of climes, in a wide range of soils, and for all kinds of purposes.[1] This exceptional tuber is the potato. It is our fourth most important food crop, a staple feeding billions of people, a mainstay of many economies, and possibly the only non-cereal crop that lays claim to having changed the world. Indeed, few if any other food plants have achieved what the seafaring, globe-trotting, mouth-watering potato has achieved. Baked, boiled, fried, or preserved, it has allowed people the wherewithal to survive, to (re)settle, and to thrive. It has made populations double and triple. It has built civilizations, states, and empires, and fueled the Industrial Revolution. It has fed peasants, kings, and armies; and it has treated pests and parasites to dinner. It has been an agent of enslavement and liberation. It has figured on art and it has been deified. It has become the object of scientific investigation and genetic improvement. It has promised to secure the food supply, create new markets, help develop the Third World, and affirm Indigenous cultures.[2]

The humble potato has really got around and done a lot of stuff, and even its absence has killed millions or put them on the move. Where the potato has been, what it has done, and who, in turn, has done what back to it is the topic of the chapter. To follow the potato's journey from its wild beginnings and Andean domestication, through pre-Columbian civilizations and colonial regimes in Peru, to Europe and beyond, and finally back to whence it came, where the modern, scientific potato confronted its traditional Andean cousins, is to see it through the eyes of history, social science, experimental science, ecology, and culture.

THE EARLY POTATO

Once upon a time, about 40 million years ago in what today is Mexico, there lived an innocuous epiphyte. When the Isthmus of Panama formed 4 million years ago, the epiphyte went exploring. It hopped south and further south, and by and by it spread along the length of the South American Andes. All the while, the little epiphyte did its favorite thing: it adapted and diversified. It moved its roots into the soil and between those and the stem, it created a starchy swelling, a tuber, with which to withstand long dry seasons. So the epiphyte evolved to become the wild ancestor of today's potato plant.[3]

That the potato plant's tiny, poisonous, bitter tubers were practically inedible to humans was irrelevant, for the place was uninhabited. But it is too soon to say that the wild potato lived happily ever after. Between 12,000 and 15,000 years ago, people crossed the Bering Strait into North America and dropped down into the formidable lowlands of South America. Then they climbed up into the inhospitable altitudes of the Andean ranges. Incredibly perhaps, these tuberous members of the poisonous nightshade family may have been the very thing that drew people into the Andes. The inhabitants domesticated the wild potato by cultivating it themselves and thus securing--or modifying--their means of survival.[4]

It is common to hear that Andeans first domesticated wild potato between 4,000 and 8,000 years ago. There was no single "domestication event" punctuating a dramatic transition from nomadic hunter-gatherers to sedentary potato farmers, as commonly portrayed in grand narratives of human progress.[5] The archeological record cannot specify how protracted, incremental, distributed, and fitful domestication proceeded; this, however, does not prevent archeologists from trying. Their evidence points to the shores of Lake Titicaca (in present-day Peru and Bolivia), at elevations of around 4,000 meters, as the very spot where Andeans first learned to cultivate a few wild potato species. Early domesticators were likely already fairly sedentary, surviving on a mixed resource base of fishing, hunting, and foraging. One can imagine that gathering of wild tubers gave way to their cultivation when people observed that new potato plants birthed from the plant's tubers. So, to plant a few of the larger, more palatable tuber seeds close to camp in soil that they knew was favorable and just when the rains were about to come, and then protect them from the elements and even manipulate those elements in their favor, may not represent a great leap forward in evolutionary history after all. Entirely intuitive was their learning of the basic principle of selection: you reap what you sow.

A good potato—and one worth replanting—is one that does not cramp your stomach, make you retch, or kill you outright. So how did the Andeans breed out the poisonous alkaloids from the wild tubers? Specifically, how did they know which were the less poisonous tubers to replant? This can only have been a process rich in experiment, story, and drama: they learned which wild tubers were less toxic by trial and error; they learned to equate bitterness and perhaps darkness with toxicity; they used their senses of smell and taste to assess risk; they licked tentatively instead of gobbling furiously; they acquired knowledge of which tubers to eat in what quantities, how to mitigate toxic effects by cooking or soaking the tubers or ingesting them with other substances (such as clay). Since the poison had long served as the plant's defense against predation, the domesticated nontoxic potato now depended on its cultivators to protect it from predators, nurture it, and encourage its reproduction. Potatoes and humans had struck a great deal.

From Lake Titicaca the edible potato spread swiftly across the high Andes, as did the people's acquired knowledge of when, where, and how to sow, tend, fertilize, harvest, cook, preserve, and store it.[6] We do not have to know much about traditional agriculture in the Andes today to affirm that, back then, seed exchange among groups, the exploitation of multiple agro-ecological levels, fallowing, and rotation prefigured as cultivation techniques. The Andean diet was complemented by maize (at lesser altitudes), quinoa, other root and tuber crops, and of course the domesticated alpaca and llama. Hunting and foraging surely continued, but due to its prominence as a foodstuff, the potato established the rhythm of Andean life.[7]

Archeologists have been able to determine that tubers were key to the emergence of early Andean Tiahuanaco (or Tiwanaku) civilization around Lake Titicaca in the Early Christian Era. Potato transported down from the mountainous hinterlands also nourished the Chimu and Nazca civilizations along the arid Pacific coast. But because harvested potato deteriorates or sprouts spontaneously, this transported, civilization-sustaining potato cannot have been simply fresh produce. Andeans had long since discovered that they could freeze-dry the bitter potato species by leaving it outside on frosty nights; this *chuño* (in Quechua) was apt for long-distance transport and long-term storage. To the extent that maize and other foods were secondary, these may represent the first non-cereal potato states.[8] Chimu pottery design and motif suggest the centrality of the potato to diet and social life, and depictions of potatoes in human form may even indicate the existence of a potato deity.[9]

Early Spanish chroniclers give us insight into the potato of the Inca civilization. Potato cultivation (alongside auxiliary crops) and the freeze-dried *chuño* participated in the astonishing expansion of the Incas.[10] After moving from Lake Titicaca to Cusco in the fourteenth century, the Incas went on to colonize up to 10 million Indigenous people via roads that radiated out of Cusco and linked the Pacific coast to the Amazonian lowlands and southern Colombia to northern Chile. That the Andeans numbered so many in the first place was itself a result of the potato. In developing an efficient administrative system, tribute labor, and produce taxes for storage- and exchange-based food security, the Incas established a more or less cohesive Andean peasantry. The Incas standardized language (Quechua and Aymara) and devised a communications technology for record-keeping (*quipu*).[11] Surely the *quipu* would record how many potatoes were harvested, the percentage given up as tax, and the number required for public works—knocking up Inca fortresses, making agricultural terraces, or stone-lining waterways.

To write of the potato in the singular is to commit a grave disservice to this characteristically underrated tuber. Over millennia, eight cultivated species emerged, each commanding its own realm of knowledge, modes of cultivation, and patterns of consumption. By virtue of the plant's adaptation to highly differentiated Andean ecological, altitudinal, and climatic niches as well as virile cross-pollination (sexual reproduction from flower seeds), thousands of landraces evolved. Andean potatoes came in all shapes, colors, textures, and tastes just as they do today; Andean people became stewards of agricultural biodiversity, not just of the potato but other domesticated food plants including scores of other tuber and root crops.[12] But under the domination of the Incas, it appears that potato diversity diminished among peasantry who produced for the state (especially for the armies); diversity flourished precisely where the state presence was weak.[13] The question of diversity within and outside the state would play out in a parallel way in modern-day Peru.

THE COLONIAL AND POSTCOLONIAL POTATO

Francisco Pizarro and his crew disembarked on Peruvian shores in 1532. When the Spanish penetrated the Andean highlands, they mistook the potato for a truffle. This truffle is "a dainty dish, even for Spaniards," exclaimed the first European to describe the odd apparition.[14] The conquistadors were quick to discover how important this food was to the Inca Empire and its vast agricultural scaffolding. The invaders' divide-and-conquer military strategy brought about the rapid collapse of Inca domination just as European disease decimated the subjected population. Wild potatoes were happily oblivious to the upheaval, but the domesticated potato only survived where people did.

When Spanish chroniclers ventured out into the potato fields they noted the ubiquity of a foot-plow, the *chaquitaclla*, used to turn over the soil. In what resonates with traditional Andean agriculture today, they described how teams of Indigenous men, chanting in unison, would move backward through the field using the bladed tool to leverage the tough Andean surface soil; a team of women would follow turning over the clods.[15] (Representations of this Andean tool figure on Chimu pottery dates from hundreds of years before the appearance of the Incas.) Chroniclers documented the "idolatry" in which agriculture was embedded, including festivals, ritual slayings, and offerings to powerful mountain deities. They banned the "satanic" activities and killed or imprisoned ritual masters and shamans. Like all colonialisms, the Spanish one was a matter of picking and choosing what to banish and what to deploy. European settlers welcomed the delicious potato into their diet. They salivated over a kind of flour made from a by-product of the freeze-dried *chuño* (*moray*, which was left for days in icy pools); Spanish housewives allegedly took to the flour with great enthusiasm.[16]

A staple food not only satiates appetites but is liable to become a player in social control and exploitation. The potato became a sinister accomplice to silver mining after the mineral was discovered in Potosí in 1545. Spaniards conscripted a native labor force of tens of thousands of Indigenous people to work the mines under soul-destroying conditions. For the duration of their truncated lifespans, the workers subsisted mainly on potato and *chuño*.[17] The circumstances under which potato was produced had of course radically altered. After the conquest, settlers concentrated the dispersed "Indians" and, eventually, dispossessed them of their lands; they established large farming estates (*haciendas*) and forced the Indigenous population to work the fields. In a cruel twist of racial fate, "Indians" grew potato under conditions of serfdom for an Indigenous labor force working the mines.

Although the Spanish introduced their own crops, farm animals, and agricultural technologies, they relied greatly on the deeply rooted Indigenous ones. On the haciendas, old Andean agriculture became mixed up with introduced crops (wheat, barley, and vegetables) and animals (horses, cows, sheep, pigs, and chickens). But on the margins of the haciendas, where native serfs were granted small parcels of land and a minimum of time to meet their subsistence needs, a purer form of Andean agriculture quietly thrived. Particularly at the highest elevations, Andean potato farming continued much as it had always done. Alongside the other Spanish and Portuguese colonies in South America, Peru was liberated from Spain in the 1820s; "Indians," though, were not liberated from haciendas; quite the contrary, serfdom was consolidated when the new science of race offered a natural explanation for native servitude.[18] Rare indeed was the autonomous highland Indigenous community when the great Russian botanist, geneticist, and explorer Nikolai Vavilov documented and collected Peru's and Bolivia's extraordinary diversity of potato species and cultivars in 1932. Vavilov perceived a sort of ecological and perhaps even cultural wealth when he recognized the Andes as a world "center of origin" of the domesticated potato and its tuberous companions. Twentieth-century political elites in Lima, however, perceived anything but wealth. Gazing up at the Indigenous and mestizo highlands from a whiter and more modern coast, they associated potato with a backwardness that permeated every facet of the highlands from its people and crops to its haciendas.[19] But before telling of how agrarian structure and highland agriculture fell to coastal intervention in the name of nation-building and development, we need to accompany the Andean potato out of Peru and into the wider world.

The Globalizing Potato

Well before the physical potato ever set sail for the Old World, its effects ricocheted around Spain, Europe, and beyond. After all, the potato was the calorific fuel behind the Potosian silver that flooded Spain. We cannot ignore the distant agency of the potato when silver paid Spain's imperial fleets and armies and drove its military expansion.[20] Unlike dazzling silver, however, the South American potato made an inconspicuous debut in Europe. And here we can justifiably revert to the singular: just one subspecies of just one potato species (*S. tuberosum*, so named in 1601 by the Leiden botanist Charles de l'Écluse) had adapted to life along the Pacific coast, and it was this individual that left behind the genetic diversity of its wild ancestors as well as its contemporary up-mountain cultivars to journey off to whence the conquistadors had come. In the 1570s the potato disembarked and began its colonizing mission in Spain.[21] The potato did not succumb to complacency. It hitched a ride to Italy on Spanish ships. Next, it traveled up the Spanish Road with troops and supplies, passing through Spain's imperial provinces as far as the Netherlands. All along the way, village folk took to growing potato. Curiously, the potato did well along the Road because villagers realized that leaving tubers in the ground was a good trick for circumventing the ravages of military requisition.[22] Foraging army contingents were unprepared to dig up their food when they could turn to barns of grain; and even when grain stores were depleted, they could not have taken all hidden tubers, as they often did with grain; exhausted soldiers would only dig up what they needed. This reduced the destructive consequences of warfare; where war met grain, there was starvation, but potatoes cushioned those consequences. So, all the more battles fought, all the greater the acreage turned over to the potato, all the way down to World War II.[23]

In the 1600s and 1700s, European notions of disease etiology made many suspect that the potato caused leprosy. Potato cultivation was even banned for a time in France. That the Bible made no mention of the potato provided many devout Christians with reason to believe that the food was not fit for humans. If such concerns retarded the infectious and heathen tuber's uptake, they paled into insignificance when compared to the nourishing potato's ability to keep peasants alive. Aristocrats, for their part, savored the potato as a delicacy or gulped it down desperately as an aphrodisiac. Rapidly but erratically, the potato extended over northern Europe with a degree of success similar to that of maize in southern Europe.[24] During the dire famine of 1709 (which coincided with the War of the Spanish Succession), people took to the potato with an appetite. But overall, the peasant potato was seldom more than a complementary food, a safeguard against grain crop failure, and a security against requisitioning. The poor potato was confined to household gardens, while fields remained the province of grains.[25]

The eighteenth century marked a turn in the potato's fortunes when it became a popular staple. Farmers were now aware of how well the potato adjusted to new soils and climes, how easily they could cultivate it with hand tools, how vigorously it grew, and how fast it matured. The potato did well on fallow land, too. Its productivity was up to four times greater than that of grains, even in sandy soils. The potato tasted good, it was nutritious, and it served as fodder. A family of six plus a cow or a pig could live on potatoes for most of the year; four kilograms of potatoes per day would satisfy the average peasant. That the potato was hailed as "the greatest gift of the New World to the Old" is hardly surprising given rising food prices, swelling populations, and many poor grain harvests. A string of famines in the eighteenth century precipitated the "triumph of the potato."[26]

On the continent, governments, kings, and landowners actively pressed potato cultivation upon peasantries while physicians now touted its health benefits. Potato became not a, but *the*, major staple. Potato jumped the garden fence and invaded the fields. Often pushing grain aside, it began to be cultivated on an unprecedented scale.[27] By enhancing the food supply, the potato began to affect the European population. Between 1750 and 1850, European numbers exploded from around 140 million to 266 million.[28] To attribute this growth to the potato, social scientists have had to annul a range of competing explanations: food supply did not increase because of the clearing and drainage of additional lands, nor because of agricultural improvements based on crop rotation, nor through the invention of new implements, nor through systematic manuring, nor because of more grain imports. In all these respects, changes were negligible prior to scientific agriculture, which came later. There was, in fact, no eighteenth-century agricultural revolution.[29] The only significant variable was the upscaling of New World crops: in northern Europe it was potato; in southern Europe it was maize.

The events surrounding the Irish potato famine illustrate the point. Basque fishermen brought the potato to Ireland's shores around 1600. After the Cromwellian Wars (1649–1652), the English forced the Irish onto smallholdings or left them landless. Peasants and laborers thrived on potatoes and not much else.[30] Many observers, including the great English demographer Thomas Robert Malthus, trembled at Ireland's population growth; between 1750 and 1845, 3 million potato-eaters jumped to 8 million.[31] The Irish people's reliance on a single crop was especially troubling when diseases afflicting the potato became more frequent in the 1800s. If, for Malthus, potato productivity was directly responsible for the demographic eruption, the converse turned out to be equally true. When blight struck in 1845, the crops blackened, leaving the potatoes inedible. Over a million Irish died of starvation or disease and by decade's end just as many again had emigrated.[32] The great famine of Ireland reminds us of the inherent vulnerability of monoculture. In the rest of northern Europe, potato shortages incurred by blight were mitigated by the broader food base. Still, food shortfalls on the continent contributed to civil unrest in 1848, which in turn set the stage for the ensuing revolutions.[33]

The story of how the potato changed history has been taken even further. Between 1780 and 1950 a number of northern European states came to dominate over most of the world by virtue of industrial, political, and military transformations, none of which could have arisen without a radically expanded food supply along the entire north-European plain from France to Russia. Once again, this most propitious tuber has everything to answer for. Over the course of a century, potato provided for healthier peasants, birth rates soared, and industrial development proceeded apace. More people, fossil fuels, and new machines, in turn, made up imperial powerful navies and armies and permitted colonization and migration. Potato historian William McNeill argues:[34]

> All this is so familiar that it somehow seems natural that European empires should have extended round the globe and that the Americas should have been repopulated from Europe.... Yet on reflection Europe's world dominance between 1750 and 1950 ought to amaze us.... An essential—but by no means the only—factor explaining the surprising rise of the west ... was the extra food that potato fields made available to the peoples of northern Europe. It is certain that without potatoes, Germany could not have become the leading industrial and military power of Europe after 1848, and no less certain that Russia could not have loomed so threateningly on Germany's eastern border after 1891. In short, the European scramble for empire overseas, immigration to the United States and elsewhere, and all the other leading characteristics of the two centuries between 1750 and 1950 were fundamentally affected by the way potatoes expanded northern Europe's food supply.[35]

Quite a career for a plant that we often treat with ridicule, McNeill concludes. In twentieth-century Europe and North America, the development and introduction of chemical fertilizers and pesticides, the mechanization of farms, and the cross-breeding of varieties all served to strengthen agriculture in general and the potato in particular.[36] As agriculture became an applied science, the potato vied for fourth position (after wheat, rice, and maize) as a world food crop. After World War II, advances in science ushered in the establishment of International Agricultural Research Centers (IAARCs).[37] And this brings us back to the Andes, for one such center was the International Potato Center (CIP), inaugurated on the outskirts of Lima in 1972.

THE SCIENTIFIC POTATO: FROM THE WORLD BACK TO PERU

If the Andean potato changed the world in the process of its globalization, the global science of potato would come back to haunt the Andean potato. In early twentieth-century Peru, nation-building coastal elites obsessed over consolidating central control over the Andean and Amazonian regions. Animated by developments in agricultural science in the United States and Europe and imagining a nationwide agricultural sector, statesmen and technocrats in Lima established a Department of Agriculture in 1904 and built up extension services. From the state's perspective, Andean agriculture equated to low productivity, poverty, and backwardness; as the dominant highland crop, the potato was firmly ensconced in that negative view. Elites were as unimpressed with the highland landownership structure (the patchwork of haciendas) as they were with the Indigenous population––neither one nor the other did anything to prosper the nation. The great diversity in potato and other tubers, recognized by Vavilov, was seen less as an environmental or cultural asset than as an economic liability.[38] Only after World War II did the state take decisive action. With Peruvian research capacity greatly strengthened, potato-collecting expeditions to all over the Andes multiplied. Hundreds of potato types were lugged back to experimental research stations to cross-breed select "native" varieties to make "improved" varieties.

Under the banner of "Third World" development, most of the funding and impetus came from the US government in conjunction with US research centers, philanthropies, and universities. US fears of communism and a rising rural class of proletarians among its southern neighbors also resulted in putting the Peruvian state under pressure to reform the agrarian structure, particularly in the highlands. Cornell University led an experiment in applied anthropology to determine what to do with the hacienda system and how best to modernize the peasantry. A large hacienda in the central Andes (Ancash) was purchased and its Indigenous occupants were placed under the direction of US social scientists. The Vicos Project

(1952–1966)--named so after the hacienda of Vicos--encompassed agricultural modernization, education, and health development. The dominant agricultural focus encouraged the cultivation of the new varieties of potato emanating from Peruvian research stations; one such station was set up on the hacienda itself.[39] Meanwhile, peasants had been quietly taking over hacienda lands wherever they could. But this process would later receive the sanction of the state. A few years after the Vicos Project concluded, the state executed a radical agrarian reform (1969–1974). The Velasco government expropriated hacienda lands and returned them, after a fashion, to the peasantry. Non-Indigenous Peruvian bureaucrats then set about organizing the newly landed peasantry into cooperatives and enterprises.

The state mandated that "Indians" be called "campesinos" in accord with national left-leaning developmentalist discourses.[40] The Green Revolution–style intervention for potato, maize, and other crops was geared to incorporate the peasantry into these state-run structures. After 1972, the International Potato Center (CIP) further impelled the taking of Andean tuber germplasm for experimentation. Of course, CIP sent its new strains abroad, but it did not forget Indigenous Peruvian highlanders. It supported state extension agencies and formative NGOs in the release, en masse, of improved varieties to replace countless native varieties. The wide distribution of high-yielding, marketable varieties of potato only consolidated the perception that native varieties were inferior, low-yielding, poverty-inducing, and inefficient. Native potatoes (*papas nativas*) were not worth maintaining in the fields, experts thought, since traditional agriculture was the source of underdevelopment; it was enough to retain the rich tuber germplasm in cold storage; as many as 3,600 varieties lay frozen at CIP alone.[41]

Back in the highlands, bureaucratic dysfunction, low production, and peasant resistance saw the cooperatives and enterprises fall apart. Peasants reassembled themselves into thousands of fairly autonomous Quechua and Aymara communities.[42] Ever determined to make of the Indigenous population "viable" market producers, the state responded by targeting the fledgling communities with rural interventions in which, again, potato was the protagonist. Next to a highly visible red revolution--a Maoist insurgency called Shining Path that lasted the better part of a decade--the Green Revolution quietly pushed its anti-communist agenda to create food abundance and a docile peasantry.

In 1997, when I arrived in Peru to undertake doctoral field research, the insurgency had been defeated but the Green Revolution was going strong. State and NGO extension agents serviced peasant communities by dispensing new potato seed, chemical fertilizers, pesticides, irrigation technologies, modern cultivation practices, and knowledge of commerce. By this stage, however, peasants had grown ambivalent about making a wholesale shift away from their traditional agriculture toward modern or market agriculture. They had learned from experience that chemical inputs damaged soils, pests had proliferated, and the new potato varieties lost their vigor after a few seasons. The economic benefits of the new agriculture often failed to materialize or were concentrated among the few who succeeded in capitalizing their farming. This did not deter extension agents, who, in abeyance to the scripture of national and overseas funding bodies, were unrelenting in their quest to press ahead with rural modernization. In doing so, they not only dismissed but also actively dismantled local Andean traditions, autochthonous modes of social organization and technologies.[43] After two intense development decades, it was clear that the results of the Green Revolution had been highly uneven. At the lower altitudes and areas closer to urban centers, the interventions had had greater impact and much of the old potato diversity and attendant knowledge had been lost, including the precise phenotype knowledge of landraces.[44] In more remote areas, the uptake of so-called improved varieties had been measured and diversity-based traditional agriculture persisted.

One often hears that traditional Andean agriculture and modern market agriculture are like oil and water: they can be mixed, but they tend to separate out. This is quite true: their respective logics, knowledge, modes of practice, and underlying values are largely incompatible (even if we find many families practicing both types, the original type for their subsistence and the new type for markets). We could say that the twentieth century divided the potato into two agricultural worlds: one modern and the other uniquely Andean.

FIGURE 21.1 Peasant farmers of a community of Paucartambo piling up their harvested native potatoes; about forty varieties constitute the pile. Photograph courtesy of CESA (Centro de Servicios Agropecuarios), © Luis Revilla Santa Cruz.

The Cultural and Environmental Potato in Peru

In the 1990s, spread thinly over the Peruvian and Bolivian highlands was a marginal contingent of NGOs with an alternative perspective on how intervention should proceed. Inspired by an organization called PRATEC (Andean Project to Support Peasant Technologies), this group took issue with the Green Revolution approach and, instead, sought to recuperate autochthonous Andean practices with a central focus on agricultural biodiversity of potato and other crops. In doing so, PRATEC and associates highlighted the importance of Andean cultural values of reciprocity, community, ecology, and spirituality. The general approach was called "cultural affirmation," and it was necessarily accompanied by a critical view of development's agricultural orthodoxy.[45] Gradually, cultural affirmation won more converts. For example, one NGO called CESA--Center for Agricultural Services--had realized that its application of the Green Revolution in Cusco's province of Paucartambo was untenable. It lamented a decade of overzealous insistence that peasants adopt improved potato varieties. Now that CESA had switched allegiance to the cultural affirmation of agrobiodiversity, it sought to reinvigorate the age-old practice of seed exchange upon which diversity in the fields had always depended. Fortunately, some communities of Paucartambo had maintained a healthy selection of native potato varieties, thus providing a starting point for CESA's facilitation of seed exchange pathways between communities. In accordance with Andean cosmology whereby Mother Earth (Pachamama) presided over an all-animate universe of living rocks, trees, rivers, and plants, CESA accorded agency to the potatoes just as the peasants had always done; it was no metaphor to say that potatoes walked--they followed seed pathways (*los caminos de las semillas*).[46]

The expansion of the native seed base across many communities preceded the relearning of many interlocking traditional knowledge practices. These covered, for example: ritual offerings to Mother Earth and mountains to ensure the arrival of the first rains; women's roles in tuber seed selection and, as harbingers of fertility, the sowing of the seed; varying, complexly patterned tillage modes and carefully sited and highly irregular farm plots (that contrasted markedly with the linear and square monocultural configurations); methods for reading and predicting weather (the tweet of a partridge signaled that it was time to sow); the transference of seed planting from middle altitudes to the higher altitudes (up to 4,300 meters) to "freshen the seed" (*refrescar la semilla*) or free it from virus; long fallow times organized around rotative sectors (*muyus*) to regenerate soil; the application of organic fertilizer and non-chemical methods for dealing with pests; the use and repair of traditional implements such as the emblematic Andean foot plow, the *chaquitaclla*; and the collective social organization including labor exchanges among the community (*faena*) and between kin (*ayni*) that was conducive to all of the above. Opposing the anti-ritual influence of the new evangelical churches in the area, CESA stressed the importance of ritual communication with Mother Earth

FIGURE 21.2 The director of CESA, Luis Revilla, emphasizes the importance of agrobiodiversity conservation in an information session with prospective "conservationists." Photograph courtesy of CESA (Centro de Servicios Agropecuarios), Cusco. © Luis Revilla Santa Cruz.

and the mountain deities (*Apus*) to promote harmony and solidarity: work was to be performed joyfully with joking, laughter, and singing, emoting a sense of empathy and fondness for fields, Nature, and, it must be emphasized, the little potatoes (referred to endearingly as *las papitas*).[47]

At the time of my first stint of fieldwork in the late 1990s, PRATEC, CESA, and similar NGOs were greatly outnumbered by Green Revolution operatives. The imbalance shifted in the new millennium when funding from the Food and Agriculture Organization (FAO) spawned a national agrobiodiversity on-farm conservation program that drew in a slew of governmental and nongovernmental actors across the Andes.[48] Participating organizations included not only the established cultural affirmationists but also standard development actors. The latter were suddenly forced to re-evaluate their entrenched mode of regarding diversity as a problem. Now they turned to the pro-Andean actors for inspiration on how to recuperate diversity and diversity-oriented farming practices. In an odd reversal, the incentivizing of traditional Andean agriculture now presented as the solution to the Green Revolution problematic. Not every organization could dispense with the market logic of the Green Revolution, however, so some endeavored to create a market for native potatoes among Western tourists grasping at cultural delicacies. Hardcore pro-Andean cultural affirmationists opposed this market solution since they considered the market to be an outside imposition, a Western construct, and not properly "Andean."[49]

Thus, the potato became the hero in manifold debates about what was Andean and what was not, what was culture and what was economy, what belonged here and what did not. The effect of on-farm conservation activities was to counterbalance the Green Revolution with a return to diversity-based practices. Precisely where the Green Revolution had floundered, cultural affirmation flourished. In these parts, one might say that on-farm conservation programs succeeded because what is now widely recognized as the Andean Culture of Biodiversity resonated with local Andean values and preferred diets; it accorded with the Quechua notion of *sumaq kausay*, living in harmony with others and with nature. Over the course of twenty years, I have seen how peasants have grown proud of their recuperated diversity. They are pleased that government and councils sponsor agricultural fairs to exhibit their beloved varieties. Farmers have taken to counting their native potato stock, and those who have the greatest number win prizes. A focus on numbers is only to be expected, since the success of on-farm agrodiversity conservation was judged not on yield and productivity but on variety counts.[50]

The funds, energy, and commitment that drove Andean cultural affirmation and the valuing of agrobiodiversity against scientific varieties gave rise to another phenomenon, the Potato Park. An NGO (ANDES--Association for Nature and Sustainable Development) helped to set up the Potato Park in 2004 up-mountain of Pisac town in the state of Cusco. The Park pulled several communities together in a collective endeavor to repatriate hundreds of potato and other tuber landraces from the International Potato Center (CIP). The varieties had allegedly been collected in the vicinity of Pisac in the 1970s and had been kept in cold storage ever since. An initial, repatriated collection of 440 tubers added to a core of locally extant ones as well as a few hundred more that had come in from communities far and wide. Episodic potato repatriations and importations followed; again, the potato was on the move. When I visited the Potato Park in 2015, ANDES reported that its 1,400 exemplars of locally cultivated potato and other tubers made it the most dense site of this type of agrobiodiversity in the world. As always, obtaining seed was one thing, reproducing it quite another. Accordingly, a team of "local knowledge experts" had been assembled to activate the stock of local knowledge surrounding potato cultivation. Community elders played an important part in making the knowledge available. ANDES framed the intervention as one imbibed in the "Andean ecological logic," which spoke of complementarity, reciprocity, and ongoing communication among people, wild nature, the Pachamama, and the mountain deities.[51]

Yet, for all the talk of cultural logics, the Potato Park was embedded in distinctly modern norms, scientific networks, vested interests, and markets. At the Park's higher elevations, scientists conducted experiments to determine which varieties could resist a hotter climate so that these could then be improved at CIP, INIA (National Institute for Agrarian Research), and university agronomy faculties. Other experiments sought varieties high in antioxidant content to meet a potential niche market with soft intellectual property rights (e.g., collective trademarks and community registers) secured for the Indigenous communities responsible for primary production. In these experiments the much-vaunted Andean tradition in potato growing often fell by the wayside. Trialed potatoes, for instance, were not planted together (*en mezcla*), as Andean tradition would dictate, but separately. Modern techniques in sexual reproduction using "true botanical seed" from the tuber plants' flowers had also replaced traditional vegetative reproduction. Science and markets were never far away in this distinctly modern rendition of traditional agriculture. It is arguable that traditional Andean culture had become the handmaiden of science and even off-farm cold storage; at the time of my last research trip in 2015, two local campesinos had boarded a plane to Norway carrying 750 varieties of jet-setting botanical seed to deposit at the Svalbard Global Seed Vault. National newspapers and in-flight magazines displayed photographs of them in ponchos at the North Pole.[52]

The Potato Park was similarly steeped in neoliberalism. One wonders whether the Park's label as an Indigenous Biocultural Heritage Territory served more as smart marketing than as genuine Andean cultural affirmation. Certainly, the focus lay on entrepreneurship more than Andean reciprocity. ANDES and local leaders chose members of the communities to conduct tours of the Park for tourists. In fact, I took part in one

FIGURE 21.3 Campesinos at the Svalbard Global Seed Vault, Norway. Photograph courtesy of ANDES (Asociación para la Naturaleza y Desarrollo Sostenible), Cusco. © Alejandro Argumedo.

such tour during which I examined the diversity and the high-altitude experimental plots. I was persuaded to pick up a *chaquitaclla*, turned over some turf, and plant a row of potato seed; I suddenly appreciated how extremely fit Andean farmers were. Over a thousand visitors had been chauffeured through the Park, generating quite an income for a few dozen key locals but considerable grief among the rest who were yet to see the spoils of their Indigenous Biocultural Heritage Territory. To create a dense hotspot of agrobiodiversity such as the Potato Park evidently had more social complications than the average potato tourist could have imagined.[53]

Conclusion

The potato was never a couch potato; it harbored a secret ambition to change the world. And so it did. The potato is a worthy subject of scholarship precisely because of its highly influential historical and contemporary place in communities and societies around the world.[54] Ever since its Andean domestication, the potato has raised communities of people, afforded ways of life, helped to establish states, accelerated population growth, and facilitated colonial expansion. The social science literature dealing with this extraordinary potato-power oscillates between two analytical tendencies. One is to attribute causal agency to the potato, which can involve demoting the significance of other factors or social forces; linear causal narratives are liable to elevate the potato to the status of a lone actor, a unitary power in its own right. The other tendency is to position the potato not as a unitary cause for given social phenomena, but as a necessary condition among many others of greater or lesser importance; here, the potato, like other food plants, presents as a social operator within a more or less complex social and technical milieu.[55] So, to what extent can we say that the potato was a causative agent in the growth of Andean communities and civilizations or European populations, states, and empires? Or, to what extent was the potato a necessary condition? In thinking about potato agency, scholars have emphasized the various attributes of plants.[56] The potato is fast-growing, high-yielding, and adaptable. It is logically as well as empirically verifiable that the potato complemented or displaced other actual or potential food sources and thus modified and stamped the crop configuration, the relationship between agriculture and other modes of making a livelihood (hunting, foraging, fishing), the quest for political power, state-making, and territorial conquest.

Power necessarily invites resistance, and in this respect the potato--like other tuber and root crops such as cassava and sweet potato--possesses a hidden agency: because the tuber lies concealed beneath the earth and can be left there intact for a considerable period, uneaten, it was preordained to participate in a strategy of opposition against dominating forces such as requisitioning armies or tax and tribute collectors.[57] Historically, the tuber has performed a socio-political, perhaps subversive, action that grains could not; it is difficult to imagine that this would not be the case today in some places. Potato agency took a new turn as capitalist logics enrolled genetics and agronomy to bolster or hijack subsistence farming (including small-scale sale of surplus) around the world. It stands to reason that a world food crop ranked fourth in terms of global consumption understandably came fourth in line--after maize, wheat, and rice--as a candidate for scientific engineering. Whether we see this as good or bad will depend on our ideological convictions about, for example, the Green Revolution, international development, and in some cases cultural survival.

The introduction of high-yielding potato varieties and the attendant technological package, of course, applies to many parts of the "underdeveloped world." In many respects, Peru and Bolivia typify the way potato development encroached upon traditional agro-food regimes. But the central Andean countries also represent a special case, for new varieties of potato impinged not only upon other crops and food in general, but also upon the potato itself and the extant, rich—but threatened—diversity in tubers. Only in this Andean context was the scientific potato turned back upon its traditional relatives; only there did the scientific potato acquire a double visibility that promised economic development but also jeopardized culture.[58] When international organizations targeted traditional agrobiodiversity for on-farm conservation, Andean preservation married ethno-environmentalism and cultural survival, thus lending the potato a distinct place in modern Indigenous politics. Indeed, wherever we look around the world, and at whichever crop and food, we will certainly see different, time- and place-specific agencies unfold in complex interaction with societies, agrarian structures, environments, and agricultural practices. In this, the potato is exemplary and potato power is undeniable. Without the potato, we might not be here; at the very least, this chapter would not exist.

Notes

* Fieldwork in Peru was supported by two Wenner-Gren Foundation post-PhD fieldwork grants for research on agrobiodiversity conservation (in 2007) and mining (in 2015). I also thank Luis Revilla of CESA and all those at PRATEC, APU, AWAY, and Chuyma Aru for their support in the field. Finally, I would like to thank Maria Scurrah for her invaluable assistance and, of course, the expert advice of Fortunata Huaman.
1. Cassava might be seen to fit this category as well. However, cassava is a root, not a tuber. Tubers are swollen extensions of the plant stem through which the plant can reproduce itself vegetatively. John Reader, *Propitious Esculent: The Potato in World History* (London: William Heinemann, 2008): 22–23.
2. Ibid.; Stephen B. Brush, "Potato," in *Encyclopedia of Latin American History and Culture*, ed. Barbara A. Tenenbaum (New York: Charles Scribner's Sons, 1996), 4:459–62.
3. John G. Hawkes, *The Potato. Evolution, Biodiversity and Genetic Resources* (London: Belhaven Press, 1990): 52; Reader, *Propitious Esculent*, 25.
4. William Langer, "American Foods and Europe's Population Growth 1750–1850," *Journal of Social History* 8, no. 2 (1975): 53; Redcliffe N. Salaman, *The History and Social Influence of the Potato. With a Chapter on Industrial Uses by W. G. Burton* (London: Cambridge University Press, 1970 [1949]): 5.

5. James C. Scott, *Against the Grain: A Deep History of the Earliest States* (New Haven, CT: Yale University Press, 2017): 37–57.
6. Reader, *Propitious Esculent*: 26–27.
7. Salaman, *The History and Social Influence of the Potato*, 45–46.
8. Cf. Scott, *Against the Grain*.
9. Brush, "Potato," 459; Salaman, *The History and Social Influence of the Potato*, 18–24.
10. William H. McNeill, "How the Potato Changed the World's History," *Social Research* 66, no. 1 (1999): 69.
11. Frank Salomon, *At the Mountain's Altar: Anthropology of Religion in an Andean Community* (London: Routledge, 2018).
12. Reader, *Propitious Esculent*, 36, 50–51; Karl S. Zimmerer, *Changing Fortunes: Biodiversity and Peasant Livelihood in the Peruvian Andes* (Berkeley: University of California Press, 1996), 10–11, 38–40.
13. Zimmerer, *Changing Fortunes*, 38–40.
14. Salaman, *The History and Social Influence of the Potato*, 36.
15. See Brush, "Potato," 460. See also Pierre Morlon, Benjamin Orlove, and Albéric Hibon, eds., *Tecnologías agrícolas tradicionales en los Andes centrales: perspectivas para el desarrollo* (Lima: COFIDE—Proyecto Regional de Patrimonio, 1982).
16. Salaman, *The History and Social Influence of the Potato*, 40.
17. Salaman, *The History and Social Influence of the Potato*, 40–41.
18. Chris J. Shepherd, "Green and Anti-Green Revolutions in East Timor and Peru: Seeds, Lies and Applied Anthropology," in *Postdevelopment in Practice: Alternatives, Economies, Ontologies*, ed. Elise Klein and Carlos Eduardo Morreo (Abingdon: Routledge, 2019).
19. Chris J. Shepherd, "Imperial Science: The Rockefeller Foundation and Agriculture in Peru," *Science as Culture: Special Issue on Postcolonial Technoscience* 13, no. 14 (2005): 122, 129; Shepherd, "Green and Anti-Green Revolutions in East Timor and Peru," 233.
20. McNeill, "How the Potato Changed the World's History," 70.
21. Langer, "American Foods and Europe's Population Growth 1750–1850," 52; Reader, *Propitious Esculent*, 27–28.
22. McNeill, "How the Potato Changed the World's History," 71.
23. Ibid., 72.
24. Langer, "American Foods and Europe's Population Growth 1750–1850," 53.
25. McNeill, "How the Potato Changed the World's History," 73.
26. Langer, "American Foods and Europe's Population Growth 1750–1850," 52–55.
27. McNeill, "How the Potato Changed the World's History," 74.
28. Langer, "American Foods and Europe's Population Growth 1750–1850," 54–56.
29. Ibid., 51–52, 54–56.
30. McNeill, "How the Potato Changed the World's History," 71, 75.
31. Langer, "American Foods and Europe's Population Growth 1750–1850," 56–57.
32. McNeill, "How the Potato Changed the World's History," 76.
33. Langer, "American Foods and Europe's Population Growth 1750–1850," 58.
34. McNeill, "How the Potato Changed the World's History," 77–80.
35. Ibid., 81–82.
36. Langer, "American Foods and Europe's Population Growth 1750–1850," 52.
37. Shepherd, "Imperial Science," 134, n13. Chris J. Shepherd, "From In Vitro to In Situ: On the Precarious Extension of Agricultural Science in the Indigenous 'Third World,'" *Social Studies of Science* 36, no. 3 (2006): 401.

38. Zimmerer, *Changing Fortunes*, 10.
39. W. Stein, *Deconstructing Development Discourse in Peru: A Meta-Ethnography of the Modernity Project at Vicos* (New York: University Press of America, 2004): 210–211.
40. See Peter S. Cleaves and Martin J. Scurrah, *Agriculture, Bureaucracy, and Military Government in Peru* (Ithaca, NY: Cornell University Press, 1980).
41. Brush, "Potato," 459; Shepherd, "From In Vitro to In Situ," 400–2.
42. Cleaves and Scurrah, *Agriculture, Bureaucracy, and Military Government in Peru*.
43. Shepherd, "From In Vitro to In Situ," 402–405.
44. J. D. van der Ploeg, "Potatoes and Knowledge," in *An Anthropological Critique of Development: The Growth of Ignorance*, ed. P. Hobart (London: Routledge, 1993).
45. See, e.g., Frédérique Apffel-Marglin, "Introduction: Knowledge and Life Revisited," in *The Spirit of Regeneration: Andean Culture Confronts Western Notions of Development*, ed. F. Apffel-Marglin (London: Zed Books, 1998); van der Ploeg, "Potatoes and Knowledge."
46. Chris J. Shepherd, "Agricultural Development NGOs, Anthropology, and the Encounter with Cultural Knowledge," *Culture and Agriculture* 27, no. 1 (2005): 36–37. Luís Pérez Baca, *Crianza de papas en Paucartambo-Qosqo* (Cusco, Perú: Centro de Servicios Agropecuarios, 1996); Grimaldo Rengifo and Jorge Ishizawa, *Los caminos andinos de las semillas* (Lima: Proyecto Andino de Tecnologías Campesinas, 1997).
47. See Morlon, Orlove, and Albéric, *Tecnologías agrícolas tradicionales en los Andes centrales*; Pérez Baca, *Crianza de Papas*; Luis Revilla Sta. Cruz, *Costumbres de las papas nativas* (Cusco, Perú: Centro de Servicios Agropecuarios, 2014).
48. See Harold Brookfield, *Exploring Agrodiversity* (New York: Columbia University Press, 2001); Stephen B. Brush, "The Issues of In Situ Conservation of Crop Genetic Resources," in *Genes in the Field: On-Farm Conservation of Crop Diversity* (Rome: International Plant Genetic Resources Institute, 2000).
49. Chris J. Shepherd, "Mobilizing Local Knowledge and Asserting Culture. The Cultural Politics of In Situ Conservation of Agricultural Biodiversity," *Current Anthropology* 51, no. 5 (2010): 217.
50. Ibid., 640–42; see also Zimmerer, *Changing Fortunes*, 20–21, 65–66.
51. See, e.g., T. Garrett Graddy, "Regarding Biocultural Heritage: In Situ Political Ecology of Agricultural Biodiversity in the Peruvian Andes," *Agriculture and Human Values* 30, no. 4 (December 2013): 587–604. Chris J. Shepherd, "Andean Cultural Affirmation and Cultural Integration in Context: Reflections on Indigenous Knowledge for the In Situ Conservation of Agrobiodiversity," in *Indigenous Knowledge: Enhancing its Contribution to Natural Resource Management* (Wallingford, UK: CABI Press, 2017).
52. Shepherd, "Andean Cultural Affirmation and Cultural Integration in Context," 137–143.
53. Ibid., 140–143.
54. Salaman, *The History and Social Influence of the Potato*.
55. See Scott, *Against the Grain*.
56. Reader, *Propitious Esculent*; Scott, *Against the Grain*, 130.
57. McNeill, "How the Potato Changed the World's History"; Scott, *Against the Grain*.
58. Apffel-Marglin, "Introduction: Knowledge and Life Revisited," 31–40.

Bibliography

Apffel-Marglin, Frédérique. "Introduction: Knowledge and Life Revisited." In *The Spirit of Regeneration: Andean Culture Confronts Western Notions of Development*, edited by F. Apffel-Marglin, 1–50. London: Zed Books, 1998.

Brookfield, Harold. *Exploring Agrodiversity*. New York: Columbia University Press, 2001.

Brush, Stephen B. "The Issues of In Situ Conservation of Crop Genetic Resources." In *Genes in the Field: On-Farm Conservation of Crop Diversity*, edited by S. B. Brush, 3–26. Rome: International Plant Genetic Resources Institute, 2000.

Brush, Stephen B. "Potato." In *Encyclopedia of Latin American History and Culture*, edited by Barbara A. Tenenbaum, 4:459–62. New York: **Macmillan Charles** Scribner's Sons, 1996.

Cleaves, Peter S., and Martin J. Scurrah, *Agriculture, Bureaucracy, and Military Government in Peru*. Ithaca, NY: Cornell University Press, 1980.

Graddy, T. Garrett. "Regarding Biocultural Heritage: In Situ Political Ecology of Agricultural Biodiversity in the Peruvian Andes." *Agriculture and Human Values* 30, no. 4 (December 2013): 587–604.

Hawkes, John G. *The Potato: Evolution, Biodiversity and Genetic Resources*. London: Belhaven Press, 1990.

Langer, William L. "American Foods and Europe's Population Growth 1750–1850." *Journal of Social History* 8, no. 2 (Winter 1975): 51–66.

McNeill, William H. "How the Potato Changed the World's History." *Social Research* 66, no. 1 (1999): 69–83.

Morlon, Pierre, Benjamin Orlove, and Albéric Hibon, eds. *Tecnologías agrícolas tradicionales en los Andes centrales: perspectivas para el desarrollo*. Lima: COFIDE—Proyecto Regional de Patrimonio, 1982.

Pérez Baca, Luís. *Crianza de papas en Paucartambo-Qosqo*. Cusco, Peru: Centro de Servicios Agropecuarios, 1996.

Reader, John. *Propitious Esculent: The Potato in World History*. London: William Heinemann, 2008.

Rengifo, Grimaldo, and Jorge Ishizawa. Los *caminos andinos de las semillas*. Lima: Proyecto Andino de Tecnologías Campesinas, 1997.

Revilla Sta. Cruz, Luis. *Costumbres de las papas nativas*. Cusco, Perú: Centro de Servicios Agropecuarios, 2014.

Salaman, Redcliffe N. *The History and Social Influence of the Potato. With a Chapter on Industrial Uses by W. G. Burton*. New York: Cambridge University Press, 1970 [first edition 1949].

Salomon, Frank. *At the Mountain's Altar: Anthropology of Religion in an Andean Community*. London: Routledge, 2018.

Scott, James C. *Against the Grain: A Deep History of the Earliest States*. New Haven, CT: Yale University Press, 2017.

Shepherd, Chris J. "Agricultural Development NGOs, Anthropology, and the Encounter with Cultural Knowledge." *Culture and Agriculture* 27, no. 1 (2005): 35–44.

Shepherd, Chris J. "Andean Cultural Affirmation and Cultural Integration in Context: Reflections on Indigenous Knowledge for the In Situ Conservation of Agrobiodiversity." In *Indigenous Knowledge: Enhancing Its Contribution to Natural Resource Management*, edited by P. Sillitoe, 130–46. Wallingford, UK: CABI Press, 2017.

Shepherd, Chris J. "From In Vitro to In Situ: On the Precarious Extension of Agricultural Science in the Indigenous 'Third World.'" *Social Studies of Science* 36, no. 3 (2006): 399–427.

Shepherd, Chris J. "Green and Anti-Green Revolutions in East Timor and Peru: Seeds, Lies and Applied Anthropology." In *Postdevelopment in Practice: Alternatives, Economies, Ontologies*, edited by Elise Klein and Carlos Eduardo Morreo: 231–246. Abingdon: Routledge, 2019.

Shepherd, Chris J. "Imperial Science: The Rockefeller Foundation and Agriculture in Peru." *Science as Culture: Special Issue on Postcolonial Technoscience* 13, no. 14 (2005): 113–137.

Shepherd, Chris J. "Mobilizing Local Knowledge and Asserting Culture. The Cultural Politics of In Situ Conservation of Agricultural Biodiversity." *Current Anthropology* 51, no. 5 (2010): 629–654.

Stein, William. *Deconstructing Development Discourse in Peru: A Meta-Ethnography of the Modernity Project at Vicos*. New York: University Press of America, 2004.

van der Ploeg, J. D. "Potatoes and Knowledge." In *An Anthropological Critique of Development: The Growth of Ignorance*, edited by P. Hobart, 209–228. London: Routledge, 1993.

Zimmerer, Karl S. *Changing Fortunes: Biodiversity and Peasant Livelihood in the Peruvian Andes*. Berkeley: University of California Press, 1996.

CHAPTER 22

COTTON

JONATHAN ROBINS

Most of our key food and fiber crops were domesticated in a single place, but our ancestors tamed cotton (*Gossypium* species) at least four times. Like many other plants, cotton plants surround their seeds with hairy fibers to protect and distribute them. In wild cottons the fiber is typically brown and short, but humans selectively developed new varieties with longer, stronger, and whiter fibers in processes that stretched over hundreds or thousands of years. The two "Old World" domesticated cottons have murky origins. *G. arboreum* ("tree cotton") was likely domesticated on the Indian subcontinent as long as 6,000 years ago. Textiles woven from its fiber have been found in Indus Valley sites dating back 5,000 years. No wild form of the plant has been conclusively identified, however. *G. herbaceum* ("Levant cotton") developed later, probably around the Red Sea some 4,500 to 3,000 years ago. Wild forms of it grow in southern Africa, but these may have emerged out of domesticated types, rather than vice versa.[1]

Both species grew as perennials in tropical and subtropical climates, and farmers cultivated them alongside food crops. Cotton yielded more fiber than other plants or animals—ten times more fiber per hectare than hemp, and twelve times more than wool—and cotton's soft bolls were easier to process than the tough stems of hemp, flax, or ramie. Much depended on the variety and how it was handled, but generally cotton textiles were strong, lightweight, and held bright dyes better than other fibers. The archeological record suggests that cotton textiles traveled far and wide in the ancient world, finding their way into elite gravesites across Asia, Africa, and eventually Europe.

Archeological finds of cotton seeds and spinning whorls—evidence of cultivation for textile production—show a more gradual diffusion of the plant itself. The biology of the plant was a limiting factor. Perennial cotton cannot tolerate cold climates. Farmers had to develop varieties that produced bolls quickly enough to be treated as annuals before cotton could spread north to China and west to Mesopotamia and beyond. Importantly, the skills of processing cotton had to move with the plant. Giorgio Riello argues that until the modern period, cotton spread through a "centrifugal" system. India was at the center, creating desires for cotton through cloth exports. Cotton seeds and knowledge about growing and processing cotton were flung outward along the same trade routes that carried cloth. Over time, China and the Middle East became major producers and exporters of cotton cloth in their own right. The "centrifugal logic" of the system meant that cotton agriculture spread outward from these new core regions, too.[2]

While the "Old World" cottons are diploids (with two sets of chromosomes), the "New World" cottons are tetraploids (with four sets of chromosomes), a fact that partly explains their diverse physical characteristics and adaptability. One species, *G. barbadense* (Sea Island, "Pima") was domesticated in Peru and Ecuador some 6,000 to 7,000 years ago. Renowned for its long and soft fibers—easy to spin and pleasant to wear—this variety spread into the Caribbean and coastal North America. By the nineteenth century it took root in the Old World, becoming the famed "Egyptian" cotton of the Nile Valley. The other New World species, *G. hirsutum* ("Upland" and many other varieties), proved even more versatile. The majority of the cotton grown today developed out of this species, first domesticated in Mexico up to 5,000 years ago. The plant quickly adapted itself to new climates and growing seasons. The sixteenth-century *Codex Mendoza* described how the plant's evolution interacted with the sophisticated tastes of spinners, weavers, and consumers during the Aztec period: "Good cotton" with long, white fiber came from irrigated farms. Cotton grown in harsher climates typically had shorter and browner fibers, with desert-grown cotton fetching the lowest prices. The *Codex* notes: "Separately the good man sells these. And he adjusts their prices. Separately he sells the yellow, separately the broken, the stretched [fibers]."[3]

The same could be said for most cotton-growing regions. Farmers balanced what the market wanted (fiber quality and cost) with what nature demanded (drought and temperature tolerance, growing periods, pest resistance, and so on). Farmers, merchants, and spinners everywhere exchanged a range of fibers identified by growing region or variety. As the *Codex Mendoza* notes, the harvesting and ginning of cotton affected its value: dirty and broken fibers were harder to spin and therefore less valuable than long, clean ones. Both Old and New World cottons could serve all sorts of needs, depending on the type: some grew short fibers fit only for rough goods like blankets; others could be spun and woven into gossamer-thin fabrics.

The spinners of the *Codex Mendoza* were not alone in processing raw material gathered across a vast empire. Ancient and medieval governments often collected raw cotton or finished cloth to tax peasants, owing to its durability and convertibility in the marketplace. The Song emperors in China took cotton tribute from the southern provinces as early as the tenth century CE, and they encouraged peasants to grow the recently arrived *G. arboreum* on drier soils. Under later Yuan and Ming governments, peasants paid taxes with raw cotton. Many households in China and across the world combined cotton growing with textile production, but by 1500 CE there was a clear trend toward a rural/urban and even interregional division of labor.[4] In India, urban manufacturers in Bengal and Madras imported cotton from dozens or hundreds of miles away.[5] By the eighteenth century some southern Indian farmers were cotton specialists, employing animal-drawn plows and wage laborers to grow cotton on black, heavy soils. Yet even these farmers balanced their cotton fields with patches of subsistence crops: food came first, no matter how lucrative cotton might be.[6]

Building a Global Division of Labor

Cotton cloth was one of the most widely traded commodities in the early modern world. A number of historians have pointed to cotton as an early marker of globalization: by the sixteenth century cotton was no longer a luxury good for elites but was becoming a staple article for the masses in Asia, Europe, Africa, and the Americas. As European powers began seizing territory in Asia, Africa, and the Americas, their focus was initially on securing the trade in cotton textiles and other valuable products, rather than controlling cotton agriculture directly. The Spanish were impressed by the quality of cotton in the defeated Aztec and Inca empires, but they made no systematic efforts to scale-up cotton agriculture. The fiber was a decidedly second-tier crop in the development of what historians call the "plantation complex" in the circum-Caribbean, marked by large-scale production for export and a near-total reliance on enslaved labor. Barbados was one of a handful of colonies to specialize in cotton from the seventeenth century; most planters found tobacco and sugar more lucrative.[7]

By the end of the century, however, cotton was becoming far more prevalent in everyday life. In Ming and Qing-dynasty China, peasant households dressed in homespun cloth or, if they did not grow cotton themselves, bought raw cotton and cotton textiles imported from as far away as India. Even the rich padded their silk garments with cotton for warmth in the winter.[8] European traders buying slaves in Africa could not do business without the right assortment of Indian cotton textiles, and captives sold in the Americas were clothed in cotton cloth bought from West African (and later, European) weavers.[9] In Europe, cotton competed with wool, linen, silk, hemp, and other fibers, inspiring protectionist measures such as an infamous 1666 English law requiring the dead to be buried in an English wool shroud. Manufacturers dodged these restrictions by spinning and weaving cotton cloth domestically, but this required raw cotton that Europe was ill suited to grow.[10]

Anatolia and the Levant offered one source of cotton for Europe's new manufacturers. Most of the cotton was grown by peasants alongside food crops, and the fiber had long supplied the region's own textile workshops. The Old World cottons grown in the region had low yields and produced a short fiber, but they were well adapted to the soils and irregular rainfall patterns of the area. Large-scale commercial farms did emerge as elites took over unused state land or consolidated peasant holdings to grow cotton, but the cost of irrigation and difficulties procuring labor slowed their expansion. Ottoman cotton exports plateaued in the early nineteenth century, unable to keep up with European demand even as the empire's own textile exports evaporated.[11]

Historians continue to debate the extent of deindustrialization in India as the British East India Company extended its grasp over the subcontinent, but like the Ottoman territories, India began to export more raw cotton and less finished cloth by the early nineteenth century.[12] This was not the inevitable result of an "invisible hand" distributing tasks to the most efficient workers. Indian spinners and weavers could turn out cheaper—and better—cloth than Europeans well into the nineteenth century. It was a political choice, a policy of re-export substitution, that led British policymakers and merchants to favor raw cotton over finished textiles.[13] British industrialization unleashed radical changes in the world of cotton, as firms adopted new machines and water- and steam-power to scale up cloth production. By the end of the nineteenth century, Europe's—and especially Britain's—competitive advantage in most types of cotton cloth was unassailable. Most raw cotton now flowed in one direction, toward the industrial centers of Europe and North America, a pattern Giorgio Riello describes as "centripetal," replacing the earlier "centrifugal" model.[14]

The "Cotton Kingdom" and Its Rivals

As Europe's new factories consumed more and more cotton, they turned to a new region for raw cotton: the southern United States. Over the course of the nineteenth century, cotton production in America shifted away from the Atlantic littoral into the interior. In the American historical canon, a machine takes center stage in this story: Eli Whitney's cotton gin. Fibers of *G. barbadense* grown in the Caribbean and on the "Sea Islands" of Georgia and South Carolina could be ginned with simple rollers. But this variety could not tolerate the colder climate inland. Georgia planters experimented with an annual *G. hirsutum* variety as early as the 1730s, but they were stymied by the difficulty of removing fiber from the hairy seed. Whitney's saw gin used sharp teeth to pull and cut fiber from the seed, though the process was far from perfect: early saw gins mangled cotton fibers.[15] Manufacturers bought the stuff reluctantly, gradually adapting their spindles to take advantage of the shorter—but cheap and plentiful—fibers.[16]

The saw gin was important, but biological and political factors figured even more prominently in the creation of a "cotton kingdom" in the American South. The key biological factor was the importation of a new type of *G. hirsutum* in 1806 smuggled out of Mexico by Mississippi planter Walter Burling.[17] It yielded more lint than the Georgia varieties, and plant breeders soon used the Mexican plant to develop new varieties adapted to the growing season and rainfall of the southwestern frontier. Annual cottons have mutations that allow them to take advantage of long summer days in subtropical and temperate zones. Though they must be grown from seed each year, requiring much more labor than perennial cottons, each plant uses that extra summer sunlight to produce more lint in a season than its perennial counterparts.[18] The new cottons spreading westward with settlers in the South were more productive, grew longer fibers, and ripened with bolls that were easier to pluck than their Mesoamerican ancestors. According to one estimate, the productivity of cotton pickers increased fourfold between 1800 and 1860, a testament to the rapid evolution of cotton in planters' fields, as well as to the socioeconomic organization of the slave-labor plantation.[19]

The southern United States became the world's leading cotton exporter in the 1820s, overtaking India. The young republic adopted a policy of conquering what was then the southwestern frontier, driving out its native inhabitants. White settlers got big tracts of "virgin" land for bargain prices. Yeoman farmers pushed the frontier westward, but it was planters and their enslaved workforce that transformed the region into the "cotton kingdom."[20] Prior to 1861, most American cotton was grown on monocultural plantations worked by slave labor. Historians continue to debate whether or not cotton—and by extension, capitalism and the Industrial Revolution—required plantation slavery. *Gossypium* did not have an opinion. In the early nineteenth century most of the world's cotton was grown by peasants in India, China, Anatolia, Egypt, and Syria, rather than slaves. Yet the slave-labor plantation proved to be the most cost-effective way of growing cotton in the American context. Cotton tolerates interplanting with food crops (as most peasants grew it), but it produces more fiber per acre in a monoculture. Transforming the South's forests into open fields, plowed in straight rows, allowed *Gossypium* to flourish without competition from native flora. These practices produced high yields, though they exhausted Southern soils, which were prone to leaching and erosion. Planters had two choices: continue marching westward, or invest more heavily on the rich floodplains along the Mississippi and other rivers.[21]

Large-scale cotton agriculture required huge amounts of labor to open up new fields, and at specific times of the year for planting, weeding, and harvesting. This was why slavery was so integral to the cotton South: few free men and women voluntarily chose to subject themselves to such work when they had alternatives. Slaves, subjected to violent punishments, white vigilantism, and the constant threat of sale and family separation, did not have much if any choice.[22] The security of slavery in the United States attracted planters from the Caribbean after the revolution in Saint-Domingue (1791), and new land bought from France and seized from Native Americans remained open to slavery even as Britain, France, and the other European powers abolished slavery in their own territories. The US ban on slave imports (1808) reduced the influx of new arrivals from Africa to a trickle, but it did nothing to stop the forced migration of hundreds of thousands of slaves from eastern states to the expanding cotton frontier.[23] Cotton would have arrived in Lancashire without plantation slavery, but not nearly as much of it would have come from the American South.

By 1860, cotton and the slave system that produced it dominated the commodity landscape of the South. Cotton served as a basis for credit, tying the fortunes of planters to distant manufacturing centers in New England and Europe.[24] That dependency on cotton continued long after the Civil War and emancipation. American cotton-growers smashed record after record in the late nineteenth century, quickly adapting to post-emancipation conditions. Yet freedmen hoping for "forty acres and a mule" found themselves working as sharecroppers, tied to fickle global prices for cotton and unable to accumulate enough land and capital to diversify away from it. The reimposition of white supremacy in the South after 1877 ensured that relatively few freedmen became smallholders. Poor white farmers also took up cotton after the Civil War, and while they enjoyed a considerable degree of racial privilege, they too labored under onerous tenancy or sharecropping arrangements. By 1900, two-thirds of all Southern cotton land was operated by white farmers, though black workers still provided a great deal of seasonal harvest labor.[25]

America's Civil War and the "cotton famine" that resulted created opportunities for farmers around the globe. Lancashire's cotton merchants and manufacturers had indeed anticipated such a crisis, founding the Cotton Supply Association (CSA) in Manchester in 1857. The CSA sent seeds, gins, and experts to India, Egypt, West Africa, South America, and even Fiji in search of new sources of long-staple cotton.[26] But the CSA had little impact on actual cotton fields. Their work highlighted and encouraged transformations in the rural economies of India, Egypt, and other parts of the world that were already well underway.

Three technologies wielded by European capitalists and imperial states—railroads, steamships, and the telegraph—helped draw cotton growers into a world market for cotton centered on Western Europe. Where these forces were weak, like the Lagos hinterland, the cotton mania of 1861–1865 was short-lived. Yoruba farmers eagerly sold cotton at high wartime prices but returned to other crops when prices fell. But in locations that had been more thoroughly captured by Europe's economic and political systems, farmers were at the mercy of prices set in Liverpool. In Egypt, Mehmet Ali and his son Ibrahim radically transformed the country to serve the cotton export economy. Landlords accumulated huge estates and compelled tenants to grow cotton, which the government monopolized and heavily taxed. When cotton prices fell, the answer was to grow even more of it. Egyptian farmers dropped fallow and crop rotation cycles as a result. Elite enthusiasm for cotton—which was celebrated and financed by European interests—led to the construction of a huge irrigation network, replacing the Nile's natural hydrological cycle with a man-made system better suited to cotton's needs. Cotton fields and the infrastructure to support them sprawled out from the Nile, displacing peasants and pastoralists to feed the export sector.[27] By the turn of the twentieth century it was clear that cotton was not making Egypt's peasants rich, and the land itself was plagued by waterlogging and salinity, as well as bilharzia and other diseases.[28]

Similar dynamics reshaped the landscape of cotton in the Indian subcontinent. While systems varied greatly from state to state, British imperial policy generally aimed to give elites the physical means (railroads, seeds, and gins) and legal tools (land surveys, legal reforms) to pursue export-oriented agriculture. Cotton did not dominate the Indian economy as it did in Egypt or the American South, but where it was the leading crop it had an immense impact on farmers. Tenancy, sharecropping, and debt pushed Indians to grow ever-greater amounts of cotton, often at the expense of food crops, forests, and pasture. While Egypt enjoyed a lucrative niche market in extra-long staple cotton, Indian farmers turned out shorter-stapled stuff that was ill-suited to Lancashire's spindles. Indian cotton exports doubled during the American Civil War, but the boom was not sustainable. Indebted peasants treated cotton with indifference, letting bales sit in the rain.[29] With dark humor Lancashire mill-hands asked God to "send us more cotton, but, O Lord, not Surat," referring to one of India's key cotton ports.[30]

Despite extensive lobbying from Lancashire's textile interests, the British government was unable and unwilling to dramatically reshape Indian farming practices or to police cotton markets to keep up quality standards. Merchants punished farmers for supplying low-quality cotton by cutting prices, but farmers responded with even worse cotton—often adulterated with water, dirt, or small stones to increase its sale weight.[31] India did send millions of bales abroad in the nineteenth century, but most went to mills in continental Europe and Japan making cheaper textiles. Importantly, Indians resisted colonial efforts to replace their hardy indigenous cottons with American varieties. *G. hirsutum* was not well adapted to the Indian climate, a fact peasants quickly recognized.[32] Lancashire spinners may not have liked their fibers, but the Old World cottons endured India's wet and dry seasons well. Importantly, they could be ginned with simple foot-rollers. Large ginneries tended to sell only for export, but hand-ginned cotton could be sold for better prices to local spinners and weavers. This local demand, along with the oil and fodder value of cottonseed, meant that the global market failed to capture the majority of India's cotton crop.

The rise of sharecropping in the American South after 1865 reflected convergence with a global pattern, ending a sixty-year era of slave-grown cotton that was only possible due to a legal system of racialized violence.[33] The world's three major groups of cotton farmers—the American sharecropper (black or white), the Indian *ryot*, and the Egyptian *fellah*—were nominally free by the turn of the twentieth century, but all were chained to cotton and the market economy. Cotton displaced their food crops, exhausted their soils, and encouraged pest invasions. While American farmers confronted the boll weevil from the 1890s onward, their counterparts battled the pink bollworm and other insects that flourished in the cotton monocultures demanded by landowners and scientific experts. When prices for cotton plunged during the long depression of the 1870s to 1890s, growers found themselves caught in a debt trap. They needed money to buy seeds and food, but low cotton prices and usurious interest rates meant that few could ever pay off their loans. While American sharecroppers faced bankruptcy or eviction, cotton growers in India, Egypt, and Brazil confronted starvation. Millions died, not so much because cotton had wrecked subsistence agricultural systems—though it had—but because governments coldly refused to intervene in rural food markets.[34]

Cotton and the "New Imperialism"

We do not have statistics for the sizable amounts of cotton grown and consumed within rural communities in the form of handicrafts, but the amount of cotton exported to major industrial centers increased more than twenty-five times between 1800 and 1914. Between 1914 and 2000, this figure nearly quadrupled. What made these massive increases possible? Yields did increase in many countries, especially after 1950, but spatial expansion was equally important. A series of market disruptions in the years leading up to 1914 inspired European manufacturers to once again seek out new sources of cotton from across the globe. A new "empire of cotton," as Sven Beckert dubbed it, emerged in African and Asian territories conquered by colonial states in the late nineteenth and early twentieth centuries.

Some colonizers tried to recreate the antebellum plantation South. In Malawi and South Africa, white settlers assumed that African labor would be cheap and abundant. In fact, Africans earned more money growing cash crops on their own or by migrating to industrial centers.[35] In Tanzania, German efforts to forcibly recruit labor for cotton plantations led to the Maji Maji rebellion of 1905–1907, which left hundreds of thousands dead from violence and famine.[36] But not all colonial powers favored the plantation model. British and French officials argued that peasant cotton represented a morally superior form of exploitation, allowing African and Asian peasants to participate in global markets without a wrenching transition to wage labor. In their eyes, the flexibility and low costs of peasant production outweighed the high yields and predictability of plantation cultivation.

Thomas Bassett describes a "toolbox" of policies used by colonial authorities to promote peasant cotton, offering a range of options that could be substituted or combined in different contexts. Distributing free seed (almost always *G. hirsutum*) or paying subsidized prices could lure farmers into the market. Marketing and cultivation rules punished farmers for selling the wrong kinds of cotton (*G. herbaceum* or *arboreum*) to the wrong people (local traders and spinners) and for growing cotton the wrong way (mixed with food crops). Taxes, production quotas, and at times outright violence forced peasants to produce for the market no matter what they thought about the prices offered for cotton.[37]

Though colonial officials used different terminology to describe it, they would have agreed with later Marxian scholars who showed that peasant cotton cultivation was cost-effective precisely because it produced commodities on the back of subsistence agriculture. Because families grew their own food, they could sell their cotton at any price. Colonial markets provided a "vent" for their "surplus" labor.[38] In reality, peasants found themselves squeezed by subsistence needs and taxation. When rain fell, insects stayed away, and the mysterious forces setting prices in distant places like Liverpool and New Orleans cooperated, peasants had food and money. When prices fell or the weather turned, peasants faced stark choices. While some colonial regimes demanded that farmers grow cotton, in other cases cotton was the only commodity that could be sold to pay tax bills and buy vital supplies. Women often bore the brunt of colonial cotton policies, laboring to grow cotton on top of necessary food crops. As a woman interviewed by Allan Isaacman in Mozambique put it, cotton was "the mother of poverty."[39]

Colonial cotton was a success story in a few places. In Uganda, peasants were forced to grow cotton by chiefs at the behest of colonial authorities but earned good incomes from it. While British interests tried to replace local cottons with *G. hirsutum*, peasants and colonial experts settled on a local variety of *G. barbadense* that fetched high prices in Lancashire. Cotton remained a profitable staple until it was displaced by coffee in the 1950s. In West Africa, French colonial officials belatedly set the stage for a "peasant cotton revolution" after 1960. During the colonial era, heavy-handed policies forced many farmers to grow cotton. Yet as independence drew near, new policies provided higher prices, subsidized fertilizer, and new tools for cotton growing. Growers experimented with new methods and social organizations and renegotiated gender roles within rural households to take advantage of attractive export prices.[40]

Under colonial rule, peasant cultivation served as a strategy to secure cheap rainfed cotton with relatively little investment. But imperial states also pursued capital-intensive irrigated cotton projects across the twentieth century. These massive projects tried to control nature as well as the people working in it. In Punjab, British colonizers built a series of "canal colonies" in what were supposedly uninhabited wastelands between 1886 and 1940, settling over a million people to grow cotton, sugar, and grain crops.[41] In Sudan, the British dammed the Blue Nile in 1925, turning the Gezira plan into an irrigated landscape for cotton and wheat.[42] At the other end of the Sahel, the French dammed the Niger to water an ancient inland delta, focused on cotton production. With few local volunteers, the French conscripted settlers from distant villages to work irrigated plots.[43] In Central Asia, Russian and Soviet engineers tried to turn arid plains into cotton monoculture, relying on experts who had done the same in California and Arizona.[44] Across all of these irrigated megaprojects, peasants became mere laborers, performing tasks scheduled by managers and often selling their produce to a single buyer.

Farmers did grow a lot of cotton with irrigation, but they balked at heavy-handed management and the fixed prices that were usually part of the package. Punjabi farmers covertly grew resilient indigenous cottons and ruined what was supposed to be a pure supply of American long-staple cotton. Sudanese men who were supposed to be yeoman tenants at Gezira wound up hiring migrant laborers and living as landlords, much to the chagrin of colonial officials. Tampering with hydrology also caused problems. It brought new diseases—as it had in Egypt decades earlier—and it had profound consequences for the environment. The most acute case was the Aral Sea, which shriveled and died as Soviet planners captured the "wasted" waters of the Amu-Darya and Syr-Darya rivers to grow cotton and rice in a desert. The sea is only beginning to recover today from half a century of desiccation and contamination from salt and pesticides carried downstream from cotton fields.

Mechanization and Change in the Cotton Industry

While cotton expanded across Europe's colonies in Africa and Asia, it also continued to grow in the American South. White yeoman and tenant farmers took up cotton across the region and carried it westward into Texas, Oklahoma, and the Southwest. At times, poor white and black farmers united against shared economic challenges. Founded in

1934, the Southern Farmers' Tenant Union fought a well-known campaign on behalf of tenant farmers in the midst of the Depression. But in many other cases, race trumped class interests in the cotton fields. South Carolina Senator "Cotton Ed" Smith famously promised to "keep the negro down and cotton [prices] up." Second-wave populist groups such as the short-lived Southern Cotton Association refused to cooperate with black farmers, and in the chaotic boom-and-bust years before and after World War I, white-hooded "night riders" attacked black and Mexican sharecroppers and laborers. White elites, pointing to the growing exodus of African Americans from the Cotton Belt, called on state and local governments to help white farmers modernize the cotton industry.[45]

Federal, state, and local initiatives provided cotton farmers in the American South with training, warehousing, and credit. Extension agents urged farmers to adopt labor-saving machines like tractors, along with fertilizers and improved cotton varieties. Their work typically benefited wealthier—and usually white—farmers who could access credit and invest in machinery. Despite this work, American cotton yields stagnated until the 1940s. American farmers failed to reach the 16 million-bale record set in 1914 until the 1990s. While several boom-and-bust cycles sent the price of cotton upward, cotton never brought the wealth it had before the Civil War.

Lynette Boney Wrenn suggests that the growth of cottonseed crushing, beginning in the late nineteenth century, kept many Southern farmers committed to cotton in face of stagnant prices. Crushed cottonseed yields oil, and the leftover seed material has value as fertilizer and animal feed. Cottonseed oil found its way into foods, first as an adulterant of other oils, and later as a celebrated ingredient in such products as Procter & Gamble's Crisco all-vegetable shortening. Though cottonseed was only worth a fraction of the value of cotton fiber, cottonseed income helped sharecroppers and tenants survive even when creditors took most of the earnings from ginned fiber. For owners of larger farms, cottonseed sales could often cover the costs of harvesting and ginning the crop, easing seasonal uncertainty around cotton fiber prices.[46]

American politicians and extension agents called on farmers to diversify into new crops or animal husbandry to reduce their dependence on cotton throughout the late nineteenth and twentieth centuries. Some farmers did switch to new crops—especially soybeans—but many fled debt and exhausted soils, joining the migration out of the rural South. White Southerners often blamed the boll weevil for their misfortune. The insect did gobble up a large share of the cotton crop in the 1920s, but the toxic mix of white supremacy and economic stagnation that characterized "New South" society was the bigger culprit.[47]

Despite the boll weevil and immiserating prices for raw cotton, American farmers turned out an average of 13 million bales in the 1930s, more than triple what India, the next-largest producer, grew. Farmers who stayed in business through the Depression did so because they grew more cotton, not less. They benefited from a growing array of state and federal programs that helped them accumulate land, buy fertilizers and pesticides, and purchase machines to replace human hands in the fields. As American cotton farms got bigger, the pool of farm owners and operators got richer and whiter.[48]

Harvesting cotton was the most important task for machinery, and it was the last step in mechanizing cotton agriculture. But picking cotton was an art, one machines struggled to master. As economist Ralph C. Hon quipped in 1937, "A successful cotton picker has been just right around the corner for the last eighty-seven years."[49] A practiced hand can dexterously pull clean lint out of a boll, but an inexperienced picker often grabs fragments of the boll, leaves, and other debris along with the lint. This "trash" reduces the value of cotton and plays havoc with finely tuned gins and spinning machines. Early mechanical harvesters used rakes, tines, rotating spindles, and even vacuums to pull out lint, but they all gathered an unacceptable amount of trash. When a workable cotton harvester finally arrived during the severe labor shortages of World War II, ginneries had to be retooled to clean the trash out of machine-picked lint.

The harvester saved a great deal of labor in picking cotton, and its adoption triggered other labor-saving interventions. Farmers already applied fertilizers and sprayed pesticides by the 1940s, but they added defoliants and other "harvest aids" to their repertory to help the harvesting machines do their work. Flame-weeders and herbicides rounded out the turn to chemical agriculture, eliminating the need to "chop" cotton with hand tools.[50] California farmers were among the earliest adopters of the new machines in the 1950s. With a typical farm covering much more land than in the South, mechanization offered major economies of scale. It was also a way to combat growing labor militancy among the predominantly Mexican labor force.[51] Mechanization spread slower in the South, but by the end of the 1960s more than 90 percent of the US cotton crop was picked by machine. For sharecroppers, mechanization meant eviction. Fragmented holdings—many of them the remnants of antebellum slave plantations—became newly consolidated "neo-plantations."[52]

Mechanization was not an exclusively American phenomenon. Wherever land holdings were large enough to make machine-harvesting plausible, machines rumbled forward, accompanied by a veritable flood of chemicals. Managers in the Soviet Union set astronomically high targets for cotton production and called for the forcible transformation of a Central Asian peasant cotton landscape into one dominated by mechanized collective farms.[53] By the 1950s, Soviet engineers deployed tractors and harvesters to grow millions of pounds of cotton in Central Asia. Yet the Soviet case shows that mechanization was not inevitable: by the 1980s the amount of cotton land being harvested mechanically actually declined. Farmers proved reluctant to give up their small private allotments within collective farm units and instead chose to hand-pick their plots.[54] The post-Soviet government in Uzbekistan gained notoriety for policies that compelled students and urban residents to work as seasonal cotton-pickers, though by 2014 it announced a new set of policies encouraging a return to mechanical harvesting.

There is a pressing need for more historical research on China's twentieth-century cotton industry, which presents an even more complex case than the Soviet Union. Today China produces about 30 percent of the world's cotton fiber, using only 15 percent of global land under cotton. China's cotton belt is marked by a paradoxical combination of labor-intensive practices (hand-pruning and double- or even triple-cropping) and capital-intensive ones (plastic weed barriers and mechanized planting of seedlings).

Smallholders and big state-owned plantations coexist in the cotton market, and both are voracious consumers of fertilizer, pesticides, and new cotton varieties. Most cotton is picked by hand, though mechanical harvesters are spreading as rural wages increase.[55]

Chinese farmers eagerly adopted one of the most significant technological innovations since the mechanical harvester: Bt cotton. Farmers had been using the toxin produced by *Bacillus thuringiensis* as an insecticide since the 1920s, but in 1996 the Monsanto seed company started selling a genetically modified (GM) variety of *G. hirsutum* with genes from the bacterium spliced into cotton's own genome. The controversial plant produces its own toxins, killing bollworms and other pests. Shortly thereafter, Monsanto scientists added herbicide-resistant genes to the mix, allowing farmers to chemically weed fields with glyphosate.

Bt cotton was made for large-scale, mechanized cotton agriculture, the kind that has dominated what is left of the American Cotton Belt since the 1960s. But the high-tech plant has been popular—and controversial—among small-scale farmers around the globe. Indian farmers pioneered "Green Revolution" techniques using fertilizers, irrigation, pesticides, and hybrid seeds in earlier decades, and many were happy to have GM seeds. Critics warned that farmers would be in thrall to Monsanto for seeds once they had adopted the full chemical/GM crop regimen. Monsanto did win a case protecting its patents for GM cotton in India, but the multinational agreed to cap royalty payments and allowed Indian firms to produce GM seeds under license. Farmers did not wait for that development: "illegal" breeders grew their own seeds from GM plants, flouting Monsanto's patents.[56] Despite the appearance of Bt-resistant Pink Bollworms and dire warnings about threats to biodiversity and the environment posed by GM crops and the chemicals used to grow them, Indian farmers are set to grow more GM cotton than ever in the future.

Burkina Faso offered another case of small-scale farmers adopting GM cotton. Partnering with Monsanto, state-owned firms distributed Bt seeds to farmers in 2003, inserting the Bt genes in a popular local variety of cotton in 2008. Despite the cost of the seeds, farmers reportedly earned 50 percent more than they did growing conventional cotton. They also sprayed less pesticide, saving time and money. But Burkina Faso reversed course in 2016: Monsanto's GM cotton had lost some of the fiber qualities that made Burkinabe cotton so desirable in international markets. Losing access to customers who valued anti-GM labeling on their products didn't help either.[57]

Conclusion

Despite several millennia of intensive cultivation and breeding, *Gossypium* remains an unruly plant. The genetic qualities that made it so amenable to breeding and hybridization have let farmers "pirate" biotech genes from corporate giants and experiment in their own fields. But there still isn't a perfect cotton. Industrial needs and consumer tastes demand a range of cotton fibers, from long and soft hand-picked *G. barbadense* cottons to the short, strong, and cheap fibers of *G. hirsutum* cottons. These two species have swept Old World varieties out of the global market, but breeders are keenly interested in finding genes for higher yields and great environmental resilience across all cotton species.

While the commodity market for cotton is more globally integrated than ever, cotton agriculture remains as diverse as the plant. From American agribusiness giants running million-dollar machines to Ivoirian peasants cultivating with iron hoes, cotton growers work under a wide range of economic, political, and environmental conditions. The cotton industry survived the challenge of synthetic fibers, and cotton remains the most widely consumed natural fiber around the world, far ahead of its plant and animal competitors. Perhaps the biggest change for farmers across the globe has been the retreat of the state from cotton agriculture. As Sven Beckert argues, the "empire of cotton" was built out of subsidies, tariffs, and violent conflict. The diminishing role of the state in agriculture and the growing importance of multinational commodity traders will present historians of cotton with many new stories to examine in coming decades.

Notes

1. Giorgio Riello, *Cotton: The Fabric That Made the Modern World* (Cambridge: Cambridge University Press, 2013); Colleen E. Kriger, *Cloth in West African History* (Lanham, MD: AltaMira Press, 2006).
2. Riello, *Cotton*, 6, 39.
3. Frances F. Berdan, "Cotton in Aztec Mexico: Production, Distribution and Uses," *Mexican Studies/Estudios Mexicanos* 3, no. 2 (July 1, 1987): 237–238, https://doi.org/10.2307/1051808.
4. Harriet Zurndorfer, "The Resistant Fibre: Cotton Textiles in Imperial China," in *The Spinning World: A Global History of Cotton Textiles, 1200–1850*: ed. Giorgio Riello and Prasannan Parthasarathi (Oxford: Oxford University Press, 2009): 43–62; and see other essays in this volume for other parts of the world.
5. K. N. Chaudhuri, *The Trading World of Asia and the English East India Company: 1660–1760* (Cambridge: Cambridge University Press, 1978): 271.
6. Prasannan Parthasarathi, *The Transition to a Colonial Economy: Weavers, Merchants and Kings in South India, 1720–1800* (Cambridge: Cambridge University Press, 2001): 64–65.
7. Barbara Gaye Jaquay, "The Caribbean Cotton Production: An Historical Geography of the Region's Mystery Crop" (PhD diss., Texas A&M University, 1997).
8. Francesca Bray, *Technology and Gender: Fabrics of Power in Late Imperial China* (Berkeley: University of California Press, 1997): 213.
9. Kriger, *Cloth in West African History*.
10. Riello, *Cotton*, 123–26; see essays in Giorgio Riello and Tirthankar Roy, eds., *How India Clothed the World: The World of South Asian Textiles, 1500–1850* (Leiden: Brill, 2009); and for the well-documented British case of wool vs. cotton see Beverly Lemire, *Fashion's Favourite: The Cotton Trade and the Consumer in Britain, 1660–1800* (Oxford: Pasold Research Fund, 1991).
11. Sevket Pamuk, "The Decline and Resistance of Ottoman Cotton Textiles, 1820–1913," *Explorations in Economic History* 23, no. 2 (1986): 205; Suraiya Faroqhi, "Ottoman

Cotton Textiles: The Story of a Success That Did Not Last, 1500–1800," in *The Spinning World: A Global History of Cotton Textiles, 1200–1850*: ed. Giorgio Riello and Prasannan Parthasarathi (Oxford: Oxford University Press, 2009): 89–104; Özgür Teoman and Muammer Kaymak, "Commercial Agriculture and Economic Change in the Ottoman Empire during the Nineteenth Century: A Comparison of Raw Cotton Production in Western Anatolia and Egypt," *Journal of Peasant Studies* 35, no. 2 (April 2008): 314–34, https://doi.org/10.1080/03066150802151074.
12. Riello, *Cotton*, 253–63.
13. J. E. Inikori, *Africans and the Industrial Revolution in England: A Study in International Trade and Development* (Cambridge: Cambridge University Press, 2002).
14. Riello, *Cotton*, 186.
15. Angela Lakwete, *Inventing the Cotton Gin: Machine and Myth in Antebellum America* (Baltimore: Johns Hopkins University Press, 2003).
16. Edmund Russell, *Evolutionary History: Uniting History and Biology to Understand Life on Earth* (Cambridge: Cambridge University Press, 2011).
17. Alan L. Olmstead and Paul W. Rhode, "Biological Innovation and Productivity Growth in the Antebellum Cotton Economy," *Journal of Economic History* 68, no. 4 (2008): 1123–1171.
18. Philip W. Porter, "A Note on Cotton and Climate: A Colonial Conundrum," in *Cotton, Colonialism, and Social History in Sub-Saharan Africa*, ed. Allen F. Isaacman and Richard Roberts (Portsmouth, NH: Heinemann, 1995): 43–49.
19. Olmstead and Rhode, "Biological Innovation and Productivity Growth in the Antebellum Cotton Economy."
20. Sven Beckert, *Empire of Cotton: A Global History* (New York: Knopf, 2014).
21. Erin Mauldin, *Unredeemed Land: An Environmental History of the Civil War and Emancipation in the Cotton South* (Oxford: Oxford University Press, 2018).
22. Edward E. Baptist, *The Half Has Never Been Told: Slavery and the Making of American Capitalism* (New York: Basic Books, 2016); but see critique in Alan L. Olmstead and Paul W. Rhode, "Cotton, Slavery, and the New History of Capitalism," *Explorations in Economic History* 67 (January 1, 2018): 1–17, https://doi.org/10.1016/j.eeh.2017.12.002.
23. Beckert, *Empire of Cotton*; Walter Johnson, *River of Dark Dreams: Slavery and Empire in the Cotton Kingdom* (Cambridge, MA: Harvard University Press, 2013).
24. Harold D. Woodman, *King Cotton & His Retainers; Financing & Marketing the Cotton Crop of the South, 1800–1925* (Lexington: University of Kentucky Press, 1968).
25. Steven Hahn, *The Roots of Southern Populism: Yeoman Farmers and the Transformation of the Georgia Upcountry, 1850–1890*, 2nd ed. (Oxford: Oxford University Press, 2006); Susan E. O'Donovan, *Becoming Free in the Cotton South* (Cambridge, MA: Harvard University Press, 2009).
26. Peter Harnetty, *Imperialism and Free Trade: Lancashire and India in the Mid-Nineteenth Century* (Vancouver: University of British Columbia Press, 1972); Ricky-Dale Calhoun, "Seeds of Destruction: The Globalization of Cotton as a Result of the American Civil War" (PhD diss., Kansas State University, 2012).
27. Timothy Mitchell, *Colonising Egypt* (Cambridge: Cambridge University Press, 1988): 16.
28. Edward Owen, *Cotton and the Egyptian Economy, 1820–1914: A Study in Trade and Development* (Oxford: Clarendon Press, 1969); Edward Roger John Owen, *The Middle East in the World Economy, 1800–1914*, rev. ed. (London: I. B. Tauris, 1993); Corey Ross, *Ecology and Power in the Age of Empire: Europe and the Transformation of the Tropical World* (Oxford: Oxford University Press, 2017), ch. 1.

29. Laxman D. Satya, *Cotton and Famine in Berar, 1850–1900* (New Delhi: Manohar, 1997).
30. Zach Sell, *Trouble of the World: Slavery and Empire in the Age of Capital* (Chapel Hill: University of North Carolina Press, 2020): 132–34.
31. Harnetty, *Imperialism and Free Trade*.
32. Sandip Hazareesingh, "Territories of Conquest, Landscapes of Resistance: The Political Ecology of Peasant Cultivation in Dharwar, Western India, 1818–1840," *Journal of Historical Geography* 42 (2013): 88–99; Sandip Hazareesingh, "'Your Foreign Plants Are Very Delicate': Peasant Crop Ecologies and the Subversion of Colonial Cotton Designs in Dharwar, Western India, 1830–1880," in *Local Subversions of Colonial Cultures*, ed. Sandip Hazareesingh and Harro Maat (Basingstoke: Palgrave Macmillan, 2015): 1–9.
33. See Beckert, *Empire of Cotton*, 292–93.
34. Mike Davis, *Late Victorian Holocausts: El Niño Famines and the Making of the Third World* (London: Verso, 2001).
35. Matthew Schnurr, "The Boom and Bust of Zululand Cotton, 1910–1933," Journal of Southern African Studies 37, no. 1 (2011): 119–134; Jonathan Robins, *Cotton and Race across the Atlantic: Britain, Africa, and America, 1900–1920* (Rochester, NY: University of Rochester Press, 2016), 112–114.
36. Thaddeus Sunseri, "The Baumwollfrage: Cotton Colonialism in German East Africa," *Central European History* 34, no. 1 (2001): 31–51.
37. Thomas J. Bassett, *The Peasant Cotton Revolution in West Africa* (Cambridge: Cambridge University Press, 2001); Robins, *Cotton and Race*; Allen F. Isaacman and Richard Roberts, eds., *Cotton, Colonialism, and Social History in Sub-Saharan Africa* (Portsmouth, NH: Heinemann, 1995).
38. See Jan S. Hogendorn, "The Cotton Campaign in Northern Nigeria, 1902–1914: An Early Example of a Public/Private Planning Failure in Agriculture," in *Cotton, Colonialism, and Social History in Sub-Saharan Africa*, ed. Allen F. Isaacman and Richard L. Roberts (Portsmouth, NH: Heinemann, 1995): 50–70; Jan S. Hogendorn, "Economic Initiative and African Cash Farming: Pre-Colonial Origins and Early Colonial Developments," in *Colonialism in Africa, 1870–1960: The Economics of Colonialism*, ed. Lewis H Gann and Peter Duignan, Hoover Institution 127 (Cambridge: Cambridge University Press, 1975). 283–328; for the Marxian critique see Michael J. Watts, *Silent Violence: Food, Famine, & Peasantry in Northern Nigeria*, 2nd ed. (Athens: University of Georgia Press, 2012).
39. Elias Coutinho Mandala, *Work and Control in a Peasant Economy: A History of the Lower Tchiri Valley in Malawi, 1859–1960* (Madison: University of Wisconsin Press, 1990); Allen F. Isaacman, *Cotton Is the Mother of Poverty: Peasants, Work, and Rural Struggle in Colonial Mozambique, 1938–1961* (Portsmouth, NH: Heinemann, 1996).
40. Bassett, *Peasant Cotton Revolution*.
41. Imran Ali, *The Punjab Under Imperialism, 1885–1947* (Princeton, NJ: Princeton University Press, 1988).
42. Maurits Ertsen, *Improvising Planned Development on the Gezira Plain, Sudan, 1900–1980* (London: Palgrave, 2016), https://www.palgrave.com/gp/book/9781137568175; Victoria Bernal, "Cotton and Colonial Order in Sudan: A Social History with Emphasis on the Gezira Scheme," in *Cotton, Colonialism, and Social History in Sub-Saharan Africa*, ed. Allen F. Isaacman and Richard L. Roberts (Portsmouth, NH: Heinemann, 1995):   96–118; T. Barnett, *The Gezira Scheme: An Illusion of Development* (London: F. Cass, 1977).
43. Monica M. van Beusekom, *Negotiating Development: African Farmers and Colonial Experts at the Office du Niger, 1920–1960*, Social History of Africa (Portsmouth, NH: Heinemann,

2002); Richard L. Roberts, *Two Worlds of Cotton: Colonialism and the Regional Economy in the French Soudan, 1800–1946* (Stanford, CA: Stanford University Press, 1996).

44. Maya Peterson, "US to USSR: American Experts, Irrigation, and Cotton in Soviet Central Asia, 1929–32," *Environmental History* 21, no. 3 (July 2016): 442–466, https://doi.org/10.1093/envhis/emw006.

45. Michael Schwartz, *Radical Protest and Social Structure: The Southern Farmers' Alliance and Cotton Tenancy, 1880–1890* (Chicago: University of Chicago Press, 1988); Neil Foley, *The White Scourge: Mexicans, Blacks, and Poor Whites in Texas Cotton Culture* (Berkeley: University of California Press, 1998); Greta de Jong, "'With the Aid of God and the F.S.A.': The Louisiana Farmers' Union and the African American Freedom Struggle in the New Deal Era," *Journal of Social History* 34, no. 1 (2000): 105–139; Robins, *Cotton and Race*, ch. 4.

46. Lynette Boney Wrenn, *Cinderella of the New South: A History of the Cottonseed Industry, 1855–1955* (Knoxville: University of Tennessee Press, 1995); Benjamin R. Cohen, *Pure Adulteration: Cheating on Nature in the Age of Manufactured Food* (Chicago: University of Chicago Press, 2019), ch. 5.

47. James C. Giesen, *Boll Weevil Blues: Cotton, Myth, and Power in the American South* (Chicago: University of Chicago Press, 2012).

48. Loren Schweninger, "A Vanishing Breed: Black Farm Owners in the South, 1651–1982," *Agricultural History* 63 (1989): 41–60; Gilbert Courtland Fite, *Cotton Fields No More: Southern Agriculture, 1865–1980* (Lexington: University Press of Kentucky, 1984).

49. Donald Holley, *Second Great Emancipation: The Mechanical Cotton Picker, Black Migration and How They Shaped the Modern South* (Little Rock: University of Arkansas Press, 2000): 37.

50. Pete Daniel, *Breaking the Land: The Transformation of Cotton, Tobacco, and Rice Cultures since 1880* (Urbana: University of Illinois Press, 1985), 239–55; Pete Daniel, *Toxic Drift: Pesticides and Health in the Post–World War II South* (Baton Rouge: Louisiana State University Press, 2007).

51. Dennis Nodín Valdés, "Machine Politics in California Agriculture, 1945–1990s," *Pacific Historical Review* 63, no. 2 (1994): 203–224, https://doi.org/10.2307/3640866.

52. Fite, *Cotton Fields No More*; Daniel, *Breaking the Land*, ch. 11; Jeannie M. Whayne, *A New Plantation South: Land, Labor, and Federal Favor in Twentieth-Century Arkansas* (Charlottesville: University of Virginia Press, 1996).

53. See Adrienne Lynn Edgar, *Tribal Nation: The Making of Soviet Turkmenistan* (Princeton, NJ: Princeton University Press, 2004).

54. Richard Pomfret, "State-Directed Diffusion of Technology: The Mechanization of Cotton Harvesting in Soviet Central Asia," *Journal of Economic History* 62, no. 1 (2002): 170–188.

55. Jianlong Dai and Hezhong Dong, "Farming and Cultivation Technologies of Cotton in China," *Cotton Research*, November 9, 2016, https://doi.org/10.5772/64485.

56. Ronald J. Herring, "State Science, Risk and Agricultural Biotechnology: Bt Cotton to Bt Brinjal in India," *Journal of Peasant Studies* 42, no. 1 (2015): 159–186; Ron Herring, "Persistent Narratives: Why Is the 'Failure of Bt Cotton in India' Story Still with Us?," *AgBioForum* 12, no. 1 (2009): 14–22; Andrew Flachs, *Cultivating Knowledge: Biotechnology, Sustainability, and the Human Cost of Cotton Capitalism in India* (Tucson: University of Arizona Press, 2019).

57. Brian Dowd-Uribe and Matthew A. Schnurr, "Briefing: Burkina Faso's Reversal on Genetically Modified Cotton and the Implications for Africa," *African Affairs* 115, no. 458 (January 1, 2016): 161–172, https://doi.org/10.1093/afraf/adv063; Brian Dowd-Uribe,

Dominic Glover, and Matthew Schnurr, "Seeds and Places: The Geographies of Transgenic Crops in the Global South," *Geoforum* 53 (January 1, 2014): 145–148, https://doi.org/10.1016/j.geoforum.2013.09.017.

Bibliography

Bassett, Thomas J. *The Peasant Cotton Revolution in West Africa*. Cambridge: Cambridge University Press, 2001.
Beckert, Sven. *Empire of Cotton: A Global History*. New York: Knopf, 2014.
Daniel, Pete. *Breaking the Land: The Transformation of Cotton, Tobacco, and Rice Cultures since 1880*. Urbana: University of Illinois Press, 1985.
Ertsen, Maurits. *Improvising Planned Development on the Gezira Plain, Sudan, 1900–1980*. London: Palgrave, 2016.
Fite, Gilbert Courtland. *Cotton Fields No More: Southern Agriculture, 1865–1980*. Lexington: University Press of Kentucky, 1984.
Flachs, Andrew. *Cultivating Knowledge: Biotechnology, Sustainability, and the Human Cost of Cotton Capitalism in India*. Tucson: University of Arizona Press, 2019.
Giesen, James C. *Boll Weevil Blues: Cotton, Myth, and Power in the American South*. Chicago: University of Chicago Press, 2012.
Isaacman, Allen F., and Richard Roberts, eds. *Cotton, Colonialism, and Social History in Sub-Saharan Africa*. Portsmouth, NH: Heinemann, 1995.
Johnson, Walter. *River of Dark Dreams: Slavery and Empire in the Cotton Kingdom*. Cambridge, MA: Harvard University Press, 2013.
Kriger, Colleen E. *Cloth in West African History*. Lanham, MD: AltaMira Press, 2006.
Lakwete, Angela. *Inventing the Cotton Gin: Machine and Myth in Antebellum America*. Baltimore: Johns Hopkins University Press, 2003.
O'Donovan, Susan. *Becoming Free in the Cotton South*. Cambridge, MA: Harvard University Press, 2007.
Owen, Edward. *Cotton and the Egyptian Economy, 1820–1914: A Study in Trade and Development*. Oxford: Clarendon Press, 1969.
Riello, Giorgio. *Cotton: The Fabric That Made the Modern World*. Cambridge: Cambridge University Press, 2013.
Satya, Laxman D. *Cotton and Famine in Berar, 1850–1900*. New Delhi: Manohar, 1997.
Wrenn, Lynette Boney. *Cinderella of the New South: A History of the Cottonseed Industry, 1855–1955*. Knoxville: University of Tennessee Press, 1995.

CHAPTER 23

TOBACCO

MELISSA N. MORRIS

A 1622 treatise exhorted Virginia planters to grow profitable, useful crops such as grapes and to abandon their devotion to that "smoakie Witch," tobacco.[1] Just a few years later, tobacco cultivation was banned in the Ottoman Empire amid fears about the corrupting influence of a foreign drug.[2] In the eighteenth century, Chinese bureaucrats argued that tobacco wasted land that might instead be devoted to grain.[3] In diverse cultures, tobacco cultivation has been criticized on a variety of counts: it exhausts soil; it is prone to boom-and-bust cycles; it uses land that might otherwise be devoted to more useful crops; consumption of its product is an unhealthy vice. Yet tobacco is a plant that has been cultivated for centuries because its distinct properties have suited the needs of individuals, nations, and empires. Tobacco has prevailed against its detractors to become a global commodity, and skilled agriculturalists have aided its rise.

Tobacco is indigenous to the Americas. Native Americans cultivated it extensively in the Pre-Colombian period. Certain characteristics of the plant led to its near-universal adoption. First, tobacco grows in a diverse array of climates and soils. As agriculture spread throughout the Americas, tobacco's tolerance of a wide variety of environments allowed widespread adoption. On the eve of European arrival, tobacco was cultivated at the northern and southern extremes of viable cultivation. It was also planted most places in between, including the Caribbean islands.

A second reason for the widespread use of tobacco is the numerous effects it has on the human body. Taken in small quantities, tobacco produces a relaxing effect. In larger doses, it produces hallucinations and even death. It is a natural hunger suppressant, analgesic, and antiseptic. These properties led to its incorporation into religious, diplomatic, social, and medicinal practices of peoples from Canada to Patagonia. The Tlingit, Blackfoot, and Crow cultures all planted tobacco and little or nothing else. Among the Taíno of Hispaniola, it was inhaled by a medicine man who then exhaled the smoke onto a sick patient. The Iroquois used it to predict the coming of rain, prepared it with other plants as a treatment for insanity, and cleansed wounds with it. The Apalachee of Florida smoked it before playing ball games, while the Aztecs incorporated it into religious rituals. The Tupinamba of Brazil smoked it in council as they debated.[4] Tobacco's diverse effects on the mind and body made it adaptable to the cultural needs of many groups.

Generations of anti-tobacco writers labeled the plant a "weed," implying that its cultivators were unskilled. Although it can grow wild under the right conditions, by 1492, tobacco cultivation was already an advanced agricultural practice. Indigenous people of the Americas were not merely taking advantage of nature's bounty; they were skilled agriculturalists who cared and tended to their "weed." One type of tobacco, *Nicotiana rustica*, was grown from Quebec to the Chiloé Province in southern Chile, or roughly 75 degrees from the equator in either direction, "almost to the farthest limits of American agriculture."[5] If a particular climate could nurture any plants, *N. rustica* was among them. Centuries, perhaps even a millennium ago, an Indigenous cultivator developed a new strain. *Nicotiana tabacum* is a hybrid of two species of tobacco with no overlapping natural range.[6] This intrepid agriculturalist took one of *N. tabacum*'s parents to another location, probably the eastern valleys of the Andes. The resulting *N. tabacum* hybrid was a plant that cultivators very intentionally grew. *N. tabacum* is a somewhat mild strain, with moderate nicotine content and large leaves, all qualities that probably made it appealing to its cultivators. From the Andes, its use spread along the Amazon, into the Guianas, and out to the Caribbean. Europeans first learned about it in those same places, from the Arawaks, Carib, Tupí, and other *N. tabacum* users. If you have ever smoked tobacco, it was most certainly *N. tabacum*.

Europeans observed Indigenous tobacco use almost from their first meeting. Christopher Columbus wrote in his diary of being offered it. Columbus inferred that these "dried leaves . . . must be a thing highly valued by them."[7] Amerigo Vespucci described native peoples chewing a mixture of ground shells and tobacco on Margarita Island. In the first published descriptions of the plant, he noted they used "a certain green herb which they chewed like cattle to such an extent that they could scarcely talk. . . . When we wondered at this act we could not clearly understand the cause and secret of it."[8] In most other sixteenth-century accounts of the Americas, Europeans recorded tobacco use.

Tobacco was consumed in a variety of ways, and was incorporated into a range of diplomatic, religious, and social practices in diverse cultures. Some of these uses facilitated its introduction to Europeans, while others discouraged it. Europeans who first came to the Americas were intensely interested in native plants and were eager to learn about their potential uses. Columbus, after all, was initially on a search for spices. Tobacco, however, did not catch on right away. Europeans had several reasons for their reluctance. First, in the places where they initially encountered its use, smoking was the predominant form of consumption. Among Europeans, only the most intrepid of travelers might have seen smoking before, and they struggled to describe it. In fact, before English-speakers settled upon "to smoke" as a verb, they instead might say someone was drinking a pipe of tobacco.[9] Had tobacco been merely a medicinal plant, used in familiar ways, Europeans probably would have more readily adopted it. While early modern herbals did indeed evaluate it as a medicine, the deeper cultural meanings of tobacco use made it seem more foreign and suspicious than other new crops. More than other plants, tobacco was thoroughly embedded in Indigenous cultural practices. The association of tobacco with pagan idolatry impeded European adoption. James I of England asked if people who adopted a fondness for tobacco might not take on other traits of Indigenous peoples: "Why doe we not as well imitate them in walking naked as they doe? in preferring glasses, feathers, and such toyes, to golde and precious stones, as they do? yea why do we not denie God and adore the Devill, as they doe?"[10] The supposed taint of this connection remained even after it became popular and appeared in anti-tobacco rhetoric throughout the seventeenth century.

Atlantic Africans, by contrast, were early adopters who consumed and raised tobacco long before it gained favor with Europeans. The Spanish historian Gonzalo Fernández de Oviedo y Valdés mentioned enslaved Africans smoking and growing tobacco in the Americas in his 1535 book.[11] Seville physician Nicolás Monardes also observed its popularity. In a 1571 work on tobacco, he wrote that Africans used it as the Indians did, to ward off fatigue and make their labor easier. They adopted it earlier than their masters, who Monardes reports forbade them from smoking tobacco and burned it, forcing the enslaved to sneak off and use it "in the forests and hidden places."[12] Some Africans were quicker to adopt tobacco, in part because they were more comfortable with its various uses. As Monardes suggests, Africans also worked and lived alongside Indigenous peoples in many parts of the Spanish Empire and so learned how to use tobacco from them. In parts of West Africa, some cultures already smoked and chewed marijuana and other leaves. These stimulants were included in religious ceremonies, as in the Americas.[13] For these reasons, some Africans on both sides of the Atlantic readily embraced tobacco. Europeans were initially puzzled by the ways tobacco was consumed and troubled by its connection to Indigenous religious practices and this impeded their adoption of it. For many West Africans, the way tobacco was used and consumed was instead familiar.[14]

Growing familiarity with tobacco eventually helped ease its acceptance in Europe as well. Sailors, priests, and other travelers to the Americas were among the first to bring the plant back to Europe. Tobacco reached the Iberian Peninsula before 1530, and by the 1560s it was growing in medicinal and academic gardens in Western Europe.[15] Accordingly, for most of the sixteenth century, Europeans primarily evaluated tobacco for its medicinal, rather than its recreational, merits. By the late sixteenth century, several varieties of tobacco had been independently introduced to and were growing in Western European gardens.

It was only after tobacco became more familiar in Europe that writers there took greater notice of it. The Flemish botanist Rembert Dodoens's 1553 encyclopedia of plants contains the first published image of a tobacco plant.[16] The illustration's accuracy suggests that Dodoens's artist drew it from life, using a plant grown in Antwerp. In 1570, Frenchman Charles Estienne published *L'agriculture et maison rustique*, offering readers a full chapter on the plant, along with an image.[17] After these early works were published, other authors began incorporating these same descriptions and images into their own works.

By the late sixteenth century, smoking tobacco was becoming a fashionable habit among some Europeans. The English were particularly fond of it. Paul Hentzner, a German traveling in England in 1598, wrote that, "everywhere . . . the English are constantly smoking Tobacco."[18] Tobacco was popular in the Netherlands, too. In *Tabacologia*, his book on the herb, author Johann Neander recalled smoking it as a student in Leiden in the 1590s, a sign that smoking had moved from the fringes of society to its elite youth.[19]

As tobacco gained wider acceptance in Europe, ships started to come to the Americas to trade for it. The early tobacco trade developed out of the piracy and illicit trading of the English, French, and Dutch in the late sixteenth and early seventeenth centuries. Some of the first cultivators to satisfy the growing European demand were Indigenous. On their way to establish the doomed colony at Roanoke, the English settlers stopped at the Caribbean island of Dominica to trade for tobacco. Its cultivation also appealed to colonists and others living in marginal places of the Spanish Empire. On Hispaniola's fertile north coast, impoverished colonists aided by Africans and natives started a trade in tobacco that attracted Dutch and French privateers. Along the Venezuelan coast and the nearby island of Trinidad, another lively illicit trade developed. Tobacco drew interlopers to Spanish colonies.[20] When non-Iberians began to establish colonies in the seventeenth century, tobacco was the first crop they grew.

The global demand for tobacco, set alongside the desire among empires to find profitable resources to extract, led to dramatic changes in its cultivation. In the Pre-Columbian period, cultivators grew tobacco on small plots and for local or perhaps regional consumption. Over the course of the seventeenth century, some colonies turned to intensive tobacco cultivation with an eye to transatlantic export. Plantations multiplied and grew in size.

Yet despite its wide cultivation range, not all environments were well suited for plantation agriculture. Many Caribbean islands that Europeans colonized were initially devoted to tobacco. St. Christopher, a small island with both French and English settlements, reportedly had good soil to grow tobacco. Until 1625, Bermuda was sending more tobacco back to England than Virginia.[21] Yet colonizers soon discovered tobacco exhausts the soil—a problem anywhere, but particularly on small islands, where geography limits arable land. By the mid-seventeenth century, the more-profitable sugar replaced tobacco in such places. Tobacco instead came to be grown most often in temperate continental places, like Virginia, that could not produce more lucrative tropical commodities like sugar and coffee. Tobacco saved the struggling English colony at Jamestown, where settlers replaced the native variety with a strain imported from Spanish America, and its cultivation spread from there throughout the Chesapeake. Yet tobacco's deleterious effects on soil were still consequential. The constant need for new tobacco fields hastened conflict between colonizers and Indigenous peoples.

Tobacco as a Global Commodity

Tobacco spread around the world with surprising speed. Dried tobacco made its way to China by the late sixteenth century, perhaps arriving on Portuguese ships. The plant itself was likely first introduced into Fujian Province, which had historically been both a source of and a destination for migrants. This, coupled with the intensive migrations that typified the Ming-Qing transition of the seventeenth century, meant that knowledge about tobacco agriculture and the seeds and plants themselves spread quickly. Migrants who grew and smoked tobacco brought it with them.[22]

Tobacco consumption conformed to Chinese cultural beliefs about the benefit of smoke for the body, mind, and soul.[23] Thus, as among Africans, it was perhaps more readily accepted. Chinese farmers took quickly to tobacco, in part because it commanded a higher price than most other crops. As in many other places, when tobacco was first introduced the authorities attempted to curb what they saw as the cultivation of a useless crop. But in China, as elsewhere, governments came to terms with tobacco once they realized it was taxable. Although early modern Europeans typically smoked tobacco grown on distant plantations by enslaved laborers, Chinese consumers relied upon a domestic source. Tobacco was grown on small farms spread through much of China. Thus, while New World–style plantations provided a lot of the global tobacco in the seventeenth through nineteenth centuries, other models also prevailed.

Tobacco also quickly spread to the Middle East. By the mid-seventeenth century, enough cultivators in Iran had taken up tobacco farming that it was no longer reliant upon imports to satisfy the increased demand. Growers in south-central Iran specialized in a finer type of tobacco used in water pipes, while those in the west grew tobacco for standard pipes. Some of this tobacco was then exported to India and the Ottoman Empire.[24] Nor was the rest of Asia immune to tobacco's charms: by the seventeenth century, it was being cultivated and consumed in the Philippines, Java, Japan, and Korea.[25] The quick turn to specialization suggests that tobacco agriculture involved more skills than just putting seeds in the ground.

Tobacco was even cultivated commercially in Europe. In England, farmers grew it from the early seventeenth century. Joan Thirsk has noted that tobacco in England quickly won favor with poorer farmers, a group typically disinclined to gamble on novel crops.[26] An early work on tobacco praised this development and advised that English smokers ought to smoke English-grown tobacco. In 1622, however, the crown gave a monopoly on tobacco to the company that colonized Virginia and Bermuda and made tobacco cultivation in England illegal. Farmers grew tobacco in parts of France, Germany, and in pockets throughout the continent. One of the biggest producers was, perhaps surprisingly, the Netherlands.

The rise of global trade led to necessary changes in production and consumption. When tobacco is produced and used locally, users might consume it in a number of ways. To survive a long journey, however, the leaves must be dried out, or cured, limiting the types of use. Consumption practices involving dried leaves—smoking, snuff-taking—predominated. As tobacco became a global commodity, cultivation also became increasingly divorced from the later stages of production. Dried leaves were sent to Europe where they were made into cigars, snuff, or other end products.

Tobacco, Labor, and Expertise

In the colonial Americas, where most of the global supply of tobacco was produced, Indigenous Americans, Africans, and Europeans labored on plantations. Over the course of the seventeenth century, however, tobacco, like other plantation commodities, became increasingly synonymous with enslaved African labor. Enslaved workers grew tobacco in the Americas from the late sixteenth century and quickly became the majority of the workforce in the Caribbean. Slavery became the predominant form of labor on tobacco plantations in Cuba and Brazil, too. In the Chesapeake region of North America, it was only by the beginning of the eighteenth century that slaves outnumbered free laborers and indentured servants. There, Bacon's rebellion in 1676 was a turning point, as indentured servants' political and economic demands put pressure on wealthy plantation owners and enslaved Africans became more available there.

Not only was tobacco produced by enslaved workers, but it was an important commodity for the slave trade itself. In Bahia, Brazil, tobacco planters specialized in a type of tobacco that was twisted into ropes and soaked in molasses. This rolled tobacco became popular along the Gold Coast of Africa, where it was traded for slaves and other goods. Bahian tobacco was so preferred that when the Dutch supplanted the Portuguese as the primary European power along the Gold Coast, they still had to allow in Portuguese ships to trade it. Likewise, English, French, and Danish ships looking to procure slaves first had to get a supply of Bahian tobacco. In the 1770s, English trader Richard Miles warned his employer in England that the Akan with whom he traded would only accept fresh, Bahian tobacco.[27] The cultivation and production techniques perfected in Bahia made it a highly desirable commodity.

Tobacco's history has been one of continual adoption by new groups and refinement of agricultural techniques to grow and manufacture a product that suits (and drives) existing tastes. This was true in the pre-Columbian period, when a constellation of consumption habits dictated a variety of cultivation practices. Those who grew tobacco had to know how to get the result they desired. The coopting of tobacco cultivation by Europeans has sometimes been treated simply as a matter of throwing seeds in the ground, but Europeans who sought to grow tobacco had to learn specific agricultural skills. Early documents about tobacco cultivation and trade routinely complained of a poorly cured product. John Rolfe, who helped introduce *N. tabacum* to Virginia, wrote in 1616 that colonists there had more still to learn before they would know how to grow tobacco well. Perhaps it is no coincidence that this colonist who unlocked the secrets to cultivation married an Indigenous woman, Pocahontas. On Bermuda, English settlers decided simply to take Africans with tobacco cultivation experience from Spanish colonies. Savvy consumers recognized poorly grown and processed tobacco and desired specific products. This concern with quality is why European empires involved in the slave trade could not easily find a substitute for the well-regarded Bahian tobacco in demand along the Gold Coast.

Abundant evidence documents efforts to learn to grow tobacco across centuries and in disparate places. Dutch settlers in the North American colony of New Netherland, trying to start tobacco plantations of their own in the 1630s, recruited assistance from already-established planters in both the Netherlands and Virginia.[28] An eighteenth-century German manual for potential tobacco farmers instead suggests they lay their fields out how an Indian would—and includes a diagram.[29] In 1903, a Rhodesian colonist was sent to Virginia to learn to grow and cure tobacco. He subsequently published a "how-to" guide in a local agricultural journal. Even so, it took the colonists years to properly produce the type of tobacco most in demand at that time.[30]

Just as Indigenous peoples of the Americas carefully cultivated tobacco, so too did subsequent laborers. Sources about tobacco cultivation from the seventeenth century through the twentieth repeatedly describe it as an intense task requiring careful attention and experience. Tobacco is hardy but presents challenges. Tobacco seeds are very small and susceptible to overcrowding by weeds. Over time, many cultivators started the seeds in seedbeds, which were later transplanted to fields, a labor-intensive task. After the plants are established, they require weekly cultivation and constant attention to prevent pests or disease. Since many of these new cultivators grew tobacco to smoke or take as snuff, advice books warned new cultivators that it needed to be more ripe-looking than food crops before it was ready. The leaves mature at different times, so planters had to watch each plant carefully to know when it was mature and cut it at just the right time and place. In the earliest days of cultivation, farmers might have left leaves in the field to dry out, but the process varied from place to place. Thus, tobacco required great care, but diligent students could pick it up easily. Learning to grow tobacco in the Americas initially meant attentively observing and learning from Indigenous groups. As tobacco became a global commodity, the sorts of specialized varieties mentioned thus far meant that cultivators had to refine their techniques. Growing tobacco was not just a set of steps learned once but a process continuously developed.[31]

Tobacco in the Nineteenth Century

By the late nineteenth century, tobacco production and cultivation saw some major changes. As slavery was abolished in the Americas, new forms of labor emerged. In the US South, Cuba, and Brazil, sharecropping became increasingly popular after emancipation. Under this system, farmers were paid wages in crops. In the United States, tenant farming was another alternative, in which farmers paid rent in crops. Both systems trapped laborers (including many white farmers) in a cycle of indebtedness. Thus, slavery was replaced with new exploitative labor regimes that kept workers tied to the land.[32]

Yet despite the strong association of tobacco with large plantations and exploitative labor systems, many regions of small-scale production continued to exist. In Bahia, Brazil, the end of slavery coupled with global economic depression led many formerly enslaved people to turn away from sugar production (which had been more popular in the region) and toward tobacco agriculture.[33] In the Appalachian region of the eastern United States, where tobacco agriculture spread after the American Revolution, small family farms were the norm. And, in much of the world outside the Americas, smaller farms were typical.

Farmers shifted their cultivation practices to keep up with trends in consumption. In the seventeenth and eighteenth centuries, pipe smoking and snuff-taking were the most popular ways to take tobacco. Divergent tastes led to regional specializations. Cuban tobacco, for example, became synonymous with cigars because cigars were more popular in Spain and its empire than elsewhere. In the early decades of the nineteenth century, cigar smoking became more popular in Europe, while pipes, snuff, and chewing tobacco all declined. This led to changes in cultivation practices. By the 1840s, Bahian farmers, for example, shifted from twisting their tobacco into ropes that could be chewed or smoked in pipes to growing more typical leaf tobacco.[34]

The biggest global shift in both consumption and agricultural practices came in the late nineteenth century, with the simultaneous rise of cigarettes and so-called bright tobacco. The rise of the "cigarette century" illustrates perfectly how cultivators have continually retooled tobacco agriculture to accommodate shifts in the global market. It led to both an increase in tobacco consumption and the spread of its cultivation to previously unsuitable places. In the late nineteenth century, US tobacco magnate Buck Duke set out to popularize the cigarette both at home and abroad. The cigarette is somewhat like a cigar but smaller and wrapped in paper rather than in a tobacco leaf. Cigarettes were expensive to produce because they were hand-rolled. There were also cultural barriers to their adoption: in the United States, they were considered effeminate. Duke overcame the first issue by investing in mechanical cigarette rollers, which dramatically decreased their cost. Duke also invested in advertising campaigns that aimed to recruit new smokers and convert existing ones to the cigarette.

Social changes also aided the rise of the cigarette. They were an ideal way to consume tobacco for a growing number of urban workers because they are portable and require little extra paraphernalia. In the United States, new immigrant groups did not hold the same prejudices against cigarettes. World War I, which brought tobacco-using soldiers from diverse cultures together, also helped spread the popularity of cigarettes. By the early decades of the twentieth century, they had become the preferred way to consume tobacco worldwide.

Just as Duke was popularizing the cigarette, farmers were developing a new sort of tobacco. Before the nineteenth century, tobacco was cured either in the open air or over a fire. Curing was a necessary step for tobacco to be shipped long distances and become a global commodity. Yet the existing curing methods sometimes left the crop unevenly cured and with a heavy flavor. In the 1840s, farmers in the Piedmont region of the southern United States started to experiment with flue curing. This process involved directing heat from a furnace into a curing shed. This innovation gave cultivators greater control over the amount of heat introduced into the process, allowing for a more uniform cure. The result was "bright tobacco," a lighter type of tobacco easier to inhale and with a brighter color, hence its name. Rather than being a distinct strain of tobacco, bright tobacco is the result of a particular type of soil and set of technologies.

Bright tobacco's qualities quickly led to its being the preferred sort of cigarette tobacco. Because bright tobacco requires light, sandy soil, large-scale tobacco cultivation spread to regions of the world previously considered unsuitable. The innovation of bright tobacco and the increase in the cigarette's popularity were not coincidental. The product and the agricultural process were codependent developments. Bright tobacco also led to other changes in cultivation. Growers started harvesting tobacco leaf by leaf, rather than harvesting the entire stalk at once. In this new method, each individual leaf was allowed to ripen, improving overall quality. It was, however, more labor-intensive because only around a fourth of the plant's leaves were harvested at a time. Cigarettes also aided the rise of another new varietal, burley, an air-cured tobacco. Farmers in Appalachian Ohio and Kentucky initially pioneered burley in the years after the Civil War. Soon, its cultivation spread to other parts of the globe. Like bright tobacco, burley has a relatively mild flavor, which facilitates its being blended with other types for use in cigarettes.

In the modern era, tobacco continued to be deployed as a tool of settler colonialism. In parts of nineteenth-century Africa, colonial powers encouraged tobacco cultivation to further their own aims. The Portuguese hoped Angolans would grow tobacco to make up for the loss of Brazil after its 1822 independence. Missionaries among the Tlhaping of South Africa introduced tobacco to encourage agriculture. Rhodesian (modern Zimbabwe) officials hoped tobacco would facilitate whites taking land from Africans and establishing their own farms.[35] In Malawi and Zambia (formerly Nyasaland and Northern Rhodesia, respectively), African farmers had long cultivated tobacco for use as a regional trade good. As European colonization intensified, settlers took over tobacco farming and introduced flue-curing to produce a more marketable global commodity. Tobacco cultivation in Africa continued to expand throughout the twentieth century, often alongside settler colonialism. Zimbabwe and Malawi were the biggest African exporters by the century's close, but tobacco cultivation is important to the economy of a number of other nations.

Mechanization

Mechanization has become an increasingly important part of tobacco production since the invention of the automatic cigarette roller in the latter half of the nineteenth century. While other forms of agriculture started mechanizing much earlier, tobacco agriculture resisted mechanization until the mid-twentieth century. This was as much due to culture as technology. In his book *Cuban Counterpoint*, anthropologist Fernando Ortiz posited an antagonistic relationship between his country's two chief agricultural products, tobacco and sugar. Among the many differences he outlines is one of mechanization. Whereas "tobacco requires delicate care," sugar, by contrast, "can look after itself." Tobacco needs the "delicacy" that can only be provided by human touch, sugar is suited to the "brute force" of machines.[36] Ortiz was writing about Cuba, but elsewhere, too, tobacco farmers saw their crop as one unsuited to mechanization. Indeed, this was cast as a virtue and evidence of their own skilled labor: not just anyone could grow tobacco.

In the United States, structural factors likewise ensured that workers, not machines, directly harvested the majority of tobacco until the 1970s. By the twentieth century, tobacco farms tended to be smaller and made use of extended family labor, precluding the large capital outlays mechanization required. As elsewhere, cultural factors led to a widely held belief that machines simply could not harvest tobacco properly. In the United States, this belief was also upheld in laws that disallowed bulk curing. By the mid-twentieth century, however, mechanization triumphed because of a convergence of factors: dwindling population in tobacco-growing regions, an increase in farm size, a rise in the number of farmers who had attended agricultural colleges, and legal changes that encouraged the introduction of machinery. In 1968, new legislation allowed farmers of bright tobacco to sell their tobacco loose, rather than hand-tying leaves together. This thus removed the last remaining manual task and encouraged farmers to invest in mechanical harvesters.[37]

The turn to mechanization had a more immediate impact on farm families, but there were other consequential changes afoot. By the 1960s, doctors and public health officials were taking the risks of tobacco use more seriously. In developed countries, tobacco consumption began to decline—though not perhaps as quickly as health officials might have hoped. In the United States, about 42 percent of adults smoked in the 1960s; in 2021, by contrast, only about 14 percent did. Explicit warning labels, restrictions on advertising, and bans on smoking in public places all helped to reduce the smoking rate in developed countries. In the United States and elsewhere, a decline in domestic tobacco sales hurt farmers.

Globally, however, tobacco use rose. Thus, despite increased awareness of the dangers of its consumption, tobacco production actually increased over the second half of the twentieth century. The number of acres devoted to tobacco in the United States and Europe has steadily declined, however, over the last half century as cigarette manufacturers have turned to developing countries not just for new smokers but also for a new source of tobacco. Malawi, China, India, Tanzania, and Indonesia have joined Brazil and the United States as the world's top tobacco-growers. In the United States, this foreign competition led to a drop in prices. This was further exacerbated in 2004, when the federal government ended the Federal Tobacco Program, which had subsidized the tobacco industry. The end of price controls for tobacco accelerated a decades-long decline in the number of acres under cultivation.

In the twenty-first century, public health officials worry that electronic cigarettes, which first became popular among young people, will reverse the decline in smoking rates. For tobacco cultivators, they present a different challenge. Because e-cigarettes use nicotine extracted from tobacco, there is no advantage in turning to special varietals. The quality of the leaf is of no importance—only the presence of nicotine. The e-cigarette thus threatens the body of knowledge developed by cultivators over centuries. More than governmental restrictions, general disdain for their product, or mechanization, it undermines their claims to be skilled cultivators of a product that people enjoy precisely because of cultivators' diligent efforts.

Conclusion

In his 1604 treatise *A Counterblaste to Tobacco*, King James I of England warned that its use was, among many other distasteful things, "dangerous to the Lungs." By the mid-twentieth century, mounting evidence suggested he had indeed been right, and that tobacco use posed more dangers besides. Throughout its history, tobacco agriculture has been maligned, but has nevertheless persisted. In the years that followed James I's treatise, Virginia planters grew tobacco as investors and officials in England repeatedly demanded they focus on more useful crops. As tobacco was introduced to new places around the globe, it was nearly always met with suspicion. Thanks in part to its addictive properties, tobacco prevailed over its detractors. Yet the people who have grown tobacco might well argue that being merely addictive was not enough. It was also important to have high-quality tobacco, grown under the watchful eye of an experienced cultivator, and carefully harvested, cured, and finished with the goal of making a superior product. Many tobacco users would agree. The rise of electronic cigarettes might well bring about major changes to its cultivation, but despite half a millennium of criticism, there is little to suggest that tobacco will cease to be grown any time soon.

Notes

1. John Bonoeil, *His Majesties Gracious Letter to the Earl of Southhampton, Treasurer, and to the council and company of Virginia here, commanding the present setting up of silk works, and planting of vines in Virginia* (London, 1622): 61.
2. Rudi Matthee, *The Pursuit of Pleasure: Drugs and Stimulants in Iranian History, 1500–1900* (Princeton, NJ: Princeton University Press, 2005).
3. Carol Benedict, *Golden Silk-Smoke: A History of Tobacco in China, 1550–2010* (Berkeley: University of California Press, 2011): 8.

4. Hans Staden records their doing so while deciding if they should eat him. Hans Staden, *Warhaftige Historia und beschreibung* (Marburg, 1557).
5. Carl O. Sauer, "Cultivated Plants of South and Central America," in *Handbook of South American Indians, Volume 6: Physical Anthropology, Linguistics, and Cultural Geography of South American Indians*, ed. Julian H. Steward (Washington, DC: US Government Printing Office, 1948): 523.
6. The two parents of *N. tabacum* are *N. sylvestris*, native to northern Argentina, and *N. tomentosum*, native to parts of Peru and Bolivia. Sauer, "Cultivated Plants," 522.
7. Clements R. Markham, ed., *The Journal of Christopher Columbus (during His First Voyage, 1492–93): And Documents Relating to the Voyages of John Cabot and Gaspar Corte Real*, Works Issued by the Hakluyt Society no. 86 (London, 1893; repr., 2010): 45.
8. Martin Waldseemuller, *Cosmographia Introdvctio* (Saint-Dié, 1507).
9. *Oxford English Dictionary Online*, "drink, v.1," Oxford University Press, https://www.oxfordlearnersdictionaries.com/us/definition/english/drink_1, accessed June 2019.
10. James I of England, *A Counterblaste to Tobacco* (London, 1604).
11. Gonzalo Fernández de Oviedo y Valdés, *The History of New Spain*, ed. Davíd Carrasco (Albuquerque: University of New Mexico Press, 2008).
12. Nicolás Monardes, *Primera y segunda y tercera partes de la historia medicinal* . . . (Sevilla, 1574), Book II, 48–49.
13. For more on the adoption of tobacco in Africa, see David Northrup, *Africa's Discovery of Europe, 1450–1850* (Oxford: Oxford University Press, 2002), 87–88; John Edward Phillips, "African Smoking and Pipes," *Journal of African History* 24, no. 3 (1983): 303–319; Allen F. Roberts, "Smoking in Sub-Saharan Africa," in *Smoke: A Global History of Smoking*, ed. Sander L. Gilman and Zhou Xun (London: Reaktion Books, 2004): 46–57.
14. Marcy Norton, *Sacred Gifts, Profane Pleasures: A History of Tobacco and Chocolate in the Atlantic World* (Ithaca, NY: Cornell University Press, 2008).
15. Joan Thirsk, "New Crops and Their Diffusion: Tobacco-growing in Seventeenth-Century England," in *Rural Change and Urban Growth: Essays in English Regional History in Honor of W. G. Hoskins*, ed. C. W. Chalkin and M. A. Halvinden (London: Longman, 1974): 77.
16. Rembert Dodoens, *Trium priorum de stirpium historia commentariorum* . . . (Antwerp, 1553).
17. Charles Estienne, *L'agriculture et maison rustique* (Paris, 1570).
18. Paul Hentzner, *Travels in England during the Reign of Queen Elizabeth* (London: Cassell, 1901): 42.
19. Johann Neander, *Tabacologia: hoc est, tabaci seu nicotianae descriptio Medico-Cheirurgico-Pharmaceutica* (Leiden, 1622); Benjamin Roberts, *Sex and Drugs before Rock 'n' Roll: Youth Culture and Masculinity during Holland's Golden Age* (Amsterdam: Amsterdam University Press, 2012): 171–74.
20. Michiel Baud, "A Colonial Counter Economy: Tobacco Production on Española, 1500–1870," *Nieuwe West-Indische Gids/New West India Guide* 65, nos. 1/2 (1991): 31.
21. Michael J. Jarvis, *In the Eye of All Trade: Bermuda, Bermudians, and the Maritime Atlantic World, 1680–1783* (Chapel Hill: University of North Carolina Press for the Omohundro Institute of Early American History and Culture, 2010): 27–28.
22. Carol Benedict, *Golden Silk-Smoke: A History of Tobacco in China, 1550–2010* (Berkeley: University of California Press, 2011): 36–44.
23. Ibid., 7.
24. Rudi Matthee, "Tobacco in Iran," in *Smoke: A Global History of Smoking*, ed. Sander L. Gilman and Zhou Xun (London: Reaktion Books, 2004): 60.

25. Benedict, *Golden Silk-Smoke*, 2.
26. Thirsk, "New Crops and Their Diffusion," 76–103.
27. George Metcalf, "A Microcosm of Why Africans Sold Slaves: Akan Consumption Patterns in the 1770s," *Journal of African History* 28, no. 3 (1987): 377–394.
28. New York State Library, *Van Rensselaer Bowier manuscripts: being the letters of Kiliaen Van Rensselaer, 1630–1643, and other documents relating to the colony of Rensselaerswyck*, (Albany: University of the State of New York, 1908): 176–81; Jaap Jacobs, *The Colony of New Netherland: A Dutch Settlement in Seventeenth-Century America* (Ithaca, NY: Cornell University Press, 2009): 124–25.
29. Anonymous, *Unterricht vom einländischen Tabacksbau* (ca. 1782).
30. Steven C. Rupert, *A Most Promising Weed: A History of Tobacco Farming and Labor in Colonial Zimbabwe, 1890–1945* (Athens: Ohio University Press for the Ohio University Center for International Studies, 1998): 3.
31. Melissa N. Morris, "Indigenous and Spanish Influences on Virginian Tobacco Cultivation," in *Atlantic Environments and the American South*, ed. Thomas Blake Earl and D. Andrew Johnson (Athens: University of Georgia Press, 2020): 157–75.
32. Adrienne Petty, "Labor," in *Tobacco in History and Culture: An Encyclopedia*, ed. Jordan Goodman (Detroit: Charles Scribner's Sons, 2005), I:291–98.
33. Michiel Baud, "Brazil," in ibid., I:88–92.
34. B. J. Brickman, *A Bahian Counterpoint: Sugar, Tobacco, Cassava, and Slavery in the Recôncavo, 1780–1860* (Stanford, CA: Stanford University Press, 1998): 32–33.
35. Steven C. Rupert, *A Most Promising Weed: A History of Tobacco Farming and Labor in Colonial Zimbabwe, 1890–1945* (Athens: Ohio University Center for International Studies, 1998), especially chs. 1 and 2.
36. Ortiz, *Cuban Counterpoint*, 6
37. Evan P. Bennett, *When Tobacco Was King: Families, Farm Labor, and Federal Policy in the Piedmont* (Gainesville: University Press of Florida, 2014): 93–94.

Bibliography

Barickman, B. J. *A Bahian Counterpoint: Sugar, Tobacco, Cassava, and Slavery in the Recôncavo, 1780–1860*. Stanford, CA: Stanford University Press, 1998.

Benedict, Carol. *Golden Silk-Smoke: A History of Tobacco in China, 1550–2010*. Berkeley: University of California Press, 2011.

Bennett, Evan P. *When Tobacco Was King: Families, Farm Labor, and Federal Policy in the Piedmont*. Gainesville: University Press of Florida, 2014.

Daniel, Pete. *Breaking the Land: The Transformation of Cotton, Tobacco, and Rice Cultures since 1880*. Urbana: University of Illinois Press, 1985.

Hahn, Barbara. *Making Tobacco Bright: Creating an American Commodity, 1617–1937*. Baltimore: Johns Hopkins University Press, 2011.

Matthee, Rudi. *The Pursuit of Pleasure: Drugs and Stimulants in Iranian History, 1500–1900*. Princeton, NJ: Princeton University Press, 2005.

Norton, Marcy. *Sacred Gifts, Profane Pleasures: A History of Tobacco and Chocolate in the Atlantic World*. Ithaca, NY: Cornell University Press, 2008.

Swanson, Drew. *The Golden Weed: Tobacco and Environment in the Piedmont South*. New Haven, CT: Yale University Press, 2014.

CHAPTER 24

SILK

A Reconsideration of "Failure" in Sericulture

LISA ONAGA

IN 1873, an opinion article appeared in the *California Farmer and Journal of Useful Sciences* that declared the United States unsuitable for "Native Silk Culture." Authored by wool manufacturers, it first lauded silk enthusiasts who endeavored to produce all the raw materials necessary for supplying raw silk for American silk manufacturers before dismissing their efforts: "We speak with authority, when we say that the most experienced and largest silk manufacturers in America, who have been led into manufacture by their experience as silk culturists, have no faith in the Indigenous production of silk upon our soil. The experiment has been tried for over a hundred years, and there is not even a glimmer of remunerating success."[1] This loss of faith had little to do with any inabilities to produce silk. No material obstacles with regard to the climate or soil actually seemed to impair the ability to coax mulberry to grow and thus rear silkworms, but the relatively perplexing underperformance of silk-making in the country compared to China, Japan, or the South of France catapulted this vehement stance to discourage the pursuit of sericulture.

The unwillingness of American sericulturists to accept the near impossibility of turning silk into a profitable crop in the United States frustrated the textile industry during the 1870s. Warnings of paltry economic returns followed earlier attempts to grow silk during the American colonial period. They also predated the more definitive decline of federal financial support for silk-growing as the United States became a dedicated consumer of Japanese raw silk in the 1920s. The one-page opinion by the Wool Manufacturer's Bulletin, intended to be read by Californian farmers, called out the persistence and failure of Californian sericulture as an example of why sericulture in the United States "does not and cannot pay." Sericulture in this context included the work of unraveling the filaments of silk threads from cocoons into the "raw material," and required importing skilled workers to help unravel silk cocoons. In comparison to other world-renowned cultures where silk-growing was a hereditary occupation, the author admonished, "How vain, then, is the expectation of engrafting this traditional skill upon

American families, except under the stimulus of great profits."[2] Silk had to have first been cultivated by every family in the manner of beans and potatoes before American manufacturers would consider the "Indigenous product."

The wool manufacturers' curious use of language to describe US-grown silk as "native" or "Indigenous" obscured settler activities by casting sericultural endeavors in California as a means to carry out protectionist choices. The framing of sericulture as a time-honored practice indicative of sophisticated know-how and skill contrasted with its framing as something that they recommended be abandoned. The California experience in sericulture represents the later end of the overall historical arc in the North American romance with sericulture. This essay examines sericulture as a technology marked by speculation, subjugation, prospecting, and experimentation. A focus on the history of sericulture as a refusal of failure in California contributes a modern case to that of earlier histories of women in sericulture. Despite the assumptions made by observers of sericulture about the relative ease of cultivating silkworms, the analysis of silk-growing in California exemplifies how the difficulties of producing silk actually served as a defining characteristic of its history of silk cultivation. Attention to women's experiences provides a critical way to comprehensively analyze the challenges that faced sericulture in California besides reasons of economic scale. Analyzing women's motivations and how they practically pursued silk cultivation in the entrepreneurial agricultural context of Californian history counterbalances accounts that characterized women as uninformed or foolhardy, unable to avoid making mistakes made by others in the past. Put another way altogether, the refusals to accept failure must be understood alongside understanding how historical actors created sericultural potential simultaneously.

Silkscape as an Inclusive History of Sericulture

"Silkscape" draws from the analytic tools and concepts of the "cropscape" developed by Francesca Bray and others.[3] They explore the movements or constraints of an assemblage of heterogeneous elements—plants, people, and pests. They also probe the technologies, skills and ideas, tastes and markets, environments and biologies, and labor and capital—that form around the making and growth of a crop. Histories of sericulture typically involve silkworms, mulberry plants (the foliage of which provide fodder for the insect larvae), and the humans associated with brokering, producing, and maintaining this silkworm-mulberry system. The static nature of this triangular relationship demonstrates that histories of sericulture can include a much more diverse cast of people, insects, plants, and pests spanning different places and time periods. By seeking out alternative perspectives from which to analyze and thus narrate any given history of sericulture, the pertinence of other plant and insect species is noticed.

Recognizing this diversity reveals basic assumptions about what constituted the establishment of sericulture, what it was for, how different human actors also related to these living things, and whom it served. This perspective calls attention to failure as a much more common experience that some may alternatively regard as experimental. While success stories single out individuals and threads of continuity, the global history of sericulture can also profit from an examination of the socioeconomic, cultural, and political phenomenon of failure to gain insights into how and why historical actors were motivated to attempt sericulture.

The silk moth (*Bombyx mori*) can be viewed as a technological living thing that connects two sets of activities, mulberry farming and the mechanical processing of cocoons into raw silk. Setting these activities in the context of a "silkscape" informs the identification of various activities, living entities, and processes that all contribute to making and unmaking sericulture over time. The centrality of the silkworm in a silkscape foregrounds the question of how human actors in California sought out silkworms to establish the technologies of sericulture. Their experience became part of a narrative of technological failure, as well as the question of which humans were responsible for these attempts to establish sericulture in the region. The botanical focus invites inquiries as to how and why crops moved, expanded, or shrank over human history.

A silkscape integrates plants and insects—not as pest or pollinator, but as producers. Thus, it parallels iconic plant-centric cases (the movement of tea from China to India in the 1830s, for example) while allowing historians to consider more specifically the animal counterparts that humans care for and harvest materials from. In the silkscape, the consumption of mulberry plant leaves by silk-moth larvae is necessary for spinning their cocoons, from which silk fibers are unraveled by human hands through a laborious procedure into skeins. Historical foci have placed most emphasis upon *Bombyx mori*, though sericulture encompasses more than one silk-moth species.

Silk and Sericulture in the New World

The time it took for mulberry to mature played a significant part in the pace of the gradual westward movement of sericulture from China to the western reaches of Europe. According to Claudio Zanier's analysis of the Eurasian "mulberry belt," climates informed the morphology of trees. While mulberry grown in China and Japan could be grown and used rather quickly, mulberry trees in Central Asia and the far western reaches of the Mediterranean and Europe required at least six years for maximum productivity.[4] Nonetheless, the appeal of silk production prompted the propagation of mulberry in new areas such as in Bursa in northwestern Anatolia, which by the sixteenth century became renowned as a center for growing several varieties of the plant.[5] The mulberry that was planted in colonial Mexico was not *Morus alba*, a common symbiont host plant of *Bombyx mori*, but the black or "Persian" mulberry (*M. nigra*, endemic to the Mediterranean), thought to be hardier and responsible for coarser quality silks.[6] In addition, the red mulberry (*M. rubra*), endemic to eastern and central America, was also used within Spanish-conquered territories.[7]

Within the New World, the geography of California suggests a middle ground where sericultural elements met. Before the convergence of silk moths, mulberry, and expertise from East Asia and Europe in the late nineteenth century, however, wild silk cultivation practices had already taken shape. Well before Iberian conquerors set foot on Caribbean islands or present-day Mexico, Indigenous societies such as the Aztec, Mixtec, and the Zapotec in Oaxaca had silk practices that involved working with the aggregate cocoons of lasiocampid moths (*Gloveria psidii*) and madrone butterflies (*Eucheira socialis*). These larvae spin collective silken shelters that resemble a bag hanging from the arbor of a tree. Humans would cut up the tissue-like silk nests and patch them together into larger fabrics and handkerchiefs.[8] The commercial and cultural value of these textile objects was considerable, and Moctezuma had even presented one such silk cloth to Cortés.[9] Analyses of objects in a pre-Columbian era burial site documented by the Spanish in 1777 have provided evidence of such silk textiles, which counterbalance historical arguments put forth by Woodrow Borah that Indigenous peoples of Mesoamerica began to use wild silk only after Spanish explorers and colonizers introduced *Bombyx mori*.[10]

Early attempts to establish European-style sericulture took place in Hispaniola and southeastern North America (now Florida) before it eventually took root in colonial Mexico. Indeed, historical traces of *Bombyx mori* silk production from the Mixteca Alta people in the late sixteenth century indicate a prospering community centered on silk cultivation. This was curtailed by imperial decisions to protect silk-making in Spain that curbed exports from Oaxaca. Silk-growing continued on a smaller scale in Oaxaca to make things for local ceremonial purposes, displacing earlier practices of working with endemic moth species' cocoons.[11]

The adaptation of foraged mulberry during the colonial era played a small but important role in the overall establishment of the American silkscape. Borah's 1943 *Silk Raising in Colonial Mexico* points out the role of endemic mulberry species (*Morus celtidifolia* or *Morus acuminata bonplandi*), which grow between 5.5 and 9 meters. These were used almost exclusively and prevented the need to wait several years before rearing silkworms, which raised the hopes of the Spanish. Accounts of abundant, weed-like mulberry in the Antilles made prospectors anticipate profitable revenues from silk. Although endemic mulberry was thought to serve as a practical bridge between sericulture in Europe and in the New World until mulberry trees from Europe were planted, the process of carrying out sericulture at this stage did not automatically lead to positive results. These failures reflected various things: the poor management of settlers, the poor survival of silkworm eggs over the Atlantic Ocean, and the uneven willingness of local Indigenous people to be enslaved to the care of silkworms.[12]

Efforts to establish sericulture in colonial Mexico reflected a jagged process mired by competing claims about what conquistador first grew silk from silkworm eggs successfully. Secretive experiments took place in different areas of colonial Mexico that primed a widespread silk fever that created conditions for complicity between colonizers and colonized. Cortés led the largest experiment in what is now the state of Morelos, paying Indigenous laborers to first gather leaves from endemic mulberry and then plant them in a formation. The first experiment failed due to a lack of understanding of how to accommodate the climate. Nonetheless, this experience functioned as a precursor to larger tree nurseries responsible for transplanting thousands of saplings in and around Cuernavaca, leading to a system of sericulture by paid labor (in gold or cacao beans). Silk cultivation radiated to other towns, where different owners of encomiendas used communities of enslaved Indigenous people. Different kinds of management principles and conditions existed over the years, from legal to violent, but it was not until the Dominicans entered the scene in the 1540s that colonial Mexican silk cultivation became more industrial and especially diffused. The Dominicans were motivated doubly by the Catholic mission and income aspirations. The value of a pound of raw silk from 1.5 to 9 pesos by the late 1570s.[13]

A closer look into the roles of organisms at the center of these industrial approaches to sericulture reveals that short-sighted assumptions were actually in play. Behind the growing industrial style of sericulture in colonial Mexico, silk production was greatly linked to challenges on the ground. Colonial entrepreneurs gradually accepted that the acclimation of living things could take more time than anticipated, which thus stressed human labor resources. As dwindling silk cultivation acreage created scarcity and higher silk prices, ideas about the inferiority of Mexican-grown silkworm eggs also grew. The encomiendas' impatience and belief in local inferiority made them favor silkworm eggs imported from Europe obscure the fact that silkworms cultivated in Mexico required time to acclimate. It took time to determine the best altitudinal range and the seasons best suited for growing silkworms.

Shortages of local human labor in Mexico, resulting from infectious diseases introduced by Europeans such as smallpox during the sixteenth century, impaired the potential of silk production in colonial Mexico. In addition, new laws that freed Indigenous people from illegal forms of enslavement dampened former enthusiasms for silk-growing. Instead, producers used Black slaves and paid Indigenous day laborers. While Mexican silk cultivation declined, production continued in some areas around present-day Mexico City, weathering through episodes of plague in 1575–1577 and 1591–1592.[14]

Sericultural technology in the New World, in short, greatly depended upon developing and exercising local knowledge of the climate, the silkworms and mulberry, and patience. Despite the significance of diverse species of mulberry and wild silk moths in the history of sericulture in Mexico, the sixteenth-century pursuit of silk cultivation in the context of Iberian conquest stresses how industrial-style sericulture in the Americas has roots as a colonial project that created a hierarchy among colonizers, the colonized, and enslaved. Over the centuries, compared to tobacco farming, sericultural history in the Americas exhibited smaller scales of exploitative labor and management practices that justified slavery and Indigenous labor.[15]

Silk-making also developed an emancipatory side as abolitionists in the United States later encouraged silk spinning as a means for women to challenge the power of slaveowners through financial independence.[16] Sericulture labor was also considered suitable for the incarcerated and for older, enfeebled slaves who could no longer perform hard labor.[17] At the same time, silk-raising's association with moral qualities gave it an aura of cultural virtue that fueled imports of *Morus multicaulis* from China via the Philippines and France to North America in the 1830s.[18] By the time women in California came to organize sericultural endeavors in the nineteenth century, the issue of success that was once anchored to the colonial labor economy had become tied more greatly to global trade with East Asia and greater efforts to understand plant and insect life.

CALIFORNIA: DREAMS OF MULBERRY AND SILKWORMS

New settlements in the American West reproduced expectations about sericulture as the appropriate work of women, children, and the elderly. During the late 1800s, for instance, making homespun silk garments in Utah served the purpose of infusing an insular economy suiting the strategies of Mormon social organization.[19] The human-mediated movement and reproduction of mulberry and silkworms in the mid-to-late nineteenth century, in other words, was linked to the morality assigned to women's labor. Northern white women had helped cement sericulture as a higher-status kind of labor requiring intelligence and delicate attention, fitting in with assumptions that women had a natural nurturing talent.[20] The moral virtues of sericulture, however extolled, did not alone sustain silk cultivation over the long term, but they did help to partially explain how different entrepreneurs pursued silkworm and mulberry cultivation in the state of California despite the economic experiences of their Atlantic counterparts.

Small-scale entrepreneurial and experimental efforts knitted people and activities together in the short history of Californian sericulture. The timeframe represented in this case illustrates key changes linked to silk trade between the mid-nineteenth century and the 1920s as the global consumption of raw silk quintupled to surpass that of wool.[21] Sericulture in California was characterized by a spirit of prospecting and experimentation alongside various challenges and hurdles similar to other instances in the country. Sericultural failure against the backdrop of international geopolitical and industrial changes of the time provided entrepreneurial sericulturists with new scenarios for comprehending how economic and moral endeavors alike encouraged the procurement of sericultural knowledge. This interest persisted especially in the absence of direct conduits to cultures that have cultivated silk for millennia.[22]

California has attracted immigrants from Europe and East Asia especially since the mid-1800s. Some, like German physician and naturalist H. Behr, "discovered" a silk moth species *Saturnia ceanothi*, which the Society of Naturalists of California studied in the 1850s. This instance of claiming the endemic moth species for scientific experimentation reflects how white settler interests continued to regard endemic living things as potential reservoirs of economic profit. The hope that the natural historians would find a way to understand this *Saturnia* species' nature and degum its tough cocoon to unwind its silk hinged upon whether they could replicate the success of Chinese producers. It could become a source of profit and pride.[23] This reference to the Chinese population referred to the largely male Chinese immigrants who arrived through the port of San Francisco at the time and managed a living by building flumes and roads. In addition to laying down the railroads that transported people and goods, including silk skeins, they also worked as cheap laboring hands in viticulture and other agriculture, including mulberry cultivation.[24]

The mulberry species that arrived in California for the purpose of silk-making arrived not with Chinese immigrants, but on a larger scale through established trade routes and other settlers. For example, the earliest known attempt to grow silk in California by Japanese people was the ill-fated Wakamatsu Tea and Silk Colony. The colony (in present-day Coloma) had shipped 50,000 three-year-old mulberry saplings in 1869, but their deaths overshadowed the promise of a productive life that the mulberry (alongside tea) represented.[25] Elsewhere, Japanese colonies were more successful, for example, the Nikkei Brazilians who have steadily exported silk to Japan throughout the early 1900s to the present day.[26]

Whereas the harsh climates tended to destroy the productivity of the mulberry-silkworm system in the North Atlantic region, a belief in the climatic parallels between the silk districts of China and California fed Gold Rush–era appetites for profit.[27] This climatological logic had also justified the importation of sheep from Australia to the West Coast.[28] Nelson Klose and Edward O. Essig characterized the Gold Rush–era enthusiasm as infused by federal appropriations directed at Californian silk culture. The decline of sericulture following the *Morus multicaulis* bubble between 1825 and 1844 did not discourage steadily growing demands for silk itself. Sericulture in California began to take shape, fueled by observations that *Morus multicaulis* fared well in the milder climate.[29] Indeed, silk manufacturers in New England considered moving to California to start anew after the mulberry bubble of the mid-1800s.[30]

The mainstream history of Californian sericulture centers upon accounts concerning Louis Prevost, an immigrant from France determined to recover sericulture suffering from the *pébrine* blight. Prevost operated a nursery and began his venture by advertising the sale of 26,000 mulberry trees in 1856. He, like other sericulturists before him, established his expertise by writing a sericultural treatise, a manual instructing and encouraging the growth of plant and insect.[31]

Federal support for sericulture was inconsistent in California's history of sericulture. Moreover, silk profits were not distributed evenly to sericulturists, and ended up in the pockets of real estate brokers, nurserymen, and those who were able to strategically fulfill requirements for coveted state bounties. Individuals like Prevost who made personal investments in silk processing machinery risked their fortunes.[32] A destructive fungus, *pébrine*, decimated silkworm nurseries and accounts for the revival of various "silk cultures" across Eurasia, from China and South Asia to the Middle East and the far reaches of the Ottoman Empire.[33] Here, cultivation began as a result of earnest efforts to replenish the landscape of blighted European silk cultivation with uninfected silk moth eggs.

By the 1870s, the silk industry had begun to decline in California due to a labor problem.[34] San Francisco continued to play a logistical role, handling and shipping eggs from Japan en route to France. In fact, as the French market for Japanese silk moth eggs dissolved, $500,000 worth of eggs stayed in San Francisco and were sold off within California in 1871.[35] State encouragement and guidance in the 1880s saw the establishment of the California Silk Culture Association, led by a group of educated women who were vested not in the incorporation of a silk industry but in small-scale cottage industry. The institutionalization of sericulture expanded with a California Silk Growers Association and a California State Board of Silk Culture, the latter of which vetted silk quality and encouraged competition until it ceased in 1888.[36]

Self-promoting experimenters like Joseph Neumann appealed regularly to Congress for support in California and even convinced Governor Haight to commission his factory to produce two silk American flags, which would then be exhibited around the United States and later in Vienna, to propagandize California silk. Neumann also explored the potential of the *Ailanthus* silk moth and made efforts to locate endemic mulberry species, resulting in the identification of a wild holly that grew in the mountain ranges. These wild *Ailanthus* plants faced very little challenge from the environment, leading Neumann to believe that they would provide perfectly for silk moth caterpillars to lay their eggs and increase yields, or even prove useful for paper-making.[37]

Prevost and Neumann figure as ready protagonists in the effort to establish silk culture in California in the nineteenth century. However, a larger cast of women shape the fuller history of the constant anticipation surrounding silk and provided the practical actions that sustained silkworm and mulberry cultivation. Historian Evelyn Pattiani has detailed the business of the Ladies' Silk Culture Society of California, which began their project of producing, manufacturing, and using silk by planting 750 *Morus alba* trees in Piedmont of Alameda County in December 1884.[38] The historical study of silk-making has understandably focused on the role of artisans who developed many new silk-weaving technologies, including the manufacture of laces and other fineries, but sericulture also depended upon female leadership, expertise, and labor, even in the late nineteenth and early twentieth centuries. The obfuscation of women's identities has been perpetuated by historians including Pattiani. For example, when writing about leaders in the Ladies' Silk Culture Society of California extensively, she used the given and surnames of their husbands, preceded by "Mrs."[39]

The founder of the California Silk Culture Association (and president of the Ladies' Silk Culture Society in 1885), Elise Christine Wiehe Hittell, was a daughter of a German field surgeon. She emigrated to San Francisco with a plan to teach German and also brought with her a fervor for science. Hittell encouraged training schools, established the San Francisco Foundling Asylum, wrote occasional articles for *Science*, and was one of the first three women admitted to the California Academy of Sciences. She may have benefited from her husband's name, Theodore H. Hittell, but her work on the applied science of silkworm cultivation stands apart from the interests of the newspaper journalist (later a renowned California historian and politician).[40]

Hittell had a respectable command of sericultural knowledge, shown in her treatise, *The California Silk Grower's Instructor*.[41] The state's promotion of sericulture also encouraged the publication of other instructional manuals by women, such as the 1887 publication by Louise Rienzi of Berkeley, the "Secretary, Instructress, and Silk Expert" of the State Board of Silk Culture based in San Jose.[42] These women led organizations and mobilized book-learned and home-grown expertise to lobby for their needs. The State Board of Silk Culture appealed to the Department of Agriculture for experiment stations in California akin to the kind of support Italy provided to the provinces of Lombardy and Piedmont. The Silk Culture Association helped develop sericulture in California through its organizational and experimental work that involved working with local soil professors and interaction with merchants as well as the Chinese consulate.[43]

High-minded efforts to make silk work in California could not deal with the perennial mismatch between labor needs and infrastructural costs on the one hand, and profitable sericulture on the other. The Silk Culture Association eventually sold their land in Piedmont containing their experiment station and mulberry plots.[44] Perhaps this was to be expected, for there had been a precedent already of entrepreneurs edging out smallholder women silk farmers.[45] While state and congressional appropriations were used to support the earlier years of California's sericulture, after 1890, the society carried on without state support and moved to Rutherford, Napa, in 1909, where they received the assistance of St. Joseph's Agricultural Institute.[46]

The mid-nineteenth and early twentieth-century growth of sericulture in California followed a convoluted path led by educated white women who had to navigate real estate dynamics and speculations about new profitable agricultural endeavors such as the raisin industry. These socioeconomic-political demands in the capitalist economy forced women's silk associations to develop organizational structures that could correspond effectively with male-dominated state and national legislators. They simultaneously studied every aspect of sericulture, from the control of silkworm disease to timing of planting and picking mulberry.[47] The dedication to silk signified by the can-do optimism of the Silk Culture Association showed a determination to establish a cottage industry, the encouragement of newcomers to sericulture, and the necessity of sericultural work to supplement incomes. Despite moments of positive growth, the women's sericulture movement in California faced many structural obstacles, since the national legislature tended to lend greater support to US importers of raw silk rather than to raw silk producers.[48] To wit, by 1910, nearly four-fifths of the raw silk volume arriving from China and Japan entered the United States through ports of the Pacific Coast. Only a relatively small number of factories in California produced woven silk goods using imported raw silk apart from the Los Angeles Silk Works, established around 1905 by D. I. Newton, who modeled it after the Paterson, New Jersey, silk factories.[49]

By the time of the Panama-Pacific International Exposition in 1915, claims of the ideal California climate accompanied samples of silk on display in the Ferry Building. Hopes of encouraging sericulture sufficiently in order to tap into a $100 million market ran high while sericulturists countered the reality of competing with imported raw silk. At the onset of World War I, the women's group justified the need for seri-labor in the name of humanity, industry, and self-sufficiency from foreign suppliers.[50] The Japanese government predictably discouraged California's independent silk culture by the end of the decade. American dependence on imports made it the world's largest consumer of Japanese silk by the 1920s.[51] Californian sericulturists eventually joined a boycott against Japanese raw silk as the country invaded Manchuria in the 1930s. The fervor for sericulture grew quiet, snuffed in part by the development of nylon.

Failure as Integral Part of Sericultural Experimentation

The plant and insect life that appeared in the experimental silkscape of California did not settle into place simply due to the hospitable climate. *Bombyx mori* eggs had become appealing thanks to market and logistic contingencies, along with purpose-driven choices that encouraged their cultivation instead of selling them to others for cash. Imported mulberry plants propagated readily and obviated the need for endemic caterpillar food alternatives, but their uses expanded as shade plants, especially to border tracts of land used in viticulture.[52] A look into the various challenges that confronted the cultivation of silkworms and mulberry demonstrates how disparate timing, beings, and things provided the material scaffolding for which economic, political, and social issues mattered to the continuity of sericulture in the state.

Tracing the arc of silk culture in California has raised a broader recognition that failure was a norm. Modernizing themes in the twentieth century have indicated an intimate historical tie between sericulture and industrialization.[53] Sericultural cultivation experiments were not limited to physiological acclimatization tests or other similar tests to determine the best-suited species and varieties of mulberry. The experiments in sericulture in California entwined agriculture and technology, and they represented a much broader test of the larger visions of economic production organized by governmental or quasi-governmental entities that exceeded the scale of individual amateurs or entrepreneurial silk farmers. While the sericultural failures defined Californian risk-taking optimism, they also created space for reimagining agricultural enterprises in the state and how private and public entities should vest their resources, if not into sericulture, then into other more seemingly lucrative agricultural options. Viewing experiments as having a purpose beyond an immediate answer to a technical question permits a new framework that brings different historical concerns together, while also widening the scope of established gentlemanly or courtly practices or expansionist ideals alone.

Analyses of the production of sericultural literature parallels the production of sericultural failures and other scientific experimentation. The failures mentioned across historical accounts can be understood collectively as evidence of such trials and errors made alongside the movement of the symbiotic relationship between mulberry plants and silkworms.[54] Importantly, failure served different functions in societies known for having centuries of sericulture. For example, in China, where mulberry had predictive value as indicators of imperial statecraft, the destruction of mulberry by frost or other detrimental factors indicated the loss of potential revenues as well as the stability of the empire itself.[55]

Histories of silk cultivation can project an impression of the past that regards failure as anomalous, but it is important to distinguish an anticipated failure from one that was made unfathomable. In recent syntheses about sericultural motivations of the Spanish, English, and French in the Americas, scholar Benjamin Marsh has reconstructed the history of Atlantic sericulture as an experiment. This conceptualization involved borrowing hired expertise from Italy and the East Indies, alongside the improvement of and reinterpretation of theories, technologies, and diagrammatic representations.[56]

Experiments in sericulture were motivated by profit. Such experiments functioned to determine the cultivation potential of particularly valuable crops linked to textile production (cotton, jute, mulberry, indigo) or sugar. While modeled after the relatively successful case of Bengal, sericulture in Punjab did not take hold, owing to a completely different climate. Historian Jagjeet Lally has explained that failure of sericulture in Punjab also pointed to a broader economic experiment altogether. The creation of entities like the Agri-Horticultural Society had organized the colonial sericultural scheme.[57]

In other instances, histories of silk aligned with modernization theories have often traced institutions (schools, societies, experiment stations) as part of efforts to defray commercial risk for peasant households supplementing their incomes via sericulture. For instance, the experimentation by Japanese sericultural experts who worked closely with university-trained scientists in the late nineteenth century shows how the pursuits of learned entrepreneurial men overlapped with and contributed to knowledge in service of a growing state.[58] Such a paternalistic approach to sericulture also afforded little room for failure.

The California Silk Board of the 1880s could not acquire appropriations from the state government, but offers were made instead to build a silk school in San Rafael and employ a teacher and a director with discretionary funds to purchase all of the cocoons he deemed necessary.[59] However, the short-lived availability of government appropriations eventually ensured that California's sericulture would be much less centralized. As a result, women's associations played an important social role in the sharing of knowledge related to mulberry cultivation and silkworm rearing and for encouraging the institutionalization of sericulture. A lack of political commitment contributed to the repeated failures of sericulture in the antebellum period and presaged the decline of silk in California. Indeed, historian Emily Pawley has emphasized the destructive impact of a lack of political support on the social support system for growing mulberry and rearing silkworms.[60] Nonetheless, the networks of sericultural knowledge, on the one hand fragile and prone to rupture, and on the other hand resilient, perpetuated episodic cultivation of silk in California.

The value of scholarly attention to the role of women in sericulture cannot be overstated.[61] Even if American sericulture did not to take local hold in the way of other plantation crops, its patchy persistence of has greatly depended on women. Historian Benjamin Marsh stresses the great range of the roles of different kinds of women in the history of silkworm and mulberry cultivation. This included the moral mobilization of a variety of women: "idle" women in the employment of silk-throwing in England and later in Virginia in the seventeenth century; silk-spinning "Indian women" in French Louisiana; and enslaved African women in Georgia. It also included European women settlers and slaves not yet involved in plantation work (of later spring and summer) in South Carolina.[62]

Such historical attention has helped show how women played a part in shaping the development and later decline of silk commodity flows between the Americas and Europe. The example of eighteenth-century Pennsylvanian women experimenters who sought to advance sericulture shows how failure fulfilled a purpose as a necessary component of experimentation.[63] Various contingencies generated by the specialization of sericultural work over the centuries had encouraged remarkable integration of diverse economies into a capitalist system and had notably challenged the movement of sericultural know-how. Although specialization had specifically contributed to the creation of a silk industry in Europe, this situation had consequences for how people, especially women, learned and taught sericulture in the Americas. A decrease in gendered agency during the Industrial Revolution has tended to reinforce understandings about the deskilling of women, stripped of sericultural knowledge by machines and men.[64]

The interest in silk cultivation among Californian women illustrates their capacity to persist in sericulture despite the challenges of capitalist sericulture enterprises using industrial labor. Sericulture faced numerous obstacles in California, including the failure of the state to appropriate funds to encourage new silk enthusiasts. This was compounded by the belief that the industry could not succeed. Nevertheless, in the early 1900s the prospect of making sericulture work was revisited. In 1917, the California Development Board hired Guy Wilkinson to determine "once and for all [sericulture] could be profitably carried on in the State." While his initial skepticism was noted, Wilkinson concluded that silk culture in California would be practical and bring employment to thousands of women and men and, most important, keep millions of dollars in the country. He went on to incorporate a silk company on 800 acres of land, built roads, and prepared to plant 175,000 mulberry cuttings.[65] His willingness to make such an investment and refusal to admit the possibility of failure, should receive scholarly attention.

The role of women in the early 1900s cannot be overlooked for their contribution to the material continuity of silk work. By engaging in the practices of producing silk from the ground up—from mulberry cultivation, rearing silkworms, the weaving of cloth, as well as the writing of sericultural manuals—knowledges that had traveled with silkworms and mulberry, through books, or as taught by earlier cultivators, continued to become concretely localized within the state.[66]

Failures in agricultural projects occur on many different scales and have different explanations. The same can be said for the reasons as to why one may engage in a refusal to admit the possibility of failure in sericulture. The historian's attention to the entwined issues of agriculture and technology foregrounds a responsibility to learn about various actors in the enterprise. In places like California, a huge cast of characters, including silkworms, played a significant role in how capitalism developed. Californian sericulture reflects a newer instance of experimentation characterized by a series of refusals to give up sericulture. It provides a case with which to consider a methodology of writing histories of agriculture that not only includes but centers on the analysis of women.

Notes

1. Wool Manufacturer's Bulletin, "The Native Silk Culture in the United States Unpromising," *California Farmer and Journal of Useful Sciences* 39, no. 14 (May 15, 1873): 106.
2. Ibid.
3. Francesca Bray, Barbara Hahn, John Bosco Lourdusamy, and Tiago Saraiva, "Cropscapes and History: Reflections on Rootedness and Mobility," *Transfers* 9, no. 1 (2019): 20–41.
4. Claudio Zanier, "The Silk Cycle in China and its Migration," in *Seri-Technics: Historical Silk Technologies*, ed. Dagmar Schäfer, Giorgio Boriello, and Luca Mola (Berlin: Max Planck Research Library for the History and Development of Knowledge, 2020): 13–31. See 14–15 for discussion of Verson and Quajat, 1896.
5. Frédéric Hitzel, "Production et techniques de tissage de la soie à Bursa aux XVe et XVIe siècles," *Rives nord-méditerranéennes* 29 (2008): 16; Suraya Faroqhi, "Declines and Revivals in Textile Production," in *The Cambridge History of Turkey* (Cambridge: Cambridge University Press, 2006), 3:363; Fahri Dalsar, *Türk sanayi ve ticaret tarihinde Bursa'da ipekçilik* (İstanbul: İstanbul Üniversitesi, 1960): 361, 386 doc 299. Thanks to Aleksandar Shopov for these references.
6. Woodrow Borah, *Silk Raising in Colonial Mexico* (Berkeley: University of California Press, 1943): 54, 69, notes that prematurely hatched larvae were sometimes fed lettuce, blackberry, or banewort . Scientific silkworm feeding studies also discuss lettuce-eating. See Lisa Onaga, "A Matter of Taste: Making Artificial Silkworm Food in 20th Century Japan," in *Nature Remade*, ed. Michael Dietrich, Tiago Saraiva, Luis Campos, and Christopher Young (Chicago: Chicago University Press, 2021): 115–134.
7. John Feltwell, *The Story of Silk* (New York: St. Martin's Press, 1991): 92–94.
8. Margarita de Orellana, "Mexican Silk," *Artes de México*, no. 142 (1971): 88–89; Richard S. Peigler, "Wild Silks of the World," *American Entomologist* 39, no. 3 (1993): 151–162.
9. Charles Leonard Hogue, *Latin American Insects and Entomology* (Berkeley: University of California Press, 1993): 328, citing F. Cowan, *Curious Facts in the History of Insects* (Philadelphia: Lippincott, 1865), and E. Wittlich, H. Beyer, and F. Damm y Palacio, *Wissenschaftliche Festschrift zu Enthüllung des Deuten Seiner Majestät Kaiser Wilhelm II, dem mexikanischen Volke zum Iubiläum seinen Unabhängigkeit gestimmt Humboldt-Dankmals* (México: Müller Enos., n.d.): 149–173; Terrence D. Fitzgerald, *The Tent Caterpillars* (Ithaca, NY: Cornell University Press, 1995): 18–20.
10. Alejandro de Avila, "Threads of Diversity: Oaxacan Textiles in Context," in *The Unbroken Thread: Conserving the Textile Traditions of Oaxaca*, ed. Kathryn Klein (Los Angeles: The

Getty Conservation Institute, 1997), 125–28; Manuel Esparza, ed., *Relaciones geográficas de Oaxaca, 1777–1778* (Oaxaca: Centro de Investigaciones y Estudios Superiores en Antropología Social and Instituto Oaxaqueño de las Culturas, 1994): 59; for Borah, see fn 23.

11. The Indigenous Oaxacan silks produced today differ on a technical level from textiles woven from "raw silk" even though they come from cocoons spun by the same species. De Avila, "Threads of diversity," 126–29.

12. Borah, *Silk Raising in Colonial Mexico*, 53; "Mexican Silk," *Artes de México*, no. 142 (1971): 88–89.

13. Mixtecan silk production endured as a cash-generator well after the boom period. Adobe-walled Mixtecan silkworm nurseries could fit 350–400 trays of silkworms each. See Borah, *Silk Raising in Colonial Mexico*, 15–25, 69.

14. Ibid., 27–30. Monovoltine silkworms were widespread by the 1570s because February–April crops did not conflict with labor needs for growing crops such as maize, beans, and squash. See also 87 for more discussion.

15. Benjamin Marsh, *Unravelled Dreams: Silk and the Atlantic World, 1500–1840* (Cambridge: Cambridge University Press, 2020).

16. Jacqueline Field, Marjorie Senechal, and Madelyn Shaw, *American Silk, 1830–1930: Entrepreneurs and Artifacts* (Lubbock: Texas Tech University Press, 2007), 31–40.

17. Emily Pawley, *Nature of the Future: Agriculture, Science, and Capitalism in the Antebellum North* (Chicago: Chicago University Press, 2020): 109–11.

18. Elizabeth Hawes Ryland, "America's 'Multicaulis Mania,'" *William and Mary Quarterly* 19, no. 1 (1939): 25–33; Amy Chambliss, "The Mulberry Craze," *Georgia Review* 14, no. 2 (1960): 156–164.

19. Clark S. Monson, "Mulberry Trees: The Basis and Remnant of the Utah Silk Industry," *Economic Botany* 50, no. 1 (1996): 130–138.

20. Pawley, *Nature of the Future*, 109–11.

21. Giovanni Federico, *An Economic History of the Silk Industry, 1830–1930* (Cambridge: Cambridge University Press, 1997): 43–60.

22. Robert Marks, *Tigers, Rice, Silk, and Silt: Environment and Economy in Late Imperial South China* (Cambridge: Cambridge University Press, 1998), 118–20.

23. "The California Silk-Worm: *Saturnia Ceanothi*," *Hutching's California Magazine*, July 1856, reprinted in "Pages from the Past: The California Silk Worm," *California History* 58, no. 1 (1979): 76–77, https://doi.org/10.2307/25157890.

24. Sucheng Chan, *This Bittersweet Soil: The Chinese in California Agriculture, 1860–1910* (Berkeley: University of California Press, 1989), 19–20, 329. The Japanese *issei* generation followed in the footsteps of the Chinese immigrants, often facing similar prejudices. Masakazu Iwata, "The Japanese Immigrants in California Agriculture," *Agricultural History* 36, no. 1 (1962): 25–37.

25. Though led by Matsudaira Katanori, the group's Prussian sponsor Henry Schnell. Daniel A. Métraux, *The Wakamatsu Tea and Silk Colony Farm and the Creation of Japanese America* (Lanham, MD: Rowman & Littlefield), 2019.

26. Christopher A. Reichl, "Stages in the Historical Process of Ethnicity: The Japanese in Brazil, 1908–1988," *Ethnohistory* 42, no. 1 (1995): 31–62.

27. T. A. Kendon, *Treatise on Silk and Tea Culture and Other Asiatic Industries Adapted to the Soil and Climate of California* (San Francisco: A. Roman & Co., 1870).

28. *California Farmer and Journal of Useful Sciences* 3, no. 8 (February 22, 1855): 58.

29. Nelson Klose, "Sericulture in the United States," *Agricultural History* 37, no. 4 (October 1, 1963): 225–34; E. O. Essig, *Silk Culture in California* (Berkeley: University of California, College of Agriculture, Agricultural Experiment Station, 1945).

30. Marjorie Senechal, "The Invention of Machine Twist the Nonotuck Silk Company, from Moths to Millions," *Textile Society of America Symposium Proceedings* 545 (2002): 213.
31. Louis Prevost, *California Silk Grower's Manual* (San Francisco: H. H. Bancroft, 1866).
32. Eugene T. Sawyer, *History of Santa Clara County California with Biographical Sketches of the Leading Men and Women of the County Who Have Been Identified with Its Growth and Development from the Early Days to the Present* (Palo Alto, CA: Bay Microfilm, Inc., 1922).
33. Kayoko Fujita, "Changing Silk Culture in Early Modern Japan: On Foreign Trade and the Development of 'National' Fashion, from the Sixteenth to Nineteenth Century," in *Threads of Global Desire: Silk in the Pre-Modern World*, ed. Dagmar Schäfer, Giorgio Riello, and Luca Molà (Woodbridge: Boydell Press, 2018): 295–321; Claudio Zanier, "Tradition and Change in the Early Marketing of Japanese Silkworm Eggs: The First Large-scale Japanese Inroad into Western Markets (1863–1875)," in *Japan's Socio-Economic Evolution: Continuity and Change*, ed. Sarah Metzger-Court and Werner Pascha (Sandgate, Folkestone, Kent: Japan Library, 1996): 50–65; Claudio Zanier, *Semai: Setaioli italiani in Giappone (1861–1880): interpretare e comunicare senza tradurre* (Padova: CLEUP, 2006); Debin Ma, ed., *Textiles in the Pacific, 1500–1900* (Aldershot: Ashgate/Variorum, 2005); Lisa Onaga, "Bombyx and Bugs in Meiji Japan: Toward a Multispecies History?," *S&F Online* 11, no. 3 (2013), http://sfonline.barnard.edu/life-un-ltd-feminism-bioscience-race/bombyx-and-bugs-in-meiji-japan-toward-a-multispecies-history/; Showkat Ahmad Naik, "Revival of Silk Industry in Kashmir During the Dogra Period," *Proceedings of the Indian History Congress* 75 (2014): 697–707.
34. "Suspension of California Silk Manufactories," *New York Times*, March 22, 1873.
35. "A Consignment of Silk-Worms.: The Largest That Ever Arrived Here-a Valuable Cargo," *New York Times*, December 21, 1879; Nelson Klose, "California's Experimentation in Sericulture," *Pacific Historical Review* 30, no. 3 (1961): 213–27.
36. Essig, *Silk Culture in California*; Nelson Klose, "Louis Prevost and the Silk Industry at San Jose," *California Historical Society Quarterly* 43, no. 4 (1964): 309–317; Klose, "California's Experimentation in Sericulture," *Pacific Historical Review* 30, no. 3 (August 1, 1961): 213–227;
37. Klose, "California's Experimentation in Sericulture," 1961; Joseph Neumann, *History of the Discovery in California of a Native Silk Worm* (San Francisco: Woodward & Co., 1887); Joseph Neumann, "Report of Joseph Neumann," in *Women's Silk Culture Association*, ed. US Department of Agriculture (Washington, DC: Government Printing Office, 1890), 28–30; Alessandro Martelli, *The Silkworm and Its Food: An Essay towards Introduction of Sericulture into the Australian Colonies, with Special Reference to Raising of Cocoons for Exportation* (Melbourne: Clarson, Shallard & Co., 1863).
38. Evelyn Craig Pattiani, "Silk in Piedmont," *California Historical Society Quarterly* 31, no. 4 (1952): 335–342.
39. Ibid., 337.
40. "In Memoriam: Theodore Henry Hittell, Born April 5, 1830, Died February 23, 1917," in *Proceedings of the California Academy of Sciences* 7, no. 1, (June 17, 1918), 1–25, pi. 1.
41. Elise C. Wiehe Hittell and California Silk Culture Association, *The California Silk Growers' Instructor* (San Francisco: California Silk Culture Association, 1881).
42. Louise Rienzi, *General Instructions for Rearing Silkworms, With a Treatise on Securing Health Silkworm Eggs. Also, a Sketch of the Habits and Structure of the Silkworm* (Sacramento, CA: State Office, P. L. Shoaff, supt. state printing, 1887); California Legislature Assembly, *The Journal of the Assembly, During the . . . Session of the Legislature of the State of California* (1895), 926–927.

43. Pattiani, "Silk in Piedmont."
44. Essig, *Silk Culture in California*; Pattiani, "Silk in Piedmont."
45. "Silk Growing; New Company: Only Plant in California to Be Near Here; Well-Known Men Take Interest in New Industry and Buy from Mrs. Williams of San Diego—Farm Already Started a Few Miles South of the City," *Los Angeles Times*, March 31, 1907, sec. Editorial.
46. "Pioneers Would Make California a Silk-Producing State," *Los Angeles Times*, January 30, 1914, 11.
47. Richard B. Rice et al., *The Elusive Eden: A New History of California*, 5th ed. (Long Grove, IL: Waveland Press, 2019), 212–15; Paul W. Rhode, "Learning, Capital Accumulation, and the Transformation of California Agriculture," *Journal of Economic History* 55, no. 4 (1995): 773–800; "Orchard and Farm Rancho and Stockyard: Rural Life in Southern California," *Los Angeles Times*, January 28, 1893.
48. Special Correspondence of the *Times*, "Silk Culture in California: Renewed Attention Is Being Given the Subject; California Has a Climate Well Adapted to the Best Growth of the Silk Worms—Factories of the United States Import $50,000,000 of Reeled Silk," *Los Angeles Times*, October 28, 1906, sec. Arts and Leisure.
49. "Silk Manufacture in California: The Pioneer Establishment Near Los Angeles Receives Highest Award for Its Product," *Los Angeles Times*, April 10, 1910, V19.
50. *Memorial of the Ladies' Silk Culture Society, of California* [California], 1885; Ladies' Silk Culture Society of California, *Sericulture Exhibit: Panama-Pacific International Exposition* (San Francisco: Ladies' Silk Culture Society of California, 1915).
51. California et al., *Report of the Assembly Interim Committee to Inquire into the Possibilities of Silk Production and Industry in California: To the Assembly, California Legislature* (Sacramento, CA: The Assembly, 1945): 3–4.
52. Cletus E. Daniel, *Bitter Harvest, a History of California Farmworkers, 1870–1941* (Berkeley: University of California Press, 1982): 48.
53. Lillian Li, *China's Silk Trade: Traditional Industry in the Modern World, 1842–1937* (Cambridge, MA: Council on East Asian Studies Harvard University, 1981); Lillian M. Li, "Silks by Sea: Trade, Technology, and Enterprise in China and Japan," *Business History Review* 56, no. 2 (1982): 192–217.
54. Ben Marsh, "'The Honor of the Thing': Silk Culture in Eighteenth-Century Pennsylvania," and Carolina Hutková, "A Global Transfer of Silk Reeling Technologies: The English East India Company and the Bengal Silk Industry," in *Threads of Global Desire*, ed. Schäfer, Riello, and Molà, 265–94.
55. Recent multidisciplinary digital historical methods using a corpus of local gazetteers dated roughly before and during the Columbian Exchange era are illustrated in Dagmar Schäfer, Shih-pei Chen, and Qun Che, "What Is Local Knowledge? Digital Humanities and Yuan Dynasty Disasters in Imperial China's Local Gazetteers," *Journal of Chinese History* 4, no. 2 (July 2020): 391–429, https://doi.org/10.1017/jch.2020.31.
56. Marsh, "The Honor of the Thing," 265–80.
57. British colonial sericultural experiments in the late 1850s and 1860s encouraged sericulture in Punjab modeled on the historical experiences and material resources of Bengal. Jagjeet Lally, "Trial, Error and Economic Development in Colonial Punjab: The Agri-Horticultural Society, the State and Sericulture Experiments, c. 1840–70," *Indian Economic & Social History Review* 52, no. 1 (2015): 1–27.

58. Tessa Morris-Suzuki, "Sericulture and the Origins of Japanese Industrialization," *Technology and Culture* 33, no. 1 (1992): 101–121; Onaga, "Bombyx and Bugs in Meiji Japan: Toward a Multispecies History?," Lisa Onaga, "More than Metamorphosis: The Silkworm Experiments of Toyama Kametarō and His Cultivation of Genetic Thought in Japan's Sericultural Practices, 1894–1918," in *New Perspectives on the History of Life Sciences and Agriculture*, ed. Denise Phillips and Sharon Kingsland (Cham, Switzerland: Springer International Publishing, 2015): 415–37.
59. "California Silk Culture: The Offer of the United States Commissioner of Agriculture," *Los Angeles Times*, November 1, 1884, p. 1.
60. Pawley, *The Nature of the Future*, 109–11.
61. Joan W. Scott, "Gender: A Useful Category of Historical Analysis," *American Historical Review* 91, no. 5 (1986): 1053–75; Nancy Stepan, *The Hour of Eugenics: Race, Gender, and Nation in Latin America* (Ithaca, NY: Cornell University Press, 1991); Francesca Bray, *Technology and Gender: Fabrics of Power in Late Imperial China* (Berkeley: University of California Press, 1997).
62. Marsh, *Unravelled Dreams*, 77, 103, 140–47, 193–95, 261–65, 303.
63. Marsh, "'The Honor of the Thing,'" 265–80.
64. Industrializing silk production employed scores of women in places ranging from Japan (which modeled its first silk filature and reeling factory after the French) to Ottoman Turkey. Akram Fouad Khater, "'House' to 'Goddess of the House': Gender, Class, and Silk in 19th-Century Mount Lebanon," *International Journal of Middle East Studies* 28, no. 3 (1996): 325–48; E. Patricia Tsurumi, *Factory Girls* (Princeton, NJ: Princeton University Press, 1992); Elyssa Faison, *Managing Women: Disciplining Labor in Modern Japan* (Berkeley: University of California Press, 2007); Zanier, "Silk Cycle in China and Its Migration," 21–25.
65. C. S. Walton, "The Possibilities of the Silk Industry in the Golden State: The Silk Industry," *Los Angeles Times*, November 28, 1920, sec. Farm and Tractor Section, p. IX3; Klose, "Sericulture in the United States."
66. Carrie Williams, *Complete Instruction in Rearing Silkworms Also How to Build and Furnish Cocooneries, How to Plant, Prune, and Care for Mulberry Trees: Together with Much Valuable Information as to the Silk Industry in General* (San Francisco: Whitaker and Ray Co., 1902).

Bibliography

Borah, Woodrow. *Silk Raising in Colonial Mexico*. Berkeley: University of California Press, 1943.

Bray, Francesca, Barbara Hahn, John Bosco Lourdusamy, and Tiago Saraiva. "Cropscapes and History: Reflections on Rootedness and Mobility." *Transfers* 9, no. 1 (March 1, 2019): 20–41. https://doi.org/10.3167/TRANS.2019.090103.

Essig, E. O. *Silk Culture in California*. Berkeley: University of California, College of Agriculture, Agricultural Experiment Station, 1945.

Klose, Nelson. "Sericulture in the United States." *Agricultural History* 37, no. 4 (October 1, 1963): 225–234.

Marsh, Ben. *Unravelled Dreams: Silk and the Atlantic World, 1500–1840*. Cambridge: Cambridge University Press, 2020.

Onaga, Lisa. "More than Metamorphosis: The Silkworm Experiments of Toyama Kametarō and His Cultivation of Genetic Thought in Japan's Sericultural Practices, 1894–1918." In *New Perspectives on the History of Life Sciences and Agriculture*, edited by Denise Phillips and Sharon Kingsland, 415–37. Archimedes 40. Springer International Publishing, 2015. http://link.springer.com/chapter/10.1007/978-3-319-12185-7_20.

Schäfer, Dagmar, Giorgio Riello, and Luca Molà. *Threads of Global Desire: Silk in the Pre-Modern World*. Edinburgh: Boydell Press, 2018.

Zanier, Claudio. *Semai: Setaioli Italiani in Giappone (1861–1880): Interpretare e comunicare senza tradurre*. Padova: CLEUP, 2006.

PART IV

KEY TRANSITIONS AND CHALLENGES

CHAPTER 25

WATERSHED MOMENTS
Turning Points in Hydro-Agricultural Development

CHRISTOPHER L. PASTORE

Efforts to control water for agriculture have fundamentally shaped human history and global ecology. Draining, damming, and diverting water stabilized growing conditions and helped control flooding, thereby increasing agricultural production. Food security created population growth and allowed for the development of more sedentary, specialized, and politically cohesive societies.[1] Historians, including, most notably, Karl Wittfogel, have argued that water engineering was so important that it stimulated state development. Others, challenging that claim, have observed that some of the ancient world's most organizationally complex societies, including those in Mesopotamia, China, and Mexico, developed before they had implemented irrigation systems, or that sophisticated hydro-agricultural techniques were developed in the absence of centralized authority altogether.[2] Perhaps irrigation created states, perhaps it derived from them, or perhaps it did not require political organization at all. But when humans began to reshape waterways in service of cultivation, they nevertheless forged new relationships with the natural world and each other. Irrigation and the effort that went into developing it wed people to the land in more permanent ways. It created new interdependencies among communities. And it shaped new forms of collective identity.[3] But at a more basic level, the creation and maintenance of irrigation systems gave people powerful new roles in shaping their environments. As the historian Veronica Strang has explained, "[T]he control of water, more than anything else changed humankind's relationship with other species on Earth and asserted the primacy of human agency."[4]

Some, however, gained more agency than others. Offering a typology for the development of "irrigation societies," or those whose economies were predicated on irrigation-based agriculture, historian Donald Worster described a "local subsistence mode" of water management, whereby planning authority was dispersed across the community and water-delivery technologies were usually small-scale and temporary. Worster's second model, or the "agrarian state mode," required a more elaborate bureaucracy to manage more intricate water systems. Decision-making power, he showed, grew more concentrated among an elite few while the labor required to create and maintain irrigation systems was shouldered by the many. Finally, a "capitalist state mode" of water management ceded control to both government officials and private interests, rendering authority "faceless and impersonal, so much so in fact that many are unaware it exists."[5] Whether controlled collectively or by a powerful few, in personal or detached ways, or with cooperative or coercive intensions, the effort to bring order to an element that continually resisted it has long shaped the contours of human society.

Social forces shaped the global hydrosphere in return. As humans created new hydraulic technologies, they transformed watershed geometries. Beginning with the dawn of agriculture and concluding in the present, this chapter examines three turning points in human-water interactions. The first was the Neolithic Revolution, which brought about a shift from hunter-gatherer to agricultural economies. Fueling dramatic population growth and unleashing a burst of innovative energy, the invention of agriculture and development of irrigation systems to support it ultimately ushered in the historic period. During the late medieval and early modern periods, the second turning point saw feudal agricultural systems transformed by capitalism. In the pursuit of profit, farmers drained swamps and marshes the world over, converting forsaken fenlands into productive farmlands. Finally, the twentieth century's Green Revolution, which, with the help of new industrial technologies, shifted most of the world's usable freshwater toward agricultural production, marks a third turning point. In aggregate, these "watershed moments" in hydro-agricultural development reveal the ways by which humans have over the long sweep of time dissolved the distinctions between culture and nature, thereby establishing a hybridized world.[6]

Acknowledging the deep history and transformative capacity of human-water interactions may help us rethink the "age of man." In 2000, Paul Crutzen and Eugene Stoermer posited that industrialization and the shift to fossil fuels in the late eighteenth century had ushered in a new geological epoch they called the "Anthropocene."[7] Since then, scientists and humanists have been grappling with the term and its implications, offering in some cases alternative dates for the Anthropocene's origins.[8] Some have identified a "Great Acceleration" in anthropogenic environmental change beginning in 1945, as nuclear fallout and new industrial pollutants entered the geological record.[9] But others have looked back in time. Soil scientists Giacomo Certini and Riccardo Scalenghe, for instance, have argued that the Anthropocene should begin about 2,000 years ago, when farming practices began reshaping the earth's surface in substantive ways.[10] Paleoclimatologist William Ruddiman argued that the Anthropocene began when people commenced clearing forests, thereby elevating greenhouse gases roughly 7,000 years ago.[11] Still others have proposed that the domestication of plants and animals between 9,000 and 11,000 years ago launched the era.[12]

Recognizing that numerous signals could mark the Anthropocene's beginnings, Ruddiman and colleagues later questioned whether a formal start date was necessary at all.[13] Echoing that sentiment, literary scholar and ecocritic Steve Mentz suggested that perhaps now is the time to "break up the Anthropocene." He offered a "composting model" of anthropogenic environmental change, one in which "human history . . .

represents the accumulation and thickening of anthropogenic pressures as human populations expand in numbers and geographic range." If scientists have been searching for a single stratigraphic "golden spike," such as elevated carbon dioxide, methane, or pollen levels, to mark the opening of the Anthropocene, Mentz imagines *narrative* as an "essential technology" for sifting through the age of man's many layers.[14]

Stories may also hold the power to divine a watershed model for the Anthropocene, one in which hydro-agricultural tinkering high in the hills, cumulatively and over time, came to reshape hydrologic processes at river basin, continental, and global scales. Although identifying a definitive start date for this process remains elusive, a closer look at the history of hydro-agricultural development may help us, at the very least, establish human-water interactions as an important marker of the Anthropocene. But understanding how local systems of water use connect to global processes may also help us rethink our approaches to water governance moving forward.

THE HYDRO-NEOLITHIC REVOLUTION

Settling near waterways, possibly in response to climatic change, early Neolithic people developed villages even before the invention of agriculture.[15] With so many archeological sites scattered across such a broad geographic area, constructing a clear chronology for Near Eastern hydraulic development poses many challenges.[16] But all indications are that with the shift from hunting and gathering to agriculture around 10,000 BCE, communities began to develop small-scale irrigation systems, ostensibly with the goal of expanding food production. By about 7700 BCE, cereal pollens began settling over the Near East, the abundance of which, some have suggested, signal that limited irrigation technologies had come into use.[17] By the sixth millennium BCE, the archeological record provides more direct evidence of early irrigation channels in what is now eastern Iraq.[18] As the vast marshes of southern Mesopotamia began to recede after about 4000 BCE, the cities that had sprouted within them were forced to expand their canal networks.[19]

Over time and across the wider region, the implementation of irrigation reshaped watershed geometries. Gravity-fed canal systems extended the waters of the Euphrates into the surrounding desert, while levees buffered areas of human habitation from damaging floods.[20] Nearby, in western Arabia, natural winter runoff, or *seil*, was diverted for irrigation purposes, and in some cases the ground was prepared to control water movement and storage. By about 3000 BCE, the people of Jawa in northeastern Jordan, for instance, had adapted natural basalt structures to store their *seil*, and near the Dead Sea in western Jordan the people of Bab edh-Dhra constructed a similar water storage system.[21] Communities in Khuzestan, along the Persian Gulf, implemented small-scale irrigation systems, which they made more complex and expanded geographically over time.[22] Early Egyptians also began cutting canals.[23] As satellite remote sensing has shown, by about 1200 BCE, irrigation systems extended into northern Mesopotamia.[24] By 300 BCE the waters of the Tigris River had been integrated into these irrigation networks.[25]

Irrigation fueled population growth across the Near East. In a study of Syria's Balikh Valley, through which flows a tributary of the Euphrates, T. J. Wilkinson showed that rain-fed agriculture had sustained small, scattered communities but that by the late second and early first millennium BCE settlement patterns and population growth had become tied directly to irrigation.[26] If the Tigris-Euphrates lowlands supported a population of only 25,000 in 4100 BCE, that number had grown to 240,000 by 1100 BCE.[27] After about 1000 BCE, irrigation technology spread across Mesopotamia and the Middle East. The extension of canal systems at once expanded irrigation capacity and facilitated transportation.[28] Over time, moreover, canal systems that had initially been constructed to irrigate water-deficient areas were built to supply rain-fed areas, likely in efforts to stabilize growing conditions and increase crop yields.[29]

By the end of the Bronze Age, water engineering had reshaped both the landscape and distribution of people across the central Near East. By the first millennium BCE, the Assyrians had begun to direct the flow of water into cities and across the surrounding countryside. Urban centers grew, while people, both by force and of their own volition, spread out across the landscape via expanded road and canal systems. Beginning in the ninth century BCE the Assyrians built an aqueduct at Jerwan, a dam at Khinis, and a sprawling system of canals, some of which were more than 100 kilometers long.[30] The city of Nimrud, on the east bank of the Tigris River, irrigated its meadowlands and built a canal to the Upper Zab River, creating an intricate hydrologic network that nurtured orchards and plow agriculture.[31] As Jason Ur has posited, "Nearly the entire hydrology of the Nineveh region had been modified by its engineers, diverting water from the rivers and moving it to the capital cities but more importantly, making it accessible for irrigation throughout the hinterland."[32] As evidenced by its art, architecture, and the geographic extent of its influence, by the eighth and seventh centuries BCE the Assyrians had developed into one of, if not the most, powerful empires the world had ever known.[33]

Strong administrative states had developed networks of water infrastructure that transformed the Near East into the Fertile Crescent. After about 1200 BCE, the Assyrian Empire extended its irrigation networks, often across multiple river catchments.[34] Due in part to irrigation advances and the resultant expansion of agriculture, by the turn of the Common Era the population of Mesopotamia had climbed to 750,000.[35] By about the third century CE, cultivation extended clear across the Mesopotamian plains.[36] At roughly the same time, imperial Rome had pushed into North Africa and the Middle East, adding its hydraulic technologies and expertise across the region.[37] By channeling water through canals, pipes, tunnels, and elevated aqueducts, the Romans had also created one of the ancient world's largest cities in Europe.[38]

Elsewhere in the world, irrigation technologies transformed agricultural production. In 256 BCE, Qin Dynasty engineers constructed levees and irrigation works along the Min River in Sichuan Province and a decade later diverted water from the Ching River to irrigate more than 200,000 acres of farmland. The wealth produced from hydraulic engineering may have helped Emperor Qin Shi Huang unify China in 221 BCE and placed water management at the center of Chinese imperial policy moving forward.[39] In the Americas, irrigation practices enter the historical record in Mexico's Tehuacán

Valley with construction of the Purrón Dam Complex, which began around 700 BCE and continued into the Common Era. Populations expanded rapidly with the adoption of canal irrigation.[40] To the north, the Hohokam began to irrigate the Salt and Gila River valleys of Arizona sometime between 450 and 650 CE.[41] In some places, they constructed weirs of brush and sand. In others they built canals, which they likely dug deeper and wider over time, creating a network that stretched nearly 250 kilometers across the landscape. Although they built and maintained their hydraulic systems without centralized authority, the Hohokam nevertheless established what one historian called "the only true irrigation culture in prehistoric North America."[42]

The development of irrigational technologies boosted agricultural production, thereby supporting population growth and urban development. But irrigation also reshaped the human relationship to the natural world. Even if the shift to agriculture antedated hydraulic engineering, the human ability to control hydrologic processes created firmer linkages between the land and culture, creating *agri-culture* as we have come to know it. The Neolithic Revolution marked an important turning point in the Anthropocene, as human engineering brought water to more lands, extending human influence across a greater portion of the globe. This process continued through the ancient and medieval periods. But as the locus of political power shifted toward temperate regions during the early modern period, hydro-agricultural regimes shifted in response.

THE GREAT DRAINAGE

If the Neolithic Revolution was shaped by efforts to deliver water, the Agricultural Revolution of the late medieval and early modern periods was marked by efforts to remove it. Historians have emphasized the ways that crop rotation and the introduction of new technologies created an English Agricultural Revolution in the eighteenth and early nineteenth centuries, but close focus on Europe's early modern hydraulic transformations could situate the revolution much earlier and over a wider geographic area.[43] From roughly 650 to 1350 the population of Europe more than doubled, thereby pushing human settlement into more marginal areas. To reclaim lands for husbandry and cultivation, farmers drained marshes, bogs, and fenlands, a process that peaked in the sixteenth and seventeenth centuries.[44] As European empires expanded across the globe, they established "neo-Europes" by, in part, implementing Old World agricultural regimes.[45] This expanded the scope and hastened the pace of global hydrologic change.

The Dutch were the great early modern movers of water and land. Indeed, the English word "landscape" derives from the Frisian (in the marshy northern Netherlands) for "land" and "schop," or shovel, so meaning quite literally shoveled land "thrown up against the sea."[46] Between the eleventh and fourteenth centuries, the Dutch began draining their coastal marshes and peat bogs, reclaiming agricultural lands in what historian Jan de Vries has characterized as an "internal colonization movement."[47] To manage these earth and waterworks, the Dutch established drainage boards, which over time assumed legal authority to manage the construction of dams and dikes.[48] Although some landowners failed to maintain their embankments, leaving their tenants vulnerable to flooding, during the sixteenth century Dutch water authorities expanded the dam and dike systems and implemented several transformative technologies, including mechanized sluices and windmills, which helped drain tidal wetlands.[49] With land prices rising during the first half of the seventeenth century, wealthy Dutch merchants funded numerous drainage projects.[50] So successful were their efforts that by the mid-seventeenth century, Dutch agricultural productivity was double that of Eastern Europe and Scandinavia.[51] Radically remade by human technology and capital, at once connected to the European continent and an expanding Atlantic world, the Low Countries grew into a global entrepôt.

By the 1580s, Dutch hydraulic expertise was creating new agricultural lands across Europe.[52] The Dutch drained the Russian flatlands, Poland's Vistula Valley, northern Germany's *Marschen*, and the wetlands of Italy.[53] So transformative were Dutch-led drainage projects in early modern France that they helped consolidate royal authority and internationalize the French economy.[54] But probably the most ambitious Dutch-guided drainage projects occurred in southeastern England, where hundreds of thousands of fenland acres were converted into farmland. From the meres of Holderness to the mouth of the Thames River estuary, tidal wetlands were drained to expand cultivation.[55]

Supporting fishing, fouling, and limited grazing and tillage during the medieval period, the fenlands had long been ecotonal landscapes connecting land and sea. Typically characterized as "wastes," these soggy wetlands were often held in common by smallhold farmers and landless cottagers. The unruly nature of the fens also attracted unruly people, including drifters and outlaws. Possibly due to climatic variations associated with the Little Ice Age, flooding grew increasingly unpredictable by the end of the sixteenth century.[56] Climatic changes could have also diminished crop yields, causing grain prices to rise. As the population of England expanded, so too did the demand for food. For all these reasons, by the early seventeenth century many sought to "improve" the fenlands by enclosing and draining them, thereby removing their unseemly inhabitants while making the lands more orderly and productive.[57]

Drainage also helped to consolidate state power.[58] In March 1593 the Dutch-born engineer Humphrey Bradley submitted a plan to drain the fens across central England. Anticipating the difficult task of reconciling the "diversity of tenures and leases," the proposal sought an Act of Parliament to see the project to completion.[59] State intervention, his application argued, would clear legal roadblocks, providing a benefit to all. In 1601, Parliament passed the General Drainage Act, which sought to make "dry and p[ro]fitable of those surrounded [inundated] Groundes" with the goal of bringing "greate and inestimable benefite" to the Crown.[60] Just as water delivery shaped the formation of empire in the ancient world, drainage shaped state aspirations in the early modern.

Drainage, many believed, would also help England actualize its full economic potential. In 1630, Francis Russell, the fourth Earl of Bedford, commissioned the Dutch engineer Sir Cornelius Vermuyden to drain the Great Level, a 1,300 square kilometer tract of fenland in southeastern England.[61] Vermuyden's work was so promising that the Drainage Act of 1649 anticipated cornucopian results. In addition to agricultural output, the Act explained that drainage would also "increase Manufactures, Commerce and Trading at home and abroad, will relieve the poor, by setting them on work, and will many other ways redound to the great advantage and strengthening of the Nation."[62]

But many fenlanders resisted drainage efforts. Protestors across the Great Level complained that drainage had made conditions worse, particularly after landowners enclosed portions of the fens in 1651 and again in 1653. Many also opposed the presence of the foreigner Vermuyden and the continental laborers whom he had hired to complete the work.[63] Riots broke out in Cambridgeshire and Norfolk, causing such disruption that Oliver Cromwell was forced to deploy troops to keep the peace.[64] Vermuyden ended his work on the Great Level in 1655, pursuing at least one other drainage project before he died in 1677, but draining the English fenlands continued throughout the early modern period, opening thousands of acres of farmland and fundamentally changing the way water flowed across southern England.[65]

As the Dutch and English empires extended their global reach, they drained their newly acquired possessions. In 1624 the Dutch began draining lower Manhattan in their nascent colony of New Netherland. In 1643 they increased their efforts by carving canals, creating new pastures, and opening new transportation routes into their growing city. When the English took control of New York in 1664 and then again (and for good) in 1675, they transformed Manhattan's marshy landscape yet again. As Ted Steinberg has explained, "Rather than building canals and internalizing the waterfront as the Dutch had, the British focused on extending the existing littoral outward." Moving great heaps of stone and soil, the English began displacing American waters by filling its coastal wetlands.[66]

That process extended up and down North America's Atlantic coast and was integral to the development of its major colonial cities.[67] For instance, soon after arriving in 1630, Boston's English settlers began draining the fens and filling the mudflats that surrounded the Shawmut Peninsula.[68] The first settlers of Newport, Rhode Island, also prioritized draining the marshes surrounding their new harbor.[69] In Charleston, South Carolina, settlers filled and drained the wetlands surrounding the Ashley and Cooper Rivers to build their city.[70] And it was draining, filling, damming, and diking that made New Orleans habitable.[71] Over the course of the early modern period, the combination of hydraulic engineering, forest clearing, and even beaver hunting did much to transform what had been a marshy coastal margin into a dryer, more clearly defined edge or "coastline," a term that first came into use around the end of the eighteenth century.[72]

THE BLUE DIMENSIONS OF THE GREEN REVOLUTION

By the mid-twentieth century, new agricultural technologies brought about a third "watershed moment," a transformation widely known as the "Green Revolution," whereby synthetic fertilizers, pesticides, and high-yield plant varieties boosted global food production. While historians have shown how the synergies among big banks, powerful governments, and industrial chemical and seed companies reshaped global systems of cultivation, they have spent less time on the role that hydraulic engineering played in the process, possibly because, as Avinash C. Tyagi, former secretary-general of the International Commission on Irrigation and Drainage, has observed, the Green Revolution was "driven through the pioneering work on HYV [high-yield varieties]," while "supporting sectors and services like irrigation and drainage were made to follow and fulfill the expected demands."[73] But water innovations were integral to the expansion of agricultural production. If the Neolithic Revolution had reshaped watersheds across the Near East, and the early modern Agricultural Revolution had reshaped watersheds wherever European empires extended their reach, the shift from rainfed "green water" agriculture to "blue water" systems that drew heavily from rivers, reservoirs, and aquifers did more to reshape the global hydrosphere than any other agricultural transformation in history.

Agricultural water use surged during the second half of the twentieth century. Between 1960 and 2000, global freshwater withdrawals doubled to 3,600 cubic kilometers, 70 percent of which was directed toward irrigation.[74] As the volume of water withdrawals increased, so too did the geographic extent of irrigated land, which nearly doubled to 301 million hectares.[75] Global food production grew 2.5 to 3 times, with 40 percent of that growth attributed directly to irrigation.[76] Nowhere was the expansion of irrigation more pronounced than in Asia, where nearly two-thirds of the world's irrigated lands came to consume almost half of the planet's available water, and in the United States, Canada, and Europe, which collectively consumed another third.[77] Irrigation extended the geographic range of arable lands, pushing them farther north and in some places providing additional growth cycles.[78]

The seeds of this irrigation boom were sown in service of empire. For instance, the Dutch had used irrigation to assert authority across colonial Indonesia.[79] The British used irrigation to impose centralized bureaucracies in India, Egypt, and the Sudan.[80] Russian and later Soviet imperial schemes sought to "civilize" Central Asia by diverting the waters of the Aral Sea.[81] The French sought but never fully achieved an agricultural empire in Mali because irrigation alienated people from their ancestral lands, thereby hampering production.[82] Even as Europe's imperial ambitions crumbled, water engineering played a central role in making the United States the "principal seat of the world-circling American Empire."[83]

Integral to the expansion of irrigation agriculture and ever a symbol of imperial persistence was the "big dam." Taller than 15 meters, or if shorter having a water-storage capacity in excess of 3 million cubic meters, big dams changed the movement of water on a global scale. If only a handful of big dams had been built by 1900, 5,000 were completed by 1950, and another 40,000 across nearly half of the world's rivers by the turn of the twenty-first century.[84] Beginning in the American West, the Hoover (1935) and Grand Coulee (1941) dams expanded the possibilities of irrigation agriculture. By mid-century, three new dams along the Yaqui River Valley in Sonora ushered in Mexico's Green

Revolution.[85] But it was China that embraced big dams more than any other nation. In 1949, China had only 100 dams, but today its rivers hold 22,000, or nearly half the global total.[86] Big dams now provide between 30 and 40 percent of irrigation worldwide.[87]

But big dams came with environmental and social costs. In the same way that the architects of early modern drainage depicted fenlanders as wild and rebellious to justify enclosure, twentieth-century dam builders often described river valley inhabitants as wasteful and inept, people desperately in need of modernization and therefore removal.[88] In other cases, big dams effected environmental changes that forced people to flee. For example, after dams were built in the lower Indus Valley between 1962 and 1997, the number of days without water increased from zero to eighty-five. Farmers could no longer function, and many migrated to cities. In other areas, big dams reshaped floodplains, decimated fish stocks, and created disease environments.[89] The best estimates suggest that worldwide big dam construction has displaced between forty and eighty million people.[90]

The Green Revolution also sent farmers deep into the earth in search of "blue water." Across the southern Great Plains in the United States, farmers dug wells into the Ogallala aquifer, allowing them to shift production from wheat and sorghum to more profitable but more water-dependent crops, such as corn, sugar beets, and alfalfa. But farmers sucked more water from the earth than was returned, causing water tables to drop.[91] A similar fate befell China, which began tapping its groundwater in the 1960s. From 1965 to 2003, the number of Chinese wells jumped from 200,000 to 4.7 million. As the water table fell and water grew less accessible, local communities abandoned collective modes of well maintenance in favor of privatization. This led to unequal water access.[92] While the wealthy watered their crops, the poor's withered nearby.

Water scarcity encouraged hydraulic engineers to divert, pump, and channel water over long distances. Inter-basin water transfers have become so commonplace that it is expected they will deliver a quarter of all blue-water withdrawals by 2025.[93] But inter-basin transfers can introduce invasive species and alter the volume and chemical composition of water, making it more susceptible to algal and bacterial blooms.[94] In one of the most ambitious efforts to reshape watershed geometries, India has advanced a plan to link river basins across the Himalayas with those of the peninsula. Although the social, ecological, and economic costs of the plan have hampered progress, the National River Linking Project, if fully implemented, would fundamentally reshape the hydrology of South Asia.[95]

As pumps and canals created new material linkages between river basins on a continental scale, global trade has integrated hydrologic systems on a planetary scale. When in 1993 the geographer Tony Allan reimagined the water used to produce agricultural commodities as "virtual water," he described a globally integrated system in which water-poor countries, such as those in the Middle East and North Africa, could meet their food needs by importing agricultural products from regions with water surpluses. As Allan explained, "[S]erious local water shortages could be very effectively ameliorated by global economic processes."[96] By connecting distant watersheds "virtually," the logic held, market-driven efficiencies could stave off scarcity-induced strife.

By the millennium, 16 percent of worldwide agricultural water use went into producing export commodities.[97] North and South America exported the most virtual water, while Central and South Asia imported the most—drawing roughly 80 billion cubic meters of virtual water from North America alone.[98] Where surpluses support exports of virtual water, trading partnerships can produce political and economic benefits. But when those virtual-water flows create environmentally destructive deficits, political and social unrest often follows.

Shaping a Future Global Hydrosphere

Humans have been managing freshwater resources to meet their needs since the dawn of agriculture. Damming, draining, and diverting water played integral roles in advancing the Neolithic Revolution, which reshaped patterns of human subsistence and, in turn, the structures of ancient societies. Food surpluses fueled urban growth and the expansion of empires. As populations grew across medieval and early modern Europe, farmers drained marshes and fens, creating new land for grazing and cultivation, both at home and among their imperial peripheries. Their efforts ushered in a new age of hydraulic control, which grew in influence during the nineteenth century as Europeans spread across the globe. Even after their empires began to erode in the twentieth century, the West came to wield new hydraulic technologies that were so effective in their ability to reshaped watersheds that they fundamentally altered the global hydrosphere.

Even the oceans responded to these powerful drivers of hydrologic change. Global warming has done its part to melt ice caps and induce the thermal expansion of seawater, but the long history of surface water drainage combined with more recent groundwater withdrawals have also played important roles in elevating sea levels. The best estimates show that between 1930 and 2000 water engineering caused an annual sea-level rise of 0.54 mm per year.[99] If anthropogenic causes flushed more fresh water into the sea, the proliferation of impoundments—roughly 45,000 large and possibly another 800,000 small dams—served to slow the flow.[100] Even if by the turn of the twenty-first century the net change to continental runoff had approached zero, the alterations to the hydrologic cycle were pronounced. In some cases, the timing and magnitude of river flows (and, in turn, sediment transport) was altered. In others, the chemical composition of water changed as it aged.[101]

Politics and the promise of profit also altered the flow of water. Recognizing that irrigation was capable of increasing food production between two- and fourfold, the World Bank devoted more than half of its agricultural lending to irrigation projects between the 1960s and 1980s.[102] Since irrigation serves as an economic multiplier, the irrigation boom benefited not only food production, but also health, education, and transportation.[103] But policymakers also recognized that irrigation had significant social and environmental costs. Irrigation dislocated communities, polluted waterways, and created the conditions for disease. Moreover, as irrigation technologies grew more expensive while food prices declined, irrigation could also saddle communities with debt. As a result, by the 1980s public investment in irrigation slowed, giving way in some cases to private development.[104] In other cases, governments ceded control of irrigation systems to local communities, encouraging farmers to integrate new efficiencies into existing systems.[105] But unless those efficiencies can be implemented on a global scale, agricultural water consumption is expected to rise 20 percent by 2050.[106] Indeed, data shows that a growing population combined with increasing water demand could apply more pressure to global water systems than climate change.[107]

But to be sure, climate change is also taking a toll. The 2008 Intergovernmental Panel on Climate Change explained that global warming "has been linked to changes in the large-scale hydrological cycle." Their report showed that patterns of precipitation had changed, making storms more intense and some areas more susceptible to flood and drought.[108] And those with the fewest resources would be the hardest hit. Acknowledging that rising atmospheric temperatures could dramatically alter water availability, the 2018 IPCC report recommended that farmers respond by increasing irrigation efficiency. But rather than implementing "large-scale infrastructural interventions," the report concluded that those improvements would be more likely achieved by way of "well-designed... community-based adaptation."[109] A global group grappling with global problems recognized that local-level efforts could have far-reaching hydrologic effects.

Although many small hydraulic changes have accrued over thousands of years, it was three watershed moments—the Neolithic Revolution, the early modern Agricultural Revolution, and the Green Revolution—that in aggregate connected those local changes with global transformations. A closer look at these important shifts in human-water relations—both the benefits they brought and the damages they wrought—may challenge the fatalistic "grand narratives" that define the Anthropocene solely in terms of decline.[110] Perhaps, instead, acknowledging the ways that water, one of the most powerful forces in nature, often checked human efforts to dominate natural systems may help us recast the "age of man" as an ongoing negotiation between culture and nature, one in which humans surely stumbled in some cases but built resilience into natural systems in others. And perhaps a historical perspective, one that embraces the power of stories, may help us affirm the ability of local people, regardless of their means, to effect meaningful change. Conceivably, this could lead us toward a new watershed moment, one that defines a more equitable and sustainable way to provide water and grow food for the future.

Notes

1. V. Gordan Childe, *Man Makes Himself* (London: Watts & Co., 1936); Kent V. Flannery, "The Origins of the Village as a Settlement Type in Mesoamerica and the Near East: A Comparative Study," in *Man, Settlement, and Urbanism*, ed. Peter J. Ucko, Ruth Tringham, and G. W. Dimbleby (London: Duckworth, 1972): 23–53.

2. Julian Steward, *Irrigation Civilizations: A Comparative Study* (Washington, DC: Pan American Union, 1955); Karl Wittfogel, *Oriental Despotism: A Comparative Study of Total Power* (New Haven, CT: Yale University Press, 1957); Robert L. Carneiro, "A Theory of the Origin of the State," *Science* 169, no. 3947 (August 21, 1970): 733–738; Carl H. Kraeling and Robert M. Adams, eds., *City Invincible: A Symposium on Urbanization, and Cultural Development in the Ancient Near East Held at the Oriental Institute of the University of Chicago, December 4–7, 1958* (Chicago: University of Chicago Press, 1960), 37, 281; William P. Mitchell, "The Hydraulic Hypothesis: A Reappraisal," *Current Anthropology* 14, no. 5 (December 1973): 532–541.
3. Henry D. Wallace and Jenny L. Adams, *Roots of Sedentism: Archaeological Excavations at Valencia Vieja, a Founding Village in the Tucson Basin of Southern Arizona* (Tucson, AZ: Center for Desert Archaeology, 2003).
4. Veronica Strang, *Water: Nature and Culture* (London: Reaktion, 2015): 86.
5. Donald Worster, *Rivers of Empire: Water, Aridity, and the Growth of the American West* (New York: Pantheon, 1985): 30–52.
6. Paul S. Sutter, "The World with Us: The State of American Environmental History," *Journal of American History* 100, no. 2 (June 2013): 94–119.
7. Paul J. Crutzen and Eugene F. Stoermer, "The 'Anthropocene,'" The International Geosphere-Biosphere Programme (IGBP) *Global Change Newsletter* 41 (2000): 17–18; Paul J. Crutzen, "Geology of Mankind," *Nature* 415 (January 3, 2002): 23.
8. Will Steffen, Paul J. Crutzen, and John R. McNeill, "The Anthropocene: Are Humans Now Overwhelming the Great Forces of Nature?" *Ambio* 36, no. 8 (December 2007): 614–621; Jason M. Kelly, et al. eds., *Rivers of the Anthropocene* (Berkeley: University of California Press, 2018).
9. W. Steffen, A. Sanderson, P. D. Tyson, J. Jäger, P. A. Matson, B. Moore III, F. Oldfield, K. Richardson, H. J. Schellnhuber, B. L. Turner II, and R. J. Wasson, *Global Change and the Earth System: A Planet under Pressure* (Berlin: Springer-Verlag, 2004): 131; J. R. McNeill and Peter Engelke, *The Great Acceleration: An Environmental History of the Anthropocene since 1945* (Cambridge, MA: Harvard University Press, 2014); Jan Zalasiewicz et al., "When Did the Anthropocene Begin? A Mid-Twentieth Century Boundary Level Is Stratigraphically Optimal," *Quaternary International* 383 (October 5, 2015): 196–203.
10. Giacomo Certini and Riccardo Scalenghe, "Anthropogenic Soils Are the Golden Spikes for the Anthropocene," *The Holocene* 21, no. 8 (2011): 1269–1274.
11. William R. Ruddiman, "The Anthropocene," *Annual Review of Earth and Planetary Sciences* 41 (2013): 45–68.
12. Bruce D. Smith and Melinda A. Zeder, "The Onset of the Anthropocene," *Anthropocene* 4 (December 2013): 8–13.
13. William F. Ruddiman, Erle C. Ellis, Jed O. Kaplan, and Dorian Q. Fuller, "Defining the Epoch We Live In: Is a Formally Designated 'Anthropocene' a Good Idea?" *Science* 348, no. 6230 (April 3, 2015): 38–39.
14. Steve Mentz, *Break Up the Anthropocene* (Minneapolis: University of Minnesota Press, 2019): 4.
15. Lewis R. Binford, "Postpleistocene Adaptations," in *New Perspectives in Archeology*, ed. Sally R. Binford and Lewis R. Binford (Chicago: Aldine, 1968), 313–41; Trevor Watkins, *The Birth of the Gods and the Origins of Agriculture* (Cambridge: Cambridge University Press, 2000): 18–19.
16. Ian Kuijt, "Life in Neolithic Farming Communities: An Introduction," in *Life in Neolithic Farming Communities: Social Organization, Identities, and Differentiation* (New York: Kluwer Academic/Plenum, 2000): 8.

17. Robert Miller, "Water Use in Syria and Palestine from the Neolithic to the Bronze Age," *World Archaeology* 11, no. 3 (February 1980): 331–341.
18. T. J. Wilkinson, *Archeological Landscapes of the Near East* (Tucson: University of Arizona Press, 2003): 73.
19. Jennifer Pournelle, "Marshland of Cities: Deltaic Landscapes and the Evolution of Early Mesopotamian Civilization" (PhD thesis, University of California, San Diego, 2003).
20. Thomas M. Whitmore et al., "Long-Term Population Change," in *The Earth as Transformed by Human Action: Global and Regional Changes in the Biosphere over the Past 300 Years*, ed. B.L. Turner II et al. (New York: Cambridge University Press, 1990): 29–30.
21. Neil Roberts, "Water Conservation in Ancient Arabia," *Proceedings of the Seminar for Arabian Studies*, Vol. 7, Proceedings of the Tenth Seminar For Arabian Studies held at The Middle East Centre, Cambridge on 12th–14th (1777): 136; Walter E. Rast and R. Thomas Schaub, "Survey of the Southeastern Plain of the Dead Sea, 1973," *Annual of the Department of Antiquities of Jordan* 19 (1974): 5–53.
22. Robert M. Adams, "Agriculture and Urban Life in Early Southwestern Iran," *Science* 136, no. 3511 (April 13, 1962): 109–122.
23. Karl W. Butzer, *Early Hydraulic Civilization in Egypt: A Study in Cultural Ecology* (Chicago: University of Chicago Press, 1976): 20–21, 107.
24. Louise Rayne and Daniel Donoghue, "A Remote Sensing Approach for Mapping the Development of Ancient Water Management in the Near East," *Remote Sensing* 10, no. 2042 (December 14, 2018): 1–21.
25. Whitmore et al., "Long-Term Population Change," 29.
26. T. J. Wilkinson, "Water and Human Settlement in the Balikh Valley, Syria: Investigations from 1992–1995," *Journal of Field Archaeology* 25, no. 1 (1998): 63–87.
27. Whitmore et al., "Long-Term Population Change," 29.
28. Stephanie Rost, "Navigating the Ancient Tigris: Insights into Water Management in an Early State," *Journal of Anthropological Archaeology* 54 (2019): 31–47.
29. Tony James Wilkinson and Louise Rayne, "Hydraulic Landscapes and Imperial Power in the Near East," *Water History* 2 (2010): 115–144.
30. T. J. Wilkinson et al., "Landscape and Settlement in the Neo-Assyrian Empire," *Bulletin of the American Schools of Oriental Research* 340 (November 2005): 23–56.
31. David Oates, *Studies in the Ancient History of Northern Iraq* (London: The British Academy, 1968): 42–48.
32. Jason Ur, "Water for Arbail and Nimrud," in *Water for Assyria*, ed. Hartmut Kühne (Wiesbaden, Germany: Harrassowitz, 2018): 57–58.
33. Wilkinson et al., "Landscape and Settlement in the Neo-Assyrian Empire," 23; Roger Matthews, *The Archeology of Mesopotamia: Theories and Approaches* (New York: Routledge, 2003): 132–142.
34. Dan Lawrence et al., "Long Term Population, City Size and Climate Trends in the Fertile Crescent: A First Approximation," *PloS ONE* 11, no. 3 (March 2016): 1–16.
35. Whitmore et al., "Long-Term Population Change," 29.
36. T. J. Wilkinson, *Archeological Landscapes of the Near East* (Tucson: University of Arizona Press, 2003): 95, 97.
37. Ibid., 94.
38. David Sedlak, *Water 4.0: The Past, Present, and Future of the World's Most Vital Resource* (New Haven, CT: Yale University Press, 2014): 2–3.

39. Brian Fagan, *Elixir: A History of Water and Humankind* (New York: Bloomsbury, 2011): 229–230.
40. Kjell I. Enge and Scott Whiteford, *The Keepers of Water and Earth: Mexican Rural Social Organization and Irrigation* (Austin: University of Texas Press, 1989): 60–63.
41. M. Kyle Woodson, *The Social Organization of Hohokam Irrigation in the Middle Gila River Valley, Arizona* (Sacaton, AZ: Gila River Indian Community, Anthropological Research Papers, 2016); Zhu Tianduowa, Kyle C. Woodson, and Maurits W. Ertsen, "Reconstructing Ancient Hohokam Irrigation Systems in the Middle Gila River Valley, Arizona, United States of America," *Human Ecology* 46 (2018): 735–746.
42. R. Douglas Hurt, *American Agriculture: A Brief History* (West Lafayette, IN: Purdue University Press, 2002): 21–23.
43. Lord [Roland Prothero] Ernle, *English Farming Past and Present* (1912; London: Heinemann, 1961); J. D. Chambers and G. E. Mingay, *The Agricultural Revolution, 1750–1880* (London: Batsford, 1966); Eric Kerridge, *The Agricultural Revolution* (New York: A. M. Kelley, 1967), argued that the Agricultural Revolution occurred in the sixteenth and seventeenth centuries. Joan Thirsk, *England's Agricultural Regions and Agrarian History, 1500–1750* (London: Macmillan, 1987), expanded the chronology of agricultural transformation while emphasizing regional differences. For a succinct historiographical analysis of the English Agricultural Revolution, see J. V. Beckett, *The Agricultural Revolution* (Oxford: Basil Blackwell, 1990): 1–10.
44. Jan de Vries, *The Dutch Rural Economy in the Golden Age, 1500–1700* (New Haven, CT: Yale University Press, 1974), 2–3, 26–27; Salvatore Ciriacono, *Building on Water: Venice, Holland and the Construction of the European Landscape in Early Modern Times* (New York: Berghahn, 2006): 3–4; Mark Overton, *Agricultural Revolution in the England: The Transformation of the Agrarian Economy, 1500–1850* (Cambridge: Cambridge University Press, 1996), 5.
45. Alfred Crosby, *Ecological Imperialism: The Biological Expansion of Europe, 900–1900* (Cambridge: Cambridge University Press, 1986).
46. John Stilgoe, *What Is Landscape?* (Cambridge, MA: MIT Press, 2015), 2.
47. de Vries, *The Dutch Rural Economy in the Golden Age*, 26.
48. Ibid., 29.
49. Tim Soens, "Resilient Societies, Vulnerable People: Coping with North Sea Floods before 1800," *Past and Present* 241 (November 2018): 143–77; Petra J. E. M. van Dam, "Ecological Challenges, Technological Innovations: The Modernization of Sluice Building in Holland, 1300–1600," *Technology and Culture* 43, no. 3 (July 2002): 517–520.
50. de Vries, *The Dutch Rural Economy in the Golden Age*, 193–95.
51. Ciriacono, *Building on Water*, 177.
52. Raphaël Morera, "Environmental Change and Globalization in Seventeenth-Century France: Dutch Traders and the Draining of French Wetlands (Arles, Petit Poitou)," *International Review of Social History* 55 (2010): 80.
53. Ciriacono, *Building on Water*, ch. 5; David Blackbourn, *The Conquest of Nature: Water, Landscape, and the Making of Modern Germany* (New York: W. W. Norton, 2007).
54. Ciriacono, *Building on Water*, ch. 5.
55. Overton, *The Agricultural Revolution in England*, 89–90.
56. Eric Ash, "Reclaiming a New World: Fen Drainage, Improvement, and Projectors in Seventeenth-Century England," *Early Science and Medicine* 21 (2016): 449–451.
57. Eric H. Ash, *The Draining of the Fens: Projectors, Popular Politics, and State Building in Early Modern England* (Baltimore: Johns Hopkins University Press, 2017): 47–49.

58. James C. Scott, *Seeing like a State: How Certain Schemes to Improve the Human Condition Have Failed* (New Haven, CT: Yale University Press, 1998).
59. Mary Anne Everett Green, ed., *Calendar of State Papers, Domestic Series, Elizabeth, 1591–1594* (London: Longmans, Green, Reader, & Dyer, 1867): 334–35.
60. *Statutes of the Realm*, Vol. IV, Part II, 43° Elizabeth, c. 10, 11 (London: Dawsons of Pall Mall, 1963): 977–78.
61. Dorothy Summers, *The Great Level: A History of Drainage and Land Reclamation in the Fens* (London: David & Charles, 1976): 63–73.
62. *An Act for the Draining of the Great Level of the Fens, Extending itself into the Counties of Northampton, Norfolk, Suffolk, Lincoln, Cambridge and Huntington, and the Isle of Ely, or some of them* (London: John Field for Edward Husband, August 1, 1649): 561.
63. H. C. Darby, *The Changing Fenland* (Cambridge: Cambridge University Press, 1983), 73–74.
64. Ash, *The Draining of the Fens*, 270–275.
65. Darby, *The Changing Fenland*, 75.
66. Ted Steinberg, *Gotham Unbound: The Ecological History of Greater New York* (New York: Simon & Schuster, 2014): 12–14, 20.
67. Ann Vileisis, *Discovering the Unknown Landscape: A History of America's Wetlands* (Washington, DC: Island Press, 1997).
68. Christopher L. Pastore, "Filling Boston Commons: Law, Culture, and Ecology in the Seventeenth-Century Estuary," in *Fluid Frontiers: Exploring Oceans, Islands, and Coastal Environments*, ed. John Gillis and Franziska Torma (Cambridge: White Horse Press, 2015): 27–38.
69. Carl Bridenbaugh, *Cities in the Wilderness: The First Century of Urban Life in America 1625–1742* (New York: Alfred A. Knopf, 1955): 19.
70. Christina R. Butler, *Lowcountry at High Tide: A History of Flooding, Drainage, and Reclamation in Charleston, South Carolina* (Columbia: University of South Carolina Press, 2020).
71. Lawrence N. Powell, *The Accidental City: Improvising New Orleans* (Cambridge, MA: Harvard University Press, 2013).
72. Christopher L. Pastore, *Between Land and Sea: The Atlantic Coast and the Transformation of New England* (Cambridge, MA: Harvard University Press, 2014).
73. Avinash C. Tyagi, "Toward a Second Green Revolution," *Irrigation and Drainage* 65 (2016): 388–389.
74. Charles J. Vörösmarty et al., "Fresh Water," in *Ecosystems and Human Well-Being: Current States and Trends*, Vol. 1: *Millennium Ecosystem Assessment Report*, ed. Rashid Hassan, Robert Sholes, and Neville Ash (Washington, DC: Island Press, 2005): 174.
75. Kathleen Neumann et al., "Exploring Global Irrigation Patterns: A Multilevel Modelling Approach," *Agricultural Systems* 104 (2011): 703–713.
76. Food and Agricultural Organization of the United Nations, *The State of the World's Land and Water Resources for Food and Agriculture: Managing Systems at Risk* (Abingdon: Earthscan, 2011): 4.
77. Vörösmarty et al., "Fresh Water," 174; Neumann et al., "Exploring Global Irrigation Patterns," 703.
78. Mark I. L'vovich et al., "Use and Transformation of Terrestrial Water Systems," in *The Earth as Transformed by Human Action*: 242.
79. Mauritz W. Ertsen, *Locales of Happiness: Colonial Irrigation in the Netherlands East Indies and Its Remains, 1830–1980* (Delft: VSSD Press, 2010).

80. Elizabeth Whitcomb, *Agrarian Conditions in Northern India*, Vol. 1: *The United Provinces under British Rule, 1860–1900* (Berkeley: University of California Press, 1972); Ian Stone, *Canal Irrigation in British India: Perspectives on Technological Change in a Peasant Economy* (Cambridge: Cambridge University Press, 1984): 8; Nicholas S. Hopkins, "Irrigation in Contemporary Egypt," in *Agriculture in Egypt from Pharaonic to Modern Times*, ed. Alan K. Bowman and Eugene Rogan (Oxford: Oxford University Press, 1999), 381; Mauritz W. Ertsen, *Improvising Planned Development on the Gezira Plain, Sudan, 1900–1980* (New York: Palgrave Macmillan, 2016).
81. Maya K. Peterson, *Pipe Dreams: Water and Empire in Central Asia's Aral Sea Basin* (Cambridge: Cambridge University Press, 2019).
82. Laurence C. Becker, "An Early Experiment in the Reorganisation of Agricultural Production in the French Soudan (Mali), 1920–1940," *Africa* 64, no. 3 (1994): 373–390.
83. Worster, *Rivers of Empire*, 15.
84. Sanjeev Khagram, "Neither Temples nor Tombs," *Environment* 45, no. 4 (2003): 28–37.
85. Gerrit Schoups et al., "Water Resources Management in the Yaqui Valley," in *Seeds of Sustainability: Lessons from the Birthplace of the Green Revolution*, ed. Pamela A. Matson (Washington, DC: Island Press, 212): 198–200.
86. Thayer Scudder, *The Future of Large Dams: Dealing with Social, Environmental, Institutional and Political Costs* (London: Earthscan, 2005): 2.
87. World Commission on Dams, "Dams and Development: A New Framework for Decision-Making," International Institute for Environment and Development, no 108 (London: Earthscan, 2001): 2.
88. Rutgert Boelens, *Water Justice in Latin America. The Politics of Difference, Equality, and Indifference. Inaugural Lecture* (Amsterdam: CEDLA & University of Amsterdam, 2015).
89. Thayer Scudder, *The Future of Large Dams: Dealing with Social, Environmental, Institutional and Political Costs* (London: Earthscan, 2005), 230–31; William Jobin, *Dams and Disease: Ecological Design and Health Impacts of Large Dams, Canals and Irrigation Systems* (London: E & FN Spon, 1999).
90. World Commission on Dams, "Dams and Development," 3.
91. Hurt, *American Agriculture*, 339–41.
92. Jinxia Wang et al., *Managing Water on China's Farms: Institutions, Policies and the Transformation of Irrigation under Scarcity* (Cambridge, MA: Academic Press, 2016): 101–2.
93. J. Gupta and P. van der Zaag, "Interbasin Water Transfers and Integrated Water Resource Management: Where Engineering, Science and Politics Interlock," *Physics and Chemistry of the Earth* 33 (2008): 28–40.
94. Belinda Gallardo and David C. Aldridge, "Inter-basin Water Transfers and the Expansion of Aquatic Invasive Species," *Water Research* 143 (2018): 282–91; Stuart E. Bunn and Angela H. Arthington, "Basic Principles and Ecological Consequences of Altered Flow Regimes for Aquatic Biodiversity," *Environmental Management* 30, no. 4 (2002): 492–507; Roberta Fornarelli and Jason P. Antenucci, "The Impact of Transfers on Water Quality and the Disturbance Regime in a Reservoir," *Water Research* 45 (2011): 5873–5885.
95. Pallava Bagla, "India Plans the Grandest of Canal Networks," *Science* 345, no. 6193 (July 11, 2015): 128.
96. J. A. Allan, "Virtual Water—the Water, Food, and Trade Nexus Useful Concept or Misleading Metaphor," *Water International* 28, no. 1 (March 2003): 4–11.
97. Arjen Y. Hoekstra and Ashok K. Chapagain, *Globalization of Water: Sharing the Planet's Freshwater Resources* (Malden, MA: Blackwell Publishing, 2008): 67.

98. Ibid., 25.
99. Dork Sahagian, "Global Physical Effects of Anthropogenic Hydrological Alterations: Sea Level and Water Redistribution," *Global and Planetary Change* 25 (2000): 39–48.
100. Vörösmarty et al., "Fresh Water," 167.
101. Charles J. Vörösmarty and Dork Sahagian, "Anthropogenic Disturbance of the Terrestrial Water Cycle," *BioScience* 50, no. 9 (September 2000): 753–765.
102. Jean-Marc Faurès, Mark Svendsen, and Hugh Turral, "Reinventing Irrigation," in *Water for Food, Water for Life*, ed. David Molden (Washington, DC: Earthscan, 2007): 358; M. W. Rosegrant and M. Svendsen, "Asian Food Production in the 1990s: Irrigation Investment and Management Policy," *Food Policy* 18, no. 1 (1993): 13–32.
103. Faurès et al., "Reinventing Irrigation," 361.
104. Ian Carruthers, Mark W. Rosegrant, and David Seckler, "Irrigation and Food Security in the 21st Century," *Irrigation and Drainage Systems* 11 (1997): 83–101.
105. Douglas L. Vermillion, *Impacts of Irrigation Management Transfer: A Review of the Evidence*, Research Report 11 (Colombo, Sri Lanka: International Irrigation Management Institute, 1997).
106. United Nations World Water Assessment Programme, *United Nations World Water Development Report 2016: Water and Jobs* (Paris: UNESCO, 2016): 22.
107. Charles J. Vörösmarty et al., "Global Water Resources: Vulnerability from Climate Change and Population Growth," *Science* 289, no.5477 (2000): 284–88.
108. Bryson Bates et al., eds., *Climate Change and Water*, Technical Paper of the Intergovernmental Panel on Climate Change (Geneva: IPCC Secretariat, 2008): 3.
109. V. Masson-Delmotte et al., eds., *Global Warming of 1.5°C: An IPCC Special Report on the Impacts of Global Warming of 1.5°C above Pre-Industrial Levels and Related Global Greenhouse Gas Emission Pathways, in the Context of Strengthening the Global Response to the Threat of Climate Change, Sustainable Development, and Efforts to Eradicate Poverty* (Geneva: Intergovernmental Panel on Climate Change, 2019): 41.
110. Celia Deane-Drummond, "Rivers at the End of the End of Nature: Ethical Trajectories of the Anthropocene Grand Narrative," in *Rivers of the Anthropocene*, ed. Jason M. Kelly et al. (Berkeley: University of California Press, 2018): 55–62.

Bibliography

Ash, Eric H. *The Draining of the Fens: Projectors, Popular Politics, and State Building in Early Modern England*. Baltimore: Johns Hopkins University Press, 2017.
Blackbourn, David. *The Conquest of Nature: Water, Landscape, and the Making of Modern Germany*. New York: W. W. Norton, 2007.
Fagan, Brian. *Elixir: A History of Water and Humankind*. New York: Bloomsbury, 2011.
Ciriacono, Salvatore. *Building on Water: Venice, Holland and the Construction of the European Landscape in Early Modern Times*. New York: Berghahn, 2006.
Crutzen, Paul J., and Eugene F. Stoermer. "The 'Anthropocene.'" The International Geosphere-Biosphere Programme (IGBP) *Global Change Newsletter* 41 (2000): 17–18.
de Vries, Jan. *The Dutch Rural Economy in the Golden Age, 1500–1700*. New Haven, CT: Yale University Press, 1974.
Hoekstra, Arjen Y., and Ashok K. Chapagain. *Globalization of Water: Sharing the Planet's Freshwater Resources*. Malden, MA: Blackwell, 2008.

Hurt, R. Douglas. *American Agriculture: A Brief History*. West Lafayette, IN: Purdue University Press, 2002.
Kelly, Jason M., Philip Scarpino, Helen Berry, James Syvitski, and Michel Meybeck, eds. *Rivers of the Anthropocene*. Berkeley: University of California Press, 2018.
McNeill, J. R., and Peter Engelke. *The Great Acceleration: An Environmental History of the Anthropocene since 1945*. Cambridge, MA: Harvard University Press, 2014.
Mentz, Steve. *Break Up the Anthropocene*. Minneapolis: University of Minnesota Press, 2019.
Overton, Mark. *Agricultural Revolution in the England: The Transformation of the Agrarian Economy, 1500–1850*. Cambridge: Cambridge University Press, 1996.
Pastore, Christopher L. *Between Land and Sea: The Atlantic Coast and the Transformation of New England*. Cambridge, MA: Harvard University Press, 2014.
Scudder, Thayer. *The Future of Large Dams: Dealing with Social, Environmental, Institutional and Political Costs*. London: Earthscan, 2005.
Strang, Veronica. *Water: Nature and Culture*. London: Reaktion, 2015.
Turner, B. L., II, William C. Clark, Robert W. Kates, John F. Richards, Jessica T. Matthews, and William B. Meyer, eds. *The Earth as Transformed by Human Action: Global and Regional Changes in the Biosphere over the Past 300 Years*. New York: Cambridge University Press, 1990.
Vileisis, Ann. *Discovering the Unknown Landscape: A History of America's Wetlands*. Washington, DC: Island Press, 1997.
Vörösmarty, Charles J., Christian Lévêque, Carmen Revenga, Robert Bos, Chris Caudill, John Chilton, Ellen M. Douglas, Michel Meybeck, Daniel Prager, Patricia Balvanera, Sabrina Barker, Manuel Maas, Christer Nilsson, Taikan Oki, and Cathy A. Reidy. "Fresh Water." In *Ecosystems and Human Well-Being: Current States and Trends*, Vol. 1: *Millennium Ecosystem Assessment Report*, edited by Rashid Hassan, Robert Sholes, and Neville Ash, 165–207. Washington, DC: Island Press, 2005.
Wilkinson, T. J. *Archeological Landscapes of the Near East*. Tucson: University of Arizona Press, 2003.
Wittfogel, Karl. *Oriental Despotism: A Comparative Study of Total Power*. New Haven, CT: Yale University Press, 1957.
Worster, Donald. *Rivers of Empire: Water, Aridity, and the Growth of the American West*. New York: Pantheon, 1985.

CHAPTER 26

THE ISLAMIC AGRICULTURAL REVOLUTION

MICHAEL J. DECKER

The Islamic conquest of the southern Mediterranean basin, the Iranian plateau, and portions of Central Asia created one of the largest unified polities and economies in world history. Among the great changes marked among the cultures of the former lands of the Roman and Sasanian empires that fell to Arab Islamic control, scholars have argued for an "Islamic Agricultural Revolution" in which a host of new crops and technologies were introduced by Islamic farmers and landowners over large areas of western Eurasia and Africa. Economist Andrew Watson was the first to argue for a medieval "green revolution" of this kind.[1] In Watson's view, Muslim farmers, merchants, and rulers spread major food plants westward, where they were adopted as part of European and African culture included rice, banana (and plantain), sugar cane, durum wheat, sorghum, lemon (and lime). Secondary, but still important, crops transferred at the same time include sour orange, colocasia (taro), coconut, eggplant (aubergine), spinach, shaddock, artichoke, and watermelon. Additionally, cotton, now globally the most important plant for cloth production, was part of this panoply of early Muslim attention and distribution.

This attempt to impart deeper symbolic meanings and create historical narrative via plants as proxy is not new; decades ago, scholars recognized the massive import of the great Columbian Exchange of the fifteenth and sixteenth centuries in which people (along with their attendant ideas, cultures, and technologies), crops, animals, and diseases were transferred among Europe, West Africa, and the Western Hemisphere.[2] Similarly, the Islamic Agricultural Revolution entailed not only the physical adoption of plants, but the technologies and knowledge required to adapt them to new climates and exploit them as food or industrial products. Such consumption of these plants and their products resulted in a fundamental reordering of how many people lived, how they worked the land, and how they ate. Few acts are as symbolic and central to life as eating; beyond the needs of nourishing the body, the meal and diet is deeply revealing about society as a whole, and scholars have long sought larger connotations in observing table manners, in feasting, and in the nature, causes, and reactions to famine. It thus scarcely needs explaining why Watson felt comfortable calling the trends he detected in the early medieval Muslim world a "revolution."[3]

Revolutions fascinate as often as they disappoint. The idea of rapid social transformation has held considerable appeal for historians, whose craft is founded upon noting and explaining change in past societies. A rapid turn in something as crucial as the farming regimen of Eurasia affecting millions of people is therefore bound to attract the scholarly and popular imagination. The first and best-known farming revolutions is the so-called Neolithic Revolution, or First Agricultural Revolution, which witnessed the rise of agriculture, via the domestication of a bevy of plants and animals; these have formed the foundation of societies ever since. Slightly less well-known is the Agricultural Revolution of eighteenth- and nineteenth-century Europe, especially in the British Isles, where new techniques and technologies led to rapid improvements in stock and plants with significant rise in yields and the carrying capacity of the landscape. Much less expected, however, was an agricultural revolution (or anything revolutionary for that matter) appearing from the medieval era, which since the Renaissance has often been viewed as a time of social upheaval, technological and scientific regression, and generally low standards of living.

Thus, when, in a 1974 article, "The Arab Agricultural Revolution and Its Diffusion, 700–1100," Watson first posited the notion of a "medieval green revolution" that transformed world history, people were quick to take notice.[4] Subsequently, Watson expanded the thesis in a number of publications.[5] It is perhaps no surprise that the claims Watson forwarded were both enthusiastically welcomed and durable, as a generation of scholars, especially from the French *Annales* school, had recently done much to begin the rehabilitation of the medieval era. Such work encouraged students of history to approach the period on its own terms, while scholars such as Maurice Lombard had begun the long and challenging task of modifying Western perceptions of the medieval Islamic world.[6]

Watson identified the outcome of the "Revolution": the relatively swift adoption and access to a range of new foods and clothing and industrial crops to large populations to which these items had previously been unavailable. He also identified the driving forces behind this massive shift, namely the growth and vibrancy of cities within the Muslim world, as well as facets of human agency behind the transformation.[7] Peasants, he argued, were likely the dominant agents in changing the planting types of a given region.[8]

That many elements of Watson's argument are quite problematic did not occupy most scholars then or now.[9] Fifty years on, it is safe to assert that the Watson thesis of "Islamic Agricultural Revolution" has been adopted wholesale into the historical canon. This is, of course, unsurprising; after all, history for most is popular history and popular history tends toward reductionism. The vision Watson ascribed to medieval Muslim farmers, merchants, landowners, and botanical experts in the diffusion and cultural embrace of plants that would become staple foods for billions of people is attractive on many levels. The Watson thesis stresses progress via peaceful exchange and positive transformations and a major role for those who often have no voice in history—namely, the peasants who silently till the earth. The compelling story of the Islamic Agricultural Revolution, however, has sometimes advanced to the detriment of the careful interrogation of the evidence.

Agricultural Expansion in the Early Islamic Centuries

Migration of Arab settlers during the conquest era of the seventh and eighth centuries spread knowledge of indigenous farming traditions, techniques, and crops from the Arabian Peninsula to the far corners of the caliphate, which, by 750, extended from Central Asia through western India and westward through Egypt and North Africa, the Maghrib, and most of the Iberian Peninsula (Arabic al-Andalus). Migration of Arabs, Berbers, and other groups continued throughout the Islamic period, culminating in the migrations of the Oghuz Turks into Iran and thence into Iraq and the Levant, with momentous consequences for world history.[10]

When Watson formulated his thesis, he had resort to relatively little archeological evidence. Since the 1990s, scholars have made considerable progress in understanding multiple facets of the material culture of the early Islamic world. Their finds support the view that in the eighth through eleventh centuries many cities the Mediterranean enjoyed prosperity under Muslim rule. While cities like Antioch, Alexandria, Carthage, and Ctesiphon faded in importance, they were replaced in many instances by new Islamic foundations. During and after the initial conquests of the seventh century, Arab Muslims settled in garrison (Arabic amsar; sing., misr) throughout their newly won lands. Individual misr served a variety of functions, primarily as army bases, administrative centers, and domestic settlements and markets for the Arab elite. Prominent amsar were founded at Kufa and Basra, both in southern Mesopotamia. In the early eighth century the Umayyad governor of Iraq, al-Hajjaj ibn Yusuf, founded another important city in the region, Wasit on the Tigris. Similar amsar were built at Anjar in Lebanon, Ramla and Ayla in Palestine, Chalcis in Syria, Fustat in Egypt, and Kairouan in North Africa.[11] The 'Abbasid foundations of Baghdad and Samarra entailed a massive reconfiguration of settlement in Iraq. Thousands of Arab Muslim males, their families, and their clients and slaves moved into the amsar and the lands around them. Throughout the lands conquered during the early conquests, Arab Muslims were joined by the movement of tens of thousands more allies and prisoners of war taken as slaves who took with them ideas and likely plants and animals as well. The settlement or resettlement by colonists confessing the new faith in places like Kairouan and Tunis in North Africa, Granada and Almería in al-Andalus, and Fustat, Babylon, and Cairo in Egypt disrupted older economic patterns and replaced these with new networks and often with new economic foci. The effects of such wide-ranging settlements, with their mixed populations, renovation of old urban spaces or building anew, the reworking of old landscapes and the opening of new ones, the breakdown of former networks and the forging of new connections in their place, all these are hallmarks of the early Islamic period and form the backdrop for social dynamism that affected all areas of life, including diet and farming. While much was new, the settlers in their new lands no doubt maintained key core cultural markers, among them the foods and clothing to which they were accustomed.

Labor is the foundation of any agrarian regime. The nature of the early Islamic movement and political apparatus favored the maintenance of prevailing community structures. Arab armies offered cities in their path the choice to resist, submit and pay taxes, or convert to Islam, and the conquest narratives imply that nearly all places were conquered or surrendered, with conversion following only many decades or event centuries later. Christians remained the great majority of the population throughout the Levant and Egypt, and this fact alone supports the view that the tendency of the early caliphs and then the Umayyads was toward settlement stability and taxation inside the Dar al Islam.[12] Most villages continued to be owned by individual landlords or, in rarer cases, by free peasants. In the Qom region, Muslim (mostly Arab) landowners invested in dryland irrigation to open new lands and expand their economic base. The landlords claimed surpluses from the inhabitants recruited to live there while the villagers themselves remained free.[13]

In the medieval Islamic world, as in all societies at that time, a significant portion of labor was unfree. There is little to support the notion that agricultural slavery was not a major component of the economy, even if most studies have focused on domestic slaves, concubines, and other forms of servitude. Often war and the slave trade in non-Muslim captives transported people from one end of the caliphate to the other. From the later seventh century on, Bantu-speaking slaves from East Africa (*Zanj*) were imported by Muslim landowners and worked to reclaim lands in southern Iraq. The intricate irrigation network employed by the Sasanians had frayed during the social and political chaos of the early and mid-seventh century.[14] With a growing population and a hunger for land, elites in the Umayyad and 'Abbasid eras turned to bringing derelict lands back into cultivation. In Iraq, Arab Muslims under the Umayyads began one of the largest agricultural reclamation projects of medieval history; the draining of the southern marshlands formed by the slowing of the great rivers Euphrates and Tigris. Within fifty years of the conquest of Sasanian Mesopotamia, east African slaves were already present in sufficient number to mount revolts, first in 689–690 CE, once more in 694, and, most seriously, in 869–883, in which the 'Abbasid authorities faced considerable difficulty in quelling the rising.[15] Ibn Hawqal, the tenth-century geographer, noted numerous black slaves who worked the fields around Shabur in the Nile Delta, and on most large estates of the Islamic west, as early as the eleventh century, carefully managed gangs of slaves worked the crops.[16] The eleventh-century Persian traveler Nasr-i Khusraw observed that the Ismaili Qarmatians in eastern Arabia at the oasis of al-Ahsa kept 30,000 Zanzibari and Abyssinian slaves who worked the fields and orchards; the surplus thus extracted supported the whole free population of the oasis, which must have been substantial.[17]

The once common view that the first centuries of Islam were ones of overall economic decline or stagnation is increasingly untenable. In the south of Syria, however, in the former Roman provinces of Palestine, the economy seems to have continued its relatively high level of prosperity. In South Arabia, for example, in the lands of the former kingdom of Himyar, which had declined prior to the birth of the Prophet Muhammad (ca. 570 CE), the region seems to have remained depressed economically. Portions of Arabia were likewise slow to recover from a deep recession of the Sasanian period.

At the end of antiquity the Roman-Persian wars of the sixth and seventh century led to the movements—some permanent, others temporary—of hundreds of thousands of soldiers and their dependents. Alongside them moved their supply trains and merchants who flocked to the camps. In their wake, these armies left thousands of civilians stripped of their lands and livelihood and, worse still, dragged thousands into a captivity whence most never returned. Like all ancient wars, the wars of the early Muslim conquests led to the displacement of peasant populations, the plundering of their property and their bodies, and the sale of many into slavery or their settlement as colonists far from their original homes.[18] Human plunder was one of the most common forms of loot, and by this means slaves were acquired from among non-Muslim populations. Though there are no sure numbers we can derive from the sources of the first three centuries of Islam, the migrations of free Arabs and their families, of allied soldiers who joined them, and of their slaves and captives was truly massive. Numerous Arab tribal groupings numbering in the thousands migrated into former Persian and Roman territory from Syria and Egypt to North Africa, Central Asia, and the Iberian Peninsula. Women and dependents eventually settled in and around the new garrison cities, and many males were repeatedly sent to fight in regions far from the tribal home areas where they eventually settled as colonists.

A new Islamic Arab elite sought land, the foundation of all wealth in pre-industrial societies. Since many wealthy landowners and functionaries seem to have remained in place in both the Sasanian and Roman empires, and there was no formal policy to dispossess them, Arabs who wished to invest in land had to look to deserted or derelict lands. Both Roman and Sasanian law had structures in place to govern the recovery and cultivation of such spaces, including exemption from taxation and safeguarding possession.[19] New settlements, new market opportunities, and new cultural patterns conditioned the expansion and intensification of farming in many regions of the caliphate, especially in Iraq. There, the desert could be reclaimed through irrigation, while in the south, fertile land could be created through the arduous draining of the marshes and removal of the salt-laden topsoil. In the middle Euphrates, during the reign of 'Abd al-Malik (685–705), the Umayyads constructed a large canal by the city of Balis (ancient Barbalissos); this project was one of many in which the early caliphs restored or built anew a network of transverse canals in the lands that lay between the Euphrates and Tigris, thus maintaining and, in some areas, expanding the pre-Islamic arable agricultural base. Without colossal investments in hydraulic infrastructure to water the crops of Iraq, tenth-century Baghdad could not have grown to a city of more than a million and a half.[20]

Irrigation on the scale and intensity described above was one of the fundaments on which the Islamic Agricultural Revolution is predicated. From ca. 700 to 1100, several technologies spread from Arabia and the Middle East into portions of the Muslim Mediterranean. The Islamic period transfer of hydraulic gear and tools has always been seen with most clarity in the Iberian Peninsula, where, prior to the arrival of Islamic rule, there is not much evidence for the employment of irrigation machinery.[21]

Across North Africa and Spain, the Romans built numerous dams, aqueducts, and canal systems that regulated floods and provided water to cities and farms. They also employed irrigation machinery, though present evidence suggests that the main technologies that are hallmarks of Islamic Agricultural "Revolution" did greatly intensify during the first centuries of Islamic rule. Of these technologies, the most important technologies are the *qanat, saqiya,* and *noria*. Though its frequency of distribution in the early Islamic world is unknown, farmers of the early Muslim world also used the *delu*, an animal-driven bucket pulley that allowed one to draw much more water from a well than by human-powered labor alone. The qanat is a chain of wells linked together via a horizontal underground channel; the wells thus linked effectively mine aquifers and free water that can be directed, sometimes over tens of kilometers, via gravity flow. The fields are generally at the terminal points of the qanat, where the horizontal channel emerges near ground level for distribution. The saqiya is an ancient technology widely employed in the Roman east, which converted the horizontal motion of a treading ox or other large animal into vertical power to raise water, usually via ceramic vessels linked in a rope chain and installed over a large well, wherefore the machines are sometimes referred to as "chains of pots" or "pot garlands." Saqiyas allowed the exploitation of deep wells—as deep as 20 meters in some cases, and the raising and use of much more water than possible with human power; a single saqiya could provide sufficient irrigation to 2–13 hectares. These machines did not need running water or massive investments like dams or large-scale canal networks, but they permitted efficient, individual plot irrigation for orchards and high-value crops, like cotton and sugar, which would return the investment required to build, operate, and maintain the machines.

The *noria* is a waterwheel generally, but the important type attributed to the expansion of Islam is the large (up to 20 meters in diameter) type of wooden waterwheel. On major streams and rivers the noria, via wooden or ceramic buckets, lifted water and discharged it at the maximum height of the wheel, allowing distribution of water by gravity over a large area (up to 75 hectares) where canals were either expensive or impossible to build.

It should be stressed that none of the technologies that supported the innovation and expansion of the early Islamic centuries was new: the *qanat* had been employed for many centuries in Persia and was widely diffused over portions of North Africa for centuries prior to the arrival of Islam, while the *saqiya* had been fundamental to agricultural intensification in Egypt and the Levant prior to Islam.[22] However, at issue is the frequency of use, and this question has yet to be adequately investigated in the fine-grained way it requires. What is visible in places like southern Andalus is an intensively farmed, highly developed landscape where these water management technologies were folded into a complex system dependent on the production of crops year round, even during the dry season, a taste for the new commodities and sufficient specialization, and urban demand from a buoyant population to keep the intensive farming economy functioning.

For dryland agriculture, the effects of the arrival and widespread application of qanat and saqiya technologies cannot be easily overlooked. In a large portion of the landscapes of the Eurasia, water is the prime limiting factor. Digging wells is not sufficient to provide moisture to large plantations of thirsty crops of the variety the Muslim farmers grew for urban markets—orchards and cotton plantings required regular watering and thrived over the summer months. Investment in irrigation allowed not only an extension of farmland into desert areas where cropping was previously limited or nonexistent, but it also supported the extension of the growing season into the hot, dry summer months. If fertility could be maintained through manuring and careful cropping, as the agronomic manuals suggest, then an additional harvest could be made during the hot season, which had previously been a fallow time.[23]

The introduction and successful integration of new crops into the landscapes of the Muslim Mediterranean and North Africa required thriving cities. Urban centers were home to political leaders, great landowners, and merchants, the wealthiest of whom attracted specialist production and owned or benefited from small-scale manufacturing themselves. Many citizens, especially salaried individuals in government employ, such as administrators and soldiers, also consumed exotics, among them new plants and their products. Men with access to wealth from salaries, inheritance, or merchant activities tended to invest in land and commerce. These activities made individuals parts of networks of knowledge and exchange.[24]

In directing our attention to the thriving urban centers and agrarian role of wealthy town dwellers of the Islamic world, Watson advanced an important perspective supported by a growing body of textual and archeological evidence. After all, one of the main preoccupations of medieval historians is the fate of the city and the rise of new urban centers, especially in northern Europe. The economic center of early medieval western Eurasia lay first in Damascus under the Umayyad dynasty (661–750 CE) and then Baghdad, in Iraq, under the 'Abbasids (750–1258 CE). Also important, though, was the caliphal court at Cordoba in Spain, where by the year 1000 the urban population was at least 150,000 and perhaps three times larger prior to the political dissolution of the caliphate in 1031.[25] Major cities like Cairo in the Fatimid period (909–1171 CE) grew to house up to more than 200,000 by no later than 1200. Vital to the sustenance of networks required to support the exchange of plants and the transmittal of technical knowledge of how to grow them were centers of knowledge and consumption provided by major urban centers. The foundation of new urban centers such as the Moroccan imperial cities founded by the Almoravids and Almohads, Fez, Marrakesh, Meknes, and Rabat, helped diffuse plants and the network of knowledge needed to manage them. In the Muslim west, great cities like Cordoba as well as such secondary cities as Toledo, Seville, Granada, and Málaga in al-Andalus and Palermo in Sicily (to name but a few) comprised important nodes of Muslim culture and knowledge. Prior to its capture by the Normans in 1072, Palermo boasted a population of at least 115,000. Though much smaller, perhaps 40,000, Toledo was home to a thriving Islamic court with an important chancery and extensive libraries.[26] The capture of these cities only rarely overturned the intensive practices introduced (or reintroduced) by Muslim patrons and cultivators.

Cities not only drove demand for the produce of the land required to keep non-farmers victualled but also served to foster a climate of scholarship in urban courts, social circles, and among educated citizens.[27] With political expansion and fragmentation came the multiplication of the courts of amirs and other local rulers, all of which were modeled on the caliphal court in Baghdad and thus included patronage of poets, doctors, and literati, many of whom doubled as functionaries within the governments. Perhaps the best-known example of this is the constellation of *taifa* kingdoms of the Iberian Peninsula, which succeeded the downfall of the Umayyad caliphate in 1031, but there are other examples, as in the formation of the small principalities such as the tenth-century Shia Hamdanids of Aleppo. In many ways then the decentralization of court life led to emulation and thus wider dissemination of information needed to sustain the parks, gardens, and palace life of the nobility.

The interest in plants, animal husbandry, and estate management is clear from Arabic works on agriculture and medicine, especially in the *filāha* (agronomy) literature. These technical handbooks, intended both as works of general reference and as guides for estate overseers, offered guidance on the practicalities of soil types, finding water and plantings and nurseries, grafting, and planting, care, and harvesting of an array of grains, trees, vegetable, herbs, and other useful advice. Among the most impressive of these is a vast encyclopedic work compiled by Ibn Waḥšiyya, *al-Filāha al-Nabatiyya* (*Nabataean Agriculture*), which depended in no small part on the treatise of the fifth-century Roman agronomer Vindanius Anatolius of Berytus (modern Beirut), who himself collected material into an agronomic handbook written in Greek.[28] The material in Anatolius' work represents something of a summation of Hellenistic thought on farming after more than 1,000 years of Hellenic colonization and political involvement in the landscape of the Levant and Mesopotamia. In turn, there can be little doubt that Hellenic thought in agrarian matters was informed by earlier Near Eastern and Mesopotamian traditions. But to date we know little about the kernels of this knowledge, nor how it was successively transmitted and received by various estate managers and scholars including the tenth-century writer and translator Ibn Waḥšiyya. The richness of the *Nabataean Agriculture*, which must represent authentic Syriac and earlier Mesopotamian traditions, indicates that while some material survived and passed into Arabic from the pre-Islamic east, much more did not.

The *Nabataean Agriculture* stands then not merely as a fossil from the ancient and late antique peasant milieu of rural Mesopotamia, but as an encyclopedia of inherited agronomic knowledge in the heartland of Iraq around the turn of the first millennium. Even if Ibn Waḥšiyya was motivated to translate the *Nabataean Agriculture* from Syriac to Arabic because he himself was an Aramaic-speaking Nabataean and his interests were both personal and antiquarian, his Arabic book became a standard in the Islamic world for centuries to follow. This multilayered aspect of the *filāha* (agronomy) literature presents both challenges and opportunities; while the handbooks provide windows in the transmission of texts and who was reading them in a given place and time, their usefulness as markers of the wider application of such knowledge is limited. In determining this, we must look further afield, to other textual sources and to the material record. However, it is worth nothing that while major treatises like the *Nabataean Agriculture* were produced prior to 1100, change in the agrarian regime of the far west of the Muslim world is found in texts such as the so-called *Calendar of Cordoba* (Spain) attributed to the 'Arib b. Sa'd al-Katib al-Qurtubi and presented to the caliph al-Hakam II around the time of his accession in 961.[29] The *Calendar of Cordoba* and the works of the eleventh-century writer Ibn Wāfidin Toledo are joined by later authorities, including Ibn Baṣṣāl. Together their writings comprise the earliest examples of a tradition that would flourish in al-Andalus, especially, until the end of Islamic rule in the fifteenth century. At the close of the twelfth century, the Umayyad caliphate had long succumbed, and al-Andalus itself was under grave threat from the Christian north when in Seville Ibn al-'Awwām produced the best organized and most thorough of all medieval treatises on agriculture, the *Kitāb al-filāḥa* ("Book of Agriculture").[30]

Cookbooks offer us additional insights into urban high cuisine of the upper classes of Islamic society forming in and emanating from Baghdad.[31] A tenth-century recipe book from Iraq includes preparations calling for sugar, coconut, eggplant, lemon, and banana.[32] Thus contemporary Baghdadi elites enjoyed these luxury foods that were generally available (likely at a steep price) in the marketplace and had found a place in the eclectic imperial cuisine of the capital. Around the same time in al-Andalus, in the farthest west part of the caliphate, the Arabic almanac referred to as *The Calendar of Cordoba* includes times for the planting and harvesting schedule of cotton, eggplant, sugar cane, and banana, which indicates that these crops were at least known in Andalusia by this time. By the thirteenth century, foods such as sugar, lemon, sour orange, banana, and other products of Muslim culinary culture were commonplace in cookbooks, though they probably remained the purview of the middle and upper strata of Islamic society.[33] Courtiers and wealthy landowners and merchants throughout the caliphate imitated the diet and feasts of the caliphal court, and regional breakaway princes styled themselves as caliphs in miniature. Regional rulers claimed as status symbols the trappings of the 'Abbasid court, among them foods, plants, and gardens.

Watson rightly observed that the great devotion shown by Islamic elites to gardens was one of the cultural choices that helped spread new plants and ideas. While he lived beyond the chronological boundaries of the Watson thesis, Fakhr ad-Din Razi expressed a sentiment shared by many Muslim elites: "The world is a garden, whose gardener is the state."[34] The Qur'an described paradise as a garden and earthly rulers and elites built gardens for pleasure in symbolic mirroring of the afterlife.[35] For the earthly observer the well-ordered, usually walled garden was filled with fruit trees, water, and places of repose where one sheltered from summer heat; all these were features of the garden of heaven, but these also served as symbols of the well-managed state.[36] Gardens provided enclosed spaces where medicinal and other foreign plants could be closely observed, carefully tended to, and their acclimation to their new environments best attained. The variety of plants contained in the horticultural handbooks of Andalusia, for instance, is far higher than contemporary works from the Latin-speaking world; Ibn Basal, who wrote in Toledo from 1075 to 1080, mentions more than 1100 plants.[37] This biodiversity is important evidence suggesting great potential variety in the crops available in the diet, and of a host of herbal and pharmacological products derived from plant sources.

But beyond the kitchens, kitchen gardens, and pleasure gardens of the upper echelons of society, there were practical economics in play as well. To date, the best case study in support of Islamic era agricultural change is that of Richard Bulliet from the territory around Qom in the drylands of the Iranian plateau approximately 140 kilometers south of modern Tehran. The region receives about 140 millimeters of rainfall annually, making dry farming of cereals impossible. The soils of the region favor irrigation by qanat, which permit perennial irrigation of sizable areas for cropping, but are laborious to build and maintain. Muslim landowners, mostly Arab newcomers in the ninth century, moved into the region and began investing heavily in qanat irrigation and recruited peasants in their newly founded villages. Given favorable economic terms, peasant laborers shifted to their new tenancies. The crop that permitted such a rational investment strategy was cotton.

Cotton, while grown in some regions of the Sasanian world prior to the rise of Islam, was not a major crop prior to the arrival of the conquerors. Guided by Muslim prohibitions against the ostentation of silk, and a preference for cotton over linen and wool, cotton garments soon became markers of practitioners of the new faith; these dress habits were soon adopted in imitation by clients of elite Muslims and no doubt by non-Muslims as well. As home to the largest concentration of Muslims in the central Islamic lands, the metropolis of Baghdad created a large market for cotton clothing. The cotton boom that resulted ended only in the eleventh century with the advent of a prolonged period of cool temperatures and the arrival of the Turks from Central Asia, which triggered a period of nomadization, urban decline, and the flight of the educated classes.[38]

While beyond the period of Watson's proposed "revolution," Richard Eaton investigated Muslim landowners in eastern Bengal. There, by the mid-fourteenth century, Muslim landowners invested in the clearing and cultivation of new lands, which converted large tracts of former forest to rice paddy agriculture. The Islamic Turkic rulers monetized the economy, and their quest for silver to mine drove settlement further into the interior of Bengal. The production of cotton, like in Iran of the earlier Islamic era, was complex, driven in part by local culture and urban demand, but also partly by an active trade with China.[39]

Conclusion

The concept of a medieval Islamic agricultural revolution has proved a durable and important contribution to world history. Though there is little or no evidence for the spread of tropical plants like coconut, sugar, rice, banana, and sorghum prior to the rise of Islam, by the later Middle Ages, there is suggestive evidence scattered in texts and in archeological contexts supporting the notion that seismic shifts had occurred in dietary culture, in farming techniques, and in consumption patterns over much of the Islamic world.

The primary drivers of these changes were the Muslim colonists of the conquest period who revived old urban centers or established new cities from the Hindu Kush. Regional dynasts, such as the Almoravids, Almohads, Buyids, Idrisids, and Fatimids, reconfigured urbanism with the foundation of new royal capitals, often in response to new realities in demography and resources. The spectacular growth and dynamism of large cities like Baghdad, Cordoba, Fustat, Cairo, Palermo, and Marrakesh ultimately derived, at least in the first instance, from royal patronage. The demand of such centers for luxury goods, including foods, stimulated production of plants like cotton and sugar. The constellation of royal courts both attracted and motivated the training of functionaries and skilled craftsmen. Regional dynasts imitated 'Abbasid court life, among the hallmarks of which were garden culture and an international, eclectic "imperial" cuisine that drew on the vast plant varieties of the empire, especially the warm-weather "exotics" that had previously been only narrowly grown and consumed. Court functionaries and literate elites invested in land, and they took at least some interest in the management and profitability of their estates, as attested by the significant volume of agronomic literature.

Due to the vagaries of the conquest and the complex situation of land tenure in many of the conquered territories, Muslim elites from the Umayyads onward frequently made significant investments in derelict or desert lands, especially through the application of perennial irrigation. Old technologies, such as the delu, noria, saqiya, and qanat, spread throughout the Muslim lands through the agency of landowners and their tenants.

However, when one delves deeper into the specifics of the "Islamic Agricultural Revolution," one quickly discovers that the term is a misnomer. Much more work has been done on subjects related to Watson's large vision, such as cooking, medicine, and archeology, and the time for a reassessment, at least of certain pieces, has certainly arrived. The spread of new plants was often slow and fitful. While overall the bevy of plants and technologies entrenched themselves permanently in some areas, the best evidence for this comes in the thirteenth and fourteenth centuries, hundreds of years later than Watson proposed. Progress was not linear. Instead we must consider each region and its products in chronological context. The movement of ideas and crops was sometimes interrupted by periods of climate change, economic or demographic retrenchment, or external conquest. Nonetheless, the adaptation of new plants to new environments spread to enough regions that they were picked up by the successors to the Muslims on the landscape, notably in places like Sicily and Iberia, whence they were eventually, centuries later, diffused to the whole of the Mediterranean and into the New World beyond. In this sense, the Muslim medieval farming tradition represents a revolution not circumscribed by limited time but marked by the tremendous effects on global diets and economies centuries into the future.

Notes

1. Andrew M. Watson, *Agricultural Innovation in the Early Islamic World: The Diffusion of Crops and Farming Techniques, 700–1100* (Cambridge: Cambridge University Press, 1983); Watson, "A Medieval Green Revolution: New Crops and Farming Techniques in the Early Islamic World," in *The Islamic Middle East, 700–1900: Studies in Economic and Social History*, ed. A. Udovitch (Princeton, NJ: Darwin Press, 1981); Watson, "The Arab Agricultural Revolution and Its Diffusion, 700–1100," *Journal of Economic History* 34, no. 1 (1974).
2. Alfred W. Crosby, *The Columbian Exchange: Biological and Social Consequences of 1492* (Westport, CT: Greenwood Press, 1972).
3. Watson, *Agricultural Innovation in the Early Islamic World*, 123ff.
4. Watson, "The Arab Agricultural Revolution and Its Diffusion, 700–1100."
5. Watson, *Agricultural Innovation in the Early Islamic World*, and "A Medieval Green Revolution." The shift from "Arab" to "Muslim" is notable and important. Historians of early Islam still grapple with the question of how to characterize the early community and its political agents.
6. Maurice Lombard, *L'islam dans sa première grandeur (Viiie–Xie siècle)*, Vol. 59 (Paris: Flammarion, 1971).
7. Watson, *Agricultural Innovation in the Early Islamic World*, 99–101.
8. Ibid., 87–88.
9. Michael Decker, "Plants and Progress: Rethinking the Islamic Agricultural Revolution," *Journal of World History* 20, no. 2 (2009): 187–206.
10. Claude Cahen, *The Formation of Turkey: The Seljukid Sultanate of Rum: Eleventh to Fourteenth Century*, trans. P. M. Holt (Harlow, England: Longman, 2001): 1–3.
11. Sylvia Denoix, "Founded Cities of the Arab World from the Seventh to the Eleventh Centuries," in *The City in the Islamic World*, ed. Salma Khadra Jayyusi et al. (Leiden: Brill, 2008): 115–139.
12. Michael Philip Penn, *Envisioning Islam: Syriac Christians and the Early Muslim World* (Philadelphia: University of Pennsylvania Press, 2015).
13. Richard W. Bulliet, *Cotton, Climate, and Camels in Early Islamic Iran: A Moment in World History* (New York: Columbia University Press, 2011): 24–25.
14. Peter Christensen, *The Decline of Iranshahr: Irrigation and Environments in the History of the Middle East, 500 BC to AD 1500* (Copenhagen: Museum Tusculanum, 1993).
15. G. S. P. Freeman-Grenville and A. Popovic, "Al-Zandj," in *Encyclopaedia of Islam*, 2nd ed., ed. P. Berman et al. (Leiden: Brill, 1960–2007) https://referenceworks.brillonline.com/entries/encyclopaedia-of-islam-2/al-zandj-COM_1379?s.num=0&s.f.s2_parent=s.f.book.encyclopaedia-of-islam-2&s.q=Freeman-Grenville+and+A.+Popovic, accessed Sept. 2, 2023.
16. Ralph A. Austen, "The Mediterranean Islamic Slave Trade out of Africa: A Tentative Census," *Slavery and Abolition* 13, no. 1 (1992): 214–48; Lucie Bolens, "The Use of Plants for Dyeing and Clothing," in *The Legacy of Muslim Spain*, ed. Salma Khadra Jayyusi and Manuela Marín (Leiden: Brill, 1992): 1000–1015.
17. Nasir-i Khusraw states that the oasis was protected by 20,000 soldiers; if this is correct the population of the oasis must have numbered around 100,000: Wheeler M. Thackston, *Nasir-i Khusraw's Book of Travels* (London: Mazda, 2001): 111–112.
18. John R. Perry, A. Shaphur Shahbazi, and Erich Kettenhofen, "Deportations," https://www.iranicaonline.org/articles/deportations, accessed Sept. 2, 2023.

19. Decker, "Plants and Progress."
20. 'Abd al-'Aziz Duri, "BagHDād," in *Encyclopaedia of Islam*, 2nd ed., ed. P. Berman et al. (Leiden: Brill, 1960–2007) https://referenceworks.brillonline.com/search?s.f.s2_parent=s.f.book.encyclopaedia-of-islam-2&search-go=&s.q=BagHDad, accessed Sept. 2, 2023.
21. Thomas F. Glick, *Irrigation and Society in Medieval Valencia* (Cambridge, MA: Belknap Press of Harvard University Press, 1970).
22. Decker, "Plants and Progress."
23. Watson, *Agricultural Innovation in the Early Islamic World*, 103–111.
24. Ibid., 99ff.
25. Lower estimate: Josiah Cox Russell, *Medieval Regions and Their Cities* (Newton Abbot: David & Charles, 1972); higher figures: Robert Hillenbrand, "The Ornament of the World: Medieval Córdoba as a Cultural Centre," in *The Legacy of Muslim Spain*, ed. Salma Khadra Jayyusi and Manuela Marín (Leiden: Brill, 1992).
26. Russell, *Medieval Regions and Their Cities*; Toledo's population in the early Islamic centuries was likely much larger if it is true that 15,000 families were exiled following the revolt against the caliph al-Hakam I (796–822 CE).
27. Watson, *Agricultural Innovation in the Early Islamic World*, 99–102.
28. Jaakko Hämeen-Anttila, *The Last Pagans of Iraq: Ibn Waḥshiyya and His Nabatean Agriculture* (Leiden: Brill, 2006), 52ff.
29. Ch Pellat, "Rabī' B. Zayd," in *Encyclopaedia of Islam*, 2nd ed., ed. P. Berman et al. (Leiden: Brill, 1960–2007) https://referenceworks.brillonline.com/search?s.f.s2_parent=s.f.book.encyclopaedia-of-islam-2&search-go=&s.q=%E2%80%9CRab%C4%AB%CA%BF+B.+Zayd&s.rows=20, accessed Sept. 2, 2023.
30. Nawal Nasrallah, *Annals of the Caliphs' Kitchens: Ibn Sayyar Al-Warraq's Tenth-Century Baghdadi Cookbook*, vol. 70 (Leiden: Brill, 2007).
31. David Waines, "'Luxury Foods' in Medieval Islamic Societies," *World Archaeology* 34, no. 3 (2003): 571–580.
32. Nasrallah, *Annals of the Caliphs' Kitchens*, 70, 191, 234, 375.
33. Charles Perry, *Scents and Flavors: A Syrian Cookbook*, vol. 47 (New York: New York University Press, 2017).
34. Richard Maxwell Eaton, *The Rise of Islam and the Bengal Frontier, 1204–1760*, vol. 17 (Berkeley: University of California Press, 1993): 22.
35. Qur'an 9.72
36. G. Marçais, "Būstān," in *Encyclopaedia of Islam*, 2nd ed., ed. P. Berman et al. (Leiden: Brill, 1960–2007) https://referenceworks.brillonline.com/search?s.f.s2_parent=s.f.book.encyclopaedia-of-islam-2&search-go=&s.q=B%C5%ABst%C4%81n&s.rows=20, accessed Sept. 2, 2023..
37. John H. Harvey, "Garden Plants of Moorish Spain: A Fresh Look," *Garden History* 20, no. 1 (1992).
38. Bulliet, *Cotton, Climate, and Camels in Early Islamic Iran*, 138.
39. Eaton, *The Rise of Islam and the Bengal Frontier*, 17, 94–96.

Bibliography

Austen, Ralph A. "The Mediterranean Islamic Slave Trade out of Africa: A Tentative Census." *Slavery and Abolition* 13, no. 1 (1992): 214–248.

Bolens, Lucie. "The Use of Plants for Dyeing and Clothing." In *The Legacy of Muslim Spain*, edited by Salma Khadra Jayyusi and Manuela Marín, 1000–15. Leiden: Brill, 1992.

Bulliet, Richard W. *Cotton, Climate, and Camels in Early Islamic Iran: A Moment in World History*. New York: Columbia University Press, 2011.

Christensen, Peter. *The Decline of Iranshahr: Irrigation and Environments in the History of the Middle East, 500 BC to AD 1500*. Copenhagen: Museum Tusculanum, 1993.

Decker, Michael. "Plants and Progress: Rethinking the Islamic Agricultural Revolution." *Journal of World History* 20, no. 2 (2009): 187–206.

Denoix, Sylvia. "Founded Cities of the Arab World from the Seventh to the Eleventh Centuries." In *The City in the Islamic World*, edited by Salma Khadra Jayyusi, Renata Holod, Antillio Petruccioli, and André Raymond, 115–39. Leiden: Brill, 2008.

Eaton, Richard Maxwell. *The Rise of Islam and the Bengal Frontier, 1204–1760*. Berkeley: University of California Press, 1993.

Glick, Thomas F. *Irrigation and Society in Medieval Valencia*. Cambridge, MA: Belknap Press of Harvard University Press, 1970.

Hämeen-Anttila, Jaakko. *The Last Pagans of Iraq: Ibn Waḥshiyya and His Nabatean Agriculture*. Leiden: Brill, 2006.

Harvey, John H. "Garden Plants of Moorish Spain: A Fresh Look." *Garden History* 20, no. 1 (1992): 71–82.

Nasrallah, Nawal. *Annals of the Caliphs' Kitchens: Ibn Sayyar Al-Warraq's Tenth-Century Baghdadi Cookbook*. Vol. 70. Leiden: Brill, 2007.

Perry, Charles. *Scents and Flavors: A Syrian Cookbook*. Vol. 47. New York: New York University Press, 2017.

Waines, David. "'Luxury Foods' in Medieval Islamic Societies." *World Archaeology* 34, no. 3 (2003): 571–580.

Watson, Andrew M. *Agricultural Innovation in the Early Islamic World: The Diffusion of Crops and Farming Techniques, 700–1100*. Cambridge: Cambridge University Press, 1983.

Watson, Andrew M. "The Arab Agricultural Revolution and Its Diffusion, 700–1100." *Journal of Economic History* 34, no. 1 (1974): 8–35.

Watson, Andrew M. "A Medieval Green Revolution: New Crops and Farming Techniques in the Early Islamic World." In *The Islamic Middle East, 700–1900: Studies in Economic and Social History*, edited by A. Udovitch, 29–58. Princeton, NJ: Darwin Press, 1981.

CHAPTER 27

WET RICE IN EAST ASIA
A Long Revolution

FRANCESCA BRAY

IN the history of monsoon Asia, wet-rice farming and civilization went hand in hand. While states and kingdoms might rise and fall, across the zone, whether in Bengal or Bali, Java or Japan, Cambodia or China, the demands and benefits of organizing wet-rice cultivation contributed to overarching continuities, in foodways, farming technology, the sculpting of landscapes, visions of social order, and patterns of creation and distribution of wealth.[1] Once wet-rice farming was established as the mainstay of the economy, its requirements and affordances structured long-term patterns of social organization and material growth.

It was the unique allure of rice that made it such a potent historical player. Asians grew many other reliable and nourishing indigenous staples—millets or yams, for instance—yet none acquired the universal appeal of rice. Throughout the region, wherever social hierarchies emerged, rice was considered the queen of cereals, the food of gods, kings, and priests. The delicious jade-white grain was the sacred food of rituals and festivals—all aspired to eat it, even though many tasted it only at weddings or festivals.[2] Rice shaped the cuisine and marked the status of ruling elites and urban populations, distinguishing them from the peasants who supplied the rice as taxes or rents, while often surviving themselves on a diet of "coarse foods" such as millets, tubers, or beans.[3]

Monarchs, officials, and landowners encouraged or enforced rice growing not simply because rice was delicious, but because it was productive: paddy fields could be coaxed into high yields unmatched by other crops.[4] The hard work involved in intensive rice farming was not a burden that farmers always took on joyfully—sometimes they grew it only because it was a condition of their access to land, as when governments or landlords insisted that taxes or rents be paid in rice.[5] Sometimes there were markets for rice or for the sideline products that rice farming typically supported, such as silk yarn, cotton textiles, or citrus, that made rice farming attractive in itself. The gradual spread of zones of intensive wet-rice farming across monsoon Asia powered the rise of kingdoms and empires and nourished the trading networks that connected them to each other and to the world. Paddy fields generated the grain surpluses necessary to accumulate wealth, feed armies, officials, and workforces, support the growth of population, manufactures, or commercial farming, and expand into new territories.

The intensification of rice production has often been identified as a vector of long-term growth. What can be learned from comparing the two closely connected cases where this historical process is most obvious, best documented and the object of most heated debate about the nature and potential of rice economies, namely late imperial/early modern China, and early modern/modern Japan? From the ninth century onward, the intensification of wet-rice farming in key zones and its spread into new areas catalyzed the rise and shaped the evolution of China, the country that by 1400 was firmly established (along with India) as the major economic powerhouse of the emerging early modern global economy.[6] Importing rice-farming expertise and technology from China, Tokugawa Japan (1603–1868) rose to riches through a pattern of rice-based production and commerce that drove the spectacularly successful Meiji (1868–1912) program of industrialization and institutional modernization and still shapes the economic and political landscape of Japan today.[7]

THE RICE ECONOMY OF LATE IMPERIAL CHINA

In 1127 the map of China was turned upside down. The defeat of the Northern Song state (960–1127) by Jurchen invaders marked a watershed moment, a historic recentering in which the rice-growing provinces of the South permanently replaced the millet and wheat landscapes of the North as the economic, political, and cultural heart of the empire.[8]

The Song defeat was catastrophic. The Jurchen armies besieged and captured the capital, Kaifeng, a city of more than half a million inhabitants located in the center of the huge and fertile Yellow River plain. The emperor and his officials fled Kaifeng and the ravaged Northern provinces for Jiangnan, the Lower Yangzi region, a thousand kilometers to the south. Despite the devastating defeat, the loss of lives and lands, the disruption of government, and the difficulties of financing defense and state-building with state coffers drained by years of war, in just a few decades the displaced dynasty was restored to stability, wealth, and brilliance.

Although confined to roughly half its former territory, the fledgling Southern Song state (1127–1279) managed to feed a population swollen by millions of refugees. Rapid increases in agricultural output not only fed the extra mouths but fueled the expansion and diversification of the economy into a commercial and manufacturing powerhouse, a prosperous society, famed worldwide for its luxurious porcelains and silks, with a population steadily growing in numbers and prosperity, in which even humble households could afford regular purchases of oil, soy sauce, vinegar, and tea. The new

Song capital, Hangzhou, located in the heart of Jiangnan's fertile rice-lands, soon counted a million inhabitants; its palaces and temples, shops, and markets outshone all the splendors of Kaifeng.

What made this astonishing resilience and recovery possible? The answer is wet-rice cultivation. Not only was Jiangnan's rice economy capable of absorbing the huge shock of the 1127 defeat: it structured the pattern of imperial China's economic development, population growth, and territorial expansion for the next seven centuries. This watershed moment marked such a radical change in China's economic and political trajectory that historians speak of the "Song Agricultural Revolution."[9] Yet, like most revolutions, it was not a sudden transformation but a change long in the making.

Nowadays it is widely but wrongly believed that the Chinese have all eaten rice as their staple since time immemorial. In fact, through two millennia of political unification and division, between 1000 BCE and 1000 CE, the northern plains were the symbolic and material heartland of China's principal ethnic group, the Han. Southern states, however powerful, were considered alien and lacked cultural legitimacy. Imperial China's traditional agrarian statecraft, administrative attention, and technical concern focused on the dry-land farming systems of the north, organized around millets as the staple food and primary tax grain. In myth and literature, millets featured as the foundation of Chinese civilization, its history, institutions, wealth, customs, and values. Prince Millet was the legendary ancestor of the imperial line, millet porridge was the staple food, and millet beer was the drink offered in ancestral rituals and passed around at feasts, poets' gatherings, or everyday meals. In consequence, while numerous early agricultural treatises, several still extant today, provide elaborate technical details about northern millet farming, the first works detailing rice-farming techniques appeared only in the 1130s and 1140s, just after the Song dynasty's retreat to the south. The transformation of priorities was, however, rapid and radical. Almost overnight, southern rice farming replaced northern millet farming as the accepted model for good husbandry and as both official and popular icon of virtuous labor.[10]

Ironically, then, it was non-Han populations who developed the rice-farming system later identified as the quintessence of dominant Han Chinese civilization. Wet-rice grown in paddy fields was an ancient staple dating back millennia in southern China and what is now northern Vietnam, domesticated and developed by Tai and other non-Han ethnic groups who then inhabited the region.[11] Wet-rice farming sustained Neolithic societies and powerful early states in the Viet (Yue) region of the southern coasts and along the whole course of the Yangzi from its delta up into Sichuan. Two thousand years ago, when northern and southern states were unified into a single empire under the Qin (221–206 BCE) and then the Han dynasty (206 BCE–220 CE), the southern territories were already known to envious northerners as "lands of fish and rice," regions of natural bounty where it seemed that food could be harvested by indolent natives without effort.

Here a brief characterization of different rice-farming systems is in order. Swidden farming, or shifting cultivation, involves clearing small patches of hillside by felling and burning trees and vegetation. The cleared ground is uneven and sloping. Seeds of rice or other crops are dropped into deep pockets made with a digging-stick, the ash fertilizes the soil, and rain provides water. Once the land has been cleared, little work is involved; the plots give good yields for four or five years, after which the goodness of the ash is exhausted and the farmer abandons the plot and clears new land. The forest typically takes ten to twelve years to renew.[12] Contrary to modern opinion, it is not an inherently unsustainable system: groups of swidden farmers move through their territory from one set of plots to another in regular cycles.[13] Wet-rice, by contrast, is grown in permanent fields surrounded by low earthen bunds to retain the water. In some places, rice farming depends on natural rainfall, in which case farmers grow just one crop of rice in the monsoon season but may also plant the field with another kind of crop in the dry season. In other places fields are irrigated: farmers build small or large tanks to gather water, divert streams, or pump water up from a nearby river. If the supply of irrigation water is sufficient, more than one crop can be grown in a year, independent of rainfall. In terms of intensity of land use, then, swidden is at the bottom of the scale, rain-fed wet-rice farming in the middle, and irrigated wet-rice farming at the top.

Northern Chinese may have imagined that their southern neighbors enjoyed bounteous harvests for little effort, but in fact, although swidden farming was certainly practiced in many parts of the south, the rise of the great southern states depended on intensive wet-rice farming. Southern rulers had long encouraged or enforced more intensive methods, well aware that rice output (and the potential to levy taxes and feed armies) rose significantly where farmers invested labor in building and maintaining an infrastructure of paddy fields and water supplies, and in cultivation techniques that increased yields and intensified cropping patterns. Pottery grave-models from two thousand years ago depict rows of transplanted seedlings standing in bunded rice fields fed by small water-tanks containing fish and water chestnuts.[14] Farming households could build these small tanks themselves, but in hilly terrain, communities across South China cooperated to build terraces, "ladder fields" (*titian*), fed by rainwater or streams; along gentle slopes or in valleys they diverted water into small canals to irrigate gently sloping banks of fields. At a larger scale of operation, a regular strategy for southern rulers seeking to strengthen and enrich their states was to build sea walls, dikes, reservoirs, and irrigation canals to expand the area of paddy fields.[15] Although irrigation blocks might be large, individual fields were most productive when kept small: adjusting the depth of the water as the plant went through its growth cycle, and controlling water flow through the field to regulate temperature, were important factors in ensuring good yields.

Other key techniques for intensifying output included transplanting, multiple cropping, and intercropping. For transplanting, the rice seed is sown in a well-manured nursery bed; when it has grown to 20 or 25 cm high it is pulled up, trimmed, and replanted in carefully spaced rows in the main field. Transplanting allows farmers to select the healthiest seedlings, encourages vigorous rooting and tillering (multiple stems and seed heads from a single plant), and facilitates weeding; all these increase the yield. An additional advantage is that transplanting reduces the time the crop spends in the main field by a month or six weeks, often allowing time for a second crop, which might be rice, wheat, or barley, or other crops depending on local climate and markets.

FIGURE 27.1 "Transplanting rice seedlings"; *Gengzhi tu* (Pictures of Tilling and Weaving) by Lou Shou, ca. 1140; 1462 Imperial edition, reproduced in Otto Franke, *Keng Tschi T'u: Ackerbau und Seidenwinnung in China*, Hamburg: L. Friederichsen, 1913.

The potential for double or multi-cropping is increased where farmers have bred quick-ripening rice varieties. Chinese references to double-cropping of rice in what is now Vietnam go back to around 100 CE. Quick-ripening varieties gradually spread north into southern and central China. Centuries later, the so-called Champa (Vietnamese) rice varieties, distributed to Jiangnan farmers by the Northern Song government in 1020, were in fact imported from next-door Fujian Province, where they had been routinely cultivated for some time.[16]

Although the most sophisticated rice-farming techniques were probably still confined to just a few areas, by the late Han dynasty the southern wet-rice landscapes were sufficiently productive to accommodate not only the needs of local populations and governments but also large influxes of northern refugees from the wars that marked the disintegration of the Han Empire. By the time the empire was reunited under the Sui (581–618) and Tang (618–906) dynasties, both the southern population and the acreage under wet-rice cultivation were expanding rapidly and the south was becoming more solidly incorporated into the imperial polity. Migrants from the crowded northern plains continued to stream south in search of land, and now tax-rice also flowed north to the capital and to the heavily defended northern frontier along new or improved north-south axes of communication, including the Grand Canal, completed in 609. By the mid-Tang, southern taxes in rice were beginning to match northern taxes in millet.[17] By 1100, two-thirds of China's population were already living in the southern rice-growing zones, a reversal of population distribution four centuries earlier.[18]

During the Tang and early Song the acreage and the productivity of southern wet-rice farming increased steadily. Not all southern wet-rice farming was intensive. In many areas the rice was not sown in nursery beds and transplanted, but sown directly into the main field; often paddy fields were rain-fed, not irrigated, and left to fallow one year in two. (In fact, extensive rice farming persisted throughout the imperial period, in newly opened frontier zones, for example, where labor was scarce.)[19] But in the core regions of Jiangnan and Lingnan (Canton and the southern coasts), the material contours of China's characteristic wet-rice landscape were already clearly traced. Here, intensive techniques had become routine, setting norms for the improvement of rice cultivation elsewhere, and providing the foundation for further refinement over the centuries.[20]

In just a few years after the loss of the north in 1127, perceptions of the relative importance of the northern and southern rural economies were permanently transformed. The new Southern Song government embraced the local Jiangnan landscape as its home and gave rice a prominent symbolic role in official discourse, establishing the virtues and skills of rice farming as icons of a quintessentially Chinese social order.

The new political cult of the rice economy was vividly illustrated in the *Gengzhi tu* (Pictures of tilling and weaving), a set of forty-five charming paintings and poems depicting each technical process in the most advanced methods of rice and silk production. Painted during the 1130s by Lou Shou, the magistrate of Yuqian County in the prosperous rice-and-silk region surrounding Hangzhou, the *Gengzhi tu* was enthusiastically received by the emperor. In Chinese statecraft, the emperor and his officials were responsible for ensuring the welfare of the people by promoting agriculture (*quannong*). The *Gengzhi tu* was a perfect token of this ideal of governance. The Song emperor immediately had it reproduced in woodblock prints and distributed; soon it was famous around the country, its lively and engaging scenes entering popular visual culture as ceramic motifs and colorful New Year prints. A long imperial love affair with the *Gengzhi tu* ensued: new versions were commissioned by a number of emperors, in particular by the first three Qing (1644–1911) emperors, who as alien Manchu conquerors were particularly anxious to establish their credentials as proper Confucian rulers.[21]

The scenes of rural life in the *Gengzhi tu* depict dense patchworks of tiny rice fields dotted with plantations of mulberry trees. Up to their knees in water, peasant farmers work the mud to silken softness, aided by cheerful water buffalo pulling the plows and harrows; bent double, they transplant the delicate seedlings, weed them, and weed them again. In some scenes a daughter brings a welcome basket of food and tea; in others, an official or a landlord watches the reapers or directs the filling of the granary. While the men toil in the fields the women toil indoors, washing and sorting silkworm eggs, caring for the voraciously munching worms as tenderly as delicate infants until the time comes to boil them alive in their cocoons. The women's labors do not end with the heaps of golden cocoons: next, they must spin off the filaments, twist and reel the yarn, and weave it into cloth.

The *Gengzhi tu* was the first work to celebrate the indispensable role of the irrigated Jiangnan landscape in supporting the imperial order, and to idealize the skills, hard work, technical sophistication, and gendered divisions of labor that made this contribution possible. But it is no coincidence that only a few years later, in 1149, an elderly Jiangnan gentleman-farmer named Chen Fu completed a short but richly detailed agricultural treatise that also systematically described the local rice-and-silk farming system, not in pictures and verse, but in the sober prose style that had been developed several centuries earlier for technical description. The treatise is divided into three sections, the first on rice cultivation, the second on caring for the indispensable water buffalo, and the third on sericulture. While earlier treatises had included chapters on fiber crops, Chen's was the first in a long series of influential treatises, some officially sponsored, some private, to highlight farming as a gender partnership, giving equal space to men's and women's work. Starting with Chen Fu, writers were also likely to include calculations of whether it was more profitable to plant different kinds of land with rice or with mulberries, and how the wages of female servants compared with the profits they brought by reeling and spinning.

Whether they were high-ranking officials or peasants choosing a New Year's print, to the late imperial Chinese the busy fields and mulberry groves of the *Gengzhi tu* portrayed a landscape that was at once a material and a moral ideal: in a society where farming was the foundation not simply of the economy but of the social, moral and cosmic order of the imperial state, these scenes of intensively worked land and disciplined skills represented more than a source of material abundance. A landscape in which "men plowed and women wove" (*nan geng nü zhi*) was also a setting in which humans acted out in microcosm the essential interflow of *yin* (female) and *yang* (male) energies that sustained cosmic harmony and social order, each sex producing food and clothing for the family and the grain and cloth in which taxes were paid. Throughout the late imperial era, long after tax payments had been commuted to cash (a process begun in the Song and completed by 1580), the Chinese state remained committed to supporting and disseminating this ideal gendered landscape as both a goal and a tool of government, investing heavily in policies and projects to develop versions of this technical-moral landscape across its territories.

To the government, agricultural development was both a material and a civilizing project. As officials sought to implant the elements of the Jiangnan landscape into new territories, they not only offered technical improvements to rice farming but also folded in projects to teach local women sericulture or cotton weaving. Teaching local men and women the skills needed to plow and weave the Chinese way would not only improve local peasants' living standards, but it would also impart the moral mindset of proper Chinese subjects, of which proper gender norms were an essential element, along with paying taxes.[22]

The term "Song Agricultural Revolution" is apt in two senses. First, like the so-called Agricultural Revolution in eighteenth-century Britain, farming improvements catalyzed huge changes in urbanization, manufacturing, and commerce. Second, like

FIGURE 27.2 "The silkworm's second sleep"; *Gengzhi tu* (Pictures of Tilling and Weaving) by Lou Shou, ca. 1140; 1742 Imperial edition, reproduced in Otto Franke, *Keng Tschi T'u*.

the Green Revolution of the 1960s and 1970s, its initial phases were facilitated by coordinated state development programs.[23]

For a century before the loss of the North, Song officials, striving to strengthen the economy and national defenses, had actively encouraged the development and dissemination of improved rice technology in the southern provinces. One strand of policy was to disseminate best practice from technically advanced regions. Another was to invest in material and financial infrastructure. The Northern Song government financed new irrigation works and land reclamation projects, supplied draft animals (the tractors of the time) where they were in short supply, and provided low-interest loans and tax rebates for farmers who opened up new rice land.[24]

The Northern Song government's introduction into Jiangnan's rice regions of an early-ripening Vietnamese varietal of rice known as "Champa" illustrates a technical model for "promoting agriculture" practiced until the end of the empire.[25] The new seeds were distributed to farmers through the district *yamen*. Written instructions on their cultivation methods and related innovations were circulated to magistrates and to literate "master farmers" (*nongshi*) chosen for their skill and experience to fill a minor official post that carried the duty of improving farming techniques and organizing mutual aid in their village. The adoption of quick-ripening rices transformed production patterns, allowing two crops of grain to be grown in a year as in the south—not of rice, this far north, but a summer crop of rice followed by a winter crop of wheat or barley. As Northern immigrants preferred wheat noodles and breads to rice, there was a ready market for the winter crops. This encouraged farmers to put in the extra effort, particularly as the government chose not to tax the second crop. Over time, quick-ripening, drought- and salt-tolerant rices proved so useful for reducing risk or occupying new ecological niches that Chinese farmers developed hundreds or even thousands of varieties. In one flood-prone region of Jiangnan, sixteenth-century farmers succeeded in breeding a "fifty-day rice."[26]

The successful Song government program established a trend. Between 1000 and 1900, China's intensive rice landscapes steadily expanded from Jiangnan to cover most of the south. As population grew in the core zones, migrant farmers helped carry the frontiers forward, their skills typically serving in lieu of capital. State officials also played a central role in promoting local projects to develop rice farming. Over the centuries we observe a ripple effect as rice-surplus zones shifted from early centers like Jiangnan and the Canton region, where farmers turned from rice to more profitable commercial crops or manufactures, to hinterland river basins upstream, which now supplied rice-deficit zones. Here, in regions typically occupied by other ethnic groups, new frontiers of rice farming and of Han-style culture and social organization opened up. Thanks to a panoply of water-control devices (including tanks, canals, flumes, and pumps) and land-reclamation techniques (polders, terracing, etc.) that permitted all kinds of land to be converted into muddy rice paddies, rice farming also spread across elevations, extending from easily managed river basins up into steep terraced hillsides or down into reclaimed land along the coast or in marshy floodplains, where continual pumping or the construction of sea walls might be necessary.[27]

Running a rice farm effectively did not require large or expensive equipment. The basic tool repertory—a small buffalo plow and iron-tined harrow, hoes, mattocks, and sickles, perhaps a wooden chain pump and winnowing fan or a small mill for grinding sugar cane or oil-seeds—was made cheaply by the local carpenter and smith, as were the looms or reels needed for women's work. Small field size enhanced efficient water management. Oil-cake and other manufacturing wastes that began to be used as fertilizers in the sixteenth century could be purchased in small quantities, as could new seed. This farming system was not capital-intensive, nor did it have economies of scale: instead it was *skill-oriented* and functioned best at household scale. In Jiangnan by the 1600s, 10 *mu* (0.7 hectare) of rice fields were sufficient to feed a household. As methods intensified and land rose in value, landlords often acquired vast tracts but did not seek to consolidate their holdings into large farms. Instead, they let it out to tenants: "There is a proverb which says 'It is better to have good tenants than good land.' . . . There are three advantages in having good tenants, namely that they are on time with plowing and sowing, they are energetic in fertilizing, and they are resourceful in conserving every drop of water."[28]

Whether initiated by officials, peasant farmers, or landlords, the steady diffusion of intensive rice farming propelled long-term economic development and integration. Higher output generated food surpluses that supported population growth and urbanization. It was not just that rice fields became more productive: the focused land and labor demands of rice growing meshed easily with commercial cropping and household or small-scale rural industry. Outside the two peak periods of transplanting and harvesting, the men in rice-farming households could tend crops grown on drier land or nearby hillsides, like tea, timber, oranges, bamboo, cotton, or mulberries for silk production, while rice paddies could be planted off-season with wheat, beans, or vegetables. Women, who normally did not work in the fields, could raise silkworms, reel silk, spin and weave cotton, raise poultry or pigs, brew, or make pickles inside their homes. At a slightly larger scale than household manufacturers, villages across South China began setting up small factories processing goods like sugar, rice wine, or paper. Market towns and merchant networks sprang up to service rural producers and distribute their goods.

Late imperial rice-based farming systems supported a regime of commercial cropping and small-scale manufacturing that famously made early modern China the world's largest economy, its biggest exporter of manufactured goods and importer of silver.[29] The rice-farming landscape served as the matrix for a thriving and versatile system of small-scale commodity production. Commodities that were plantation crops in European colonies, including rice, cotton, tea, and sugar, were grown on peasant smallholdings, processed domestically or in small local factories, and distributed by merchant networks through China's vast internal markets as well as abroad—a system effective in assuring foreign markets for Chinese smallholders producing goods like tea or sugar, even after the rise of colonial competition.[30]

The rice trade was the lifeblood sustaining both government and commerce. Continuously expanding in scale and scope from Song times, the rice market enabled farmers to choose how to use their land and labor in response to markets. The household-scale cotton industry and imperial silk manufactures of Jiangnan, the porcelain factories of Jingdezhen, peasant tea farmers in Fujian, and paper workshops in the Sichuan mountains all depended on efficient flows of rice. As home-grown rice surpluses fell below internal demand, the network of rice merchants and millers expanded beyond China's frontiers to control imports from countries like Siam and Burma that became regular suppliers. The rice market increasingly integrated all of Chinese imperial territory and its many trading partners across East and Southeast Asia.[31] Shaped by rice production and fueled by the rice trade, late imperial China was, then, a rice economy in every sense.

Involution or Industrious Revolution?

In 1178 the Song official Zhou Qufei wrote disapprovingly that the rice farmers of Qinzhou (upriver from Canton) were very careless in their methods, simply breaking up the soil into clods rather than working it till it was smooth, dibbling the seed into the field directly rather than transplanting, and neglecting to weed or irrigate—"they simply leave Nature to take care of the crop." In the late seventeenth century, Qu Dajun described how the farmers of the same region coaxed a continual sequence of

FIGURE 27.3 "Plowing"; *Gengzhi tu* (Pictures of Tilling and Weaving) by Lou Shou, ca. 1140; 1742 Imperial edition, reproduced in Otto Franke, *Keng Tschi T'u*.

rice, indigo, melons, oil-seed, or cotton from the soil, not only providing for their own subsistence but also exporting large volumes of food and raw materials down-river to Canton: "The people are all *extremely industrious* and devote themselves so *diligently* to their farming that truly *no patch of land is wasted and no hands are ever idle*."[32]

One influential school of historians has qualified the long-term intensification of the Chinese rice-based, skill-oriented economy as *involutionary*: a process of "growth without development" that supported increasingly dense populations by absorbing labor, but lacked the capacity to increase labor productivity through the kinds of mechanical innovation and scale economies that revolutionized the industrial West.[33] By this reckoning, imperial China's rice economy was a failure: it expanded and evolved for a thousand years, during which it succeeded in meshing together a political, moral, and material order that survived invasions and other disasters—but ultimately it failed to transform itself.

Southern China's rice-powered era began around 800, reaching a zenith of prosperity and global impact in around 1750. By then, China's agriculture was indeed nearing its territorial, demographic, and environmental limits.[34] Degradation set in through the nineteenth century as the last imperial government struggled to resist colonial aggression and internal rebellions, eventually falling in 1911. In contrast, Japan was a relative latecomer on the scene of intensive rice farming, which began there in around 1600.

But unlike China's nineteenth-century breakdown, in Japan the rice economy served as a springboard to successful modernization. Today it is claimed as one of the miracle ingredients that makes modern Japan exceptional. At the core of this model of Japan's success is the concept of a rural, household-scale, skill-oriented, rice-based *industrious revolution*, a radical change perceived as drawing its strength precisely from the habits of diligence, skill, and thrifty use of scarce resources that Qu Dajun approved in the Qinzhou farmers.

Post–World War II Japanese sociologists, historians, and philosophers have elaborated the theory of Japan as a rice economy in ways that fundamentally challenge Western-centered historical periodizations and geographies. For a start, they assert that the Japanese path to industrial modernity was quite distinct from the path of the West. In Japanese models of *longue durée* history and paths to modernity, *industrious revolution* specifically denotes an economic transformation based on the constellation of managerial, technical, and financial skills associated with the complex of small-scale rice farms, crafts, and manufactures that clustered in the early modern Japanese countryside. Starting in the seventeenth century, in a parallel trajectory to the rice regions of late imperial China, these characteristic resources led Japan, it is argued, on a rurally rooted, rice-based path of economic growth in which households increased both output *and income* by working harder; capital assets or inputs (machines, livestock) dwindled in importance as the quality of labor improved.[35]

Before about 1600, rice was a prestige crop rather than a popular staple in Japan.[36] But under Tokugawa rule (1603–1867), Chinese intensive rice systems and the associated agronomic expertise were imported to Japan. Agricultural treatises proliferated, new varieties of rice and other crops were bred, fertilizing methods were improved, and multi-cropping expanded, fueling the dynamic economic and manufacturing growth, the commercialization, and urbanization that built the foundations for nineteenth-century modernization.[37] When the Meiji government was formed in 1868, in reaction to the threat of invasion by Western powers it determined to pursue a policy of rapid modernization, militarization, and industrialization mobilizing Western expertise. The platform for this takeoff, however, was the productive and versatile Tokugawa rice-scape, not transformed but rather dynamized by Western agronomic science, chemical fertilizers, mechanized pumps, breeding programs, etc.[38] The rise of Meiji Japan depended on national rice production. A ruthless regime of extraction from the rice-farming peasantry was veiled by an agrarian ideology extolling the small farmer as a loyal and productive citizen. It was the surpluses of food and labor extracted from increasingly immiserated rice farmers in Japan and its colonies of Taiwan and Korea that fueled Japan's rise between 1870 and 1940 as a military-industrial power.

In early modern Japan as in late imperial China, industrious revolution did not, in itself, lead toward industrialization. However, when the Meiji government decided that the nation must industrialize in short order, the assets of the industrious revolution were deployed to fashion a model of industrialization quite different from the classic models of Britain or the eastern United States. In Japan the rural economy was not *reactive to*, but *constitutive of,* development trajectories. Furthermore, rural skills and creativity were not marginalized or displaced by Western-inspired technical expertise, but mobilized and developed in the service of a characteristically Japanese repertory of modernizing techniques. There is a broad consensus among historians and social scientists that these deep-rooted resources and dynamics gave a distinctive shape to Meiji Japan's modernization, and continue to shape the organization of the economy and of production in Japan today, as well as its politics and culture.[39]

Clearly, the Japanese state's successive manipulations of the moral-material landscape of intensive wet-rice farming, and the kinds of political subject it fashioned, were—although rooted in the same technology—very different from the social compact between state and peasant envisaged by elites in imperial China. The reconfiguring of rice farmers as self-sacrificing patriots was a significant factor in Japan's capacity to successfully integrate the rice economy with modern institutions and mobilize it to meet nationalist ambitions. However, the broader concept of "industrious revolution," with its analysis of how industrious Japan became industrial Japan, soon attracted historians rethinking paths to modernity elsewhere.

In the case of China, recasting late imperial history as a story not of involution but of industrious revolution takes us out of the contentious analytical framework of comparative history, with its implicit guiding question: "why was the West best?," and into the more open arena of global history.[40] Once we focus attention on the diverse ways in which China's local rice-anchored landscapes and its overarching rice economy sustained the many-stranded commercial and financial networks that both knit together the country's regions and shaped China's role in the evolving global economy through the early modern, colonial, and modern periods, then—as in the case of Japanese history viewed through its rice economy—we are prompted to rethink ruptures, transitions, and continuities.

To give just one example: beginning in the 1840s, Western colonial powers exercised increasing political and economic control over imperial China's territories and government. From that perspective, China was clearly in decline as a world power. Yet at precisely the same time, as colonial exploitation of Southeast Asia expanded and intensified and with it markets for and production of rice, it was Chinese rice-merchant dynasties, with a long history of operating import-export businesses across the region, who took control of almost every step of the burgeoning international rice trade. In addition, their networks, strong local connections, and flexibility in moving and mobilizing capital allowed them to rival or even outcompete colonial states and enterprises in developing mines, rubber, and other colonial commodity production, for which they provided capital, managers, and labor force (migrants recruited in South Chinese villages). They also established banks to handle regional transfers of funds that included, as well as transfers of remittances and overseas investments, substantial loans to governments. In Southeast Asia, Chinese merchant associations had a significant role in state-building that paradoxically had been historically denied them in China itself.[41] The long history of Chinese business and its special contributions to global capitalism reminds us firstly that China's place in shaping the modern world has to be thought of in terms other than isolation and involution, and secondly that rice wove the Asian world together in complex ways that we are only beginning to appreciate.

Asian Rice Mosaics

From the great temple complexes and irrigation tanks of Angkor Wat and other Hindu empires across South India and Southeast Asia, to the cascading terraces of Bali and southwest China, some of Asia's most spectacular landscapes are monuments to the bounties of wet-rice farming, and to the investments of labor involved.

The buildup to a full-fledged intensive rice economy always took time. Bali is a case in point. Its spectacular rice terraces and temple-based irrigation associations (*subak*) date back over a thousand years. Political ecologists argue that the *subak* is "best understood as an emergent *complex adaptive system*" in which evolving environmental changes have triggered successive social responses.[42] First documented in inscriptions from about 880 CE, as demands on land and water diversified and increased, the organizing principles and methods of the *subak* were adapted to accommodate increasingly complex challenges of material and social management; the institution remains in vigorous health today.[43]

The incomparable Angkor Wat, the world's largest religious monument, was erected around 1100 CE by King Suryavarman II, ruler of the Khmer Empire (ca. 800–1450 CE). The temple is set between two enormous *baray* or artificial reservoirs, built a couple of centuries earlier. Angkor's towers and the surrounding waters embodied a Brahmanic cosmic-political landscape modeled on sacred Mount Meru rising from the Sea of Milk, the source of divine and human sustenance.[44] Angkor's *baray* each measure roughly eight kilometers by two. Led through a network of canals, reservoirs, channels, and embankments, their waters irrigated a grid of small rice fields that at the height of the Khmer Empire expanded to cover an area of over 1,000 square kilometers, populated by about 750,000 people.[45] The huge amounts of wealth and labor needed to build Angkor's *baray* in the first place came from surpluses of rice generated by an earlier system of paddy fields. These fields were fed not by grand hydraulic works but by natural water flow; they were built on shallow slopes along the dense network of rivers and streams flowing down into the nearby inland sea of Tonlé Sap. These less-intensive systems of irrigated rice farming had in turn been developed and elaborated over centuries.[46]

The expansion and intensification of irrigated rice farming supported the rise of medieval powers like the Khmer Empire and of ambitious modernizing monarchs like the late nineteenth-century kings of Siam.[47] It has been persuasively argued that India's rise as a major early modern economic power was, like that of early modern China, founded on the dynamics of its wet-rice economy.[48] The development of intensively worked "monotonous rice bowls" in their colonies in Java, Burma, and Cochinchina sustained the intricate flows of food, labor, and commodities that made Dutch, English, and French imperialism so lucrative.[49]

Rice farming was not destiny, however. It would be wrong to claim that rice farming always intensified over time, that intensification inevitably triggered growth, or that there was a simple relationship between volume of rice produced and number of mouths fed. Only in some circumstances did rice farming underpin the long-term historical developments we have noted for China and Japan. At any point in history, including the present day, rice-farming societies in Asia present not a steadily unfurling wave of "best practice," but rather a complex mosaic of systems, operating at various levels of intensity and rhythms of change and supporting different types of social organization.

Not surprisingly, it is the spectacular sites and the larger, more elaborate rice economies that have attracted the attention of historians and archeologists, and furnished sufficient material and documentary records to permit their study, ensuring recognition of their historical significance.

But rice is extraordinarily versatile: in Asia it is grown in upland slash-and-burn fields, in rain-fed or irrigated paddies, and in swamplands where it keeps pace with rising floodwaters. Rice paddies, fixed in place, help governments to count and control farmers, extracting surpluses through taxation. Shifting cultivation of upland rice in forested mountains offered food and camouflage to those who wished to elude such control. Outlaws or guerrilla troops paddled through swamps to snatch harvests of floating rice from under the noses of officials or occupying armies.[50] Historians estimate that until the nineteenth century the majority of Southeast Asia's farming population lived off swidden cultivation.[51] But by their very nature these societies leave few traces. They remained nearly invisible in history—until recently historians realized how many valuable global commodities (forest products, pepper, opium, and rubber) were produced as cash crops by swidden farmers, often outcompeting production on large-scale plantations.[52]

Although we know relatively little of their history, we may be sure that these were anything but "timeless" communities. Meshed into one or more circuits of the prevailing global trading networks by sales of sea or forest products or household production of high value, portable crops such as pepper, they responded actively to changing configurations of commercial or political regimes. Yet where rice farming was concerned, low-intensity production, sufficient to meet subsistence needs and buffer livelihoods against fluctuations in commodity markets, typically survived long-term, well into the modern era.[53]

In other words, Asia's rice mosaic was far more than a pattern composed of separate units. It was, in the terminology of STS (Science and Technology Studies), an *assemblage*: to understand the configuration of any individual element at a specific point in time we need to factor in not just internal factors but the connections that shaped it, its linkages in a global network.[54] What is historically significant about Asian rice farming viewed in regional rather than local perspective is how the many different types of source and flow converged as the lifeblood for circuits of long-distance as well as local trade. The production and circulation of rice linked impressive civilizations and tiny, remote communities alike into networks of commerce that steadily intensified as the early modern and modern world economy gathered strength.

Epilogue

In addressing the multiple temporalities of history, Fernand Braudel famously distinguished between the short-term impact of political and other similarly episodic phenomena, the "froth" of history, and long-term (*longue durée*) structural temporalities, such as the slow growth of trading networks or farming systems.[55] Wet-rice agriculture played this long-term systemic role in Chinese history, serving as a buffer to the vicissitudes of politics, climate, or patterns of world trade. For about a thousand years, between 800 and 1800 CE, however dramatic the immediate impact of the rise and fall of dynasties, palace coups or wars, famines or plagues, these setbacks proved short-lived disturbances in a long-term trend of growth, nurtured and structured by the characteristics and potential of China's wet-rice economy.[56]

The impressive intensification of rice farming during the Song has been described by historians as a "revolution." Indeed, the level of state intervention, and the components of the technical packages involved (hydraulic projects, distribution of seeds, technical instruction, and loans to farmers) invite comparison with the Green Revolution of the 1960s and 1970s. But unlike the modern Green Revolution, the intensification of the Jiangnan system of rice farming, and its dissemination through southern China and eventually into Japan, was not a sudden transformation but a revolution with deep roots, long in the making and in its unfolding—lasting for a thousand years in China, and still powerfully shaping Japan's culture, economy, and global claims today.

The modern Green Revolution was a universalizing project, designed to increase productivity (and promote food supplies for cities and industries) by producing homogenized, simplified, and specialized landscapes, developing zones of intensive rice monoculture through a universal technical package combining large-scale irrigation schemes with laboratory-bred seed (HYVs: high-yielding varieties) and chemical fertilizers.[57] The Jiangnan rice system, in contrast, owed its astonishing long-term success to its infinite flexibility, its ability to incorporate farmers' improvements or initiatives, to adapt to different conditions, and to combine with a host of complementary crops and economic activities. It was this flexibility that allowed the diffusion of the Jiangnan model across East Asia, not just as a source of food and the anchor of a model of economic growth, but as a moral icon, and the foundation of a long-lasting mode of governance.

One reason why the Green Revolution failed to meet expectations in Asia's rice-growing zones was precisely its rigidity and uniformity: it prioritized rice output over a working rice economy with its multiple, flexible opportunities for gainful employment.[58] Indeed it has been suggested that what our overcrowded planet needs today is not another Green Revolution, but Chinese- or Japanese-style "industrious revolutions" that would allow rural populations to prosper on the land while contributing fully to national economic growth.[59] Is this realistic? Whether it be the potential of early modern Jiangnan's rice economy to solve today's hollowing-out of the countryside, the supposed immunity of "free," "egalitarian" swidden farmers to the moral perils of capitalist intrusion, or the power of modern science's magic wand to transform hunger into plenty, we must beware of romanticizing complex solutions past as answers to the equally complex dilemmas of the present.[60] Yet the many histories of rice in Asia, large-scale or small, and the ways in which they have interwoven over the centuries, undoubtedly constitute a rich resource for thinking critically about alternative futures.

Notes

1. On the "order-legitimacy-wealth" concept of long-term civilization overarching shorter-term political change, see Miriam T. Stark, "Inscribing Legitimacy and Building Power in the Mekong Delta," in *Counternarratives and Macrohistories: New Agendas in Archaeology and Ancient History*, ed. Geoff Emberling (Cambridge: Cambridge University Press, 2015), 75–105. For Bengal see Lauren Minsky, "Of Health and Harvests: Seasonal Mortality and Commercial Rice Cultivation in the Punjab and Bengal Regions of South Asia," in *Rice: Global Networks and New Histories*, ed. Francesca Bray et al. (Cambridge: Cambridge University Press, 2015): 245–274, and for South India Kathleen D. Morrison, "Archaeologies of Flow: Water and the Landscapes of Southern India Past, Present, and Future," *Journal of Field Archaeology* 40, no. 5 (October 1, 2015): 560–580 https://doi.org/10.1179/20424582 15Y.0000000033; for Java, van Setten van der Meer, *Sawah Cultivation* (Canberra: ANU Press, 1979); for Siam, Yoneo Ishii, *Thailand: A Rice-Growing Society*, trans. Peter Hawkes and Stephanie Hawkes (Honolulu: University of Hawai'i Press, 1978). China and Japan, Cambodia, and Bali are discussed in more detail later.
2. Roy W. Hamilton, ed., *The Art of Rice: Spirit and Sustenance in Asia* (Los Angeles: UCLA Fowler Museum of Cultural History, 2004).
3. Morrison, "Archaeologies of Flow"; Sui-Wai Cheung, "A Desire to Eat Well: Rice and the Market in Eighteenth-Century China," in *Rice: Global Networks and New Histories*, ed. Francesca Bray et al. (Cambridge: Cambridge University Press, 2015): 84–98; Hsiao-t'ung Fei and Chih-i Chang, *Earthbound China: A Study of Rural Economy in Yunnan* (London: Routledge & Kegan Paul, 1948); Charlotte von Verschuer and Wendy Cobcroft, *Rice, Agriculture, and the Food Supply in Premodern Japan* (London: Routledge, 2016).
4. D.H. Grist, *Rice* (London: Longman, 1975); Francesca Bray, *The Rice Economies: Technology and Development in Asian Societies*, 2nd ed. (Berkeley: University of California Press, 1994).
5. James C. Scott, *The Art of Not Being Governed: An Anarchist History of Upland Southeast Asia* (New Haven, CT: Yale University Press, 2010).
6. André Gunder Frank, *ReOrient: Global Economy in the Asian Age* (Berkeley: University of California Press, 1998); Francesca Bray, "Instructive and Nourishing Landscapes: Natural Resources, People and the State in Late Imperial China," in *Technology, Gender and History in Imperial China: Great Transformations Reconsidered* (Abingdon: Routledge, 2013), 57–89; Ravi Palat, *The Making of an Indian Ocean World-Economy, 1250–1650: Princes, Paddy Fields, and Bazaars* (Basingstoke: Palgrave Macmillan, 2015).
7. Penelope Francks, "Rice and the Path of Economic Development in Japan," in *Rice: Global Networks and New Histories*, ed. Francesca Bray et al. (Cambridge: Cambridge University Press, 2015): 318–34.

8. Bray, "Instructive and Nourishing Landscapes"; Richard von Glahn, *The Economic History of China: From Antiquity to the Nineteenth Century* (Cambridge: Cambridge University Press, 2016).
9. Mark Elvin, *The Pattern of the Chinese Past: A Social and Economic Interpretation* (Stanford, CA: Stanford University Press, 1973).
10. Bray, "Instructive and Nourishing Landscapes," 59–65.
11. Chi Zhang and Hsiao-chun Hun, "The Emergence of Agriculture in Southern China," *Antiquity* 84, no. 323 (2010): 11–25.
12. Derek Freeman, *Report on the Iban* (London: Bloomsbury Academic, 1970); Anthony Reid, *A History of Southeast Asia: Critical Crossroads* (New York: John Wiley & Sons, 2015): 13.
13. Michael R. Dove, "Theories of Swidden Agriculture, and the Political Economy of Ignorance," *Agroforestry Systems* 1, no. 2 (1983): 85–99, https://doi.org/10.1007/BF00596 351; Anabel Ford and Ronald Nigh, *The Maya Forest Garden: Eight Millennia of Sustainable Cultivation of the Tropical Woodlands* (Walnut Creek, CA: Left Coast Press, 2016).
14. Bray, *The Rice Economies*, figs. 2.1, 3.3.
15. Ibid., 69–100; Bray, "Agriculture," 371–73.
16. Bray, "Instructive and Nourishing Landscapes," 75.
17. Bozhong Li, *Tangdai Jiangnan nongye di fazhan (Agricultural Development in Tang Dynasty Jiangnan)* (Beijing: Agriculture Press, 1990): 285–293.
18. von Glahn, *Economic History*, 209.
19. Evelyn Sakakida Rawski, *Agricultural Change and the Peasant Economy of South China*, Harvard East Asian Series 66 (Cambridge, MA: Harvard University Press, 1972).
20. Li, *Agricultural Development in Tang*; Bozhong Li, *Agricultural Development in Jiangnan, 1620–1850* (London: Macmillan, 1998).
21. Roslyn Lee Hammers, *Pictures of Tilling and Weaving: Art, Labor and Technology in Song and Yuan China* (Hong Kong: Hong Kong University Press, 2011); Francesca Bray, "Agricultural Illustrations: Blueprint or Icon?," in *Technology, Gender and History in Imperial China: Great Transformations Reconsidered* (Abingdon: Routledge, 2013), 219–52. The original is lost but there is a surviving twelfth-century copy in the Sackler Collection: https://asia.si.edu/object/F1954.20/ and https://asia.si.edu/object/F1954.21/, accessed December 28, 2019.
22. Francesca Bray, *Technology and Gender: Fabrics of Power in Late Imperial China* (Berkeley: University of California Press, 1997): 242–252.
23. Elvin, *Pattern*, 113–30; Bray, *The Rice Economies*, 152.
24. Peter J. Golas, "Rural China in the Song," *Journal of Asian Studies* 39, no. 2 (1980): 291–325, https://doi.org/10.2307/2054291; Dagmar Schäfer and Yi Han, "Great Plans: Song Dynastic (960–1279) Institutions for Human and Veterinary Healthcare," in *Animals through Chinese History: Earliest Times to 1911*, ed. Roel Sterckx, Martina Siebert, and Dagmar Schäfer (Cambridge: Cambridge University Press, 2018), 160–80, https://doi.org/10.1017/9781108551571.
25. Francesca Bray, "Science, Technique, Technology: Passages Between Matter and Knowledge in Imperial Chinese Agriculture," *British Journal for the History of Science* 41, no. 3 (2008): 319–344, https://doi.org/10.1017/S0007087408000873; William T. Rowe, *Saving the World: Chen Hongmou and Elite Consciousness in Eighteenth-Century China* (Stanford, CA: Stanford University Press, 2001); Peter B. Lavelle, *The Profits of Nature:*

Colonial Development and the Quest for Resources in Nineteenth-Century China (New York: Columbia University Press, 2020).
26. Ping-Ti Ho, "Early-Ripening Rice in Chinese History," *Economic History Review* 9, no. 2 (1956): 200–218, https://doi.org/10.2307/2591742.
27. Bray, *The Rice Economies*, 28–42; Li, *Agricultural Development 1620–1850*.
28. Zhang Ying, *Hengchan suoyan* (Remarks on real estate), probably completed 1697, trans. Beattie, *Land and Lineage in China*, 149; see also Francesca Bray, *Science and Civilisation in China*, Vol. 6: *Biology and Biological Technology*, Part 2: *Agriculture* (Cambridge: Cambridge University Press, 1984): 82–85.
29. Frank, *ReOrient*; Robert Marks, *Tigers, Rice, Silk, and Silt: Environment and Economy in Late Imperial South China*, Studies in Environment and History (Cambridge: Cambridge University Press, 1998).
30. Robert Gardella, *Harvesting Mountains: Fujian and the China Tea Trade, 1757–1937* (Berkeley: University of California Press, 1994); Sucheta Mazumdar, *Sugar and Society in China: Peasants, Technology, and the World Market* (Cambridge, MA: Harvard University Press, 1998).
31. Marks, *Tigers, Rice, Silk, and Silt*; Sui-Wai Cheung, *The Price of Rice: Market Integration in Eighteenth-Century China* (Bellingham, WA: Center for East Asian Studies, 2008); Sarasin Viraphol, *Tribute and Profit: Sino-Siamese Trade, 1652–1853* (Cambridge, MA: Harvard University Press, 1997).
32. Bray, *Agriculture*, 1984, 510, 509, emphases added.
33. Elvin, *Pattern*; Philip C. C. Huang, *The Peasant Family and Rural Development in the Yangzi Delta, 1350–1988* (Stanford, CA: Stanford University Press, 1990).
34. Mark Elvin and Ts'ui-jung Liu, eds., *Sediments of Time: Environment and Society in Chinese History* (Cambridge: Cambridge University Press, 1998); Marks, *Tigers, Rice, Silk, and Silt*.
35. Akira Hayami, *Japan's Industrious Revolution: Economic and Social Transformations in the Early Modern Period* (Tokyo: Springer Japan, 2015); Osamu Saito, "An Industrious Revolution in an East Asian Market Economy? Tokugawa Japan and Implications for the Great Divergence," *Australian Economic History Review* 50, no. 3 (2010): 240–261, https://doi.org/10.1111/j.1467-8446.2010.00304.x; Bray, *The Rice Economies*, 113–39: 210–217.
36. von Verschuer and Cobcroft, *Rice, Agriculture and Food*.
37. Thomas C. Smith, *The Agrarian Origins of Modern Japan* (Stanford, CA: Stanford University Press, 1959); Tessa Morris-Suzuki, *The Technological Transformation of Japan: From the Seventeenth to the Twenty-First Century* (Cambridge: Cambridge University Press, 1994).
38. Penelope Francks, *Technology and Agricultural Development in Pre-War Japan* (New Haven, CT: Yale University Press, 1984).
39. Morris-Suzuki, *Technological Transformation*; Francks, "Rice and the Path of Economic Development"; Emiko Ohnuki-Tierney, *Rice as Self: Japanese Identities through Time* (Princeton, NJ: Princeton University Press, 1994); Francesca Bray, "Health, Wealth, and Solidarity: Rice as Self in Japan and Malaysia," in *Moral Foods: The Construction of Nutrition and Health in Modern Asia*, ed. Angela Ki Che Leung and Melissa L. Caldwell (Honolulu: University of Hawai'i Press, 2019): 23–46.
40. Kenneth Pomeranz, *The Great Divergence: Europe, China, and the Making of the Modern World Economy* (Princeton, NJ: Princeton University Press, 2000); R. Bin Wong, *China Transformed: Historical Change and the Limits of European Experience*

(Ithaca, NY: Cornell University Press, 1997); Giovanni Arrighi, Takeshi Hamashita, and Mark Selden, *The Resurgence of East Asia: 500, 150 and 50 Year Perspectives* (London: Routledge, 2003).

41. Wu Xiao An, *Chinese Business in the Making of a Malay State, 1882–1941: Kedah and Penang* (London: Routledge, 2003); Rajeswary Ampalavanar Brown, ed., *Chinese Business Enterprise in Asia* (London: Routledge, 1995); Peter A. Coclanis, "Distant Thunder: The Creation of a World Market in Rice and the Transformations It Wrought," *American Historical Review* 98, no. 4 (1993): 1050–1078, https://doi.org/10.2307/2166598.
42. J. Stephen Lansing et al., "A Robust Budding Model of Balinese Water Temple Networks," *World Archaeology* 41, no. 1 (2009): 213, https://doi.org/10.1080/00438240802668198.
43. J. Stephen Lansing, *Priests and Programmers: Technologies of Power in the Engineered Landscape of Bali*, 2nd ed. (Princeton, NJ: Princeton University Press, 2007).
44. Roland Fletcher et al., "Angkor Wat: An Introduction," *Antiquity* 89, no. 348 (December 2015): 1388–1401, 1395. https://doi.org/10.15184/aqy.2015.178.
45. Ibid., 1396.
46. Scott Hawken, "Designs of Kings and Farmers: Landscape Systems of the Greater Angkor Urban Complex," *Asian Perspectives* 52, no. 2 (2013): 347–367, https://doi.org/10.1353/asi.2013.0010; Fletcher et al., "Angkor Wat"; Stark, "Inscribing Legitimacy."
47. Ishii, *Thailand*.
48. Palat, *The Indian Ocean World-Economy*.
49. Peter Boomgaard, "From Riches to Rags?: Rice Production and Trade in Asia, Particularly Indonesia, 1500–1950," in *The Wealth of Nature: How Natural Resources Have Shaped Asian History, 1600–2000*, ed. Greg Bankoff and Peter Boomgaard (London: Palgrave Macmillan, 2007), 185–204; Coclanis, "Distant Thunder."
50. Scott, *The Art of Not Being Governed*; David Biggs, "Promiscuous Transmission and Encapsulated Knowledge: A Material-Semiotic Approach to Modern Rice in the Mekong Delta," in *Rice: Global Networks and New Histories*, ed. Francesca Bray et al. (Cambridge: Cambridge University Press, 2015), 118–137.
51. Reid, *A History of Southeast Asia*, 14; R. D. Hill, *Rice in Malaya: A Study in Historical Geography*, 2nd ed. (Singapore: National University of Singapore Press, 2012).
52. Dove, "Swidden Agriculture."
53. Reid, *A History of Southeast Asia*, 46.
54. Aihwa Ong and Stephen J. Collier, eds., *Global Assemblages: Technology, Politics, and Ethics as Anthropological Problems* (Oxford: Blackwell, 2005); Coclanis, "Distant Thunder."
55. Fernand Braudel, *La Méditerranée et le monde méditerranéen a l'époque de Philippe II*, 2 vols. (Paris: Armand Colin, 1966); Fernand Braudel, *Civilization and Capitalism, 15th–18th Century*, Vol. 1: *The Structures of Everyday Life*, trans. Sian Reynolds (London: William Collins, 1981).
56. von Glahn, *Economic History*.
57. Jonathan Harwood, "Global Visions vs. Local Complexity: Experts Wrestle with the Problem of Development," in *Rice: Global Networks and New Histories*, ed. Francesca Bray et al. (Cambridge: Cambridge University Press, 2015): 41–55; Raj Patel, "The Long Green Revolution," *Journal of Peasant Studies* 40, no. 1 (2013): 1–63, https://doi.org/10.1080/03066150.2012.719224.

58. B. H. Farmer, "Perspectives on the 'Green Revolution' in South Asia," *Modern Asian Studies* 20, no. 1 (1986): 175–199, https://doi.org/10.1017/S0026749X00013627; Gordon Conway, *The Doubly Green Revolution: Food for All in the Twenty-First Century* (Ithaca, NY: Cornell University Press, 1999); Francesca Bray, "Feeding the Farmers, Feeding the Nation: The Long Green Revolution in Kelantan, Malaysia," in *Handbook of Food and Anthropology*, ed. James L. Watson and Jakob A. Klein (London: Bloomsbury, 2016): 173–199.
59. Giovanni Arrighi, *Adam Smith in Beijing: Lineages of the Twenty-First Century* (London: Verso, 2007); Shaohua Zhan, *The Land Question in China: Agrarian Capitalism, Industrious Revolution and East Asian Development* (Abingdon: Routledge, 2019).
60. Tania Murray Li, *Land's End: Capitalist Relations on an Indigenous Frontier* (Durham, NC: Duke University Press, 2014).

Bibliography

Biggs, David. *Quagmire: Nation-Building and Nature in the Mekong Delta*. Seattle: University of Washington Press, 2011.

Bray, Francesca. *The Rice Economies: Technology and Development in Asian Societies*. 2nd ed. Berkeley: University of California Press, 1994.

Bray, Francesca. *Science and Civilisation in China: Volume 6, Biology and Biological Technology, Part 2, Agriculture*. Cambridge: Cambridge University Press, 1984.

Bray, Francesca. "Agriculture," in *The Six Dynasties 220-581*, edited by Albert E. Dien and Keith N. Knapp, vol 2, pp. 355–373. Cambridge History of China. Cambridge and New York: Cambridge University Press, 2019.

Bray, Francesca, Peter A. Coclanis, Edda L. Fields-Black, and Dagmar Schäfer, eds. *Rice: Global Networks and New Histories*. Cambridge: Cambridge University Press, 2015.

Elvin, Mark. *The Pattern of the Chinese Past: A Social and Economic Interpretation*. Stanford, CA: Stanford University Press, 1973.

Fei, Hsiao-t'ung. *Peasant Life in China: A Field Study of Country Life in the Yangtze Vally*. London: Routledge, 1939.

Francks, Penelope. *The Japanese Consumer: An Alternative Economic History of Modern Japan*. Cambridge: Cambridge University Press, 2009.

Grist, D. H. *Rice*. London: Longman, 1975.

Hamilton, Roy W., ed. *The Art of Rice: Spirit and Sustenance in Asia*. Los Angeles: UCLA Fowler Museum of Cultural History, 2004.

Hammers, Roslyn Lee. *Pictures of Tilling and Weaving: Art, Labor and Technology in Song and Yuan China*. Hong Kong: Hong Kong University Press, 2011.

Hill, R.D. *Rice in Malaya: A Study in Historical Geography*. 2nd ed. Singapore: National University of Singapore Press, 2012.

Lansing, J. Stephen. *Priests and Programmers: Technologies of Power in the Engineered Landscape of Bali*. 2nd ed. Princeton, NJ: Princeton University Press, 2007.

Li, Bozhong. *Agricultural Development in Jiangnan, 1620–1850*. London: Macmillan, 1998.

Marks, Robert. *Tigers, Rice, Silk, and Silt: Environment and Economy in Late Imperial South China*. Cambridge: Cambridge University Press, 1998.

Ohnuki-Tierney, Emiko. *Rice as Self: Japanese Identities through Time*. Princeton, NJ: Princeton University Press, 1994.
Palat, Ravi. *The Making of an Indian Ocean World-Economy, 1250–1650: Princes, Paddy Fields, and Bazaars*. Basingstoke: Palgrave Macmillan, 2015.
Scott, James C. *The Art of Not Being Governed: An Anarchist History of Upland Southeast Asia*. New Haven, CT: Yale University Press, 2010.
Smith, Thomas C. *The Agrarian Origins of Modern Japan*. Stanford, CA: Stanford University Press, 1959.
Van Setten van der Meer, N.C. *Sawah Cultivation in Ancient Java*. Canberra: ANU Press, 1979.
Verschuer, Charlotte von, and Wendy Cobcroft. *Rice, Agriculture, and the Food Supply in Premodern Japan*. London: Routledge, 2016.

CHAPTER 28

THE ATLANTIC PLANTATION

TREVOR BURNARD

THE plantation complex was a global institution that was especially prominent in the Atlantic world, areas such as Brazil, the Caribbean, and the American South. Karl Marx depicted plantations as inherently economically backward and a way station on the march from feudalism to capitalism. The great but flawed film *Gone with the Wind* exemplified and perpetuated the image of them as hybrid feudal estates with picturesque slave quarters and enslaved people working in mills and fields overseen by stern (but benign) masters. This view of plantations was a misconception. These were modern capitalist institutions marked by extreme violence and designed to enable complex and sophisticated chains of production. The most efficient of them tended to be run by masters unconstrained by either morality or outside pressure, as in the eighteenth-century killing fields of the Greater Antilles. Such brutality condemns the complex. Marcus Rediker describes how death stalked the Atlantic slave trade, the mechanism by which labor was provided to fuel the plantations' insatiable desire for labor. Plantations ate up unfortunate individuals enmeshed in the system through forced hard work and poor material conditions. He concludes, chillingly: "Another way to look at the loss of life would be to say that an estimated 14 million people were enslaved to produce a 'yield' of nine million longer-surviving Atlantic workers."[1]

Typically depicted as a tropical organizational form, the plantation functioned as a frontier institution.[2] The driving force of the plantation was not its tropical location but expanding world capitalism. The "plantation"—an English term—originated when the English began exploiting Ireland. It expanded in the eighteenth century to tropical countries as large agricultural enterprises, managed for profit, that produced an export crop for sale in Europe and elsewhere. The hierarchically stratified labor force was usually of African descent. In short, the frontier facilitated the use of cheap land and coerced or enslaved labor and allowed the plantation form to flourish without regard to latitude. It is also a form that tends toward environmental vandalism. The history of plantations in colonial settings has been one of terrible environmental destruction, justifying the German term for plantation as *Raubbau*, or "robber agriculture." As Sidney Mintz observed, "forests, water, animal and plant life and the soil itself were sacrificed repeatedly to garner quick profits." This environmental vandalism was notably true for sugar-producing plantations in the Caribbean. The ecological changes brought by the sugar boom that started in Barbados after 1640 made the Caribbean a deadlier and sicklier place, with sugar plantations providing an ideal habitat for the *Aedes aegypti* mosquito, the primary vector of yellow fever. In the American South, malaria, brought on by the *Anopheles* mosquito, was a major killer. Sugar plantations were great for mosquitoes but hell for humans. Plantations were marked by demographic disaster for Europeans and Africans alike.[3]

Philip Curtin outlines six features that define the mature plantation complex. The most important feature was the labor force, from the middle of the seventeenth century normally African, though in several places and times the plantation relied on European and Native American labor. The populations, except in North America and the United States from the mid-eighteenth century, was not demographically self-sustaining and thus relied on a regular supply of fresh labor through the Atlantic slave trade. Plantations, as noted above, were capitalist enterprises, even if in sixteenth-century Brazil that capitalist orientation was tempered by older understandings of master-slave relations informed by paternalism. Nineteenth-century American plantations similarly adopted an ideology of paternalistic concern for slaves, although that paternalism hardly stopped planters from resorting to the whip and seeking profit. These enterprises produced for distant markets in Europe and thus were dependent on the vagaries of long-distance trade for their success of failure. Finally, plantation societies were colonial societies, with political control resting in European imperial systems. Plantation societies thus did not grow autonomously but were part of empires, these being in Western Europe, notably in Iberia, Britain, France, and the Netherlands.[4]

The use of the word "plantation" to describe what Curtin called the "plantation complex" has become recently a contested term. Peter Wood and Edward Baptist suggest that scholars should think of alternating (Wood) or replacing (Baptist) the word "plantation" with "slave labor camp." They contend that "plantation" is a word redolent in the United States of "magnolia and moonshine" nostalgia, which obscures the harsh treatment meted out to enslaved workers. Baptist and Wood's preferred term "slave labor camps" avoids that historical romanticism. They stress the extent to which plantation profits relied on the exploitation of coerced workers in ways similar, they believe, to the horrific gulags of twentieth-century Soviet Russia and the concentration camps of Nazi Germany.[5]

Their thought-provoking and powerful arguments make clear that New World plantations were sites of violence and misery and that the work enslaved people did was both involuntary and inadequately rewarded. Their argument, however, is anachronistic. Slave labor camps were twentieth-century institutions designed for punishment rather than production. Plantations, by contrast, existed in order to make profits for their owner, rather than principally to punish enslaved people. They were also embedded within the structures of European colonialism, located outside Europe but producing goods mostly for European or North American consumers.

A new special construct of the early modern English Atlantic, the "plantation" originated as a way to describe people on the Celtic frontiers of England. The term, coined in fifteenth-century Scotland to describe efforts to reform the Highlands, was then transferred to Elizabethan Ireland. As exploitation of New World colonies expanded in the seventeenth century, the term was adopted in British America and then in the tropical holdings of other European empires, notably the French and Dutch. As Paul Musselwhite notes, the concept of the "plantation" was rooted in Renaissance humanist ideas about civility as a justification for colonization and was a means of replacing "uncivil" populations like Scottish and Irish Gaels and Native Americans. Colonists at first saw the plantation as a means of justifying the appropriation of Native American land.[6]

By the eighteenth century, plantations were distinctive agricultural places. They were privately owned farms that grew tropical crops for long-distance trade using bound labor. Some of that bound labor in the seventeenth century was European indentured servants; occasionally it involved Native American servants and slaves. By the end of the seventeenth century, in English, Dutch, and French America, bound laborers on plantations were overwhelmingly men and women either born in Africa and sent to the New World in the cruel Atlantic slave trade or their descendants, born into New World slavery.

The plantation is a less stable form of enterprise than is commonly supposed. It is best described as a powerful but unstable form of colonial place—space being vital for how plantations were organized and conceived. The plantation was neither inherently feudal nor decidedly capitalist but was a fusion of both forms, as Marxist historians have always insisted.[7] A liminal colonial space that became increasingly capitalist over time, the plantation took some time to move away from its original communal definition to become a place of private profit-making and coerced labor.

Plantations tended to grow first near the coasts of islands. Jamaica and Saint-Domingue were classic examples of this kind of development, with settlement not going into the mountainous interiors until fifty to eighty years after initial European settlement by the British and French. Slavery was not always the first kind of economic organization developed, with plantations in Barbados, for example, beginning when the dominant element in the labor force was indentured servants. But slavery soon began to dominate, with slaves sourced overwhelmingly from West Africa and brought to America in the horrific conditions of the Middle Passage.

Sustained by pervasive violence, something crucial to the plantation system, plantation societies were divided socially and economically in ways that made them qualitatively different from European or African societies. They tended to be intellectual backwaters, deficient in every respect except for the wealth they produced, wealth that tended to increase for plantations in more southerly locations, especially in the Caribbean. Eventually, European societies came to see their colonial societies in which plantations were prevalent as being not just backward but evil. Many Europeans came to view the treatment of enslaved people as intolerable. But Europeans were at least as concerned about what the horrors of slavery revealed about the cruelty of Europeans to non-Europeans as they were about what enslaved people had to endure.

Plantation crops fueled the expansion of European empires and the growth of European and American economies. In the case of England, the principal seventeenth-century plantation crops—tobacco and sugar—expanded from virtually nothing to becoming household items by the end of the seventeenth century. Tobacco imports into England were valued at just 1,000 pounds in 1616 but were over 1 million pounds by the 1640s. The great Barbadian sugar boom of the 1640s meant that as early as the 1650s, England was importing 5,000 tons of sugar worth £50,000 sterling per annum. As early as the mid-seventeenth century, the tobacco and sugar trades were a major part of England's external commerce. They employed hundreds of ships and thousands of seamen while attracting the interests of the country's richest merchants. By 1686, tobacco and sugar accounted for 76 percent of the value of all imports from the Americas.[8] Both crops, especially sugar, became more important within the European economy in the eighteenth century, with sugar becoming an indispensable part of eating cultures. Annual consumption of sugar in Britain increased twenty-five-fold between 1650 and 1800. By 1800, everyone in Britain and most people in Europe and the Americas had access to sugar at low prices and to tropical goods generally through effective and extensive domestic trading networks.

In the late eighteenth century, cotton came to rival sugar as a preeminent Atlantic plantation crop. That it did so is a little surprising because cotton was far from being a mainly Atlantic commodity. The invention of the cotton gin in 1794 by Eli Whitney allowed the production of cotton to boom to 55 pounds per day from a much lower previous number. Up to that point, cotton had been primarily a product sourced from South Asia. After the adoption of the cotton gin, the staple began to be grown by enslaved people, largely in the US South. It replaced Indian cotton very quickly, a process that was nearly completed by 1810. This reflected a major shift that occurred after the late eighteenth-century British Industrial Revolution when British manufactures, notably in Manchester, began to produce their own cloth in new cotton mills, using American cotton. The United States was ideally suited for producing cotton. It had abundant land in the Deep South that was perfect for cotton cultivation.

Production in the United States surged from virtually nothing before 1794 to world dominance by the 1840s. It jumped from 334,000 bales in 1820 to 2.4 million bales in 1850, with over half of all cotton produced in Alabama, Louisiana, and Mississippi. It fueled an intensive internal slave trade in America, with perhaps 850,000 enslaved people sold to planters in the Lower South from the Upper South. Eventually, the United States created its own cotton industry in New England, starting in the first half of the nineteenth century. Nevertheless, America's major market remained the industrial heartland of Lancashire, England. In 1841, 70 percent of 1,105 cotton mills in Britain were in Lancashire, employing 40,000 workers. The adoption of new and easier to pick and process varieties of cotton allowed for higher yields but also kept the price of raw cotton low. Additional productivity gains also resulted from declining transportation costs and increased speed in getting cotton to Britain.

Sugar enabled Britons to live better than they had done before and satisfied their strong sweet tooth. Cotton did more than this, however. It became essential to the growth of British manufacturing. It enabled this small island to develop an economy several times larger than the needs of its own people required, thus playing a central role in what historians call the Great Divergence—the time from around 1800 where the wealth of Western Europe for the first time exceeded the wealth of China. Giorgio Riello explains that the advantages that the cotton industry provided to Britain "stimulated backward linkages to other parts of the country's manufacturing economy, in particular iron, coal, and the mechanical industry; it facilitated the building of internal infrastructures in shipping and engineering and enabled the development of insurance and financial intermediaries."[9]

Before industrialization, most plantation productivity gains resulted from changes in labor organization, notably the shift from European indentured servants to enslaved African. This transition permitted planters, emboldened by the racism against Africans that pervaded European thinking in the seventeenth century, to ignore the conventions they had brought with them across the Atlantic about overworking and excessively punishing indentured servants. Enslaved people were not allowed rest periods in the middle of the day and had to work more regularly on Saturdays and on traditional English holidays. Moreover, the shift to slavery encouraged planters to overcome their reluctance to assign women to field work. African women were made to work in plantation fields from the mid-seventeenth century in Virginia and Barbados. Planters relied on racist stereotypes of black women being ideally suited to laboring in the heat, as being more similar to animals than to humans, and as important as workers as they were as mothers supposedly giving birth easily and without pain.[10] Planters used these stereotypes to force enslaved women to work in the same jobs, and as hard, as did enslaved men, in ways that made plantation slavery different from agricultural work in either Africa or Europe.

Indeed, one of the distinctive features of plantation slavery in the Americas was that it was exceptionally harsh for enslaved women. In the sugar plantations of the Caribbean and in Brazil, where most Africans arriving in the slave trade were placed after being purchased, almost 90 percent of enslaved women performed arduous field work. Required to perform such labor until ill-health forced them forced them out of the fields, they transitioned to work as nurses or became invalids. By contrast, only about 60 percent of enslaved men were employed as field workers by the second half of the eighteenth century. The only other occupation on the plantation open to enslaved women was domestic servant, and only a few women were ever required for that occupation. By contrast, men were frequently trained to be tradesmen. They looked after animals, performed high-skill tasks such as boiling sugar, and, mainly due to planters' patriarchal prejudices as to how people were deployed, were promoted into supervisory positions such as drivers—the black equivalents of white overseers.

Contrary to planter presumptions, hard field labor for women, especially in the brutal regime of sugar, was devastating for female health and disastrous for female reproductive capacities. The physical demands of sugar cultivation weighed heavily upon women in their twenties, their prime childbearing years when they performed the hardest labor on plantations. Hoeing (digging holes to plant sugar cane) and manuring fields from daylight to dark, they were overworked and underfed. This arduous work regime greatly reduced fertility and increased infant mortality rates. Moreover, planters seldom gave enslaved pregnant women much relief and extended them little help once they had given birth, forcing them to return quickly to heavy labor and hindering them from nursing their children properly.[11]

Abolitionist pressure in the early nineteenth century forced planters in the Caribbean to engage in self-serving ameliorationist practices. They hoped to improve the dire demographic situation of Caribbean slavery, where between 4 to 5 percent of the enslaved population during the period of the African slave trade died each year without being replaced by new births. Without the slave trade, Caribbean enslaved populations would have decreased rapidly. Even with ameliorationist policies designed to lessen the punishment of women by confining whipping only to enslaved males and some assistance to women during pregnancy and early motherhood, enslaved populations everywhere in the Caribbean, with the partial exception of early nineteenth-century Barbados, continued to decline.[12]

Because planters viewed women as workers rather than as mothers, their main concern was to keep women in the field, working on increasing crops rather than becoming mothers of children. They understood that most children would die before adulthood, rendering an enslaved child a burden rather than a potential addition to the workforce. The main exception to this general rule was in the Upper South of the United States from the mid-eighteenth century onward. Because work in tobacco was supplemented by working in mix-grain production, a relatively benign work environment existed there, and this led to considerable population growth within the enslaved population. Selling "excess" enslaved people became an important source of income. Teenagers were particularly valuable commodities, but estate sales to pay off the excessive indebtedness of planters were commonplace. Even prominent planters like Presidents Thomas Jefferson, James Madison, and James Monroe left their heirs with substantial debt who relied on the sale of large parcels to satisfy creditors. Such additional income was crucial as the tobacco industry began to falter in the early nineteenth century and dealt a serious blow to planters in the Upper South. Planters there had an economic incentive to try to improve the conditions under which enslaved women reproduced in ways that did not occur in other slave regimes—their incentive, however, was motivated more by economic necessity than by moral concern for improving slave welfare.

Economic incentives dictated planter actions toward the abolition of the Atlantic slave trade in 1807–1808 in the British Empire and the United States. Planters in Virginia wanted the Atlantic slave trade to be closed, mainly because they believed that if the supply of enslaved people from Africa was reduced, then they would get better prices for their surplus enslaved people in a slave system with strong demographic growth. In South Carolina, where demographic growth among the enslaved was less pronounced, planters were more ambivalent, accepting the closure of the slave trade but importing a record number of slaves in the five years prior to the end of the slave trade. By contrast, planters in the West Indies realized that the end of slave trade, in a slave system unable to maintain a stable population without the addition of fresh laborers from Africa, would be disastrous for plantation profits, and they fought as hard as they could to stop the abolitionist onslaught against them.[13]

Richard Dunn studied the demographic histories of two large enslaved populations on a sugar estate in Jamaica and a mixed-farming large farm in tidewater Virginia in the early nineteenth century. Dunn attributes demographic performance mainly due to the type of work that enslaved people were forced to do. He compares the life histories of two women—Sarah Affir (1767–after 1833) of Mesopotamia, Jamaica, and Winney Grimshaw (1826–after 1866) of Mount Airy, Virginia, both of whom started work young (just seven years of age in the case of Sarah and fourteen for Winney) and spent their lives as enslaved women in arduous and varied kinds of work. Both became lost to the historical record after emancipation in 1834 in Jamaica and 1865 in the American South. Both also gave birth to mixed-race children, presumably in short-term relationships with white overseers, illustrating another aspect of plantation work for enslaved women that men did not have to face.[14]

Sarah, who was also known as Affy, led a life that was filled with overwork, poor living conditions, and subsequent poor health for herself and her truncated family. She spent most of her life as a field hand, performing taxing and hazardous labor. Dunn describes Affy working six days a week, in a slave gang that "did everything in unison and by hand, with no reliance on draft animals or labor-saving tools."[15] Jamaican field hands had to dig holes to plant cane, cut those canes when harvest arrived, and take those canes to boiling houses that operated twenty-four hours a day. There was little variety in what they did, except according to the rhythm of sugar cane growth, and enslaved people worked together, rather than separately. For many Jamaican enslaved people, this arduous agricultural regimen was so intolerable that they ran away. Running away was a major managerial problem for planters, one that they partially overcame by a system of militarized surveillance that turned sugar estates into semi-military enterprises from the middle of the eighteenth century.

Observers often noted that enslaved workers formed "armies," and military metaphors about the regimented nature of sugar production abounded. Most enslaved people ran away only under intense stress, as this action attracted severe punishment. But enslaved workers engaged in multiple kinds of everyday resistance, designed to frustrate planter efforts to maximize productivity. Such everyday resistance included working slowly, deliberately destroying property, and insisting on their "rights" in what enslaved people considered a moral economy where the work they did for planters entitled them to adequate food, housing, and time to themselves. Planters seldom recognized this sense of moral economy, leading to frequent conflict, conflict that intensified after emancipation (from 1834 in the British Empire and from 1848 in the French Empire) as freed workers refused to work exactly as they had done during enslavement. One demand that was common on plantations as enslavement turned to freedom was that women and children need to be given special consideration and that family life had to be considered, not ignored, when working out how people were to be employed.

Winney Grimshaw, by contrast, had a much more varied work life, as she was a craft and domestic worker and only occasionally involved in field work. She also had a larger and more flourishing family, some of whom were mixed-race children. They received advantages in what sort of work they were assigned that was based on their racial position. Winney started work as a domestic at age seventeen in 1843 and was employed as a spinner and weaver of locally produced wool and cotton. Three years later she was transferred, along with her infant son but not with her husband, who as a skilled tradesman was too valuable to be transformed into a field hand, to a property in Alabama that grew cotton. There, she picked cotton until she was freed in 1865, after which time we lose track of her movements.

Winney worked when she lived in Virginia in the early 1840s on a large estate that produced corn and wheat and tended livestock. Enslaved people on the well-managed Mount Airy estate did not work in gangs, or collectively at all, except for two weeks in late June and early July when everyone joined in the grain harvest. Otherwise, they labored at separate jobs, which varied by season and which depended on the skills of the enslaved. Many men were craftsmen, and even when they were assigned to bring in the harvest, they were assigned to the most skilled job, which was cutting grain with a cradle scythe—very hard work and needing great skill to do properly. Enslaved women in the Chesapeake, by contrast, were forced into increasingly burdensome work routines as a result of modernization on Chesapeake plantations that allowed farmers to improve their wheat and corn outputs. Female laborers had to do drudge jobs such as hoeing, weeding, and grubbing while the new skill jobs such as plowing, harrowing, and carting were taken up by enslaved men. And, like everywhere in the plantation world, craft and artisanal work were monopolized by men.

Recent scholarship on antebellum American slavery suggests that one reason for increased plantation productivity in the nineteenth century was increasingly harsh treatment of enslaved people. Edward Baptist and Walter Johnson go so far as to contend that planters perfected techniques of terror and torture that made enslaved people work ever harder to reach increasingly onerous work quotas.[16] Their argument is unconvincing, as all the evidence points to conditions of slavery being especially harsh in the starting period of large-scale plantation slavery in the late seventeenth century. As Ira Berlin put it, "the demand for slaves was greater, the importation of slaves more massive, and degradation of black life swifter and deeper." They lived lives of greater desperation in both Carolina and the Chesapeake after 1700 than before and faced the constant threat of violence more than Anthony Johnson had done. As Berlin continues, "Chesapeake slaves faced the pillory, whipping post, and gallows far more frequently and in far larger numbers than before." Those punishments were both cruel, ingenious, and humiliating as when the Virginian great planter William Byrd forced a bedwetting slave to drink a "pint of piss."[17]

Slavery got no easier psychologically for enslaved people as the frontier conditions of the seventeenth century receded in places like Virginia and South Carolina and as planters developed techniques of controlling enslaved people that involved not so much the application of raw force as the application of methods of domination intended to demean enslaved people and keep them in awe of planter power. But the raw brutality of the plantation system in the period of the Atlantic slave trade, when most enslaved people were Africans rather than Creoles (people born in the Americas), became less obvious over time, especially in settled regions of North America and to an extent on plantations in the Caribbean and in Brazil.

Philip Morgan has described how this process unfolded for eighteenth-century Virginia plantations. Enlightenment beliefs encouraged planters to move from rigid patriarchalism, enforced by vicious punishment, to what Morgan calls an ethos of paternalism. Although planters stressed order and authority as essential to plantation operations, they were more inclined after the mid-eighteenth century than planters of an earlier generation to emphasize their solicitude to enslaved people, a solicitude that sometimes slipped into sentimentality. Paternalistic masters appealed to their enslaved people through calculated assertions of their benevolence rather than threatening them with violence. They came to celebrate enslaved family life and encouraged Christian conversion. The rise of humanitarianism made people aware of the worst excesses of planter cruelty.[18] It did not mean that enslaved people worked less hard, and, in some ways, it was a more all-encompassing form of subordination that imposed massive psychological stresses on enslaved people, with systematic racism taking the place of unvarnished force as a negative part of enslaved people's daily lives. But it did mean that in most places in the nineteenth-century Atlantic world, slavery was ameliorated over time into something less notably violent and more obviously devoted to modern agricultural methods.[19]

That modernization impulse was significant in improving agricultural productivity. As Justin Roberts shows, the adoption of scientific methods of slave management from the late eighteenth century onward put plantations in the New World at the forefront of some, though not all, of the "improving" features of the age. Planters prided themselves on how forward-thinking they were as they devised ever more effective ways of managing slaves, measuring output, and improving production processes. They attempted as much as was possible in very different environmental and labor circumstances to follow in the footsteps of contemporary British agricultural reformers by making plantation management more rational, more systematic, and more scientific.[20]

Roberts argues that the most significant work innovation in the plantation regime was the development of the gang system of labor. This system flourished in the Caribbean from the seventeenth through to the nineteenth century and in Virginia until the start of the nineteenth century, when changing crop patterns away from tobacco and an enslaved population that was Creole rather than African made gang labor less necessary or desirable, and on the antebellum cotton plantations of the lower Mississippi River Valley. It was never prominent in more marginal plantation economies and was seldom practiced in the rice and cotton plantation regimes of the Lower South of America. There enslaved people worked according to the "task system," in which slaves were allocated a daily work quota they had to complete before being released to work on their own account.

Work in the gang system was closely supervised and conducted rhythmically to maximize the ability of enslaved people to work together in unison. It made individual laborers interchangeable, all working at the same pace and doing the same work. Such regimentation made it very hard for older or unhealthy enslaved people, as the system was designed to stop stragglers. The system was flexible enough to change over time and to vary by crop type. According to Roberts, the gang system was a fundamental product of Enlightenment beliefs, and the Enlightenment search for universal rules and processes led to a more efficient form of slavery that would make life better for enslaved people.[21]

The latter belief was laughably misplaced. Enslaved people hated gang labor because of its monotony, lack of individuality, and the tendency of planters to push enslaved people beyond endurance in order to obtain outstanding crops. Plantation management was beset by short-term thinking rather than long-term planning, in which the welfare of laborers came a distant second to extracting as much profit from the soil as quickly as possible. It was also a system characterized by harsh discipline, with the whip used liberally. One of the principal objectives of formerly enslaved persons after emancipation was to eliminate the whip from their work experience.

Workers were divided on large plantations into several gangs. On the vast Parnassus Estate in Jamaica in 1779, eight drivers supervised 147 adult field hands and many other workers (children and the "superannuated") in a workforce of 457 enslaved people. The "great gangs" on sugar estates contained between 50 and 80 slaves, on average, and did hard physical labor, while second gangs with less healthy and with older slaves did weeding and transporting trash. Children worked from about the ages of seven on Caribbean plantations, gathering grass for livestock. The one constant was the length of time worked—from sunup to sundown, six days a week. Roberts notes that this form of labor organization resembled in many ways labor in the early stages of factory production in the British Industrial Revolution. Both planters and factory owners, for example, used clock time to regulate and track their laborers' work. And enslaved people in good harvest years worked almost as many hours as did early factory workers. As in factories, work was divided into many small tasks, which facilitated greater repetition of movement, specialization, and synchronization of labor tasks. Even more significant, productivity increases in both areas of work "were caused in large part by increasing labor discipline and the rising number of hours of labor."[22]

An examination of the extensive records kept by some planters reveals the scientific nature of plantation management. They had, Caitlin Rosenthal observes, an obsession with collecting data, seeking to determine how much labor enslaved people could perform in a given amount of time and pushing them to achieve that maximum. In short, "the soft power of quantification supplemented the driving force of the whip." The point of the accounting practices employed on plantations was like how enslaved people were supervised—planters sought control, so they could manage with great precision, transport people to distant plots of land, and manipulate labor processes in minute ways. As Rosenthal concludes, "slavery became a laboratory for the development of accounting because the control drawn on paper matched the reality of the plantation more closely than that of almost any other early American business enterprise."[23] Planters' obsession with data has provided historians with masses of evidence about how planters monitored time and motion of their enslaved laborers so as to maximize production.

Alan Olmstead and Paul Rhode, for example, surveyed 602,219 individual daily cotton-picking records in antebellum America, which enabled precise summaries of productivity within the cotton industry.[24]

Other productivity gains on plantations came early in the development of the plantation system in what Russell Menard terms the birth of the large integrated plantation as a characteristic New World form of agricultural organization.[25] That form of plantation organization was one that emerged in mid-seventeenth Barbados. It replaced a system that existed in Brazil in the sixteenth century where small farmers grew cane that they took to the owners of large sugar mills who processed that cane. What Barbadians did, and which was revolutionary, was to combine all parts of the growing and processing of sugar cane into one operation. It led to the classic eighteenth- and nineteenth-century plantation that both tended toward self-sufficiency and in which there was a high degree of integration of all aspects of the plantation process prior to sending tropical raw products to Europe to be manufactured. These classic plantations tended to have large labor forces, especially on Caribbean, Brazilian, and Louisiana sugar plantations, with a median number of around 200 enslaved persons being common. Tobacco plantations in the Chesapeake were much smaller, with only a third of enslaved laborers being in workforces of over twenty people. The rice plantations of South Carolina had labor forces that were larger than those on tobacco plantations but smaller than those on sugar plantations, with over 50 percent of rice plantations in the eighteenth-century Lowcountry having more than fifty enslaved workers.[26]

The size of workforces brought economies of scale that allowed for substantial efficiencies in production, such as refining sugar in boiling houses on plantations. Over time, planters refined this process of making sugar so that additional refining could use molasses that could also be transformed into rum—a product that became an essential part of the North American diet in the eighteenth century in the form of rum punch. Tobacco planters similarly adapted new techniques of cultivation, which meant that mean crops per hand rose from 900 pounds in the 1640s to nearly 1,900 pounds by the 1690s. Over the seventeenth century, farmers and planters along the Tobacco Coast of the Chesapeake developed ways of farming that blended European, Native American, and African practices along with new methods that were developed from a Chesapeake form of husbandry that was learning-by-doing.[27]

The excellent records of the Virginian planter, Daniel Parke Custis, whose widow Martha married George Washington, provides insight into the functioning of a large planter in tidewater Virginia with over 17,000 acres and 283 enslaved laborers. His main crop was tobacco, with field hands making about 800 pounds of high-quality tobacco per annum. Custis paid great attention to making sure this tobacco met very high standards, spending lots of time on seed selection, on how tobacco was packed for shipping, and to continuous improvement in tobacco based on criticisms made by his British factors. He also raised corn and wheat for local and Caribbean markets as well as many oats. Annual output per laborer was 13 barrels of corn and 9 bushels of wheat, excluding seeds. He produced this crop, worth in the late 1750s £4,581 per annum, without the use of plow but using hoes, and increasing production by making slaves work longer hours.

Custis was also keen on cultivating livestock, owning nearly 1,000 cattle, 117 sheep, and more than 600 pigs. Lorena Walsh estimates that the sale of surplus meat, butter, wool, and breeding stock accounted for 11 percent of his income. He began to use new methods of British husbandry, but as in many plantation areas where labor was relatively cheap compared to Britain, he was slow to use technology to replace human labor. He managed his plantations through nine overseers but was himself an active manager. His death proved unfortunate for his plantation: his heirs did not pay the attention Custis did to ensuring his tobacco was of the highest standard, and without Custis's substantial inherited assets, great planting skill, and unusual fiscal discipline, George Washington, who gained eighty-five slaves from his marriage to Custis's widow, had to put all his profits into developing his farms and get money from plantation profits alone rather than the profits from moneylending that Custis had enjoyed. Custis's death was even more disastrous for his enslaved laborers, who were divided among Custis's heirs, with many having to move far away from their tidewater homes.[28]

Recent work on plantations has moved away from planter actions to thinking about how enslaved people experienced work on plantations. Neil Oatsvall and Vaughn Scribner suggest that we should think of work on plantations as a form of energy transfer and thus see the plantation system as a series of interconnected energy flows rather than merely being a collection of shared human experiences, important though cataloguing such experiences might be as a means of understanding the pressures of working in plantation settings. Using Caribbean sugar plantations as an example, they suggest that sugar cane "worked" just as did humans. They note that the energy transfers required to produce a commodity such as rum included making sugar cane grow; providing human labor to plant, tend, harvest, and process the sugar cane; and, finally, doing microbial work for the yeast to take sugar and ferment it into alcohol. The environment, in this reading, was central to making plantation products and the energy of enslaved people, acting against them at every turn through heat, disease, and even gravity.[29]

The plantation environment was challenging for enslaved people. But it was the owners of enslaved people who were their principal enemies. They made their workers' lives miserable. A study of living standards for the enslaved in Jamaica around 1774 shows both massive income inequality, with planters among the richest people in the world and enslaved people among the poorest, and extreme poverty for the 90 percent of the population who were enslaved. Slaves were kept, deliberately, at below subsistence level and were forced to grow their own food in addition to being worked excessively hard. One sign of their impoverishment can be seen in data on heights, one of the clearest indications for premodern populations about nutritional sufficiency. Enslaved Jamaican Creoles were much shorter and lived shorter lives than either agricultural or industrial workers elsewhere in the Americas or in Western Europe. Jamaica, like other eighteenth-century American plantation societies, was a source of great wealth that made its most privileged inhabitants rich and was financially beneficial to the imperial state. But that wealth went only to the fortunate few who owned plantations. Their wealth was based on the systematic exploitation and under-compensation of their laborers for the work that they did—this under-compensation forming the rationale for contemporary claims for reparative justice. If the farms in the northern colonies of British North America could be celebrated by polemicists such as Benjamin Franklin as "the best poor man's place," the most fully developed plantation societies of the Atlantic world—the plantation societies of Saint-Domingue, Jamaica, and Cuba in the Greater Antilles in the second half of the eighteenth century and the first half of the nineteenth century—were hell on earth.[30]

That hell was an experience that most enslaved people were forced to endure, especially before the birth of abolitionism in the latter half of the eighteenth century, when planter power was almost complete and was fully supported by all the authority of imperial and colonial states. The risks of resistance were very real—when revolts failed, as they inevitably did, rebellious slaves were treated as traitors and were subject to all the harsh punishment that European empires and American republics could devise for treachery. The horrors of enslavement, however, were such that some brave or desperate enslaved men (slave rebellion was heavily masculine) risked resistance against planters and escaped the plantations and created semi- or fully autonomous runaway communities that in places like Jamaica, Brazil, and the Guianas became maroon societies that formed states-within-states in plantation societies. And on occasion, large-scale slave revolts broke out, as in 1760 in Jamaica, 1763 in Berbice, and most famously in Saint-Domingue in 1791. The last of these ended in the creation of the first black republic in the Americas and the destruction of the most profitable plantation economy that ever existed. Even when slave revolts were not successful, as in Demerara in 1823 and in Jamaica in 1831–1832, they often galvanized support from abolitionists in Europe and the Americas, showing that planter statements that enslaved people liked working on plantations were lies.[31]

The plantation as a modern form of economic organization brought many benefits to the world. The commodities produced on plantations, including sugar, coffee, cotton, and tobacco, were highly desirable to consumers all over the world and made people happier. But these benefits came at great cost: the environmental destruction of vast areas; the immiseration of the workers who produced such products; and lasting division between the owners of plantations and their workers in ways that accentuated global inequality and heightened racial tensions. Despite its modernity, the plantation was not a positive innovation in world history. It remained, however, a remarkably persistent phenomenon.

Notes

1. Marcus Rediker, *The Slave Ship: A Human History* (London: Penguin Books, 2007), 218–220.
2. Edgar Tristram Thompson, *The Plantation*, rev. ed. (Columbia: University of South Carolina Press, 2010).
3. Todd Savitt, *Medicine and Slavery: The Diseases and Health Care of Blacks in Antebellum South* (Urbana: University of Illinois Press, 1981): 7–25; Sidney Mintz, *Three Ancient Colonies: Caribbean Themes and Variations* (Cambridge, MA: Harvard University Press, 2010).

4. Philip D. Curtin, *The Rise and Fall of the Plantation Complex: Essays in Atlantic History* (New York: Cambridge University Press, 1990).
5. Peter H. Wood, "Slave Labor Camps in Early America: Overcoming Denial and Discovering the Gulag," in *Inequality in Early America*, ed. Carla Gardina Pestana (Hanover, NH: Dartmouth College Press, 1999): 230–231; Edward E. Baptist, *The Half Has Never Been Told: Slavery and the Making of American Capitalism* (New York: Basic Books, 2014).
6. Paul Musselwhite, "Private Plantation: The Political Economy of Land in Early Virginia," in *Virginia 1619: Slavery and Freedom in the Making of English America*, ed. Musselwhite, Peter C. Mancall, and James Horn (Chapel Hill: University of North Carolina, 2019): 150–172.
7. Robin Blackburn, *The Making of New World Slavery: From the Baroque to the Modern, 1492–1800* (London: Verso, 2010).
8. Nuala Zahedieh, "Overseas Expansion and Trade in the Seventeenth Century," in *The Oxford History of the British Empire: Origins of Empire*, ed. Nicholas Canny (Oxford: Oxford University Press, 2001): 410.
9. Giorgio Riello, *Cotton: The Fabric That Made the Modern World* (Cambridge: Cambridge University Press, 2013): 271–72.
10. Lorena S. Walsh, "Slave Life, Slave Society, and Tobacco Production in the Tidewater Chesapeake, 1620–1820," in *Cultivation and Culture: Labor and the Shaping of Slave Life in the Americas*, ed. Ira Berlin and Philip D. Morgan (Charlottesville: University of Virginia, 1993): 170–203; Jennifer Morgan, "Gender and family Life," in *The Routledge History of Slavery*, ed. Gad Heuman and Trevor Burnard (London: Routledge, 2010): 138–152.
11. Kenneth Morgan, "Slave Women and Reproduction in Jamaica, c. 1776–1834," *History* 91 (2006): 231–253.
12. Sasha Turner, *Contested Bodies: Pregnancy, Childrearing, and Slavery in Jamaica* (Philadelphia: University of Pennsylvania Press, 2017).
13. Edward B. Rugemer, *Slave Law and the Politics of Resistance in the Early Atlantic World* (Cambridge, MA: Harvard University Press, 2018), ch. 6.
14. Richard S. Dunn, *A Tale of Two Plantations: Slave Labor in Jamaica and Virginia* (Cambridge, MA: Harvard University Press, 2014): 74–130.
15. Ibid., 81–82.
16. Baptist, *The Half Has Never Been Told*; Walter Johnson, *River of Dark Dreams: Slavery and Empire in the Cotton Kingdom* (Cambridge, MA: Harvard University Press, 2013)
17. Ira Berlin, *Many Thousands Gone: The First Two Centuries of Slavery in North America* (Cambridge, MA: Harvard University Press, 1998).
18. Philip D. Morgan, *Slave Counterpoint: Black Culture in the Eighteenth-Century Chesapeake & Lowcountry* (Chapel Hill: University of North Carolina Press, 1998), 288.
19. Ibid, 280–308.
20. Justin Roberts, *Slavery and the Enlightenment in the British Atlantic, 1750–1807* (Cambridge: Cambridge University Press, 2013).
21. Ibid., 132.
22. ibid., 288.
23. Caitlin Rosenthal, *Accounting for Slavery: Masters and Management* (Cambridge, MA: Harvard University Press, 2018).
24. Alan L. Olmstead and Paul W. Rhode, "Biological Innovation and Productivity Growth in the Antebellum Cotton Economy," *Journal of Economic History* 68 (2008): 1123–1171.
25. Russell R. Menard, *Sweet Negotiations: Sugar, Slavery, and Plantation Agriculture in Early Barbados* (Charlottesville: University of Virginia Press, 2006).

26. Morgan, *Slave Counterpoint*, 40–41.
27. Russell R. Menard, "Plantation Empire: How Sugar and Tobacco Planters Built Their Industries and Raised an Empire," *Agricultural History* 81 (2007): 320.
28. Lorena Walsh, *Motives of Honor, Pleasure, and Profit: Plantation Management in the Colonial Chesapeake, 1607–1763* (Chapel Hill: University of North Carolina Press, 2010): 448.
29. Neil Oatsvall and Vaughn Scribner, "'The Devil Was in the Englishman that He Makes Everything Work': Implementing the Concept of 'Work' to Reevaluate Sugar Production and Consumption in the Early Modern British World," *Agricultural History* 92 (2018): 464, 467.
30. Trevor Burnard and John Garrigus, *The Plantation Machine: Atlantic Capitalism in French Saint Domingue and British Jamaica* (Philadelphia: University of Pennsylvania Press, 2016); Laura Panza Burnard and Jeffrey Williamson, "Living Costs, Real Incomes and Inequality in Colonial Jamaica," *Explorations in Economic History* 71 (2019): 55–71.
31. Rugemer, *Slave Law and the Politics of Resistance*; Stephanie M. H. Camp, *Closer to Freedom: Enslaved Women and Everyday Resistance in the Plantation South* (Chapel Hill: University of North Carolina Press, 2004).

Bibliography

Burnard, Trevor, and John Garrigus. *The Plantation Machine: Atlantic Capitalism in French Saint Domingue and British Jamaica*. Philadelphia: University of Pennsylvania Press, 2016.
Camp, Stephanie M. H. *Closer to Freedom: Enslaved Women and Everyday Resistance in the Plantation South*. Chapel Hill: University of North Carolina Press, 2004.
Curtin, Philip D. *The Rise and Fall of the Plantation Complex: Essays in Atlantic History*. New York: Cambridge University Press, 1990.
Dunn, Richard S. *A Tale of Two Plantations: Slave Labor in Jamaica and Virginia*. Cambridge, MA: Harvard University Press, 2014.
Edelson, S. Max. *Plantation Enterprise in Colonial South Carolina*. Cambridge, MA: Harvard University Press, 2006.
Higman, B. W. *Plantation Jamaica 1750–1850: Capital and Control in a Colonial Economy*. Kingston, Jamaica: University of the West Indies Press, 2005.
James, C. L. R. *The Black Jacobins: Toussaint L'Ouverture and the San Domingo Revolution*. 2nd ed. New York: Vintage, 1963.
Menard, Russell R. *Sweet Negotiations: Sugar, Slavery, and Plantation Agriculture in Early Barbados*. Charlottesville: University of Virginia Press, 2006.
Mintz, Sidney. *Three Ancient Colonies: Caribbean Themes and Variations*. Cambridge, MA: Harvard University Press, 2010.
Morgan, Philip D. *Slave Counterpoint: Black Culture in the Eighteenth-Century Chesapeake & Lowcountry*. Chapel Hill: University of North Carolina Press, 1998.
Musselwhite, Paul. "Private Plantation: The Political Economy of Land in Early Virginia." In *Virginia 1619: Slavery and Freedom in the Making of English America*, ed. Musselwhite, Peter C. Mancall, and James Horn, 150–72. Chapel Hill: University of North Carolina, 2019.
Rediker, Marcus. *The Slave Ship: A Human History*. London: Penguin Books, 2007.

Riello, Giorgio. *Cotton: The Fabric That Made the Modern World.* Cambridge: Cambridge University Press, 2013.
Roberts, Justin. *Slavery and the Enlightenment in the British Atlantic, 1750–1807.* Cambridge: Cambridge University Press, 2013.
Rosenthal, Caitlin. *Accounting for Slavery: Masters and Management.* Cambridge, MA: Harvard University Press, 2018.
Walsh, Lorena. *Motives of Honor, Pleasure, and Profit: Plantation Management in the Colonial Chesapeake, 1607–1763.* Chapel Hill: University of North Carolina Press, 2010.

CHAPTER 29

AGRICULTURE, THE ATLANTIC PLANTATION, AND THE ENVIRONMENT IN THE US SOUTH

JEANNIE WHAYNE

THE Atlantic plantation complex was the vehicle through which British mercantilism matured and global capitalism emerged. Tobacco was the original crop that bound the fate of colonists to Britain, but cotton supplanted it in the early nineteenth century and thus elongated a British role in the Southern economy. Regardless of crop grown, the plantation developed into an exploitative institution that captured control of land, labor, and natural resources. It adapted to changing circumstances and survived into the twenty-first century. Regardless of time or place, the plantation led to environmental degradation and retarded economic development beyond that which supported the production of commercial crops for an international market. Planters, through their influence with governmental authorities at all levels, leveraged resources for the sole purpose of securing profits. Although free market ideology and common sense would suggest that planters would conserve their most precious resource—the landscape—they failed to do so. They intensively cultivated crops that robbed the soil of nutrients, moved into forested areas when their farmland was made worthless by overproduction, and wantonly destroyed natural habitats.

At its creation, the plantation complex included expenditure of capital from investors in England, the production of commercial crops in the colonies of Virginia and the Caribbean, and the use of unfree labor. An inhospitable natural environment proved to be one of their greatest early challenges. Whether settling the island of Jamaica or the lowland swamps in the Chesapeake region, they suffered illness and death, largely because of waterborne diseases like dysentery and typhoid and mosquito borne diseases like malaria and yellow fever. On the other hand, in introducing commercial agricultural practices, the British played havoc with the forested wetlands. In Virginia, for example, they felled trees, cleared land, and proceeded to wear out the soil growing tobacco. Once the British took formal possession of Jamaica in 1870, they promoted the cultivation of sugar cane, which not only had deleterious effect on the soil but required even greater deforestation as fuel for the sugar mills as well as expansion.

Even as British settlers in the Americas began their careless farming practices, an agricultural revolution was underway in Britain. At the beginning of the seventeenth century, British farmers began developing techniques to preserve their agricultural land and feed a growing population crowding into London and other cities. Among the many improvements that occurred over the next two centuries was the adoption of the four-field system. By rotating from cereals and grasses to legumes, British farmers accomplished two very important objectives. They allowed soil that had been robbed of nutrients because of the cultivation of cereals and certain grasses to be restored by the nutrient-fixing qualities of legumes. And, by moving from one crop to another annually, they were lessening the problem of pests. Continuous growth of any crop is an open invitation to pathogens or predators that are attracted to specific plants. British farmers understood that failure to control pests reduced yields and could lead to economic calamity. British farmers also began to employ the use of guano from the Americas to fertilize their fields. Guano restores nitrogen to exhausted soils and otherwise fixes nitrogen in soils that are heavily farmed. The output of British farmers increased as these and other improvements were made, but there was a limit to what that relatively small island could produce. In the Chesapeake, Britain secured additional acreage in the form of ghost acres to which it could expand by proxy. By requiring their colonists in the Americas to market their crops through Britain, they expanded the home country's agricultural production.[1]

Plantations versus Small Farming: The Environment

It was through the adoption of the plantation model of development that planters in the colonies were able to achieve so much production, but only at a high price. In all places where the plantation came to dominate, it proved to be detrimental to the environment and inhibited other economic activities. Because planters captured control of the most fertile land nearest rivers that could transport their crops to market, they rarely supported infrastructure improvements beyond what was required to ship their crops to market. Planters also enjoyed a beneficial relationship with the government and were able to influence officials to enact policies and practices that served their interests. The pursuit of profits was augmented by harsh labor regimes marked by slavery or some other form of unfreedom, and government officials and law enforcement could be counted upon to maintain planter control over labor. Driven by the pursuit of profits and often buffeted by rising and falling agricultural prices, they failed to practice careful agricultural stewardship.[2] By the late eighteenth century, farmers like Thomas Jefferson and George Washington became attuned to the advances in agriculture made in England and adopted the use of guano. A small literature on the topic of agricultural stewardship appeared, but even the greatest defender of early nineteenth-century planters admitted that when prices were high, most planters threw caution to the wind.[3]

Planters were hardly the only agriculturalists, and the role played by small farmers in doing damage to Southern soils warrants scrutiny. The presence the planters drove the price of land so high that small farmers usually settled outside of areas dominated by the plantation. They practiced a safety-first strategy in their farming enterprises, meaning they produced what was essential for their survival and bartered with their neighbors for what they themselves did not produce. They did grow crops for the market—usually a local or regional one—in order to pay their taxes, purchase new land, or hire labor, but they were rarely engaged in commercial agriculture. Small farmers might sell their own labor, in fact, to planters or large farmers in their community. The conventional wisdom suggests that, operating on the margins and closely connected to the land they worked, small farmers more carefully husbanded their soil, but there is some reason to doubt the universality of this truism. Among the agriculturalists who laid waste to the Georgia Piedmont were many small farmers. Within a few decades of cultivation, the Piedmont region was heavily eroded and, as Paul Sutter suggests, some of it was made over into gullies. Those who would argue that small farmers lived lightly on the soil must also reckon with the migration patterns of such farmers from the East to the western reaches of the South from the seventeenth through the nineteenth centuries. Just as planters wore out their soils and moved on, so too did small farmers. To be fair to them, however, small farmers typically occupied the least fertile and thinner soils, as planters cornered the market for the richer land. The most fertile and desirable lands were given over to plantation agriculture; thus planters did the greatest damage to the best land the South had to offer.[4]

Tobacco and the Plantation

The verdant land in the Chesapeake and a growing market for tobacco constituted the perfect circumstances within which to extend Britain's agricultural output in the seventeenth century. Because the growers were required to send their crops to Britain for resale, the British government, business interests, and shippers benefited from tobacco sales. Thus, Britain became an exporter of a highly sought-after commodity and could command favorable trading exchanges in Europe and elsewhere.[5] However, the British first had to establish a foothold in North America, and that began in 1607 when a small group of settlers landed at the southern edge of what has since been known as the Chesapeake Bay. They established the settlement of Jamestown on a peninsula to the north because it afforded protection from Spanish attacks and because it had waters deep enough to provide easy access for British shipping.[6]

The landscape encountered by the Jamestown settlers was at once both forbidding and promising. It was heavily forested, and to the British seemed undeveloped and thus open for exploitation. A long coastal plain stretched southward from Chesapeake Bay; much of it was naturally well drained, but some of it was given over to swamps, including the nearly impenetrable Great Dismal Swamp. As British settlement increased and planters moved inland, they encountered the Piedmont region where clay soils existed, some of them thinner and more subject to erosion. The earliest tobacco planters preferred the well-drained sandy soils along the Chesapeake, but as the population expanded, they pushed deeper into Native American lands.[7]

Native Americans along the Chesapeake had long cultivated small fields growing corn, beans, and squash, a combination that had the advantage of providing a complete protein. But this grouping also had other benefits. Growing beans, a legume, restored nitrogen to the soil and thus balanced out the nitrogen-robbing qualities of corn. Native Americans supplemented their diets by hunting, fishing, and the gathering of wild plants. There was considerable diversity among the various Native American groups, with some of them relying more heavily on agriculture because the specific area they occupied was more suitable to it than others. Most of them grew small amounts of tobacco for consumption but understood its negative effects on the soil and allowed fields overworn by its production to lay fallow periodically. Thus, their interaction with the landscape impacted the environment, but in a more limited way. Human agency introduces a new element that influences and, in some cases, accelerates these alterations. Native American agriculture constituted a relatively light interaction with the environment that resulted in small, if steady, ecological changes. The arrival of the British marked an end to the mildly intrusive practices of Native Americans.[8]

The British initially adopted some aspects of Native American agricultural practices as they adapted to conditions in the Chesapeake. They used the Native American practice of the long fallow, a process by which exhausted acreage is taken out of production and allowed to remain fallow for eight to twenty years. Had they failed to do so, the consequences would have been dire. Southern soils and climate conditions were unlike anything the British were accustomed to. Thin soils together with a wet, hot climate caused organic matter to deteriorate rapidly, making it necessary to take steps to replenish fertility. These conditions also made land far more vulnerable to erosion. The use of the long fallow was a good solution, but taking a large number of acres out of production periodically had the effect of making expansion of British plantation operations into new lands absolutely necessary. To reap the profits to be had from the tobacco market, planters expanded continually, thus subjecting even greater acreage to intensive agriculture. In the process, the British pushed Native Americans farther and farther away, seized their land, and engaged in massive deforestation.[9]

In order to pursue commercial agriculture, planters cleared forests and in the process destroyed the abundant wildlife habitats that existed there. Dependent upon the forest floor for life-sustaining nourishment in forests, animals hunted by the Native Americans ranged further away and increasingly out of reach. The impact was greater than might be imagined. Native Americans depended upon more than just the protein to be had from animals. They used every part of the animals – meat, bones, fur, teeth— to provide clothing, tools, fat, and more. Any Native Americans able to remain in the region would have had to adapt to a vastly different ecosystem, one that was far less amenable to their traditional lifeways.[10]

The destruction of forests also had ecological implications for those engaged in intensive agricultural production. Although the colonists' use of the long fallow allowed land to restore its nutrient content naturally, the abundant rainfall typical of the Southern climate played a role in causing erosion. Coming at the wrong time, rain could interrupt planting or harvesting, but if too much rain landed on fallow land that was not properly maintained with restorative cover crops, the result could be disastrous. The problem was particularly acute on hillsides, but even flatlands could suffer if planters were careless.[11]

The colony first established by the British in Virginia was only the opening wedge of exploitation of the environment in the southern reaches of North America. By the end of the seventeenth century, British planters had also extended tobacco production into Maryland and North Carolina and carved out rice plantations in the coastal areas of the Carolinas and Georgia. Louisiana, while still a French colony, launched sugar plantation agriculture that competed somewhat favorably with that of the British, French, Portuguese, and Spanish producers of that product in the Caribbean and Brazil. Once the cotton crop began to supply the British textile industry in the early nineteenth century, the demand for cotton soon outpaced that of any other crop. Although the South was no longer a creature of the British commonwealth after the American Revolution, planters there began to deliver cotton to the British textile industry. In providing the raw materials, they played an important role in facilitating a new industrial revolution in Britain and the establishment of global capitalism. All the while, the Southern agricultural landscape paid the price through fertility reduction and soil erosion.[12]

Plantation Labor

A crucial feature of the establishment of a successful plantation system in the Southern colonies was securing and maintaining an abundant and cheap supply of labor. The plantation could not have functioned without labor to work the soil and cut the forests. Colonists first attempted to use Native Americans, but the tribes were too dispersed and far too disinclined to subject themselves to such a labor regime. They could escape to the hinterlands, rejoin their own or another Native American group, and become a threat to plantation operations. British indentured servitude seemed a logical alternative labor force, and it had the added advantage of drawing upon the excess—and largely impoverished—population in Britain. Planters convinced British citizens to sell themselves into servitude for five to seven years in return for the promise of earning acreage upon completing their contract. Characterized as an opportunity for enterprising British subjects, it was initially well received.[13]

Once indentured servants arrived, however, they confronted a disease environment to which they had little or no immunity. As tillers of the soil and agents of deforestation, they would visit disaster on the ecosystem, but an invisible enemy in the form of bacteria exacted its revenge. The brackish water in the Chesapeake led to serious outbreaks of dysentery and typhoid, which decimated their ranks, and to make matters worse, planters were ruthless in imposing a grueling work regime. They had purchased the services of these indentured servants and treated them like slaves. Ceaseless labor combined with the disease environment led to a mortality rate of roughly 50 percent of indentured servants, and those who survived were often at least partially disabled. When word of poor treatment and disease filtered back to England, the supply began to decline. Because of protests and appeals, the General Assembly in Virginia enacted laws to prevent harsh treatment and provide sufficient food, stirring fears among planters that the need to do so would further diminish the flow of labor from England.[14]

African people had been in the colony since 1619, but their numbers grew slowly until British merchants became dominant in the slave trade. Once that occurred, Africans became more affordable, and their numbers increased from roughly 300 in Virginia and Maryland in 1650 to over 300,000 in Virginia alone by 1790. For Virginia planters desperate for a cheap source of labor, they were the perfect choice. Africans had the advantage of being enslaved for life and because of natural increase, enslaved people in the Southern colonies made themselves into a self-replicating labor force. When the intermarriage of some enslaved Africans with indentured servants or with Native Americans led to confusion over the status of children born of these unions, Virginia passed a statute in 1662 establishing that the children born of enslaved mothers would themselves be enslaved and were the property of the planter for whom the mother labored. This constituted an approach to ownership that had seldom been seen in global history. The planter grip on the lives of African enslaved people had tightened.[15]

Africans also possessed another trait that served the interests of the planters. They had a genetic anomaly—the sickle cell trait scientists would later discover—which gave them apparent resistance to malaria and yellow fever. Malaria is caused by a parasite transmitted by the *Anopheles* mosquito, while the yellow fever virus is carried by the *Aedes aegypti* mosquito. An abundant supply of both varieties of mosquitoes already existed in the swamps of Virginia. All it took was for one sailor or enslaved person from Africa to land in Virginia carrying either the parasite or the virus for the diseases to become problematic there. The African resistance to malaria and yellow fever was observed by planters, and they soon opined that this made them the preferable labor force in a harsh environment. In fact, it served as a further justification for the pernicious institution.

Africans brought something of far greater importance to the agricultural enterprise in the colonies than their resistance to disease, however. They had experience with girding and burning trees, an efficient means of forest removal, and they knew how to process lumber for use. They had herded livestock in Africa, and their ability to maintain cattle during the early settlement period proved invaluable and eventually ended the colonies' dependence on cattle imports from the Caribbean. Of greatest importance were their agricultural skills. By the time that British turned away from indentured servants and began importing greater numbers of Africans, tobacco had been introduced to Africa. Thus, at least by 1650, Africans were growing tobacco, and many were already familiar with its cultivation by the time they arrived in the Chesapeake. Had it not been for the skills that Africans brought to the British colonies, tobacco planters would not have achieved early prosperity.[16]

Rice Plantations

As British settlers moved into the coastal areas of Carolinas and Georgia, they discovered that the clay subsoil there was well suited wet for rice agriculture, but British citizens had little to no knowledge of rice cultivation. Africans, on the other hand, had been cultivating rice for at least three thousand years. The variety introduced to the British colonies in the seventeenth century, *O. sativa*, had been cultivated in coastal West Africa for a few centuries at the time the slave trade began. Thus, many of the African enslaved people came to the colonies with knowledge of cultivating rice in swampy conditions like those that existed in the Carolinas and Georgia. Three types of rice cultivation arose there, depending on specific conditions: dryland culture, irrigated upland rice culture, and hydraulic, tidal rice culture (typically referred to as wet-rice agriculture).[17]

The adoption of wet-rice agriculture in coastal Carolina and Georgia did not necessarily result in extensive loss of fertility, but significant landscape revision occurred. The construction of canals and deforestation destroyed habitats that had maintained a rough equilibrium of plants, animals, and microbes. The successful production of rice depended upon the quality of the water and the length of time it stood upon the crop. Flooding rice fields with polluted water could be disastrous, but even good water standing too long on the fields could block the absorption of oxygen and negatively affect the soil's productive capacity. However, carefully timed flooding of rice fields had the advantage of reducing pests and thus eliminated one important impediment to producing high yields.[18]

The activities of upstream farmers and planters in the Georgia Piedmont demonstrate how chance developments could bring both good and ill to rice planters along the coast. As Mart Stewart demonstrates in a pathbreaking 1996 book, in the late eighteenth century when upstream settlers in Georgia cut back vegetation next to rivers, they caused erosion of their own topsoil and inadvertently benefited the lowland rice planters. The root system of trees keeps soil in place and absorbs rainwater. When heavy rains came—as they inevitably did in the Southern climate—the Georgia upcountry's topsoil flowed downriver to the rice plantations, flooding rice fields with water that was rich in topsoil and silt.[19] As settlement in the upcountry increased and farmers there removed even more trees and other vegetation along the rivers, eroding banks sent rivers of red clay mud to the Georgia coastal plantations. As they had cleared fields, they removed trees whose root systems held the soil in place and absorbed rainwater. The red clay mud inundated canals and rice fields and wreaked havoc on rice production.[20] When river levels were low in coastal Georgia, however, a different kind of problem emerged. In times of drought, salt water would reach further upriver from the ocean and increase the salinity of the river water planters used to flood their fields.[21] Enslaved workers were called upon to dig new canals to bring fresh water to the fields. These time-consuming efforts were a necessary but costly distraction from producing the crop. In the final analysis, abundant labor was essential.[22]

The problems associated with growing rice and maintaining the labor necessary to both cultivate the crop and perform remedial tasks when necessary did not undermine the success of the rice plantation enterprise. It was relatively efficient and made planters wealthy. The need for a clay subsoil to hold the water, however, limited rice's expansion into the interior. On the other hand, tobacco could be produced in many different soil types, but tobacco prices were notoriously unstable. For the plantation system to expand into the interior, planters needed a marketable crop that grew well there.

COTTON AND THE ENVIRONMENT

Cotton would prove to be the crop of planters' dreams. It also served to tie the fate of Southern planters to the British economy long after the revolution freed the colonies—the United States—of British mercantile demands. Long-staple cotton had been grown on the coast, but for a small market and was unsuitable for soils in the interior. It was a delicate plant producing a fine fiber that was typically made into expensive cloth. With the emergence of the British textile industry in the late eighteenth century, however, demand grew for a courser fiber suitable for the cheaper cloth required by the British textile mills. Short-staple cotton suited the requirements of the textile industry in producing inexpensive products, and it answered the planters' need for a studier plant that grew well in the interior. A hybrid variety of cotton, *Gossypium bardadense* (Petit Gulf cotton), noted for its hardiness, became the dominant strain grown, particularly in the frontier South along the Mississippi River valley. The only impediment to short-staple cotton's mass production was the difficulty of pulling the seeds from the harvested cotton. Following the 1791 invention and use of the cotton gin, a device that could much more efficiently remove seeds, westward expansion increased substantially. The only thing standing in the way was Native Americans. Federal policies emerging in the early nineteenth century and accelerating in the late 1820s and 1830s eliminated that obstacle. Planters proved to be remarkably mobile and moved ever westward in search of land to replace that which had been exhausted by intensive cultivation.

Cotton, like tobacco, robbed the soil of nitrogen, but the economic incentive to produce for the expanding market was too great to encourage caution. The familiar pattern of soil exhaustion, the need for new lands to exploit, and deforestation repeated itself. However, when cotton planters moved into the Mississippi River valley in the early nineteenth century, they faced an environmental issue that was not entirely of their own making. Although the deep and fertile soil in the valley rendered the issue of soil exhaustion far less acute, the river too often delivered an unwelcome gift: floods that overwhelmed meager levees and inundated newly cultivated fields. The increasingly devastating floods were the result of the forest-clearing activities of farmers along the Upper Mississippi River and the Ohio River. Removing the trees thus caused rainwater to run more quickly into the Mississippi River. The floods increased not only in frequency but also in ferocity in the Lower Mississippi River valley just as new planters were establishing their plantation enterprises.[23]

The backswamps of the river valley, moreover, were ripe for breeding the bacteria or mosquitoes that brought dysentery, yellow fever, and malaria. Malaria would become so endemic in the region that it was rare to find a plantation household located near the swamps that remained healthy. It was an unforgiving and brutal environment, and only the most ambitious planter willing to put profits ahead of all else dared venture there. Nevertheless, the Mississippi River valley was the location of the last great cotton plantation frontier before the Civil War. By 1860, the American South was producing two-thirds of the world's cotton supply, much of it coming from this region.

Enslaved People and the Environment

Enslaved labor was the chief means by which planters manipulated the environment. Whether growing tobacco, rice, cotton, or sugar cane, enslaved people bore the responsibility to plant, cultivate, and harvest crops. There were some chores that were common to most crops, but there were specific tasks connected to each of them. Tobacco had to be cultivated in seedbeds, carefully protected from the elements in its early stage of growth and thinned in a later stage. The crop required constant attention until it reached maturity when it had to be topped—the flowers and seeds removed—in order to promote growth of the all-important tobacco leaves. Constant vigilance was required throughout the process to guard against pests, especially the damaging hornworm. Lacking effective poisons to remedy the situation, the pests had to be carefully picked off by hand. Once harvested, the tobacco leaves had to be cured and another series of time-consuming tasks performed to bring the crop to market.

On rice plantations, enslaved people worked closely with the soil too, planting, hoeing, and harvesting. Wet-rice workers also constructed canals to bring water to or divert water from the fields. Those who worked in sugar cane fields in Louisiana took on additional challenges. Cutting cane roughly six inches from the ground was a dangerous activity. They hacked away at the cane with curved machetes that could maim them in a careless moment. They then loaded it on wagons for transport to nearby mills or to the port if the plantation was not large enough to have its own mill. Work in the boiling house connected to the mill was equally grueling, as these ran for twenty-four hours during the harvest season.[24] Cotton was simple in comparison but strenuous nonetheless. Breaking the soil, seeding the field in rows, hoeing around the plant when the inevitable weeds appeared, thinning the crop, and harvesting it were all essential elements of the process. Scouting the field for signs of the cotton worm and then removing the pest by hand was tedious and time-consuming. After all of this had occurred, the real work had only just begun. Picking cotton required bending low over the stalks and moving down rows with an increasingly heavy cotton sack strapped to the back. Laborers then hauled it to wagons that transported it to a cotton gin so that it could be processed into clean fiber that could be turned into cloth in textile mills in faraway England.

Enslaved people not only interacted with the land they were cultivating, but they also engaged intimately with the forested areas of the edges of plantations. In the best of situations, planters kept up to a third of their acreage in crops, with the rest laying fallow or in reserve forests for later use.[25] These forested areas provided a temporary refuge for enslaved people across the South, from the Carolinas and Georgia to the Mississippi River valley. It was there they could find sustenance by hunting, fishing, and trapping.[26] They not only diversified their diets through their own efforts in these forested spaces, but they also secured much needed nutrition. Planters typically issued only salt pork and corn to the quarters. In gathering wild plants and berries, and in procuring fresh fish and meat, enslaved people maintained a better standard of health and well-being than was otherwise possible.[27]

Did planters know what enslaved people were doing in these hinterlands? Almost certainly, but not necessarily when, where, or how. To be sure, they had good reason to expect their enslaved people to venture there when instructed because there were duties for them to perform in the forests. Planters maintained the practice of allowing their cattle and hogs to graze freely in the forests; thus enslaved people were periodically dispatched to either survey or bring livestock in for inspection or slaughter. Still, enslaved people used these hinterlands for their own purposes, and they cherished the space they occupied there free of the planter's gaze. However, to keep those spaces as a refuge from planter interference, they needed to obscure the extent of their hunting and gathering activities from the planters. To overharvest plants and animals would have drawn unwanted attention that might have endangered their other activities.[28]

These semi-covert places were also used as opportunities for social activities that included enslaved workers living on nearby plantations. These interactions enabled them to meet—and even marry—others outside their small communities. Because plantations in the southern regions of the United States were small, typically twenty to fifty enslaved people on a given plantation, they needed these social spaces to find mates. Thus, the nourishment they secured there was far more than diet and nutrition. It provided them social relationships that sustained and fortified them.[29]

Forests and swamplands also provided corridors of escape. Enslaved people found the densely forested, swampy eastern Arkansas delta, for example, an ideal habitat for clandestine meetings. Like enslaved people elsewhere, they used it as a place to seek either temporary or permanent freedom. Although heavily engaged in the arduous work of cutting old-growth forests, they turned the knowledge of these hinterlands to their advantage when they could.[30] Planters realized the danger soon enough and sometimes took extreme measures to retain their slave "property." One Union scout in Arkansas reported during the Civil War that enslaved people attempting to run to Union lines were killed by an overseer who hoped to instill fear in others who might follow suit.[31] Despite the odds, the Civil War provided enslaved people the greatest opportunity to seize freedom and at the same time deliver a severe blow to the Confederate South and the institution of slavery. Their familiarity with the geography through their association with enslaved people from nearby plantations in the forested areas played a critical role in undermining the Confederacy.

THE CIVIL WAR AND ENVIRONMENTAL VULNERABILITIES

Planters recognized that opposition to the expansion of slavery posed a serious threat to the viability of the Southern plantation, and most shrewd planters understood the standoff between the South and the federal government in the late antebellum era in those terms. The agricultural system functioned in a precarious balance of exhausted lands laying fallow, agricultural acreage in intensive cultivation, and forested lands in reserve. Although political considerations—such as the balance of power in the US Senate—were ever present, the desire for additional land was a central characteristic of Southern planters. The idea that expansion was necessary to their survival did not simply reside in the imaginations of fire-eating secessionists; it was a cold statement of fact. Without new lands to exploit, the plantation would weaken, and men would lose money and status. Southerners also knew, however, that close to 80 percent of the cotton feeding Great Britain was Southern-grown. Once the South seceded, planters were convinced that Britain would recognize the Confederacy and offer aid. But British textile mill owners had been watching with growing alarm as events spiraled out of control in the United States in the 1850s and began stockpiling cotton. The British government also began promoting cotton cultivation in Indian and Egypt. The slaveowners were playing a much weaker hand than they imagined.[32]

The planters most immediate blow though was not the British failure to recognize the legitimacy of the Confederacy. Enslaved people departed plantations in great numbers as soon as the Union army drew near, throwing plantation operations into jeopardy. It is estimated that 400,000 self-freed men, women, and children walked off plantations during the Civil War. Approximately 180,000 of 200,000 of the African Americans who wore Union blue were, in fact, self-freed men. While Southern planters saw these Black soldiers as renegade slaves, self-freed men understood themselves to be fighting for freedom. They played a crucial role in not only ending slavery but also in winning the war for the Union.[33]

From the time the first enslaved people reached Union lines at Fortress Monroe, Virginia, in May 1861, they began to influence federal policymaking. When Southern planters demanded that General Benjamin Butler return these self-people to their custody, he refused and declared them "contraband of war." Three months later, Congress virtually ratified Butler's solution to the problem by passing a Confiscation Act, and in June 1862, declared enslaved people free if they reached Union lines. Those who abandoned plantations essentially forced federal policy on emancipation, but they also threw plantation operations into disarray. Losing a labor force so integral to both the production of the crop and the mitigation of the damage resulting from intensive agricultural practices was a devastating blow. And what was barely manageable under normal circumstances became impossible to maintain under the extraordinary conditions applying during wartime.[34]

A new group of historians led by Lisa Brady, Erin Mauldin, Judkin Browning, and Timothy Silver have inspired a new generation of scholars to probe the environmental toll the Civil War took on the landscape.[35] Because most battles were fought on Southern soil, the ramifications were far-reaching. Although many areas of the South were untouched by the war, the heart of the cotton-producing areas of the old southeastern plantation sector faced battle after battle. Sustained sieges and military campaigns had a devastating impact not only on embattled soldiers but also on the landscape. The construction of defensive works around cities and in the countryside during protracted battlefield engagements were common practices but on Southern soils had lasting implications. Soil structures are complex and even if left untouched by human hands can be seriously damaged by natural phenomenon. The act of digging trenches and other earthworks common in warfare could cause compaction of soils, a situation where soil particles are pressed tightly together. Such a process can reduce nutrient content and impede the absorption of water. In the worst cases, it can reduce soil fertility and thus crop yields. To make matters worse, battlefields marked by cannon fire and over which thousands of troops engaged in combat were cleared of vegetation that made them ill-prepared to withstand the abundant rainfall that, under these circumstances, can wash away topsoil. Repeated engagements by troops could leave land barren of vegetation and result in soil erosion, a problem that outlasted the war.[36]

Southern forests were also subject to devastation, and their destruction had tremendous implications for farmers. Because planters depended upon moving into forested areas when agricultural lands were exhausted, the ruination of these reserve forests was not merely an incidental inconvenience. As armies encamped or prepared for battle, forests were frequently cut down to build breastworks, to shore up trenches, and to construct a variety of temporary huts for army personnel. If they were not harvested for these purposes, trees could be seriously damaged by shot and shell. Enormous amounts of wood were consumed for fuel for campfires and cookstoves. Their destruction furthered the problem with soil erosion as devastated cut-over lands eroded quickly and failed to serve the purposes for which they were intended. Held in reserve to be used when intensive cultivation wore out cotton fields, they were made worthless for that purpose but also for another important task. Southern planters did not pen their livestock but allowed them to range in the forests. Without forests they would have to turn to a Northern model of livestock-raising: fencing their herds. After the war, the need to construct fence posts further depleted the forests. Southern states began to pass laws requiring farmers to keep their herds of hogs and cattle fenced in rather than allowing them to range freely, as had been the custom. These new laws were far from universally popular with rural residents in the post–Civil War South.

Post–Civil War South

Although the Civil War resulted in the liberation of nearly four million people held in bondage, federal policy decisions made during the war ensured that the plantation system would survive. Some plantations remained in operation with federal permission during the war, and the cotton produced on them stamped with a seal signaling its legality. Run by Northern entrepreneurs or Southern planters who took an oath of allegiance, they were farmed by self-freed people who worked under a contract negotiated between the army—later the Freedmen's Bureau—and the individual freed person.

As the most highly traded commodity produced in the United States, cotton provided handsome returns not only to Southern planters but also to Northern companies, shippers, and financiers. Its elimination was simply not an option. A few Radical Republicans promoted confiscation and redistribution of plantations, but that never received serious consideration by Congress. Given nothing but freedom, freed people found few options available to them other than to continue to work on plantations. Planters found they could only push them so far. They could not force them to do the remedial work that enslaved people had performed in addition to cultivating crops under the antebellum plantation system.

As slavery gave way to the contract labor system and then to the sharecropping system, planters found it impossible to maintain a labor regime that included not only agricultural work but mitigation activities. Under slavery, African American laborers worked in gangs and were heavily supervised by overseers armed with the power of the lash. The sharecropping system functioned very differently. Freed people moved away from the old slave quarters and onto small parcels of land that they worked, often as a family, in return for a share of the crop. They reconstituted their families, established African American churches, and gained a semblance of independence from the planter's control. Sharecroppers understandably refused to engage in uncompensated labor such as moving into forested areas to break new ground.[37]

Furthermore, the quest for maintaining profits in the postwar period necessitated the elimination of the reserve forested lands that remained, those undeveloped places African Americans enslaved people had used to their advantage. For a few decades, freed people would continue to carve out places in remote areas outside the gaze of hostile southern whites but the intensification of deforestation in the late nineteenth century largely eliminated those spaces. As planters turned to the timber industry as a means of realizing profits, particularly along the Lower Mississippi River valley, they also opened up these lands for agriculture. The implications were enormous for those who would use them to supplement their diets.[38]

Even without their forests as reserve lands, planters were determined to restore their lagging fortunes after the Civil War by returning to monocrop agriculture and intensive cultivation practices. However, cotton planters had to calculate the implications of the failure of Cotton Diplomacy during the Civil War. When Britain began securing its cotton from India and Egypt, it altered the calculus that planters would be operating under in the postwar years. Although Southern planters would recover their share of the cotton market, the price of cotton rarely returned to its pre–Civil War high. Planters could no longer count on the profit margins that had enriched them in the 1850s.

The failure to incorporate a soil restoration regimen in their operations took a heavy toll, but the emergence of agricultural sciences in the late nineteenth century permitted them to avoid total collapse. Initially, however, Southern states and planters were lukewarm to what they perceived as a federal intrusion. Southern congressmen in the antebellum period had prevented the passage of legislation that would have created land-grant institutions designed to promote the agricultural sciences, but once Southern congressmen left the Union to join the Confederate rebellion, the Morrill Land-Grant Act passed in 1862. When the Confederate states were restored to the Union, they began to establish land-grant colleges authorized under the act, but Southern state legislatures were reluctant to appropriate state funds to fully fund their operations. Only when a formidable pest threatened cotton production in the early twentieth century did planters enthusiastically embrace the experts and the measures advocated by them.[39]

The appearance of the devastating boll weevil infestations that destroyed cotton crops in the early twentieth century convinced planters of the value of the agricultural sciences. Even as the weevil revealed the folly of dedication to monocrop cotton cultivation, planters doubled down and grew more cotton in 1921 than they had in 1892.[40] Agricultural specialists had introduced better cotton seed varieties and fertilization practices; small farmers who had never grown cotton had moved into the market, in part because merchants would only extend credit if they grew a marketable crop like cotton; and new cotton lands were opening up in the Far West. During World War I cotton prices regained their pre–Civil War highs, but only briefly. Prices plummeted in 1919 and the situation worsened in the 1920s. Still, acres devoted to cotton in the South increased between 1919 and 1929 by 26.3 percent while the number of bales harvested increased by 23.3 percent.[41] Meanwhile, the American West increased its production from a mere 204,257 to 647,936 (+217 percent) bales. In fact, the cotton industry's days were numbered. Demand was declining even as production was increasing, and its decreasing importance in the British and global economy meant that the cotton would soon be eclipsed by other crops.

The Great Depression and World War II ushered in a new era, and the crop that fed the British textile industry faced challenges from synthetic fibers. Planters continued to grow cotton but shared space on Southern plantations with soybeans and rice. The agribusinesses of the twenty-first century have been able to achieve record levels of production through use of chemicals and genetically modified seeds, but questions have arisen about the environmental damage that heavy concentrations of chemicals can cause. The depletion of water tables may become the greatest concern of agriculturalists in the near future. Meanwhile, if the British were the purveyors of agricultural colonialism in the seventeenth century, the United States, Europe, and China have played that role in Africa at the beginning of the third millennium. They have disrupted traditional agriculturalists on that continent and posed new environmental challenges, ones that greatly eclipse those caused by the British four centuries ago.

Acknowledgements

I am very grateful to Melissa Walker and Patrick Williams who read multiple drafts of this chapter and offered excellent advice.

Notes

1. Kenneth Pomeranz, *The Great Divergence* (Princeton, NJ: Princeton University Press, 2000); and Gary M. Pecquet, "British Mercantilism and Crop Controls in the Tobacco Colonies: A Study of Rent-Seeking Costs," *Cato Journal* 22, no. 3 (Winter 2003): 467–484.
2. Mitch Aso, "Plantations: Economies, Societies, and Environments, 1850–1950," Academia.com, https://www.academia.edu/1834380/Plantations_Economies_societies_and_environments_1850-1950, accessed February 18, 2021; Philip D. Curtin, *The Rise and Fall of the Planation Complex: Essays in Atlantic History* (New York: Cambridge University Press, 1990); Trevor Burnard, "Plantation Societies," 262–282 in *The Cambridge World History*, Vol. 2, ed. Jerry H. Bentley, Sanjay Subrahmanyam, and Merry E. Wiesner-Hanks (Cambridge: Cambridge University Press, 2015); Trevor Burnard, *Planters, Merchants, and Slaves: Plantation Societies in British America, 1650–1820* (Chicago: University of Chicago Press, 2015); George L. Beckford, *Persistent Poverty: Underdevelopment in Plantation Economies of the Third World* (Kingston, Jamaica: University of West Indies Press, 1972); Stuart B. Schwartz, ed., *Tropical Babylons: Sugar and the Making of the Atlantic World, 1450–1680* (Chapel Hill: University of North Carolina Press, 2004).
3. Carville Earle, "The Myth of the Southern Soil Miner: Macrohistory, Agricultural Innovation, and Environmental Change," in Donald Worster, ed., *The Ends of the Earth* (Cambridge University press, 1988): 177–178; and John E. Wennersten, "Soil Miners Redux: The Chesapeake Environment, 1680–1810," *Maryland Historical Magazine* 91, no. 2 (Summer 1996): 157–179.
4. Paul Sutter, *"Let Us Now Praise Famous Gullies": Providence Canyon and the Soils of the South* (Athens: University of Georgia Press, 2015): 147.
5. Pomeranz, *The Great Divergence*.
6. Timothy Silver, *A New Face on the Countryside: Indians, Colonists, and Slaves in South Atlantic Forests, 1500–1800* (Cambridge: Cambridge University Press, 1990); and William Cronon, *Changes in the Land: Indians, Colonists, and the Ecology of New England* (New York: Hill & Wang, 1983).
7. Silver, *A New Face on the Countryside*.
8. Ibid., 35–66.
9. Ibid.
10. Silver, *A New Face on the Countryside*.
11. Ibid.; and Sutter, *"Let Us Now Praise Famous Gullies."*
12. Sven Beckert, *Empire of Cotton: A Global History* (New York: Alfred A. Knopf, 2015).

13. Edmund S. Morgan, *American Slavery, American Freedom: The Ordeal of Colonial Virginia* (New York: W. W. Norton, 1975).
14. Ibid.
15. Ibid.
16. Silver, *A New Face on the Countryside*, 106–107, 145, 173–174; Sutter, "Let Us Now Praise Famous Gullies," 145–150.
17. Peter Wood, *Black Cargo: Negroes in Colonial South Carolina from 1670 through Stono Rebellion* (New York: W. W. Norton, 1974); Silver, *A New Face on the Countryside*, 108, 144, 152.
18. Mart A. Stewart, *"What Nature Suffers to Groe": Life, Labor, and Landscape on the Georgia Coast, 1680–1920* (Athens: University of Georgia Press, 1996): 154–55.
19. Ibid., 155–156.
20. Jeannie Whayne, *Delta Empire: Lee Wilson and the Transformation of Agriculture in the New South* (Baton Rouge: Louisiana State University Press, 2011): 65–69.
21. Stewart, *What Nature Suffers to Groe*, 154–157, 193–196.
22. Peter Coclanis, *The Shadow of a Dream: Economic Life and Death in the South Carolina Low Country, 1670–1920* (New York: Oxford University Press, 1989): 97.
23. Whayne, *Delta Empire*, 65–69.
24. Mart Stewart, "Slavery and the Origins of African American Environmentalism," in *"To Love the Wind and the Rain": African Americans and Environmental History*, ed. Diane D. Glave and Mark Stoll (Pittsburgh: University of Pittsburgh Press, 2006): 11.
25. Judkin Browning and Timothy Silver, *An Environmental History of the Civil War* (Chapel Hill: University of North Carolina Press, 2020): 181.
26. Stewart, "Slavery and the Origins of African American Environmentalism," 12.
27. Ibid., 10, 12; Anthony E. Kaye, *Joining Places: Slave Neighborhoods in the Old South* (Chapel Hill: University of North Carolina Press, 2007); and Kelly E. Jones, *A Weary Land: Slavery on the Ground in Arkansas* (Athens: University of Georgia Press, 2021).
28. Jones, *A Weary Land*.
29. Stewart, "Slavery and the Origins of African American Environmentalism," 12; Kaye, *Joining Places*.
30. Jones, *A Weary Land*.
31. David Schieffler, "Civil War in the Delta: Environment, Race, and the 1863 Helena Campaign" (PhD diss., University of Arkansas, 2017): 163
32. Beckert, *Empire of Cotton*, 260–65.
33. Steven Hahn, "Did We Miss the Greatest Slave Rebellion Ever," in Hahn, *The Political Wars of Slavery and Freedom* (Cambridge, MA: Harvard University Press, 2009).
34. Eric Foner, *Reconstruction: America's Unfinished Revolution, 1863–1877* (New York: Harper & Row, 1988): 5; Erin Mauldin, *Unredeemed Land: An Environmental History of Civil War and Emancipation in the Cotton South* (New York: Oxford University Press, 2018): 146–148.
35. Lisa Brady, *War upon the Land: Military Strategy and the Transformation of Southern Landscapes during the American Civil War* (Athens: University of Georgia Press, 2009); Browning and Silver, *An Environmental History of the Civil War*.
36. Mauldin, *Unredeemed Land*, 46–51.
37. Roger Ransom and Richard Sutch, *One Kind of Freedom: The Economic Consequences of Emancipation* (New York: Cambridge University Press, 1977); Leon Litwack, *Been in a Storm so Long: The Aftermath of Slavery* (New York: Knopf, 1979); and Harold D. Woodman, *New South, New Law: The Legal Foundations of Credit and Labor Relations in the Postbellum Agricultural South* (Baton Rouge: Louisiana State University Press, 1995).

38. Mauldin, *Unredeemed Land*, 147.
39. Ibid., 158–159; see also David Danbom, *Born in the Country: A History of Rural America* (Baltimore: Johns Hopkins University Press, 1995); James C. Giesen, *Boll Weevil Blues: Cotton, Myth, and Power in the American South* (Chicago: University of Chicago Press, 2011); and R. Douglas Hurt, *American Agriculture: A Brief History*, rev. ed. (West Lafayette, IN: Purdue University Press, 2002).
40. John Gray, "Arkansas Forest History," Forest History, Arkansas Forestry Association, 1993, https://www.arkforests.org/page/foresthistory, accessed August 27, 2020; Ted Ownby, "The Defeated Generation at Work: White Farmers in the Deep South, 1865–1890," *Southern Studies* 23, no. 4 (Winter 1984): 325–347.
41. U.S. Census of Agriculture, 1930, Vol. 2, Reports by States, Summaries, Table V, p. 16.

Bibliography

Beckert, Sven. *Empire of Cotton: A Global History*. New York: Alfred A. Knopf, 2015.

Brady, Lisa. *War upon the Land: Military Strategy and the Transformation of Southern Landscapes during the American Civil War*. Athens: University of Georgia Press, 2009.

Browning, Judkin, and Timothy Silver. *An Environmental History of the Civil War*. Chapel Hill: University of North Carolina Press, 2020.

Coclanis, Peter. *The Shadow of a Dream: Economic Life and Death in the South Carolina Low Country, 1670–1920*. New York: Oxford University Press, 1989.

Curtin, Philip D. *The Rise and Fall of the Planation Complex: Essays in Atlantic History*. New York: Cambridge University Press, 1990.

Foner, Eric. *Reconstruction: America's Unfinished Revolution, 1863–1877*. New York: Harper & Row, 1988.

Hurt, R. Douglas. *Blackwell's Companion to American Agriculture*. Hoboken, NJ: Wiley, 2022.

Jones, Kelly E. *A Weary Land: Slavery on the Ground in Arkansas*. Athens: University of Georgia Press, 2021.

Litwack, Leon. *Been in a Storm so Long: The Aftermath of Slavery*. New York: Knopf, 1979.

Morgan, Edmund S. *American Slavery, American Freedom: The Ordeal of Colonial Virginia*. New York: W. W. Norton, 1975.

Mauldin, Erin. *Unredeemed Land: An Environmental History of Civil War and Emancipation in the Cotton South*. New York: Oxford University Press, 2018.

Pomeranz, Kenneth. *The Great Divergence*. Princeton, NJ: Princeton University Press, 2000.

Ransom, Roger, and Richard Sutch. *One Kind of Freedom: The Economic Consequences of Emancipation*. New York: Cambridge University Press, 1977.

Schwartz, Stuart B., ed. *Tropical Babylons: Sugar and the Making of the Atlantic World, 1450–1680*. Chapel Hill: University of North Carolina Press, 2004.

Silver, Timothy. *A New Face on the Countryside: Indians, Colonists, and Slaves in South Atlantic Forests, 1500–1800*. Cambridge: Cambridge University Press, 1990.

Stewart, Mart A. *"What Nature Suffers to Groe": Life, Labor, and Landscape on the Georgia Coast, 1680–1920*. Athens: University of Georgia Press, 1996.

Sutter, Paul *"Let Us Now Praise Famous Gullies": Providence Canyon and the Soils of the South*. Athens: University of Georgia Press, 2015.

Woodman, Harold D. *New South, New Law: The Legal Foundations of Credit and Labor Relations in the Postbellum Agricultural South*. Baton Rouge: Louisiana State University Press, 1995.

CHAPTER 30

THE BRITISH AGRICULTURAL REVOLUTION

RICHARD HOYLE

For generations of historians, it followed logically and naturally that an industrial revolution was mirrored by an agricultural revolution. If they had looked, they would also have found contemporary awareness of radical change. It was not merely reform-minded writers like Arthur Young and William Marshall who were searching out and publicizing the new techniques used by improving farmers. An essay published in 1790 by Joseph Wimpey of North Bockhampton in Dorset itemized "the improvements in agriculture that have been successfully introduced into this kingdom within the past fifty years" under eight headings.[1] These were all alterations in the management of land that paid for themselves through increased net profits.

The first innovation was superior standards of tillage and the preparation of the ground, and from this followed the second, the invention of new implements of husbandry. Wimpey noted an improvement in plows, the best of which reduced the number of horses and men needed to operate them while giving a much better tilth. Third, Wimpey saw drilling machines as a major innovation. They reduced the amount of seed that needed to be sown and made it possible to hand- or horse-how between the lines of seeds. Fourth, Wimpey felt that the increase in the range of crops available to farmers now allowed them to grow what suited their soil rather than growing what would fetch the best price at market. Fifth, it was the "rotation of most beneficial succession of crops" that "comprehends improvements of great magnitude and extent." Wimpey distinguished between crops that left the soil exhausted (cereals), and those that replenished it (legumes and roots). The judicious use of "ameliorating" crops after "exhausting" crops allowed for continuous cropping. Sixth, the soil itself was improved by the use of soil improvers (marl, chalk, shells, and lime. Wimpey does not say anything about animal manures.) His seventh innovation was the "successful introduction of many new articles into field culture." Turnips, potatoes, cabbages, carrots, and parsnips had been cultivated for domestic use for much longer than fifty years, "but the field culture of these articles for the feed of cattle in any considerable degree is quite a modern practice." Wimpey particularly stressed the use of artificial grasses, Sainfoin and

Lucerne, and made especially large claims for the former. Finally, Wimpey commented that the use of turnips for the feed of sheep and the fattening of cattle was now so general that it required no comment and mused whether the potato would come to have a similar role as animal feed. He could doubtless have suggested other improvements. Drainage, for instance, was a matter of great interest at the end of the eighteenth century but was not mentioned by him, nor was enclosure, either of open fields or commons.

Other late eighteenth-century accounts of change can be found, but much of the literature of the time was not so much congratulatory as striving for further improvement, for more enclosure, better drainage, greater efficiency in farming, and new machinery. It is replete with accounts of how to get more for less. Contemporaries thought they were living through a time when change was not only possible but happening around them. They had the evidence of their eyes: enclosure, new farmsteads, new crops, more cattle in the fields, and a higher standard of living for farmers.

The Board of Agriculture—not a government department but a pressure group of enthusiasts in receipt of a government grant—was established in 1793.[2] Its members were driven by the conviction that English agriculture was failing because imports of grain had, since about 1765, been steadily rising. The answer was to enclose and extend the area under cultivation. What they could not have foreseen in 1793 was that the following two decades would be marked by high prices, two years of harvest failure and near famine, and the interruption to imports caused by war. As prices were high, rents and the value of land rose. Investment in agriculture promised good returns. This was a golden age for farming, and for farmers.

After 1813 the agricultural boom collapsed. In a great tour d'horizon given as a speech in the House of Commons in April 1816, Henry Brougham, later Lord Chancellor, argued that agricultural expansion over the previous twenty years had far exceeded what was prudent. Agriculture was overextended. Capital had been poured into it which could not be recovered:

> [T]he work both of men and cattle has been economized, new skill has been applied, and a more dexterous combination of different kinds of husbandry been practised, until, without at all comprehending the waste lands wholly added to the productive territory of the island, it may be safely said, not perhaps that two blades of grass now grow where one only grew before, but I am sure, that five grow where four used to be; and that this kingdom which foreigners were wont to taunt as a mere manufacturing and trading country, inhabited by a shopkeeping nation, is in reality, for its size, by far the greatest agricultural state the world.[3]

He does not use the words, but here is an agricultural revolution.

Historiography

Historians have tried to digest and understand these changes ever since the domestic agrarian economy started to decline under the weight of cheap imports of American wheat, South American beef, and New Zealand lamb after 1880 or so. Two schools of thought can be identified. Following Marx, some historians place a great emphasis on enclosure and the social ills it brought with it: the decline of the small landowner, the emergence of large capitalist farms, the pauperization of commoners and laborers and their enforced migration into towns. This was an approach that perhaps found its apogee in the writings of J. L. and Barbara Hammond on the eve of World War I.[4] The view that enclosure was a legalized form of dispossession of the vulnerable still has its advocates among historians and a prominent place in the popular understanding of history.[5]

A quite different school of historians stressed the technical innovations that enclosure permitted. The foremost advocate of an agricultural revolution (although he seems not to have used the phrase) along these lines was R. E. Prothero (Lord Ernle). His *English Farming Past and Present* bestrode the field for over half a century after its first publication in 1912: the sixth posthumous edition appeared as late as 1961. Prothero placed an emphasis on parliamentary enclosure's breaking the restraints on agricultural progress. He saw early eighteenth-century agriculture as little different from its medieval precursor. In his view, enclosure unleashed the entrepreneurial spirit of the farmer. Freed from the dead weight of the collective farming of open fields, farmers were then free to draw on a range of new crops—artificial grasses, turnips—all integrated into new systems of rotation, new livestock breeds, and new labor-saving machines. These possibilities were publicized by heroic pioneers—Robert Bakewell of Dishley, T. W. Coke of Holkham, Viscount Townshend ("Turnip Townshend") of Raynham, Jethro Tull—and word of them was further circulated by William Marshall, Arthur Young, and the publications of the Board of Agriculture. For many people this heroic account remains the agricultural revolution.

Agriculture before 1750 had never been static but was constantly adapting to price signals and new opportunities. Prothero's view of a discontinuity in practice about the third quarter of the eighteenth century fell out of favor with the realization that the innovations he attributed to that time were often known a century and more earlier. If obscure, the history of the turnip was both longer and more complicated than he understood. Clover was also known well before 1750. There were simply not enough of the new breeds of cattle and sheep to make any great difference to the national herd and flock. Only about 21 percent of the land area of England was enclosed by parliamentary statute. In some counties virtually none was; in others over half of the land area was subject to enclosure by act.[6]

The developing knowledge of agrarian practices before 1760 and the fundamentally unquantitative nature of the debate led to the idea of an agricultural revolution being stretched over several centuries. Some historians abandoned the concept altogether or declared it to be unhelpful. In a well-known survey of 1966, Chambers and Mingay argued for an agricultural revolution stretching from about 1760 to the onset of depression around 1880, a long, thin agricultural revolution.[7] The sixth volume of the *Agrarian History of England and Wales* covering 1750–1850, edited by Mingay and published in 1989, dismissed the notion of an agricultural revolution in the first paragraph of the first page, where the incremental improvement of agriculture over a much longer period was noted and the idea of the agricultural revolution ("if [it] has any validity") reserved for the years after 1945.[8] Early attempts at quantification were also dismissive of the idea of a late eighteenth-century agricultural revolution, suggesting that the rate of increase in productivity in the eighteenth century was far from impressive and actually declined later in the century.[9]

Mingay's volume of the *Agrarian History* was perhaps the low point in the historiography of the agricultural revolution, although others continue to eschew both the term and the concept. An attractive and well-informed study of agriculture, landscape, and agricultural buildings of 2004 that placed a stress on change never used the term and took refuge in the more neutral word "improvement."[10] Tides come in and tides go out, and in 1996 Mark Overton published a paper summarizing the quantitative materials that he and others had been gathering over the previous decade and more from probate inventories, and restated the traditional view that the experience of the later eighteenth century saw a real break with its past on a scale worthy of the epithet "revolution." Overton's book of the same year took the title *Agricultural Revolution in England*, the lack of a definite article being both a tease and a caution.[11]

In his 1996 paper, estimating agricultural output by a number of methods and extending his pool of inventories, Overton showed that on a number of criteria, output rose by about a quarter between 1700 and 1750 and continued to grow over the next century. And so he concluded by saying that "evidence overwhelmingly favours the century after 1750 as the period of most rapid and fundamental change in output and productivity, which were associated with equally unprecedented and fundamental changes in husbandry."[12]

Having given some quantitative underpinning to the view that the late eighteenth century was qualitatively different from what had preceded it, Overton went on to explain the characteristics of his agricultural revolution. Some of the features that he identified were not novel but had long been a staple of the literature, so turnips and clover, but he also showed a much higher density of animals and, following on from this, he demonstrated a reduction in the area of fallow. These ideas were developed further with a stronger statistical backing in a later publication, but after Overton's 1996 paper, the idea of an agricultural revolution has been part of the currency of debate.

The idea was confronted head-on by Michael Turner, John Beckett, and Bethanie Afton in their book of 2004.[13] This was primarily a study of farm productivity seen through the records of individual farmers, but the new data they assembled was placed firmly in the context of agricultural revolution. Their conclusion was that there was a revolution but that it was between 1815 and 1850. They identified an increase in acreage of 56 percent between those dates but a rise in output of 120 percent, showing that yields per acre substantially increased.

Here we might reflect on a paper of 1968 prompted by Chambers and Mingay's book. F. M. L. Thompson argued that the years after the end of the postwar depression should be seen as a second agricultural revolution that stretched through to the onset of depression about 1880.[14] The first agricultural revolution had been marked by a physical reorganization of the landscape by enclosure, by increased cultivation, increased capitalization, and a greater market orientation. But farms remained mixed (i.e., both arable and pastoral) and largely self-sufficient in nutrients. They were a closed system that produced wheat and barley for sale, livestock for slaughter, and some wool. The roots and clovers the farm produced, together with its hay, were essentially for internal consumption. Thompson perhaps minimized the external inputs to make this system work—he acknowledged the need for clover seed but not the requirement for a supply of young beasts to feed up—but he was surely right when he saw the second agricultural revolution as being driven by much greater farm inputs of nutrients, starting with bone meal, oil-seed cake, then from ca. 1840 guano, mineral phosphates, and nitrates, and this created the prospect of a farm with neither cattle or rotations, but continuous cropping, as has become normal in our own times. This chapter adopts a largely Thompsonian perspective.

THE AGRICULTURAL REVOLUTION AS A REGIONAL PHENOMENON

Previous authors have all tended to view the agricultural revolution as a national phenomenon. One of the reasons why the agricultural revolution is so hard to pin down is that rapid innovative change came to different places at different times. There is an argument to be made that what determined the timing was not the market but the soil and, to a lesser degree, location. (A third factor, prices, we will address in a moment.) The classic agricultural revolution—the sowing of artificial grasses for fallows, turnips for winter animal fodder, the adoption of the Norfolk four-course rotations, the investment in new farm buildings to house cattle—developed earliest and proceeded furthest on light soils. Downlands and heathlands were broken up, enclosed and brought into cultivation. Turnips were much less suited to heavy clay soils. Hence turnip cultivation may have allowed agriculture to bound ahead in areas where they could be advantageously grown while in other areas agriculture languished.

Before 1793 this gave heavy land areas a price incentive to enclose to enable arable to be converted to grassland, with a switch into dairying and beef production. After 1793 much of this heavy land was once again plowed. This was high-cost arable land whose innate disadvantages could be overcome when prices were high, but where the plow could not be sustained in the low-price years after 1815. In any case, contemporaries in the postwar years often recognized that this land was exhausted from overcultivation. The problem of how to make a living out of this land in adverse conditions was summarized in the reported objectives of James Loch, appointed steward to the Sunderland estates in the northwest Midlands in 1813. In 1818 it was said that his mission was to "introduce as good a system of farming upon the stiff lands of the country as exists upon the light and turnip soils."[15] This is as clear a recognition as we might hope to find that these districts had missed out on the rapid advances of the eighteenth century on the lighter soils, not because their farmers were ignorant of them or willfully resistant to change, but because rotations based around roots would not work in their local conditions. In fact, the long-term direction of change on heavy soils was toward grass, cattle rearing, and dairying and the chief means of improvement may be identified as improved drainage and deep plowing. Because cattle were integral, farming continued to be mixed because animal dung offered a route to arable fertility.

If we accept that the agricultural revolution was a succession of regional phenomena, with differing local chronologies, forms, and outcomes, then we should avoid falling into the trap of seeing corn production as the sole measure of success of English agriculture. We need to give weight to the contribution of the meat and dairy sectors of the economy. It was entirely rational for the English agricultural economy to optimize its *total* output (and income) by some areas shifting to animal and dairy production while drawing in increasing quantities of imported corn to feed domestic markets. An overconcentration on bread grains—and measuring the success of agriculture by the level of imports, as the Board of Agriculture and its circle did in the 1780s and 1790s—gives a wholly misleading view of agricultural achievement in the country.

For present purposes we would define the agricultural revolution as starting in the third quarter of the eighteenth century but ending fairly abruptly in 1814–1815. The onset of war in 1793 and a run of poor harvests in the 1790s and the first decade of the new century distinguish the war years from what had preceded them, being marked by very high prices. By 1815, the enclosure of open fields had more or less run its course. After the end of war, the domestic agrarian economy was plunged into depression for a decade or more, and in many respects it marked time until the appearance of "High Farming," the capital-intensive, machine-driven, off-farm nutrient-dependent farming regime that characterized the middle years of the century, Thompson's "second agricultural revolution." Turner, Beckett, and Afton have warned us, though, not to underestimate the capacity of farmers to squeeze more out of the existing agrarian systems in the postwar years.

The Agricultural Revolution in a British Context

It is all too easy to see the agricultural revolution as a purely English phenomenon. The term has never really been deployed in modern discussions of agricultural change in either Scotland or Ireland. Of course, Scotland suffered the Highland Clearances in which poor arable and pastoral farmers were cleared off their land to make way for sheep. Enforced migration engendered a bitterness that lingers. But this is never called an "agricultural revolution," perhaps because it only involved a change in land use and not technological innovation. In the Scottish lowlands, the enclosure and reorganization of arable farming by landlords was commonplace in the middle years of the eighteenth century but is much less well known than later changes in the Highlands. In many respects what happened here was much more severe than enclosure in England, lowland Scots farmers generally having no rights in their land, but again the phrase "agricultural revolution" is never used of this dramatic transformation in the modern literature.[16] Much less is known about Irish conditions in the eighteenth century, but in the century after 1750 Ireland was transformed from being a marginal importer of English grain to a major exporter of grain into England (on one estimate contributing about one-sixth of English consumption). Again, the phrase "agricultural revolution" is rarely, if ever, used of Irish conditions, although one suspects that change in the east of the island was every bit as dramatic as anything that happened in Britain. The key difference between England and Wales on the one hand and Scotland and Ireland on the other is that in the latter, enclosure never became a public process. In all three nations landlords who had unity of ownership could enclose pretty much at will. This was less common in England and Wales, and for that reason public legal processes (described below) had to be employed. Enclosure here is well (but partially) documented where in Scotland and Ireland the reorganization of tenant land and the enclosure of commons could be achieved at the landlord's command and for that reason is much less historically visible. But it needs to be emphasized that the "agricultural revolution" is a British and Irish phenomenon. To view it as a purely English one (as is usual) is grossly misleading. Both Britain and Ireland were able to take advantage of the growing English, southern Welsh, and Scottish urban markets to transform their rural economies.

THE LIMITS OF QUANTIFICATION

One of the reasons why there has always been a tendency to view the agricultural revolution in terms of personalities and new techniques is that until recently we lacked hard quantitative data on agricultural production in Britain before the mid-nineteenth century. The British government collected no statistics on agricultural output or performance before 1866 (but from 1847 in Ireland). Throughout the eighteenth century it was happy to leave the market in agricultural products to market forces operating within the framework of the Corn Laws (the body of legislation that regulated the import and export of grain according to the prices prevailing in the domestic market.[17]) The one area in which the government did collect and publish statistics throughout was for imports and exports, but relating these trade flows to the state of the domestic market is not straightforward. They did, however, exercise a great hold over Young and his contemporaries, who thought it wrong that the country should be drawing in imports when it could achieve near-self-sufficiency. Failing to grasp larger changes in the economy, they saw rising imports as evidence of agrarian failure.

Fairly solid data exists for four areas of the economy that bear on the agricultural revolution. There are reliable estimates for English population by Wrigley and Schofield, and these can be scaled up to become estimates of British population. We have comprehensive price data, statistics for imports and exports, and the area enclosed by parliamentary enclosure. All bring problems of accuracy and meaning. Overton pioneered the use of probate inventories to secure yield and other farm-level data, but the procedure of the probate courts changed about 1740 and thereafter inventories are no longer available in large numbers after mid-century.

The quantitative basis of any assessment of the agricultural revolution has therefore been extremely weak in the past, and while much improved by the recent work of Overton and others, it remains far from satisfactory. If we move any study of the agricultural revolution along from great men, enclosure, and new techniques, we must decide the criteria we would use to assess whether an agricultural revolution had taken place. The first and most obvious is the extension of the cultivated area. Parliamentary enclosure may be taken as the most obvious evidence for this, but any such assumption needs heavy qualification. Nonetheless, it is clear enough that eighteenth-century enclosure transformed that part of the landscape *which was not already enclosed*. The second criteria would be that total output increased, and given the scale of population growth between 1750 and 1850, it makes immediate sense to suppose that it did. This is not necessarily a sign of a revolution. Total output could rise because of a recourse to labor-intensive spade agriculture on what contemporaries (such as Malthus) took to be an Irish model and therefore regressive and undesirable. Declining output per head is not evidence of an agricultural revolution. Overall, it is not easy to arrive at a quantitative, as opposed to qualitative, assessment.

An examination of measures of productivity per unit area or productivity per individual employed in agriculture—if they could be calculated—might confirm a revolution. Enclosure might well have actually reduced the productivity per cultivated area: much of the land enclosed had little agricultural potential under the techniques then being employed. A leap forward in agricultural techniques was necessary to get the best out of the addition to the stock of cultivated land. Labor productivity is even more problematic. It is just about possible to arrive at a head count of male agricultural laborers, but much harder to ascertain how many days of the week they worked and for what hours, or what the contribution of female labor was to the overall pool of labor.

The Supply of the Domestic Market

Contemporaries were aware that population was growing after 1750, but they had only a rough idea of the number of people in Britain until 1801, and even then, the rate of growth before that date remained a matter of speculation. The modern and generally accepted estimates for England are those by Wrigley and Schofield (Figure 30.1).

Population growth had an obvious impact on agriculture. The three chief grains all served different markets: wheat being used for bread and confectionary, barley for brewing, and oats for feeding to horses. Before about 1770, England was normally self-sufficient in all three grains and had a surplus to export. This surplus may have arisen

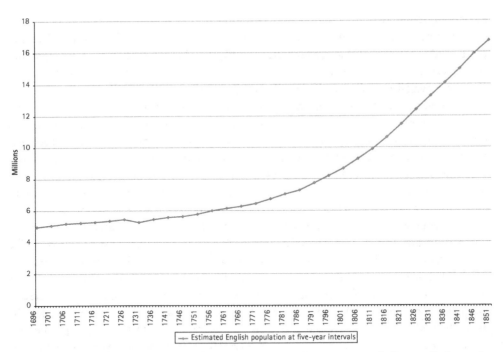

FIGURE 30.1 Estimated English population, 1696–1851, at five-year intervals. Source: Estimates by back projection from E. A. Wrigley and R. S. Schofield, *A Population History of England, 1541–1871* (London: Edward Arnold), Table A3.1.

from the development of light downland soils, often on chalk, whose cultivation may have been permitted by the development of rotations that maintained and even enhanced the fertility of these thin soils. Defoe remarks on this in the second decade of the century. The same developments were taking place on the light heathland soils of the Holkham estate in Norfolk.[18] The author of the first *General View* for Gloucestershire (1794), commented how

> Probably no part of the kingdom has been more improved in the past forty years than the Cotswold Hills. The first enclosures are about that standing [so ca. 1750]; but the greater part are of a later date. Three parishes are now enclosing, and out of about 13, which still remain in the common field state, two I understand are taking the requisite measures for an inclosure; the advantages are very great, rent more than doubled, the produce of every kind proportionably increased. In the open field state, a crop and fallow was the usual course. What is here called the "seven field husbandry" now generally obtained, that is about a seventh part sainfoin, and the remainder under the following routine; turnips, barley, seeds [grass or clover] two years, wheat, oats.[19]

All of this served to increase the cultivated area. So too did the second drainage of the Fenland after ca. 1770, when the work of the seventeenth-century drainers was brought to a satisfactory conclusion.[20]

The improvement of downland and fenland shifted the cultivation of corn to new locations and produced an oversupply on the market. The problem of low domestic prices was a long-standing one and was initially answered by subsidized exports (the "Bounty"), but it also forced producers of corn on heavy soils into forms of animal husbandry that produced better profits. In turn, this entailed enclosure, conversion to grass, and depopulation. It was this sequence of changes that shaped the public perception of enclosure until late in the century.[21] The surplus for export progressively disappears, and by the end of the eighteenth century, Britain was consistently a net importer of grain.

The data presented in figure 30.2 for imports and exports has been cited on several occasions and is taken to be authoritative. It is not certain, however, on what basis it was calculated. It is not clear, for instance, whether the earlier data includes Scotland. The table says that it includes trade with Ireland. The data does, however, illustrate the point that a relatively low level of exports before 1765 grew to a high level of imports thereafter.

Contemporaries read rising imports as a failure of English agriculture where we might read it as a rational response to farmgate prices. The need to reduce imports by plowing up land was a preoccupation in the circles of the Board of Agriculture: hence the chapter in the *General Report on Enclosures* (1808) entitled "Produce of the Country Insufficient

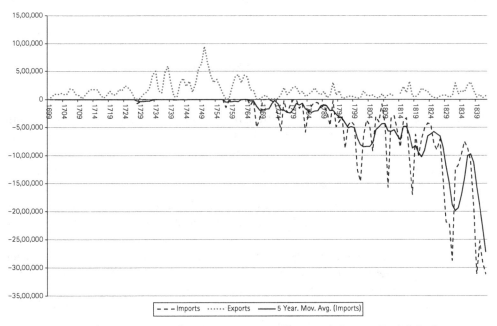

FIGURE 30.2 Wheat imports and exports, 1697–1842 (quarters). Source: British Parliamentary Papers 1843, House of Commons paper, 177, LIII, 9. Corn. *Returns to an address of the Honourable the House of Commons, dated 23 March 1843; ordered to be printed 7 April 1843*, Table 12, p. 58, "Total quantities of wheat and wheat flour imported into and exported from Great Britain in each year from 1697 to 1842."

for Its Consumption." This referred solely to grain: the Board and its members had a blind spot over pastoral production.[22]

So while the background to the classic agricultural revolution was population growth at home, there was much more to it than population growth. A rising standard of living among at least a part of the population made for a higher per capita consumption of meat and cheese. With more money in their pockets, people increased their consumption of beer and spirits, leading to an increased demand for barley. Increasing numbers of horses for traction required more provender for their sustenance. Increased demand of corn in particular was met in part by imports. In 1773, with the memory of the harvest failure of 1765 and the disturbances of 1766 in mind, the Corn Law was reconfigured to encourage imports in order to maintain domestic peace in high-price years. The domestic corn market it created did not serve the needs of English farmers very well in the twenty years after 1773 and encouraged a recourse to pasture. But from 1793, in the years of war, prices became extremely high, imports were disrupted, and farmers received a considerable incentive to convert pasture to arable land and adopt new techniques to meet a hungry market. All this came crashing down with the excellent harvest of 1813 and the end of the war. Farm incomes fell precipitately and a revision to the Corn Law was enacted in 1815 to maintain grain prices, but at a fraction of their wartime levels. Brougham was doubtless right to identify the wartime years as a bubble, an overextension of the cultivated area, with a vigorous market in land at inflated prices that had left many landowners with insurmountable debts as rents fell postwar.

Enclosure

Enclosure lies at the heart of the agricultural revolution as it is normally understood. But enclosure is also perhaps the most misunderstood process in English history, in part because we use a single word for an experience that everywhere went through but that had different characteristics, legal forms, and implications according to when and where it took place. In sum, it is the process of taking land over which multiple rights existed and vesting it solely in a single individual (in severalty), whose rights are not qualified by the seasonal rights of others to graze the land. The land itself is enclosed by fences, hedges, or walls.

In the case of open-field land ("sub-divided arable"), then the rights of a landowner within the open-fields were tempered by their collective management and the use of the land, normally for one year in three, as a fallow when there was a general right to graze. The opponents of common fields always maintained that this system was inflexible and the entrepreneurial spirit of improving farmers was restrained by their more conservative neighbors. This may have been true in many cases, but there are also examples of the fallows in open fields being used to grow clover and turnips. It would now be accepted that open fields were not as inflexible as hostile observers maintained, but what is more material is that a farmer who wanted to put down his land to grass could not easily do so because he was trapped in a cooperative system of arable farming. In openfield enclosure, land was reallocated, so the holdings of an individual ceased to be scattered and were normally consolidated into one compact, ring-fenced holding.

Commons were grazing land shared between a range of people in the village. They might be closely controlled by stints, in which specific individuals owned the right to graze a specified number of animals. Where manorial control had broken down, a common might be more of a free-for-all. In this last circumstance, overgrazing often resulted and a "tragedy of the commons" ensued. In enclosure the right of common is abolished. The whole area subject to common was divided into parcels of land held in severalty. As these might be too small to be useful and located at a distance from their owner's house, they are often sold to larger landowners and so the enclosure of commons acts as a mechanism to bring about the consolidation of ownership.

Parliamentary enclosure in England was a specific stage in a much longer process. Its characteristic was that the owners of the land sought a private act of parliament to appoint commissioners to undertake the enclosure. But where the land belonged to a single landlord, there was no need to seek public sanction to enclose. Where the number of proprietors was small and they trusted each other, again, there was no need to seek an act of parliament. But the fear was always that where the ownership of an open field or common was shared between several proprietors, one of them might claim that the proposed arrangements were disadvantageous to them and exercise a veto, or, at a later date, they might try to withdraw their consent in an attempt to unravel what had been done. And some proprietors could not consent to an agreement, especially if they were minors, clergy owning glebe, or the life tenants of land. Hence there was the need for a way of binding the parties to an agreement. Up to about 1750 a decree in Chancery was deemed sufficient: from about that time lawyers recommended a private act. But at no point was all the land being enclosed subject to enclosure by an act: land continued to be enclosed by unity of ownership, by agreement between the owners and by encroachment.

A private act brought another advantage as well. Where there was no consensus among the landowners that enclosure was desirable, a private act could be secured if the majority of the landholders, or the owners of a majority of the land, consented to it. Hence a private act could force enclosure on the owners of property who did not seek or welcome it.

It is insufficiently appreciated is that enclosure did not start with parliamentary enclosure. Most of the country was already enclosed by 1750. Rather than seeing parliamentary enclosure as the apogee of an extended process, it is better to see it as its tail end, mopping up the enclosure of parishes that had remained unenclosed for one or more of a number of reasons: divided ownership, the failure to achieve a consensus that enclosure was desirable, or the legal problems posed by landowners who could not consent to enclosure—or where the investment that enclosure entailed was unlikely to make any return.

While the legal process remained the same, in practice parliamentary enclosure meant different things in different places. There was barely any parliamentary enclosure in some counties. Nationally, Turner has shown that there were two marked periods of parliamentary enclosure with an intermission in between. Enclosure in the 1760s and 1770s was largely the enclosure of open field arable in a band of Midland counties stretching through Lincolnshire to the East Riding of Yorkshire. This was recognized by contemporaries as depopulating enclosure, that is, it involved conversion to pasture and a reduced need for labor. In the second period, after 1793, enclosure was more scattered but included the enclosure of open fields in the south Midland counties and East Anglia, and commons and waste in the northwestern counties.[23]

Young and his circle in the Board of Agriculture and his contributors to *Annals of Agriculture* were fixated on enclosure. Rather than see "waste" as land that was used for common for a reason, they saw it as a wasted opportunity. Plowing up commons would obviate the need to import grain. They saw the existing legal process of enclosure as an impediment and so pressed for a general enclosure act. A bill along these lines was passed in 1800 but fell far short of the Board's aspirations. Nonetheless, enclosure proceeded at a pace in the wartime years.

So long as enclosure was fashionable, its advantages were seen to be compelling. It increased the cultivated area in the way that Young and his circle thought desirable. It also increased the area under cultivation in a second way by permitting farmers to have green rather than bare fallows. It allowed arable land to be put down to grass. It probably reduced labor inputs by decreasing the time spent traveling between a farmer's dispersed land in an open field, but advocates of enclosure also pointed to the costs of planting and then maintaining hedges. (Overall, far fewer laborers were needed if a farm was converted to pasture.) It allowed drainage to take place within the confines of a single farm where arranging drainage in an open field was more difficult and perhaps impossible. For landlords, it allowed them to break the existing terms of tenancy and raise rents to what they saw as realistic levels. Its disadvantages, such as they were, largely fell on the poor and laboring classes who lost property rights (where they had them) and employment opportunities.[24]

A review of the contemporary literature shows that its advocates were unspecific about the productivity gains that accrued from enclosure. They occasionally produced elaborate (and implausible) calculations of the quantity of additional grain that might be produced by the general enclosure of wastelands. There was a general agreement, though, that enclosed land paid higher rents than unenclosed and that enclosure could be expected to produce a once-off bonanza for the landlord. This does not directly equate with greater productivity but resulted in part from a resetting of tenurial relationships and an increase in the cultivated area: enclosed commons paid rent where open commons did not.

Modern attempts to calculate productivity gains, no matter how sophisticated, have been largely unconvincing.[25] In fact it is virtually impossible to calculate gains without making some heroic assumptions about information that was never collected by contemporaries. Moreover, enclosure before 1793 often involved conversion to pasture, so in many instances there is no direct comparison to be made about productivity pre- and post-enclosure. Likewise, it is impossible to separate the effects of enclosure from that of a booming wartime agrarian economy.

Technological Change

The agricultural revolution involved a considerable investment in reorganizing the landscape through enclosure and in the necessary costs that followed. It is hard to establish whether it also brought about technological changes that improved productivity.

When the Board of Agriculture launched its *General Views* in 1793, it called on its reporters to gather information about the implements and the tools being used by farmers. *Annals of Agriculture* also regularly carried descriptions of new technical innovations. Though all this evidence deserves fuller and cross-county examination, at the moment it is hard to conclude that improvements in farm equipment increased either labor productivity or the efficiency of horse traction. A number of reporters to the Board discussed the Rotherham plow, but if this was still being adopted in some counties, it was also hardly new, having allegedly been patented in the 1720s.[26] The agricultural engineering trade, supplying farmers with standardized equipment made from wrought iron, only really emerged after 1825 so that in the late eighteenth century, farmers were still buying wooden equipment fabricated by village or small town manufacturers who may—or may not—have been influenced by developments in design.[27]

The machine that at a later date bore the blunt of laborers' anger was the threshing machine.[28] Early threshing machines appeared in Scotland in the 1780s. There is evidence that they were quite common in Scotland in the 1790s, and it is reported that by 1811 there were no fewer than seventy-five in the Isle of Man. There seems to have been less eagerness to adopt in England, particularly southern England. William Mavor, discussing Berkshire in 1809, dates the take-up of threshing machines in the county to after 1805, although he thought that their use in northern England was "usual."[29] The obvious explanation is that reductions in the number of laborers paid by farmers would only bring about an increase in the poor rates. Seen in this light, threshing machines were a zero-sum game, doing nothing to reduce costs while poisoning social relations. In recognition of this, there are some instances of farmers deciding collectively not to employ them.

The tentative conclusion must be that the agricultural revolution did not produce any breakthrough in the adoption of machinery or other labor-saving devices. That said, the cumulative contribution made by seed drills, horse-drawn harrows and hoes, and better carts needs to be taken seriously, even if small and impossible to quantify.

The Totality of Agricultural Production

Our inability to quantify most aspects of the agricultural revolution forces us to adopt a largely qualitative approach. But we need to consider the recent work of Broadberry,

Campbell, Klein, Overton, and van Leeuwen in *British Economic Growth, 1270–1870*,[30] which provides a quantitative backbone for British agriculture over the long term based on careful estimation from the available datasets. The data is presented only at fifty-year intervals, so it is impossible to derive any close chronology from it.

Fundamental to their work are new estimates of the area under arable and its cropping (Table 30.1). This table shows first of all that the total arable area increases progressively after 1700, with the greatest gains after 1800 (and, one supposes, largely achieved by 1815), and second, within the acreage deployed as arable, the area used as fallow—so in a traditional three-course rotation—progressively declines. In short, farmers found better uses for their fallow by sowing it with roots and artificial grasses, thus increasing the amount of feed available to their animals and allowing higher stocking rates.

Table 30.2 gives Broadberry et al.'s estimates as to how this arable land was used. It is suggested that between 1650 and 1750 there was little increase in the area devoted to wheat. In 1800 the area devoted to wheat is a quarter more than in 1750, but then falls back by 1830. Rye, as appears from the table, was never important. There is noticeably less acreage devoted to barley in 1800 than 1700 but a greater acreage of oats (reflecting the demand for horse provender rather than human needs). But these figures reflect

Table 30.1 Estimates of the extent of arable land, 1700–1836 (in millions of acres)

Date	Total arable (m. acres)	Percent fallow	Total sown area
1700	9.56	20.0	7.64
1750	10.51	15.1	8.92
1801	11.35	11.2	10.08
1836	13.87	9.4	12.57

Source: Stephen Broadberry, Bruce M. S. Campbell, Alexander Klein, Mark Overton, and Bas van Leeuwen, *British Economic Growth, 1270–1870* (Cambridge: Cambridge University Press, 2015), Table 2.10.

Table 30.2 Composition of arable land use, 1270–1871 (millions of acres)

Date	Wheat	Rye/maslin	Barley/dredge	Oats	Pulses	Potatoes	Other crops	Total sown
1700	1.99	0.42	1.82	1.15	0.98	0.00	1.30	7.64
1750	1.95	0.06	1.5	1.82	0.98	0.08	2.53	8.92
1800	2.51	0.06	1.46	1.97	0.83	0.17	2.90	9.91
1830	2.12	0.06	1.81	1.27	0.63	0.26	4.46	10.62

Source: Adapted from Broadberry et al., *British Economic Growth, 1270–1870*, Table 3.03.

only half of the agrarian economy. The estimates for animal numbers (Table 30.3) show an increase of between three and four times between the 1700s and the 1800s.

Acreage and numbers do not readily transfer to yields of dry goods such as corn and the volume of animal products. In Table 30.4 we can see how wheat output increases by roughly a half between the 1750s and the 1800s (we would expect the figure to be less if the figures were for the 1750s and 1790s), while the output of rye, barley, and oats remained pretty static. It is in the production of animal products that we see the great leap forward. Milk (meaning ultimately butter and cheese) increased by about 70 percent between mid-century and end of century. Beef, mutton, and pork more or less doubled (Table 30.5).

Constant 1700 prices take the computed volumes at each successive datum and calculates the value of those volumes of production in the prices current in 1700. (This is a method to factor out differential commodity price inflation, that is, if the price of, say, meat goes up much more than the price of grain, a calculation based on current prices will exaggerate the scale of growth in the production of meat.)

Broadberry et al. supply a further body of data. Working out the value of the products of the arable and animal sectors, they found that the pastoral sector increased its share over the eighteenth century and on into the nineteenth (Table 30.6). There are several explanations for their finding. One would be that bread became less of a staple for

Table 30.3 Estimates of livestock numbers, 1700s–1850s

Date	Milk cattle (m.)	Beef cattle (m.)	Calves (m.)	Sheep (m.)	Swine (m.)
1700s	0.24	0.22	0.24	17.36	0.78
1750s	0.57	0.52	0.57	13.58	1.20
1800s	0.84	0.76	0.84	20.21	1.78
1850s	1.12	1.01	1.12	22.88	2.31

Adapted from Broadberry et al., British Economic Growth, 1270–1870, Table 3.11.

Table 30.4 Total arable output (net of seed and animal consumption, 10-year average given as million bushels)

Date	Wheat	Rye	Barley	Oats	Pulses
1700s	27.94	6.70	35.20	5.70	8.25
1750s	31.48	1.51	39.67	13.03	9.03
1800s	46.32	1.36	42.67	14.06	11.07
1850s	73.69	1.09	58.23	15.93	9.57

Adapted from Broadberry et al., British Economic Growth, 1270–1870, Table 3.07.

Table 30.5 Estimated total outputs

Date	Milk (m. gallons)	Beef (m. lbs)	Mutton (m. lbs)	Pork (m. lbs)	Wool (m. lbs)
1700s	59.10	21.16	211.92	39.93	39.09
1750s	163.19	62.94	217.12	84.40	34.12
1800s	279.75	115.99	422.49	170.63	56.62
1850s	434.05	192.64	616.27	297.43	71.66

Adapted from Broadberry et al., British Economic Growth, 1270–1870, Table 3.15. Veal and hides are omitted from the original table.

Table 30.6 Current- and constant-price shares of arable and livestock outputs in English agriculture, 1700s to 1850s (%)

	Current prices		Constant 1700 prices	
Date	Arable	Livestock	Arable	Livestock
1700s	59.7	40.3	61.5	38.5
1750s	57.8	42.2	54.6	45.4
1800s	48.5	51.5	45.3	54.7
1850s	44.8	55.2	44.2	55.8

Adapted from Broadberry et al., British Economic Growth, 1270–1870, Table 3.18.

people who ate more butter, cheese, and meat. But there is also a fundamental shift: that English agriculture over time was less concerned with providing bread grains because the domestic price was disadvantageous to domestic growers who made better profits from supplying meat and valued-added dairy products. Hence a higher proportion of the bread the population ate came from imported grain. There is an argument to be made that the arable sector was in decline even before 1793, by which time the advantages of sourcing wheat from abroad were doubtless clear enough. The prevailing argument in the 1790s stressed self-sufficiency and the balance of trade. The high prices of the Napoleonic wars doubtless concealed the direction of change, but the question after 1813 is that which remains today: how can domestic arable agriculture flourish as a high-cost producer when corn prices in international markets are lower?

The answer, then as now, was to place domestic industry behind high tariff barriers. This was done in a further revision of the Corn Laws in 1815 (and amended subsequently). Having made imports difficult, for a quarter of a century English farmers largely monopolized English markets. In a way, this was a halcyon period in which, as

Turner, Beckett, and Afton have argued, low prices forced farmers to be more productive by increasing not only the sown area but also the yield per acre.[31] But the political costs were high, and an increasingly urbanized society resented the favoring of the interests of domestic landlords over consumers. It could not be sustained indefinitely. In 1846 the Corn Laws were repealed, and while this did not bring about any immediate effect, it left British agriculture vulnerable to imports of first American and then Russian wheat.

So these estimates all point to a considerable growth in production in the later eighteenth century and after, achieved first by the extension of the cultivated area by enclosure, the better use of fallows in rotations that integrated cattle into them, and second by the emergence of the specialist dairy farm. There is no great technological breakthrough evident either in these figures or the historiography: power continued to be provided by humans and horses, most farms remained self-reliant in nutrients and soil improvers, and yet there was the constant tread of improvement.

Conclusion

In the end, the agricultural revolution is rather like hill walking. From the flat plain, the first hills look like a great challenge, but from their top a vista emerges of higher hills, and from that second ridge there emerges a view of mountains. The agricultural revolution is like that. From the perspective of the eighteenth century, there plainly was a great deal of change, not least in the reorganization of the landscape (where this had not happened before), perhaps the most visible feature for contemporaries, but also less obvious alterations including the development of rotations that gave higher levels of stocking of animals. Agriculture came to run at new levels of production—if not productivity—before 1815. The second agricultural revolution after 1840 was a second ridge, which again produced new achievements in output brought about by steam technology and imported fertilizers before it was knocked back by imports after 1880. The mountains might well be the revolution in machinery, new strains of plants and animals, and artificial fertilizers that took place after 1945.[32]

Notes

1. Joseph Wimpey, "On the Improvements in Agriculture That Have Been Successfully Introduced into This Kingdom within the Last Fifty Years," in *Letters and Papers on Agriculture, Planning etc. Addressed to the Society at Bath* (1790; 2nd ed., Bath: R. Cruttwell, 1793), V:1–24.
2. Rosalind Mitchison, "The Old Board of Agriculture (1793–1822)," *English Historical Review* 74 (1959): 41–69.
3. Henry Brougham, *Parliamentary Debates (Commons)* [Hansard], first ser. 33, cols. 1086–1119 (sitting April 9, 1816): the quotation from col. 1094.
4. J. L. Hammond and B. Hammond, *The Village Labourer, 1760–1832. A Study of the Government of England before the Reform Bill* (London: Longman, 1911; repr. 2005).

5. The most recent work to take this approach is J. M. Neeson, *Commoners: Common Right, Enclosure and Social Change in England, 1700–1820* (Cambridge: Cambridge University Press, 1993).
6. M. E. Turner, *English Parliamentary Enclosure* (Folkestone: Dawson, 1980): 32–34.
7. J. D. Chambers and G. E. Mingay, *The Agricultural Revolution, 1750–1880* (London: B. T. Batsford, 1966).
8. G. E. Mingay, ed., *The Agrarian History of England and Wales*, Vol. 6: *1750–1850* (Cambridge: Cambridge University Press, 1989). E. L. Jones was dismissive of an eighteenth-century agricultural revolution in 1981, regarding change in that century as being "more like a tide, its turn only just discernible, submerging under its waves a group of islands one by one." E. L. Jones, "Agriculture, 1700–80," in *The Economic History of Britain since 1700*, Vol. 1: *1700–1860*, ed. R. Floud and D. McCloskey (Cambridge: Cambridge University Press, 1981): 85.
9. Crafts, in a pioneering assessment, found a lower rate of agricultural growth in the second half of the eighteenth century to the first. N. F. R. Crafts, *British Economic Growth during the Industrial Revolution* (Oxford: Clarendon Press, 1985): 38–44; Mark Overton, *Agricultural Revolution in England. The Transformation of the Agrarian Economy, 1500–1850* (Cambridge: Cambridge University Press, 1996): 84–86.
10. Susanna Wade Martins, *Farmers, Landlords and Landscapes. Rural Britain, 1720 to 1870* (Macclesfield: Windgather Press, 2004).
11. Mark Overton, "Re-establishing the English Agricultural Revolution," *Agricultural History Review* 44 (1996): 1–20; Overton, *Agricultural Revolution in England*.
12. Overton, "Re-establishing," 20.
13. M. E. Turner, J. V. Beckett, and B. Afton, *Farm Production in England, 1700–1914* (Oxford: Oxford University Press, 2001).
14. F. M. L. Thompson, "The Second Agricultural Revolution, 1815–1880," *Economic History Review* 21 (1968): 62–77.
15. Cited by R. W. Sturgess, "The Agricultural Revolution on the English Clays," *Agricultural History Review* 14 (1966): 107–108.
16. T. M. Devine, *The Transformation of Rural Scotland, Social Change and the Agrarian Economy, 1660–1815* (Edinburgh: Edinburgh University Press, 1994); Devine, "The Highland and Lowland Clearances," in *Clearance and Improvement. Land, Power and People in Scotland, 1700–1900* (Edinburgh: John Donald, 2006), 93–112; but cf. the older work of James E. Handley, *The Agricultural Revolution in Scotland* (Glasgow: Burns, 1963).
17. Donald Grove Barnes, *A History of the English Corn Laws from 1660–1846* (London: G. Routledge & Sons, 1930).
18. For references to downland improvement, J. Thirsk, ed., *The Agrarian History of England and Wales*, vol. 6. (Cambridge: Cambridge University Press, 1984), i, 213, 333–34, 336, n. 81. R. A. C. Parker, *Coke of Norfolk. A Financial and Agricultural Study, 1707–1842* (Oxford: Clarendon Press, 1975), ch. 4; also Susanna Wade Martins and Tom Williamson, *Roots of Change. Farming and the Landscape in East Anglia, c. 1700–1870* (Exeter: British Agricultural History Society, 1999): 43–46.
19. George Turner, *General View of the Agriculture of the County of Gloucester* (London, 1794): 10–11.
20. H. C. Darby, *The Changing Fenland* (Cambridge: Cambridge University Press, 1983), 141–43.
21. S. J. Thompson, "Parliamentary Enclosure. Property, Population and the Decline of Classical Republicanism in Eighteenth-Century Britain," *Historical Journal* 51 (2008): 621–642.
22. Board of Agriculture [i.e., Arthur Young], *General Report on Enclosures* (London: 1808, repr. 1971), ch. 4.

23. Turner, *English Parliamentary Enclosure*.
24. Neeson, *Commoners*.
25. Robert C. Allen, *Enclosure and the Yeoman. The Agricultural Development of the South Midlands, 1450–1850* (Oxford: Clarendon Press, 1992), is the fullest attempt.
26. Messrs Rennie, Broun, and Shirreff, *General View of the Agriculture of the West Riding of Yorkshire* (London, 1794): 33–34, 97–98.
27. David Grace, "The Agricultural Engineering Industry," in *Agrarian History*, ed. Mingay, 6:520–45.
28. E. J. T. Collins, "The Diffusion of the Threshing Machine in Britain, 1790–1880,' *Tools and Tillage* 2 (1972): 16–33.
29. William Mavor, *General View of the Agriculture of Berkshire* (London, 1809), 129–36. See too the comments of Wade Martins and Williamson on the slow take-up in Norfolk: *Roots of Change*, 117.
30. Stephen Broadberry, Bruce M. S. Campbell, Alexander Klein, Mark Overton, and Bas van Leeuwen, *British Economic Growth, 1270–1870* (Cambridge: Cambridge University Press, 2015). For an extended review of the chapters on agriculture, R. W. Hoyle, "A Harvest Gathered In: Some Implications of *British Economic Growth 1270–1870* for Agricultural History," *Agricultural History Review* 66 (2018): 112–131.
31. Turner et al., *Farm Production*, 221.
32. A case made in Paul Brassley, David Harvey, Matt Lobley, and Michael Winter, *The Real Agricultural Revolution. The Transformation of English Farming, 1939–1985* (Woodbridge: Boydell Press, 2021).

Bibliography

Allen, Robert C., *Enclosure and the Yeoman. The Agricultural Development of the South Midlands, 1450–1850*. Oxford: Clarendon Press, 1992.
Beckett, J. V. *The Agricultural Revolution*. Oxford: Blackwell, 1990.
Broadberry, Stephen, Bruce M. S. Campbell, Alexander Klein, Mark Overton, and Bas van Leeuwen. *British Economic Growth, 1270–1870*. Cambridge: Cambridge University Press, 2015.
Mingay, G. E., ed. *The Agrarian History of England and Wales*. Vol. 6: *1750–1850*. Cambridge: Cambridge University Press, 1989.
Neeson, J. M. *Commoners: Common Right, Enclosure and Social Change in England, 1700–1820*. Cambridge: Cambridge University Press, 1993.
Overton, Mark, *Agricultural Revolution in England. The Transformation of the Agrarian Economy, 1500–1850*. Cambridge: Cambridge University Press, 1996.
Thompson, F. M. L. 'The Second Agricultural Revolution, 1815–1880.' *Economic History Review* 21 (1968): 62–77.
Turner, M. E. *English Parliamentary Enclosure. Its Historical Geography and Economic History*. Folkestone: Dawson, 1980.
Turner, M. E., J. V. Beckett, and B. Afton. *Farm Production in England, 1700–1914*. Oxford: Oxford University Press, 2001.
Wade Martins, Susanna, and Tom Williamson. *Roots of Change, Farming and the Landscape in East Anglia, c. 1700–1870*. Exeter: British Agricultural History Society, 1999.

CHAPTER 31

FRONTIER AGRICULTURE AND THE CREATION OF GLOBAL NEO-EUROPES

JONATHAN DALY[*]

IN 1986, Alfred Crosby observed that four countries—Canada, the United States, Argentina, and Australia—dominated global trade in the world's most abundantly produced and exported crop, wheat. He called such lands Neo-Europes because European settlers found these countries' temperate climates congenial to their lifestyle and farming traditions. In 1982 they accounted for 30 percent of world agricultural exports—and 72 percent of exports of wheat.[1] Back in 1909–1913, those countries, plus pre-revolutionary Russia, had exported 62.7 percent of wheat (and also accounted for 50 percent of its total global production).[2] This made them breadbaskets for a dramatically expanding world population.

Why these specific countries? Given their rich, deep chernozem soils, temperate climate, and moderate rainfall patterns, they are home to the best lands for growing wheat, barley, rye, and other bread-making grains. Growing wheat in particular is a highly efficient use of agricultural land. Farmers can derive from cattle grazing on one hectare of natural grassland only one-fortieth as much nourishment as from the same area planted with wheat.[3]

Scholars have argued about environmental impacts on historical development. The late nineteenth century produced many advocates of geographical determinism, including Sergei Solov'ev in Russia and Frederick Jackson Turner in the United States, who argued that climate and topography strongly influence historical evolution.[4] Most later scholars questioned such interpretations. After all, the five countries considered here experienced diverse pathways to their status of global breadbaskets. The state was the most active in promoting agricultural settlement in the Russian steppe, and the least on the Argentinian pampa. Rugged smallholders played the biggest role in Canada, while big landed estates produced most of the exportable wheat in Argentina. Individualism and fierce competition were the norm on the US frontier more than elsewhere.[5] Argentina exported 65 percent of its total wheat production; the United States, only 14 percent.[6] That all five became and remain global breadbaskets despite these differences suggests that, historically speaking, geography is akin to fate.

Ten thousand years ago, Middle Easterners domesticated the major grains, including wheat. Humans thus gained access to massive stores of nutrients derived from the soil and the atmosphere.[7] Grain cultivation spread in every direction across Afro-Eurasia, resulting in population growth, the emergence of cities and civilization, and the pursuit of new frontiers to open.[8]

Yet the richest grasslands remained unplowed for millennia. The major grasslands of Eurasia became pathways (the famed "Silk Road") for nomadic horsemen, who fostered exchanges of goods, people, fauna, ideas, inventions, and microbes.[9] Only the development of heavier plows and the in-migration of well-armed Europeans, beginning a few centuries ago, made their cultivation possible.[10] This was true in all five regions, despite their disparate geographical locations. Likewise, only the discovery of synthetic fertilizer enabled them to contribute significantly to colossal population growth.[11] Those regions had always had the physical preconditions to become breadbaskets, but only rapid industrialization and urbanization in nineteenth-century Europe, America, and Japan, drove armies of farmer-entrepreneurs to produce and market grain.

As the Second Industrial Revolution got underway, Great Britain increased food imports in order to focus on manufacturing. By 1900, British farmers could supply only about 17 percent of domestic requirements.[12] Steamships, railroads, the telegraph, and the commercial press made possible a flood of inexpensive grain from newly developed grasslands to Europe, raising the standard of living in both.[13] Likewise, high wheat prices stimulated railroad construction and the steady settlement and expansion of land sown to wheat, contributing strongly to a global economic boom.[14] Declining factor costs created a single global price and a unified world market for wheat.[15]

Once the temperate frontiers opened up fully, between roughly 1865 and 1914, foreign investment, chiefly from Europe, flowed into them.[16] These New Worlds also attracted most of the overseas European migration, for they offered seemingly boundless opportunities to settle on some of the richest farmland in the world.[17] This settlement destroyed the natural economy of the earlier inhabitants of the fertile grasslands. This was a tragic outcome. Yet it was also a causal factor in the subsequent dramatic increase in human population.

Russia

Russia first developed in northern forests with infertile soils and a short growing season, where climatic variations could cause dire economic hardship.[18] Russian peasants therefore avoided risky agricultural innovation. To the south and southeast, the steppe beckoned with rich soils that had been building up nutrients for centuries. This land boasts extraordinary biodiversity: at least 5,000 vascular plant species—roughly the same number that inhabit the North American prairie.[19]

After Ivan the Terrible conquered the Tatar strongholds of Kazan and Astrakhan on the Volga River in the mid-1500s, the Russian state built successively further defensive lines against nomadic incursions. Across them a slow trickle of settlers passed.[20] Peter I and his immediate successors promoted a more orderly settlement, but as of 1719 only around 200,000 male souls inhabited the steppe.[21] Toward the end of the century, Catherine II defeated the Ottoman Empire, subdued the northern Black Sea coastal region, and promoted its peopling. Some half-million migrants, including 100,000 from Europe, settled in the region.[22] Settlers received various exemptions, usually temporary, from taxation and military conscription. Here was a distinctive feature of Russian grassland settlement: the government deprecated migration within the empire, preferred foreign (especially German) immigrants, imposed heavy liabilities on settlers following a grace period, and exerted tight administrative supervision on migration and settlement.[23] Gradually, Russia became a significant exporter of grain, its share of world grain exports rising from 2.9 percent in 1710 to 20 percent in the early 1800s, thanks in part to lower import tariffs in Spain, France, and Britain.[24]

Settlers in Russia, as on the other four frontiers, both struggled to survive and rejoiced when they thrived. Boosters in all five areas extolled the virtues of the pioneer spirit. Yet the Russian steppe frontier remained for most Russians an alien land, at once of Russia and yet distinct from it at the same time.[25] It is hard to imagine the American or Canadian prairie or the Argentine pampas described in this manner.

Migrants to the Russian steppe brought agricultural techniques and crops similar to those of the Europeans, but they did not create Neo-Europes. First, the Indigenous nomads were no strangers to the staple grains and livestock of western Eurasia. In fact, their horsemanship had made it hard for sedentary peoples to break into their territory. Second, the steppe inhabitants had immunity to the pathogens that devasted populations of the New World and Australia.[26] Nevertheless, Russian settlers gradually conquered and peopled these lands, as the nomads had once overwhelmed sedentary peoples on the margins of the grasslands. From 1871 to 1896, roughly two million migrants, mostly from central Russia and Left-Bank Ukraine, settled in the steppe region.[27] This increased the total population to roughly ten million settled farmers.[28] Demand for wheat from the industrializing countries, especially the UK, pushed up prices and created a "wheat boom." In Russia, the expanding railroad network and the convertibility of the gold-backed ruble enabled farmers to take part in this first era of true globalization. Improved agricultural methods and technology increased output and drove exports.[29]

Yet not all was well on the steppe. Most decades witnessed drought-induced crop failures. (Such was true of all the other fertile grassland regions, because of sparse annual rainfall, but the problem was especially acute on the steppe.) The years 1891–1892 were catastrophic. Agricultural experts began to worry about anthropogenic damage to grassland ecosystems. Others, such as Vasilii Dokuchaev, the pioneering worldwide expert on black earth soils, articulated an early vision of sustainable agriculture.[30]

During this timeframe, 1861–1914, Russia was the world's largest exporter of wheat. After Britain repealed its protective Corn Laws in 1846, grain flooded in from around the world. The steppe regions north of the Black Sea and the Caucasus Mountains, which had weak legacies of serfdom, were highly dynamic.[31] Here roughly 40 percent of the agricultural land in 1905 consisted of large estates over 200 *desiatiny* (or some 544 acres).[32] These large operations produced higher yields, for example, 14.6 bushels per acre of winter wheat in 1893–1903, compared to only 11.3 bushels per acre on peasant farms.[33] Nevertheless, even peasant farmers with communal landholding arrangements adopted improved agricultural techniques.[34] Although Russia had few grain elevators at the turn of the century, and its wheat exports contained a high level of impurities, the cost of shipment from both northern and southern Russian ports to British markets bested those from the United States, thanks in part to highly sophisticated trading firms.[35] In 1909–1913, Russia accounted for 20.03 percent of global wheat exports, with the United States a distant second at 12.52 percent.[36] At the same time, grain consumption in Russia increased per capita by 31 percent in 1885–1913,[37] thanks to steadily expanding acreage devoted to the crop.[38]

The Russian Revolution dramatically curtailed grain exports, as peasants seized the big estates and the Bolsheviks nationalized (and then collectivized) the land. From 1924 to 1928, the other four major exporters seized a whopping 83.79 percent share (down to an average of 74.6 in the subsequent decade, amid the Great Depression), while Russia managed only an annual average of 3.34 percent from 1924 to 1938.[39] In the 1950s, Nikita Khrushchev promoted migration to the furthest southeastern steppe, where some 300,000 Soviet citizens plowed up nearly 89 million acres.[40] Unfortunately, such vast bureaucratic projects proved no more successful than Stalin's devastating collectivization drive.[41] Beginning in 1964, the USSR became a net importer of wheat (and ceased exporting grain to its Eastern European satellites), the amount imported each year depending on weather and other conditions. Russia, which had been the largest exporter of grain in the early 1900s, became the world's largest importer by the mid-1980s, purchasing over 15 percent of world grain exports, such that fully one-third of baked goods in the late USSR was made from imported grain.[42] Only after the fall of communism—and the collapse of the centralized command economy and attendant rise in local decision-making, entrepreneurship, resultant market efficiencies, and integration into the world agricultural economy—could Russia gradually retake its place as the world's biggest exporter.

THE UNITED STATES

The native peoples of North America did not live "in balance, stasis, or perfect harmony," according to the environmental historian Geoff Cunfer, but were "constantly in flux, constantly in conversation with the natural world."[43] Sometimes the interaction was deadly, as when they hunted hundreds of megafauna species to extinction, including giant armadillos and saber-tooth tigers. More recently, natives set fires to assist with landscape management and hunting. Among their main quarry were the roughly 28 million bison roaming on the North American Great Plains in 1500.[44] Indigenous people learned to domesticate and ride horses introduced by Spanish explorers, reinventing themselves as "equestrian nomads."[45] Mounted Comanche and Cheyenne outfought and outhunted their rivals.[46] European settlers joined in the hunt, beginning in the 1840s, for both food and trade, as bison products gained popularity out East. By the late 1860s, when Euro-American settlers began migrating in large numbers to the Plains, the bison were well on their way to destruction, leaving the grasslands wide open for herds of cattle and grain cultivation. Native peoples continued to resist white incursions through most of the 1870s but gradually accepted treaties imposed on them by the US government and retreated to reservations comprised largely of poor land.[47] The American government and society partly justified taking native land by claiming to bring civilization and economic development to empty wilderness and to people unwilling or unable to improve the land using modern methods.[48]

The Euro-American migrants found the Great Plains not only far more fertile than land in Europe but even better suited to grain cultivation, thanks to more favorable rainfall patterns, than on the Russian steppe.[49] The thirteen British colonies had already become a breadbasket to Europe decades before the founding of the Republic and its absorption of the Great Plains. Improvements in mail service, logistics, and insurance methods and a decline of piracy fueled a high level of international market integration, though the French Revolution and Napoleonic Wars interrupted it for several decades.

As the population of the early Republic steadily expanded and intensive farming depleted the relatively poor soils of the eastern region, settlers migrated west. The Land Ordinance, adopted by the Congress of the Confederation in 1785, established rules for the sale of federal lands. The price was high and minimum parcels large, as Alexander Hamilton advocated. But over the next decades, Congress slashed both prices and acreage, following the preference of Thomas Jefferson. By 1832, one could buy a forty-acre farm for $50, or roughly half the average annual per capita income. Alexis de Tocqueville considered this land policy fundamental to "American democracy and equality."[50] The policy culminated in a series of laws, most notably the Homestead Act of 1862, which aimed at providing "homes for the homeless and land to the landless."[51] The law enabled applicants to receive free of charge 160 acres of land in exchange for inhabiting and improving it for a period of five years. In 1869, both the Transcontinental Railroad and the Suez Canal opened, knitting the earth together into a global trading network, with wheat among the major objects of international trade. Within decades, tens of millions of acres on the American prairie had devolved to pioneer farmers, but also to land speculators.[52]

The failure rate was high, living conditions harsh: endless flat land, scarce building material, inadequate water supplies, few neighbors, and extraordinarily dense soil. Nevertheless, an extensive study drawing on records of 1,571 households in Kansas, Nebraska, and the Dakota Territory, many of which must have benefited from the Homestead Act, found that migrants to the frontier enjoyed greater financial success than those who remained in the East (though settlers arriving before 1860 accumulated more wealth than those who came later).[53]

Amendments to the law eased tenure requirements. Thus, the standard allotment for far western states increased to 320 acres in 1909, and the required period of tenure was reduced to three years in 1912.[54] By contrast, the largest allotments granted under analogous Russian laws did not exceed 80 acres, with far more obligations.[55] No wonder some 12,000 German settlers (from the earlier wave of in-migration during the reign of Catherine II) left the Russian Empire for Kansas in the 1870s, and at least 50,000 emigrated to other Neo-Europes from 1870 to 1900.[56] These immigrants imported Russian varieties of hard winter wheat, with enormous success thanks to its resistance to drought and disease.[57] Ironically, much of the 400 million bushels of US wheat sold to the USSR in 1972 was the "offspring" of Russian seeds imported decades before.[58]

The "wheat frontier" expanded rapidly across the Great Plains, as improved land increased from 78 million acres in 1870 to over 250 million in 1910. Already in the early 1890s, in the spring wheat region of Minnesota, North Dakota, and South Dakota, nearly 70 percent of farmland was planted to wheat and almost 85 percent of the resultant crop was exported.[59] Thanks to automation, Minneapolis became the leading flour-milling center in the world, surpassing Budapest in 1884, and expanding its output from 3 million bushels in 1882 to over 7 million in 1890.[60]

The Great Plow-Up was an extraordinary undertaking. With horses—roughly one per fifty-three acres of farmland—individual farmers plowed and harrowed a couple dozen acres each year and typically kept 45 percent of their land in pasture.[61] Horses were invaluable resources around the farm and, after the cost of land, the most expensive capital input. From the 1920s, tractors began to replace horses, mules, and many human laborers on American farms. (The number of tractors on the southern Great Plains increased from fewer than 300 in 1915 to 10,000 in the early 1930s.[62]) In 1924–1928, the United States reached its high point of wheat and wheat flour exports as a percentage of the world total, at 21.36 percent.[63]

Although the prairie soil was among the richest in the world—and farmers conducted crop rotations, used manure produced by their livestock, and planted nitrogen-fixing crops for animal fodder—the soil steadily lost nitrogen.[64] By the 1890s, American farmers and agronomists, like their Russian counterparts, began to worry about sustainability. Also, as in Russia, the Great Plains experienced cyclical dry spells, though at less frequent intervals. The worst in recorded history, called the Dust Bowl, struck in the 1930s.[65] One storm picked up and spread over the eastern United States and the Atlantic Ocean more dirt than was excavated to build the Panama Canal. Donald Worster, a leading environmental historian, called it "the most severe environmental catastrophe in the entire history of white man on this continent."[66]

Despite the narrative of the Great Plains as dominated by industrialized agriculture, and the reality of some immense farms, the average farmsteads on the Great Plains were small and family-operated, typically producing a variety of crops and livestock for both personal consumption and marketing.[67] Moreover, the Dust Bowl did not permanently stunt agricultural development in the region. The wheat harvest in 1945 was nearly as immense as it had been in 1930, and five years later farmers sowed 50 percent more land to wheat: 59.5 million acres, compared to 36 million in 1945 and 38 million in 1930, the previous high point. It seems likely that, while human activity contributed to the Dust Bowl, shifting weather patterns were the main causal factor. Massive dust storms occurred both before the introduction of European-style farming and in places where such farming had not occurred, suggesting that they are, according to Cunfer, "normal forms of ecological disturbance on the southern plains."[68]

Subsequently, Great Plains farmers deployed two principal methods to boost output. They dramatically increased the use of synthetic fertilizer (though at a lower rate than elsewhere in the United States, since the prairie soils remained comparatively more fertile), and they tapped into the Ogallala Aquifer to irrigate their fields. As the water table fell, they turned to dry-farming techniques, a pattern that repeated itself in all the grassland breadbaskets as farmers expanded wheat cultivation into more arid regions. These methods, along with better technology and agricultural practices, helped grow wheat yields from an average of 14 bushels per acre in 1950 to 39 bushels in 1987—an almost threefold increase.[69] Since then, wheat yields have increased still further, reaching an all-time high in 2016 of 52.7 bushels per acre.[70]

Of course, humans have had an impact on the Great Plains. The plowing up of grasslands dramatically reduced biodiversity. One study in Nebraska showed that thirteen species of bird made a home on untilled land but only two in adjacent cultivated fields.[71] Early narratives of frontier agriculture told stories of pioneers on the Great Plains battling natives and a hostile wilderness and establishing democratic institutions and a productive economic system. Later accounts have emphasized destructive impacts on native cultures and natural environments. Both aspects of the story are true. But a more balanced interpretation probably needs to see humans less as alien interlopers than as citizens of the land community, alongside countless other species striving to fit in and making their mark.[72]

CANADA

About 5 percent of Canadian land is suitable for agriculture; the best is in the prairie provinces of Alberta, Manitoba, and Saskatchewan,[73] which contain over 80 percent of Canada's croplands.[74] The Canadian government, looking to the example of its southern neighbor (and also to prevent Canadians from migrating south), adopted its own homesteading policy, the Dominion Lands Act, in 1872.[75] By then, the bison were all but gone from the Canadian prairie; consequently, European immigrants did not significantly participate in their decimation.[76] The Canadian government did institute policies that devastated communities of human natives on the prairie with a series of treaties beginning in 1871 that squeezed them into highly restrictive reserves.[77] Canadian homesteaders received 160 acres, though unlike in the United States women could usually not apply.[78] To foster economic development, the government also offered land grants to facilitate the building of a transcontinental railroad (completed in 1885) and established research stations, extension services, and grain elevators.[79] Family farms became the norm. The model was so attractive, tens of thousands of Americans migrated to the Canadian prairie to benefit from the program.[80]

The Canadian government was quite restrictive in its immigration policy, favoring Ukrainians, Germans, and Britons, while rejecting Spaniards, Italians, and Greeks.[81] The main reason was that immigrants from southern Europe tended to shuttle between the Old World and the New, whereas those from northern and eastern Europe were more likely to settle permanently, which the Canadian government considered a predictor of eventual economic success.[82] Immigrant farmers on the Canadian prairie were indeed successful. By 1911, 90 percent owned their own land. It helped that Canadian prairie farmers had access to extensive credit, both formal and informal, permitting them to acquire more land and livestock and purchase labor-saving machinery.[83]

Government promotion of economic development on the Canadian prairie, described in promotional literature as "the largest flower garden on the continent," was driven by hopes of building a flourishing egalitarian society in the wilderness. Despite the availability of relatively free land, much of it extraordinary fertile, many homesteaders failed in Canada, for example 57 percent in Saskatchewan from 1911 to 1931.[84] This was not surprising. Pioneer life was backbreaking, lonely, and full of privation. Moreover, the Canadian government provided very little assistance to individual farmers, as it sought to promote rugged self-reliance. The most successful pioneers on the Canadian prairie were American citizens loaded with experience and requisite equipment, as well as Mennonites, Ukrainians, and others who formed tight-knit and mutually supportive communities.[85]

As Canada's wheat cultivation tripled to over ten million acres in 1890–1914, it was often (and nearly always between 1924 and 1938) the main exporter to the UK, the world's biggest wheat market.[86] During World War I, the UK imported more wheat than ever, and its government pressured Canada to increase its output and exports. Farmers raced to sow more wheat. The Canadian government, for its part, imposed stricter regulations and control.[87] After the war, these controls were eased, and Canada became the world's largest wheat exporter, achieving 35.15 of total global exports in 1924–1928.[88] The worldwide economic downturn, compounded by a multiyear drought in the 1930s, hit Canada hard, as it found itself sitting on huge surpluses of unsalable wheat. Some 247,000 farmers abandoned the prairie provinces between 1931 and 1934.[89] The government stepped in to purchase and liquidate the excess grain, a policy that continued into World War II.[90] It also increased its provision of expertise, resources, infrastructure development, and other forms of support to prairie agriculture.[91]

As in the United States, agriculture has dramatically altered prairie ecology. Researchers found that a twenty-seven-acre tract of wild land in Saskatchewan provided a habitat for twice as many species of butterflies as in the vast stretch of surrounding cropland.[92] Likewise, agricultural pursuits have dissipated some 36–50 percent of the natural nutrient content of Canada's prairie soils. As in the United States, such environmental harm has been countered with heavy applications of synthetic fertilizer. Thanks to improved farming methods, in the early twenty-first century Canada was a top exporter of all the major Middle Eastern grains, and between 1989 and 2007 it exported 62 percent of its entire crop production.[93] It is without a doubt one of the great agricultural and broadly economic success stories of modern history.

Argentina

The same cannot be said of Argentina, though its story began auspiciously. Spanish missionaries introduced horses and cattle to the Argentine pampas beginning in 1580. By 1700, millions of the beasts roamed the fertile grasslands.[94] With easy livings thus to be made from animal husbandry, farming developed late in Argentina. In fact, until it became possible to export jerked beef in the late 1700s, meat had almost no value in Argentina. Even the best horses could be acquired for a pittance. This extraordinary abundance fostered a lifestyle of leisure and enjoyment among the gauchos, the iconic European inhabitants of the pampas.[95]

It seems that Argentina was cursed with an extraordinary and valuable abundance of one resource, which as in some oil-rich countries, prevented the development of others. Or as Edward B. Barbier, an environmental and resource economist, has argued, "there is no iron law associating natural resource abundance with national industrial strength."[96] Those who undertook farming usually did not devote their lives to learning best practices for cultivating wheat—the main crop—on the pampas. Likewise, Argentine farmers had little savings to invest in essential farm implements. Few could even afford to put up sheds or barns, and fencing was usually installed by cattleman to protect their precious herds, not farmers to protect their crops from trampling. Consequently, Argentina was not integrated into the world grain market until relatively late in the nineteenth century.[97] Then, suddenly bumper harvests in 1893 and 1894 suggested to *Harper's Weekly* that Argentina would soon "become the greatest wheat producing country in the world."[98] It also helped that trade factor costs—including insurance rates, handling costs, and tariffs—dramatically declined in the same era.[99] Indeed, from 1909 to 1938, Argentina was consistently the world's second or third biggest exporter of wheat, even though its proportion of world production was the second smallest (after Australia) of the five major producers.[100]

Argentina and Canada had a lot in common but also important differences. Each enjoyed enviable resource endowments, including some of the best arable grassland in the world, but with sparse populations. Rainfall in both regions was sometimes insufficient for wheat production, but more so in Argentina.[101] The grasslands in both countries were inhabited by mounted native warriors, often equipped with firearms, who dominated until Europeans with superior firepower pushed them off the range. Until the 1870s, neither country attracted much interest among European investors. As the worldwide demand for meat expanded later in the century, especially in the UK, however, Great Britain became the major source of investment for both countries.[102]

From 1890 to 1914, both countries attracted millions of European immigrants. In fact, Argentina attracted more than Australia or Canada in 1881–1910.[103] Political leaders looked to the United States as a model for development, though neither the central nor the provincial Argentine governments did much to promote farming.[104] Wheat became their primary export, within an export-driven economic development strategy. Indeed, arable land sown to wheat in Argentina expanded in 1880–1929 from 73,100 to 9,219,000 ha.[105] "Yet in the long run," the prominent economic historian Jeremy Adelman notes, "Canada's salutary performance in subsequent decades is almost as notorious as Argentina's failure."[106]

The key distinction, he argues, had to do with property relations. Immigrant farmers found no open prairie in Argentina but rather a region dominated by well-established ranchers. Most farmers in Canada owned their own land, whereas in Argentina most were leaseholders and tenants. In Canada, the government worked hard to distribute public land widely. State intervention kept land prices low in Canada, whereas land became nearly unaffordable for recent immigrants in Argentina, where most public land ended up concentrated in large estates.[107] While immigrants to Canada expected to own their means of production (farms), most immigrants to Argentina only hoped for high wages and profits from leasing and working the land, rather than owning it. Nor did Argentine's ruling landed elites opt for a homesteading program, preferring to attract southern European laborers who were willing to work for low wages and often did not remain in Argentina.[108] Eighty percent of immigrants to Argentina from 1857 to 1924 came from Italy and Spain. Few had experience of land ownership, and less than half of the 4.5 million Europeans who moved to Argentina between 1890 and 1914 remained in the country, the rest returning home with their earnings. By contrast, nearly all immigrants to Canada stayed out on the distant prairie, which took days to reach by train. The dense grid of Argentine railroads and close proximity of the pampas to big cities, by contrast, made it easy to shuttle back and forth without putting down roots.[109]

Credit institutions existed on the pampas, but their main focus was lending to large landowners. After all, tenants typically had no collateral to put up. Consequently, Argentine wheat farmers found it far more difficult to acquire labor-saving and productivity-increasing machinery than their Canadian counterparts. Saskatchewan farmers' investments in farm machinery per hectare, for example, bested those of their Argentine counterparts by a factor of 6.2.[110] Moreover, insufficiently developed infrastructure, handling capacity, storage devices, railroad stock, and other capital-intensive factors made for significant loss of wheat through spoilage on its way from field to ship, though conditions improved in the decade or so after 1900.[111]

On the eve of World War I, Argentina achieved export levels per capita similar to those of Canada and Australia.[112] The war itself brought hardship, as the UK reduced its imports of grain and impeded Argentine exports to its second biggest trading partner, Germany.[113] When Soviet Russia curtailed its wheat exports, however, Argentina benefited, its share of world wheat exports climbing to 19.48 percent in 1934–1938.[114] During World War II, Argentine wheat exports contracted by 30 percent, in part because Britain favored Australian grain.[115] This trend continued in subsequent decades.

Australia

Before Europeans arrived, Australian natives had hunted the indigenous megafauna—including two-ton marsupials—to extinction. European migrants found an entirely unfamiliar environment. Vast tracts of extraordinarily fertile soils, scarcely scratched by agriculturalists or trampled by wild beasts, beckoned the newcomers.[116] Sheep introduced into New South Wales in 1792 had grown into herds totaling twelve million by 1854.[117] A population boom stimulated by the Gold Rush of 1851 drove a corresponding expansion in wheat production along the southeast, south, and southwestern coastal regions.[118]

In 1895 to 1903, intermittent dry weather conditions in southern Australia, called the Federation Drought, devastated the agricultural sector. Australians responded in three principal ways. First, they applied natural and artificial fertilizers and introduced higher-yielding seed varieties and land-management techniques.[119] Second, they diversified the economy toward industry, which supported agriculture with technological innovation and development.[120] Finally, the government promoted agricultural development in the vast wheatbelt region just inland from the southwestern Australian Coast.[121] Consequently, Australian wheat farming steadily expanded in the 1920s.

All the world's main wheat-exporting countries were competing against each other by 1930, which produced a major glut and a consequent decline in prices. Instead of retrenching, however, most Australian farmers continued to expand their acreage. Thus, in New South Wales, 1930 was declared the "Grow More Wheat" year.[122]

As a result of improvements in agricultural techniques, technologies, and seed varieties, and expanded acreage devoted to wheat, Australia's proportion of world exports increased from 6.26 percent in 1909–1913 to 16.30 percent in 1934–1938.[123] The worldwide economic downturn in the 1930s had a powerful negative effect on Australia and the other major exporters, yet there was an upside to the economic devastation. A dramatic decrease in land sown to wheat (in the range of 20–30 percent) resulted in the concentration of wheat production in the most productive lands, boosting yields.[124]

Conclusion

Today, Canada, the United States, Argentina, and Australia remain leading wheat exporters. Thanks to the collapse of communism, however, Russia is again the biggest exporter. The biggest wheat exporters do not necessarily produce the most wheat. The European Union, mainland China, and India are currently the leading producers (together they account for just over half of the world production of roughly 750 million tons), but most of their output is consumed, and only the European Union is a leading exporter (the third biggest). Exports constitute a tiny fraction of total worldwide production, with Russia accounting in 2018–2021 on average for 36 million tons, the European Union for 29 million, the United States for 26 million, Canada for 25 million, Ukraine for 18 million, Australia for 13 million, and Argentina for 11 million, numbers that were projected to hold roughly steady through 2023 (with Ukraine's production dramatically falling, due to Russia's invasion of Ukraine).[125] Thus, the highly fertile, temperate grasslands plowed up starting a century and a half ago remain today the same global breadbaskets, suggesting something like geographical determinism, especially given these countries' diverse evolutionary pathways.

Questions of sustainability nevertheless arise. The ecological transformation has been dramatic with a loss of biodiversity, contamination of soil and groundwater, and other costs. Indeed, only some 10 percent of the world's natural grassland remain intact.[126] The human impact has been equally extreme, including the decimation of native peoples and grassland agriculture's significant contribution to the world population explosion from 1.2 billion in 1850 to 8 billion today. More and more people depend on these regions' output: over 50 percent of countries globally import more grain than they produce for themselves.[127] For example, Indonesians scarcely ate wheat until the United States included some in its package of food aid in 1969. They now import seven million tons of wheat and wheat flour annually.[128] An extraordinary aspect of this story is the decline in the number of farmers producing grain from more than half the populations of those five countries to under 1 percent (6.7 percent in Russia) today. Of course, the major reason for increased productivity is the energy-intensive application of synthetic fertilizer and farm machinery. Scholars question whether this trend can be sustained.[129] The answer depends in large part on the world's breadbaskets.

Their ability to produce depends on geopolitics. Russia's invasion of Ukraine in February 2022 drove grain prices to record highs and prompted fears of global food shortages.[130] A trade deal reached in July permitted Ukrainian grain exports through the Black Sea, easing fears of food scarcity in the developing world, and bringing wheat prices back down. The agreement was extended in November for another three months.[131] In July 2023, Russia abrogated the deal, and its military bombarded the Ukrainian ports and grain-handling infrastructure, driving up Chicago wheat futures 9 percent.[132] Such actions further underscored the importance of frontier agriculture.

Notes

* I am grateful to participants in the Chicago Russian History Workshop for invaluable comments on an earlier draft of this chapter.
1. Alfred W. Crosby, *Ecological Imperialism: The Biological Expansion of Europe, 900–1900*, 2nd ed. (New York: Cambridge University Press, 2004): 3–4.

2. Gema Aparicio and Vicente Pinilla, "International Trade in Wheat and Other Cereals and the Collapse of the First Wave of Globalization 1900–1938," *Journal of Global History* 14, no. 1 (2010): 55.
3. Jeremy M. B. Smith, "Grassland," in *Encyclopædia Britannica* (October 25, 2002), https://www.britannica.com/science/grassland, accessed July 3, 2019.
4. Mark Bassin, "Turner, Solov'ev, and the 'Frontier Hypothesis': The Nationalist Significance of Open Spaces," *Journal of Modern History* 65, no. 3 (September 1993): 473–511.
5. John C. Weaver, *The Great Land Rush and the Making of the Modern World, 1650–1900* (Montreal: McGill-Queen's University Press, 2003): 265.
6. Aparicio and Pinilla, "International Trade," 55. Australia exported 55 percent of its total production, Canada 46 percent, and Russia 21 percent.
7. Geoff Cunfer, "Manure Matters on the Great Plains Frontier," *Journal of Interdisciplinary History* 34, no. 4 (Spring 2004): 540.
8. Hugh Brody, *The Other Side of Eden: Hunters, Farmers and the Shaping of the World* (New York: North Point Press, 2001): 147–148.
9. Andrew C. Isenberg, "Seas of Grass: Grasslands in World Environmental History," in *The Oxford Handbook of Environmental History*, ed. Andrew C. Isenberg (Oxford: Oxford University Press, 2014): 141.
10. J. R. McNeill and Verena Winiwarter, "Breaking the Sod: Humankind, History, and Soil," *Science*, n.s., 304, no. 5677 (June 11, 2004): 1627–1629.
11. Vaclav Smil, *Enriching the Earth: Fritz Haber, Carl Bosch, and the Transformation of World Food Production* (Cambridge, MA: MIT Press, 2004).
12. Gerald Friesen, *The Canadian Prairies: A History* (Toronto: University of Toronto Press, 1987): 327.
13. Kevin H. O'Rourke, "The European Grain Invasion, 1870–1913," *Journal of Economic History* 57, no. 4 (1997): 775–801; Mette Ejrnæs and Karl Gunnar Persson, "The Gains from Improved Market Efficiency: Trade before and after the Transatlantic Telegraph," *European Review of Economic History* 14, no. 3 (December 2010): 361–381.
14. Edward B. Barbier, *Scarcity and Frontiers: How Economies Have Developed through Natural Resource Exploitation* (New York: Cambridge University Press, 2011): 369.
15. André Magnan, *When Wheat Was King: The Rise and Fall of the Canada-UK Grain Trade* (Vancouver: University of British Columbia Press, 2016): 30.
16. Gregg Huff, "Globalization, Natural Resources, and Foreign Investment: A View from the Resource-Rich Tropics," *Oxford Economic Papers* 59 (October 2007): i127–i155.
17. Jeremy Adelman, *Frontier Development: Land, Labor, and Capital in the Wheat Lands of Argentina and Canada, 1890–1914* (Oxford: Clarendon Press, 1994): 20.
18. David Moon, "Land and Environment," in *The Oxford Handbook of Modern Russian History*, ed. Simon Dixon (New York: Oxford University Press, 2013): 4.
19. Jennifer S. F. Reinecke et al., "Land Use of Natural and Secondary Grasslands in Russia," in *Grasslands of the World*, ed. Victor R. Squires et al. (Boca Raton, FL: CRC Press, 2018), 127; Candace Savage, *Prairie: A Natural History*, 2nd ed. (Vancouver: Greystone Books, 2011): 225.
20. John F. Richards, *The Unending Frontier: An Environmental History of the Early Modern World* (Berkeley: University of California Press, 2003), 256–66.
21. Willard Sunderland, *Taming the Wild Field: Colonization and Empire on the Russian Steppe* (Ithaca, NY: Cornell University Press, 2004): 45.
22. Ibid., 74, 77.

23. Ibid., 115.
24. Rafael Dobado-González, Alfredo Garcîa-Hiernaux, and David E. Guerrero, "The Integration of Grain Markets in the Eighteenth Century: Early Rise of Globalization in the West," *Journal of Economic History* 72, no. 3 (September 2012): 675.
25. Sunderland, *Taming*, 173.
26. David Moon, "Peasant Migration and the Settlement of Russia's Frontiers, 1550–1897," *Historical Journal* 40, no. 4 (1997): 881–882.
27. Sunderland, *Taming*, 180.
28. David Moon, "Agriculture and the Environment on the Steppes in the Nineteenth Century," in *Peopling the Russian Periphery: Borderland Colonization in Eurasian History*, ed. Nicholas Breyfogle, Abby Schrader, and Willard Sunderland (London: Routledge, 2007): 81.
29. Oscar Sanchez-Sibony, *Red Globalization: The Political Economy of the Soviet Cold War from Stalin to Khrushchev* (New York: Cambridge University Press, 2014): 30.
30. David Moon, "The Environmental History of the Russian Steppes: Vasilii Dokuchaev and the Harvest Failure of 1891," *Transactions of the Royal Historical Society* 15 (2005): 149–174.
31. Leonard G. Friesen, *Rural Revolutions in Southern Ukraine: Peasants, Nobles, and Colonists, 1774–1905* (Cambridge, MA: Harvard University Press, 2008): 198.
32. Mark Cohen, "Reforming States, Agricultural Transformation, and Economic Development in Russia and Japan, 1853–1913," *Comparative Studies in Society and History* 60, no. 3 (July 2018): 741.
33. Barry K. Goodwin and Thomas J. Grennes, "Tsarist Russia and the World Wheat Market," *Explorations in Economic History* 35, no. 4 (October 1998): 407.
34. Michael Kopsidis, Katja Bruisch, and Daniel W. Bromley, "Where Is the Backward Russian Peasant? Evidence against the Superiority of Private Farming, 1883–1913," *Journal of Peasant Studies* 42, no. 2 (2015): 434–435.
35. Goodwin and Grennes, "Tsarist Russia," 410, 413.
36. Aparicio and Pinilla, "International Trade," 55.
37. Boris N. Mironov, "The Myth of a Systemic Crisis in Russia after the Great Reforms of the 1860s–1870s," *Russian Studies in History* 47, no. 4 (Spring 2009): 43.
38. M. E. Falkus, "Russia and the International Wheat Trade, 1861–1914," *Economica* 33, no. 132 (November 1966): 422–424.
39. Aparicio and Pinilla, "International Trade," 55.
40. Moon, "Peasant Migration," 892.
41. Andrei Suslov, "'Лучше перегнуть, чем недогнуть': 'Dekulakization' as a Facet of Stalin's Social Revolution (The Case of Perm Region)," *Russian Review* 78 (July 2019): 391.
42. Yegor Gaidar, *Collapse of an Empire: Lessons for Modern Russia* (Washington, DC: Brookings Institution Press, 2007): 95, 98.
43. Geoff Cunfer, "Overview: The Decline and Fall of the Bison Empire," in *Bison and People on the North American Great Plains: A Deep Environmental History*, ed. Geoff Cunfer and Bill Waiser (College Station: Texas A&M University Press, 2016): 1.
44. Geoff Cunfer, *On the Great Plains: Agriculture and Environment* (College Station: Texas A&M University Press, 2005): 39.
45. Isenberg, "Seas of Grass," 143.
46. Elliott West, *The Contested Plains: Indians, Goldseekers, and the Rush to Colorado* (Lawrence: University Press of Kansas, 1998).
47. Robert Wooster, *The American Military Frontiers: The United States Army in the West, 1783–1900* (Albuquerque: University of New Mexico Press, 2009).

48. Julia M. L. Laforge and Stéphane M. McLachlan, "Environmentality on the Canadian Prairies: Settler-Farmer Subjectivities and Agri-Environmental Objects," *Antipode* 50, no. 2 (2018): 363.
49. David Moon, "In the Russians' Steppes: The Introduction of Russian Wheat on the Great Plains of the United States of America," *Journal of Global History* 3 (July 2008): 208.
50. J. Atack, F. Bateman, and W. N. Parker, "Northern Agriculture and the Westward Movement," in *The Cambridge Economic History of the United States*, Vol. 2, ed. S. L. Engerman and R. E. Gallman (Cambridge: Cambridge University Press, 2000): 285–328 (statistics: 292, quotation: 297).
51. Lawrence B. Lee, "The Homestead Act: Vision and Reality," *Utah Historical Quarterly* 30, no. 1 (1962): 220.
52. Fred A. Shannon, *The Farmer's Last Frontier Agriculture, 1860–1897*, vol. 5 of *The Economic History of the United States* (London: Routledge, 2015 [1945]): 51–52.
53. James I. Stewart, "Migration to the Agricultural Frontier and Wealth Accumulation, 1860–1870," *Explorations in Economic History* 43 (2006): 547–577.
54. Lee, "Homestead Act," 234.
55. Sunderland, *Taming*, 87.
56. Moon, "Russians' Steppes," 213 (12,000); Sunderland, *Taming*, 188 (50,000).
57. Winter wheat, which is planted in the fall, is cultivated primarily in Kansas, Oklahoma, southern Nebraska, eastern Colorado, and northern Texas. The spring wheat belt encompasses North Dakota, northern Montana, and a large swath of Alberta, Saskatchewan, and Manitoba.
58. Moon, "Russians' Steppes," 224.
59. Barbier, *Scarcity*, 395–96.
60. David Danbom, "Flour Power: The Significance of Flour Milling at the Falls," *Minnesota History* 58 nos. 5–6 (Spring/Summer 2003): 271–85 (1884: 273); Alfred D. Chandler Jr., *The Visible Hand: The Managerial Revolution in American Business* (Cambridge, MA: Belknap Press of Harvard University Press, 1977): 253 (1890).
61. Cunfer, *Great Plains*, 18 (pasture), 115 (horses).
62. Isenberg, "Seas of Grass," 146.
63. Aparicio and Pinilla, "International Trade," 55.
64. Cunfer, "Manure Matters," 544.
65. Sterling Evans, *Bound in Twine: The History and Ecology of the Henequen-Wheat Complex for Mexico and the American and Canadian Plains, 1880–1950* (College Station: Texas A&M University Press, 2007): 182.
66. Donald Worster, *Dust Bowl: The Southern Plains in the 1930s*, 25th anniversary ed. (New York: Oxford University Press, 2004), 18 (Panama Canal), 24 (severe).
67. Kenneth Sylvester and Geoff Cunfer, "An Unremembered Diversity: Mixed Husbandry and the American Grasslands," *Agricultural History* 83, no. 3 (Summer 2009): 357; Cunfer, *Great Plains*, 76–86.
68. Cunfer, *Great Plains*, 86 (acres), 163 (quotation).
69. Cunfer, *Great Plains*, 200 (irrigation); Cunfer, "Manure Matters," 563 (fertile, yields).
70. USDA, National Agricultural Statistics Service, *Crop Production, 2018 Summary* (February 2019), 25.
71. Savage, *Prairie*, 230.
72. Cunfer, *Great Plains*, 234.
73. D. F. Acton, "Development and Effects of Farming in Canada," in *The Health of Our Soils: Toward Sustainable Agriculture in Canada*, ed. D. F. Acton and L. J. Gregorich (Ottawa: Agriculture and Agri-Food Canada, 1995), 11.

74. Meidad Kissinger and William E. Rees, "Footprints on the Prairies: Degradation and Sustainability of Canadian Agricultural Land in a Globalizing World," *Ecological Economics* 68 (2009): 2310.
75. Peter A. Russell, *How Agriculture Made Canada: Farming in the Nineteenth Century* (Montreal: McGill–Queen's University Press, 2012): 198.
76. Cunfer, "Overview," 24.
77. Laforge and McLachlan, "Environmentality," 364.
78. Bill Waiser, *Saskatchewan: A New History* (Calgary, AB: Fifth House, 2005), 101.
79. Barbier, *Scarcity*, 405.
80. Russell, *How Agriculture Made Canada*, 205 (migrated), 207 (norm).
81. Laforge and McLachlan, "Environmentality," 366.
82. Jeremy Adelman, "The Social Bases of Technical Change: Mechanization of the Wheatlands of Argentina and Canada, 1890 to 1914," *Comparative Study of Society and History* 30, no. 1 (April 1992): 277.
83. Adelman, "Social Bases," 278 (statistic), 280–91 (credit).
84. Friesen, *Canadian Prairies*, 302 (quotation), 309 (statistic).
85. Waiser, *Saskatchewan*, 105 (self-reliance), 110–11 (successful).
86. B. R. Mitchell, *Abstract of British Historical Statistics* (Cambridge: Cambridge University Press, 1971), 102. In other years, Russia, the United States, or Argentina, and occasionally Australia or India, held that distinction.
87. Magnan, *When Wheat Was King*, 34 (acreage), 39 (1909), 46–50 (control).
88. Aparicio and Pinilla, "International Trade," 55.
89. Evans, *Bound in Twine*, 183.
90. Magnan, *When Wheat Was King*, 50–60.
91. Laforge and McLachlan, "Environmentality," 369–71.
92. Savage, *Prairie*, 229.
93. Kissinger and Rees, "Footprints," 2312–2313.
94. Isenberg, "Seas of Grass," 142.
95. Richard W. Slatta, *Gauchos and the Vanishing Frontier* (Lincoln: University of Nebraska Press, 1992), 23–27.
96. Barbier, *Scarcity*, 427.
97. Elinor G. K. Melville, "Global Developments and Latin American Environments," in *Ecology and Empire: Environmental History of Settler Societies*, ed. Tom Griffiths and Libby Robin (Edinburgh: Keele University Press, 1997): 185–198.
98. James R. Scobie, *Revolution on the Pampas: A Social History of Argentine Wheat, 1860–1910* (Austin: University of Texas Press, 1964): 71–88 (quotation: 86).
99. Vicente Pinilla and Agustina Rayes, "How Argentina Became a Super-Exporter of Agricultural and Food Products during the First Globalisation (1880–1929)," *Cliometrica* 13 (2019): 465.
100. Aparicio and Pinilla, "International Trade," 55.
101. Adrián Gustavo Zarrilli, "Capitalism, Ecology, and Agrarian Expansion in the Pampean Region, 1890–1950," *Environmental History* 6, no. 4 (October 2001): 565.
102. Adelman, *Frontier Development*, 4.
103. Barbier, *Scarcity*, 406.
104. Adelman, *Frontier Development*, 19 (model); Slatta, *Gauchos*, 152–54 (promote).
105. Pinilla and Rayes, "Super-Exporter."
106. Adelman, "Social Bases," 271.

107. Slatta, *Gauchos*, 22.
108. Adelman, *Frontier Development*, 143.
109. Adelman, "Social Bases," 276–79.
110. Ibid., 298.
111. Scobie, *Revolution*, 92–99.
112. Vicente Pinilla and Gema Aparicio, "Navigating in Troubled Waters: South American Exports of Food and Agricultural Products in the World Market, 1900–1938," *Revista de historia económica* 33, no. 2 (2015): 229.
113. Tait Keller, "The Ecological Edges of Belligerency: Toward a Global Environmental History of the First World War," *Annales. Histoire, sciences sociales*, English ed., 71, no. 1 (March 2016): 73.
114. Aparicio and Pinilla, "International Trade," 55.
115. Pinilla and Aparicio, "Navigating," 241.
116. Eric Rolls, "The Nature of Australia," in *Ecology and Empire: Environmental History of Settler Societies*, ed. Tom Griffiths and Libby Robin (Edinburgh: Keele University Press, 1997): 36, 37, 39.
117. Isenberg, "Seas of Grass," 145.
118. Dmytro Ostapenko, "Golden Horizons: Expansion of the Wheat-Growing Industry in the Colony of Victoria in the 1850s," *Agricultural History* 87, no. 1 (Winter 2013): 35–56.
119. Emily O'Gorman, James Beattie, and Matthew Henry, "Histories of Climate, Science, and Colonization in Australia and New Zealand, 1800–1945," *WIREs Climate Change* 7 (November/December 2016): 900–928.
120. Barbier, *Scarcity*, 410–11.
121. R. A. Morgan, "Farming on the Fringe: Agriculture and Climate Variability in the Western Australian Wheat Belt, 1890s to 1980s," in *Climate, Science, and Colonization: Histories from Australia and New Zealand*, ed. J. Beattie, E. O'Gorman, and M. Henry (New York: Palgrave Macmillan; 2014): 159–176.
122. David Wood, "Limits Reaffirmed: New Wheat Frontiers in Australia, 1916–1939," *Journal of Historical Geography* 23, no. 4 (1997): 473.
123. Rajabrata Banerjee and Martin Shanahan, "The Contribution of Wheat to Australian Agriculture from 1861 to 1939," *Australian Economic History Review* 56, no. 2 (July 2016): 125–50, 132–36 (acreage); Aparicio and Pinilla, "International Trade," 55 (statistics).
124. Daniel F. Calderini and Gustavo A. Slafer, "Changes in Yield and Yield Stability in Wheat during the 20th Century," *Field Crops Research* 57 (1998): 340.
125. Food and Agricultural Organization of the United Nations, *Food Outlook: Biannual Report on Global Food Markets* (Rome: FAO, 2022): 15.
126. Kaitlin Sullivan, "Only 10 Percent of the World's Grasslands Are Intact," *Popular Science* (Summer 2019), https://www.popsci.com/grasslands-disappearing-chart, accessed October 3, 2021.
127. Kissinger and Rees, "Footprints," 2310.
128. Gunnar Rundgren, "Food: From Commodity to Commons," *Journal of Agricultural and Environmental Ethics* 29, no. 1 (February 2016): 104.
129. Mitchell C. Hunter et al., "Agriculture in 2050: Recalibrating Targets for Sustainable Intensification," *BioScience* 67, no. 4 (April 2017): 386–91.
130. Carol Ryan, "Insecurity in the World's Food Supply Grows," *Wall Street Journal*, March 16, 2022, B13.

131. Victoria Kim, "Ukraine-Russia Grain Export Deal Is Extended," *New York Times*, November 18, 2022, A8.
132. Marc Santora, Matthew Mpoke Bigg, and Joe Rennison, "Kremlin Warns it Will Enforce Naval Blockade," *New York Times*, July 20, 2023, A1.

Bibliography

Adelman, Jeremy. *Frontier Development: Land, Labor, and Capital in the Wheat Lands of Argentina and Canada, 1890–1914*. Oxford: Clarendon Press, 1994.

Crosby, Alfred W. *Ecological Imperialism: The Biological Expansion of Europe, 900–1900*. 2nd ed. New York: Cambridge University Press, 2004.

Cunfer, Geoff. *On the Great Plains: Agriculture and Environment*. College Station: Texas A&M University Press, 2005.

Davidson, B. R. *European Farming in Australia: An Economic History of Australian Farming*. Amsterdam: Elsevier Scientific, 1981.

Dunsdorfs, Edgars. *The Australian Wheat-Growing Industry, 1788–1948*. Melbourne: Melbourne University Press, 1956.

Isenberg, Andrew C. "Seas of Grass: Grasslands in World Environmental History." In *The Oxford Handbook of Environmental History*, edited by Andrew C. Isenberg, 133–53. Oxford: Oxford University Press, 2014.

Magnan, André. *When Wheat Was King: The Rise and Fall of the Canada-UK Grain Trade*. Vancouver: University of British Columbia Press, 2016.

Moon, David. *The Plough That Broke the Steppes: Agriculture and Environment on Russia's Grasslands, 1700–1914*. Oxford: Oxford University Press, 2013.

Russell, Peter A. *How Agriculture Made Canada: Farming in the Nineteenth* Century. Montreal: McGill-Queen's University Press, 2012.

Scobie, James R. *Revolution on the Pampas: A Social History of Argentine Wheat, 1860–1910*. Austin: University of Texas Press, 1964.

Slatta, Richard W. *Gauchos and the Vanishing Frontier*. Lincoln: University of Nebraska Press, 1992.

Sunderland, Willard. *Taming the Wild Field: Colonization and Empire on the Russian Steppe*. Ithaca, NY: Cornell University Press, 2004.

Worster, Donald. *Dust Bowl: The Southern Plains in the 1930s*. 25th anniversary ed. New York: Oxford University Press, 2004.

CHAPTER 32

CONTESTATIONS OVER AGRICULTURAL PRODUCTION IN COLONIAL AFRICA

CASSANDRA MARK-THIESEN

GROWING markets for raw agricultural commodities were a key factor behind the launch of colonial projects in Africa in the late nineteenth century, and agriculture would remain at the heart of colonial economies until (and into) the period of independence.[1] Some eyewitnesses to European expansionism and the frenzy over African agricultural and mineral commodities in the late nineteenth and early twentieth centuries were based on the coast of West Africa in the black-led state of Liberia, a country that was founded by the American Colonization Society as a colony in 1822 and had been independent since 1847. In 1881, one observer there reported how "Foreigners are fighting for entrance into this Continent on the north and on the south, on the east and on the west."[1] These foreigners were far from the first to attempt to exploit the region. Beginning in the first quarter of the nineteenth century and continuing during the slow end of the transatlantic slave trade, British, Dutch, and Portuguese traders penetrated the region and began to export agricultural products. By the final quarter of the century, a rising number of European and African traders were significantly boosting agricultural exports, and colonial officials were soon to follow. In 1903, the Liberian president noted the "eagerness with which all the leading nations of the world are seeking to grasp the advantages offered by agricultural pursuits, and the number of Europeans who leave their homes for Africa."[2]

Though agricultural exports from colonial Africa only ever made up a small share of the global market, their enduring transformative effects on the continent's development trajectories is undeniable. Yet, by the dawn of political independence, the following questions remained in dispute: to what extent and under which circumstances had

---

[1] This work has been supported by the Swiss National Science Foundation under PMPDP1_164485.

Africans been beneficiaries of this wealth, and which Africans had benefited? Historians of Africa (and the globe) are currently faced with the challenge of disentangling the complex economic, social, political, and spiritual outcomes of colonial agricultural intervention. Resulting contestations and negotiations had an impact at the continental level, as well as the level of lived experience. The nature of the agricultural transition during the colonial period is best observed by viewing a few instances of Africans' encounters with colonial state interventions on the ground.

The origins of the "cash crop revolution" that accompanied the colonial period had in fact long preceded formal colonial occupation. A. G. Hopkins, an economic historian of Africa and the globe, has framed it as part and parcel of "an ambitious program of modernization that affected, or at least touched, not only . . . Africa but also the rest of the globe in the nineteenth century." Beginning in 1815, some years after the legal end of the transatlantic slave trade, a growing number of African traders and producers were invited to participate in global markets in an alternative manner under the banner of "legitimate" commerce. At the time, African agricultural commodities were forecast to increase in value, opening the way, it was hoped, for a greater alignment of European and African property rights, patterns of consumption, and social and moral values.[3] The actual encounter proved to be much more complex.

Colonial Conquest

The motivations for European colonial conquest in Africa in the late nineteenth century were multifaceted, being political, moral, and economic in nature. In West Africa, colonial conquest occurred at a moment of economic depression and commercial chaos that was being driven by the rising number of foreign traders. During this period, this group was gaining unprecedented access to (such as information about) the hinterland, including its agricultural and mineral resources. The drive to expand commerce and trade guided actions between capital and colonial authorities and sustained the collaborative nature of conquest. The evangelizing mission and the desire to "civilize" what were viewed as backwards peoples, who were coincidentally increasingly viewed as racially inferior as during this era, further informed the colonial encounter. But just as colonialism took on a variety of manifestations from one territory to the next across Africa, so too did colonial authorities' engagement with differing agricultural systems across the continent. This incoherence becomes evident when we compare empirical evidence across, or even within, many colonial states—whether ruled by Britain, France, Portugal, Germany, Belgium, or other European powers. Adding to this muddled picture were Africa's diverse physical landscapes, climates, and ecologies as well as its territories' varying population densities, histories, and sociopolitical structures. Regional studies have tended to categorize early colonial agricultural production systems as follows: smallholders deploying family or communal labor (prevalent in West Africa), sharecroppers on settler estates (especially in Southern and East Africa), and wage (and occasionally forced) labor on the large-scale plantations of chartered companies (in Central Africa and, to some extent, South Africa). Throughout the colonial period, it would remain difficult to discern the actual terms and mechanisms of agricultural "progress" given the divergent and contradictory needs and priorities of the key actors involved in these different contexts: African producers, white settlers, trading companies, and imperial and colonial agents, to name a few.

To maximize the potency of colonial governance, the authorities in many instances aimed to transform production, cultivation, and pastoral-nomadic migration patterns. Furthermore, they introduced new seeds and seedlings and set new marketing standards for produce directed at foreign markets. At the time of conquest, the reconstruction of agrarian economies all over Africa was primarily intended to bring wealth to the colonial state via custom duties, but it was also assumed that it would better the living standards of colonial subjects. As such, authorities placed an urgent emphasis on involving Africans in cash cropping for domestic and overseas markets through the cultivation of a limited number of commodities. Among these were cocoa, coffee, cotton, tea, tobacco, timber, peanuts, palm oil, groundnuts, and rubber—the demand for which was mostly being driven by the industrial revolution in Europe. Colonial authorities believed that advances away from small-scale farming, especially subsistence food production, were a necessary step in delivering measured change to local peoples, the kind of change that would not pose a threat to colonial law and order.

Colonial engagements with local agriculture tended to follow a guiding principle of "improvement," with significant disregard for preexisting agricultural systems, such as shifting cultivation and bush fallowing, which were both rooted in the slash-and-burn practices that were widespread across the continent.[4] This practice would nevertheless remain prevalent. For most of the colonial period, the authorities and specialists regarded it as—while perhaps serving as a cost-effective means for small-scale producers to fertilize their soil (with phosphorous)—an undeniably "primitive" and destructive practice for the forests and valuable commodities contained therein, such as timber.[5] In British-ruled colonial Ghana, where a "laissez-faire" policy had previously determined colonial governance, the state's campaign against shifting production dragged on for multiple decades and with limited acknowledgment of African farmers' wealth of knowledge on local ecosystems and natural resources. In 1936, the director of agriculture, G. G. Auchinleck, remained optimistic, insisting that a "turn of the tide" lay just ahead given what he had observed as an emerging trend toward the commercialization of land. His proposal was to use demonstration farming in the rural areas to popularize permanent farming (coupled with a persisting schedule of rotational planting across multiple plots).[6] Another reason that shifting cultivation was targeted in this manner was because it was a practice closely associated with land clearance for food crops intended for local consumption, which de facto deprioritized colonial export commerce and development.

Imperial and colonial authorities generally preferred commercial methods of agricultural production. Instilling this kind of change, however, was evidently far more complicated at the local level. The experience of agricultural transformation took on a particular shape in the settler colonies (colonial South Africa, Namibia, Kenya, Zimbabwe, North Africa, Mozambique, and Angola) in the late nineteenth and early twentieth centuries. The colonial authorities in these territories implemented land alienation and labor mobilization measures that clearly favored white commercial farmers over African producers, heightening competition between white-owned firms for these resources. Small-scale African producers, who depended on access to land for their economic, spiritual, and social well-being, figured less frequently in policy papers concerned with commerce. They did, however, make an appearance where they were subjected to strategies of exclusion by the colonial state that artificially rendered them uncompetitive in relation to other categories of producers. This was evident, for instance, in the case of colonial Kenya, where up until the 1930s Africans had been prohibited from selling the valuable commodity of coffee. In contrast, including during the Great Depression, white settlers were able to arrange public subsidies and loans for growing coffee and other types of cash crops.[7] Furthermore, throughout the colonial period, the white settler population was able to exert increasing pressure on the government to maintain their access to most arable land. British and French colonial authorities in the non-settler colonies were just as convinced of the improvement potential of plantation economies; yet securing regular labor for wage work was a formidable challenge in this region for most of the colonial period given the ease of local access to land. In addition, this interest was offset by the formidable drawbacks associated with European migration to West Africa, in particular the potential financial and administrative burden that large numbers of sick and unemployed white settlers could place on colonies struggling to maintain financial self-sufficiency. In several West African territories (such as colonial Ghana and French West Africa) but also elsewhere (such as parts of colonial Tanzania),[8] a pro-peasant rhetoric on the part of colonial authorities eventually gained in strength, although in reality farmers in these areas only ever experienced minimal levels of government support. In accordance with their inability to closely regulate many of the markets in these territories, the colonial authorities were initially less optimistic about the prospects for cash cropping. Still, they hedged their bet by developing some marketing incentives and minimal infrastructure to facilitate cash crop production, a decision that would a bet that would eventually pay off. Above all else, the cocoa boom from the 1890s to the 1930s in colonial Ghana was testament to the entrepreneurial spirit of African small-scale farmers, most of whom were migrants to the area.[9] The colonial authorities' laissez-faire and risk-averse strategy was rewarded in the end.

It should also be noted that African small-scale farmers and European settler planters coexisted in many areas. In such locations, the former group competed directly with planters for labor (including their own). The contest worsened for African producers when putting the same items up for sale as the plantations.

The transformation of African labor relations was a slow but decisive process. Generally, if the post-1815 economic order (as described earlier) disfavored the use of slave labor, this preference was not immediately apparent on the ground—not even during the colonial period. Colonial agricultural systems, whether they were governed by Britain, France, Germany, Portugal, or other European powers, accommodated a wide range of labor relations, including slave labor. An abstract preference for "free labor" also did not mean that colonial officials were above resorting to coercive cultivation, for instance by means of the dictates of local authorities or taxation.[10] The ideal of "free labor" was regularly sacrificed in favor of greater output, especially since forced labor was claimed to have an "educational" effect on the "child-like" African. Only gradually did growing regional and international markets for local agricultural commodities open up more opportunities for hired agricultural labor (frequently formerly enslaved African men and women).[11] The use of forced labor was most widespread and longest lasting in the Belgian Congo, a personal fiefdom of King Leopold II from 1885 to 1909. The authorities there were particularly brutal in enforcing rural dwellers' adherence to daily quotas for rubber production. Torture became routine within the existing rubber regime, with the hands of noncompliant individuals severed as a matter of policy, to name only one example. Compulsory cultivation continued under state rule, albeit with less extreme penalties. At times this involved the pressurizing or bribing of rural chiefs to compel young men and women in their communities to plant specific crops and bring them to market in compliance with the colonial state's output demands, as witnessed in many other parts of the continent.

Cotton, which was already a favored agricultural commodity in missionary circles prior to the late nineteenth century, became arguably the premier colonial crop.[12] Aiming to suppress the price of this commodity, manufacturers in Britain, Germany, France, and Belgium drove colonial efforts to integrate African producers into the global value chain. Experiments to improve cotton yields that were conducted together with African producers, some of whose participation was more voluntary than others, occurred all across the continent, from colonial Côte d'Ivoire to colonial Malawi, Portuguese Mozambique to British Uganda, to name just a few territories. At the same time, the demand for increased cotton output tended to come at the long-term expense of local manufacturing, including weaving, spinning, and dyeing, the end products of which many colonial officials deemed to be too labor-intensive, overly expensive, and of lesser quality than what could be imported from the industrial center of Lancashire, or elsewhere in Europe.[13] Indeed, European textile manufacturers went to great lengths to cater to local tastes and aesthetics.[14] Cotton production would draw in a complex network of migrant workers, sharecroppers, and independent smallholders, some resisting involvement in the crop's cultivation more than others. According to scholars such as Andrew Zimmerman, the category of race was central to the expansion of the cotton frontier in Africa, Africans being conveniently assessed as especially adept at harvesting this labor-intensive crop decades after the end of the American Civil War.[15]

The cash crop revolution also placed different demands on African men and women. While wage work, including on plantations, was expected to lift colonized populations to a new stage of consumption and "civilization," it remained the duty of the small-scale farmer to provide food for the domestic market. However, as part of their attempts to diminish the significance of small-scale farming and the production of food crops, colonial authorities further relegated this activity to the category of "women's work," while their male counterparts expected to take on various seasonal jobs on the plantations, mines, or railways or to become more intimately involved in commerce and consumption. Wealthy (male) farmers, chiefs, and marabouts (or traditional healers), for instance, were especially well equipped to participate in new agricultural markets, as they received prime access to new seeds and seedlings as well as education and training through government programs. In contrast, it has been argued in the historiography of South Africa, in particular, that women's agricultural productivity in labor-sending rural areas (such as in colonial Malawi, Zambia, and Mozambique) subsidized the urban colonial economy by allowing European employers to lower wages artificially in South Africa.[16] African producers did not always respond to colonial demands and expectations. Still, overall the political regime here and elsewhere put in place meaningful obstacles to African women's accumulation of wealth. This trend did not relent in the context of the intensification of commercial agriculture that followed World War I.

The Interwar Years

An influx of European and American capital penetrated colonial African agricultural markets after World War I as the demand for African agricultural produce rose further on the global market. But even as notable achievements were recorded in independent, small-scale farming, colonial authorities continued to focus on the prospects for large-scale plantations' future profitability under European supervision. This was in keeping with a vision to advance industrialization after 1918 for the sake of, among other aims, returning prosperity to war-ridden European metropoles. Several colonial governments also sought to boost levels of productivity and revive profitability in these territories; this while the notion of French and British "trusteeship" over Germany's former colonies also sparked colonial developmentalism in its earliest form. More generally, the technocratic capacity of colonial states began to grow at a faster pace and become more specialized, with scientific knowledge being hailed as the key to "modern" agriculture. By the 1930s, the British Colonial Office in particular had placed a large number of technical and scientific experts in its colonies to assist in agrarian affairs and, more generally, to solve various economic, ecological, and social problems. With these changes, the contact and exchange between African farmers or farmworkers and the colonial state grew in frequency.

While the establishment of some agricultural departments had preceded the war, by the end of the interwar period the general consensus was, in the words of Liberian agricultural expert George S. Best, that "No Tropical country can consider itself as functioning properly unless it has a well-equipped and competently staffed department of agriculture."[17] Most African farmers, whether working on mid-size or small farms, did not have the time to complete formal training. But this is where the experts would come in: departments of agriculture would make science work for the farmers by imposing new methods for fighting pests, discerning different soil types, and predicting the weather.

Colonial states across the continent, increasingly with corporate and philanthropic backing, deployed extension workers to assist and train village leaders and agricultural aides. In this context of mass (adult) education, they provided rural dwellers with lectures on "improved" farming and land cultivation methods. The advantages of agricultural diversification and permanent farming methods were exhibited on various demonstration farms that were located close to villages. This form of mass education was frequently accompanied by public health initiatives that prioritized the prevention of disease in order to promote health, wealth, and, of course, productivity.[18] Experimental schemes grew in significance during this period as scientists aimed to create more robust crops that would ensure that Africa made its contribution to expanding world markets.

Besides the expansion of extension work and other "low technology" rural development schemes, this was also the era of "high modernist" development projects.[19] Large-scale schemes, such as the Office du Niger (in French West Africa) and the East Africa Ground Nut scheme (in colonial Tanzania), were initiated to improve irrigation and stimulate plantation cultivation, while others focused on the construction of dams, such as the Kariba Dam (in colonial Zambia). Yet, such large-scale projects were frequently plagued by defunct imported machinery, a high turnover of staff, and other related challenges. They also regularly caused chronic ecological damage and had a devastating social impact on those who were forced to relocate from the areas where these new constructions were built, not to mention those with little choice but to continue living near them.[20] Large machinery, such as tractors, and draft animals, such as oxen, helped to transform agriculture in many parts of the continent. Their implementation was less useful in the forest belt in West Africa, by way of comparison.

A meaningful share of agricultural education also began to move to a classroom setting after World War I. This shift marked an official denunciation of the bookishness of missionary education, as public education began to expand. For example, another American philanthropic organization, the Jeanes Foundation, established a number of rural schools in Britain's African colonies. In certain instances, vocational education that placed emphasis on agricultural and manual training did prepare African secondary school students for some degree of semi-skilled wage labor on foreign-owned plantations or mines, but more often than not it served the purpose of keeping poorer rural dwellers on the land and in their home regions.[21] The American philanthropic Phelps-Stokes Fund's 1920 African Education Commission and the resulting publication by the organization's director, Jesse Jones's *Education in Africa: A Study of West, South, and Equatorial Africa*, underscored the importance of "adapted" (namely, agricultural and industrial) education for interwar colonized societies in Africa. But colonial states all over Africa also adopted its agenda as the best strategy for improving "native" lifestyles without attracting rural populations to urbanizing areas. Vocational training was not new to the continent, but some scholarship has argued that the new curricula had been explicitly "adapted" from the education aimed at African Americans in the United States,[22] attesting to the colonial states' new, optimistic perspective on the economic behavior of African workers. Agricultural and industrial education eventually lost favor as it gradually fell out of sync with the educational and professional desires and demands of post–World War II African communities.

While the filling of positions in the colonial civil service had long been given some priority, there was less of a rush to equip African students with the skills needed to take on positions in the upper echelons of higher education and industry. The agricultural sciences, which subsumed both the research-based and applied sciences as well as the study of social and economic interventions, expanded in step with the growth of empire in the late nineteenth and early twentieth centuries, while also being advanced by corporations and academia itself. Many of the research institutions established after World War I were preceded by others that had been broadly preoccupied with spreading a vague notion of "scientific" agriculture.[23] But the number of specialized agricultural research stations only grew substantially after the global conflict, with those run by the French and British leading the way. In 1929, the *Educational Outlook* newspaper in Liberia reprinted a recent speech by the retired British administrator Frederick Lugard, in which he had announced the following: "Steps are being taken to create a large inter-Colonial research fund and to establish a chain of research stations to investigate diseases of men, animals and plants, which have caused so great a loss of human and animal life, and the waste of so substantial a part of the potential products of Africa."[24] Modernization without research became unthinkable for many individuals linked to government, and the ultimate aim of those working at such institutes was to improve local production techniques through botanical and biological engineering in fields such as plant breeding and genetics, horticulture, soil science, and entomology. Certain scientists even engaged with the viability and benefits of indigenous practices and instruments in relation to enhancing the agricultural, forest, and food sciences.[25] Though Britain did lead the pack in giving Africans access to scientific training in agriculture, only a small share of trained African scientists managed to find positions at colonial agricultural research stations.[26] At best, European and American agricultural scientists dominated agenda-setting positions in their field, while most African scientists were relegated to extension or experimental work.

The Great Depression heightened a number of new debates on agricultural productivity. For one, colonial authorities began to concentrate their efforts on the production of food crops. A multipage appeal in the *Nigerian Eastern Mail* by the Nigerian colonial government, which was later reprinted in Liberia's *Weekly Mirror* newspaper on October 4, 1940, demonstrated this precisely. Against the backdrop of increasing food imports, officials urged Nigerians to engage in food production in order to feed themselves and "try to export our surplus of production of foodstuffs to our neighboring colonies in order that they may not need to import from outside of West Africa."[27] Also during the interwar period, however, new state institutions and practices to supposedly lighten the burden of African producers ended up imposing the heavy hand of colonial governments. State-run agricultural marketing boards in colonial Nigeria and Ghana became a vital, albeit controversial, fiscal tool. Over time, many African producers no longer viewed them as providing protection from the vicissitudes of the market. Rather they perceived them as a further tool of colonial exploitation that counteracted market liberalization through their monopolizing strategies.

Ecological changes could frustrate the plans of both the colonial state and producers. New conservation practices enacted by the colonial state impinged upon the livelihoods and agricultural systems of African farmers in particular. Environmental concerns took a prominent place on the colonial agenda during this era, in rare instances even trumping the emphasis on cash cropping; in contrast to the continent's depletable raw mineral reserves, agricultural commodities promised the further advantage of renewable long-term wealth if properly managed. Colonial authorities tried to make sense of various forms of environmental degradation by pointing to supposedly "irrational" and "irresponsible" African planting, foraging, and livestock raising methods as well as poverty and overcrowding. In plenty of cases, soil erosion was presented as evidence of environmental mismanagement, with colonial officials showing little understanding for why farmers acted in the ways they did.[28] "In other words," as Ramutsindela explains for the Southern African case, "farmers were deemed to have little or no knowledge of their biophysical environment and therefore needed to be educated and disciplined so they could use the land properly."[29] It remains difficult to assess to what extent the tensions of this era fed directly into rising anti-colonial and nationalist sentiments after 1940.

From World War II to Independence

As World War II neared its end, "developmentalism" became a guiding concept for colonial states in Africa, with French- and British-ruled territories at the forefront. Long-term development plans were formed that were partially dependent on public funds from Europe. The boosting of agricultural exports became a focal point of many of these schemes, including Britain's 1940 Colonial Development and Welfare Act, which was expanded in 1945; France's 1946 Fonds d'investissement pour le développement économique et social des territoires d'outre-mer (FIDES); Belgium's 1949 Plan décennal pour le développement économique et social du Congo belge; and Portugal's 1953 Planos de Fomento.

By 1940, Africa's terms of trade were back at their 1800 levels, but this did not deter colonial states from forecasting that agriculture would become profitable.[30] During the so-called second colonial occupation, agricultural productivity was meant to generate wealth for postwar reconstruction. Even more important, it was projected that it would improve standards of living among Africans, with colonial states convinced that investing unprecedented amounts in the socioeconomic development of "the colonial subject" would be a useful strategy for maintaining control over their colonies. New colonial programs explicitly targeted food production, the building of infrastructure such as train networks, and improving the financing of cooperatives. Moreover, unlike before, these programs were to be implemented directly by colonial authorities. Nevertheless, tensions mounted as agricultural experts attempted to render local producers and their harvests more predictable and productive, often at the expense of their own ideological politics, which included the pretense of a mutually beneficial engagement.

After 1940, in parallel with many colonial states' growing interest in providing greater protections for farmers and other workers, both groups also began to become increasingly engaged with broader political questions. Not only were local producers using cooperatives (also known as farmers' unions) to gain access to a greater share of resources, such as credit, these organizations also boosted the political clout of participating farmers.[31] This new progressive sentiment gained a life of its own as it became consolidated by nationalist leaders in different colonial territories.

Some colonial officials and white settler planters, however, dragged their heels and even vigorously resisted African independence. In 1961, for instance, the international press reported on atrocities committed by Portuguese planters in colonial Angola and Mozambique with the aid of Portuguese military personnel. Citing a source within the foreign board of missions of the Methodist church in Angola, an article first published in the Associated Negro Press and reprinted in the *Liberian Age* newspaper revealed details of brutal massacres committed against small-scale African farmers near the cities of Luanda and Dondo. The article reported "wholesale slaughter of innocent and unarmed African villagers," observing how "the field of operation of these white terrorists is the geographic area in which they have commercial or agricultural interests." It continued in graphic detail:

> One report from Coio, halfway between Lucala and Samba Caju, on the main north road to the Congo, told of the arrival of armed civilians and soldiers early one morning in mid-May. All the able-bodied men were lined up in two lines, about 16 in each. Those on one side were shot in cold blood, one after another, with their wives and children looking on. Those on the other side were carted off to prison and have not been heard of since. The wives of the dead men were then ordered to bury their husbands at the edge of the village where they fell.[32]

According to the same article, a "Dutch mining engineer working in the Dembos area at the outbreak of the war [Mozambican War of Independence] interpreted the merchants' and planters' ill-will as being against the educational programme of missions, which was helping develop too rapidly the ability of the African population to defend itself against financial and labour abuses."[33] As such, the empowerment of African farmers was perceived as standing in direct competition with settlers' commercial success.

Overall, the 1950s and 1960s were marked by higher wages and greater social welfare protections for African workers. African producers benefited from a slight recovery in the global market for agricultural exports, while those in settler colonies specifically managed to gain a greater market share. By the 1960s, however, African farmers had reached the peak of their wealth accumulation. They were now confined to specializing in the production of a few types of agricultural commodities that offered diminishing returns.[34] Moreover, the continuation of state-led development into the postcolonial era coexisted with a growing suspicion of, as well as a desire to control, politically active organizations such as the farmers' unions. After political independence, meager earnings were consequently coupled with political suppression.

Conclusion

Agricultural transition during the colonial period was a dynamic, multilayered, and heterogeneous process. The story of the agricultural frontier in colonial Africa was one of a narrowly focused, export-oriented commercial intensification that followed two separate tracks—peasant and plantation farming. Monocultural economies that catered to foreign consumers left African colonies particularly vulnerable to the whims of the global market. This chapter has attempted to show the shifts in colonial policy that helped to shape African economies in this regard. With a particular eye on African farmers, most of whom reached the peak of their wealth accumulation during the 1950s and 1960s, this chapter has been careful to discuss both contestation and negotiation, resistance as well as indifference to colonial intervention. At the same time, there has been an interest in illustrating how different actors (e.g., African producers, white settlers, or foreign firms) were involved in this process. Moreover, agricultural education was highlighted as a further space of contestation.

Colonial commerce and development programs were rarely implemented with cultural sensitivity or a sense of modesty. Assessing such interventions, however, is a complex matter. They created winners and losers, the identities of whom could change over time. The accumulation of wealth for broad segments of the population could be temporarily facilitated by the same mechanisms that would subsequently hamper them or that would benefit only a small section of the population over the long term. African manufacturers, craftspeople, and small-scale farmers struggled to maintain their relevance in a globalized context.

African responses to these transformations were unsurprisingly diverse. Defending their existing lifestyles, methods of land tenure, family structures, and social communities inspired action on the part of many, at times with greater or less success. Some actors had neither the means nor the power to protect themselves from a state that conducted forced removals and enforced compulsory cultivation. Others were more optimistic about what the modernization program, with its promise of commercial intensification, had to offer.

Notes

1. "President Anthony W. Gardner's Speech to the National Legislature on 20 December 1881," reprinted in D. Elwood Dunn, *The Annual Messages of the Presidents of Liberia 1848–2010: State of the Nation Addresses to the National Legislature* (Berlin: De Gruyter Saur, 2011): 323.

2. "President Garretson Wilmot Gibson's Speech to the National Legislature on 16 December 1903," reprinted in Dunn, *The Annual Messages of the Presidents of Liberia*, 427.
3. Hopkins describes leaders in Britain, in particular, as being at the forefront of this "modernisation programme which continued throughout the colonial period." Antony G. Hopkins, "The New International Economic Order in the Nineteenth Century: Britain's First Development Plan for Africa," in *From Slave Trade to "Legitimate" Commerce: The Commercial Transition in Nineteenth-Century West Africa*, ed. Robin Law (Cambridge: Cambridge University Press, 2002): 258–259.
4. Zeleza identifies seven agricultural methods and techniques in nineteenth-century Africa: shifting cultivation, intercropping, agro-forestry, terracing, wetland farming, irrigated farming, and mixed farming. Paul Tiyambe Zeleza, *A Modern Economic History of Africa: The Nineteenth Century* (Kenya: East African Publishers, 1997): 86–87.
5. In the 1960s and 1970s, scholars were similarly divided on the issue of shifting cultivation. While some did indeed consider it an outdated practice and uneconomical in terms of its use of labor power (see, e.g., Ester Boserup, *The Conditions of Agricultural Growth: The Economics of Agrarian Change under Population Pressure* [London: Routledge, 2014 (1965)]; K. Newton, "Shifting Cultivation and Crop Rotations in the Tropics," *Papua and New Guinea Agricultural Journal* 13 [1960]: 81–118), others defended its value for tropical ecology (Brian Hopkins, *Forest and Savanna: An Introduction to Tropical Terrestrial Ecology with Special Reference to West Africa* [Ibadan: Heinemann, 1977 (1974)]).
6. Public Records and Archives Administration Department of Ghana (PRAAD), CSO8/1/160, "Shifting Cultivation (Report for 1935)," April 1, 1936.
7. See, e.g., Kenneth P. Vickery, "Saving Settlers: Maize Control in Northern Rhodesia," *Journal of Southern African Studies* 11 (1985): 212–234; Klaus Deininger and Hans P. Binswanger, "Rent Seeking and the Development of Large-Scale Agriculture in Kenya, South Africa, and Zimbabwe," *Economic Development and Cultural Change* 43 (1995): 493–522.
8. Thaddeus Sunseri, "Labour Migration in Colonial Tanzania and the Hegemony of South African Historiography," *African Affairs* 95 (1996): 581–598.
9. Polly Hill, *The Migrant Cocoa-Farmers of Southern Ghana: A Study in Rural Capitalism* (Münster: LIT Verlag, 1997); Gareth Austin, "The Emergence of Capitalist Relations in South Asante Cocoa-Farming, c. 1916–33," *Journal of African History* 28 (1987): 259–279.
10. The colonial state also compelled African producers to cultivate certain crops to the detriment of their own nutrition and at the cost of advanced environmental degradation to their land. See, e.g., Elias Mandala, "'We Toiled for the White Man in Our Own Gardens': How the Self-Regulating Market Came to Colonial Malawi," in *Cotton, Colonialism, and Social History in Sub-Saharan Africa*, ed. Allen F. Isaacman and Richard L. Roberts (Portsmouth, NH: Heinemann, 1995): 285–305; Jamie Monson, "Rice and Cotton, Ritual and Resistance: Cash Cropping in Southern Tanganyika in the 1930s," in ibid., 268–84.
11. Austin, "Cash Crops and Freedom: Export Agriculture and the Decline of Slavery in Colonial West Africa," *International Review of Social History* 54 (2009): 1–37.
12. Allen F. Isaacman, *Cotton Is the Mother of Poverty: Peasants, Work, and Rural Struggle in Colonial Mozambique, 1938–1961* (Portsmouth, NH: Heinemann, 1996); Richard L. Roberts, *Two Worlds of Cotton: Colonialism and the Regional Economy in the French Soudan, 1800–1946* (Stanford, CA: Stanford University Press, 1996).
13. See, e.g., Judith A. Byfield, *The Bluest Hands: A Social and Economic History of Women Dyers in Abeokuta (Nigeria), 1890–1940* (Portsmouth, NH: D. Philip, 2002), ch. 1.

14. Christopher B. Steiner, "Another Image of Africa: Toward an Ethnohistory of European Cloth Marketed in West Africa, 1873–1960," *Ethnohistory* 32 (1985): 91–110.
15. Andrew Zimmerman, *Alabama in Africa: Booker T. Washington, the German Empire, and the Globalization of the New South* (Princeton, NJ: Princeton University Press, 2012).
16. See, e.g., Cherryl Walker, "Gender and the Development of the Migrant Labour System c. 1850–1930," in *Women and Gender in Southern Africa to 1945*, ed. Cherryl Walker (Cape Town: David Philip Publishers, 1990): 168–196.
17. Observing the institutional framework of colonial agriculture from an outside perspective, George S. Best, who would be appointed chief of the Bureau of Agriculture in Liberia in 1936, called on Liberian officials to finally invest appropriately in agricultural development. George S. Best, "Liberian Agriculture," *Croizerville Observer 1* (December 1930): 2.
18. See, e.g., Caroline Authaler, *Deutsche Plantagen in Britisch-Kamerun: Internationale Normen und lokale Realitäten 1925 bis 1940* (Cologne: Böhlau Verlag, 2018), ch. 6; Helen Tilley, *Africa as a Living Laboratory: Empire, Development, and the Problem of Scientific Knowledge, 1870–1950* (Chicago: University of Chicago Press, 2011), ch. 4.
19. For an original discussion on the manifestations of these two schemes, see James Scott, *Seeing like a State: How Certain Schemes to Improve the Human Condition Have Failed* (New Haven, CT: Yale University Press, 2020).
20. Julia Tischler, *Light and Power for a Multiracial Nation: The Kariba Dam Scheme in the Central African Federation* (Basingstoke: Palgrave Macmillan, 2013); Heather J. Hoag, *Developing the Rivers of East and West Africa: An Environmental History* (London: Bloomsbury Publishing, 2013).
21. Julia Tischler, "Education and the Agrarian Question in South Africa, c. 1900–40," *Journal of African History* 57 (July 2016): 251–270.
22. Donald Spivey, *The Politics of Miseducation: The Booker Washington Institute of Liberia, 1929–1984* (Lexington: University Press of Kentucky, 1986).
23. Tilley, *Africa as a Living Laboratory*.
24. Albert Porte Papers 1902–1973, Baron Lugard, "Problem of Tropical Africa [reprint from a recent address]," *The Educational Outlook* 1 (April 1929): 8.
25. Rather than perpetuating the divisive concept of "colonial science," scholars such as William Beinart and Helen Tilley have argued in favor of conceiving science itself as a "contact zone," in which progress is inherently achieved through entanglement and exchange. William Beinart, "African History and Environmental History," *African Affairs* 99 (April 2000): 269–302; Tilley, *Africa as a Living Laboratory*.
26. For a discussion on African experts in colonial science, see William Beinart, Karen Brown, and Daniel Gilfoyle, "Experts and Expertise in Colonial Africa Reconsidered: Science and the Interpenetration of Knowledge," *African Affairs* 108 (July 1, 2009): 413–433.
27. "The Governor of Nigeria Gives Nigerians Advice Which Liberians Would Do Well to Follow," *Weekly Mirror* 10 (October 4, 1940): 1–3.
28. Sara Berry, *No Condition Is Permanent: The Social Dynamics of Agrarian Change in Sub-Saharan Africa* (Madison: University of Wisconsin Press, 1993); Henrietta L. Moore and Megan Vaughan, *Cutting Down Trees: Gender, Nutrition, and Agricultural Change in the Northern Province of Zambia, 1890–1990*, Social History of Africa (Portsmouth, NH: Heinemann, 1994); Sara Berry, "Debating the Land Question in Africa," *Comparative Studies in Society and History* 44 (October 2002): 638–668.

29. Maano Ramutsindela, "Political Dynamics of Human-Environment Relations," in *The Politics of Nature and Science in Southern Africa*, ed. Maano Ramutsindela, Giorgio Miescher, and Melanie Boehi (Basel: Basler Afrika Bibliographien, 2016).
30. Ewout Frankema, Jeffrey Williamson, and Pieter Woltjer, "An Economic Rationale for the African Scramble," *VoxEU.Org* (blog), July 14, 2015, https://voxeu.org/article/economic-rationale-african-scramble.
31. Catherine Boone, *Political Topographies of the African State: Territorial Authority and Institutional Choice*, Cambridge Studies in Comparative Politics (Cambridge: University Press, 2003), ch. 4; Frederick Cooper, *Africa since 1940: The Past of the Present* (Cambridge: Cambridge University Press, 2002): 24.
32. "In Angola: Merchants, Farmers in Plan to Decimate Africans," *The Liberian Age*, September 22, 1961.
33. Other observers suspected a link to "reprisals following the massacre in mid-March of a thousand whites in the coffee growing area of northern Angola." Others blamed the weakness of the Salazar regime for this breakdown of law and order. "In Angola: Merchants, Farmers in Plan to Decimate Africans," *The Liberian Age*, September 22, 1961.
34. Ewout Frankema, Jeffrey Williamson, and Pieter Woltjer, "An Economic Rationale for the African Scramble." *VoxEU.Org* (blog), July 14, 2015, https://voxeu.org/article/economic-rationale-african-scramble.

Bibliography

Austin, Gareth. "Cash Crops and Freedom: Export Agriculture and the Decline of Slavery in Colonial West Africa." *International Review of Social History* 54, no. 1 (2009): 1–37.

Authaler, Caroline. *Deutsche Plantagen in Britisch-Kamerun: Internationale Normen und lokale Realitäten 1925 bis 1940*. Köln: Böhlau Verlag, 2018.

Beinart, William, Karen Brown, and Daniel Gilfoyle. "Experts and Expertise in Colonial Africa Reconsidered: Science and the Interpenetration of Knowledge." *African Affairs* 108, no. 432 (July 1, 2009): 413–433.

Berry, Sara. "Debating the Land Question in Africa." *Comparative Studies in Society and History* 44, no. 4 (October 2002): 638–68.

Byfield, Judith A. *The Bluest Hands: A Social and Economic History of Women Dyers in Abeokuta (Nigeria), 1890–1940*. Portsmouth, NH: James Currey 2002.

Deininger, Klaus, and Hans P. Binswanger. "Rent Seeking and the Development of Large-Scale Agriculture in Kenya, South Africa, and Zimbabwe." *Economic Development and Cultural Change* 43, no. 3 (1995): 493–522.

Hill, Polly. *The Migrant Cocoa-Farmers of Southern Ghana: A Study in Rural Capitalism*. Münster: LIT Verlag, 1997.

Hoag, Heather J. *Developing the Rivers of East and West Africa: An Environmental History*. London: Bloomsbury, 2013.

Hopkins, Antony G. "The New International Economic Order in the Nineteenth Century: Britain's First Development Plan for Africa." In *From Slave Trade to "Legitimate" Commerce: The Commercial Transition in Nineteenth-Century West Africa*, edited by Robin Law, 240–64. Cambridge: Cambridge University Press, 1995.

Isaacman, Allen F. *Cotton Is the Mother of Poverty: Peasants, Work, and Rural Struggle in Colonial Mozambique, 1938–1961*. Portsmouth, NH: Heinemann, 1996.

Mandala, Elias. "'We Toiled for the White Man in Our Own Gardens': How the Self-Regulating Market Came to Colonial Malawi." In *Cotton, Colonialism, and Social History in Sub-Saharan Africa*, edited by Allen F. Isaacman and Richard L. Roberts, 285–305. Portsmouth, NH: Heinemann, 1995.

Monson, Jamie. "Rice and Cotton, Ritual and Resistance: Cash Cropping in Southern Tanganyika in the 1930s." In *Cotton, Colonialism, and Social History in Sub-Saharan Africa*, edited by Allen F. Isaacman and Richard L. Roberts, 268–84. Portsmouth, NH: Heinemann, 1995.

Moore, Henrietta L, and Megan Vaughan. *Cutting Down Trees: Gender, Nutrition, and Agricultural Change in the Northern Province of Zambia, 1890–1990*. Portsmouth, NH: Heinemann, 1994.

Ramutsindela, Maano. "Political Dynamics of Human-Environment Relations." In *The Politics of Nature and Science in Southern Africa*, edited by Maano Ramutsindela, Giorgio Miescher, and Melanie Boehi, 20–36. Basel: Basler Afrika Bibliographien, 2016.

Spivey, Donald. *The Politics of Miseducation: The Booker Washington Institute of Liberia, 1929–1984*. Lexington: University Press of Kentucky, 1986.

Tilley, Helen. *Africa as a Living Laboratory: Empire, Development, and the Problem of Scientific Knowledge, 1870–1950*. Chicago: University of Chicago Press, 2011.

Tischler, Julia. "Education and the Agrarian Question in South Africa, c. 1900–40." *Journal of African History* 57, no. 2 (July 2016): 251–270.

Zeleza, Paul Tiyambe. *A Modern Economic History of Africa: The Nineteenth Century*. Dakar, Senegal: CODESRIA/East African Publishers, 1997.

Zimmerman, Andrew. *Alabama in Africa: Booker T. Washington, the German Empire, and the Globalization of the New South*. America in the World. Princeton, NJ: Princeton University Press, 2012.

CHAPTER 33

THE GLOBAL GREEN REVOLUTION

MARK B. TAUGER

THE Green Revolution originated in mid-twentieth-century Europe, reached its full expression in the Third World, and expanded to a global network of agricultural research. It has had many critics and it achieved limited outcomes. While the Green Revolution had origins in fascist, communist, and several different democratic systems, its personnel were highly apolitical: they recognized and utilized scientific achievement from any source to improve food production, socioeconomic relations, and environmental conditions in farming everywhere they could.

The initial concept of the Green Revolution involved the crossing Asian dwarf varieties of rice and wheat with other international varieties to breed "semidwarf" varieties with larger "spikes" or ears of grain and short and sturdy stems that would be much less likely to "lodge"—break and collapse—from rain, wind, and heavier spikes. These altered plants produced much larger yields and were called "high-yielding varieties" (HYVs) or modern varieties (MVs). They were also bred to resist plant diseases and insects, to be less sensitive to day length, and to have other characteristics promoting higher yields.

After the development of varieties in Italy and the USSR, teams led by American agronomists Norman Borlaug in Mexico and Henry Beachell in the Philippines in the 1950s and 1960s developed successful HYVs of wheat and rice, respectively, supported mainly by the Rockefeller Foundation. This success persuaded a group of international organizations to form an overarching agency, the Consultative Group for International Agricultural Research (CGIAR), to attract funding and establish more research centers for other crops and geographical regions and address issues of biodiversity and government policies. This agency oversaw the expansion of the Green Revolution to many more crops and regions. It transformed the Green Revolution into a vast international network of research centers but faced problems with financing, organization, relations with large agribusiness connections, and many criticisms.

Critics of the Green Revolution argued that HYVs polarized social and economic relations between the wealthier farmers who could afford all of the components of HYV cultivation and poor farmers who ended up working as laborers. They argued that HYVs displaced local crops and reduced diversity, criticisms that ignored the innate diversity of new varieties and the large seed collections of the CGIAR. More serious criticisms concerned the effects of pesticides, fertilizers, and irrigation on the environment and human health, which are problems throughout world agriculture. And despite the increased food production of the Green Revolution, there are still approximately a billion extremely poor and hungry people in the world. The Green Revolution's work is far from over.

First Stages of the Green Revolution: Italy and the USSR

The origins of the Green Revolution lay in early dwarf varieties of wheat and rice developed centuries ago in India and China that spread to Korea, Japan, and Taiwan by the late nineteenth century. The first Western country to employ these varieties was Italy, which relied on wheat as its main food source. Italy's wheat varieties had relatively low yields and were subject to lodging; the country had to import wheat every year. The key figure in Italy was the agronomist Nazareno Strampelli, who in 1903 became the head of the Rieti agricultural research station in central Italy.[1] While breeding wheat for lodging resistance, a seed company in 1911 sent him seeds of the Japanese dwarf wheat Akakomugi, which was itself an international hybrid. Strampelli saw its potential to reduce lodging by passing on genes for short growth and sturdy stems. He began crossing it with varieties he had acquired from several countries, based on Mendelian genetics. By 1920 he had bred several semidwarf wheat varieties, including Ardito and Mentana, that were much more resistant to lodging and to rust and produced much larger yields than previous tall varieties.[2]

Italy's new dictator Benito Mussolini, facing the old problem of crop failures and importing wheat, declared a "Battle for Wheat" in 1925 and recruited Strampelli to lead this program. Strampelli accepted this post as an opportunity to help the poor and improve agriculture.[3] He utilized Italy's existing agricultural extension system, the *cattedra ambulanti*, a group of agricultural scholars and specialists who traveled in the countryside to provide assistance to smaller-scale farmers. They organized lectures and publications about his varieties, planted sample plots to demonstrate them, and provided incentives for farmers to adopt them. Their use spread from the more commercial northern and central provinces to the poor southern provinces. In 1932, a wheat rust epidemic reduced harvests from central Europe to the Volga, but much less in Italy, because by then about half of Italy's farmers were growing Strampelli's highly rust-resistant varieties.[4]

During the 1930s, Italy went for several years without importing wheat. Strampelli spread his varieties with a guidebook that explained how to grow them and advised significant applications of fertilizer and then available pesticides. These guidelines were very similar to those later employed by Borlaug in the "package" methods for growing HYVs.[5] Strampelli's program also increased wheat production without significantly increasing the wheat area, which left more land for other crops and livestock.[6] The "Battle for Wheat" could not eliminate poverty and malnutrition in Italy by the 1940s, because of entrenched social inequities, but it reduced them somewhat.[7] Strampelli's varieties were used widely in several countries in Europe, Argentina, and China.[8]

World War II disrupted Strampelli's work, and he died in 1942, but his varieties survived and influenced world agriculture. After the war, the new Italian government repudiated fascism and with it the "Battle for Grain." Scholars revived the memory of Strampelli only decades later. Yet Italian farmers and wheat breeders continued to use his varieties. While the wheat area in Italy declined, production was stable and even grew. Since the war, most European wheat varieties have become semidwarf or dwarf HYVs, most have dwarfing genes from Akakomugi, and Strampelli was the first breeder to introduce these in Europe.[9]

The second country to develop wheat HYVs was the USSR.[10] The Russian Empire had a long history of serious famines, almost entirely from natural disasters and the many crop failures they caused. In the nineteenth century the Russian government established an extensive system of famine relief and supported an expanding program of agricultural science research, which by the early twentieth century reached international levels in certain areas.[11] Nonetheless, crop failures and food shortages recurred and were important causes of the 1917 revolutions and of food supply problems during the Civil War that followed (1918–1921).

During the first decade of Soviet rule, the USSR had three crop failures and famines, and the government formed relief agencies and imported food for famine victims. Soviet scientists tried to address these problems by seeking new varieties in 1920s. The biologist Nikolai Vavilov and his associates at the Bureau of Applied Botany collected more than 200,000 grain and other crop varieties from around the world and employed research stations to determine how they adapted to Soviet environmental conditions. One center was near Krasnodar in the North Caucasus, where a young plant breeder Pavel Panteleimonovich Luk'ianenko (1901–1973) worked with other specialists on this project.[12]

Soviet leaders attributed these famines mainly to backward peasant farming, and in response to the third famine, in 1928–1829, decided they had to modernize peasant farming to prevent famines. This modernization involved collectivization, a forced land reform that converted the prevailing medieval interstripped fields into consolidated fields on the model of industrial-style American farms. These reformed villages were farmed cooperatively and called "collective farms," or *kolkhozy*. The regime also established larger industrial farms called *sovkhozy*.[13] The regime also undertook to modernize peasants' traditional methods by applying the advancements of agronomy. In 1929, Soviet authorities brought all the agricultural research agencies under an All-Union Academy of Agricultural Sciences (VASKhNiL) headed by Vavilov.

In 1931 the USSR was struck by severe drought, and then in 1932 by plant diseases, especially rust (part of the Europe-wide infestation that Strampelli's wheat withstood), smut, ergot, and insects. These disasters resulted in small harvests, crop failures, and widespread starvation. The Soviet government recognized the drought, but high officials never mentioned the disasters of 1932, mistakenly attributing the famine to mismanagement, peasant resistance, and nationalism. The regime undertook significant famine relief, though several million people died of starvation and related diseases.[14] The agronomist Luk'ianenko understood the real causes of the crop failures. He published a long article on the rust infestation and the lack of Soviet wheat varieties resistant to rust, as did other Soviet agronomists.[15] Luk'ianenko set out to breed rust-resistant wheat using Vavilov's world plant collection, which included Strampelli's varieties, and following Vavilov's advice regarding the characteristics of the ideal wheat variety, anticipating the approach of the Green Revolution.[16] Luk'ianenko developed rust-resistant varieties in the 1930s, but his institute had to flee the Nazi occupation of the Kuban, and when they returned after the war they began work again almost from scratch. In 1948 the fraudulent scientist Trofim Lysenko rose to power over Soviet agricultural sciences and tried to suppress genetics. Leading scientists in Moscow and Leningrad had to abandon their work and careers. Luk'ianenko, however, was almost 1,000 miles away, and like many other plant breeders continued to use genetics and avoided interaction with Lysenko and his cronies. After Stalin's death in 1953, Lysenko's power declined, and Luk'ianenko's work accelerated.[17]

In 1955, Luk'ianenko and his team developed an extremely high-quality semidwarf variety, Bezostaia 1, based on varieties bred by Strampelli and by an Argentine breeder who used Strampelli's varieties as a source, and certain American varieties that Vavilov had identified as highly rust-resistant. Bezostaia 1 was high-yielding and resistant to rust and to lodging. Over the next decades it was grown on millions of hectares in the USSR, Eastern Europe, and Turkey, where it was ranked very highly in an international comparative trial in 1969–1970. Meanwhile Luk'ianenko continued to breed more semidwarf HYV varieties that produced up to ten tons per hectare. He used varieties that Norman Borlaug (see below) used as well, and in 1971 Borlaug traveled to Krasnodar to meet Luk'ianenko.[18] By Luk'ianenko's death in 1973, other Soviet grain breeders were using his varieties and his approaches for their own breeding, developing semidwarf rye and other crops.[19] VASKhNiL provided the national network to support the wide development and cultivation of improved varieties.

The Italian and Soviet breeding of semidwarf wheat anticipated the Green Revolution in technology, but neither country had the wealth, global reach, or larger humanitarian and political objectives of the United States after World War II.

The US-Supported Green Revolution after World War II

The postwar Green Revolution derived from several factors. The work of the Rockefeller Foundation to improve health in Latin America and Asia led to growing awareness that its efforts were leading to rapid population growth in countries with backward agriculture that could not produce enough food for the whole population. US foreign policy officials during the peak of the Cold War feared that inadequate food supplies could radicalize the population of poor and newly decolonized countries.[20] These concerns persuaded the US government and private funders to begin new programs for agricultural development, based on the rapid advances in US agricultural and nutritional sciences in the early twentieth century.

Mexico in 1940 faced a crisis like those of Italy and the USSR. The new president in 1940, Manuel Camacho, began to break away from previous leaders' focus on peasants and land reform and shifted policies toward industrialization. He viewed agriculture as a resource for industrial growth.[21] He came to the United States in 1941 seeking assistance to make Mexico self-sufficient in food to free up funds for industrialization. Also, from 1939 to 1942 Mexican wheat harvests were reduced by rust infestations, which required more imports and threatened US wheat crops.[22]

The US government sent the Mexican officials to the Rockefeller Foundation (RF), which had begun agricultural programs in several countries. The RF recruited leading agricultural specialists, including the rust specialist Ervin Stakman from the University of Minnesota, to study Mexico firsthand, and their investigations led to an agreement between the RF and Mexico that established the Mexican Agriculture Program (MAP) to improve maize, wheat, and certain other crops. The program did improve corn production, but the more important breakthrough came in wheat. Stakman's former student Norman Borlaug became head of the wheat program in 1945 and set out to develop rust-resistant wheats. He accumulated many resistant varieties from Mexico, the United States, and other countries, including Strampelli's variety Mentana, and crossed them until he obtained much better varieties.[23]

In the process he employed an innovative approach: "shuttle breeding"—growing one generation of crossings at MAP headquarters in Chapingo and nearby Toluca, near Mexico City, then shipping them north to a research center in Ciudad Obregon, in Sonora state near the US border, to grow the next generation immediately, rather waiting a year to grow it in central Mexico. This cut breeding time in half. Also, because the two centers were hundreds of miles apart in latitude, their day lengths were different. Shuttle breeding thereby produced varieties that were photo-insensitive and could grow well in different regions.

Using these methods, by the mid-1950s Borlaug and his team produced higher yielding rust-resistant wheats that he persuaded many farmers in Mexico to grow. By the late 1950s, Mexico became self-sufficient in wheat and corn. Borlaug also trained many Mexican scientists and plant breeders to work directly in the fields, rather than relying on laborers, which made them actively involved in the breeding processes. This work took place during a new stem rust outbreak in the United States and Mexico. In response, Borlaug proposed an international cooperative effort to set up spring wheat nurseries in several countries to find and develop new local resistant varieties. These nurseries played an important role in developing new varieties.[24]

The key breakthrough of the Green Revolution began in 1953, when Orville Vogel, a leading plant breeder at Washington State University, send Borlaug samples of a hybrid dwarf wheat, Norin-10, developed by Japanese breeders in the 1930s.[25] Borlaug realized that these Japanese varieties could reduce lodging by passing on genes for short growth and sturdy stems. The process of breeding new semidwarf varieties took several years and more than 8,000 crosses, but by the early 1960s Borlaug's group had genuine semidwarf HYVs such as Sonora 64 and Lerma Rojo 64. Mexican farmers grew them extensively, and by 1963, Mexico produced more than two million tons of wheat, six times the amount produced in 1944.[26]

By the 1960s, the Food and Agricultural Organization of the United Nations (FAO) had begun farming improvement programs in the Middle East, Africa, Asia, and Latin America, using Mexican HYVs. Borlaug, however, argued that these countries also needed well-trained and experienced specialists to educate farmers in the new technologies and assist governmental personnel. Borlaug called them "apostles" and persuaded the FAO to work with the RF to bring young specialists from all over the world to study at the MAP plant-breeding programs. In addition, the Mexican president, Adolfo López Mateos, impressed with the early work of the International Rice Research Institute (IRRI), proposed to the RF that MAP breeding centers be institutionalized into a similar international program. The RF accepted this proposal, and in 1963 an international agreement renamed the MAP centers the International Center for the Improvement of Maize and Wheat, known by the Spanish acronym CIMMYT, serving as a training center and a source of new wheat varieties.[27]

In 1962–1964, agricultural specialists from India and Pakistan, including M. S. Swaminathan, the director of the Indian Agricultural Research Institute, asked Borlaug to help their countries. Both countries had serious food supply problems and were importing millions of tons of wheat every year. These countries' agricultural research centers had great difficulties developing higher-yielding wheats.[28] Borlaug visited in 1963 and won the support of the minister of food and agriculture, Chidambaram Subramaniam, for the transfer of HYV technology to India. From 1962 to 1965, Pakistan and India imported thousands of tons of Mexican varieties, tested them, and began crossing them with many local varieties.[29]

In 1965–1966, India suffered two droughts from the failure of the monsoons to deliver their usual abundant rainfall, causing massive crop failures and deaths from starvation, despite importing more than 10 million tons of food.[30] This crisis persuaded the government to import tens of thousands of tons of Mexican HYVs with the hope that they would produce high yields in Indian conditions. The Indian project focused on several regions that had irrigation and good soils, especially Punjab in the northwest. The result in 1968 was an unprecedented harvest of 17 million tons of wheat in India, despite a partial monsoon failure. Pakistan also made great progress: its harvest of 8 million tons in 1968 made it self-sufficient in wheat. India reached that point in 1972.[31] Borlaug also trained many Indian and Pakistani scientists.

By this time, at least ten more countries had acquired HYV wheats and rice varieties from IRRI, produced much larger grain harvests than before, and were approaching self-sufficiency. In a speech in March 1968, William Gaud, head of the US Agency for International Development, described these developments as a "Green Revolution," in contrast to a violent "Red Revolution" that shortages could have caused. In 1970 the Swedish Nobel Committee awarded Borlaug the Nobel Peace Prize, which he accepted as a representative of "an army of hunger fighters around the world."[32] CIMMYT and IRRI also won the UNESCO science prize. In the 1980s, Borlaug with private financial support established a World Food Prize to give recognition to many other agricultural specialists.[33]

The IRRI similarly began with the philanthropic campaigns of the Rockefeller and Ford Foundations, the Cold War policies of the United States, and an appeal by a country in need.[34] While running the MAP, the RF was also investigating the possibility of supporting agriculture in Asia. Nelson Rockefeller led a US government committee in 1950 that proposed substantial US support for agricultural development in poor and newly independent countries, in line with President Harry Truman's goals of expanding US trade and deterring communist subversion. The RF had run an agricultural program in China since 1924, and in the postwar period came to focus on Asia as the main region in need of agricultural development, and rice as the key crop. In 1951 the secretary of agriculture and natural resources of the Philippines learned about the MAP and wrote to the RF appealing for aid in agricultural development. After considerable debate, during 1958–1962 the two foundations agreed to construct an international center in Los Baños, the location of the University of the Philippines. When the Ford Foundation allotted the future IRRI $6.9 million in 1959, the foundation's vice president W. H. Ferry called improving rice harvests a "Green Revolution."[35]

IRRI relied on rice research and improvements by scientists, breeders, and farmers across Asia.[36] Japanese farmers in the late nineteenth century had developed *rono* varieties (those grown by skilled farmers), some of which had a short growth pattern and produced higher yields when fertilized. After conquering Taiwan, Japan bred high-yielding rice for export to Japan. One was a Chinese dwarf variety, Dee Geo Woo Gen, from which Taiwanese breeders in 1956 bred a semidwarf variety called Taiching Native 1, grown on a million hectares by 1968 in several Asian countries. The Indian Central Rice Research Institute in the 1950s also bred short-growing rice varieties by crossing Indian and Japanese varieties.

In 1962, breeders at the newly established IRRI, including the American Henry Beachell, made several crosses with Taiching Native 1 and an Indonesian variety, Peta, and found one variety, which they called IR8, that was low-growing, with sturdy stems, produced very large heads of rice when fertilized, and matured in three-fourths of the time of other varieties. In 1966, an Indian agronomist at IRRI, Sumit Kumar de Datta, showed that IR8 produced 5 tons of rice per hectare with no added fertilizer, much more than traditional Philippine varieties, and up to 10 tons per hectare with fertilizer.[37]

IR8 was soon grown widely, but it tasted bad, broke easily, and was subject to pests, especially the brown planthopper. IRRI breeders made thousands of additional crosses, every few years developing new more resistant varieties, but sooner or later the insects and diseases mutated in response, requiring yet more breeding. In 1976 they released

IR36, which tasted better, matured even faster, and resisted several pests and diseases; by the 1980s, it was being grown all over Asia. In 1985, IRRI produced IR64, which had cooking quality "matching that of the best varieties available," as well as resistance to blights and the brown planthopper, followed by an even better variety, IR72, in 1990.[38] IRRI also supported national rice-breeding and agricultural development programs in many countries by training scientists and others, sharing resources, and helping them cross IRRI varieties with local ones to suit local conditions.[39]

The success of CIMMYT and IRRI led the Ford and Rockefeller Foundations to establish new centers for tropical agriculture in Nigeria (IITA) and Colombia (CIAT). By 1970, these centers' funding needs exceeded the capacity of the foundations.[40] To address this issue, representatives of the foundations, several governments, and international funding agencies, including Robert McNamara, president of the World Bank, met in Bellagio, Italy, and in 1971 established the Consultative Group for International Agricultural Research, an international organization to attract funding to these centers and help establish new ones.[41] The group held regular meetings of representatives from countries and research centers around the world, developed priorities, and evaluated proposals, relying especially on a technical advisory committee (TAC) of specialists from developing and developed countries.

In its first two decades, the CGIAR founded centers on many aspects of agriculture, including preservation of plant genetic resources, specific crops, livestock, geographic regions, and food policies. The CGIAR based its work on principles of "donor sovereignty"—donors could fund any center or the CGIAR as a whole and could specify their funds' uses—and center autonomy, allowing each center to set its own research agendas.[42] The centers worked on the basis of free exchange of ideas and plant varieties with national agricultural research centers.[43] The Green Revolution spread to many countries and crops, and world food production substantially increased, except in Africa.[44]

From the 1970s, food crises, such as the droughts of 1972 and 1985 and the economic crises of 1997 and 2008, a renewed focus on markets and prices as the root of poverty, environmental and sustainability concerns, and the growing role of agribusiness and biotechnology companies all began to turn funders' attention away from the original Green Revolution goals.[45] CGIAR encountered a funding shortfall by the 1990s, and it began to seek support from biotechnology corporations. Syngenta became a CGIAR board member in 2002, which provoked international protests by La Vía Campesina, an international peasant network, and other grass-roots groups demanding food sovereignty. The CGIAR repeatedly altered its mission statement to reflect the new focuses on poverty, sustainability, and biodiversity, setting up new centers on these issues while closing others. During the 2000s the CGIAR restructured itself, added objectives such as food sovereignty and environmental and market systems to its mission statements, and brought Monsanto and the Bill and Melinda Gates Foundation onto its governing board.[46]

Sub-Saharan Africa in the 1980s became the last regional focus of the Green Revolution. Borlaug worked with Ryoichi Sasakawa, a Japanese magnate, to form the

Sasakawa-Global 2000 partnership to breed and distribute high-yielding crops to thousands of farmers in fifteen African countries.[47] In 2006, the Gates Foundation launched the Alliance for a Green Revolution in Africa (AGRA), which has funded hundreds of small-scale projects in Africa. Yet Africa's population is the fastest-growing in the world, and specialists disagree over whether these programs can solve Africa's food crisis.[48]

The People's Republic of China (PRC) also participated in the Green Revolution.[49] China had Strampelli's wheat varieties and was breeding new rice varieties before World War II. In 1966, Pakistani officials brought samples of Mexican-Pakistan HYV wheat to China; after testing them, in 1970 the PRC bought 5,000 tons of Mexican HYV wheat from Pakistan. In 1974, Borlaug and other US agricultural scientists visited China and found it had an effective program of grain improvement. The rice scientist Yuan Longping, head of the China National Hybrid Rice Research and Development Center, began breeding high-yielding hybrid rice in the 1960s, and He Kang guided China's agricultural modernization as agriculture minister and head of a major research center; both received the World Food Prize. From the 1960s to the 1980s, China had among the largest increases in grain yields and production of any Green Revolution country. In 1983, based on its overall economic growth, the PRC became a donor member of CGIAR.

As a result of the efforts of the CGIAR and its centers to address the growing complexity of the world food system, the Green Revolution evolved from the heroic initiative of a relatively small group of scientists in a few places into "big science." It now comprised a vast global network of international and national research centers employing tens of thousands of specialists, whose work advanced beyond the original goal of breeding new grain varieties into programs to analyze and improve agricultural systems, alleviate poverty, ameliorate environmental problems, and prepare farming and food systems for climate change.

On the macroeconomic level, the Green Revolution worked. Production of basic staple crops grew substantially from the 1950s to the 2000s. World population more than doubled from 3 billion in 1960 to 7.7 billion (2019), but food production kept pace: there were no famines in the Americas and in Asia except in North Korea. Government policies in North Korea emphasized heavily mechanized production that relied on fuel imports from the USSR. When the USSR fell, those imports were stopped, and North Korea could not maintain its former food production. Hunger and malnutrition now seemed clearly to be results of maldistribution, poverty, and policy rather than shortages. Yet some grass-roots movements and NGOs in developing countries and First World scholars and humanitarian movements began to find problems in the ways the Green Revolution was implemented and its effects on farmers and the local environment.

Early in the Green Revolution, researchers found that better-off peasants and landlords disproportionately benefited from the new technologies. In Mexico in the 1950s and 1960s, HYV wheat was grown mainly by farmers with large landholdings able to afford fertilizer, pesticides, and irrigation. Small farmers and tenants usually could not afford the initial expenses, even with government subsidies, found themselves unemployed in their villages, and often left the land for the industrializing cities, which was one of President Camacho's goals for the policy. From the 1970s, large-scale industrial and agricultural capitalists shifted Mexico's farming toward an export orientation, and Mexico again began importing food.[50]

In India, small farmers often went into debt to local moneylenders to finance purchases of inputs. From the 1980s, many thousands of farmers faced growing debts and the threat of losing their land, and some committed suicide by drinking the very pesticides they had purchased. In Pakistan, the government limited the size of landholdings, but big landlords evaded the limits by "selling" some of their holdings to neighbors who were actually family members. They also evicted their tenants, who often became laborers working on those same allotments. Small farmers could not afford the initial expenses of HYVs, and either used them without adequate fertilizer or relied on their old varieties.[51]

These patterns of higher benefits to better-off social groups applied to whole regions. In India in the 1960s, one of the priority regions for growing the new HYVs was the northwest state of Punjab, which had an advanced irrigation network and entrepreneurial Sikh farmers. Punjab became one of India's richest states, while a larger state in east India, Bihar, remained poor even though it had better soil and weather conditions. Many critics argued that despite assertions by plant breeders and Green Revolution centers that they aimed to reduce poverty, implementation of their programs actual worsened poverty for many groups in the villages and sometimes radicalized them.

Other investigations, however, raised questions about these criticisms. A study of the Green Revolution in Bangladesh found that small farmers adopted HYV rice varieties at rates comparable to those of larger farmers and even produced higher yields.[52] A thirty-year study in Punjab found poverty declined significantly during the Green Revolution.[53] Other studies have found that small farms still dominate world agriculture, showing that most small farmers can survive these economic difficulties.[54] These inequalities also long predated the Green Revolution and reflected socioeconomic patterns and attitudes difficult to change over a few decades.[55]

After numerous publications reported poor and small farmers' difficulties in participating in the Green Revolution, funding agencies and CGIAR centers began to reorient their programs to benefit those groups. Borlaug told a CGIAR meeting in 1995 that despite its successes, the Green Revolution "has not solved the problem of poverty and chronic under-nutrition afflicting hundreds of millions of people around the world."[56] World Bank president Robert McNamara in 1973 proposed a program of small loans to help 100 million poor farmers, which neglected the much larger numbers of landless working class groups.[57] In 1986 the CGIAR committed itself to improving "the general economic well-being of low-income people," and the centers have similar commitments in their mission statements online.[58]

Some critics of the Green Revolution criticized it for reducing or even "destroying" biodiversity, describing HYV varieties as genetically "narrow," and claiming that their use has led to the "loss" of hundreds or thousands of traditional varieties.[59] They claimed that some local traditional varieties, or landraces, had yield potential equal or superior to that of HYVs. Landraces are varieties that had been bred and grown in the region for centuries, and even if they were lower-yielding, they had resistance to pests, aridity, and other threats. These critics argued that the HYVs needed substantial irrigation, fertilizer, and pesticides or their yields would be worse than those of traditional varieties. They imply that the Green Revolution was unnecessary and an imposition of "Western science" on a functional traditional agriculture.

The repeated imports of millions of tons of food by Mexico, India, and Pakistan before the Green Revolution casts doubt on these critics' views of traditional agriculture. As to the number of traditional varieties used, farmers in developing countries and colonial areas, including India and Mexico, before the Green Revolution frequently relied on very few varieties, often developed by local breeding centers, because they were better than landraces.[60] HYVs were widely used in the 1960s and afterward for the same reason: farmers preferred them. The HYVs also were not "narrow" but embodied biodiversity: they derived from crossings of dozens of varieties, including landraces, selected for possession of certain specific characteristics, such as dwarfing, or resistances to plant diseases, insects, and aridity.[61] HYVs were almost always more resistant to pests and often other environmental hazards than traditional varieties, because breeders sought crossed landraces and earlier hybrids with greater resistance to transfer that resistance to new HYVs.[62] Also, since the HYVs were bred for shorter growth and high yield, they had higher yields than landraces at every level of fertilizer and irrigation.[63]

Some landraces did become extinct, but that was a result of floods and droughts, and urbanization that paved over farms, pastures, and forests as much as from farming. Some specialists argue that farmers using HYVs are contributing to biodiversity by using the genetically complex HYVs.[64] The critics also tend to ignore the enormous numbers of landraces and other plants that the Green Revolution centers collected. CIMMYT, IRRI, and the other crop-oriented centers all established programs to collect and preserve local varieties, grow and study them to detect their unique characteristics, and use them to breed new varieties. Soon after CGIAR was founded, it established the International Board for Plant Genetic Resources in 1974 to coordinate and support formation of "genebanks." It was renamed Biodiversity International as part of the CGIAR reforms.[65]

The CGIAR, the FAO, and agricultural ministries and research centers in many countries around the world have preserved millions of traditional and wild varieties of grains, legumes, forage crops, vegetables, and fruits, including many that were thought lost but were discovered in unexpected places.[66] The biggest collection is the Svalbard Global Seed Bank in Spitsbergen, Norway. These vast collections can prevent the erosion of genetic diversity caused not only by farmers' decisions to use few varieties but also by disasters, such as the forced flight of the International Center for Agricultural Research in the Dry Areas (ICARDA) from Syria at the beginning of the civil war in 2011. ICARDA, now based in Lebanon and Morocco, had to request the Svalbard Seed Bank to provide duplicates of many seeds it had to abandon in Syria.[67]

A much more serious criticism of the Green Revolution is environmental pollution caused by increased use of fertilizers, pesticides, and other agricultural chemicals.

Concerns about these problems arose independently of the Green Revolution, particularly with the publication of biologist Rachel Carson's *Silent Spring* (1962). NGOs also criticized the Green Revolution and CGIAR for their easy acceptance of pesticide use and collaboration with the corporations.

Like farmers in the developed world, farmers in Green Revolution who could afford chemicals resorted to their use with little or no hesitation in order to raise large crops. By the 1980s, the use of chemicals caused serious pollution, especially of drinking water. Increasing cases of cancers and other diseases emerged in regions with heavy pesticide use, as in heavy pesticide-contaminated regions from California to Pakistan. Also, as in other regions, heavy pesticide use led to the evolution of resistant insects, which farmers tried to combat by using even more pesticides.[68]

CGIAR meetings soon included representatives of chemical companies who tried to minimize the risks from these chemicals. Borlaug, who began his career working on agricultural chemicals for DuPont in the 1930s, wrote an article in 1972 that dismissed *Silent Spring* and other criticisms as one-sided, incomplete, and inaccurate, and argued that pesticides were essential for feeding the world's growing population. Several scientists responded critically to his essay.[69] One article defending the Green Revolution attributed chemical pollution to greed on the part of farmers and chemical companies and dealers, and insisted that the Green Revolution was not responsible for these abuses.[70] On the other hand, M. S. Swaminathan, who worked with Borlaug in the 1960s and afterward, wrote and spoke repeatedly of the need for an "evergreen revolution" that emphasized sustainability.[71] In the 1980s, CGIAR and its centers made sustainability and insect resistance part of their mission statements. As of 2019, all the centers are addressing these problems in their work, especially because funders like the Gates Foundation are proposing projects with a focus on organic farming and integrated pest management.

A related environmental problem concerns the most important input, water. During the 1960s, for example, farmers across South Asia drilled tens of thousands of tube wells to irrigate the new HYVs. Within a decade or two, more and more of these farmers found that they had to drill much deeper to get necessary water, and sometimes the wells went dry. India and Pakistan are now facing the most serious water crises in their history, in large part because of irrigation.[72] Depletion of aquifers, like pesticide contamination, is not unique to Green Revolution regions, but is common to many farming areas in advanced countries as well.

The Green Revolution began three times in the twentieth century: in fascist Italy in the 1920s, in the communist USSR in the 1950s, and in multiple countries (Mexico, the Philippines, communist China, and elsewhere) in the second half of the century. Political leaders viewed these programs as supporting their political systems: American leaders said the Green Revolution would stop "Red Revolution," while Chinese leaders saw their Green Revolution as supporting their Red Revolution. The scientists involved were apolitical and tried to avoid dealing with political issues, seeking only to exchange germplasm and improve production and food supply. Their indifference and even challenge to political concerns was exemplified among other ways in the awarding of the

World Food Prize to two Communist Chinese figures—a government official and a rice breeder, both of whom did much of their work under Mao Zedong.

The Green Revolution has grown from local programs to breed semidwarf high-yielding crops into a global and interlinked network of agricultural research programs and farming systems that underlies food supplies for most of the world's population. At its peak in the 1970s, the Green Revolution centers relied on teams of thousands of scientists who used scientific agriculture to increase food production to avert famine in poor countries with rapidly growing populations, and thereby reduce the risk of hunger rebellions and communist subversion. Now most of the world directly or indirectly depends on the work of this global network and its affiliated national agricultural research systems.

After initially ignoring or minimizing the social and environmental repercussions of their agricultural projects, these centers and agencies are now addressing the social and environmental issues that still hinder elimination of hunger and poverty. The websites of CIMMYT and IRRI, for example, show a much more sophisticated and complex approach to their work than in the 1960s. They highlight research programs that are environmentally and socially conscious and focused on addressing broader real-world issues. Yet they still work on breeding high-yielding varieties and addressing agricultural crises, such as a new virulent rust variety Ug99, discovered in 1998 and still considered a major threat to world wheat supplies.

Notes

1. Sergio Salvi, *L'uomo che voleva nutrire il mondo: I primi 150 anni di Nazareno Strampelli* (Treia, Italy: Accademia Georgica, 2016); Roberto Lorenzetti, *Wheat Science: The Green Revolution of Nazareno Strampelli* (Rome: Journal of Genetics and Breeding, 2000); and several primary sources from the period.
2. Strampelli explained this in a commemorative volume on his work, Strampelli et al., *Origini, sviluppi, lavori e risultati* (Rome: Istituto nazionale di Genetica per la Cerealicoltura, 1932), 53ff, which also contains illustrations and agronomic descriptions of several of his semidwarf wheat varieties.
3. Ibid., 103–4.
4. The *New York Times*, September 4, 1932, and *Wall Street Journal*, September 26, 1932, reported that forecasts had been lower because of "extensive rust damage," but also that Italy had an unprecedently large harvest. Heavy rains also caused less lodging of crops in Italy than elsewhere in Europe; *Wall Street Journal*, August 3, 1932. These do not appear to have been propaganda reports because the Italian government openly reported lower harvests in previous years. On rust in Europe in 1932 see also Tauger, *Natural Disaster and Human Action in the Soviet Famine of 1931–1932* (Pittsburgh: University of Pittsburgh, 2001).
5. "Phenomenal Wheat Crops Grown by Italian Farmers," *Daily Sentinel* (Rome, NY), March 12, 1935, citing *Country Home*, an American farm journal. I am grateful to Sergio Salvi for sharing this source with me.
6. Alexander Nützenadel, "Economic Crisis and Agriculture in Fascist Italy, 1927–1935: Some New Considerations," *Rivista di storia economica*, no. 3 (2001): 289–312.

7. *Baltimore Sun*, February 25, 1940, column by Philip MacKenzie.
8. Lorenzetti, *Wheat Science*, 112–45, 190–203.
9. Katarina Borojevic and Ksenija Borojevic, "The Transfer and History of 'Reduced Height Genes' (Rht) in Wheat from Japan to Europe," *Journal of Heredity* 96, no. 4 (2005): 455–59.
10. This section is based on Mark Tauger, "Pavel Pantelimonovich Luk'ianenko and the Origins of the Soviet Green Revolution," in *The Lysenko Controversy as a Global Phenomenon*, Vol. 1: *Genetics and Agriculture in the Soviet Union and Beyond*, ed. William deJong-Lambert and Nikolai Krementsov (Cham, Switzerland: Palgrave Macmillan, 2017), and other works cited.
11. See, among several studies, A. L. Ivanov et al., *Ocherki po istorii agronomii* [Outline history of agronomy] (Moscow: Rossel'khozakademiia [Russian Academy of Agricultural Sciences], 2008), especially ch. 6–7; and Ol'ga Elina, *Ot tsarskikh sadov do sovetskikh polei*, 2 vols. [From tsarist gardens to Soviet fields] (Moscow: Akademiia Nauk [Russian Academy of Sciences], 2008).
12. See I. G. Loskutov, *Vavilov and His Institute: A History of the World Collection of Plant Genetic Resources in Russia* (Rome: IPGRI, 1999); and Aleksandr Fedorenko, *Luk'ianenko* (Moscow: Molodaia Gvardiia, 1984), 105ff.
13. See Tauger, "Stalin, Soviet Agriculture, and Collectivization," in *Food and Conflict in Europe in the Age of the Two World Wars*, ed. Frank Trentmann and Fleming Just (New York: Palgrave Macmillan, 2006), 109–42.
14. On the causes of the 1931–1933 famine, see Tauger, "The 1932 Harvest and the Famine of 1933," *Slavic Review* 50, no. 1 (Spring 1991): 70–89; and Tauger, *Natural Disaster and Human Action*; R. W. Davies and S. G. Wheatcroft, *The Years of Hunger: Soviet Agriculture 1931–1933* (London: Palgrave Macmillan, 2004), presents considerable detail on the actions and attitudes of leaders but minimizes the environmental factors. A politicized literature, especially associated with Ukrainian nationalists, asserts the famine was "man-made" but ignores or denies environmental factors; see, e.g., Anne Applebaum, *Red Famine* (New York: Doubleday, 2017), and the following review: Tauger, "Review of Anne Applebaum's *Red Famine: Stalin's War on Ukraine*, History News Network, https://historynewsnetwork.org/article/169438.
15. P. P. Lukianenko, *O stepeni ugneteniia gibridov ozimoi pshenitsy buroi rzhavchinoi v 1932 g. v sviazi s rezul'tatami selektsii na immunitet* [On the susceptibility of winter-wheat hybrids to *Puccinia triticina Erikss.* during 1932 in connection with results obtained in breeding for immunity] (Rostov-na-Donu: Severo-Kavkazskii selektsionnyi tsentr Soiuzsemenovodob"edineniia [North Caucasus selection center of seed-growers association 'Edinenie'], 1934); P. K. Artemov, "K voprosu o porazhaemosti sortov zernovykh kul'tur grybnymi bolezniami" [On the question of infestation of grain crop varieties to fungal diseases], *Trudy po prikladnoi botanike, genetike i selektsii, seriia A: Sotsialisticheskoe rastenievodstvo*, no. 7 (Leningrad, 1933): 75–90.
16. N. I. Vavilov, *The Scientific Basis of Wheat Breeding* (Moscow: Gosudarstvennoe izdatel'stvo sovkhoznoi i kolkhoznoi literatury [state publisher of sovkhoz and kolkhoz literature], 1935), translated in *The Origin, Variation, Immunity, and Breeding of Cultivated Plants: Selected Writings of N. I. Vavilov*, edited and translated by K. Starr Chester, *Chronica Botanica* 13, no. 1/6 (1949–1950): 170–314.
17. On these points see Fedorenko, *Luk'ianenko*; Valery Soyfer, *Lysenko and the Tragedy of Soviet Science* (New Brunswick, NJ: Rutgers University Press, 1994); Ol'ga Elina, "Mezhdu nauchnoi teoriei i sel'skokhoziaistvennoi praktikoi. Selektsionery i Lysenko [Between

scientific theory and agricultural practice. Plant breeders and Lysenko] (1948–1955 gg.),″ in *Za "Zheleznym zanevesom": mify i realii sovetskoi nauki*, ed. E. I. Kolchinskii et al. (St. Petersburg: DB, 2002): 376–392.
18. On these points see Tauger, "Luk'ianenko"; A. A. Romanenko et al., eds., *Bezostaia 1—50 Let Triumfa* (Krasnodar: Krasnodar Agriculture Research Institute and Russian Academy of Agricultural Sciences, 2005).
19. Ivanov et al., *Ocherki po istorii agronomii*, 366ff.
20. The main sources on these points are John Perkins, *Geopolitics and the Green Revolution* (New York: Oxford University Press, 1997); and Nick Cullather, *The Hungry World: America's Cold War Battle Against Poverty in Asia* (Cambridge, MA: Harvard University Press, 2010).
21. See Perkins, *Geopolitics*, and Stephen Niblo, *War, Diplomacy, and Development: The United States and Mexico, 1938–1954* (Lanham, MD: Rowman & Littlefield, 1995).
22. Lennard Bickel, *Facing Starvation: Norman Borlaug and the Fight against Hunger* (Pleasantville, NY: Reader's Digest Press, 1974): 116–117.
23. Bickel, *Facing Starvation*, 93–228. Norman Borlaug, "Mexican Wheat Production and Its Role in the Epidemiology of Stem Rust in North America," *Phytopathology* 44 (1954): 398–404, provides an interim report by Borlaug that notes his use of Strampelli's Mentana.
24. Leon Hesser, *The Man Who Fed the World: And His Battle to End World Hunger* (Dallas: Durban, 2009): 61.
25. L. P. Reitz and S. C. Salmon, "Origin, History, and Use of Norin 10 Wheat," *Crop Science* 8, no. 6 (November 1968): 686; and Bickel, *Facing Starvation*, 217–28.
26. Bickel, *Facing Starvation*, 236–40.
27. Ibid., 229–36; Carl Pray, "The Green Revolution as a Case Study in Transfer of Technology," *Annals of the American Academy of Political and Social Science* 458 (November 1981): 68–80; Hesser, *The Man Who Fed the World*, 70.
28. Christopher Baker, "Frogs and Farmers: The Green Revolution in India, and Its Murky Past," in *Understanding Green Revolutions*, ed. Tim P. Bayliss-Smith and Sudhir Wanmali (Cambridge: Cambridge University Press, 1984): 37–53.
29. Swaminathan reported on this work in a paper in 1964; M. S. Swaminathan, *50 Years of Green Revolution: An Anthology of Research Papers* (Singapore: World Scientific, 2017): 1–8.
30. Ibid., 85.
31. Hesser, *The Man Who Fed the World*, 100, 203.
32. Bickel, *Facing Starvation*, 345.
33. Hesser, *The Man Who Fed the World*, 136–46.
34. A good objective study of this history is Robert S. Anderson, "The Origins of the International Rice Research Institute," *Minerva* 29, no. 1 (March 1991): 61–89; see also Robert F. Chandler Jr., *An Adventure in Applied Science: A History of the International Rice Research Institute* (Manila: IRRI, 1992).
35. Mark Dowie, *American Foundations: An Investigative History* (Cambridge, MA: MIT Press, 2002): 112.
36. On this background, see Randolph Barker et al., *The Rice Economy of Asia*, Resources for the Future and IRRI, Washington, DC (Baltimore: Johns Hopkins University Press, 1985), vol. 2.
37. S. K. De Datta et al., "Effect of Plant Type and Nitrogen Level on Growth Characteristics and Grain Yield of Indica Rice in the Tropics," *Agronomy Journal* 60 (1968): 643–647.
38. On these developments, see Genetic Evaluation and Utilization Program, *Parentage of IRRI Crosses IR1-IR50,000*, Manila: IRRI, 1985; *IR36: The World's Most Popular Rice*, IRRI

(n.d. but apparently 1980s); David Mackill, Gurdev Khush, "IR64: a high-quality and high-yielding mega variety," *Rice (N Y)*, 9 April 2018, 2018; 11:18.
39. See, e.g., Thomas Hargrove and Victoria Cabanilla, "The Impact of Semidwarf Varieties on Asian Rice-Breeding Programs," *BioScience* 29, no. 12 (December 1979): 731–735.
40. Hesser, *The Man Who Fed the World*, 65; Selçuk Özgediz, *The CGIAR at 40: Institutional Evolution of the World's Premier Agricultural Research Network* (Washington, DC: CGIAR, 2012), ix–x.
41. Özgediz, *The CGIAR at 40*, 1–11.
42. Ibid., xi, 94.
43. Hesser, *The Man Who Fed the World*, 72, 211.
44. See especially Robert Evenson, "Food and Population: D. Gale Johnson and the Green Revolution," *Economic Development and Cultural Change* 52, no. 3 (April 2004): 543–569.
45. Courtney Kramer, "Exposing Biases in Agricultural Research: The CGIAR and the Evolution of Global Approaches to Food and Agriculture," *Pardee Periodical Journal of Global Affairs* 1, no. 2 (Fall 2016): 17–34; Hessel, *The Man Who Fed the World*, 120ff, 179ff, 211.
46. Özgediz, *The CGIAR at 40*, xvi–xxiii; 31–110.
47. Hesser, *The Man Who Fed the World*, 160–69.
48. See, from among a large literature, Alejandro Nin-Pratt and Linden McBride, "Agricultural Intensification in Ghana: Evaluating the Optimist's Case for a Green Revolution," *Food Policy* 48 (2014): 153–67; Eric Holt-Giménez et al., *Ten Reasons Why the Rockefeller and the Bill and Melinda Gates Foundations' Alliance for Another Green Revolution Will Not Solve the Problems of Poverty and Hunger in Sub-Saharan Africa*, Policy Brief No. 12 (Oakland, CA: Institute for Food and Development Policy, 2006); Keijiro Otsuka, "Why Can't We Transform Traditional Agriculture in Sub-Saharan Africa?," *Review of Agricultural Economics* 28, no. 3 (Autumn 2006): 332–337.
49. Hesser, *The Man Who Fed the World*, 147–55; Sigrid Schmalzer, *Red Revolution, Green Revolution: Scientific Farming in Socialist China* (Chicago: University of Chicago Press, 2016).
50. David Sonnenfeld, "Mexico's 'Green Revolution,' 1940–1980: Towards an Environmental History," *Environmental History Review* 16, no. 4 (Winter 1992): 34–38.
51. Rashid Amjad, "A Critique of the Green Revolution in West Pakistan," *Pakistan Economic and Social Review* 10, no. 1 (June 1972): 17–41.
52. Mahabub Hossain, *Nature and Impact of the Green Revolution in Bangladesh*, International Food Policy Research Institute and Bangladesh Institute of Development Studies, Research Report 67, July 1988.
53. H. S. Shergill and Gurmail Singh, "Poverty in Rural Punjab," *Economic and Political Weekly* 30, no. 25 (June 24, 1995): A80–A83.
54. Sarah Lowder et al, "The Number, Size, and Distribution of Farms, Small Holder Farms, and Family Farms Worldwide," *World Development* 87 (2016): 16–29; Benjamin Graeub et al., "Family Farms in the World," *World Development* 87 (2016): 1–15.
55. Kusum Nair, *In Defense of the Irrational Peasant: India after the Green Revolution* (Chicago: University of Chicago Press, 1979), uses historical research and interviews to document these social patterns in Punjab and Bihar.
56. Hesser, *The Man Who Fed the World*, 171.
57. Ernest Feder, "McNamara's Little Green Revolution," *Economic and Political Weekly* 11, no. 4 (April 3, 1976): 532–41.
58. Swaminathan, *50 Years*, 339–41; Evenson, "Food and Population," 548.

59. See, e.g., Vandana Shiva, *The Violence of the Green Revolution: Third World Agriculture, Ecology, and Politics* (London: Zed Press, 1991).
60. Melinda Smale, "The Green Revolution and Wheat Genetic Diversity: Some Unfounded Assumptions," *World Development* 25, no. 8 (1997): 1260–1261.
61. Prabhu Pingali, "The Green Revolution and Crop Biodiversity," in *The Routledge Handbook of Agricultural Biodiversity*, ed. Danny Hunter et al. (London: Routledge, 2017), 217ff; Smale, "Green Revolution and Wheat Genetic Diversity," 1262–63.
62. Smale, "Green Revolution and Wheat Genetic Diversity," 1263–66; Swaminathan, *50 Years*, 136–39.
63. Swaminathan, *50 Years*, 119ff; De Datta et al., "Effect of Plant Type," cited above.
64. Smale, "Green Revolution and Wheat Genetic Diversity," Pingali, "Green Revolution and Crop Biodiversity." There is a large literature documenting the diverse causes of biodiversity decline.
65. Özgediz, *The CGIAR at 40*, 15.
66. Susan Dworkin, *The Viking in the Wheat Field* (New York: Walker, 2009), has a list of the holdings of gene banks of CGIAR and many countries, 204–10, and discusses the processes and disputes involved in establishing and running them, 97–116, 139–42 (at CIMMYT), and 177–87 (regarding the Norwegian Gene Bank).
67. This article from the Nordic Genetic Resources Centre describes the process by which ICARDA was able to recover its seedbank from the duplicates stored at the Global Seed Vault: https://www.nordgen.org/en/icarda-seeds-day/.
68. There is a large literature on agricultural chemicals, especially pesticides, cancers, and other diseases. See, e.g., Sean Gallagher, "The Poisoning of Punjab," at the website of the Pulitzer Center, https://pulitzercenter.org/reporting/poisoning-punjab; Sarojeni Rengam, "The Struggle against Pesticides," in *Women and IPM: Crop Protection Practices and Strategies*, ed. Elske van de Fliert and Jet Proost (Amsterdam: Royal Tropical Institute, 1999): 15–22; Azizullah et al., "Water Pollution in Pakistan and Its Impact on Public Health—A Review," *Environment International* 37, no. 2 (February 2011): 479–97, among many others.
69. Norman Borlaug, "Mankind and Civilization at Another Crossroad: In Balance with Nature—A Biological Myth," *BioScience* 22, no. 1 (January 1972), 41–44; 22, no. 5 (May 1972): 273–74; 22, no. 7 (July 1972): 393.
70. Swaminathan, *50 Years*, 341.
71. See several essays on the "evergreen revolution," ibid.
72. This is again a topic with a vast literature; see, e.g., S. T. Somashekhara Reddy, "Declining Groundwater Levels in India," *International Journal of Water Resources Development* 5, no. 3 (1989): 183–90; Sami Bouarfa and Marcel Kuper, "Groundwater in Irrigation Systems: From Menace to Mainstay," *Irrigation and Drainage* 61, no. 51 (2012): 1–13.

Bibliography

Bickel, Lennard. *Facing Starvation: Norman Borlaug and the Fight Against Hunger.* Pleasantville, NY: Reader's Digest Press, 1974.

Chandler, Robert F., Jr. *An Adventure in Applied Science: A History of the International Rice Research Institute.* Manila: IRRI, 1992.

Cullather, Nick. *The Hungry World: America's Cold War Battle against Poverty in Asia.* Cambridge, MA: Harvard University Press, 2010.

Dworkin, Susan. *The Viking in the Wheat Field*. New York: Walker, 2009.
Hesser, Leon. *The Man Who Fed the World: And His Battle to End World Hunger*. Dallas: Durban, 2009.
Lorenzetti, Roberto. *Wheat Science: The Green Revolution of Nazareno Strampelli*. Rome: Journal of Genetics and Breeding, 2000.
Özgediz, Selçuk. 2012. *The CGIAR at 40: Institutional Evolution of the World's Premier Agricultural Research Network*. Washington, DC: World Bank. https://openknowledge.worldbank.org/handle/10986/23845 License: CC BY 3.0 IGO.
Perkins, John H. *Geopolitics and the Green Revolution*. New York: Oxford University Press, 1997.
Salvi, Sergio. *L'uomo che voleva nutrire il mondo: i primi 150 anni di Nazareno Strampelli*. Treia, Italy: Accademia Georgica, 2016.
Schmalzer, Sigrid. *Red Revolution, Green Revolution: Scientific Farming in Socialist China*. Chicago: University of Chicago Press, 2016.
Swaminathan, M. S. *50 Years of Green Revolution: An Anthology of Research Papers*. Hackensack, NJ: World Scientific, 2017.
Tauger, Mark. "Pavel Pantelimonovich Luk'ianenko and the Origins of the Soviet Green Revolution." In *The Lysenko Controversy as a Global Phenomenon*, Vol. 1: *Genetics and Agriculture in the Soviet Union and Beyond*, ed. William deJong-Lambert and Nikolai Krementsov, 97–127. New York: Palgrave Macmillan, 2017.

CHAPTER 34

FAMINE

JENNY LEIGH SMITH

Mass starvation events are not exclusively associated with agricultural societies, but the expansion of agriculture during the Neolithic Revolution led to a dramatic increase in famines in world history.[1] Before settled agriculture became widespread, hunting and migratory pastoralism supported smaller communal groups. At times these groups sometimes starved due to bad weather or scarce prey, but because of their smaller populations, the scale of hunger and its effect on hunting societies was slight when compared to more recent famines. Today famines are rarely triggered by an absolute shortage of food, but in pre-agricultural societies, catastrophic shortfalls were the main cause of periods of hunger and starvation. Far more common than death by starvation in these pre-agrarian societies were stunted growth (and likely stunted intellect) and immunologic frailty induced by chronic malnutrition.

The rise of agriculture during the Neolithic Revolution presents a paradox; there is overwhelming archeological evidence that separate cultural groups in different parts of the world shifted from nomadic hunting to settled agriculture. It seems likely this shift was made because it increased the amount and quality of food in these early communities. In other words, many people in many different places all decided that farming would benefit them and their descendants. However, once the transition to agriculture was complete, agricultural societies tended to experience more food insecurity, malnutrition, and famines than earlier pre-agrarian communities had. This instability and increase in food insecurity endured for hundreds, sometimes thousands of years. Why did they choose farming over hunting? Historians and archeologists have many theories on this topic, but no final answers.

In spite of rising food insecurity and general precarity, human populations in farming communities steadily increased. Agriculture supported larger communities than hunting did, and these communities left artifacts, artistic relics, and written accounts of their experiences. Famines became touchstone events for early agrarian societies, and the cultural and economic impact of famines endures in the material cultures that remain of these ancient civilizations. The earliest famine depicted in art is a wall carved with pictographs of dead and suffering famine victims on the pyramid of Unas in Sakkara, created in about 3500 BCE.[2] Numerous civilizations in Europe, Asia, and Africa endured a century-long megadrought, also known as the 4.2 kiloyear event, that occurred between 2200 BCE and 2100 BCE. Surviving records from at least four different early civilizations in Egypt, Mesopotamia, and eastern China show evidence of famine and food strain during this century, including artworks that depict emaciated people and livestock, account books that register sharp spikes in grain prices, and architectural ruins that demonstrate that existing storehouses were hastily expanded, presumably to increase emergency grain stores.[3] A similar megadrought occurred in North and South America between 900 and 1000 CE and may have led to a series of famines that destabilized the Mayan Empire and Anasazi settlements in the American Southwest. However, in these civilizations there is only archeological proof of sudden and dramatic population decrease in the centuries following the megadrought; there is no direct evidence of famine as a primary cause.[4]

Famines increased in agrarian settings, and in response, early farmers adopted strategies to avoid or reduce their impact. Because these strategies were partially effective at shoring up the survival of early farming systems, they have become key components of modern agriculture. In particular, three adaptations ancient farmers made to avoid famines are worth noting: the mixed husbandry system, the systematic diversification of crops, and building and managing community granaries.

Archeological evidence indicates that farming and pastoralism coevolved, with many early farmers switching between these livelihoods or engaging in a mixed husbandry system. Maintaining crops and domestic animals, particularly domestic animals who could provide either milk or meat as additional food resources, proved to be a better hedge against famine than field crops alone. The first and most important dairy products to be exploited were fermented products such as yogurt and cheese in the early agrarian cultures of Mesopotamia. Archeologists believe these were the most useful early dairy products because they could be stored and used during lean times and also because the fermentation process for these products broke down indigestible milk sugars.[5] Some farming groups would eventually develop lactase persistence, or the ability to digest milk sugars into adulthood, thus allowing human bodies to more efficiently exploit the nutrients in fresh dairy products, but there is no evidence of this trait from the first 4,000 years of agriculture.

Once lactase persistence evolved in adult humans, it shored up the survival of some farming populations, especially in marginal environments, including Northern Europe, present-day Ireland, and the highlands of southern France. The overwhelming majority of people from these regions have inherited lactase persistence, which probably indicates it was a significant survival advantage for people born with this trait. Lactase persistence evolved in different populations for different reasons, but one likely reason for its presence in Ireland, northern Europe, and the highlands of Western Europe is because of the survival advantage that mixed husbandry, specifically with dairying, bestowed.

Selective breeding of animals created some of the earliest regional breeds of livestock that were well adapted to a niche environment but also maximally productive at converting the plants they consumed into milk and meat. Selective breeding was even more important for field crops. A thousand years after the first signs of agricultural activity the earliest cultivated crops, einkorn and triticale, show evidence of selective breeding. Grains were selected in ancient times for many of the same reasons that prevail today: survival, abundance, and environmental resilience, especially to temperature extremes and drought. By 8000 BCE there were regionally specific forms of millet and amaranth found across Asia Minor and East Asia, and every major agrarian society in North America, South America, Europe, Africa, and Asia shows evidence of selective breeding.

The Russian geographer V. I. Vavilov was the first Western agricultural expert to note that well-adapted local varieties were important, but that planting a range of plant varieties was a safer technique. Early farmers tended a variety of grains, but as farming became more specialized, famine was far less likely among societies with a robustly diversified crop base. Cultures that practiced radical diversification fared the best. This was not an invention or innovation, but a survival strategy that had evolved first among pre-agrarian hunter-gatherers who tended patches of semi-domesticated grains, fruits, and seeds along their migration routes. Farmers in present-day Peru initially domesticated a single variety of potato 7,000 to 10,000 years ago, but built up a library of more than 3,000 potato varieties by the height of the Inca Empire.[6] Incidences of famine in the region dropped once it became common for farmers to plant dozens, or even hundreds, of varieties in one region. If a disease or a weather event destroyed part of the crop, the entire harvest would not fail.

Finally, the logic of farming and settled agriculture required safe, reliable access to grains. Since many field crops were harvested just once a year, the ability to store these crops for the remainder of the year, or at least for as long as possible, was essential, and thus granaries were important architectural features in agricultural communities. The size and construction of granaries varied dramatically by region and ecology, but in general granaries needed to do three things: they needed to protect harvested grains from rotting, they needed to protect them from being eaten by pests such as insects and rats, and they needed to protect grain from theft by other humans.

Over time, agrarian populations expanded and created more sophisticated forms of government. This was true very early in agrarian history in East Asia, where wet rice agriculture along the floodplains of the Yangtze and other major rivers made agriculture especially productive. With larger populations came the potential for more dramatic food crises. Centralized state governments that agricultural societies helped to support were expected to offer assistance to subjects affected by harvest shortfalls or weather disasters like floods or droughts. The earliest famine code was likely written in the third or fourth century BCE during the Zhou Dynasty in present-day eastern China. It included twelve actions the state pledged to take to help its subjects in times of famine. These included loaning out seeds and money, eliminating customs duties and market taxes, and reducing the number of festivals and rituals, such as marriage, that typically involved expensive displays of tribute.[7]

While the Zhou code described a planned state response to famines, it is an unusual document because it is so ancient. For the most part, famines that occurred before about 400–500 CE are poorly chronicled and evidence about how they were experienced has been passed down through art, architecture, and archeological remains rather than through written narratives. On the other hand, the period between 400 and 1500 CE contains some of the earliest precise narrative descriptions of famines. Famines during this period are characterized by two common themes. The first was a shift from famines resulting from absolute scarcity to those that were the result of shifting entitlements. The second was the rise in prestige and power of charitable institutions. Most of these charities were associated with churches and other religious orders. The central role of charity and stewardship in religious organizations evolved in part as a response to food insecurity and epidemic diseases that devastated agricultural communities during this time.

Early modern famines were most often created by what economist Amartya Sen has called the entitlement theory of famine, rather than absolutely short supply.[8] The notion of entitlement here stems from a narrow definition used by economists that is worth explaining in plain language. While the more straightforward meaning of entitlement comes from the notion that someone has the right or claim to some resource, for economists the term describes the relationship between people and resources, specifically the way that laws, social obligations, and cultural norms influence this relationship. When food was abundant in medieval Europe, for example, peasants who labored on vassal estates had an entitlement with their lord to a portion of the annual grain harvest that would provide adequate calories for their household. However, this relationship changed from year to year; in abundant years the entitlement might mean peasants received surplus grain, but in years of harvest scarcity their entitlement would result in a decrease of the harvest share. Entitlements were a side effect of powerful central states that could and did control access to food as a means of controlling their populations, and in autocratic societies where power was attained by wealth and the seizure of valuable assets, entitlement was always stacked against poor people and in favor of the rich.

The famines associated with the end of the Roman Empire are a good example of this situation. Although much of the Roman Empire's political strength was derived from its robust agricultural output, especially from its colonies in North Africa, France, and Spain, the redistribution of this food was unequal and only the wealthiest Roman classes were free from food insecurity.[9] Many famines in this era, while still often triggered by scarcity, were amplified by war, particularly the siege of fortified cities and dwellings. One of the earliest narrative accounts of famine comes from St. Jerome's account of the 408 CE siege of Rome: "nay more famine was beforehand with the sword and but few citizens were left to be made captives. In their frenzy the starving people had recourse to hideous food; and tore each other limb from limb that they might have flesh to eat."[10] Long-term siege was a new tactic of warfare for Europe during this period, and though sieges could be violent attacks on a fortified structure, they were more often long-term blockades, intended to starve the occupants of the fortification into surrender.

Rotting human remains in a besieged city could trigger infectious disease epidemics. A Baghdadi physician visiting the fortified city of Cairo during a famine in 1201–1202 described the risks of mass putrefaction; "the corpses lay unburied in the sureties and a virulent pestilence spread over the delta."[11] The famine historian Cormac Ó Gráda has described this combination of an initial period of starvation followed by a larger, more deadly epidemic of contagion as a classic "one-two punch" of large-scale famines.[12] The death toll in a famine is often disputed; one reason is the uncertain classification of diseases that emerge in the wake of famines. The "one-two punch" pattern has endured and remains a major risk during contemporary famines.

St. Jerome's earlier description of the behavior of Rome's starving reflects a popular and enduring preoccupation with the rise of cannibalism during famines. In turn, this reflects a fascination with the grotesque and the taboo. Stories of famine-induced cannibalism are also moral tales that indicate a profound disruption in traditional social order. After witnessing a famine in Shaoxing, China, He Xiaoqin wrote: "fathers eat their sons and sons also kill their fathers and eat them. Or husbands eat their wives and wives also slaughter their husbands and eat them."[13] He's description is not designed to maximize revulsion, but to emphasize the extraordinary breakdown of social relations this famine triggered. Fathers and husbands killing and consuming their children and wives is terrible, but for children and wives to turn on their parents and husbands is both horrifying *and* a clear perversion of well-established social hierarchical norms.

In addition to becoming more common, more severe, and more frequently used as a tool of war, famines in the early modern era reflect one of the most important social influences of the time, religious-based charity. These groups established soup kitchens in Europe and rice-porridge stations in East Asia. The guiding principle was that during times of scarcity a free hot meal was offered to anyone in need. Initially developed as a way to respond to short-term crisis situations, soup kitchens are still common charitable fixtures in contemporary cities. Developed to fight famines, soup kitchens now play a broader role in reducing urban food insecurity.

Charitable hot meals were most often (although not always) sponsored and distributed by religious orders and other non-state organizations. Granaries, by contrast, were typically managed by a local or national government authority. China's ancient granaries, established perhaps as early as 5000 BCE, were described in detail in Chen Huan-Chang's economic history of China, published in English in 1911. Chen, one of Columbia University's first Chinese graduates, described in detail how ancient granaries were constructed, managed, and allocated in times of need.[14] His work served as an inspiration for Henry A. Wallace, the United States secretary of agriculture during the 1930s who helped create the policies of strategic national grain reserves to ensure food security and price stability in US agricultural markets.

China was early but not exceptional; evidence of storerooms or storehouses created to guard against famine appear in most urbanizing agrarian societies. Stone granaries abutted palaces and temples throughout ancient Egypt by 3000 BCE. Their construction was so robust and enduring that the Roman state still kept grain in them 3,500 years later. The *Florentine Codex*, a sixteenth-century ethnographic account of the Aztec

Empire, describes Petlacalco, a vast city of storehouses. Petlacalco stored grains, beans, and quinoa that had been collected as tribute from farms across the empire.[15]

Releasing storehouse inventory during famines and other disasters was strategic; these releases helped stabilize the economy and shore up state power. Grain was directly dispensed to needy households only occasionally. The main purpose of a storehouse was not charity but social stability. Granaries help to control price inflation, allowing poor people to continue to purchase necessary staples. In contemporary society, granaries and strategic food reserves remain important state-controlled resources that serve this same function. Created to prevent or reduce famine emergencies, national food stockpiles are an important tool that helps control not only the price of the food supply, but also prices for other commodities linked to food and agriculture. Most nations maintain stockpiles of staple grains, but many also store strategic supplies of soap, sugar, salt, pork bellies, and cotton, among many other products.

Advances in navigation and ship construction expanded international trade and the rise of global capitalism. The period between 1500 and 1900 was marked by robust global trade in agricultural commodities. The wealth and poverty this new economic pattern engendered ultimately created a dark, brutal era of extreme famines. Britain and a small number of other wealthy European countries promoted unequal and exploitative trade and labor relationships with much of the rest of the world, colonizing some countries, promoting chattel slavery in others, and negotiating usurious trade deals with still others. While two or three twentieth-century famines have the highest overall number of fatalities, those in this earlier era killed far more people in terms of percentages of the population. Early modern famines, while often triggered by natural disasters such as droughts or floods, were made much worse by emerging market-oriented legal and social structures.

For example, in the period immediately before British colonization, during the Mughal Empire, India experienced unprecedented growth and quality-of-life improvement. In 1765 the average lifespan of a subject of the Mughal Empire was thirty-five years, one year longer than that of a contemporary Western European. Urbanization and robust artistic and literary cultures flourished across India. This period of growth was partially due to a more stable food supply. During these centuries, advances in agricultural technology and improved plant varieties made Indian farmers more productive and the country more resilient to disasters. While famines were not unheard of in the Mughal period, most were small-scale (500,000 or fewer deaths) and they did not make a major demographic impact. This changed for the worse. First, the British-sponsored East India Company and then the British government directly sought trade monopolies and influence over much of India's agricultural and industrial production. British colonization in India focused on increasing plantation-style agriculture, and on promoting the production of three inedible but commercially valuable commodities—tea, silk, and cotton. With less land dedicated to food production, years of drought and harvest failure became food crises. In 1769 in the southern state of Bengal, monsoon rains did not reach the continent, and this triggered a four-year period of famine and mass death. This was relatively early in India's colonial project, but Bengal had been managed for a decade by the East India Company, and company policies in the state directly contributed to a higher death toll and a more prolonged period of suffering.

The most problematic policies the East India Company adopted were raising taxes on farmers and abandoning long-standing grain storage practices that had kept the Bengal state free of wide-scale famine for centuries. Bengal households traditionally maintained personal storehouses for their rice harvests. These were small-scale structures that held just enough rice for a household for a few months in case of harvest or market failures. In the decade before the 1770 famine, Bengal farmers had been discouraged from hoarding harvest surpluses and encouraged to sell this rice immediately after harvesting it.[16] Misguided, profit-driven British policies in Bengal created famine in a state that had not experienced widespread famine for at least two centuries. Amartya Sen has described this famine as completely "man-made." Although triggered by a drought, the high loss of life in the Bengal famine of more than 2 million people was primarily caused by the damaging policies of the East India Company.[17]

British policies also contributed to the Great Irish Famine, which affected Ireland between 1847 and 1856. After Britain annexed Ireland in 1801, the wealth differences between absentee Anglican landowners and local Catholic tenant farmers expanded. The famine killed at least 1 million people and forced the exodus of another 2 million. Ireland's dense population, the vast disparities between the landed gentry and working poor, and its export-based agricultural economy meant that during the nineteenth century, the Irish population was chronically food-insecure. The physical impact was striking: higher infant and childhood mortality, physical stunting from chronic malnutrition, and shorter life expectancies across the population. However, the occupied Irish population avoided widespread famine during this period. This was in no small part due to a switch in staple crop. Over the course of the preceding century, Irish farmers had switched their household subsistence production from oats and barley to the cheaper and more productive New World crop of potatoes. Relying on just one variety of this single staple food made Ireland's poorest farmers uniquely vulnerable when the potato crop succumbed to a devastating fungal blight.

In 1845 a North American strain of potato fungus, *Phytophthora infestans*, arrived in Ireland and began to spread. The impact was rapid and dramatic. By 1846 the blight affected 60 percent of the crop, and famine deaths began. The crisis peaked in 1847, but deaths from starvation and related "second punch" diseases like typhus and cholera lingered until 1856. The Irish Famine is best remembered as a slow-motion catastrophe that could have been alleviated by good governance on the part of the British. Prevailing market-friendly economic theories supported a laissez-faire attitude toward food pricing. Although Ireland experienced a genuine scarcity of food at the end of 1846 and the beginning of 1847, by the second half of 1847 enough grain had been shipped into the country to prevent hundreds of thousands of deaths.[18] However, Britain was not able or willing to prevent these deaths and instead mismanaged distributing the relief grain and operating relief kitchens and other forms of charity.

In this way global capitalism in the nineteenth century helped redefine the experience of famine. In the future very few famines would be based on absolute scarcity. In the twentieth century, famines were largely caused by the relationship between people and the abstract concept of the economy. Access to food in this new era was mediated primarily by money, power, and personal connections. Britain was not the only instigator of a pro-market logic that left many farmers hungry and frequently in crisis, but the vast wealth the country accumulated in this period made its role in intensifying and amplifying the experience of famine particularly striking.

Britain was not the only country whose policies during this period made famines worse. However, unique in the early nineteenth century, long-standing principles of charitable assistance and economic support that had reduced suffering and death during past famines were suspended by Britain during the Irish famine in the interests of fiscal prudence. Thus, grain was not released from English storehouses to save Irish subjects, and while soup kitchens operated in the winter and spring of 1847, they were dismantled by the end of the summer in spite of the fact that deaths from starvation continued for another three years. Britain also allowed Irish landlords to evict impoverished residents from their tenant farms. Losing their homes and access to land increased poverty and food insecurity. Additionally, once food imports arrived in the country in late 1847, the government placed no cap on the price nor made any efforts to distribute the grain to the parts of the country that were suffering the most.

Finally, the Great Irish famine was the first famine to elicit the emotion of famine fatigue. This was a phenomenon brought on by the news cycle—in this case, daily newspapers—in which constant updates about a tragic situation eventually make the reader emotionally numb. This term originated over the summer of 1847.[19] In the twenty-first century, this phenomenon remains a significant obstacle to effective long-term famine relief. While the English-speaking public was initially moved by accounts of starvation across Ireland, continued Irish misery after the most acute period of the famine ended in August 1847 meant many politicians and potential donors became bored with the cause. Quaker and Catholic charity groups in the United States persevered for much longer in sending supplies and remittances to Ireland, but even for these groups the campaign lost its sense of immediacy by 1848 and charity dropped off every year in spite of the fact that malnutrition persisted.

The Great Irish famine may be the most remembered and memorialized famine in the English-speaking world, but it was a forerunner of a series of famines in China and India in the second half of the nineteenth century that were collectively the deadliest set of mass starvation events of the modern era. The historian Mike Davis has called these famines late Victorian holocausts, and he has written extensively about how the cyclical weather event ENSO combined with British colonial and expansionist policies and the introduction of capitalist marketing practices to overwhelm the regions and maximize fatalities. Davis uses the term "synergistic virulence" to describe the relationship between extreme weather, colonial policies, and food supplies in India and China during the second half of the nineteenth century. Even his most conservative estimate, of 36 million dead globally between 1856 and 1902, indicates a new scale of demographic catastrophe. Mass-scale famines would occur several times over the course of the twentieth century.[20]

Famines of the late nineteenth century are also significant for the ways in which they were managed by the government. In colonial India, the British Raj established Famine Codes that were increasingly narrow in their definition of what constituted a famine. Communities that experienced harvest shortfalls and malnutrition needed to be assessed by famine officers, who were under enormous pressure from their overseas supervisors to downplay and to normalize the risks of food insecurity. During this period, Britain was pledged, in theory, to a policy of humanitarian intervention in colonies that experienced famine, but in practice the Famine Codes provided a way for colonial administrators to "unsee" famine.

In China, famine relief was often initiated by community organizations, religious organizations, and diasporic networks. In these networks, successful and established immigrant communities, still feeling tied to their home county or village, helped to organize shipments of emergency supplies and cash payments back to these areas. This same strategy had been an essential lifeline for Irish farmers who survived the initial starvation period in 1847, but were too poor to emigrate or to re-establish a self-sufficient plot of land. Remittances from emigrant communities and organizations became essential for many subjects of the Qing Empire in China as well. One of the unanticipated aspects of the burst of economic migration in the nineteenth century was an enormous increase in the number of people who maintained social, cultural, and economic ties in at least two very different parts of the world. Famines and other crises made these ties more visible, as emigrants struggled to ensure relatives and others from their ancestral villages had access to the charitable resources they donated.

The historic connections between agriculture and large military forces and farming's focus on land as sovereign property make the history of hunger intimately tied to that of war. The vast majority of twentieth-century famines are associated with wars, Both world wars engendered serious famines: during World War I there were famines in Lebanon, Persia, Russia, Germany, Kazakhstan, and East Africa; during World War II, in the Netherlands, the Soviet Union, Vietnam, Java, Iran, India, the Philippines, and Poland.

Ironically, the two most deadly twentieth-century famines were inspired by civil wars in which governments that were struggling to maintain power over vast and unruly rural areas resorted to rule by terror, manufacturing famines that rapidly broke the independent and separatist spirits of these regions. Under the guidance of Stalin, and in the name of agricultural collectivization, the Soviet Union between 1929 and 1932 attacked its agricultural heartland, especially those borderland territories in Ukraine and Southern Russia with the strongest regional identities. The USSR purposely cleared storehouses and approved the complete state appropriation of grain harvests. The People's Republic of China launched a "Great Leap Forward" campaign between 1958 and 1961. This campaign sought to modernize the country and suppress rural resistance to the new urban and industrial focus of the republic. Much like the Soviet collectivization drive, which was carried out most vigorously in regions that had resisted being incorporated into the Soviet Union during the Russian civil war of 1919–1922, in PRC China, grain quotas and famine deaths were highest in provinces that had been loyal to the anti-Communist KMT during the 1946–1949 civil war.[21] Both campaigns are best thought of as a new and deadly form of punitive civil war, targeting regions, political groups, and ethnicities that were perceived as challenges to the current government. Both campaigns killed tens of millions of citizens and are widely regarded as major tragedies. Although the level of their manufacture is still disputed, the historical record is clear that humans rather than nature played the greatest role in sponsoring these events of mass death.

Support for larger-scale international nongovernmental organizations gained traction in the period between the two world wars, and a level of international prominence after the United Nations was founded in the wake of World War II. NGOs organized around a variety of topics but several groups tackled hunger and malnutrition. These groups believed that a neutral and well-funded NGO could potentially organize a more rapid and effective response to famines than the government. Herbert Hoover was an early adopter of this perspective, which he eventually expanded into strong support for the United Nations.

Hoover gained much of his experience in international organizations as program director for the American Relief Association (ARA), a charitable organization formed in 1919. Like the Red Cross before it, the ARA was funded by both the US government and private donations. The organization initially worked in Western Europe, helping to feed and resettle citizens in the aftermath of World War I. The ARA expanded its operation into Soviet Russia in 1921 and it spent two years in the country working to reduce the death toll of a major famine that hit the Volga region of southern Russia. At the peak of the program's operation during the winter of 1921–1922, ARA staff were providing hot meals for 10 million people a day. Their intervention did not prevent a large-scale famine in the region—millions died—but it is just as certain that the intervention did prevent millions more from starving.[22]

The success of the ARA and the positive publicity that Hoover, a well-connected future American president, arranged for the program meant that the interwar years were a period of optimism and growing faith in the efficacy of large-scale interventions. Hoover's well-coordinated, "industrial" approach to famine management reflected a strong belief in progress and a faith that modern science, technology, and logistics could reform the chaotic and underdeveloped worlds in which famines occurred.

World War II would test this optimism, as dozens of countries experienced extreme food shortages during and immediately after the war. Some of these famines were famous. In the siege of Leningrad, the blockaded population experienced perhaps as many as a million deaths, but city officials were able to keep morale in the city high. In 1942 a famine hit colonial Bengal, triggered by multiple natural disasters. The slow and incompetent British response to the emergency escalated the death toll and became a rallying point for India during its postwar campaign for independence. Many wartime and postwar famines faded into the general chaos and misery of the era. Japan's occupation of China, Indochina, and present-day Indonesia engendered major famines in all of these regions, but these disasters went virtually unreported by Western news agencies. A famine in the postwar Soviet Union, occurring just as Cold War alliances were solidifying, was downplayed and was mostly ignored by the USSR's former war allies.

In the optimism and global restructuring of the postwar period, two important trends in famine response emerged. First was a focus on the science of nutrition and a search for the most economical and effective feeding programs to reverse acute malnutrition. Second was a redefinition of famine, away from a focus on food shortages and price spikes, and toward a concern with issues of overpopulation and crowding.

To their horror, the British soldiers first tasked with liberating and feeding starving concentration camp survivors discovered that camp inmates initially suffered acute stomach pains and even died after eating the military rations the soldiers had with them. This negative reaction was refeeding syndrome; after months of a watery and inadequate diet, normal food was dangerous to medically frail inmates.[23] What was the best way to renourish the critically sick? The quest for the best therapeutic refeeding diet began.

Following established nutrition guidelines for invalids and small children, physiologists, nutritionists, and food chemists all researched best practices of refeeding in the postwar era. These programs sought to improve upon the soups and porridges that soup kitchens had provided. Some of the earliest programs built on the work of nutritionists who devised military rations and quartermaster protocols for soldiers during World War II. Ancel Keys, inventor of the K-ration, also wrote the first reference handbook on stages of malnutrition and therapeutic refeeding, *The Biology of Human Starvation*.[24] Published in 1950 and based on research conducted on volunteer subjects during World War II, Keys's research classified and described stages of malnutrition, the effects of caloric deprivation on various systems of the body, and the impact of differently paced refeeding programs. A generation of nutrition scientists and medical personnel who treated famine victims would use it as a definitive reference guide.

Improvements in therapeutic refeeding were incremental; for most of the twentieth century, state-of-the-art refeeding substances were still thick slurries based on boiled grain and some combination of sugar, salt, and protein. Refeeding formulas used cheap, high-protein ingredients like soymeal and whey and increased their palatability by adding sugar and fat. By the mid-1960s, the go-to product for food crises was the nourishing but decidedly unappetizing Corn-Soy-Blend cereal, referred to as CSB. CSB would remain a staple product of humanitarian agencies for the rest of the twentieth century.

Palatability in therapeutic refeeding protocols was a thorny problem; while substances might pass an initial taste-test in the laboratory, in real-life settings famine victims tended to be suspicious of new and unfamiliar foods. Scientists and health practitioners working in the field in famine-struck regions initially underestimated the powerful links between food and culture, assuming hungry people would not be picky eaters. This was wrong, and early field experiences soon demonstrated that there was not going to be a single refeeding formula that would be appropriate and acceptable to all people in all places. People overwhelmingly preferred therapy foods that tasted familiar and that were based on staple grains of the region. CSB was an effective but almost universally unpopular famine relief product for much of the second half of the twentieth century.

Some of the first famine aid workers to measure the impact of new formulas for therapeutic refeeding in field settings were the health professionals working for a new charity called Oxfam, a portmanteau of the Oxford Committee on Famine Relief. Oxfam was formed during World War II to send famine aid and medical supplies into Nazi-blockaded Greece. At war's end, Oxfam's mission was still relevant. In the postwar era the organization expanded and professionalized, and because of its strong connections with Oxford University it developed a policy of sending doctors and nurses as well as food aid to various places experiencing food shortages. This new wave of humanitarian medical professionals replaced Herbert Hoover's teams of logistical managers. Oxfam workers were able to document the efficacy and shortcomings of the first generation of therapeutic refeeding substances.[25] Earlier charities and government famine rescue missions had focused simply on getting food to hungry people. Oxfam's approach treated communities hit by famines as the public health disasters they were and combined primary health care with therapeutic feeding. This new approach and the logic behind it were so effective that many other charities and NGOs concerned with hunger alleviation adopted it in the coming decades, including the International Red Cross, CARE, Catholic Relief Services, and the United Nations World Food Programme.

Another significant postwar trend affected social science rather than medical science. This was a preoccupation with the world's population. In part because of improved techniques of population analysis, demographers and other social scientists began to think of the rising world population as a potential global problem. This approach to the world as a crowded place with limited food resources affected food security policy and famine relief policy for the second half of the twentieth century.[26] Often the concern with overpopulation focused specifically on rising populations of non-white populations. Theories of overpopulation linked famines and food insecurity with newly defined notions of development and underdevelopment. Famines could be interpreted as events triggered by food shortages or by price fluctuations that reduced access to food, but they could also be seen as Malthusian events. This view of famines as biological "corrections" that targeted locations with the highest birth rates would persist into the late twentieth century.

Historically high birth rates in the sixteenth through eighteenth centuries triggered famines and exacerbated their severity in Asia and Europe, a trend Malthus recognized in his most famous work.[27] However, in the mid-twentieth century this phenomenon was virtually extinct. Agricultural production capacity in most parts of the world had increased dramatically since Malthus's time, and food processing, strategic reserves, transportation networks and cold storage made food supplies far more stable, predictable, and secure than they had ever been before. Food insecurity and malnutrition were still scourges of the world's poor, and many of the world's poor lived in countries with high birth rates, but this was a case where correlation was not causation; the two phenomena were linked, but they were not completely dependent on one another.

Since the 1970s, two further phenomena have influenced the severity and pattern of contemporary famines. The first of these is the recurring Sahelian drought. In the Sahel, inflated human and animal populations have intensified the experience of drought in the region, turning what might have otherwise been a lean period for marginal farmers into mass starvation events for a much larger portion of the population. In contrast to the neo-Malthusians, who saw demographic surpluses across wide swaths of Africa, South Asia, and East Asia, Sahelian population surpluses are limited to the narrow strip of land across northern Africa that separates the Sahara desert from the much wetter southern continent. Droughts are not a new phenomenon in the Sahel, but in the past fifty years they have been more frequent and more severe than they had been for the previous two centuries. The Sahel region has experienced five periods of multiyear drought since 1970. Each of these droughts resulted in famines. Major famines in Ethiopia, Sudan, and Somalia and smaller famines in Mali, Niger, Burkina Faso, South Sudan, and Yemen have exacerbated preexisting political tensions. At times, governments and military forces have restricted access to food as a tactic of war, much as in the medieval sieges of Europe and the Middle East centuries earlier.

In the Sahel drought, there were also mass human and livestock migrations. For these African countries, some 40 to 65 percent of the population farms, and most of these farms raise both crops and livestock as a way to bolster food security. During Sahelian droughts most surface water sources disappear, and farmers are forced to migrate with their herds to the few remaining wells and oases. The die-off of animals during these migrations is severe, and these die-offs further impoverish farmers. Mass migration and the refugee populations they create, not just in the Sahel because of drought, but around the world for a variety of economic and political reasons, are the second significant phenomenon affecting contemporary famines. Refugees strain regional goodwill, and at times surges of refugees cause or exacerbate regional wars.

Two recent famine interventions have significantly reduced famine deaths in the past generation. The first is a tool of surveillance, the USAID-sponsored FEWS Net, the Famine Early Warning Systems Network. The FEWS Net monitors key indicators of agricultural productivity and other food security indicators in twenty critical locations around the globe. This approach has been successful in part because the network monitors factors like weather and rainfall as well as variables like political stability, price spikes, and overall regional dependency on agricultural sales. FEWS Net is not infallible. For example, FEWS Net completely missed the "Arduous March" famine of 1994–1995 in North Korea because that country makes so little of its food production and price data available. However, assuming accurate information is available, FEWS Net has been a valuable tool for predicting and mitigating famines. While not a particularly happy ending, there are persuasive reasons to be optimistic that famines that kill tens of millions of people have been eliminated, famines with millions of victims will become rare, once-in-a-decade events, and food resources and humanitarian aid will primarily be dedicated to completely eliminating seven-figure famines over the course of the next century.

The second recent development is a new emergency food product, and perhaps more importantly, a new method of producing and distributing the product. Referred to generically as a ready-to-use-therapeutic food, or RUTF, the gold standard RUTF is a product called Plumpy'nut. Plumpy'nut is a sweet, peanut-flavored paste that comes packaged in single-use foil sachets. Unlike the majority of mid-twentieth century therapeutic products, which relied on research and development from charitable foundations and government programs, Plumpy'nut was developed by a small private company in France, Nutriset, which now licenses the formula and oversees quality control at dozens of Plumpy'nut production facilities.

RUTFs have some significant advantages over earlier therapeutic foods: they require no cooking, they are shelf-stable, and they remain sealed in sterile packaging until they are consumed. All these factors eliminate the very serious risk of contamination. Because RUTFs are based on a sweet paste rather than a hot cereal, they have a much higher rate of acceptance among hungry populations. Critically, babies can eat RUTFs since they do not need to be chewed. RUTFs also allow severely malnourished people to treat their own illness in a home setting; affected populations visit a clinic or healthcare provider once every week for a medical checkup to make sure their health is improving and to pick up new sachets. In the twentieth century, famine feeding programs have evolved once again. In terms of cost, most RUTFs are no more expensive than other refeeding programs. No longer relying on centralized soup kitchens of the early modern period or on the directly supervised medical model Oxfam workers pioneered in the post–World War II era, twenty-first century refeeding programs are more autonomous, decentralized, and, critically, affordable than they have ever been before.

Can we eliminate famines? This was a stated goal of numerous governmental and nongovernmental groups throughout the twentieth century. Yet famines, just like agriculture, are likely here to stay as long as humans endure on earth. This does not mean they will always be as devastating as the worst famines of the nineteenth and twentieth centuries. Global climate change has made weather patterns more unpredictable, and the world food supply is increasingly challenged by supply chain interruptions. These pose real risks to food security for hundreds of millions, perhaps billions of people. However, famines appear to be growing less severe, and the tools scientists and medical personnel have to predict and respond to famines are far more effective than at any previous point in history. There is reason to be cautiously optimistic that severe famines will be smaller, more isolated, and more infrequent events in the future.

Notes

1. Clark Spencer Larsen, "The Agricultural Revolution as Environmental Catastrophe: Implications for Health and Lifestyle in the Holocene," *Quaternary International* 150, no. 1 (2006): 12–20; Stephen Shennan, Sean S. Downey, Adrian Timpson, et al., "Regional Population Collapse Followed Initial Agriculture Booms in Mid-Holocene Europe," *Nature Communications* 4, no. 1 (2013): 2486, https: doi.org/10.1038/ncomms3486; Christopher R. Gignoux, Brenna M. Henn, and Jenna L. Mountain, "Rapid, Global Demographic Expansions after the Origins of Agriculture," *Proceedings of the National Academy of Science* 108, no. 15 (2011): 6044–6049, https://doi.org/10.1073/pnas.0914274108.
2. Bill Manley, "Famine and Food Shortages, Pharaonic Egypt," in *The Encyclopedia of Ancient History*, ed. Roger S. Bagnall, Kai Brodersen, Craige B. Champion, Andrew Erskine, and Sabine R. Huebner (2023), https://doi.org/10.1002/9781444338386.wbeah15155.
3. "4.2 ka BP Megadrought and the Akkadian Collapse," in *Megadrought and Collapse: From Early Agriculture to Angkor*, ed. Harvey Weiss (New York: Oxford University Press, 2017), 93–160, Jean-Daniel Stanley et al., "Nile Flow Failure at the End of the Old Kingdom, Egypt: Strontium Isotopic and Petrologic Evidence," *Geoarchaeology* 18, no. 3 (2003): 395–402.

4. Billie Turner II and Jeremy A. Sabloff, "Classic Period Collapse of the Central Maya Lowlands: Insights about Human-Environment Relationships for Sustainability," *Proceedings of the National Academy of Sciences of the United States of America* 109, no. 35: 13908–13914, https://doi.org/10.1073/pnas.1210106109.
5. Pascale Gerbault, Anke Liebert, Yuval Itan, et al., "Evolution of Lactase Persistence: An Example of Human Niche Construction," *Philosophical Transactions. Biological Sciences* 366, no. 1566 (2011): 863–877.
6. Robert Hijmans and David Spooner, "Geographic Distribution of Wild Potato Species," *American Journal of Botany* 88, no. 11 (November 2001): 2101–2112.
7. Ulrich Theobald, "Zhouli 周禮," https://www.chinaknowledge.de, accessed August 31, 2020.
8. Amartya Sen, *Poverty and Famines: An Essay on Entitlement and Deprivation* (Oxford: Oxford University Press, 2013): 45–51.
9. Dionysios Stathakopoulos, *Famine and Pestilence in the Late Roman and Early Byzantine Empire: A Systematic Survey of Subsistence Crises and Epidemics* (Farnham: Ashgate, 2017), ch. 3.
10. St. Jerome in *Select Library of the Nicene and Post-Nicene Fathers of the Christian Church*, Vol. 6: *The Principal Works of St. Jerome*, ed. Phillip Schaff and Henry Wace, trans. William . Fremantle (New York: Christian Literature Company, 1893): 257.
11. Abd-el-Latíf, quoted in Stanley Lane-Pool, *The Story of Cairo* (London: J. M. Dent & Sons, 1918): 195.
12. Cormac Ó Gráda, *Ireland's Great Famine: Interdisciplinary Essays* (Dublin: University College Dublin Press, 2007): 20.
13. He Xiaoqin, as quoted in Jennifer Eileen Downs. *"Famine Policy and Discourses on Famine in Ming China, 1368–1644"* (PhD diss., University of Minnesota, 1995).
14. Henry A. Wallace derived his "Ever Normal Granary" theory from this thesis. Chen Huan-Chang, *The Economic Principles of Confucius and His School* (PhD diss., Princeton University, 1911).
15. Fr. Bernardino de Sahagún, *Florentine Codex: General History of the Things of New Spain; Book 8—Kings and Lords*, no. 14, Part IX, ed. and transl. Arthur J. O. Anderson and Charles E. Dibble (Santa Fe and Salt Lake City: School of American Research and the University of Utah, 1951): 44.
16. William Dalrymple. *The Anarchy: The Relentless Rise of the East India Company* (New York: Bloomsbury Publishing, 2019), ch. 6.
17. Amartya Sen, "Imperial Illusions," *New Republic*, December 31, 2007, https://newrepublic.com/article/61784/imperial-illusions.
18. Cormac Ó'Grádá, *Black '47 and Beyond: The Great Irish Famine in History, Economy, and Memory* (Princeton, NJ: Princeton University Press, 2000).
19. "Signs of Famine Fatigue Increase," *Irish Times*, August 1847, republished in Brendan Ó Cathaoir, *Famine Diary* (Dublin: Irish Academic Press, 1998).
20. Mike Davis, *Late Victorian Holocausts: El Niño Famines and the Making of the Third World* (New York: Verso, 2002): 44.
21. Frank Dikötter, *Mao's Great Famine: The History of China's Most Devastating Catastrophe, 1958–1962* (London. Bloomsbury, 2010); Xun Zhou, *Forgotten Voices of Mao's Great Famine, 1958–1962. An Oral History* (New Haven, CT: Yale University Press, 2014); Jisheng Yang et al., *Tombstone: The Great Chinese Famine, 1958–1962* (New York: Farrar, Straus & Giroux, 2013).
22. Bertrand M. Patenaude, *The Big Show in Bololand: The American Relief Expedition to Soviet Russia in the Famine of 1921* (Palo Alto, CA: Stanford University Press, 2002).
23. Tom Scott-Smith, *On an Empty Stomach: Two Hundred Years of Hunger Relief* (Ithaca, NY: Cornell University Press, 2020): 103.

24. Ancel Keys, *The Biology of Human Starvation*, 2 vols. (Minneapolis: University of Minnesota Press, 1950).
25. Maggie Black, *A Cause for Our Times: Oxfam, the First 50 Years* (Oxford: Oxfam Great Britain, 1992): 233.
26. The rationale for this is best set out in Paul R. Ehrlich, *The Population Bomb* (New York: Ballantine Books, 1968), https://archive.org/details/populationbomb00ehrl.
27. Thomas Robert Malthus, *An Essay on the Principle of Population, as It Affects the Future Improvement of Society* (London: J. Johnson, 1798), https://archive.org/details/essayonprinciploomalt.

Bibliography

Applebaum, Anne. *Red Famine: Stalin's War on Ukraine*. New York: Doubleday, 2017.
Bose, Sugata. "Starvation amidst Plenty: The Making of Famine in Bengal, Honan, and Tonkin, 1942-44," *Modern Asian Studies* 24, no. 4 (1990): 699–727.
Cameron, Sarah. *Hungry Steppe: Famine, Violence, and the Making of Soviet Kazakhstan*. Ithaca, NY: Cornell University Press, 2020.
Clapp, Jennifer. *Hunger in the Balance; The New Politics of International Food Aid*. Ithaca, NY: Cornell University Press, 2012.
Conquest, Robert. *The Harvest of Sorrow: Soviet Collectivization and the Terror-Famine*. New York: Oxford University Press, 1987.
Davis, Mike. *Late Victorian Holocausts: El Niño Famines and the Making of the Third World*. London: Verso, 2002.
De Waal, Alexander. *Mass Starvation: The History and Future of Famine*. Cambridge: Polity, 2018.
Keneally, Thomas. *Three Famines: Starvation and Politics*. New York: Public Affairs, 2011.
Ladurie, Emmanuel Le Roy. *Times of Feast, Times of Famine: A History of Climate since the Year 1000*. Trans. Barbara Bray. New York: Noonday Press, 1988.
Mukerjee, Madhusree. *Churchill's Secret War the British Empire and the Ravaging of India during World War II*. New York: Basic Books, 2010.
Ó Gráda, Cormac. *Famine: A Short History*. Princeton, NJ: Princeton University Press, 2010.
Sathyamala, C. "Nutritionalizing Food: A Framework for Capital Accumulation." *Development and Change* 47, no. 4 (2016): 818–39. doi:10.1111/dech.12250.
Scott-Smith, Tom. *On an Empty Stomach: Two Hundred Years of Hunger Relief*. Ithaca, NY: Cornell University Press, 2020.
Sen, Amartya. *Poverty and Famines: An Essay on Entitlement and Deprivation*. Oxford: Oxford University Press, 2013.
Smith, Jenny Leigh. "The Awkward Years: Defining and Managing Famines, 1944–1947." *History and Technology*, 31, no. 3 (2005): 206–219. DOI: 10.1080/07341512.2015.1129810.
Sorokin, Pitirim A., and T. Lynn Smith. *Hunger as a Factor in Human Affairs*. Gainesville: University Presses of Florida, 1975.
Winick, Myron, ed. *Hunger Disease: Studies by the Jewish Physicians in the Warsaw Ghetto*. New York: Wiley & Sons, 1979.
Xun Zhou. *Forgotten Voices of Mao's Great Famine, 1958–1962. An Oral History*. New Haven, CT: Yale University Press, 2014.
Yang, Jisheng, et al. *Tombstone: the Great Chinese Famine, 1958–1962*. New York: Farrar, Straus & Giroux, 2013.

CHAPTER 35

FOREST TRANSITION THEORY

BRETT M. BENNETT AND GREGORY A. BARTON

Humans have destroyed forests for millennia to create settlements and farms, but the onset of modern deforestation since the 1600s has no historical equivalent in terms of the total forest that has been destroyed. From 1500 to 1985, an immense amount of forests, 1.39 billion hectares, was cleared globally.[1] Naturalists, early scientists, began to warn about the environmental consequences of rapid deforestation in the 1600s and 1700s when they witnessed the destruction of tropical forests on tropical islands; they argued that the process of deforestation changed local climate by decreasing rainfall, causing erosion, and lowering the water table. Concerns about global deforestation in the 1850s to 1900s instigated the conservation movement, the first global effort to set aside forests into state-controlled reserves. More recent alarm about the loss of rainforest and old-growth forests in the Pacific Northwest of the United States has fueled the rise of modern environmentalism since the late 1970s and continues to do so. Concerns of deforestation continue to be raised by international leaders, such as when the French president Emmanuel Macron warned about Brazilian deforestation at the 2019 G7 meeting.

The pervasiveness of public and scientific anxieties about deforestation has to a large extent obscured from the public eye the stabilization and regrowth of forests in large swaths of the world. Although deforestation is well recognized as a process, few understand that there has been a complex but persistent reforestation trend in many parts of the world that previously experienced deforestation. During the past century and a half, many parts of the world have been experiencing a regrowth of forest cover and trees. The Western countries that industrialized first—Britain, France, and the eastern United States—experienced gains in naturally regenerated and planted forests in the twentieth century after experiencing high rates of deforestation in the run-up to industrialization. Asian countries that industrialized later—Japan, South Korea, and then China—have experienced forest regrowth at later periods due to a time lag in development. This process may be playing itself out in tropical developing countries, such as Thailand and Brazil, which are now experiencing forest regrowth in certain areas. Deforestation rates continue to slow, although there does not seem to be an end in sight given that extensive tropical forest in Africa, the Amazon, and Asia are currently being cut down or degraded.

Forest transition theory (FTT) is both a historical observation and a theoretical model used in sociology, economics, and development studies that helps explain the stopping and reversal of deforestation. Forest transition can be visualized using a U-shaped curve that plots when forests shift from loss to gain. Researchers have linked these transitions with the processes of urbanization, industrialization, and globalization. Historical studies have shown that industrialization and rapid urbanization have in most countries led to a significant decline in overall forest cover during periods of demographic and economic expansion.

Shifts toward a post-industrial economy, and the increase of political regulation and imports from newly developing regions, have also led to a regrowth of some (but usually not all) natural forests. In many instances, the planting of trees for commercial timber plantations composed of one or a limited number of species causes the increase of overall forest cover, but these forests tend to have lower biodiversity than preexisting natural forests. Researchers have identified at least twenty countries with reliable data of forest cover showing a transition including: Bangladesh, China, Costa Rica, Cuba, Denmark, Dominican Republic, France, Gambia, Hungary, Ireland, Peninsular Malaysia, Morocco, New Zealand, Portugal, Rwanda, Scotland, South Korea, Switzerland, and the United States. More countries may be added to this list in the coming decades.

Alexander Mather, a Scottish geographer, first developed the concept of the forest transition in his 1990 book *Global Forest Resources*, and he elaborated it in his 1992 article, "The Forest Transition," in the geography journal *Area*.[2] Mather drew on evidence from geography, forestry, economics, and history in Europe and in developing countries to trace the process of forest transition in a variety of countries from the onset of industrialization and urbanization. Mather further developed this theory with a variety of collaborators who used modeling and historical examples to support the theory. Researchers in the fields of geography, forestry, economics, history, political science, and agriculture have used or debated the concept to describe changes to forest cover in developed and developing countries. FTT is part of a longer debate about developmental pathways and sustainability. FTT finds resonances with economists using an environmental Kuznets curve model, a U-shaped curve that posits that economic development precedes sustainable resource utilization.

The FTT concept, though popular in some social scientific fields, has received criticism, especially among cultural geographers. Mather recognized that every instance of forest transition had multiple drivers that differed from other examples. As a result, some critics have gone further by arguing that the concept lacks theoretical clarity and that it is not useful analytically because every instance differs considerably in drivers and details. The suggestion that there is a common pathway of economic and ecological development has led others to criticize the theory for mirroring modernization theory, an idea (largely challenged and, for many, discredited) in developmental politics and economics that suggests that there is a universal model of economic progress.

FTT potentially implies that the regrowth is equivalent to the forest lost, but it has been pointed out in most cases that corresponding regrowth lacked the biological diversity of forests that had been destroyed. Researchers agree broadly that a global forest transition is happening, but the transition does not mark a turn backward in time but rather reflects the formation of new forest types that face uncertain futures. For instance, some Central European forests have experienced ecological collapse because of changing management regimes, pests, and increased temperatures, so there is considerable uncertainty about the resilience of some replanted forests. FTT has, despite criticism and modification, remained a useful concept to explain, and possibly even predict, forest-cover change in different countries and regions.

Developing FTT

In 1992, Mather proposed his theory of forest-area transition, which he defined as "the change from decreasing to expanding forest areas that has taken place in many developed countries."[3] FTT developed in response to key forest trends that can be traced to the 1980s: growing concerns about tropical deforestation, shifts within forestry production, and the divergent patterns of forest use in developed and developing countries.

Few scholars pursued global analyses of forest trends prior to the 1980s due to limitations in data and a lack of scientific and public interest in global (as opposed to national) trends. Mather, an expert on the United Nations Food and Agricultural Organization (FAO) *Production Yearbook*, lamented in 1992 that "Statistical coverage of forest areas and their trends is lacking in both reliability and comprehensiveness."[4] Growing awareness of tropical deforestation through media and scientific efforts to quantify the ecological and climatic impacts of tropical deforestation began to shift attention to the problem of deforestation to the developing world. Mather, like many researchers, responded to these alarms: "For the first time in history, concern about the forest resource has become a global—as opposed to a national or regional-issue. The fate of the tropical forest in particular is the focus of unprecedented worldwide concern."[5]

Mather drew on the work of pre–World War II geographers who studied other types of resource transitions. The German Ernst Friedrich posited a model whereby resources followed the sequence DEPLETION → HUMAN NEED → CONSERVATION → RESTORATION.[6] In 1941, J. R. Whitaker developed a "depletion-melioration" model that saw resource use fall to a "base level" when it rebounded. Whitaker's model could be described with a U-shape. Whitaker argued that the destruction of resources was faster than recovery, a point Mather held to be generally but not always correct.[7]

In the late 1980s, the American forest economist Roger Sedjo argued that a "management transition" was reshaping forestry worldwide. Sedjo pointed out that forest productivity had increased due to advancements in breeding, site selection, fertilizers, and technological and labor efficiencies as well as the expansion of intensive timber plantations grown in warm climates that favored faster growth. Mather explored key trends in forest cover in articles in the late 1980s and his 1990 book *Global Forest Resources*. The book offered a global assessment of forests based on a synthesis of national and regional data. Mather observed general historical trends that had occurred in temperate developed countries and were just beginning to happen in developing tropical countries.

Mather proposed a three-stage model of forest-use history to explain the use of forests and their changing value in society. In the pre-industrial stage, forests were utilized by communities for a variety of uses, economic, cultural, and spiritual. Forests were often held in communal property arrangements. The emergence of market economies, and the demand for timber products, ushered in an era of industrial forests where trees were valued for their timber and wood became a commodity. The industrial era ushered in private property ownership and saw the modern state enter as a manager of forest resources. People living in areas that had experienced significant destruction of forests for industry began to value forests for their noneconomic services—recreation, conservation, aesthetics, species richness—as much or more than timber. Mather described these as post-industrial forests.

Most, but certainly not all, post-industrial forests had been significantly modified by humans. Protected and isolated forests, such as the inner part of Białowieża Forest in Central Europe and Yellowstone National Park, were spared the worst from industrial-scale harvesting due to being protected against the most destructive aspects of industrialization. Still, the post-industrial phase of forests reflected the awareness that industrialization had destroyed many forest ecosystems and the people and livelihoods associated with them.

In his 1992 *Area* article, Mather described an "areal transition" when declining forests started to grow again as a global trend. He pointed to developed countries, mostly in Europe but also in the United States and Japan, to highlight this trend. The areal forest transition occurred for a variety of reasons, but population growth, the use of forest products, and changes to human valuations of nature were the three most important. Mather noted that the rate of deforestation peaked at times of increased population growth. As growth rates slowed, forests often stabilized or began to grow back before population stabilized.

In Mather's definition, "forest" regrowth described a variety of ecosystems, which includes the spontaneous regrowth of indigenous forests (as in the eastern United States and mountainous parts of France) on abandoned farmlands, replanting efforts including native species found in neighboring regions (such as the Norway spruce, *Picea abies*, now planted throughout Central Europe, Britain, and eastern France), human-created timber plantations composed of exotic species (in South Africa and southern China), and agro-forestry efforts mixing crops and plantations (most popular in Asia and Africa). Mather noted that the regrowth rarely equaled the forest diversity of the original forest, a point that is worth remembering lest his theory be interpreted as a celebration of development. In many places, so many species had already been made locally extinct that the resulting regrowth had far fewer species.[8] FTT offered no panacea, but it nonetheless shifted views on global forest loss.

Early Case Studies: France, Switzerland, and Scotland

The strongest case for forest transition, and the earliest example of transition, occurred in Europe, the first part of the world to undergo industrialization. Mather wrote a series of case studies of Europe to illustrate his FTT concept. These case studies focused on France, Switzerland, and Scotland, countries that exemplified key trends in population growth, forest loss, and then legislative reform coupled with industrialization and urbanization.

National data on French forests presented significant challenges to making accurate assessments of historical forest-cover change. Before the advent of scientific forestry in the nineteenth century, surveys of the forest estate of France were "rough estimates that were both sporadic and of varying degrees of reliability."[9] The first detailed forest survey was completed only in 1878, right when the forests of France were beginning to recover, so the full extent of France's forests had to be roughly estimated. Mather et al. relied on research by historians to reconstruct demographic and forest cover prior to the 1800s.

Estimates suggested that approximately 60 percent of France was under forest cover in the tenth century. From 1050 to 1300 a phase of population growth led to the concomitant loss of forest. French history highlighted how forest growth and destruction responded to a variety of factors, not simply population growth. For instance, forest destruction had already started to decline before the Black Plague in the mid-1300s because the French elite maintained forests for hunting and their own profit. The death of people during the plague allowed forests to take over farms abandoned by those who died or could not support the farm. Briefly, the forests grew, something of an early forest transition. From the mid-1500s the population of France continued to grow steadily, as did the expansion of farms.

Alarms about the loss of timber began to be voiced in the 1600s in increasingly strident terms, although efforts to legislate the protection of forests had little success in the face of pressing demand for timber for war and industry and food for a growing population. The mid-1700s to early 1800s represented the peak of forest clearing: high prices, war with Britain, and the destruction of protected forest during the French revolution led to soaring wood prices and increasingly strident calls for conservation. Mathers et al. agreed that this ecological crisis encouraged, but did not single-handedly cause, the French Revolution. During the Revolution, French people disregarded royal forestry laws. Farmers, charcoal-makers, and iron forgeries expanded into forested mountains. The loss of forests—and state control—later supported foresters' warnings about erosion and flooding in the nineteenth century.

France's recovery began in the early nineteenth century. Mather et al. described the transition using a "crisis-response model." Intense deforestation exacerbated environmental and economic conditions, while scientific concerns about the impact of deforestation gained ascendency throughout Europe. A shift in consciousness about the value of forests occurred when the chaos of the Napoleonic era abated in 1815. Influenced by Enlightenment ideas of science and the development of expertise, in this case foresters and hydrologists, the French state gained greater control over forests. The establishment of the powerful Code Forestier in 1827, amended and upheld by elite French foresters, led to greater protection of state forests and eventually ushered in large tree-planting initiatives. Forest protection was aided by the increase of urbanization, the abandonment of farms on marginal lands, and the growing use of coal rather than wood for industry and fuel.

The calculations of Mather et al. were reassessed in 2006 by another team, including Mather and Sedjo.[10] The team highlighted how France's forest cover grew by one-third from the 1830 to 1950, at the same time that the population increased from 32 million in 1830 to 42 million in 1950. France continued to gain another one-quarter of forest cover in the second half of the twentieth century despite the population expanding more rapidly, from 42 to 61 million from 1950 to 2005.

An analysis of the forest transition in Switzerland reinforced the crisis model developed based on French history. Mather and Fairbairn traced how Switzerland's forest cover declined to 15 percent of the country's total surface by the mid-nineteenth century, but forests have subsequently doubled to 30 percent. The Swiss model mirrored France in that population growth in highland areas created the perception of environmental degradation and flooding. Foresters justified the state takeover of mountains and catchments based on the idea that forests moderated flooding, an idea that was used in a variety of countries—the United States, South Africa, and India, to name a few—to justify the state control of land. They concluded: "The lesson from the Swiss case is that a jolt into forest sustainability is more likely than a smooth, crisis-free passage."[11]

In 2004, Mather offered a case study of Scotland, his home country. Mather grew up and lived within 30 kilometers of Aberdeen, Scotland, and he studied and worked at Aberdeen University's geography department for his entire career. His earliest work focused on Scotland's landscape before he started analyzing FAO global forest assessments. Scotland's peak deforestation occurred in the early modern era, and by 1600 forests clothed possibly as little as 5 percent of the land area, compared to a potential maximum of 50 percent. Scotland's forests grew slightly in the 1700s and 1800s due to tree planting on aristocratic estates, but the creation of planted forests was offset by continued loss of native forests for the expansion of farms. Scotland by the late nineteenth century imported a large amount of its timber, a situation that put it in a precarious situation during World War I when wood imports were cut off.

As in France, legislation encouraged a forest transition. World War I led to skyrocketing timber prices and a domestic shortage in Britain. During the war, the government set up a Forestry Sub-Committee of the Reconstruction Committee in 1916, otherwise known as the Acland committee. The Acland committee advised domestic planting, and the recommendations set up the Forestry Act of 1919, which established the British Forestry Commission. Scotland, like the whole of Britain, gained timber until World War II, when another shortage occurred due to the slowing down of sea-based wood shipments from the Baltic. World War II strengthened the Forestry Commission's efforts to plant. Incentives to private landowners and state planting led to a rapid reforestation using a limited number of species. As in France and Switzerland, crisis acted as a trigger. Scotland's forest cover, mostly timber plantation, increased threefold in the twentieth century.

Theoretical and Empirical Development, 1995–2007

The forest transition theory gained popularity and must be contextualized within broader academic discussions about forests and global sustainability that emerged in the 1990s and early 2000s. Fears of deforestation were heightened by scientific warnings of global warming and the loss of biodiversity, much of it caused by the destruction of tropical forests. The forest transition raised the hope that perhaps tropical forests would not suffer the same fate as other forests or would rebound. In a popular book published in 1997, Gregg Easterbrook pointed to the growth of forests as part of a "coming age of environmentalism optimism" encouraged by capitalist economic cycles (a view that many scientists and environmentalists disagreed with at the time because it, among other things, it downplayed the loss of biodiversity in clear-cut western US forests and extinctions in forests in the country's east).[12] In the late 1990s, economists began to test the forest transition using an environmental Kuznets curve (EKC), a hypothesized, U-shaped relationship between economic development and environmental degradation. Easterbrook's optimism was not borne out by modeling from economists who applied the EKC to deforestation. Simulations by Stern et al. suggested that global environmental degradation would continue to increase rather than decrease into the near future.[13]

In 1998, T. K. Rudel offered an early empirical assessment of Mather's forest transition. He drew on global forest estimates beginning in 1922, but he had to throw out early estimates of forest cover in developing countries because in many instances they were guesses with little basis in fact. The number of countries he analyzed increased from the year 1922, when 60 countries produced valid data, to 138 in the year 1990. Definitions of forest cover changed considerably during this period. The first authoritative global survey, by Zon and Sparhawk in 1923, defined forests conservatively as closed canopy. At the other extreme, some FAO definitions allowed as little as 10 percent forest canopy cover. The spread of remote sensing in the 1990s and 2000s gave a more reliable estimate of overall forest cover, but the coarseness of the images could not identify timber plantations or fragmentation. Nonetheless, new methods provided a firm foundation for estimating national forest cover.[14]

Rudel's work situated the forest transition in a wider scholarly debate about development and modernization. Rudel drew from Karl Polanyi's *The Great Transformation*, published in 1944. Polanyi sought to explain the transformations that led Britain to become the first nation to become a "market society" where market dynamics replaced older social relationships. The twin engines of urbanization and industrialization kickstarted this process. People moved to cities which allowed for more efficient use of farmland. Industrialization rationalized production, increased output, and entrenched capitalist relationships. By the nineteenth century, laissez-faire capitalism and free trade had reshaped Britain, as it later would much of the world. Polanyi ascribed self-regulating powers to markets, a concept that influenced the ideas of other on modernization (Walt Rostow, for instance) and globalization.[15]

The rationality of markets, imbedded within Polanyi's *The Great Transformation* and other liberal economic works on modernization, has been used to explain the process of forest transition. The rise of market societies encouraged efficient allocation of forest resources after a prolonged period of destruction during the most destructive, intense phases of urbanization and industrialization. In this model, forests that were cut for farming could grow back due to more efficient farming, and the production of timber became concentrated in areas of high productivity. Farmers in areas of lower productivity would thus move to cities and abandon their land. Thus, forests would recover or be planted. Mather and Needle (1998) modeled how increased efficiency in farming would, over time, lead to an overall decline in production area and an increase or stability of food production.[16]

Rudel et al. (2005) suggested two pathways of forest transition based on empirical and theoretical analyses to date. First, they described an "economic development path" that fit with Mather's original conception. This model corresponded with research in economics on environmental Kuznets curves. In this scenario, farmers caused deforestation, eventually people started moving to cities, and the resulting urbanization and industrialization (often involving a shift to coal from wood) allowed for forest regrowth.[17]

A second "forest scarcity path" posited that the rising price of wood could induce private landowners, communities, and the state to plant trees. This model applied to regional areas in Indian and Bangladesh, places where community and social forestry initiatives sought to alleviate wood (often for fuel) shortages. Mather did not discuss the forest scarcity path because of his focus on regions that had undergone industrialization, whereas countries such as India and Bangladesh had not yet fully undergone industrialization and urbanization.

According to this model, Europe and Asia, the two regions with the most complete data, experienced different types of forest transition. Rudel et al. emphasized the regional character of these forest transition processes. For instance, much of Asia experienced a forest scarcity path whereas European countries underwent an economic development path. A few societies did not experience transitions. Without urbanization and industrialization, farmers were "trapped" and could not move to cities, and they continued to expand farms into forest. Continued loss of forests occurred in small, poor countries, such as Haiti, where neither pathway occurred. Rudel downplayed the possibility that transition would save remaining untouched forest. After all, forest transitions usually occurred after peak forest loss.

A multiauthor review led by Kauppi in the *Proceedings of the National Academy of Sciences*, including Mather (in his last paper), offered the most comprehensive empirical analysis of forest cover trends globally to show a forest transition. They argued, "Among 50 nations with extensive forests reported in the Food and Agriculture Organization's comprehensive Global Forest Resources Assessment 2005, no nation where annual per capita gross domestic product exceeded $4,600 had a negative rate of growing stock change."[18] Their paper modeled various forest transitions trajectories using a Forest Identity equation (Q = A × D × B × C based on carbon in forests [Q] equaling forest area [A], growing forest stock [D], density of biomass [B], and carbon density per biomass unit [C]).

Asia

In his early work, Mather raised the prospect of forest transitions happening elsewhere in the world, especially Asia. East Asia's rapid economic development occurred a century after the industrialization of Europe and the United States. Japan was the first East Asian country to develop a large-scale industrial economy, followed by Taiwan, South Korea, Singapore, and Hong Kong. The opening up of China to global trade in the 1980s and the liberalization of world trade then allowed for the expansion of economies in Southeast Asia, especially Thailand, Indonesia, Malaysia, and Vietnam.

In the United States and Europe, most of the forest transition occurred because farmers abandoned less-productive farmland and forests rebounded. In China, as well as in India and Vietnam, forest transition has been achieved largely by additional factors, as Rudel noted. These factors include the establishment of timber plantations composed of exotic species or a monoculture, payment to regional authorities for watershed afforestation, bans on logging certain forest regions, and a cultural predilection for forest gardens and other areas that use trees for aesthetic purposes. The economic development that accompanies globalization and state forest policies have all impacted the process of forest transition in these countries. Multi-country research by Liu et al. in 2017 found, however, that even low-income countries are able to achieve forest transition if state interventions that protect forest regions and promote afforestation efforts are vigorous.[19]

Japan was the first Asian country to experience forest transition. Cutting during World War II led to the destruction of much of the island's native forest. The Forest Law promulgated in 1951 spawned a Forestry Planning System and Forest Owners Cooperative System that promoted widespread plantings of conifers. These largely replaced the broad-leafed deciduous forests with Japanese cedar, larch, fir, and pine, all of which grew straight and produced usable timber for industrial purposes. Generous subsidies encouraged private owners to expand timber plantations and forest cover that saw significant gains from the 1950s through the 1980s. Replanted forests favored a handful of species and lowered overall diversity.

China represents a particularly striking forest transition. In 1949, China had only 12.5 percent of its original forest cover. From the 1980s to 2015, however, China increased its forest cover to 22 percent, due largely to state policy that advocated participatory forestry, industrialization, and afforestation programs. Between 1949 and 1952, timber plantations in many cases doubled as shelterbelts to protect against soil erosion and to halt the incursion of desertification. In 1954, the government launched timber production schemes in the South. Aerial seeding met with mixed success to rehabilitate larger regions. Environmental reforms also played a part in tree planting. Between 1950 and the 1970s, 24 million hectares were planted to protect riverbanks, catchment areas, and fight flooding, and to stop sand dune encroachment.

India has gone through the classic U-shaped curve of deforestation and then reforestation from the 1950s to the 1980s. Factors that reduced deforestation were agricultural intensification, state intervention, social forestry, and the growth of timber plantations. Forest decline and afforestation happened at the same time in India. India provides something of a challenge to the FTT. The causes of deforestation were similar to those in East Asia: the conversion of forest land to agriculture, increasing population, exploitation of forests to provide timber to urban areas, and "forest dependency," that is, the use of the forest for daily fuel for cooking and heating. Attempts were made to notify private landowners that their forest lands must be properly managed under state-sponsored working plans and regulation. This conservation effort often resulted in owners fearing their resources would soon be taken, and thus hastened logging. Factors that reduced deforestation were agricultural intensification, state intervention, social forestry, and the growth of timber plantations.

But these traditional FTT pathways are complicated by India's unique characteristics. Its population is still growing, and thus greater agricultural production only partially offsets population pressure on agricultural land and on forests. In addition, though forest areas are counted in forest inventory, these inventories do not capture forest degradation, which is still growing. The problems that led to deforestation in India are still very much present, and it is not possible to confidently predict that forest transition is stable or a certainty for the future. In other words, forest decline and afforestation are occurring simultaneously in India. Given the fact that natural forests do not provide the revenue that once occurred in Europe, and that economic processes are not static but change over time (e.g., an industrial phase may never happen in some countries), the FTT that arose from the observation of the European forest transition may not be as applicable to places like India.

Vietnam highlights the dynamics of Southeast Asian forest transition. Since 1992, Vietnam has seen regrowth of its forests. This has been cited as an example of how forest transition occurs in an area well outside the original examples of FTT in Europe and North America. However, scholars have argued that this reforestation has been achieved by adding to the displacement of forests illegally harvested in neighboring Southeast Asian countries (e.g., illegal timber imports from Cambodia and Laos to Vietnam have led to the loss of forest cover in the region). Meyfroidt and Lambin argue that almost 40 percent of Vietnam's regrowth can be attributed to illegal harvesting that is not properly accounted for by official statistics.[20]

Questioning the Forest Transition

The concept of a forest transition relies primarily on an agreement about what constitutes a "forest." Mather and many forest-transition scholars have relied on somewhat narrow definitions used by the FAO during the 1990s and 2000s, which defined a forest simply as anywhere where trees provided a minimum of 10 percent cover. To assess this 10 percent, the FAO relied on national statistics of forest cover that it has collected since 1948.

Relying on government statistics to define forest transition presents two major problems. First, the data may not even be accurate. The FAO became serious about verifying forest statistics, especially from developing countries, only in the 1980s, because of growing concerns about tropical deforestation. Even today, data collected by governments is treated with suspicion. Many researchers, such as the institution Global Forest Watch, prefer to use satellite rather than government statistics because they believe some governments downplay the rate of deforestation and forest degradation.

Second, forest statistics do not clearly distinguish between different types of forests, such as a native forest or a timber plantation. The primary forests, whether old growth or regrowth, contains a complexity and diversity that the secondary vegetation or timber plantation replacing it lacks. Primary forest contains more carbon and biomass. Thus, diverse native forests are replaced by secondary forests that lack diversity. Many species that thrive in the primary forests do not thrive in the secondary. Hence replacing forests with croplands of timber plantations, broken canopies, dislocated enclosures, and native species with exotic hardwoods in plantations genetically designed for chipping is hardly the equivalent to the primary forest that was lost. Stephen Perz points out that Brazil's Atlantic forest is now destroyed except for remnants, while the Amazon forest risks being replaced by secondary growth and farms.[21] The continued use of fire along the edges of the Amazon fundamentally alters it ecology, making the possibility of a full restoration in the future difficult, if not impossible.

In the past, FAO made no distinction between different kinds of forest cover. Hence when plantations displace natural forests, advocates of FTT record an end to deforestation and often an increase in forest cover. China's forest transition offers one striking example of the replacement of native forest by timber plantations. Southern China's Hainan Island and Xishuangbanna regions recorded an increase forest cover during the 1980s because plantations and regrowth expanded more rapidly than native forests which were destroyed. Natural forests declined in Xishuangbanna, largely due to the increase in rubber plantations. Sloppy terminology for the definition of "forests" may detract attention from continued deforestation of an important and essential type of forest cover.

Researchers using FTT and critics both recognize that forests that grow back during a transition rarely equal those that were previously lost. Forest transition describes a broad process, but it does not return forests to a previous condition, which may be impossible to achieve given the fundamental altering of ecosystem processes that sometimes occurred over hundreds of years. Forest transition usually causes an increase biomass and the fixing of carbon in the soil, especially in the early years of growth. But the ecological complexity and species diversity of primary forests take decades or centuries to recover, if it ever does. In Japan and Central Europe, forest transition occurred because of the planting of a limited number of species that are native to a region (this is particularly significant in Central Europe and Japan) but that were not indigenous to the sites they were planted on.

The planting of a small number of species created a number of ecological problems that have been compounded by changing management regimes and increased temperatures and prolonged droughts. For instance, forests in Central Europe now dominated by Norway spruce (*Picea abies*) have lower diversity and are more prone to ecological collapse from pests (bark beetle) than the mixed forests that existed before foresters planted them in the 1600s to 1900s. In southern China, southern Africa, and parts of eastern Brazil, forest transitions occurred in part due to the planting of exotic species, such as eucalyptus from Australia. Forest transition in many developing countries reflect the expansion of timber plantations more than the regrowth of native forests, a dynamic that has received little attention from historians.

One of the most telling criticisms of FTT involves implications it raises about the costs of capitalist development. Some are concerns that FTT creates the assumption that capitalism has a natural developmental cycle, and thus it implies that capitalism will not ultimately destroy nature. Critics note FTT's resemblance to modernization theory, an idea suggesting that societies follow universal patterns of development. Many academics and environmentalists are highly critical of capitalism, and FTT is seen as to some extent justifying the destruction of primary forest because a regrowth is expected.

Meanwhile, the vagueness of FTT has led some to criticize its analytic value. FTT offers an overly general framework that does not explain specific instances and relies on limited examples. General frameworks do not explain the site-specific factors that led to forest recovery. For instance, in Japan the state pursued an extensive postwar planting effort, whereas on the American east coast, forest regrowth followed the abandonment of farm and the expansion of privately owned farms and plantations. In many regions, the forest transition involved the planting of vast exotic plantations of eucalyptus or pines. These exotic trees displaced indigenous vegetation and did little to supply food or even labor to local communities. In India, protestors uprooted eucalyptus saplings and planted mangos to highlight how privately owned timber plantations were displacing people and their food supplies.

Ultimately, case studies do not always capture global trends. A global analysis of FTT suggests that the regrowth of forests has been more than offset by deforestation in other parts of the world. Paul Robbins and Alistair Fraser argue that developed countries offset their deforestation to developing regions and thus the forest transition concept must be assessed globally and not on a country-by-country basis. This is especially clear in the rise of Japan and then China. Peter Dauvergne has described Japan's forest regrowth as "shadow deforestation" because it required steady imports to offset the lack of domestic timber supply. China closed its native forests but has continued to import native forests from Southeast Asia, Africa, and the Americas to feed its domestic and export markets.

Global Forest Transition Trends since 2000

Research into forest transitions offers some cautious optimism that the worst of global deforestation may be over for many regions and slowing (but not certainly stopping) in developing countries. Assessments of forest cover suggest that the global rate of deforestation has slowed since the early 2000s, although tropical Africa, Southeast Asia, and South America continue to experience overall forest loss. An important review in 2011 by Patrick Meyfroidt and Eric F. Lambin confirmed that national-scale forest transitions had occurred throughout large parts of the world.[22] The increase in forests in different countries came from a range of processes: natural regeneration, the expansion of native and exotic timber plantations, and planting by individual landowners and communities in a range of agroforestry and tree farm models.

The review identified the economic drivers of globalization as a key factor in the onset of transitions in developing tropical countries. For instance, Brazilian deforestation of the Amazon can be correlated to the price of beef. Increased beef prices globally lead to an increase in the value of agricultural land. Correspondingly, declines in beef prices are correlated with a conversion of farmland back to forest for timber plantations of commercially valuable species, conservation, or ecotourism. Shifts in consumer preference, and the ability to certify the sustainability of farms and forests, have the potential to improve protection of forests against destruction for farming.

Forest transitions have different drivers depending on a mix of local and global circumstances. In Central America and the Caribbean, reforestation is more common on abandoned farmland. In South America, private forest plantations are key drivers of increase. In much of Asia, native forests have regrown as a result of stricter protection and the expansion of large timber plantations composed of exotic species. In southern Africa, forest transitions happened in countries where trees are outcompeting grass, government policies have produced exotic timber plantations, and abandoned farmland is returning to forest conditions. These variations show that FTT is contingent on local circumstances and does not follow a universal or evolutionary pattern.

A significant amount of reforestation since the 2000s has been driven by timber plantations, at industrial scale (especially in China and Brazil) and in small holdings (especially in parts of Southeast and South Asia). Brett Bennett argues that the bifurcation of forests into plantations and protected areas is one of the major trends reshaping forests.[23] Favorable economic and climatic conditions in many developing tropical countries have provided for the rapid expansion of timber plantations. In the developing tropics, a combined high demand for wood, an abundance of cheap labor, propitious growing conditions with rainfall and warm weather, and export-focused economic orientations have driven the expansion of tree plantations. In some cases, local community control led to replanting in small holdings (such as in South Asia), whereas in Brazil and China the drive for commercial profit by corporations and the state led to utilization of deforested land areas with plantations. In most cases, centralized government policy, including tax incentives, mandated tree planting, and restrictions on timber harvesting, have encouraged small holders, corporations, or the state to develop plantations.

Not all transitions involve large forests. Forests have transitioned also through growth of small woodlands, gardens, orchards, agroforestry, and other small and fragmented areas where vegetation has rebounded. Often regrowth occurs on former pastures and farmlands that are no longer economically viable. Agroforestry is defined as the integration of crops and trees, which can mean anything from farmland with planted trees, or woodlands, gardens that contain trees, or forests that have been modified by special plantings of native or exotic origin, but still retain the characteristics of a natural forest. This kind of forest transition is often not caught by satellite imagery and is often undercounted.

Tree plantations in arid regions are also contributing to forest transitions. While climate variations affect forest cover, so too in the Mediterranean afforestation occurred when economic growth fed urbanization and a stream of labor evacuated rural areas. Reforestation also occurred with the planting of plantations in those regions where timber production and exports provided employment and profit. Other arid regions, such as North Africa and the Middle East, have also continued to experience some reforestation after 1990. Grassland, savanna, and Mediterranean-climate ecologists are warning about the dangers of tree planting in areas without forest because many landscapes have been forestless for millions of years.[24] It is essential that transitions only occur in areas where forests previously existed. Given alarms about climate change, and the push to plant trees for carbon sequestration, this will remain a pressing concern for years to come.

CONCLUSION

Many scholars are optimistic that forest transition will continue to reduce deforestation rates globally, but there is no clear end in sight. Others claim that forest transition will merely outsource deforestation from developed regions to developing regions. The rate of deforestation has declined, but the overall loss of biodiversity continues because of the overall impact of humans. With the impact of global warming being seen increasingly in forest fires, outbreaks of pests, and species migration (and possible extinction), one wonders to what extent the world's native forests will exist as we know them in the future. Despite uncertainties, critics and adherents to FTT agree that the world's forests are continually changing due to globalization and the changing needs of human society. There are some reasons to be cautiously optimistic, but we are still living through an age of global biodiversity loss that is occurring even in sites of forest regrowth.

Notes

1. Michael Williams, *Deforesting the Earth: From Prehistory to Global Crisis* (Chicago: University of Chicago Press, 2003): 396.
2. Alexander Mather, *Global Forest Resources* (London: Belhaven Press, 1990); Mather, "The Forest Transition," *Area* 24, no. 2 (1992): 367–379.
3. Mather, "The Forest Transition," 367.
4. Ibid., 368.
5. Ibid., 367.
6. Ibid., 367.
7. Ibid., 377.
8. Ibid., 377.
9. A. S. Mather, J. Fairbairn, and C. L. Needle, "The Course and Drivers of the Forest Transition: The Case of France," *Journal of Rural Studies* 15 (1999): 66.
10. Pekka E. Kauppi, Jesse H. Ausubel, Jingyun Fang, Alexander S. Mather, Roger A. Sedjo, and Paul E. Waggoner, "Returning Forests Analyzed with the Forest Identity," *Proceedings of the National Academy of Sciences of the United States of America* 103 (2006): 17574.
11. A. S. Mather and J. Fairbairn, "From Floods to Reforestation: The Forest Transition in Switzerland," *Environment and History* 6 (2000): 400.
12. Gregg Easterbrook, *A Moment on the Earth: The Coming Age of Environmental Optimism* (New York: Viking, 1995).
13. D. Stern, M. S. Common, and E. B. Barbier, "Economic Growth and Environmental Degradation: The Environmental Kuznets Curve and Sustainable Development," *World Development* 24 (1996): 1151–1160.
14. T. K. Rudel, "Is There a Forest Transition? Deforestation, Reforestation, and Development," *Rural Sociology* 63 (1998): 533–552.
15. Karl Polanyi, *The Great Transformation: The Political and Economic Origins of Our Time* (New York: Farrar & Rinehart, 1944).
16. A. X. Mather and C. L Needle, "The Forest Transition: A Theoretical Basis," *Area* 30 (1998): 117–124.
17. Thomas Rudel, Oliver Coomes, Emilio Moran, Frederic Achard, Arlid Angelsen, Jianchu Xu, and Eric Lambin, "Forest Transitions: Towards a Global Understanding of Land Use Change," *Global Environmental Change* 15 (2005): 23–31.
18. Kauppi et al., "Returning Forests Analyzed with the Forest Identity," 17574.
19. Jinlong Liu, Ming Liang, Lingchao Li, Hexing Long, and Wil De Jong, "Comparative Study of the Forest Transition Pathways of Nine Asia-Pacific Countries," *Forest Policy and Economics* 76 (2017): 25–34.
20. Patrick Meyfroidt and Eric F. Lambin, "Forest Transition in Vietnam and Displacement of Deforestation Abroad," *Proceedings of the National Academy of Sciences* 106 (2009): 16139–144.

21. Stephen Perz, "Grand Theory and Context-Specificity in the Study of Forest Dynamics: Forest Transition Theory and Other Directions," *The Professional Geographer* 59 (2007): 105–114.
22. Patrick Meyfroidt and Eric F. Lambin, "Global Forest Transition: Prospects for an End to Deforestation," *Annual Review of Environment and Resources* 36 (2011): 343–371.
23. Brett Bennett, *Plantations and Protected Areas: A Global History of Forest Management* (Cambridge, MA: MIT Press, 2015).
24. William Bond, "Ancient Grasslands at Risk," *Science* 351 (2016): 120–122.

Bibliography

Bennett, Brett M. *Plantations and Protected Areas: A Global History of Forest Management*. Cambridge MA: MIT Press, 2015.
Bond, William, "Ancient Grasslands at Risk." *Science* 351 (2016): 120–122.
Boomgaard, Peter. "The Forests of Southeast Asia, Forest Transition Theory and the Anthropocene, 1500–2000." In *Economic Development and Environmental History in the Anthropocene: Perspectives on Asia and Africa*, edited by Gareth Austin, 179–198. London: Bloomsbury, 2017.
Chazdon, Robin L. "Beyond Deforestation: Restoring Forests and Ecosystem Services on Degraded Lands." *Science* 320 (2008): 1458–1460.
De Jong, Wil. "Forest Rehabilitation and Its Implication for Forest Transition Theory." *Biotropica* 42 (2010): 3–9.
Kauppi, Pekka E., Jesse H. Ausubel, Jingyun Fang, Alexander S. Mather, Roger A. Sedjo, and Paul E. Waggoner. "Returning Forests Analysed with Forest Identity." *Proceedings of the National Academy of Sciences of the United States of America* 103 (2006): 17574–17579.
Liu, Jinlong, Ming Liang, Lingchao Li, Hexing Long, and Wil De Jong. "Comparative Study of the Forest Transition Pathways of Nine Asia-Pacific Countries." *Forest Policy and Economics* 76 (2017): 25–34.
Mather, A. S. "The Forest Transition." *Area* 24, no. 2 (1992): 367–379.
Mather, A. S., and J. Fairbairn. "From Floods to Reforestation: The Forest Transition in Switzerland." *Environment and History* 6 (2000): 399–421.
Mather, A. S., J. Fairbairn, and C. L. Needle. "The Course and Drivers of the Forest Transition: The Case of France." *Journal of Rural Studies* 15 (1999): 65–90.
Meyfroidt, Patrick, and Eric F. Lambin. "Forest Transition in Vietnam and Displacement of Deforestation Abroad." *Proceedings of the National Academy of Sciences* 106 (2009): 16139–16144.
Meyfroidt, Patrick, and Eric F. Lambin. "Global Forest Transition: Prospects for an End to Deforestation." *Annual Review of Environment and Resources* 36 (2011): 343–371.
Perz, Stephen. "Grand Theory and Context-Specificity in the Study of Forest Dynamics: Forest Transition Theory and Other Directions." *The Professional Geographer* 59 (2007): 105–114.
Polanyi, Karl. *The Great Transformation: The Political and Economic Origins of Our Time*. New York: Farrar & Rinehart, 1944.
Rudel, Thomas K. "Is There a Forest Transition Deforestation, Reforestation, and Development." *Rural Sociology* 63 (1998): 533–552.
Rudel, Thomas, Oliver Coomes, Emilio Moran, Frederic Achard, Arlid Angelsen, Jianchu Xu, and Eric Lambin. "Forest Transitions: Towards a Global Understanding of Land Use Change." *Global Environmental Change* 15 (2005): 23–31.

Stern, David I., Michael S. Common, and Edward B. Barbier. "Economic Growth and Environmental Degradation: The Environmental Kuznets Curve and Sustainable Development." *World Development* 24 (1996): 1151–1160.

Williams, Michael. *Deforesting the Earth: From Prehistory to Global Crisis*. Chicago: University of Chicago Press, 2003.

Zhai, Deli, Jianchu Xu, Zhicong Dai, and Dietrich Schmidt-Vogt. "Lost in Transition: Forest Transition and Natural Forest Loss in Tropical China." *Plant Diversity* 39 (2017): 149–153.

Index

For the benefit of digital users, indexed terms that span two pages (e.g., 52–53) may, on occasion, appear on only one of those pages.

Tables and figures are indicated by *t* and *f* following the page number

Africa
    Agrarian capitalism in, 118
    agricultural labor, 117, 228
    colonialism, 3–4, 15, 35, 120, 189, 229, 570–80
    drought and, 615
    famines and, 603–4, 606, 611, 614–15
    free trade and, 124
    global markets, 124, 207–8
    Green Revolution and, 123, 590, 592–93
    Indigenous labor and, 120, 121
    land, 42–43, 80
    livestock, 79–80
    neoliberalism and, 124
    plantations, 220, 401, 622
    Silk Road, 12
    subsistence farming and, 43
    water and, 453–54
    women, 154–56
Age of Discovery, 3–4, 5, 9, 10–11, 14
agrarian capitalism, 118, 119, 121, 123
agrarian change, 129, 133, 490
agrobiology, 182, 394–95
agrochemistry, 27–28
agribusiness, 117, 123–24, 125, 197, 201–4, 205, 207–8, 528–29, 585–86, 592
agricultural labor (farm labor)
    agrarian capitalism and, 113–114, 118–19
    agromedicine and, 235–36
    Alabama Sharecroppers Union (ASU), 122
    Cesar Chavez and, 238
    coercion, 117
    Cold War and, 238
    colonialism, 117, 119–21, 230, 231, 236
    corporate-capitalist agriculture, the state and, 122
    hazards of, 8–9, 115, 118–19, 188, 226, 227, 228, 233, 234–35, 238, 239
    land, 118
    markets and, 117
    mechanization and, 152–53
    National Farm workers Association and, 237–38
    neoliberal policies and, 261
    peasant resistance and, 116
    plantations and, 233–34, 235
    Southern Tenant Farmers Union (STFU), 122
    technology and, 121–24, 172
    United Farm workers Union, 123, 238
    women and, 115, 148, 149–50, 151, 152, 156
    World Health Organization and, 236–37
agrobiodiversity, 384, 385*f*, 385–86, 387–88, 389
agrochemistry, 27–28
agro-food regimes, 389
agronomy, 386–87, 388–89, 470–71, 587
ANDES, 117, 288, 374–75, 376, 378, 381–82, 385–88, 412. *See also* Peru
Angkor, 490
Angkor Wat, 490
Anthropocene, 3, 16–17, 304–5, 446–47, 449, 455
aquifer, 46, 452, 468, 558, 596
Asia
    agrarian capitalism and, 118, 121
    agricultural corporations and, 8–9
    agricultural labor, 236, 237, 239
    colonialism and, 230

Asia (*cont.*)
  commodity frontiers and, 216
  drought in, 603–5
  export market, 120
  famine in, 593, 607, 614–15
  farmer suicides in, 232
  fertilizer use in, 231
  foreign companies in, 124
  forests, 622, 626, 627–29
  globalization, 121, 124
  grain cultivation in, 553
  Green Revolution and, 64, 123, 585, 588–89
  International Rice Research Institute in, 591–92
  irrigation in, 295, 452, 453–54, 469, 596
  Islamic conquest, 463, 464, 465, 467
  livestock in, 77, 554
  locusts, 103–4
  markets and, 186
  peasants and, 135
  pesticides, 232, 238
  plantations, 228–29, 237–38, 631–32
  rice, 229–30, 286–87, 289, 290–92, 293–94, 296, 297, 298–300
  Rockefeller fund and, 591
  seed, 66–67
  silk and, 426–27, 428–31, 472
  Silk Road and, 12
  small-scale farmers and pastoralists in, 113, 121, 141–42
  soy in, 11, 304, 305, 306f, 312–13
  subsistence farming and, 43, 58–59
  UN food programs in, 590
  wet rice, 304–493, 605
  women, 152
Atlantic plantation, 14, 327, 329–30, 331, 336–37, 499–511, 515
Atlantic slave trade, 253, 294–95, 499, 500, 501, 504–5, 506–7, 570, 571
Atlantic World, 449–50, 499, 507, 510–11

Bali, 286, 477, 490
banana
  agricultural labor, 364
  Banana Massacre, 368
  capitalism and, 361
  Chiquita label, 362–63, 369, 370, 371, 372
  CIA activity and, 369
  Columbian worker revolt and, 367–68
  company production of, 363, 364–66
  Gros Michel, 366, 367, 369–70
  Guatemalan worker revolt, 368
  Honduras, 26–27
  Indonesia, in, 361–62
  Islamic Agricultural revolution and, 463, 472–73
  plant disease, 365–67, 369–70
  Southeast Asia, in, 361–62
  Standford Fruit company and, 363
  Taiwan and, 372
  The Calendar of Cordoba and, 471
  trade, 362–63, 365, 371–72
  transportation of, 362–63, 365
  United Fruit, 31, 367–69, 370–71
  US and, 366–69, 371–72
  varieties, 366, 367, 369–70, 371, 372
biodiversity
  agrobiodiversity, 385–86, 387–88, 389
  Andean people and, 376–77, 386
  Association for Nature and Sustainable Development and, 386
  Atlantic plantation and, 14
  biotechnology in corn and, 263
  Consultative Group for International Agricultural Research and, 585, 592
  corporations and, 8
  cotton and, 405
  environmental impact on, 14
  Food and Agriculture Organization (FAO) and, 385–86
  forests, 620, 625, 632–33
  good crisis and, 592
  Great Plains and, 558
  Green Revolution and, 68, 585–86, 592
  high yielding varieties (HYVs) and, 595
  Indigenous biocultural Heritage Territory, 387–88
  Islamic Agricultural Revolution and, 471–72
  loss of, 46, 317–18, 563, 592
  plant diversity and, 54
  potato and, 384, 386–87
  Rockefeller Foundation and, 585
  Russia and, 553–54
  soils and, 46, 52

biogeochemistry, 53
Black Rice, 294
Borlaug, Norman, 15–16, 281, 585, 586–87, 589, 590–91, 593, 594, 596
botany, 4, 41, 58–59, 60, 62, 64, 65, 67, 68, 587
breeding
   Africa and, 577
   agricultural science and, 179, 180, 185, 197
   California Fruit Growers and, 202
   chickens and, 186
   China and, 593
   China National Hybrid Rice Research and Development Center, 593
   coffee and, 349–50
   corn and, 251–52, 256, 258–59
   cotton and, 405–6, 589
   crop yields and, 604–5
   Food and Agricultural Organization of the United Nations and, 590
   forests and, 621–22
   GMOs and, 262–63
   Green Revolution and, 586, 588, 590
   high yielding varieties and, 591–92, 593, 595, 597
   hybrid corn and, 201–2
   inbreeding and, 185–86
   International Rice Research Institute and, 591–92
   livestock and, 4, 79, 86, 179, 190, 197, 604–5
   Mexico and, 589
   plantations and, 336–37
   potatoes and, 381
   rice and, 484–85, 488
   Rockefeller Foundation Mexican Agriculture Program and, 189
   sugar cane and, 336–37
   wheat and, 586, 589

Combined Feeding Operations (CAFO), 85–87
capitalism
   Agrarian capitalism, 114, 116, 118–19, 121, 123, 251–52, 256
   agricultural commodities and, 8
   agricultural expertise and, 206–7
   agricultural labor and, 226
   agricultural transformation and, 265
   bananas and, 361
   British, 515, 519
   China, 189–90, 489–90
   commodities and, 212, 215, 222–23, 276
   conflict and, 119–20
   corn and, 251
   cotton and, 10–11, 212, 398
   critique of, 222–23, 279
   cycles and, 215
   dependence on new resources and, 215
   ecological degradation and, 212
   emergence of, 213–14
   expansion of, 214, 218, 608
   famine and, 16, 609–10
   free labor and, 121
   frontiers of, 221–22
   global, 214, 218–19, 446
   Green Revolution and, 231
   land, 29, 220
   market transformation and, 625–26
   peasant farming and, 132, 134, 137, 139, 141
   plantations and, 499–500
   resistance, 213–14, 217
   rice and, 299
   silk and, 436
   soy and, 318–19
   subsistence farmers and, 114
   technology and, 218–19
cattle
   antibiotics and, 86, 259
   Argentina and, 560
   Armour and Company, 203, 204
   atlantic plantation and, 510
   breeding developments and, 186, 197
   British Agricultural Revolution and, 361–62, 532–33, 534, 535–36, 547*t*, 549
   British colonies and, 520–21
   Confined Animal Feeding Operations (CAFO) and, 85–86
   corn and, 259
   cowpox and, 235–36
   diseases, 79, 84–85, 235–36
   enslaved Africans and, 520–21
   environmental degradation and, 80
   Estancieros and, 275–76
   famine and, 101–2
   feed and, 4–5, 85, 532–33

cattle (*cont.*)
  fencing and, 526–27, 560
  free range and, 78–79, 524
  grass seed and, 79–80
  grasslands and, 81–82
  grazing, 77, 229, 552
  growth hormones and, 85, 86
  Hereford, 184
  market incentives and, 229
  methane emission and, 87
  Mexico and, 258
  Native Americans and, 78
  planters and, 524
  railroads and, 82
  stockyards and, 84, 85
  Swift and Company and, 203
  water and, 80
  windmills and, 218–19
  women and, 149
Cavendish (tobacco), 369–70, 371, 372
chemistry, 27–28, 40, 41, 178, 179, 198, 205,
    335–36, 365
China
  agrarian capitalism and, 118
  collectivization and, 231
  corn and, 9–10, 254
  cotton and, 10–11, 394–95, 396, 398, 404–5
  dams and, 452–53
  deforestation and, 619–20, 622
  drought and, 603–4
  famine and, 231, 603–4, 605, 607–8,
    610, 611–12
  forests, 627, 628, 629, 630–32
  Green Revolution and, 189–90, 586,
    593, 596–97
  industrialization and, 154
  irrigation and, 445
  rice and, 9, 13–14, 230
  Rockefeller Foundation, and, 589, 591, 592
  silk and, 12, 424, 426–27, 428–29, 430–31,
    432, 433–34
  soy and, 11, 42–43, 305–9, 314–15, 319
  sugar cane and, 32, 326, 327–28, 330–31
  tobacco and, 415, 420–21
  water and, 448–49, 453
  wheat and, 280–81, 569, 586–87
Civil War (American)
  British textile mills and, 213
  cotton, 399, 528
  emancipation and, 527
  enslaved people and, 119–20, 524–25
  environmental toll and, 526
  grain prices and, 163
  plantations and, 14
  wheat acreage and, 81
climate change
  agricultural hazards and, 240
  Anthropocene and, 16
  biotechnology and, 264
  challenge to farmers, 1
  changes in precipitation and, 43
  coffee and, 355, 356
  famines and, 616
  forests and, 632
  Middle East and, 473
  mitigation of, 41
  preparing for, 593
  rice and, 289, 301
  threat to agriculture, 5
  water scarcity and, 289, 454–55
coffee
  Africa and, 205, 255, 572
  Brazilian plantations and, 26–27
  Caribbean and, 183
  commodity, 213–14, 511
  Costa Rica and, 31
  Global South and, 220
  globalization, 343
  impact of in colonies, 15
  Kenya and, 120, 572–73
  Latin America and, 205
  Middle East origins and, 10
  Sumatra and, 221–22
Cold War, 33–34, 189, 216, 237–38, 305, 319, 352,
    353–54, 588–89, 591, 612
colonialism
  Africa and, 419, 528–29, 571–72
  agricultural labor, 119, 226, 230–31
  Belgian Congo and, 228
  British and, 500
  capitalism and, 230
  colonialism, 3–4
  commercialization and, 118
  corn and, 253
  Cuba and, 217
  Europe and, 116, 500

France and, 230
Indigenous populations and, 95
Java and, 217
Latin America and, 95, 106
markets and, 121
Mekong delta and, 230
plantations and, 217, 500
rebellion and, 220–21
rice and, 230
rural England and, 118
settler colonialism, 237, 272, 419–20
Spain and, 377
tobacco and, 419
unhealthy agricultural practices and, 230
United States and, 500
violence and, 228, 237
Columbian exchange, 2, 9–12, 319, 463–64
commodification, 133, 190, 212, 256–57, 258, 263, 265
commodity
　Atlantic and, 502
　brokers and, 202–3
　chain, 305, 343
　coffee as, 64, 343, 344–45, 354–55
　colonial production and, 489–90
　corn, 47, 206, 254–55, 256
　cotton, 47, 203, 398–99, 401, 406, 527, 574
　creation of simplified landscape and, 183
　cultures and, 269, 276, 277–78
　ecological catastrophes and, 276–81
　energy transfers necessary to produce, 510
　frontiers and, 8
　global and, 251, 297, 305
　grade, 350
　grain and, 254–55
　industrialized and, 256
　issues and, 273
　land and, 30, 317–18
　livestock as, 76
　market, 255, 354–55, 406, 491
　plantations and crops as, 202–3
　plants as, 183
　prices, 187, 355, 547
　regime and, 319
　shipping and, 418–19
　silk as, 435
　slave trade and, 416
　small-scale and, 486

soy as, 11, 304–5, 314–15, 318–19
sugar as, 325–26
timber products as, 622
tobacco as, 10, 202–3, 411, 415–16, 417, 419, 517
traders, 406
web and, 314–15
wheat as, 47, 269, 272
commodity frontier
　agronomic power and, 218–19
　chains and, 214, 219, 221
　domains and, 215–16
　ecological conditions and, 213
　expansion and, 214, 215, 220–21, 307
　frictions and fixes, 217
　global capitalism and, 222
　global integration and, 218–19
　labor and, 213, 219–20
　land use and, 213
　markets and, 216, 218–19
　plantations and, 221–22
　production, 213–14, 219, 220, 222
　regimes and, 217, 221, 222
　Saint-Domingue and, 213
　slavery, 221
　smallholders and, 221–22
　South America and, 216
　Southeast Asia and, 216
　soy and, 318–19
　trade and, 216, 218–19
　United States and, 216
　women, 234
　zones and, 219–20
Consultant Group for International Agricultural Research (CGIAR), 585–87, 592, 593, 594, 595–96
corn (maize)
　agribusiness and, 261–62
　agricultural experimentation and, 183
　biofuels and, 260
　blight and, 258–59
　breeders and, 60–61
　British Corn Laws and, 274, 538, 542, 548–49, 555
　capitalism and, 251–52, 256, 265
　characteristics of, 204, 251
　companion crops and, 254, 265, 518
　Corn Belt (US), 42–43, 312–14

corn (maize) (*cont.*)
　corn syrup and, 259–60
　corn-based foods and, 254, 255
　drought and, 254–55
　enslaved people and, 50, 506
　feed lots and, 259
　flex crop and, 251, 253, 260–61
　food and feed as, 253
　food regime, 251–52, 255–56, 259, 261
　genetically modified organisms, 262, 264, 265
　global markets and, 124
　Global South and, 255, 261–62, 264
　Green Revolution and, 257–58, 453, 589
　hybrid and, 64, 180, 185–86, 187–88, 201–2, 205–6, 256–59, 265, 312–13
　livestock production and, 312
　locusts and, 93, 96, 101–3, 104
　marketing and, 185–86
　mechanization of, 167–69, 171
　Mesoamerica and, 253–54
　Mexico and, 206, 257–58, 589
　Midwest (US) and, 203–4, 256
　neoliberal agricultural and trade policies, 262
　nitrogen rates and, 47, 518
　plantations and, 509
　processed food and, 205, 251
　Russian steppe and, 277
　seed and, 63–64, 189, 201–2
　soy rotation and, 310
　United States and, 60
　wheat rotation and, 269
　women and, 151, 152
　World Bank and, 261–62
　World Trade Organization and, 261
cotton
　Africa, 572, 574
　African American women and, 151
　agricultural labor, 233–34
　agricultural research and, 255
　American South, 515, 519, 522
　Atlantic plantation, 502
　biotech and, 264
　boll weevil, 528
　British Textile industry and, 10–11, 522
　brokers and, 202–3
　China and, 395, 396
　Civil War and, 213, 525
　Codex Mendoza, 395
　commodity culture and, 276
　commodity frontier and, 213–14
　cotton diplomacy, 528
　cotton gin, 10–11, 164, 522
　Egypt, 399
　enslaved labor, 202–3, 523–24
　environmental impact of, 14, 526
　fertilizers and, 47
　frontiers and, 212
　global expansion of cotton and, 10–11
　Great Depression, 528–29
　growing conditions and, 10–11
　indentured servants and, 119
　India and, 213, 399–400, 603
　long staple and, 10–11, 12, 522
　mechanical cotton picker and, 7, 173
　mechanization, 402–5
　Mexico and, 264
　Middle East and, 472–73
　Mississippi River Valley, 522–23
　multinationals, 406
　Muslim farmers, 463
　New Deal and, 11, 312–13
　new imperialism, 400–2
　nitrogen robbing and, 10–11, 522
　plantations and, 14, 202–3
　reformers and, 152
　sharecropping and, 122, 229, 399, 400
　short staple and, 10–11, 522
　silk, 463
　Southern planters and, 11
　sugar, 502
　textile production and, 395, 396–97
　The Calendar of Cordoba, 471
　United States, 397–99
　USSR and, 212
　water, 11–12, 469
　World War II and, 7, 528–29

dams, 452–53, 454, 576
deskilling, 12–13, 84, 435, 452, 453, 468
disease. *See also* epidemic
　Africa and, 577
　agricultural colleges and study of, 198–99, 200

agricultural laborers and, 226, 228–29, 230, 233, 234–35, 236, 237–38, 240, 364, 510, 576
banana and, 25, 365–67, 368–69, 372
chemicals and, 596
chickens and, 5
coffee and, 349–50, 352–53, 355, 356
Columbian Exchange and, 463–64
corn and, 59, 198, 205–6, 254
cotton and, 399, 402
famines and, 5, 228, 606, 607, 609
floods and, 453, 454–55
forests, 186
Green Revolution, 585, 587–88, 591–92, 595, 596
Indigenous communities and, 120, 273, 377, 428, 576
land and, 25–26
livestock and, 79, 80, 83–85, 86, 186, 200, 314–15
locust outbreaks and, 94, 95, 96, 97, 99, 100–1, 105, 106
malaria, 520
monocrop agriculture and, 365–66
plantations and, 510
potato and, 379, 380
rice and, 334
Russia, plant disease and, 605
seeds and, 63
silkworm and, 432
soil-borne and, 34, 35, 45
tobacco and, 417
wheat and, 189, 205–6, 257–58, 273, 557
diversification, 179, 478–79, 571–72, 573, 604, 605, 607
domestication of plants and animals, 10, 76, 258, 286–87, 289, 293, 374, 375, 388, 446, 477–78
drainage
  British Agricultural Revolution and, 532–33, 536–37, 540, 544
  British and, 450–51
  climate change and, 454
  deforestation and, 628
  Dutch and, 449–51
  environmental impact of, 14
  experimentation with, 200
  famine, 604–5, 607, 614–15

Green Revolution and, 451–52
Neolithic period and, 449
New Netherland and, 452
nineteenth century and, 197
North America's Atlantic coast and, 451
plantations and, 14
potato and, 379–80
rice and, 295
rice domestication and, 305
sericulture (silk), 427, 428–30
soy, 305, 309, 312
sugar and, 336
tobacco and, 364, 366–67
wetlands and, 14

ecological nutrient management, 52–53
Egypt
  Aedes aegypti mosquito (yellow fever) and, 499–500, 520
  amsar (cities) and, 465–66
  coffee, 344–45
  corn, 254
  cotton, 395, 398, 399, 400, 402, 525, 528
  famine and, 5, 603–4, 607–8
  irrigation, 447, 452
  Islamic expansion and, 465
  rice, 287, 288, 293–94, 297
  saqiya (mechanical water device), 468–69
  sugar, 212
  tribal migrations and, 467
  wheat, 270
empires
  agricultural sciences and the growth of empires, 577
  Assyrian Empire and hydrology, 448
  Aztec (Mexica) and, 97, 396
  Aztec empire and famine, 607–8
  British Empire, 451, 504–5
  Chinese Empire and soy, 307
  colonialism and, 78, 81–82, 95, 230, 233–34, 451–52
  Cotton Empire and, 395, 400–1, 406
  Dutch empire and hydrology, 451
  European empire, 350, 380, 416–17, 449, 450–51, 500, 501, 502, 511
  French Empire and the abolition of slavery, 333

empires (*cont.*)
  hydrology and, 450
  Inca empire, 377, 396, 605
  irrigation, 452, 454
  Islamic empire and agriculture, 473
  Mayan Empire, drought, and famine, 603–4
  Mughal Empire and famine, 608–9
  Ottoman Empire and coffee, 344–45, 346–47, 396, 411, 431, 433–34
  plantation empire, 363
  potatoes and, 374, 388
  Qing Empire and famine, 611
  Roman Empire and Arab Islamic control, 13, 116, 463, 467, 606
  Russia Empire, 274, 275, 282, 554, 557, 587
  Sasanian Empire, 463, 467
  settler colonists and, 255
  Spanish Empire, 413, 414, 415, 418
  transnational companies and, 226
  United Fruit, 31
  wheat, 269–70
enclosure
  agricultural revolution and, 542–45
  agro-industries and, 219
  British, 535–36, 537–38, 539
  contraction of land rights and de-peasantization, 215–16
  dam building and, 453
  displacement of smallholders and, 317–18
  drainage and, 533
  Global South and, 219
  Land Enclosure Act of 1773, 14–15
  open fields and, 537
  Scottish lowlands and, 537–38
  Sixteenth century England and, 78
  soy farms and, 317–18
  Wales and, 537–38
entitlement, 28–29, 238–39, 606
entomology, 97, 577
epidemic, 95, 96, 97–98, 100–1, 105, 106, 607.
  See also disease
experiment stations
  California programs and, 202
  coffee rust and, 350, 352–53
  Dutch, coffee rust and, 352–53
  East Asia and, 312
  French and, 181

  Germany and, 180
  Hatch Act of 1877 in U.S. and, 180, 200
  Mexican agricultural colleges and, 205–6
  Portugal, coffee rust, and, 352–53
  Russia and, 180–81
  silk and, 432, 434
  U.S., 60, 179, 180, 200
expert networks. *See also* expertise
  agri-business and, 201–3
  Chicago and, 203
  contract farming and, 205
  Europe and, 7–8, 198–99
  Germany and, 198
  Green Revolution and, 205–6
  Midwestern U.S. and, 203–4
  modern farmer and, 7–8
  North Africa and, 469
  scientists and, 264, 347, 386–87
  sericultural knowledge and, 434
  U.S. and, 198, 201
expertise. *See also* expert networks
  Chicago and, 203
  cooperatives and associations and, 202
  ideas about, 196–97
  Midwestern farmers and, 203
  Nepali farmers and, 196
  research stations and, 187
  scientific and, 187
  soil conservation and, 35
  southern plantations in the 19th century and, 202–3
  technology and, 203–4
exports
  African colonialism and, 570–71, 572, 577–78, 579–80
  agro-food globalization and, 319
  agro-industrial outputs and, 219
  Atlantic plantation, 14
  bananas and, 366, 368–70, 372
  beef and, 560
  biomaterial, pollution and, 217
  British, 541
  China and, 307–8, 630–31
  coffee and, 347–48, 351–52
  colonialism, slave labor and, 120
  corn, 255, 259
  cotton and, 374, 394–95, 396–97, 398, 399, 400

enslaved Africans as, 295
exploitation of resources and, 180
famine and, 609
food production, markets and, 207–8
grains, 206, 254–55, 261, 537–38
Green Revolution and, 206, 591, 593–94
land reform, Brazil Movement of Landless Rural Workers and, 34
Latin America, livestock hides, and, 82–83
market incentives, cattle production, and Africa, 229
Mexico, fruits and vegetables and, 261–62
monoculture and, 120, 121
nontraditional foods, the Global South and, 261
pesticides and, 232
plantations and, 499–500, 632
rice, 289, 294, 295–96, 299, 300, 489–90
silk, 427, 430
soil, 48, 52–53
soy and, 11, 307–8, 314–16, 318–19
sugar and, 327
taxes, 135
timber and, 631–32
tobacco, 10, 414, 415, 419–20
U.S. Civil War, cotton and, 399
water and, 453–54
wetland reclamation, crop production of crops for, 81
wheat and, 552–53, 554, 555, 557, 559–61, 562–63
extractive economies, 211–12

family farm
Canadian programs and, 558–59
coffee and, 345
corn and, 252
corporate agriculture and, 187
global markets and, 124
labor and, 227, 228, 229–30, 232, 240
modernization, pesticides and, 200–1
peasantry and, 130, 131, 134
soy production and, 310, 313
tobacco and, 418
wheat and, 276, 277
women and, 148, 154, 155, 172
famine
adaptation to, 25

agricultural output and, 238–39
Bengal and, 608–9
British policies and, 609, 610
cannibalism and, 607
China and, 309, 492, 607–8, 610, 611–12
China relief and, 611
collectivization and, 231
concentration camps and, 613
crop failure and, 16–17, 533
drought and, 615
East India Company policies and, 609
entitlements and, 238–39
entitlement theory of, 606
expansion of agriculture and, 603–4
famine codes and, 611
farmer ill health and, 227–28
fatigue, 610
feeding programs and, 613
FEWS Net and, 615
Florentine Codex, 81
food production and, 230–31
forest habitats and, 16
global capitalism and, 609–10
global climate change and, 616
global trade and, 608
globalism capitalism and, 609–10
granaries and, 604, 605, 608
Green Revolution and, 189, 597
immigration and, 611
importance of local plant varieties and, 605
India and, 379–80, 608–9, 611
Irish Famine, 609, 610, 611
locust infestations and, 96, 97, 100–1, 102–3, 105
Mughal period and, 608–9
national food stockpiles and, 608
NGO response to and, 593–612
North Korea and, 593
overpopulation and, 614
Oxfam Committee on Famine Relief, 613–14
potato, 379, 609
refeeding programs and, 613–14
religious-based charities and, 607
rice and, 9–10
Roman empire and, 606
Russia and, 180–81, 587
RUTF and, 615

famine (*cont.*)
   Sahelian drought and, 614–15
   science of nutrition and, 613
   Soviet Union and, 33, 587, 612
   strategies of early farmers and, 604
   surveillance as preventative and, 615
   Tanzania and, 401
   therapeutic food products and, 615
   therapeutic refeeding diets and, 613–14, 615
   triggers of, 5, 10, 15–16, 299–300, 603, 606, 607, 608–9
   twentieth century wars and famine, 611–12
   war and, 611–12
   world population growth and, 614
   World War II and, 612
   Zhou famine code, 605–606
fanning mills, 161–62
farm labor. *See* agricultural labor
fertilizer use
   4Rs, (*see* 4Rs Nutrient Management Stewardship Framework)
   agrochemistry and, 28
   Aleksandr Engel'gardt studies and, 180
   chemical plants harmful practices and, 188
   commercial and, 31–32
   corn and, 256
   corporations and, 219
   dangers of, 231
   dependence upon and, 43
   GPS satellite guidance systems and, 171
   Green revolution and, 593–94
   guidelines and, 181
   John Bennet Lawes and, 179
   Justus von Liebig, 27–28
   landraces and, 594–95
   livestock and, 77–78
   mineral and, 34
   Mussolini's Italy and, 586–87
   nitrogen and, 44–45, 185, 188–89
   organic agriculture and, 52, 386
   peasants and, 189
   productivity and, 563
   replacement of manure with synthetic and, 252
   research and, 185
   rice and, 591
   runoff from, 257
   small farmers and, 594
   soil health and, 49, 51–52
   soy and, 309
   subsidized and, 401–2
   synthetic fertilizers, 35, 257, 558
   transformation of corn production and, 257
   yields in the U.S. and, 259
feudalism, 29–30, 33, 115–16, 117, 136, 446, 499, 501, 615
fiber, 59, 76, 177, 227, 271, 426, 483
flex crop, 251, 258–59, 260–61, 265, 305
floods, 1, 25, 97, 447, 468, 522–23, 595, 605, 608
food regimes, 215, 314–15, 319, 389
food security, 5, 95, 106, 134, 201, 219, 239, 376, 445, 603–4, 615, 616
food supply
   agribusiness claims and, 8–9
   biofuels adverse effect on, 260–61
   British population growth and, 608–9
   climate change and, 616
   Europe and, 380
   expansion of, 380
   famines and, 608
   Green Revolution and, 596–97
   India and, 590
   locust threat to, 5, 95, 106
   Pakistan and, 590
   potatoes and, 374, 379–80
   smallholders as largest producers of, 6
   Virgin Islands campaign and, 278–79
   war and, 587
Ford, Henry, 167, 168
forest transition
   agroforestry and, 632
   Asia and, 627
   China and, 628
   Europe and, 623
   Forestry Act of 1919, 624–25
   France and, 623–24
   global estimates and, 625–26
   Global Forest Resources Assessment and, 627
   globalization and, 631
   India and, 628
   Japan and, 627
   Kuznets curve and, 625

pathways of, 626
process of, 626
Scotland and, 624–25
Switzerland and, 624
timber plantations and, 631–32
United States and Europe and, 627
Vietnam and, 628–29
forests
   Anthropocene and, 446–47
   banana, 364, 366, 367
   coffee and, 343–44
   colonialism, 572
   commercial agriculture and, 518–19
   cotton, 398, 399
   dangers to, 349–51, 356, 500, 518–19, 595
   enslaved people and, 524–25
   famine and, 16
   livestock and, 77–78, 80
   plantation, 234–35, 519, 524
   Russia and, 553–54
   soy, 315
   sugar, 333–34
   war and, 526–27
frontier
   Africa and, 574, 580
   agriculture and, 558, 563
   Atlantic plantation and, 499–500, 501
   coffee and, 345–46, 347, 348, 350, 351–52, 354
   cotton and, 397–98
   enslaved people and, 506–7
   Europe and the Americas, 553
   food regimes and, 304–5
   frontier agriculture, 15, 27, 552
   globalization and, 305
   rice and, 481–82, 485, 486
   Russia and, 554
   soy and, 307–9, 310, 312–13, 316–17, 319
   US frontier, 552–53
   wheat and, 272, 273, 274, 275, 557
   women and, 234

gender. *See also* women
   agricultural labor and, 8–9, 125
   balance and, 232–33
   China and, 483
   cotton and, 401–2

   farm families and, 152
   farming partnerships and, 483
   irrigation and, 483
   land conflicts and, 30
   mechanization and, 169, 313
   migrants and, 233
   plantations and, 234
   rice cultivation and, 291–92
   roles and, 6
   silk and, 435
   worker health and, 227
genetically modified organisms (GMOs), 4–5, 262–63, 264
genetics, 62, 68, 180, 181–82, 186, 287, 295, 388–89, 577, 586, 587–88
global countryside, 214, 219, 222
globalization
   agro-foods and, 305, 319–20
   burdens of, 318–19
   changes to countryside and, 132–33
   chemicals and, 2–3
   coffee and, 343
   cotton and, 396
   economic development and, 627
   forest transition and, 620, 631, 632–33
   frontier expansions and, 305, 627
   modernization and, 625–26
   peasantry's end and, 132
   peasants and, 141
   potato and, 381
   Russia and, 554
   soy and, 305, 319–20
gluten, 259–60, 269, 271, 273, 277
grains. *See also* wheat
   Africa and, 254–55
   Australia and, 276
   Britain and, 533, 538, 541, 547–49, 553
   Brokers and, 201–2
   Chicago and, 197, 203
   China and, 593
   climate conditions and, 450
   colonization and, 272
   combine harvester and, 170
   commodity culture and, 278
   conflicts between raisers and shepherds, 77
   control of market and, 314–15
   corn laws and, 538, 542

grains (*cont.*)
   Cyrus Hall McCormick and, 162
   displacement of other crops and, 311–12
   Dust Bowl and, 279
   enclosure and, 544
   enslaved people and, 506
   expansion and, 274
   experts and, 203, 206
   famine and, 603–13
   farm programs and, 259
   farmers marginalization and, 274
   global markets and, 300, 563
   Global North, 261
   Global South, 261
   Green Revolution and, 585
   HYV and, 590–91
   imports, 36, 380
   indigenous people and, 271
   industrialization and urbanization's impact on production and, 553
   Ireland, 537–38
   Italy, 587
   John Deere & Company corn head attachment and, 171
   Labor needs and, 170
   livestock finishing and, 85–86
   markets and, 273, 275–76, 539–40
   mechanization and, 161, 162, 163–66
   Mexico and, 258
   Middle East and, 553, 559–60
   Middleman and, 203–4
   monoculture and, 279
   Native Americans and, 556
   neolithic period and, 269, 270
   North African crop failure of, 63
   Obed Hussey and, 162
   pastoral production and, 541–42
   potatoes, 378–79, 388–89
   protein content and, 272
   quick ripening varieties and, 484–85
   reapers and, 162–63, 164
   rotation and, 317
   Russia and, 554, 563
   seeds, 58, 59, 61, 62–59, 197–98
   Soviet Dust Bown and, 278–79
   tariffs and, 548–49
   taxes and, 479
   Tobacco and, 411
   tractors, 164, 166–69, 171, 173
   trade, 273
   transgenic corn and, 263–64
   US and, 555–56
   USSR and, 587, 588
   wheat and, 270, 271
   whole-grain movement, 271–99
   world grain markets and, 560
   World War I and, 561
granaries, 59, 65, 271, 604, 605, 607–8
Green Revolution
   Africa, 592–93
   agribusiness and, 123–24
   agricultural production and, 64, 188–89
   Andean Project to Support Peasant Technologies and, 384, 385–86
   anti-communist agenda and, 382
   Asia, 281, 298, 590, 591
   China and, 484, 492–93, 593
   coffee and, 352
   consolidation of power and, 190, 219
   cotton, 405
   criticisms of and, 67, 585–86, 594–95, 596–97
   East Africa, 590
   environmental concerns, 595–96
   global agricultural production and, 15–16
   hunger and poverty and, 123–24
   India and, 206, 590, 594
   Indigenous farming resistance and, 16
   Italy and, 586–87, 592
   labor and, 230
   land reform pressures and, 34
   Latin America, 590
   Luk'ianenko, Pantelimonovich, 587–88
   medieval version and, 463, 464
   Mexico and, 182, 205–6, 257–58, 589–90
   Middle East and, 590
   NGOs and, 585
   North Korea, 593
   Pakistan, 590, 594
   peasants and, 382
   Peru and, 382–83
   Philippines, 591
   proponents of, 189–90
   small farmers and, 594

Strampelli, Nazareno, 586–88, 593
subsistence peasant farmers, 257–58
sustainability of food production and, 41
Taiwan, 591
USSR and, 587–88
water and, 446, 451–52, 453, 455
Guatemala, 29–30, 93, 95, 96, 100–1–, 102–4, 255, 264, 363, 368–69, 371

homestead, 65–66, 151, 558–59, 561
homestead act, 152, 275–76, 556–57
humanitarianism, 105, 507
hunger, 96, 102–3, 106, 123, 188–89, 190, 205–6, 257–58, 411–12, 492–93, 590–91, 593, 597, 603, 611, 612, 613–14
Hussey, Obed, 162–63, 169–70
hybrid
    corn, 63–64, 68, 180, 185–86, 187–88, 201–2, 205–6, 256–57, 258–59, 265
    cotton, 405–6, 522
    grains, 201–2
    rice, 585, 593
    seeds, 4, 16, 62, 185, 186, 201–2, 207, 595
    soy, 305, 312–13, 353
    tobacco, 412, 446
    wheat, 9, 205–6, 269–70, 586, 590
hydro-agricultural development, 13, 446, 447
HYV (high yielding varieties), 231, 451–52, 462, 492, 585, 586–87, 588, 590–91, 593–94, 596

Iberia, 293, 413, 414, 417, 427, 428, 465, 467, 468, 470, 473, 500, 570, 575, 577–78
imperialism, 78–79, 183, 238, 255, 272, 400–1, 490
improvement
    4Rs and, 48
    Africa and, 572–73
    agricultural, 7, 464, 562
    agricultural labor and, 121, 235, 237–38
    Britain and, 516, 532–33, 534–35, 536–37, 541, 545, 549
    chemicals, 1
    colonial engagements and, 572
    corn and, 255
    crop and, 281
    damaged ecosystems and, 47

enclosure and, 78
famine and, 608–9
farm machinery and, 14–15, 163, 168
fertilizers and, 48
four-field system, 516
Green Revolution and, 590, 591, 593
guano and, 516
hydrology and, 455
infrastructure and, 516–17
limits to, 26
open field system, 14–15
potatoes, 374, 379–80
rice and, 230–31, 235, 482, 483–84, 492
science and technology and, 335
seeds, 60–61
silk and, 434
soil and, 52, 55, 197, 198
sugar, 337–38
therapeutic refeeding and, 613
tobacco and, 509
transportation and communication and, 299
wheat and, 206, 281
inbreeding, 179, 185–86
Incas, 117–32, 376–77
Indians, 273, 368, 377, 378, 382, 399, 413. See also Native Americans and indigenous people
Indigenous people. See also
    Indians and Native Americans
    Africa and, 577
    Africans and, 413
    Andean agriculture, 377, 378
    animals and, 77–78
    colonialism and, 95, 119
    conflict with Europeans, 414
    displacement of, 220
    Europeans and, 3–4, 78, 96, 252–53
    exploitation of, 2, 8
    farmers and, 15–16, 465
    Great Plains and culture, 281
    Green Revolution and, 382–83
    hunting and, 562
    incas and, 376
    labor and, 120–21, 234, 237, 349
    land, 30, 80, 120, 315–16, 317–18, 381–82
    locusts and, 95, 96, 97–98, 101–3, 104, 105–6
    mining and, 377

Indigenous people (*cont.*)
  potatoes and, 374
  rights organization, 264
  Russia and, 554, 555–56
  silk and, 424–25, 427–28
  soy, 316
  subsistence agriculture and, 5
  tobacco cultivation and, 412, 414, 416–17
  transnational corporations and, 221
  wheat and, 272, 273
  women and, 6, 147–48
Indigenous plants, 205–6, 251, 252–53, 254, 264, 400, 402, 411, 477, 622, 630
Indochina, 227–28, 234–35, 236, 237–38, 612
industrial agriculture, 41, 45, 58–59, 114, 125, 134–35, 190, 229, 238–40, 251, 255–56
industrialization
  Agrarian capitalism and, 119, 251–52
  agriculture and, 252, 255–56, 292
  animal production, worker health and, 233
  Anthropocene and, 446
  deforestation and, 589, 619–20, 622
  deindustrialization in India and, 396–97
  East Asia and, 627
  Japan and, 478, 488–89
  Mexico and, 258, 589
  plantations and, 503
  rice and, 299
  sericulture and, 259
  soy and, 315–16
  sugar and, 337
Industrial Revolution
  Anthropocene and, 3
  British food imports and, 553
  coffee and, 10
  commodity regimes, 215–16, 217, 218–19
  cotton and, 10–11, 398, 519
  Europe and, 572
  livestock and, 81, 83, 431–32
  potato and, 374
  sugar and, 508
inequality, 32, 33–34, 118, 125, 230–31, 309–10, 316–17, 338, 511
insects
  agricultural labor illness and, 238
  chemicals, agricultural labor and, 231
  corn and, 60

  cotton and, 400, 401
  crop damage and, 5
  DDT and, 7
  destructiveness of, 93–94
  early efforts to curb, 94–95, 101–2, 106
  famines and, 100–1
  grains and, 59
  harvested grains and, 605
  HVYs and, 585, 595, 596
  locust swarms and, 96–269
  rice and, 591–92
  silk and, 12, 425, 426
  sugar and, 336
  wheat and, 587–88
intensification
  commercial agriculture in colonial Africa and, 574–75, 580
  commodified land rights and, 220
  deforestation and, 527
  economic penetration of Europe and Euro-American economies and, 299
  Egyptian agriculture and, 468–69
  irrigated rice fields and, 490
  Islamic expansion and, 467
  locust swarms and, 95
  production and, 51–52
  rice production and, 478, 487, 491, 492
  state interventions in deforestation and, 628
  sugar production and, 333
inter-basin transfers, 453
Iran, 270, 290, 463, 465, 472, 576–77, 611
Iraq, 465–66, 467, 469–70, 471, 483–84
irrigation
  African plantations and, 576
  agricultural revolutions and, 449–51
  agricultural science and, 188–89, 205–6
  Arab, 466, 468, 469, 472, 473
  bananas and, 364, 366–67
  centralized state in China and, 230
  coffee and, 345–46
  cotton and, 396, 399, 402, 405
  global hydrosphere, 446, 452, 454–55
  Green Revolution and, 123–24, 451–54, 585–86, 590, 593–94, 595, 596
  hydro-agricultural development and, 445–46
  neolithic revolution and, 447–49

plantations and, 234
potatoes and, 382–83
reliance upon, 42–43
rice (dry) and, 289–91, 295, 298
Romans and, 468
sugar and, 327–28, 331, 334–35
unfree labor and, 230
wet rice and, 13–14, 480, 484–85, 490, 492
Islamic, 97, 344–45, 463–76

Japan
agricultural laborer and, 230, 233–34
cotton and, 400
deforestation and, 619–20
famine and, 612
forests, 622, 627, 630–31
Green Revolution, 586, 590, 591, 592–93
land, 29–30, 230
livestock and, 305
rice and, 230, 286, 287, 297–98
silk and, 424–25, 426–27, 430, 431, 432–33, 434
soy and, 11, 307–9, 310–12, 315–16, 319
sugar and, 327, 328, 330–31, 333
tobacco and, 415
wet rice agriculture and, 13–14, 477, 478, 487–89, 491, 492–93
World War II and destruction of agriculture and, 205

Kuznets curve, 620, 625, 626

laboratories, 26, 62, 177–78, 179, 185, 199
land grant system, 7–8, 185, 199–201, 275, 528
land markets, 31–32, 220
land ownership
concentration of, 14, 124
farmers movements and, 240
patterns, 30, 215–16, 332
planters and, 329–30
political and socioeconomic asset, 35
Siam's system of, 136
titles to, 220
US decrease of, 240
women and, 154
land reform
Brazil and, 34

Cold War and, 33–34
Cuba and, 33–34
Estonia and, 33
French revolution and, 33
Global South and, 34
Green revolution and, 33–34
Japan and, 33
Mexico and, 589
modern history and, 32
Ottoman rule and, 33
Soviet collectivization and, 587
Ukrainian "Holodomor" and, 33
Zimbabwe and, 34
landraces, 63, 64–65, 67, 68–69, 190, 376–77, 383, 386, 594–95
Latin America
agricultural corporations and, 8
agricultural laborers and, 113, 120
bananas and, 362–63, 365–66, 367, 370
biotech crops and, 263
coffee and, 205, 348, 352, 353
colonization, 120
commercialization of agriculture and, 121
corn and, 253, 254, 255, 257–58, 264
global markets and, 124
Green Revolution and, 64, 123, 588–89, 590
land, 33–34, 222
locust swarms and, 95, 106
plantations and, 121
rice and, 286, 297
seed banks and, 66–67
soy and, 306f
sugar and, 327–28, 335
United Fruit and, 29–30
wheat and, 281
levees, 447, 448–49, 522–23
Liebig, Justice von, 7, 27–28, 182–83, 198, 199, 333, 335–36
livestock
Africa and, 520–21, 578
agricultural chemicals and, 188
agricultural labor and, 233
agrochemical drift and, 317–18
Argentine pampas and, 275–76
British Agricultural Revolution and new breeds, 534
British closed system and, 536

652   INDEX

livestock (*cont.*)
   Canada and, 559
   colonialism, 79–81
   diseases and, 84–85, 186
   domestication and, 76
   enslaved people, 506, 508
   expert knowledge and, 197
   famine and, 603–5, 615
   Green Revolution and, 586–87, 592
   imperialism, 78, 184
   Industrial Revolution and, 81
   land-grant system advice and, 200
   livestock and augmentation of production and, 77–78
   management of and, 76–77
   marketing, 82–83
   pastures and, 77
   plantations and, 510, 524, 526–27
   Russian agriculture and, 554, 557–58
   scientific advances and, 85–87, 190
   sedentary agriculture and, 77–78
   slaughtering and, 83–84
   South Australia and, 276
   soy and, 312–13
   sugar and, 325, 328
   transhumance and, 77
   wet rice and, 488
locust, 1, 5, 16, 93–106

maize. *See also* corn
malaria, 228, 230, 231, 233, 234–35, 364, 499–500, 515–16, 520, 523
malnutrition, 226, 227–28, 233, 234–35, 261, 586–87, 593, 603, 609, 610, 611, 613
McCormick, Cyrus Hall, 6–7, 162–64, 169–70
meat
   agricultural labor, packing plants and, 233
   Argentina and, 560
   British economy and, 537
   Canada and, 560–61
   consumption, 86, 261, 310–11, 314–15, 542
   Dutch agriculturalists and, 35–36
   enslaved people and, 518–19, 524
   famine and, 604–5
   global surface allocated to, 42*f*
   industrialization of agriculture and, 255–56, 258
   laws and, 81
   middlemen and, 209
   packing plants and, 203
   refrigerator cars, 203
   regulations on, 203–4
   slaughterhouses and, 83, 84
   technology development and, 84
   World War II rationing, 205
mechanization
   binders, 162, 163–64
   combines, 168–69, 170–71, 277–78, 312–13
   reapers, 6–7, 162–64, 167, 168, 482
   steam traction engines, 164, 165–66
   threshing machines, 7, 161, 162, 164, 218–19, 545
   tractors, 164, 165–69, 291, 403, 404, 557, 576
   women and, 152–53
Mendelism, 181–82
Mexico
   agricultural self-sufficiency, 589
   agronomists attempts to reshape peasant farm practices, 182
   anti-GMO activism, 263
   coffee, 349, 354–55
   corn, 59, 67, 79–80, 260, 264
   cotton, 10–11, 395, 397
   dams within, 452–53
   farmer suicides over DDT, 232
   free trade leads to poverty among small producers, 124
   Green Revolution and, 258, 595, 596–97
   Gulf of Mexico "dead zone," 47, 188
   hybrid corn seed, 64
   HYVs of wheat and rice within, 585
   importation of corn from US, 255, 258, 259, 262
   International Monetary Fund (IMF)'s structural adjustment policies and, 261–62
   irrigation within, 448–49
   labor migration within and across international borders into US and Canada, 262
   locust, 93, 94–95, 96, 97, 99, 100–1, 106
   Mexican Agricultural Program (MAP), 205–6, 257–58, 589–90
   migrant workers from, 237

North American Trade Agreement
(NAFTA), 258
potato and, 374–75
sheep's impact on land, 78–79
silk production, 426–28
water, 445
wheat, 189, 281, 593–94
women, 152
Middle Ages, 30, 81, 212, 472–73
Middle East
banana and Muslim trade routes, 362
barley diversity within, 63
cotton, 394–95
Green Revolution, 64, 590
hybridization of wheat within, 9
irrigation technology, 448, 468
reforestation within, 632
rice cultivation within, 287, 292, 293–94, 298–99, 300
Roman hydraulic technologies and, 448
sericulture (silk) within, 430–31
Silk Road linkages, 12
sugar cane production in, 10
tobacco production within, 415
virtual water, 453–54
migration
Africa and, 572–73
Arab migrations, 465, 467
British Agricultural Revolution and, 537–38
capitalism and, 265
Chinese knowledge of tobacco agriculture and seeds and, 415
colonization and, 380
corn and, 256
famine and, 605, 611, 615
global warming and, 632–33
Han Chinese and, 307
Mexico, 97, 262
Middle Ages, 30
networks of, 233–34
New Zealand and, 533–34
peasants and, 317–18
rural poverty and, 125
Russian migration, south to north, 309
Russia, 554
Russification and, 275
shaping of the countryside and, 132–33

soil exhaustion in US South and, 517
USSR promotion of to the steppe, 555
women, 153–54
modernization
African agriculture and, 571
agricultural, 29, 180–81, 507
Brazil, 314–16
cotton and, 6–7
drainage and, 453
forest transition theory and, 630
HYV rice and China's agricultural modernization, 593
impact on the peasantry and, 129, 132–33
introduction of problems and, 200–1
plantations and delay of, 14
potatoes and, 383
research and, 577
silk and, 434
soviet collectivization and, 587
Vicos Project (Andes) and, 381–82
wet rice and, 13–14, 478, 488–89
wheat and, 282
Moore, Hiram, 169–70

Native American agriculture. *See also* Indians and Indigenous people
agricultural colleges for, 199
appropriation of land and, 501, 518
cultivation practices and, 501, 518
division of labor among as interpreted by colonizers, 147–48
federal policy and removal, 522
forest use, 518–19
intermarriage with enslaved people, 520
knowledge of soil type, 197–98
land seizures by colonizers, 398
plantation labor and, 500, 518–19
tobacco, 411
Neo-Europes, 449, 552, 554, 557
neoliberalism, 124–25, 137, 265, 315, 316–17, 387–88
Neolithic Revolution, 26, 269, 286–87, 362, 446, 447, 449–52, 454, 455, 464, 603
North Africa
agricultural expansion, 465
Asian rice and, 293–94
banana cultivation and, 362

North Africa (*cont.*)
  emergence of garrison cities (amsar), 465–66
  famine and the unequal distribution of food under Roman empire, 606
  introduction of new crops, 469
  Islamic foundations, 465–66
  reforestation and, 632
  Roman dams, aqueducts, canals, 468–69
  seed banks and barley, 63
  settler colonies and commercial agriculture, 572–73
  virtual water and, 453–54
  water infrastructure and, 448
  wheat, 270
North America
  bananas and, 363, 364–65
  bison, 556
  British colonies, 14, 510–11, 519
  coffee and, 348
  commodity cultures, 269
  cotton, 395, 396–400
  drainage, 451
  forest transition theory, 628–29
  GMOs and, 258
  indigenous people, 6, 114–15, 146–47, 254, 273, 555–56
  industrial commodity corn, 256
  irrigation, 448–49
  plantations, 500
  potatoes, 375, 381, 609–10
  rice and, 294, 295, 299
  scientific ideas applied to agriculture, 201
  seasonal workers within, 562
  selective breeding, 604–5
  silk, 425, 427, 429
  soy and, 305, 306*f*
  sugar and, 329–30, 509
  tobacco, 416–17, 517
  virtual water, 453–54
  wheat, 273, 274, 277, 279, 280, 553–54
  women and contribution to agriculture, 227
nutrition (animal), 186
nutrition (people)
  agricultural development, 588–89
  agricultural workers and, 226, 227–28
  chronic under-nutrition, 594, 603
  diseases and, 230, 234–35
  enslaved people and, 524
  famine, 16, 609, 610, 611, 612, 613, 614
  GMOs and, 262–63, 264
  maize and, 254, 257–58
  malnutrition, 235, 236, 239, 586–87, 593, 603
  premodern populations and, 510–11
  soybean, 304, 310–11
  wheat, 271, 281
nutrition (plants), 27–28, 31–32, 76–77, 184–85

O glaberrima (rice species), 287, 293, 294
O. sativa (rice species), 287, 293–94, 295, 521
occupational health, 226
Oxfam, 613–14, 616

paddy fields, 290–92, 296–97, 477–78, 479, 480, 482
pampas, 80, 275–76, 554, 560–61
panama disease, 31–32, 366–67, 368–70, 372
peasants and peasantry
  agrarian capitalism and, 118–19
  Agrarian ideology and rice production, 488
  agricultural biotechnology and, 263, 264
  China, 185
  colonialism and, 120–21, 401–2, 406, 580
  cotton, 395
  countryside changes in, 132–33, 361–411
  dispossession, 219, 255, 467
  European experiment stations and, 180
  famine and, 606
  globalization, 396, 398, 399–80
  Green Revolution and, 189–90, 257–58, 593–94
  Guatemala, 368–69
  La Via Campesina (The Peasant Way), 68, 134–35, 592
  Mexico and, 589
  migration of, 30
  political force, 134–35
  politics, agricultural science and Mexican peasants, 182
  potato and the Andean, 376–77, 379–80, 381–432
  property rights and, 317–18
  resistance, 58–59, 115–17, 219–21
  revolutions and land reforms, 33
  rice, 178, 477, 482, 483, 485–86

Russian peasants, 553–54, 555
silk cultivation and, 434
social compact, rice and, 489
Soviet Union and, 587–61
soy production and, 305, 309–10
subsistence and, 117
sugar cane cultivation and, 327–28, 329, 332, 333
Thailand and, 135–40
wheat production and, 272
Persia, 212, 287, 426–27, 468–69, 611
Peru, 10–11, 67, 354–55, 374–89, 395, 605. *See also* Andes
pesticides
    agricultural science, 177, 200, 206
    bananas, 371–72
    biological innovation, 185
    climate change, 240
    cotton, 403, 404–5
    dependence upon, 122, 218–19
    environmental consequences, 125, 188–89, 231–32, 239, 301, 402
    expense of, 123–24, 187–88, 206, 219, 230, 232–33, 239, 252
    global production, 451–52
    GMOs, 4, 405
    Indigenous farmers, 16, 382–83
    locusts, 5
    organic farming and, 239
    potato, 381
    problems of, 122, 188, 219, 231, 232–33, 353, 371, 585–86, 594–96
    rice, 298
    wheat, 586–87
physical injury, 226, 233
pig, 35–36, 76, 77–79, 80, 81, 82, 84, 85–86, 101–2, 148, 207, 378, 379, 486, 510
plant breeding, 58–59, 62, 67–68, 180, 185, 189, 205–6, 251–52, 256, 262–63, 336–37, 577, 590
plantations
    Africa, 573, 575, 576–77
    Atlantic plantation, 499
    Atlantic slave trade, 500
    banana, 31–32, 363, 364–65, 370
    coffee, 347–48, 349
    colonialism, 121, 571–72, 574–75
    commodity crops, 202–3, 213–14
    compulsion of labor, 328–29
    corporate, 2–3, 371
    cotton, 14, 398, 401, 405, 522–23
    diseases, 234–35, 236
    enslaved laborers, 329, 415, 416
    environment, 333–34, 516–19, 523–25
    fertilizers, 371–72
    forests, 620–30, 631–32
    gang labor, 507–8
    gendered division of labor, 506
    government and, 367
    Guatemala, 368
    harsh treatment, 506
    health and, 236, 238, 240, 329
    indigenous people, 120, 416
    Islamic, 469
    land acquisition, 120, 215, 233–34
    machinery, 337
    malnutrition and, 235
    modernization, 507
    neo-plantations, 404
    overseers, 510
    plant diseases, 366–67
    productivity, 509
    resistance to, 236, 511
    rice, 295, 482, 491, 521–22
    rubber, 228, 233–34
    scientific principles, 335–37, 507
    soil fertility, 335–36
    sugar, 26–27, 82–83, 96, 327, 329, 330–31, 333
    tea, 31–32
    tobacco, 414, 415, 417, 418
    violence, 500, 501
    water, 469
    women, 150, 503–4, 505
plow-up, 279–80, 557
potato, 10, 53, 102–3, 297, 374–93, 532–33, 546t, 605, 609
prairie, 45, 77–78, 167, 273, 277–79, 310, 553–54, 556–57, 558–60, 561, 562
public health, 83–84, 95, 100, 104, 105, 228–29, 273, 420, 421, 576, 613–14

range management, 184–85
reapers, 7, 163, 164, 169–70
refeeding, 613–14, 616

INDEX

resistance (human) 122, 186, 214, 215–16, 217, 218, 220–21, 222–23, 264, 382, 388–89, 505, 511, 520–348, 580, 611–12
resistance (non-human), 7, 43–44, 59, 63, 177, 186, 187–88, 317, 352–53, 355, 369–70, 395, 557, 591–92, 594–95, 596
rice, 286
    agricultural labor, 229–30
    agricultural science, 183
    Asia, 230
    climate change, 301
    colonialism, 230–31
    conditions for growth, 288–90
    dangers, 233–34
    domestication, 286–87
    environment, 212–13
    geography of rice, 292–96
    Green Revolution, 123, 230
    hybridization, 206
    irrigation, 290
    labor intensity, 291
    markets and trade, 296–300
    mechanization, 164, 168–69
    peasants, 131, 135, 136, 139, 178
    plantations, 202–3, 331
    seeds, 64
    sowing and harvesting, 291–92
    U.S. government programs, 124, 185–86
    varieties, 287, 293–94
    women, 152, 153, 155
    yields, 292
rice (wet), 477
    Asian Mosaics, 490–91
    canals, 523–24
    double or multi-cropping, 481
    environmental consequences, 521
    expansion, 482, 490
    famine, 605
    irrigation, 480, 523–24
    Japan, 489
    plantations, 521–22
    productive capacity, 481–82
    size of production, 479
    song government policies, 484–85
    territorial expansion and, 479
    zones, 478

Rockefeller Foundation, 15–16, 123, 185, 189, 205–7, 281, 585, 588–89, 591, 592
scientific agriculture, 1, 3–4, 7–8, 183–85, 187, 380, 577, 597
seeds
    agribusiness, 201–2
    banana, 361–62, 367
    banks, 63–65
    capitalist agriculture, 218–19
    China, 605
    coffee, 346
    colonialism, 197–98, 572, 574–75
    corporations, 122, 123–24
    cotton, 394–95, 397, 399, 400, 401, 403, 404–405–5, 522, 523, 528–29
    diversity, 65, 66, 68–69
    global bank, 595
    Global Crop Diversity Trust, 68–69
    GMO, 2–3, 4, 7, 262–63, 264
    hybridized, 16, 205–6
    HYV, 33–34, 231, 451–52, 462, 492, 585, 586–87, 588, 590–91, 593–94, 596
    Italy, 586
    keeping, 58
    land grant system, 200
    marketing, 61–62
    mechanization, 532–33, 545
    native seeds/SEARCH, 66
    NGOs, 66
    non-native seeds, 184
    potatoes, 375, 376, 382–83, 384–85, 386–87, 387f
    rice, 479–80, 481f, 482, 484–85, 486–87, 492
    Rural Advancement International, 66–67
    Russia, 605
    selection, 509
    soy, 309, 312, 317, 319
    storage, 59–61
    The True Seed Exchange (Seed Savers), 65–66
    tobacco, 415, 416–17, 452
    Via Campesina, 68
    wheat, 557, 562

silk (sericulture)
  California, 425, 429–33, 435
  capitalism, 436
  China, 426–27, 482
  commodity flows, 435
  Japan, 56
  making, 428–29
  mulberry, 425
  origins, 12
  practices, 427–28
  process, 426
  silkworms, 434, 482, 484f, 524
  traders, 396
  U.S. 424
  women, 270, 424, 428–29, 435, 482
sharecropper, 122, 169, 398–99, 400, 402–3, 404, 527, 571–72, 574
slash and burn, 114, 115, 290–91, 491
slavery, 2, 121, 152–53, 216, 229, 327, 329, 398, 416, 418, 499, 501–4, 506–7, 516–17, 525
soil
  4Rs Nutrient Stewardship, 47, 48
  chemistry, 34, 43–44, 179, 182–83, 198, 305
  conservation, 35
  damage to, 14, 31–32, 42–43, 46, 262
  ecological nutrient management, 52–56
  fertility, 4, 41, 43–45
  fertilizer, 44–45
  health, 49–52
  industrial agriculture, 45
  science, 181, 196
soy
  biofuels, 260
  Brazil, 213–14, 314–18
  global capitalism, 318–20
  global demand for, 86–87, 304–5, 307–10
  GM soybeans, 264
  Great Acceleration, 305
  mechanization, 171
  United States, 310–14
sugar
  agricultural labor and, 238, 327–32
  colonialism, 119, 120, 183, 212–13
  environmental, 332–35
  global commodity, 325
  origins, 10, 326
  process, 326–27
  technology, 335–38

technology
  animals and, 84
  British, 549
  frontier expansion, 215, 218–19
  GMOs, 261–65
  irrigation, 448
  locusts and, 102–3
  machines, 161–73
  modernization, 200–1
  productivity, 26
  Russia, 554
  soy, 312–16
  sugar, 335–38
  women, 154
Tobacco, 26–27, 149–50, 229, 411–21, 502, 509–10, 517–19, 523

United Fruit Company, 362–63, 367
United States
  agricultural research, 60–61, 63–64, 180, 207–8
  Cold War policies, 33–34, 368–69
  cotton, 397–401
  Green Revolution, 188–90, 591
  land grant system, 199–201
  mechanization, 165, 166, 172
  modern environmentalism, 619–20
  multinational corporations, 11–12
  neoliberalism and labor, 124–25
  seed networks, 65–66
  soil research, 35, 178
  water use, 452
  worker health, 226, 237

Western Europe
  colonization, 213–14, 500
  commodity chains, 305
  cotton, 399
  Great Divergence, 502–3
  GMOs, 264
  land, 3–4
  tobacco, 413

wheat. *See also* grain
   colonizer, 272–76
   ecological implications, 276–81
   expertise, 205–6
   frontier agriculture, 552
   Green Revolution, 585, 586–88, 589, 593
   mechanization, 161–64, 165, 169–70
   Mexican Agricultural Program, 257–58
   origins, 9, 269–70
   research, 180, 184
   Russia, 555

women. *See also* gender
   central role in agriculture, 6, 146–56, 384–85
   enslaved, 212–13, 503–6
   labor, 115, 227, 231, 234, 309, 377, 573–75
   land, 30, 327–28
   mechanization, 169, 313
   pesticide poisoning, 232–33
   sericulture, 425, 435, 483
   women and agricultural, 155–56